HANDLING
FEDERAL ESTATE
and
GIFT TAXES
LAW • PRACTICE • PROCEDURE

by

HOMER I. HARRIS

Mount Kisco, N. Y.
BAKER, VOORHIS & CO., INC.
1959

Harris

To My Wife

PREFACE

The past thirty odd years of probate practice have witnessed a veritable revolutionary change in taxation. Whereas thirty years ago the average general practitioner rarely was required to file a Federal Estate Tax Return, intervening inflation and changes in the law have produced many estates subject to the Federal tax. In that time there has also been introduced the first workable Federal Gift Tax Statute. These changes have created a basic need by the lawyer for a knowledge of these statutes which year by year and amendment by amendment have become more complex.

The writer's thesis in his first legal text, that the value of such a work is determined by its practicality, has been fortified by the reception accorded four subsequent efforts.

Precept and example are the best teachers. The Federal Estate and Gift Tax statutes are involved and in many instances incomprehensible to the uninitiated. It has been the writer's purpose to simplify the complexities and make the statute understandable.

The approach to this task has been to assume that the reader has little or no knowledge of Federal Estate and Gift Tax law, practice and procedure. Enough history of the statute has been furnished to give an understanding of the basis of the tax and to establish a feeling for the subject. Then step by step we have proceeded with each of the details required to guide an estate through a tax proceeding. In every case examples are furnished so that the reader may see exactly what he must know to prepare a return, how the return is prepared, computations made, and the tax paid. Pitfalls to be avoided are clearly marked. The same has been done in the case of the Gift Tax.

Once the return has been filed, procedure in the Internal Revenue Service is delineated. If the result there be unsatisfactory, further steps which may be taken either in the Tax Court, the United States Court of Claims, or the United States District Court are exemplified.

By this method of treatment, it is hoped that the reader will be able to conduct an Estate or Gift Tax case with a minimum of difficulty.

Since practicality is the guide, no attempt has been made to collate all of the authorities but merely the leading cases. A lawyer needs only a lead. In keeping with the desire for practicality, all forms are complete and intended to cover as many situations as possible, and computations, both complex and simple, are furnished.

In addition to the table of cases and statutes, the writer has attempted to describe subjects in the indices not only in the technical statutory terms and by descriptive words of art, but also in terms by which the uninitiated might be likely to describe a subject. In order to add utility, as a ready reference there are set forth in the Appendices, the texts of the Rules of Practice of the Tax Court of the United States and the Estate Tax and Gift Tax Regulations.

The writer acknowledges with thanks the suggestions of Samuel A. Brander, formerly Estate and Gift Tax Supervisor, Internal Revenue Service, First District, New York, the cooperation of Joseph Billo, assistant to the President of Baker, Voorhis & Co. Inc., as well as the help of the staff of the Printing Division and Proofreading Department of the Lawyers Co-operative Publishing Company. Thanks are also due C. West Jeffrey, Vice-President of Baker, Voorhis & Co., for his uncanny ability to grasp the essence of a legal text and his presentation thereof.

To my secretary, Ida Braverman, my sincerest thanks for her devotion to a difficult task.

Finally, to my long suffering wife and daughters, my grateful appreciation for their understanding, patience and cooperation.

HOMER I. HARRIS

149 Broadway
New York 6, N. Y.
March, 1959

TABLE OF STATUTES

INTERNAL REVENUE CODE OF 1954

INTERNAL REVENUE CODE OF 1954—Continued

INTERNAL REVENUE CODE OF 1954—Continued

INTERNAL REVENUE CODE OF 1954—Continued

INTERNAL REVENUE CODE OF 1939

INTERNAL REVENUE CODE OF 1939—Continued

UNITED STATES CODE
TITLE 28

UNITED STATES CODE JUDICIARY AND JUDICIAL PROCEDURE

MISCELLANEOUS STATUTES PUBLIC LAWS AND REVENUE ACTS

DISTRICT OF COLUMBIA CODE
TITLE 14

FEDERAL RULES OF CIVIL PROCEDURE

REGULATION 70

REGULATION 78

REGULATION 79

REGULATION 105

REGULATION 108

26 CODE FEDERAL REGULATIONS, PART 20
ESTATE TAX

26 CODE FEDERAL REGULATIONS, PART 20
ESTATE TAX—Continued

26 CODE FEDERAL REGULATIONS, PART 20
ESTATE TAX—Continued

26 CODE FEDERAL REGULATIONS, PART 25
GIFT TAX—Continued

26 CODE FEDERAL REGULATIONS PART 301
ADMINISTRATIVE REGULATIONS

26 CODE REGULATIONS, PART 301
ADMINISTRATIVE REGULATIONS—Continued

REVENUE RULINGS AND REVENUE DECISIONS

REVENUE RULINGS AND REVENUE DECISIONS—Continued

RULES OF UNITED STATES COURT OF CLAIMS

RULES OF UNITED STATES COURT OF CLAIMS—Continued

RULES OF PRACTICE OF THE TAX COURT OF THE UNITED STATES

RULES OF PRACTICE OF THE TAX COURT OF THE UNITED STATES
—Continued

SMALL BUSINESS TAX REVISION ACT OF 1958

TECHNICAL AMENDMENTS ACT OF 1958

TABLE OF CASES

(References are to sections)

(References are to sections)

(References are to sections)

(References are to sections)

(References are to sections)

(References are to sections)

(References are to sections)

(References are to sections)

(References are to sections)

(References are to sections)

(References are to sections)

(References are to sections)

(References are to sections)

TABLE OF CONTENTS

CHAPTER 1

GENERAL PRINCIPLES

CHAPTER 2

GROSS ESTATE

CHAPTER 3

TAXABLE ESTATE

CHAPTER 4

COMPUTATION OF TAX

CHAPTER 5

PRACTICE AND PAYMENT

CHAPTER 6

GENERAL PRINCIPLES OF FEDERAL GIFT TAX

CHAPTER 7

TRANSFERS SUBJECT TO FEDERAL GIFT TAX

CHAPTER 8

FEDERAL GIFT TAX EXCLUSIONS
AND DEDUCTIONS

CHAPTER 9

COMPUTATION OF FEDERAL GIFT TAX

CHAPTER 10

PRACTICE AND PAYMENT OF FEDERAL GIFT TAX

CHAPTER 11

PRELIMINARY TO ESTATE OR GIFT
TAX LITIGATION

CHAPTER 12

JURISDICTION OF TAX COURT

CHAPTER 13

PLEADINGS AND MOTION PRACTICE
IN TAX COURT

CHAPTER 14

PROCEEDINGS PREPARATORY TO TRIAL

CHAPTER 15

TRIAL IN THE TAX COURT

CHAPTER 16

PROCEEDINGS AFTER TRIAL IN TAX COURT

CHAPTER 17

ACTIONS FOR REFUND

APPENDIX A

APPENDIX B

APPENDIX C

HANDLING
FEDERAL ESTATE
and
GIFT TAXES

LAW   PRACTICE   PROCEDURE

CHAPTER 1

GENERAL PRINCIPLES

§ 1. Scope of Chapter.

While for many members of the bar the need at one time for
familiarity with the Federal Estate Tax statutes was not too
important, with the passage of time and continuing inflation,
more and more decedents' estates have required the preparation
and filing of a Federal Estate Tax return, even though there may
be no tax payable. From the viewpoint of the practicing lawyer,
the important thing is to know what is required to be done, who
is required to do it, when it must be done, and most importantly
how it is to be done. It is the purpose of the writer to answer
each of these questions from a practical point of view, demonstrating by example, so that the example may be applied to the
concrete situation with which the lawyer is faced. History and
theory will be explored only to the extent necessary for an understanding of the subject and to develop a feel for the subject
matter. We shall proceed through the steps necessary to complete a Federal Estate Tax proceeding from the initial notice, the
preparation of schedules, payment of the tax, and an appeal if
that be necessary. The Federal Gift Tax statute will also be
treated, since that tax is allied to and in many ways is an adjunct
to the Estate Tax statute. Before preparing an Estate Tax return there is required preliminarily an understanding of certain
matters upon which the entire scheme of taxation is based. This
chapter will be devoted to an exposition of such matters.

§ 2. Nature.

Although the tax is designated an estate tax, it is not, as that
title would imply, a tax on the estate or property of a decedent,

2   [Harris]

but is a tax on the *right* to transfer such property.[1] By whatever name the tax be called, whether death, legacy, estate, transfer, inheritance or succession tax, all such laws rest in essence on the principle that death is the generating source from which the particular taxing power takes its being, and that it is the power to transmit, or the transmission from the dead to the living, on which such taxes are rested.[2] Another theory on which such taxes are sustained is that since the government has the right to impose conditions on the right of transmission of property by descent or devise, which is not a natural right, it may tax such right.[3] The tax may be based either on the right of the decedent to transmit property or on the beneficiary's right to receive it. The Federal Estate Tax is classified as one on the former right.[4] It is the shifting of economic benefits which generates the tax.[5] Such tax is not a direct tax within the meaning of the Constitution, but is a duty or excise.[6] Estate taxes and income taxes are in different categories and are not mutually exclusive, although imposed on the same subject matter.[7] As has been pointed out, the phrases "transfer", "estate" and "succession" taxes and "death duties" are somewhat indiscriminately used to designate two wholly different forms of tax, that on the privilege of transmission being a transfer tax and that on the privilege of receiving being a succession tax.[8] It is also said that the Estate Tax is directed against the transfer by the decedent, while an inheritance tax is directed against the receipt of property by the beneficiary.[9] The United States Supreme Court has held that a true Estate Tax is not directed against the benefits received.[10] So far as the United States is concerned, the fact that the tax reduces the amount received by the beneficiary is of no importance.[11] Since the tax is an excise tax, the theory is that the tax imposed is the fund excised from the de-

1. Knowlton v Moore, 178 US 41, 44 L ed 969, 20 S Ct 747 (1900).

2. Note 1, supra.

3. Magoun v Illinois Trust & Savings Bank, 170 US 283, 42 L ed 1037, 18 S Ct 594 (1898).

4. Note 1, supra.

5. Landman v Comm. 123 F2d 787 (CCA10), cert den 315 US 810, 86 L ed 1209, 62 S Ct 799 (1942); Chanler v Kelsey, 205 US 466, 51 L ed 882, 27 S Ct 550 (1906).

6. Note 1, supra; Scholey v Rew, 23 Wall 331, 23 L ed 99 (1874).

7. Bull, 7 BTA 993 (1927).

8. Coolidge v Long, 282 US 582, 75 L ed 562, 51 S Ct 306 (1931).

9. McGrath, 191 Wash 496, 71 P2d 395, cert den 303 US 651, 82 L ed 1111, 58 S Ct 749 (1937).

10. Young Men's Christian Assn. v Davis, 264 US 47, 68 L ed 558, 44 S Ct 291, affg 106 Oh 366, 140 NE 114 (1923).

11. Zahn, 188 M 856, 69 NYS2d 289, revd other grounds 273 AD 476, 77 NYS 2d 904, affd 300 NY 1 (1947).

cedent's property and appropriated at the instant of death by the sovereign as its toll and which never passes into the ownership of the beneficiary.[12] The states may relieve the beneficiaries from the hardship arising from the imposition of the tax by providing for apportionment among those benefited. In considering the Federal Estate Tax, the shares which the beneficiaries will receive are not a matter of concern.[13] The tax is one upon the estate and not upon the beneficiaries.[14]

§ 3. Statutory Structure and History.

Legacy and inheritance taxes in general are of ancient origin, dating back to the Roman Empire and according to some writers to a time before that.[15] In the United States the first Federal inheritance tax was a stamp tax on estates, enacted July 6, 1797.[16] The imposition of the tax was postponed and the law repealed June 30, 1802.[17] Probate taxes imposed during the Civil War[18] were repealed by 1870.[19] The Income Tax Bill of 1894[20] included an inheritance tax, but the act was declared unconstitutional[1] and the inheritance feature fell with the act. An inheritance tax on personal property passed during the Spanish American War[2] was repealed in 1902.[3] It may be noted in passing, however, that both the act passed during the Civil War[4] and that passed during the Spanish American War[5] sustained attacks on their constitutionality.

The first Federal Estate Tax was imposed by the Act of September 8, 1916 and amended by the Act of March 3, 1917 and the Act of October 3, 1917. Subsequent changes in the law took place by the Revenue Act of 1918, the Revenue Act of 1921 and the Revenue Act of 1924.

In 1926 there was a revision of the entire structure and the Revenue Act of 1926 appeared, which is the foundation upon

12. Harjes, 170 M 431, 10 NYS2d 627 (1939); note 11, supra.

13. Sherman, 179 AD 497, 166 NYS 19, affd 222 NY 540 (1917).

14. Hamlin, 226 NY 407, affg 185 AD 153, 172 NYS 787, cert den 250 US 672, 63 L ed 1200, 40 S Ct 14 (1919).

15. See Hanson's Death Duties; Dowell's History of Taxation; Dos Passos; 3 Smith, Wealth of Nations.

16. 1 Stat 527 (1797).

17. 2 Stat 148 (1802).

18. 12 Stat 432 (1862); 13 Stat 223 (1864); 14 Stat 98 (1866).

19. 16 Stat 256, 257 (1870).

20. 28 Stat 509 (1894).

1. Pollock v Farmers Loan & Trust Co, 157 US 429, 39 L ed 759, 15 S Ct 673 (1894).

2. 30 Stat 448 (1898).

3. 32 Stat 97 (1902).

4. Scholey v Rew, note 6, supra.

5. Knowlton v Moore, 178 US 41, 44 L ed 969, 20 S Ct 747 (1900).

which the present estate tax statute was built. That act was amended in 1928[6] and 1931.[7] The yoke of the tax grew heavier with the introduction of the additional estate tax in 1932[8] which imposed a tax in addition to the tax imposed under the 1926 Act as amended, but using the latter as a basis. Further amendments took place in 1934,[9] 1935,[10] 1936,[11] and 1938.[12] In 1939 the 1926 Act as variously amended was replaced by the Internal Revenue Code, commonly referred to as the 1939 Code.[13] This in turn was amended every year, with the exception of 1952, until 1954, when the estate tax law was re-written and became the Internal Revenue Code of 1954, applying to the estates of decedents dying *on and after August 17, 1954*. Two minor changes were made to this Code in 1956.[14] Further changes were made by the Technical Amendments Act of 1958. The significance of this panoply of changes lies in the fact, as we shall see, that *the law applicable to a particular estate depends upon the date of the decedent's death*. A transfer made by a decedent dying at one time might not be taxable, whereas it would be if the death were at a later time. The right to a deduction may similarly depend upon the date of death.

§ 3A. Outline of the Tax.

While, as we shall see, the Estate Tax statute abounds with complexities, the basic provisions of the law are not difficult to comprehend. Essentially it is a tax upon the right to transmit or the right of transmission of property. While it is not a tax on the property, it is measured by the property. There is first determined the gross estate of a decedent. This includes not only property to which the decedent technically had title, but includes property in which the decedent had an interest. There are thus encompassed certain transfers which a decedent made during his lifetime as well as other interests which have the indicia of testamentary transfers. From the gross estate thus determined the statute provides for the deduction of certain enumerated items, designated deductions, and an exemption. The remainder is the taxable estate. The tax is computed upon this remainder, or taxable estate, by applying the graduated rates according to

6. Rev Act of 1928 (Part I, Title II).
7. Pub Res No. 131, 71st Congress.
8. Rev Act of 1932 (Title II).
9. Rev Act of 1934 (Titles II, III).
10. Rev Act of 1935.
11. Rev Act of 1936.
12. Rev Act of 1938.
13. IRC (1939), Chap 3.
14. PL 901, Aug. 1, 1956; PL 1011, Aug. 6, 1956.

the brackets in which the taxable estate falls. Against the tax as thus computed certain credits are allowable. Prior to the adoption of the Internal Revenue Code of 1954 it was necessary to compute the tax under two different tables, for the basic tax and the tentative tax separately. The 1954 Code combined the rates so that computation is now required under but a single table. There is a separate table for the computation of the maximum credit for state death taxes. Each of the elements entering into the determination of the tax will be treated hereinafter.

§ 4. Constitutionality.

Even as former inheritance tax laws have been attacked,[15] so was the first Federal Estate Tax. Such attacks were of two kinds. The first was directed to the law itself. Thus, it was claimed that it was unconstitutional as a direct tax. The Supreme Court held that the tax was an indirect tax and did not require apportionment.[16] Subsequent attacks established other propositions. The Federal Estate Tax provisions are not unconstitutional for lack of uniformity nor are they a deprivation of property without due process of law.[17] The constitutionality of the acts must be considered as of the date of the enactment.[18] The Federal Estate Tax laws prevail over conflicting provisions in state laws or state constitutions.[19] And it has been pointed out that while frequently there are differences which are sanctioned by the Federal government, such sanctions do not infringe the constitutional prohibition against delegating taxing power or the requirements of geographical uniformity.[20] It is a general proposition that the tax law requirements are read into contracts such as insurance policies. A consequence of this is that the Estate Tax Law has been held not to violate the contract impairment clause of the Constitution.[1] However, where rights have become vested they cannot be affected by subsequent tax legislation.[2] Where an amendment to a tax law is intended to be retroactive,

15. See § 3, supra.

16. New York Trust Co. v Eisner, 256 US 345, 65 L ed 963, 41 S Ct 506 (1921).

17. Gottlieb v White, 69 F2d 792 (CCA1), cert den 292 US 657, 78 L ed 1505, 54 S Ct 867 (1934).

18. Note 17, supra.

19. Florida v Mellon, 273 US 12, 71 L ed 511, 47 S Ct 265 (1927).

20. Note 17, supra.

1. Guaranty Trust Company of New York v Blodgett, 287 US 509, 77 L ed 463, 53 S Ct 244 (1933).

2. Coolidge v Long, 282 US 582, 75 L ed 562, 51 S Ct 306 (1931); see also Blackstone v Miller, 188 US 189, 47 L ed 439, 23 S Ct 277 (1902).

it can be sustained unless it is unreasonable, arbitrary, capricious and unjust.[3]

Other attacks have been leveled at particular sections of the statute. These will be discussed in connection with the treatment of such provisions.

§ 5. Statutory Construction.

In the interpretation of the Federal Estate Tax statute there are applied the usual rules of statutory construction. The controlling and final authority is, of course, the United States Supreme Court, and its decisions are binding on the lower Federal courts.[4] Its decisions are likewise binding upon state courts.[5] While it is said that the decisions of different circuit courts should tend to uniformity rather than creating situations where one circuit overthrows the view of another,[6] certainly in tax cases the admonition appears to be observed in the breach rather than in the performance. The courts will avoid applying tax laws retroactively unless constrained to do so.[7] The goal should be to carry out the intention of Congress.[8] In this regard it has been pointed out that an amendment should not be held to indicate legislative construction of prior acts.[9] But the legislative intent should not be based upon conjecture.[10] Oppressive consequences should be avoided if possible.[11] This is equally true of double taxation.[12] Coming down to a more detailed consideration, punctuation should not be permitted to assume too great an importance.[13]

§ 6. Law Applicable.

The estates which are subject to the Federal Estate Tax originate in the several states and are governed by the intestate laws or probate provisions of such states. The validity of the inter-

3. Peo ex rel. Beck v Graves, 280 NY 405, 21 NE2d 371 (1939).

4. Ballard v Hepburn, 9 F Supp 812, affd 85 F2d 613 (CCA6) (1936).

5. See Amoskeag v Dartmouth, 89 NH 471, 200 A 786 (1938).

6. Note 17, supra.

7. See Bingham v U. S. 76 F2d 573 (CCA1), revd 296 US 211, 80 L ed 160, 56 S Ct 180 (1935); see also Knox v McElligott, 258 US 546, 66 L ed 740, 42 S Ct 396 (1921).

8. Del Drago, 317 US 95, 87 L ed 106, 63 S Ct 109; granting cert from 287 NY 61, revg 175 M 489, 23 NYS 943 (1942).

9. See Manning v Board of Commrs., 46 RI 400, 127 A 865 (1925).

10. Note 9, supra.

11. See Paul, 303 Pa 330, 154 A 503, cert den 284 US 630, 76 L ed 536, 52 S Ct 13 (1931).

12. Note 11, supra.

13. Coffee, 19 Cal2d 248, 120 P2d 661 (1941); see also U. S. v Isham, 17 Wall 496, 84 US 496, 21 L ed 728 (1873).

ests is determined by the state courts, but the question of what is subject to the Federal tax is determined by the Federal law.[14] In other words, while the state court decides the nature of the interest of a beneficiary, the Federal government determines whether such interest is taxable.[15]

Whether a particular estate is subject to taxation under a prior or subsequent statute depends upon the effective date of the statute.[16] A statute which is not particularly and properly retroactive does not apply to an estate which has arisen and come into existence prior to its effective date. The same principle applies where the question arises upon the effect of the repeal of a statute.[17] Thus, where an estate is taxable under a particular law, it is not relieved from the tax where the act is repealed after the death of the decedent.[18]

The appointment of guardians and the transmission of property is generally governed by the law of the situs of the property.[19]

While Federal laws and decisions generally control in the construction of similar provisions of a state statute,[19a] some courts have taken the position that the decisions of the United States Supreme Court are controlling on the state courts,[20] while others have hedged on the question.[1] There are, however, two matters entirely within the jurisdiction of the states. These are the apportionment of the tax among the beneficiaries and the distribution of the assets to those entitled thereto, and are entirely separate and apart from the tax problem.[2] The right of the state to provide for apportionment of the tax has been held not to violate the requirement of geographical uniformity, nor the supremacy provision of the United States Constitution.[3]

14. Rogers, 320 US 410, 88 L ed 134, 64 S Ct 172, affg 135 F2d 35 (CCA2) (1943).

15. Allen v Henggeler, 32 F2d 69 (CCA8), cert den 280 US 594, 74 L ed 642, 50 S Ct 40 (1929).

16. Guaranty Tr. Co. 16 BTA 314 (1929).

17. Harris, 5 BTA 41 (1926).

18. Hertz v Woodman, 218 US 205, 54 L ed 1001, 30 S Ct 621 (1909).

19. Clarke v Clarke, 178 US 186, 44 L ed 1028, 20 S Ct 873 (1899).

19a. Anderson, 171 M 795, 13 NYS2d 504 (1939).

20. Porter, 197 M 472, 94 NYS2d 887 (1945); Rogers, 269 AD 551, 56 NYS2d 289, affd 296 NY 676 (1945); Anderson, 171 M 795, 13 NYS2d 504 (1939).

1. Larkin, 183 M 1052, 50 NYS2d 500 (1944).

2. McKay v Lauriston, 204 Cal 557, 269 P 519 (1928); Williams v State, 87 NH 341, 125 A 661 (1938); Bernheimer, 352 Mo 91, 176 SW2d 15 (1943).

3. Note 8, supra.

§ 7. Domicile; Residence.

The question of whether the decedent was a resident or citizen of the United States or a nonresident alien is of substantial importance, since taxability, deductions and the amount of exemption depend upon the answer to the question. The determination of domicile is that of a question of fact, and there is much case law on the subject.[4] There is involved not only the problem of residence and nonresidence, but also that of citizen or alien.[5] These questions are answerable in the same manner as when the question arises in any proceeding involving domicile in the state courts. While the statute does not define the terms "resident" and "nonresident", the Regulations define the term "resident" as meaning a decedent who at the time of his death had his domicile in the United States, and "nonresident" as a decedent who at the time of his death had his domicile outside the United States. They further state the criteria for the determination of domicile.[6] The same questions of the decedent's intention, change of domicile and proof to establish the acquisition of domicile arise and are solved as where the question is raised in a probate or other proceeding when it is claimed that a decedent was or was not domiciled in a particular state. The decisions of the Supreme Court in cases which have arisen between the several states where each has claimed that the decedent was a domiciliary of the state will be found helpful in furnishing both the factual situations and the law applicable.[7]

4. See Farmers Loan & Trust Co. v Morrison, 60 F2d 618 (1932); Cooper v Reynolds, 24 F2d 150 (1927); Rodiek, 33 BTA 1020, affd 87 F2d 328 (1937); McMillan, 27 BTA 318 (1932); Lyons, 4 TC 1202 (1944); Fisher, 36 BTA 534 (1937); Jeffress, 25 BTA 507 (1931); Rogers, 17 BTA 570 (1929); Rosenberg, 2 BTA 720 (1925); Herenden, 5 BTA 1272 (1927); Nienhuys, 17 TC 1149 (1952); Fokker, 10 TC 1225 (1948); Bowring v Bowers, 24 F2d 918 (CCA2) (1928); Smallman, 21 BTA 330 (1930); Smallwood, 11 TC 740 (1949).

5. Note 4, supra.

6. Reg § 20.0–1(b).

7. See Texas v Florida, 306 US 398, 83 L ed 817, 59 S Ct 563 (1939); Dor-rance, 287 US 660, 77 L ed 569, 53 S Ct 222, 288 US 617, 77 L ed 990, 53 S Ct 507 (1932); Central Hanover Bank v Kelly, 319 US 94, 87 L ed 1282; 63 S Ct 945 (1943); City Bank Farmers Trust Co. v Schnader, 293 US 112, 79 L ed 228, 55 S Ct 29 (1934); First Nat. Bank of Boston v Maine, 284 US 312, 76 L ed 313, 52 S Ct 174 (1931); Baldwin v Missouri, 281 US 586, 74 L ed 1056, 50 S Ct 436 (1930); Farmers Loan & Trust Co. v Minnesota, 280 US 204, 74 L ed 749, 48 S Ct 410 (1929); Frick v Pennsylvania, 268 US 473, 69 L ed 1058, 45 S Ct 603 (1925); Mitchell v U. S. 21 Wall 350, 88 US 350, 22 L ed 584 (1874).

§ 8. Construction of Will.

The necessity for construction of a will may present itself in Federal taxation as well as in state estate taxation. In many cases it is necessary to determine the nature of the interest of a beneficiary before the audit of the estate may be completed. In such case the same canons and rules of construction apply in determining the intention of the testator, and the fact that it involves the determination of the Federal tax effects no change. As in any will construction, the primary question is what the testator intended, and the Federal courts follow the general rule of examining the words used in their setting.[8] Their right to do so is undoubted.[9] The taxing authorities may determine whether an interest is a life estate or a contingent interest.[10] They have passed upon such complex questions as the violation of the Rule against Perpetuities,[11] and determined the amount of the net taxable estate by construing the will.[12] Where land is concerned, the general rule is that the law of the situs governs.[13]

§ 9. Authority for Proceedings.

While the Estate Tax Law is the basis for all procedure under it, the provisions therefor in the Revenue Act of 1954 have been grouped together under the title of "General Requirements for Returns." The statute then proceeds to authorize the Secretary of the Treasury or his delegate to formulate Regulations in more detail.[14] Pursuant to this authority the Secretary has prepared Regulations[15] which not only prescribe in detail the procedure for filing the returns required by the law, but more importantly expand upon the statutory language and explain it. The practicing lawyer will find these Regulations extremely helpful in answering many of his questions, particularly with respect to some of the more involved provisions of the law. The Estate Tax Regulations will be found in the Appendix at the end of the text herein. It may be pointed out that the purpose of the Regulations is to clarify the law, but are not the law itself. Reg-

8. See Beals v Hiagens, 307 Mass 547, 31 NE2d 20 (1948).

9. Hinkley v Art Students' League, 37 F2d 225 (CCA4), cert den 281 US 733, 74 L ed 1149, 50 S Ct 248 (1930).

10. Kahn v U. S. 257 US 244, 66 L ed 215, 42 S Ct 85 (1921).

11. Henderson, 45 BTA 1080 (1941).

12. Lamport, 28 BTA 862 (1933).

13. De Vaughan v Hutchinson, 165 US 566, 41 L ed 827, 17 S Ct 461 (1896).

14. IRC, §§ 6011, 6018, 6036, 6061, 6064, 6065, 6071, 6075, 6091, 6151, 6155, 6161, 6163, 6165 (1954 Code).

15. Estate Tax Regulations.

ulations cannot create a tax or enlarge a taxing statute.[16] Reasonably clear revenue statutes cannot be extended or restricted by administrative regulations. To the extent that the Regulations clarify the law they are proper and helpful. In most instances they serve this purpose. When they do not explain, but legislate, they will be rejected by the courts.[17] Another source of assistance in the preparation of the returns and schedules is the instructions which are part of each return. These contain detailed information as to the manner of preparation of the return, the necessary supplemental documents which may be required and examples of both preparation and computations.

§ 10. Applicable Statutes.

Since August 17, 1954 the statute applicable to the estates of decedents dying on and after such date is Chapter 11 of the Internal Revenue Code of 1954, commonly referred to as the 1954 Code. Subchapter A of Chapter 11 treats with the estates of citizens or residents, whereas Subchapter B of Chapter 11 treats with the estates of nonresidents not citizens of the United States. It is a basic tenet of estate taxation that the taxing statute which is in effect at the date of death of a decedent determines and controls the taxation of his estate.[18] *It is, therefore, of the utmost importance to determine in every case what statute was in effect at the date of the decedent's death.*

Prior to the enactment of the Internal Revenue Code of 1954 and from February 11, 1939 the Internal Revenue Code of 1939 was effective. This is commonly referred to as the 1939 Code. It must also be borne in mind that whether an estate is taxable under either the 1939 Code or the 1954 Code, such codes are periodically, if not annually, amended. It is important to determine in any case whether a particular provision of the Code has been amended between the date of death and the date of preparation of the return. This has two facets. The first is, that as the result of an amendment, items may become tax-

16. Missouri Packing Co. v Hellmich, 12 F2d 978 (CCA8), aff'd 273 US 242, 71 L ed 628, 47 S Ct 395 (1926).

17. See Comm. v Clark, 202 F2d 94 (1953).

18. Alker v U. S. 47 F2d 229, aff'g 38 F2d 879, cert den 283 US 842, 75 L ed 1452, 51 S Ct 489 (1931); Ewbank v U. S. 50 F2d 409, aff'g 37 F2d 383, cert den 284 US 657, 76 L ed 557, 52 S Ct 35 (1931); Burrows v U. S. 56 F2d 465 (1932); Schoenheit v Lucas, 44 F2d 476 (1930); O'Brien v Sturgess, 45 F2d 1017, aff'g 39 F2d 950 (1931); Page v Skinner, 293 F 468, aff'd 298 F 731 (1924); Flannery v Willcuts, 25 F2d 951 (1928).

able or nontaxable which before the amendment were nontaxable or taxable. Examples of this are the marital deduction amendment of 1948,[19] the Technical Changes Acts of 1949[20] and 1953,[1] the Powers of Appointment Act of 1951[2] and the changes made in the statute by the 1954 Code. The second facet is that in reading case law on particular questions, if the reader is not aware that the statute has been amended, he may be misled into believing that a decision applies to his case, which does not. Examples of this are the many cases decided under the 1939 Code denying the marital deduction for legal life estates not in trust,[3] or portion trusts,[4] and which disqualification was removed by the 1954 Code.

§ 11. Definitions; Gross Estate; Taxable Estate; Executor; Transferee.

While the Estate Tax provisions of the 1954 Code contain definitions of various taxable interests, emphasis is placed upon four terms. These are "gross estate," "taxable estate," "executor," and "transferee."

The value of the *gross estate* of the decedent shall be determined by including to the extent provided for in Part III of the statute, *the value at the time of death* of all property, real or personal, tangible or intangible, wherever situated, *except* real property situated outside of the United States.[5] This is not any change in substance of the provision under the 1939 Code.

The value of the *taxable estate* shall be determined by deducting from the value of the gross estate the exemption and deductions provided for in Part IV of the statute.[6] This is a substitution of the term "taxable estate" for the prior term "net estate." Both terms have the same meaning.[7]

The term "executor" wherever it is used in connection with the Estate Tax, means the executor or administrator of the decedent, or, if there is no executor or administrator appointed, qualified, and acting within the United States, then any person

19. Rev Act of 1948, Apr. 2, 1948.

20. PL 378, 81st Congress.

1. § 811(c)(1)(3)(4), Aug. 15, 1953.

2. §§ 811(f), 1000(c), 82nd Congress, 1st Sess.

3. Pipe, 23 TC 99, aff'd 241 F2d 210 (CA2) (1956); Evilsizor, 27 TC 710 (1957).

4. Rev Rul 54-20, 1954-1 CB 195; Hoffenberg, 22 TC 1185, aff'd 223 F2d 470 (CA2) (1954); Melamid, 22 TC 966 (1954); Shedd, 23 TC 41, aff'd 237 F2d 347 (CA9) (1954).

5. IRC, § 2031(a) (1954 Code).

6. IRC, § 2051 (1954 Code).

7. Sen Fin Comm Report (1954 Code).

in actual or constructive possession of any property of the decedent.[8] The definition was the same under the 1939 Code.[9]

The term "transferee" includes donee, heir, legatee, devisee, and distributee, and with respect to estate taxes, also includes any person who is personally liable for any part of such tax.[10]

The 1939 Code also contained definitions of the terms "month" and "collector."

These definitions are in the case of several of them, and additional ones, further explained by the Regulations.[11]

§ 12. Definitions; Citizens; Residents; Nonresidents Not Citizens.

Under state inheritance tax laws a distinction is made between residents and nonresidents. The distinction under the Federal statute differs. It provides in Subchapter A that the tax shall be imposed on the transfer of the taxable estate of every decedent, *citizen or resident* of the United States.[12] Subchapter B contains special provisions for the taxation of the estates of every decedent *nonresident not a citizen* of the United States.[13]

While the statute does not define the terms, the Regulations define "resident" as a decedent who, at the time of his death, had a domicile in the United States, which includes only the States, the Territories of Alaska and Hawaii, and the District of Columbia, and a "nonresident" as a decedent who, at the time of his death, had his domicile outside the United States.[13a] This will cover the admission of Alaska to the United States.

In the case of a resident of the United States, whether or not he is a citizen, his estate is subject to taxation under the general provisions of the statute, except for real estate having a foreign situs.[14] In the case of a nonresident alien, however, only his gross estate situated in the United States at the time of his death is taxable.[15] Included within residents are missionaries in foreign service.[16]

It having been held that a citizen of the United States who at the time of his death was domiciled in the Virgin Islands was

8. IRC, § 2203 (1954 Code).
9. IRC, § 930(a) (1939 Code).
10. IRC, § 6901(h) (1954 Code).
11. Reg, §§ 20.0-2(b)(2), 20.2031-1 (a), gross estate; Reg, §§ 20.0-2(b)(3), 20.2051-1, taxable estate; Reg. § 20.-2203-1.

12. IRC, § 2001 (1954 Code).
13. IRC, § 2101(a) (1954 Code).
13a. Reg, § 20.0-1(b).
14. IRC, § 2033 (1954 Code).
15. IRC, § 2103 (1954 Code).
16. IRC, § 2202 (1954 Code).

not a citizen of the United States for the purpose of the Estate Tax,[16a] there has been added to the 1954 Code a provision[16b] to overcome this decision. The new section provides that a decedent who was a citizen of the United States and a resident of a possession thereof at the time of his death shall, for purposes of the Estate Tax, be considered a "citizen" of the United States within the meaning of that term wherever used in the Estate Tax statute *unless* he acquired his United States citizenship solely by reason of (1) his being a citizen of such possession of the United States, or (2) his birth or residence within such possession of the United States. *The provision applies only to estates of decedents dying on and after September 2, 1958.* The effect is that a United States citizen who moves from the United States to one of the possessions will be treated for Estate Tax purposes in the same manner in which he would have been treated if he had remained in the United States.

§ 13. Outline of Procedure.

The Federal Estate Tax proceedings progress by stages from the initial notice to payment of the tax.

The first step is the requirement that a preliminary notice be filed by the fiduciary with the Internal Revenue Service within two months of the decedent's death or the appointment of the fiduciary.

The second step is the filing of the Estate Tax return, in which are set forth the assets comprising the gross estate, the deductions and exemption and the computation of the tax. The fiduciary is permitted fifteen months for compliance with this requirement.

The third step is the audit of the return by the Internal Revenue Service and the determination of the tax.

If additional tax is determined to be due, after it has been assessed in the form of a deficiency assessment, there may be conferences or appeal, and payment or nonpayment of the deficiency, depending upon the result.

§ 14. Preliminary Notice; Statutory Provision.

Whereas the 1939 Code specifically provided that the fiduciary

---

16a. Fairchild, 24 TC 408 (1956); see also Smallwood, 11 TC 740 (1949); Rivera, 214 F2d 60 (CA2), affg 19 TC 271 (1954).

16b. IRC, § 2208 (1954 Code), added by Technical Amendments Act of 1958, § 102(a), HR 8381, 75th Cong, 2nd Sess.

must give notice to the collector within two months after the decedent's death, or within a like period after qualifying as such,[17] the 1954 Code provides that such notice shall be given in such manner and at such time as may be required by regulations of the Secretary of the Treasury or his delegate.[18] Pursuant to this authorization, the Regulations provide for the filing of the notice of qualification, which is designated "Preliminary notice," within the same period as was required by the 1939 Code.[19] The notice is provided for in the case of a resident or citizen of the United States and also in the case of a nonresident not a citizen.[20]

§ 15. Preliminary Notice; When Required.

It is a common experience to discover that there has been a failure to file the preliminary notice because of unfamiliarity with the requirements. It is not the *net estate* which determines whether the notice must be filed, but the *value of the gross estate* of the decedent at the date of death. A preliminary notice is required to be filed on Form 704 in the case of every *citizen or resident* of the United States whose gross estate exceeded *$60,-000* in value at the date of death, and on Form 705 in the case of every *nonresident who is not a citizen* if that part of his gross estate which was situated in the United States exceeded *$2,000* in value at the date of death. *The value of the gross estate at the date of death* governs with respect to the filing of the notice, regardless of whether the value of the gross estate is, at the executor's election, finally determined as of a date subsequent to the date of death.[1] This latter is a reference to the election given the fiduciary to value the estate as of the date of death or as of a date one year after the date of death, formerly known as optional valuation and under the 1954 Code called alternate valuation.[2]

There are many estates in which the notice is required to be filed although no tax will be payable. Thus, where a gross estate of $120,000 is bequeathed to the surviving spouse, the marital deduction and the specific exemption will result in a nontaxable estate. The same situation exists where the gross estate is $70,-000, but is subject to the payments of debts and administration

---

17. IRC, § 820 (1939 Code).
18. IRC, § 6036 (1954 Code).
19. Reg, § 20.6071-1.

20. Reg, §§ 20.6036-1, 20.6071-1.
1. Reg, § 20.6036-1(a).
2. IRC, § 2032 (1954 Code).

expenses of $15,000. In each of these cases a preliminary notice must be filed because the gross estate exceeds $60,000.

Since the notice is primarily informatory, if there is any doubt as to whether the gross estate will exceed $60,000 or $2,000, as the case may be, the notice should be filed as a matter of precaution in order to avoid the possibility of penalties attaching.[3] Since the preparation of the notice is a comparatively simple matter and consumes little time, if a rough estimate of the assets of the estate indicate that they may exceed the above amounts the notice should be filed.

§ 16. Preliminary Notice; Timeliness; Purpose.

As noted, the Regulations require that the preliminary notice be filed within two months.[4] They provide that if a duly qualified fiduciary of the estate of a decedent who was a resident or a citizen of the United States qualifies within two months after a decedent's death, or if a duly qualified fiduciary of the estate of a nonresident not a citizen qualifies within the United States within two months after the decedent's death, the preliminary notice must be filed within two months after his qualification. If no such fiduciary qualifies within that period, the preliminary notice must be filed within two months of the decedent's death.[5] The Regulations under the 1939 Code made the filing of the notice mandatory,[6] but Regulations under the 1954 Code do not so provide, since the statute on which the Regulations are based grants discretion to the Secretary of the Treasury in this regard.[7]

As the Regulations note, the primary purpose of the preliminary notice is to advise the Government of the existence of taxable estates, and filing should not be delayed beyond the two months' period merely because of uncertainty as to the exact value of the assets. The estimate of the gross estate called for by the notice should be the best approximation of value which can be made within the time allowed.[8]

In spite of the particularity of the Regulations, and the still greater particularity of the preliminary notice and the instructions on the back thereof, the Internal Revenue Service is more interested in receiving the notice than the details thereof. The writer has seen notices accepted which merely stated that the

3. Note 1, supra.
4. § 14, supra.
5. Note 19, supra.
6. Reg 105, § 81.58.
7. Note 18, supra.
8. Note 1, supra.

gross estate exceeded the minimum amount without any details as to the assets.

§ 17. Preliminary Notice; Who Files.

The statute requires the preliminary notice to be filed by the executor.[9] Executor, however, includes not only a fiduciary of the estate, but within the meaning of that term as used and defined in the statute, any person in actual or constructive possession of any property of the decedent.[10] In all except the unusual case, the notice is filed by the fiduciary after his qualification. As the instructions on the return indicate, he must file the notice unless at the time of his qualification the notice has already been filed.[11]

The Regulations provide that in the estate of a citizen or resident of the United States the preliminary notice must be filed by the duly qualified fiduciary, or if none qualifies within two months after the decedent's death, by every person in actual or constructive possession of any property of the decedent at or after the time of the decedent's death. In the case of a nonresident not a citizen, the notice must be filed by every duly qualified fiduciary within the United States, or if none qualifies within two months after the decedent's death, by every person in actual or constructive possession of any property of the decedent at or after the time of the decedent's death.[12]

Persons in actual or constructive possession of property of a decedent include custodians, fiduciaries, transferees, joint owners, partners, distributees, debtors, agents, factors, brokers, bankers, safe deposit companies, and warehouse companies.[13] Such persons are relieved from the necessity for filing the notice if the fiduciary qualifies within two months of the decedent's death.[14]

§ 18. Preliminary Notice; Execution of.

The preparation of the preliminary notice presents no great difficulty. It is primarily an information return and does not fix tax liability. The notice must be prepared upon the official forms[15] which may be obtained from the District Director.[16] The

9. Note 18, supra.
10. See § 11, supra.
11. Instructions on Preliminary Notice.
12. Reg, § 20.6036–1(b).
13. Note 11, supra.
14. Note 11, supra.
15. Reg, §§ 20.6011–1(a), 20.6011–2.
16. Note 15, supra.

fact that a fiduciary has not been furnished with copies of the forms will not excuse him from filing the notice.[17] The Regulation provides that the executor should carefully prepare the preliminary notice so as to set forth fully and clearly the data called for therein, since a notice which has not been so prepared will not be accepted as meeting the requirements of the Regulations.[18]

While in practice the Internal Revenue Service is not as strict as the Regulations would indicate, it is no more difficult to prepare the notice in accordance with the instructions than not to do so. All that is required is *approximate* values. All the information required by the form is ordinarily in the possession of the fiduciary within a short time after his appointment. If assets are discovered after the notice has been filed, no great harm is done, since the Estate Tax return will set them forth. The instructions are not printed here but are treated in preceding and succeeding sections.

FORM NO. 1

Estate Tax Preliminary Notice; Estate of Citizen or Resident of the United States

(To be executed and filed by executor or person in possession of property—observe instructions on reverse side)

Name of decedent   WINTHROP BENSON
Date of death   Jan. 10, 1960   Citizenship (nationality)   United States
Place of death   Riverhead, L. I., N. Y.
Residence (domicile) at time of death   100 Elm Street, Riverhead, L. I.,
     N. Y.   March 1, 1960

DISTRICT DIRECTOR OF INTERNAL REVENUE,
     Brooklyn, N. Y.

1. Pursuant to the requirements of sections 6036 and 6018 (a) of the Internal Revenue Code, notice is hereby given that: (*Executors or administrators fill in (a); custodians, joint owners, distributees, etc., fill in (b)*)

(*a*) The undersigned qualified as executrix/administrat.... of the estate of the above-named decedent in the Surrogate's Court at Suffolk County, New York on the 20th day of January, 1960.

(*b*) The undersigned, on or subsequent to the date of the decedent's death, had actual or constructive possession of property or of an interest

---

17. Reg, § 20.6011–2.   18. Note 17, supra.

[Harris]

in property which constituted a part of the decedent's gross estate, within the meaning of the estate tax law. The description and approximate value of such property at the time of death were as follows:

Description	Value
....	$.........
....	....
....	....

2. To the best of the undersigned's knowledge the *approximate* values of the various classes of property (including any property not in possession of the undersigned) constituting the decedent's gross estate at date of death were as follows:

Real estate	$38,000.00	Jointly owned property	$ 5,000.00
Stocks and bonds	75,000.00	Transfers during decedent's	
Mortgages, notes, and cash	18,000.00	life	2,000.00
Insurance on decedent's life	57,700.00	General powers of appointment	10,000.00
Annuities	....	All other property	150,000.00
Total of above items			$355,700.00

3. The names and addresses of the legal representatives of the estate and their attorneys insofar as known to the undersigned are:

	Name	Address
Executors Administrators	Katherine Benson	100 Elm Street, Riverhead, L. I., N. Y.
Attorneys	Daniel Webster Clay	100 Broadway, Riverhead, L. I., N. Y.

The undersigned HEREBY CERTIFIES that the instructions on the reverse side of this form have been carefully read and that all the statements made herein are correct to the best of the undersigned's knowledge and belief.

(Address) 100 Elm Street, Riverhead, L. I., N. Y.

(Signature) Katherine Benson
(Designation) Executrix

(Executor/administrator/custodian/ or other person—see instructions on back, "Persons required to file notice")

NOTICE.—Failure to file a required return on Form 706 within 15 months from the date of death may render executors, administrators, and persons in actual or constructive possession of the decedent's property liable for penalties.

Attention must be directed to two items in the above form. Paragraph "1" has two subdivisions. The first, (a), is for use when the notice is being executed by the duly qualified fiduciary of the estate. The second, (b), is for use when the notice is being executed by one in actual or constructive possession of property of the decedent.[19]

The itemization set forth in paragraph "2" of the above form represents the assets comprising the gross estate. The details of the items constituting the gross estate are treated in the next chapter, which may be consulted as an aid in completing the above notice. If the notice is being filed by a person in actual or constructive possession of property of the decedent, an unusual situation, it will necessarily be less complete, containing only information as to assets held by such person. When it is being filed by the fiduciary it may be anticipated that it will be as complete as the information available to the fiduciary. The anticipation is not always realized. Where several persons are required to file the notice, the signature of one executor or administrator is sufficient.[20] In the case of a nonresident not a citizen the notice must be filed by *every* duly qualified executor or administrator.[1]

§ 19. Preliminary Notice; Place of Filing.

If the decedent was a resident of the United States, the preliminary notice must be filed with the District Director in whose district the decedent had his domicile at the date of death. If the decedent was a nonresident (whether a citizen or not a citizen), the notice must be filed with the Director of International Operations, Internal Revenue Service, Washington 25, D. C., or with such other office as the Commissioner may designate.[2]

§ 20. Preliminary Notice; Gross Estate.

Examination of the preliminary notice discloses that it is concerned with obtaining notice of qualification of the fiduciary, the items comprising the gross estate and the names and addresses of the fiduciary and attorney. The most important of these is the second mentioned, since the primary purpose of the notice, is as stated,[3] to advise the Government of the existence of taxable estates. This is also indicated by the fact that almost half of the instructions are devoted to an explanation of property which comprises the gross estate. In the succeeding chapter the subject of the gross estate is considered in detail. As a matter of convenience, however, the official instructions con-

19. See § 17, supra.
20. Reg, § 20.6036–1(b).
1. Note 20, supra.

2. Reg, § 20.6091–1.
3. Reg, § 20.6036–1(a).

tained in the preliminary notice are set forth here. The answers to any questions raised by the instructions will be found in the next chapter.

The gross estate, as defined by section 2031(a) of the Internal Revenue Code, comprises property wherever situated, except real property outside the United States, and includes—

1. Property in which the decedent at the time of his death had any beneficial interest.

2. Interest of surviving spouse, as dower, curtesy, or estate in lieu thereof.

3. Property transferred by the decedent during his life, by trust or otherwise (other than by bona fide sale for an adequate and full consideration in money or money's worth) as follows: (1) Transfers made in contemplation of death are includible only if made within 3 years prior to death; (2) transfers intended to take effect in possession or enjoyment at or after the decedent's death; (3) transfers under which the decedent reserved or retained (in whole or in part) the use, possession, rents, or other income, or enjoyment of the transferred property, for his life, or for a period not ascertainable without reference to his death, or for a period of such duration as to evidence an intention that it should extend to his death; including also the reservation or retention of the use, possession, rents, or other income, the actual enjoyment of which was to await the termination of a transferred precedent interest or estate; (4) transfers under which the decedent retained the right, either alone or in conjunction with another person or persons, to designate who should possess or enjoy the property or the income therefrom; and (5) transfers under which the enjoyment of the transferred property was subject at decedent's death to a change through the exercise, either by the decedent alone or in conjunction with another person or persons, of a power to alter, amend, revoke, or terminate, or such a power was relinquished in contemplation of decedent's death.

4. Annuities received by any beneficiary by reason of surviving the decedent.

5. Property owned *jointly* or in *tenancy by the entirety,* with right of survivorship.

6. Property subject to a general power of appointment, including property with respect to which the decedent exercised or released the power during his lifetime.

21

7. Insurance upon the life of the decedent, including insurance receivable by beneficiaries other than the estate.

These instructions contain a summary of the interests constituting the gross estate, the details of which are found in the statute and the Regulations, and treated hereafter.[4]

§ 21. Preliminary Notice; Lien of Tax.

The discussion of the lien of the tax is reserved for treatment hereinafter.[5] It should be noted, however, that the instructions for the preparation of the preliminary notice contain the advice that unless sooner paid in full, the tax is a lien for 10 years upon the entire gross estate, except such part thereof as is used for payment of charges against the estate and expenses of its administration allowed by any court having jurisdiction.[6]

§ 22. Preliminary Notice; Penalties.

While the statute has many provisions for penalties, the official instructions on the preliminary notice refer to only two. The first states that the penalty for knowingly making any false statement in the notice is a fine not to exceed $1,000, or imprisonment, or both. This is provided for in the 1954 Code[7] as it was in the 1939 Code.[8] The second states that the penalty for failure to file the notice as required is a sum not to exceed $500 and cost of suit. This is also provided for in the 1954 Code[9] as it was in the 1939 Code.[10] It is questionable whether the latter provision has ever been invoked.

§ 23. Preliminary Notice; Delinquency.

The instructions provide that in the event of failure to file the preliminary notice within the time prescribed, a detailed explanation under oath or under the penalties of perjury should accompany the notice when filed.[11] In spite of this statement, in practice, almost any excuse for failure to file in time will suffice. The important thing is that the notice be filed, and the Internal Revenue Service is lenient in the case of late filing of the preliminary notice. *The same thing does not apply to the Estate Tax return,* as we shall see.[12]

---

4. §§ 37 et seq, infra.
5. See §§ 348 et seq, infra.
6. Note 11, supra.
7. IRC, § 7207 (1954 Code).
8. IRC, §§ 894(b)(2), 3793(b) (1939 Code).

9. IRC, § 7269 (1954 Code).
10. IRC, § 894(b)(1) (1939 Code).
11. Instructions on Preliminary Notice.
12. § 34, infra.

§ 24. Preliminary Notice; Nonresident Not a Citizen.

In the case of a nonresident not a citizen of the United States the preliminary notice is filed on Form 705, which while different in form in some respects, is substantially the same as the notice in the estate of a resident. The taxing authorities are primarily interested in the names of the fiduciary and the date and place of qualification, the items comprising the gross estate situated in the United States and the name and address of the fiduciary and attorney for the estate. As in the resident notice there is provision for the information to be furnished either by the duly qualified fiduciary or the person in actual or constructive possession of property of the decedent. It is much more common for the latter to file such notice in the case of a nonresident not a citizen than in the case of a resident. While the former form required the notice to be filed with the District Director at the Custom House, New York, this place of filing has been changed, as noted. It is now filed with the Director of International Operations, Internal Revenue Service, Washington 25, D. C.[13]

These have been discussed previously the time within which the preliminary notice must be filed,[14] estates in which the notice is required to be filed,[15] the persons required to file the same,[16] and the execution of the notice.[17] As noted, in the case of a nonresident not a citizen, the notice must be executed by every duly qualified executor or administrator.[18]

FORM NO. 2

Estate Tax Preliminary Notice; Estate of Nonresident Not a Citizen of the United States

---

(To be filed by executor or person in possession of property— observe instructions on reverse)

Name of decedent   HENRI BOUISSON
Date of death   Jan. 10, 1960   Citizenship (nationality)   French
Place of death   St. Germain en Lais, Paris, France
Residence (domicile) at time of death   100 Rue Robillard, Paris, France
March 1, 1960

13. Reg, § 20.6091–1.
14. §§ 13, 16, supra.
15. § 15, supra.
16. § 17, supra.
17. § 18, supra.
18. Note 20, supra.

DISTRICT DIRECTOR OF INTERNAL REVENUE,

    Baltimore, Maryland.

1. Pursuant to the requirements of sections 6036 and 6018 (a) (2) of the Internal Revenue Code, notice is hereby given that (*fill in (a) or (b) as facts warrant*):

(*a*) The undersigned qualified as execut..../administrat.... of the estate of the above-named decedent in the .... Court at .... on the .... day of ...., 19..

(*b*) The undersigned, on the date of the decedent's death, had actual or constructive possession of property or of an interest in property which constituted part of the gross estate, within the meaning of the estate tax law, situated within the United States, of the decedent named above; or, the undersigned came into actual or constructive possession of such property or of an interest in such property on the 15th day of Jan. 1960. The description and approximate value of such property at the time of death were as follows:

Description	Value
Premises, the Elms, Augusta, Maine	$10,000.00
....	....
....	....

2. To the best of the undersigned's knowledge the *approximate* value at the date of death of the property (including any property not in possession of the undersigned) constituting the part of the gross estate situated in the United States was as follows:

Property beneficially owned by decedent (not classifiable below) $10,560.00

Property held by decedent as *joint tenant* or *tenant by the entirety,* with
    right of survivorship ....

Community property owned by decedent and surviving spouse ....

Annuities ....

Property transferred during life for less than adequate and full considera-
    tion in money or money's worth ....

Property subject to a general power of appointment possessed, exercised or
    released by decedent ....

3. The names and addresses of the legal representatives of the estate and their attorneys, agents, or other representatives, insofar as known to the undersigned, are:

Executor or administrator	Attorneys, agents, or other representatives
In United States Charles Boissevain	Daniel Webster Clay
(Address) 980 Park Avenue, N. Y. C.	80 Broad Street, N. Y.
Outside United States Katherine Bouisson	Mlle. Marcelle Cannes
(Address) 100 Rue Robillard, Paris, France	10 Rue Chatillon, Paris, France

The undersigned HEREBY CERTIFIES that the instructions on the reverse of this form have been carefully read and that all the statements made herein are correct to the best of the undersigned's knowledge and belief. (Address) 980 Park Avenue, N. Y.

(Signature) Charles Boissevain

(Designation) Ancillary Administrator

(Executor/administrator/custodian/or other person—see sec. 3 of instructions)

NOTICE.—Failure to file a required return on Form 706NA or Form 706 within 15 months from the date of death may render executors, administrators, and persons in actual or constructive possession of the decedent's property liable for penalties.

As a matter of convenience the following is the property situated in the United States which must be considered in preparing the notice.

This notice is required only with respect to property having a situs in the United States, i.e., the States, the Territories of Alaska and Hawaii, or the District of Columbia. Property transferred during the decedent's life, and includible in the gross estate, is deemed situated within the United States if such property was so situated either at the time of the transfer or at the time of death.

Except as otherwise provided by treaty, the following rules are applicable in determining whether property is situated in the United States:

(*a*) Real estate and tangible personal property are within the United States if physically located therein.

(*b*) Stocks of corporations organized in or under the laws of the United States constitute property within the United States, irrespective of where the stock certificates are physically located.

(*c*) Other written evidences of intangible property which are treated as being the property itself, such as bonds of a domestic or foreign corporation (but not certificates of stock of a foreign corporation), are property situated in the United States if physically located therein.

(*d*) Intangible personal property, the written evidence of which is *not treated as being the property itself,* such as a simple debt or open account, constitutes property within the United States if consisting of a property right issuing from or enforceable against a resident of the United States or a domestic corporation (public or private).

25

(*e*) Proceeds of insurance on the life of a nonresident alien decedent are deemed situated outside the United States.

(*f*) Moneys deposited with any person carrying on the banking business, by or for a nonresident alien decedent who was not engaged in business in the United States at the time of his death are deemed situated outside the United States.

The United States has entered into treaties relating to the estate tax with certain countries. In the case of a decedent who was a resident of such a country, the situs of property is governed by the rules of situs set forth in the applicable treaty. In such a case the treaty and the regulations issued pursuant thereto should be consulted.

This is a condensation of the statute[19] and the Regulations.[20] The official instructions also set forth the items constituting the gross estate,[1] which are the same as those set forth in the instructions for the preliminary notice of a resident,[2] but in the case of a nonresident alien direct attention to the fact that *if such decedent was not engaged in business in the United States* at the time of his death, the gross estate does not include obligations of the United States issued prior to March 1, 1941.[3] As in the case of residents the gross estate does not include real property situated outside the United States. These instructions similarly are a condensation of the Regulations.[4] The final admonition is that failure to file the Estate Tax return within fifteen months from the date of death may render the executors, administrators and persons in actual or constructive possession of the decedent's property liable for penalties.[5] This would apply only if the gross estate exceeds $2,000.[6]

§ 25. Information Return by Corporation or Transfer Agent.

The Regulations provide that upon notification from the Internal Revenue Service, a corporation (organized or created in the United States) or its transfer agent is required to file a return disclosing the following information pertaining to stocks or bonds registered in the name of a nonresident decedent (regardless of citizenship): (1) the name of the decedent as registered; (2) the date of the decedent's death; (3) the decedent's

19. IRC, §§ 2104, 2105 (1954 Code).
20. Reg. §§ 20.2104–1, 20.2105–1.
1. Official Instructions on Preliminary Notice.
2. See § 20, supra.

3. Note 1, supra.
4. Note 20, supra.
5. Notice, Estate Tax Preliminary Notice.
6. IRC, § 6018(a)(2) (1954 Code).

residence and his place of death; (4) the names and addresses of executors, attorneys, or other representatives of the estate, within and without the United States; and (5) a description of the securities, the number of shares or bonds and the par values thereof.[7] Form 714 is furnished by the Internal Revenue Service for this purpose. The Regulation is promulgated under the authority of the statute.[8]

§ 26. Return; Statute and General Instructions.

The United States Estate Tax Return for a citizen or resident of the United States, and which may also be required in the case of a nonresident not a citizen in an exceptional situation, is a formidable document. It comprises forty pages, almost half of which is devoted to instructions both general and specific. It begins with a statement of the decedent's name, date of death, residence or domicile at the time of death, and his citizenship or nationality at the time of death. Although the computation of the tax is the last thing to be done, it is contained on the first page of the return for convenience in auditing. There then follow general instructions which are particularly valuable to the uninitiated, since they describe the statute and the general nature and description of the tax, when a return is required, where and when it must be filed, payment of the tax, execution of the return, representation of the estate by an attorney or agent, and the penalties in regard to the return. As the instructions point out, the tax is imposed by Chapter 11 of the Internal Revenue Code of 1954. *It is not an inheritance tax.* It is imposed upon the transfer of the *entire taxable estate* and not upon the share received by a particular beneficiary and is determined by taking the value of the gross estate and deducting therefrom the total amount of the deductions authorized by the statute.[9] They further direct attention to the fact that different provisions control the determination of the tax liability of the estates of citizens or residents of the United States and the estates of nonresidents not citizens.[10] The form is numbered "706" and is generally referred to as the 706.

The United States Nonresident Alien Estate Tax Return, designated Form 706NA is considerably less complicated than the above form. It consists of four pages, two of which are

---

7. Reg, § 20.6001–1(d).
8. IRC, § 6001 (1954 Code).

9. Return, Page 2.
10. Note 9, supra.

entirely devoted to instructions. This contains a statement of the decedent's name, date of death, residence or domicile at time of death, citizenship or nationality at time of death, business or occupation, name, title, and address of person filing the return, a series of questions, hereafter discussed,[11] computation of the tax and declaration on the first page.[12] The second page contains two schedules and general information and the balance of the form is devoted to instructions. These instructions are similarly valuable, since they chart the course in the usual estate. It is this form which is used in the great majority of nonresident alien estates, *but it is important to note that it cannot be used,* it being required that the return be made on Form 706 under the following circumstances:

(1) In case the decedent made any transfer during life or possessed, exercised, or released any power of appointment with respect to property situated in the United States, requiring any disclosure or affirmative answer under Schedule G or H of Form 706.

(2) In case of a deduction for charitable, public, and similar gifts and bequests, credit for Federal gift taxes, or credit for tax on prior transfers is claimed.

(3) In case the decedent was a resident of France or a citizen or resident of Greece and a prorated allowance authorized by treaty extends beyond the specific exemption, such as a prorated deduction for a bequest to a foreign charity.[13]

§ 27. Return; Estates for Which Required.

The Federal Estate Tax statute requires that in the case of citizens or residents of the United States a return shall be made in all cases where the gross estate *at the death* of the decedent exceeds $60,000.[14] In the case of nonresidents not citizens of the United States a return is required if that part of the gross estate which is situated in the United States exceeds $2,000.[15]

Form 706 provides that the return must be filed for the estate of every citizen or resident of the United States whose gross estate as defined by the statute exceeded $60,000 in value *at the*

11. §§ 187, 298, infra.

12. Nonresident Alien Estate Tax Return.

13. Additional Instructions for Estates of Nonresidents Not Citizens of the United States, Form 706, p. 39; Instruction No. 2, Form 706NA; Reg, § 20.6018–1(b).

14. IRC, § 6018(a)(1) (1954 Code).

15. IRC, § 6018(a)(2).

date of death.[16] Form 706NA provides that an Estate Tax return must be filed for the estate of a nonresident alien if the part of his gross estate situated in the United States exceeded a value of $2,000 at the date of death.[17] Both Form 706 and the Regulations[18] further note that the value of the gross estate at the date of death governs with respect to the filing of the return regardless of whether the value of the gross estate is, at the executor's election, finally determined as of a date subsequent to the date of death pursuant to the provisions of section 2032 of the Code. For some strange reason the same admonition does not appear on Form 706NA nor in the Regulation[19] with respect to returns of nonresident aliens, although it does appear on the preliminary notice in the case of nonresident aliens.[20]

§ 28. Return; Time and Place for Filing.

The statute provides that the Estate Tax Return shall be filed within fifteen months after the date of the decedent's death.[1] The Regulation provides similarly, unless an extension of time is granted.[2] The due date is the date on or before which the return is required to be filed, i.e. fifteen months after the death of the decedent, or the last day covered by an extension granted by the District Director. Unless an extension of time for filing has been granted, the due date is the day of the fifteenth calendar month after the decedent's death numerically corresponding to the day of the calendar month on which death occurred, except that if there is no numerically corresponding day in such fifteenth month, the last day of the fifteenth month is the due date. For example, if the decedent died on August 31, 1955, the due date is November 30, 1956. When the due date falls on Saturday, Sunday, or a legal holiday, the due date for filing the return is the next succeeding day which is not Saturday, Sunday, or a legal holiday. If the return is placed in the mails it should be posted in ample time to reach the office of the District Director under ordinary handling of the mails, on or before the date on which the return is required to be filed. If the return is made and placed in the mails in due course, properly addressed and postage paid, in ample time to reach the office of the District Director on or before the due date, no penalty will attach should the return

16. Form 706, p. 2.
17. Reg, § 20.6011–2.
18. Reg, § 20.6018–1(a).
19. Reg, § 20.6018–1(b).

20. Instruction No. 1, Form 705.
1. IRC, § 6075(a) (1954 Code).
2. Reg, § 20.6075–1(a).

not actually be received by the District Director until after the due date. If a question may be raised as to whether the return was posted in ample time to reach the office of the District Director on or before the due date, the envelope in which the return was transmitted will be preserved by the District Director and attached to the return.[3] The Administrative Regulations further define timely mailing[4] and time for performance of acts where the last day falls on Saturday, Sunday, or legal holidays.[5] If this appears to be an unduly long Regulation to cover the simple matter of time of filing, we shall see that there is good reason therefor because of the results flowing from late filing or failure to file.[6]

The place for filing the return, if the decedent was a resident of the United States, is with the District Director in whose district the decedent had his domicile at the date of death. If the decedent was a nonresident (whether a citizen or not a citizen), the return must be filed with the Director of International Operations, Internal Revenue Service, Washington 25, D. C.[7] The Regulation is pursuant to the statute.[8] The place indicated for filing on the present nonresident return should be disregarded.

It may be noted that payment of the tax is required to be made at the time and place fixed for filing the return.[9]

§ 29. Return; Who Files.

The statute provides that the return shall be made by the executor.[10] It must be recalled that this term is not used in the sole sense of the fiduciary, but includes any person in actual or constructive possession of property of the decedent. The Regulation provides that the duly qualified executor or administrator shall file the return. If there is more than one executor or administrator, unlike the preliminary notice, the *return* must be made jointly by *all*. If there is no executor or administrator appointed, qualified and acting within the United States, every person in actual or constructive possession of any property of the decedent situated in the United States is constituted an executor for purposes of the tax, and is required to make and file a return.[11]

3. Reg, § 20.6075–1(b).
4. See Reg, § 301.7502.
5. See Reg, § 301.7503.
6. See §§ 34, 35, infra.
7. Reg, § 20.6091–1.

8. IRC, § 6091(b)(3).
9. IRC, § 6151 (1954 Code).
10. IRC, § 6018 (1954 Code).
11. Reg, § 20.6018–2.

§ 30. Return; Execution.

The Regulations treat of the preparation of the return in some detail. After noting the duty of the executor to keep such complete and detailed records of the affairs of the estate as will enable the District Director to determine accurately the amount of the Estate Tax liability[12] they point out the further duty of the executor to furnish copies of any documents in his possession relating to the estate and render any written statement in respect thereto which the District Director may require for the determination of the tax.[13] Other persons are also required to furnish information,[14] as are corporations and transfer agents.[15] The return must be made upon the prescribed form, Form 706 or 706NA, as the case may be, and other forms are provided for.[16] The use of the prescribed forms is made mandatory.[17] The contents of the returns for both citizens or residents and nonresidents not citizens is then particularized, following in general the schedules of the returns.[18] The documents which must accompany the returns are then set forth.[19]

The returns may be obtained from the office of the District Director. In some cases, certain offices insist that the preliminary notice be filed before they will issue copies of the return. Formerly it was required that the return be filed in duplicate, but this is no longer so.

The general instructions on Form 706 are most explicit as to mechanical details, and provide:

This form consists of 40 pages numbered in consecutive order. For convenience in typing carbon copies, the sets as issued may be readily separated and the corresponding sheets matched. When completed, the return must be permanently fastened together with all sheets in proper order. Any suitable type of paper fastener may be utilized for this purpose. Ordinary wire staples are recommended for the return of average size. All pages provided, numbered 1 through 40, must be included.

Write only on one side of each sheet of paper. If there is not sufficient space for all entries under any of the printed schedules, use additional sheets of the same size, and insert in the proper order in the return. All information required as indicated under "General Information" must be supplied in the spaces provided.

12. Reg, § 20.6001–1(a).
13. Reg, § 20.6001–1(b).
14. Reg, § 20.6001–1(c).
15. Reg, § 20.6001–1(d).

16. Reg, § 20.6011–1.
17. Reg, § 20.6011–2.
18. Reg, § 20.6018–3.
19. Reg, § 20.6018–4.

The questions asked under each schedule must be specifically answered, and if the decedent owned no property of any class specified for the schedule, the word "None" should be written across the schedule.

It will be found that the most practical way to deal with the forms is to remove the staples and slit the sheets, which are already serrated to expedite such action, since any attempt to handle the double sheet in typing copies has horrendous results. The execution of the declaration is treated hereafter.[20]

§ 31. Return; Persons Dying Before August 17, 1954.

The return issued at the present time is applicable to estates of decedents dying on or after August 17, 1954, the effective date of the Internal Revenue Code of 1954. As the return indicates, if the decedent died prior to the effective date of the latter statute, Form 706, Revised December 1953 should be used.[1] Any attempt to use the present form for estates of decedents taxable under the 1939 Code would result in much needless confusion because of the many changes which were made in the schedules and the instructions under the 1954 Code.

§ 32. Return; General Information.

Before taking on the preparation of the schedules required to be completed in the return, two pages of general information are required of the person preparing the return. The information required is set forth in some twenty-two questions, in turn subdivided. The final question is not so much a question as an election by the executor as to whether the estate is to be valued as of the date of death or as of the alternate date or dates provided by the statute. The election, now designated "alternate valuation" was designated "optional valuation" under the 1939 Code. It will be noted that these pages, as well as all the pages listing information, have at the bottom a line for the name of the estate.

FORM NO. 3

General Information

1. Address of decedent at time of death (Number, street, city, zone, and State)   1500 Lake Shore Drive, Chicago 10, Illinois

2a. State in which domiciled at time of death   Illinois

---

20. § 330, infra.

1. Title, Form 706, p 1; Title, Form 706NA, p 1.

2b. Year in which this domicile was established   June 8, 1902

3. Date of marriage to surviving spouse   August 31, 1938

4. Domicile at date of marriage to surviving spouse   Chicago, Illinois

5. Citizenship (nationality) at date of death   United States

6a. Place of death   Chicago, Illinois

6b. Cause of death   Cardiac decompensation

6c. Length of last illness   3 months

7. Decedent's physicians

Names	Addresses (Number, street, city, zone, and State)
Dr. Walter Lang	1500 Lake Shore Drive, Chicago, Ill.

8. If decedent was confined in a hospital during his last illness or within 3 years prior to his death, give name and address of hospital   Shore Hospital   Lake Shore Drive, Chicago, Illinois

9a. Date of birth   Sept. 15, 1892.

9b. Place of birth (City and State or country, if other than United States)   Chicago, Illinois

10a. Business or occupation   Fraternal supplies

10b. If retired, state former business or occupation

10c. Business address (Number, street, city, zone, and State)   100 State Street, Chicago, Illinois

11. Marital status at date of death

[x] Married   [ ] Single   [ ] Separated   [ ] Widowed   [ ] Divorced

12a. If widowed, give name of deceased spouse

12b. Date of death   March 15, 1960

13. Number of children   2

14. Heirs, next of kin, devisees, and legatees (If more than five, only the names of the five principal ones are required)

Name	Relationship	Address (Number, street, city, zone, and State)
Katherine Benson	Widow	1500 Lake Shore Drive, Chicago 10, Ill.
George Benson	Brother	84 Paradise Blvd., Los Angeles, Cal.
James Benson	Son	11 Laurel Drive, Tuckahoe, N. Y.

15. Did the decedent die testate?   [x] Yes   [ ] No

16a. Were letters testamentary or of administration granted for this estate?   [x] Yes   [ ] No

16b. Date granted   March 30, 1960

16c. Case No.   P1608–1960

16d. Name of court   Probate Court, Cook County, Ill.

16e. Location of court   Chicago, Ill.

16f. To whom granted?   (Designate whether executor, executrix, administrator, or administratrix.   Explain if different from the person or persons filing return)

Name	Designation	Address (Number, street, city, zone, and State)
Katherine Benson	Executrix	1500 Lake Shore Drive, Chicago 10, Ill.

Estate of WINTHROP BENSON

17a. Did the decedent at date of death own property in any State or country other than that of his last domicile? [ ] Yes [x] No
If "Yes," state place of ancillary probate proceedings
17b. Name of ancillary administrator or executor   None
17c. Address of ancillary administrator or executor (Number, street, city, zone, and State)   None
18a. Did the decedent at the time of his death have a safe deposit box held either alone or in the joint names of himself and another?
[x] Yes   [ ] No
If "Yes," state location
Fiduciary Trust Company, Chicago, Illinois
18b. If held jointly, give the name of the joint depositor   Katherine Benson
18c. Relationship of joint depositor to decedent   Widow
18d. If the decedent had a safe deposit box at the time of his death, indicate under what schedules in this return the contents are listed B, C, E and F
18e. If any of the contents of the safe deposit box are omitted from the schedules, explain why   None
19. Did the undersigned person or persons filing return make diligent and careful search for property of every kind left by the decedent? [x] Yes   [ ] No
20. Did the same undersigned make diligent and careful search for information as to any transfers of the value of $5,000 or more made by the decedent during his lifetime without an adequate and full consideration in money or money's worth?   [x] Yes [ ] No
21. Did the same undersigned make diligent and careful search for the existence of any trusts created by the decedent during his lifetime or any trusts created by other persons under which the decedent possessed any power, beneficial interest, or trusteeship?
[x] Yes   [ ] No
22a. Name of attorney representing estate, if any   Daniel Webster Clay
22b. Address (Number, street, city, zone, and State) 250 W. Madison Street, Chicago 2, Ill.
22c. Telephone No.   MA 2–0500

ALTERNATE VALUATION

(These instructions apply only if alternate valuation is elected.
For further information on this subject, see
General Instructions on page 4)

23. An election to have the gross estate of the decedent valued as of the alternate date or dates is made by entering a check mark in the box set forth below.
[x] The executor elects to have the gross estate of this decedent valued

                    [Harris]

in accordance with values as of a date or dates subsequent to the decedent's death as authorized by section 2032 of the Code.

The election cannot be exercised unless it is shown upon the return, Form 706, and the return is filed within 15 months after the decedent's death or within the period for filing the return as extended by the District Director.

The due date for the filing of the return is the day of the 15th calendar month after the decedent's death numerically corresponding to the day of the calendar month in which death occurred, except that, if there is no numerically corresponding day in such 15th month, the last day of such 15th month is the due date. For example, if the decedent died on August 31, 1954, the due date is November 30, 1955. If placed in the mails the return must be posted in ample time to reach the District Director's office, under ordinary handling of the mails, on or before the date on which the return is required to be filed.

Estate of WINTHROP BENSON

§ 33. Return; Extension of Time.

The statute provides that the Secretary of the Treasury or his delegate may grant a reasonable extension of time for filing any return, declaration, statement, or other document required by the statute or regulations. Except in the case of taxpayers who are abroad, no such extension shall be for more than six months.[2]

The Regulation provides that in case it is impossible or not practicable for the executor to file a reasonably complete return within fifteen months from the date of death, the District Director may, *upon a showing of good and sufficient cause,* grant a reasonable extension of time for filing the return. Unless the executor is abroad, the extension may not be for more than six months from the date required for filing, that is, twenty-one months from the date of the decedent's death. The extension may, of course, be for a lesser period of time.[3]

The application for an extension of time for filing the return should be addressed to the District Director for the district in which the return is to be filed, and must contain a *full recital of the causes for the delay.* It must be made before the expiration of the time within which the return otherwise must be filed. It should, where possible, be made sufficiently early to permit the District Director to consider the matter and reply before what otherwise would be the due date of the return.[4]

2. IRC, § 6081(a) (1954 Code).   4. Reg, § 20.6081–1(b).
3. Reg, § 20.6081–1(a).

It should be noted that while an extension of time will permit the amendment of the return within the extension period so as to elect the alternate valuation,[5] it does not extend the time for payment of the tax.[6]

§ 34. Return; Failure to File; Delinquency.

The failure to file the Estate Tax return entails a number of penalties. If the failure is a willful one the person required to make the return is subject to fine and imprisonment.[7] He is also personally liable to civil suit by the United States.[8] These, however, are unusual situations. More common are the cases of delinquency, rather than willful failure to file. Such delinquency has a number of consequences. The first is that in case of failure to file a return on the date prescribed therefor, unless it be shown that such failure is due to reasonable cause and not due to willful neglect, there shall be added to the amount required to be shown on such tax return 5% of the amount of such tax if the failure is for not more than one month, with an additional 5% for each additional month or fraction thereof during which such failure continues, not exceeding 25% in the aggregate. The addition to the tax is computed upon the net amount of the tax remaining unpaid.[9] The addition so incurred is treated as part of the tax.[10]

The next result of failure to file the return in time is that the election for alternate valuation is lost.[11] Finally the limitations on assessment and collection of the tax do not apply in the case of failure to file the return.[12]

While, as we have indicated, the Internal Revenue Service is lenient in the case of late filing of the preliminary notice, it adheres strictly to the statute and the Regulation in the case of delinquency in the filing of the Estate Tax Return.[13] The preliminary notice does not constitute the filing of a return so as to avoid the penalty.[14]

5. Reg, § 20.6081–1(c); Rev Rul 54–445, 1954–2 CB 301.

6. Reg, § 20.6081–1(c).

7. IRC, § 7203 (1954 Code).

8. IRC, § 7269 (1954 Code).

9. IRC, § 6651 (1954 Code); Reg, § 301.6651–1.

10. IRC, § 6659 (1954 Code); Reg, § 301.6659–1.

11. Downe, 2 TC 967 (1943).

12. IRC, § 6501(C)(3) (1954 Code).

13. See Flinchbaugh, 1 TC 653 (1942); Szilagye, 9 TC 853 (1947); Werbelovsky, 9 TC 689 (1947); Wilson, 2 TC 1059 (1943); McCue, 5 TCM 141 (1945); Curie, 4 TC 1175 (1945); Reinhold, 7 TCM 697 (1946); Cronin, 7 TC 1403 (1946).

14. Goldstein, 6 TCM 899 (1946).

A taxpayer who wishes to avoid the addition to the tax for failure to file a tax return must make an affirmative showing of all facts alleged as a reasonable cause for his failure to file such return on time in the form of a written statement containing a declaration that it is made under penalties of perjury. Such statement should be filed with the District Director with whom the return is required to be filed. If the District Director determines that the delinquency was due to a reasonable cause and not to willful neglect, the addition to the tax will not be assessed. If the taxpayer exercised ordinary business care and prudence and was nevertheless unable to file the return within the prescribed time, then the delay is due to a reasonable cause.[15]

Failure to file in reliance on an attorney has usually been held to be reasonable cause,[16] but not always.[17] Estoppel has been invoked against the Commissioner.[18] Each case must necessarily depend upon its own facts. When the return is not filed within the prescribed time, the statement should, as the Regulation provides, make an affirmative showing of all *facts* alleged as a reasonable cause for the delay. A perfunctory statement will not suffice. Being too busy or mistakenly believing that the return had been filed does not constitute reasonable cause.[19]

§ 35. Return; Incomplete Return.

If the executor is unable to make a complete return as to any part of the gross estate of the decedent, he shall include in his return a description of such part and the name of every person holding a legal or beneficial interest therein. Upon notice from the Secretary of the Treasury or his delegate, such person shall in like manner make a return as to such part of the gross estate.[20] This is intended to cover cases where the property of the decedent may never come into the possession of the executor, such as insurance, joint bank accounts and the like. It is a rarity for the executor to be unable to obtain the necessary information for the purpose of the return.

§ 36. Return; Supplemental Documents.

The Federal Estate Tax statute requires every person liable

15. Reg, § 301.6651–1(a)(3).

16. Rohmer, 21 TC 1099 (1954); Fisk v Comm. 203 F2d 358 (CA6) (1953); Reichers, 9 TCM 403 (1947); McColgan, 10 BTA 958 (1928).

17. Cronin, note 13, supra.

18. Stockstrom v Comm. 190 F2d 283 (CA DC) (1951).

19. Reinhold, note 13, supra.

20. IRC, § 6018(b) (1954 Code); Reg, § 20.6018–2.

for the tax imposed to keep such records, render such statements, make such returns and comply with such rules and regulations as the Secretary of the Treasury or his delegate may from time to time prescribe.[1] Unlike the 1939 Code,[2] the 1954 Code contains no provision for the filing of supplemental data. The Regulation does, however, provide in detail for the documents to accompany the return. It provides:

(a) All documents and vouchers used in preparing the return should be retained by the executor until the expiration of the period of limitations for assessment of the tax so as to be available for inspection whenever required.

(b) A *certified* copy of the will, if the decedent died testate, must be submitted with the return, together with such other documents as are required in Form 706 and in the applicable sections of the Regulations.

(c) There may also be filed copies of any documents which the executor may desire to submit in explanation of the return.

(d) In the case of an estate of a *nonresident citizen,* the executor should also file the following documents with the return:

(1) a copy of any inventory of property and the schedule of liabilities, claims against the estate and expenses of administration filed with the foreign court; and

(2) a copy of any return filed under any applicable foreign inheritance, estate, legacy or succession tax act, *certified* by a proper official of the foreign tax department.

(e) In the case of an estate of a *nonresident not a citizen,* the executor must also file with the return, *but only if deductions are claimed,* a copy of the inventory of property filed under the foreign death duty act; or if no such inventory was filed, a *certified copy* of the inventory filed with the foreign court of probate jurisdiction.

(f) For every policy of life insurance listed on the return, the executor must procure a statement, on *Form 712,* by the company issuing the policy and file it with the return.

(g) If pursuant to section 2032, the executor elects to have the estate valued at a date or dates subsequent to the time of the decedent's death, the executor should file with the return evidence in support of any statements made by him in the return as to distributions, sales, exchanges, or other dispositions of property during the one year period which followed the de-

1. IRC, § 6001 (1954 Code).   2. IRC, § 821(a)(1) (1939 Code).

cedent's death. If the court having jurisdiction over the estate makes an order or decree of distribution during that period, a *certified* copy thereof may be submitted as part of the evidence. The District Director may require the submission of such additional evidence as is deemed necessary.

(h) In any case where a transfer, by trust or otherwise, was made by a written instrument, a copy thereof should be filed with the return if

(1) the property is included in the gross estate, or

(2) the executor has made a disclosure of the transfer on the return but has not included its value in the gross estate in the belief that it is not includible. If the written instrument is of public record, the copy should be *certified,* or if it is not of record, the copy should be *verified.* If the decedent was a *nonresident not a citizen* at the time of his death, the copy may be either certified or verified.

(i) If the executor contends that the value of property transferred by the decedent within a period of three years ending with the date of the decedent's death should not be included in the gross estate because he considers that the transfer was not made in contemplation of death, he should file with the return

(1) a copy of the death certificate, and

(2) a statement, containing a declaration that it is made under the penalties of perjury, of all the material facts and circumstances, including those directly or indirectly indicating the decedent's motive in making the transfer and his mental and physical condition at the time. However, this data need not be furnished with respect to transfers of less than $1,000 in value unless requested by the District Director.[3]

The above itemization of documents which may be required to accompany the return may be used as a check list. Many of these will be discussed at greater length hereafter in applicable situations. Since many tax cases are won or lost depending upon the thoroughness with which they are prepared, the subject of necessary evidence and the documents in support thereof is of vital importance. As a matter of economy of effort, it is usual in preparing the state tax return to prepare a sufficient number of copies of affidavits and exhibits so that they will be available for the Federal return.

3. Reg, § 20.6018-4.

CHAPTER 2

GROSS ESTATE

§ 37. Scope of Chapter.

In the preceding chapter we have been introduced to the
Federal Estate Tax. All which has been done has been in preparation for presenting the facts and figures upon which the amount
of tax ultimately payable will be determined. The logical place
for the beginning of that task is the schedules in which are
enumerated the assets of the decedent, the starting point for determination of the tax. That is the gross estate. The statute
in that respect begins by stating that "the value of the gross
estate shall include",[1] and then proceeds to enumerate the property so included. We shall, therefore, treat generally of the
subject of valuation, and then discuss each of the items of the
gross estate, together with the method of enumeration and valuation of particular assets.

There are two subjects which require special consideration,
since they are found in the Federal Estate Tax statute and not
generally requiring consideration in state estate taxation. These
are community property and alternate valuation.

1. IRC, § 2033 (1954 Code).

§ 38. Property Subject to Tax.

In the consideration of the Federal Estate Tax, state lines have no effect. Under that statute the value of the gross estate includes the value of all property (*except real property situated outside of the United States*) to the extent of the interest therein of the decedent at the time of his death.[2] This is an inclusive definition, since with the exception of real property situated outside of the United States, it includes *all property* if the decedent had an *interest therein,* and provided he had that interest at the *time of his death*. As we shall see, such interest need not be a property interest in the usual sense. Simple as the statute, which is substantially similar to previous versions, appears, the meaning of it has been the subject of much litigation.

It is also provided that the value of the gross estate of the decedent shall be determined by including to the extent provided for in the statute, the value at the time of his death of all property, real or personal, tangible or intangible, wherever situated, except real property situated outside of the United States.[3]

The Regulation provides further explanation of property in which the decedent had an interest.[4] Such property will be found to include not only usual assets of a decedent such as real estate, stocks and bonds, business interests, mortgages, notes, cash in bank, personal effects and property, but also dower, curtesy, certain lifetime transfers, annuities, joint property, powers of appointment and insurance, each of which will be severally treated hereafter.

§ 39. Valuation; Fair Market Value.

The Estate Tax statute, with the exception of unlisted stocks and securities,[5] states no method for the valuation of the gross estate, merely providing that the value of the gross estate is includible as of the date of death.[6] The Regulation, however, provides that in the valuation of property in general, the value of every item of property includible in a decedent's gross estate is its *fair market value* at the time of his death, except that if the alternate valuation is elected, it is the fair market value at the latter date, as adjusted. The fair market value is the price at which the property would change hands between a willing

2. Note 1, supra.
3. IRC, § 2031(a) (1954 Code).
4. Reg, § 20.2033–1.

5. IRC, § 2031(b) (1954 Code).
6. Note 3, supra.

buyer and a willing seller, neither being under any compulsion
to buy or to sell and both having reasonable knowledge of relevant facts. It is not to be determined by a forced sales price.
The value is generally to be determined by ascertaining as a basis
the fair market value as of the applicable valuation date of each
unit of the property. All relevant facts and elements of value
shall be considered in every case.[7]

This is merely a statement of the rules generally applicable to
valuation. The value furnished should be fair and reasonable.[8]
But it must be remembered that what is market value is a question of fact.[9] The rules laid down by the Internal Revenue Service are not formulae, but elements which furnish a basis for
arriving at a fair valuation. Valuation of particular assets are
dealt with at length in the Regulations and will be discussed hereafter in connection with each of such items of property. A word
of advice is in order. Many of the disagreements as to value are
adjusted by compromise in conference. Placing absurdly low
values on assets is unlikely to receive a reasonable response from
the agent, now called examiner, auditing the return. Common
sense dictates that values submitted be not unreasonable.

§ 40. Valuation; Alternate; Generally.

Since the normal date for valuation of the property of a decedent under inheritance tax statutes is the date of death, when
there is a depression, the tax on the estate of a decedent who died
before the crash is likely to exceed the amount which can be
realized from the assets of the estate at the time of payment of
the tax. This was the case after 1929. Because of the unfair-
ness of such situations, the then statute[10] was amended[11] in 1935
to grant to the executor an election to value the property of the
decedent either as of the date of death, or as of a date one year
after the decedent's death. This was known as the optional valuation and was carried over into the 1939 Code.[12] The 1954 Code,
while re-wording the statute, and changing the name from "optional" valuation to "alternate" valuation, made no substantive
change in the law.[13]

The value of the gross estate may be determined, *if the ex-*

7. Reg, § 20.2031–1(b).
8. Hunt v Comm, 12 BTA 396 (1928).
9. Minnesota Rate Cases, 230 US 352, 57 L ed 1511, 33 S Ct 729 (1912).
10. § 302, Rev Act of 1926.
11. § 202(a), Rev Act of 1935.
12. IRC, § 811(j) (1939 Code).
13. IRC, § 2032 (1954 Code).

ecutor so elects, by valuing all the property included in the gross estate as follows:

(1) *In the case of property distributed, sold, exchanged, or otherwise disposed of, within one year* after the decedent's death such property shall be valued *as of the date of distribution, sale, exchange or other disposition.*

(2) In the case of property *not distributed, sold, exchanged or otherwise disposed of, within one year* after the decedent's death such property shall be valued *as of the date one year after* the decedent's death.

(3) Any *interest or estate* which is *affected by mere lapse of time* shall be included at its *value as of the time of death* (instead of the later date) *with adjustment* for any difference in its value as of the later date not due to mere lapse of time.[14]

As the Regulation states, it is the purpose of the statute to permit a reduction in the amount of tax that would otherwise be payable if the gross estate has suffered a shrinkage in its aggregate value in the year following the decedent's death.[15] But while that is stated to be its purpose, there is nothing in the statute to prevent an election to value the property as of the alternate date.[16] This may be desirable for the purpose of acquiring a higher income tax cost basis, even though it results in a larger estate tax. But it may not be used for this purpose unless the gross estate is $60,000 or more.[17]

It will be noted that the statute takes a practical and sensible approach to the matter. If property is disposed of within a year of the decedent's death, the value at which it was so disposed of is the best evidence of its value, and therefore, that value is taken. If it has not been disposed of, an arbitrary date, one year after the date of death is selected. If it is an asset, such as a remainder in the estate of another, the decrease in value due to lapse of time is not the decrease or shrinkage the statute was intended to relieve and is not, therefore, considered. This is a fair and reasonable rule.

The operation of the statute is reserved for treatment in the chapter devoted to the subject of computation of the tax.[18]

The statute further provides special rules with respect to deductions when the alternate valuation date is elected.[19] These

14. IRC, § 2032(a) (1954 Code).
15. Reg § 20.2032–1(b)(1).
16. Rev Rul 55–333, 1955–1 CB 449.
71. Rev Rul 56–60, 1956–1 CB 443.
18. §§ 260 et seq, infra.
19. IRC, § 2032(b) (1954 Code).

apply to deductions and are treated hereafter in the chapter devoted to the taxable estate. They are discussed in the sections discussing losses,[20] deductions in the estates of nonresidents not citizens,[1] and the marital[2] and charitable[3] deductions.

At this point there must be emphasized the fact that the election provided for in the statute must be exercised by the executor on his return if filed within the time prescribed by law or before the expiration of any extension of time granted pursuant to law for the filing of the return.[4] The Regulation points out that if the alternate valuation method is to be used, the executor must so elect on the Estate Tax return, filed within 15 months from the date of the decedent's death, or within the period of any extension of time granted by the District Director.[5] The *election* may be *made or revoked in an amended return* filed within such time, but it *cannot be made or revoked after the expiration of such time.* If the election is made, it *applies to all the property* included in the gross estate and cannot be applied to only a portion of the property.[6] The Regulation is a condensation of the case law and Revenue Rulings.[7]

It must also be noted that the alternate valuation method *must be elected* and is not automatic.[8] It is, of course, a condition precedent to the exercise of the election that the property constituting the gross estate be determined.

§ 41. Community Property; Generally.

Until the enactment of the Revenue Act of 1942 the statute was silent as to community property, but as the result of case law, half of the community property was taxed in the estate of the spouse first dying, with certain exceptions, under the general provisions of the statute.[9] The revenue Act of 1942 amended the 1939 Code so as to include in the gross estate the entire value of the community property, except to the extent that it could be shown that the property had been received as compensation for personal services actually rendered, or derived

20. § 221, infra.
1. § 258, infra.
2. § 244, infra.
3. § 252, infra.
4. IRC, § 2032(c) (1954 Code).
5. See § 33, supra.
6. Reg, § 20.2032–1(b)(2).
7. ET 14, 1940–1 CB 221; Trust Co. of

Ga. v Allen, 164 F2d 438 (CCA 5) (1947); Rev Rul 54–445, 1954–2 CB 301; Flinchbaugh, 1 TC 653 (1952); Downe, 2 TC 967 (1943); Doriss, 3 TC 219 (1944).
8. Note 15, supra.
9. IRC, § 811(a) (1939 Code).

originally from such compensation, or from separate property of the surviving spouse.[10] The Revenue Act of 1948, whose purpose was to extend the tax advantage which taxpayers in community property states enjoyed, to the citizens of non-community property states, introduced the concept of the marital deduction, repealed the provisions for inclusion of community property interests in the gross estate, as to persons dying after December 31, 1947,[11] and thus restored the rule in effect prior to the 1942 Act. The result was that as to persons dying on and after January 1, 1948, one half of the community property was generally includible in the gross estate. The 1954 Code made no change in this respect. There are special rules for the computation of the marital deduction in the case of community property which are treated hereafter.[12]

At the present time eight states[13] have community property laws. Prior to the Revenue Act of 1948 five others[14] and Hawaii adopted such laws to afford their citizens its tax advantages. All except Pennsylvania repealed their laws after 1948 and the Pennsylvania statute was declared unconstitutional.[15]

In considering the estates of residents of community property law states it must be borne in mind that there may be community property, separate property, and community property which was converted into separate property after January 1, 1943. In California, a determining date is July 28, 1927. Different taxability results, depending upon which kind of property the decedent had an interest in at the time of his death. Insofar as separate property is concerned it is treated in the same way as property in which decedents, residents of noncommunity property states, had an interest at the time of death. The Estate Tax statute includes such separate property in its entirety in the gross estate of its owner, in any case where the same property would be included in the estate of a citizen of a non-community property state. The marital deduction is similarly available.

The *general* theory of community property is that all property acquired and the income and the increase thereof, or exchanges

---

10. IRC, § 811(e)(2) (1939 Code).
11. Rev Act of 1948, § 351.
12. § 285, infra.
13. Arizona, California, Idaho, Louisiana, Nevada, New Mexico, Texas, Washington.

14. Michigan, Nebraska, Oklahoma, Oregon, Pennsylvania.
15. Wilcox v Penn Mutual Life Ins. Co. 357 Pa 581, 55 A2d 521 (1947).

during the marriage, is community property, and to be managed by the husband pursuant to the particular statute, which varies from state to state. Each spouse has the right to dispose by will of his or her interest. But there are differences between states. Each spouse may have separate property, which consists of property owned by either prior to the marriage and property acquired during the marriage by gift, descent, or devise, together with the income, increases and exchanges. In some states the income from separate property is considered community property.

The fact that the decedent was a resident of a non-community property state does not foreclose the possibility of his owning community property. Thus either by agreement,[16] or residence in a foreign country,[17] or a community property state, or the purchase of realty in such state,[18] community property laws may apply.

It will be seen from the foregoing that community property requires consideration, since it may arise in connection with various types of assets. It will be adverted to as necessary hereafter.

§ 42. Preparation of Schedules; Generally.

The Federal Estate Tax Return, Form 706, contains nine separate schedules for listing the items making up the gross estate. The admonition of the Regulation[19] that the instructions on the return should be carefully followed may well be heeded. Estate Tax Examiners are human beings, whatever one may think to the contrary of some, and burdened with heavy case loads. When the schedules are carefully prepared, all necessary information and documents furnished, and values or claims substantiated by affidavits and documentary proof, his digestive processes are considerably improved. His approach to preparing his report is different than if the schedules are carelessly prepared, and much needed information is not available at once. He must then do a double job of collating a list of the information or documents required and advising the attorney to that effect. Where he has discretion, he is unlikely to exercise it favorably in the latter case. *Many Estate Tax cases are lost because of the*

16. See Rodiek v Helvering, 87 F2d 328 (CCA 2) (1937).

17. Comm v Cadwallader, 127 F2d 547 (CCA 9) (1942).

18. Rev Rul 55–461, IRB 1955–2 CB 608.

19. Reg, § 20.6018–3(a).

failure to prepare schedules properly so as to substantiate claims or values. Statements that the decedent had only a half interest in joint property, that a transfer was not made in contemplation of death, that a debt due is not worth its face value, or that property found in the decedent's safe deposit vault is the property of another, are worthless without carefully prepared supporting proof.

The general instructions on the return advise that the *items should be numbered* under every schedule and a *separate enumeration* should be used for *each schedule.* The *total* for each schedule should be shown *at the bottom of the schedule. The total should not be carried forward from one schedule to another,* but the total or totals for each schedule should be entered under the Recapitulation, Schedule O.

For every item of principal, *any income accrued* thereon at the date of the decedent's death must be *separately entered* under the column headed "Value at date of death"; and if the alternate valuation is adopted, any includible income with respect to each item of principal, as explained thereafter, must be separately entered under the column headed "Alternate value."

The information indicated by the columns headed *"Subsequent valuation date"* and *"Alternate value" should not be shown* unless the executor adopts the alternate valuation. If such alternate valuation is not adopted, the space in the columns headed "Subsequent valuation date" and "Alternate value" may be utilized for descriptive matter, as indicated in the example shown under the instructions for Schedule A. Similar information should be omitted in the space provided therefor under the Recapitulation, Schedule O, if the alternate valuation is not adopted.[20]

While both the instructions[1] and the Regulation[2] indicate that a return which does not contain all the information required will not be considered the filing of a complete return as required by the statute, it would only be so held if the return was so incomplete as to amount to fraudulent misrepresentation and concealment.[3] But, as we have noted, filing a properly prepared return has advantages other than legal.

20. General Instruction, Form 706.
1. Note 20, supra.

2. Reg, § 20.6011–2.
3. See Wilson, 2 TC 1059 (1943).

§ 43. Schedule A; Real Estate; What Included.

Since real estate situated in the United States is property in which the decedent has an interest, it is within the meaning of the statute includible in the gross estate.[4]

The Regulation provides that the gross estate of a decedent who was a citizen or resident of the United States at the time of his death, includes the value of all property, whether real or personal, beneficially owned by the decedent at the time of his death, *except* real property situated outside of the United States. Real property situated in the United States is included whether it came into the possession and control of the executor or administrator or passed directly to heirs or devisees.[5] The same rule applies in the case of a nonresident not a citizen of the United States.[6] Ordinarily there is no question about the taxability of such real estate if it stands solely in the name of the decedent.[7] In such cases parol evidence has been held inadmissible to raise a constructive trust.[8] Where the property was acquired in the wife's name and subsequently transferred into the husband's name and at all times controlled by him, it was held his property and includible in his gross estate.[9] Mere execution and recording of a deed, without a completed gift, has the same result.[10] An interest in real property which ceases on the death of the decedent is not includible.[11] Real estate within the meaning of the statute has been held to include, crops growing thereon,[12] oil producing properties, mineral rights and royalties, as well as fixtures and equipment affixed to the ground and used for the production of oil, which under state law was deemed real property,[13] a leasehold exchangeable for a 999 year interest,[14] and Cuban "hipotecas".[15] In the latter two cases, however, the property was not includible because it was situated outside of the United States.

Taxable real estate is basically controlled by the law of the state in which the decedent had his domicile. It is the general rule that findings of state courts of the decedent's ownership, in the absence of fraud, collusion or a determination not on the

4. IRC, §§ 2031, 2033 (1954 Code).
5. Reg, § 20.2033–1(a).
6. Reg, § 20.2103–1.
7. Montedonico, 12 BTA 572 (1928).
8. Elliott, 23 BTA 354 (1931).
9. Murphy, 16 BTA 1351 (1929).
10. Mortimer, 17 TC 579 (1951).

11. Field, 22 BTA 915 (1931).
12. Peebles, 5 BTA 386 (1926); but see Martin v US, 52–1 USTC ¶ 10,844.
13. Umpsted v US, 35–1 USTC ¶ 9130.
14. De Perigny, 9 TC 782 (1947).
15. Fair v Comm, 91 F2d 218 (CCA 3) (1937).

merits in an adversary proceeding, will be binding in tax proceedings.[16] Prior to the 1926 Act, from which the present statute derives, property was only includible in the gross estate to the extent to which it was subject under state law to the payment of charges and the expenses of administration of the decedent's estate. Many cases decided under the prior statutes on the question of includibility or nonincludibility are today only of historical interest.[17]

As noted,[18] prior to 1942 community property was included to the extent of one half, in the estate of the spouse first dying. The law was returned to that status in 1948 and continues thus to date.

Where the decedent has conveyed the real estate prior to his death bona fide and for a full consideration, it is not includible in his gross estate.[19] This usually depends upon a contract[20] based on a fair and full consideration.[1] If the consideration is not a full consideration in money or money's worth, the real estate is includible in the gross estate.[2] Whether title actually vested in another, prior to the death of the decedent, is important in the determination of includibility.[3] If it is clearly the property of another, it should not be included in the decedent's gross estate.[4]

Whether property be real estate or other property, if the decedent transferred it prior to his death as a *completed gift,* and the transfer was not in contemplation of death or intended to take effect at death, it will not be includible in his gross estate.[5]

16. Sharp v Comm, 303 US 624, 32 L Ed 1087, 58 S Ct 748 (1938); Dysart v US, 95 F2d 652 (CCA 8) (1938); Helvering v Rhodes, 117 F2d 509 (CCA 8) (1941); Comm v Childs, 147 F2d 368 (CCA 3) (1945); Security First Nat Bank, 38 BTA 425 (1938).

17. See Continental Illinois Bank & Tr. Co. 65 F2d 506 (CCA 7) (1933); Tait v Dante, 78 F2d 303 (CCA 4) (1935); First Trust Co. of Omaha v Allen, 60 F2d 812 (CCA 8) (1932); Bretzfelder v Comm, 86 F2d 713 (CCA 2 (1936); note 13, supra; Ballard v Helburn, 9 F Supp 812 (1935); Bishop Trust Co. v US, 38–1 USTC ¶ 9271; Safe Deposit & Trust Co. v Tait, 54 F2d 387 (1932); Crooks v Harrelson, 282 US 55,

75 L ed 156, 51 S Ct 49 (1930); US v Willcox, 73 F2d 781 (CCA 4) (1934); McFadden v US, 10 F Supp 286 (1935); 13 F Supp 766 (1936).

18. § 41, supra.

19. Beeler v Motter, 33 F2d 788 (1929).

20. Lincoln v US, 65 Ct Cls 198.

1. Montague, 23 BTA 800 (1931).

2. Sheets v Comm, 95 F2d 727 (CCA 8) (1938).

3. Williams, 25 BTA 1078 (1932).

4. MacKenzie, 8 BTA 740 (1927).

5. Owen v Comm, 53 F2d 329 (CCA 9) (1932); Rose v Comm, 65 F2d 616 (CCA 6) (1933); Black v US, 68 F Supp 74 (1946); Norris v US, 7 F Supp 415 (1943); True v US, 51 F Supp

As to property in the name of the decedent which is claimed to belong to another, the burden of proof is on the one so contending.[6]

§ 44. Schedule A; Real Estate; Description.

The Regulation provides that a legal description should be given of each parcel of real estate, and, if located in a city, the name of the street and number, its area, and, if improved, a short statement of the character of the improvements.[7] It is not necessary that a description by metes and bounds be given, because as the instructions point out, real estate should be so described and identified that upon investigation by an Internal Revenue officer it may be readily located for inspection and valuation. The instructions go further than the Regulation and direct that for city or town property the street and number, ward, subdivision, block and lot, etc., be furnished, and for rural property the township, range, landmarks, etc.[8]

Although the Regulation does not refer to rent accrued and unpaid on real property at the date of death, the example in the instructions contains such item, which is correct, since such item is an asset of the decedent at the date of death. But rent accruing after the date of death is not includible.[9]

720 (1943); Schwartz, 9 TC 229 (1947); Miller, 40 BTA 138 (1939); Hartley, 3 TCM 3 (1944); Gaffney, 36 BTA 610 (1937); City Bank Farmers Trust Co. 23 BTA 663 (1931); Foster, 13 BTA 496 (1928); Blodgett, 18 BTA 1050 (1929).

6. Emery, 21 BTA 1038 (1931); McRae, 30 BTA 1087 (1934).
7. Reg, § 20.6018-3(c)(1).
8. Instructions, Schedule A, Form 706.
9. Saks v Higgins, 312 US 443, 85 L Ed 940, 61 S Ct 631, revg 111 F2d 78 (CCA 2), affg 29 F Supp 996 (1940).

FORM NO. 4

Schedule A; Real Estate

Did the decedent, at the time of his death, own any real estate in the United States? [x] Yes [ ] No

(Where the alternate valuation is not adopted; date of death, January 1, 1955)

Item No.	Description	Subsequent valuation date	Alternate value	Value at date of death
1	House and lot, 1921 William Street NW., Washington, D. C. (lot 6, square 481). Rent of $900 due at end of each quarter, February 1, May 1, August 1, and November 1. Value based on appraisal, copy of which is attached			$36,000
	Rent due on item 1 for quarter ending November 1, 1954, but not collected at date of death			900
	Rent accrued on item 1 for November and December 1954			600
2	House and lot, 304 Jefferson Street, Alexandria, Va. (lot 18, square 40). Rent of $100 payable monthly. Value based on appraisal, copy of which is attached			12,000
	Rent due on item 2 for December 1954, but not collected at date of death			100

(Where the alternate valuation is adopted; date of death, January 1, 1955)

Item No.	Description	Subsequent valuation date	Alternate value	Value at date of death
1	House and lot, 1921 William Street NW., Washington, D. C. (lot 6, square 481). Rent of $900 due at end of each quarter, February 1, May 1, August 1, and November 1. Value based on appraisal, copy of which is attached. Not disposed of within year following death	1/1/56	$30,000	$36,000
	Rent due on item 1 for quarter ending November 1, 1954, but not collected until February 1, 1955	2/1/55	900	900
	Rent accrued on item 1 for November and December 1954, collected on February 1, 1955	2/1/55	600	600
2	House and lot, 304 Jefferson Street, Alexandria, Va. (lot 18, square 40). Rent of $100 payable monthly. Value based on appraisal, copy of which is attached. Property exchanged for farm on December 1, 1955 ...	12/1/55	10,000	12,000
	Rent due on item 2 for December 1, 1954, but not collected until February 1, 1955	2/1/55	100	100
	TOTAL (also enter under the Recapitulation, Schedule O)		$41,600	$49,600

(If more space is needed, insert additional sheets of same size)

Estate of WINTHROP BENSON

§ 45. Schedule A; Real Estate; Subject to Mortgage.

In reporting real estate owned by the decedent, which was subject to a mortgage for which the estate was liable at the date of his death, it is not the equity value which is returned in Schedule A, *but the full value, undiminished by the mortgage.* The amount of the mortgage is allowed as a deduction.[10] If the decedent's estate *is not so liable,* only the value of the equity of redemption (or value of the property, less the mortgage or indebtedness) need be returned as part of the value of the gross estate.[11] Although the Regulation is entitled "Deduction for unpaid mortgages", it applies not only to mortgages but to any other indebtedness in respect of the property.[12] The instructions expand on this and explain that by the estate being liable is meant that the indebtedness is enforceable against other property of the estate not subject to such mortgage, or if the decedent was personally liable therefor.[13] Both the Regulation and the instructions point out that no deduction is allowable for mortgages on real property situated outside the United States, since such property is not includible in the gross estate.[14]

It will be noted that it is not mandatory that the equity value be reported in Schedule A where the estate is not liable for the mortgage. The usual practice, whether or not the estate is liable, is to report the full value in Schedule A and take the deduction for the mortgage in Schedule K. It is easier to do so in states which require reporting in this manner, and there is then no need for changing the schedules.

10. Reg, § 20.2053–7.
11. Note 10, supra.
12. Note 10, supra.

13. Note 8, supra.
14. Note 10, supra; Instructions, Schedule K, Form 706.

FORM NO. 5

Schedule A; Real Estate; Subject to Mortgage

Item No.	Description	Subsequent Valuation date	Value under option	Value at date of death

3	Improved real estate located at 45 Kilburn Road, Garden City, Nassau County, New York, S 33, B 74, Lots 9–10–11, improved with a one family brick veneer and frame dwelling and two car garage
	Assessed Value 1960.
	    Land $2,160
	    Building 7,040
	
	          $9,200
	
	Appraised at $10,500, subject to mortgage reduced to $8,910, leaving an equity of $1,590.00 ....
				$10,500.00

In the foregoing form, it was assumed no optional valuation was used.

§ 46. Schedule A; Real Estate; Contract to Purchase.

The instructions require that real property which the decedent has contracted to purchase should be listed in Schedule A. The full value of the property and not the equity must be extended in the value column. The unpaid portion of the purchase price should be deducted under Schedule K of the return.[15] Upon execution of the contract the purchaser becomes the equitable owner of the property, and it is therefore part of his gross estate, subject to the deduction for the balance due. Where it is the seller whose estate is concerned, the balance due is personal property.

FORM NO. 6

Schedule A; Real Estate; Contract to Purchase

Item No.	Description	Subsequent Valuation date	Value under option	Value at date of death
4	Decedent was the purchaser under contract with one George Hall to purchase premises 1921 William Street, NW., Washington, D. C. (lot 5, square 481). Said contract is dated the 20th day of Dec., 1959, and the consideration therein is the sum of $8,000. Decedent paid on account thereof the sum of $1,000. Value based on appraisal, copy of which is attached.			$8,000.00

15. Note 8, supra.

§ 47. Schedule A; Real Estate; Dower; Curtesy.

The statute provides that the value of the gross estate shall include the value of all property (except real property situated outside of the United States) to the extent of any interest therein of the surviving spouse, existing at the time of the decedent's death as dower or curtesy, *or* by virtue of a statute creating an estate in lieu of dower or curtesy.[16]   The Regulation further points out that the statute includes any interest created by statute in lieu of dower or curtesy, although such interest may differ in character from dower or curtesy, and that the full value of such property is included in the decedent's gross estate, without deduction of such an interest of the surviving husband or wife, and without regard to when the right to such an interest arose.[17] The instructions are still more explicit and state that the value of dower, curtesy, or a statutory estate created in lieu thereof, is taxable, and no reduction on account thereof or on account of homestead or other exemptions should be made in returning the value of the real estate.[18]

The theory on which such interests are included in the gross estate is that the surviving spouse succeeds to such interest at the time of the death of the other spouse.[19]   The contention that such interest was not a transfer by the decedent and therefore not includible in the gross estate has not been sustained.[20]   The fact that an interest may be excluded in the state where the property is situated has no effect so far as the Federal statute is concerned.[1]   It does not matter that the particular provision is an antenuptial agreement which is a substitute for the right of dower,[2] nor that a will disposes of real property without reserving dower.[3]   A bequest in lieu of dower cannot be diminished by the value of the dower interest.[4]

16. IRC, § 2034 (1954 Code).

17. Reg, § 20.2034–1.

18. Note 8, supra.

19. Mayer v Reinecke, 130 F2d 350 (CCA 7), cert den 317 US 684, 87 L ed 548, 63 S Ct 255 (1942).

20. Crooks v Hibbard, 33 F2d 567 (CCA 8), cert den 280 US 608, 74 L Ed 651, 50 S Ct 157 (1930); US v Waite, idem; McMullin, 20 BTA 527 (1930); Kirkwood, 23 BTA 955 (1931); Mercantile Trust Co. 13 BTA 85 (1928); Garrison, 21 BTA 904 (1930); Nyberg v US, 66 Ct Cls 153, cert den 278 US 646, 73 L Ed 559, 49 S Ct 81 (1928); Allen v Henggeler, 32 F2d 69 (CCA 8) (1929); US v Dietz, 33 F2d 576 (CCA 8) (1929); Brock, 16 BTA 1358 (1929).

1. Faber, 40 BTA 1070 (1939).

2. Empire Trust Co. v Comm, 94 F2d 307 (CCA 4) (1938).

3. Scott v Comm, 25 BTA 131, modfd & revd 69 F2d 444 (CCA 8) (1932).

4. Title Guarantee & Trust Co. v Edwards, 290 F 617 (1922).

§ 48. Schedule A; Real Estate; Community Property.

As previously discussed,[5] in the case of a resident of one of the community property states, dying after December 31, 1947, one half of the community property is generally includible in the gross estate of the spouse first dying. Only if the decedent died between October 21, 1942 and January 1, 1948 would a different rule apply. It is unlikely that enough such estates are pending at this late date to warrant discussion of that situation.

The general rule of inclusion of one half of the community property in the gross estate of the spouse first dying applies only if under the state law, the decedent has a vested interest at the date of death. In the case of a wife in New Mexico, her interest ceases at her death, and therefore her interest in the community property is not includible in her gross estate.[6] This was the situation in California prior to the amendment of the California Code in 1927.[7] That amendment, however, was held not to be retroactive.[8] The result is that in that state as to community property acquired before July 29, 1927, the whole of the community property is includible in the husband's estate,[9] while none of it is includible in her estate.[10] There may also be a conversion of community into separate property. The problem in such case is whether the transaction was one in contemplation of death, which will be treated hereafter.[11] The holding of property as community property also affects the marital deduction, for which the statute makes special provision.[12]

At this point we are interested in real property which is community property. Prior to the repeal of the community property provisions of the statute, the instructions for Schedule A contained the requirement for the inclusion of the entire property. Since 1948, however, there is no need therefor, since the interest of a decedent, resident of a community property law state, in real property, is reported to the extent of the interest held, usually one half thereof. It is reported no differently than if a decedent was a tenant in common of real estate. If the decedent owned any real estate as separate property, it is reported

5. § 41, supra.

6. Hernandez v Becker, 54 F2d 542 (CCA 10) (1931).

7. § 161a, amended effective July, 1927.

8. Silverburg, 20 BTA 716 (1930).

9. Gump, 42 BTA 197, affd 124 F2d 540 (CCA 9), cert den 316 US 697, 86 L Ed 1766, 62 S Ct 1292 (1942).

10. Talcott v US, 23 F2d 897 (CCA 9) (1928).

11. § 154, infra.

12. § 285, infra.

in the same way as such property owned by a resident of a non-community property state.

The community property does not include property which is the separate property of either spouse,[13] nor property which has been conveyed.[14] The scope of inclusion may be abridged by waiver.[15] Where the wife never had any interest in the community property it is all includible in the husband's gross estate.[16]

§ 49. Schedule A; Real Estate; Valuation.

The Estate Tax statute, except in the case of unlisted stocks and securities[17] and the matter of alternate valuation[18] does not define the manner in which property of a decedent shall be valued, leaving the subject entirely to the Regulations. The Regulations merely provide that the fair market value, according to the willing seller-willing buyer rule be applied to any valuation, and further that property shall not be returned at the value at which it is assessed for local tax purposes unless that value represents the fair market value.[19] But the courts have had much to say on the question of valuation of real estate.

As we have noted, value is a matter of opinion, so that no yardstick may be used by which a particular parcel may be fitted and measured. There have, however, evolved general rules which are applicable.

The Regulation states the rule distilled from the cases that fair market value is the price which a seller willing to sell at a fair price will accept from a buyer willing to buy at a fair price, neither being under any compulsion and both having a reasonable knowledge of the facts.[20] The usual and most satisfactory method of proving the value of a parcel of real estate is by submitting a real estate appraisal by a recognized expert,[1] in affi-

---

13. Hill, 24 BTA 1144 (1931).

14. US v Goodyear, 99 F2d 523 (CCA 9) (1938).

15. Pacific Nat Bank of Seattle, 40 BTA 128 (1939).

16. Melczer, 23 BTA 124, app dism 63 F2d 1010 (CCA 9) (1931).

17. IRC, § 2031(b) (1954 Code).

18. IRC, § 2032 (1954 Code).

19. Reg, § 20.2031–1(b).

20. O'Brien v US 57–2 USTC ¶ 11,704 (1957); Seaboard Citizens Nat. Bank of Norfolk v US, 58–1 USTC ¶ 11,738 (1957); Chicago Ry Equipment Co. v Blair, 20 F2d 10 (CCA 7), second hearing 13 BTA 471, affd in part, revd in part 39 F2d 378 (CCA 7), revd 282 US 295, 75 L ed 349, 51 S Ct 137 (1927).

1. Dillon, 3 BTA 1139 (1925).

davit form.[2] Such proof is usually acceptable,[3] although not necessarily binding on the court.[4]

Since it is rare that the factors entering into value will be the same in any two parcels, the factors which have been considered as affecting value will bear examination. Thus general real estate activity, prior to and subsequent to death,[5] physical condition, location, difficulty of sale and age,[6] historical interest,[7] improvements,[8] leases,[9] mortgages,[10] lack of rental or market,[11] options,[10] rents,[13] and as noted, the testimony of witnesses,[14] have all been considered. On the other hand, assessed valuation is not generally acceptable,[15] although this is not necessarily so if it is shown that the assessed value is based on fair market value or is a percentage thereof.[16]

The thing to be borne in mind is that the expert's affidavit must set forth *the facts* on which he bases his opinion. If he is not a qualified expert or his affidavit is vague, it is of no value.[17] The importance of facts in the supporting affidavits of value will be repeated many times hereafter. State inheritance tax appraisals may[18] or may not[19] be acceptable.

Where a state return is necessary, it is usual for the appraiser to furnish enough copies of his affidavit for use on both state and Federal returns.

2. Fincham, 16 BTA 1418 (1929).

3. See Rosenbaum, 3 TCM 925 (1944); note 1, supra.

4. See Bernstein, 3 BTA 1280 (1925).

5. Wilson, 5 BTA 615 (1926); Cary, Jr. 7 TCM 731 (1946).

6. McDermott, 12 TCM 481 (1949).

7. Blow, 16 BTA 872 (1929).

8. Hoover, 20 BTA 906 (1930); Cary, Jr. note 5, supra.

9. Meader, 26 F Supp 925 (1939); Van Dyke v Kuhl, 78 F Supp 698 (1945); Wolfe, 13 TCM 22 (1949).

10. France, 18 BTA 442 (1929); Rosenbaum, note 3, supra.

11. Fisher, 3 BTA 679 (1925); note 6, supra.

12. Prouty, 5 BTA 107 (1926).

13. McBride, 8 BTA 435 (1927).

14. Note 2, supra; Hauptfuhrer, 9 TCM 974 (1947); Lavelle, 8 BTA 1150 (1927); Lippincott, 27 BTA 735 (1933).

15. Lippincott, note 14, supra; Sochalski, 14 TCM 72 (1950).

16. Kelly, 18 BTA 1049 (1930); Cary, Jr, note 8, supra.

17. Cronin v Comm, 164 F2d 561 (CCA 6) (1947); Hauptfuhrer, note 14, supra.

18. Buck, 25 BTA 780 (1932); First Nat. Bank v Comm, 125 F2d 157 (CCA 6) (1942).

19. Powel, 10 BTA 166 (1928).

FORM NO. 7

Affidavit of Real Estate Appraiser

In the Matter of the Appraisal
  of the Estate of
      WINTHROP BENSON,
                    Deceased.

STATE OF OHIO   }
                       } ss:
COUNTY OF HAMILTON   }

CHARLES HORN, being duly sworn, deposes and says:

That he is an appraiser and President of Charles Horn, Inc., a licensed real estate broker, with offices located at 550 Huron Road, Cincinnati, Ohio.

That he has resided in the City of Cincinnati for over 40 years and now resides at 1508 Pine Street in said city and has been and is fully familiar with conditions of the real estate and mortgage markets in said city.

That he is a member of the Cincinnati Real Estate Board; an affiliated member of the American Institute of Real Estate Appraisers, of the National Association of Real Estate Boards; an appraiser for the City of Cincinnati in condemnation proceedings; a director and member of the Executive Committee of the Inland National Bank; that he has been retained as an appraiser by various banks and financial institutions in the City of Cincinnati, and that he has duly qualified as an appraiser in the United States Court for the Southern District of Ohio.

That for the past 31 years your deponent has bought, sold, appraised and managed real property throughout the City of Cincinnati, including the type of premises hereinafter appraised and is now actively engaged in appraising all types of real estate throughout said city.

That your deponent's employment and compensation for making this appraisal is in no manner contingent upon the amount of the appraisal, nor is your deponent concerned with the purpose for which said appraisal is made. The value as hereinafter given is in all respects applicable to the time of death of decedent, to wit: January 10, 1960.

That your deponent has on numerous occasions personally inspected the parcel hereinafter appraised; That he is thoroughly familiar with the physical conditions and other details concerning same.

100 Elm Street—Situate on east side of Elm Street, 200 feet North of Davis Road, in the City of Cincinnati, State of Ohio; improvements consist of a 2 story and cellar, detached, brick, 1 family dwelling 25' × 60' on lot 200' × 100' erected in 1936; containing eight rooms and three baths, of ordinary construction; poured concrete foundation; gable roof of slate; equipped with modern plumbing; electric refrigeration; "Richardson" steam boiler, burning oil, supplies heat; separate hot water heater connected to monel metal storage tank; present rental income $250.00 per month; street paved and has all improvements and utilities; convenient to schools, churches and transit.

1959 Assessed valuation is land $15,000.00, improvement $10,000.00, total $25,000.00.

In my opinion the land is worth $20,000.00

Improvement adds to the value of the land 20,000.00
_____
Total appraised value $30,000.00

Your deponent has not based his appraisal of said premises in any manner on the assessed valuation, for the reason that deponent does not substitute for his own judgment the varying abilities of the county assessors.

CHARLES HORN

Sworn to before me this 22nd
day of February, 1960
    ALFRED A. ADAMS
    Notary Public
    Hamilton County

§ 50. Schedule A; Real Estate; Valuation; Fractional Interests.

The valuation of fractional interests in real estate presents a special problem. Neither the statute nor the Regulations offer any guidance, other than the provision in the latter that all relevant facts and elements of value as of the applicable valuation date shall be considered in every case.[20]

The mere fact that the decedent owned a fractional interest in real property is not in and of itself sufficient to warrant a reduction in value.[1] The fact is, that because of the difficulty of disposing of such an interest, it is not usually worth its aliquot share of the whole value. But reduction in value is largely determined by divisibility.[2] Where sufficient proof is furnished by expert evidence that such fractional interest is worth less than its aliquot share of the entire value, it has been held that discounts of between ten to fifteen percent are allowable.[3] When,

20. Reg, § 20.2031–1(b).

1. McColgan, 10 BTA 958 (1928).

2. Henry, 4 TC 423, affd but not on point, 161 F2d 574 (CCA 7) (1947); Natl City Bank of New York, 2 BTA 696 (1925); Cook, 2 BTA 126 (1925).

3. Stewart, 31 BTA 201 (1935); Campanari, 5 TC 488 (1947); Herter, 13 TCM 298 (1949); Eggleston, 6 TCM 400 (1946); Henry, note 2, supra.

therefore, it is claimed that the decedent's fractional interest is entitled to a discount it is advisable to substantiate the claim by an affidavit of an expert.

§ 51. Schedule A; Real Estate; Valuation; Miscellaneous Interests.

There are various types of interests which may be real property or personal property depending upon state law, or which while not usually thought of as real estate, are in fact so. Thus timber licenses may[4] or may not[5] be considered real estate. The same is true of leaseholds.[6] Growing crops, as has been pointed out, are real estate and valued accordingly.[7] Oil royalty interests and lessee or working interests have been valued on the average daily oil production over a period of three months and based on the price per barrel on the date of valuation.[8] The value of a Texas oil lease was valued on the basis of comparative sales, other factors affecting value and the testimony of experts.[9] In the case of leaseholds, the usual method is capitalization of earnings.[10] For Gift Tax purposes a citrus grove was valued on the basis of expert testimony and actual sales of comparable property at or about the time in question.[11]

§ 52. Schedule B; Stocks and Bonds; Generally.

Stocks and bonds are an important part of the general personal assets of the decedent which are required to be reported in the Estate Tax schedules provided they are owned by the decedent at the date of his death, regardless of situs, and unless exempt by statute.[12] As in the case of all other property, the first question to be determined is whether the decedent had a beneficial interest therein at the time of his death.[13] If he did, they must be reported.[14] Even though a transfer of the securities may have been made during the decedent's lifetime, they must be reported if he retained control,[15] although not reportable in

4. Laird v US, 115 F Supp 931 (1953).

5. Rev Rul 65, 1953-1 CB 391.

6. See Leeser, 17 BTA 226 (1929); De Perigny, 9 TC 782 (1947).

7. Tompkins, 13 TC 1054 (1949).

8. Brown v US, 16 AFTR 1084 (1935).

9. Humphrey, 5 TCM 34 (1944).

10. See Van Dyke v Kuhl, 78 F Supp

698 (1945); see also McMichaels Appraising Manual, 4th Ed.

11. Carlton v Comm, 190 F2d 183 (CA 5) (1951).

12. Reg, § 20.2033-1 (a); see also Greiner v Lewellyn, 258 US 384, 66 L Ed 676, 42 S Ct 324 (1921).

13. Reg, § 20.2033-1 (a).

14. Foster, 13 BTA 496 (1928).

15. Union Trust Co. of Detroit v US,

Schedule B. If there is a divided ownership, the fiduciary reports the extent of the decedent's interest.[16]

Securities which have been the subject of a lifetime transfer which was not in contemplation of death nor intended to take effect at death are not a part of the gross estate.[17] Where there has been a transfer creating a divided interest, such as a tenancy in common, the securities may not need to be reported in full.[18] The same applies where the decedent at the time of death was holding the securities as fiduciary.[19] Between husband and wife, where she holds as a dummy for her husband, they have been held not part of her gross estate.[20] The same applies where the husband is holding securities for the wife.[1] Where a transfer intended as a gift fails for insufficiency, the securities will be held to be part of the gross estate of the transferor.[2]

In determining whether to include or exclude securities from the gross estate, the law applicable at the date of death must be considered.[3] The state law is important on the question of what are estate assets.[4] Includibility may or may not be determined by the determination of the state courts.[5] But allowances for the surviving spouse do not escape taxation because under state law they are not deemed assets of the decedent.[6] The decisions of the state court as to the ownership of securities have been followed by the Federal taxing authorities.[7]

§ 53. Schedule B; Stocks and Bonds; Description.

The Regulation provides that a description of bonds should include the number held, principal amount, name of obligor, date of maturity, rate of interest, date or dates on which interest is payable, series number if there is more than one issue, and the

73 Ct Cls 315, 54 F2d 152, cert den 286 US 547, 76 L Ed 1284, 52 S Ct 500 (1932).

16. Harvey v US, 185 F2d 463 (CA 7) (1950).

17. US v Union Trust Co of Indianapolis, 90 F2d 702 (CCA 7) (1937); City Bank Farmers Trust Co, 23 BTA 663 (1931).

18. Helvering v Miller, 75 F2d 474 (CCA 2) (1935).

19. Holt, 14 BTA 564 (1929).

20. McCann v Comm, 87 F2d 275 (CCA 6) (1937).

1. True v US, 51 F Supp 720 (1943).

2. Sizer v US, 65 Ct Cls 450.

3. Henry, 4 TC 423, affd 161 F2d 574 (CCA 7) (1947).

4. O'Neill, 4 BTA 78 (1926).

5. See Elliott, 23 BTA 354 (1931); Smith v Comm, 140 F2d 759 (CCA 3) (1944); Du Puy, 9 TC 276 (1947).

6. Waldman, 46 BTA 291 (1942); Jacobs, 8 TC 1015 (1947); Faber, 40 BTA 1070 (1939); Mayer v Reinecke, 130 F2d 350 (CCA 7), cert den 317 US 684, 87 L Ed 548, 63 S Ct 255 (1942).

7. Du Puy, note 5, supra; Norris v US, 7 F Supp 415 (1934).

[Harris]—5

principal exchange on which listed, or the principal business office of the corporation, if unlisted.

Description of stocks should include number of shares, whether common or preferred, and, if preferred, what issue, par value, quotation at which returned, exact name of corporation, and, if the stock is unlisted, the location of the principal business office and the State in which incorporated and the date of incorporation, or if the stock is listed, the principal exchange upon which sold.[8]

The instructions for Schedule B set forth the same requirements in substantially identical language.[9] The fiduciary has an election to value the estate assets either as of the date of death or the alternate valuation date, and the return will reflect this. The instructions contain an example of the manner in which securities are to be listed under both methods of valuation.

FORM NO. 8

Schedule B; Stocks and Bonds

1. Did the decedent, if a resident or citizen of the United States, own any stocks or bonds, regardless of physical location, at the time of his death? [x] Yes   [ ] No
2. Did the decedent, if a nonresident not a citizen of the United States, own, at the time of his death, any stocks of corporations organized in the United States or bonds situated in the United States as explained in the instructions? [ ] Yes   [ ] No

(Where the alternate valuation is not adopted; date of death, January 1, 1955)

Item No.	Description (including face amount of bonds or number of shares)	Par	Unit value	Subsequent valuation date	Alternate value	Value at date of death
1	$60,000—Arkansas Railroad Co. first mortgage 4%, 20-year bonds, due 1966. Interest payable quarterly on Feb. 1, May 1, Aug. 1, and Nov. 1, N. Y. Exchange	1,000	100			$60,000
	Interest coupons attached to bonds, item 1, due and payable on Nov. 1, 1954, but not cashed at date of death					600
	Interest accrued on item 1, from Nov. 1, 1954, to Jan. 1, 1955					400
2	500 shares Public Service Corp., common ex dividend, N. Y. Exchange	100	110			55,000
	Dividend on item 2 of $2 per share declared Dec. 10, 1954, payable on Jan. 10, 1955, to holders of record on Dec. 30, 1954					1,000

8. Reg., § 20.6018–3 (c)(2).   9. Instructions, Schedule B, Form 706.

(Where the alternate valuation is adopted; date of death, January 1, 1955)

Item No.	Description (including face amount of bonds or number of shares)	Par	Unit value	Subsequent valuation date	Alternate value	Value at date of death
1	$60,000—Arkansas Railroad Co. first mortgage 4%, 20-year bonds, due 1966. Interest payable quarterly on Feb. 1, May 1, Aug. 1, and Nov. 1, N. Y. Exchange on date of death ..	1,000	100			$60,000
	$30,000 of such bonds distributed to legatees on Aug. 1, 1955, N. Y. Exchange		99	8/1/55	$29,700	
	$30,000 of such bonds sold by executors on Sept. 1, 1955		99	9/1/55	29,700	
	Interest coupons attached to bonds, item 1, due and payable on Nov. 1, 1954, but not cashed at date of death. Cashed by executor on Feb. 1, 1955			2/1/55	600	600
	Interest accrued on item 1, from Nov. 1, 1954, to Jan. 1, 1955. Cashed by executor on Feb. 1, 1955			2/1/55	400	400
2	500 shares Public Service Corp., common. N. Y. Exchange. Ex dividend on date of death	100	110			55,000
	Not disposed of within year following death		90	1/1/56	45,000	
	Dividend on item 2 of $2 per share declared Dec. 10, 1954, and paid on Jan. 10, 1955, to holders of record on Dec. 30, 1954			1/10/55	1,000	1,000

TOTAL (also enter under the Recapitulation, Schedule O) $106,400 $117,000

(If more space is needed, insert additional sheets of same size)

Estate of WINTHROP BENSON   Schedule B—Page 9

§ 54. Schedule B; Stocks and Bonds; Valuation; Generally.

The objective to be achieved in valuing securities for Estate Tax purposes is the determination of fair market value, which is the interpretation of the statutory term "value".[10] Fair market value is the value in money of the stocks or bonds as between one who wishes to purchase and one who wishes to sell where both have reasonable knowledge of the facts.[11] Where the securities are listed on a stock exchange there is ordinarily little difficulty in evaluation. If there is a market for stocks or bonds, on a stock exchange, in an over-the-counter market, or otherwise, the *mean* between the highest and lowest quoted selling prices on the valuation date is the fair market value per share or bond. *If there were no sales on the valuation date,* but there were sales

10. Gamble v Comm, 101 F2d 565 (CCA 6), cert den 306 US 664, 83 L ed 1060, 59 S Ct 788 (1939); Reg, § 20.2031-2 (a).

11. Wood v US, 29 F Supp 853 (1939).

on dates within a reasonable period both before and after the valuation date, the fair market value is determined by taking a weighted average of the means between the highest and lowest sales on the nearest date before and the nearest date after the valuation date. The average is to be *weighted adversely* by the respective numbers of trading days between the selling dates and the valuation date. For example, assume that sales of stock nearest the valuation date (Friday, June 15) occurred two trading days before (Wednesday, June 13) and three trading days after (Wednesday, June 20) and that on these days the mean sale prices per share were $10 and $15, respectively. The price of $12 is taken as representing the fair market value of a share of the stock as of the valuation date, arrived at by adding the product of 3 multiplied by 10 to the product of 2 multiplied by 15, and dividing the total of 60 by 5, the sum of 3 and 2. If, instead, the mean sale prices per share on June 13 and June 20 were $15 and $10, respectively, the price of $13 is taken as representing the fair market value, arrived at by adding the product of 3 multiplied by 15 to the product of 2 multiplied by 10, and dividing the total of 65 by 5. If the decedent dies on Sunday, and Saturday and Sunday are not trading days, but the mean sale price per share on Friday was $20 and $23 on Monday following, then the fair market value per share as of the valuation date is $21.50.[12] It is to be observed that *only trading days* before and after the valuation date are to be considered.

If stocks or bonds are listed on more than one exchange, the records of the exchange where the stocks or bonds are principally dealt in should be employed.[13]

In the absence of unusual facts the best evidence of the value of stock listed on an exchange is the price at which it sells on the valuation date.[14] And where it is sold on two exchanges the value may be determined by taking the mean between the highest bid and the lowest asked on the two exchanges.[15]

Where the stock has not been fully paid for at the date of death, it is taxable to the extent of the equity actually paid for,[16] but this does not affect the question of valuation, the balance due being a proper deduction.[17]

12. Reg, § 20.2031–2 (b).
13. Note 12, supra.
14. Spencer, 5 TC 904 (1945).
15. Blossom, 45 BTA 691 (1941).
16. Gump v Comm, 42 BTA 197, aff'd 124 F2d 540 (CCA 9), cert den 316 US 697, 86 L Ed 1766, 62 S Ct 1292 (1940).
17. Linde, 8 TCM 1102 (1947).

The size of a block of stock may have an important bearing on its value, and that subject is treated in the succeeding section.

In valuing listed securities, the fiduciary should be careful to consult accurate records to obtain values as of the applicable valuation date.[18] The usual method is to obtain a letter from a stock brokerage house, furnishing the necessary information.

§ 55. Schedule B; Stocks and Bonds; Valuation; Blockage.

The so-called "blockage rule," i.e., that a large block of listed securities has a lesser value than a fewer number of shares because of the difficulty of disposing of it without depressing the market value, has been the subject of much litigation and discussion. It must first be understood that it is neither a rule nor a presumption. The Internal Revenue Service at one time attempted to outlaw it by a Regulation which provided that the size of a block of securities was not a relevant factor in determining its value.[19] The Regulation was held invalid.[20]

As the Board of Tax Appeals said, blockage is not a law of economics, a principle of law, nor a rule of evidence. If the value of a given number of shares is influenced by the size of the block, *this is a matter of evidence* and not of doctrinaire assumption.[1]

Although the Service vigorously opposed for many years the contention that the size of a block of stock listed on an exchange affected its value, in the Regulations issued under the 1954 Code for the first time the effect of blockage is recognized, but reluctance is also indicated, in that not only the adverse effect is considered, but also the favorable effect.

The Regulation provides that the size of the block of securities to be valued in relation to the numbers of shares changing hands in sales is relevant in determining whether or not selling prices reflect fair market value. Thus, if the block is so large in relation to the existing market that it could not be liquidated in a reasonable time without depressing the market, the price at which the block could be sold as such outside the usual market, as through an underwriter, may be a more accurate indication of the value than market quotations. *On the other hand,* if the

18. Note 12, supra.
19. Reg 79, Art 19.
20. Comm v Shattuck, 97 F2d 790 (CA 7) (1938); Helvering v Safe De- posit & Trust Co of Baltimore, 95 F2d 806 (CCA 4) (1938).
1. Walters, 35 BTA 259 (1936).

block to be valued represents a controlling interest in a going business, the price at which small lots change hands may have little relation to its true value.[2]

The Tax Court and other courts have recognized that the fair market value of a large block of stock is not necessarily the quoted price. The result is that the size of holdings may be an important consideration. *But merely proving that the decedent was the owner of a large block of stock is not sufficient.* Expert testimony will be required that it cannot be sold at the quoted price and evidence must be presented of all factors which will result in a lower valuation. Before returning a value below the quoted price on an exchange, because of the size of the block of securities, the fiduciary will do well to prepare his evidence carefully, for the courts have fixed a value below the quoted price *when the facts warranted*[3] and have refused to do so when they did not.[4]

The fact to be borne in mind is that valuation by the Commissioner is prima facie correct, and it is the obligation of the taxpayer to create an issue of fact by the presentation of appropriate evidence.[5]

§ 56. Schedule B; Stocks and Bonds; Valuation; Bid and Asked Prices.

If actual sales are not available during a reasonable period beginning before and ending after the valuation date, the fair market value may be determined by taking the mean between the bona fide bid and asked prices on the valuation date, or if none, by taking a weighted average between the bona fide bid and asked prices on the nearest trading date before and the nearest trading date after the valuation date, if both such near-

2. Reg, § 20.2031–2 (e).

3. Dupont, 26 F Supp 773 (1939); Helvering v Maytag, 125 F2d 55 (CCA 8), cert den 316 US 689, 86 L ed 760, 62 S Ct 1280 (1942); Fleming, 10 TCM 764 (1948); Lunken, 4 TCM 610 (1944); Avery, 3 TC 963 (1944); Havemeyer v US, 59 F Supp 537 (1943), cert den 326 US 776, 90 L Ed 456, 66 S Ct 138 (1945); Standish, 8 TC 1204 (1947).

4. Mott v Comm, 139 F2d 317 (CCA 6) (1944); Newberry, 39 BTA 1123 (1939); Groff v Smith, 34 F Supp 319 (1943); Bull v Smith, 119 F2d 490

(CCA 2) (1941); Phipps v Comm, 12 F2d 214 (CCA 10) (1942), cert den 317 US 645, 87 L ed 519, 63 S Ct 38; Richardson v Comm, 151 F2d 102 (CA DC) (1945), cert den 326 US 796, 90 L ed 485, 66 S Ct 490; Clause, 5 TC 647, affd 154 F2d 655 (CCA 3) (1945); Allen, 3 TC 1224 (1944).

5. McKitterick, 42 BTA 130 (1940); Gamble v Comm, 101 F2d 565 (CCA 6), cert den 306 US 664, 89 L Ed 1060, 59 S Ct 708 (1939); Krauss v US, 51 F Supp 388, affd 140 F2d 510 (CCA 5) (1944).

est dates are within a reasonable period. The average is to be determined in the same way as previously discussed[6] in the case of listed stock on an exchange where there are no sales on the valuation date.[7] This Regulation provides for the valuation of securities which are not quoted on a high and low basis, but on a bid and asked basis. One example of such are bank stocks. This has been the standard method of evaluation.[8] It should be noted that adverse weighting and trading days are similarly to apply.

§ 57. Schedule B; Stocks and Bonds; Valuation; Incomplete Selling Prices or Bid and Asked Prices.

In the case of certain securities infrequently traded, there is the possibility that there have been no sales either within a reasonable period either before or after the date of valuation. In such case, it is provided that if there are no actual sales prices or bona fide bid and asked prices available on a date within a reasonable period before the valuation date, but such prices are available on a date within a reasonable period after the valuation date, or vice versa, then the mean between such highest and lowest available sales prices or bid and asked prices may be taken as the value.[9]

§ 58. Schedule B; Stocks and Bonds; Valuation; Sales Price Not Reflecting Value.

As we have seen, normally the sales price of a security is the best evidence of its value. But there may be situations in which this is not so. The Regulations take cognizance of this fact. It is provided that if it is *established* that the value of any bond or share of stock determined on the basis of selling prices or bid and asked prices does not reflect the fair market value thereof, then some reasonable modification of that basis or other relevant facts and elements of value are considered in determining the fair market value.[10] While the Regulation furnishes as an example of the case referred to, the case of a large block of securities,[11] there is nothing in the Regulation to indicate that this is the only situation to which it applies. It

6. § 54, supra.
7. Reg, § 20.2031–2(c).
8. Maxwell, 3 TCM 1207 (1944); Vandenhoeck, 4 TC 125 (1944).

9. Reg, § 20.2031–2(d).
10. Reg, § 20.2031–2(e).
11. See § 55, supra.

may apply where there are isolated sales,[12] limited market-ability,[13] or the stock is speculative and sold sporadically.[14]

§ 59. Schedule B; Stocks and Bonds; Valuation; Close Corporation.

Former Regulations[15] referred to "close corporations" and "inactive stocks." The instructions for Schedule B still use the terms.[16] The Regulations under the 1954 Code are more general in character and the Code itself has a provision with respect to unlisted stocks and securities.[17] The 1954 Code provides that in the case of stocks and securities of a corporation the value of which, by reason of their not being listed on an exchange and by reason of the absence of sales thereof, cannot be determined with reference to bid and asked prices or with reference to sales prices, the value thereof shall be determined by taking into consideration, in addition to all other factors, the value of stock or securities of corporations engaged in the same or a similar line of business which are listed on an exchange.[18]

The Regulation provides that if the provisions for valuation of securities regularly traded are inapplicable because actual sales prices and bona fide bid and asked prices are lacking, then the fair market value shall be determined by taking the following factors into consideration:

(1) In the case of corporate or other bonds, the soundness of the security, the interest yield, the date of the maturity, and *other relevant factors.*

(2) In the case of shares of stock, the company's net worth, prospective earning power and dividend-paying capacity, and *other relevant factors.*

Some of the *other relevant factors* referred to are:

(1) The good will of the business.

(2) The economic outlook in the particular industry.

(3) The company's position in the industry and its management.

(4) The values of securities of corporations engaged in the

---

12. See Walter, 2 BTA 453 (1925).

13. See Bank of California v Comm, 133 F2d 428 (CCA 9) (1943); Schnorbach v Kavanagh, 102 F Supp 828 (1952).

14. Note 8, supra.

15. Reg 80, Art 10C.

16. Instructions, Schedule B, Form 706.

17. IRC, § 2031(b) (1954 Code).

18. Note 17, supra.

same or similar lines of business which are listed on a stock exchange.

However, the weight to be accorded such comparisons or any other evidentiary factors considered in the determination of a value *depends upon the facts of each case.* Complete financial and other data upon which the valuation is based should be submitted with the return, including copies of reports in any case in which examinations of the company have been made by accountants, engineers, or any technical experts as of or near the applicable valuation date.[19]

A Revenue Ruling defines the term "close corporation" in the words of a decision,[20] as meaning a corporation in which the stock is held in few hands, or in few families, and wherein it is not at all, or only rarely dealt in by buying or selling.[1] The same Ruling sets forth some of the fundamental factors in evaluation of such stock. These factors are:

(1) The nature of the business and the history of the enterprise.

(2) The economic outlook in general and the condition and outcome of the specific industry.

(3) Book value and financial condition.

(4) Earning capacity.

(5) Dividend-paying capacity.

(6) Good will.

(7) Sales of the stock and the size of the block.

(8) Market price of similar stocks which are listed on an exchange.

We thus have general rules but no formula. The term "relevant factors" covers a host of matters. Valuation is determined by the application of the general rules to the *facts* of each case. As the Revenue Ruling referred to points out, a sound valuation will be based upon all relevant facts, but the elements of common sense, informed judgment and reasonableness must enter into the process of weighing these facts and determining their aggregate significance.[2] Valuations have been based upon the following in particular cases: net worth,[3] book value,[4] business

19. IRC, § 2031(f) (1954 Code).
20. Brooks v Willcuts, 78 F2d 270 (CCA 8) (1935).
1. Rev Rul 54-77, IRB 1954-1 CB 187.
2. Note 1, supra.

3. Richardson v Comm, 151 F2d 102 (CCA 2) (1945), cert den 326 US 796, 90 L Ed 485, 66 S Ct 490 (1946); Bank of California v Comm, 133 F2d 428 (CCA 9) (1943).
4. O'Bryan Bros v Comm, 127 F2d

conditions,[5] capitalization of earnings,[6] comparison with stock
of other corporations,[7] competitive risks,[8] dividends,[9] earnings,[10]
expert testimony,[11] financial condition of the company,[12] future
prospects,[13] the fact of minority interest,[14] restrictions on sale,[15]
sales,[16] management capacity,[17] and the history of the company.[18]
The only useful purpose that such cases serve is for the knowledge of the factors which have been considered. As has been
said, the question of fair market value is one of fact and not of
formula.[19] Each case must depend upon its own facts, but the
knowledge of what have been considered to be relevant factors
is important in collating proof to sustain a valuation.

There is another factor which frequently causes difficulty
in evaluating the stock of close corporations, that is, whether
in addition to any other factors affecting value, there is excess
earning value. In the final analysis, earning capacity determines whether or not there is good will. The presence of good
will and its value depends upon the excess of net earnings over
and above a fair return on the net tangible assets. Capitalization of such excess earnings at an appropriate rate is one method
for determining good will, but is not the controlling basis. While
the element of good will may be based primarily on earnings,
such factors as the prestige and renown of the business, the
ownership of a trade or brand name, and a record of successful
operation over a prolonged period in a particular locality, also
may furnish support for the inclusion of intangible value.[20]

645 (CCA 6) (1942), cert den 317 US
647, 87 L Ed 526, 63 S Ct 46; True v
US, 51 F Supp 720 (1943).

5. Aufiero, 13 TCM 182 (1949); Spitzer, 6 TCM 332 (1946); Horlick v Kuhl,
62 F Supp 168 (1945).

6. Parker, 4 TCM 449 (1944); Wishon
v Anglim, 42 F Supp 359 (1942).

7. Plant v Mumford, 188 F2d 543
(1951); Aufiero, note 5, supra.

8. Joslin, 5 TCM 410 (1945).

9. O'Bryan Bros v Comm, note 4,
supra; Schlegel v US, 164 F2d 276
(CCA 2) (1948).

10. Abrams, 4 TCM 392 (1944);
Morse v Comm, 10 TCM 636 (1948).

11. Lingo, 13 TCM 436 (1949); Metcalf, 12 TCM 1428 (1949).

12. Heppenstall, 8 TCM 136 (1947);
Reinhold, 7 TCM 697 (1946).

13. Heppenstall, note 12, supra; note
8, supra.

14. Lingo, note 11, supra; Pabst, 6
TCM 1186 (1946).

15. James v Comm, 148 F2d 236
(CCA 2) (1945); Rev Rul 189, IRB
1953-2 CB 294.

16. Cotton v Comm, 165 F2d 987
(CCA 9) (1948); Stowers, 6 TCM 1330
(1946).

17. Montgomery, 12 TCM 1380
(1949); McDermott, 12 TCM 481
(1949).

18. Aufiero, note 5, supra; note 8,
supra.

19. Burda, 2 TCM 497 (1944).

20. Rev Rul 54-77, IRB 1954-1 CB
187.

There are three accepted methods for the evaluation of good will, namely, capitalization of earnings, the Federal Income Tax method and the years' purchase method.

Under the capitalization of earnings method, the net profits *for a representative number of years* are averaged and the result multiplied by 10 or 15, depending upon the business. The product is the value of the business, including good will.

The second method[1] adopted under the early Income Tax statute is to deduct from the average net profits a percentage of the net tangibles and capitalize the result by multiplying by a fixed number. Adding the product to the net tangibles furnishes the total value.

The years' purchase method is to take 6% or 8% of the average capital invested over a representative number of years and deduct it from the average net profits for the same period of time. The result is multiplied by a fixed number and added to the net worth as good will.

It is important to note that the above are *methods* of valuing good will. The fact is, *there is no rule* for such valuation.[2]

The two elements which present the greatest problem are the matters of what is a representative number of years and the fixed number to be used. There is no definitive answer, it depending, as has been said, on the nature of the business, the risk involved, and the stability or regularity of earnings.[3] The usual practice is to furnish balance sheets for the five years preceding the death of the decedent.[4] *If these years are not representative* of earnings, such as being abnormally high, there should be no hesitation in submitting balance sheets and profit and loss statements for any greater period which it is claimed truly represents normal earnings. As in all cases of valuation, the proof submitted should be full and complete enough to support the fiduciary's claim of value. The important thing is to furnish sufficient evidence,[5] for failure to do so results in the Commissioner's valuation being sustained.[6] The certification of the accountant who prepared the financial evidence

1. ARM 34, 2 CB 31, June 1920.
2. Fish, 1 BTA 882 (1924).
3. Note 20, supra.
4. Dougherty, 4 BTA 1232 (1926).
5. McBride, 8 BTA 435 (1927).
6. Gessell v Comm, 41 F2d 20 (CCA 7) (1930).

should be furnished,[7] and any witness used should be well qualified.[8]

FORM NO. 9

Affidavits as to Value; Balance Sheets and Computation

In the Matter of the Appraisal
   of the Estate of
       WINTHROP BENSON,
                     Deceased.

STATE OF MISSOURI   ⎱
COUNTY OF JACKSON   ⎰ ss:

KATHERINE BENSON, being duly sworn, says: That I am the Executrix under the Last Will and Testament of Winthrop Benson, late of the County of Jackson, Deceased. That said decedent was my husband and I have been acquainted with his connection with Winthrop Benson, Inc., ever since the inception of the company in 1941.

That the decedent was the owner of 120 shares of the preferred stock of the said corporation of a total of 240 shares issued, and of 150 shares of the common stock of said corporation out of a total of 200 shares issued.

Said business was instituted by the decedent as a mail order business. That the sole and only person who was and is thoroughly familiar with all of the details of said business from the financial, buying and selling point of view was the decedent. There was no other person capable of carrying on the said business and his loss, therefore, will have an extremely adverse effect upon the business, since it is questionable whether it can be continued without him. Efforts have been made to obtain a buyer for his interest, but the same have been unsuccessful since there is no market for the same. The business is that of fraternal goods and supplies for which there is a limited demand, so that the number of people who might be interested in purchasing the business is few.

There are annexed hereto computations of the value of the stock of the corporation based upon the average net worth for five years. Although the volume of the business has increased, the profit from operations was small and in the year ending December 31, 1958, a loss of $2,999.58 was sustained.

The average earning power of the business was, over a period of five

7. Fairchild, 9 BTA 416 (1927).   8. Sensenbrenner v Comm, 134 F2d 883 (CCA 7) (1943).

years, $83.82, an insufficient amount to pay dividends on preferred stock. There were no dividends paid on the common stock.

On the basis of averaging the book value and earnings capitalized at 8% the common stock is worth less than par and is of the fair market value of $38.35 per share.

KATHERINE BENSON

Sworn to before me this 18th day
of June, 1959

       Andrea Hayes
       Notary Public
       Jackson County

WINTHROP BENSON, INC.

Comparative Summarized Balance Sheets as at December 31, 1954, 1955, 1956, 1957, 1958

	As at Dec. 31, 1954	As at Dec. 31, 1955	As at Dec. 31, 1956	As at Dec. 31, 1957	As at Dec. 31, 1958
ASSETS					
Current Assets					
Cash in Bank and on Hand	$ 3,773.50	$ 9,937.57	$ 5,135.01	$ 6,540.05	$31,024.91
Accounts Receivable (Less Reserve for Bad Debts)	35,557.54	46,618.46	49,257.36	55,883.56	58,533.81
Advances Receivable	215.00	75.00	309.82	1,092.87	461.92
Notes Receivable	....	....	50.00	....	200.00
Accounts Payable—Debit Balances	....	....	....	....	1,125.25
Net Cash Surrender Value—Life Insurance Policies	619.38	1,036.93	1,585.47	4,531.25	430.00
Merchandise Inventory	46,154.87	50,665.64	55,170.98	60,017.98	99,203.62
	$86,320.29	$108,333.60	$111,508.64	$128,065.71	$190,999.51
Fixed Assets					
Furniture, Fixtures, Equipment and Alterations (Less Reserve for Depreciation)	3,272.04	3,220.81	3,802.07	3,697.68	3,330.23
Deferred Charges					
Unexpired Insurance Premiums	450.42	556.78	557.90	593.81	1,371.20
	$90,042.75	$112,111.19	$115,868.61	$132,357.20	$195,709.94

WINTHROP BENSON, INC.

Comparative Summarized Balance Sheets as at December 31, 1954, 1955, 1956, 1957, 1958

LIABILITIES AND CAPITAL	As at Dec. 31, 1954	As at Dec. 31, 1955	As at Dec. 31, 1956	As at Dec. 31, 1957	As at Dec. 31, 1958
Liabilities					
Notes Payable	$ 2,918.80	$ 4,930.64	$ 5,200.00	$ 9,267.42	$ 7,640.80
Acceptances Payable	3,255.96	6,310.91	2,310.92	3,092.06	5,014.36
Vouchers Payable—Trade	31,130.13	41,837.99	40,432.70	28,196.84	49,924.36
Accrued Liabilities	....	342.79	....	....	....
Winthrop Benson, President, and Estate of Winthrop Benson	18,435.07	20,533.71	21,335.91	29,555.26	38,264.02
James Benson, Vice-President	342.61*	2,033.38	6,191.31	13,056.02	20,738.08
Walter Ward, Secretary and Treasurer	365.42*	1,787.00	5,245.15	12,489.45	20,747.54
Accounts Receivable—Credit Balances	....	....	....	....	1,342.86
Reserve for Taxes	....	....	631.97	911.53	220.13
	$55,031.93	$ 77,776.42	$ 81,347.96	$ 96,568.58	$143,892.15
Capital Stock					
Authorized and Issued					
Common—200 shares	$ 1,000.00	$ 1,000.00	$ 1,000.00	$ 1,000.00	$ 1,000.00
Preferred—240 shares	24,000.00	24,000.00	24,000.00	24,000.00	24,000.00
	25,000.00	25,000.00	25,000.00	25,000.00	25,000.00
Surplus	10,010.82	9,334.77	9,520.65	10,788.62	26,817.79
	$90,042.75	$112,111.19	$115,868.61	$132,357.20	$195,709.94

* Red figures.

WINTHROP BENSON, INC.

Comparative Summarized Statement of Income Profit and Loss and Surplus—For the Years Ending December 31, 1954, 1955, 1956, 1957 and 1958

	Year Ending December 31, 1954	Year Ending December 31, 1955	Year Ending December 31, 1956	Year Ending December 31, 1957	Year Ending December 31, 1958
Net Sales	$236,418.04	$279,900.43	$306,623.84	$350,661.48	$380,949.53
Cost of Sales—					
Inventory at Beginning of Year	$ 53,666.58	$ 46,154.87	$ 50,665.64	$ 55,170.98	$ 60,017.98
Purchases and Import Expenses	154,799.18	198,893.28	208,116.53	238,814.49	289,363.81
	$208,465.76	$245,048.15	$258,782.17	$293,985.47	$349,381.79
Less: Inventory at Year-End	46,154.87	50,665.64	55,170.98	60,017.98	99,203.62
	162,310.89	194,382.51	203,611.19	233,967.49	250,178.17
Gross Profit	$ 74,107.15	$ 85,517.92	$103,012.65	$116,693.99	$130,771.36
Store, Office and General Expenses—					
Salaries—Officers	$ 22,324.54	$ 25,871.00	$ 29,169.12	$ 33,163.98	$ 38,581.97
Others Including Commissions	22,694.26	23,927.48	29,850.32	32,087.04	39,646.76
Rent Paid — (less Rent Received)	2,558.50	4,116.00	4,311.00	4,311.00	4,731.00
Repairs to Building and Elevator	344.46	529.71	392.95	364.34	872.71
Travelling Expenses	2,934.72	3,969.49	5,139.12	5,697.05	4,852.05
Advertising Expenses	6,129.10	8,419.12	9,100.85	12,621.54	14,770.74
Advertising	1,175.16	1,654.96	1,149.21	1,681.14	1,640.85
Shipping and Selling Expenses	4,848.26	4,515.89	4,580.93	5,095.88	5,680.03
Trucking and Expressage	1,866.99	1,838.90	2,061.29	2,051.16	2,108.73
Light and Heat	901.36	907.57	1,083.61	1,128.59	1,212.14

WINTHROP BENSON, INC.

Comparative Summarized Statement of Income Profit and Loss and Surplus—For the Years Ending December 31, 1954, 1955, 1956, 1957 and 1958

	Year Ending December 31, 1954	Year Ending December 31, 1955	Year Ending December 31, 1956	Year Ending December 31, 1957	Year Ending December 31, 1958
Telephone and Telegraph	$1,242.73	$1,438.33	$1,325.60	$1,385.42	$1,435.04
Letter Postage	2,879.31	3,494.21	4,335.91	4,541.32	3,207.43
Sundry Office and General Expenses	1,053.19	1,465.26	1,604.91	1,474.14	1,731.34
Insurance on Merchandise and Equipment	1,101.75	773.99	675.65	578.35	1,731.34
Depreciation of Furniture and Equipment	3,106.42	1,008.94	3,116.09	4,127.09	7,083.22
Provision for Bad Debts	12.80	58.40	734.39	1,322.88	1,145.12
Taxes—Federal		385.91	396.57	813.10	1,619.89
State		156.93	111.79	135.77	133.16
City					
	75,573.55	84,532.09	99,139.31	112,579.79	131,125.80
Other Income and Deductions from Income	$ 1,466.40*	$ 985.83	$ 3,873.34	$ 4,114.20	
Cash Discount (Net)	$ 469.60	$ 602.60	$ 125.36	$ 1,445.54	$ 1,646.60
Miscellaneous Income and Adjustments	422.61	779.38	224.02*	108.15*	504.88
Interest Paid	1,191.11*	1,426.67*	1,660.99*	2,107.99*	4,178.96*
	298.90*	44.69*	1,759.65*	770.60*	2,027.48*
Net Profit or Loss From Operations	$ 1,765.30*	$ 941.14	$ 2,113.69	$ 3,343.60	$ 2,381.92*

* Red figures.

WINTHROP BENSON, INC.

Comparative Summarized Statement of Income Profit and Loss and Surplus—For the Years Ending December 31, 1954, 1955, 1956, 1957 and 1958

	Year Ending December 31, 1954	Year Ending December 31, 1955	Year Ending December 31, 1956	Year Ending December 31, 1957	Year Ending December 31, 1958
Special Profit and Loss Credits and Charges					
Life Insurance Premiums on Officers —Less Cash Surrender Value	$ 86.19	$ 117.19*	487.82*	635.63*	617.66*
Proceeds of Insurance Policy on Life of Winthrop Benson — Less Cash Surrender Value					20,468.75
Net Profit or Loss for Year Transferred to Surplus	$ 1,679.11*	$ 763.95	$1,625.88	$ 2,707.97	$17,469.17
Surplus at Beginning of Year	$13,129.93	$10,010.82	$9,334.77	$9,520.65	$10,788.62
Deduct: Dividends on Preferred Stock	1,440.00	1,440.00	1,440.00	1,440.00	1,440.00
	11,689.93	8,570.82	7,894.77	8,080.65	9,348.62
Surplus at Year-End	$10,010.82	$ 9,334.77	$9,520.65	$10,788.62	$26,817.79

* Red figures.

82

[Harris]

Certification by Accountant

Winthrop Benson, Inc.
220 State Street
Kansas City, Mo.

We made an examination of accounts pertaining to the assets and liabilities of Winthrop Benson, Inc., as of December 31, 1958. Inventories taken and certified by the Company, were tested by us as to prices, computations and footings. Materials and supplies and inventory were based on the basis of the lower of cost or market.

On the above basis and information furnished us, more fully commented on in our detailed report of examination, it is our opinion that the accompanying statement shows the financial condition of the Company at the date stated. The statements for preceding years were prepared on the same basis as above.

HAND & HAND
Certified Public Accountants

Method 1

COMPUTATION OF VALUE OF COMMON STOCK

Year		*Surplus*
1954	....	$10,010.82
1955	....	9,334.77
1956	....	9,520.65
1957	....	10,788.62
1958	....	26,817.79

	5⟩	$66,472.65

Average surplus	....	$13,294.53
Capital stock	....	25,000.00

Average capital invested	....	$38,294.53
Value of preferred stock	....	24,000.00

Book value of common stock	....	$14,294.53
	200⟩	$14,294.53

Book value per share	....	$71.47

	Profit	*Loss*
1954	....	$1,679.11
1955	....	$763.95
1956	....	1,625.88
1957	....	2,707.97
1958 (after deducting insurance received on decedent's life) .		2,999.58

	$5,097.80	$4,678.69
	4,678.69	

	5⟩	$419.11

Average net profit	....	$83.82
Average capital invested	....	$38,294.53
		.06

		$2,297.6718
Average net profit	....	83.82
6% average capital invested	....	2,297.67

		None
Number of year purchase	....	x 5

Good will	....	None

Good will per share	....	None
Book value per share	....	$71.47
Value per share	....	$71.47

Method 2

Average net earnings of common stock capitalized at 8%		$83.82
		12.5
		41910
		16764
		8382
	200)	$1,047.750
Value per share on net earnings at 8%		$5.23
Net earning basis		$5.23
Book value plus good will basis		71.47
	2)	$76.70
Value per share		$38.35

§ 60. Schedule B; Stocks and Bonds; Valuation; No Value.

Infrequent is the estate not possessing stock that has only decorative value. While the Regulations make no reference to such securities, the instructions advise that securities returned as of no value, nominal value, or obsolete, *should be listed last,* and the address of the company and the State and date of incorporation should be stated. Copies of the correspondence or statements used as the basis for return at no value should be attached.[9]

It should not be taken for granted that stock is worthless because it is not listed or information is not generally available about it. There are firms dealing in such securities, and if they are worthless, such firms will furnish a letter of the facts supporting their opinion. Copies of such letters are customarily annexed to the return.

§ 61. Schedule B; Stocks and Bonds; Valuation; When Pledged.

The full value of securities pledged to secure an indebtedness of the decedent is included in the gross estate. If the decedent had a trading account with a broker, all securities belonging to the decedent and held by the broker at the date of death must be included at their fair market value as of the applicable valuation date. Securities purchased on margin for the decedent's account and held by a broker must also be returned at their

9. Instructions, Schedule B, Form 706.

fair market value as of the applicable valuation date. The amount of the decedent's indebtedness to a broker or other person with whom securities were pledged is allowed as a deduction from the gross estate.[10] The Regulation states the summary of the case law on the subject.[11] The fact that securities have been pledged has no effect on their value.[12] The proper practice is to list each security in Schedule B and list the amount due in Schedule K.

§ 62. Schedule B; Stocks and Bonds; Valuation; Subject to Option or Contract to Purchase.

In the "close corporation" there is quite likely to be found a buy-and-sell agreement or an option agreement which has been entered into between the decedent and the other stockholders.

The Regulation provides that another person may hold an option or a contract to purchase securities owned by the decedent at the time of his death. The effect, *if any*, that is given to the option or contract price in determining the value of the securities for Estate Tax purposes depends upon the circumstances of the particular case. Ordinarily, *no effect* will be given to an *option or contract* under which the *decedent is free to dispose* of the underlying securities at any price he chooses *during his life*. Such is the effect of an option or contract to purchase whatever shares of stock the decedent may own at the time of his death, or an agreement amounting only to a right of first refusal during the decedent's life. Even though the decedent's right to dispose of the underlying securities during his life is restricted, *if full and adequate consideration* in money or money's worth was not given for the option or contract, the option or contract price will be disregarded in determining the value of the securities. An agreement will *ordinarily* be presumed to have been entered into for *full and adequate consideration* in money or money's worth if it was arrived at as a result of *arm's length bargaining between strangers. However, this presumption does not apply* if the agreement is entered into *by the decedent* and those who are, directly or indirectly, the *natural objects of his bounty,* as for example, an agreement entered into

10. Reg, § 20.2031–2(g).

11. See City Bank Farmers Trust Co v Bowers, 2 F Supp 883, pet for rev dism 68 F2d 909 (CCA 2) (1933); Lyman v Comm, 83 F2d 811 (CCA 1) (1936); Borland, 38 BTA 598 (1938); Hartford Nat Bank & Trust Co v Smith, 54 F Supp 579 (1941).

12. Borland, note 11, supra; Lyman v Comm, note 11, supra.

by the decedent and a corporation controlled by the decedent and his family.[13]

The Regulation is new and to a large extent is a statement of case law. Not every agreement for the disposition of a stockholder's stock will fix the value of the stock for Estate Tax purposes. In order for an agreement to do so it must

(1) Be an arm's length transaction, *and*

(2) *Restrict* the sale of the interest *during life* unless first offered to the other interested parties, and upon death, *either* with option to the survivor to buy at a price fixed by the agreement,

or

(3) Provide for a binding agreement for sale by the deceased and purchase by the survivor.

Thus, the value is fixed for Federal Estate Tax purposes only under two kinds of agreement. The first is one in which the parties agree that *they will not sell their stock during life* without giving the other party the right to purchase, and if owned at the time of death, giving the other *an option* to purchase, at a price fixed by the agreement in either case.[14] The agreement fixes the price even if the survivor does not exercise the option.[15]

The second is where the parties have contracted that upon death the owner's estate is bound to sell his stock and the survivor is bound to buy it at the agreed price.[16]

The fact that the purchase price at the date of death is less than the fair market value does not affect the question of bona fides if the price was a fair price at the time the agreement was made.[17] But a price which indicates, together with other circumstances, that the agreement was a substitute for a testamentary disposition, will not be sustained.[18]

If, *instead of the survivor having the option* to purchase, *the estate has the option* to offer the stock to the survivor, and must offer it to the survivor before selling to any one else, the price

13. Reg, § 20.2031-2(h).

14. Wilson v Bowers, 57 F2d 682 (CCA 2) (1932); Lomb v Sugden, 82 F2d 166 (CCA 2) (1936); May v McGowan, 194 F2d 396 (CA 2) (1952); Salt, 17 TC 92 (1952); Broderick v Gore, 224 F2d 892 (CA 10) (1955).

15. Wilson v Bowers, note 14, supra.

16. Mitchell, 37 BTA 1 (1938);

Riecker, 3 TCM 1294 (1944); Third Nat. Bank v US, 64 F Supp 198 (1946); Newman, 31 BTA 772 (1934); Weil, 22 TC 1267 (1954).

17. May v McGowan, note 14, supra; Comm v Bensel, 100 F2d 639 (CCA 3) (1939).

18. Trammell, 18 TC 662 (1952).

fixed in such agreement *does not fix the value* for Federal Estate Tax purposes.[19] It may, however, have an effect upon the value.[20]

If the agreement gives an option to purchase, or binds the estate to sell and the survivor to purchase, but the parties *may dispose of their stock during their lives,* the agreement *does not fix* the Federal Estate Tax value.[1]

It will be observed that the Regulation injects the element of "full and adequate consideration in money or money's worth" into the consideration of the question. To the extent that the Regulation involves the question of whether the agreement was a substitute for a testamentary disposition there can be no disagreement. If it is intended to establish a test of equivalency of value between the parties to such an agreement, it is questionable whether the courts will sustain it.

It may be observed, that the rule applicable under the Federal Estate Tax statute is followed in only a few states.[2] In the other states in which the question has arisen, it has been held "that no agreement by a property owner fixing the value can oust the jurisdiction of or control the Commonwealth's appraisers; such agreement does not create a limitation on the value binding the Commonwealth but it will be considered with the other evidence."[3] A number of states have adopted this position either judicially or by opinions of the Attorney General.[4]

In cases in which it is claimed that the value of stock has been fixed for the purpose of the Federal Estate Tax by an agreement, a copy of the agreement, certified as a true and correct copy, should be annexed to the return.

§ 63. Schedule B; Stocks and Bonds; Interest; Dividends.

Dividends *declared* on shares of stock *prior to the death* of the decedent but *payable* to stockholders of record on a date *after his death* are not includible in his gross estate for Federal Estate

19. City Bank Farmers Trust Co, 23 BTA 663 (1931); Michigan Trust Co, 27 BTA 556 (1932); Koch, 28 BTA 363 (1933); Worcester County Trust Co v Comm, 134 F2d 578 (CCA 1) (1943).

20. Worcester County Trust Co v Comm, note 19, supra; Chamberlin, 2 TCM 469 (1943).

1. Mathews, 3 TC 525 (1944); Hoffman, 2 TC 1160 (1943); note 18, supra.

2. (Maryland) Ruling of Attorney General, May 4, 1950; (Mississippi) Strange v State Tax Commr, 192 Miss 765, 7 So2d 542 (1942); (New York) Fieux, 241 NY 277, 149 NE 857 (1925); Miller, 191 M 784, 79 NYS2d 372 (1948); (Wisconsin) Banta, 77 NW2d 739 (1956).

3. McLure, 347 Pa 481, 32 A2d 885 (1943).

4. DC; Ky; Mass; NJ; NC; Ohio; Tenn; Wash.

Tax purposes.[5] However, in a case where the stock is being traded on an exchange and is selling ex-dividend on the date of the decedent's death, the amount of the dividend should not be included in the gross estate as a separate item but should be added to the ex-dividend quotation in determining the fair market value of the stock as of the date of the decedent's death.[6]

Interest on bonds and dividends on stock are required to be shown separately in the schedule.[7] As each security is listed it is followed by an appropriate entry of any interest or dividends accrued prior to death. The amount is carried into the value column.[8]

Where the fiduciary elects the alternate valuation, interest and dividends may accrue before the alternate valuation date, or before the property is distributed, sold, exchanged or otherwise disposed of. Such interest and dividends are "excluded property"[9] and are not includible in the gross estate.[10]

§ 64. Schedule B; Stocks and Bonds; Community Property.

Where stocks and bonds are community property they are includible in the gross estate to the extent of the decedent's interest under the applicable law of the State, Territory, or possession of the United States, or of the foreign country.[11] What the extent of ownership of community property is in particular states has been discussed heretofore.[12] The usual case requires that the interest in stocks or bonds be reported in the same way as if the decedent was the owner, as tenant in common of the securities.

§ 65. Schedule C; Mortgages; Notes.

Mortgages, notes, contracts by the decedent to sell land and cash in possession and in bank are listed separately in the order given, in Schedule C.[13] In the case of mortgages it is required that there be stated (1) face value and unpaid balance, (2) date of mortgage, (3) date of maturity, (4) name of maker, (5) prop-

5. Instructions, Schedule B, Form 706; Lockie, 21 TC 64 (1954); Rev Rul 54–399, 1954-2 CB 279.

6. Instructions, Schedule B, Form 706; Reg, § 20.2031-2(j); Rev Rul 54–399, 1954-2 CB 279.

7. General Instructions, Form 706; Instructions, Schedule B, Form 706.

8. See Form No. 8; § 53, supra.

9. Reg, § 20.2032-1(d)(1)(2).

10. Maas v Higgins, 312 US 443, 85 L Ed 940, 61 S Ct 631 (1941).

11. General Instructions, Form 706.

12. See §§ 41, 48, supra.

13. Instructions, Schedule C, Form 706.

erty mortgaged, and (6) interest dates and rate of interest. Similar data is required in the case of notes.[14]

The Regulations make no reference to mortgages, merely providing for the valuation of notes.[15] This is undoubtedly because a mortgage is in substance in the nature of a secured note.

The fair market value of notes, secured or unsecured, is *presumed* to be the amount of unpaid principal, plus interest, *unless* the *executor establishes* that the value is lower or that the notes are worthless. However, items of interest shall be separately stated on the Estate Tax return. *If not returned at face value,* plus accrued interest, satisfactory evidence must be submitted that the note is worth less than the unpaid amount (because of the interest rate, date of maturity, or other cause), or that the note is uncollectible, either in whole or in part (by reason of the insolvency of the party or parties liable, or for other cause), and that any property pledged or mortgaged as security is insufficient to satisfy the obligation.[16]

During the depression years the valuation of mortgages was of great importance and an E.T. or Estate Tax Decision[17] was issued which promulgated rules for the valuation of mortgages or mortgage participation certificates which were claimed to be worth less than face value. At the same time there was devised Form No. 947 to be completed in such cases. The form is no longer in use, but the same information is furnished by affidavit. If it is claimed that a mortgage is worth less than face value because of the insufficiency of the security, the mortgage will be valued upon the basis of the fair market value of the property, less back taxes, estimated foreclosure expenses, and, where justified, the expense of rehabilitation.[18] It must be emphasized that the *presumption* is that a mortgage is worth the face amount.[19] Unless the fiduciary furnishes proof to the contrary, the presumption will prevail.[20] The question is one of fact, and when *the facts* establish that a mortgage is worth less than face value, the courts will act accordingly.[1]

The valuation of promissory notes presents many more problems than do mortgages, and the subject has been considerably

14. Note 13, supra; Reg, § 20.6018-3 (c)(2).

15. Reg, § 20.2031-4.

16. Note 15, supra.

17. E T 8, XV-2 CB 297 (1936).

18. Note 17, supra.

19. Hartley, 3 TCM 3 (1944).

20. Low, 2 TC 1114, aff'd 145 F2d 832 (CCA 2) (1945); note 19, supra.

1. Dibble, 6 BTA 732 (1927); Proctor v Hassett, 52 F Supp 12 (1943).

litigated. The problem may be complicated by the fact that the notes are installment notes and the necessity for determining the value of the unpaid installments.[2] Collection may be barred by the Statute of Limitations.[3] If such note is secured by collateral, it is includible in the gross estate,[4] but only to the extent of the value of the collateral.[5]

A note indorsed by the decedent to a bank in payment of an indebtedness has been held not to be an asset of the decedent's estate.[6] Where the note is payable only upon a contingency which does not occur, it is valueless.[7] Although it has been held that where a note is valueless at death, and a small percentage of the value was recovered several years thereafter, that such value is not includible,[8] it has also been held that collection in full five years after death on a note outlawed at the date of death, warranted inclusion of the note at face value.[9]

Primarily, the value of a note depends upon the facts in each case. If it is established by the fiduciary that the maker is insolvent,[10] or for any other reason the note is uncollectible,[11] there will be no value placed upon it. But in the absence of such proof it will be included at full value.[12] The opinion expressed of the value of a note by the state appraiser is not binding on the Federal authorities.[13]

2. Gump v Comm, 124 F2d 540 (CCA 9), cert den 316 US 697, 86 L Ed 1766, 62 S Ct 1292 (1942).

3. Philbrick v Manning, 57 F Supp 245 (1944).

4. United States Trust Co, 14 BTA 312 (1928).

5. Walker, 4 TC 390 (1945); see also Harper, 11 TC 717 (1948).

6. Donalson, 6 BTA 455 (1927).

7. Oliver v Comm, 148 F2d 210 (CCA 3) (1945).

8. Millikin v Magruder, 55 F Supp 895, affd 149 F2d 593 (CCA 4) (1944).

9. Buck v Helvering, 73 F2d 760 (CCA 9) (1934).

10. Note 8, supra; Lincoln, 1 TCM 326 (1942); Malloch Westover, 51-1 USTC ¶10,816 (1951); Scott v Hendrickson, 41-2 USTC ¶10,098 (1941).

11. Walker, 4 TC 390 (1944); Henry, 7 BTA 172 (1927).

12. Cross, 5 BTA 621 (1926); Hill, 8 BTA 1277 (1921); Burr, 4 TCM 1054 (1945).

13. Hill, note 12, supra.

FORM NO. 10

Schedule C; Mortgages, Notes, and Cash

Did the decedent, at the time of his death, own any mortgages, notes, or cash? [x] Yes [ ] No

Item No.	Description	Subsequent valuation date	Alternate value	Value at date of death
1	First mortgage bond and mortgage in the face amount of $10,000.00, unpaid balance $9,-000.00, dated July 15, 1958, due July 14, 1963, executed by Henry Field, upon premises 216 Catalpa Avenue, San Diego, Cal., interest 5%, payable Jan. 15th and semiannually.			$9,000.00
	Interest accrued on Item 1 from July 15, 1959 to date of death			12.50
	(See affidavit of valuation annexed.)*			
2	$500 note, unpaid balance $500, dated Sept. 15, 1959, due March 15, 1960, executed by John Benson, interest 6%.			500.00
	Interest accrued on Item 2 from Sept. 15, 1959 to date of death			9.59
3	$1,000 note, unpaid balance $1,000, dated Oct. 12, 1955, payable on demand, executed by Henry Benson, interest 6%.			no value
	(See affidavit annexed.)			
4	The decedent on Dec. 15, 1959 contracted to sell to James Woods the following property: (*describe as in Item 1, Form No. 851, § 4414, supra*). The sale price thereof is $15,000.00, of which $2,500.00 was paid upon contract. The balance due as of decedent's death, without interest.			4,296.70
5	Cash in possession of decedent			35.60
6	Account San Diego Savings & Loan Assn., 2687 Verdugo Avenue, San Diego, Cal., Account number 897654.			2,875.40
	Interest on Item 6 from Jan. 1, 1960 to date of death			1.60
7	Account Bank of America NTSA, San Diego, Cal., checking account.			1,262.85
	TOTAL (also enter under the Recapitulation, Schedule O)			$17,994.24

* *When mortgage worth less than face value.*

(If more space is needed. insert additional sheets of same size)

Schedule C—Page 11

Estate of WINTHROP BENSON

FORM NO. 11

Affidavit Mortgage Worth Less Than Face Value

STATE OF CALIFORNIA
COUNTY OF SAN DIEGO } ss:

KATHERINE BENSON, being duly sworn, says:

I am the Executrix under the Last Will and Testament of Winthrop Benson, deceased.

That Item 1, Schedule C is a bond, secured by a mortgage on premises 216 Catalpa Avenue, San Diego, California, in the face amount of $10,000, reduced at the date of the decedent's death to the sum of $9,000.

That the assessed value of the said premises for the year 1959 is $8,000. At the date of the decedent's death there were arrears of interest due for 8 months and of taxes for one year. As appears from the annexed affidavit of B. Washburn Fielding, a duly licensed real estate appraiser, the value of said premises does not exceed the sum of $7,500, and the value of said bond is therefore the sum of $7,500. That Henry Field, the mortgagor, was adjudicated a bankrupt in the United States District Court for the Southern District of California, on the 20th day of January, 1959, and listed among his liabilities his obligation upon the said bond. No dividend was paid in the said bankrupt's estate.

KATHERINE BENSON

Sworn to before me this 19th day
of March, 1960.

        Marsha Hayes
        Notary Public
        San Diego County

FORM NO. 12

Affidavit Note of No Value

STATE OF CALIFORNIA
COUNTY OF SAN DIEGO } ss:

KATHERINE BENSON, being duly sworn, says:

I am the Executrix under the Last Will and Testament of Winthrop Benson, deceased.

That Item 3, Schedule C, is a promissory note executed by Henry Benson, the brother of the decedent, in the face amount of $1,000, payable on demand. That said note is dated October 12th, 1955. The said Henry Benson is insolvent and unable to pay the said note or any part thereof.

Judgments have been recovered against Henry Benson by various persons, aggregating in excess of $30,000. No part of any of said judgments has been paid, although the last of said judgments was recovered in 1958, and in proceedings for the collection thereof the said debtor disclosed no assets, means, or ability to pay.

I, therefore, verily believe that the aforesaid note is of no value.

KATHERINE BENSON

Sworn to before me this 19th day
of March, 1960
        Marshall A. Hahn
        Notary Public
        San Diego County

§ 66. Schedule C; Contract by the Decedent to Sell Land.

A description of the seller's interest in land contracts should include name of buyer, date of contract, description of property, sale price, initial payment, amounts of installment payments, unpaid balance of principal and accrued interest, interest rate and date prior to decedent's death to which interest had been paid.[14]

An acceptable method of determining the value of such contract is by a schedule of adjustments as of the date of death, in the same manner as upon closing of title.

FORM NO. 13

Adjustments on Contract by Decedent to Sell Land

All adjustments as of date of death, January 10, 1960

Credits		Debits	
Paid on contract	$2,500.00	Purchase Price	$15,000.00
First mortgage	8,000.00	Insurance	182.70
Interest on first mortgage, 6%, 2 months	160.00		
Taxes	212.00		
Water rates	14.00		
Total credits	$10,886.00	Total debits	$15,182.70
		Total credits	10,886.00
		Balance payable	$ 4,296.70

14. Reg, § 20.6018–3(c)(2); Instructions, Schedule C, Form 706.

§ 67. Schedule C; Cash; Bank Accounts.

A description of bank accounts should disclose name and address of depository, amount on deposit, whether a checking, savings, or a time-deposit account, rate of interest, if any payable, amount of interest accrued and payable, and serial number.[15] The instructions further advise that cash in possession should be listed separately from bank deposits and if statements are obtained from banks they should be retained for inspection by an Internal Revenue agent,[16] now Estate Tax examiner.

The amount of cash belonging to the decedent at the date of his death, whether in his possession or in the possession of another, or deposited with a bank, is included in the decedent's gross estate. If bank checks outstanding at the time of the decedent's death and given in discharge of bona fide, legal obligations of the decedent, incurred for an adequate and full consideration in money or money's worth are subsequently honored by the bank and charged to the decedent's account, the balance remaining in the account may be returned, but only if the obligations are not claimed as deductions from the gross estate.[17] Obviously a bank account cannot be reduced by checks cashed by the bank after the decedent's death and a further deduction taken.[18]

Cash includes many items such as refunds for electric bills, safe deposit fees, insurance and the like. It includes a bonus payment[19] and executor's fees to which the decedent has become entitled as an estate fiduciary.[20]

§ 68. Schedule C; Community Property.

As in the case of other assets of a decedent held as community property, mortgages, notes and cash are reported to the extent of the interest of the decedent.[1]

§ 69. Schedule D; Insurance; Defined.

The statute has never defined what insurance is. The Regulations use the same description as formerly, namely, that the term "insurance" refers to life insurance of every description, including death benefits paid by fraternal beneficial societies

---

15. Reg, § 20.6018–3 (c)(3).
16. Instructions, Schedule C, Form 706.
17. Reg, § 20.2031–5.
18. Hauptfuhrer, 9 TCM 974 (1947).
19. McKitterick, 12 BTA 130 (1940).
20. McGlue, 41 BTA 1199 (1940).
1. See §§ 41, 48, supra.

operating under the lodge system.[2] The insurance must be upon
the life of the decedent.[3] It must have a contractual basis,[4] and
result in a settlement of the contract.[5] Judicial decisions have
held that it includes accidental death benefits,[6] annuity and life
insurance combinations,[7] group insurance,[8] health insurance,[9]
death benefits in addition to retirement benefits,[10] stock exchange benefits,[11] war risk insurance,[12] and National Service life
insurance.[13]

There are a number of benefits, which while considered by
many to be insurance, are not life insurance, and are included
under other sections of the Code. Examples of these are annuities,[14] Civil Service death benefits,[14a] retirement system benefits,[14b] pension fund payments,[14c] premium refunds,[14d] and insurance policies which are equivalent to a bequest.[14e]

§ 70. Schedule D; Insurance; Statutory Provisions.

Estate taxation of insurance under the Federal statutes has
periodically varied, and it is doubtful that the end is in sight.
Prior to 1918, insurance was not includible in the gross estate.[15]
Thereafter and until 1942, insurance payable to the estate of a
decedent was includible in the gross estate to the full extent
thereof, but insurance payable to designated beneficiaries was

2. Reg, § 20.2042–1 (a)(1).

3. Ballinger, 23 BTA 1312 (1931).

4. Illinois Merchants Trust Co. 12 BTA 818 (1928).

5. Chew v Comm, 148 F2d 76 (CCA 5), cert den 325 US 882, 89 L Ed 1997, 65 S Ct 1575 (1945).

6. Ackerman, 15 BTA 635 (1929).

7. Bohnen v Harrison, 199 F2d 492 (CA 7), affd 345 US 946, 97 L ed 1370, 73 S Ct 836 (1953); but see Rev Rul 54–552, IRB 1954–2 CB 284 to the contrary, and cases cited. See however, § 152, infra.

8. Old Colony Trust Co, 39 BTA 871 (1939).

9. Goodenough, 29 BTA 211 (1933).

10. Snyder, 4 TCM 957 (1944).

11. Comm v Treganowan, 182 F2d 288 (CA 2) (1950).

12. US Trust Co v Comm, 307 US 57, 83 L Ed 1104, 59 S Ct 692 (1939).

13. Deputy Commissioner's Letters, Nov. 11, 1944, Mar. 14, 1946.

14. Comm v Clise, 122 F2d 998 (CCA 9), cert den 315 US 821, 86 L ed 1218, 62 S Ct 919 (1941); Helvering v Le Gierse, 39 BTA 1134, affd 110 F2d 734 (CCA 2), revd 312 US 531, 85 L ed 996, 61 S Ct 646 (1941); Mearkle v Comm, 45 BTA 894, affd 129 F2d 386 (CCA 3) (1941).

14a. E T 11, 1937–2 CB 470.

14b. Wilson, 42 BTA 1196 (1940); Kernochan v US, 29 F Supp 86 (1939); Knight v Finnegan, 74 F Supp 900 (1947).

14c. Note 4, supra.

14d. Note 5, supra.

14e. First Trust & Deposit Co v Shaughnessy, 134 F2d 940 (CCA 2), cert den 320 US 744, 88 L ed 442, 64 S Ct 46 (1943).

15. See Mimnaugh v US, 66 Ct Cls 411, cert den 280 US 563, 74 L ed 617, 50 S Ct 24 (1929); Guettel v US, 67 Ct Cls 613.

includible only to the extent that it exceeded $40,000. The Revenue Act of 1942 among other changes eliminated this provision and made a number of other changes with respect to insurance. Prior to that time the payment of premiums test for includibility of insurance was formulated.[16] The result of these amendments was that insurance proceeds were includible in the decedent's gross estate if

(1) receivable by the executor,

(2) receivable by other beneficiaries

(a) where it was purchased with premiums or other consideration paid *directly or indirectly,* by the decedent, and in the proportion that the premiums paid by the decedent bore to the total premiums paid

(b) where the decedent possessed at the time of death any of the *incidents of ownership,* exercisable either alone or in conjunction with any other person.

"Incident of ownership" did not include a reversionary interest.[17]

The 1954 Code made two changes, the most revolutionary of which was to eliminate from the decedent's gross estate the proceeds of insurance upon which he paid the premiums. The other change was to include as an "incident of ownership" the retention of a reversionary interest by the decedent, if the value of such interest exceeds 5% of the value of the policy *immediately before* the death of the insured, and whether arising from express provision therefor or by operation of law.

The statute now provides for the inclusion in the gross estate of a decedent

(1) To the extent of the amount receivable by the *executor* as insurance under policies on the life of the decedent.

(2) To the extent of the amount receivable by *all other beneficiaries* as insurance under policies on the life of the decedent with respect to which the *decedent possessed at his death any of the incidents of ownership,* exercisable either alone or in conjunction with any other person.

The term "incident of ownership" includes a *reversionary interest* (whether arising by the express terms of the policy or other instrument or by operation of law) *only if* the *value* of such reversionary interest *exceeded 5%* of the value of the policy

16. TD 5032, 1941–1 CB 427, Jan. 10, 1941.

17. IRC, § 811 (g) (1939 Code).

immediately before the death of the decedent. The term "reversionary interest" includes a possibility that the policy or the proceeds of the policy, may return to the decedent or his estate, or may be subject to a power of disposition by him.[18]

The statute thus establishes the same test of a reversionary interest as in the case of transfers taking effect at death.[19]

Each of the matters affecting the inclusion of insurance on the life of the decedent are treated in succeeding sections.

§ 71. Schedule D; Insurance; Constitutionality.

As might be anticipated, estate taxation of insurance was subject to attack on the ground of unconstitutionality from the very beginning. When the Revenue Act of 1918[20] for the first time taxed insurance as property includible in the gross estate, while it was held that the provision did not apply retroactively, the Supreme Court did not pass upon the constitutionality of the statute.[1] After the enactment of the Revenue Act of 1924, if insurance was taken out at any time by the decedent and he had an incident of ownership at the time of his death, it was included in his gross estate.[2] The constitutionality of the statute has been sustained in a number of decisions.[3] Until recently the estate taxation of life insurance appeared immune to attack upon constitutional grounds. But the Seventh Circuit, in a decision[4] which as to decedents dying after the 1954 Code is academic held that the premium payment test as applied to insurance transferred by the decedent during his life, was a direct tax in violation of the Constitution. Since, as we have seen, the premium payment test has been eliminated, unless it is restored, which is not an unlikely prospect, the decision is of historical interest only, except in cases still pending under the 1939 Code. The Commissioner has announced that the decision will not be

---

18. IRC, § 2042 (1954 Code).

19. See IRC, § 2033 (1954 Code); see also § 145, infra.

20. § 402(f), Rev Act 1918.

1. Lewellyn v Frick, 268 US 238, 69 L ed 934, 45 S Ct 487, affg 298 F 803 (1925); see also Helvering v St Louis Union Trust Co, 296 US 39, 80 L ed 29, 56 S Ct 74 (1935); Becker v St Louis Union Trust Co, 296 US 48, 80 L ed 35, 56 S Ct 78 (1935).

2. Levy v Comm, 65 F2d 412 (CCA 2) (1933); Schongalla v Hickey, 149 F2d 687 (CCA 2) (1945); Broderick v Keefe, 112 F2d 293 (CCA 1) (1940).

3. Chase Nat Bank of NY v US, 278 US 327, 73 L ed 405, 49 S Ct 126 (1929); Levy v Comm, note 2, supra; Colonial Trust Co v Kraemer, 63 F Supp 866 (1946).

4. Kohl v US, 226 F2d 381 (CA 7) (1955).

considered a precedent, although no review was sought because of procedural defects.[5]

§ 72. Schedule D; Insurance; the Regulations; Generally.

The Treasury Regulations with respect to life insurance are complete and informative. After generally pointing out that insurance receivable by or for the benefit of the estate and by other beneficiaries is includible in the gross estate, they define insurance as previously noted.[6] There is then directed to attention a fact which might be overlooked by those not familiar with the statute. *Proceeds of life insurance which are not includible in the gross estate under Section 2042* (the section dealing with insurance) *may,* depending upon the facts of the particular case, *be includible under some other section of the Estate Tax Law.* For example, if the decedent possessed incidents of ownership in an insurance policy on his life but gratuitously transferred all rights in the policy in contemplation of death, the proceeds would be includible under Section 2035. Section 2042 has no application to the inclusion in the gross estate of the value of rights in an insurance policy on the life of a person other than the decedent, or the value of rights in a combination annuity contract and life insurance policy on the decedent's life (i.e., a "retirement income" policy with death benefit or an "endowment" policy) under which there was no insurance element at the time of the decedent's death.[7] The latter provision has been discussed previously.[8]

The Regulations further discuss in detail the amount to be included,[9] the meaning of "receivable by or for the benefit of the estate"[10] and "receivable by other beneficiaries,"[11] insurance in community property states,[12] "incidents of ownership,"[13] and a "reversionary interest."[14] The Proposed Regulation had a provision with respect to partnership or corporate insurance under buy-and-sell agreements,[15] which happily has been deleted from the Regulations. Each of these provisions will be treated in succeeding sections.

---

5. Rev Rul 56–250, 1956–1CB 659.
6. Reg, § 20.2042–1 (a)(1).
7. Reg, § 20.2042–1 (a)(2).
8. § 69, supra.
9. Reg, § 20.2042–1 (a)(3).
10. Reg, § 20.2042–1 (b).
11. Reg, § 20.2042–1 (c)(1).
12. Reg, § 20.2042–1 (b)(2).
13. Reg, § 20.2042–1 (c)(2)(3)(4)(5).
14. Reg, § 20.2042–1(c)(3).
15. Proposed Reg, § 20.2042–1(c)(6).

§ 73. Schedule D; Insurance; What Included.

The first consideration in the preparation of Schedule D is that the insurance reported be upon the life of the decedent.[16] The next is that it must in fact be insurance and not an item resembling insurance.[17] If the latter, the item must be reported in other schedules.[18] These questions having been answered, then all insurance receivable by or for the benefit of the decedent's estate, and all insurance receivable by all other beneficiaries with respect to which the decedent possessed at his death any of the "incidents of ownership" exercisable either alone or in conjunction with any other person, including a reversionary interest, whether arising under the express terms of the policy or an instrument or by operation of law, provided the reversionary interest exceeds 5% of the value of the policy immediately before the death of the decedent,[19] is includible in the gross estate.

The amount to be included in the gross estate is discussed hereafter.[20]

As we have noted,[1] between 1918 and 1942 insurance payable to designated beneficiaries was not includible to the full extent, but that has not been so since 1942. It is also to be observed that the statute was changed in 1954. As to decedents who died prior thereto the statute in force at the time should be followed.

§ 74. Schedule D; Insurance; Receivable by the Executor.

The statute refers to insurance under policies on the life of the decedent *receivable by the executor*.[2] As the Regulation points out, the term "executor" is not used in the usual sense. The statute requires the inclusion in the gross estate of the proceeds of insurance on the decedent's life receivable by the executor or administrator in his representative capacity, or payable to the decedent's estate. It makes no difference whether the estate is the beneficiary under the terms of the policy or as a matter of fact. Thus, if under the terms of an insurance policy the proceeds are receivable by another beneficiary but are subject to an obligation, legally binding upon the other beneficiary, to pay taxes, debts, or other charges enforceable against the estate,

16. Note 6, supra; § 69, supra.
17. See § 69, supra.
18. See note 7, supra.
19. IRC, § 2042 (1954 Code).

20. § 83, infra.
1. § 70, supra.
2. IRC, § 2042 (1) (1954 Code).

then the amount of such proceeds required for the payment in full (to the extent of the beneficiary's obligation) of such taxes, debts or other charges is includible in the gross estate. Similarly, if the decedent purchased an insurance policy in favor of another person or corporation as collateral security for a loan or other accommodation, its proceeds are considered to be receivable for the benefit of the estate. The amount of the loan outstanding at the date of the decedent's death, with interest accrued thereon to that date, will be deductible in determining the taxable estate.[3]

Prior to the Revenue Act of 1942, the question of whether insurance was receivable by the decedent's estate or by other beneficiaries was of greater importance than it is today, since if it was then receivable by the estate the entire proceeds were includible in the gross estate, while if receivable by other beneficiaries it was only includible to the extent that it exceeded $40,000. The only importance the question has today is that if it is receivable by the decedent's estate, taxability is unquestioned, whereas if it is receivable by another beneficiary it is only taxable if the decedent possessed an "incident of ownership." Decisions on the question, therefore, have a bearing on the determination in the latter case.

It is not necessary that the policy be payable to the estate of the decedent to come within the statute. It is considered payable to the estate whether it is payable to the estate in so many words,[4] or whether it is payable to the executor,[5] an executor and trustee,[6] or executors, administrators and assigns.[7] It is sufficient that the amounts are receivable by the executor or other representative.[8] The fact that it is payable to the estate is not necessarily controlling, if under state law the proceeds are in fact receivable by one or ones other than the estate.[9] State law controls.[10] Where it is payable to a trustee, the question is whether the latter is obligated to pay debts and other charges[11]

---

3. Reg, § 20.2042–1 (b)(1).

4. Bodell v Comm, 47 BTA 62, affd 138 F2d 553 (CCA 1), cert den 321 US 778, 88 L Ed 1071, 64 S Ct 619 (1944).

5. Proutt, 41 BTA 1299 (1940).

6. US v First Nat Bank & Trust Co of Minn, 42–1 USTC ¶10,164, affd 133 F2d 886 (CCA 8) (1943).

7. Merrill Trust Co, 21 BTA 970 (1931).

8. Matthews, 3 TC 525 (1944).

9. Webster v Comm, 120 F2d 514 (CCA 5) (1941); Nyemaster, 2 TCM 1183 (1943); Comm v Jones, 62 F2d 496 (CCA 6) (1933).

10. Comm v Jones, note 9, supra.

11. Morton, 23 BTA 236 (1931).

or may do so in his discretion.[12] Where the insurance is security for a debt it is includible to the extent that it is so applied.[13]

§ 75. Schedule D; Insurance; Receivable by Other Beneficiaries.

The second kind of insurance includible in the gross estate of the decedent is that receivable by *all other beneficiaries* as insurance on the life of the decedent *with respect to which the decedent possessed at his death any of the incidents of ownership.*[14]

This raises the question at once whether the decedent at the time of his death possessed an incident of ownership, a truly troublesome question. That subject is discussed in the succeeding section.

The phrase "all other beneficiaries" has been construed to include an assignee who did not pay an adequate consideration for the assignment.[15] Where the assignment of the policy took place prior to the death of the insured and it was cashed in by the owner, there being no proceeds payable at the death of the insured, the assignee was not a beneficiary of the policy within the meaning of the statute.[16]

The status of the beneficiary is not important. Thus it is not necessary that the beneficiary be an individual. Insurance for the benefit of a partnership or corporation has been held includible in the gross estate.[17] Where a creditor collected the proceeds of insurance and applied them to his debt, the proceeds were held part of the gross estate.[18] Where the decedent had a refusal right over a trust containing insurance on his life, even though he had not purchased the insurance, it was held includible in his estate.[19]

The Regulation states the case law on the subject, and provides that the statute requires the inclusion in the gross estate of the proceeds of insurance on the decedent's life not receivable by or for the benefit of the estate, if the decedent possessed at

12. Old Colony Trust Co, 39 BTA 871 (1939); Wade, 47 BTA 21 (1942).

13. Hofferbert, 46 BTA 1101 (1942); note 8, supra; Reinhold, 3 TCM 285 (1944).

14. IRC, § 2042(2) (1954 Code).

15. Billings, 35 BTA 1147 (1937); Rosenstock, 41 BTA 635 (1940); Pritchard, 4 TC 204 (1944).

16. Hutchinson, 20 TC 479 (1953).

17. Mitchell, 37 BTA 1 (1938); Legallet, 41 BTA 294 (1940); Dobrzensky, 34 BTA 305 (1936); Tompkins, 13 TC 1054 (1949).

18. Hofferbert, note 13, supra.

19. Karagheusian, 233 F2d 197 (CA 2), revg 23 TC 806 (1956).

the date of his death any of the incidents of ownership in the
policy, exercisable either alone or in conjunction with any other
person. However, if the decedent did not possess any of the
incidents of ownership at the time of his death nor transfer them
in contemplation of death, no part of the proceeds would be includible in his gross estate. Thus, if the decedent owned a
policy of insurance on his life and, four years before his death,
irrevocably assigned his entire interest in the policy to his
wife, retaining no reversionary interest therein, the proceeds
of the policy would not be includible in his gross estate.[20]

§ 76. Schedule D; Insurance; Incidents of Ownership.

That portion of the Federal Estate Tax Law taxing insurance
proceeds which has been most fruitful of litigation has involved
the question of what is an incident of ownership.

As noted in the preceding section, insurance on the life of
the decedent is includible in the gross estate when it is receivable by beneficiaries other than the decedent's estate if the
decedent possessed at the time of his death any of the incidents
of ownership, exercisable either alone or in conjunction with
any other person. The statute further provides that an "incident of ownership" *includes a reversionary interest* (whether
arising by the express terms of the policy or other instrument
or by operation of law) *only if* the value of the reversionary
interest *exceeded 5%* of the value of the policy immediately
before the death of the decedent. The term "reversionary interest" *includes a possibility* that the policy or the proceeds
of the policy, *may* return to the decedent or his estate, or *may
be* subject to a power of disposition by him.[1]

The test of includibility on the grounds of a retention of a
reversionary interest is a partial return to the doctrine of
Bailey vs. United States,[2] which followed the holding in Helvering vs. Hallock.[3] As we shall see,[4] the 5% limitation was
caused by the inequitable decision in Spiegel vs. Comm.[5] The
Helvering vs. Hallock case taxed lifetime transfers in which
the decedent *expressly* retained a reversionary interest. As
the Committee Report on the present statute points out, in

20. Reg, § 20.2042-1(c)(1).
1. Note 14, supra.
2. 31 F Supp 778, cert dism on stipulation, US Sup Ct, Sept. 27, 1940.
3. 309 US 106, 84 L ed 604, 60 S Ct
444 (1939).
4. See § 120, infra.
5. 335 US 701, 93 L ed 330, 69 S Ct
30 (1948).

order to place life insurance policies in an analogous position to other property, it was necessary to make the 5% reversionary interest rule, applicable to other property, also applicable to insurance.[6]

Since the elimination of the payment of premiums as a test of includibility of insurance, the primary question in the estates of decedents dying on and after August 17, 1954 is, what is an "incident of ownership". The question usually arises when the decedent has made a lifetime transfer of the policy, neither in contemplation of death nor intended to take effect at death, but it is claimed that he has retained an incident of ownership.

The test is whether the decedent has retained to himself at the date of his death any power of control over the proceeds, or any substantially beneficial interest, so as to shift economic benefits from the dead to the living.[7] The obvious situations are those where the decedent retained the right to change the beneficiary, either alone,[8] or with the consent of the beneficiary,[9] to surrender and cancel and to pledge the policies as security for loans,[10] and to borrow on the policies.[11] The less easily recognized cases are those where the decedent has a power of revocation[12] or a veto,[13] or the insurance is pledged for the payment of alimony.[14] The proceeds in such case have been included in the gross estate. The same has been held where the proceeds are devoted to the payment of funeral and administration expenses.[15] Whether the proceeds are subject to payment of debts or not is another consideration.[16]

Whereas under the 1939 Code a reversionary interest was not deemed an incident of ownership,[17] as we have seen, the retention of a reversionary interest is an incident of ownership under the present statute, *but only* if it exceeds 5% of

6. House Committee Report, IRC, § 2042 (1954 Code).

7. Ballard v Helburn, 9 F Supp 812, affd 85 F2d 613 (CCA 6) (1936).

8. Singer v Shaughnessy, 198 F2d 178 (CA 2) (1952); Wilson, 10 TCM 750 (1948).

9. Godfrey v Smyth, 50–1 USTC ¶ 10,753, affd 180 F2d 220 (CA 9) (1950); note 19, supra.

10. Chase Nat. Bank v US, 278 US 327, 73 L ed 405, 149 S Ct 126 (1928).

11. Chase Nat. Bank v Hickey, 42–2 USTC ¶10,208.

12. Reed 24 BTA 166 (1931).

13. Note 19, supra.

14. Mason, 43 BTA 813 (1941).

15. Pacific Nat. Bank of Seattle, 40 BTA 128 (1939).

16. Comm v Lyne, 90 F2d 745 (CCA 1) (1937); Comm v Jones, 62 F2d 496 (CCA 6) (1933).

17. IRC, § 811(g)(2) (1939 Code).

the value of the policy *immediately before the decedent's death.*
This does not mean 5% of the proceeds of the policy. The usual
case in which this occurs is where the decedent is the contingent beneficiary if the transferee predeceases him.[18] It will
be noted that the reversionary interest exists whether it is expressly retained or accrues by operation of law, such as intestacy.
It includes not only an easily identifiable reversionary interest
but one where there is a *possibility* that the policy or proceeds
may either return to the decedent or his estate or be subject
to *a power of disposition* by him.[19]

The date of the issuance of the policy has no bearing on the
possibility of reverter.[20]

§ 77. Schedule D; Insurance; Incidents of Ownership; Regula-
tions.

The Regulations are most helpful in pointing out the situations in which an incident of ownership may exist. The term
"incidents of ownership" is not limited in its meaning to ownership of the policy in its technical legal sense. Generally speaking, the term has reference to the right of the insured or his estate to the economic benefits of the policy. Thus, it includes
the power to change the beneficiary, to surrender or cancel
the policy, to assign the policy, to revoke an assignment, to
pledge the policy for a loan, or to obtain from the insurer a
loan against the surrender value of the policy. Similarly, the
term includes a power to change the beneficiary reserved to a
corporation of which the decedent is sole stockholder.[1]

The term "incident of ownership" also includes a reversionary interest in the policy or its proceeds, whether arising
by the express terms of the policy or other instrument or by
operation of law, but only if the value of the reversionary interest immediately before the death of the decedent exceeded
5% of the value of the policy. The term "reversionary interest"
includes a possibility that the policy or its proceeds may return
to the decedent or his estate and a possibility that the policy or
its proceeds may become subject to a power of disposition by

18. See Brous, 10 TC 597 (1948);
Newbold, 4 TCM 568 (1945); Schongalla
v Hickey, 149 F2d 687 (1945), cert den
326 US 736, 90 L ed 439, 66 S Ct 46
(1945); Thierot, 7 TC 1119 (1949);
Donan, 6 TCM 185 (1946).

19. IRC, § 2042(2) (1954 Code).
20. Bodell v Comm, 138 F2d 553 (CCA
1), cert den 321 US 778, 88 L ed 1071,
64 S Ct 619 (1944).
1. Reg, § 20.2042-1(c)(2).

him. In order to determine whether or not the value of a reversionary interest immediately before the death of the decedent exceeded 5% of the value of the policy, the principles contained in the Regulations for the valuation of a reversionary interest in the case of property included in the gross estate because a reversionary interest causes property to be so included as a transfer taking effect at death, apply.[2] In that connection there must be specifically taken into consideration any incidents of ownership held by others immediately before the decedent's death which would affect the value of the reversionary interest. For example, the decedent would not be considered to have a reversionary interest in the policy of a value in excess of 5% if the power to obtain the cash surrender value existed in a designated beneficiary immediately before the decedent's death and was exercisable by such beneficiary alone and in all events. The terms "reversionary interest" and "incidents of ownership" do not include the possibility that the decedent might receive a policy or its proceeds by inheritance through the estate of another person, or as a surviving spouse under a statutory right of election or a similar right.[3]

A decedent is considered to have an "incident of ownership" in an insurance policy held in trust if, under the terms of the policy, the decedent (either alone or in conjunction with another person or persons) has the power (as trustee or otherwise) to change the beneficial ownership in the policy or its proceeds, or the time or manner of enjoyment thereof, even though the decedent has no beneficial interest in the trust. Moreover, such a power may result in the inclusion in the decedent's gross estate under Sections 2036 or 2038 of the Internal Revenue Code of the other property held in the trust, if for example, the decedent has the power to surrender the insurance policy and if the income used to pay premiums on the policy would be currently payable to a beneficiary of the trust in the event that the policy were surrendered.[4]

As an additional step in determining whether or not a decedent possessed any incidents of ownership in a policy or any part of a policy, regard must be given to the effect of State or other applicable law upon the terms of the policy. For example, assume that the decedent purchased a policy of insurance on

---

2. Reg, § 20.2037–1(c)(3)(4).

3. Reg, § 20.2042–1(c)(3).

4. Reg, § 20.2042–1(c)(4).

his life with funds held by him and his wife as community property, designating their son as beneficiary but retaining the right to surrender the policy. Under the local law, the proceeds upon surrender would have inured to the marital community. Assuming that the policy is not surrendered and that the son receives the proceeds on the decedent's death, the wife's transfer of her half interest in the policy was not considered absolute before the decedent's death. Upon the wife's prior death, half of the value of the policy would have been included in her gross estate. Under these circumstances, the power of surrender possessed by the decedent as agent for his wife with respect to half of the policy is not, for purposes of the section, an "incident of ownership", and the decedent is, therefore, deemed to possess an incident of ownership in only half of the policy.[5]

It will be observed that the Regulation is a combination of a statement of the statute and court decisions on the subject.[6]

§ 78. Schedule D; Insurance; Change of Beneficiary.

Unquestionably, the most important right in connection with a policy of insurance is the right to change the beneficiary. It has been described as a right and not as property.[7] It has been one of the most frequently litigated questions on the taxability of insurance. Since the test of includibility is the retention of control over the proceeds so as to shift economic benefits from the dead to the living,[8] it is obvious that the retention of the right to change the beneficiary is squarely within that category.

The proceeds of policies have been repeatedly held includible in the gross estate where the decedent reserved the right to change the beneficiary.[9] This has been held under all previous

5. Reg, § 20.2042–1(c)(5).

6. See §§ 70, 73, 76, supra and § 81, infra.

7. Dimock v Corwin, 19 F Supp 56, affd 99 F2d 799 (CCA 2), affd 306 US 363, 83 L ed 763, 59 S Ct 551 (1937).

8. Ballard v Helburn, 9 F Supp 812, affd 85 F2d 613 (CCA 6) (1933).

9. Heiner v Grandin, 44 F2d 141, amended, 56 F2d 1082 (CCA 3), cert den 286 US 561, 76 L ed 1294, 52 S Ct 643 (1936); Liebes v Comm, 63 F2d 870 (CCA 9) (1933); Chase Nat Bank of NY v Brown, 278 US 327, 73 L ed 405, 49 S Ct 126 (1929); Richardson, 20 BTA 728 (1930); Cook v Comm, 66 F2d 995 (CCA 3) (1933); Levy v Comm, 65 F2d 412 (CCA 2) (1933); Igleheart v Comm, 77 F2d 704 (CCA 5) (1935); Schongalla v Hickey, 60 F Supp 814, affd 149 F2d 687 (CCA 2), cert den 326 US 736, 90 L ed 439, 66 S Ct 46 (1945); Scott v Comm, 69 F2d 444 (CCA 8) (1934); Anthracite Trust Co v Phillips, 49 F2d 910 (CCA 3) (1931); Brown v Comm, 95 F2d 184 (CCA 6), cert den 305 US 674, 83 L ed 437, 59 S Ct 246 (1938); Singer v Shaughnessy, 198 F2d 178 (CA 2) (1952); Comm v Washer, 127 F2d 446 (CCA 6), cert den 317 US 653, 87 L ed 525, 63 S Ct 49 (1942).

acts since 1918. The proceeds have been held includible even
though at the time the policy was issued the proceeds of insurance were not taxable, but were at the time there was a change
of beneficiary.[10] It is sufficient that the right be reserved and
there is no necessity that it be exercised to incur incidence of
the tax.[11] The right to change the beneficiary need not be retained by the decedent alone, since taxability will result if he
may exercise the right with the consent of any other person or
persons.[12]

It must be noted, however, that while retention of the
right to change the beneficiary will result in the inclusion of the
proceeds of the policy in the decedent's gross estate, the fact
that he has parted with such right, in and of itself does not result
in non-inclusion, since the proceeds may be included on a number
of other grounds, such as other incidents of ownership or by
reason of contemplation of death and the like.

§ 79. Schedule D; Insurance; Assignment.

A complete assignment of the policy may or may not result
in non-inclusion of the proceeds in the estate of the decedent.
Even though the decedent may have retained no incident of
ownership the proceeds may still be includible in his gross estate
as a transfer made in contemplation of death. The inclusion is
not based on any of the provisions for the taxation of the proceeds of insurance, but on other provisions which tax lifetime
transfers made in contemplation of death[13] or intended to take
effect at death.[14]

10. Keefe v US, 46 F Supp 1016, cert den 318 US 768, 87 L ed 1139, 63 S Ct 759 (1943).

11. Feuerbacher, 22 BTA 734 (1931).

12. Godfrey v Smyth, 50–1 USTC ¶10,753, affd 180 F2d 220 (CA 9) (1950); Bank of New York v US, 115 F Supp 375 (1953).

13. Davidson v Comm, 158 F2d 239 (CCA 10) (1946); Diamond v Comm, 159 F2d 672 (CCA 2) (1947); First Trust & Deposit Co v Shaughnessy, 134 F2d 940 (CCA 2), cert den 320 US 744, 88 L ed 441, 64 S Ct 45 (1943); Garrett v Comm, 180 F2d 955 (CA 2) (1956); Slifka v Johnson, 161 F2d 467 (CCA 2), cert den 332 US 758, 92 L ed 343, 68 S Ct 57 (1947); Sloan v Comm, 168 F2d 470 (CCA 2) (1948); Vanderlip v Comm, 155 F2d 152 (CCA 2), cert den 329 US 728, 91 L ed 630, 67 S Ct 83 (1946).

14. Helvering v LeGierse, 312 US 531, 85 L ed 996, 61 S Ct 646 (1941); Burr v Comm, 156 F2d 871 (CCA 2) (1946); Bohnen v Harrison, 345 US 946, 97 L ed 1371, 73 S Ct 863 (1953); Hutchinson, 20 TC 749 (1953); Conway v Glenn, 193 F2d 965 (CCA 6) (1952); Fidelity Philadelphia Trust Co. v Smith, 142 F Supp 561, revd 241 F2d 690 (CA 3), revd 356 US 274, 2 L ed2d 765, 78 S Ct 730 (1956).

§ 80. Schedule D; Insurance; Payment of Premiums.

Where the decedent died prior to August 17, 1954, even though he might have divested himself of all of the incidents of ownership and the transfer of the policy was neither made in contemplation of death nor intended to take effect at death, the proceeds were still includible in his gross estate to the extent of the amount receivable purchased with premiums, or other consideration, paid directly or indirectly by the decedent, in proportion that the amount so paid by the decedent bore to the total premiums paid for the insurance.[15] This was the so-called "payment of premiums test". There was much litigation on the question of who paid the premiums under the facts of a particular case. It was further complicated by the fact that there were cut-off dates. Happily for all concerned with the subject, the Internal Revenue Code of 1954 interred the test. The House Committee Report[16] states that Section 2042 of the 1954 Code revises existing law so that payment of premiums is no longer a factor in determining the taxability under the section of insurance proceeds.

As to all decedents dying on and after August 17, 1954, it makes no difference who paid the premiums for insurance on the life of the decedent. While it is to be hoped that the payment of premiums test will remain interred, it is a lively ghost, and there have already been suggestions for a return to the former rule in some form or other.

§ 81. Schedule D; Insurance; Community Property.

In the case of insurance upon the life of a decedent in a community property law state, cognizance must be taken of the particular state law applicable. As the Regulation points out, as an additional step in determining whether or not a decedent possessed any incidents of ownership in a policy or any part of a policy, regard must be given to the effect of the State or other applicable law upon the terms of the policy.[17] This means that it is necessary to determine just what the decedent's interest was in a policy under the law of his domicile. The Regulation further notes that if the proceeds of an insurance policy made payable to the decedent's estate are community assets

15. IRC, § 811(g)(2) (1939 Code). 17. Reg, § 20.2042–1(c)(5).
16. House Committee Report, IRC, § 2042 (1954 Code).

under the local community property law and, as a result, half of the proceeds belongs to the decedent's spouse, then only half of the proceeds is considered to be receivable by or for the benefit of the decedent's estate.[18]

As we have noted,[19] the laws of the community property law states are not identical, so that it is necessary to determine the ownership of the policy before determining the taxability of the proceeds. In Texas one half of the proceeds of insurance purchased with community funds is community property.[20] In California, if premiums are paid from community funds, unless the wife is the beneficiary, the proceeds are community property.[1] If she is the beneficiary the proceeds are her separate property or she has a vested interest therein.[2] The same rule applies in Washington.[3] In Louisiana and New Mexico if the policy was acquired before marriage the proceeds do not become community property, but do, if acquired during marriage.[4]

It will be seen from the above that it is necessary in each case to determine whether the decedent was married at the time of issuance of the policy, whether premiums were paid from separate or community funds, and the insured and beneficiary under the policy. Where the policy is acquired prior to marriage and premiums thereafter are paid from separate property there is no problem. Where premiums are paid from community funds, one state holds that no part of the proceeds are community property if there has been no fraud upon the wife,[5] others apportion the proceeds,[6] and others hold the proceeds separate property.[7] Some have not passed upon the problem.

The next question is what effect does the naming of particular beneficiaries have on the proceeds where the premiums are paid

18. Reg, § 20.2042–1(b)(2).

19. §§ 41, 48, supra.

20. Womack v Womack, 172 SW2d 307 (1943).

1. Mundt v Conn General Life Ins Co, 35 Cal App2d 416, 95 P2d 966 (1939); Union Mutual Life Ins Co v Broderick, 196 Cal 497, 238 P 1034 (1925); McBride v McBride, 23 Cal App2d 77, 71 P2d 1117 (1937).

2. Dobbel, 104 Cal 432, 38 P 87 (1894); N Y Life Ins Co v Bank of Italy, 60 Cal App 602, 214 P 61 (1923); Travelers Ins Co v Fancher, 219 Cal 351, 26 P2d 482 (1933).

3. Occidental Life Ins Co v Powers, 74 P2d 27 (1937).

4. Berry v Franklin State Bank, 186 La 623, 173 So 126 (1937); White, 43 NM 202, 89 P2d 36 (1939).

5. Rowlett v Mitchell, 52 Tex Civ App 589, 114 SW 845 (1908).

6. Modern Woodman v Gray, 113 Cal App 729, 299 P 754 (1931); Small v Bartyzel (Wash) 117 P2d 391 (1937).

7. Berry v Franklin State Bank, note 4, supra; White, 41 NM 631, 73 P2d 316 (1937).

from community funds. If the decedent's estate is the beneficiary the proceeds are either community property,[8] or one half is paid to the widow and one half to the estate.[9] Where the wife is named beneficiary, Texas holds the proceeds are her separate property if she is irrevocably designated,[10] California, Louisiana and New Mexico, that they are her separate property,[11] and Washington, that they are community property.[12] Where a third party is named the beneficiary, Washington holds such designation void.[13] Texas, Arizona and Nevada, in the absence of fraud, validate the designation,[14] California requires half of the proceeds to be paid to the wife,[15] and Louisiana in one case upheld the designation.[16]

There is another factor which must be considered in connection with insurance in community property law states. Where insurance on the life of one spouse is community property, upon the death of the one who is not the insured, there is includible in the estate one half of the replacement value of the policy.[17] This is includible not under the provisions pertaining to the proceeds of insurance on the life of the decedent, but under the general provisions for the taxation of all property in which the decedent had an interest at the time of death.[18]

The determining test will still be the retention of an "incident of ownership".

§ 82. Schedule D; Insurance; Funding Buy-and-Sell Agreement.

We have previously discussed the subject of valuation as affected by agreements between stockholders of a close corporation to dispose of their interests to the other stockholders.[19] It has become common practice to fund such agreements with life

8. Lee v Lee, 112 Tex 392, 247 SW 828 (1923); Castagnola, 68 Cal App 732, 230 P 188 (1924); LeBlanc, 142 La 27, 76 So 223 (1917); Miller, 44 NM 214, 100 P2d 908 (1940).

9. Towey (Wash), 155 P2d 273 (1945).

10. Davis v Magnolia Petroleum Co, 105 SW2d 695 (1937).

11. Dobbel, note 2, supra; Putnam v N Y Life Ins Co, 42 La Ann 739, 7 So 602 (1890); White, note 4, supra.

12. Note 3, supra.

13. Note 3, supra.

14. Note 5, supra; Grisby v Hudgens, 23 Ariz 339, 203 P 569 (1922); Nixon v Brown, 46 Nev 439, 214 P 524 (1923).

15. N Y Life Ins Co v Bank of Italy, note 2, supra.

16. Pearce v National Life and Accident Ins Co, 12 La App 608, 125 So 776 (1930).

17. Carroll, 29 BTA 11 (1934); US v Ryerson, 312 US 260, 85 L ed 819, 61 S Ct 479 (1941).

18. IRC, § 2033 (1954 Code); see also Reg, § 20.2042–1(c)(5).

19. § 62, supra.

insurance. For the first time the Proposed Regulations treated of the subject.[20] The Proposed Regulation with respect to insurance stated that life insurance policies frequently form a part of arrangements for the purchase of partnership interests or corporate shares from a decedent's estate. If such an arrangement was a binding agreement for full and adequate consideration in money or money's worth entered into in good faith and at arm's length providing for the use of proceeds of insurance on the decedent's life for the purchase of his partnership interest or corporate shares, the value of the interest or shares (as affected by the agreement) and not the value of the insurance, was to be included in the decedent's gross estate. However, if the insurance was owned by or payable to the partnership or corporation, or a trust created by it or for its benefit, the proceeds of insurance were considered as an asset of the partnership or corporation for the purposes of first, determining whether the agreement was supported by full and adequate consideration in money or money's worth and, second, determining the value of the decedent's interest or shares if the agreement was not considered to have been entered into in good faith and at arm's length. The principles described in the Proposed Regulation for determining the effect to be given to the value fixed in a buy-and-sell agreement[1] were to be applied in determining whether the agreement was supported by the full and adequate consideration in money or money's worth. If the agreement was not supported by full and adequate consideration in money or money's worth, there was to be included in the decedent's gross estate both the value of the decedent's interest or shares (determined without regard to the agreement) and, if otherwise includible, the proceeds of the insurance (except to the extent that the proceeds were included in the value of the interest or shares).[2]

To the extent that the Proposed Regulation stated the prevailing case law it was unobjectionable. It is established that the estate taxation of the proceeds of insurance upon the life of a party to a binding buy-and-sell agreement depends upon whether the decedent had an incident of ownership in the policy or they were payable to his estate. If either fact is present the proceeds will be includible in his gross estate.[3] If the insurance is pay-

---

20. Reg, § 20.2031–2(h), Proposed Reg, § 20.2042–1(c)(6).

1. Reg, § 20.2031–2(h).

2. Proposed Reg, § 20.2042–1(c)(6).

3. Scovell, 30 BTA 669 (1934); Dobrzensky, 34 BTA 305 (1936); Mitchell, 37 BTA 1 (1938); Tompkins, 13 TC 1054 (1949); Maddock, 16 TC 324

able to a designated beneficiary, such as the partnership, corporation, or a trustee for the benefit of either, the proceeds will not be includible in the decedent's gross estate.[4] But the Regulation went beyond the case law and injected an element of doubt by the provisions as to consideration in money or money's worth. It was doubtful that this form of legislation by Regulation would be sustained. There was much objection to the Proposed Regulation and it has been deleted from the Regulations promulgated.

§ 83. Schedule D; Insurance; Valuation.

We are not here concerned with the valuation of insurance policies on the life of another in which the decedent had incidents of ownership. Such asset is not returnable in Schedule D but as miscellaneous property under Schedule F. The valuation of insurance on the life of the decedent is provided for in the Regulations.

The amount to be included in the gross estate is the full amount receivable under the policy. If the proceeds of the policy are made payable to a beneficiary in the form of an annuity for life or for a term of years, the amount to be included in the gross estate is the one sum payable at death under an option which could have been exercised either by the insured or by the beneficiary, or if no option was granted, the sum used by the insurance company in determining the amount of the annuity.[5] Where the insurance proceeds are payable in installments it has been held that the amount included is the commuted value of the installments,[6] but where the payments consist only of interest, the face value is includible,[7] as it is where the proceeds are to be paid in three deferred installments with monthly payments meantime.[8] The one sum payable under an option which could have been exercised by the decedent is the amount includible when that amount is not less than the cost of an annuity contract similar to the rights receivable under the option.[9]

As the result of the inclusion of insurance in which the decedent had a reversionary interest in excess of 5% of the value

---

(1951); Letter of D. S. Bliss, Deputy Commr, Nov 24, 1947.

4. Newell v Comm, 66 F2d 102 (CCA 7) (1933); Wilson v Crooks, 52 F2d 692 (1931); Ealy, 10 TCM 431 (1948); Weil, 22 TC 1267 (1954).

5. Reg, § 20.2042-1(a)(3).

6. Chisholm, 37 BTA 167 (1938); Blacksher, 38 BTA 998 (1938); Goldblatt, 16 TC 204 (1951); McKelvy, 31 BTA 1206 (1934).

7. Allentown Nat Bank, 37 BTA 750 (1938); Willis, 28 BTA 152 (1933).

8. Schongalla v Hickey, 60 F Supp 814 (1944).

9. Walker, 8 TC 1107 (1947).

of the policy immediately before his death, it is necessary to determine whether the statutory amount has been exceeded. Such valuation is determined under the principles for the valuation of a reversionary interest,[10] hereafter treated,[11] taking into consideration any incidents of ownership held by others immediately before the decedent's death which would affect the value of the reversionary interest.[12] This is not the valuation of insurance proceeds.

§ 84. Schedule D; Insurance; Return.

The only references in the Regulations as to the form of the return for life insurance on the life of the decedent is the requirement for giving the name of the insurer and beneficiary, number of the policy and the amount of the proceeds and for obtaining a statement on Form 712 from the company issuing the policy and filing it with the return.[13] The instructions on the return are, however, more detailed. It is first required that all insurance payable either to the estate of the decedent or to beneficiaries other than the estate be included. Instructions for execution of the schedule provide that under "Description" there be shown the name of the insurance company, number of policy, name of beneficiary, face amount of the policy, principal amount of any indebtedness to the insurance company deductible in determining the net proceeds, and the interest on such indebtedness accrued to the date of death. The value to be entered on Schedule D is the face amount of the policy less the indebtedness and accrued interest. *Accumulated dividends*[14] (including interest payable thereon), *post mortem dividends,*[15] *and returned premiums are to be entered on Schedule F and not Schedule D.* In addition to the insurance shown on the return as part of the gross estate, *complete information must be submitted as to any insurance on the decedent's life which the executor believes is not includible in the gross estate.*[16]

10. Reg, §§ 20.2037–1(c)(3)(4), 20.-2031–8.

11. § 115, infra.

12. Reg, 20.2042–1(c)(3).

13. Reg, §§ 20.6018–2(c)(3), 6018–4 (d).

14. Parker, 30 BTA 342, affd 84 F2d 838 (CCA 8) (1936).

15. Chase Nat Bank of N Y v US, 28 F Supp 947 (1939).

16. Instructions for Execution of Schedule D, Form 706.

FORM NO. 14

Schedule D; Insurance

1a. Was any insurance on life of decedent receivable by his estate?
[x] Yes   [ ] No

1b. By beneficiaries other than estate?   [x] Yes   [ ] No

2. Was there any insurance on the decedent's life which is not included in the return as a part of the gross estate?   [x] Yes   [ ] No
If "Yes," a complete explanation as to all such insurance must be submitted.

Item No.	Description	Subsequent valuation date	Alternate value	Value at date of death
1.	Prudential Insurance Company of America, Newark, N. J., Policy No. 608423, payable to estate of decedent, face amount $25,000.			$25,000.00
2.	Home Life Insurance Company, 256 Broadway, New York City, Policy No. 108965, payable to Katherine Benson, face amount $10,000			10,000.00
3.	Metropolitan Life Insurance Company, New York, Policy No. 874309, payable to Winthrop Benson, Inc., face amount $100,000. Decedent held no incidents of ownership in said policy. (See affidavit of Charles Benson, annexed.)			
4.	Equitable Life Assurance Society of U. S., New York, Policy 765432, payable to George Benson, face amount $10,000, subject to loan of $1,200 and interest accrued to date of death of $38.14.			8,761.86
	TOTAL (also enter under the Recapitulation, Schedule O)			$43,761.86

(If more space is needed, insert additional sheets of same size)

Estate of WINTHROP BENSON

Schedule D—Page 13

There must be procured for every policy of life insurance listed on the return a statement, on Form 712, the Life Insurance Statement, which must be filed with the return.[17] This may be obtained from the company issuing the policy, upon request. It is not necessary to send the form to the company, since they are supplied therewith.

17. Reg, § 20.6018–4(d).

FORM NO. 15

Life Insurance Statement

U. S. TREASURY DEPARTMENT—INTERNAL REVENUE SERVICE

LIFE INSURANCE STATEMENT

(To be filed by Executor with Federal Estate Tax Return, Form 706)

Enter these items on Schedule D, Form 706

1. Name of insurance company: Prudential Insurance Company of America.
2. Name of decedent *(Insured)*: Winthrop Benson.
3. Kind of policy: Ordinary life.
4. No. of policy: 608423.
5a. Names of beneficiaries: Estate of Winthrop Benson.
5b.
5c.
5d.
6. Face amount of policy: $10,000.
7. Principal of any indebtedness to the company deductible in determining net proceeds:
8. Interest on indebtedness *(Item 7)* Accrued to date of death:
9. Amount of proceeds if payable in one sum: $10,270.00
10. Value of proceeds as of date of death *(If not payable in one sum)*:
11. Date of death of insured: January 10, 1960.
12. Date of issue of policy: August 12, 1937.
13. Amount of premium: $465.80.

Enter these items on Schedule F, Form 706

14. Amount of accumulated dividends: NONE.
15. Amount of post mortem dividends: $270.00.
16a. Provisions of policy with respect to the deferred payments or to the installments *(NOTE: Where marital deduction under Code section 812(e) involved, if other than lump sum settlement authorized, copy of insurance policy should be attached)*:
16b. Amount of installments:
16c. Date of birth and name of any person the duration of whose life may measure the number of payments:
16d. Amount applied by the insurance company as a single premium representing the purchase of installment benefits:
16e. Basis *(Mortality table and rate of interest)* Used by insurer in valuing installment benefits:
17. Was the insured the annuitant or beneficiary of any annuity contract issued by the company? [ ] Yes [x] No
18. Names of companies with which decedent carried other policies and amount of such policies if this information is disclosed by your records: Home Life Insurance Company, $25,000.

The undersigned officer of the above-named insurance company hereby certifies that this statement sets forth correct and true information.

19. Date of certification:
20. Signature:
21. Title:

Instructions

PURPOSE OF STATEMENT.—The information shown by this statement is required for the purpose of determining the statutory gross estate of the insured for Federal estate tax purposes.

STATEMENT OF INSURER.—This statement must be made, on behalf of the insurance company which issued the policy, by an officer of the company having access to the records of the company.

DUTY TO FILE.—It is the duty of the executor to procure this statement from the insurance company and file it with the return. However, if specifically requested, the insurance company should file this statement direct with the official of the Internal Revenue Service making the request.

SEPARATE STATEMENTS.—A separate statement must be filed for each policy listed on the return.

§ 85. Schedule E; Jointly Owned Property; Statutory Provisions.

The Internal Revenue Code of 1954 made no substantive changes in the provisions for the Federal estate taxation of jointly owned property. The statute divides such property into three categories and provides that there shall be included in the gross estate of a decedent the value of all property to the extent of the interest therein

(1) held as joint tenants by the decedent and any other person, *or*

(2) as tenants by the entirety by the decedent and spouse, *or*

(3) deposited, with any person carrying on the banking business, in their joint names and payable to either or the survivor.[18]

The fact that property is jointly owned does not necessarily mean that the decedent originally owned all of it. The fact may be that he contributed none or only a part. In recognition of this the statute *excepts from its operation* such part thereof as

18. IRC, § 2040 (1954 Code).

may be shown to have originally belonged to such other person and never to have been received or acquired by the latter from the decedent for less than an adequate and full consideration in money or money's worth.[19] It is further provided that where such property or any part thereof, or part of the consideration with which such property was acquired, is shown to have been at any time acquired by such other person from the decedent for less than an adequate and full consideration in money or money's worth, there shall be excepted only such part of the value of such property as is proportionate to the consideration furnished by such other person.[20]

The statute takes further cognizance of the fact that while in the usual case of tenancy by the entirety or joint tenancy, the entire consideration is furnished by one spouse or joint tenant, that is not so where the property has been acquired by gift, bequest, or devise. A further exception is therefore provided that where any property has been acquired by gift, bequest, devise, or inheritance, as a tenancy by the entirety by the decedent and spouse, then there shall be included one half of the value of such property, or, where so acquired by the decedent and any other person as joint tenants and their interests are not otherwise specified or fixed by law, then there shall be included in the decedent's gross estate the value of a fractional part to be determined by dividing the value of the property by the number of joint tenants.[1] Thus, in the case of tenancy by the entirety so acquired, one half of the value of the property would be included in the decedent's gross estate, and in the case of joint interests so acquired there would be included one half, one third or such other amount as represented the decedent's interest in the property.

Prior to Jan. 1, 1948 the 1939 Code included within the provisions for the taxation of jointly owned property, community property. The enactment of the marital deduction in 1948 made the provisions in that respect superfluous. Since the interest of a deceased spouse in such property is generally one half thereof, and such interest is taxable under other provisions of the Code, the subdivision was repealed.[2]

19. Note 18, supra.
20. Note 18, supra.
1. Note 18, supra.

2. IRC, § 811(e)(2) (1939 Code), repealed by § 351, Rev Act of 1948.

§ 86. Schedule E; Jointly Owned Property; Property Includible.

In general the property held jointly at the time of the decedent's death by the decedent and another person or persons with right of survivorship is includible in his gross estate:

(1) To the extent that the property was acquired by gift, devise, bequest, or inheritance, the decedent's fractional share of the property.

(2) In all other cases, the entire value of the property, except such part as is attributable to the amount of consideration in money or money's worth furnished by the other joint owner or owners.[3]

"Property held jointly" specifically covers property held jointly by the decedent and any other person or persons, property held by the decedent and spouse as tenants by the entirety, and a deposit of money, or a bond or other instrument, in the name of the decedent and any other persons and payable to either or the survivor. *It applies to all classes of property, whether real or personal, and regardless of when the joint interests were created.* Furthermore, it makes no difference that the survivor takes the entire interest in the property by right of survivorship and that no interest therein forms a part of the decedent's estate for purposes of administration.[4]

The determining date is that of the decedent's death and not that upon which the tenancy was created.[5]

§ 87. Schedule E; Jointly Owned Property; Value Reported.

In the absence of evidence that jointly owned property was not acquired entirely with consideration furnished by the decedent or by gift, bequest, devise or inheritance, *the entire value of such property* is included in a decedent's gross estate.[6] The full value of the property must be included in the gross estate unless it can be shown that a part of the property originally belonged to the other tenant or tenants and was never acquired or received by the other tenant or tenants from the decedent for less than an adequate and full consideration in money or money's worth.[7] This is merely a statement of the case law.[8] It will be

3. Reg, § 20.2040–1(a).
4. Reg, § 20.2040–1(b).
5. US v Jacobs, 306 US 363, 83 L Ed 763, 59 S Ct 551 (1939).
6. Note 4, supra.

7. Instructions, Schedule E, Form 706.
8. City Bank Farmers Trust Co, 23 BTA 663 (1931); American Security & Trust Co, 24 BTA 334 (1931); Reese, 25 BTA 38 (1931); Tenant, 8 TCM 143

noted that the rule only applies in the absence of evidence that the other joint owner or owners contributed to the value. Both the statute and the Regulation recognize that it would be unfair to include in the decedent's gross estate property for which he furnished no part of the consideration. As we have seen, the statute excepts that part of such property as may be shown to have originally belonged to the other joint tenant and never to have been acquired by the latter from the decedent for less than an adequate and full consideration in money or money's worth.[9] The Regulation phrases the same thought by excluding from the decedent's gross estate such part of the entire value as is attributable to the amount of consideration in money or money's worth furnished by the other joint owner or owners.[10]

As the Regulation points out, the entire value of jointly held property is included in a decedent's gross estate unless the executor submits *facts* sufficient to show that property was not acquired entirely with consideration furnished by the decedent, *or* was acquired by the decedent and the other joint owner or owners by gift, bequest, devise, or inheritance. Each case therefore ultimately depends upon the factual situation.

§ 88. Schedule E; Jointly Owned Property; Original Ownership.

The statute uses as a determinant for the exclusion of part or all of joint property, original ownership of such excluded part by the other joint owner, except in the case of property acquired by gift, bequest, devise or inheritance.[11] The problem of original ownership has many ramifications, which the Regulation spells out.

Examples of the application of the statute are as follows:

(1) If the decedent furnished the entire purchase price of the jointly held property, the value of the entire property is included in his gross estate.[12]

(2) If the decedent furnished a part only of the purchase price, only a corresponding portion of the value of the property is so included.[13]

(1947); McGrew v Comm, 135 F2d 158 (CCA 6) (1943).

9. Note 18, supra.

10. Note 3, supra.

11. Note 18, supra.

12. Note 8, supra.

13. Brandt, 8 TCM 820 (1947); Howard, 9 TC 1192 (1947); Smith, 45 BTA 59 (1941); Giuliani, 11 TCM 673 (1948).

(3) If the decedent furnished no part of the purchase price, no part of the value of the property is so included.[14]

(4) If the decedent, before the acquisition of the property by himself and the other joint owner, gave the latter a sum of money or other property which thereafter became the other joint owner's entire contribution to the purchase price, then the value of the entire property is so included, notwithstanding the fact that the other property may have appreciated in value due to market conditions between the time of the gift and the time of acquisition of the jointly held property.[15]

(5) If the decedent, before the acquisition of the property by himself and the other joint owner, transferred to the latter for less than an adequate and full consideration in money or money's worth other income-producing property, the income from which belonged to and became the other joint owner's entire contribution to the purchase price, then the value of the jointly held property less that portion attributable to the income which the other joint owner did furnish is included in the decedent's gross estate.[16]

(6) If the property originally belonged to the other joint owner and the decedent purchased his interest from the other joint owner, only that portion of the value of the property attributable to the consideration paid by the decedent is included.[17]

§ 89. Schedule E; Jointly Owned Property; Consideration.

The test of original ownership discussed in the preceding section has another facet. While there is excepted from inclusion in the decedent's gross estate jointly owned property, except such part thereof as may be shown to have originally belonged to the other joint owner, *it is further provided* that the property must never have been received or acquired by the latter from the decedent *for less than an adequate and full consideration* in money or money's worth.[18] Therefore, the fact of original ownership alone will not be sufficient to exclude jointly owned property from a decedent's gross estate, unless the other joint owner paid the decedent an adequate and full consideration for his

---

14. Koussevitsky, 5 TC 650 (1945).
15. Note 18, supra; but see Harvey v US, 185 F2d 463 (CA 7) (1950).
16. See Harvey v US, note 15, supra; see also Rev Rul 56–519, 1956–2 CB 123; Reg, § 20.2040–1(c)(5).

17. Waterman, BTA memo op Dec 11, 351–D (1940); Reg, § 20.2040–1(c).
18. IRC § 2040 (1954 Code).

interest. If he did not, there will be excluded only such part of the value of such property as is proportionate to the consideration furnished by the other owner.[19] As the Regulation points out the entire value of jointly owned property is included except such part of the entire value as is attributable to the amount of the consideration in money or money's worth furnished by the other owner. In determining the consideration furnished by the other joint owner or owners, there is taken into account only that portion of such consideration which is shown not to be attributable to money or other property acquired by the other joint owner or owners from the decedent for less than a full and adequate consideration in money or money's worth. (Property will not be treated as having been acquired from the decedent for less than an adequate and full consideration in money or money's worth if it represents income from property acquired from the decedent. For this purpose, gain (whether realized or unrealized) resulting from appreciation in the value of property is not "income" from property.)[20]

Whether or not a full and adequate consideration has been furnished depends of course upon the facts in each case. The most common situation is that in which there are either joint holdings or a tenancy by the entirety between husband and wife. When the husband furnishes the consideration, there is no question about taxability.[1] But it may be claimed that the wife made a contribution of services or released rights which constituted consideration. Where the services have been the usual wifely ones such as nursing the husband,[2] contributing toward the upkeep of the home and the education of the children,[3] or assisting in the management of investments,[4] they have not been deemed an adequate and full consideration. When there has been a joint participation together in business the services have been deemed an adequate and full consideration.[5]

19. Note 18, supra.

20. The last two sentences were deleted from the proposed Regulation. But Example 5, Reg, § 20.2040-1(c) and Harvey v US, note 15 supra, would appear to make it applicable.

1. McCrady v Heiner, 19 F Supp 575 (1937); Hornor v Comm, 130 F2d 649 (CCA 3) (1942); Fox v Rothensies, 115 F2d 42 (CCA 3) (1940); US v Jacobs, 306 US 363, 83 L ed 763, 59 S Ct 551 (1939); Foster v Comm, 90 F2d 486 (CCA 9), affd 303 US 618, 82 L ed 1083, 58 S Ct 525 (1937).

2. Loveland, 13 TC 5 (1949).

3. Fox v Rothensies, note 1, supra.

4. Bushman v US, 8 F Supp 694 (1934).

5. Berkowitz v Comm, 108 F2d 319 (CCA 3) (1939); Richardson v Helvering, 80 F2d 548 (CA DC) (1935); see also Awrey, 5 TC 722 (1945); Ferry

Insofar as the release of marital rights is concerned, the statute provides that a relinquishment or promised relinquishment of dower or curtesy, or of a statutory estate created in lieu of dower or curtesy, or of other marital rights in the decedent's property or estate shall not be considered to any extent a consideration "in money or money's worth."[6] While the Gift Tax statute provides that a transfer of property in settlement of marital rights pursuant to an agreement of separation or divorce, where the divorce takes place within two years thereafter, is a transfer for an adequate and full consideration,[7] there is no such provision in the Estate Tax law.

It has been held that an interest acquired in jointly owned property in exchange for a waiver of marital rights was not an acquisition for an adequate and full consideration.[8] The question is confused, however, by a ruling that while relinquishment of dower, curtesy or a statutory right in lieu thereof does not constitute consideration, to the extent that transfers are made in satisfaction of support rights they are made for adequate and full consideration.[9] It would appear that to the extent that the interest in joint property represented the value of the right of support it would be excluded from the decedent's gross estate.

§ 90. Schedule E; Jointly Owned Property; Tenancy by Entirety.

A tenancy by the entirety may arise either by purchase or by gift, bequest, devise or inheritance. Property held by the entirety at the death of one of the tenants,[10] is generally includible in his gross estate and taxable.[11] The constitutionality of such taxation has been upheld.[12] The date of the creation of the tenancy

v Rogan, 154 F2d 974 (CCA 9) (1946); Singer v Shaughnessy, 198 F2d 178 (CA 2) (1952).

6. IRC § 2043(b) (1954 Code).

7. IRC, § 2516 (1954 Code).

8. Sheets v Comm, 95 F2d 727 (CCA 8) (1938).

9. E T 19, 1946–2 CB 166.

10. Provident Trust Co, 281 US 497, 74 L ed 991, 50 S Ct 356, revg 35 F2d 339 (CCA 3), affg 5 BTA 1004 (1930); see also Fox v Rothensies, note 1, supra.

11. Gwinn v Comm, 287 US 224, 77 L

ed 270, 53 S Ct 157 (1932); Putnam v Burnet, 63 F2d 456 (CA DC) (1933); Third Nat Bank & Trust Co of Springfield v White, 45 F2d 911, affd 58 F2d 1085 (1930), affd 287 US 577, 77 L ed 505, 53 S Ct 290 (1931); Morton, 23 BTA 236 (1931); Blood, 22 BTA 1000 (1931); Comm v Emery, 21 BTA 1038, revd 62 F2d 591 (CCA 7) (1931); Dann, 20 BTA 42 (1930); Paul v US, 127 F2d 64, affd 317 US 329, 87 L ed 304, 63 S Ct 297 and 317 US 338, 87 L ed 312, 63 S Ct 302 (1942).

12. Tyler v US, 281 US 497, 74 L Ed

has no effect on taxability, provided that the tenancy existed at the date of death,[13] since it is the change of ownership on death which is taxed.[14]

The test of original ownership applies to estates by the entirety, as it does to other jointly owned property.[15] This test is met by proof of the contribution by the other spouse.[16] But in the absence of such proof the entire value of the property will be included in the gross estate of the spouse who originally furnished the consideration.[17]

Under certain circumstances the effect of state law may operate to exclude the proceeds of property held as tenants by the entirety. Where there is no estate by the entirety in personal property, the proceeds of such a tenancy will be deemed to be held as tenants in common and includible to the extent of one half.[18] It has been held that Federal law will relate back to an original gift to overcome the presumption created by state law that jointly held personalty is a holding in common.[19] And it has been held that such presumption is not conclusive.[19a] A presumption of state law that parties taking under a tenancy by the entirety furnished an equal consideration is not indulged by the Federal statute and the survivor has the burden of showing the consideration furnished.[20]

A variety of mesne conveyances have not been effective to exclude property from the estate of a decedent from whom the original consideration flowed.[1]

§ 91. Schedule E; Jointly Owned Property; Acquired by Gift, Bequest, Devise, or Inheritance.

As previously noted, a major exception to the taxation of joint interests is that *where any property has been acquired by gift,*

991, 50 S Ct 356 (1930); Robinson v Comm, 63 F2d 653 (CCA 6) (1933).

13. US v Jacobs, note 1 supra; note 11, supra.

14. US v Jacobs, note 1, supra; Levy v Comm, 65 F2d 412 (CCA 2) (1933).

15. Kelley, 22 BTA 421 (1931); Reese, 25 BTA 38 (1932); Derby, 20 TC 164 (1953); Hornor v Comm, note 1, supra; McCrady v Heiner, note 1, supra; Bowditch, 23 BTA 1265, vacated 62 F2d 1065 (CCA 1) (1937); Stuart v Hassett, 41 F Supp 905 (1941).

16. McCrady v Heiner, note 1, supra;

Drummond v Paschal, 75 F Supp 46 (1947); Leoni, 7 TCM 759 (1946).

17. Blood, note 11, supra; Bowditch, note 15, supra; Kelley, note 15, supra; Bremer v Luff, 7 F Supp 148 (1933).

18. Slocum, 21 BTA 169 (1931); Dennis, 26 BTA 1120 (1932).

19. Bremer v Luff, note 17, supra.

19a. Reese, note 15, supra.

20. Butzel, 21 BTA 188 (1930).

1. Hornor v Comm, 130 F2d 649 (CCA 3) (1942); Derby, note 15, supra; Stuart v Hassett, note 15, supra.

bequest, devise, or inheritance, as a tenancy by the entirety by the decedent and spouse, such property is includible in the decedent's gross estate to the extent of one half of the value thereof, or, where so acquired by the decedent and any other person *as joint tenants* and their interests are not otherwise specified or fixed by law, then to the extent of the value of a fractional part to be determined by dividing the value of the property by the number of joint tenants.[2] Thus, to the extent that joint property was acquired by the decedent and the other joint owner or owners by gift, devise, bequest, or inheritance, the decedent's fractional share of the property is included in his gross estate.[3]

As an example, if the decedent and his spouse acquired the property by will or gift as tenants by the entirety, half of the value of the property is includible in his gross estate. If the decedent and his two brothers acquired the property by will or gift as joint tenants, a third of the value of the property is so included.[4]

§ 92. Schedule E; Jointly Owned Property; Proration Among Joint Tenants.

The statute provides two situations in which less than the full value of jointly owned property is to be included in the gross estate. One is the case where the joint property was acquired by gift, or by will, and the method of proration of interests in such case has been previously discussed.[5] The other is the case in which the surviving joint tenant has acquired his interest from the decedent for less than adequate and full consideration in money or money's worth. *In such case, there is excluded from the decedent's gross estate only such part of the value of such property as is proportionate to the consideration furnished by the survivor.*[6]

This presents two problems. The first is to determine the amount of the consideration furnished by the survivor and the total consideration. The second part presents merely a matter of mathematical computation.

The portion to be excluded from the decedent's gross estate

2. IRC, § 2040 (1954 Code).
3. Reg, § 20.2040–1(a)(1).
4. Reg, § 20.2040–1(c)(7)(8); Carter v English, 15 F2d 6 (CCA 9) (1926); Comm v Fletcher Savings & Trust Co,

59 F2d 508 (CCA 7) (1932); Drummond v Paschal, note 16, supra.
5. § 91, supra.
6. IRC, § 2040 (1954 Code).

is that portion of the entire value of the property at the decedent's death or at the alternate valuation date which the consideration in money or money's worth furnished by the other joint owner or owners bears to the *total cost of acquisition and capital additions.* In determining the consideration furnished by the other joint owner or owners, there is taken into account only that portion of such consideration which is shown not to be attributable to money or other property acquired from the decedent for less than a full and adequate consideration in money or money's worth.[7] The proposed Regulation provided that property will not be treated as having been acquired from the decedent for less than adequate and full consideration in money or money's worth if it represents *income* from property acquired from the decedent. For this purpose, *gain* (whether realized or unrealized) resulting from appreciation in the value of property is not "income" from property. This provision has been deleted from the Regulation.

However, in Harvey vs. U. S.,[8] the decedent made gifts to his wife which through investments resulted in gain and were invested in other property. Such investments were made from both income and profits, and the wife's contributions from income were deemed her separate property and not includible in the decedent's gross estate. The court indicated that if the original gift and profits had been reinvested, a different result would have been effected. Example 5 of the Regulation recognizes this.

In varying factual situations, where the proof established the contribution of the survivor, different proportionate amounts have been held to have been contributed by the survivor.[9]

§ 93. Schedule E; Jointly Owned Property; Bank Accounts.

Because bank accounts are most frequently the subject matter of joint ownership, the cases dealing with such accounts are collated in this section. In order to include the proceeds of a joint bank account in the estate of a decedent it must have

7. See note 20, § 89, supra.
8. 185 F2d 463 (CA 7) (1950).
9. See Brandt, 8 TCM 820 (1947); Bendet, 5 TCM 302 (1945); Howard, 9 TC 1192 (1947); Brockway v Comm, 18 TC 488 (1952); Singer v Shaughnessy, 198 F2d 178 (CA 2) (1952); Giulani, 11 TCM 673 (1948); Ferry v Rogan, 154 F2d 974 (1946); Berkowitz, 108 F2d 319 (CCA 3) (1939); McCrady v Heiner, 19 F Supp 575 (1937); Drummond v Paschal, note 16, supra; Leoni, note 16, supra; Seleeman, 9 TCM 997 (1947); Thompson, 7 TCM 142 (1946); Bank of America NTSA, 43 BTA 695 (1941).

originally belonged to him.[10] In other words, the entire amount of the joint account will be included except the part originally belonging to the survivor.[11] The effect of this cannot be avoided by withdrawal of the funds by the survivor shortly before the decedent's death.[12] The fact that the parties are husband and wife does not change the tax effect.[13] The constitutionality of such taxation has been upheld.[14] Bank accounts created by a decedent in trust for another are not joint property, but taxable as transfers with possession or enjoyment retained.[15] Such accounts are reported in Schedule G.

As in the case of any other joint property, proof that all of the funds in the account were not contributed by the decedent will result in their exclusion from his gross estate.[16] But it is a *fact* to be established[17] and a state presumption of equal ownership will not prevail.[18]

§ 94. Schedule E; Jointly Owned Property; Evidence and Burden of Proof.

The statute taxing joint interests begins by creating a presumption that all joint interests are includible in a decedent's gross estate, by providing for taxation *unless it is shown*

(1) to have originally belonged to the survivor and never acquired from the decedent for less than an adequate and full consideration in money or money's worth.[19]

The Regulation is even more specific in stating that the entire value of jointly held property is included in a decedent's gross estate unless the executor submits *facts sufficient to show* that property was not acquired entirely with consideration furnished by the decedent, or was acquired by the decedent and the other joint owner or owners by gift, bequest, devise, or inheritance.[20] Therefore, when the surviving joint owner claims that he contributed to the joint property, the fiduciary has the burden of overcoming the statutory presumption.[1]

10. Koussevitsky, 5 TC 650 (1945).
11. Robinson v Comm, 63 F2d 653 (CCA 6) (1953).
12. Grant, 1 TC 731 (1942); Sullivan, 10 TC 961 (1948).
13. City Bank Farmers Trust Co, 23 BTA 663 (1931).
14. Dime Trust & Safe Deposit Co v Phillips, 284 US 160, 76 L ed 220, 52 S Ct 46 (1931).
15. Wasserman, 139 F2d 778 (CCA

1) (1944); Helfrich v Comm, 143 F2d 43 (CCA 7) (1944).
16. Brandt, note 9, supra; Bendet, note 9, supra.
17. See § 94, infra.
18. Robinson v Comm, 63 F2d 652 (CCA 6) (1933).
19. Note 6, supra.
20. Reg, § 20.2040-1(a).
1. Foster v Comm, 90 F2d 486 (CCA 9), affd 303 US 618, 82 L ed 1083, 58

The claim is constantly made by the surviving joint owner or tenant by the entirety that he or she either contributed some or all of the consideration. There is the naive belief among many people that all that is needed in such case is an affidavit containing that bald statement of fact. *This is far from sufficient.* What is required is proof.[2] In the absence of such proof the entire amount will be deemed to belong to the decedent and taxed accordingly.[3] The evidence must be testimonial, documentary, or by affidavit. Except in the unusual case it is supplied by affidavit. It should be as complete as possible. Thus, it may be shown that money in an account is in fact the property of another, the contribution made by the survivor, that the survivor's income contributed to the property, that the property was acquired by will or gift, or any other fact which will establish that the survivor did not acquire his interest, in any of the ways which as previously discussed would result in the inclusion of it in the decedent's gross estate.

In marshalling facts for an affidavit to establish the fact that the decedent was not the owner of all of the joint property, they should be of the same quality as would be presented to a court upon the trial of the issue. It must not be assumed that because the proof is submitted by affidavit and is not testimonial proof that a lesser quantum or quality will suffice. The hurdle created by the statutory presumption is no mean obstacle to overcome. The reason is that owners of joint property do not usually keep any exact records of their individual contributions and withdrawals. Digging for the facts will frequently strike pay dirt. If the property is real estate there will be a closing statement with a record of the source of payment or receipt of the fund. These may then be traced to particular savings or check accounts. In such case, a copy of the closing statement should be annexed to the return and the dates and amounts of payments, the particular bank account from which the funds were withdrawn or in which they were deposited set forth. The exact facts, so far as available, should be detailed. If the joint property is a bank account, it may be part of an inheritance, in which case the name of the

S Ct 525 (1937); Stuart v Hassett, 41 F Supp 905 (1941).

2. Giulani, note 9, supra.

3. Clarke v Welch, 7 F Supp 595 (1934); Stephenson, 27 BTA 850 (1933); Tennant, 8 TCM 143 (1947);

Foster v Comm, 303 US 618, 82 L ed 1083, 58 S Ct 525 (1937); Heidt, 8 TC 969, aff'd 170 F2d 1021 (CA 9) (1948); Bremer v Luff, 7 F Supp 148 (1934); Thompson, note 9, supra.

decedent, the amount of the bequest, the date of payment and deposit in the joint account should be set forth. If the deposits are periodic and from earnings, details of the employment, compensation and relation to deposits should be furnished. Every possible fact which will connect the survivor with the contribution should be given. Few cases are lost because of surplusage of detail, many because of lack thereof.

FORM NO. 16

Affidavit to Establish Ownership of Jointly Owned Property

In the Matter of the Estate Tax
  in the Estate of
      WINTHROP BENSON,
           Deceased.

STATE OF FLORIDA   } ss:
COUNTY OF DADE

KATHERINE BENSON, being duly sworn, says:

I am the widow of the decedent above named. That Account No. 6023 in the Miami Beach Federal Savings & Loan Association is in the name of Winthrop Benson and Katherine Benson, jointly, payable to either or the survivor. Said account was opened on March 8, 1958, by transferring thereto $1,000 from Account No. 6221 in the name of Winthrop Benson, and $2,000 from Account No. 5725 in my name. That there have been no withdrawals from the said account and that the sum of $1,000, therein was and is my individual property and was not and is not an asset of Winthrop Benson.

or

That I am the sister of Winthrop Benson. That all of the funds in Account No. 6843 in the Miami Beach Federal Savings & Loan Association are my property and not an asset of the estate of Winthrop Benson. That said account was originally an account in my individual name. I am an invalid and unable to get about. In order that money might be drawn from such account for my use I caused the account to be changed to its present joint form so that my brother could conveniently make withdrawals from time to time at my request, which he did. That none of the deposits in said account were made from funds of my brother, but were deposits of bond coupons and dividends upon securities owned by me and as set forth in the annexed schedule. Except when I gave my brother the bank book for the purpose of making a deposit or withdrawal, the same was in my possession and was not among his effects at the time of his death.

or

That title to premises 66 Poinciana Drive, Hollywood, Florida is in the name of Winthrop Benson and myself as tenants by the entirety. That the said premises were purchased on July 8, 1957 from Alfred A. Adams for the sum of $30,000. As appears from the annexed closing statement prepared by my attorney at the time of closing title, the consideration paid on closing was the sum of $14,870.94. Of that sum I contributed the sum of $7,435.47 from my savings account in the Miami Federal Savings & Loan Association. The sum on deposit in said account totalled $10,000, the amount of a bequest made to me under the will of my Father, Gregory Thompson, who died a resident of Genesee County, New York on the 12th day of April, 1955. As appears from the annexed affidavit of Kenneth P. Gross, the Executor of my father's estate, payment of the legacy was made to me on the 18th day of August, 1955 and deposited by me the following day in the account referred to.

KATHERINE BENSON

Sworn to before me this 18th day
of October, 1959
        Andrea Hayes
        Notary Public
        Dade County

§ 95. Schedule E; Jointly Owned Property; Contemplation of Death.

The Proposed Regulation dealing with jointly owned property had a subdivision dealing with the subject of such property transferred in contemplation of death[4] or severed in contemplation of death. It appeared strange to find the subject dealt with under jointly owned property, but it reflected several fairly recent cases.

It provided that if a decedent's fractional interest in joint tenancy property *is given away in contemplation of death, his fractional interest* is nevertheless includible in his gross estate under the provisions of the Internal Revenue Code dealing with transfers includible in the gross estate because made in contemplation of death.[5] This recognized that a joint owner may dispose of only his fractional interest generally.[6]

4. IRC, § 2035 (1954 Code).
5. Proposed Reg, § 20.2040–1(d).
6. Sullivan v Comm, 175 F2d 657 (CA

9) (1949); Brockway, 18 TC 488, aff'd 219 F2d 400 (CA 9) (1954).

It further provided that if a joint tenancy in property *is severed* during the decedent's life *in contemplation of death,* as by converting it into a tenancy in common, *the fractional interest of the other* owner (or owners) is not included in the decedent's gross estate either as a transfer in contemplation of death nor as jointly owned property if the decedent has no remaining interest in or control over such interest, even though the decedent furnished the entire consideration for the property.[7] This similarly was based on the determination by the Tax Court that the decedent's interest in the property at the time of the transfer was one half, and since the severance vested one half of the entire property in him outright, nothing additional could be included in his gross estate as a transfer in contemplation of death.[8]

It would appear from the deletion of the provision in the Regulation as adopted, that the Commissioner will further litigate the issue.

§ 96. Schedule E; Jointly Owned Property; Tenancy in Common.

While tenancies in common are frequently discussed in the same group as joint tenancies and tenancies by the entirety, they are not only legally distinct, but for Estate Tax purposes are reportable in different schedules and taxable under different sections of the Internal Revenue Code. Both the Regulation and the Instructions for Schedule E emphasize that Section 2040 of the Code has no application to property held by the decedent and any other person or persons as tenants in common.[9] Property in which the decedent held an interest as tenant in common should not be listed under Schedule E, but the value of his interest therein should be returned under Schedule A, if real estate, or if personal property, under such other appropriate schedule.[10]

§ 97. Schedule E; Jointly Owned Property; Interest in Partnership.

While an interest in a partnership is an interest in property with another person or persons, it is not jointly owned property. The decedent's interest in a partnership should not be included

---

7. Note 5, supra.

8. Borner, 25 TC 584 (1955); Carnall, 25 TC 654 (1955).

9. Reg, § 20.2040–1(b).

10. Instructions, Schedule E, Form 706.

under Schedule E, but should be shown under Schedule F, "Other miscellaneous property."[11]

§ 98. Schedule E; Jointly Owned Property; Community Property.

As we have previously noted,[12] the Revenue Act of 1948 repealed the provisions for inclusion of community property interests in the gross estate as to persons dying after Dec. 31, 1947, so that where death occurred on and after Jan. 1, 1948, one half of the community property is generally includible in the estate of each spouse. The exceptions to the rule have also been treated heretofore.[13] In the case of community property there is a special provision for computation of the marital deduction, which subject is discussed hereafter.[14]

In the current return it is pointed out that community property held by the decedent and spouse should be returned under the appropriate Schedules A to I.[15] Thus, community real estate would be reported in Schedule A to the extent of the decedent's interest, similarly with stocks and bonds in Schedule B, or transfers during the decedent's life in Schedule F. Such assets are not jointly owned property, since there is no right of survivorship, and should not therefore be reported in Schedule E.

§ 99. Schedule E; Jointly Owned Property; Return.

We have previously discussed the situations in which only a part of the jointly owned property may be includible in the decedent's gross estate. The Instructions establish the requirement that *in every instance* a statement under the column headed "Description" must disclose whether the whole or only a part of the property is included in the gross estate. *If only a part of the property is included* in the gross estate, *the fair market value of the whole must be shown under "Description."*[16] Thus if there is a parcel of real estate valued at $30,000, which had been devised to the decedent and his two brothers, the "Description" column would show the value of $30,000, but only $10,000 would be reflected in the valuation column.

11. Note 10, supra.
12. § 41, supra.
13. § 48, supra.

14. § 285, infra.
15. Note 10, supra.
16. Note 10, supra.

FORM NO. 17

Schedule E; Jointly Owned Property

1. Did the decedent, at the time of his death, own any property as a joint tenant or as a tenant by the entirety, with right of survivorship? [x] Yes [ ] No

If "Yes," state the name and address of each surviving cotenant.

NAME   ADDRESS (Number, Street, City, Zone, State)

Katherine Benson, 66 Poinciana Drive, Hollywood Beach, Florida.

George Benson, 865 Fifth Avenue, New York City.

Sylvia Benson, 100 Bender Street, San Diego, California.

Item No.	Description	Subsequent valuation date	Alternate value	Value at date of death
1	House and lot, 66 Poinciana Drive, Hollywood Beach, Fla. (lot 18, block 1042). Value based on appraisal, copy of which is attached, $30,000, subject to mortgage of $10,000, acquired by devise under will of Horace Sayre, as per annexed affidavit. Title held by decedent and Katherine Benson, His wife, as tenants by the entirety.			$10,000.00
2	Account Emigrant Industrial Savings Bank, New York City, Account number 206875. Balance at date of death $4,500, in the name of the decedent and George Benson, jointly, and the survivor. $2,000 was contributed to said account by George Benson. See annexed affidavit.			2,500.00
	Interest accrued on Item 2.			18.78
3	Account San Diego Savings & Loan Assn., San Diego, Cal., Account number 6549. Balance at date of death $3,280.96 in the name of decedent and Sylvia Benson.			3,280.96
	Interest accrued on Item 3.			34.90
	TOTAL (also enter under the Recapitulation, Schedule O)			$15,834.64

(If more space is needed, insert additional sheets of same size)

Estate of WINTHROP BENSON

Schedule E—Page 15

§ 100. Schedule F; Miscellaneous Property; Generally.

Schedule F of the Federal Estate Tax Return is a catch-all schedule. There is no provision in the statute or the Regulations for particularization of schedules, this matter being left to the Secretary of the Treasury.[17] In order to expedite the audit of estates there have been devised the forms in use. The various schedules of property included in the gross estate are intended to

17. IRC, § 6011 (1954 Code).

group together property similar in nature. There are, however, many items which do not fit into any of these categories, but which are includible. All of these are lumped together for reporting in the miscellaneous schedule. As the Instructions direct, there is to be listed under Schedule F all items of the gross estate not returnable under any other schedule, such as the following: Debts due the decedent; interests in business; insurance on the life of another; accumulated dividends (including interest payable thereon), post mortem dividends, and returned premiums on the insurance policies listed on Schedule D; claims; rights; royalties; pensions; leaseholds; judgments; reversionary or remainder interests; shares in trust funds; household goods and personal effects, including wearing apparel; farm products and growing crops; livestock; farm machinery; automobiles; etc.[18]

As the "etc." indicates, the list of miscellaneous property enumerated does not exhaust the possibilities, since there are also included unpaid annuity payments,[19] a bonus for services,[20] income tax refunds,[1] contract rights,[2] retirement system benefits,[3] salary,[4] undistributed profits,[5] and fiduciary commissions.[6] If an item will not fit into any other schedule of the return, it should be reported in Schedule F.

§ 101. Schedule F; Miscellaneous Property; Debts Due Decedent.

Upon the death of the decedent there will be numerous items due the decedent which will be collected by the fiduciary. There will be various deposits with utilities, the balance of his salary,[7] refunds,[8] and the like. He may also be entitled to receive payments under contracts,[9] outstanding loans,[10] promises to pay

---

18. Instructions, Schedule F, Form 706.

19. Millard v Maloney, 121 F2d 257 (CCA 3), cert den 314 US 636, 86 L ed 510, 62 S Ct 69 (1941).

20. McKitterick, 42 BTA 130 (1940).

1. Bank of Cal v Comm, 133 F2d 428 (CCA 9) (1943).

2. Rainger, 12 TC 483, aff'd 183 F2d 587 (CA 9) (1950).

3. Kernochan v US, 29 F Supp 860, cert den 309 US 675, 84 L ed 1019, 60 S Ct 711 (1937).

4. Leoni, 7 TCM 759 (1946).

5. Nichols v US, 64 Ct Cls 241, cert den 277 US 584, 72 L ed 99, 48 S Ct 432 (1927); McClennen v Comm, 131 F 2d 165 (CCA 1) (1942).

6. McGlue, 41 BTA 1199 (1940).

7. Note 4, supra; Davis v Comm, 11 TCM 814 (1948).

8. Security First Nat. Bank, 35 BTA 815 (1936); note 1, supra.

9. Note 2, supra; Parrott, Jr v Comm, 30 F2d 792 (CCA 9), cert den 279 US 870, 73 L ed 1006, 49 S Ct 512 (1929); Nevin, 11 TC 59 (1948).

10. Hamlin, 9 TC 676 (1947); **Todd v US,** 46 F2d 589 (Ct Cl) (1931).

obligations,[11] or settlement claims.[12] All of these are reportable in Schedule F.

But not every debt is worth the face amount. As in the case of a note, the debtor may be insolvent. In such event an affidavit of the facts should be annexed. Where the facts have warranted, accounts receivable[13] and contract rights[14] have been valued at less than face value. The form of affidavit used in connection with notes claimed to be worth less than face value may be adapted for this purpose.[15]

§ 102. Schedule F; Miscellaneous Property; Interests in Business.

The interest of the decedent either as sole proprietor[16] or as a member of a partnership[17] is, of course, includible in his gross estate. Few assets of a decedent present as many problems of valuation as that of the business of the deceased sole proprietor or member of a partnership. The Instructions direct that when an interest in a copartnership or unincorporated business is returned, there must be submitted a statement of assets and liabilities as of the valuation date and for the five years preceding, and statements of the net earnings for the same five years. Good will must be accounted for. In general, the same information should be furnished and the same methods followed as in valuing close corporations.[18] We have previously discussed the subject of such valuation.[19]

The Regulation provides that the fair market value of any interest of a decedent in a business, whether a partnership or a proprietorship, is a net value equal to the amount which a willing purchaser whether an individual or a corporation would pay for the interest to a willing seller, neither being under any compulsion to buy or sell. The net value shall be determined on the basis of all relevant factors including—

(a) A fair appraisal as of the applicable valuation date of all

11. Welch v Hall, 134 F2d 366 (CCA 1) (1943).

12. Equitable Trust Co of NY, 31 BTA 329 (1934); note 19, supra.

13. Brown v US, 38 F Supp 444 (1941); Schnorbach v Kavanaugh, 102 F Supp 828 (1952); Rosskam v US, 64 Ct Cls 272 (1927).

14. Farmer's Bank & Trust Co, 10 BTA 43 (1928); Skinker, 13 BTA 846 (1928).

15. Form 12, § 65, supra.

16. Britt, 9 TCM 26 (1947).

17. Kihchel v US, 105 F Supp 523 (1952); McClennen v Comm, 131 F2d 165 (CCA 1) (1942).

18. Instructions, Schedule F, Form 706.

19. § 59, supra.

the assets of the business, tangible and intangible, *including good will.*

(b) The demonstrated earning capacity of the business; and

(c) The other factors set forth in Regulation § 20.2031–2(f) and (h) relating to the valuation of corporate stock, *to the extent applicable.*

Special attention should be given to determining an adequate value of the good will of the business in all cases in which the decedent has not agreed, for an adequate and full consideration in money or money's worth, that his interest passes at his death to his surviving partner or partners. Complete financial and other data upon which the valuation is based should be submitted with the return, including copies of reports in any case in which examination of the business has been made by accountants, engineers, or any technical experts as of or near the applicable valuation date.[20]

The Regulation is a combination of an inclusion of some of the provisions for the valuation of stock of close corporations and a repetition of some of the matter contained in the Regulation for valuation thereof. The effect of buy-and-sell agreements on valuation, which is referred to, has been treated heretofore.[1]

The first thing to bear in mind in valuing an interest in a sole proprietorship or a partnership is that, like wills, few businesses have twin brothers. Each case is determined upon its own facts, so that the fact that one method of valuation, such as assets value,[2] or book value,[3] or sale value,[4] is used in one case, is no assurance that the same rule can be applied to another and different factual situation. In the case of a partnership, the decedent may be possessed of four different interests in the firm. There is his interest in the firm capital, any profits which have not been withdrawn, possible interest in future profits, and finally, there may be, and often is, good will. All of these interests, if present, enter into valuation. There is no fixed rule for valuation of a business interest, and the Regulation recognizes this fact by the statement that "the net value shall be determined on the basis of all relevant factors."[5] In attempting to fix value, the fact that the Instructions refer to statements for five years does

20. Reg, § 20.2031–3.

1. § 62, supra.

2. McColgan, 10 BTA 958 (1928); Brandt, 8 TCM 820 (1947).

3. First Nat Bank of Richmond, 19 BTA 288 (1930); Degener v Comm, 26 BTA 185 (1932); Kaffie, 44 BTA 843 (1941).

4. Stern, 2 BTA 102 (1925).

5. Note 20, supra.

not mean that such number of years is the only number which may be used. If they are not representative, the number of years which is, should be submitted. If such years are abnormal, *that fact is a relevant factor* and should be submitted.

Profits paid to the decedent's estate as a matter of grace have been held not includible in the decedent's gross estate.[6] In case of a partnership, insurance on the decedent's life, owned by the partnership is includible in valuing his interest therein.[7] It is generally the rule that the partnership assets as such are not part of the decedent's estate, but that which is valued is his interest, including his share of partnership profits.[8] To the extent that he has an interest, it is intangible property subject to the Estate Tax.[9]

§ 103. Schedule F; Miscellaneous Property; Interests in Business; Good Will.

Good will is one of the most intangible of intangibles. We have previously discussed the subject of valuation of good will in the case of stock of close corporations.[10] As the Regulation for the valuation of interests in businesses point out, among the relevant factors to be considered are the same factors considered in the valuation of such stock.[11] Therefore, all which has been said previously applies, *to the extent applicable,* to the valuation of business interests. But the Regulation referred to directs that special attention should be given to determining an adequate value of the good will of the business, except where there is a binding buy-and-sell agreement.

While generally, the loss to a corporation of an officer by death, does not affect valuation of its stock,[12] the death of a partner or of the proprietor of a business has been considered in valuation.[13] But various factors have been considered, such as the effect of the decedent's death, offers to purchase and potential competition,[14] the good will vesting by agreement in the survivors,[15] and the earning record of the business for several years, the business location, reputation for fair dealing, type of clientele,

6. US Trust Co of NY, 9 BTA 514 (1928).
7. Atkins, 2 TC 332 (1943).
8. McColgan, note 2, supra.
9. Blodgett v Silberman, 277 US 1, 72 L ed 749, 48 S Ct 410 (1928).
10. § 59, supra.
11. Reg, § 20.2031-3(c).
12. Newell v Comm, 66 F2d 102 (CCA 7) (1933).
13. Brandt, note 2, supra; Gannon, 21 TC 1073 (1953); First Nat Bank of Memphis v Henslee, 74 F Supp 106 (1947); Rubenstein, 10 BTA 864 (1928).
14. Rubenstein, note 13, supra.
15. Blodgett, 18 BTA 1050 (1929).

quality of merchandise, amount and kind of advertising, and public esteem.[16] Good will has also been valued by subtracting 8% of the invested capital from the average net profit for five years, and capitalizing the balance on a three year basis.[17] The income tax formula[18] previously referred to, was rejected and the Court took into consideration the outmoded nature of the business premises, the low rent charged by the decedent as owner, the effect of the location of the business, the competence and efficiency of management, and the effect on profits of the prevailing seller's market for seven years.[19] The Court has also determined good will by taking the average earnings in excess of a return upon the average tangible assets for ten years, with adjustments in net income on account of unusual war conditions and inadequate rentals and salaries.[20] This again indicates that, as has been said, *there is no rule,* for the valuation of good will.[1]

Whether or not there is good will depends upon the evidence presented. The facts may be such as to indicate that there is no good will.[2]

§ 104. Schedule F; Miscellaneous Property; Interests in Business; Valuation; Subject to Option or Contract to Purchase.

We have previously discussed the effect on Estate Tax valuation of an agreement between stockholders of a close corporation for the sale of their interests.[3] All which has been said thereunder applies equally to agreements between partners or in the case of a sole proprietor who has agreed to sell to employees.

The Regulation for the valuation of an interest in a business recognizes such agreements, by providing that special attention be given to the valuation of good will *in all cases in which the decedent has not agreed, for an adequate and full consideration in money or money's worth, that his interest passes at his death to his surviving partner or partners.*[4]

If the agreement is an arm's length transaction with either an option or a binding agreement to sell at an agreed price both during life and at death, it will fix the value for Estate Tax pur-

16. Trammell, 18 TC 662 (1952).

17. Danley v Deal, 54–1 USTC ¶10,936.

18. See § 59, supra.

19. Bluestein, 15 TC 770 (1950).

20. Watson, Sr, 7 TCM 74 (1946).

1. Fish, 1 BTA 882 (1924).

2. See Brandt, 8 TCM 820 (1947); Bendet, 5 TCM 502 (1945); Gumpel, 2 BTA 1127 (1925).

3. § 62, supra.

4. Reg, § 20.2031–3.

poses.[5] If it does not meet these requirements, it will not fix the value.[6]

§ 105. Schedule F; Miscellaneous Property; Insurance on Life of Another.

With the transfer of insurance policies to the ownership of one other than the insured, which has been encouraged by the removal of the payment of premiums test, such policies are more likely to be found among estate assets. The policies which are reportable in Schedule F, are not policies on the life of the decedent in which he has an incident of ownership. Such latter policies are returned in Schedule D. Where, however, the decedent owns policies on the life of a person other than himself, such policies are includible in his gross estate. The same details as to name of company, number of policy, beneficiary, face amount and indebtedness is set forth in Schedule F, but the valuation is not the face value but the replacement value, using the same method as that applied in the case of Gift Taxes.[7] The Gift Tax rule laid down in Guggenheim vs. Rasquin[8] and Powers vs. Comm.[9] has been set forth in the Regulation.[10]

The value of a contract for the payment of an annuity, or an insurance policy on the life of a person other than the decedent, issued by a company regularly engaged in the selling of contracts of that character is established through the sale by that company of comparable contracts. An annuity payable under a combination annuity contract and life insurance policy on the decedent's life (e.g., a "retirement income" policy with death benefit) under which there was no insurance element at the time of the decedent's death is treated like a contract for the payment of an annuity for purposes of Section 2031.[11]

As valuation through sale of comparable contracts is not readily ascertainable when, at the date of the decedent's death, the contract has been in force for some time and further premium payments are to be made, the value may be approximated by adding to the interpolated terminal reserve at the date of the

5. Tompkins, 13 TC 1054 (1949); Weil, 22 TC 1267 (1954); Maddock, 16 TC 324 (1951); Broderick v Gore, 224 F2d 892 (CA 10) (1955); Mandel v Sturr, 57–1 USTC ¶11,688.

6. Hoffman, 2 TC 1160 (1943); Straus, 8 TCM 442 (1947).

7. Telegraphic Ruling, July 22, 1948; Dupont, 18 TC 1134 (1952).

8. 312 US 254, 85 L ed 813, 61 S Ct 507 (1941).

9. 312 US 259, 85 L ed 817, 61 S Ct 509 (1941).

10. Reg, § 20.2031–8.

11. Reg, § 20.2031–8(a).

decedent's death the proportionate part of the gross premium last paid before the date of the decedent's death which covers the period extending beyond that date. If, however, because of the unusual nature of the contract such an approximation is not reasonably close to the full value of the contract, this method may not be used.[12]

The Regulation furnishes examples of the method of computation, which will be discussed under Gift Taxes, where it has greater application. The practical method of obtaining such valuation for Estate Tax purposes is to request from the insurance company which issued the policy or annuity contract the information required, which it will furnish on Form 938, the form used in connection with the Gift Tax return.

It should be noted that the annuity referred to and reportable in Schedule F is not an annuity based upon the life of the decedent. Such annuities are reportable in Schedule I. The distinction should be kept in mind and the two not confused.

§ 106. Schedule F; Miscellaneous Property; Royalties; Pensions; Leaseholds; Judgments.

Royalties,[13] pension rights,[14] leaseholds[15] and judgments[16] are property in which the decedent had an interest at the time of his death and are therefore includible in his gross estate. The Regulations contain no reference to any of these except judgments, as to which it is required that they be described by giving the title of the cause and the name of the court in which rendered, date of judgment, name and address of the judgment debtor, amount of judgment, and rate of interest to which subject, and stating whether any payments have been made thereon, and, if so, when and in what amounts.[17]

In the case of royalties and leaseholds, it will depend upon whether under local law such are real property or personal property.[18] If the latter, they are reportable in Schedule F. If the former, they are reported in Schedule A. In the case of pension rights, if they are of the joint and survivor type, they will be reported in Schedule I, discussed hereafter.[19]

The valuation of oil and mineral royalties and leaseholds has

12. Reg, § 20.2031–8(b).
13. Umsted v US, 35–1 USTC ¶9130; Rainger, 12 TC 483, affd 183 F2d 587 (CA 9) (1952).
14. GCM 27242, 1952–10, p 21; Casilear, 4 TCM 970 (1944).

15. Leser, 17 BTA 266 (1929).
16. Reg, § 20.6018–2(c)(5).
17. Note 16, supra.
18. See § 51, supra.
19. § 177, infra.

been previously treated.[20] When patents and copyrights are to be valued, the usual method is to capitalize the average royalties earned. Such valuation is largely a matter of bargaining with the Estate Tax examiner.[1]

If it is claimed that a judgment has no value, the same factual substantiation should be furnished as when it is claimed that a note is valueless.[2]

§ 107. Schedule F; Miscellaneous Property; Share in Trust Fund.

Where the decedent has been the beneficiary of a trust, if there is any interest in the fund to which he is entitled at his death it must be reported in Schedule F. In the usual case such interest is income unpaid at his death,[3] but may, on occasion include some part of the corpus.[4] Whatever the interest, it is required to be scheduled. The interests in trusts includible as miscellaneous property, are those in trusts created by one other than the decedent. Interests in trusts created by the decedent are reported in Schedule F, if the corpus of such trust is includible in the decedent's gross estate.

§ 108. Schedule F; Miscellaneous Property; Household Goods; Personal Effects; Wearing Apparel; Etc.

Household furnishings and effects are the most common type of miscellaneous property. By some strange coincidence, if the husband dies first, the household effects are found to be the property of the wife, and vice versa. An early Treasury Decision pointed out that household effects and personal property used by husband and wife in the marriage relation are presumed to be the property of the husband and in the absence of evidence overcoming the presumption, must be returned as part of the husband's gross estate.[5] In the usual estate it does not make much difference, since the value of such articles is not great. In whose name the property is insured should be investigated before reporting the property.

20. Note 18, supra; see also Craig, 8 TCM 1019 (1947).

1. See Rainger, note 13, supra; Rohmer, 21 TC 1099 (1953); Perini Machinery, 22 BTA 450 (1931); Wright's Automatic, 1 BTA 1260 (1924); Modern Inventions, 16 BTA 1267 (1929).

2. See § 65, supra.

3. Equitable Trust Co, 31 BTA 329 (1934); Pratt, 1 TCM 627 (1942).

4. Equitable Trust Co, note 3, supra; Earle, 5 TC 991, affd 157 F2d 501 (CCA 6) (1946).

5. TD 2529, Oct 4, 1917.

The Regulation is quite specific with respect to the valuation of such items. The general rule is that the fair market value is the price which a willing buyer would pay to a willing seller, neither being under any compulsion to buy. A room by room itemization of household and personal effects is desirable. All the articles should be named specifically, except that a number of articles contained in the same room, none of which has a value in excess of $100, may be grouped. A separate value should be given for each article named. In lieu of an itemized list, the executor may furnish a written statement containing a declaration that it is made under penalties of perjury setting forth the aggregate value as appraised by a competent appraiser or by appraisers of recognized standing and ability, or by a dealer or dealers in the class of personalty involved.[6]

If there are included among the household and personal effects articles having marked artistic or intrinsic value of a total value in excess of $3,000 (e.g., jewelry, silverware, paintings, etchings, engravings, antiques, books, statuary, vases, oriental rugs, coin or stamp collections), the appraisal of an expert or experts, under oath, should be filed with the return. The appraisal should be accompanied by a written statement of the executor containing a declaration that it is made under the penalties of perjury as to the completeness of the itemized list of such property and as to the disinterested character and the qualifications of the appraiser or appraisers.[7] It will be observed that the tax authorities are also interested in etchings.

If it is desired to effect distribution or sale of any portion of the household or personal effects of the decedent in advance of an investigation by an officer of the Internal Revenue Service, information to that effect shall be given to the District Director. The statement to him shall be accompanied by a verified appraisal of such property and by a written statement of the executor containing a declaration that it is made under the penalties of perjury regarding the completeness of the list of such property and the qualifications of the appraiser. If a personal inspection by an officer of the Internal Revenue Service is not deemed necessary, the executor will be so advised. This procedure is designed to facilitate disposition of such property and to obviate future expense and inconvenience to the estate by affording the District Director an opportunity to make an

6. Reg, § 20.2031-6(a).   7. Reg, § 20.2031-6(b).

investigation should one be deemed necessary prior to sale or distribution.[8]

If expert appraisers are employed, care should be taken to see that they are reputable and of recognized competency to appraise the particular class of property involved. In the appraisal, books in sets by standard authors should be listed in separate groups. In listing paintings having artistic value, the size, subject, and artist's name should be stated. In the case of oriental rugs, the size, make, and general condition should be given. Sets of silverware should be listed in separate groups. Groups or individual pieces of silverware should be weighed and the weights given in troy ounces. In arriving at the value of silverware, the appraisers should take into consideration its antiquity, utility, desirability, condition, and obsolescence.[9]

The requirements of the Regulation appear to make the valuation of household and personal effects an arduous task. The fact is that they are enforced in the spirit of and not to the letter of the Regulation. Unless such articles are valuable, in the usual case the examiner will accept a nominal value of $50 or $100. Where they are worth substantially more, the practice is to have a qualified appraiser furnish an inventory and affidavit of value. Such appraisers abound, as any attorney who has filed a petition for administration or probate knows. Where a qualified appraiser is selected the examiner will rarely, if ever, raise any question. It is the writer's practice when there are assets which are likely to cause a difference of opinion as to value, such as a rare art work or valuable jewelry, to arrange with the appraiser in the office of the District Director to be present at the time of appraisal. Such instances are rare and in more than thirty years the writer has never experienced a case in which the executor's expert and that of the Service were unable to agree upon a value.

Included in miscellaneous effects are automobiles,[10] yachts, horses, carriages and like personal possessions. The appraiser selected will value all of these and furnish all necessary affidavits of appraisal and inventory for submission with the return.

There is one further matter in connection with personal and household effects which must be noted. Frequently, upon opening the decedent's safe deposit vault there will be found jewelry,

8. Reg, § 20.2031–6(c).
9. Reg, § 20.2031–6(d).
10. American Security Trust Co, 35 BTA 815 (1936).

bonds or other property which is claimed to be owned by some other member of the family. Or other property may have been used by other members of the decedent's family. *An adequate affidavit of the facts* will prevent its inclusion in the estate where ownership is proven. But the burden of proving that property which is ostensibly owned by the decedent belongs to another is upon the executor.[11] When such claim is made and supported by affidavit, the item must nevertheless be set forth in the schedule, but no value is placed thereon and the statement made that the property is not that of the decedent.

§ 109. Schedule F; Miscellaneous Property; Crops; Livestock; Farm Machinery.

As we have previously noted,[12] growing crops are part of the real estate and are reported in Schedule A. Although the instructions require the inclusion in Schedule F of farm products and growing crops,[13] the latter refers to crops severed from the land. Livestock and farm machinery are similarly included. Such items are easily appraised at their fair market value.

§ 110. Schedule F; Miscellaneous Property; Community Property.

Prior to January 1, 1948 miscellaneous property owned as community property was reportable in Schedule F.[14] The only situation in which this would still apply today is where California community property was acquired prior to July 29, 1927.[15]

§ 111. Schedule F; Miscellaneous Property; Annuities; Life, Remainder, Reversionary Interests.

At the time of his death a decedent may have been entitled to receive annuity benefits or have a life, remainder or reversionary interest in property. Such interests are includible in his gross estate, but which schedule they are to be reported in presents problems, because it will depend upon the nature of the interest whether it is taxable under the general provisions of the statute which includes all property in which the decedent had an interest at the time of his death,[16] the provisions dealing

---

11. McIlhenny, 22 BTA 1093 (1931); Hogdon, 11 TCM 898 (1948).

12. § 51, supra.

13. Instructions, Schedule F, Form 706.

14. IRC, § 811(a) (1939 Code).

15. See §§ 41, 48, supra.

16. IRC, § 2033 (1954 Code).

with property includible because of a transfer taking effect at death,[17] that taxing joint and survivor annuities,[18] or those including property because of inadequate consideration.[19]

In the case of annuities, there is reportable in Schedule F generally, annuities payable to the decedent during the life of another, annuities for a term of years, and refund annuities.[20]

If the decedent had an interest for the life of another or for a term of years, such interest is reportable in Schedule F. If the interest was for his life, all that is included is any balance due at his death.[1] Interests which terminate on his death are not includible.[2] Vested remainder interests are likewise includible in Schedule F.[3] And that is so whether the recognition comes after the decedent's death[4] or results from an intestacy under the instrument of transfer.[5]

In the case of reversionary interests we again have a situation in which there may be confusion because of the use of the same word in different sections of the statute. A reversionary interest in insurance or other property transferred during life by the decedent may result in the inclusion of such property in his estate.[6] In such cases it is not the reversionary interest which is included, but the entire property, if the value of the reversionary interest is in excess of the statutory amount. In any event it must be valued to determine such fact, and if less, will be reported in Schedule F.

§ 112. Schedule F; Miscellaneous Property; Annuities; Life, Remainder, Reversionary Interests; Valuation; Generally.

The Regulation for the valuation of annuities, life estates,

17. IRC, § 2037 (1954 Code).
18. IRC, § 2039 (1954 Code).
19. IRC, § 2043 (1954 Code).
20. See Equitable Trust Co, 31 BTA 329 (1934); Millard v Maloney, 121 F 2d 257 (CCA 3), cert den 314 US 636, 86 L ed 511, 62 S Ct 100 (1941); as to taxability, under IRC, § 2037; see Goldstone v US, 325 US 687, 89 L ed 1871, 65 S Ct 1323 (1945); Wishard v US, 143 F2d 704 (CCA 7) (1944); Tips v Bass, 21 F2d 460 (1927); Polk v Miles, 268 F 175 (1920); Philadelphia Trust Co v Smith, 241 F2d 690 (CA 3) (1957); under IRC, § 2039, see § 4504A,

infra; under IRC, § 2043, see Updike v Comm, 88 F2d 807 (CCA 8), cert den 301 US 708, 81 L ed 1362, 57 S Ct 941 (1937); Rev Rul 55–378, 1955–1 CB 447.

1. Martin v US, 52–1 USTC ¶10,844.
2. Frew v Bowers, 12 F2d 625 (CCA 2) (1926); Helvering v Rhodes, 117 F 2d 509 (CCA 8) (1941).
3. Frazer v Comm, 162 F2d 167 (CCA 3) (1947).
4. Dickson, 13 TC 318 (1949).
5. Chemical Bank v Early, 67 F Supp 530 (1946).
6. See § 77, supra and § 145, infra.

terms for years and remainders and reversions furnishes complete details, with concrete examples as guides, and the tables to be used in the ordinary case. Since January 1, 1952 the tables applicable to persons dying thereafter use the $3\frac{1}{2}\%$ rate. A pamphlet entitled "Actuarial Values for Estate and Gift Tax," is available from the Superintendent of Documents, United States Printing Office, Washington 25, D. C., for 35 cents and is an excellent investment. It is very detailed, with examples of varying interests and computations showing how the amount of each such interest is computed. It treats of income and remainder factors involving two lives, factors involving one life and a term of years, annuity factors involving two lives and more, together with formulae and tables.

The use of such tables has been sustained by the courts,[7] and it has been said that when compelled to take present action based upon forecasts of a man's life, courts have long been accustomed to use mortality tables.[8] But mortality tables are evidentiary only and must give way to the proven facts, the Tax Court has held,[9] even though prior thereto the Supreme Court had held that in determining the present value of a life interest, mortality tables should be used, though the life beneficiary had died before the time for filing the return,[10] in effect reversing previous decisions to the contrary.[11]

The fair market value of annuities, life estates, terms for years, remainders and reversions is their present value determined under the Regulation, *except* in the case of annuities under contracts issued by companies regularly engaged in their sale. The valuation of such commercial annuity contracts is determined under Regulation § 20.2031–8.[12]

The present value of an annuity, life estate, remainder or reversion determined under Regulation § 20.2031–7 which is dependent on the continuation or termination of the life of one person is computed by the use of Table I in paragraph (f) of

7. Simpson v US, 252 US 547, 64 L ed 709, 40 S Ct 367 (1920); Herold v Kahn, 163 F 947 (CCA 3) (1948).

8. Bankers Trust Co v Higgins, 137 F2d 477 (CCA 2) (1943).

9. Denbigh, 7 TC 387 (1946); Jennings, 10 TC 323 (1948); Douglas, 12 TCM 347 (1949); Hanley v US, 63 F Supp 73 (1945); Huntington Nat Bank of Columbus, 13 TC 760 (1949).

10. Ithaca Trust Co v US, 279 US 151, 73 L ed 647, 49 S Ct 291 (1929).

11. Boston Safe Deposit & Trust Co v Nichols, 18 F2d 660 (1927); Herron v Heiner, 24 F2d 745 (1928); Owens v Heiner, 19 F2d 362 (1927).

12. Reg, § 20.2031–7(a)(1); see also § 105, supra.

the section. The present value of an annuity, term for years, remainder or reversion dependent on a term certain is computed by the use of Table II in paragraph (f). If the interest to be valued is dependent upon more than one life or there is a term certain concurrent with one or more lives, the pamphlet referred to above is used. For purposes of the computations described, the age of a person is to be taken as the age of that person at his nearest birthday.[13]

Where the computation cannot be made with the use of the tables following or those set forth in the pamphlet "Actuarial Values for Estate and Gift Tax" because a special factor is required, the Commissioner will furnish the factor upon request. The request must be accompanied by a statement of the date of birth of each person, the duration of whose life may affect the value of the interest, and by copies of the relevant instruments.[14]

TABLE I

[As to estates of decedents dying after December 31, 1951]

Table, single life, 3½ percent, showing the present worth of an annuity, of a life interest, and of a remainder interest

1	2	3	4	1	2	3	4
		Life				Life	
Age	Annuity	Estate	Remainder	Age	Annuity	Estate	Remainder
0	23.9685	.83890	.16110	24	21.7902	.76266	.23734
1	24.9035	.87162	.12838	25	21.5950	.75582	.24418
2	24.8920	.87122	.12878	26	21.3942	.74880	.25120
3	24.8246	.86886	.13114	27	21.1878	.74157	.25843
4	24.7378	.86582	.13418	28	20.9759	.73416	.26584
5	24.6392	.86237	.13763	29	20.7581	.72653	.27347
6	24.5326	.85864	.14136	30	20.5345	.71871	.28129
7	24.4188	.85466	.14534	31	20.3052	.71068	.28932
8	24.2982	.85044	.14956	32	20.0699	.70245	.29755
9	24.1713	.84600	.15400	33	19.8288	.69401	.30599
10	24.0387	.84135	.15865	34	19.5816	.68536	.31464
11	23.9008	.83653	.16347	35	19.3285	.67650	.32350
12	23.7600	.83160	.16840	36	19.0695	.66743	.33257
13	23.6161	.82656	.17344	37	18.8044	.65815	.34185
14	23.4693	.82143	.17857	38	18.5334	.64867	.35133
15	23.3194	.81618	.18382	39	18.2566	.63898	.36102
16	23.1665	.81083	.18917	40	17.9738	.62908	.37092
17	23.0103	.80536	.19464	41	17.6853	.61899	.38101
18	22.8511	.79979	.20021	42	17.3911	.60869	.39131
19	22.6870	.79404	.20596	43	17.0913	.59820	.40180
20	22.5179	.78813	.21187	44	16.7860	.58751	.41249
21	22.3438	.78203	.21797	45	16.4754	.57664	.42336
22	22.1646	.77576	.22424	46	16.1596	.56559	.43441
23	21.9801	.76930	.23070	47	15.8388	.55436	.44564

13. Reg, § 20.2031–7(a)(2).   14. Reg, § 20.2031–7(e).

TABLE I—Continued

1	2	3 Life Estate	4	1	2	3 Life Estate	4
Age	Annuity	Estate	Remainder	Age	Annuity	Estate	Remainder
48	15.5133	.54297	.45703	77	5.6201	.19670	.80330
49	15.1831	.53141	.46859	78	5.3345	.18671	.81329
50	14.8486	.51970	.48030	79	5.0572	.17700	.82300
51	14.5101	.50785	.49215	80	4.7884	.16759	.83241
52	14.1678	.49587	.50413	81	4.5283	.15849	.84151
53	13.8221	.48377	.51623	82	4.2771	.14970	.85030
54	13.4734	.47157	.52843	83	4.0351	.14123	.85877
55	13.1218	.45926	.54074	84	3.8023	.13308	.86692
56	12.7679	.44688	.55312	85	3.5789	.12526	.87474
57	12.4120	.43442	.56558	86	3.3648	.11777	.88223
58	12.0546	.42191	.57809	87	3.1601	.11060	.88940
59	11.6960	.40936	.59064	88	2.9648	.10377	.89623
60	11.3369	.39679	.60321	89	2.7788	.09726	.90274
61	10.9776	.38422	.61578	90	2.6019	.09107	.90893
62	10.6186	.37165	.62835	91	2.4342	.08520	.91480
63	10.2604	.35911	.64089	92	2.2754	.07964	.92036
64	9.9036	.34663	.65337	93	2.1254	.07439	.92561
65	9.5486	.33420	.66580	94	1.9839	.06944	.93056
66	9.1960	.32186	.67814	95	1.8507	.06477	.93523
67	8.8464	.30962	.69038	96	1.7256	.06040	.93960
68	8.5001	.29750	.70250	97	1.6082	.05629	.94371
69	8.1578	.28552	.71448	98	1.4982	.05244	.94756
70	7.8200	.27370	.72630	99	1.3949	.04882	.95118
71	7.4871	.26205	.73795	100	1.2973	.04541	.95459
72	7.1597	.25059	.74941	101	1.2033	.04212	.95788
73	6.8382	.23934	.76066	102	1.1078	.03877	.96123
74	6.5231	.22831	.77169	103	.9973	.03491	.96509
75	6.2148	.21752	.78248	104	.8318	.02911	.97089
76	5.9137	.20698	.79302	105	.4831	.01691	.98309

TABLE II

[*As to estates of decedents dying after December 31, 1951*]

Table showing the present worth at 3½ percent of an annuity for a term certain, of an income interest for a term certain, and of a remainder interest postponed for a term certain

1 Number of Years	2 Annuity	3 Term Certain	4 Remainder	1 Number of Years	2 Annuity	3 Term Certain	4 Remainder
1	0.9662	.033816	.966184	11	9.0016	.315054	.684946
2	1.8997	.066489	.933511	12	9.6633	.338217	.661783
3	2.8016	.098057	.901943	13	10.3027	.360596	.639404
4	3.6731	.128558	.871442	14	10.9205	.382218	.617782
5	4.5151	.158027	.841973	15	11.5174	.403109	.596891
6	5.3286	.186499	.813501	16	12.0941	.423294	.576706
7	6.1145	.214009	.785991	17	12.6513	.442796	.557204
8	6.8740	.240588	.759412	18	13.1897	.461639	.538361
9	7.6077	.266269	.733731	19	13.7098	.479844	.520156
10	8.3166	.291081	.708919	20	14.2124	.497434	.502566

Table II—Continued

1 Number of Years	2 Annuity	3 Term Certain	4 Remainder	1 Number of Years	2 Annuity	3 Term Certain	4 Remainder
21	14.6980	.514429	.485571	26	16.8904	.591162	.408838
22	15.1671	.530849	.469151	27	17.2854	.604988	.395012
23	15.6204	.546714	.453286	28	17.6670	.618346	.381654
24	16.0584	.562043	.437957	29	18.0358	.631252	.368748
25	16.4815	.576853	.423147	30	18.3920	.643722	.356278

§ 113. Schedule F; Miscellaneous Property; Annuities; Valuation.

The value of an annuity will vary depending upon whether it is payable annually at the end of the year, at the end of, or at the beginning of, stated periods. The Regulation furnishes the factor to be used in such cases.

If an annuity is payable annually at the end of each year during the life of an individual (as for example if the first payment is due one year after the decedent's death) the amount payable is multiplied by the figure in column 2 of Table I[15] opposite the number of years in column 1 nearest the age of the individual whose life measures the duration of the annuity. If the annuity is payable annually at the end of each year for a definite number of years, the amount payable is multiplied by the figure in column 2 of Table II[16] opposite the number of years in column I representing the duration of the annuity.[17]

Thus, if the decedent received under the terms of his father's will, an annuity of $10,000 a year payable annually for the life of his elder brother, and at the time he died, an annual payment had just been made, and at which time the brother was 40 years 8 months old, the value of the annuity would be computed as follows: The figure in column 2 of Table I opposite the brother's age of 41 years is 17.6853. The present value of the annuity is therefore $10,000 × 17.6853 = $176,853. If the decedent was entitled to receive the same amount annually throughout a term certain, and if at the time he died an annual payment had just been made, with five more payments to be made, the value of the payments still to be made would be found by taking the figure in column 2 of Table II opposite five years, or 4.5151 and multiplying it by $10,000, the result being $45,151.[18]

If an annuity is payable at the *end* of semi-annual, quarterly,

15. § 112, supra.
16. § 112, supra.
17. Reg, § 20.2031–7(b)(1).
18. Examples, note 17, supra.

monthly, or weekly periods during the life of an individual (as for example if the first payment is due one month after the decedent's death), the result in the examples above would be multiplied by the following factors:

1.0087 for semiannual payments,

1.0130 for quarterly payments,

1.0159 for monthly payments, and

1.0171 for weekly payments.[19]

If the first payment of an annuity for the life of an individual is due at the *beginning* of the annual or other payment period rather than at the end (as for example if the first payment is to be made immediately after the decedent's death), the value of the annuity is the sum of (a) the first payment plus (b) the present value of a similar annuity, the first payment of which is not to be made until the end of the payment period.[20] Thus, if decedent was entitled to receive an annuity of $50 a month for the life of a person aged 50 at the former's death, the value of the annuity, if the decedent died on the day the payment was due would be $50 + ($50 × 12 × 14.8486) × 1.0159 = $9,100.82.

If the first payment of an annuity for a definite number of years is due at the *beginning* of the annual or other payment period, the applicable factor to be applied is as follows:

1.0350 for annual payments,

1.0262 for semiannual payments,

1.0218 for quarterly payments,

1.0189 for monthly payments, and

1.0177 for weekly payments.[1]

Thus, if the decedent was the beneficiary of an annuity of $50 a month and died on the day a payment was due, with 300 payments still to be made, the computation would be $50 × 12 × 16.-4815 (from column 2, Table II, opposite 25 years) × 1.0189 = $10,075.80.

§ 114. Schedule F; Miscellaneous Property; Life Estates and Terms for Years; Valuation.

If the interest to be valued is the right of a person for his life, or for the life of another person, to receive the income of certain property, or to use non-income-producing property, the value

19. Reg, § 20.2031–7(b)(2).

20. Reg, § 20.2031–7(b)(3).

1. Reg, § 20.2031–7(b)(3)(ii).

of the interest is the value of the property multiplied by the figure in column 3 of Table I[2] opposite the number of years nearest to the actual age of the measuring life. If the interest to be valued is the right to receive income of property or to use non-income-producing property for a term of years, column 3 of Table II[3] is used.[4]

Thus, the decedent or his estate was entitled to receive the income from a fund of $50,000 during the life of his elder brother, aged 31 years at the decedent's death. By reference to Table I, the figure in column 3 opposite 31 years is .71068. The present value of decedent's interest is, therefore, $50,000 × .71068 = $35,534.

§ 115. Schedule F; Miscellaneous Property; Remainders or Reversionary Interests; Valuation.

If a decedent had, at the time of his death, a remainder or a reversionary interest in property to take effect after an estate for the life of another, the present value of his interest is obtained by multiplying the value of the property by the figure in column 4 of Table I[5] opposite the number of years nearest to the actual age of the person whose life measures the preceding estate. If the remainder or reversion is to take effect at the end of a term for years, column 4 of Table II[6] is used.[7]

Thus, if the decedent was entitled to receive property worth $50,000 upon the death of his elder brother, to whom the income was bequeathed for life, and at the date of the decedent's death the brother was 31 years old, the value of the decedent's remainder interest would be $50,000 × .28932 (the figure opposite 31 years in column 4, Table I) = $14,466.

The necessity for determining the value of a reversionary interest has become more frequent because of the inclusion in the decedent's gross estate of property transferred by a decedent in which he had a reversionary interest immediately preceding his death of a value in excess of 5% of the value of such property.[8]

2. § 112, supra.
3. § 112, supra.
4. Reg, § 20.2031–7(c).
5. § 112, supra.

6. § 112, supra.
7. Reg, § 20.2031–7(d).
8. See § 111, supra.

§ 116. Schedule F; Miscellaneous Property; Tenancy in Common.

A tenancy in common involving personal property must be reported in the schedule appropriate to the type of property concerned. In consequence, where such personal property is miscellaneous property of the kind reported in Schedule F, the decedent's interest should be reported in that schedule.

§ 117. Schedule F; Miscellaneous Property; Return.

In reporting the items includible as miscellaneous property we have discussed the information required with respect to insurance on the life of another,[9] judgments,[10] and household effects.[11] In describing an annuity, the name and address of the grantor of the annuity should be given, or, if the annuity is payable out of a trust or other funds, such a description as will fully identify it. If the annuity is payable for a term of years, the duration of the term and the date on which it began should be given, and if payable for the life of a person other than the decedent, the date of birth of such person should be stated.[12] When an interest in a copartnership or unincorporated business is returned, there must be submitted a statement of assets and liabilities as of the valuation date and for the 5 years preceding, and statements of the net earnings for the same 5 years.[13] In case of an interest in a trust fund, a copy of the trust instrument should be submitted.[14]

As to the other items of Schedule F, neither the Regulations nor the return contain any instructions other than the general requirement that in listing property upon the return it should be described so that the property may be readily identified for the purpose of verifying the value placed on it by the executor.[15]

FORM NO. 18

Schedule F; Other Miscellaneous Property

1. Did the decedent, at the time of his death, own any interest in a copartnership or unincorporated business? [x] Yes   [ ] No

9. § 105, supra.
10. § 106, supra.
11. § 108, supra.
12. Reg, § 20.6018–3(c)(4).

13. Instructions, Schedule F, Form 706.
14. Note 13, supra.
15. Reg, § 20.6018–3(a).

2. Did the decedent, at the time of his death, own any miscellaneous property not returnable under any other schedule? [x] Yes [ ] No
3. Was there any insurance which the decedent owned on the life of another which is not included in the return as a part of the gross estate? If "Yes," full details must be submitted under this schedule. [x] Yes [ ] No
4. State whether the decedent's estate, his spouse, or any other person, has received, or will receive, any bonus or award as a result of the decedent's employment or his death. If "Yes," full details must be submitted under this schedule. [x] Yes [ ] No

Item No.	Description	Subsequent valuation date	Alternate value	Value at date of death
1	Decedent was the sole proprietor of Elite Hardware Co. Annexed hereto are balance sheets and profit and loss statements of said business for the 5 years preceding his death			$34,678.90
2	Household and personal effects as per annexed inventory and affidavit of appraisal			3,351.80
3	Decedent owned policy of insurance on the life of Katherine Benson, State Insurance Company, #176,543, the gross annual premium is $2,811. Said policy was issued 9 years 4 months before decedent's death. At date of issuance Katherine Benson was 35 years of age. See statement of value annexed.			15,384.33
4	Decedent received under will of Winthrop Benson, Sr., admitted to probate in Probate Court, Middlesex County, N. J. June 15, 1957, an annuity of $10,000 per year for the life of Henry Benson. At the date of decedent's death Henry Benson was 40 years 8 months old. Value of annuity			148,610.20
5	Bonus received from Benson Holding Corp. ..			10,000.00

TOTAL (also enter under the Recapitulation, Schedule O) $212,025.23
(If more space is needed, insert additional sheets of same size)
Estate of WINTHROP BENSON
Schedule F—Page 17

§ 118. Schedule G; Transfers During Life; The Problem.

Not only does the law favor the alienability of property, real or personal, but it goes further, and prohibits suspension of alienability for more than a prescribed period, as witness the Rule Against Perpetuities. The purpose of that rule has been stated that it is to prevent restraints on free transfer of property in commerce.[16] That being so, there is nothing to prevent a per-

16. Mayfield v Parks (Tex) 57 SW2d 885 (1933); Chilcott v Hart, 23 Colo 40, 45 P 391 (1896); Pulitzer v Livingston, 89 Me 359, 36 A 635 (1896); Edgerly v Barker, 66 NH 434, 31 A 900 (1891).

153

son divesting himself of any property he may acquire, even to the extent of disposing of all of his assets, subject to the payment of any Gift Taxes incurred thereby. By so doing he may transfer all of his property to the natural objects of his bounty, or others, and thereby leave no taxable estate. So far as the taxing authorities are concerned there is only one limitation, in addition to Gift Tax liability, and that is that he may not do so for the purpose of defeating the Estate Tax under the circumstances we are about to discuss.

The Regulations require that there be reported enumerated transfers made by the decedent during his life, by trust or otherwise, other than sales for an adequate and full consideration in money or money's worth.[17] The purpose of such requirement is to determine whether the decedent made a transfer of property which under the pertinent provisions of the statute is taxable. The statute is not concerned with transfers made for an adequate consideration. Examination of the amendments to the statute indicate that from the first Revenue Act in 1916 taxing lifetime transfers[18] there has been a continuing battle of wits between the taxing authority and the taxpayer with respect to taxable transfers. The taxpayer by ingenious devices, attempted to exclude himself from the purview of the statute, and the taxing authorities attempted inclusion. As the taxpayer discovered a loophole in the law, the law was amended. Amendment followed amendment, since few are so diligent as those seeking to avoid taxation. The present statute, the result of more than thirty years of experience, is almost foolproof.

Although the instructions[19] refer to the transfers we shall discuss in succeeding sections as "Transfers During Decedent's Life" and the Regulations[20] dealing with them are grouped under "Transfers During Lifetime," there are embraced within these descriptive terms many transfers not usually thought of as taxable, but which are within the contemplation of the statute. There are included transfers in contemplation of death, transfers with retained life estates, transfers taking effect at death and revocable transfers.

The statute specifically provides for the inclusion in a decedent's gross estate of all property which he transferred during

17. Reg, §§ 20.2035–1, 20.2036–1, 20.2037–1, 20.2038–1.

18. Rev Act of 1916, § 202(b).

19. Instructions, Schedule G, Form 706.

20. Reg, §§ 20.2035–1 et seq.

his lifetime where, either dominion in any degree is retained by him at the date of his death over the property transferred, or he relinquishes such dominion within three years of his death. The underlying theory of such taxation is that so long as the donor retains a string attached to the gift until his death, it will be included in his estate.[1] It is, therefore, necessary to understand the statute in order to solve the problem of whether the string is or is not attached under the facts of a particular case. The problem is by no means easy of solution. It will be the purpose of succeeding sections to furnish the necessary guidance to that end.

§ 119. Schedule G; Transfers During Life; Statutory Scheme.

Few sections of the Estate Tax statute have been the subject of so much litigation as those dealing with transfers designated in general "transfers in contemplation of death." The basic provisions for taxing lifetime transfers under the provisions of the Estate Tax Law stem from the Revenue Act of 1926. Those provisions have, however, been frequently amended to avoid the effect of various constructions by the courts. Even the enactment of the Provisions of the Internal Revenue Code of 1954 dealing with such transfers made further amendments, and there has been one minor and restricted amendment since.

The statute at present divides such transfers into four classes. First are transactions in contemplation of death.[2] This includes transfers of property or the relinquishment, exercise or release of a general power of appointment. Second are transfers with a retained life estate.[3] Third are transfers taking effect at death.[4] Finally are revocable transfers.[5] In the case of certain of these transfers there are cut-off dates which provide for different taxability before and after such dates, which will be discussed hereafter under the appropriate section.

As we shall see, the statutory scheme is intended to embrace transfers which are substitutes for testamentary disposition, or in which a decedent has retained the fruits from the property or such control that there is not in fact a transfer until his death. Like it or not, it must be conceded that it is realistic and com-

1. Comm v Field, 324 US 113, 89 L ed 786, 65 S Ct 511 (1945); Fidelity Philadelphia Trust Co v Rothensies, 324 US 108, 89 L ed 782, 65 S Ct 508 (1945).

2. IRC, § 2035 (1954 Code).
3. IRC, § 2036 (1954 Code).
4. IRC, § 2037 (1954 Code).
5. IRC, § 2038 (1954 Code).

prehensive. In effect the statute says that you cannot eat your cake and also have it.

§ 120. Schedule G; Transfers During Life; Evolution of Statute.

As we have observed, the history of taxable transfers is the history of the duel of wits between taxing authorities and the taxpayer, or more accurately the taxpayer's tax counsel. The Revenue Act of 1926 included as taxable transfers, any transfer in trust or otherwise, in contemplation of or intended to take effect in possession or enjoyment at or after death.[6] This was construed by the Treasury Department to include irrevocable transfers in trust in which the transferor retained the income or the right to designate the person who should possess or enjoy the property or the income.

In March, 1931, however, the United States Supreme Court held that such transfers were not taxable.[7] Thereupon, at the request of the Acting Secretary of the Treasury, by joint resolution on March 3, 1931, Congress amended the law to tax such transfers.[8] The section was further amended by the Revenue Act of 1932 to include transfers in which the decedent retained the use, possession, right to income or enjoyment for any period not ascertainable without reference to his death or which did not in fact end before his death.[9] There were also amendments in 1934,[10] and 1936.[11] The 1932 Act also amended the provisions of Section 303(d) of the 1926 Act.[12]

The amendments were held not to be retroactive.[13] The Supreme Court then decided in 1940 that transfers with a retained possibility of reverter were taxable.[14] The decision, commonly referred to as the Hallock case, created doubt as to whether it had overruled May vs. Heiner,[15] which had held that transfers prior to March 3, 1931 in which the settlor divested himself of all ownership but retained income rights were not taxable. Finally in the Church case[16] and the companion Spiegel case,[17]

6. IRC, § 302(c) (Rev Act 1926).

7. Burnet v Northern Trust Co, and McCormack v Burnet, 283 US 784, 75 L ed 1413, 51 S Ct 343 (1931).

8. H J Res 529, amending IRC § 302 (c) (Rev Act 1926).

9. Rev Act 1932, § 803(a).

10. Rev Act 1934, §§ 401, 404.

11. Rev Act 1936, § 805(a).

12. Rev Act 1932, § 804.

13. Hassett v Welch, 303 US 308, 82 L ed 858, 58 S Ct 559 (1938).

14. Helvering v Hallock, 309 US 106, 93 L ed 1446, 60 S Ct 444 (1940).

15. 281 US 238, 74 L ed 826, 50 S Ct 286 (1929).

16. Comm v Church, 335 US 632, 93 L ed 288, 59 S Ct 322 (1949).

in addition to overruling May vs. Heiner, the Supreme Court subjected to tax any transfer in which there was retained a possibility of reverter, whether by operation of law or otherwise, and no matter how remote or small in value. In the Spiegel case, the retention of a reversionary interest valued at $70 upon a corpus of $1,000,000, resulted in the imposition of a $450,000 tax.

Because of the unjustness of retroactive application of the principles enunciated, Congress enacted the Technical Changes Act of 1949.[18] Congress interred the rule enunciated in the Church case by enactment of the Technical Changes Act of 1953[19], which freed from tax transfers prior to March 3, 1931 with income retained, no matter when the decedent died, provided the transfer was not otherwise taxable. In re-writing the statute in the Internal Revenue Code of 1954 Congress substantially re-enacted Section 811 of the 1939 Code, which in turn had followed the provisions of Section 302 of the 1926 Act. In so doing the former subdivisions of the single section were made separate sections, and certain other changes were made, to be discussed hereafter. In addition, a new section dealing with annuities was enacted, such transfers having been previously taxed as transfers taking effect at death.

These details of history, if they were only that, might be interesting, but quickly forgotten. They are furnished for *two reasons*. The first, is that an understanding of the basic approach to taxable lifetime transfers may be obtained. Secondly, and more important, is the fact that *the tax statute in effect at the date of death controls taxability*. If in a pending estate the decedent died prior to August 17, 1954 the applicable statute should be consulted.

§ 121. Schedule G; Transfers During Life; Transactions in Contemplation of Death; Generally.

From the very beginning of the Estate Tax Law in 1916 transfers in trust or otherwise in contemplation of or intended to take effect in possession or enjoyment at or after the death of the transferor were included in his gross estate.[20] Substantially the same provision in the 1954 Code requires the inclusion in

---

17. Spiegel v Comm, 335 US 701, 93 L ed 330, 69 S Ct 301 (1949).

18. PL 378–81st Congress, approved Oct. 25, 1949.

19. PL 287, Aug. 15, 1953, 83rd Congress.

20. Rev Act 1916, § 202(b).

the gross estate of property of which the decedent has at any time made a transfer (except in case of a bona fide sale for an adequate and full consideration in money or money's worth), by trust or otherwise, in contemplation of his death.[1] The statute further creates presumptions discussed hereafter.[2]

The provision has been the subject of extensive litigation, in the course of which general principles have developed. There is further embraced within transfers in contemplation of death, the relinquishment of a power, or the exercise or release of a general power of appointment under such circumstances.[3]

Such transfers are taxable if made within three years of death and are not a bona fide sale for an adequate and full consideration in money or money's worth.[4]

There is thus presented the question of what is meant by the term "in contemplation of death". Contemplation of death as used in the statute means a present apprehension from some existing bodily condition or impending peril, known to the decedent, creating a reasonable fear that death is near at hand. It is not the general knowledge of all men that they must die at some time. It is only when contemplation of death is the motive without which the transfer would not have been made and is the controlling motive in making the gifts, that the transfer is taxable.[5] The same idea has been phrased in many different ways. Thus, it has been said that gifts in contemplation of death are gifts motivated by the same consideration as lead to testamentary dispositions and made as substitutes therefor.[6] It is not necessary that death be near at hand[7] or imminent.[8] The phrase is not confined to gifts causa mortis, the indicia of which are imminent death, revocability and a return of the subject of the gift if the donor survives. The statute embraces gifts inter vivos which are fully executed, irrevocable and indefeasible.[9]

As a consequence of these definitions, the shorter the period

1. IRC, § 2035(a) (1954 Code).
2. § 123, infra.
3. IRC, § 2035(b) (1954 Code).
4. Note 3, supra.
5. US v Wells, 283 US 102, 75 L ed 867, 51 S Ct 446 (1931).
6. Milliken v US, 283 US 15, 75 L ed 809, 51 S Ct 324 (1931); Dierks v US, 86 F Supp 832 (1949); Trust Co, of Georgia v Allen, 55 F Supp 269, aff'd 149 F2d 120 (CCA 5), aff'd 326 US 630,

90 L ed 367, 66 S Ct 389 (1944); Flannery v Willcuts, 25 F2d 951 (CCA 8) (1928); Reeves v Comm, 180 F2d 829 (CA 2), cert den 340 US 813, 95 L ed 598, 71 S Ct 41 (1950); Loetscher v Burnet, 46 F2d 835 (CA DC) (1931).
7. Russell v US, 38 F Supp 438 (1941).
8. Rengstorff v McLaughlin, 21 F2d 177 (1927).
9. Note 5, supra.

between the gift and the date of death, the more likely is it to be held as made in contemplation of death. The statute has removed the time element, however, to a very large degree, by creating a presumption which has removed the cause of much, but by no means all, of the litigation concerning such transfers.

The Regulation, however, goes along with the courts' interpretation of the statute part way. It states that a transfer in contemplation of death is a disposition of property prompted by the thought of death (though it need not be solely so prompted). A transfer is prompted by the thought of death if it is made with the purpose of avoiding the tax, or as a substitute for a testamentary disposition of the property, or for any motive associated with death. The bodily and mental condition of the decedent and all other attending facts and circumstances are to be scrutinized to determine whether or not such thought prompted the disposition.[10] The persistence of the Commissioner in applying standards which the courts have refused to follow has resulted in seemingly endless litigation, and the Commissioner's record of success in such cases is far from good.

Essentially, whether a transfer was made in contemplation of death is a question of fact.[11] This means that *facts* will determine the issue. It is the job of the lawyer to collate the facts to establish the position of the executor. Which facts will accomplish the desired result of excluding a transfer are treated in succeeding sections.

§ 122. Schedule G; Transfers During Life; Transactions in Contemplation of Death; Presumption.

The statute provides that if the decedent *within a period of three years* ending with the date of his death (*except* in case of a bona fide sale for an adequate and full consideration in money or money's worth)

(1) transferred an interest in property,

(2) relinquished a power, *or*

(3) exercised or released a general power of appointment, such transfer, relinquishment, exercise or release shall, *unless shown to the contrary,* be deemed to have been made in contemplation of death within the meaning of the section and the sec-

10. Reg, § 20.2035–1(c). 8) (1932); Garvan, 63 F2d 685 (CCA 1)
11. Neal v Comm, 53 F2d 806 (CCA   (1933); note 5, supra.

tions relating to revocable transfers[12] and powers of appointment;[13] *but no such transfer, relinquishment, exercise, or release made before such 3 year period shall be treated as having been made in contemplation of death.*[14]

This statutory conclusive presumption *in favor of the taxpayer* first appeared in the predecessor[15] of the present statute and became effective September 24, 1950. Prior to that time a transfer within two years of death was presumed to be in contemplation of death, while transfers made more than two years before death could be attacked by the tax authorities. The two year presumption was rebuttable however.[16] In fact, the attempt to make the presumption in favor of the government a conclusive one was held in violation of the Constitution as being so arbitrary and unreasonable as to deny due process.[17]

Under the present statute, as to all irrevocable transfers made *more than three years prior to death,* no claim that they were made in contemplation of death may be made by the tax authorities. The possibility of attack upon gifts made *within three years of death* still remains however, since they are subject to the presumption in favor of the Commissioner that they were made in contemplation of death.

Where a transfer has been made within the statutory period, the taxpayer has the burden of establishing that it was not made in contemplation of death,[18] and the Commissioner may raise the question for the first time in the Tax Court,[19] or other court.[20] The Commissioner's finding is presumptively correct[1] and failure to overcome it results in taxability.[2] The presumption is prima facie only, and cannot stand in the face of proof to the contrary.[3] The question is one of fact[4] and doubts must be resolved in favor of the taxpayer.[5] This explains to some extent the Commissioner's lack of success in such cases. When the tax is paid and suit

12. IRC, § 2038 (1954 Code).

13. IRC, § 2041 (1954 Code).

14. Note 3, supra; Reg, § 20.2035–1 (d).

15. IRC, § 811(c)(1)(A) (1939 Code).

16. Heiner v Donnan, 285 US 312, 76 L ed 772, 52 S Ct 358 (1932); Dupont v Comm, 285 US 352, 76 L ed 793, 52 S Ct 371 (1932).

17. Note 16, supra.

18. Lippincott, 27 BTA 735 (1933); Belyea v Comm, 206 F2d 262 (CA 3) (1953); Rickenberg, 11 TC 1 (1948).

19. McCue, 5 TCM 141 (1945).

20. Orvis v Higgins, 80 F Supp 64 (1948).

1. Hornor, 44 BTA 1136 (1941); Maxwell, 3 TCM 1207 (1944); note 20, supra.

2. Pennsylvania Co., 21 BTA 176 (1931).

3. US v Wells, 283 US 102, 75 L ed 867, 51 S Ct 446 (1931).

4. Note 11, supra.

5. Norris v Goodcell, 17 F2d 181 (1927).

brought in the District Court, juries are reluctant to find contemplation of death. It must not be assumed however that the presumption is easily rebutted. If the facts repel death as the motive for the transfer, taxability may be avoided. The succeeding sections will particularize the facts which determine the question.

§ 123. Schedule G; Transfers During Life; Transactions in Contemplation of Death; Motive.

While other factors enter into the determination of whether a transfer has been made in contemplation of death, the primary question for decision and the essential test is to be found in the decedent's motive.[6] If the thought of death is the impelling or dominant motive,[7] and it is one associated with thought of death[8] and testamentary disposition,[9] then the transfer will be deemed made in contemplation of death within the meaning of the statute. The immediacy of death is not necessarily a conclusive factor,[10] nor the fact that death ensues shortly after the transfer.[11]

What is in fact determined in each case involving whether a transfer has been made in contemplation of death is the decedent's intention, which essentially calls for an examination of his state of mind at the time of transfer.[12] The determination of the question is further complicated by the fact that there may be mixed motives, in which case the dominant motive will determine the question.[13] There are no calipers into which the

6. Note 3, supra; Allen v Trust Co of Georgia, 326 US 630, 90 L ed 367, 66 S Ct 389 (1946); City Bank Farmers Trust Co v McGowan, 323 US 594, 89 L ed 483, 65 S Ct 496 (1945); Becker v St Louis Union Trust Co, 296 US 48, 80 L ed 35, 56 S Ct 78 (1935).

7. Note 6, supra; Comm v Colorado Nat Bank of Denver, 95 F2d 160 (CCA 10), revd other grounds 305 US 23, 83 L ed 20, 59 S Ct 48 (1938); Belyea v Comm, note 18, supra; Rickenberg v Comm, 177 F2d 114 (CA 9), cert den 338 US 949, 94 L ed 585, 70 S Ct 487 (1949).

8. Allen v Trust Co of Georgia, note 6, supra; Bradley v Smith, 114 F2d 161 (CCA 7) (1940); Comm v Colorado Nat Bank of Denver, note 7, supra; Tait v Safe Deposit & Trust Co of Baltimore, 74 F2d 851 (CCA 4) (1935); Bell v US, 74 F Supp 295 (1947).

9. Pate v Comm, 149 F2d 669 (CCA 8) (1945); Updike v Comm, 88 F2d 807 (CCA 8), cert den 301 US 708, 81 L ed 1362, 57 S Ct 942 (1937); Bradley v Smith, 114 F2d 161 (CCA 7) (1940); Comm v Colorado Nat Bank of Denver, note 7, supra; Russell v US, 39 F Supp 438 (1941).

10. Comm v Colorado Nat Bank of Denver, note 7, supra.

11. Routzahn v Brown, 95 F2d 766 (CCA 6) (1938).

12. Flack v Holtegel, 93 F2d 512 (CCA 7) (1938).

13. Omaha Nat Bank v O'Malley, 69 F Supp 354 (1937).

facts may be fitted and whereby an answer is given. The facts, and the facts alone, will establish whether the controlling motive was the thought of death without which the transfer would not have been made.[14] The absence of the requisite motive must lead to a finding that there was not present in a transfer the element of contemplation of death.[15]

§ 124. Schedule G; Transfers During Life; Transactions in Contemplation of Death; Time Element.

Standing alone, the length of time between the transfer and the date of death has no significance. Examination of the decided cases indicate this fact. Transfers within the following periods before death have been held not in contemplation of death: two months,[16] a few days,[17] one month,[18] a few months,[19] shortly before,[20] less than two years,[1] one year,[2] one day,[3] and three days.[4] On the other hand, before the present three year conclusive presumption in favor of the taxpayer, when there was a rebuttable presumption that transfers more than two years before death were not in contemplation of death, the Commissioner overcame the presumption in the case of transfers made two years,[5] three years,[6] four years,[7] and five years[8] before death.

The cases indicate that while the time of the transfer in relation to death is a fact to be considered, its importance will depend upon the other facts present.

14. US v Wells, note 3, supra; Diamond v Comm, 159 F2d 672 (CCA 2) (1947); Rogan v Ferry, 154 F2d 974 (CCA 9) (1946).

15. Safford v US, 66 Ct Cls 242 (1928).

16. Lavelle, 8 BTA 1150 (1927); Schumacher, 2 TCM 1018 (1943).

17. Beeler v Comm, 33 F2d 788 (1929); Mather v McLaughlin, 57 F2d 223 (1932).

18. Koussevitsky, 5 TC 650 (1945); Heipershausen, 18 BTA 218 (1929).

19. True v US, 51 F Supp 720 (1943); Kaufman v Reinecke, 68 F2d 642 (CCA 7) (1934); Proctor v Hassett, 52 F Supp 12 (1943).

20. Hammond v Westover, 97 F Supp 753 (1951); Kneeland, 34 BTA 816 (1936).

1. Cherry, 5 TCM 495 (1945); Greer v Glenn, 64 F Supp 1002 (1946).

2. White, 21 BTA 500 (1931).

3. Comm v Sharp, 91 F2d 804 (CCA 3) (1937).

4. Lohman, 6 TCM 1071 (1946).

5. Walton, 42 BTA 300 (1940).

6. Burns v Comm, 177 F2d 739 (CA 5) (1949).

7. Gross v Rothensies, 65 F Supp 92 (1946).

8. Commonwealth Trust Co v Driscoll, 50 F Supp 949, aff'd 137 F2d 653 (CCA 3), cert den 321 US 764, 88 L ed 1061, 64 S Ct 521 (1943).

§ 125. Schedule G; Transfers During Life; Transactions in Contemplation of Death; Health.

The standard enunciated for the determination of whether a transfer has been made in contemplation of death includes a present apprehension from some existing *bodily condition* or impending peril, *known to the decedent.*[9] The physical condition of the donor, or his state of health therefore becomes an important factor in the determination.

Knowledge that a disease is incurable carries with it the thought of death[10] and is an important factor.[11] While fear of ill health is not a determining factor, when there are other facts present it may be.[12] The habit of going to doctors frequently is not a sign of ill health, if such visits are merely precautionary.[13]

The fact that the donor was suffering from a heart condition,[14] cancer,[15] paralytic strokes whether singly[16] or in series,[17] paresis,[18] pernicious anemia and other ailments,[19] or arteriosclerosis and myocardial degeneration[20] gives rise to an affirmative inference that the transfer was in contemplation of death.

Where the donor was in good health although elderly at the time of transfer, the tendency of the courts is to find that it was not made in contemplation of death.[1] The fact that the donor died shortly after the gift is not of great importance.[2] Conversely, bad health at the time of the transfer, particularly at a time when it was growing gradually worse is almost a cer-

9. US v Wells, 283 US 102, 75 L ed 867, 51 S Ct 446 (1931).

10. Ward, 3 BTA 879 (1925).

11. Travelers Bank & Trust Co, 29 BTA 88 (1934).

12. Liebmann v Hassett, 50 F Supp 537, affd 148 F2d 247 (CCA 1) (1943).

13. True v US, note 19, supra; Burr, 4 TCM 1054 (1945); McCormick, 13 BTA 423 (1928).

14. Harris Trust & Sav Bank v US, 29 F Supp 876, cert den 310 US 632, 84 L ed 1042, 60 S Ct 1074 (1929); Worcester County Trust Co v US, 35 F Supp 970 (1940); Stubblefield v US, 6 F Supp 440 (1934); Springer, 45 BTA 561 (1941); Diamond v Comm, 159 F2d 672 (CCA 2) (1947).

15. Turner v Hassett, 37 F Supp 996 (1941); Basset v Comm, 170 F2d 916 (CA 2) (1948); Gilson, 47 BTA 529 (1942).

16. Russell v US, 38 F Supp 438 (1941).

17. Walton, 42 BTA 300 (1940).

18. Wheelock, 13 BTA 828 (1928).

19. Humphrey v Comm, 162 F2d 1 (CCA 5), cert den 332 US 817, 92 L ed 394, 68 S Ct 157 (1947).

20. Harris Trust & Sav Bank v US, note 14, supra; Wright, 43 BTA 551 (1941).

1. Wishard v US, 143 F2d 704 (CCA 7) (1944); McGregor v Comm, 82 F2d 948 (CCA 1) (1936); Selling, 24 TC 191 (1955); Fidelity & Columbia Trust Co v Lucas, 7 F2d 146 (1925); Orvis v Higgins, 80 F Supp 64, revd other grounds 180 F2d 537 (CA 2), cert den 340 US 810, 95 L ed 595, 71 S Ct 37 (1948); Talbot, 42 BTA 1081 (1940).

2. Llewellyn v US, 40 F2d 555 (1930).

tain guarantee that there will be a finding of contemplation of death.[3]

But there are two situations in which there may be ill health, but there is nothing in the condition to create a fear of death. The first is where the condition exists and has existed for many years,[4] and the other is where the condition exists but the donor has no knowledge of it.[5] Once again we have a factual question for determination.

§ 126. Schedule G; Transfers During Life; Transactions in Contemplation of Death; Activity; Longevity; Plans.

Since the bodily and mental condition of the donor is an element in the determination of whether his transfer was made in contemplation of death, it is natural that if he was active in the affairs of business and otherwise, such fact would indicate that the imminence of death was not in his mind. Thus, it has been one of the important considerations in negativing contemplation of death that the donor was actively engaged in business at the time of the transfer.[6] As has been said, such fact militates against considering that the transfer was so made.[7]

The fact that at the time of the transfer the donor was looking forward to life, as evidenced by the fact that he was making plans for the future, has also been held indicative of the fact that there was no contemplation of death present.[8]

Where the decedent was a member of a family which had a history of longevity, that fact has been considered in repelling the claim of contemplation of death.[9]

3. Hunter v US, 14 F Supp 523 (1936); Lawrence v Anderson, 17 F Supp 357 (1937); Stubblefield v US, note 14, supra; Kahn, 4 BTA 1289 (1926); Ader, 40 BTA 581 (1939).

4. Note 2, supra; Atwater, 3 TCM 1223 (1944); Terrell v US, 64 F Supp 418 (1946); Ferry v Rogan, 154 F2d 974 (CCA 9) (1944); note 13, supra.

5. Levi v US, 14 F Supp 513 (1936); Eckhart, 33 BTA 426 (1935); Proctor v Hassett, 52 F Supp 12 (1943); Browarsky, 148 F Supp 665 (1956); Serrien, 7 BTA 1129 (1927); Gimbel, 11 BTA 214 (1928).

6. Fidelity & Columbia Trust Co v Lucas, note 1, supra; Levi v US, note 5, supra; Wishard v US, note 1, supra;

Howard v US, 65 Ct Cls 332; Hennings v Smith, 63 F Supp 834 (1946); Orvis v Higgins, note 1, supra; Wier, 17 TC 409 (1952); Coffin, 9 TCM 1129 (1947); Ford, 4 TCM 321 (1945); Johnston, 2 TCM 299 (1943); Hodgkins v Comm, 44 F2d 43 (CCA 7) (1931).

7. Wishard v US, note 1, supra.

8. US v Wells, note 9, supra; Hammond v Westover, 97 F Supp 753 (1951); Oliver v Bell, 23 F Supp 30, affd 103 F2d 760 (CCA 3) (1938).

9. Lozier, 7 BTA 1050 (1927); Blakeslee v Smith, 26 F Supp 28, affd 110 F2d 364 (CCA 2) (1940); Orvis v Higgins, note 1, supra; Lineberger, 13 TCM 252 (1949).

§ 127. Schedule G; Transfers During Life; Transactions in Contemplation of Death; Age Element.

Advanced age is not in itself sufficient evidence to show that a transfer was made in contemplation of death.[10] While it is a factor to be considered, it is not in itself decisive.[11] It is interesting to observe how many octogenarians and even nonagenarians who make gifts, are healthy, active in business and look forward to many years of life. The fact is that many such gifts have been held not to have been made in contemplation of death.[12]

But age, coupled with other factors, such as sickness,[13] a continued illness,[14] the last illness,[15] a prospective operation,[16] or execution of a will on the same day as the transfer,[17] has been held indicative of a death motive. The ultimate test is whether the motives of the donor are associated with life rather than death.[18] Age is important only to the extent that it throws light on the motive.[19]

§ 128. Schedule G; Transfers During Life; Transactions in Contemplation of Death; Tax Avoidance.

Where the motive is tax avoidance there is a strange dichotomy of thought on such fact being indicative of a transfer in contemplation of death. While it has been said that the desire to avoid Estate Tax does not establish that a transfer was in contemplation of death[20] and standing alone cannot be deemed conclusive of a mental state such as is contemplated by the statutory phrase "contemplation of death",[1] where the dominant or con-

10. Flack v Holtegel, 93 F2d 512 (CCA 7) (1938); Updike v Comm, 88 F2d 807 (CCA 8) cert den 301 US 708, 81 L ed 1362, 57 S Ct 942 (1937); Kaufman v Reinecke, 68 F2d 642 (CCA 7) (1934); Hackney v Fahs, 62 F Supp 926 (1945); Smith v US, 16 F Supp 397, affd 92 F2d 704 (CCA 1) (1936).

11. Duncan v US, 148 F Supp 264 (1957).

12. (75) Gillette v Comm, 182 F2d 1010 (CA 9) (1950); (83) Gaither v Miles, 268 F 692 (1920); (72) First Nat Bank of Kansas City v Nee, 67 F Supp 815 (1946); (82) Brewer v Hassett, 49 F Supp 501 (1943); (80) Howell, 1 TCM 481 (1942); (87) Schumacher, 2 TCM 1081 (1943); (94) Johnson, 10 TC 680 (1948; (82) Comm v Nevins, 4 F2d 478 (CCA 3) (1931); (85) Bradley v Smith, 114 F2d 161 (CCA 7) (1940).

13. Lawrence v Anderson, 17 F Supp 337 (1937).

14. Kunhardt v Bowers, 57 F2d 1064 (1932).

15. Kengel v US, 57 F2d 929 (1932).

16. Gregg v US, 13 F Supp 147 (1936).

17. O'Neal v Comm, 170 F2d 219 (CA 5) (1948); Old Colony Trust Co v Delaney, 69 F Supp 495 (1947).

18. Flack v Holtegel, note 10, supra.

19. Land Title & Trust Co v McCaughn, 7 F Supp 742 (1934).

20. Allen v Trust Co of Georgia, 326 US 630, 90 L ed 367, 66 S Ct 389 (1946).

1. Denniston v Comm, 106 F2d 925 (CCA 3) (1939).

trolling motive is the avoidance of Estate Taxes it is invariably held that the transfer is taxable,[2] and in fact it is held that such purpose is sufficient to make the transfer one in contemplation of death.[3]

On the other hand where the motive was to avoid the effect of the proposed Gift Tax law,[4] or an increase in Gift Tax rates,[5] or a state property tax,[6] such tax avoidance is held not a motive indicative of a transfer in contemplation of death. And the desire to realize Income Tax savings, which is another form of tax avoidance, no other motives being present, is practically a guarantee that the transfer will not be held to have been made in contemplation of death.[7] The strange fact is that where such is the motive, the courts have found no contemplation of death, even though there were other facts indicating motive.[8]

The distinction is based on the theory that a desire to avoid Estate Taxes is evidence that the donor has death in mind, whereas avoidance of other taxes indicates that the donor is looking to his own future. There appears little logic to the distinction. A desire to avoid taxes is not illegal and Estate Taxes should not be singled out in this manner. As one of the factors to be considered it is unobjectionable, but as a sole criterion, it is not sustained by reason.

2. Farmers Loan & Trust Co v Bowers, 68 F2d 916 (CCA 2), 98 F2d 794, cert den 306 US 648, 83 L ed 1047, 59 S Ct 589 (1938); Turner v Hassett, 37 F Supp 996 (1941); Commonwealth Trust Co v Driscoll, 50 F Supp 949, affd 137 F2d 653 (CCA 3), cert den 321 US 764, 88 L ed 1061, 64 S Ct 521 (1943); Hill, 23 TC 588, affd 22 F2d 327 (CA 2) (1954); Vanderlip v Comm, 155 F2d 152 (CCA 2) (1946); Slifka v Johnson, 63 F Supp 289 (1945); Satuloff, 6 TCM 1246 (1946); First Trust & Safe Deposit Co v Shaughnessy, 134 F 2d 940 (CCA 2), cert den 320 US 744, 88 L ed 441, 64 S Ct 45 (1943).

3. Rickenberg v Comm, 177 F2d 114 (CA 9) (1949); Larzelere, 13 TCM 455 (1949).

4. Howell, 1 TCM 481 (1942); Hardesty, 11 TCM 359 (1949); Kneeland, 34 BTA 816 (1936).

5. Fair v US, 59 F Supp 801 (1945); Baker, 6 TCM 1249 (1946); O'Neal, 6 TCM 713 (1946); Scheide, 6 TCM 1271 (1946).

6. Taft, 33 BTA 671 (1936); Gamble v US, 65 F Supp 114 (1946); US v Tonkin, 56 F Supp 817, revd on other grounds 150 F2d 531 (CCA 3), cert den 326 US 771, 90 L ed 466, 66 S Ct 176 (1944).

7. White, 21 BTA 500 (1931); Bell v US, 74 F Supp 295 (1948); First Nat Bank of Kansas City v Nee, 67 F Supp 815 (1946); Minzesheimer, 13 TCM 760 (1949); Hardesty, note 4, supra; Haley, 10 TCM 805 (1948); Farnum, 14 TC 884 (1950); US v Tonkin, note 6, supra.

8. See Farnum, note 8, supra; Harnischfeger, 31 BTA 224 (1934); Kneeland, 34 BTA 816 (1936); Proctor v Hassett, 52 F Supp 12 (1943).

§ 129. Schedule G; Transfers During Life; Transactions in Contemplation of Death; Business Transactions.

Transfers of an interest in a business are always subject to inquiry as to whether the transfer was made in contemplation of death. Where it is shown that there was a legitimate business purpose for the transfer, such gifts have been held uniformly not to be in contemplation of death. Thus, where the purpose is to give a person closely related and engaged in the business a greater incentive,[9] to induce him to enter the business,[10] as a reward for services to the business,[11] or for other family or business purposes,[12] gifts of stock or other interest in the business have been held not to have been made in contemplation of death.

Other reasons which have been held not to make the transfers taxable as in contemplation of death have been, the desire to relinquish control,[13] to retire,[14] or to release oneself from burdens.[15]

§ 130. Schedule G; Transfers During Life; Transactions in Contemplation of Death; Consideration.

It will be recalled that the statute includes transactions as transfers in contemplation of death only to the extent that such transfers are not made for an adequate and full consideration in money or money's worth.[16] Only the excess of the fair market value over the consideration received, is taxable.[17] Therefore, if full consideration has been paid it makes no difference whether the transaction was in contemplation of death. Such transactions as transfer of a leasehold for release of responsibility,[18] transfer of land in return for an agreement to carry on business at reduced cost to the transferor,[19] a sale of stock for a full consideration,[20] an option to purchase similarly,[1]

9. Hausman, 5 BTA 199 (1926); Wilfley v Hellmich, 56 F2d 845 (1932); True v US, 51 F Supp 720 (1943).

10. Cooper, 7 TC 1236 (1946); Merchants Nat Bank of Cedar Rapids, 38 BTA 1343 (1934); Cherry, 5 TCM 495 (1945).

11. Myers, BTA memo op Dec. 12, 218-E (1941); Goldberg, 10 TCM 977 (1941).

12. Kaufman v Reinecke, 68 F2d 642 (CCA 7) (1934); Hammond v Westover, 97 F Supp 753 (1951); Cushman, 40

BTA 948 (1939); Atwater, 3 TCM 1223 (1944); Sessoms, 8 TCM 1056 (1947); Fry, 9 TC 503 (1937); Bradley, 2 TCM 609 (1943); Douglas, 10 TCM 970 (1948).

13. Harnischfeger, note 8, supra.

14. Rogers, 21 BTA 1124 (1931).

15. Artman, 38 BTA 1020 (1938).

16. IRC, § 2035(b) (1954 Code).

17. Schoenheit, 14 BTA 33 (1929).

18. Siegel, 19 BTA 683 (1930).

19. Mills, 5 TCM 768 (1945).

20. Black v US, 68 F Supp 74, affd

repayment of loans,[2] an annuity in exchange for securities,[3] have all been held transfers for an adequate consideration.

It is to be noted in this connection that a relinquishment or promised relinquishment of dower or curtesy, or of a statutory estate created in lieu of dower or curtesy, or of other marital rights in the decedent's property or estate, shall not be considered to any extent a consideration in money or money's worth.[4]

§ 131. Schedule G; Transfers During Life; Transactions in Contemplation of Death; Family Purposes.

The courts look with a kindly eye on transfers motivated by family reasons. Where the transfer is made to overcome objections to a parent's marriage,[5] to promote family harmony,[6] to provide financial independence,[7] to provide for children or grandchildren,[8] to help children in business,[9] to provide for the education of children,[10] to provide a dowry,[11] to equalize gifts,[12] to provide funds for needy members of the family,[13] to make children independent,[14] to provide for a spouse,[15] they have all generally been held to indicate motives associated with life and not taxable as transfers in contemplation of death.

164 F2d 96 (CCA 6) (1946); Macdonald, 10 TCM 1038 (1948); note 17, supra.

1. Comm v Bensel, 100 F2d 639 (CCA 3) (1938); May v McGowan, 194 F2d 396 (CA 2) (1952).

2. Hunt, 19 BTA 624 (1930); Goldman, 11 BTA 92 (1928); Root v US, 56 F2d 857 (1932).

3. US Nat Bank of Portland v Earle, 54–1 USTC ¶ 10,937.

4. IRC, § 2043(b) (1954 Code); see also § 47, supra.

5. Note 19, supra; Gillette v Comm, 182 F2d 1010 (CA 9) (1950).

6. Fidelity Phila Trust Co, 17 BTA 910 (1929); Stinchfield, 4 TCM 511 (1944); Halsey, 42 BTA 607 (1940); Welch v Hassett, 15 F Supp 692 (1936); Jacobsen, 9 TCM 1112 (1947); Morr, 47 BTA 765 (1942); Tillotson, 44 BTA 644 (1941); Atwater, note 12, supra.

7. Atwater, note 12, supra; Welch v Hassett, note 6, supra.

8. Brehmer, 9 BTA 423 (1928); Sessoms, note 12, supra; Wilson, 13 TC 869 (1949); Wier, 17 TC 409 (1951).

9. Commercial Nat Bank, 36 BTA 239 (1937); Siegel, 19 BTA 683 (1930); Goldberg, note 11, supra.

10. Kroger, 2 TCM 644 (1943); Spiegle, 11 TCM 1004 (1948); Coffin, 9 TCM 1129 (1947).

11. Block-Sulzberger, 6 TCM 1201 (1946); Schmucker, 10 TC 1209 (1948).

12. Awrey, 5 TC 222 (1945); Engel, 6 TCM 70 (1946); Mills, 5 TCM 768 (1945); Stitt, 7 TCM 920 (1946).

13. Llewellyn v US, 40 F2d 555 (1930); Orvis v Higgins, 80 F Supp 64 (1948); Engel, note 12, supra; Cook, 9 TC 563 (1947); Haley, 10 TCM 805 (1948).

14. St Louis Union Trust Co v Becker, 296 US 48, 80 L ed 34, 56 S Ct 78 (1936); Handy v Delaware Trust Co, 285 US 352, 76 L ed 793, 52 S Ct 371 (1932).

15. McGregor v Comm, 82 F2d 948 (CCA 1) (1936); Hinds, 11 TC 314 (1949); Hofford, 4 TC 542, mod other grounds 4 TC 790 (1944); McCulloch, 8 TCM 110 (1947).

§ 132. Schedule G; Transfers During Life; Transactions in Contemplation of Death; Vesting.

In the matter of contemplation of death, unlike transfers taking effect at death,[16] the fact that title to and dominion over the property transferred has vested in the donee does not prevent such property being included in the gross estate of the donor. The fact that a Gift Tax has been paid on the transfer also does not prevent such property being included.[17] In fact, the Estate Tax Law specifically provides for just such an eventuality.[18] Transfers in contemplation of death are not taxed on the theory of legal ownership, but on the avoidance of the tax. As the Regulation points out, the result is not affected by the fact that at the time of the transfer the decedent parted absolutely and immediately with his enjoyment of and title to the property.[19]

§ 133. Schedule G; Transfers During Life; Transactions in Contemplation of Death; Preservation of Property.

That a transfer has been made for the purpose of preserving the property transferred has in a large number of cases been held to indicate that the compelling motive was one associated with life. Thus, where the transfer was for the purpose of placing the property beyond the reach of an estranged spouse,[20] or a judgment levy,[1] or because of fears of incompetency,[2] demands from members of the family which could not be resisted,[3] disagreements among beneficiaries,[4] loss through speculation,[5] marital difficulties,[6] business hazards,[7] or a will contest,[8] it has been held not made in contemplation of death. Where the transfer is made to a trust in order to preserve the property the courts have held similarly.[9]

---

16. §§ 139 et seq, infra.
17. Steere, 22 TC 79 (1954).
18. IRC, § 2012 (1954 Code).
19. Reg, § 20.2035-1(a).
20. Hunter, 26 BTA 417 (1932).
1. Hunt, 14 TC 1182 (1950).
2. Chemical Bank & Trust Co, 37 BTA 535 (1938).
3. Higgins, 9 TCM 426 (1947); Gilbert, 14 TC 349 (1950).
4. Ferry v Rogan, 44-2 USTC ¶10,125.
5. Colorado Nat Bank of Denver v Comm, 305 US 23, 83 L ed 20, 59 S Ct 48 (1938); Boswell, 37 BTA 970 (1938); Thacher, 20 TC 474 (1953);

Farnum, 14 TC 884 (1950); Hopper, 22 TC 138 (1954).
6. First Nat Bank of Memphis v Henslee, 74 F Supp 106 (1947); Jacobsen, 9 TCM 1112 (1947), Lindsay, 11 TCM 514 (1949); Barad, 13 TCM 223 (1949).
7. Lehman, 39 BTA 17 (1939); Richards, 20 TC 904 (1953); McClung, 39 BTA 667 (1939); note 1, supra; Cronin v Comm, 164 F2d 561 (CCA 6) (1947); Wilson, 13 TC 869 (1949); Spiegle, 11 TCM 1004 (1948).
8. Green, 6 BTA 278 (1929).
9. Smith v US, 16 F Supp 397 (1936); Farnum, note 5, supra; Se-

§ 134. Schedule G; Transfers During Life; Transactions in Contemplation of Death; Amount of Transfer.

Prior to the amendment of 1950 the 1939 Code provided that the two-year presumption applied[10] where the transfer was of a *material part* of the donor's property.[11] The Regulation also provided that all transfers of $5,000 or more made at any time were required to be reported.[12] The 1954 Code[13] contains no such provision, nor do the Regulations,[14] but the instructions[15] and the Regulation[16] require that all transfers made within three years of death of the value of $1,000 or more and all transfers made at any time of a value of $5,000 or more be reported. The only purpose in requiring the reporting of transfers in excess of $5,000, is that although such may not be taxable as transfers in contemplation of death, they may be taxable under other sections of the statute, such as if there were a retained right to income or a reversionary interest.

While in and of itself the amount of the transfer may not be determinative of the question of contemplation of death, it is a fact throwing light on the decedent's motives. Five or six percent has been held to be a material portion of the estate.[17] The fact of the substantiality of the transfer *together with other facts* has tipped the scale in favor of taxability.[18] On the other hand other factors have outweighed the fact that a major portion of the donor's assets were transferred.[19]

§ 135. Schedule G; Transfers During Life; Transactions in Contemplation of Death; Date of Will.

The relation of the decedent's will to transfers made by the decedent is an important factor in the determination of whether a transfer was made in contemplation of death. Where the transfers are made at or about the time the decedent executed

curity First Nat Bank, 36 BTA 633 (1937); US Trust Co of NY v US, 23 F Supp 476, cert den 307 US 633, 83 L ed 1515, 59 S Ct 1031 (1938); Israel, 3 TCM 1301 (1944); Hopper, 22 TC 138 (1954).

10. See § 122, supra.
11. IRC, § 811 (c)(1939 Code).
12. Reg 105, § 81.16.
13. IRC, § 2035 (1954 Code).
14. Reg, § 20.2035–1.
15. Instructions, Schedule G, Form 706.

16. Reg, § 20.6018–2(c)(7).
17. Boggs, 11 BTA 824 (1928).
18. See McClure v Comm, 56 F2d 548 (CCA 5), cert den 287 US 609, 77 L ed 529, 53 S Ct 12 (1932); Signor, 6 TCM 1059 (1946); Bradbury, 5 TCM 788 (1945); Springer, 45 BTA 561 (1941); Budd, 4 TCM 601 (1944); Bassett, 6 TCM 887 (1946); Northern Trust Co v Comm, 116 F2d 96 (CCA 7) (1940).
19. Johnson, 10 TC 680 (1948); Selling, 24 TC 191 (1955).

his will and in much the same proportions as the testamentary distributions, it is strong evidence that the decedent's motives were associated with death.[20] It has been stated to be an important factor.[1] It is not, however, controlling.[2]

The longer the period between the transfers and the will the greater the chance of exclusion,[3] it having been held that it was improper for the Tax Court to consider the decedent's intent in executing his will, where the transfers had taken place six years prior.[4] Where the transfers are subsequent to the execution of the will, there is more easily discernible a testamentary substitute.[5] It may be said that where the gifts and the will indicate a complete plan for the distribution of a decedent's estate, such gifts are likely to be found to have been made in contemplation of death.[6] Any transfer which is a testamentary substitute will be included in a decedent's gross estate as such transfer.[7]

§ 136. Schedule G; Transfers During Life; Transactions in Contemplation of Death; Miscellaneous Factors.

In the preceding sections we have discussed the factors which are generally to be considered in the determination of whether a transfer has been made within contemplation of death within the meaning of the statute. These are the factors most often found present in such cases. But they are by no means all of the possible ones. As we have noted, the Regulation states that in addition to motive, the bodily and mental condition of the decedent *and all other attendant facts and circumstances* are to be scrutinized in order to determine whether or not such thought (of death) prompted the disposition.[8]

20. Oliver v Bell, 103 F2d 760 (CCA 3) (1939); Diamond v Comm, 159 F2d 672 (CCA 2) (1947); Travelers Bank & Trust Co, 29 BTA 88 (1934); Purvin v Comm, 96 F2d 929 (CCA 7) (1938); Igleheart v Comm, 77 F2d 704 (CCA 5) (1935); Davidson v Comm, 158 F2d 239 (CCA 10) (1946); Flick, 6 TCM 72, revd on other grounds 166 F2d 733 (CCA 5) (1948); O'Neal v Comm, 170 F2d 217 (CCA 5) (1948).

1. Satuloff, 6 TCM 1246 (1946).

2. See O'Neal, 6 TCM 713 (1946); Farnum, 14 TC 884 (1950); Flynn, 3 TCM 1287 (1944); Johnson, 10 TC 680 (1948); Du Puy, 9 TC 276 (1947); Cronin v Comm, 164 F2d 561 (CCA 6)

1947; Smith, 1 TCM 518 (1942); Hinds, 11 TC 314 (1949); Sessoms, 8 TCM 1056 (1947); Roddenburg, 8 TCM 781 (1947).

3. Farnum, note 2, supra; Johnson, note 2, supra; Cronin v Comm, note 2, supra; Roddenburg, note 2, supra.

4. Garrett v Comm, 180 F2d 955 (CA 2) (1950).

5. Flick, note 20, supra.

6. Davidson v Comm, 158 F2d 239 (CCA 10) (1946); Davis, 1 TCM 476, affd 142 F2d 450 (CCA 6) (1944).

7. Patton, 10 TCM 1066 (1948); Worcester County Trust Co v US, 35 F Supp 970 (1941); Thomas v Graham, 158 F2d 561 (CCA 5) (1947).

8. Reg, § 20.2035–1(c).

This recognizes that the question is one of fact to be decided by all the facts.[9] *Any fact* which will throw light on the question of whether the donor was prompted by thoughts of life or of death is relevant. Many other facts have been considered on the question, such as that the transfer was to aid the decedent's estate after his death,[10] they were made as Christmas gifts,[11] pursuant to a promise,[12] as distribution of inherited property to adjust inequities,[13] in execution of an expressed intention,[14] because of a moral obligation,[15] because it had long been planned,[16] in fulfillment of a promise,[17] pursuant to a habit of making gifts,[18] or a family precedent to that effect.[19]

§ 137. Schedule G; Transfers During Life; Transactions in Contemplation of Death; Summary.

We have discussed at some length the subject of transfers which are taxable as having been made in contemplation of death. To facilitate reference to such transfers and as a ready means of testing their taxability, the following concise summarization is offered:

(1) Any transfer made by a decedent within three years of his death which is not made for an adequate consideration in money or money's worth is prima facie taxable.[20]

(2) Any such transfer made more than three years before the decedent's death cannot be taxed as a transfer in contemplation of death.[1] *It may be taxable under some other provision of the statute.*

9. Neal v Comm, 53 F2d 861 (CCA 8) (1932); First Nat Bank of Boston v Welch, 63 F2d 685 (CCA 1) (1933).

10. Sloan v Comm, 168 F2d 470 (CCA 3) (1948).

11. Wilson, 13 TC 869 (1949); Hopper, 22 TC 138 (1954); Mills, 5 TCM 768 (1945).

12. Boggs, 11 BTA 824 (1928); Byram, 9 TC 1 (1947).

13. Talbott, 42 BTA 1081 (1940); Stinchfield, 4 TCM 511 (1944); Keck, 10 TC 1121 (1948).

14. Hicks, 9 BTA 1226 (1928); Comm v Nevins, 47 F2d 478 (CCA 3) (1931).

15. Barad, 13 TCM 223 (1949); Rosebault, 12 TC 1 (1949); Sessoms, 8 TCM 1056 (1947).

16. Brown v Comm, 74 F2d 281 (CCA 10) (1935); True v US, 51 F Supp 720 (1943); Dierks v US, 86 F Supp 832 (1949); Flannery v Willcuts, 25 F 2d 951 (CCA 8) (1928).

17. Heipershausen, 18 BTA 218 (1930); True v US, note 16, supra; Pate v Comm, 149 F2d 669 (CCA 8) (1945).

18. US v Wells, 283 US 102, 75 L ed 867, 51 S Ct 446 (1931); Loetscher v Burnet, 46 F2d 835 (CA DC) (1931); Johnson, 10 TC 680 (1948).

19. Topliffe, 39 BTA 13 (1939).

20. § 121, supra.

1. § 122, supra.

(3) The presumption referred to is rebuttable, but the executor has the burden in that respect.[2]

(4) Contemplation of death means a present apprehension from some existing bodily condition or impending peril, known to the decedent, creating a reasonable fear that death is near at hand and not the general knowledge that all men must die at some time. *It is only when contemplation of death is the motive without which the transfer would not have been made and is the controlling motive, that the transfer is taxable.*[3]

(5) The essential question for determination is the motive of the donor.[4] In seeking the motive the following factors will be considered:

(a) The time between the transfer and death,[5]

(b) The health of the donor at the time of transfer,[6]

(c) His activities, family longevity and plans for the future at the time of transfer,[7]

(d) His age,[8]

(e) Whether he was motivated by the desire for Estate Tax avoidance,[9]

(f) Whether the gift had a business purpose,[10]

(g) The extent of consideration,[11]

(h) Whether the gift was motivated by family reasons,[12] or

(i) Was for the purpose of conserving the property,[13]

(j) The amount of the transfer in proportion to the donor's assets,[14]

(k) The proximity of the transfer to the date of the donor's will,[15] and

(l) Miscellaneous factors.[16]

There has been discussed previously the subject of transfers of jointly owned property given away in contemplation of death, or severed in contemplation of death.[17]

The subject of relinquishment of a power, or the exercise or release of a general power of appointment is treated hereafter.[18]

2. § 122, supra.
3. § 121, supra.
4. § 123, supra.
5. § 124, supra.
6. § 125, supra.
7. § 126, supra.
8. § 127, supra.
9. § 128, supra.
10. § 129, supra.
11. § 130, supra.
12. § 131, supra.
13. § 133, supra.
14. § 134, supra.
15. § 135, supra.
16. § 136, supra.
17. See § 95, supra.
18. § 150, infra.

§ 138. Schedule G; Transfers During Life; Transactions in Contemplation of Death; Evidence.

In an examination of cases dealing with the subject of evidence in cases of transfers claimed to have been made in contemplation of death, it must be borne in mind that many such were decided in the cases of decedents dying before September 23, 1950. Cases holding that the Commissioner had the burden of proof in some cases where the transfer took place more than two years before death and that the Commissioner's finding is presumptively correct have had no application since 1950. As previously noted,[19] the only transfers which may be attacked as having been made in contemplation of death are those made within three years of the decedent's death. As to all others, the facts are of no importance on the question, since they cannot be taxed under that section of the statute. Today, therefore, we are concerned only with transfers made within three years of death, and as to those, the presumption is that they were made in contemplation of death. The burden of proving otherwise is on the executor.[20] He must establish by a fair preponderance of the evidence that the transfer was not made in contemplation of death.[1]

Since the inquiry concerns the state of mind of the donor at the time of the transfer, the best evidence of that is statements made by him at the time and the circumstances surrounding the transaction.[2] Thus, statements of the reason for the transfer and the health and plans of the donor are material.[3] Statements of the insured's purpose in letters of his broker to insurance companies,[4] evidence of property donated to the donees by others,[5] articles relating to proposed increases in Estate Taxes in papers habitually read by the decedent,[6] proof

19. § 122, supra.

20. Humphrey v Comm, 162 F2d 1 (CCA 5), cert den 332 US 817, 92 L ed 394, 68 S Ct 157 (1947); McGrew v Comm, 135 F2d 158 (CCA 6) (1943); First Trust & Safe Deposit Co v Shaughnessy, 134 F2d 940 (CCA 2), cert den 320 US 744, 88 L ed 442, 64 S Ct 46 (1943).

1. Farmers' Loan & Trust Co v Bowers, 98 F2d 794 (CCA 2), cert den 306 US 648, 83 L ed 1047, 59 S Ct 589, motion denied 307 US 651, 83 L ed 1529, 59 S Ct 1036, rehg den 308 US 634,

84 L ed 528, 60 S Ct 117 and 310 US 657, 84 L ed 1421, 60 S Ct 1083 (1938); Flack v Holtegel, 93 F2d 512 (CCA 7) (1938).

2. Gross v Rothensies, 56 F Supp 340 (1944).

3. Note 2, supra.

4. Slifka v Johnson, 161 F2d 467 (CCA 2), cert den 332 US 758, 92 L ed 344, 68 S Ct 57 (1947).

5. Smails v O'Malley, 127 F2d 410 (CCA 8) (1942).

6. Oliver v Bell, 103 F2d 760 (CCA 3) (1939).

of increased needs of the decedent's family,[7] the wealth of the donor,[8] have all been held relevant. Where it is claimed that the motive was to avoid state taxes, whether such taxes were paid by the decedent has been held material.[9] But where the motive involved was that of the court in the case of an incompetent, the state court's order and testimony of the judge who ordered the transfer, was not competent.[10] And a witness who never discussed the reason for the transfer with the donor, may not testify as to his intention,[11] nor may a Revenue Agent testify as to his reasons for holding a transfer to have been made in contemplation of death.[12] It was also held improper for the Tax Court to consider the decedent's intent in making transfers in 1923 and a will in 1935, in determining whether a transfer in 1929 was made in contemplation of death.[13] An affidavit annexed to a Gift Tax return alleging that the transfer was not in contemplation of death was held to have no effect one way or the other.[14]

Decisions of the state courts on the same transfers, while entitled to weight, are not conclusive.[15]

As we have repeatedly stressed, the question of whether a transfer was made in contemplation of death is a question of fact. That being so, when the transfer has been made within three years of death, it is necessary to collate the facts to overcome the presumption and present them in affidavit form. As the Regulation states, if the executor believes that such a transfer is not subject to the tax, a brief statement of the pertinent facts should be made.[16]

7. Note 6, supra.

8. Note 5, supra.

9. Schwab v Doyle, 269 F 321, revd on other grounds 258 US 529, 66 L ed 747, 42 S Ct 391 (1920).

10. City Bank Farmers Trust Co v McGowan, 43 F Supp 790, affd 142 F 2d 599, affd in part and revd in part on other grounds 323 US 594, 89 L ed 483, 65 S Ct 496 (1942).

11. Northern Trust Co v Comm, 116 F2d 96 (CCA 7) (1940); note 6, supra.

12. Kentucky Trust Co v Glenn, 217 F2d 462 (CA 6) (1954).

13. Garrett v Comm, 180 F2d 955 (CA 2) (1950).

14. Engel, 6 TCM 70 (1946).

15. Comm v Nevin, 47 F2d 478 (CCA 3), cert den 283 US 835, 75 L ed 1447, 51 S Ct 485 (1931); Rogers, 21 BTA 1124 (1931); Phillips, 7 BTA 1054 (1927); Harnischfeger, 31 BTA 224 (1934).

16. Reg, § 20.6018-3(c)(7).

FORM NO. 19

Transfers During Life; Affidavit

In the Matter of the Estate Tax
  on the Estate of
      WINTHROP BENSON,
                      Deceased.

COMMONWEALTH OF PENNSYLVANIA ⎱
COUNTY OF PHILADELPHIA   ⎰ ss:

KATHERINE BENSON, being duly sworn, says:

I am the Executrix of the above named decedent and his widow.

On August 15, 1958, the decedent transferred to me 100 shares of the common capital stock of Winthrop Benson, Inc.

The decedent's net worth at the time was approximately $200,000, and the value of the property so transferred was $25,000, or approximately 12½% of his property.

At the time thereof, the decedent was 55 years old. The immediate cause of the decedent's death was cardiac decompensation with pulmonary oedema, the result of rheumatic disease of the mitral valve. His last illness was of three months' duration, prior to which time he suffered from no incapacitating illness of any kind and was actively engaged in the conduct of his business. He dictated all the policies thereof and was the guiding hand therein. He was actively interested as an officer in the Benevolent and Protective Order of Elks, Elkins Park Lodge, as Exalted Leading Knight, and was the Senior Deacon of Fraternity Lodge, No. 1111, Free and Accepted Masons.

The decedent suffered from no bodily or mental condition which would have created the fear of imminent death and looked forward to many years of normal life. He was keen mentally, cheerful of demeanor and suffered from no illness confining him to bed, other than possibly a cold or indisposition of a day or two. Just prior to his death he had purchased tickets for a European trip and had made reservations in various foreign countries for hotel accommodations.

At the time of the transfer herein, the decedent and your deponent prepared and filed appropriate Gift Tax returns, and the Gift Tax thereon was paid. A copy of both the donor's and donee's return are annexed hereto.

The decedent transferred the stock for the purpose of assuring me an independent income and pursuant to a plan he had long contemplated.

That from the date of said transfer the said stock has been in my possession and I have received the income therefrom and deposited the dividends thereon in my individual bank account.

The said gift was further made pursuant to my husband's custom of making regular gifts to his family, he having made gifts to our son James and myself in the sum of $1,000 on each Christmas since the year 1946.

That the said transfer was not made in contemplation of death, but at a time when he looked forward to many years of life, both of his parents having lived to be more than eighty years of age.

There are annexed hereto and made a part hereof, the affidavits of Dr. Alfred A. Adams, Kenneth Gross, Minnie Grittle, Estelle Main, Leo Key and John Ward, persons closely associated with the decedent, either socially or in business, corroborating the facts above stated.

KATHERINE BENSON

Sworn to before me this 12th
day of January, 1959
  MARSHA HAYES
  Notary Public
  Philadelphia County

§ 139. Schedule G; Transfers During Life; Transfers with Retained Life Estate; The Problem.

Few aspects of estate taxation are as confused and confusing as that involving lifetime transfers, largely due to court decisions overruling what was considered established law, and the many amendments made to the statute in an attempt to clarify the law and avoid the effect of some of the decisions.

From the beginning of the Estate Tax statute in 1916 there were taxed transfers in contemplation of or intended to take effect in possession or enjoyment at or after the decedent's death.[17] But the interpretation of the statute has varied widely.

Transfers in contemplation of death, as we have seen, present principally factual questions. But in the case of transfers intended to take effect in possession or enjoyment at or after the decedent's death, there are embraced two kinds of transfers. Subsequent amendments of the original statute have recognized this fact by providing different sections for their taxation. The first includes transfers in which the property itself is the subject of a lifetime transfer, but the beneficial enjoyment of the property is retained by the donor. Such transfers are designated transfers with retained life estate,[18] but the phrase is more comprehensive than the title indicates.

The general theory of taxation in such case is that there is a shifting of economic benefits as a result of the death, which

17. Rev Act 1916, § 202(b).   18. IRC, § 2036 (1954 Code).

attracts the tax.[19] Judged by this standard, the methods devised to circumvent the tax, namely, by the creation of irrevocable trusts with retention of income or other lesser rights than the whole, were doomed to failure. But that fact did not appear for a long time and after much litigation and amendment of the statute.

§ 140. Schedule G; Transfers During Life; Transfers with Retained Life Estate; Evolution of the Statute.

In connection with many sections of the Estate Tax Law its history is interesting but unimportant. In the case of transfers taking effect at or after death, within which designation transfers with retained life estates were originally embraced, it is impossible to understand the law without a knowledge of its background.

Under the 1916 statute as noted,[20] transfers in contemplation of death and those taking effect in possession or enjoyment at or after death were lumped together. Until 1930, under the statute, transfers in which the donor retained a life interest were taxed. In that year the Supreme Court held that such transfers were not taxable.[1] The following year this same determination was made by the Court.[2] The Acting Secretary of the Treasury thereupon requested an amendment of the statute, which was done by a joint resolution of Congress just before the session ended.[3] There was an amendment the following year.[4] It was then held that the amendment of 1931 did not affect irrevocable transfers with retained income where the transfer took place before the passage of the Joint Resolution of 1931.[5] From 1938 until 1949 if the decedent had made an irrevocable transfer before March 3, 1931 and retained a life estate, the property was not includible in his gross estate. In the latter year the Supreme Court in Comm. vs. Church,[6] reconsidered May vs. Heiner[7] and Hassett vs. Welch,[8] and overruled them, holding that a transfer

---

19. § 2, supra.

20. Note 17, supra.

1. May v Heiner, 281 US 238, 74 L ed 826, 50 S Ct 286 (1930).

2. McCormick v Burnet, 283 US 784, 75 L ed 1413, 51 S Ct 343 (1931); Morsman v Burnet, 283 US 783, 75 L ed 1412, 51 S Ct 343 (1931); Burnet v Northern Trust Co, 283 US 782, 75 L ed 1412, 51 S Ct 342 (1931).

3. H J Res 529, Mar. 3, 1931.

4. Rev Act of 1932, § 803(a).

5. Hassett v Welch, 303 US 303, 82 L ed 858, 58 S Ct 559 (1938).

6. 335 US 632, 93 L ed 288, 69 S Ct 322 (1949).

7. Note 1, supra.

8. Note 5, supra.

with a retained life estate was taxable no matter when the transfer had taken place.

Because of the situation thus created and the injustice of retroactive application of the principles enunciated, Congress enacted the Technical Changes Act of 1949[9] and limited the operation of the rule enunciated in the Church case to persons dying before the Act and required other persons to release their income rights before 1951 if they wished to escape taxability. The statute was again amended in 1951 to cover the cases of persons dying before January 1, 1951.[10] The effect of the Church rule was completely eliminated by the Technical Changes Act of 1953[11] which removed the necessity for the relinquishment of retained right to income where the transfer was made prior to March 4, 1931, and prior to June 7, 1932, in cases where the transfer would not have been taxable under the Joint Resolution of 1931, but would have been taxable under the 1932 Revenue Act.

All of these amendments were reflected in the 1939 Code[12] and have been carried over into the 1954 Code.[13] They will be discussed in the succeeding sections. The effect of the various amendments is to restore the rule in effect prior to the Church case.

§ 141. Schedule G; Transfers During Life; Transfers with Retained Life Estate; Statutory Scheme.

The present statute[14] provides for the inclusion in the gross estate of a decedent the value of all property (except real property situated outside of the United States) to the extent of any interest therein of which the decedent *has at any time* made a transfer (except in case of a bona fide sale for an adequate and full consideration in money or money's worth), *by trust or otherwise,* under which he has retained

(1) for his life, *or*

(2) for any period not ascertainable without reference to his death, *or*

(3) for any period which does not in fact end before his death

(a) the possession or enjoyment of, *or* the right to the income from the property, *or*

9. PL 378, 81st Congress, approved Oct 25, 1949.
10. Rev Act of 1951, § 609.
11. PL 287, Aug 15, 1953, 83rd Congress.
12. IRC, § 811(c)(1)(B) (1939 Code).
13. IRC, § 2036 (1954 Code).
14. Note 13, supra.

(b) the right, *either alone or in conjunction with any person,* to designate the persons who shall possess or enjoy the property or the income therefrom.[15]

Application of the rule is limited to exclude from its operation such transfers made before March 4, 1941, or after March 3, 1931 and before June 7, 1932, unless the property transferred would have been includible in the decedent's gross estate by reason of the amendatory language of the Joint Resolution of March 3, 1931.[16]

The words "or for any period not ascertainable without reference to his death" are intended to reach a transfer, where for example, decedent reserved to himself semi-annual payments of income in a trust which he created, which provided that no part of the trust income between the last payment and his death should be paid to him or his estate.[17]

The words "or for any period which does not in fact end before his death" are intended to reach a transfer where for example a 70-year-old donor reserves the income for an extended period and dies before the term, or a contingent right to income becomes vested before his death.[18]

If the decedent retained or reserved a right with respect to all of the property transferred by him, the amount to be included in his gross estate is the *value of the entire property,* less only the value of any outstanding income interest which is not subject to the decedent's right and which is actually being enjoyed by another person. If the decedent retained or reserved a right with respect to a part only of the property transferred by him, the amount to be included in his gross estate is only a corresponding proportion of the amount described in the preceding sentence. An interest or right is treated as having been retained or reserved if at the time of the transfer there was an understanding, express or implied, that the interest or right would later be conferred.[19]

The Regulation states the results of case law. If the decedent retains the right to all of the income from all of the property the full value is includible in his gross estate. If he retains

15. IRC, § 2036(a)(1954 Code).
16. IRC, § 2036(b)(1954 Code).
17. Senate Report No 665, 72nd Cong, 1st Sess 1939, 1 CB (Part 2) 532; Reg, § 20.2036–1(b)(i).

18. Note 17, supra; see also Fry, 9 TC 503 (1947); Comm v Nathan, 159 F2d 546 (CCA 7) (1947), cert den 334 US 843, 92 L ed 1767, 68 S Ct 1510 (1948); Reg, § 20.2036–1(b)(ii).
19. Reg, § 20.2036–1(a).

the right to part of the income and another person has a partial life estate, the value of that estate will be deducted from the entire value. If the decedent transfers property, in part of which he retains the income, that part of the property will be included.

§ 142. Schedule G; Transfers During Life; Transfers with Retained Life Estate; Possession or Enjoyment.

The statute taxes not only property transferred when the decedent retains or reserves the right to the income therefrom, but also where he retains or reserves the possession or enjoyment of the income therefrom.[20] The determination of when he has retained the right to income presents little difficulty. But when he retains *possession or enjoyment* of the income is not as simple.

The "use, possession, right to the income, or other enjoyment of the transferred property" is considered as having been retained by or reserved to the decedent *to the extent* that the use, possession, right to the income, or other enjoyment is to be applied (or an *enforceable right* exists to cause it to be applied) toward a *legal obligation* of the decedent, *or otherwise for his pecuniary benefit*. The term *legal obligation* includes a legal obligation to support a dependent during the decedent's lifetime.[1] This is a spill-over from the income tax field of the legal obligation concept.

If the decedent retained or reserved an enforceable right to have the income from the transferred property applied toward the discharge of his legal obligation, such as support of his wife or minor children, the property is includible in his gross estate.[2] The fact that he does not directly receive the income is of no consequence, since the effect is the same as if he did. If, however, the application of income is not obligatory and is in the discretion of one who has no such legal obligation, it is not includible.[3] Where the donor enjoys incidental benefits at the sufferance of the owner, the property will not be includible.[4]

20. IRC, § 2036(a)(1) (1954 Code).
1. Reg, § 20.2036–1(b)(2).
2. Comm v Dwight, 205 F2d 298 (CA 2), cert den 346 US 871, 98 L ed 380, 74 S Ct 121 (1953); Helvering v Mercantile Commerce Bank, 111 F2d 224, cert den 310 US 654, 84 L ed 1418, 60 S Ct 1104 (1926); Hooper, 41 BTA 114 (1940); McKeon, 25 TC 697 (1956).
3. Burr, 4 TCM 1054 (1945); Flynn, 3 TCM 1287 (1944); Scheide, 6 TCM 1271 (1946); Sessoms, 8 TCM 1056 (1947); Comm v Douglas, 143 F2d 961 (CCA 3) (1941); Barad, 13 TCM

As previously noted,[5] if the decedent retains or reserves only a part of the use, possession, income or enjoyment of the property, then only a corresponding portion of the property is includible.[6]

While most of the decided cases deal with property transferred in trust, the statute covers transfers in trust *or otherwise*. Thus, the transfer may be outright, but so long as the right to the income or possession or enjoyment of it is retained, as by agreement, the property will be includible in the decedent's gross estate.[7] The fact that the decedent is the trustee does not affect taxability, if he does not have the right to the income nor is it usable to discharge his legal obligation.[8] He must further not have the right to designate who shall enjoy the property or income therefrom.[9] Where the decedent was not the settlor of a trust, but transferred property to it, and he was the income beneficiary, the property transferred was includible in the decedent's gross estate.[10]

§ 143. Schedule G; Transfers During Life; Transfers with Retained Life Estate; Right to Designate Enjoyment.

The use, possession, right to the income, or other enjoyment of transferred property is not the only indicia of beneficial ownership. The right to designate the person or persons who shall enjoy either the income from or the property itself is another indicia. Thus, where the decedent transfers property but retains the right to designate those who shall enjoy it, it is not until his death that a final determination of economic benefits is made. The statute therefore taxes such transfers, since death creates the taxable event.

Where the decedent retains or reserves for his life, or for any period not ascertainable without reference to his death, or for any period which does not in fact end before his death,[11] the

223 (1949); McCullough v Granger, 128 F Supp 611 (1955); Colonial American Nat Bank of Roanoke v US, 243 F 2d 312 (CA 4) (1957).

4. Nichols v Coolidge, 274 US 531, 71 L ed 1184, 47 S Ct 710 (1927); Burr, note 3, supra; Flynn, note 3, supra; Green, 4 TCM 286 (1944); Sherman, 9 TC 594 (1947); Scheide, note 3, supra.

5. § 142, supra.

6. See Comm v Dwight, note 2, supra.

7. See Fry, 9 TC 503 (1947); Seward, 6 TCM 510, affd 164 F2d 434 (CCA 4) (1947); Touhy, 14 TC 245 (1950); Morton, 12 TC 380 (1949); Schwartz, 9 TC 229 (1947).

8. Hays v Comm, 181 F2d 169 (CA 5) (1950).

9. See § 143, infra.

10. Liebmann, 3 TCM 303 (1944).

11. See § 141, supra, as to distinctions.

right, *either alone or in conjunction with any other person* or persons, to designate the person or persons who shall possess or enjoy *the transferred property or the income therefrom,* the property is includible in the decedent's estate.[12]

The phrase "right . . . to designate the person or persons who shall possess or enjoy the transferred property or the income therefrom" includes a power to designate the person or persons to receive the income from the transferred property, or to possess or enjoy non-income-producing property, during the decedent's life or during any other period described in the statute. With respect to such a power, it is immaterial

(i) whether the power was exercisable alone or in conjunction with another person or persons, whether or not having an adverse interest;

(ii) in what capacity the power was exercisable by the decedent or by another person or persons in conjunction with the decedent; and

(iii) whether the exercise of the power was subject to a contingency beyond the decedent's control which did not occur before his death (e.g., the death of another person during the decedent's life).

The phrase, however, does not include a power over the transferred property itself not affecting the enjoyment of the income received or earned during the decedent's life. Such property may be includible as a revocable transfer under Section 2038. Nor does the phrase apply to a power held solely by a person other than the decedent. But, for example, if the decedent had the unrestricted power to remove or discharge a trustee at any time and appoint a new trustee, including himself, the decedent is considered as having the powers of the trustee.[13]

It must first be noted that, although the section is entitled "Transfers with retained life estate,"[14] it also embraces transfers in which the decedent retained control over corpus as well as income.[15] In such case that portion of the principal over which the decedent retained the power is included.[16] If it is limited to income in a specific amount, only that portion of the corpus necessary to produce such income is includible.[17] The fact that

12. IRC, § 2036(a)(2) (1954 Code); Reg, § 20.2036–1(a)(ii).

13. Reg, § 20.2036–1(b)(3).

14. IRC, § 2036 (1954 Code).

15. Du Charme v Comm, 164 F2d 959 (CCA 6) (1947).

16. Note 15, supra.

17. Industrial Trust Co v Comm, 165 F2d 142 (CCA 1) (1948).

the power is not exercisable under the trust instrument but by will does not prevent taxability.[18]

Where the power of designation is retained by the decedent individually,[19] as sole trustee,[20] or, as one of several trustees,[1] the property is includible, *unless the trustee's power is subject to definite standards* which could be enforced in court by the beneficiaries.[2] But standards such as "best interest",[3] or where the income could be accumulated or distributed in the discretion of the trustee,[4] do not qualify as definite standards. Where the power to accumulate is the usual discretionary one in a spendthrift trust, it has been held not such as to subject to tax.[5]

§ 144. Schedule G; Transfers During Life; Transfers Taking Effect at Death; Evolution of the Statute.

If the history of transfers during life was confused and confusing, that part thereof dealing with transfers taking effect at death has been the ultimate in that respect. What started out with a simple provision taxing transfers intended to take effect in possession or enjoyment at or after the decedent's death,[6] and embraced all taxable lifetime transfers, and required ten lines for definition, has been so expanded that but one facet of such transfers, those taking effect at death, takes twenty-five lines of definition and is the subject of a separate section of the 1954 Code.

We have previously discussed the development of the law in respect to transfers with retained life estates.[7] During this time the Commissioner was attacking transfers in which the decedent had a reversionary interest on the ground that they were transfers taking effect at death. In Klein vs. U.S.,[8] a transfer in which the decedent had retained a contingent reversionary interest so that the transferee did not obtain ownership unless she survived the transferor, was held taxable as taking effect at death. Four years later, on the basis of local

---

18. Cooper, 7 TC 1236 (1946).

19. Exton, 33 BTA 215 (1935); note 18, supra.

20. Note 17, supra.

1. Note 15, supra; Yawkey, 12 TC 1164 (1949).

2. Jennings v Smith, 161 F2d 74 (CCA 2) (1947); Budlong, 7 TC 756 (1946); Frew, 8 TC 1240 (1947); Wier, 17 TC 409 (1951).

3. Wier, note 2, supra.

4. McDermott, 12 TCM 481 (1949); note 17, supra; Hager, 5 TCM 972 (1945).

5. Note 8, supra.

6. Rev Act of 1916, § 202(b).

7. § 140, supra.

8. 283 US 231, 75 L ed 796, 51 S Ct 398 (1931).

property law to the effect that a contingent reversionary interest was a vested interest subject to divestment and the fact that the transfers were complete, with a reserved reversionary right, the Supreme Court held that the transfers were not taxable.[9] The practical distinction between the cases was so nebulous that there was difficulty in reconciling them, if indeed they could be logically rather than legalistically distinguished. The court therefore considered the question again in Helvering vs. Hallock[10] which involved facts similar to the St. Louis Trust Co. cases, and this time the court held the transfers taxable as taking effect at death, thus overruling those cases.

The Hallock case created doubt as to whether it had also overruled May vs. Heiner[11] and Hassett vs. Welch.[12] It was eleven years before the doubt was resolved. In the intervening years the Commissioner attacked transfers in which there were reversionary interests or possible reverters and there were a series of decisions which did not settle the doubts.[13] At this time there developed the concept that if the decedent retained a string to a transfer it would be included in his gross estate.[14] Finally in Comm. vs. Church[15] and the companion case of Spiegel vs. Comm.,[16] the Supreme Court overruled May vs. Heiner[17] and Hassett vs. Welch[18] and subjected to tax any transfer, no matter when made, if the decedent retained a possible reversionary interest, whether by operation of law or by express agreement, and no matter how small. This led to the series of amendments which we have previously discussed[19] and to the present statute.

9. Helvering v St Louis Union Trust Co, 296 US 39, 80 L ed 29, 56 S Ct 74 (1935); Becker v St Louis Union Trust Co, 296 US 48, 80 L ed 35, 56 S Ct 78 (1935).

10. 309 US 104, 84 L ed 604, 60 S Ct 444 (1940).

11. 281 US 238, 74 L ed 826, 50 S Ct 286 (1929).

12. 303 US 308, 82 L ed 858, 58 S Ct 559 (1938); see also §§ 4472A, 4486A, supra.

13. Fidelity Philadelphia Trust Co v Rothensies, 324 US 108, 89 L ed 783, 65 S Ct 508 (1945); Comm v Field, 324 US 113, 89 L ed 786, 65 S Ct 511 (1945); Goldstone v US, 325 US 687, 89 L ed 1871, 65 S Ct 1323 (1945).

14. Comm v Field, note 13, supra; Comm v Kellog, 119 F2d 54 (CCA 3) (1941); Lloyd v Comm, 141 F2d 758 (CCA 3) (1944); Comm v Hall, 153 F2d 172 (CCA 2) (1946).

15. 335 US 632, 93 L ed 288, 69 S Ct 322 (1949).

16. 335 US 701, 93 L ed 330, 69 S Ct 301 (1949).

17. Note 11, supra.

18. Note 12, supra.

19. § 120, supra.

§ 145. Schedule G; Transfers During Life; Transfers Taking Effect at Death; Statutory Scheme.

A transfer without an adequate and full consideration is includible in the gross estate of a decedent as a transfer taking effect at death, where he has *at any time after September 7, 1916* made a transfer *by trust or otherwise,* if

(1) possession or enjoyment of the property can, through ownership of such interest, be obtained only by surviving the decedent, *and*

(a) *if made after October 8, 1949,* the decedent has retained a reversionary interest in the property (*either by operation of law or by the express terms of the instrument*) and the value of such reversionary interest immediately before the death of the decedent exceeds 5% of the value of the property, and

(b) *if made before October 8, 1949,* the decedent has retained a reversionary interest in the property *by the express terms of the instrument* and the value of such reversionary interest immediately before the death of the decedent exceeds 5% of the value of the property.[20]

"Reversionary interest" includes a *possibility* that property transferred by the decedent (1) may return to him or his estate *or* (2) may be subject to a power of disposition by him, *but does not* include a possibility that the income alone from such property may return to him or be subject to a power of disposition by him. The value of such interest immediately before the decedent's death is to be determined by usual methods of valuation, including the use of mortality tables and actuarial principles as if it were a possibility that such property may return to the decedent or his estate.[1]

An interest transferred shall not be included in the donor's gross estate if possession or enjoyment of the property could have been obtained by a general power of appointment exercisable immediately before the decedent's death.[2]

As can be seen, the statute is the distillation of extensive litigation and amendments of prior law and is directed to so-called "Spiegel" and "Hallock" transfers.[3]

A "Spiegel" transfer is one in which the possibility exists that a transfer made by the donor may return to him or his estate

---

20. IRC, § 2037(a)(1)(2) (1954 Code).

1. IRC, § 2037(b)(1)(2) (1954 Code).

2. IRC, § 2037(b)(2) (1954 Code).

3. Spiegel v Comm, note 16, supra; Helvering v Hallock, note 10, supra.

or be subject by him to a power of disposition *by operation of law*. A "Hallock" transfer is one in which the donor *expressly* retains a reversionary interest.

The reason for the percentage limitation, as we have previously noted, is that in the Spiegel case a reversionary interest valued at $70 in a fund of $1,000,000 resulted in a tax of $450,000.

It will be observed that the crucial date is October 8, 1949. If the transfer was made *prior* to that date it is includible in the decedent's gross estate only if possession or enjoyment of the property depends upon surviving the decedent, *and* the latter *expressly retained* a reversionary interest in excess of 5% of the value of the property. If made *on or after* October 8, 1949 it is includible if possession or enjoyment of the property depends upon surviving the decedent, *and* there is *either* an express retention of a reversionary interest, *or* if the reversionary interest arises by operation of law *and in either case exceeds 5%* of the value of the property. The *reversionary interest* even though 5% or less is taxable,[4] although the rest of the transfer is not.

It is to be noted that whether the transfer is before or after October 8, 1949, both survival of the beneficiary *and* a reversionary interest must be present for taxability. Thus, if survival is a condition for enjoyment, but the reversionary interest does not exceed 5%, the corpus is not includible in the decedent's gross estate. If the survival is not a condition for enjoyment and the reversionary interest exceeds 5%, the reversionary interest is includible, but not the entire corpus.

§ 146. Schedule G; Transfers During Life; Transfers Taking Effect at Death; Condition of Survivorship.

One of the statutory conditions for taxability as a transfer taking effect at death is that possession or enjoyment of the transferred property can, through ownership of such interest, be obtained only by surviving the decedent.[5] It is further provided that an interest so transferred, shall not be included in the decedent's gross estate if possession or enjoyment of the property could have been obtained by any beneficiary during the decedent's life through the exercise of a general power of appointment which in fact was exercisable immediately before the decedent's death.[6]

4. IRC, § 2033 (1954 Code).
5. IRC, § 2037(a)(1) (1954 Code).
6. IRC, § 2037(b)(2) (1954 Code).

The Regulation[7] restates the statutory rule, but further points out that property is not includible in the decedent's gross estate, if immediately before the decedent's death, possession or enjoyment of the property could have been obtained by any beneficiary either by surviving the decedent or through the occurrence of some other event such as the expiration of a term of years or the exercise of a power of appointment. However, if a consideration of the terms and circumstances of the transfer as a whole indicates that the "other event" is unreal and if the death of the decedent does, in fact, occur before the "other event", the beneficiary will be considered able to possess or enjoy the property only by surviving the decedent.

As examples of this, if the decedent transfers property at the age of 30, with income to be accumulated for 20 years or until his death, with principal and accumulated income payable to his son if then surviving, and he dies before the expiration of the 20 years, the son will be considered able to possess or enjoy the property without surviving the decedent. If the decedent were 70 years old at the time of the transfer the son would not be so considered. If a decedent transfers property, with the income to be accumulated for his life, and upon his death the principal and accumulated income to be paid to his then surviving children, with an unrestricted power in the decedent's wife to alter, amend, revoke, or terminate the trust, the property is not includible, since the wife has a general power of appointment exercisable immediately before the decedent's death, which is within the statutory exception.[8]

The 1939 Code[9] specifically provided for the "other event" referred to in the Regulation, whereas the 1954 Code does not. But decisions under the former provisions with respect to survivorship will undoubtedly still apply under the 1954 Code.[10]

It must be borne in mind that survivorship is only part of the test of taxability, since if it is not coupled with a reversionary interest in excess of 5% of the value of the property, there is no taxability under this section.[11]

7. Reg, § 20.2037–1(b).
8. Reg, § 20.2037–1(f), Examples (5)(6).
9. IRC, § 811(c)(3)(B) (1939 Code).
10. See Dominick v Comm, 152 F2d 843 (CCA 2) (1946); Nettleton, 5 TCM 127 (1945); Comm v Marshall, 203 F2d 534 (CCA 3) (1953).
11. IRC, § 2037 (1954 Code).

§ 147. Schedule G; Transfers During Life; Transfers Taking Effect at Death; Reversionary Interest.

The statute provides as a condition for taxability of transfers to take effect at death, in addition to survivorship, that the decedent shall have retained a reversionary interest in the property, other than the income alone, and that the value of such interest shall exceed 5% of the value of the property.[12] A distinction is made, however, between transfers made *prior to October 8, 1949* and those made thereafter. In the case of *transfers* made *before that date,* taxability results only if the *reversionary interest* arises by the *express terms of the instrument.* Transfers *after that date* are includible whether the reversionary interest arises *either* by the *express terms* of the instrument *or by operation of law.* Thus, if before October 8, 1949 the decedent created a trust with income payable to his wife for the decedent's life, and the remainder to the decedent's then surviving descendants, there is a possibility that he might die with no issue surviving, so that there is a possible reversion by operation of law. It would not be taxable even though the interest exceeded 5% of the value of the transfer. If the transfer were made after October 8, 1949 it would be taxable.[13]

The term "reversionary interest" includes a *possibility* that property transferred by the decedent may return to him or his estate and a possibility that property transferred by him may become subject to a power of disposition by him. The term is not used in a technical sense, but has reference to any reserved right under which the transferred property shall or may be returned to the grantor. The term "reversionary interest", however, *does not include* rights to income only, such as the right to receive income from a trust after the death of another person. Such property may be included because of the retention of a life estate.[14] Nor does the term "reversionary interest" include the possibility that the decedent during his life might have received back an interest in transferred property by inheritance through the estate of another person. Similarly, a statutory right of a spouse to receive a portion of whatever estate a decedent may leave at the time of his death is not a "reversionary interest".[15]

A reversionary interest may arise in many ways and under varying circumstances. It need not necessarily be the result of

12. Note 11, supra.
13. Reg, § 20.2037–1(g)(1).
14. See §§ 139 et seq, supra.
15. Reg, § 20.2037–1(c)(2).

specific language, but may be found from the form of the transaction,[16] and in the case of such interests arising by operation of law there may be many different situations resulting in such reversionary interest existing.[17]

It should be remembered that a reversionary interest is an incident of ownership under the provisions for the taxation of the proceeds of insurance.[18]

§ 148. Schedule G; Transfers During Life; Transfers Taking Effect at Death; Five Percent Limitation.

We have seen that in addition to the survivorship condition for includibility of transferred property as a transfer taxable as one taking effect at death, there must also be a reversionary interest.[19] It is further required that such interest be valued in excess of 5% of the value of the entire property *immediately before the decedent's death*.[20]

For purposes of Section 2037, the value of the decedent's reversionary interest is computed as of the moment immediately before his death, without regard to whether or not the executor elects to have the gross estate valued as of the alternate valuation date and without regard to the fact of the decedent's death. The value is ascertained in accordance with recognized valuation principles for determining the value for Estate Tax purposes of future or conditional interests in property.[1] For example, if the decedent's reversionary interest was subject to an outstanding life estate in his wife, the interest is valued according to the actuarial rules set forth in the Regulation[2] for the valuation of annuities, life estates, remainders and reversions. On the other hand, if the decedent's reversionary interest was contingent on the death of his wife without issue surviving and if it cannot be shown that the wife is incapable of having issue (i.e., an interest not subject to valuation according to actuarial rules) his interest is valued according to the general rules for the valuation of property.[3] A possibility that the decedent may be able to dispose of property under certain condition is considered to

---

16. See Gilbert, 14 TC 349 (1950); Slade v Comm, 190 F2d 689 (CA 2) (1951); Thacher, 20 TC 474 (1953); Mullikin v Magruder, 149 F2d 593 (CCA 4) (1945).

17. Chemical Bank & Trust Co. v Early, 67 F Supp 530 (1946); Beachy, 15 TC 136 (1950).

18. See §§ 76, 77, supra.
19. §§ 146, 147, supra.
20. IRC, § 2037(a)(2)(1954 Code).
1. See § 115, supra.
2. Reg, § 20.2031–7.
3. Reg, § 20.2031–1.

be as valuable as a right of the decedent to the return of the property under the same conditions.[4]

Where the value could not be determined the court has fixed it at zero.[5] It has also held that a reversionary interest had no determinable value.[6] And in the absence of proof of the value the court will assume that it is in excess of 5%.[7]

In order to determine whether or not the decedent retained a reversionary interest in transferred property of a value in excess of 5%, the value of the reversionary interest is compared with the value of the transferred property, including interests therein which are not dependent upon survivorship of the decedent. For example assume that the decedent A, transferred property in trust with the income payable to B for life and with the remainder payable to C if A predeceases B, but with the property to revert to A if B predeceases A. Assume that A does in fact, predecease B. The value of A's reversionary interest immediately before his death is compared with the value of the trust corpus, without deduction of the value of B's outstanding life estate. If, in the above example, A had retained a reversionary interest in half only of the trust corpus, the value of his reversionary interest would be compared with the value of half of the trust corpus, again without deduction of any part of the value of B's outstanding life estate.[8]

If separate interests in property are transferred to one or more beneficiaries, the provisions of the Regulation[9] are to be separately applied with respect to each interest. For example, assume that the decedent transferred an interest in property which could be possessed or enjoyed only by surviving the decedent, and also transferred another interest in the same property which could be possessed or enjoyed only on the occurrence of some event unrelated to the decedent's death. Assume also that the decedent retained a reversionary interest in the property in excess of 5%. Only the value of the interest first transferred is includible in the decedent's gross estate. Similar results would obtain if possession or enjoyment of the entire property could have been obtained only by surviving the dece-

4. Reg, § 20.2037–1(c)(3).

5. Slade v Comm, 190 F2d 689 (CA 2) (1952).

6. Hill v Comm, 193 F2d 734 (CA 2) (1952).

7. Gilbert, note 16, supra; Thacher, note 16, supra.

8. Reg, § 20.2037–1(c)(4).

9. Reg, § 20.2037–1(a)–(c).

dent, but the decedent retained a reversionary interest in a part only of such property.[10]

In order for an outstanding life interest to be deductible, in computing the value of the reversionary interest it must be one presently enjoyable and not one to take effect at the decedent's death.[11] If there are intervening life estates they are deducted provided they are vested.[12] If the decedent retains the power to vary the amount payable,[13] to revoke,[14] or the life estate is contingent upon the beneficiary remaining married to the decedent,[15] the intervening interest is not deductible in computing the value.

The determination of the value of the reversionary interest is primarily for the purpose of deciding whether the interest exceeds the statutory amount of 5%, in which case the *entire property* to which the interest relates is included in the decedent's gross estate. But even where the value of the reversionary interest is less than 5%, that amount is includible in the gross estate.[16]

§ 149. Schedule G; Transfers During Life; Revocable Transfers.

A further lifetime transfer which is includible in the decedent's gross estate is one in which the decedent has at any time made a transfer, except for an adequate consideration, by trust or otherwise, where the enjoyment thereof was subject at the date of his death to any *change through the exercise of a power,* (in whatever capacity exercisable) *either by* the decedent *alone or in conjunction with any other person* (without regard to when or from what source the decedent acquired such power), to alter, amend, revoke, or terminate, or where any such power is relinquished in contemplation of death.[17]

The above applies to all transfers made after June 22, 1936.

In the case of such transfers made prior to that date, the phrases in parentheses are eliminated.[18] The reason for the

10. Reg, § 20.2037–1(d).

11. Fidelity Philadelphia Trust Co v Rothensies, 324 US 108, 89 L ed 783, 65 S Ct 508 (1945); Central Hanover Bank & Trust Co v Nunan, 56 F Supp 147 (1947); Forbes, 3 TCM 283 (1944); Gaston, 2 TC 672 (1943); Kitchen, 3 TCM 877 (1944); Dominick v Comm, 152 F2d 843 (CCA 2) (1946).

12. Nettleton, 5 TCM 127 (1945); Comm v Schwartz, 74 F2d 712 (CCA 2) (1935); Central Nat Bank of Cleveland v US, 41 F Supp 239 (1941); Sinclair, 6 TC 1080 (1946).

13. Weadock v Cavanaugh, 45–2 USTC ¶10,220.

14. Omaha Nat Bank v O'Malley, 69 F Supp 354 (1947).

15. Corbett, 12 TC 163 (1949).

16. See § 111, supra.

17. IRC, § 2038(a)(1) (1954 Code); Reg, § 20.2038–1(a).

18. IRC, § 2038(a)(2) (1954 Code).

difference is that it had been held that a decedent who had been reappointed trustee after the resignation of another trustee had not *reserved* the power and there was no taxability.[19] This is reflected in the Regulation.[20] The statute was amended in 1936 as a result of the decision above.[1]

For the purposes of the section, the power to alter, amend, revoke, or terminate is considered to exist on the date of the decedent's death even though the exercise of the power is subject to a precedent giving of notice or even though the alteration, amendment, revocation, or termination takes effect only on the expiration of a stated period after the exercise of the power, whether or not on or before the date of the decedent's death notice has been given or the power has been exercised. In such cases proper adjustment is made representing the interests which would have been excluded from the power if the decedent had lived, and for such purpose, if the notice has not been given or the power has not been exercised on or before the date of his death, such notice is considered to have been given, or the power exercised, on the date of his death.[2]

The 1954 Code eliminated the provision under the 1939 Code where there was a failure to relinquish, Gift Tax free, reserved powers where there was a disability.[3]

It will be noted that taxability depends upon the retention of the power by the decedent exercisable by him *in any capacity* and whether by him alone or in conjunction with any person. It is immaterial (i) in what capacity the power was exercisable by the decedent, *or* by another person or persons *in conjunction with* the decedent; (ii) whether the power was exercisable alone or only in conjunction with another person or persons, whether or not having an adverse interest (unless the transfer was made before June 2, 1924) and (iii) at what time or from what source the decedent acquired his power (unless the transfer was made before June 22, 1936). The section is applicable to any power affecting the time or manner of enjoyment of property or its income, even though the identity of the beneficiary is not affected. For example it is applicable to a power reserved by the grantor of a trust to accumulate income or distribute it to A, and to distribute corpus to A, even though the remainder is vested in A

19. White v Poor, 296 US 98, 80 L ed 80; 56 S Ct 66 (1935).

20. Reg, § 20.2038–1 (d).

1. Rev Act of 1936, § 805.

2. IRC, § 2038(b) (1954 Code); Reg, § 20.2038–1(b).

3. IRC, § 811(d)(4) (1939 Code).

or his estate, and no other person has any beneficial interest in the trust.[4]

The best way of understanding whether a power is one embraced within the statute is to consider the powers in cases which the courts have decided. Retained powers which have been held to incur taxability are: to change beneficiaries or their shares,[5] to speculate with trust property as if the decedent's own,[6] to change benefits by will,[7] discretion to invade principal for the beneficiary,[8] but, not if contingent upon a condition which had not occurred,[9] to change enjoyment, even though the power is not exercised,[10] to substitute securities without restriction as to kind or value,[11] to revoke,[12] to accelerate the remainder by termination,[13] and whether prior notice is,[14] or is not,[15] required for termination, prohibited powers, where even though by state law the beneficiary is entitled to the property,[16] to appoint the decedent successor trustee, with right to terminate,[17] but not when the right is to appoint a successor who has the right of termination, unless the exercise of discretion is governed by recognizable external standards,[18] or the right is not exercised before death,[19] prohibited powers even though under state law there is a right to revoke,[20] to borrow upon or surrender a life insurance policy,[1] or excessive management powers.[2]

4. Reg, § 20.2038–1(a).

5. Guggenheim v Helvering, 117 F2d 469 (CCA 2), cert den 314 US 621, 86 L ed 499, 62 S Ct 66 (1941); Union Trust Co v Driscoll, 137 F2d 152 (CCA 3), cert den 321 US 764, 88 L ed 1061, 64 S Ct 521 (1943).

6. Comm v Hager, 173 F2d 613 (CA 3), pet for cert dism 337 US 937, 93 L ed 1742, 69 S Ct 1515 (1949).

7. Cooper, 7 TC 1236 (1946); Korn, 35 BTA 107 (1937); Moon, 34 BTA 614 (1936).

8. Mollenberg, 173 F2d 698 (CA 2) (1949); Nettleton, 4 TC 987 (1944).

9. Markson, 3 TC 309 (1944); Fiske, 5 TCM 42 (1945).

10. Korn, note 7, supra; Halberstamm, 13 TCM 1081 (1949).

11. Commonwealth Trust Co v Driscoll, 43–1 USTC ¶10,011, ¶10,016, affd 137 F2d 653 (CCA 3), cert den 321 US 764, 88 L ed 1061, 64 S Ct 521 (1943).

12. Reinecke v Northern Trust Co, 278 US 339, 73 L ed 410, 49 S Ct 123 (1928).

13. Comm v Holmes, 326 US 480, 90 L ed 228, 66 S Ct 257 (1946); Lober v US, 346 US 335, 98 L ed 15, 74 S Ct 98 (1953).

14. Mellon v Driscoll, 117 F2d 477 (CCA 3), cert den 313 US 579, 85 L ed 1536, 61 S Ct 1100 (1941).

15. Mollenberg, note 8, supra.

16. Lober v US, note 13, supra.

17. Loughridge v Comm, 183 F2d 294 (CA 10) cert den 340 US 830, 95 L ed 609, 71 S Ct 67 (1950).

18. Wilson, 13 TC 869, affd 187 F2d 145 (CA 3) (1951).

19. Rev Rul 55–393, IRB 1955–1 CB 448.

20. Howard v US, 125 F2d 986 (CCA 5), affg 40 F Supp 697 (1942); contra, Newhall v Casey, 18 F2d 447 (1927).

1. Wishard v US, 143 F2d 704 (CCA 7) (1944).

[Harris]

Retained powers held not to subject the transferred property to tax are: to direct the trustee to issue voting proxies and to sell, exchange, invest and reinvest the fund,[3] to control payment of the dividends of the corporation whose stock was transferred,[4] to amend as to mechanics or details,[5] such as administrative matters,[6] designation of income or capital,[7] or investment power,[8] to add to the trust,[9] to postpone payment after the death of the life beneficiary, where the latter survived the settlor,[10] where exercise of the power extinguished it,[11] to change the manner of distribution of income,[12] where the change was slight or trivial,[13] or to change certain provisions for termination.[14]

The term "any other person", which was the former language, does not differ in meaning from the present "any person", and was construed to include a beneficiary.[15] Thus tax liability arises whether the power is exercisable by the decedent as transferor or trustee alone, or in either of such capacities in conjunction with others, whether they be trustee, beneficiaries or disinterested parties. Where, however, *all of the parties* interested in a trust, both vested and contingent interests, have the right to terminate a trust, such reservation in the instrument does not make the power taxable under the section.[16]

Where the power to alter extends to only a part of the trust, only that part is includible.[17]

Where under the law of a community property state the husband has powers equivalent to any of those referred to in the statute, the transfer of community property is includible.[18]

It should be noted that a transfer of property under one of the Acts for expediting gifts to minors is included within the

2. Note 6, supra.
3. Downe, 2 TC 967 (1943).
4. Burr, 4 TCM 1054 (1945).
5. Storer, 41 BTA 1156 (1940).
6. Neal, 8 TC 237 (1947).
7. Fiske, 5 TCM 42 (1945).
8. Johnston, 2 TCM 299 (1943); Fifth Ave Bank v Nunan, 59 F Supp 753 (1945); Hall, 6 TC 933 (1946).
9. Central Trust Co v US, 167 F2d 133 (CCA 6) (1948); Johnston, note 8, supra.
10. Helvering v Tetzlaff, 141 F2d 8 (1944).
11. Burney, 4 TC 449 (1944).

12. McFadden v US, 20 F Supp 625 (1937).
13. Dominick, 4 TCM 226 (1944); Theopold v US, 164 F2d 404 (CCA 1) (1948).
14. See Helvering v Helmholtz, 296 US 93, 80 L ed 76, 56 S Ct 68 (1936).
15. Helvering v City Bank, 296 US 85, 80 L ed 62, 56 S Ct 70 (1936).
16. Note 14, supra; Reg, § 20.2038–1 (a)(2).
17. Dravo v Comm, 40 BTA 309 (1939).
18. Showers, 14 TC 902 (1950), settled by stipulation.

section if the transferor dies before the minor attains his majority.[19]

The Regulation points out one further exception in the case of transfers made before June 2, 1924, the date of the Revenue Act of 1924. If an interest in property was transferred by a decedent before the enactment of the Revenue Act of 1924, and if a power reserved by the decedent to alter, amend, revoke, or terminate was exercisable by the decedent only in conjunction with a person having a *substantial adverse interest* in the transferred property, or in conjunction with several persons, some or all of whom held such an adverse interest, there is included in the decedent's gross estate only the value of any interest or interests held by a person or persons not required to join in the exercise of the power plus the value of any insubstantial adverse interest or interests of a person or persons required to join in the exercise of the power.[20] Where the transfer was made after June 2, 1924, adversity of interest has no bearing on taxability.

§ 150. Schedule G; Transfers During Life; Revocable Transfers; Relinquishment of Power.

The relinquishment of a power to alter, amend, revoke, or terminate is taxable under the provisions of Section 2038 of the 1954 Code, as it was under prior statutes if it is made in contemplation of death.[1] The effect is, that as to such relinquishment within three years of death, the provisions of Section 2035 of the 1954 Code apply, creating a presumption of a transfer in contemplation of death.[2] Section 2035 also specifically provides that the relinquishment of a power within such period shall be treated as having been made in contemplation of death.[3]

If a power to alter, amend, revoke, or terminate would have resulted in the inclusion of an interest in property in a decedent's gross estate under Section 2038 if it had been held until the decedent's death, the relinquishment of the power in contemplation of the decedent's death within three years before his death results in the inclusion of the same interest in property

---

19. Showers v Comm, 51–2 USTC ¶10,832; Rev Rul 57–366, IRB 1957–32 p 20.

20. Reg, § 20.2038–1(e); see White v Poor, 296 US 98, 80 L ed 80, 56 S Ct 66 (1935); note 14, supra; Rev Rul 55–683, 1955–2 CB 603.

1. IRC, § 2038 (1954 Code); Reg, § 20.2038–1(f).

2. See §§ 121 et seq, supra.

3. IRC, § 2035(b) (1954 Code); Reg, § 20.2035–1(b).

in the decedent's gross estate.[4] In the case of a transfer made before June 23, 1936, Section 2038 applies only to a relinquishment made by the decedent. However, in the case of a transfer made after June 22, 1936, Section 2038 also applies to a relinquishment made by a person or persons holding the power in conjunction with the decedent, if the relinquishment was made in contemplation of the decedent's death and had the effect of extinguishing the power.[5]

The same standards for determining contemplation of death would apply in the case of a relinquishment as in any other transfer.[6]

Whether the relinquishment of a power to amend may not make the transfer includible in the gross estate is questionable in spite of Allen vs. Trust Co. of Georgia,[7] which held that it was not under the facts in that case, which were not subject to review. The fact that the power to amend is not for the benefit of the decedent has no effect on taxability.[8]

§ 151. Schedule G; Transfers During Life; Reciprocal Trusts.

It is the purpose of the sections of the Estate Tax Law which we have been discussing, to reach transfers to which the transferor has retained a string. Fertile imaginations have invented tax devices designed to avoid the effect of the statute and at the same time to permit the decedent to enjoy transferred property. One of these was the reciprocal trust whereby A created a trust for B, retaining no rights which would make the property includible in his estate, but granting such rights to B. In turn, B would create a similar trust for A. The question in such case is which party is the settlor of which trust.

In Lehman vs. Commissioner[9] it was determined that where two persons each create trusts and grant the other rights, which if he had retained would make the property includible in his estate, if the facts indicate that each trust was set up in consideration of the creation of the other, the property could be included

4. Reg, § 20.2038–1(f)(1).

5. Reg, § 20.2038–1(f)(2); see also § 4491, supra.

6. Note 2, supra; see also Denniston v Comm, 106 F2d 925 (CCA 3) (1939); Allen v Trust Co of Georgia, 326 US 630, 90 L ed 367, 66 S Ct 389 (1946); Boyle Trust & Investment Co v US, 43–1 USTC ¶10,021; Central Nat Bank of Cleveland v US, 41 F Supp 239 (1941); Rev Rul 56–324, 1956–2 CB 999.

7. Note 6, supra.

8. Porter v Comm, 288 US 436, 77 L ed 880, 53 S Ct 451 (1933).

9. 109 F2d 99 (CCA 2), cert den 310 US 637, 84 L ed 1406, 60 S Ct 1080 (1940).

in the beneficiary's estate as property in which he had an interest at the date of his death. The rule has even been applied to savings and loan certificates with husband and wife each trustee for the other.[10]

The decision created such an impression that the Technical Changes Act of 1949[11] permitted persons who had created such trusts to release their rights without penalty. If the right was not released before December 31, 1950, a relinquishment thereafter may be claimed to be in contemplation of death if made within three years of death.

Whether or not such property is includible in a decedent's gross estate depends upon whether it is in fact reciprocal, that is, each trust being created in consideration of the creation of the other. Where reciprocity is established, the property is taxable,[12] and where reciprocity is negatived there is no taxability.[13]

§ 152. Schedule G; Transfers During Life; Annuity Combined with Life Insurance.

It will have been observed that the same transfer may be taxable under different sections of the statutes dealing with transfers during life. One of these is the combination annuity and life insurance, which has attempted to be utilized to avoid Estate Tax. Under this plan the annuitant purchases a single premium life insurance and annuity contract. Such life insurance contract would not be issued alone. The purchaser then assigns the policy so that he no longer has any of the incidents of ownership.

The Supreme Court had held that the proceeds of such a policy *were not insurance* since there was no element of risk involved.[14] That decision had been widely followed,[15] with one exception.[16]

10. Harvey v US, 86 F Supp 609 (1949).

11. PL 378, 81st Cong, Oct 25, 1959.

12. Lehman v Comm, note 9, supra; Newberry, 6 TCM 455, aff'd 172 F2d 220 (CA 3) (1948); Neal, 2 TCM 1137 (1943); Fish, 45 BTA 120 (1941); Moreno, 28 TC 98 (1957).

13. Lueders v Comm, 164 F2d 128 (CCA 3) (1947); Comm v Dravo, 119 F2d 97 (CCA 3) (1941); Newberry v Comm, 201 F2d 874 (CA 3) (1953); Ruxton, 20 TC 487 (1953).

14. Helvering v Le Gierse, 312 US 531, 85 L ed 996, 61 S Ct 646 (1941).

15. Keller v Comm, 312 US 543, 85 L ed 1032, 61 S Ct 651 (1943); Burr v Comm, 156 F2d 871 (CCA 2), cert den 329 US 785, 91 L ed 673, 67 S Ct 298 (1946); Conway v Glenn, 193 F2d 965 (CA 6) (1952); Hutchinson, 20 TC 749 (1953); Tyler v Helvering, 312 US 657, 85 L ed 1105, 61 S Ct 729 (1941); Mearkle v Comm, 129 F2d 386 (CCA 3) (1942); Blackard v Jones, 62 F Supp 234 (1944); Reynolds, 45 BTA 44 (1941).

The proceeds had been included in the decedent's estate as a transfer in contemplation of death,[17] or one to take effect at death.[18] In the one exception, the Seventh Circuit held that since the decedent had retained no reversionary interest, nor retained any control over possession or enjoyment, the insurance proceeds were not includible in the decedent's gross estate. The Supreme Court affirmance was by a court divided 4–4, and the Internal Revenue Service therefore refused to follow that case, claiming it was not authority for the determination of other cases involving similar situations.[19] The Estate Tax status of such combinations was therefore in doubt. Such doubt was resolved by the Supreme Court recently,[20] holding as it had been held previously by the Tax Court,[1] that where the policies were assigned and cashed in by the owners, the proceeds were not includible in the decedent's gross estate. Where the decedent made a gift of the cost of both contracts to his wife and she purchased them, the annuity being payable to him, the proceeds were not includible.[2] This approval by the Supreme Court will result in substantial use of the device.

§ 153. Schedule G; Transfers During Life; Overlapping Taxability of Reserved Powers.

As may be noted from the preceding sections, and as the Regulation points out, there is considerable overlap in the application of Sections 2036 through 2038 with respect to reserved powers, so that transferred property may be includible in the decedent's gross estate in varying degrees *under more than one* of these sections.[3]

The customary practice is for the Commissioner to claim taxability under both Section 2036(a)(2) as a transfer in which the decedent retained the right to designate the persons to enjoy the property or the income, and also under Section 2038 as a transfer in which the decedent retained the right to alter, amend,

---

16. Bohnen v Harrison, 199 F2d 492 (CA 7), affd 345 US 946, 97 L ed 1371, 73 S Ct 863 (1952).

17. US v Tonkin, 150 F2d 531 (CCA 3), cert den 326 US 771, 90 L ed 465, 66 S Ct 176 (1945).

18. Note 15, supra.

19. Rev Rul 54–552, IRB 1954–2 CB 284.

20. Fidelity Philadelphia Trust Co v Smith, 58–1 USTC ¶11,761, 4/28/58, revg 57–1 USTC ¶11,683 (CA 3), revg 142 F Supp 56.

1. Hutchinson, 20 TC 749 (1953) (Non acq).

2. Dundore, BTA memo op Dec 12, 244 B (1942); Dickson v Smith, 45–2 USTC ¶10,226 (1945).

3. Reg, § 20.2031(a)(2).

revoke, or terminate. In the ordinary case there is little difference under which section a transfer is taxed, but there may in some cases be a practical difference, where the amount includible is different under the sections. Section 2036 taxes the entire interest, whereas 2038 taxes the value of the interest to which the power to alter, etc. relates. Section 2036 taxes where the right is *retained,* while 2038 taxes where the decedent has the power *without regard to from what source he acquired the power.* The distinction has been observed.[4] When it is advantageous taxwise, these fine distinctions may be of value.

§ 154. Schedule G; Transfers During Life; Community Property.

As we have noted previously,[5] community property is generally includible to the extent of one half of the property in the estate of each owner. The exceptions have also been noted. Such interest is reported in the appropriate schedule of the return. It therefore follows that if one of the spouses makes a lifetime transfer which comes within one of the provisions taxing such a transfer, it must be reported.

The same considerations affect transfers of community property when it is claimed that the transfer was in contemplation of death,[6] the decedent retained a life estate,[7] or the power to alter or amend is retained.[8]

§ 155. Schedule G; Transfers During Life; Insufficient Consideration.

It will have been noted that each of the sections of the 1954 Code dealing with taxable lifetime transfers which we have been discussing contain the identical provision, excepting such transfers from taxation *in case of a bona fide sale for an adequate and full consideration in money or money's worth.*[9]

4. Industrial Trust Co v Comm, 7 TC 756, affd in part and revd in part 173 F2d 613 (CCA 1) (1948).

5. §§ 41, 48, supra.

6. See Humphrey v Comm, 162 F2d 1 (CCA 5), cert den 332 US 817, 92 L ed 394, 68 S Ct 157 (1947); Hammond v Westover, 97 F Supp 753 (1951); Larsh, 8 TCM 799 (1947).

7. See Wier, 17 TC 409 (1952); Comm v Hinds, 180 F2d 930 (CA 5) (1950);

Gray, 14 TC 390 (1950); Scofield v Bethea, 170 F2d 934 (CA 5) (1948).

8. See Sampson v Welch, 23 F Supp 434, vacated on authority of US v Goodyear, 99 F2d 523 (CCA 9) (1938), vacatur proper, 138 F2d 417 (CCA 9) (1943); Showers, 14 TC 902 (1950); vacated on stipulation (CA 5) 51-2 USTC ¶10,832; Zirjacks v Scofield, 197 F2d 688 (CA 5) (1952).

9. IRC, §§ 2035–2038 (1954 Code).

The subject of consideration is recurrent in estate taxation, as we have seen in connection with buy-and-sell agreements,[10] insurance to fund the same,[11] jointly owned property,[12] and transactions in contemplation of death.[13] In the case of lifetime transfers a specific section of the statute is devoted to the subject.

If any one of the transfers, trusts, interests, rights, or powers enumerated and described in Sections 2035 to 2038 inclusive, and Section 2041 is made, created, exercised, or relinquished for a consideration in money or money's worth, but is not a bona fide sale for an adequate and full consideration in money or money's worth, there shall be included in the gross estate only the excess of the fair market value at the time of death of the property otherwise to be included on account of such transaction, over the value of the consideration received therefor by the decedent.[14]

The statute further expressly provides, as previously noted in connection with jointly owned property,[15] that a relinquishment or promised relinquishment of dower or curtesy, or of a statutory estate created in lieu of dower or curtesy, or of other marital rights in the decedent's property or estate, shall not be considered to any extent a consideration "in money or money's worth."[16]

Adequacy of consideration determines whether lifetime transfers which would otherwise be taxable escape taxation. If consideration is lacking the entire transfer will be included in the decedent's gross estate.[17] If the price was less than an adequate consideration, only the excess of the fair market value of the property (as of the applicable valuation date) over the price received by the decedent is included in ascertaining the value of his gross estate.[18] On the other hand, where the considera-

10. § 62, supra.
11. § 82, supra.
12. § 89, supra.
13. § 130, supra.
14. IRC, § 2043(a) (1954 Code).
15. § 89, supra.
16. IRC, § 2043(b) (1954 Code).
17. Armstrong v Comm, 146 F2d 457 (CCA 7) (1945); Mollenberg v Comm, 173 F2d 698 (CA 2) (1949); Barnard, 5 TC 971 (1945); Phillips v Gnicktel,

27 F2d 662 (CCA 3) (1928); Safe Deposit Trust Co v Tait, 295 F 429 (1924); Giannini v Comm, 148 F2d 285 (CCA 9), cert den 326 US 730, 90 L ed 434, 66 S Ct 38 (1945).

18. Reg, § 20.2043–1(a); Schoenheit, 14 BTA 33 (1928); McDonald, 19 TC 672 (1953); Pritchard, 4 TC 204 (1944); Schwing, 3 BTA 697 (1925); Comm v Erickson, 74 F2d 327 (CCA 1) (1935).

tion is adequate, none of the transferred property will be included.[19]

The question of consideration arises more frequently in cases involving the Gift Tax and will be dealt with at further length hereafter.[20]

§ 156. Schedule G; Transfers During Life; Instructions on Return.

The instructions for Schedule G, although entitled "Transfers During Decedent's Life", groups all such transfers under a subhead "Transfers made in contemplation of death", but then enumerates all taxable lifetime transfers which must be reported.

Where a part of the property transferred is included, it is required that the entire value be shown and an explanation given of the proportionate inclusion.[1]

All transfers made by the decedent within three years prior to death of a value *of $1,000 or more and all transfers* made by the decedent *at any time* during his life of a value *of $5,000 or more,* except bona fide sales for an adequate and full consideration in money or money's worth must be disclosed in the return, *whether the executor regards such transfers as subject to the tax or not.* If the executor believes that the transfer is not subject to tax a statement of the pertinent facts should be made.[2]

There has previously been noted the kind of statement which should be furnished.[3]

It may be noted that whether a transfer is taxable may involve questions of law as well as those of fact. In such case, in addition to an affidavit of the facts, it is advisable to submit a memorandum of law with the return and not wait until the legal questions are raised by the Estate Tax examiner.

§ 157. Schedule G; Transfers During Life; Valuation.

All of the Proposed Regulations covering taxable lifetime transfers contained the same provision that the value of an

19. McDonald, 2 BTA 1295 (1925); Siegel, 19 BTA 683 (1930); Bergan, 1 TC 543 (1943); Mills, 5 TCM 768 (1945); Black v US, 68 F Supp 74, affd 164 F2d 96 (CCA 6) (1946); McDonald, 10 TCM 1038 (1948); Hunt, 19 BTA 624 (1930); Goldman, 11 BTA 92 (1928); Root v US, 56 F2d 857 (1932); Belknap, 10 TCM 769 (1948).

20. See §§ 4662B.30 et seq, infra.

1. Instructions, Schedule G, Form 706.

2. Note 1, supra.

3. § 138, supra.

interest in transferred property includible in a decedent's gross estate was the value of the interests as of the applicable valuation date, and if the transferee had made improvements or additions to the property, any resulting enhancement in the value of the property was not considered in ascertaining the value of the gross estate. Similarly, neither income received subsequent to the transfer nor property purchased with the income was considered.[4]

This provision has been deleted from all of the Regulations dealing with lifetime transfers, except transfers in contemplation of death.[4a] It is recognition of the case law that as to transfers in contemplation of death, the value of the property is that as of the applicable valuation date and not as of the time of the transfer,[5] and additions by the transferee, whether of income or otherwise, are not to be considered.[6]

Where property has been transferred, there may be many changes between the date of transfer and the date of death. If the property is converted into other property the value is that of such other property.[7] There is included so much of the original transfer as is retained, and property or the proceeds of the sale of part of the property, as of the applicable valuation date.[8] Where an insurance policy was transferred in contemplation of death, there was deducted from the proceeds the proportionate amount of insurance purchasable with the premiums paid by the transferee.[9] The fact that the property is diminished or injured as the result of the transferee's actions has no bearing on valuation.[10] In the case of a transfer in trust, the cost of an accounting has been allowed as a deduction.[11]

§ 158. Schedule G; Transfers During Life; Meaning of Adequate Consideration.

We have seen that there is excepted from taxation in the case of lifetime transfers otherwise taxable, such part thereof as is

4. Proposed Reg, §§ 20.2035–1(e); 20.2036–1(e); 20.2037–1(e); 20.2038–1 (e).

4a. Reg, § 20.2035–1(e).

5. Igleheart v Comm, 77 F2d 704 (CCA 5) (1935).

6. Burns v Comm, 177 F2d 739 (CA 5) (1949); Comm v Gidwitz, 196 F2d 813 (CA 7) (1952).

7. Kroger, 2 TCM 644 (1943).

8. Howard v US, 125 F2d 986 (CCA 5) (1942).

9. Liebmann v Hassett, 148 F2d 247 (CCA 1) (1945).

10. Humphrey v Comm, 162 F2d 1 (CCA 5) (1947).

11. Rev Rul 293, 1953–2 CB 257.

based upon a bona fide sale for an adequate and full consideration in money or money's worth.[12]

To constitute a bona fide sale for an adequate and full consideration in money or money's worth, the transfer must have been made in good faith, and the price must have been an adequate and full equivalent reducible to a money value.[13] The money equivalency test is taken from the Gift Tax law.[14] It may be noted that the Estate Tax and the Gift Tax are pari materia, and, it is held, should be construed with reference to each other.[15]

Common law consideration is not the consideration referred to in the statute.[16] The subject of adequate consideration will be discussed at greater length in the sections dealing with the Gift Tax, where it has been more frequently adjudicated.[17]

We have also noted that a relinquishment or promised relinquishment of dower, curtesy, or of a statutory right in lieu thereof is not adequate consideration.[18] The Proposed Regulation pointed out that a transfer of property which is to be used in the future to discharge a decedent's obligation to support a dependent is not a transfer for a consideration in money or money's worth, unless under local law the transfer operates completely to discharge the decedent's obligation. The decedent's obligation is discharged pro tanto as each payment for support is made, and not by the original transfer. Therefore, for example, property transferred in trust for the support of a dependent was stated to be includible under Section 2036(a)(1) if the trust continued in existence until the decedent's death and if the dependency relationship existed at that time, since in such a case the decedent retained the benefit of the property or its income during his life. However, if such a transfer is made to carry out a decree or order of a court of competent jurisdiction, entered in a divorce, separate maintenance, or annulment proceeding, or if made in advance of such a decree or order, is later incorporated or approved therein, or is contingent thereon, the includible amount is decreased by the value at the date of the decedent's death of any of the beneficiaries' continuing right of support as fixed or approved by the court. In this connection, continuing right of support does not include provisions made

12. § 155, supra.

13. Reg, § 20.2043-1(a).

14. Comm v Bristol, 121 F2d 129 (CCA 1) (1941).

15. Merrill v Fahs, 324 US 308, 89 L ed 963, 65 S Ct 655 (1945).

16. Note 14, supra.

17. Note 20, supra.

18. § 130, supra.

for payments to children of the decedent beyond the date on which the decedent's obligation of support would have ceased in the absence of the decree or order and had he lived.[19] This proposed provision carried over partly the effect of Harris vs. Comm.[20] from the Gift Tax field, and has been deleted in the Regulation as adopted. That statute[1] provides that a property settlement incorporated within a divorce decree within two years thereafter shall be deemed a transfer for an adequate consideration. There is no such provision in the Estate Tax statute. But it has been held that when the provision for support rights is incorporated in a court decree the value thereof is deductible.[2] If it is not so incorporated, so that enforcement of the right is not dependent upon the decree, it is not deductible.[3]

§ 159. Schedule G; Transfers During Life; Preparation of Schedule.

Once it has been determined that there are lifetime transfers required to be reported, there must be set forth in the schedule the name of the transferee, date and form of the transfer, and a complete description of the property. Rents and other income must be included as in the case of any other property required to be included in a decedent's gross estate.[4]

Many transfers required to be reported in this schedule are the subject of a trust or agreement, in which case a copy of the instrument of transfer must be filed with the return. If of public record, the copy should be certified; if not of record, the copy should be verified.[5]

As previously noted, if only part of the property is claimed to be includible, the entire property will be described in the column headed "Description" and the part includible carried out into the appropriate value column, with an explanation of the reason for noninclusion. If none of the transfer is claimed to be includible the entire transfer will be set forth in the "Description" column, with a short statement that the property is not taxable, and nothing is carried out to the appropriate value column.

19. Proposed Reg, § 20.2043-1(b).
20. 340 US 106, 95 L ed 111, 71 S Ct 181 (1950).
1. IRC, § 2516 (1954 Code).
2. Fleming v Yoke, 53 F Supp 552, affd 145 F2d 472 (CCA 4) (1944); Comm v Swink, 155 F2d 723 (CCA 4) (1946); Watson, 20 TC 386 (1953); Maresi, 6 TC 582 (1946).
3. Bank of New York v US, 115 F Supp 375 (1953).
4. Instructions, Schedule G, Form 706.
5. Note 4, supra.

FORM NO. 20

Schedule G; Transfers During Decedent's Life

1. Did the decedent make any transfer described in the first paragraph (including the six subparagraphs) of the instructions for this schedule? [x] Yes   [ ] No

2a. Did the decedent, at any time, make a transfer of an amount of $5,000 or more without an adequate and full consideration in money or money's worth, but not believed to be includible in the gross estate as indicated in the first paragraph (including the six subparagraphs) of the instructions for this schedule? [x] Yes   [ ] No
   If "Yes," furnish the following information:

2b. Date	2c. Amount or value	2d. Character of transfer
May 15, 1952	$25,000	Trust for benefit of children
March 17, 1950	$50,000	Trust for benefit of mother

3a. Did the decedent, within 3 years immediately preceding his death, make any transfer of his property without an adequate and full consideration in money or money's worth? [x] Yes   [ ] No
   If "Yes," and the transfer was of an amount of $1,000 or more, furnish the following information:

3b. Date	3c. Amount or value	3d. Character of transfer
July 1, 1957	$5,000	Gift

3e. Motive which actuated decedent in making transfer
   Reward for services

4. Were there in existence at the time of the decedent's death any trusts created by him during his lifetime? [x] Yes   [ ] No

Item No.	Description	Subsequent valuation date	Alternate value	Value at date of death
1	On March 17, 1950 the decedent transferred to Provident Trust Co. the sum of $50,000, in trust to pay the income to Minna Benson, his mother, for her life, and upon her death to pay the remaining principal to Charles Benson. Decedent retained no rights in such property. Copy of trust instrument is annexed.			
2	On July 1, 1957 the decedent made a gift of $5,000 to his son, Winthrop Benson, Jr. as a reward for services rendered in the operation of the decedent's business. Such gift is claimed not to have been made in contemplation of death. See affidavit annexed.			
3	On May 15, 1952 the decedent transferred to the Provident Trust Co. the sum of $25,000, in trust, to accumulate the income and pay same and principal to his children, with a retained reversionary interest in the decedent of a value less than 5% of the corpus. Copy of trust instrument annexed, with computation of reversionary interest.			
4	Account No. 8862, Provident Trust Co. in trust for Katherine Benson			$5,628.89

TOTAL (also enter under the Recapitulation, Schedule O) $5,628.89

(If more space is needed, insert additional sheets of same size)

Estate of WINTHROP BENSON

Schedule G—Page 19

§ 160. Schedule H; Powers of Appointment; General Considerations.

It has been said that the power of appointment is the most efficient dispositive device that the ingenuity of Anglo-American lawyers has ever worked out.[6] While powers of appointment have been in use for centuries, the Revenue Acts of 1942 and 1948 focused more attention on them. Their taxation has frequently been confusing. The framers of the Powers of Appointment Act of 1951, which is the basis for the present taxation of powers, stated that the most important consideration of the bill was "to make the law simple and definite enough to be understood and applied by the average lawyer."[7]

A power of appointment is in essence a device by which the owner of property or the right to dispose of property, reserves to himself, or grants to another person or persons, the power

6. Powers of Appointment, Leach, 24 ABAJ 807 (1938).

7. Senate Finance Comm Rep on PL 58, 82nd Cong, 1st Sess, (HR 2084) approved June 28, 1951.

to designate, within such limits as the person granting the power may prescribe, the persons who shall receive the property, or the shares which they may receive.[8]

The lawyer unfamiliar with powers is inclined to think of the kind of power used in the marital deduction trust, or other trust, in which a power is clearly recognizable. But there are many other powers which are in fact powers of appointment, not so clearly indicated. Many of these are taxable and must be identified. Their identification is treated hereafter.[9] Reference is made to the problem at the outset, to alert the lawyer to the necessity for examining trust instruments in which the decedent had any interest, or any will or trust instrument in which he may have been a fiduciary, with such fact in mind, to determine whether he had any power which may be claimed to be taxable, and not to rely on the nomenclature customary in granting powers of appointment.

So far as other nomenclature is concerned, the same designation of the donor, donee, appointee and appointive property is utilized in the Estate Tax Law, but the distinction is between general and nongeneral powers, rather than general and special powers.

§ 161. Schedule H; Powers of Appointment; Statutory Provisions Generally.

Although the framers of the Powers of Appointment Act of 1951 stated it as their purpose to provide simplification, the statute is a complex one. The present statute divides powers of appointment for purposes of estate taxation into those created *prior to October 21, 1942,* and *subsequent* to that date. The statute further does not refer to powers as general and special or limited. It refers only to powers which are general powers of appointment and those which are not deemed general powers. This distinction should be noted, because the statutory definition determines whether a power of appointment is taxable as a general power within the meaning of the law, and not its definition under state law.[10]

General powers within the meaning of the statute are taxable under the circumstances provided in the statute, while nongen-

8. See Restatement, Property, § 318 (1) (1940).

9. § 164, infra.

10. Morgan v Comm, 309 US 78, 84 L ed 585, 60 S Ct 424 (1940); Reg, § 20.2041–1(b)(1).

eral powers are not, with the exception that a nongeneral power of appointment created after October 21, 1942 may become taxable when exercised by creating another power of appointment.[11]

The section then proceeds to define the terms "general power of appointment" together with exceptions to the definition,[12] and the meaning of "lapse of a power",[13] and since the date of October 21, 1942 is crucial on the question of taxability, the date to be considered as the creation date of a power.[14]

It will be seen that the statute embraces many diverse questions. For ease of comprehension the component parts of the statute will be treated severally in the succeeding sections.

§ 162. Schedule H; Powers of Appointment; Evolution of the Statute.

The manner in which the present statute taxing powers of appointment evolved will be found helpful to an understanding of the subject. The first statute in 1916 contained no reference to powers of appointment, and an attempt to subject the property subject to the power to taxation on the theory that the exercise of a general power is a disposition of property in which the decedent has an interest equivalent to ownership, was unsuccessful.[15] The Revenue Act of 1918 contained a provision taxing property passing under general powers of appointment exercised by the decedent.[16] Under that statute it was held that property did not *pass* within the meaning of the statute if the beneficiaries took under the will of the donor,[17] but was taxable if the property was received under the exercise of the power.[18] Thus it was only the *exercise* of a *general power* of appointment which subjected to tax.

This was the law until 1942, in which year the Revenue Act was amended so as to tax powers, whether exercised or not, with the exception that powers created prior to October 21, 1942 were not taxable if they were special powers and were not exercised, or if they were general powers and were released prior to January 1, 1943, or the donee died before that date without exercising

11. IRC, § 2041(a) (1954 Code).
12. IRC, § 2041(b)(1) (1954 Code).
13. IRC, § 2041(b)(2) (1954 Code).
14. IRC, § 2041(b)(3) (1954 Code).
15. US v Field, 255 US 257, 65 L ed 617, 41 S Ct 256 (1921).

16. Rev Act of 1918, § 402(e).
17. Helvering v Grinnell, 294 US 153, 79 L ed 825, 55 S Ct 354 (1935).
18. Rogers v Helvering, 320 US 410, 88 L ed 134, 64 S Ct 172 (1943).

the power. The cut-off date was extended from year to year until 1951. Powers created after October 21, 1942 were taxed only if they were general powers. There were also excepted certain powers limited in their exercise or in which the donee's power was nonbeneficial.[19] Taxability under that statute did not depend either upon the fact that a power was general or special, or exercise or nonexercise, but solely on the decedent possessing the power at his death.

The statute presented so many complexities in its operation that it prompted Congress in the Powers of Appointment Act of 1951[20] to substantially abandon the taxation of unexercised powers created prior to October 21, 1942.[1] As the Senate Finance Committee Report noted, the then law was artificial and complicated to apply and tended to force property dispositions into narrow and rigid patterns.[2] The Internal Revenue Code of 1954 substantially re-enacted Section 811(f) of the 1939 Code in present Section 2041.

The present statute eliminates taxation of unexercised powers created *before 1942*, by providing that they shall be taxable only if they are *general* and are *exercised*. Powers are divided into general and nongeneral, and those created before October 21, 1942 and after that date.[3] It applies to the estates of persons dying after October 21, 1942. The statute is a codification of the law as it existed prior to 1942, so far as powers created before that date, but differs in its treatment of unexercised powers, in that renunciation by the appointee will not relieve from tax.

§ 163. Schedule H; Powers of Appointment; Constitutionality.

As in the case of many other sections of the Estate Tax Law, the taxation of powers of appointment was attacked upon the ground that a particular statute violated the Constitution. It was held that taxation resulting from the exercise of a power created prior to the taxing statute was invalid.[4] The attack was unsuccessful. Subjecting property passing under a power of

19. IRC, § 811(f) (1939 Code) as amended by § 403(a) Rev Act of 1942.

20. PL 58, 82nd Congress, 1st Sess (HR 2084) approved June 28, 1951.

1. IRC, § 811(f) (1939 Code) as amended by note 20, supra.

2. Sen Fin Comm Report, 1942–2 CB 674.

3. IRC, § 2041 (1954 Code).

4. Lee v Comm, 57 F2d 399 (DC App), cert den 286 US 563, 76 L ed 1295, 52 S Ct 645 (1932).

appointment exercised by will to estate taxation was held not violative of due process.[5]

§ 164. Schedule H; Powers of Appointment; Definition.

The statute provides that the value of the gross estate shall include the value of all property (except real property situated outside of the United States)

(1) To the extent to which a *general power* of appointment created on or before October 21, 1942, is exercised by the decedent—[6]

(2) To the extent of any property with respect to which the decedent had at the time of his death a *general power* of appointment created after October 21, 1942 * * * * * * * *.[7]

The first determinant of taxability, therefore, is whether the decedent has at any time had a general power of appointment. There is a single exception, limited in its application to a single state, which is discussed hereafter.[8]

The statute then defines the term "general power of appointment" to mean a power which is exercisable in favor of (a) the decedent, (b) his estate, (c) his creditors, or (d) the creditors of his estate. *There is excepted from the definition certain powers which might otherwise be considered general powers and which are treated in the succeeding section.*

The term "power of appointment" includes all powers which are in substance and effect powers of appointment regardless of the nomenclature used in creating the power and regardless of local property law connotations.[9] For example, if a trust instrument provides that the beneficiary may appropriate or consume the principal of the trust, the power to consume or appropriate is a power of appointment. Similarly, the power given to a decedent to affect the beneficial enjoyment of trust property or its income by altering, amending or revoking the trust instrument or terminating the trust is a power of appointment. If the community property laws of a State confer upon the wife a power of testamentary disposition over property in which she does not have a vested interest she is considered as having a power of appointment. A power in a donee to remove or dis-

---

5. Stratton v US, 50 F2d 48 (CCA 1), cert den 284 US 651, 76 L ed 552, 52 S Ct 31 (1931); see also Wooster, 9 TC 742 (1947); Thompson v US, 148 F Supp 910 (1957).

6. IRC, § 2041(a)(1) (1954 Code).
7. IRC, § 2041(a)(2) (1954 Code).
8. § 167, infra.
9. Note 10, supra; note 18, supra.

charge a trustee and appoint himself, may be a power of appointment. For example, if under the terms of a trust, the trustee or his successor has the power to appoint the principal of the trust for the benefit of individuals including himself, and the decedent has the unrestricted power to remove or discharge the trustee at any time and appoint any other person or class which could include himself, the decedent is considered as having a power of appointment. However, the decedent is not considered to have a power of appointment if he only had the power to appoint a successor, including himself, under limited conditions which did not exist at the time of his death, without an accompanying unrestricted power of removal. Similarly, a power to amend only the administrative provisions of a trust instrument, which cannot affect the beneficial enjoyment of the trust property or income, is not a power of appointment. The mere power of management, investment, custody of assets, or the power to allocate receipts and disbursements as between income and principal, exercisable in a fiduciary capacity, whereby the holder has no power to enlarge or shift any of the beneficial interests therein except as an incidental consequence of the discharge of such fiduciary duties is not a power of appointment. Further, the right in a beneficiary of a trust to assent to a periodic accounting, is not a power of appointment if the right of assent does not consist of any power or right to enlarge or shift the beneficial interest of any beneficiary therein.[10]

The Regulation states that the term "general power of appointment" as defined in the statute means any power of appointment exercisable in favor of the decedent, his estate, his creditors or the creditors of his estate, with the exceptions to be discussed hereafter.[11] A power of appointment exercisable to meet the Estate Tax, or any other taxes, debts, or charges which are enforceable against the estate is included within the meaning of a power of appointment exercisable in favor of the decedent, his estate, his creditors or the creditors of his estate. A power of appointment exercisable for the purpose of discharging a legal obligation of the decedent or for his pecuniary benefit is considered a power of appointment exercisable in favor of the decedent or his creditors. However, for purposes of §§ 20.2041–1 through 20.2041–3, a power of appointment is not treated as a general power of appointment merely by reason of the fact that

10. Reg, § 20.2041–1(b)(1).   11. Reg, § 20.2041–1(c)(1).

an appointee may, in fact, be a creditor of the decedent or his estate.

A power of appointment is not a general power if by its terms it is either—

(a) Exercisable only in favor of one or more designated persons or classes other than the decedent or his creditors (if the power is exercisable during life), or his estate or the creditors of his estate, or

(b) Expressly not exercisable in favor of the decedent or his creditors (if the power is exercisable during life), his estate, or the creditors of his estate.[12]

A decedent may have two powers under the same instrument, one of which is a general power of appointment and the other of which is not. For example, a beneficiary may have a power to withdraw trust corpus during his life, and a testamentary power to appoint the corpus among his descendants. The testamentary power is not a general power of appointment.[13]

A right to designate the beneficiary under a pension plan,[14] or the retention of the right to dispose of a trust fund by will, the donor and donee being the same person,[15] are powers of appointment. A power to fix values in connection with authority to distribute in kind may be construed to create a power of appointment in the trustee. Where under applicable local law the beneficiary, one of the trustees, may not participate in a decision to distribute trust principal to herself, neither she nor the trustee will be deemed to have a general power of appointment.[16]

Both the statutory definition and the examples in the Regulation have developed from much prior case law, much of it under the Gift Tax statute.[17] The theme of "beneficial enjoyment" and "beneficial interest" is recurrent, as well as decedent's control of such rights. It is again, essentially, the test of the "string"

12. Reg, § 20.2041–1(c)(1)(a)(b).
13. Note 11, supra.
14. GCM 27242, IRB 1952–1 CB 160.
15. Valentine, 21 BTA 197 (1930).
16. Rev Rul 54–153, IRB 1954–1 CB 185.
17. See Morgan v Comm, 309 US 78, 84 L ed 585, 60 S Ct 424 (1940); Comm v Solomon, 124 F2d 86 (CCA 3) (1941); Fidelity Trust Co v McCaughn, 1 F2d 987 (1924); Clauson v Vaughan, 147 F2d 84 (CCA 1) (1945); Johnstone v Comm, 76 F2d 55 (CCA 9), cert den 296 US 578, 80 L ed 408, 56 S Ct 89 (1935); Rose v McCaughn, 21 F2d 164 (CCA 3) (1927); Penn Co v US, 69 F Supp 577 (1947); Lee v Burnet, 57 F2d 399 (CA DC), cert den 286 US 563, 76 L ed 1295, 52 S Ct 644 (1932).

to the property, to which reference has been made in the case of lifetime transfers.

§ 165. Schedule H; Powers of Appointment; Exceptions to Definition.

After defining a general power of appointment as one exercisable in favor of the decedent, his estate, his creditors, or the creditors of his estate, the statute proceeds to except from that definition, three powers which would otherwise be considered general powers. The following, for purposes of the statute *shall not* be deemed *general powers* of appointment:

(1) A power to consume, invade, or appropriate property for the benefit of the decedent, which is limited by *an ascertainable standard* relating to the health, education, support or maintenance of the decedent.

(2) A power created *on or before October 21, 1942* exercisable only by the decedent *in conjunction with another person.*

(3) A power created *after October 21, 1942* only *in conjunction with another person, and*

(a) such other person is the creator of the power, *or*

(b) such other person has a *substantial interest* in the property, subject to the power, which is *adverse* to exercise of the power in favor of the decedent, a person who, after the death of the decedent has the power to appoint the property to himself, being deemed as having an adverse interest in the property.[18]

If such other person does not have a substantial adverse interest against the exercise of the power, it will be deemed a general power of appointment only in respect of a fractional part of the property subject to the power, determined by dividing the value of the property by the number of persons, including the decedent, in favor of whom the power is exercisable.[19]

The test of whether a power is exercisable in favor of such person is that for the determination of a general power of appointment.

The exceptions in turn present two terms which require definition, i.e., "ascertainable standard" and "adverse interest". The question of what is an ascertainable standard has been determined in many cases in connection with charitable gifts. It

18. IRC, § 2041(b)(1) (1954 Code).   19. IRC, § 2041(b)(1)(C)(iii).

has been construed to mean a standard which is fixed in fact and capable of being stated in definite terms of money.[20] Provisions which establish comfort, welfare or happiness as a standard have invariably been held insufficient to meet the test.[1] The Regulation provides that a power is limited by an ascertainable standard if the extent of the holder's duty to exercise and not to exercise the power is reasonably measurable in terms of his need for health, education, or support (or any combination of them). The words "support" and "maintenance" are synonymous. While their meaning is not limited to the bare necessities of life, and includes other reasonable living expenses, it does not necessarily extend to all expenditures that might be considered customary in the decedent's position in life. A power to use property for the comfort, welfare, or happiness of the holder of the power is not limited by the requisite standard. Examples of powers which are limited by the requisite standard are powers exercised for the holder's "support", "support in reasonable comfort", "reasonable comfort and support", "maintenance in health and reasonable comfort", "education, including college and professional education", "health", and "medical, dental, hospital and nursing expenses and expenses of invalidism". In determining whether a power is limited by an ascertainable standard, it is immaterial whether the beneficiary is required to exhaust his other income before a power can be exercised. The fact that the governing instrument gives the holder of a power discretion to determine amounts to be distributed under the power is not in itself an indication that the power is not limited by the requisite standard.[2] The Regulation codifies the results of many cases in which the question of what an ascertainable standard is has been determined.[3] But the fact that the words "comfort", "welfare" or other similar words are used is not

20. Merchant's Nat Bank of Boston v Comm, 320 US 256, 88 L ed 35, 64 S Ct 108 (1943).

1. Henslee v Union Planters Nat Bank & Trust Co, 335 US 595, 93 L ed 259, 69 S Ct 290 (1949); Industrial Trust Co v Comm, 151 F Supp 592 (CCA 1) (1945); Schumacher, 2 TCM 1018 (1943); note 20, supra.

2. Reg, § 20.2041-1(c)(2).

3. Jack, 6 TC 241 (1946); Runyan, 5 TCM 531 (1945); Briggs, 5 TCM 1114 (1945); Elmer, 6 TC 94 (1946); Jennings, 10 TC 323 (1948); Ithaca Trust Co v US, 279 US 151, 73 L ed 647, 49 S Ct 291 (1929); Comm v Wells Fargo Bank & Union Trust Co, 145 F2d 130 (CCA 9) (1944); Comm v Bank of America NTSA, 133 F2d 753 (CCA 9) (1943); Wells Fargo Bank v Comm, 145 F2d 132 (CCA 9) (1944); Berry v Kuhl, 174 F2d 565, (CA 7) (1949); Lincoln Rochester Trust Co v Comm, 181 F2d 424 (CA 2) (1950).

the sole indicia, so long as there are other words in the governing phrase which set an ascertainable standard.[4]

The second term which is used in connection with the exceptions to the definition of a general power of appointment is "substantial adverse interest", and refers only to powers created after October 21, 1942. Unlike the Income Tax statute[5] which defines an adverse party, the Estate Tax statute does not in terms define the phrase. But the Regulation points out examples of powers which are considered adverse. A taker in default of appointment has a substantial adverse interest, but not a permissible appointee or a co-holder of the power, except that a co-holder who may appoint to himself, his estate, his creditors, or the creditors of his estate, after the other co-holder's death has such an interest.[6] The term has been adjudicated in connection with revocable transfers, and the Regulation reflects the cases.[7] A trustee does not have an adverse interest.[8] An interest adverse to the exercise of a power is considered as substantial if its value in relation to the total value of the property subject to the power is not insignificant.[9] This is hardly a helpful definition of substantiality.

There is a further exception in the statute, but it does not relate to the definition of a general power of appointment. It deals with a *nongeneral* power and is discussed hereafter.[10]

§ 166. Schedule H; Powers of Appointment; Created Prior to October 21, 1942.

There is includible in the gross estate of a decedent any property with respect to which a *general power* of appointment *created on or before October 21, 1942, is exercised* by the decedent

(1) by will, *or*

(2) by a disposition which is of such nature that if it were a transfer of property owned by the decedent, such property would

---

4. See Berry v Kuhl, note 3, supra; Blodget v Delaney, 201 F2d 589 (CA 1) (1953).

5. IRC, § 672 (1954 Code).

6. Reg, § 20.2041–3(c)(2).

7. Reinecke v Northern Trust Co, 278 US 339, 73 L ed 410, 49 S Ct 123 (1929); MacKay v Comm, 94 F2d 558 (CCA 2) (1938); Comm v Flanders, 111 F2d 117 (CCA 2) (1940).

8. Reinecke v Smith, 289 US 172, 77 L ed 1109, 53 S Ct 570 (1933); Stewart, 28 BTA 256, revg 27 BTA 593, affd 70 F2d 696 (CCA 2), cert den 293 US 582, 79 L ed 678, 55 S Ct 96 (1934); Union Trust Co of Pittsburgh v Comm, 138 F2d 152 (CCA 3) (1943).

9. Note 6, supra.

10. § 167, infra.

be includible in the decedent's gross estate under Sections 2035 to 2038 inclusive.[11]

The subject of nonexercise[12] or release[13] of such powers is discussed hereafter, as well as the effect of disclaimer or renunciation of a power.[14]

Suffice it to say, that if the power of appointment was created *before October 21, 1942,* only if it is a *general power,* and only if it is *exercised,* is the property subject to the power includible in the gross estate of the decedent. A nongeneral power, whether created before or after October 21, 1942, will not cause the property subject to the power to be includible in the gross estate of the decedent, with the single exception that a nongeneral power created after October 21, 1942, if exercised by creating another power will result in taxability.[15]

§ 167. Schedule H; Powers of Appointment; Created Subsequent to October 21, 1942.

There is includible in the gross estate of a decedent any property with respect to which the decedent *has at the time of his death,* a *general power* of appointment *created after October 21, 1942,* or with respect to which the decedent has *at any time exercised or released* such power of appointment by a disposition which is of such a nature that if it were a transfer of property owned by the decedent, such property would be includible in the decedent's gross estate *under Sections 2035 to 2038,* inclusive. For purposes of the paragraph, the power of appointment is considered to exist on the date of the decedent's death, even though the exercise of the power is subject to a precedent giving of notice, or even though the exercise of the power takes effect only on the expiration of a stated period after its exercise, whether or not on or before the date of the decedent's death notice has been given or the power has been exercised.[16] Here again the reference is to a general power of appointment.

There is one instance in which a *nongeneral power* of appointment created after October 21, 1942 may become taxable. There is includible in the decedent's gross estate any property with respect to which the decedent (1) by will, or (2) by a disposition which is of such nature that if it were a transfer of property

11. IRC, § 2041(a)(1) (1954 Code).
12. § 170, infra.
13. § 171, infra.
14. § 172, infra.

15. See § 167, infra.
16. IRC, § 2041(a)(2) (1954 Code); Reg, § 20.2041–3(a)(b).

owned by the decedent such property would be includible in the decedent's gross estate under Sections 2035, 2036, or 2037, exercises a power of appointment created after October 21, 1942, *by creating another power* of appointment which under the applicable local law can be validly exercised so as to postpone the vesting of any estate or interest in such property, or suspend the absolute ownership or power of alienation of such property, for a period ascertainable without regard to the date of the creation of the first power.[17] The purpose of this provision is to prevent property being handed down from generation to generation without ever paying Estate Tax.[18] The statute is directed at powers created under the laws of Delaware, where the date of the exercise of a power determines the date of the beginning of the allowable period of suspension of alienation. The provision only applies where the nongeneral power is so exercised.

The subject of disclaimer or renunciation of a general power of appointment created after October 21, 1942 is treated hereafter.[19]

It will be observed that in the case of a general power of appointment created *after October 21, 1942,* unlike such power created prior thereto, it is only necessary that the power exist on the date of death, and that the decedent have such power. However, a power which by its terms is exercisable only upon the occurrence during the decedent's lifetime of an event or a contingency which did not in fact take place or occur during such time is not a power in existence on the date of the decedent's death. For example, if a decedent was given a general power of appointment exercisable only after he reached a certain age, or only if he survived another person, or only if he died without descendants, the power would not be in existence at the date of the decedent's death if the condition precedent to its exercise had not occurred.[20] The fact is, that in each of the examples above, the decedent does not have the power at the time of death. They are not cases such as are covered by the statute, where the decedent has the power, but it does not become effective until notice.

17. IRC, § 2041(a)(3); (1954 Code) Reg, § 20.2041-3(e).
18. Sen Fin Comm Report PL 58, 82nd Congress, June 28, 1951.
19. § 172, infra.
20. Reg, § 20.2041-3(b).

§ 168. Schedule H; Powers of Appointment; Date of Creation of Power.

A power of appointment created by a will executed on or before October 21, 1942, shall be considered a power created *on or before such date* if the person executing such will died before July 1, 1949, without having republished such will by codicil or otherwise after October 21, 1942.[1] This is an exception to the general rule that testamentary powers speak from the death of the testator. In all other cases the power will be considered created after October 21, 1942.

A power of appointment created by an inter vivos instrument executed on or before October 21, 1942, is considered as created after that date, if on that date the instrument was *revocable,* or was *amendable* in a manner which could substantially affect the terms of the power or the identity of its holders, other than by or with the consent of the holder of the power. However, a power is not considered as created after October 21, 1942, merely because the power is not exercisable or the identity of its holders is not ascertained until after that date. If the power is acquired by the holder by reason of the failure of some other person to exercise a power of appointment in such other person, or upon the happening of some event, contingency or condition, within the unrestricted control of some other person, including the settlor of a trust or the trustee, the power is not deemed to be created until the event, contingency or condition takes place or becomes fixed. However, where an irrevocably fixed power of appointment is acquired only by reason of the exercise of a right in the trustee, or his successor (other than the settlor), to appoint a successor or additional trustee (not consisting of a right to establish a power of appointment or to change the extent or quality of a previously existing power), the power will be deemed to be created when the power is fixed.[2]

§ 169. Schedule H; Powers of Appointment; Exercise.

We have seen that it is only as to powers of appointment created before October 21, 1942 that the question of exercise of the power is material, except in the case of the exercise of a nongeneral power by creating another power. In such cases

---

1. IRC, § 2041(b)(3) (1954 Code).
2. Reg, § 20.2041–1(e); see also Simmons v US, 135 F Supp 461, affd 227 F2d 168 (CA 2) (1955); Rev Rul 278, 1953–2 CB 267.

the question may arise whether the decedent exercised the power. The common law rule was that a power was not exercised by a will unless the intent to do so could be gathered from the will. In seventeen states[3] and the District of Columbia by statute a residuary clause is deemed to exercise a power. In the majority of states, the intent to exercise the power must be found from the instrument claimed to exercise it.[4] In Massachusetts[5] and Pennsylvania[6] in the absence of evidence to the contrary there is a presumption of intent to exercise.

The will may have been executed before the creation of the power. In such case, if the will contains a blanket exercise of powers, or purports to pass a property interest which is identifiable as an interest over which the donee had a power, or extraneous circumstances indicate an intent to exercise it, or there is a judicial or statutory presumption, the will will be deemed an exercise of the power. In the absence of any of the above it will not.[7]

The Regulation states that local law may determine whether a power has been exercised, but regardless of local law, a power of appointment is considered as exercised even though the exercise is in favor of the taker in default, and irrespective of whether the appointed interest and the interest in default are identical, or whether the appointee renounces any right to take under the appointment. A power is also considered as exercised even though the exercise cannot take effect until the occurrence of an event after the exercise takes place, if the exercise is *irrevocable* and, as of the time of the exercise, the condition was not impossible of occurrence. Thus, if property is left in trust to A for life, with a power in B to appoint the remainder by will, and B dies before A, exercising his power by appointing the remainder to C, in the event that C survives A, B is considered to have exercised his power if C survives B. On the other hand, a testamentary power is not considered as exercised if it is exercised subject to the occurrence during the decedent's

3. California, Kentucky, Maryland, Michigan, Minnesota, Montana, New York, North Carolina, North Dakota, Oklahoma, Pennsylvania, Rhode Island, South Carolina, South Dakota, Utah, West Virginia, Wisconsin.

4. Johnston v Knight, 117 NC 122, 23 SE 92 (1895).

5. King v Walsh, 250 Mass 462, 146 NE 33 (1925).

6. Provident Trust Co v Scott, 335 Pa 231, 6 A2d 814 (1940).

7. 5 American Law of Property, § 23.1 (1952).

life of an express or implied condition which did not in fact occur. Thus if in the example above, C dies before B, B's power of appointment would not be considered to have been exercised. Similarly, if a trust provides for income to A for life, remainder as A appoints by will, and A appoints a life estate to B and does not otherwise exercise his power, but B dies before A, A's power is not considered to have been exercised.[8]

§ 170. Schedule H; Powers of Appointment; Failure to Exercise; Lapse.

The statute provides that as to powers of appointment created *on or before October 21, 1942,* the *failure to exercise* such a power *shall not be deemed an exercise* thereof.[9] As to powers created *after October 21, 1942,* the *lapse* thereof during the life of the individual possessing the power *shall be considered a release* of such power, but only *to the extent, during any calendar year,* that the property which could have been appointed by exercise of such lapsed power, *exceeds* at the time of such lapse, *the greater of*

(1) $5,000, or

(2) 5% of the aggregate value, at the time of such lapse, of the assets out of which, or the proceeds of which, the exercise of the lapsed powers could have been satisfied.[10]

The above provision is aimed at unexercised annual powers of invasion. During the life of the donee, the failure to exercise the power of invasion will not subject to tax unless the extent to which invasion is permitted is more than $5,000 or 5% of the fund, whichever is greater.

Thus, a power to draw down $15,000 of principal annually from a fund of $200,000, if the power were not exercised, would require the inclusion in the donee's gross estate in the year of his death of the amount of $15,000, or such part thereof as had not been drawn during the year, *and in addition,* that portion of the appointive fund, in the proportion that the excess of the amount subject to withdrawal greater than $5,000, or 5% of the appointive fund valued in each year, bears to the total value of the fund in each year in which there is a lapse, each year being determined separately. The includible amount cannot exceed the value of the appointive fund.

8. Reg, § 20.2041–1(d).
9. IRC, § 2041(a)(1) (1954 Code); Reg, § 20.2041–2(d).
10. IRC, § 2041(b)(2) (1954 Code).

Since each lapse is treated as though the holder of the power had exercised dominion over the trust property by making a transfer of principal, reserving the income therefrom, that proportion of the trust property is includible in the decedent's estate.[11]

Thus, in the above situation, $15,000 would be includible in the decedent's estate, and in addition $2\frac{1}{2}\%$ of the value of the appointive property as of the applicable valuation date would also be includible in his gross estate, i.e., 5000/200,000, and a similar proportion based upon the greater of $15,000 or 5% of the fund in the particular year would be includible for each year of lapse.[12]

§ 171. Schedule H; Powers of Appointment; Release or Partial Release.

As we have noted, donees of general powers of appointment were afforded an opportunity to escape tax on the exercise of powers created *before October 21, 1942,* by releasing them so that they were no longer general powers.[13]   As to such general powers the statute provides that if before November 1, 1951, or within six months after the termination of a legal disability, the donee partially released such power so that it was no longer a general power of appointment, the subsequent exercise of such power shall not be deemed to be the exercise of a general power of appointment, nor shall the complete release, as in the case of a failure to exercise the power, be deemed an exercise thereof.[14]

With respect to powers of appointment created *after October 21, 1942,* there is includible in the decedent's gross estate any property with respect to which he released a general power of appointment by a disposition which is of such a nature that if it were a transfer of property owned by him, such property would be includible in his estate under Sections 2035 to 2038 inclusive.[15]

§ 172. Schedule H; Powers of Appointment; Disclaimer or Renunciation.

A disclaimer or renunciation of a general power of appoint-

11. Reg, § 20.2041–3(d)(3)(5).

12. Reg, § 20.2041–3(d)(4).

13. § 162, supra.

14. IRC, § 2041(a)(1) (1954 Code); Reg, § 20.2041–2(d)(e).

15. IRC, § 2041(a)(2) (1954 Code); see §§ 118 et seq, supra, as to circumstances under which §§ 2034–2038 apply; see also § 173, infra; Reg, § 20.2041–3(d).

ment created after October 21, 1942 is not deemed a release of such power.[16]

While in effect, a disclaimer or renunciation is a release of the right to exercise the power, the reason for the exception is that the donee of a power, particularly under an inter vivos trust, often does not learn that he has the power until long after the trust was created. Inter vivos trusts and wills frequently give powers of appointment to persons not born, or unascertainable, at the time when the trust was created. The framers of the Powers of Appointment Act of 1951 took cognizance of this fact and made provision therefor.

The statute does not so provide, but both the Regulation and the Senate Finance Committee Report on the 1951 Act both provide that the disclaimer or renunciation must be unequivocal and effective under local law. A disclaimer is a complete and unqualified refusal to accept the rights to which one is entitled. There can be no disclaimer or renunciation of a power after its acceptance. In any case where a power is purported to be disclaimed or renounced as to only a portion of the property subject to the power, the determination of whether or not there has been a complete and unqualified refusal to accept the rights to which one is entitled will depend on all the facts and circumstances of the particular case, taking into account the recognition and effectiveness of such a disclaimer under local law. Such rights refer to the incidents of the power and not to other interests of the decedent in the property. If effective under local law, the power may be disclaimed or renounced without disclaiming or renouncing such other interests. In the absence of facts to the contrary, the failure to renounce or disclaim within a reasonable time after learning of its existence will be *presumed* to constitute an acceptance of the power.[17] There is thus written into the Regulation a presumption which does not appear in the statute.

The Proposed Regulation contained the statement that a disclaimer of a power over only a portion of the property subject to the power was not a complete and unqualified refusal to accept the rights to which one was entitled. This was deleted from the final Regulation, and the question is now made to depend on the facts and circumstances of the particular case, taking into ac-

16. IRC, § 2041(a)(2) (1954 Code).   17. Reg, § 20.2041–3(d)(6).

count the recognition and effectiveness of such a disclaimer under local law.

§ 173. Schedule H; Powers of Appointment; Exercise or Release Taxable Under Other Sections.

It will have been noted that there is includible in the gross estate of a decedent not only property with respect to which the decedent exercised or released a power of appointment or possessed a power of appointment, but the statute also includes reference to "a disposition which is of such a nature that if it were a transfer of property owned by the decedent, such property would be includible in the decedent's gross estate under Sections 2035 to 2038, inclusive."[18] Thus, if the decedent exercised a general power of appointment created on or before October 21, 1942, or exercised or released a general power of appointment created after October 21, 1942, in contemplation of death,[19] or retained a life estate,[20] or the transfer was intended to take effect at death,[1] or he retained the right to alter, amend, revoke or terminate,[2] the property which was the subject of the exercise or release would be taxable in his estate.

The provisions of Sections 2035 to 2037 are also made applicable in the case of successive powers.[3]

It will be recalled that Section 2035 of the 1954 Code refers specifically to the relinquishment of a power, or exercise or release of a general power of appointment. The relinquishment of a power to alter, amend, revoke, or terminate is also specifically provided for in Section 2038.[4]

If a Gift Tax has been paid on the prior transfer there would be a Gift Tax credit to the estate.

§ 174. Schedule H; Powers of Appointment; Legal Disability.

As to a general power of appointment created on or before October 21, 1942, if it has been partially released so that it is no longer a general power, the exercise of such power shall not be deemed the exercise of a general power of appointment if the donee of such power was under a legal disability to release such

18. IRC, §§ 2041(a)(1)(B), 2041(a)(2) (1954 Code); see also IRC, § 2041(a)(3) (1954 Code); Reg, § 20.2041-2(c), § 20.2041-3(d).

19. §§ 121 et seq, supra; see Rev Rul 56-324, 1956-2 CB 999.

20. §§ 139 et seq, supra.

1. §§ 144 et seq, supra.

2. §§ 149 et seq, supra.

3. IRC, § 2041(a)(3) (1954 Code); Reg, § 20.2041-3(e).

4. See § 150, supra.

power on October 21, 1942, and such partial release occurred not later than six months after the termination of such legal disability.[5] We have discussed the matter of partial release previously.[6] Since persons under a legal disability on October 21, 1942, where such disability continued after the date on which they might have released the power tax free by reducing it to a nongeneral power, were unable to do so, the statute extends the period of release for them.

The legal disability referred to is determined under local law and may include the disability of an insane person, a minor or an unborn child. The fact that the type of general power of appointment possessed by the decedent actually was not generally releasable under the local law does not place the decedent under a legal disability within the meaning of the statute. In general, however, it is assumed that all general powers of appointment are releasable, unless the local law on the subject is to the contrary, and it is presumed that the method employed to release the power is effective, unless it is not in accordance with the local law relating specifically to releases, or, in the absence of such local law, is not in accordance with the local law relating to such transactions.[7]

Although in the absence of statutory authority it appears that all powers, general or special, and either presently exercisable or testamentary powers may be released,[8] there was some doubt, and many states adopted special legislation to remove any doubt.[9]

It is to be observed that the provision applies *only to pre-1942* general powers and not to those created thereafter.[10] Mental incapacity cannot be claimed to effect a partial release by implication,[11] nor can it be claimed, in the case of a post-1942 power that disability creates a limitation by an ascertainable standard.[12]

5. IRC, § 2041(a)(1)(B)(ii) (1954 Code).

6. § 171, supra.

7. Reg, § 20.2041-2(e).

8. 5 American Law of Property, §§ 23.26–23.28(1952).

9. Alabama, California, Colorado, Connecticut, Delaware, Florida, Georgia, Hawaii, Illinois, Indiana, Iowa, Kentucky, Maryland, Massachusetts, Michigan, Minnesota, Mississippi, New Hampshire, New Jersey, New York, North Carolina, Ohio, Oregon, Pennsylvania, Rhode Island, South Dakota, Texas, Virginia, Washington, West Virginia, Wisconsin.

10. See Reg, § 20.2041-3(b).

11. Simmons v US, 135 F Supp 461, affd 227 F2d 168 (CA 2) (1955).

12. Rev Rul 55–518, 1955–2 CB 384.

§ 175. Schedule H; Powers of Appointment; Amount Includible.

If a power of appointment exists as to part of an entire group of assets or only over a limited interest in property, the statute applies only to such part or interest. Thus if a trust created by S grants the income from the fund to A for life, then to B for life, with a power in A to appoint the remainder, and A dies before B, the section applies only to the value of the remainder reduced by W's life estate. If the power related to only half of the remainder, the section would apply to only half.[13]

In the case of powers created on or *before October 21, 1942,* if the power is exercised only as to a portion of the property subject to the power, the section is applicable only to the value of that portion. Thus, if the fund to which the power related was valued at $200,000 and the decedent exercised the power by appointing only $100,000, only that amount would be includible in his gross estate.[14]

Where the power is created on or *before October 21, 1942* and is exercised by a disposition making the property subject to Sections 2035 to 2038, the property to which the power is subject is valued and includible in the same way as are other taxable lifetime transfers.[15] If there is a lifetime exercise of part of the power, that part will be includible.[16]

The subject of the amount includible upon lapse of a power created *after October 21, 1942* has been discussed previously.[17]

In the case of successive powers, the value of the property subject to the second power of appointment is considered to be its value unreduced by any precedent or subsequent interest which is not subject to the second power.[18]

§ 176. Schedule H; Powers of Appointment; Summary of Taxability.

For ease of reference and testing of questions involving powers of appointment, the taxability for Estate Tax purposes of property subject to a power of appointment may be summarized as follows:

With a single exception, only *general powers* of appointment will subject to tax.[19] *Nongeneral* powers will not.

13. Reg., § 20.2041–1(b)(3).
14. Reg., § 20.2041–2(f).
15. § 157, supra; Reg., § 20.2041–2 (c).
16. Reg., § 20.2041–2(d).
17. § 170, supra.
18. Reg., § 20.2041–3(e).
19. § 161, supra.

[Harris]

A general power of appointment is one which is exercisable in favor of the (a) decedent, (b) his creditors, (c) his estate, or (d) the creditors of his estate,[20] *except* that

(a) a power so exercisable, which is limited by an *ascertainable standard, or*

(b) a *pre-1942* power exercisable by the decedent in *conjunction* with another person, *or*

(c) a *post-1942* power exercisable only by the *decedent* with the consent of the *creator of the power, or in conjunction* with a person having a *substantial adverse interest*[1] shall not be deemed a general power of appointment.

Property subject to a general power is includible in the decedent's gross estate, *if*

(1) It is a *pre-1942* power and is *exercised.*[2]

(2) It is a *post-1942* power and is *held* by the decedent *at his death.*[3]

(3) *Whether or not a general power* created after October 21, 1942 it is *exercised by creating another power.*[4]

(4) It is a *post-1942* power and *lapses,* but only to the extent such proportion of the appointive property valued at the applicable valuation date, as the amount of the power exceeds the greater of $5,000 or 5% of the fund, bears to the appointive fund in the year of lapse.[5]

(5) It is a *post-1942* power and the decedent *exercises or releases* the power under such circumstances that if it were a gift by the donee it would be taxable in his estate.[6]

§ 177. Schedule H; Powers of Appointment; Return.

The instructions for the preparation of Schedule H are excusably scanty. If the decedent *ever possessed* a general power of appointment, the executor is advised to examine the Regulations to ascertain whether the value of the property subject to the power is includible in the gross estate.[7] If the decedent *ever possessed* a power of appointment it must be examined to determine whether it was a general power, and whether it was ever exercised or released. It is also necessary to determine the date of the creation of the power.

20. § 164, supra.
1. § 165, supra.
2. § 166, supra.
3. § 167, supra.
4. Note 3, supra.
5. § 170, supra.
6. § 173, supra.
7. Instructions, Schedule H, Form 706.

The instructions further require that if the decedent *ever possessed* a power of appointment, a certified or verified copy of the instrument granting the power, together with a certified or verified copy of any instrument by which the power was exercised or released must be filed with the return. *These copies must be filed even though it is contended that the power was not a general power* of appointment, and that the property is otherwise not includible in the gross estate.[8] Note that *any power* of appointment possessed at any time must be reported. If it is claimed for any reason that it is not such as to require inclusion of the property subject to the power, the facts may be set forth in the return or an affidavit.

FORM NO. 21

Schedule H; Powers of Appointment

1a. Did the decedent, at the time of death, possess a general power of appointment created after October 21, 1942? [x] Yes [ ] No
1b. On or before such date? [x] Yes [ ] No
2a. Did the decedent, at any time, by will or otherwise, exercise or release (to any extent) a general power of appointment created after October 21, 1942? [x] Yes [ ] No
2b. On or before such date? [x] Yes [ ] No
3. Were there in existence at the time of the decedent's death any trusts not created by him under which he possessed any power, beneficial interest, or trusteeship? [x] Yes [ ] No

8. Note 7, supra.

Item No.	Description	Subsequent valuation date	Alternate value	Value at date of death
			$	$
1	Decedent was the donee of a power of appointment under the will of Winthrop Benson, Sr., to appoint a fund of $50,000 to his issue. Said will was admitted to probate in the Probate Court of Sussex County, New Jersey on the 20th day of March, 1950. Decedent appointed the said fund to his son James Benson. (See annexed Exhibits.) The Executrix contends that such power was a nongeneral power.			
2	Decedent was the donee of a power of appointment under Indenture of Trust, dated July 31, 1938, created by Winthrop Benson, Sr. Said power was not exercised by the decedent. (See annexed Exhibits.)			
3	Decedent was the donee of a power of appointment under the will of Grace Benson. Said will was admitted to probate in the Probate Court of Sussex County, New Jersey on the 31st day of August, 1956. Decedent released said power more than three years prior to his death and retained no interest of any nature therein. (See annexed Exhibits.) The Executrix contends that the property subject to such power is not includible in decedent's gross estate.			
4	Decedent was the donee of a general power of appointment under Trust Indenture created by Winthrop Benson, Sr. on June 8, 1940. Decedent partially released such power by release annexed hereto on March 2, 1950. (See annexed Exhibits.) The Executrix contends that such power was reduced to a nongeneral power.			

TOTAL (also enter under the Recapitulation, Schedule O) ...... $

(If more space is needed, insert additional sheets of same size)

§ 178. Schedule I; Annuities; Generally.

Prior to the Internal Revenue Code of 1954 there was no provision in the statute specifically referring to survivorship annuities, or other annuities under which further annuity payments were to be made to others after the death of the primary annuitant. They were taxed on the general theory that there was a shifting of economic benefits as the result of death.[9] This applied only if there was not consideration.[10] It was not clear,

9. Comm v Clise, 122 F2d 998 (CCA 9), cert den 315 US 821, 86 L ed 1217, 62 S Ct 914 (1941); Mearkle v Comm, 129 F2d 386 (CCA 3) (1942).

10. Hirsh v US, 35 F2d 982 (1929); Security Trust & Savings Bank, 11 BTA 833 (1928).

however, whether such annuities payable under pension plans or other employee's trusts were taxable.[11]

The 1954 Code specifically provides that the gross estate shall include the value of an *annuity or other payment* receivable by any beneficiary by reason of surviving the decedent under any form of contract or agreement entered into after March 3, 1931[12] (*other than as insurance under policies on the life of the decedent*), if, under such contract or agreement,

(1) An annuity or other payment was payable to the decedent, *or*

(2) The decedent possessed the right to receive such annuity or payment, *either alone or in conjunction with another*

(a) for his life, *or*

(b) for any period not ascertainable without reference to his death, *or*

(c) for any period which does not in fact end before his death.[13] Note the similarity of the phraseology to that taxing transfers with retained life estates.[14]

The statute then furnishes the rule for the determination of how much of such annuity shall be includible in the gross estate depending upon the decedent's contribution,[15] and a provision for exemption of such annuities in the case of certain employee plans.[16]

There should be noted that the section does not apply to an amount which constitutes proceeds of insurance under a policy on the decedent's life.[17] It also does not apply to annuities payable to the decedent during the life of another, annuities for a term of years, or refund annuities.[18]

§ 179. Schedule I; Annuities; Definition of Terms.

The term "annuity or other payment" as used with respect to both the decedent and the beneficiary has reference to one or

11. See Higgs v Comm, 184 F2d 427 (CA 3) (1950); Howell, 15 TC 224 (1950); Comm v Twogood, 194 F2d 627 (CA 2) (1952); Miller, 14 TC 657 (1950); Leoni, 7 TCM 759 (1946); Stake, 11 TC 817 (1948); Saxton, 12 TC 569 (1949); Hanner v Glenn, 11 F Supp 52, affd 212 F2d 483 (CA 6) (1953); GCM 27242, 1952–1 CB 160; Nevin, 11 TC 59 (1949).

12. The date fixed by the Technical Changes Act of 1953 for liability for tax of irrevocable transfers with income retained.

13. IRC, § 2039(a) (1954 Code).

14. IRC, § 2036(a) (1954 Code); see §§ 139 et seq, supra.

15. IRC, § 2039(b) (1954 Code); § 180, infra.

16. IRC, § 2039(c) (1954 Code); § 181, infra.

17. Reg, § 20.2039–1(a).

18. See § 111, supra; Reg, § 20.2039–1(d).

more payments extending over any period of time. The payments may be equal or unequal, conditional or unconditional, periodic or sporadic.

The term "contract or agreement" includes any arrangement, understanding or plan, or any combination of arrangements, understandings or plans arising by reason of the decedent's employment.

An annuity or other payment "was payable to the decedent", if at the time of his death, the decedent was in fact receiving an annuity or other payment, whether or not he had an enforceable right to have payments continued.

The decedent "possessed the right to receive" an annuity or other payment if, immediately before his death the decedent had an enforceable right to receive payments at some time in the future, whether or not, at the time of his death, he had a present right to receive payments.[19]

The term "for his life or for any period not ascertainable without reference to his death or for any period which does not in fact end before his death" has been previously treated.[20]

The Senate Finance Committee Report furnishes five illustrations of contracts to which the section applies, but not necessarily the only form of contracts to which it applies.

(1) A contract under which the decedent immediately before his death was receiving or was entitled to receive for the duration of his life an annuity, or other stipulated payment, with payments thereunder to continue after his death to a designated beneficiary if surviving the decedent.

(2) A contract under which the decedent immediately before his death was receiving or was entitled to receive, together with another person, an annuity, or other stipulated payment payable to the decedent and such other person for their joint lives, with payments thereunder to continue to the survivor following the death of either.

(3) A contract or agreement entered into by the decedent and his employer under which the decedent immediately before his death and following retirement was receiving or was entitled to receive an annuity or other stipulated payment, payable to the decedent for the duration of his life and thereafter to a

19. Reg, § 20.2039-1(b).   20. § 141, supra.

designated beneficiary, if surviving the decedent, whether the payments after the decedent's death are fixed by the contract or subject to an option or election exercised or exercisable by the decedent.

(4) A contract or agreement entered into by the decedent and his employer under which at the decedent's death, prior to retirement or prior to the expiration of a stated period of time, an annuity or other payment was payable to a designated beneficiary if surviving the decedent.

(5) A contract or agreement under which the decedent immediately before his death was receiving or was entitled to receive an annuity for a stated period of time, with the annuity or other payment to continue to a designated beneficiary, upon the decedent's death prior to the expiration of such period, if surviving the decedent.[1]

A combination annuity contract and life insurance policy may be subject to the section, depending upon whether there is any insurance element in the contract at the date of death. If there is none, and it has become a survivorship annuity, it will be. If the decedent dies before the terminal reserve value equals the death benefit, it will be taxed as insurance. If the decedent dies after the terminal reserve value equals the death benefit, it may be taxable as an annuity under the section, or may be taxable under some other provision of the statute.[2]

§ 180. Schedule I; Annuities; Amount Includible.

Not all of the value of a survivorship annuity is necessarily includible in the decedent's gross estate. The statute provides that subsection (a) shall apply to only such part of the value of the annuity or other payment receivable under such contract or agreement as is proportionate to that part of the purchase price thereof contributed by the decedent. Any contribution by the decedent's employer or former employer to the purchase price of such contract or agreement (whether or not to an employee's trust or fund forming part of a pension, annuity, retirement, bonus or profit-sharing plan) shall be considered to be contributed by the decedent *if made by reason of his employment*.[3] There is excepted from this provision contributions made by an

---

1. See also examples in Reg, § 20.-2039-1(b).

2. Reg, § 20.2039-1(d); see also § 152, supra.

3. IRC, § 2039(b) (1954 Code).

employer pursuant to "qualified plans", which is discussed in the succeeding section.[4]

There is embraced in the foregoing provision two situations. The first is where the decedent contributes part of the purchase price of a survivorship annuity with another person. If he contributed half of the cost, half of its value at his death would be includible in his gross estate.[5] The second is where both the decedent and his employer contribute to a fund to provide a retirement annuity for him for life, and a similar annuity to his designated beneficiary. If the plan is not a "qualified plan" the entire value of the annuity would be includible, and this would be so even if the entire contribution were made by the employer.[6] A contribution by the employer is considered made by reason of the decedent's employment if, for example, the annuity or other payment is offered by the employer as an inducement to employment, or a continuance thereof, or if the contributions are made by the employer in lieu of additional compensation or other rights, if so understood by employer and employee whether or not expressly stated in the contract of employment or otherwise.[7]

Contributions made by an employer pursuant to a pension, stock bonus or profit-sharing plan *qualified* under Section 401 (a) of the 1954 Code, or a retirement annuity contract *qualified* under Section 401(a)(3), (4), (5), (6) are not considered made by reason of the decedent's employment.[8] The Technical Amendments Act of 1958 amended the Code with respect to annuities by extending the benefits accorded other annuities under qualified plans, to annuities purchased by educational, charitable and religious organizations referred to in Section 503(b)(1), (2), or (3), and which are exempt from tax under Section 501(a).[8a] In such case there is excluded from the decedent's gross estate an amount which bears the same ratio to the value at the decedent's death of the annuity or other payment receivable by the beneficiary as the employer's contribution (or a contribution made on his behalf) to the plan on the employee's account, bears to the total contributions to the plan on the employee's account. Where there is a separate account kept of the contributions of

4. § 181, infra.
5. Reg, § 20.2039–1(c).
6. Note 5, supra.
7. Sen Fin Comm Report.
8. § 181, infra.

8a. IRC, § 2039(c)(3) (1954 Code), as added by Technical Amendments Act of 1958, § 23, HR 8381, 85th Cong, 2nd Sess.

the employer and employee the proportion is easily ascertainable. When this is not so, and the employer's contributions are not credited to the account of individual employees the Regulation explains the method of proration. If the value of the annuity at the time of the decedent's retirement was $40,000, and at the date of death his wife's annuity was valued at $16,000, and the decedent contributed $10,000 to the annuity, the employer's contribution is presumed to be the value at retirement, $40,000, less the employee's contribution of $10,000, or $30,000. There is thus excludible ($30,000 ÷ $40,000) × $16,000, or $12,000.[9] Where no part of the contribution is made by the employee to such a qualified plan, no part of the annuity is includible in his gross estate.[10]

The value of the annuity is determined in the same way as is provided for the valuation of such interests generally.[11]

§ 181. Schedule I; Annuities; Exemptions Under Qualified Plans.

It has become the policy of the Congress to encourage "qualified" employee benefit plans. The employer's contributions are deductible,[12] the pension or profit sharing trust is tax exempt,[13] and the employer's contribution is not taxable to the employee in the year of contribution, except to the extent that any part is used to purchase life insurance on the employee's life.[14]

In keeping with this policy, in the enactment of the provisions for the estate taxation of survivorship annuities it is provided that notwithstanding the provisions of Section 2039 or any provision of law, there shall be excluded from the gross estate the value of an annuity or other payment receivable by any beneficiary (other than the executor) under—

(1) An employee's trust (or under a contract purchased by an employee's trust) forming part of a pension, stock bonus, or profit-sharing plan which, at the time of the decedent's separation from employment (whether by death or otherwise), or at the time of termination of the plan if earlier, *met the requirements of Section 401a; or*

(2) A retirement annuity contract purchased by an employer (and not by an employee's trust) pursuant to a plan which, at

9. Reg, § 20.2039–2(c).
10. Reg, § 20.2039–2(b).
11. See §§ 112, 113, supra.

12. IRC, § 404(a) (1954 Code).
13. IRC, § 501(a) (1954 Code).
14. Rev Rul 55–747, 1955–2 CB 228.

the time of decedent's separation from employment (by death or otherwise), or at the time of termination of the plan if earlier, *met the requirements of Section 401(a)(3), (4), (5), (6).*[15]

The plans referred to in the section are designated "qualified plans", or, in the statutory language, have met the requirements of the provisions of the statute for exemption of income either as a trusteed or non-trusteed employees' benefit plan.

While the other subdivisions of Section 2039 apply only to the estates of persons dying on and after August 17, 1954, the provisions of subdivisions (c)(1) and (c)(2) are specifically made applicable to the estates of decedents dying after December 31, 1953,[16] while the provisions of subdivision (c)(3), which was added by the Technical Amendments Act of 1958,[16a] is applicable to the estates of persons dying after December 31, 1957.[16b] This latter subdivision also, as in the case of qualified plans, excludes from the gross estate the value of an annuity or other payment receivable by any beneficiary (other than the executor) under a retirement annuity contract purchased for an employee by an employer which is an organization referred to in Section 503(b)(1), (2), or (3), and which is exempt from tax under Section 501(a).[16c] The organizations referred to are educational, charitable and religious ones.

While the Proposed Regulation excluded from the exemption by implication, lump sum payments, and specifically, payments made upon insurance purchased by the trustee of a qualified plan, for the benefit of an employee, the Regulation as adopted reverses this position.[16d] The Proposed Regulation did not express the meaning or intent of the statute, which makes no such distinction.

The result of the exemption provided can be appreciable when the amount includible in the decedent's estate is compared in cases where all contributions are made by the employer to a qualified plan and one not qualified.[17]

15. IRC, § 2039(c) (1954 Code).

16. Note 15, supra.

16a. Technical Amendments Act of 1958, § 23, HR 8381, 85th Cong, 2nd Sess.

16b. Technical Amendments Act of 1958, § 23(g), HR 8381, 85th Cong, 2nd Sess.

16c. IRC, § 2039(c)(3) (1954 Code) as added by Technical Amendments Act of 1958, § 23(e), HR 8381, 85th Cong, 2nd Sess.

16d. Reg, § 20.2039-2(b), Examples 2, 3.

17. Compare Examples Reg, § 20.-2039-1(b) and Reg, § 20.2039-2(b).

The extent to which effect is given to the employer's contribution has been discussed previously.[18]

§ 182. Schedule I; Annuities; Return.

The instructions for Schedule I contain a summary of the Regulations. The value to the survivor is the value of the annuity immediately following the decedent's death.[19]

In describing an annuity, the name and address of the grantor of the annuity should be given, or if payable out of a trust or other fund, such a description as will fully identify it. If payable for a term of years, the duration of the term and the date on which it began should be given, and if payable for the life of a person other than the decedent, the date of birth of such person should be stated.[20]

Although the instructions do not so state, there may be much other information required to be furnished. If the annuity was purchased with funds partly contributed by the decedent, there should be proof of the respective contributions of the contributors. If the annuity is receivable under a qualified plan, a copy of the plan should be furnished together with information as to the time and place of qualification. When part of the annuity was purchased with the employer's contribution, there should be shown the respective contributions of the employer and employee. Computations of the includible or excludible amount may be set forth in an exhibit annexed to the return. In any particular situation all the information which the Estate Tax examiner will need to make his report should be furnished with the return.

FORM NO. 22

Schedule I; Annuities

1a. Was the decedent, immediately before his death, receiving an annuity
     as described in paragraph 1 of the instructions? [x] Yes   [ ] No
1b. If "Yes," was that annuity paid pursuant to an approved plan as
     described in paragraph 4 of the instructions? [x] Yes   [ ] No
1c. If the answer to "1b." is "Yes," state the ratio of the decedent's
     contribution to the total purchase price of the annuity.   28.6%

18. § 180, supra.   20. Note 19, supra.
19. Instructions, Schedule I, Form
706.

2a. If the decedent was employed at the time of his death, did an annuity or other payment as described in paragraph 3(d) of the instructions become payable to any beneficiary by reason of the beneficiary's having survived the decedent? [x] Yes [ ] No

2b. If "Yes," state the ratio of the decedent's contribution to the total purchase price of the annuity. None

Item No.	Description	Subsequent valuation date	Alternate value	Value at date of death
1	Decedent at his death was receiving an annuity from Winthrop Benson, Inc., 100 Main Street, Salina, Kansas for his life, and upon his death to Katherine Benson for life. (See annexed copy of plan).			
2	Decedent at the time of his death was employed by Winthrop Benson, Inc. There was receivable by Katherine Benson by reason of surviving the decedent an annuity of $5,000 per annum. Katherine Benson at the date of decedent's death was 50 years of age. (See annexed copy of annuity agreement). Value of annuity as per annexed computation			$74,243.00

TOTAL (also enter under the Recapitulation, Schedule O) $74,243.00

(If more space is needed, insert additional sheets of same size)

Estate of WINTHROP BENSON

Schedules H and I—Page 21

§ 183. Former Schedule I; Property Previously Taxed.

Prior to the Internal Revenue Code of 1954 a deduction was allowable for property previously taxed.[1] The details required for the computation were set forth in the schedule designated Schedule I. Under the 1954 Code there is no longer a deduction for property previously taxed, but there is a credit for taxes paid on prior transfers which will be treated hereafter.[2] However, the credit applies only to the estates of persons dying on and after August 17, 1954, while the provisions of the deduction for property previously taxed apply to the estates of persons dying prior thereto. Since there are such estates presently pending it will be necessary to explain the workings of the deduction which will be treated in the chapter dealing with computation of the tax.[3]

§ 184. Nonresidents Not Citizens; Gross Estate; Generally.

Unlike the 1939 Code, the 1954 Code defines the gross estate of every decedent nonresident not a citizen of the United States

1. IRC, § 812(c) (1939 Code).
2. § 315, infra.
3. §§ 276 et seq, infra.

as that part of his gross estate (determined as provided in Section 2031) *which at the time of his death is situated in the United States.*[4]

It will be noted that this differs from the case of a resident decedent which includes all property except real property situated outside of the United States. The "entire gross estate" wherever situated of a nonresident who was not a citizen of the United States at the time of his death is made up in the same way as the "gross estate" of a citizen or resident of the United States. As in the case of a citizen or resident of the United States it does not include real property situated outside the United States. However, in the case of a nonresident not a citizen, only that part of the entire gross estate which is *situated in the United States* is included in his taxable estate. In fact, property situated outside the United States need not be disclosed on the return unless certain deductions are claimed or information is specifically requested.[5]

There is thus presented as the test of inclusion whether property is situated within the United States[6] or without the United States.[7]

It having been held that a citizen of the United States who at the time of his death was domiciled in the Virgin Islands was not a citizen of the United States for the purpose of the Estate Tax,[7a] there has been added to the 1954 Code a provision[7b] to overcome this decision. The new section provides that a decedent who was a citizen of the United States and a resident of a possession thereof at the time of his death shall, for purposes of the Estate Tax, be considered a "citizen" of the United States within the meaning of that term wherever used in the Estate Tax statute *unless* he acquired his United States citizenship solely by reason of (1) his being a citizen of such possession of the United States, or (2) his birth and residence within such possession of the United States. *The provision applies only to estates of decedents dying on and after September 2, 1958.* The effect is that a United States citizen who moves from the United States to one of the possessions will be treated for Estate Tax

---

4. IRC, § 2103 (1954 Code).

5. Reg, § 20.2103–1.

6. § 185, infra.

7. § 186, infra.

7a. Fairchild, 24 TC 408 (1956); see also Smallwood, 11 TC 740 (1949);

Rivera, 214 F2d 60 (CA 2), affg 19 TC 271 (1954).

7b. IRC, § 2208 (1954 Code), added by Technical Amendments Act of 1958, § 102(a), HR 8381, 85th Cong, 2nd Sess.

purposes in the same manner in which he would have been treated if he had remained in the United States.

§ 185. Nonresidents Not Citizens; Property within the United States.

It is provided that for purposes of Subchapter B of Chapter 11, the provisions dealing with the estates of nonresidents not citizens,

(1) Shares of stock owned and held by such decedents shall be deemed property within the United States *only if issued by a domestic corporation.*

(2) Any property of which the decedent has made a transfer, by trust or otherwise, within the meaning of Sections 2035 to 2038, inclusive, shall be deemed to be situated in the United States, if so situated *either at the time of transfer or at the time of the decedent's death.*[8]

The 1954 Code retained the rule that stock of domestic corporations, no matter where physically located, was deemed situated within the United States,[9] but changed the rule that stock of foreign corporations if physically located here, were so situated.[10] Under the present statute, stock of foreign corporations, *no matter where situated* are not property within the United States. The change was motivated by the desire to conform to the tax conventions the United States has entered into with many countries and to remove any deterrent to the use of United States banks and trust companies as depositories.[11]

The Regulation expands upon the subject, as the statute refers to only two kinds of property and presents no other criteria. Property of a nonresident who was not a citizen of the United States at the time of his death is considered to be situated in the United States if it is—

(1) Real property located in the United States.[12]

(2) Tangible personal property located in the United States,[13] except certain works of art on loan for exhibition.[14]

(3) Written evidence of intangible personal property which

8. IRC, § 2104 (1954 Code).

9. Nienhuys, 17 TC 1149 (1952); Verderhoeck, 4 TC 125 (1944).

10. Burnet v Brooks, 288 US 378, 77 L ed 844, 53 S Ct 457 (1933); First Nat Bank of Boston v Comm, 63 F2d 685 (CCA 1) (1933).

11. House Committee Report on IRC § 2104 (1954 Code).

12. Johnstone, 19 TC 44 (1952).

13. See Delaney v Murchie, 177 F2d 444 (CA 1) (1949); Rev Rul 55-143, 1955-1 CB 455.

14. IRC, § 2105(c) (1954 Code).

is treated as being the property itself, such as a bond for the payment of money, if physically located in the United States,[15] except obligations of the United States[16] (but not its instrumentalities)[17] issued before March 1, 1941, *if the decedent was not engaged in business in the United States at the time of his death.*

(4) Intangible personal property the written evidence of which is not treated as being the property itself (other than corporate shares,[18] amounts receivable as insurance on the decedent's life,[19] and moneys deposited in the United States with any person carrying on the banking business),[20] if it is issued by or enforceable against a resident of the United States or a domestic corporation or governmental unit.[1]

(5) Shares of stock issued by a domestic corporation, regardless of the location of the certificates.[2]

(6) Moneys deposited in the United States with any person carrying on the banking business by or for the decedent,[3] *if the decedent was engaged in business in the United States at the time of his death.*[4]

Property of which the decedent has made a transfer taxable under Sections 2035 through 2038 is deemed to be situated in the United States if it is determined under the provisions above, to be so situated either at the time of transfer or at the time of the decedent's death.[5]

The situs rules described in the Regulation may be modified for various purposes under the provisions of an applicable death duty convention with a foreign country.[6] There are presently in effect Death Tax Conventions with twelve countries[7] and others pending with ten others.[8] These establish situs rules which should be consulted when estates of nonresident aliens who are

15. Note 10, supra; Equitable Trust Co of NY, 31 BTA 329 (1934).

16. Jandorf v Comm, 171 F2d 464 (CA 2) (1948); IRC, § 2106(c) (1954 Code).

17. Resch, 20 TC 171 (1953); Worthington, 18 TC 796 (1952).

18. IRC, § 2104(a) (1954 Code).

19. IRC, § 2105(a) (1954 Code).

20. IRC, § 2105(b) (1954 Code).

1. Todd v US, 46 F2d 589 (1930); Rosenblum v Anglim, 135 F2d 512 (CCA 9) (1943); Wodehouse, 19 TC 487 (1953).

2. Note 18, supra.

3. IRC, § 2105(b) (1954 Code).

4. Reg, § 20.2104–1(a).

5. Reg, § 20.2104–1(b).

6. Reg, § 20.2104–1(c).

7. Australia, Canada, Finland, France, Greece, Ireland, Italy, Japan, Norway, South Africa, Switzerland, United Kingdom.

8. Mexico, Philippines, Colombia, Brazil, Cuba, Argentina, Uruguay, Israel, Austria, Belgium.

citizens or subjects of such countries are involved. U. S. Treasury Department Internal Revenue Service Publication No. 228 contains an outline of Death Duty and Gift Tax Treaties which will be found helpful.

§ 186. Nonresidents Not Citizens; Property without the United States.

The statute provides that for the purposes of Subchapter B of Chapter 11, there shall not be deemed property within the United States of a nonresident not a citizen, (a) the amount receivable as insurance on his life, (b) any moneys deposited with any person carrying on the banking business, by or for such alien, *if the latter was not engaged in business in the United States at the time of his death,* and (c) works of art on loan for exhibition, under specific conditions.[9]

The Regulation enumerates property which is considered to be situated outside of the United States, as

(a) Tangible personal property located outside the United States.

(b) Works of art owned by the decedent if they were—

(1) Imported into the United States solely for exhibition purposes,

(2) Loaned for those purposes to a public gallery or museum, no part of the net earnings of which inures to the benefit of any private shareholder or individual, and

(3) At the time of the death of the owner, on exhibition, or en route to or from exhibition, in such a public gallery or museum.

(c) Written evidence of intangible personal property which is treated as being the property itself, such as a bond for the payment of money, *if it is not physically located in the United States.*

(d) Obligations of the United States issued before March 1, 1941, even though physically located in the United States, *if the decedent was not engaged in business in the United States at the time of his death.*

(e) Intangible personal property the written evidence of which is not treated as being the property itself (other than corporate shares, amounts receivable as insurance on the decedent's

---

9. IRC, § 2105 (1954 Code).

life, and moneys deposited in the United States with any person carrying on the banking business), if it is not issued by or enforceable against a resident of the United States or a domestic corporation or governmental unit.

(f) Shares of stock issued by a corporation which is not a domestic corporation, *regardless of the location of the certificates.*

(g) Amounts receivable as insurance on the decedent's life.

(h) Moneys deposited in the United States with any person carrying on the banking business by or for the decedent, *if the decedent was not engaged in business in the United States at the time of his death.*[10]

It will be observed that the Regulation with respect to property without the United States is a combination of the statutory provisions and the converse of many of the statements in the Regulation treating property within the United States.

The largest amount of litigation has involved moneys deposited with any person carrying on the banking business. Thus it has been held that moneys deposited in an agency account,[11] in a custody account,[12] in a customer's ledger account,[13] assets converted into cash and held on deposit,[14] deposits made by a prior decedent which the decedent inherited,[15] moneys deposited with an express company,[16] deposited by another for the decedent,[17] held by the City Treasurer,[18] trust funds held in an account for the decedent,[19] and cash on deposit representing an undistributed interest in an estate, where the amount to which the decedent was entitled was determined,[20] were not includible in the alien's estate. On the other hand loans made to a partnership,[1] funds held in an active trust for the benefit of an alien,[2] moneys held in trust where the consent of the trustee was required for withdrawal,[3] funds on deposit in savings and loan

10. Reg, § 20.2105–1.
11. Gade, 10 TC 585 (1948); Melotte, 7 TCM 208 (1946).
12. Letter of Deputy Comm, Mar 7, 1944.
13. Forni, 47 BTA 76 (1942).
14. Davey, 10 TC 515 (1948).
15. DeEissengarthen, 10 TC 1277 (1948); Bradford-Martin, 18 TC 544 (1952).
16. Rev Rul 54–14, 1954–1 CB 204.
17. Weiss, 6 TC 227 (1946).

18. Joachim, 22 TC 875 (1954).
19. DeGuebriant, 14 TC 611 (1950), revd on other grounds 186 F2d 307 (CA 2) (1951).
20. Worthington, 18 TC 796 (1952).
1. Todd v US, 46 F2d 589 (1931).
2. Loewenstein, 17 TC 60 (1952).
3. City Bank Farmers Trust Co v Pedrick, 168 F2d 618 (CCA 2), cert den 335 US 898, 93 L ed 433, 69 S Ct 300 (1948).

associations,[4] funds in a safe deposit vault,[5] and moneys on deposit with the Treasurer of the United States, as successor to the Alien Property Custodian, who held such funds under the vesting provisions,[6] have all been held not within the exemption of the statute. The words "by and for" in the alternative, as used in the statute is construed to mean that when money is deposited either by a nonresident for the benefit of himself, or by a third person for the benefit of a nonresident, exemption is available if all the other requirements are satisfied.[7]

It will be noted that the requirement that the decedent be not engaged in business in the United States at the time of his death, applies only to subdivisions (d) and (h) above. Whether he was so engaged is a question of fact which has been adjudicated in a number of cases.[8]

There has been discussed previously the question of real estate situated outside the United States.[9] Bonds, even though of domestic corporations, held abroad,[10] the proceeds of insurance,[11] and obligations of the United States issued before March 1, 1941[12] are not includible, provided the other provisions of the statute are met.

§ 187. Nonresidents Not Citizens; Return.

In the case of a resident, whether citizen or alien, the Estate Tax Return required to be used is Form 706.[13] But in the case of a nonresident not a citizen, whether that form is to be used or Form 706NA depends upon whether any of the following circumstances exist:

(a) If the decedent made any transfer during his lifetime (without an adequate and full consideration in money or money's worth) of property of the value of $5,000 or more, any part of which was situated in the United States either at the time of the transfer or at the time of death.

(b) If there were in existence at the time of the decedent's

4. Rev Rul 54–624, 1954–2 CB 16; This does not include savings banks, Rev Rul 54–623, 1954–2 CB 14.

5. Rev Rul 55–143, 1955–1 CB 465.

6. Rev Rul 56–421, 1956–2 CB 602.

7. Swan v Comm, 247 F2d 144 (CA 2), revg 24 TC 829 (1957).

8. See Turner v McCuenn, 2 USTC ¶572 (1930); Banac v Comm, 17 TC 748 (1951); Pinchot v Comm, 113 F2d

718 (CCA 2) (1940); Tarafa y Armas, 37 BTA 19 (1938); Rev Rul 56–52, 1956–1 CB 448.

9. § 43, supra.

10. Holsten, 36 BTA 568 (1936); Tarafa y Armas, note 8, supra.

11. Nienhuys, 17 TC 1149 (1952).

12. Jandorf v Comm, 171 F2d 464 (CA 2) (1948).

13. Reg, § 20.6018–1(a).

death any trusts created by him during his lifetime, any part of the property of which was situated in the United States either at the time the trust was created or at the time of death.

(c) If the decedent at the time of his death, possessed a general power of appointment over property situated in the United States or, at any time, by will or otherwise, exercised or released such a power.

(d) If a deduction is taken for the value of property of the gross estate transferred by the decedent for public, religious, charitable, scientific, literary, or educational purposes to corporations or associations created or organized in the United States or to trustees for use within the United States.

(e) If credit is taken for United States Gift Tax paid by or on behalf of the decedent in respect of property included in the part of the gross estate situated within the United States.

(f) If credit is taken for United States Estate Tax paid in connection with the transfer of property to the decedent from a transferor who died within a period of 10 years before (or 2 years after) the decedent.

(g) If the decedent was a resident of France or a citizen or resident of Greece and a prorated allowance authorized by treaty extends beyond the specific exemption, such as a prorated deduction for a bequest to a foreign charity.[14]

If any one of the above circumstances is found in the estate of a nonresident not a citizen of the United States, Form 706, the same form, the details of which we have been discussing in this chapter, must be used. If they are not, then Form 706NA, which is a single sheet, may be used. This is the form which is used in the greater number of estates.

In listing property within the United States, the same method is used as in listing property of a resident. The instructions for preparation of the return are very complete and list property which is and is not considered situated in the United States. Values must be substantiated in the same way as in the case of a resident, and valuation must be in dollars.[15] There is also the right to elect alternate valuation.[16] The supplemental documents required to be filed with the return have been discussed previously.[17]

14. Instructions, Form 706NA
15. Note 11, supra.

16. IRC, §§ 2032, 2106(a)(2)(F)(1) (1954 Code).
17. See § 36, supra.

Since Form 706NA is a single double sheet, which contains the items of the gross estate, the taxable estate and the computation of the tax, the completed schedule will be found in the chapter on computation of the tax.[18]

§ 188. Missionaries in Foreign Service.

Missionaries duly commissioned and serving under boards of foreign missions of the various religious denominations in the United States, dying while in the foreign missionary service of such boards, shall not, by reason merely of their intention to permanently remain in such foreign service, be deemed non-residents of the United States, but shall be presumed to be residents of the State, the District of Columbia, Alaska, or Hawaii wherein they respectively resided at the time of their commission and their departure for such foreign service.[19]

18. § 326, infra.

19. IRC, § 2202 (1954 Code); Reg, § 20.2202-1.

CHAPTER 3

TAXABLE ESTATE

§ 189. Scope of Chapter.

In the preceding chapter we have dealt with all of the items of property in which a decedent may have had an interest which must be reported in the gross estate. In determining the tax which will be payable, however, that is merely the starting point, since we are interested in determining the amount of the estate upon which the tax will be paid. In arriving at that amount it is necessary to ascertain all the items which are allowable to reduce the gross estate. It is the purpose of this chapter to examine each of these items and thus arrive at the amount of the taxable estate.

§ 190. Taxable Estate; Definition.

The value of the *taxable estate* shall be determined by deducting from the value of the gross estate the exemption and deductions provided for in the statute.[1] Under the 1939 Code the term used was "net estate", but there is no difference in meaning between the two terms.

The taxable estate of a decedent who was a citizen or resident of the United States at the time of his death is determined by subtracting the total amount of the deductions authorized by the statute and the Regulations thereunder, from the total of the amounts which must be included in the gross estate. These deductions are in general as follows:

(1) An exemption of $60,000.;

(2) Funeral and administration expenses and debts (including certain taxes and charitable pledges);

(3) Losses from casualty or theft during the administration of the estate;

(4) Charitable transfers; and

(5) The marital deduction.[2]

§ 191. General Considerations.

In considering the matter of the statutory deductions the statutory definition controls[3] and not that under any general rule of law or statutes governing the administration of estates. There is no inherent right to a deduction, but the right must be found in the statute.[4] Whether deductions shall be allowed depends

1. IRC, § 2051 (1954 Code).
2. Reg, § 20.2051–1.
3. Porter v Comm, 288 US 436, 77 L ed 880, 53 S Ct 451 (1933).

4. US v Ramsay, 130 F2d 938 (CCA 10) (1942).

on legislative grace,[5] which is wholly within the power of Congress,[6] so that unless there is a clear provision authorizing a deduction it cannot be allowed.[7] One seeking a deduction must show that he comes clearly within the terms of the statute.[8]

While the statute permits the enumerated deductions if allowed by local law, it does not follow that all deductions allowed by local law are deductible for purposes of the Federal Estate Tax. If the statute does not provide for a particular deduction, it is not allowable, no matter what the local law is.[9] If it is, then the local law must be looked to for determination of whether a claim is proper.[10]

The fact that the exact amount of a deduction has not been finally determined at the time of audit does not mean that the deduction cannot be allowed. An item may be entered on the return for deduction though its exact amount is not then known, provided it is ascertainable with reasonable certainty, and will be paid. No deduction may be taken upon the basis of a vague or uncertain estimate.[11] Thus, commissions[12] and attorney's fees[13] are regularly estimated and allowed. If not determinable with reasonable certainty at the time, application may be made thereafter for refund.[14]

The Internal Revenue Code of 1954 made one substantial change in the provisions with respect to deductions. This was to permit the deductions enumerated in the statute although they exceeded the amount of the property in the estate subject to claims, provided they were paid before the expiration of the period for filing the return,[15] which is discussed in the following section. There was also provided in the Income Tax Law au-

5. Empire Trust Co v Comm, 94 F2d 307 (CCA 4) (1938); First Trust Co of St Paul v Reynolds, 46 F Supp 497, affd 137 F2d 518 (CCA 8) (1942); Conner v Bender, 125 F2d 796 (CCA 6) (1942).

6. Comm v Ames, 88 F2d 338 (CCA 7) (1937).

7. First Trust Co of St Paul v Reynolds, note 5, supra.

8. Empire Trust Co v Comm, note 5, supra.

9. Reg, § 20.2053–1(b); Goodwin v Comm, 201 F2d 576 (CA 6) (1953).

10. Towner v Comm, 182 F2d 903 (CA 2), cert den 340 US 912, 95 L ed 659, 71 S Ct 293 (1950); Nashville Trust Co v Comm, 136 F2d 148 (CCA 6) (1943); First Mechanics Nat Bank of Trenton v Comm, 117 F2d 127 (CCA 4) (1940); Vaccaro v US, 55 F Supp 932, affd 149 F2d 1014 (CCA 5) (1944); U. S. v Security First Nat Bank of Los Angeles, 30 F Supp 113 (1939).

11. Reg, § 20.2053–1(b)(3).

12. Larkin, 13 TC 173 (1949); Kaufman, 5 BTA 31 (1926); Loetscher, 14 BTA 228 (1928); Lohman, 6 TCM 1071 (1946); Burney, 4 TC 449 (1944).

13. Burney, note 12, supra; Lohman, note 12, supra.

14. Note 11, supra.

15. IRC, § 2053(b)(c)(2) (1954 Code).

thority for the deductions permitted under the Estate Tax Law to be taken as deductions thereunder. The fiduciary is therefore given an election to use the deduction for either Estate Tax or Income Tax, whichever will be most beneficial.[16]

§ 192. Deductions; Property Subject to Claims.

Prior to 1942, under the 1939 Code, deductions were allowed to the extent they were contracted bona fide for an adequate consideration and were allowable under local law. Therefore, when the amount of claims exceeded the probate or distributable estate, they were nonetheless allowed against the tax estate.[17] The Revenue Act of 1942 amended the Code to limit the deductions for administration expenses and claims to the amount in the estate subject to claims.[18]

This distinction was felt to be arbitrary, when administration expenses and claims were actually paid,[19] and the 1954 Code removed the limitation where the amounts are paid prior to the time prescribed for the filing of the Estate Tax return.

In the case of funeral expenses, administration expenses, claims against the estate, and unpaid mortgages on, or any indebtedness in respect to, property included in the gross estate there shall be disallowed the amount by which such deductions exceed the value, at the time of the decedent's death, of property subject to claims, *except to the extent that such deductions represent amounts paid before the date prescribed for the filing of the Estate Tax return.*[20]

In the case of other administration expenses, such as trustees' principal commissions and attorneys' fees in connection therewith, there shall be deducted such expenses incurred in administering property not subject to claims which is included in the gross estate to the same extent such amounts would be allowable as a deduction under subsection (a) of Section 2053 if such property were subject to claims, and such amounts are paid be-

---

16. IRC, §§ 642(g), 691(b) (1954 Code); see § 223, infra.

17. Comm v Hallock, 102 F2d 1 (CCA 6) (1939); Union Guardian Trust Co, 32 BTA 996 (1935); Comm v Strauss, 77 F2d 401 (CCA 7) (1935); Reichers, 9 TCM 403 (1947); Small, 1 TCM 885 (1942); Comm v Ames, 88 F2d 338 (CCA 7) (1937); Comm v Lyne, 90 F2d 745 (CCA 1) (1937).

18. IRC, § 812(b) (1939 Code) as amended by §§ 405(a) and 406(a) of Rev Act of 1942, effective October 22, 1942.

19. House Committee Report, § 2053 (1954 Code).

20. IRC, § 2053(c)(2) (1954 Code).

fore the expiration of the period of limitation for assessment provided in Section 6501.[1]

These provisions apply only to the estates of persons dying on and after August 17, 1954.

The term "property subject to claims" means property includible in the gross estate of the decedent which, or the avails of which, would under the applicable law, bear the burden of payment of such deductions in the final adjustment and settlement of the estate, except that the value of the property shall be reduced by the amount of the deduction for losses during administration attributable to such property.[2]

The Regulation furnishes examples of the operation of the statute. Thus, the only item in the gross estate is real property valued at $250,000. held by the decedent and his wife as tenants by the entirety. The property is not subject to claims under local law. Funeral expenses of $1,200. and debts of $1,500. are allowable under local law. Before the date for filing the return the widow paid the funeral expenses and $1,000. of the debts, and $500. of the debt after such time. There is allowable as a deduction only the $2,200. paid before the date for filing the return and not the $500. paid thereafter.[3]

The estate consisted of a bank account of $20,000. and insurance payable to the wife in the amount of $150,000., and the executor paid out of a total of $30,000. of funeral expenses and debts, $10,000. before the date for the filing of the return, of which $5,000. was contributed by the wife. Thereafter the executor paid the balance of the debts in the amount of $20,000. with the balance of the estate funds and $5,000. contributed by the widow. The total allowable deduction would be $25,000., the amount of the estate assets, $20,000., and the amount contributed and paid by the widow before the date for the filing of the return, i.e., $5,000.[4]

It should be noted that the limitation described above is made applicable to funeral expenses, administration expenses, claims against the estate, and mortgage or other property indebtednesses, and other administration expenses and not to other statutory deductions.

1. IRC, § 2053(b) (1954 Code).
2. Note 20, supra.
3. Reg, § 20.2053–1(c), Example 1.
4. Reg, § 20.2053–1(c), Example 2.

§ 193. Effect of Court Decree.

The statute provides that there shall be allowed as deductions for funeral expenses, administration expenses, claims, and mortgages such amounts as are allowable by the laws of the jurisdiction, whether within or without the United States, under which the estate is being administered.[5]

The Regulation states that the decision of a local court as to the amount and allowability under local law of a claim or administration expense will ordinarily be accepted if the court passes upon the facts upon which deductibility depends.[6] If the court does not pass upon those facts, its decree will, of course, not be followed.[7] For, example, if the question before the court is whether a claim should be allowed, the decree allowing it will ordinarily be accepted as establishing the validity and amount of the claim. However, the decree will not necessarily be accepted even though it purports to decide the facts upon which deductibility depends. It must appear that the court actually passed upon the merits of the claim.[8] This will be presumed in all cases of an active and genuine contest.[9] If the result reached appears to be unreasonable, this is some evidence that there was not such a contest, but it may be rebutted by proof to the contrary. If the decree was rendered by consent, it will be accepted, provided the consent was a bona fide recognition of the validity of the claim—and not a mere cloak for a gift—and was accepted by the court as satisfactory evidence upon the merits.[10] It will be presumed that the consent was of this character, and was so accepted, if given by all parties having an interest adverse to the claimant. The decree will not be accepted if it is at variance with the law of the state; as, for example, an allowance made to an executor in excess of that prescribed by statute.[11] On the other hand, a deduction for the amount of a bona fide indebtedness of the decedent, or of a reasonable expense of administration, will not be denied because no court decree has been entered[12] if the amount would be allowable under local law.[13]

5. IRC, § 2053(a) (1954 Code).

6. First Mechanics Nat Bank of Trenton v Comm, 117 F2d 127 (CCA 4) (1940).

7. Cross, 5 BTA 621 (1926).

8. Smith v US, 16 F Supp 397, affd 92 F2d 704 (CCA 1) (1936).

9. Goodwin v Comm, 201 F2d 576 (CA 6) (1953); Erickson v Smyth, 108 F Supp 412 (1952); Flick, 6 TCM 72.

10. Goodwin v Comm, note 9, supra.

11. See Fidelity Phila Trust Co v Smith, 135 F Supp 331 (1955).

12. Erickson v Smyth, note 9, supra.

13. Reg, § 20.2053–1(b)(2).

The word "allowable" in the statute does not mean allowed and paid.[14] It has previously been noted that the amount may be estimated.[15] Whether or not a claim is deductible depends upon allowance under state law, which in turn depends upon whether it is enforceable against the estate under the state law.[16]

§ 194. Exemption.

Before the enactment of the Internal Revenue Code of 1954 since there were two taxes, the basic tax under the 1926 Act[17] and the additional tax,[18] there were two exemptions. Under the basic tax there was an exemption of $100,000.,[19] and under the additional tax an exemption of $60,000.[20] These exemptions apply only to the estates of persons dying before August 17, 1954 who were citizens or residents of the United States.

The 1954 Code revised the method of computation of the tax and allows a single exemption of $60,000. in the estates of all citizens and residents of the United States who died on and after August 17, 1954.[1] This exemption is a specific exemption and is allowable to the estate, the amount thereof not depending on the relation of any beneficiary as in the case of exemptions allowable under certain state death tax laws.

Various exemptions existing under other Federal or state laws do not apply to the Estate Tax. Thus, bonds which may be exempt from other taxes such as state and municipal bonds,[2] United States savings bonds,[3] homestead rights,[4] Indian lands,[5] a widower's allowance,[6] or property set aside as an exemption for the benefit of the family,[7] are not exempt from the Estate Tax.

There is an exemption which applies to members of the Armed Forces dying during an induction period, which is discussed in the succeeding section.[8]

The specific exemption referred to, of $60,000., applies only to the *estate of a resident or citizen* who died on and after August

---

14. Comm v Lyne, note 17, supra.

15. § 191, supra.

16. Smyth v Erickson, 221 F2d 1 (CA 9) (1955); note 6, supra.

17. IRC, § 810 (1939 Code).

18. IRC, § 935 (1939 Code).

19. IRC, § 812(a) (1939 Code).

20. IRC, § 935(c) (1939 Code).

1. IRC, § 2052 (1954 Code).

2. Greiner v Lewellyn, 258 US 384, 66 L ed 676, 42 S Ct 324 (1922).

3. Mim 5202, 1941–2 CB 241.

4. Hinds, 11 TC 314 (1949).

5. Rev Rul 54–168, 1954–1 CB 182; Landman v Comm, 123 F2d 787 (CCA 10), cert den 315 US 810, 86 L ed 1209, 62 S Ct 799 (1941).

6. Jacobs, 8 TC 1015 (1947).

7. Waldman, 46 BTA 291 (1942); Faber, 40 BTA 1070 (1939); Mayer v Reinecke, 130 F2d 350 (CA 7), cert den 317 US 684, 87 L ed 549, 63 S Ct 257 (1942).

8. § 195, infra.

17, 1954. In the case of a nonresident not a citizen, there is a different exemption discussed hereafter.[9]

§ 195. Members of the Armed Forces.

While the "additional tax" to which we have referred has been eliminated for all other purposes, it is provided that the additional Estate Tax shall not apply to the transfer of taxable estates of citizens or residents of the United States dying during an induction period, while in active service as a member of the Armed Forces of the United States, if such decedent—

(1) was killed in action while serving in a combat zone, as determined under Section 112(c); or

(2) died as the result of wounds, disease, or injury suffered, while serving in a combat zone (as determined under Section 112(c), and while in line of duty, by reason of a hazard to which he was subjected as an incident of such service.[10]

"Induction period" means any period during which individuals are liable for induction, for reasons other than prior deferment, for training and service in the Armed Forces of the United States.[11]

Service is performed in a combat zone only—

(1) If it is performed in an area which the President of the United States has designated by Executive Order for purposes of Section 112(c) as an area in which the forces of the United States are, or have, engaged in combat, and

(2) It is performed on or after the date designated by the President by Executive Order as the date of the commencing of combatant activities in such zone and on or before the date designated by the President by Executive Order as the date of termination of combatant activities in such zone.[12]

If the official record of the branch of the Armed Forces of which the decedent was a member at the time of his death states that the decedent was killed in action while serving in a combat zone, or that death resulted from wounds or injuries received or disease contracted while in line of duty in a combat zone, this fact shall, in the absence of evidence establishing the contrary, be presumed to be established for the purposes of the exemption. Moreover, wounds, injuries or disease suffered while in line of duty will be considered to have been caused by a hazard to which

---

9. § 258, infra.
10. IRC, § 2201 (1954 Code).

11. Reg, § 20.2201–1(b).
12. Reg, § 20.2201–1(c).

the decedent was subjected as an incident of service as a member of the Armed Forces, unless the hazard which caused the wounds, injuries, or disease was clearly unrelated to such service.[13]

A person was in active service as a member of the Armed Forces of the United States if he was at the time of his death actually serving in such forces. A member of the Armed Forces in active service in a combat zone who thereafter becomes a prisoner of war or missing in action, and occupies such status at death or when the wounds, disease, or injury resulting in death were incurred, is considered for purposes of the section as serving in a combat zone.[14]

The exemption from tax granted by the section does not apply to the basic Estate Tax as defined in Section 2011(d).[15]

As the result of the statute, there would be no tax payable in the estate of such a person unless the estate exceeded $100,000., and if in excess of that amount, there would be an exemption of $100,000. and only the basic tax would apply. The section does not apply to civilians attached to the Armed Forces, but only to those technically and formally in the military or naval forces of the United States.[16]

§ 196. Schedule J; Funeral Expenses.

Though the specific exemption is deductible in determining the taxable estate, it is not technically a deduction, the first such named in the statute being that for funeral expenses.[17] The term is not limited in meaning to funeral, but includes a *reasonable* expenditure for a tombstone, monument or mausoleum, or for a burial lot, either for the decedent or his family, including a *reasonable* expenditure for its future care, provided such expenditure is allowable by local law. Included in funeral expenses is the cost of transportation of the person bringing the body to the place of burial.[18] This is a statement of prevailing case law.[19] The Regulation points out that such amounts for funeral expenses are allowed as deductions as are actually expended and would be properly allowable out of property subject to claims under the laws of the local jurisdiction. Thus, if perpetual care

13. Reg, § 20.2201–1(d).
14. Reg, § 20.2201–1(e).
15. Reg, § 20.2201–1(f).
16. Dupont, 18 TC 1134 (1952).
17. IRC, § 2053(a)(1) (1954 Code).
18. Reg, § 20.2053–2.

19. Tate v O'Malley, 52 F Supp 834 (1943); Lee, 11 TC 141 (1948); Comm v Cardeza, 173 F2d 19 (CA 3) (1949); Loeb v McCaughn, 20 F2d 1002 (1927); McGugan v Comm, 47 BTA 658 (1942); Audenried, 26 TC 120 (1956).

is not deductible under local law it cannot be allowed,[20] nor if the decedent was not buried in the plot.[1] Whether the amount expended is a reasonable amount is, of course, a question of fact in each case. What is and is not allowable as a funeral expense will be found substantially the same in most states, with some variances.

§ 197. Schedule J; Administration Expenses; Executors' Commissions.

Schedule J breaks administration expenses down into three categories; executors' commissions, attorneys' fees, and miscellaneous administration expenses. The statute refers only to administration expenses[2] and other administration expenses.[3]

The Regulation provides that the fiduciary, in filing the return, may deduct his commissions in such an amount as has actually been paid, or in an amount which at the time of the filing of the return may reasonably be expected to be paid, but no deduction may be taken if no commissions are to be collected. If the amount of the commissions has not been fixed by decree of the proper court, the deduction will be allowed on the final audit of the return, to the extent that all three of the following conditions are satisfied:

(1) The District Director is reasonably satisfied that the commissions claimed will be paid;

(2) The amount entered as a deduction is within the amounts allowable by the laws of the jurisdiction in which the estate is being administered; and

(3) It is in accordance with the usually accepted practice in the jurisdiction to allow such an amount in estates of similar size and character.[4]

The first thing to note is that the commissions of an executor need not have been paid, but may be estimated,[5] which is the usual procedure, since at the time of the audit of the return it would be a rarity for a decree to have been entered. The commissions must, however, be such as are allowable under state

20. Igleheart v Comm, 77 F2d 704 (CCA 5) (1935).
1. Gillespie, 8 TC 838 (1947); Rev Rul 57–530, IRB 1957–45, p 71.
2. IRC, § 2053(a)(2) (1954 Code).
3. IRC, § 2053(b) (1954 Code).
4. Reg, § 20.2053–3(b)(1).

5. Larkin, 13 TC 173 (1949); Kaufman, 5 BTA 31 (1926); Loetscher, 14 BTA 228 (1928); Nicholson, 21 BTA 795 (1931); Claiborne, 40 BTA 722 (1939); Lohman, 6 TCM 1071 (1946); Burney, 4 TC 449 (1944).

law where the estate is being administered.[6] There is a diversity of opinion on the question of whether commissions in excess of usual may be allowed when such commissions have been paid. Some courts have held that they are[7] and others to the contrary.[8] Where additional commissions have been allowed by the Probate Court for extraordinary services, they have been allowed as a deduction.[9] Prolongation of the period of administration may not be used to increase commissions.[10] Commissions are to be computed on the basis of rates prevailing at the date of the decedent's death[11] and there are not included commissions on income after death.[12] The amount allowed as a deduction by the state tax authorities is not controlling.[13]

A bequest or devise to an executor in lieu of commissions is not deductible. If, however, the decedent fixed by his will the compensation payable to the executor for services to be rendered in the administration of the estate, deduction may be taken to the extent that the amount so fixed does not exceed the compensation allowable by the local law or practice.[14]

If the deduction is allowed in advance of payment and payment is thereafter waived, it shall be the duty of the executor to notify the District Director and to pay the resulting tax, together with interest.[15] Where the commissions are waived, but the waiver is withdrawn a deduction will be allowed,[16] and where one executor waives and his share goes to the others, the entire amount will be allowed.[17]

When there is no necessity for administration, commissions paid cannot be deducted,[18] but this is not so where it is necessary to complete the fixation and payment of the tax.[19]

Where commissions have been allowed by the court having jurisdiction of the estate,[20] or are unpaid, but allowable by the

6. Lewis v Bowers, 19 F Supp 745 (1937); Voelbel, 7 BTA 276 (1927); Werbelovsky, 11 TC 525 (1948); Hartley, 5 TC 645 (1945).

7. Freed, 6 TCM 216 (1946); Cardeza, 5 TC 202, affd on other issue 173 F2d 19 (CA 3) (1949).

8. Fidelity Phila Trust Co v U. S. 122 F Supp 551, affd 222 F2d 377 (CA 3) (1954).

9. Howard, 2 TCM 1075 (1943).

10. Peckham, 19 BTA 1020 (1930); Jackson, 18 BTA 875 (1929).

11. Lewis v Bowers, note 6, supra.

12. Note 11, supra; Levy, BTA memo op Dec 11, 740-G (1941), but see Hubbard, 26 TC 183 (1956).

13. Audenried, 26 TC 120 (1956).

14. Reg, § 20.2053-3(b)(2); see Moore, 5 BTA 255 (1926).

15. Reg, § 20.2053-3(b)(1).

16. Siegel, BTA memo op Dec 10, 464-B (1938).

17. Burney, note 5, supra.

18. Chapman, 8 BTA 1071 (1927).

19. Helis, 26 TC 143 (1956).

20. Power, 11 BTA 1313 (1928); Henry, 7 BTA 172 (1927); Hunt, 12

laws of that jurisdiction,[1] they will be deductible, but there must be proof of the amount.[2]

Two statements in the instructions for Schedule J bear emphasis. "If the commissions claimed have not been paid at the time of the final audit of the return, the amount deducted must be supported by an affidavit, or statement signed under the penalties of perjury, of the executor, stating that such amount has been agreed upon and will be paid." "Executors should note that executors' commissions constitute taxable income and that the amounts received or receivable by them as such compensation are cross-referenced for Income Tax purposes."[3] This is a polite reminder that if a fiduciary takes a deduction for commissions he had better remember to return the amount in his Income Tax return. The usual procedure is for the Estate Tax examiner to request such an affidavit.

FORM NO. 23

Affidavit for Allowance of Executors' Commissions

U. S. TREASURY DEPARTMENT
INTERNAL REVENUE SERVICE
FIRST DISTRICT OF NEW YORK

In the Matter of the Estate Tax
on the Estate of
    WINTHROP BENSON,
            Deceased.

STATE OF NEW YORK $\Big\}$ ss:
COUNTY OF NEW YORK

KATHERINE BENSON, being duly sworn, says: I am the Executrix under the Last Will and Testament of the above named decedent, having duly qualified and am presently acting as such.

That I have been advised by my attorney that the statutory commissions to which I shall be entitled as Executrix is the sum of $6,533.87.

That I reasonably expect that said commissions which have been agreed upon, will be paid to me during the year 1959. That I shall file, if my

BTA 396 (1928); Huntington, 36 BTA 698 (1937); Vaughan, 10 BTA 140 (1928).

1. Goldschmidt, 14 BTA 1010 (1929); Larkin, note 5, supra; Degener, 26 BTA 185 (1932); Sweeney, 15 BTA 1287 (1929); Lamport, 28 BTA 862 (1933); Leewitz v U. S. 75 F Supp 312 (1948); Bensel, 36 BTA 246 (1937).

2. Potter, BTA memo op Dec 10, 514-G (1938); Stinchfield, 4 TCM 551 (1944).

3. Instructions, Schedule J, Form 706.

[Harris]

entire taxable income requires the filing of a Federal Income Tax Return, such return in the First District of New York and shall include the receipt of said commissions or such amount as I shall receive in that year, and such other amounts, if any, which I may receive in the year of receipt thereof.

KATHERINE BENSON

Sworn to before me this 15th
day of June, 1959.
  ANDREA HAYS
  Notary Public
  New York County

§ 198. Schedule J; Administration Expenses; Trustees' Commissions; Other Administration Expenses.

We have previously discussed the subject of property subject to claims and the changes made in respect thereto by the 1954 Code.[4] As to decedents dying on and after August 17, 1954 it is provided that subject to meeting the requirements of adequate consideration and the other limitations of Section 2053(c)(1), there shall be deducted in determining the taxable estate amounts representing expenses incurred in administering property not subject to claims which is included in the gross estate to the same extent such amounts would be allowable as a deduction under subsection (a) if such property were subject to claims, and such amounts are paid before the expiration of the period of limitation for assessment provided in Section 6501.[5]

The reason for the inclusion of the provision was stated that it was to allow a deduction for expenses incurred in administering property not subject to claims if paid prior to the expiration of the period set forth. Such expenses include such items as commissions paid in respect of trust property included in the gross estate and attorneys' fees incurred to contest the inclusion of the trust property in the decedent's gross estate.[6]

The effect of the section and the cases dealing with the deductibility of trustees' commissions is likely to be confusing unless the distinction between the trustees' commissions referred to in the section, and trustees' commissions generally, is understood. The Regulation points out that except to the extent that a trustee is in fact performing such services with respect to property subject to claims *which would normally be performed by an ex-*

4. § 192, supra.
5. IRC, § 2053(b) (1954 Code).

6. Senate Comm Report on IRC, § 2053 (1954 Code).

ecutor, amounts paid as trustees' commissions do not constitute expenses of administration.[7] What the Regulation says is that if a trustee in fact acts in the capacity of an executor the commissions he receives are for settling the estate preliminary to turning it over to individual beneficiaries or the trustee, as trustee,[8] and are deductible.[9] But if after the estate is settled the trustee administers the trust, such commissions as he earns in that capacity are "not in settlement of a dead man's affairs" and are not deductible.[10]

But where the decedent created a trust during his life and it is necessary to account and terminate it on his death, the expenses in connection therewith reduce the amount of the property includible in the gross estate. In such cases some courts held that the charges were deductible[11] and others that they were not.[12]

Under the present statute not only the commissions of the trustee, but other expenses such as attorneys' fees, special guardians' fees, accountants' fees and the like, in administering property not subject to claims, but which is included in the gross estate, are deductible if incurred in settling the decedent's interest in the property or vesting good title in the beneficiaries.[13] These expenses must meet the same requirements as to reasonableness, allowance by local law, etc., as any other claim. In the case of such deductions,[14] as in the case of other claimed administration expenses,[15] if they are incurred for the individual benefit of the heirs, legatees, or devisees, they may not be taken as deductions.

§ 199. Schedule J; Administration Expenses; Attorneys' Fees.

The fiduciary, in filing the return, may deduct such an amount of attorneys' fees as has actually been paid, or an amount which at the time of filing may reasonably be expected to be paid. If on

7. Reg, § 20.2053–3(b)(3).
8. Reg, § 20.2053–3(a).
9. Comm v Bronson, 32 F2d 112 (CCA 8) (1929); Clark, 1 TC 663 (1942).
10. Sharpe v Comm, 148 F2d 179 (CCA 3) (1945); Central Hanover Bank & Trust Co v Comm, 118 F2d 270 (CCA 2) (1941); Bretzfelder v Comm, 86 F2d 713 (CCA 2) (1936); Smith, 6 BTA 911 (1927); Braun v Lewellyn, 38 F2d 477 (1930).
11. Comm v Davis, 132 F2d 644 (CCA 1) (1943); Chemical Bank & Trust Co v Early, 67 F Supp 530 (1946); Reed, 8 TCM 303 (1947); Clark, 1 TC 663 (1943); Fidelity Phila Trust Co v U. S. 222 F2d 379 (CA 3) (1955); Lincoln, 1 TCM 326 (1942).
12. Reynolds, 45 BTA 44 (1941); Baldwin, 44 BTA 900 (1941).
13. Reg, § 20.2053–8.
14. Reg, § 20.2053–8(a).
15. Reg, § 20.2053–3(a).

the audit of the return the fees claimed have not been awarded by the proper court and paid, the deduction will, nevertheless, be allowed if the District Director is reasonably satisfied that the amount claimed will be paid and that *it does not exceed a reasonable remuneration* for the services rendered, taking into account the size and character of the estate, and the local law and practice. If the deduction is disallowed in whole or in part on final audit, the disallowance will be subject to modification as the facts may later require.[16]

A deduction for attorneys' fees incurred in contesting an asserted deficiency or in prosecuting a claim for refund should be claimed at the time the deficiency is contested or the refund claim is prosecuted. A deduction for reasonable attorneys' fees actually paid in contesting an asserted deficiency or in prosecuting a claim for refund will be allowed even though the deduction as such, was not claimed in the Estate Tax return or in the claim for refund. A deduction for these fees shall not be denied, and the sufficiency of a claim for refund shall not be questioned, solely by reason of the fact that the amount of fees to be paid was not established at the time that the right to the deduction was claimed.[17]

Attorneys' fees incurred by beneficiaries incident to litigation as to their respective interests do not constitute a proper deduction, inasmuch as expenses of this character are incurred on behalf of the beneficiaries personally and are not administration expenses.[18]

The primary test of the allowance of attorneys' fees is reasonableness, taking into account the amount involved, time and effort expended, seriousness of the problems, results obtained, and experience and ability of the attorney.[19] Normally, if the fee has been allowed by the probate court, it will be allowed for tax purposes,[20] but not where the amount was excluded from a court decree.[1] If the amount is allowed by law,[2] or paid or agreed to be paid,[3] it will be allowed. The usual procedure is to esti-

16. Reg, § 20.2053–3(c)(1).
17. Reg, § 20.2053–3(c)(2).
18. Reg, § 20.2053–3(c)(3).
19. Schnorbach v Kavanagh, 102 F Supp 828 (1951).
20. Schmalstig v Conner, 46 F Supp 531 (1942); Bell, 3 BTA 1172 (1925); Bensel, 36 BTA 246 (1937).

1. Commercial Nat Bank of Charlotte v U. S. 196 F2d 182 (CA 4) (1952).
2. Loetscher, 14 BTA 228 (1929); Howard, 2 TCM 1075 (1943).
3. Leewitz v US, 75 F Supp 312 (1948); Sessoms, 8 TCM 1056 (1947); Stewart, 31 BTA 201 (1934); Belzer, 1 TCM 539 (1942); Lamport, 28 BTA 862 (1933); Larzelere, 13 TCM 455 (1949).

mate the amount, and if reasonable, it will be allowed.[4] Fees incurred in connection with estate litigation, such as contested tax proceedings, are properly deductible,[5] but after conclusion of a suit for refund, the question of res judicata may arise.[6] It will depend upon whether the facts were known at the time of the first refund action.

As in estate administration generally, if the legal services are rendered for the benefit of individual beneficiaries and not for the estate, since it is not a proper administration charge, it will not be allowed as a deduction.[7]

Attorneys' fees in connection with an accounting have been allowed as a deduction,[8] and under a Revenue Ruling as an allowance.[9] This has been discussed in connection with trustees' commissions previously.[10]

In the absence of evidence of the reasonableness of the fee,[11] or the amount of services,[12] a deduction cannot be allowed.

As in the case of a fiduciary, it is required that the attorney furnish an affidavit that the fee has been agreed upon and will be paid, and attention is also directed to the cross reference for Income Tax purposes.[13] *An attorney should report on the return not the amount which he hopes to receive, but the actual amount which has been agreed upon.*

4. Burney, 4 TC 449 (1944); Lohman, 6 TCM 1071 (1946).

5. Humphrey, 5 TCM 34 (1945); Bob, 4 TCM 34 (1944).

6. Guettel v U. S. 95 F2d 229 (CCA 8) (1938); Cleveland v Higgins, 148 F2d 722 (CCA 2) (1945); Van Dyke v Kuhl, 171 F2d 187 (CA 7) (1948), but see Magruder v Safe Deposit Trust Co, 159 F2d 913 (CCA 4) (1947); Martin v Brodrick, 49-2 USTC ¶ 10,742 (CA 10) (1949); First Nat Bank of Atlanta v Allen, 100 F Supp 133 (1951); Goyette v US, 59-2 USTC ¶11,710 (1957).

7. Bottle, 1 BTA 1167 (1924); Reed, 4

TCM 889 (1945); Wright, 8 TC 531 (1937).

8. Clark, 1 TC 663 (1942); Haggart v Comm, 182 F2d 514 (CA 3) (1950); Abbett, 17 TC 1293 (1951); Reed, 8 TCM 303 (1947).

9. Rev Rul 293, 1953-2 CB 257.

10. § 198, supra; see also Baldwin, 44 BTA 900 (1941); Wright, 8 TC 531 (1947).

11. Hunt, 11 TC 984 (1948).

12. Loetscher, 14 BTA 228, affd 36 F 2d 835 (CA DC) (1928).

13. Instructions, Schedule J, Form 706.

FORM NO. 24

Affidavit for Allowance of Attorneys' Fees

U. S. TREASURY DEPARTMENT
INTERNAL REVENUE SERVICE
FIRST DISTRICT OF NEW YORK

In the Matter of the Estate Tax
  on the Estate of
    WINTHROP BENSON,
          Deceased.

STATE OF NEW YORK   ⎰
COUNTY OF NEW YORK ⎱ ss:

DANIEL WEBSTER CLAY, being duly sworn, says: I am an attorney at law duly admitted to practice in and for the State of New York.

That I have been retained by the Executrix in the above-entitled estate to act as attorney to said estate and am personally acting as such. That the fee agreed to be paid to me as and for the services rendered and to be rendered in connection with the same is the sum of $10,000.

That I reasonably expect to receive said fee during the year 1959. That I file my individual Federal Income Tax Return in the First District of New York and shall include the receipt of such fee in the return or returns to be filed by me for the year 1959 and thereafter until the total fee shall have been received.

DANIEL WEBSTER CLAY

Sworn to before me this
15th day of June, 1959
  MARSHA HAYS
  Notary Public
  New York County

§ 200. Schedule J; Administration Expenses; Miscellaneous.

There are many miscellaneous expenses other than fiduciaries' commissions and attorneys' fees. They include such expenses as court costs, surrogates' fees, accountants' fees, clerk hire, etc. Expenses necessarily incurred in preserving and distributing the estate are deductible, including the cost of storing or maintaining property of the estate, if it is impossible to effect immediate distribution to the beneficiaries. Expenses for preserving and caring for the property may not include outlays for additions or improvements; nor will such expenses be allowed for a longer period than the fiduciary is reasonably required to retain the property. A brokerage fee for selling property of the estate is deductible if the sale is necessary in order to pay the decedent's debts, the expenses of administration, or taxes, or to effect distribution. Other expenses attending the sale are deductible, such as the fees of an auctioneer, if it is reasonably necessary to employ one.[14] The Regulation states the effect of the decisions.[15]

There have been allowed, salaries paid to office help, engineers and accountants, in a difficult estate,[16] expenses on a claim for refund,[17] expenses of office rent, secretary and accountant,[18] discount, premium and note issuance and redemption expenses of a note to pay estate taxes,[19] notarial and stenographic fees,[20] witness fees,[1] court costs,[2] disbursements,[3] special guardian's fee,[4] traveling expenses,[5] the cost of an investment advisory service,[6] and brokerage.[7] It must be borne in mind, however, that certain expenses which will be deductible in one estate may not be in another. In a small estate a secretary, or an investment service, would not be a necessary expense. Whether or not a prolonged administration would have any effect on allowance of a deduction would depend upon the facts.[8]

On the other hand, there has been disallowed as a deduction, amounts paid to procure the discharge of the administrator of another estate,[9] the amount estimated as the cost of the record on appeal,[10] and a tax service for the executors.[11]

The subject of administration expenses incurred in connection

14. Reg, § 20.2053–3(d).

15. Blossom, 45 BTA 691 (1941); Scott v Comm, 69 F2d 444 (CCA 8) (1934); Reed, note 7, supra; Chemical Bank & Trust Co v Early, 67 F Supp 530 (1946); Singer, 4 TCM 960 (1945); note 8, supra.

16. Adams v Comm, 110 F2d 578 (CCA 8) (1940).

17. Bourne v U. S., 2 F Supp 228 (1933).

18. Chisholm, 37 BTA 167 (1938).

19. Huntington, 36 BTA 698 (1937).

20. Richardson, 1 BTA 1196 (1924).

1. Wright, 43 BTA 551 (1941); Chemical Bank & Trust Co v Early, note 15, supra.

2. Bluestein, 15 TC 770 (1950); Kohl v U. S. 128 F Supp 902, affd 226 F2d 381 (CA 7) (1955).

3. Kohl v US, note 2, supra.

4. Kings County Trust Co, BTA memo op Dec 10, 554-C (1938); Chemical Bank & Trust Co v Early, note 15, supra; Ruxton, 20 TC 487 (1953).

5. Chemical Bank & Trust Co v Early, note 15, supra.

6. Lehman, 39 BTA 17 (1939).

7. Allison, 5 TCM 992 (1945); Sternberger v Comm, 18 TCM 836, affd 207 F 2d 600 (CA 2) (1953).

8. See Adams v Comm, note 16, supra; Peckham, 19 BTA 1020 (1930).

9. Vereen v Allen, 75 F Supp 406 (1947).

10. Note 9, supra.

11. Note 9, supra.

with property included in the gross estate has been discussed previously.[12]

§ 201. Schedule J; Administration Expenses; Taxes.

While the statute refers to various kinds of taxes which are deductible from the gross estate, and others which are not, the only tax deductible as an administration expense is an excise tax incurred in selling property of a decedent's estate if the sale is necessary in order to pay decedent's debts, expenses of administration, or taxes, or to effect distribution. Excise taxes incurred in distributing property of the estate in kind are also deductible.[13] Accrued property, gift, and income taxes are debts and deductible in the schedule treating therewith,[14] and are discussed hereafter.[15] It is to be noted that not all excise taxes are deductible as administration expenses, but only such as are incurred in selling a decedent's property. As we shall see, a state estate tax, while an excise tax, is not deductible,[16] except in one case.[17] On the other hand, a liquor tax due at the date of death is a debt, and deductible.[18]

§ 202. Schedule J; Return.

Schedule J is the schedule for listing funeral expenses and expenses incurred in administering *property subject to claims.* It should be noted that expenses incurred in administering *property not subject to claims* should not be listed in this schedule but in Schedule L.[19] If, for example, part of the administration expenses were paid out of property subject to claims and part out of property not subject to claims, there should be listed in Schedule J, only such items as were paid out of property subject to claims, or were paid within fifteen months of death.[20]

As we have noted, an item may be entered for deduction though the exact amount is not known at the time the return is filed, provided it is ascertainable with reasonable certainty, and will be paid. No deduction may be taken upon the basis of a vague or uncertain estimate.[1] The instructions advise that all vouchers and receipts should be preserved for inspection by an Estate Tax

12. § 198, supra.
13. Reg, § 20.2053-6(c).
14. Reg, § 20.2053-6(b)(d)(f).
15. §§ 212, 215, infra.
16. IRC, § 2053(c)(B) (1954 Code).
17. IRC, § 2053(d) (1954 Code).
18. McCue, 5 TCM 141 (1945).
19. Instructions, Schedule J. Form 706.
20. See § 192, supra.
1. Note 19, supra; Reg, § 20.2053-1 (b)(3); § 190, supra.

examiner. They further repeat much of the material which we have been discussing.

The schedule is divided into four categories; executors' commissions, attorneys' fees, funeral expenses, and miscellaneous administration expenses. In the case of funeral and administration expenses, they should be itemized, giving the names and addresses of persons to whom payable, and exact nature of the particular expense.[2] As noted, if commissions or attorneys' fees are estimated there must be an affidavit in respect thereto.[3]

FORM NO. 25

Funeral Expenses and Expenses Incurred in Administering Property Subject to Claims

NOTE.—Do not list on this schedule expenses of administering property not subject to claims. In connection with such expenses, see Schedule L.

If executors' commissions, attorneys' fees, etc., are claimed and allowed as a deduction for estate tax purposes, they are not allowable as a deduction in computing the taxable income of the estate for Federal income tax purposes.

Item No.	Description	Amount
1	Executors' commissions—amount estimated/agreed upon/paid. (Strike out words not applicable)	$6,533.87
2	Attorneys' fees—amount estimated/agreed upon/paid. (Strike out words not applicable)	10,000.00
	(FUNERAL EXPENSES)	
3	Morticians, Inc., 200 Ann Street, Des Moines, Iowa, funeral expenses of decedent.	750.00
4	Picayune-Times, Des Moines, Iowa, publication of death notices.	12.00
5	Rev. J. B. Tyler, 100 Willow Street, Des Moines, Iowa, religious services at funeral.	100.00
6	Stone & Co. Des Moines, Iowa, for monumental work on decedent's grave (estimated).	500.00
	(MISCELLANEOUS ADMINISTRATION EXPENSES)	
7	Incidental disbursements (estimated).	100.00
8	Chas. Horn, 100 Pear Street, Des Moines, Iowa, appraisals.	150.00
9	Thomas J. Sands, 100 Main Street, Des Moines, Iowa, brokerage on sale of decedent's business.	250.00

TOTAL (also enter under the Recapitulation, Schedule O) $18,395.87

(If more space is needed, insert additional sheets of same size)

Schedule J—Page 23

Estate of WINTHROP BENSON

2. Note 19, supra.
3. See Forms, §§ 197, 199, supra.

§ 203. Schedule K; Claims against Estate; Generally.

The statute provides for the allowance of a deduction for claims against the estate as are allowable by the laws of the jurisdiction, whether within or without the United States, under which the estate is being administered.[4]

The amounts that may be deducted as claims against a decedent's estate are such only as represent personal obligations of the decedent existing at the time of his death, whether or not then matured,[5] and interest thereon which had accrued at the time of death.[6] Only interest accrued at the date of the decedent's death is allowable even though the executor elects the alternate valuation method.[7] Only claims enforceable against the decedent's estate may be deducted.[8] Except as otherwise provided with respect to pledges or subscriptions, the allowance of a deduction for a claim founded upon a promise or agreement is limited to the extent that the liability was contracted bona fide and for an adequate and full consideration in money or money's worth.[9] Liabilities imposed by law[10] or arising out of torts are deductible.[11]

As in the case of other deductions, if the state court passed upon the claim on the merits it is deductible,[12] but if not, the state court determination is not binding.[13]

Whereas prior to the 1954 Code claims against the estate were deductible only to the extent that the property subject to claims was sufficient for their payment, that is no longer so, subject to the statutory limitations.[14]

The subject of adequate consideration[15] and charitable pledges[16] are considered hereafter.

4. IRC, § 2053(a)(3) (1954 Code).

5. Guggenheim v Helvering, 117 F2d 469 (CCA 2) (1941).

6. McFadden v US, 20 F Supp 625 (1937).

7. IRC, § 2032 (1954 Code).

8. US v Mitchell, 74 F2d 571 (CCA 7) (1934); Erickson v Smyth, 108 F Supp 412 (1952); Thacher, 20 TC 474 (1953); Glascock v Comm, 104 F2d 475 (CCA 4) (1939); Comm v Kelly, 84 F 2d 958 (CCA 7), cert den 299 US 603, 81 L ed 445, 57 S Ct 230 (1936); Smyth v Erickson, 221 F2d 1 (CA 9) (1955).

9. IRC, § 2053(c)(A) (1954 Code).

10. Grinnell, 44 BTA 1286 (1941); Comm v Maresi, 156 F2d 929 (CCA 2) (1946); Smith v US, 16 F Supp 397, affd 92 F2d 704 (CCA 1) (1936).

11. Reg, § 20.2053-4(a).

12. Burton v Burke, 41-2 USTC ¶10,-091; Nashville Trust Co v Comm, 136 F 2d 148 (CCA 6) (1943); Harter, 3 TC 1151 (1944); Vose, 20 TC 597 (1953); Goodwin v Comm, 201 F2d 576 (CA 6) (1953).

13. First Mechanics Nat Bank of Trenton v Comm, 117 F2d 127 (CCA 3) (1941); Wolfsen v Smyth, 53-2 USTC ¶ 10,924.

14. See § 192, supra.

15. § 218, infra.

16. § 209, infra.

§ 204. Schedule K; Claims against Estate; Interest.

The deduction for claims against the estate includes not only the principal amount of the claim, but also interest thereon which has accrued at the date of the decedent's death.[17] And this applies even though the fiduciary elects to have the estate valued as of the alternate valuation date. Thus, where the transaction involved was an advance against the decedent's interest in a trust distribution, while the principal was not deductible, the interest required to be paid in order to obtain the advance was deductible.[18]

§ 205. Schedule K; Claims against Estate; Contracts; Generally.

The test of whether a claim is deductible is whether it is enforceable against the estate.[19] It must be founded upon an agreement and contracted for an adequate and full consideration in money or money's worth.[20] The question of consideration looms large in the allowance of claims, since if it is lacking there can be no deduction.[1] The subject of an adequate and full consideration in money or money's worth is discussed hereafter.[2]

If the claim is paid, but is not an enforceable one, it cannot be allowed as a deduction,[3] so that a contract which was barred by the Statute of Limitations would not be deductible.[4] Voluntary payment and allowance is not sufficient.[5]

Contractual claims arising out of the matrimonial relationship have been the subject of much litigation and are separately treated.[6]

Certain claims may not be deductible because they are not in fact contractual but are gifts.[7] In such cases there is also often involved the question of consideration.

17. Reg, § 20.2053–4(a).

18. McFadden v US, 20 F Supp 625 (1937).

19. Comm v Kelly, note 8, supra.

20. Glascock v Comm, note 8, supra.

1. Goldsmith, 36 BTA 1201 (1937); Nicholas, 40 BTA 1040 (1939); Garrett, 12 TCM 1142 (1949); Gray, 44 BTA 545 (1941); Biel, 11 TCM 1092 (1949); Connell, 20 TC 917 (1953); Ensley v Donnelly, 51–1 USTC ¶ 10,815 (CA 5) (1951); Friedman, 3 TCM 180 (1944); Comm v Swink, 155 F2d 723 (CCA 4) (1946).

2. § 218, infra.

3. Wolfsen v Smyth, 53–2 USTC ¶ 10,924 (1953); Thacher, note 8, supra; First Mechanics Nat Bank of Trenton v Comm, note 13, supra.

4. Brown v US, 37 F Supp 444 (1941).

5. US v Mitchell, 74 F2d 571 (CCA 7) (1934); Wolf, 29 TC 441 (1957).

6. § 208, infra.

7. Latty v Comm, 24 BTA 296 (1931); Glascock v Comm, note 8, supra; May, 8 TC 1099 (1947).

There is no requirement that the claim must have been paid in order for it to be deductible,[8] nor that it has been allowed by court decree,[9] but merely that it is a valid claim.[10] The fact that the claim has been compromised does not detract from its deductibility.[11] But settlement of a claim of heirship is not payment of a claim but payment of an inheritance, and is not a deduction.[12]

§ 206. Schedule K; Claims against Estate; Contracts; Notes and Loans.

Notes and loans, like other deductions, must be enforceable and given by the decedent for an adequate consideration in the case of notes, or an adequate consideration received, in the case of loans.[13] If any of these elements are lacking, no deduction is permissible.[14] The fact that the transaction is between husband and wife is not alone sufficient to establish lack of bona fide.[15]

Where the decedent was the endorser on a note, the amount due is deductible,[16] but only to the extent that the note remains unpaid.[17] If the estate holds collateral, only the amount in excess of the value of the collateral is deductible.[18] Where the decedent is jointly and severally liable with others, it will depend upon whether the others are financially responsible whether a deduction may be allowed. If they are not, a deduction will be allowed,[19] but if they are, there will be allowed only the decedent's share of the obligation.[20] The effect on deductibility of the al-

8. Helvering v O'Donnell, 94 F2d 852 (CCA 2) (1938); Comm v Windrow, 89 F2d 69 (CCA 5) (1937); Baer v Milbourne, 13 F Supp 998 (1936).

9. Erickson v Smyth, 108 F Supp 412 (1952).

10. Union Guardian Trust Co, 32 BTA 996 (1935).

11. McCoy v Rasquin, 102 F2d 434 (CCA 2) (1939); Smith v US, 16 F Supp 397, affd 92 F2d 704 (CCA 1) (1936); Metcalf, 7 TC 153 (1946).

12. Howard, 2 TCM 1075 (1943).

13. Earle, 5 TC 991, affd 157 F2d 501, 677, 678, 680 (CCA 6) (1945); Connell, 20 TC 917 (1953); GCM 4784, VIII-2 CB 385; Security Trust Co, 4 BTA 983 (1926).

14. Guaranty Trust Co v Comm, 98 F2d 62 (CCA 2) (1938); Fry, 9 TC 503

(1947); First Nat Bank of Birmingham v US, 25 F Supp 816 (1939); Hauptfuhrer, 9 TCM 974 (1947); Biel, 11 TCM 1092 (1948); Connell, note 13, supra; Earle, note 13, supra.

15. Johnson, 2 TCM 208 (1943).

16. Hofford, 4 TC 542, modfd other grounds 4 TC 790 (1945); Old Colony Trust Co, 39 BTA 871 (1939).

17. Atkins, 2 TC 332 (1943).

18. Eckhart, 33 BTA 426 (1935).

19. Comm v Wragg, 141 F2d 638 (CCA 5), affg 1 TCM 541 (1943); Comm v Porter, 92 F2d 426 (CCA 2) (1937).

20. Parrott v Comm, 30 F2d 792 (CCA 9), cert den 279 US 870, 73 L ed 1007, 49 S Ct 512 (1929); Schoenfeld v Comm, 103 F2d 964 (CCA 9) (1939); Du Val v Comm, 152 F2d 103 (CCA 9) (1945); note 17, supra.

lowance of the claim by a court decree depends upon whether the question was decided upon the merits.[1] A note overlooked in filing the return, may nonetheless be allowed as a deduction.[2]

§ 207. Schedule K; Claims Against Estate; Contracts; Guaranty.

Where the decedent has guaranteed obligations of another, the same question arises as where he is jointly and severally liable on an obligation. If the primary obligor is solvent, there is no enforceable claim against the decedent, and the deduction will not be allowed.[3] But when the primary obligor is insolvent, so that in effect the decedent becomes the primary obligor, the amount will be allowed as a deduction.[4] A guarantor and an endorser of a note are in exactly the same position, since the endorser is in fact a guarantor.

The question of adequate consideration enters into a guarantee by the decedent. In such case, the fact that the loan is made to one who receives the benefits thereof, even though without consideration is not the determining factor. The consideration in such case passes from the obligee, so that so long as the guarantee is a commercial transaction and not an attempted disposition of property there is an adequate consideration.[5] It is not necessary that the decedent received the consideration.[6]

§ 208. Schedule K; Claims Against Estate; Contracts; Matrimonial Obligations.

We have previously discussed the subject of marital rights and consideration in connection with inter vivos transfers.[7] The subject also occurs in connection with agreements arising from the marital relationship when a deduction is claimed on the ground that such rights are claims against the estate.

The test of whether or not amounts for the support of the wife are deductible as claims against the decedent's estate is whether the provision has been incorporated in a court decree. If the amount payable is based upon the decree *and not upon an agree-*

1. § 193, supra.
2. Hunt, 12 BTA 396 (1928).
3. Cabot, 46 BTA 225 (1942); Buck v Helvering, 73 F2d 760 (CCA 9) (1934); Du Val v Comm, note 20, supra.
4. Carney v Benz, 90 F2d 747 (CCA 1) (1937); Lang, 32 BTA 527 (1935); Dodge v Gagne, 23 F Supp 729 (1938);

McCoy v Rasquinn, 102 F2d 434 (CCA 2) (1939); Comm v Porter, note 19, supra; Hoffard, 4 TC 542 (1944); Bob, 4 TCM 592 (1944).
5. Carney v Benz, note 4, supra.
6. US v Mitchell, 74 F2d 571 (CCA 7) (1934).
7. § 158, supra.

ment, it will be allowed as a deduction.[8] The fact that there is an agreement does not deny deductibility if it is incorporated in the decree,[9] but if it is not,[10] or there is an agreement without it being incorporated in a subsequent decree,[11] the claim is not deductible. Amounts paid pursuant to an antenuptial agreement, since they are not founded upon an adequate consideration, are not deductible as claims.[12] Where alimony payments are reduced to a court decree,[13] or they are past due,[14] they are deductible.[15]

Payments made by the estate in fulfillment of the decedent's promises to support his children are deductible if they are minors,[16] but not if they are beyond the age at which the decedent was liable for their support.[17]

§ 209. Schedule K; Claims against Estate; Contracts; Charitable Pledge or Subscription.

While claims founded upon a promise or agreement must be for an adequate consideration, there is a *statutory exception.* In any case in which any claim is founded on a promise or agreement of the decedent to make a contribution or gift to or for the use of any donee described in Section 2055 for the purpose specified therein, the deduction for such claims shall not be so limited, but shall be limited to the extent that it would be allowable as a charitable deduction.[18]

Prior to 1942, where the decedent made a pledge to a charity or gave a note for a charitable pledge, the amounts paid thereon

8. Comm v State Trust Co, 128 F2d 618 (CCA 1) (1942).

9. Comm v Watson, 54–2 USTC ¶ 10,-973 (CA 2) (1954); Fleming v Yoke, 53 F Supp 552, affd 145 F2d 472 (CCA 4) (1944); Comm v Swink, 155 F2d 723 (CCA 4) (1946); Bank of New York v US, 53–2 USTC ¶10,910 (1953); Maresi, 6 TC 582, affd 156 F2d 929 (CCA 2) (1946); Watson, 20 TC 386 (1953); Forstmann, 6 TCM 1136 (1946).

10. Adriance v Higgins, 113 F2d 1013 (CCA 2) (1940); Phillips, 36 BTA 752 (1937); Weiser, 39 BTA 1144, affd 113 F2d 486 (CCA 10) (1940); Meyer v Comm, 110 F2d 367 (CCA 2), cert den 310 US 651, 84 L ed 1416, 60 S Ct 1103 (1940); Nantke v US, 59 F Supp 633 (1945); McKeon, 25 TC 697 (1956).

11. Bank of New York v US, 115 F Supp 375 (1953).

12. Empire Trust Co v Comm, 94 F 2d 307 (CCA 4) (1938); Empire Trust Co, 35 BTA 886 (1936); Central Union Trust Co, 24 BTA 296 (1931).

13. Comm v State Trust Co, 128 F2d 618 (CCA 1) (1942); Young, 39 BTA 230 (1939).

14. Mason, 43 BTA 813 (1941).

15. Reg, § 20.2053–4(a).

16. Weiser, 113 F2d 486 (CCA 10) (1940); Phillips, note 10, supra; Cherry, 5 TCM 495 (1945).

17. Markwell v Comm, 112 F2d 253 (CCA 7) (1940); Chase Nat Bank of NY v Hickey, 42–2 USTC ¶10,208.

18. IRC, § 2053(c)(1)(A) (1954 Code); Reg, § 20.2053–5.

after his death were not allowed as deductions from his estate, on the theory that the claims were not founded upon a promise or agreement supported by an adequate consideration.[19] The fact that payment was made with the approval of the court,[20] or was enforceable,[1] did not affect the question of deductibility. A distinction, however, was made by the courts where the decedent's promise was conditioned on others making similar pledges. In such case it was held that there was a consideration, which did not necessarily have to be received by the decedent, and that the pledge was properly deductible.[2] The Commissioner did not agree with many of these decisions.[3]

Such cases became a matter of history when the statute[4] was amended by the Revenue Act of 1942 to permit the deduction of such pledges if they would qualify as charitable deductions had they been bequests. The 1954 Code made no change in this respect, so that if a pledge or subscription is made by the decedent for the public, charitable or religious uses enumerated in Section 2055, it is deductible as a claim against the estate.

§ 210. Schedule K; Claims Against Estate; Torts.

Claims against the estate, although for the most part based upon contractual obligations, need not necessarily be such. Claims arising out of liabilities imposed by law or tort are also recognized as deductible.[5] Thus the decedent's liability for an assessment because of his ownership of bank stock has been held a proper deduction.[6]

§ 211. Schedule K; Claims Against Estate; Miscellaneous Claims.

There may be many other claims against an estate which are deductible, other than those we have heretofore discussed. Ex-

---

19. Taft v Comm, 304 US 351, 82 L ed 1393, 58 S Ct 891 (1938); Bretzfelder v Comm, 86 F2d 713 (CCA 2) (1936); Porter v Comm, 60 F2d 673 (CCA 2), affd 288 US 436, 77 L ed 880, 53 S Ct 451 (1932); Mechanics Bank of New Haven, 20 BTA 1033 (1930).

20. Jordan, 45 BTA 832, affd 131 F2d 435 (CCA 2) (1942).

1. Chase Nat Bank of N Y v Higgins, 42 F Supp 325, affd 124 F2d 519 (CCA 2) (1941).

2. Wade, 21 BTA 339 (1930); Comm

v Bryn Mawr Trust Co, 87 F2d 607 (CCA 3) (1937); Comm v Porter, 92 F 2d 426 (CCA 2) (1937); Helvering v Safe Deposit & Trust Co, 95 F2d 806 (CCA 4) (1938).

3. GCM 4784, VIII-2 CB 385.

4. IRC, §§ 812(b), 861(a)(1) (1939 Code).

5. Reg, § 20.2053–4(a).

6. Hays, 34 BTA 808 (1936); Smith v US, 16 F Supp 397, affd 92 F2d 704 (CCA 1) (1936).

amples of such which have been allowed are: a liability to pay an annuity under a stock purchase agreement,[7] compromise settlement of a claim,[8] claims against an includible trust estate,[9] an indebtedness of the decedent to another estate,[10] hospitalization charges for a daughter whom the decedent had no legal obligation to support,[11] an indebtedness against securities loaned to be pledged,[12] a judgment liability,[13] moneys paid to redeem property of another converted by the decedent,[14] amounts paid in settlement of a lawsuit,[15] excess amounts withdrawn by a partner,[16] and amounts improperly drawn by a life beneficiary of a trust.[17]

There is one type of claim deserving of special mention. That is a loan upon an insurance policy. Where the decedent pledges the policies with the insurance company for a loan, the amount of the loan is deducted from the policy and only the net proceeds are includible in the gross estate, so that the amount of the loan is not deductible.[18] Where the policy is pledged with a bank for a loan, the entire amount of the proceeds is includible in the gross estate and the amount of the loan is a proper deduction.[19] In the latter case the beneficiary, if he pays the loan, or the pledgee, has an enforceable right against the estate.

§ 212. Schedule K; Claims Against Estate; Taxes; Generally.

The statute provides that any Income Taxes on income received after the death of the decedent, or property taxes not accrued before his death, or any estate, succession, legacy, or inheritance taxes, shall not be deductible under the section.[20]

This limitation was reduced in the case of state death taxes insofar as transfers for charitable, educational or religious purposes were concerned, and will be discussed hereafter.[1]

7. Linde, 8 TCM 1102 (1947).
8. Rosenman v US, 53 F Supp 722 (1944).
9. Harter, 3 TC 1151 (1944); Vose, 20 TC 597 (1953).
10. Thiele, 9 TC 473 (1947).
11. Dodge, BTA memo op Dec 12, 113-H (1941).
12. Borland, 38 BTA 598 (1938); Hartford Nat Bank v Smith, 54 F Supp 579 (1941).
13. Moore, 21 BTA 279 (1930); Buck v Helvering, 73 F2d 760 (CCA 9) (1934).
14. Stewart v Comm, 49 F2d 987 (CCA 10) (1931).
15. Howard, 2 TCM 1075 (1943).
16. Gannon, 21 TC 1073 (1954).
17. Clement, 13 TC 19 (1949).
18. Kennedy, 4 BTA 330 (1926); Waterman, BTA memo op Dec 12, 220-D (1941); Marsh, BTA memo op Dec. 12, 411-F (1942).
19. Reinhold, 3 TCM 285 (1944).
20. IRC, § 2053(c)(1)(B) (1954 Code).
1. § 213, infra.

The cleavage point is the date of death. To the extent that taxes were due at the time of the decedent's death they are an obligation of his estate and a proper deduction. Since the Estate Tax is not concerned with events occurring after death, except for the purposes of the alternate valuation, taxes incurred thereafter are not obligations of the decedent, but of his estate. The single exception, as noted,[2] is excise taxes incurred in selling property of a decedent's estate. This deduction is not predicated on a claim against the decedent's estate, but as an administration expense.

The Regulation deals with, in addition to the excise taxes above, property taxes, death taxes, gift taxes, and income taxes, each of which will be treated in the succeeding sections.

§ 213. Schedule K; Claims Against Estate; Property Taxes.

Property taxes are not deductible unless they accrued *before the decedent's death*. However, they are not deductible merely because they have accrued in an accounting sense. Property taxes in order to be deductible must be an enforceable obligation of the decedent at the time of his death. Real property taxes are deductible *only if they have become a lien* on the real property *before the decedent's death.*

Personal property taxes which attach on assessment, if due at the date of death are deductible.[3] This is so even though the amount had not been determined at the date of death.[4] But if the fiduciary received a certificate of immunity against collection, it is not.[5] Partnership,[6] or liquor taxes,[7] due at the date of death, have been held deductible.

Real property taxes must be a lien at the date of death to be deductible,[8] so that those becoming a lien thereafter are not deductible.[9] The fact that they accrue before death does not affect deductibility.[10] And where the amount of tax is compromised, only the compromised amount is deductible.[11]

The deduction is no longer dependent upon the property being

2. § 201, supra.

3. Hill v Grissom, 299 F 641 (1924); Claiborne, 40 BTA 722 (1939).

4. Shelton, 3 BTA 809 (1926).

5. Jacobs, 34 BTA 594 (1936).

6. Moore, 13 BTA 864 (1928).

7. McCue, 5 TCM 141 (1945).

8. Thompson v US, 8 F2d 175 (1925); Wright v Jones, 44–1 USTC ¶10,093.

9. Klyce, 41 BTA 194 (1940); Claiborne, note 3, supra; Scott, 25 BTA 131 (1931); Seagrist, 42 BTA 1159 (1940).

10. Claiborne, note 3, supra.

11. Metcalf v Comm, 47–2 USTC ¶10,566 (CCA 6).

subject to the payment of debts, provided payment of the tax is made within fifteen months of death.[12]

§ 214. Schedule K; Claims Against Estate; Death Taxes.

No estate, succession, legacy, or inheritance tax payable by reason of the decedent's death is deductible, except certain State death taxes on charitable, public or religious gifts.[13] There is, however, a *credit* for such taxes, discussed hereafter.[14]

Under earlier statutes death taxes were deductible if the tax was a charge against the estate and not the beneficiary.[15] The statute has for many years expressly provided that death taxes, whether estate, succession, legacy, or inheritance taxes, are not deductible.[16] There is no constitutional obligation of the United States or the states to allow any deduction on account of the tax of the other.[17]

There is one exception to this rule. Most of the states do not tax transfers for charitable, public or religious purposes, but some few do. In order to provide for this situation, Congress amended the statute in 1956[18] and added a new subsection to Section 2053, *effective as to estates of persons dying after December 31, 1953*, and not August 17, 1954, as the other provisions generally of the 1954 Code apply. A deduction is allowed for the amount of any estate, succession, legacy, or inheritance tax imposed by a State or Territory or the District of Columbia upon a transfer by the decedent for public, charitable, or religious uses, within the meaning of the statute, provided the following conditions are met:

(1) Either the entire decrease in the Federal Estate Tax resulting from the allowance of the deduction inures solely to the benefit of a charitable, etc. transferee, *or*

(2) The Federal Estate Tax is equitably apportioned among all the transferees (including the decedent's surviving spouse

12. § 192, supra.
13. Reg, § 20.2053-6(c).
14. §§ 309 et seq, infra.
15. See Miles v Curley, 291 F 761 (CCA 4) (1923); New York Trust Co v Eisner, 256 US 345, 65 L ed 963, 41 S Ct 506 (1921); Lederer v Northern Trust Co, 262 F 52 (CCA 3), cert den 253 US 487, 64 L ed 1026, 40 S Ct 483 (1920); Kearns v Dunbar, 292 F 1013 (1922).
16. Note 20, supra.
17. Frick v Pennsylvania, 268 US 473, 69 L ed 1058, 45 S Ct 603 (1925).
18. PL 414 of 1956, Sec 2, changed subsection d of IRC, § 2053 to subsection e and enacted a new subsection d.

and the charitable, etc., transferees) of property included in the decedent's gross estate.[19]

It is further required that the fiduciary must make an election to take the deduction by filing a notification in writing to that effect with the District Director before the expiration of the period of limitation for assessment (usually 3 years). The election may be revoked within the same period of time.[20]

For purposes of the statute, the Federal Estate Tax is considered to be equitably apportioned among all the transferees of property included in the decedent's gross estate only if each transferee is required to bear the burden of the Federal Estate Tax in an amount, A, which bears the same ratio to B (the Federal Estate Tax payable after allowance of the credits authorized by Sections 2011 to 2014, inclusive, and Section 2102 (relating to estates of nonresidents not citizens)) as C (the value of the transfer reduced as provided in the following sentence) bears to D (the sum of the taxable estate and the exemption allowed in computing the taxable estate). If any deduction under Sections 2053(d), 2055 (charitable deduction), 2056 (marital deduction), or 2106(a)(2) (relating to estates of nonresidents not citizens) are allowed with respect to the transfer, Factor "C" of the ratio is the value at which the transfer is included in the gross estate, reduced by the amount of the deductions allowed under those sections with respect to the transfer.[1]

As will be observed, the provision is complex and requires an involved computation. The operation of the provision and examples thereof are treated in the chapter on computations.[2]

The Technical Amendments Act of 1958 added a section to the 1954 Code providing for the taxation of the estates of residents of United States' possessions who acquired their citizenship completely independently of their connections with the possessions in the same manner as if they had stayed in the United States.[2a] The statute relating to death taxes paid on public, charitable, or religious uses was accordingly amended so that taxes paid to such possessions will be treated as taxes paid to a foreign country for which there is a credit,[2b] rather than as a

---

19. IRC, § 2053(d) (1954 Code); Reg, § 20.2053–9.

20. Reg, § 20.2053–9(c).

1. Reg, § 20.2053–9(b)(2).

2. § 283, infra.

2a. See § 12, supra.

2b. §§ 309 et seq, infra.

credit for State death taxes.[2c]   The amendment applies only to the estates of decedents dying after September 2, 1958.[2d]

§ 215. Schedule K; Claims Against Estate; Gift Taxes.

Unpaid Gift Taxes on gifts made by the decedent before his death are deductible.   If a gift is considered made half by the decedent and half by his spouse under Section 2513, the entire amount of the Gift Tax, unpaid at the decedent's death, attributable to a gift in fact made by the decedent is deductible.[3]   No portion of the tax attributable to a gift in fact made by the decedent's spouse is deductible, except to the extent that the obligation is enforced against the decedent's estate and his estate has no effective right of contribution against his spouse.[4]   The latter provision would refer to a split gift, where one of the parties was insolvent.   Since the obligation in such case for payment of the tax is joint and several, the decedent's estate would be liable for the unpaid tax and it would have no effective right of contribution.

Interest on unpaid Gift Taxes accruing after death have been held not a claim against the estate and therefore not deductible.[5]

It should be noted that if the property transferred is included in the decedent's gross estate, there is a credit against the Estate Tax for the Gift Tax paid on the transfer.[6]

§ 216. Schedule K; Claims Against Estate; Income Taxes.

Unpaid Income Taxes are deductible if they are on income properly includible in an Income Tax return of the decedent *for a period before his death.*[7]   This is so, whether or not it has been paid,[8] or whether it is paid after the Estate Tax return has been filed.[9]   Taxes on income received after the decedent's death are specifically excluded as a deduction.[10]   Deficiencies assessed against the decedent because of nonrecognition of his son as a

2c. §§ 318 et seq, infra.

2d. IRC, § 2053(d) (1954 Code), as amended by Technical Amendments Act of 1958, § 102(c)(3), HR 8381, 85th Cong, 2nd Sess.

3. Rev Rul 55–334, 1955–1 CB 449.

4. Reg, § 20.2053–6(d).

5. Hornor, 44 BTA 1136, affd 130 F2d 649 (CCA 3) (1942).

6. § 304, infra.

7. Schatzinger, 12 BTA 1353 (1928); Kirkwood, 23 BTA 95 (1931); Glaser, 27 BTA 313, affd 69 F2d 254 (CCA 8) (1932); Nevin, 11 TC 59 (1949).

8. Schatzinger, note 7, supra; Kirkwood, note 7, supra; Glaser, note 7, supra.

9. Steen v US, 51–1 USTC ¶10,818.

10. IRC, § 2053(c)(1)(B) (1954 Code).

partner,[11] and Income Tax on a trust created by the decedent which is included in his estate,[12] is deductible.

When the decedent files a joint return, how much of the tax due is deductible has been a problem for the Internal Revenue Service. After modifying[13] a prior ruling,[14] further clarification was required.[15] It is now ruled that for the purposes of Section 2053 in determining the decedent's share of tax liability shown on a joint return of the decedent and his spouse for the year in which he died, there is taken into account in the computation a tax computed on the income of the decedent for the part of the year immediately prior to the date of his death (a fractional year) and tax computed on the income of the surviving spouse for the entire year. For example, assume that on the basis of a separate return the Income Tax liability of a decedent on his income for the period prior to the date of his death would have been $4,000. and the income tax liability of his spouse on the basis of a separate return for the entire year would have been $8,000. The tax liability shown on the joint return which has been filed is $11,760. The decedent's share of the tax shown on the joint return is computed as follows:

$4,000 ÷ $12,000 × $11,760 = $3,920.

§ 217. Schedule K; Claims Against Estate; Mortgages and Liens.

A deduction is allowed from the decedent's gross estate of the full unpaid amount of a *mortgage upon, or of any other indebtedness* in respect of, any property of his gross estate, including interest which had accrued thereon to the date of death, provided the value of the property, undiminished by the amount of the mortgage or indebtedness, is returned as part of the value of the gross estate.[16] If the decedent's estate is liable for the amount of the mortgage or indebtedness, the full value of the property subject to the mortgage or indebtedness must be included as part of the value of the gross estate;[17] the amount of the mortgage or indebtedness being in such case allowed as a deduction. But if the decedent's estate is not so liable, only the equity of redemption need be returned as part of the value of

11. Rev Rul 56–6, 1956–1 CB 660.
12. Rev Rul 55–601, 1955–2 CB 606.
13. Rev Rul 56–290, 1956–1 CB 445.
14. Rev Rul 54–382, 1954–2 CB 279.
15. Rev Rul 57–78, IRB 1957–9, p. 17.
16. Steedman v US, 35 F Supp 533 (1940); Scott, 25 BTA 131 (1932).
17. City Bank Farmers Trust Co v Bowers, 2 F Supp 883 (1932); Comm v Kelly, 84 F2d 958 (CCA 7) (1936).

the gross estate.[18] In no case may the deduction on account of the mortgage or indebtedness exceed the liability therefor contracted bona fide and for an adequate and full consideration in money or money's worth.[19] Only interest accrued to the date of the decedent's death is allowable even though the alternate valuation method is selected.[20] Inasmuch as real property outside the United States does not form a part of the gross estate, no deduction may be taken of any mortgage thereon, or any other indebtedness in respect thereto.[1] Where the decedent owned an undivided half interest in property subject to a mortgage, only half of the liability was held deductible.[2]

§ 218. Schedule K; Claims Against Estate; Mortgages and Liens; Consideration.

It will have been observed that throughout the preceding sections there sounds the refrain of consideration. The statute provides that the deductions allowed by Section 2053 in the case of claims against the estate, unpaid mortgages, or any indebtedness shall, when founded on a promise or agreement, *be limited to the extent that they were contracted bona fide and for an adequate and full consideration in money or money's worth,* with the single exception of pledges or subscription for charitable, public, or religious uses.[3] This is repeated throughout the Regulations in the various sections dealing with debts.[4] Both the statute[5] and the Regulation[6] refer to the fact that the relinquishment of marital rights is not a consideration in money or money's worth.

We have discussed the subject of consideration in connection with claims generally,[7] contracts,[8] notes and loans,[9] guarantees,[10] matrimonial obligations,[11] and mortgages and other indebtednesses.[12] It is emphasized at the conclusion of the subject, since it must not be taken for granted that merely because the decedent was a debtor or obligor, the amount thereof is, per se, de-

18. Johnstone, 19 TC 44 (1952).
19. Mann, 14 TC 555 (1950); Schiffman v US, 51 F Supp 728 (1943); Ashforth, 30 BTA 1306 (1934); Seagrist, note 9, supra.
20. IRC, § 2032 (1954 Code).
1. Reg, § 20.2053-7.
2. Parrott v Comm, 30 F2d 792 (CCA 9), cert den 279 US 870, 73 L ed 1007, 49 S Ct 512 (1929).

3. IRC, § 2053(c)(A) (1954 Code).
4. Reg, §§ 20.2053-4; 20.2053-7.
5. IRC, § 2053(e) (1954 Code).
6. Reg, § 20.2053-4(a).
7. § 203, supra.
8. § 205, supra.
9. § 206, supra.
10. § 207, supra.
11. § 208, supra.
12. § 217, supra.

ductible from his gross estate. If it was not contracted bona fide and for an adequate and full consideration in money or money's worth it will not be deductible. Interfamily transactions are particularly suspect and may require explanation. When such appear, the lawyer will be well advised to be prepared to show that the note held by the decedent's wife or son was given for consideration.

§ 219. Community Property; Funeral and Administration Expenses; Claims Against Estate; Mortgages and Liens.

Whether, in community property law states, all or half of the deductions we have been discussing will be allowed, depends upon the particular laws.

In Idaho funeral expenses were deductible in full and commissions and administration expenses to the extent of one half.[13]

In Texas, the entire amount of funeral expenses was deducted from the decedent's half of community property,[14] half of the commissions, accountant's and attorney's fees,[15] and half of an indebtedness of the decedent to his wife.[16]

In Louisiana the entire cost for attorney's fees, commissions, and administration expenses were deductible.[17]

In Washington half of the funeral expenses, administration expenses,[18] the expenses of the decedent's last illness,[19] and debts[20] were deductible. But attorney's fees incurred in connection with settlement of the tax liability of the decedent's portion of the estate were deductible in full from his estate.[1]

In California, the husband having conveyed his interest in the community property to his wife, his personal debts were deductible in full.[2]

All of these determinations, except for two recent cases in Louisiana, were determined before the 1948 amendment changed the taxation of community property.[3] Whether all or half of

---

13. Lee, 11 TC 141 (1948).

14. Blair v Stewart, 49 F2d 257 (CCA 5), cert den 284 US 658, 76 L ed 558, 52 S Ct 35 (1931).

15. Schuhmacher, 8 TC 453 (1947).

16. Lucey, 13 TC 1010 (1949).

17. Vaccaro v US, 55 F Supp 932 (1944); see also McCullough v US, 134 F Supp 673 (1955); Gannett, 24 TC 654 (1955).

18. Lang v Comm, 97 F2d 867 (CCA

9) (1938); Pacific Nat Bank of Seattle, 40 BTA 128 (1939).

19. Pacific Nat Bank of Seattle, note 18, supra.

20. Lang v Comm, note 18, supra.

1. Lang v Comm, note 18, supra.

2. US v Goodyear, 99 F2d 523 (CCA 9) (1938).

3. See §§ 41, 48, 64, 68, 81, 98, 110, 154, supra.

funeral and administration expenses, claims against the estate, and mortgages and indebtednesses are deductible will depend upon whether under local law the charge is against the entire community property or only the decedent's share. In the former case only one half will be deductible, while in the latter case the entire amount will be.

§ 220. **Schedule K; Claims Against Estate; Mortgages and Liens; Return.**

The instructions for Schedule K advise that if the amount of a debt is disputed or the subject of litigation, only such amount may be deducted as the estate concedes to be a valid claim. If the claim is contested, that fact should be stated.[4]

In listing notes, full details must be given, including names of payee, face and unpaid balance, date and term of note, interest rate and date to which interest was paid prior to death. Care must be taken to state the exact nature of a claim as well as the name of the creditor. If the claim is for services rendered over a period of time, the period covered by the claim should be stated.[5]

If the amount of the claim is the unpaid balance due on a contract for the purchase of any property of the gross estate, the schedule and item number of the property reported should be indicated. If the claim represents a joint and several liability, the facts must be fully stated and the financial responsibility of the co-obligor explained.[6]

All vouchers or original records should be preserved for inspection by the Estate Tax examiner.[7]

In reporting mortgages and liens, the property to which they apply should be indicated by reference to the schedule and item number where it is reported. The name and address of the mortgagee, payee, or obligee, and the date and term of the mortgage, note, or other agreement under which the indebtedness is established should be shown, as well as the face amount, the unpaid balance, the rate of interest, and the date to which the interest was paid prior to death.[8]

In the case of some of the items listed in Schedule K supplemental documentation may either be required to be submitted

4. Instructions. Schedule K, Form 706.
5. Note 4, supra.
6. Note 4, supra.
7. Note 4, supra.
8. Note 4, supra.

with the return or for presentation to the Estate Tax examiner when he audits the return. Thus, if there is a balance due on the purchase of property there should be annexed a computation of the amount due as of the date of death. In the case of Income Taxes, computation of the decedent's liability under a joint return should be furnished. If the decedent was jointly and severally liable and his co-obligor is insolvent, proof of that fact by affidavit will be required, and, as we have observed, if the obligation is due to a member of the decedent's family it is well to be prepared with proof of the adequacy of consideration.

FORM NO. 26

Schedule K; Debts of Decedent and Mortgages and Liens

Item No.	Debts of Decedent—Creditor and nature of claim	Amount
1	Rent of premises 23 Orion Drive, Salt Lake City, Utah, for balance of term of lease, Dec. 1959 to April 30, 1960 at $150 per month. ...	$750.00
2	Utah Telephone Co., final bill for telephone services	18.36
3	Salt Lake Electric Co., electric service Dec. 1959	8.49
4	Dr. George Shore, 100 Maple Street, Salt Lake City, medical services to date of death.	75.00
5	Claim of John Bowen for alleged breach of contract	2,500.00
6	Zachary Benson, claim for recovery of proceeds of Schedule C, Item 6, as alleged gift. The Executrix has rejected the said claim	2,875.40
7	Note payable to Jon Hall, dated January 5, 1959, due March 5, 1960. Interest 6%. Interest paid to Sept. 5, 1959	1,000.00
	Interest to date of death	12.86
8	Balance due upon contract for purchase of Item 3, Schedule A (See adjustments as of date of death, annexed).	6,807.14
9	Real Estate Taxes, lien upon premises Schedule A, Item 1, at the time of decedent's death	285.00
10	Director of Internal Revenue, Federal Income Taxes to date of death (See annexed computation).	3,769.54

TOTAL (also enter under the Recapitulation, Schedule O) $18,101.79

Item No.	Mortgages and liens—Description	Amount
1	Mortgage on premises Schedule A, Item 1, payable to Utah Federal Savings & Loan Assn., Salt Lake City, Utah, dated June 1, 1958, due May 31, 1973, in the face amount of $15,000. Interest 5½%, paid to Dec. 1, 1959. Balance due at date of death	14,870.00
	Interest to date of death	38.48
2	Note payable to Salt Lake City Trust Co., dated Sept. 15, 1959, due March 15, 1960. Interest 6%. Interest paid to Dec. 15, 1959. Secured by collateral, Items 3 & 4, Schedule B.	5,000.00
	Interest to date of death	12.50

TOTAL (also enter under the Recapitulation, Schedule O) $19,920.98

(If more space is needed, insert additional sheets of same size)

Estate of WINTHROP BENSON   Schedule K—Page 25

Where the decedent is the purchaser under a contract, a computation of adjustments should be annexed as shown in the case where he is the seller.[9] If the decedent filed a joint Income Tax return, adjustment should be made and shown.[10]

§ 221. Schedule L; Net Losses and Support of Dependents.

There is allowed as a deduction from the gross estate losses incurred during the settlement of the estate arising from fires, storms, shipwrecks, or other casualties, or from theft, when such losses are not compensated for by insurance or otherwise.[11]

If the loss is partly compensated for, the excess of the loss over the compensation may be deducted. Losses which are not of the nature described are not deductible. In order to be deductible a loss must occur during the settlement of the estate. If a loss with respect to an asset occurs after its distribution to the distributee it may not be deducted.[12]

Prior to the 1954 Code the statute had a provision denying a deduction of such loss for both Estate and Income Tax purposes.[13] That provision has been dropped from the Estate Tax Law and is now part of the Income Tax Law.[14]

Formerly there was a deduction for the support of the dependents of the decedent during the settlement of the estate. Subdivision 5 of paragraph b of Section 812 of the 1939 Code was repealed as to persons dying after September 23, 1950. The primary reason therefor, was that after the creation of the Marital Deduction, the original motivation for the provision for support of dependents had no validity.

Although the deduction has been repealed, the amounts allowed for the support of a wife *may qualify* for the marital deduction.[15]

§ 222. Schedule L; Expenses Incurred in Administering Property Not Subject to Claims.

Schedule L has a separate portion for listing administration expenses not subject to claims. This does not refer to property not subject to claims from which funeral, administration ex-

9. See adjustments, Form No 13, § 66, supra.
10. See § 216, supra.
11. IRC, § 2054 (1954 Code).
12. Reg, § 20.2054–1; Leewitz v US, 75 F Supp 312, cert den 335 US 820, 93 L ed 374, 69 S Ct 42 (1948); Lyman v Comm, 83 F2d 811 (CCA 1) (1936).
13. IRC, § 812(b) (1939 Code).
14. IRC, § 642(g) (1954 Code); see also § 222, infra.
15. See §§ 225 et seq, infra.

penses, debts and mortgages have been paid prior to the date for filing the Estate Tax return. Such obligations are listed in the appropriate schedule and proof submitted that payment of the same was made out of property not subject to claims.[15a] It refers to such expenses as are incurred in connection with trust property included in the tax estate in which the trust is obligated for the trustee's principal commissions and attorney's fees and other like expenses necessary to settle the decedent's interest or vest good title in the beneficiaries. We have previously discussed this subject generally.[16] The Regulation furnishes examples of the operation of the statute in this respect. In the case of such expenses, they must have been paid before the expiration of the period of limitation for assessment as provided in Section 6501, and meet the other requirements that such deductions would have to meet if they were not in the excepted class, i.e., allowance by local law, reasonableness, etc.

Thus if trust property is included in the estate and in order to dissolve the trust and make distribution, there is incurred the trustee's commissions and the attorney's fee for that purpose, both such items would be deductible.[17] If a controversy arises under the trust instrument as to the rights of remaindermen and the trustee is made a party to the suit, to the extent that attorney's fees, guardian's fees, and accountant's fees are incurred for the usual services in connection with an accounting, they will be allowed and to the extent they are incurred in connection with the suit they will be disallowed. The trustee's commissions are allowable in full.[18] If no accounting is necessary, but one is had at the request of the beneficiary of the trust, no part of the expenses will be deductible.[19] If, in accordance with local custom, where there is no administration of the estate, as for example where the only asset is insurance, and it is necessary for the protection of the trustee or other interested party to prepare the Estate Tax return and complete the tax proceedings, the expenses incurred would be deductible.[20]

§ 223. Income Tax and Estate Tax Deductions.

In the case of deductions allowable under Sections 2053 and 2054 of the 1954 Code, as under prior provisions of the 1939

15a. See § 192, supra.
16. §§ 192, 198, supra.
17. Reg, § 20.2053–8(d), Example (1).

18. Reg, § 20.2053–8(d), Example (2).
19. Reg, § 20.2053–8(d), Example (3).
20. Reg, § 20.2053–8(d), Example (4).

Code, the fiduciary has a choice of taking such deductions on either the Estate Tax return or the Income Tax return, but not on both. The 1939 Code provided specifically that net losses could only be deducted on the Estate Tax return if at the time of filing the deduction had not been taken as an Income Tax deduction.[1] It was required that if the Income Tax deduction was taken that a statement be filed that the Estate Tax deduction had not been claimed or allowed.[2] While the Estate Tax Law no longer contains such a provision under the 1954 Code, the Income Tax Law provision corresponding to former Section 162(e) is continued in the 1954 Code.[3]

The Estate Tax Regulation points out that Section 642(g) and Regulation § 1.642(g)–1 with respect to the disallowance for Estate Tax purposes of certain deductions if the right to take such deductions is waived in order to permit their allowance for Income Tax purposes should be consulted,[4] and in the case of net losses, that no deduction is allowed if the estate has waived its right to take such a deduction in order to permit its allowance for Income Tax purposes.[5]

While in most cases a double deduction may not be had, it does not mean that some deductions may not be taken both for Estate Tax and Income Tax purposes. In the case of deductions itemized in Section 691(b) of the 1954 Code a deduction may be taken in the Income Tax return and the Estate Tax return. Thus, interest deducted from policies on the life of a decedent may be both an Income and Estate Tax deduction.[6] The same would apply if the decedent made a charitable pledge.

§ 224. Schedule L; Net Losses and Expenses Incurred in Administering Property Not Subject to Claims; Return.

The instructions for Schedule L note that depreciation in the value of securities or other property does not constitute a deductible loss. In listing losses, full particulars must be given as to the loss sustained and the cause thereof. If insurance or other compensation was received on account of loss, the amount collected must be stated. The property with respect to which the loss is claimed should be identified by indicating the

---

1. Note 13, supra.
2. IRC, § 162(e) (1939 Code).
3. IRC, § 642(g) (1954 Code).
4. Reg, § 20.2053–1(d).
5. Reg, § 20.2054–1.
6. Hooks, 22 TC 502 (1954); see also IT 4048, 1951–1 CB 39.

particular schedule and item number where such property is returned under the gross estate.[7]

If the alternate valuation is adopted, deduction for any loss is limited to the extent that such loss is not in effect allowed in the valuation of the item in the gross estate.[8]

With respect to expenses incurred in administering property not subject to claims, the names and addresses of the persons to whom payable and the exact nature of the particular expense should be stated. The property with respect to which the expense was incurred should be identified by indicating the schedule and item number where such property is included in the gross estate. As in the case of other administration expenses, the instructions indicate that estimated amounts may be given provided the item is ascertainable with reasonable certainty and will be paid within the time limited,[9] and that all vouchers and receipts should be preserved for inspection by an Estate Tax examiner.[10]

Although the instructions do not so state the same affidavit will be required from the attorney and trustee when the fees and commissions are estimated, as in other cases.[11]

FORM NO. 27

Schedule L; Net Losses During Administration and Expenses Incurred in Administering Property Not Subject to Claims

Item No.	Net losses during administration	Amount
1	Bearer Bond, Item 5, Schedule B, was stolen from the residence of the decedent on January 19, 1959, after his death. Report of theft has been made to the police authorities. Said property was uninsured.	$1,000.00
	Interest to date of death	8.33
	TOTAL (also enter under the Recapitulation, Schedule O)	$1,008.33

7. Instructions, Schedule L, Form 706.
8. Note 7, supra.
9. See §§ 197, 199, 200, 202, supra.
10. Note 7, supra.
11. See Form No 23, § 197 and Form No 24, § 199, supra.

Item No.	Expenses incurred in administering property not subject to claims	Amount
1	Daniel Webster Clay, Esq., 100 Main Street, Milwaukee, Wisc., attorney's fee for settlement of account of Wisconsin Trust Co. as Trustee under trust created by the decedent and included in gross estate, Item 3, Schedule G. (estimated).	$2,500.00
2	Wisconsin Trust Co., 100 Main Street, Milwaukee, Wisc., Trustee's commissions as trustee of trust created by decedent and included in gross estate, Item 3, Schedule G (estimated).	1,874.34

TOTAL (also enter under the Recapitulation, Schedule O) $4,374.34

(If more space is needed, insert additional sheets of same size)

Estate of WINTHROP BENSON   Schedule L—Page 27

§ 225. Schedule M; Marital Deduction; Generally.

The Federal Revenue Act of 1948 introduced a completely new concept to estate taxation. In an attempt to place residents of states not having a community property law on an equal tax footing with residents of community property law states, and to remove the tax disadvantages which the former suffered, Congress created *the marital deduction,* which permitted the deduction from the gross estate, of any interest passing to a surviving spouse, in an amount not exceeding 50% of the "adjusted gross estate."[12]

As a result *double taxation* upon the property passing under the marital deduction to the surviving spouse and then to the children, is avoided. It is not, however, a complete forgiveness of the tax on the property passing to the spouse, but defers its taxation to the death of the surviving spouse, at which time, to the extent that the property has not been consumed or given away by the survivor, it will be taxed in the latter's estate, subject to the specific exemption in the estate of the survivor.

The statute is complex, and has many refinements and distinctions, which in its short life have been the source of much litigation. The 1954 Code removed two limitations which had previously existed. Prior to that statute, neither a legal life estate nor an interest in a portion of a trust qualified for the deduction.[13] Cases decided under the former statute, which held that legal life estates or portion trusts did not qualify for the marital deduction, no longer apply to the estates of persons dying on and after August 17, 1954,[14] nor as we shall see, have

12. Hamrick v Pitts, 228 F2d 486 (CA 4), affg 135 F Supp 835 (1955); Weyenberg v US, 135 F Supp 299 (1955); Buckhantz, 260 P2d 794 (Cal) (1953);

Rosenfeld, 101 A2d 684, 376 Pa 42 (1954).
13. IRC, § 812(e)(F)(G) (1939 Code).
14. See Rev Rul 54–20, 1954–1 CB,

they any further application. The 1954 Code also changed the provision with respect to property converted from community property to separate property to apply to such conversions made at any time after 1941.

As noted above, by the 1954 Code, Congress removed the limitations in the marital deduction which denied the same if the surviving spouse's share was by way of a conventional or legal life estate instead of in trust, and also if the share was of a portion of a trust instead of a separate trust. Congress has realized the injustice of this situation and by the Technical Amendment Act of 1958 has amended the 1939 Code so as to make the provisions thereof the same as under the 1954 Code.[14a] *The amendment applies to estates of decedents dying after April 1, 1948, and before August 17, 1954 (the date of the enactment of the 1954 Code).* If refund or credit of any overpayment resulting from the application of the amendment is prevented on the date of the enactment of the Act (September 2, 1958), or at any time within one year from such date, by the operation of any law or rule of law (other than Section 3760 of the Internal Revenue Code of 1939 or Section 7121 of the Internal Revenue Code of 1954, relating to closing agreements, and other than Section 3761 of the Internal Revenue Code of 1939 or Section 7122 of the Internal Revenue Code of 1954, relating to compromises), refund or credit of such overpayment may, nevertheless, be made or allowed if claim therefor is filed within one year after the date of the enactment of the Act. *No interest* shall be allowed or paid on any overpayment resulting from the enactment of the section.[14b]

The result of this amendment is that if the marital deduction was disallowed because the share of the surviving spouse was a legal life estate or a portion of a trust, application for refund may be made,[14c] *provided*

(1) the application for refund is made within one year from September 2, 1958, *and*

195; Hoffenberg, 22 TC 1185, aff'd 223 F2d 470 (CA 2) (1954); Melamid, 22 TC 966 (1954); Shedd, 23 TC 41, aff'd 237 F2d 345 (CA 9), cert den Mar 4, 1957.

14a. IRC,   § 812(e)(1)(F)   (1939 Code), as amended by Technical Amendments Act of 1958, § 93(a), HR 8381, 85th Cong, 2nd Sess.

14b. Technical Amendments of 1958, § 93(b), HR 8381, 85th Cong, 2nd Sess.

14c. See §§ 376 et seq, infra.

(2) the case was not closed *either* by a closing agreement *or* compromise.[14d]

The statute of limitations does not apply, but no interest will be paid on the refund.

It should be noted that, except as otherwise provided by a convention with a foreign country, *the marital deduction is not allowed in the case of an estate of a nonresident not a citizen of the United States.* However, if the decedent was a citizen or resident of the United States, his estate is not deprived of the right to the marital deduction by reason of the fact that his surviving spouse was neither a resident nor a citizen.[15]

The Technical Changes Act of 1953[16] made the statute apply to particular situations of decedents dying between December 31, 1947, the effective date of the marital deduction provisions under the 1939 Code and April 2, 1948, the date of their enactment.

§ 226. Schedule M; Marital Deduction; Facts Required to Establish.

In order to obtain the marital deduction with respect to any property interest it is required that *the fiduciary establish*

(1) That the decedent was survived by a spouse.

(2) That a property interest *passed* from the decedent to such spouse.

(3) That such interest is a *deductible interest.*

(4) The value of such interest.

(5) The value of the *adjusted gross estate.*[17]

The deduction is allowed only to the extent that the property is included in determining the value of the gross estate.[18] Thus real property outside the United States could not qualify.

§ 227. Schedule M; Marital Deduction; Interest in Property.

The statute uses the words *interest in property.*[19] It is not synonymous with "property". "Property" is used in a comprehensive sense and includes all objects or rights which are susceptible of ownership. "Interest" refers to the extent of ownership, i.e., to the estate or the quality and quantum of ownership. Thus, a life estate in property is an interest in property as distinguished from the property per se.[20]

14d. § 382, infra.
15. Reg, § 20.2056(a)–1(a).
16. PL 287, 83rd Cong, Aug 15, 1953.
17. Reg, § 20.2056(a)–1(b).
18. IRC, § 2056(a) (1954 Code).
19. Note 18, supra.
20. Sen Fin Comm Report No 1013, Part 2, p 4 (1948 Revenue Act).

§ 228. Schedule M; Marital Deduction; Interest in Property Passing.

The statute allows the deduction for any interest in property *which passes or has passed* from the decedent to his surviving spouse.[1] It also defines what constitutes an interest in property passing within the meaning of the statute.[2]

An interest in property shall be considered as passing from the decedent to any person *if and only if*

(1) It is bequeathed or devised to such person by the decedent.

(2) It is inherited by such person from the decedent.

(3) It is the dower or curtesy interest (or statutory interest in lieu thereof) of such person as surviving spouse of the decedent.

(4) It has been transferred to such person by the decedent at any time.

(5) At the time of the decedent's death it was held by the decedent and such person (or by them and any other person) in joint ownership with right of survivorship.

(6) The decedent had the power (either alone or jointly with another) to appoint such interest, and he appoints or has appointed such interest to such person or such person takes such interest by release or nonexercise of such power, *or*

(7) It is insurance upon the life of the decedent receivable by such person.

Where at the time of the decedent's death it is not possible to ascertain the particular person or persons to whom an interest in property may pass from the decedent, such interest shall be considered as passing from the decedent to a person other than the surviving spouse, unless it passes under (6) or (7) above or in a marital deduction life estate or trust.[3] Prior to the Technical Amendments Act of 1958 the life estate would only have qualified if the decedent died after August 16, 1954.[4] The Technical Amendments Act of 1958, however, amended the 1939 Code so as to make the marital deduction provision the same under both the 1939 Code and the 1954 Code, with the Amendment retroactive to the date of the enactment of the marital deduction.[4a]

Thus, a devise to the wife for life and then to such grandchil-

---

1. Note 18, supra.
2. IRC, § 2056(e) (1954 Code).
3. IRC, § 2056(b)(5)(6) (1954 Code).

4. Note 14, supra.
4a. See § 225, supra.

[Harris]

dren as survive the wife, but if none, to the wife's estate, does not qualify as an interest passing to the wife.

Similarly treated is a devise to the wife for life with a non-general power of appointment.

The following would constitute property passing, *if* included in the gross estate:

(1) Property interests devolving upon any person as surviving co-owner with the decedent under any form of joint ownership under which the right of survivorship existed.

(2) Property interests at any time subject to the decedent's power to appoint (whether alone or in conjunction with any person) received under the decedent's exercise of the power, or in case of lapse, release, or nonexercise of the power.

(3) Dower or curtesy (or a statutory interest in lieu thereof).

(4) Insurance received by the beneficiary.

(5) Any property interest transferred during life, bequeathed or devised by the decedent, or inherited from the decedent.

(6) The survivor's interest in an annuity included in the gross estate.[5]

A property interest is considered as passing to the surviving spouse only if it passed to her as beneficial owner, except in the case of excepted terminable interests.[6]

It will be seen that there is included property which passes not only in intestacy or by testamentary disposition, but many other interests, such as pass under trusts, powers of appointment, joint bank accounts, tenancy by the entirety, insurance, annuities, dower and curtesy, elective rights, and property transferred during life but which may have been included in the gross estate as a transfer in contemplation of death or other taxable lifetime transfer. It has also been held that an amount received as an allowance for support under local law, which is a vested right, is property passing.[7]

§ 229. Schedule M; Marital Deduction; Nondeductible Interests.

As noted,[8] one of the facts to be established by the fiduciary in order to be entitled to the marital deduction, is that the interest for which the deduction is sought is a deductible interest.

5. Reg, § 20.2056(e)–1(a).
6. Reg, § 20.2056(e)–2(a).
7. Rev Rul 83, 1953–1 CB 395; note 6, supra.
8. § 226, supra.

The statute defines both those interests which will qualify for the marital deduction and those which will not.[9] The Regulation provides that an interest passing to a decedent's surviving spouse is a "deductible interest" if it does not fall within one of the following categories of "nondeductible interests":

(1) Any property interest which passed from the decedent to his surviving spouse is a "nondeductible interest" to the extent that it is not included in the decedent's gross estate.

(2) If a deduction is allowed under Section 2053 by reason of the passing of a property interest from the decedent to his surviving spouse, such interest is, to the extent of the deduction under Section 2053 a "nondeductible interest". Thus, payments to the wife of a debt or as commissions is a "nondeductible interest."

(3) Net losses incurred during administration are "nondeductible interests".

(4) A "terminable interest" is a "nondeductible interest" to the extent specified.[10]

The statute defines the interests which will not qualify.[11] These are those

(1) where, (a) on the lapse of time, (b) on the occurrence of an event or contingency, (c) or on the failure of an event or contingency to occur, the interest passing will *terminate or fail*

(A) if an interest in such property passes or has passed (*for less than an adequate and full consideration* in money or money's worth) from the decedent to any person *other than such surviving spouse* (or the estate of such spouse) ; *and*

(B) if by reason of such passing such person (or his heirs or assigns) *may* possess or enjoy any part of such property after such termination or failure of the interest so passing to the surviving spouse;

(2) where such interest is to be acquired for the surviving spouse, *pursuant to the directions of the decedent,* by his executor or by the trustee of a trust.

For the purposes of (1) and (2), an interest shall not be considered as an interest which will terminate or fail merely because it is the ownership of a bond, note, or similar contractual obligation, the discharge of which would not have the effect of an annuity for life or for a term.[12]

9. IRC, § 2056 (1954 Code).
10. Reg, § 20.2056(a)–2(b).
11. IRC, § 2056(b)(1) (1954 Code).
12. IRC, § 2056(b) (1954 Code).

This is the "terminable interest rule". If the interest bequeathed or devised to the surviving spouse will fail either because of a time limitation, or the occurrence of an event, or the failure of the limiting event to occur, no marital deduction will be allowed. Thus, a bequest to a wife for life, or until her remarriage, a patent, copyright, or annuity contract, a lease bequeathed to a wife, which was retained out of a *gift* of the fee to a person other than the wife, or a devise to a wife and daughter, jointly, are all terminable interests.[13] In spite of the Finance Committee's examples in the foregoing statement, it was questionable that some of the interests indicated were in fact terminable interests. The Regulation recognizes this by providing that if the decedent transfers to his spouse *all the interest he ever had* in a term for years, a patent or any other terminable interest, the interest of the spouse is a deductible interest if not otherwise disqualified.[14]

The Regulation furnishes examples of deductible and nondeductible interests.[15] To the uninitiated the fine distinctions may appear puzzling. Reference to the examples will be found helpful.

It will be noted that the statute refers to property passing
(1) without consideration,
(2) to a person other than the surviving spouse (or her estate), and
(3) if by reason of such passing such person *may* enjoy the property after termination of the spouse's interest. It is not enough that the enjoyment does not in fact occur, *if it may*, the interest will not qualify.

These provisions are significant. The Regulation states that "persons other than the surviving spouse" includes the possible unascertained takers of a property interest, as for example, the members of a class to be ascertained in the future. It further states that whether there is a *possibility* that others may enjoy the property after the spouse's interest terminates is to be determined *as of the time of the* decedent's death.[16] An estate trust, that is, one in which the wife is given a life interest and the remainder is payable to her estate, qualifies for the marital deduction because there is no such possibility.

13. Sen Fin Comm Report No 1013, Part 2, pp 7-10 (1948 Revenue Act).
14. Reg, § 20.2056(b)-1(c).
15. Reg, § 20.2056(b)-1(g).
16. Reg, § 20.2056(e)-3.

The statute provides that if a terminable interest is *directed* to be acquired for the surviving spouse by the executor or trustee the deduction will not be allowed.[17]

§ 230. Schedule M; Marital Deduction; Exceptions to Terminable Interest Rule.

There are three exceptions to the "terminable interest" rule. These are

(1) Where the interest passing to the surviving spouse is terminable if the wife does not survive the decedent by more than six months, *or* in the case of death of both in a common disaster, *or* only in the case of either event *and* such termination does not in fact occur.[18]

(2) Where the interest passing to the surviving spouse is in a form under which

  (a) she is entitled *for life* to *all the income* from
    (i) the entire interest, *or*
    (ii) a specific portion thereof,
  (b) the income is *payable* not less frequently than *annually,*
  (c) she has the *sole* power to appoint the entire interest or portion *in favor of herself or her estate,*
  (d) the power to appoint is *exercisable in all events and*
  (e) it is *not subject* to a power in *any other person* to appoint any part of the interest or portion to anyone other than the wife.[19]

(3) Where the interest passing to the surviving spouse is in the form of the proceeds of a life insurance, endowment, or annuity contract, which provides

  (a) the proceeds shall be held by the insurer to pay the proceeds in installments or to pay interest thereon, *only* to the wife for life,
  (b) not less frequently than annually beginning not more than thirteen months after the decedent's death,
  (c) the wife shall have *sole* power to appoint
    (i) all the proceeds, *or*
    (ii) a specific portion thereof *to herself or her estate,*
  (d) the power to appoint is *exercisable in all events and*
  (e) it is *not subject* to a power in *any other person* to ap-

17. Note 11, supra; see also § 236, infra.
18. IRC, § 2056(b)(3) (1954 Code).
19. IRC, § 2056(b)(5) (1954 Code).

point any part of the proceeds or the specific portion thereof to anyone other than the wife.[20]

As we have noted previously, the 1954 Code permits the deduction in the case of a legal life estate and where the power to appoint applies to only a portion of a fund or the proceeds of insurance.[1] The Technical Amendments Act of 1958 applies the same rule retroactively, as noted.[1a]

Each of the exceptions are separately treated in succeeding sections.

§ 231. Schedule M; Marital Deduction; Interest in Unidentified Assets.

An allowable marital deduction may be reduced so as to be negligible or nonexistent if the assets out of which the spouse's share is to be paid includes assets which do not qualify for the marital deduction. These are commonly referred to as "tainted assets."

Where the assets (included in the decedent's gross estate) out of which, or the proceeds of which, an interest passing to the surviving spouse may be satisfied, include a particular asset or assets with respect to which no deduction would be allowed if such asset or assets passed from the decedent to such spouse, then the *value of such interest passing to such spouse shall be reduced by the aggregate value of such particular assets.*[2]

In order for the provision to apply, two circumstances must coexist. These are

(1) The property interest which passed to the surviving spouse must be payable out of a group of assets *included in the gross estate.*

(2) The group of assets out of which the property interest is payable must include one or more particular assets which if passing specifically to the surviving spouse, would be nondeductible assets.

It does not apply merely because the group of assets includes a terminable interest, but only if the interest is a nondeductible terminable interest.[3]

Thus a bequest of $50,000. to a wife, where the estate includes a term for years retained out of a *gift* of the fee to a person other

20. IRC, § 2056(b)(6) (1954 Code).

1. § 225, supra; see also §§ 234, 235, 237, infra.

1a. See § 225, supra.

2. IRC, § 2056(b)(2) (1954 Code).

3. Reg, § 20.2056(b)–2(b).

than the wife, which lease is valued at $60,000., will eliminate the marital deduction.[4] If the retained interest was after a *sale* the statute would not apply.

Where the decedent bequeaths one third of the residue of his estate to his wife, and the property passing under his will includes a right to rentals of an office building for a term of years reserved by the decedent under a deed of gift to his son, and the rentals were not specifically bequeathed, such right to the rentals passing specifically to the wife would be a nondeductible interest. If the wife's residuary interest were $80,000. and the value of the rentals $60,000., and the executor had the right either under the will or local law to assign the lease in satisfaction of the bequest, the bequest is a nondeductible interest to the extent of $60,000. If the executor could only assign one third, the bequest is a nondeductible interest to the extent of $20,000. If the decedent's will provided that his wife's bequest could not be satisfied with a nondeductible interest, the entire bequest is a deductible interest.[5]

It may be observed that careful testamentary draftsmen today invariably provide that there be allocated to the marital deduction share only such assets included in the gross estate which qualify for the marital deduction.

§ 232. Schedule M; Marital Deduction; Interest of Spouse Conditional on Survival for Limited Period.

The first exception to the terminable interest rule is that an interest passing to the surviving spouse shall not be considered as an interest which will terminate or fail on her death *if*

(1) such death will cause a termination or failure of such interest *only if* it occurs

(a) within a period *not exceeding six months* after the decedent's death, *or*

(b) as a result of *common disaster* resulting in the death of the decedent and the surviving spouse, *or*

(c) in the case of either event, *and*

(2) such termination or failure *does not* in fact occur.[6]

The statute applies to all terminable interests.[7]

Where the order of deaths of the decedent and his spouse can-

---

4. Note 13, supra.
5. Reg, § 20.2056(b)–2(d).
6. IRC, § 2056(b)(3) (1954 Code).

7. Sen Committee Report No 1622, 83rd Cong, 2nd Sess (1953).

not be established by proof, a presumption (whether supplied by local law, the decedent's will, or otherwise) that the decedent was survived by his spouse will be recognized as satisfying the requirement that the decedent was survived by his spouse *only to the extent* that it has the effect of *giving to the spouse* an interest in property includible *in her estate*.[8]

The Uniform Simultaneous Death Act has been enacted in the majority of states. In such states where there is not sufficient evidence that deaths have been other than simultaneous, the property of each spouse passes in the individual estates as if each had died first. In such case the presumption may be supplied by a will provision that it shall be deemed that one or the other spouse predeceased the other.

The statutory provision means that the presumption created by local law or will, will be effective only if under local law it gives such property to the surviving spouse, *and such property will be includible in her estate*. Of course, the presumption, like any other rebuttable presumption, will yield to proof that she did not in fact survive the decedent.

If the will provides that taking depends upon the causal relation between the accident and death, such as the spouse taking unless she dies *as the result* of a common accident or disaster, since the Regulation provides that the deduction will not be allowed if at the time of the final Estate Tax audit it has not been finally determined whether the spouse will live or die as the result of her injuries, if such fact is not determined at the time of audit, such clause will result in the loss of the deduction.[9]

Provision that the wife was to receive the testamentary benefit if she was alive at the date of distribution[10] has been held to deny the marital deduction. A distinction has been made however, where under local law, a provision for a bequest if the beneficiary be alive at the time of distribution of the estate is held to create a vested interest. In such case it is held that the condition is a condition subsequent, and if it fails, the bequest qualifies for the marital deduction.[11] It was also held that where an insurance policy provided for payment to the beneficiary only if she was

8. Reg, § 20.2056(e)–2(e).

9. Reg, § 20.2056(b)–3(e).

10. Street, 25 TC 673 (1955); Kasper v Kellar, 217 F2d 743 (CA 8) (1955); California Trust Co v Riddel, 136 F Supp 7 (1956).

11. Smith v US, 58–1 USTC ¶11,745; Kellar v Kasper, 138 F Supp 738 (1956) on remand of Kasper v Kellar, note 10, supra; Steele v US, 146 F Supp 316 (1956).

living at the time of the insurer's receipt of due proof of death, that the proceeds did not qualify for the deduction.[12] On appeal, and under the factual situation, the court decision was reversed.[12a]

The survivorship limitation period of the statute applies to trusts and life estates with general power of appointment.[13]

§ 233. Schedule M; Marital Deduction; Valuation of Interest Passing to Surviving Spouse.

The statute provides that in determining the value of the interest passing to a surviving spouse

(1) there shall be taken into account the effect which the Federal Estate Tax or *any* estate, succession, legacy, or inheritance tax, has upon the net value to the surviving spouse of such interest, *and*

(2) where such interest is encumbered in any manner, or where the surviving spouse incurs any obligation imposed by the decedent with respect to the passing of such interest, such encumbrance shall be taken into account in the same manner as if the amount of a gift to such spouse were being determined.[14]

The reason for providing that these items shall be taken into account is to insure that the marital deduction shall only be allowed to the extent that the surviving spouse actually receives property. Where any tax is chargeable to the spouse's share, or there is an encumbrance, the net amount received is less than the total reported.

Since the matter of valuation is primarily one of computation, such matters when taxes are chargeable against the marital deduction share,[15] or property is subject to an encumbrance,[16] will be discussed in the chapter on computation of the tax.

The value for the purpose of the marital deduction, of any deductible interest which passed from the decedent to his surviving spouse is to be determined as of the date of death, except that if the alternate valuation method is elected, the valuation is to be determined as of the date of death as adjusted. In determining the value of an interest in property passing to the spouse, account must be taken of the effect of any limitation upon

---

12. Rev Rul 54–121, 1954–1 CB 196; Eggleston v Dudley, 154 F Supp 178 (1957).

12a. Eggleston v Dudley, 58–2 USTC ¶11,807 (CA 3).

13. Reg, § 20.2056(b)–5(h).

14. IRC, § 2056(b)(4) (1954 Code).

15. §§ 287 et seq, infra.

16. § 286, infra.

her right to income from the property.[17] Such a limitation would be a provision in a marital deduction trust that the income from the property until the date of distribution to the trustee be used to pay administration expenses. This would not result in denial of the deduction because of the delay in payment of the income, but in reduction of the amount of the deduction.[18]

Where the interest passing is a remainder interest, the marital deduction is based upon the present value of the remainder.[19] This is computed in the same manner as previously discussed for the valuation of remainders.[20]

Thus it has been held that where insurance was subject to a loan, the amount of the loan had to be considered in valuing the marital deduction.[1] It has also been held that Estate Taxes chargeable to the spouse's share must be deducted,[2] but not if not so chargeable.[3] Where administration expenses are claimed as an Income Tax deduction, the effect is to increase the amount of the marital deduction.[4]

§ 234. Schedule M; Marital Deduction; Life Estate with Power of Appointment in Surviving Spouse.

The second exception to the terminable interest rule is that a life estate, or a life estate in trust, which are terminable interests, and would therefore not qualify for the marital deduction, *may qualify, if*

(1) The surviving spouse is entitled for life to *all the income* from

    (a) the entire interest, *or*

    (b) a specific portion thereof,

(2) such income is payable not less frequently than annually, *and*

(3) she has the *sole power* to appoint the entire interest or portion in favor of *herself or her estate,*

    (4) the power to appoint is *exercisable in all events, and*

    (5) the power is *not subject* to a power in *any other person* to

17. Reg, § 20.2056(b)–4(a).
18. Special Ruling, Carl T Palmer, Sept 20, 1957.
19. Reg, § 20.2056(b)–4(d).
20. § 115, supra.
1. Coffin, 13 TCM 1149 (1954).
2. Merchants Nat Bank & Trust Co v US, 246 F2d 410 (CA 7) (1957);
Thompson v Wiseman, 233 F2d 734 (CA 10) affg 56–1 USTC ¶11,591 (1956); Jaeger, 27 TC 861, affd 252 F2d 790 (CA 6) (1957).
3. Babcock, 234 F2d 837 (CA 3), revg 23 TC 888 (1956).
4. Rev Rul 55–225, 1955–1 CB 460.

appoint any part of the interest or portion to any one other than the surviving spouse.[5]

The effect of this exception is that if the wife is given either a legal life estate or is the income beneficiary of a trust *and in addition* she has the sole and unlimited power to appoint her interest *to herself or her estate,* the interest will qualify for the marital deduction. The Regulation formulates this in the form of five conditions which must be met, namely, (1) income for life from the entire interest or a *specific* portion, or a specific portion of income, (2) payable annually or more frequently, (3) power to appoint the interest to herself or her estate, (4) exercisable by her alone and in all events, and (5) not subject to a power in any one else.[6] The subject of a portion interest is discussed hereafter.[7]

In determining whether or not the conditions are satisfied by the instrument of transfer, regard is to be had to the applicable provisions of the law of the jurisdiction under which the interest passes and, if the transfer is in trust, the applicable law governing the administration of the trust. Silence of a trust instrument as to frequency of payment of income will not fail to satisfy the statute if local law requires payment to be made not less frequently than annually,[8] as is customary.

The surviving spouse is entitled for life to all the income if the effect of the interest granted is to give her substantially that degree of beneficial enjoyment of it during her life which the principles of trust law accord to a person who is unqualifiedly designated as the life beneficiary of such interest. Such degree of enjoyment is given only if it was the decedent's intention, as manifested by the terms of the instrument and the surrounding circumstances, that the interest should produce for the surviving spouse during her life, such an income, or that the spouse should have such use of the property as is consistent with the value of the corpus and with its preservation.[9]

Administrative provisions which evidence an intention to deprive the spouse of the beneficial enjoyment of the interest required by the statute will disqualify.[10]

An interest will not qualify if by the terms granting it the primary purpose is to safeguard property without providing the

5. IRC, § 2056(b)(5) (1954 Code).
6. Reg, § 20.2056(b)–5(a).
7. § 237, infra.

8. Reg, § 20.2056(b)–5(e).
9. Reg, § 20.2056(b)–5(f)(1).
10. Reg, § 20.2056(b)–5(f)(4).

spouse with the required beneficial enjoyment. Thus, provisions for the accumulation of income whether directly or indirectly, will disqualify. If the interest consists substantially of unproductive property, and there is no right to convert or deal with it in such a way as to make it productive, there is no such right to income as the statute contemplates.[11]

Where the gift is inter vivos, it is immaterial whether its terms satisfied the conditions prior to the decedent's death so long as they are satisfied after his death.[12]

The statutory conditions are not satisfied (1) *if* the income is required to be accumulated in whole or in part or may be accumulated in the discretion of any person other than the surviving spouse, (2) *if* the consent of any person other than the surviving spouse is required as a condition precedent to distribution of the income, (3) *if* any person other than the surviving spouse has the power to deprive such spouse of her right, or (4) *if* any person other than the surviving spouse is entitled to any part of the income from her interest during her life.[13]

The income provisions of the statute have not been the subject of any litigation. It has been held under the Gift Tax that insurance trusts which produced no income did not qualify for the marital deduction.[14] It has also been ruled that a provision for the application of the income to the payment of administration expenses did not disqualify.[15]

Many questions have been raised, however, as to whether certain usual administrative provisions would have the effect of disqualifying a marital deduction trust. The Regulations answer these questions in detail. *It is held that the following administrative provisions will not disqualify a provison for a spouse, which is otherwise qualified:*

(1) Silence of the trust instrument as to frequency of payment, unless local law permits payment to be made less frequently than annually.[16]

(2) Amortization of bond premiums.[17]

(3) Allocation to income of rents, ordinary cash dividends and interest and to corpus of the proceeds of the conversion of trust assets.

11. Reg, § 20.2056(b)-5(f)(5).
12. Reg, § 20.2056(b)-5(f)(6).
13. Reg, § 20.2056(b)-5(f)(7).
14. Smith, 23 TC 367 (1954); Halsted, 28 TC 1059 (1957).
15. Note 18, supra.
16. Note 8, supra.
17. Reg, § 20.2056(b)-5(f)(2).

(4) Charging against income, depletion, depreciation, commissions and other like charges.[18]

(5) Administrative powers subject by law to reasonable exercise thereof, such as power to

(a) allocate receipts between income and corpus,

(b) determine charges to be made against income and corpus,

(c) apply income for the benefit of the wife,

(d) retain assets passing to the trust.

(6) Permitting retention of unproductive property *if*

(a) the rules for the administration of trust property require the trustee to either make the property productive or to convert it within a reasonable time, *or*

(b) the applicable rules require the trustee to use the degree of judgment and care in the exercise of the power which a prudent man would use if he were the owner of the trust assets,[19] *or*

(c) the applicable rules require, or permit the spouse to require, that the trustee provide the required beneficial enjoyment, such as by payments to the spouse out of other assets of the trust.[20]

(7) Permitting the retention of a residence for the spouse, or other property for her personal use.[1]

(8) Granting the wife the income until the interest is terminated by her.[2]

(9) A spendthrift provision.[3]

The exception to the terminable interest rule which we have been discussing requires not only that the spouse be entitled to the income or specific portion, but also that the spouse have the power to appoint the interest to herself or her estate, and no power in any other person to appoint any part of such interest to any person other than the surviving spouse.

The power of appointment may be, *either* (1) in her own favor, at any time after decedent's death, such as an unlimited power of invasion, *or* (2) in favor of her estate, fully exercisable by deed or will, *or* (3) a combination of both, so long as at the time of her death the interest will be subject to either power.[4]

18. Reg, § 20.2056(b)–5(f)(3).
19. Note 10, supra.
20. Note 11, supra.
1. Note 10, supra.

2. Note 12, supra.
3. Note 13, supra.
4. Reg, § 20.2056(b)–5(g)(1).

The power in the surviving spouse *must be* a power to appoint her interest *to herself* as unqualified owner or to appoint the interest *as part of her estate,* that is, to dispose of it to whomsoever she pleases. Thus, an agreement by the wife to appoint only to her issue, violates the statutory condition for qualification.[5]

The power of appointment must be exercisable without the joinder or consent of any other person. It is not "exercisable in all events" if it can be terminated during the wife's life by any event other than the complete release or exercise thereof. Such a power would be one which terminated on remarriage or was restricted by local law to exercise only for the wife's support.[6]

A power is exercisable in all events *only if* it exists *immediately* following the decedent's death. Examples which do not satisfy the conditions are, a power exercisable during life or by will, but in either case, not prior to distribution of trust assets by the executor to the trustee.[7]

It does not follow that any limitation will disqualify a life estate for a spouse. Thus, the following provisions will not defeat the right to the marital deduction:

(1) A power to appoint to the spouse up to a certain age, and thereafter to her estate.[8]

(2) A power arising by local law, as where a joint devise to the spouse and another permits the spouse to sever her interest.[9]

(3) Designation of takers in default upon failure to exercise the power, or continuation for further trust in event of failure to exercise.[10]

(4) Formal limitations on the exercise of the power, such as it must be exercised.

(a) by will, or by deed,

(b) by filing with the trustee,

(c) by giving notice,

(d) at reasonable intervals between successive partial exercises,

(e) by will executed after the decedent's death,

(f) by specific reference to the power.[11]

(5) A limited power *in addition to* the power to appoint to herself or her estate.[12]

(6) A power in another which is not in opposition to that of

5. Reg, § 20.2056(b)-5(g)(2).
6. Reg, § 20.2056(b)-5(g)(3).
7. Reg, § 20.2056(b)-5(g)(4).
8. Note 4, supra.
9. Note 5, supra.
10. Note 5, supra.
11. Reg, § 20.2056(b)-5(g)(4).
12. Reg, § 20.2056(b)-5(g)(5).

the spouse, such as of a trustee to distribute corpus to the spouse, or a power in another to appoint after the spouse's death in the event of her failure to exercise her power.[13]

Whether or not particular provisions complied with the statutory requirements has been the subject of litigation which has created some questions. Thus, a life estate with power to sell, deed, and transfer the real property concerned,[14] a power to consume, but with a gift over,[15] an unlimited power in the spouse to dispose of the property during her life, but with the right in a trustee to invade for a son,[16] and an unlimited power to dispose of principal and income during life but not thereafter,[17] have all been held not to qualify for the marital deduction. In a recent case, although the spouse received all the income and the power to appoint by will, since under the law of Maryland such a power did not include the right to appoint to the spouse's estate, the interest was held not to meet the statutory requirement.[18] Where the power of appointment ceased if the spouse were legally incapacitated, the interest was not within the exception.[19]

§ 235. Schedule M; Marital Deduction; Life Insurance or Annuity Payments with Power of Appointment in Surviving Spouse.

The third exception to the terminable interest rule is that where the interest passing to the surviving spouse is in the form of proceeds of a life insurance, endowment, or annuity contract, it will qualify for the marital deduction, *if the contract provides*

(1) the proceeds shall be held by the insurer to pay the proceeds, or *a specific portion thereof,* in installments or to pay interest thereon, *only* to the spouse for life,

(2) not less frequently than annually, to begin not more than thirteen months after the decedent's death,

(3) the spouse shall have *sole power* to appoint *all* the proceeds *or a specific portion* thereof to *herself or her estate,*

---

13. Reg, § 20.2056(b)–5(j).

14. Evilsizor, 27 TC 710 (1957).

15. Howell, 28 TC 1193 (1957); Matteson v U. S., 147 F Supp 535, app dism 240 F2d 517 (CA 2) (1957); Ellis, 58–1 USTC ¶11,746 (CA 3), revg 26 TC 694 (1958).

16. Weisberger, 29 TC 217 (1957); Wheeler, 26 TC 466 (1956).

17. Pipe v Comm, 241 F2d 210 (CA 2), affg 23 TC 99 (1957); Boyd v Gray, 58–1 USTC ¶11,737.

18. Allen v Comm, 29 TC 465 (1957).

19. Tingley, 26 TC 402, affd sub nom Starrett v Comm, 223 F2d 163 (CA 1) (1955).

(4) the power is exercisable in all events, and

(5) it is *not subject* to a power in *any other person* to appoint any part of the proceeds or a specific portion thereof to anyone other than the spouse.[20]

The statute applies to proceeds of insurance upon the life of the decedent, upon the life of a person who predeceased the decedent, a matured endowment policy, or an annuity contract, but only in case such proceeds are to be held by the insurer.[1] Where the insurance is payable to a trustee with power of appointment in the spouse, the trust must meet the requirements heretofore set forth.[2]

If the five conditions above are met, even though there is a requirement for accumulation, the proceeds will not be disqualified if the spouse has the right to require distribution of the proceeds or the interest.[3]

Requiring the compliance with certain formalities, such as furnishing proof of death before the first payment is made is not a disqualification.[4] As previously noted, while it was held that if the policy required that payment be made to the spouse only if she was living at the time of receipt by the insurer of due proof of death, disqualification resulted from other statutory grounds, that decision was reversed.[5]

In determining whether the power of appointment satisfies the statutory requirements, the same rules apply as to life estates with such power.[6]

Where payments by the insurer commenced during the decedent's life, it is immaterial whether the conditions were satisfied prior to the decedent's death.[7]

Insurance proceeds held by the company with income payable to the wife and the proceeds payable to her estate qualify for the marital deduction.[8] But this is because the entire interest is in the wife,[9] and no other person than the wife has an interest.[10]

It is not necessary that the phrase "power to appoint" be used in the contract. Thus, the right to withdraw the amount remain-

---

20. IRC, § 2056(b)(6) (1954 Code); Reg, § 20.2056(b)–6(a).

1. Reg, § 20.2056(b)–6(c)(2).

2. § 234, supra; Telegraphic Ruling, July 20, 1948.

3. Reg, § 20.2056(b)–6(d).

4. Note 3, supra.

5. § 232, supra.

6. Note 1, supra.

7. Reg, § 20.2056(b)–6(c)(3).

8. Reg, § 20.2056(b)–6(e)(3).

9. Letter Ruling, July 22, 1949.

10. Telegraphic Ruling, April 14, 1948.

ing in the fund or to direct that such amount be paid to the estate of the spouse at her death, satisfies the condition.[11]

In the common type of payment provision, with the proceeds payable to the wife in installments, and any installments not paid before her death, to be paid to other contingent beneficiaries, there is a failure to comply with the statutory requirement.[12]

§ 236. Schedule M; Marital Deduction; Direction for Purchase of Terminable Interest.

Reference has been made to the fact that the statute provides that no deduction is to be allowed if a terminable interest is to be acquired for the surviving spouse, *pursuant to directions of the decedent,* by his executor or the trustee of a trust.[13] This is the situation where the decedent *directs* that his executor or trustee purchase an annuity for the surviving spouse. The statute provides that the proceeds of insurance payable to the surviving spouse shall be considered an interest in property passing.[14] But it also provides that if a terminable interest is to be acquired *pursuant to directions* of the decedent, by his executor or by the trustee of a trust, even though such an interest might not be disqualified under subparagraphs (A) and (B) of paragraph (b)(1) of Section 2056 it shall nevertheless not be allowed as a deduction.[15] This does not apply to a nonrefund joint and survivor annuity purchased by the decedent.[16]

If the provision is not mandatory the section would not apply. A general investment power, authorizing investments in both terminable interests and other property, is not a direction to invest in a terminable interest.[17]

§ 237. Schedule M; Marital Deduction; Entire Interest or Specific Portion.

Two of the exceptions to the terminable interest rule, as we have seen,[18] provide for their application if the surviving spouse receives for life *all the income from the entire interest, or* all the income from *a specific portion* thereof, in the case of property other than the proceeds of insurance,[19] and in the case of insur-

---

11. Reg, § 20.2056(b)-6(e)(4).
12. White, 22 TC 641 (1954); Reilly, 25 TC 366 (1955).
13. IRC, § 2056(b)(1)(C) (1954 Code).
14. IRC, § 2056(e)(7) (1954 Code).
15. IRC, § 2056(B)(1) (1954 Code).
16. Reg, § 20.2056(b)-1(g)(3).
17. Reg, § 20.2056(b)-1(f).
18. §§ 234, 235, supra.
19. IRC, § 2056(b)(5) (1954 Code).

ance, if *all of the proceeds or a specific portion* of the proceeds are payable in installments to the spouse for life.[20]

The qualification of a portion was new to the 1954 Code, and applied only in the case of decedents dying on and after August 17, 1954 prior to the Technical Amendments Act of 1958.[20a] Under the 1939 Code the marital deduction was denied in a number of cases in which the spouse was entitled to a portion of a trust or the proceeds of insurance.[1] In such cases as have not been closed by compromise or closing agreement, refund may be had if the application is made in time.

Since a marital deduction is allowed for each qualifying separate interest in property passing from the decedent to his spouse, each property interest in which the surviving spouse received some rights is considered separately in determining whether her rights extend to the entire interest or to a specific portion of the entire interest. A property interest which consists of several identical units of property (such as a block of 250 shares of stock, whether evidenced by one or several certificates) is considered one property interest, unless certain of the units are to be segregated and accorded different treatment, in which case each segregated group of items is considered a separate property interest. The bequest of a specified sum of money constitutes the bequest of a separate property interest if immediately following distribution by the executor, and thenceforth, it and the investments made with it, must be so segregated as to permit its identification as a separate item of property.[2]

The determination of the amount of the specific portion is more likely to present questions. If either the right to income or the power of appointment passing to the surviving spouse pertains only to a specific portion of a property interest passing from the decedent, the marital deduction is allowed only to the extent that the rights in the surviving spouse meet all the five conditions heretofore discussed.[3] While the rights over the income and the power must coexist as to the same interest in property, *it is not necessary that the right over the income or the power as to such interest be in the same proportion.* But whichever interest is

---

20. IRC, § 2056(b)(6) (1954 Code).

20a. See § 225, supra.

1. Shedd, 23 TC 41, affd 237 F2d 345 (CA 9) (1954); Hoffenberg, 22 TC 1185, affd 223 F2d 470 (CA 2) (1955); Rev Rul 54–20, 1954–1 CB 195; Sweet v

Comm, 234 F2d 401 (CA 10), affg 24 TC 488, cert den 352 US 878, 1 L ed 2d 79, 77 S Ct 100 (1956).

2. Reg, § 20.2056(b)–5(d).

3. §§ 234, 235, supra.

smaller is the extent to which the deduction is limited. Thus, if the right is to all the income, but the power of appointment applies to only half of the property, the deductible interest is limited to half. If the right is to a quarter of the income, and the power of appointment extends to all of the property, only a quarter of the interest is deductible. If there is a right to either the income or the power to appoint, but they do not both exist, there is no right to the deduction.[4]

A partial interest in property is not treated as a specific portion of the entire interest unless the rights of the surviving spouse in income and as to the power constitute a fractional or percentile share of a property interest so that such interest or share in the surviving spouse reflects its proportionate share of the increment or decline in the whole of the property interest to which the income rights and the power relate. Thus, if the right of the spouse to income and the power extend to one half or a specified percentage of the property, or the equivalent, the interest is considered as a specific portion. On the other hand, if the annual income of the spouse is limited to a specific sum, or if she has a power to appoint only a specific sum out of a larger fund, the interest is not a deductible interest. Even though the rights in the surviving spouse may not be expressed in terms of a definite fraction or percentage, a deduction may be allowable if it is shown that the effect of local law is to give the spouse rights which are identical to those she would have acquired if the size of the share had been expressed in terms of a definite fraction or percentage.[5]

In the case of insurance, the same principles for determining what constitutes a specific portion apply. However, the interest in the proceeds passing to the surviving spouse will not be disqualified by the fact that the installment payments or interest to which the spouse is entitled or the amount of the proceeds over which the power of appointment is exercisable may be expressed in terms of a specific sum rather than a fraction or a percentage of the proceeds, provided it is shown that such sums are a definite or fixed percentage or fraction of the total proceeds.[6]

4. Reg, § 20.2056(b)–5(b).
5. Reg, § 20.2056(b)–5(c).

6. Reg, § 20.2056(b)–6(b)(c)(1).

§ 238. Schedule M; Marital Deduction; Limitation on Aggregate of Deductions.

The statute provides that the aggregate amount of the deduction allowed as the marital deduction *shall not exceed* 50% of the value of *the adjusted gross estate*.[7]

For the purposes of the statute the adjusted gross estate shall be computed by subtracting from the entire value of the gross estate the aggregate amount of the deductions allowed for funeral and administration expenses, claims against the estate, mortgages and liens, and the taxes allowed as deductions and net losses.[8]

There is a special rule for computation of the marital deduction in cases involving community property, discussed hereafter.[9]

It is to be noted that the *maximum amount* allowable is 50% of the adjusted gross estate. This does not mean that the amount of the marital deduction will be 50% of the adjusted gross estate, for the amount of the deduction is either the amount *actually* passing to the spouse *or* 50% of the adjusted gross estate, whichever is *less*.

If the fiduciary decides to take administration expenses as Income Tax deductions,[10] the adjusted gross estate is determined without taking such deductions for Estate Tax purposes.[11] This will, of course, increase the amount of the marital deduction.

It must be borne in mind that the maximum amount which may be allowable may be reduced by other items.[12] Local law may have the effect of increasing the amount of the deduction.[13] The construction of the will may also affect the amount of the deduction.[14]

§ 239. Schedule M; Marital Deduction; Other Interests Which Qualify for the Marital Deduction.

We have heretofore discussed the circumstances under which terminable interests of different kinds will qualify for the marital deduction. Both the statute and the Regulations expand upon such interests. Emphasis thereon tends to obscure the fact that there are many other interests which are not terminable

7. IRC, § 2056(c)(1) (1954 Code).
8. IRC, § 2056(c)(2)(A) (1954 Code).
9. § 243, infra.
10. § 223, supra.
11. Rev Rul, 55–225, 1955–1 CB 460; Rev Rul, 55–643, 1955–2 CB 386.

12. See §§ 231, 233, supra.
13. See King v Wiseman, 147 F Supp 156 (1957).
14. Thompson v Wiseman, 233 F2d 734 (CA 10), affg 56–1 USTC ¶11,591 (1956).

interests, and which need not meet the tests applicable to the latter.

The statute provides that the marital deduction is allowed for the value of *any interest* which passes or has passed from the decedent to the surviving spouse to the extent that such interest is included in determining the value of the gross estate.[15] It then proceeds to define terminable interests and provide exceptions which will permit such interests to qualify.[16]

We have discussed the circumstances under which qualification may be had of such interests.[17] We shall now consider interests other than terminable interests which may qualify for the marital deduction.

Obviously, an outright gift, devise, or bequest will qualify.[18] Where the spouse takes her interest by intestacy, her share also qualifies.[19] A dower or curtesy interest (or statutory interest in lieu thereof) if not a terminable interest, qualifies.[20] If the surviving spouse elects to take against the will the interest so passing qualifies if it is otherwise qualified under the statute.[1] If the interest so passing is a terminable interest, not within the exceptions, no deduction is allowable. If the wife receives a property interest as the result of a will contest, it will be deductible only if it was received as a bona fide recognition of her enforceable rights in the estate, pursuant to the decision of the Surrogate's Court, *upon the merits in an adversary proceeding,* following a genuine and active contest, and only to the extent that the court passed upon the facts upon which deductibility of the property interest depends.[2] Other similar interests which qualify are: property exempted from execution and set off to the spouse,[3] a *vested* right to a widow's allowance,[4] and property held jointly by the decedent and his wife, such as joint bank accounts or estates by the entirety.[5]

15. IRC, § 2056(a) (1954 Code).

16. IRC, § 2056(b) (1954 Code).

17. §§ 230, 232, 234, 235, supra.

18. IRC, § 2056(e)(1)(4) (1954 Code).

19. IRC, § 2056(e)(4) (1954 Code).

20. IRC, § 2056(e)(3) (1954 Code); Crosby & Berry v US, 148 F Supp 910, supplemented 151 F Supp 497 (1956).

1. IRC, § 2056(e)(3) (1954 Code); Sperry v Brodrick, 123 F Supp 108 (1954); Reg, § 20.2056(e)–2(c).

2. Reg, § 20.2056(e)–2(d).

3. Rev Rul 55–419, 1955–1 CB 458.

4. Rev Rul 83, 1953–1 CB 395; Rev Rul 56–26, 1956–1 CB 447; King v Wiseman, note 13, supra; see also Rensenhouse v Comm, 27 TC 107, remanded 252 F2d 562 (CA 6) (1958); Reg, § 20.2056(e)–2(a).

5. Awtry v Comm, 221 F2d 749 (CA 8) (1955); Peterson v Comm, 56–1 USTC ¶11,597 (CA 8) (1955); Kingery v US, 56–1 USTC ¶11,587 (1956).

An interest which has passed to the surviving spouse during the decedent's lifetime, but is subsequently included in decedent's estate as a taxable lifetime transfer,[6] likewise qualifies.[7]

Where the wife acquires property from the husband because of his exercise or nonexercise of a power of appointment, the interest if otherwise qualified, is deductible.[8]

Insurance payable to the surviving spouse in a lump sum qualifies for the deduction.[9]

An example of property received outright and qualified as property passing to the surviving spouse may be found in a bequest pursuant to an antenuptial agreement.[10]

On the other hand it is held that an Income Tax refund due the decedent on a joint return, he having paid the tax,[11] the proceeds of insurance receivable under the World War Veteran's Act of 1924, or the National Service Life Insurance Act of 1940,[12] and homestead rights,[13] do not qualify for the deduction. Of course, where there are no assets in the estate after the payment of funeral and administration expenses and debts, there can be no marital deduction.[14]

§ 240. Schedule M; Marital Deduction; Disclaimers.

If a surviving spouse *disclaims* an interest which would otherwise pass to her, then such interest shall be considered as passing to the person entitled to receive the interest as the result of the disclaimer.[15]

If *in the absence of a disclaimer* by *a person other* than the surviving spouse an interest would pass to such person, and such person disclaims the interest, as a result of which the wife receives it, such interest does not qualify for the marital deduction.[16]

This is a sort of damned if you do and damned if you do not provision. A disclaimer is a complete and unqualified refusal to accept the rights to which one is entitled. If the wife disclaims a bequest of the husband and the property passes to others, it does not qualify for the deduction. If another disclaims the be-

---

6. See §§ 118 et seq, supra.

7. IRC, § 2056(e)(4) (1954 Code).

8. IRC, § 2056(e)(6) (1954 Code); Reg, § 20.2056(e)-1(a)(2).

9. IRC, § 2056(e)(7) (1954 Code).

10. Rev Rul 54-446, 1954-2 CB 303.

11. Special Ruling, August 9, 1957.

12. Rev Rul 57-423, IRB 1957-38, p 16.

13. Nelson v Comm, 232 F2d 720 (CA 5) (1956).

14. Wheeler, 26 TC 466 (1956); Hohensee, 25 TC 1258 (1956).

15. IRC, § 2056(d)(1) (1954 Code).

16. IRC, § 2056(d)(2) (1954 Code).

quest from the husband, and it passes to the wife, it does not qualify. However, if the wife disclaims a bequest, which then falls into the residue, in which she shares, her share of the bequest is entitled to the deduction, but if it becomes part of the residue because of disclaimer by another under the same circumstances, it is not entitled to the deduction.[17]

There have been no answers given to many of the questions raised by the statute. The principal question has been as to whether there may be a partial disclaimer. The Regulation does not recognize a partial disclaimer under a power of appointment,[18] and by implication does not recognize it under the provisions for the marital deduction.[19]

Where property passes under intestacy statutes, one has no right to renounce in order to avoid vesting title in himself.[20] A testamentary benefit, however, may be renounced.[1] The Gift Tax consequences of such action are not here involved.

The right of disclaimer also applies to the proceeds of insurance.[2] It should be noted that there is a distinction between the spouse disclaiming such proceeds, and accepting them but directing the insurance proceeds to be paid after her death to another. In the former case there is no deduction allowable, while in the latter there is.[3]

A renunciation of rights under a will as a result of which there is received a dower or curtesy interest will not entitle to the marital deduction, since such interest is a terminable one.[4]

It must also be pointed out that if the disclaimer is for a consideration, then there has been no refusal of the rights to which the beneficiary was entitled.[5]

§ 241. Schedule M; Marital Deduction; Election by Surviving Spouse.

One of the many questions which arise in connection with the marital deduction is the effect on its allowance when property interests pass to the surviving spouse neither under the intestacy laws, gifts, by will nor other instrument, but as the result of her

17. Sen Fin Comm Rep 1948 Rev Act, PL 471 80th Cong.
18. Reg, § 20.2041–3(d)(6).
19. Reg, § 20.2056(d)–1(a).
20. Bostian v Milens, 239 Mo App 555, 193 SW2d 797 (1946); Coomes v Finegan, 233 Ia 448, 7 NW2d 729 (1943).

1. Brown v Routzahn, 63 F2d 914 (CCA 6), cert den 290 US 641, 78 L ed 72, 54 S Ct 60 (1933).
2. Reg, § 20.2056(d)–1.
3. Note 19, supra.
4. Reg, § 20.2056(e)–2(c).
5. Note 17, supra.

claiming her marital rights under applicable law. Where the decedent makes a lesser provision for the surviving spouse than she is entitled to, either under a right of dower or curtesy, a right of election, or under community property laws, if the spouse elects to take her statutory rights in lieu of such provision, then the property interests provided by the decedent are not considered as having passed from the decedent to his spouse, but instead the property which she has under her statutory rights is considered as having so passed.[6]

Whether or not the interest which has so passed qualifies for the marital deduction depends upon whether the interest received as the result of the election is a deductible or nondeductible interest. If under applicable local law it is a terminable interest, it will not.[7] If, however, there is a vested right to the commuted value of the interest, it is a deductible interest.[8]

§ 242. Schedule M; Marital Deduction; Will Contests.

While the statute makes no reference to interests received by the spouse as the result of a will contest, or which she releases in settlement thereof, the Regulation provides that if as a result of a controversy involving the decedent's will, or involving any bequest or devise thereunder, *his surviving spouse assigns or surrenders* a property interest in settlement of the controversy, the interest so assigned or surrendered is not considered as having passed from the decedent to his surviving spouse.[9] The Tax Court has so held.[10]

If as a result of the controversy involving the decedent's will, or involving any bequest or devise thereunder, a property interest is *assigned or surrendered to the surviving spouse,* the interest so acquired will be regarded as having passed from the decedent to his surviving spouse *only if* the assignment or surrender was a bona fide recognition of enforceable rights of the surviving spouse in the decedent's estate. Such a bona fide recognition will be presumed where the assignment or surrender was pursuant to a decision of a local court *upon the merits in an adversary proceeding* following a genuine and active contest. However, such a decree will be accepted only to the extent that the court

---

6. Reg, § 20.2056(e)–2(c).
7. Rev Rul 279, 1953–2 CB 275.
8. US v Traders Nat Bank of Kansas, 248 F2d 667 (CA 8) affg 148 F Supp 278 (1957).

9. Reg, § 20.2056(e)–2(d)(1).
10. Tebb, 27 TC 671 (1957).

passed upon the facts upon which deductibility of the property interests depends. If the assignment was pursuant to a decree rendered by consent, or pursuant to an agreement not to contest the will or not to probate the will, it will not necessarily be accepted as a bona fide evaluation of the rights of the spouse.[11] The test of bona fides is substantially the same as that in the case of deductions generally.[12] This does not mean that where there has been a settlement of a will contest the amount received by the spouse will not qualify for the marital deduction. The Regulation merely states an evidentiary rule and creates a presumption in the case of property received as the result of a decree in a genuine contest. If upon the facts the settlement was the result of an arm's length transaction, it will be recognized.[13] If on the other hand there is a decree in a nonadversary proceeding which is collusive, it will not be recognized.[14]

§ 243. Schedule M; Marital Deduction; in Community Property Law States.

Since the purpose of the Revenue Act of 1948 was to equalize the tax status of citizens of community property law states and noncommunity property law states, it became necessary to establish a special rule for computing the adjusted gross estate in the case of community property, in order that a double deduction might not result in such cases.[15] This has been carried over into the 1954 Code, *except that as to persons dying on and after August 17, 1954 the conversion of community property into separate property at any time after December 31, 1941* results in such property being considered community property for the purposes of the statute,[16] whereas in the case of decedents dying prior to that date, such was the result only if the conversion took place during the calendar year 1942, or after April 2, 1948, the date of the enactment of the Revenue Act of 1948.[17]

If the decedent and his surviving spouse at any time held property as community property under the law of any state, Territory, or possession of the United States, or any foreign country, then the *adjusted gross estate* shall be determined by subtracting from the entire value of the gross estate *the sum of*

11. Reg, § 20.2056(e)–2(d)(2).
12. § 193, supra.
13. Barrett, 22 TC 606 (1954).
14. Stallworth, 16 TCM 741 (1957).

15. Note 17, supra.
16. IRC, § 2056(c)(2)(C) (1954 Code).
17. IRC, § 812(e)(2)(C) (1939 Code).

(1) the value of property which is at the time of his death held as community property; *and*

(2) the value of property transferred by the decedent during his life, if at the time of such transfer the property was held as community property; *and*

(3) the amount receivable as insurance under policies on the life of the decedent, to the extent purchased with premiums or other consideration paid out of property held as such community property; *and*

(4) an amount which bears the same ratio to the aggregate of the deductions for funeral and administration expenses, claims, debts, and losses, which the value of the property included in the gross estate diminished by the total of (1), (2) and (3), bears to the entire value of the gross estate.

For purposes of (1), (2) and (3), community property (except property which is considered as community property solely by reason of the provisions of Section 2056(c)(2)(C), that is, because of the conversion of community property into separate property after December 31, 1941) shall be considered as not "held as such community property" as of any moment of time, if in case of the death of the decedent at that moment, such property (and not merely one half thereof) would be or would have been includible in determining the value of the gross estate prior to the Revenue Act of 1942. The amount to be subtracted under (1), (2), and (3) cannot exceed the value of the interest in the property described in (1), (2) and (3), which is included in determining the value of the gross estate.[18]

The effect of this is that in computing the decedent's gross estate, his interest in community property and his separate property are totalled. There is then subtracted from that amount (1) his interest in community property, plus his interest in (2) transfers of community property includible in his gross estate because of contemplation of death or similar reasons, plus (3) his interest in the proceeds of insurance on his life purchased with community property. The ratio of the result to the property includible in the gross estate, is the extent to which deductions for funeral and administration expenses, claims, debts, and losses are permitted to reduce this result. What is left is the adjusted gross estate. The provision appears to apply particu-

18. IRC, § 2056(c)(2)(B) (1954 Code).

larly to California community property so held prior to July 29, 1927, the date of the enactment of California Code § 161a.[19]

It is immaterial whether the decedent bequeaths his interest in separate property or community property to the surviving spouse.[20] If the decedent has separate property he need not bequeath such property to his surviving spouse in order to obtain the marital deduction. As long as there is separate property upon which to allow the marital deduction, a bequest of his interest in community property qualifies. No marital deduction will be allowed if the only property included in the gross estate is community property.

If after December 31, 1941, in the case of decedents dying on and after August 17, 1954, property held as community property (unless considered as above not so held) was *converted* by the decedent and the surviving spouse, by one transaction or a series of transactions, *into separate property* (including any form of co-ownership by them), the separate property so acquired by the decedent and any property acquired at any time by the decedent in exchange therefor shall be considered as "held as such community property".[1]

Where the value at the time of such conversion of the separate property so acquired by the decedent exceeded the value at the time of the separate property so acquired by the decedent's spouse, the decedent's separate property so acquired shall be considered as community property for the purposes of (1), (2) and (3) above, only in respect to the portion of said separate property as the portion which the value of the spouse's separate property so acquired is of the value of the decedent's separate property so acquired, value being fixed as of the date of the conversion.[2]

It will be observed that the statute refers to the fact that property shall not be considered held as community property if at the death of the decedent the entire property would have been included in the gross estate.[3] The Regulation refers to this as an expectant interest.[4] This situation exists in the case of

19. See §§ 41, 48, supra.

20. Sen Fin Comm Rep 1948 Rev Act, PL 471, 80th Cong; See also California Trust Co v Riddell, 136 F Supp 7 (1955).

1. IRC, § 2056(c)(2)(C)(i) (1954 Code).

2. IRC, § 2056(c)(2)(C)(ii) (1954 Code).

3. Note 18, supra.

4. Reg, § 20.2056(c)-2(c)(d).

California community property acquired prior to July 29, 1927.[5]

The determination having been made as to which property is separate property and which is considered community property, and the maximum marital deduction determined, computation of the tax is made in the same manner as in noncommunity property estates. The method of computation is treated hereafter.[6]

§ 244. Schedule M; Marital Deduction; Return.

As might be anticipated, in view of the complexity of the marital deduction, the Instructions for preparation of Schedule M are extensive. The major portion thereof is devoted to an explanation of the statute, in condensed form. Before listing the items which qualify for the marital deduction, it will be necessary to determine whether or not they qualify. That having been determined the extent to which they are to be listed must be determined. Thus, if the property passing consists of a specific portion rather than the entire interest, the return should indicate the manner in which the value of the specific portion has been determined.

The Instructions point out that terminable interests[7] and terminable interests directed by the decedent to be purchased for the surviving spouse[8] are to be excluded from the schedule. It is further noted that there is to be included only the amount of property passing, reduced by tainted assets,[9] interests for which deductions have been allowed in Schedules J to L, inclusive,[10] and reduced by the amount of a mortgage or other encumbrance affecting the property passing.[11]

It is directed that a full description of each property interest listed be given and that the items be numbered in sequence, indicating the instrument (including clause or paragraph number if the instrument is so drawn) or provision of law under which each item passed to the surviving spouse. Where possible, the schedule and item number of the property interest as it appears in the Schedules should be shown. It has been the writer's prac-

---

5. See § 48 supra.

6. § 285, infra.

7. Instructions, Schedule M, Par 7(a) Form 706.

8. Instructions, Schedule M, Par 7 (b), Form 706.

9. Instructions, Schedule M, Par 7 (c), Form 706.

10. Instructions, Schedule M, Par 7 (d), Form 706.

11. Instructions, Schedule M, Par 7 (e), Form 706.

tice to refer to items only by the Schedule and Item number, and not to give any other description, when the entire interest is qualified. The value of each item is given without taking into account the effect thereon of the Federal Estate Tax or any other death tax. If the alternate valuation is used, the amount is set forth in the appropriate column. If there is included a bequest of the residue, or a portion of the residue of the decedent's estate, there should be submitted a copy of the computation showing how the value of such item was determined. Such computation should include a statement showing:

(a) The value of all property which is included in the decedent's gross estate but does not pass under the will, such as transfers, jointly owned property which passed to the survivor on decedent's death, and the insurance payable to specific beneficiaries.

(b) The values of all specific and general legacies or devises, with an appropriate reference in each instance to the applicable clause or paragraph of the decedent's will or codicil. (In any case where legacies are made to each member of a class, for example, $1,000. to each of decedent's employees, only the number of each such class and the aggregate value of property received by them need be furnished.)

(c) The dates of birth of all persons, the durations of whose lives may affect the value of the residuary interest passing to the surviving spouse.

(d) Any other information that may appear material, such as that relating to any claim, not arising under the will, to any part of the estate.[12]

The total of the values listed on Schedule M must be reduced by the amount of the Federal Estate Tax, and the amount of State or other death taxes, which are payable out of, or chargeable against the property interests involved. The amount of such taxes are entered at the bottom of the schedule. State death taxes claimed must be supported by an identification and computation of the amount of State or other death taxes shown in (b), at the bottom of the schedule.[13]

The computation of the amount of taxes payable out of the property passing to the surviving spouse, when the marital de-

---

12. Instructions, Schedule M, Par 8, Form 706.

13. Instructions, Schedule M, Par 9, Form 706.

ductions and taxes are interrelated is extremely complicated and is treated in the chapter on computations.[14]

If property interests passing by the decedent's will are listed in Schedule M, a *certified* copy of the order admitting the will to probate must be submitted with the return. If, at the time the return is filed, the court of probate jurisdiction has entered any decree interpreting the will or any provisions thereof affecting any of the interests listed in Schedule M, or has entered any order of distribution, a copy thereof should also be submitted with the return. If the surviving spouse has filed with the court a renunciation of the decedent's will, or an election to take under the will, or a disclaimer of any property interest, a copy thereof is required. Additional evidence to support the deduction claimed may be requested by the District Director.[15]

As in preparation of other schedules, the digestive processes of the Estate Tax examiner will be aided if he is furnished with all the evidence he needs to make his determination. One of the great disillusionments of preparation of this schedule, is that many times, after a complicated computation has been completed, the Estate Tax examiner revalues an item, thus requiring a recomputation. In such case, however, the examiner makes the recomputation and it is only necessary to check his figures.

FORM NO. 28

Schedule M; Marital Deduction

If the decedent died testate, the person or persons filing the return should answer the following questions. Only question 4 should be answered in case the decedent died intestate. If the answer to any question is "Yes," full details should be submitted with the return.

1. Has any action been instituted to contest the will or any provision thereof affecting any property interest listed on this schedule or for construction of the will or any such provision? [ ] Yes [x] No
2a. Had the surviving spouse the right to declare an election between (i) the provisions made in his or her favor by the will and (ii) dower, curtesy, or a statutory interest? [ ] Yes [x] No
2b. If answer to question 2a is "Yes," has the surviving spouse renounced the will and elected to take dower, curtesy, or a statutory interest? [ ] Yes [ ] No
2c. Elected to take under the will. [ ] Yes [ ] No

14. §§ 287 et seq, infra.

15. Instructions, Schedule M, Par 10, Form 706.

2d. Does the surviving spouse contemplate renouncing the will and electing to take dower, curtesy, or a statutory interest?
[ ] Yes   [ ] No

3. According to the information and belief of the person or persons filing the return, is any action described under question 1 designed or contemplated?   [ ] Yes   [x] No

4. According to the information and belief of such person or persons, has any person other than the surviving spouse asserted (or is any such assertion contemplated) a right to any property interest listed on this schedule, other than as indicated under questions 1 or 3?   [ ] Yes   [x] No

Item No.	Description of property interests passing to surviving spouse	Value
1	House and lot, 1921 William Street, NW, Washington, D. C., devised by Article Third of Will (Schedule A, Item 1)	$36,000.00
2	Proceeds of Home Life Insurance Company, Policy 108965 (Schedule D, Item 2)	10,000.00
3	Pecuniary bequest under Article Fourth of Will	10,000.00
4	Bequest of share of residue under Article Sixth (See computation annexed)	57,014.75

TOTAL $113,014.75

Less: (a) Federal estate tax payable out of above-listed property interests $0.00

    (b) Other death taxes payable out of above-listed property interests 0.00

Total of items (a) and (b) 0.00

Net value of above-listed property interests (also enter under the Recapitulation, Schedule O) $113,014.75

(If more space is needed, insert additional sheets of same size)

Estate of WINTHROP BENSON

FORM NO. 29

Computation of Spouse's Share in Residuary Estate

Nontestamentary property interests passing to spouse
    Proceeds of insurance $10,000.00
Gross Testamentary Estate $285,462.90

Charges

Devise under Article Third	$36,000.00	
General Legacies under Articles Fourth and Fifth	20,000.00	
Funeral and Administration Expenses	18,395.87	
Debts	18,101.79	
Mortgages	19,920.98	114,418.64

Net distributable estate before taxes $171,044.26
Surviving spouse's interest under Article Sixth—⅓ of
    residue $57,014.75

§ 245. Schedule N; Transfers for Public, Charitable, and Religious Uses; Statutory Provisions.

There is allowed as a deduction from the gross estate transfers made for public, charitable and religious uses. For the deduction to be allowed, however, it is necessary that the bequest comply with all the statutory requirements, which are many and varied.

Under the 1954 Code a deduction is allowable for the amount of all bequests, legacies, devises, or transfers (including the interest which falls into any such bequest, legacy, devise, or transfer as a result of an irrevocable disclaimer of a bequest, legacy, devise, transfer, or power, *if the disclaimer is made before* the date prescribed for the filing of the Estate Tax return)—

(1) to or for the use of the United States, any State, Territory, any political subdivision thereof, or the District of Columbia, *for exclusively public purposes;*

(2) to or for the use of any corporation organized and operated *exclusively* for religious, charitable, scientific, literary, or educational purposes, including the encouragement of art and the prevention of cruelty to children or animals, *no part of the net earnings of which inures to the benefit of any private stockholder or individual,* and *no substantial part of the activities* of which is carrying on *propaganda,* or otherwise attempting, to *influence legislation;*

(3) to a trustee or trustees, or a fraternal society, order, or association operating under the lodge system, but only if such contributions or gifts are to be used by such trustee or trustees, or by such fraternal society, order, or association, *exclusively* for religious, charitable, scientific, literary, or educational purposes, or for the prevention of cruelty to children or animals, and *no substantial part of the activities* of such trustee or trustees, or of such fraternal society, order, or association, is carrying on *propaganda,* or otherwise attempting, to *influence legislation;* or

(4) to or for the use of any veteran's organization incorporated by Act of Congress, or of its departments or local chapters or posts, no part of the net earnings of which inures to the benefit of any private shareholder or individual.

For purposes of the subsection, the complete termination before the date prescribed for the filing of the Estate Tax return of a power to consume, invade, or appropriate property for the benefit of an individual before such power has been exercised by reason of the death of such individual or for any other reason shall be considered and deemed to be an irrevocable disclaimer with the same force and effect as though he had filed such irrevocable disclaimer.[16]

This provision of the 1954 Code changed the provisions of the 1939 Code, in that veterans' organizations were added to the group qualified, and the termination of a power to consume before the filing of the Estate Tax return is deemed an irrevocable disclaimer. There should be noted the emphasis on exclusivity, the use of the gift for the benefit of individuals, and propaganda or lobbying.

Property includible in the gross estate because of a taxable power of appointment received by one of the donees described above, for purposes of the section is considered a bequest of the decedent.[17] There was added to the statute in 1956,[18] effective as to the estates of persons dying on and after August 17, 1954, a provision to allow a deduction to the extent that the donee of a testamentary power of appointment over the corpus of a trust declares by affidavit his intention, within one year of the decedent's death, to exercise the power in favor of *specified* charitable organizations and the power is exercised in the manner stated

16. IRC, § 2055(a) (1954 Code).   18. PL 1011, 84th Congress.
17. IRC, § 2055(b)(1) (1954 Code).

in the affidavit. *It applies only* if the donee of the power is *over eighty years of age* at the time of the decedent's death.[19]

The statute further provides for the reduction of the deduction by the amount of death taxes payable out of the bequest,[20] the limitations on the amount of the deduction,[1] the disallowance of the deduction in certain cases,[2] and cross references to statutes covering bequests to certain national public organizations,[3] which are discussed in the succeeding sections.

§ 246. Schedule N; Transfers for Public, Charitable, and Religious Uses; Uses Qualifying.

It will have been observed that the statute prescribes definite tests for the allowance of the deduction. It states the entities or organizations which qualify, the purposes of gifts, and those things which will disqualify. While state law will control the determination of the validity of the transfer,[4] whether or not the deduction is allowable depends upon the Federal statute.[5] It must be remembered that the fiduciary has the burden of establishing that the beneficiary is qualified.[6] While it has been held that the Commissioner is not bound by the decision of the state court as to what is a charitable corporation,[7] more recently it has been held that the state courts' determination of what is a charitable bequest is conclusive in determining Federal tax liability.[8]

Except in the case of veterans' organizations the first test is that *the gift be used exclusively* for the statutory purposes. The deduction will be denied if this element be found lacking.[9] In the

19. IRC, § 2055(b)(2) (1954 Code).
20. IRC, § 2055(c) (1954 Code).
1. IRC, § 2055(d) (1954 Code).
2. IRC, § 20755(e) (1954 Code).
3. IRC, § 2055(f) (1954 Code).
4. Newton Trust Co v Comm, 160 F 2d 175 (CCA 1) (1947); Sharpe v Comm, 148 F2d 179 (CCA 3) (1945); Watkins v Fly, 136 F2d 578 (CCA 5), cert den 320 US 769, 88 L ed 459, 64 S Ct 80 (1943).
5. Dumont v Comm, 150 F2d 691 (CCA 3) (1945); Sharpe v Comm, note 4, supra; Hendrickson v Baker-Boyer Nat Bank, 139 F2d 877 (CCA 9) (1944); Robbins v Comm, 111 F2d 828 (CCA 1) (1941); St Louis Union Trust

Co v Burnet, 59 F2d 922 (CCA 8) (1932).
6. Porter v Comm, 60 F2d 673 (CCA 2), affd 288 US 436, 77 L ed 880, 53 S Ct 451 (1932); see also Bretzfelder v Comm, 86 F2d 713 (CCA 2) (1936); Comm v Boston Safe Deposit & Tr Co, 30 BTA 679 (1934); Moore, 21 BTA 279 (1930).
7. First Nat Bank in Dallas v Comm, 45 F2d 509 (CCA 5), cert den 283 US 845, 75 L ed 1454, 51 S Ct 492 (1940).
8. Howell v Dudley, 154 F Supp 571 (1957).
9. Davison v Comm, 60 F2d 50 (CCA 2) (1932); Stoeckel, 2 TC 975 (1943); Greiss v US, 146 F Supp 505 (1956).

case of religious, charitable, scientific, literary, or educational organizations, including those for the encouragement of art and the prevention of cruelty to children or animals, as well as in the case of veterans' organizations, no part of the net earnings of the organization may inure to the benefit of a stockholder or individual. In the case of religious, charitable, scientific, literary, or educational organizations and fraternal societies, orders, or associations, the deduction will be denied if any *substantial part* of their activities is carrying on propaganda or otherwise attempting to influence legislation.[10]

The following bequests to organizations have been held qualified under the statute: to establish a fund for scholarships,[11] for the beneficial usage of the citizens of a community,[12] for benevolent purposes,[13] for erection of a city auditorium,[14] for civic purposes,[15] to a charity to be named by the decedent's widow,[16] for educational purposes,[17] to a college fraternity *solely for educational purposes*,[18] for statutory purposes, although providing for preference of the decedent's family,[19] to provide care for graduate nurses,[20] for the benefit of settlement workers,[1] to Columbia University,[2] for employee protection,[3] to an employee's welfare and retirement fund,[4] to a hospital for the purchase of iron lungs,[5] to a Federation of Women's Clubs,[6] to the New York State Bar Association Foundation,[7] to the William Nelson Cromwell Foundation,[8] to the United States Olympic Association,[9] for the promotion of practical benevolence,[10] to the Ruskin

10. Sharpe v Comm, note 4, supra; Marshall v Comm, 147 F2d 75 (CCA 2), cert den 325 US 872, 89 L ed 1991, 65 S Ct 1413, rehg den 326 US 804, 90 L ed 490, 66 S Ct 14 (1945); Vanderbilt v Comm, 93 F2d 360 (CCA 1) (1938); Old Colony Trust Co v Welch, 25 F Supp 45 (1938).

11. Sells, 10 TC 692 (1948); Blossom, 45 BTA 691 (1941).

12. Koehler v Lewellyn, 44 F2d 654 (1948).

13. St Louis Union Trust Co v Burnet, note 5, supra; Hight v US, 151 F Supp 202 (1957).

14. Sol Op 159, III–1 CB 480.

15. Boyles, 4 TC 1092 (1945).

16. Michigan Trust Co v US, 21 F Supp 482 (1937).

17. Leubuscher, 21 BTA 1022 (1931).

18. Elmira Bank & Trust Co v McGowan, 54–2 USTC ¶10,959; but see Hall, 2 BTA 931 (1925).

19. Robinson, 1 TC 19 (1942); Sells, note 11, supra.

20. Gray, 2 TC 97 (1943).

1. Wald, 3 TCM 802 (1944).

2. Meirhoff v Higgins, 42–1 USTC ¶10,185.

3. Eagan v Comm, 43 F2d 881 (CCA 5) (1930).

4. Carlson, 21 TC 291 (1953).

5. Gilbert, 4 TC 1006 (1945).

6. Huntington Nat Bank of Columbus, 13 TC 760 (1949).

7. Special Ruling, Oct 17, 1950.

8. Dulles v Johnson, 57–2 USTC ¶11,725.

9. Special Ruling, Apr 15, 1952.

10. Union & New Haven Tr Co v Eaton, 20 F2d 419 (1927).

Art Club,[11] to an association for the support of an Indian hospital and medical college,[12] to Anti-Vivisection societies,[13] to the Committee on Prisons and Prison Labor,[14] to a nurses organization for aid of student nurses,[15] for the care of a Bar Association law library,[16] for the care of neglected animals,[17] to an alumni association of a university,[18] to a cemetery,[19] and to the Board of Temperance, Prohibition and Public Morals of the Methodist Episcopal Church.[20]

The following bequests have, however, been held not deductible: to trustees to be delivered to an organization to be organized for statutory purposes,[1] to a private trust for the education of the decedent's grandchildren,[2] a bequest to a fraternal society which did not state the use thereof,[3] a bequest for a family memorial,[4] to a Consistory of the Ancient and Accepted Scottish Rite,[5] to Masonic bodies,[6] to cemetery associations,[7] to Elmira Free Academy,[8] to Waterbury Medical Association,[9] to National Women's Party,[10] to Free Thinkers of America,[11] to The Manhattan Single Tax Club,[12] a bequest to a religious communal society,[13] property passing to a religious society through its members,[14] a bequest to a bar association,[15] and to a sportsmen's club.[16]

In establishing the right to the deduction it is not enough to

11. Wadleigh, 4 TCM 664 (1944).
12. Farrington, 5 TCM 78 (1945).
13. Penn Co for Ins v Helvering, 66 F2d 284 (CA–DC) (1933); Old Colony Trust Co v Welch, 25 F Supp 45 (1938).
14. GCM 19715, 1938–1 CB 499.
15. Davis, 26 TC 549 (1956).
16. Audenried, 26 TC 120 (1956).
17. Rev Rul 55–519, 1955–2 CB 386.
18. Thayer, 24 TC 384 (1955).
19. Note 16, supra; but see Gund v Comm, 113 F2d 61 (CCA 6) cert den 311 US 696, 85 L ed 451, 61 S Ct 134 (1940).
20. Girard Trust Co v Comm, 122 F2d 108 (CCA 3) (1941).
1. ET 3, XII–2 CB 279.
2. Dorsey, 19 TC 493 (1953).
3. Levey v Smith, 103 F2d 643 (CCA 7), cert den 308 US 578, 84 L ed 484, 60 S Ct 94 (1939).
4. Taylor, 40 BTA 375 (1939).
5. McReynolds, 1 BTA 815 (1924).
6. First National Bank in Dallas v Comm, 45 F2d 509 (CCA 5) cert den 283 US 845, 75 L ed 1454, 51 S Ct 492 (1940).
7. Gund v Comm, note 19, supra; Wilber Nat Bank of Oneonta, 17 BTA 654 (1929).
8. Lande, 21 TC 977 (1954).
9. Colonial Trust Co, 19 BTA 174 (1930).
10. Vanderbilt v Comm, 93 F2d 360 (CCA 1) (1938).
11. Old Colony Trust Co v Welch, 25 F Supp 45 (1938).
12. Leubuscher v Comm, 54 F2d 998 (CCA 2) (1932).
13. Rev Rul 57–574, 1957–49 p 34.
14. Rev Rul 55–759, 1955–2 CB 607; Rev Rul 55–760, 1955–2 CB 607.
15. Dulles v Johnson, 155 F2d 275 (1957); but see Rhode Island Hospital Trust Co v US, 58–1 USTC ¶11,747.
16. Griess v US, 146 F Supp 505 (1956).

submit the charter of the organization, where there is any question raised.[17] Evidence should be produced to show that the beneficiary is in fact organized for the statutory purposes.[18]

There are special statutory provisions for the exemption or construction of bequests for the benefit of the Library of Congress, the library of the Post Office Department, the Office of Naval Records and Library, The National Park Service, the Naval Academy Museum and the National Archives Trust Fund Board, as well as for the construction of bequests to various other governmental officers or agencies.[19]

Certain charitable deductions otherwise allowable may be disallowed because of prohibited activities, discussed hereafter.[20]

§ 247. Schedule N; Transfers for Public, Charitable, and Religious Uses; When Not Deductible; Validity of Gift.

It is essential that any gift for which deduction is sought, be valid under state law. Thus, if a bequest is void because it violates the Rule against Perpetuities,[1] exceeds the amount allowable by state law to be given to charity, if the distributees raise an objection, or it violates the statutory time limit for gifts to charitable beneficiaries,[2] it cannot be allowed as a deduction. Where the bequest is voidable because it exceeds the permissible statutory amount, if the legatees do not object, the deduction will be allowed.[3] It will be allowed to the extent permissible, when there is objection.[4] Where the bequest violates a statute with respect to time, it depends upon whether such gifts are void or merely voidable. In the former case, no action of the legatees will permit the deduction.[5] But if the statute makes such gifts voidable and the legatees do not object, the deduction

17. Robertson, BTA memo op, Dec 12, 830–D (1942).

18. See Moore, 21 BTA 279 (1930); Comm v Boston Safe Deposit & Trust Co, 30 BTA 679 (1934).

19. IRC, § 2055(f) (1954 Code).

20. § 248, infra.

1. Hidden v Durey, 34 F2d 174 (1929).

2. Lancaster Trust Co, 3 BTA 298 (1925); Selig v US, 73 F Supp 886, affd 166 F2d 299 (CCA 3) (1947); Carey, 9 TC 1047, affd 168 F2d 400 (CCA 3) (1948); Riddle, 21 TC 1109 (1954).

3. Dockweiler, 30 BTA 1136 (1934); Varick, 10 TC 318 (1948); Humphrey v Millard, 79 F2d 107 (CCA 2) (1935); Dimock v Corwin, 99 F2d 799 (CCA 2) (1938); US v Jacobs, 306 US 363, 83 L ed 763, 59 S Ct 551 (1939).

4. Butler, 18 TC 914 (1952).

5. Riddle, note 2, supra; Carey, note 2, supra; Janson, 3 BTA 298 (1925); Lancaster Trust Co, note 2, supra; Selig v US, note 2, supra; Watkins v Fly, 136 F2d 578 (CCA 5), cert den 320 US 769, 88 L ed 459, 64 S Ct 80 (1943).

is allowable.[6] The deduction may also be denied because the gift is indefinite,[7] or because of failure to specify the statutory use.[8]

§ 248. Schedule N; Transfers for Public, Charitable, and Religious Uses; Disallowance for Prohibited Transactions.

The statute provides for disallowance of the deduction for gifts to public, charitable, and religious organizations, when there have been prohibited transactions by the beneficiary, by an oblique reference to Sections 504 and 681 of the Code.[9] These sections are Income Tax sections which eliminate the Income Tax exemptions of such organizations for a taxable year in which it engaged in the transactions prohibited by the statute.

As to transfers made after January 1, 1951, a deduction otherwise allowable, will be disallowed if the organization to which it is made

(1) loans any part of its income to the donor, a member of his family or a corporation controlled by either of them;

(2) makes its services available to such persons or corporation on a preferential basis;

(3) pays any compensation from corpus or income except for personal services actually rendered;

(4) buys securities with such corpus or income, or sells any substantial part of the securities from such income or corpus for other than an adequate consideration;

(5) engages in any other transaction which diverts the corpus or income to the donor, a member of his family, or a corporation controlled by either of them.[10]

Of course, the purpose of this limitation is to insure that a gift to a public, charitable, or religious organization is in fact such and not a cover for the donor.

In cases in which prior notification by the Commissioner is not required in order to limit the deduction of a trust under Section 681(b) or to deny exemption of the organization under Section 503, the deduction otherwise allowable for Estate Tax is not disallowed in respect of transfers made during the same taxable

6. Comm v First Nat Bank, 102 F2d 129 (CCA 5) (1939).

7. Taylor, 40 BTA 375 (1939).

8. Levey v Smith, 103 F2d 643 (CCA 7), cert den 308 US 578, 84 L ed 484, 60 S Ct 94 (1939); Miss Valley Trust Co v Comm, 72 F2d 197 (CCA 8), cert den 293 US 604, 79 L ed 695, 55 S Ct 119 (1934).

9. IRC, § 2055(e) (1954 Code); Reg, § 20.2055-4.

10. IRC, §§ 503, 681 (1954 Code).

year of the trust or organization in which a prohibited transaction occurred or in a prior taxable year unless the decedent or a member of his family was a party to the prohibited transaction. For the purposes of the section, the members of the decedent's family include only his brothers and sisters, whether by whole or half blood, spouse, ancestors, and lineal descendants.[11]

§ 249. Schedule N; Transfers for Public, Charitable, or Religious Uses; Pledges.

We have heretofore noted the fact that in any case in which a claim is founded upon a promise or agreement of the decedent to make a contribution or gift to or for the use of a public, charitable, religious, or veterans' organization described in Section 2055 of the Code, the deduction for such claim shall not be so limited, but shall be limited to the extent that it would be allowable as a charitable deduction.[12]

The effect of this provision is to incorporate the requirements of Section 2055 into the determination of whether a charitable pledge is allowable not as a charitable deduction, but as a deduction for a claim against the estate. The tests for a charitable deduction, heretofore discussed, must therefore be met in such case.

It has recently been held that an unpaid pledge, not supported by consideration, was not deductible, even though it had been allowed by the probate court, since it was not contested.[13]

§ 250. Schedule N; Transfers for Public, Charitable, and Religious Uses; Conditional Gifts.

In order for a charitable gift to be deductible, the amount of the gift must be determinable with reasonable certainty. Thus, if at the date of the decedent's death, a transfer for charitable purposes is dependent upon the performance of some act, or the happening of a precedent event in order that it might become effective, no deduction is allowable unless the possibility that the charitable transfer will not become effective is so remote as to be negligible. If an estate or interest has passed to or is vested in charity at the time of a decedent's death and the estate or interest would be defeated by the performance of some act

11. Reg, § 20.2055-4(c).   13. Sochalski, 14 TCM 72 (1955).
12. § 209, supra.

or the happening of some event, the occurrence of which appeared to have been highly improbable at the time of the decedent's death, the deduction is allowable.[14] It is also noted in the Regulation that the deduction is not allowed in the case of a transfer in trust conveying a present interest in income if by reason of all the conditions and circumstances surrounding the transfer, it appears that the charity may not receive the beneficial enjoyment of the interest.[15]

The allowance or disallowance of conditional charitable gifts as deductions has been the subject of much litigation. The cases are generally divisible into two categories. The first is that in which the possibility of the charity taking at all may be in doubt. The second is that in which the amount which may be received by the charity is not ascertainable. We shall treat of the first category in this section and the second in the succeeding one.

Various conditions which may make the receipt of the gift by the charity uncertain, will defeat the deduction. Thus, a lifetime gift conditioned on the charity performing certain conditions which had not been done at the time of his death,[16] a bequest to a church on compliance with certain conditions, and if not met to the decedent's heirs,[17] the creation of the fund depending upon there being sufficient future income,[18] bequests which were not specific but depended upon the discretion of the trustee,[19] or which depended upon the conduct of the beneficiary,[20] have all been held so uncertain as to disallow the deduction.

On the other hand, a fund which could be diverted to other uses if the trustee did not accept, but which he accepted,[1] and a gift to a religious organization with the right to revoke under certain conditions, have been allowed.[2] In each case there was an accomplished act.

Contingent gifts whose value cannot be determined are not

14. Reg, § 20.2055–2(b).

15. Note 14, supra.

16. US v Fourth Nat Bank in Wichita, 83 F2d 85 (CCA 10), cert den 299 US 575, 81 L ed 423, 57 S Ct 38 (1936).

17. St Louis Union Trust Co v Burnet, 59 F2d 922 (CCA 8) (1932); Delaware Trust Co v Handy, 53 F2d 1042 (1932); Churchill v U. S. 68 F Supp 267 (1946).

18. Old Point Nat Bank, 39 BTA 343 (1939).

19. Norris v Comm, 134 F2d 796 (CCA 7), cert den 320 US 756, 88 L ed 450, 64 S Ct 63 (1943); Delfridge v US, 89 F Supp 845 (1950); Delaney v Gardner, 204 F2d 855 (CA 1) (1953).

20. Note 18, supra; Helvering v Union Trust Co, 125 F2d 401 (CCA 4), cert den 316 US 696, 86 L ed 1766, 62 S Ct 1292 (1942).

1. Bishop, 23 BTA 920 (1931).

2. Brown v Comm, 50 F2d 842 (CCA 3) (1931).

deductible.[3] Such gifts are those in which the charity takes in
the event certain contingencies occur, such as the consent of
the widow,[4] if there be sufficient funds after the needs of a beneficiary are met,[5] or payments be first made to future members
of a class,[6] that the bequest be made if the selection was made
within a year.[7] Gifts to charity dependent on the possibility of
issue will be deductible if it be proven that the possibility is
extinct,[8] but not otherwise.[9] In a recent case a contingent bequest to charity if the testator did not leave issue of his contemplated marriage at the age of 73, was held deductible.[10] Apparently this was the triumph by the court, of experience over
hope, it being held that from all the facts the decedent had intended vested interests for the charity.

Where the survival of a beneficiary is the contingency, the
determination of deductibility appears to be dependent to an even
greater extent that otherwise upon whether the court deciding
the question believes that there is uncertainty. It is difficult
to reconcile the cases on any other basis.[11]

§ 251. Schedule N; Transfers for Public, Charitable, or Religious Uses; Subject to Diversion.

A second way in which a gift to a charity may be uncertain
is where the gift is of a remainder subject to a power to apply
the corpus to the needs of the primary beneficiary. This has been
the source of major litigation on the subject.

Where there is a power of invasion, in order that the deduction
may be allowed, it is necessary that a highly reliable appraisal

---

3. Humes v US, 276 US 487, 72 L
ed 667, 48 S Ct 347 (1927).

4. First Trust Co of St Paul v Reynolds, 137 F2d 518 (CCA 8) (1943).

5. Pomerene, 2 TCM 304 (1943).

6. Penn Co v Brown, 70 F2d 269
(CCA 3) (1934).

7. Burdick v Comm, 117 F2d 972 (CA
2), cert den 314 US 631, 86 L ed 506,
62 S Ct 63 (1941); Danbury Nat Bank
v Fitzpatrick, 55–1 USTC ¶11,526.

8. US v Provident Trust Co, 291
US 272, 78 L ed 793, 54 S Ct 389 (1934);
Guaranty Trust Co of NY, 27 BTA
550 (1932); City Bank Farmers Trust
Co v US, 74 F2d 693 (CCA 2) (1935);
Ninth Bank & Trust Co v US, 15 F
Supp 951 (1936).

9. Comm v Sternberger, 348 US 187,
99 L ed 246, 75 S Ct 229 (1955); Farrington v Comm, 30 F2d 915 (CCA 1),
cert den 279 US 873, 73 L ed 1008, 49
S Ct 513 (1929); Hoagland v Kavanagh, 36 F Supp 875 (1941).

10. Lloyd, 24 TC 624 (1955).

11. See Meirhof v Higgins, 129 F2d
1002 (CCA 1) (1942); Graff v Smith,
100 F Supp 42 (1951); Wood v US,
20 F Supp 197 (1937); Gardiner v Hassett, 63 F Supp 853 (1946); Dean v US,
224 F2d 26 (CA 1) (1955); Gaston,
2 TC 672 (1943); Boston Safe Deposit
& Trust Co, 20 BTA 1159 (1930), 30
BTA 679 (1934); Allen v First Nat
Bank of Georgia, 169 F2d 221 (CCA
5) (1948).

of the amount the charity will receive,[12] based upon conditions on which the extent of the invasion of the corpus is fixed by reference to some readily ascertainable and reliably predictable facts[13] which restrict it by a fixed standard based on the beneficiary's prior way of life,[14] be present. Where the uncertainty of the gift to charity is not appreciably greater than the general uncertainty attending human affairs,[15] or the possibility of invasion is remote,[16] the deduction will be allowed.

Where, however, the direction for the invasion is couched in such phrases as "for use and benefit as the trustee deems advisable",[17] "welfare, comfort, and happiness",[18] "pleasure, comfort, and welfare",[19] "comfort and pleasure",[20] "comfort and support",[1] "necessities and comforts in life",[2] "comfort and convenience",[3] "properly care for and maintain",[4] "if the trustee should deem wise",[5] and other such indefinite standards, the deduction will be denied. The courts are allergic to the words "pleasure", "comfort", and "happiness". In some instances, a standard having been stated, its effect may be negated by the addition of another phrase, such as, invasion for medical needs *or otherwise*,[6] or invasion if net income be not sufficient for the beneficiary's needs *or if for any reason* the beneficiary desired invasion.[7]

But the fact that the provision for invasion contains words which alone would deny the deduction, does not matter if there is in addition a definite standard.[8]

12. Note 3, supra.

13. Bank of America v Comm, 126 F 2d 48 (CCA 9) (1942).

14. Ithaca Trust Co v US, 279 US 151, 73 L ed 647, 49 S Ct 291 (1929).

15. Note 14, supra; Merchant's Nat Bank v Comm, 320 US 256, 88 L ed 35, 64 S Ct 108 (1943); Henslee v Union Planter's Nat Bank, 335 US 595, 93 L ed 259, 69 S Ct 290, rehg den 336 US 915, 93 L ed 1078, 69 S Ct 601 (1949).

16. Rev Rul 54–285, IRB 1954–2 CB 302.

17. Newton Trust Co v Comm, 160 F2d 175 (CCA 1) (1951).

18. Merchants Nat Bank v Comm, note 15, supra; E T 12, 2 CB 335.

19. Henslee v Union Planters' Nat Bank, note 15, supra.

20. Industrial Trust Co v Comm, 151

F2d 592 (CCA 1) cert den 327 US 788, 90 L ed 1014, 66 S Ct 807 (1945).

1. Wiggins, 3 TC 464 (1944); Price v Rothensies, 67 F Supp 591 (1946).

2. Nat Bank of Commerce v Scofield, 169 F2d 145 (CCA 5), cert den 335 US 907, 93 L ed 440, 69 S Ct 410 (1948).

3. Schumacher, 2 TCM 1018 (1943).

4. Homes, 5 TC 1289 (1945).

5. Third Nat Bank & Trust Co v US, 129 F Supp 442, affd 228 F2d 772 (CA 1) (1955).

6. McDonald v Welch, 17 F Supp 549 (1937).

7. Randall v Harrison, 40–2 USTC ¶9498; see also Schmidt, 14 TCM 451 (1944); Gammons v Hassett, 121 F2d 229 (CCA 1), cert den 314 US 673, 86 L ed 539, 62 S Ct 136 (1941).

8. See Jack, 6 TC 241 (1946); Run-

Provisions which have been held to fix a definitely ascertainable standard, are: "properly provide for support and maintenance",[9] "care and maintenance",[10] "suitably maintain in as much comfort as now enjoyed",[11] "for sickness, want or other emergency".[12] Some of the decided cases are difficult to reconcile with the weight of authority to the contrary,[13] except that it must be remembered that while whether the will establishes an ascertainable standard is a question of law depending on its wording,[14] the possibility of invasion is a factual question, as to which the estate has the burden.[15] Where there is ample income, so that no invasion is necessary,[16] or the possibility of invasion is remote,[17] the deduction will be allowed. The fact that the beneficiary is advanced in age is a strong factor in negativing the possibility of the need for invasion,[18] but not necessarily controlling.[19]

If the state court has found that there is no right of invasion, the deduction must be allowed, it has been held.[20]

§ 252. Schedule N; Transfers for Public, Charitable, and Religious Uses; Disclaimer.

The statute provides that in two cases an interest which falls into a bequest, legacy, devise, transfer, or power for the use of a public, charitable, or religious organization as the result of an irrevocable disclaimer is deductible. The first is if the disclaimer is made before the date prescribed for the filing of the Estate Tax return. The other is that the complete termination before the same date of a power to consume, invade, or appro-

yan, 5 TCM 531 (1945); Briggs, 5 TCM 1114 (1945); note 14, supra.

9. Elmer, 6 TC 944 (1946).

10. Jennings, 10 TC 323 (1948).

11. Note 14, supra.

12. Comm v Wells Fargo Bank & Union Trust Co, 145 F2d 130 (CCA 9) (1944); Comm v Bank of America NTSA, 133 F2d 753 (CCA 9) (1943); Wetherill, 4 TC 678 (1944); Lincoln Rochester Trust Co v McGowan, 217 F2d 287 (CA 1) (1954).

13. See Blodget v Delaney, 201 F2d 589 (CA 1) (1953); Comm v Robertson, 141 F2d 855 (CCA 4) (1944).

14. Price v Rothensies, note 1, supra.

15. Bank of America NTSA v Comm, 126 F2d 48 (CCA 9) (1942).

16. Mercantile Safe Deposit & Trust Co v US, 141 F Supp 546 (1946); First Nat Bank of Birmingham v Snead, 24 F2d 186 (CCA 5) (1928).

17. Gilfillan v Kelm, 128 F Supp 291 (1955); Comm v Robertson, note 13, supra; Comm v Bank of America NTSA, note 12, supra; Boston Safe Deposit & Trust Co, 21 BTA 394 (1931).

18. Kenny, 11 TC 857 (1948).

19. Henslee v Union Planters Nat Bank, 335 US 595, 93 L ed 259, 69 S Ct 290, rehg den 336 US 915, 93 L ed 1078, 69 S Ct 601 (1949).

20. Hendricksen v Baker-Boyer Nat Bank, 139 F2d 877 (CCA 9) (1944); see also Mead v Welch, 95 F2d 617 (CCA 9) (1938).

priate property for the benefit of an individual before such power has been exercised by reason of the death of such individual or for any other reason shall be considered and deemed an irrevocable disclaimer with the same force and effect as though he had filed such irrevocable disclaimer.[1]

Ordinarily a disclaimer made by a person not under any legal disability will be considered irrevocable when filed with the probate court. A disclaimer is a complete and unqualified refusal to accept the rights to which one is entitled. Thus, if a beneficiary uses these rights for his own purposes, as by receiving a consideration for his formal disclaimer, he has not refused the rights to which he was entitled. There can be no disclaimer after an acceptance of these rights, expressly or impliedly. The disclaimer of a power is to be distinguished from the release or exercise of a power. The release or exercise of a power by the donee of the power in favor of public, charitable, or religious organizations does not result in any deduction under Section 2055 in the estate of the donor of the power, but does in the estate of the donee of the power.[2]

Prior to the Revenue Act of 1942, property passing to a charity as the result of a disclaimer was held by the Commissioner not to be deductible. The 1942 Act amended the statute to permit the deduction.[3] It was held, however, that the amendment was merely declaratory of existing law.[4] In any event, since such time, a *timely* disclaimer is effective.[5] A disclaimer must be complete, unqualified and irrevocable, or it will not be sufficient.[6] Where property passes to the charity by agreement between the heirs, there is not a disclaimer, and the deduction is not allowable.[7]

The 1954 Code added the provision above that the complete termination of a power of invasion before the date for filing the Estate Tax return shall be deemed an irrevocable disclaimer.

1. IRC, § 2055(a) (1954 Code).

2. Reg, §§ 20.2055–2(c), 20.2055–1 (b).

3. IRC, §§ 812(d), 861(a)(3) (1939 Code) amended by Rev Act of 1942, § 408.

4. Comm v Macaulay, 150 F2d 847 (CCA 2) (1945); but see First Trust Co of St Paul v Reynolds, 137 F2d 518 (CCA 8) (1943).

5. Doane, 10 TC 1258 (1948).

6. Seubert v Shaughnessy, 233 F2d 134 (CA 1) (1956).

7. Selig v US, 73 F Supp 886, affd 166 F2d 299 (CCA 3) (1948); Carey, 9 TC 1047, affd 168 F2d 400 (CCA 3) (1948); Dumont, 4 TC 158, revd other grounds 150 F2d 691 (CCA 3) (1944).

§ 253. Schedule N; Transfers for Public, Charitable, or Religious Uses; Payments in Compromise.

If a charitable organization assigns or surrenders a part of a transfer to it pursuant to a compromise agreement in settlement of a controversy, the amount so assigned or surrendered is not deductible as a transfer to the charitable organization.[8]

While it has been held to the contrary in one case,[9] and under unusual facts in another,[10] it is consistently held that only the amount which the charity actually receives is allowable as a deduction.[11]

§ 254. Schedule N; Transfers for Public, Charitable, and Religious Uses; Transfers by Others Than Decedent.

It will have been observed that the statute allows the deduction for transfers for public, charitable, or religious uses, but does not specifically state that such transfers must be made by the decedent.[12] The Regulation, however, specifically so provides.[13] Thus gifts made by the beneficiaries out of estate assets are not deductible.[14] The charity must take by bequest, legacy, devise or transfer from the decedent.[15] As previously noted,[16] charitable pledges which were at one time not allowed as deductions, were disallowed on the ground that they were not bequests from the decedent.[17]

§ 255. Schedule N; Transfers for Public, Charitable, or Religious Uses; Death Taxes Payable Out of Bequests.

The statute provides that the amount of the charitable deduction shall be reduced by any death taxes which are payable from the bequest.[18] If under the terms of the will or other governing instrument, or the law of the jurisdiction imposing the particu-

8. Reg, § 20.2055-2(d).
9. Continental Ill Nat Bank & Trust Co, 38 BTA 220 (1938).
10. Dumont v Comm, 150 F2d 691 (CCA 3) (1945).
11. Gilbert, 4 TC 1006 (1945); E T 17, 1940-1 CB 231; Toeller, 6 TC 832 (1946); Rev Rul 145, 1953-2 CB 273; Irving Trust Co v US, 54-2 USTC ¶10,968; Thompson v Comm, 123 F2d 816 (CCA 2) (1941); Heim v Nee, 40 F Supp 594 (1937).
12. IRC, § 2055(a) (1954 Code).
13. Reg, § 20.2055-1(a).

14. Kirkwood, 23 BTA 955 (1931); Glaser v Comm, 69 F2d 254 (CCA 8), cert den 292 US 654, 78 L ed 1502, 54 S Ct 864 (1934); Mississippi Valley Trust Co v Comm, 72 F2d 197 (CCA 8), cert den 293 US 604, 79 L ed 695, 55 S Ct 119 (1934).
15. Dimock v Corwin, 99 F2d 799 (CCA 1), affd 306 US 363, 83 L ed 763, 59 S Ct 551 (1939).
16. §§ 209, 249, supra.
17. Taft v Comm, 304 US 351, 82 L ed 1393, 58 S Ct 891 (1938).
18. IRC, § 2055(c) (1954 Code).

lar tax, the Federal Estate Tax, or any estate, succession, legacy, or inheritance tax is payable in whole or in part out of any property transferred for the statutory uses, the sum deductible is the amount of the transferred property reduced by the amount of the tax. The section in effect provides that the deduction is based on the amount actually available for charitable uses, that is, the amount of the fund remaining after the payment of all death taxes.[19]

Taxes may be payable out of a charitable bequest either because the testator so directed, or in such states as tax charitable bequests. As to these latter, we have previously noted the 1956 amendment permitting the deduction of such taxes from the gross estate.[20] The usual situation in which taxes will reduce a charitable gift is where the charity shares in the remainder, and taxes are payable therefrom.

The computation of the amount of the charitable deduction in such cases is extremely complicated and is treated in the chapter on computations.[1]

Prior to the Revenue Act of 1924 charitable bequests were not reducible by any taxes payable therefrom.[2] The 1924 Act required this reduction.[3] The provision was repealed by the Revenue Act of 1926,[4] but restored by the Revenue Act of 1932,[5] and has continued in the 1939 Code[6] and the 1954 Code.[7] Where there is an apportionment statute, a residuary bequest to charity presents no problem. If, however, the Federal tax must be paid from the general estate, like other administration expenses, the payment of the tax upon the taxable portion of the estate will operate to reduce the nontaxable residuary gift to charity.[8]

§ 256. Schedule N; Transfers for Public, Charitable, or Religious Uses; Valuation.

Where there is a present gift to charity there is no problem in

19. Reg, § 20.2055–3(a).

20. § 214, supra.

1. § 282, infra.

2. Edwards v Slocum, 264 US 61, 68 L ed 564, 44 S Ct 293 (1924).

3. §§ 303(a)(3), 303(b)(3).

4. § 323.

5. § 807.

6. IRC, § 812(d) (1939 Code).

7. Note 18, supra.

8. Rogan v Taylor, 136 F2d 598 (CCA 9) (1943); see also Harrison v Northern Trust Co, 317 US 476, 87 L ed 407, 63 S Ct 361 (1943); Blumenthal, 182 M 137, 46 NYS2d 688, affd 267 AD 949, 47 NYS2d 652, affd 293 NY 707, 56 NE 2d 588 (1943); Brooks, 27 TC 295 (1956).

determining the amount, except in the case where part of the taxes are payable therefrom, discussed heretofore.[9]

The more usual problem presented in determining the amount receivable by the charity is that in which the gift is of a remainder subject to intervening life estates. In such case, in the absence of other proof, the value of the remainder is determined from data available at the date of death,[10] and by the use of mortality tables.[11] While it has been held that conditions known at the time of the computation should be used,[12] the Supreme Court has held that mortality tables should be used even though the life beneficiary died within the year.[13] For such computation the tables heretofore referred to may be used.[14] The value of a remainder to charity should be valued on the residue subject to the life estate and not by deducting the life estate from the total residuary estate.[15] Remainders subject to annuities are valued on the reversionary interest.[16] It has been held that where annuities were payable from the fund and it was subject to invasion, adjustment should be made for the present value of the annuities and of the amounts fixed by the trustee as reasonably necessary for support.[17]

Where the alternate valuation is elected, the amount of the deduction is determined by the value of the property with respect to which the deduction is allowed, as of the date of the decedent's death, adjusted, however, for any difference in its value as of the date one year after death, or as of the date of its distribution, sale, exchange, or other disposition, whichever first occurs. However, no such adjustment may take into account any difference in value due to lapse of time or to the occurrence or nonoccurrence of a contingency.[18]

9. § 255, supra.

10. Wells Fargo Bank & Union Trust Co v Comm, 145 F2d 132 (CCA 9) (1944); Burdick v Comm, 117 F2d 972 (CCA 2), cert den 314 US 631, 86 L ed 506, 62 S Ct 63 (1941); Delbridge v US, 89 F Supp 845 (1950); Hanley v US, 63 F Supp 73 (1945).

11. Hidden v Durey, 34 F2d 174 (1929); Millard v Humphrey, 8 F Supp 784, affd 79 F2d 107 (CA 2) (1934); US v Dean, 224 F2d 26 (CA 1) (1955).

12. Jennings, 10 TC 323 (1948); Union Trust Co of Pittsburgh v Heiner, 19 F2d 362 (1927); Boston Safe Deposit & Trust Co v Nichols, 18 F2d 660 (1927).

13. Ithaca Trust Co v US, 279 US 151, 73 L ed 647, 49 S Ct 291 (1929).

14. See §§ 112, 113, 114, 115, supra.

15. Waldman, 46 BTA 291 (1942); Hartford Nat Bank & Trust Co v US, 185 F2d 463 (1952).

16. Cromwell, 24 BTA 461 (1931); Butler, 18 TC 914 (1952).

17. Herron v Heiner, 24 F2d 745 (1928).

18. Reg, § 20.2032-1(f).

§ 257. Schedule N; Transfers for Public, Charitable, or Religious Uses; Return.

The Instructions for Schedule N in addition to very briefly referring to pertinent provisions of the statute, but for the most part referring the person preparing the same to the Estate Tax Regulations, deals largely with the mechanical details. If the transfer was made by will, a *certified* copy of the order admitting the will to probate, in addition to the copy of the will, should be submitted. If the transfer was made by any other written instrument, as for instance an inter vivos trust indenture, a copy thereof should be submitted with the return, *and if the instrument is of record* the copy should be *certified* and *if not of record* the copy should be *verified.* If the transfer was made by will, an affidavit or statement signed under the penalties of perjury, of the executor must be submitted, showing whether any action has been instituted to have interpreted or to contest the will or any provision thereof affecting the charitable deduction claimed, and whether, according to his information and belief, any such action is designed or contemplated.[19]

If claim is made for deduction of the value of the residue, or a portion of the residue, passing to charity, there should be submitted a copy of the computation, or supporting documents should include:

(1) A statement showing the values of all specific and general legacies or devises, indication whether they are for charitable or noncharitable uses, with an appropriate reference in each instance to the applicable paragraph or section of the decedent's will or codicil.

(2) The dates of birth of all life tenants or annuitants, the duration of whose lives may affect the value of the interest passing to charity.

(3) A statement showing the value of all property which is included in the decedent's gross estate but does not pass under the will, and

(4) Any other information that may appear material, such as that relating to any claim, not arising under the will, to any part of the estate, as of a spouse claiming dower, or curtesy, or similar rights, etc.[20]

19. Instructions, Schedule N, Form 706. 20. Note 19, supra.

[Harris]—22

337

If the amount of the charitable deduction is reduced by death taxes payable out of the gift, there should also be annexed a computation showing how the amount claimed as a deduction was obtained.[1]

FORM NO. 30

Schedule N; Charitable, Public, and Similar Gifts and Bequests

Item No.	Name and address of beneficiary	Character of institution	Amount
1	Federation of Women's Clubs, Washington, D. C.	Educational	$1,000.00
2	Nursing Sisters of the Poor, N. Y. C.	Religious	5,000.00
3	Alfred University, Hornell N. Y.	Educational	2,500.00
4	American Society for the Prevention of Cruelty to Animals, remainder interest in residue of estate (See computation annexed).	Prevention of cruelty to animals	93,362.35

TOTAL (also enter under the Recapitulation, Schedule O) $101,862.35

(If more space is needed, insert additional sheets of same size)

Schedule N—Page 31

Estate of WINTHROP BENSON

FORM NO. 31

Executor's Statement for Charitable Deduction

U. S. TREASURY DEPARTMENT
INTERNAL REVENUE SERVICE
FIRST DISTRICT OF NEW YORK

In the Matter of the Estate Tax
in the Estate of
    WINTHROP BENSON,
            Deceased.

STATE OF NEW YORK   }
COUNTY OF NEW YORK   } ss:

KATHERINE BENSON, being duly sworn, says: I am the executrix under the Last Will and Testament of the above named decedent, having duly qualified and am presently acting as such.

That no action or proceeding has been instituted in any court for a construction of the will of the above named decedent, nor has any action or proceeding been instituted to contest the said will or any of the provisions thereof affecting the charitable deduction claimed in Schedule N,

1. See § 282, infra.

[Harris]

of the Federal Estate Tax Return. That to the best of my knowledge, information, and belief no such action or proceeding is designed or contemplated.

KATHERINE BENSON

Sworn to before me this
18th day of April, 1960.
ANDREA HAYS
Notary Public
New York County

FORM NO. 32

Computation of Amount of Charitable Deduction Claimed

Gross distributable estate	$185,627.14
Less funeral expenses, administration expenses, debts, liens, etc.	18,542.19
Adjusted Gross Estate	$167,084.95
Legacy, Article 2 of Will $10,000.00	
Charitable Legacies, Articles 3, 4, 5 of Will 8,500.00	18,500.00
Net residue	$148,584.95

The remainder is subject to the life estate of Katherine Benson, born Jan. 15, 1898.

$148,584.95 × .62835, Value of remainder[2] $93,362.35

FORM NO. 33

Disclaimer of Bequest

SURROGATE'S COURT:
NASSAU COUNTY

In the Matter of Proving the Last
Will and Testament of
WINTHROP BENSON,
Deceased.

I, the undersigned, a legatee under the Last Will and Testament of Winthrop Benson, late of the County of Nassau, deceased, do hereby

2. See § 115, supra, for method of computing value of remainder interest.

irrevocably renounce and disclaim the legacy bequeathed to me under Article Fourth of said Last Will and Testament.

Dated the 1st day of February, 1960

GEORGE BENSON

STATE OF NEW YORK ⎫
COUNTY OF NASSAU ⎬ ss:
                ⎭

On the 1st day of February, 1960, before me personally came GEORGE BENSON, to me known and known to me to be the person described in and who executed the foregoing instrument and he acknowledged to me that he executed the same.

MARSHA HAYS
Notary Public
Nassau County

§ 258. Nonresidents Not Citizens.

The discussion in the preceding sections of this chapter deals with the deductions allowable in determining the taxable estate in the case of citizens or residents of the United States. In the case of nonresidents not citizens of the United States separate provisions of the statute provide for the deductions which are permissible and the amount of the specific exemption.[3]

There are a number of differences in the deductions allowed, the extent thereof, the amount of the specific exemption, and the information required.

In the case of funeral and administration expenses, claims, taxes, and net losses, *only that proportion thereof is allowed* which the value of the decedent's gross estate situated in the United States at the time of his death bears to the value of the decedent's entire gross estate wherever situated. It is immaterial whether the amounts to be deducted were incurred or expended within or without the United States.[4] *There is no provision for the allowance of the marital deduction,* except as otherwise provided by a convention with a foreign country.[5]

A charitable deduction is allowable for public, charitable, and religious uses in the same manner as in the case of citizens or residents, *except* that the deduction, while not limited to a proportion, is allowed only for transfers to corporations and associations created or organized in the United States, and to trustees

3. IRC, § 2016 (1954 Code).
4. Reg, § 20.2106–2(a)(2); Neinhuys, 17 TC 1149 (1952); Bordes, 19 TC 1093 (1953).

5. Reg, § 20.2056(a)–1(a).

for use within the United States. The provision of Section 2055 that the complete termination of a power to consume before exercise and before the date for filing the Estate Tax return, does not apply to nonresidents not citizens.[6]

The specific exemption in the case of a nonresident not a citizen of the United States is $2,000.,[7] instead of the $60,000. exemption in the case of a citizen or resident, unless a death duty convention provides for another amount.[8]

The statute provides that *no deduction shall be allowed* for funeral and administration expenses, claims, taxes, net losses, and transfers for public, charitable, or religious uses, *unless* the executor includes in the return required to be filed the value at the time of death of that part of the gross estate not situated in the United States.[9] This does not mean that property outside the United States must be included in the gross estate, but as the Regulation notes, merely that in order to obtain the proportionate deduction it is necessary to *disclose* such property.[10] Real property outside the United States need not be disclosed.[11]

Where real property in the United States is included, only the equity of redemption is includible if the decedent is not personally liable on a mortgage on the property, whereas if he is personally liable, only a proportionate deduction would be allowable.[12]

The provisions for alternate valuation apply to the estates of nonresidents not citizens.[13]

Adequate proof of the total gross estate wherever situated and of the claimed deductions must be submitted; otherwise, the deductions will be disallowed. There must be filed a certified copy of the foreign death tax return; or, if no such return was filed, a certified copy of the inventory of the estate, together with the schedule of debts and charges, filed in conjunction with the administration proceedings of the estate or with the foreign court of probate jurisdiction. Additional proof may be required in specific cases.[14]

If the return is made upon Form 706NA it is necessary to attach itemized schedules in order to obtain the proportionate

6. Reg, § 20.2106–1(a)(2).

7. IRC, § 2106(a)(3) (1954 Code).

8. Reg, § 20.2106–1(a)(3).

9. IRC, § 2106(b) (1954 Code).

10. Reg, § 20.2106–1(b); Jandorf, 9 TC 388 (1947).

11. Additional Instructions for Estates of Nonresidents Not Citizens of the United States, Form 706.

12. Johnstone, 19 TC 44 (1952).

13. IRC, §§ 2032, 2103 (1954 Code); Reg, § 20.2106–1(b).

14. Instructions, Form 706NA; note 11, supra.

deduction. Failure to furnish such information will result in a complete denial of any deduction.[15]

Since Form 706NA is a single double faced sheet containing the items of the gross estate, the deductions and the computation of the tax, the manner of reporting the deductions will be found in the chapter on computation of the tax.[16]

15. Jandorf, note 10, supra; but see Swan, 24 TC 829, revd in part and affd in part 247 F2d 144 (CA 2) (1955).

16. § 326, infra.

CHAPTER 4

COMPUTATION OF TAX

343

§ 259. Scope of Chapter.

In the preceding chapters it has been the purpose to familiarize the lawyer who is charged with the preparation and processing of the Estate Tax return with all of the steps required to be taken in order to arrive at the determination of the amount of tax. We have, therefore, progressed through the preliminary details which must be known before the return can be begun. We have also dealt with each of the items which must be listed in the schedules in order to determine the gross estate and all of those items which must be listed for which deduction may properly be made, so as to arrive at the figure which will represent the taxable estate. The logical next step is the computation of the tax.

In this chapter there are grouped all the mathematical computations which require solution. The computation of the tax is not the only mathematical problem presented. In connection with the determination of the items of the gross estate there are such mathematical situations as computing the value of annuities, remainders or reversionary interests, community property, business interests, and the extent to which lifetime transfers are includible in the gross estate. With respect to deductions, the outstanding problems mathematically are the computation of the amounts of the marital deduction and charitable deductions.

These computations having been made, we are in a position to determine the amount of the tax payable. But even after this has been done, there is a further computation necessary if the estate is entitled to credits for taxes paid on prior transfers, or by reason of death taxes or gift taxes which have been paid on property included in the gross estate. Each of these computations and others which may arise will be dealt with severally.

§ 260. Valuation; Alternate; Generally.

The Internal Revenue Code provides for the valuation of the property of a decedent included in his gross estate at the time of his death,[1] *or if the executor so elects,* by valuing all the property included in the gross estate as follows:

(1) In the case of property *distributed, sold, exchanged, or otherwise disposed of, within one year* after the decedent's death such property shall be valued *as of the date of distribution, sale, exchange, or other disposition.*

(2) In the case of *property not distributed, sold, exchanged, or otherwise disposed of within one year* after the decedent's death such property shall be valued *as of the date one year after the decedent's death.*

(3) Any interest which is affected by mere lapse of time shall be included at its value as of the time of death (instead of the later date) with adjustment for any difference in its value as of the later date not due to mere lapse of time.[2]

No deduction under Chapter 11 of any item shall be allowed if allowance for such item is in effect given by the alternate valuation provided by the section. Whenever in any other subsection or section of the chapter reference is made to the value of property at the time of the decedent's death, such reference shall be deemed to refer to the value of such property used in determining the value of the gross estate. In case of an election made by the executor under the section, then—

(1) for purposes of the charitable deduction under Section 2055 (applying to residents or citizens) or 2106(a)(2) (applying to nonresidents not citizens), any bequest, legacy, devise, or transfer enumerated therein, *and*

(2) for the purposes of the marital deduction under Section 2056, any interest in property passing to the surviving spouse shall be valued as of the date of the decedent's death with adjustment for any difference in value (not due to mere lapse of time or the occurrence or nonoccurrence of a contingency) of the property as of the date one year after the decedent's death (substituting, in the case of property distributed by the executor or trustee, or sold, exchanged, or otherwise disposed of, during such one year period, the date thereof).[3]

The election provided for shall be exercised by the executor on his return filed within the time prescribed by law or before the expiration of any extension of time granted pursuant to law for the filing of the return.[4]

1. IRC, § 2031(a) (1954 Code).
2. IRC, § 2032(a) (1954 Code).
3. IRC, § 2032(b) (1954 Code).
4. IRC, § 2032(c) (1954 Code).

This latter election to value as of a time other than the date of death came into the law after the Great Depression subsequent to the stock market debacle of 1929. In many estates valuations of property as of a date prior to the crash resulted in a tax many times in amount the value of the estate after the crash. In 1935[5] Congress introduced what was known as the "optional valuation." This was continued in the 1939 Code[6] and the 1954 Code made no substantial changes therein, but changed its name to the "alternate valuation."

We have previously discussed the manner in which the election must be made, and the purpose of the statute, as well as the property to which it applies.[7] At this point we are concerned with the manner in which the statute operates. As previously noted, the alternate valuation election is available to nonresidents not citizens of the United States, as well as to residents and citizens.[8]

§ 261. Valuation; Alternate; "Included Property" and "Excluded Property."

The Regulation refers to "included property" and "excluded property."[9] If the executor elects the alternate valuation, all property interests *existing at the date of the decedent's death which form a part of his gross estate* are valued in accordance with the section. Such property interests are "included property" and *remain* "included property" for the purpose of valuing the gross estate under the alternate valuation method even though they change in form during the alternate valuation period by being actually received, or disposed of, in whole or in part, by the estate.[10]

On the other hand, *property earned or accrued* (whether received or not) *after the date of the decedent's death* and during the alternate valuation period with respect to any property interest existing at the date of the decedent's death, which does not represent a form of "included property" itself or the receipt of "included property" is excluded in valuing the gross estate

5. § 302(j), Revenue Act of 1926 as added by § 202(a), Revenue Act of 1935.
6. § 811(j) (1939 Code).
7. § 40, supra.
8. § 258, supra.
9. Reg, § 20.2032–1(d).
10. Note 9, supra; Clark v US, 33 F Supp 216 (1940); Saks v Higgins, 29 F Supp 996, affd 111 F2d 78 (CCA 2), revd on other grounds 312 US 443, 85 L ed 940, 61 S Ct 631 (1939).

under the alternate valuation method. Such property is "excluded property."

This Regulation was not promulgated without an extended campaign of the Treasury to include post mortem income as "included property". It was not until the Supreme Court held a contrary Regulation invalid that it yielded.[11] It is now unquestioned that rents, dividends, and interest received after the decedent's death are not to be considered in the alternate valuation.[12]

A recent Revenue Ruling[12a] has clarified several questions by holding:

(1) Stock rights sold before the year expires are "included property".

(2) Stock rights exercised before the year expires are "included property".

(3) Stock received as a result of a stock dividend before the year expires but after the death of the decedent is "included property".

(4) Insurance policies where the beneficiary exercises her right to receive monthly payments instead of a lump sum payment are valued as of the date of death.

(5) Mortgages where principal payments are received in accordance with the terms of the note between the date of death and the expiration of one year are valued as of one year after the date of the decedent's death, to which is added any payments on principal of the mortgages, since such payments are "included property".

§ 262. Valuation; Alternate; Operation as to Real Estate, Stocks and Bonds.

The alternate valuation date may be any date after the date of death up to a date one year after the date of death. Thus if there were more than 365 different assets in the estate and each separate one of 365 was distributed, sold, exchanged, or otherwise disposed of on a different day of the year, they would each be valued on a different day, and any which had not been

11. Maas v Higgins, 312 US 443, 85 L ed 940, 61 S Ct 631 (1941).

12. Penn Co v US, 59 F Supp 667, affd 152 F2d 757 (CCA 3) (1945); Peoples Pittsburgh Trust Co v US, 54 F Supp 742 (1944); Howard v US, 40 F Supp 697, affd 125 F2d 986 (CCA 5) (1941); Stuart v Hassett, 41 F Supp 905 (1941).

12a. Rev Rul 58-576, IRB 1958-47 p 8.

so disposed of would be valued as of a date one year after the date of death. Whatever the date of valuation, the criterion is the same, namely, the fair market value.

In the case of real estate the same elements of valuation are considered as in date of death valuation.[13]

Interest bearing obligations such as bonds or notes may comprise two elements of "included property", the principal and the interest accrued to date of death. Each is separately set forth in the schedule as of the applicable valuation date, but interest between the date of death and the valuation date is "excluded property". Payments of principal after death are included as of the date of payment. This would, of course, reduce the reportable amount of the obligation.[14] The same is true of leased property.[15] In the case of noninterest bearing obligations sold at a discount, such as savings bonds, the principal is valued as of the alternate date without regard to any further increase in value due to amortized discount, the discount being amortized to the date of death and reported. The discount amortized after the date of death is equivalent to post-death income and is not reported.[16]

Stock of a corporation presents more problems. First there is involved the determination of the valuation date where there have been changes in holdings after death. It is necessary to decide whether there has been a distribution, sale, exchange, or other disposition as a result. There has been if there is a surrender of the stock for corporate assets in complete or partial liquidation of the corporation. But there has not been when there is a mere change of form, or a transfer of assets to a corporation in exchange for its stock in a transaction with respect to which there would be no gain or loss for Income Tax purposes, nor an exchange of stock or securities in a corporation for stock or securities in the same or another corporation in a transaction, such as a merger, recapitalization, reorganization, or other transaction with respect to which there would be no gain or loss for Income Tax purposes.[17] The valuation date having been determined, the value may then be fixed. Shares of stock in a corporation and dividends declared to stockholders of record on or before the date of the decedent's death constitute "included prop-

13. §§ 43 et seq, supra; see Stowers, 6 TCM 1330 (1955).

14. Reg, § 20.2032–1(d)(i); see Rev Rul 156, 1953–2 CB 253.

15. Reg, § 20.2032–1(d)(ii).

16. Reg, § 20.2032–1(d)(iii).

17. Reg, § 20.2032–1(c).

erty." *Ordinary dividends* out of earnings and profits (whether in cash, shares of the corporation, or other property) declared to stockholders of record after the date of the decedent's death are "excluded property" and are not to be valued under the alternate valuation method. If, however, dividends are declared to stockholders of record after the date of the decedent's death with the effect that the shares of stock at the subsequent valuation date do not reasonably represent the same "included property" of the gross estate as existed at the date of the decedent's death, the dividends are "included property," except to the extent that they are out of earnings of the corporation after the date of the decedent's death. For example, if a corporation makes a distribution in partial liquidation to stockholders of record during the alternate valuation period which is not accompanied by a surrender of a stock certificate for cancellation, the amount of the distribution received on stock included in the gross estate is itself "included property," except to the extent that the distribution was out of earnings and profits since the date of the decedent's death. Similarly, if a corporation in which the decedent owned a substantial interest and which possessed at the date of his death accumulated earnings and profits equal to its paid-in capital, distributed all of its accumulated earnings and profits as a cash dividend to stockholders of record during the alternate valuation period, the amount of the dividends received on stock includible in the gross estate will be included in the gross estate under the alternate valuation method. Similarly, a stock dividend is "included property".[18]

What the Regulation is saying is that the label "dividend" is not enough to exclude property when the alternate valuation method is used, but that if what is so labeled is in fact a distribution of principal, it will be so considered. In recent years the courts have been required to determine for trust accounting purposes the same question, namely, whether a corporate distribution was income or principal, or how much of it was income and how much principal.

18. Reg, § 20.2032–1(d)(iv).

FORM NO. 34

Alternate Valuation of Bonds, Real Estate and Stock

Description	Subsequent valuation date	Value under option	Value at date of death
Bond, par value $1,000, bearing interest at 4% payable quarterly on Feb. 1, May 1, Aug. 1, and Nov. 1. Bond distributed to legatee on March 1, 1960	Mar. 1, 1960	$1,000.00	$1,000.00
Interest coupon of $10 attached to bond and not cashed at date of death although due and payable Nov. 1, 1959. Cashed by executor on Feb. 1, 1960	Feb. 1, 1960	10.00	10.00
Interest accrued from Nov. 1, 1939, to Jan. 1, 1940, collected on Feb. 1, 1960	Feb. 1, 1960	6.67	6.67
Real estate. Not disposed of within year following death. Rent of $300 due at the end of each quarter, Feb. 1, May 1, Aug. 1, and Nov. 1.	Jan. 1, 1961	11,000.00	12,000.00
Rent due for quarter ending Nov. 1, 1959, but not collected until Feb. 1, 1960	Feb. 1, 1960	300.00	300.00
Rent accrued for November and December, 1959, collected on Feb. 1, 1960 ..	Feb. 1, 1960	200.00	200.00
Common stock, X Corporation, 500 shares not disposed of within year following decedent's death	Jan. 1, 1961	47,500.00	50,000.00
Dividend of $2 per share declared Dec. 10, 1959, and paid on Jan. 10, 1960, to holders of record on Dec. 30, 1959	Jan 10, 1960	1,000.00	1,000.00

§ 263. Valuation; Alternate; Operation as to Assets Affected by Mere Lapse of Time.

Certain assets become worthless, not because of any change in the fair market value according to the willing-seller, willing-buyer rule, but merely because of the passage of time. Thus, patents, life estates and like interests will be worth less one year from the decedent's death than they were at his date of death. It was not the purpose of the statute to afford a reduction in such case, but to grant relief in cases where there had been a decline in value due to market conditions. It was therefore provided that any interest or estate which is affected by mere lapse of time shall be valued as of the date of death with adjustment for any difference in value as of the alternate valuation date not due to mere lapse of time.[19] The phrase "affected by mere

19. IRC, § 2032(a)(3) (1954 Code).

lapse of time" has no reference to obligations for the payment of money, whether or not interest bearing, the value of which changes with the passing of time. However, such an obligation like any other property, may become affected by lapse of time when made the subject of a bequest or transfer which itself creates an interest or estate so affected.[20]

Thus, if the decedent was entitled to receive the remainder of property worth $50,000. at the decedent's death, after the death of the life beneficiary, who at the time of the decedent's death was 31 years old, and the property declined in value so that one year after the decedent's death the property was worth $40,000., the adjustment and valuation would be computed as below.

FORM NO. 35

Alternate Valuation of Remainder

Value of property as of alternate valuation date $40,000.00
Factor for valuation of remainder interest *age 31*[1] .... ×   .28932
_____
Value of remainder as of alternate valuation date $11,572.80

It will be observed that although the value of the property is its value as of the alternate valuation date, the age factor is the age of the life tenant as of the date of the decedent's death.[2]

In the case of a patent, if it is assumed that the patent was worth $78,000. at the date of death, at which time it had an unexpired term of ten years, and was sold six months after the date of death for $60,000., the value on the alternate valuation date would be obtained by dividing the value on that date by the proportion of the remaining life of the patent at such date to the life of the patent at the date of death. In the above illustration it would be .95.

20. Reg, § 20.2032–1(e).
1. Reg, § 20.2031–7, Table I, Column 4.

2. Reg, § 20.2032–1(e)(i); see also Welliver, 8 TC 165 (1947); Hance, 18 TC 499 (1952).

FORM NO. 36

Alternate Valuation of Patent

Value of patent at date of death $78,000.00
Life of patent at date of death .... 10 years
Value of patent six months after date of death 60,000.00
Proportionate life of patent at alternate valuation date to
  life of patent at date of death (100 — .05) .... ÷ .95
_____
Alternate valuation $63,157.89

When a trust is included in the gross estate as a taxable transfer, the division of the corpus of the trust for the purpose of facilitating payment of income is not a "distribution" within the meaning of the statute for the purpose of fixing the alternate date.[3]

Where the value of a policy of insurance on the life of another increases after the decedent's death because of the payment of premiums or interest earned, the increase is not included in the alternate valuation.[4]

§ 264. Valuation; Alternate; Deductions.

A reduction in value cannot be allowed twice. Thus, it is provided that deductions for net losses under Section 2054 or 2106 will be allowed only to the extent that they are not otherwise in effect allowed in determining the value of the gross estate. Furthermore, the amount of any charitable deduction or marital deduction is determined by the value of the property with respect to which the deduction is allowed as of the date of the decedent's death, adjusted, however, for any difference in its value as of the alternate valuation date. No such adjustment may take into account any difference in value due to lapse of time or to the occurrence or nonoccurrence of a contingency.[5]

§ 265. Real Estate.

While the primary problem in respect to real estate is one of valuation, there are a number of instances in connection therewith when computations are necessary. If the property is income-producing it is necessary to accrue rentals to the date of

3. Rev Rul 57–495, IRC 1957–43 p 31.
4. Rev Rul 55–379, 1955–1 CB 449.
5. IRC, § 2032(b) (1954 Code); Reg, § 20.2032–1(f).

death,[6] and when there is a mortgage the interest to date of death must be shown.[7] If the interest is a fractional one,[8] or a leasehold is involved,[9] there may be considerable computation required. Valuation of these interests have been treated heretofore. Where there is a contract to sell land, the computation of the value of such interest will be required.[10]

§ 266. Stocks and Bonds.

In determining the value of stocks and bonds, in the case of listed securities the only computation is averaging high and low or bid and asked prices.[11] In the case of close corporations there is need to determine value by various methods. These computations and methods have been discussed previously.[12] In the case of bonds interest must be computed to the date of death.[13] When the alternate valuation date is elected there will be the need to apportion dividends or interest so as to reflect that which is reportable.

§ 267. Mortgages, Notes, Cash.

Normally the only problem in the case of mortgages, notes and cash is one of valuation. Where the alternate valuation is elected, while cash will remain constant, the value of a mortgage or note may have changed. This will be reflected without the inclusion of post death income on such assets.[14]

When mortgages or notes are claimed to be worth less than their face value, we have previously discussed the proof required for substantiation of that fact.[15]

§ 268. Insurance.

Prior to the 1954 Code there was required computation of the extent to which insurance on the life of the decedent was includible in his gross estate by reason of the payment by him of premiums. With the removal of the payment of premiums test as to decedents dying on and after August 17, 1954 such computation is no longer required.[16]

When the decedent owns a contract of insurance on the life of

6. § 44, supra.
7. §§ 217, 218, supra.
8. § 50, supra.
9. § 51, supra.
10. § 66, supra.
11. §§ 56, 57, supra.

12. § 59, supra.
13. § 63, supra.
14. § 261, supra.
15. § 65, supra.
16. § 80, supra.

another or for the payment of an annuity on the life of another, it is necessary to compute the value thereof at the date of his death.[17] The method of computation is illustrated in the chapters on valuation in the Gift Tax, since it is used more often therein.

In such cases as it may be necessary to determine the includible amount of insurance where the decedent died prior to August 17, 1954, the Regulations under the 1939 Code furnish examples of the method of determining the includible amount.[18]

§ 269. Jointly Owned and Community Property; Entireties.

The primary problem in the case of jointly owned property, estates by the entirety, and community property is the one of proving the extent of the contribution of each owner.[19] Once the contribution of the decedent to the ownership of the property has been determined, computation of his interest in the value either as of date of death or the alternate valuation date merely requires the application of the fraction representing his share to the entire value.

§ 270. Miscellaneous Property.

So far as miscellaneous property is concerned, the only items requiring computation are the decedent's interest in a business,[20] insurance on the life of another,[1] and annuities, life, remainder, and reversionary interests.[2] We have previously illustrated the computations in the case of a business interest, and discuss hereafter the method of valuation of insurance on the life of another. The valuation of annuities, life estates and terms for years, and remainder and reversionary interests have been treated heretofore and the methods of computing the value demonstrated.[3]

§ 271. Miscellaneous Property; Annuities; Life Estates; Remainders; Reversions.

There has been demonstrated heretofore the methods used for the computation of the value of annuities,[4] life estates[5] and terms for years, and remainder and reversionary interests.[6] It

---

17. § 105, supra.
18. Reg 105, § 81.27.
19. §§ 85 et seq, supra.
20. §§ 102, 104, supra.
1. §§ 105, 268, supra.
2. §§ 111, 115, supra.
3. Annuities, § 113, supra; life es-

tates and terms for years, § 114, supra; remainder or reversionary interests, § 115, supra.
4. § 113, supra.
5. § 114, supra.
6. § 115, supra.

must be borne in mind that when the alternate valuation method is used, since such interests are such as are affected by mere lapse of time, that element must not enter into the calculation.[7]

§ 272. Transfers During Life.

In the case of property transferred by the decedent during his life and included in his gross estate, a number of computations may be necessary. If the transferee has made improvements or additions to the property, there must be deducted from the value on the applicable valuation date the value thereof.[8] If part of the property is sold and part retained, the value of such interest must be computed. Where an insurance policy is the subject of transfer and the transferee thereafter pays premiums there will be deducted the amount of insurance purchasable with such premiums.

In connection with such transfers it may also be necessary to compute how much of the transfer is includible. For example, if the decedent transfers property but retains a right which would make the property includible in his gross estate, but such right extends to only a portion of the property, then the proportion of the property to which such right attached would have to be determined in relation to the entire property.[9]

It is also necessary to compute the value of any reversionary interest which may have been retained by a decedent at the time of a transfer, since if immediately before his death it has a value in excess of 5% of the property, the entire property will be includible in his gross estate, and if it is less, the value of the reversionary interest is includible.[10]

§ 273. Powers of Appointment.

Where property subject to a power of appointment is includible in the gross estate, if the power exists as to only part of an entire group of assets or only over a limited interest in property, it will be necessary to compute the includible portion. Thus, if a trust created by S provides for the payment of income to A for life, then to W for life, with power in A to appoint the remainder by will and in default of appointment for payment of the remainder to B or his estate, and A dies before W, the power applies only to the value of the remainder interest excluding W's

7. § 263, supra.   9. Reg, § 20.2037-1(c)(4).
8. § 157, supra.   10. § 148, supra.

life estate. If A dies after W the power applies to the entire estate. In the former case it would be necessary to compute the value of the remainder interest. If the power were only over half the remainder interest, only half thereof would be includible.[11]

Where there has been a lapse of a power it is necessary to compute the amount of the unexercised power includible in the estate at the date of the donee's death and the amount of property subject to the power includible. The method of computation has been demonstrated heretofore.[12]

Where there are successive powers, the value of the property subject to the second power of appointment is computed without any reduction by any precedent or subsequent interest which is not subject to the second power.[13] Thus, if the decedent has a power to appoint by will $100,000. to a group of persons consisting of his children and grandchildren and exercises the power by making an outright appointment of $75,000. and by giving one appointee a power to appoint $25,000., no more than $25,000. will be includible in the decedent's gross estate. If, however, the decedent appoints the income from the entire fund to a beneficiary for life with power in the beneficiary to appoint the remainder by will, the entire $100,000. will be includible in the decedent's gross estate if the exercise of the second power can validly postpone the vesting of any estate or interest in property or can suspend the absolute ownership or power of alienation of the property for a period ascertainable without regard to the date of the creation of the first power.

§ 274. Survivor Annuities.

Since survivor annuities are includible in the gross estate to the extent of the amount that the decedent contributed to a qualified plan, in such case it is necessary to compute the proportionate amount of the annuity which is to be reported. It is first necessary to obtain the total amount of contributions and the amount contributed by the decedent. The method of computation in such case and also when no separate account is kept of the employer's contribution has been illustrated previously.[14]

11. Reg, § 20.2041–1(b)(3);   § 175, supra.

12. § 170, supra.

13. Reg, § 20.2041–3(e).

14. § 180, supra.

§ 275. Deductions; Generally.

While deductions for funeral and administration expenses, debts and mortgages, generally entail no computation, except the amount of the fiduciary's commissions and such cases as those obligations are not paid before the time for filing the Estate Tax return and exceed the amount of property subject to claims, the amount of the marital deduction, charitable deduction and in cases still pending in which there is a deduction for property previously taxed, involve such complex computations that they will be treated seriatim in succeeding sections.

So far as the commissions of fiduciaries are concerned, these are computed under state law and vary from state to state. In the case of the above expenses exceeding the amount of property subject to claims, computation will be necessary to determine the amount allowable as deductions, depending upon whether the same have been paid or not. We have previously considered the method by which the determination is made.[15] Where Income Taxes are due and a joint return is filed, it is necessary to compute the portion thereof which is the decedent's obligation. That computation has been illustrated.[16]

§ 276. Deduction for Property Previously Taxed; Statutory Provisions.

Prior to August 17, 1954, when a decedent died and a transferee of his property thereafter and within five years of the death of such decedent also died, in order to grant relief against the same property being taxed twice within so short a period of time, the statute provided for a deduction, designated the deduction for property previously taxed. It applied to both Estate and Gift taxes and was circumscribed by many limitations which made computation of the deduction to one not enamored of mathematics a nightmare. The relation between the deduction and the tax which had been paid was made to depend on the size of the estate rather than upon the former.[17] The deduction was reduced if the property was subject to a debt or claim and was not allowable if the property was received from the decedent's spouse.

The provision, however, still applies to the estates of decedents dying prior to August 17, 1954, except that in the case of prop-

15. § 192, supra.   17. IRC, § 812(c) (1939 Code).
16. § 216, supra.

erty transferred by a decedent to his spouse within two years of his death, if the decedent died after December 31, 1951, the credit for prior transfers created by the 1954 Code may be taken.[18] It is because there are still pending estates to which the statute is applicable that we shall deal with it and its operation.

It is provided that for the purpose of the tax the value of the net estate shall be determined *in the case of a resident or citizen of the United States* by deducting from the value of the gross estate an amount equal to the value of any property

(1) forming a part of the gross estate *situated in the United States* of any person who died *within five years prior to the death of the decedent, or*

(2) transferred to the decedent by gift *within five years prior* to his death, *where such property can be identified* as having been received by the decedent from the donor by gift, bequest, devise, or inheritance, or which can be identified as having been acquired in exchange for property so received.[19] In many cases identification presented a real problem.[20]

Property includible in the gross estate of the prior decedent under Section 811(f) (i.e., taxable powers of appointment) and property included in *total* gifts of the donor under Section 1000 (c) received by the decedent described in the section shall, for the purposes thereof, be considered a bequest of such prior decedent or gift of such donor.[1]

The deduction is allowed *only where* a Gift Tax imposed under Chapter 4, or under Title III of the Revenue Act of 1932, or an Estate Tax imposed under the Chapter or any prior Act of Congress, was finally determined and paid by or on behalf of such donor, or the estate of such prior decedent, as the case may be, and *only in the amount* finally determined as the value of such property in determining the value of the gift, or the gross estate of such prior decedent, *and only to the extent* that the value of

---

18. IRC, § 814 (1939 Code) as added by PL 417, §§ 1, 2, 84th Cong.

19. Note 17, supra.

20. See McFadden v US, 20 F Supp 625 (1937); Levi v US, 14 F Supp 513 (1936); Brawner, 15 BTA 1122 (1929); Miller, 3 TC 1180 (1944); Schroeder, 13 TC 259 (1949); Coffin, 9 TCM 1129 (1947); Horlick v Kuhl, 62 F Supp 168 (1945); Gray, 19 BTA 455 (1930); Vath, 41 BTA 487 (1940); Milburn, 6 TC 1119 (1946); Rodenbough v US, 25 F2d 13 (CCA 3) (1928); Farmers Loan & Trust Co v US, 60 F2d 618 (1932); Wiggin v Hassett, 56 F Supp 263 (1944); Van Dyke v Kuhl, 78 F Supp 698 (1945); Rolfe, 16 BTA 519 (1929); Lang, 34 BTA 337 (1936); Gladding, 27 BTA 385 (1932); Blair v Dustin, 30 F2d 774 (CCA 2) (1929).

1. Note 17, supra.

such property is included in the decedent's gross estate, *and only if* in determining the value of the net estate of the prior decedent no deduction was allowable under the subsection, Section 861(a)(2), or the corresponding provisions of any prior Act of Congress, in respect of the property or property given in exchange therefor.[2] We thus have a limitation and three conditions within a single paragraph.[3]

The statute then describes property for which the deduction may not be allowed, which includes (A) property received from a prior decedent who died after December 31, 1947, and was at the time of such death the decedent's spouse, (B) property received by gift after the date of the enactment of the Revenue Act of 1948 from a donor who at the time of the gift was the decedent's spouse, and (C) property acquired in exchange for property described in (A) or (B).[4] Where there was a split gift, one half of the gift is considered as received by the decedent from each spouse. With respect to such property we have noted that in the case of such transfers within two years of death, if the decedent died after December 31, 1951, the executor may elect to take the credit for prior transfers instead of the deduction here discussed.[5]

While the foregoing embraces all the conditions which must be met in order for the deduction to be allowed, there are two further limitations.

Where a deduction was allowed of any mortgage or other lien in determining the Gift Tax, or the Estate Tax of the prior decedent, which was paid in whole or in part prior to the decedent's death, then the deduction allowable under the subsection shall be reduced by the amount so paid. The deduction shall be reduced by an amount which bears the same ratio to the amounts allowed as deductions under subsections (a), (d), and (e) and the amounts of general claims allowed as deductions under subsection (b) as the amount otherwise deductible under the subsection bears to the property *subject to general claims.*[6]

If the property includible in the gross estate to which the deduction under the subsection is attributable *is not wholly property subject to general claims*—

2. Note 17, supra; see Horlick v Kuhl, note 20, supra; Vath, note 20, supra; Hart, 2 TC 1246 (1943); Schmidt, 19 TC 54, affd 220 F2d 63 (CA 9) (1952).

3. Reg 105, §§ 81.41(a)(3)(4)(5); 81-.41(b).

4. Note 17, supra.
5. Note 18, supra.
6. Note 17, supra.

(1) before the application of the preceding sentence, the amount of the deduction under the subsection shall be reduced by that part of such amount as the value at the time of the decedent's death, of such property (to which such deduction is attributable) subject to claims but not to general claims is of the value, at the time of decedent's death, of such property, and

(2) in the application of the preceding sentence in reducing the balance, if any, of such deduction, "the amount otherwise deductible under the subsection" shall be only that part of such amount otherwise deductible (determined without regard to clause (1) of this paragraph) as the value, at the time of the decedent's death, of such property (to which such deduction is attributable) subject to general claims is of the value, at the time of the decedent's death, of such property.

For the purposes of the two preceding sentences and this sentence, "general claims" are the amounts allowed as deductions under subsection (b) which, under the applicable law, in the final adjustment and settlement of the estate may be enforced against any property subject to claims, as defined in subsection (b), and "property subject to general claims" is the value, at the time of the decedent's death, of property subject to claims, as defined in subsection (b), reduced by the value, at the time of the decedent's death, of that part of such property against which amounts allowed as deductions under subsection (b) which are not general claims may be enforced, under the applicable law, in the final adjustment and settlement of the estate. Where the property referred to in the subsection consists of two or more items the aggregate value of such items shall be used for the purpose of computing the deduction.[7]

It is apparent why there were no tears shed when this monstrosity was interred by the 1954 Code.

§ 277. Deduction for Property Previously Taxed; Conditions.

There are five conditions set forth in the Regulation[8] which must be complied with if the deduction is to be allowed. They are:

(1) The property respecting which the deduction is sought must have been received by the decedent as a gift within five years prior to his death, or received by him by gift, bequest,

---

7. Note 17, supra.   8. Reg 105, § 81.41(a).

devise, or inheritance from a prior decedent who died within five years of the decedent's death. Notwithstanding the designation by local law of the capacity in which the decedent takes, for the purposes of this deduction, property received by gift, bequest, devise or inheritance includes property, or rights with respect to property, held by or devolving upon the decedent as spouse under dower or curtesy laws or laws creating an estate in lieu of dower or curtesy, as spouse under community property laws, as tenant of a tenancy by the entirety or joint tenancy with survivorship rights, as donee (possessor) of a power of appointment, as appointee under the exercise of a power of appointment, as remainderman under the release or nonexercise of a power of appointment, or as beneficiary of life insurance.

(2) The property must be identified either as the same property which the decedent so received or as property acquired in exchange therefor.

(3) The property must have formed a part of the gross estate, situated in the United States, of such prior decedent, or have been included in the total amount of the donor's gifts made within five years prior to the decedent's death.

(4) An Estate Tax by or on behalf of the estate of such prior decedent, or a Gift Tax by or on behalf of the donor, must have actually been paid (the mere filing of a return for such estate or donor not being sufficient). Where, under the provisions of section 1000 (f), a gift received by the decedent was considered as made one-half by the donor and one-half by the donor's spouse, the deduction may not be taken in respect of the half of the gift considered as made by the donor unless a Gift Tax was paid by or on behalf of the donor, or in respect of the half of the gift considered as made by the donor's spouse unless a Gift Tax was paid by or on behalf of such spouse.

(5) No such deduction, in respect to the property or property given in exchange therefor, must have been allowable in determining the value of the net estate of the prior decedent.

(6) The property (or property given in exchange therefor) must not have been received (by gift or otherwise) from a prior decedent who died after December 31, 1947, and was at the time of such death the decedent's spouse, and must not have been received by gift after April 2, 1948, from a donor

who at the time of the gift was the decedent's spouse. This latter condition, added by section 362 of the Revenue Act of 1948, is effective even though the decedent (surviving spouse) died after December 31, 1947, and on or before April 2, 1948; but the Estate Tax payable by the estate of such spouse is, nevertheless, not to exceed the Estate Tax which would have been imposed if the Revenue Act of 1948 had not been enacted. These conditions arise from the wording of the statutory provisions last discussed.

The sixth condition set forth in the Regulation does not reflect the 1956 amendment to which we have previously referred, which grants an election to the executor in the case of transfers between spouses within two years of death to take the credit for tax on prior transfers if the death occurred after December 31, 1951.

The first condition, in fact, contains two conditions, namely, that the property must have been the subject of a gift, bequest, devise, or inheritance,[9] and the prior decedent must have died within five years of the decedent.[10]

The second condition of identification of the property or exchanges therefor has been the major source of litigation.[11]

The third and fourth conditions are to assure that the property was included in the prior Estate or Gift Tax return,[12] and that a tax was paid thereon.[13]

The fifth condition is that the deduction may only be allowed once in the five year period. Thus, if property passed from A to B to C, all three decedents dying within a five year period, if the deduction were allowed in B's estate, it cannot again be allowed in C's estate.

The sixth condition which denied the deduction in cases where the prior decedent was the spouse of the decedent, no longer has any practical effect in view of the 1956 amendment previously discussed.[14]

9. Hart, note 2, supra; Gardner, 22 BTA 1076 (1931); Guenzel, 28 TC 59 (1957).

10. Second Nat Bank & Trust Co v Comm, 63 F2d 815 (CCA 6) (1933).

11. Note 20, supra.

12. Horlick v Kuhl, note 20, supra; Gray, 19 BTA 455 (1930); Gardner, note 9, supra; Kirkwood, 23 BTA 955 (1931); Comm v Fletcher, Savings & Trust Co, 59 F2d 508 (CCA 7) (1932); G C M 8481, X–1 CB 451; Bank of America v US, 237 F2d 942 (CA 9), affg 130 F Supp 923 (1955).

13. Note 2, supra.

14. § 276, supra.

§ 278. Deduction for Property Previously Taxed; Limitations.

There are three limitations on the deduction for property previously taxed to be considered. As stated in the Regulation[15] they are as follows:

(1) The deduction is limited to the value of the property, or the aggregate value of such property if more than one item, as finally determined for the purpose of the Gift Tax or for the purpose of the prior Estate Tax, or to the value of such property or aggregate items thereof (or property acquired in exchange therefor) included in the decedent's gross estate, whichever is the lower.[16]

(2) The deduction, as limited in (1) is reduced by the total amount paid prior to the decedent's death on any mortgage or other lien on the property previously taxed, provided such mortgage or other lien was deducted in determining the Estate Tax of the prior decedent or the Gift Tax of the donor.

(3) If the decedent died on or before October 21, 1942, the date of the enactment of the Revenue Act of 1942, the deduction is further reduced by the amount of that proportion of the deductions allowed under paragraphs (a), (b), and (d) of section 812 which the amount otherwise deductible for property previously taxed bears to the value of the decedent's gross estate. If the decedent died after October 21, 1942, the deduction (the amount ascertained after applying the limitations set forth in (b) (1) and (2) of this section of the Regulations) is to be reduced by an amount which bears the same ratio to the amounts allowed as deductions under subsections (a), (d), and (e) of section 812 and the amounts of general claims allowed as deductions under paragraph (b) of section 812 as the amount otherwise deductible for property previously taxed bears to property subject to general claims. However, before applying the rule in the preceding sentence, if the property previously taxed includible in the gross estate is not wholly subject to general claims, the amount otherwise deductible (the amount ascertained after applying the limitations set

15. Reg 105, § 81.41(b).

16. Bloedorn v US, 116 F Supp 133 (1953); Hanch, 19 TC 65 (1953); Gardner, note 9, supra; Comm v Garland, 136 F2d 82 (CCA 1) (1943); Bahr v Comm, 119 F2d 371 (CCA 5), cert den 314 US 650, 86 L ed 521, 62 S Ct 95 (1941); Central Hanover Bank & Trust Co v Comm, 159 F2d 167 (CCA 2), cert den 331 US 836, 91 L ed 1848, 67 S Ct 1518 (1947); Ransbottom v Comm, 148 F2d 280 (CCA 6) (1945); Thomas v Earnest, 161 F2d 845 (CCA 5) (1947); Plessen, 25 TC 1301 (1956).

forth in (b)(1) and (2) of this section of the Regulations) is first subject to further adjustments as hereinafter set forth.[17]

Property included in the total amount of gifts of a donor for the purpose of the Gift Tax and also included in the donee's gross estate does not embrace any portion of the gifts excluded under the annual exclusion provisions of the Gift Tax, and due allowance must be made for any such exclusions when computing the deduction for property previously taxed. Thus if a donor made a gift of property valued at $24,000. at a time when the annual exclusion was $4,000. and the property was included in the donee's estate at a value of $18,000., since only $20,000. was included in the Gift Tax return, 20,000/24,000 of $18,000., or $15,000. would be considered for the purpose of the deduction for property previously taxed.[18]

§ 279. Deduction for Property Previously Taxed; Operation.

Fortunately for those required to compute the deduction for property previously taxed, the Regulation[19] is most explicit. While the example demonstrates the method to be employed, it also demonstrates that the amount allowed as a deduction is negligible in comparison to the amount of property involved.

It is assumed that all of the conditions which we have previously discussed[20] have been complied with so that the deduction is allowable. *The computation is based upon the estate of the present decedent* and not that of the prior one. The prior decedent is Hall and the present decedent is Benson.

Benson leaves (1) a residence worth $25,000., (2) other real estate worth $30,000., (3) proceeds of life insurance totaling $50,000., (4) other property worth $105,000. The total gross estate is $210,000.

Benson's estate is entitled to the following deductions in computing the basic tax: (1) specific exemption, $100,000., (2) mortgage on residence, $9,000.; (3) homestead exemption $1,000., (4) mortgage on other real estate $35,000., (5) funeral, administration and other expenses, $4,000., (6) charitable bequests $6,000. The total deductions are $155,000.

Assume that the residence was valued at $20,000. in Hall's estate and that the $9,000. mortgage was placed on it after Hall died and after Benson had inherited it.

17. Emanuel, 9 TC 779 (1947); Hirsch, 14 TC 509 (1950); Haggett, 14 TC 325 (1950).

18. Note 15, supra.
19. Note 15, supra.
20. § 277, supra.

Assume also that the insurance is exempt from claims of creditors. Note that the other real estate ($30,000.) is subject to a mortgage of $35,000. If the mortgage is not satisfied out of Benson's other real estate it will remain unpaid to the extent of $5,000. Assume that the $5,000. balance is payable out of other property.

Deduction for property previously taxed is claimed for the residence received by Benson from Hall. Up to this point, the residence is valued at $20,000., its appraised value in the prior estate of Hall.

Since the residence is not wholly subject to general claims of creditors, because its equity is reduced by a mortgage of $9,000. an adjustment is necessary. The proportion is as follows: the mortgage ($9,000.) is to the value of the residence in Benson's estate ($25,000.) as the reduction is to the value of the residence in Hall's estate ($20,000.). Or 9,000 : 25,000 : : X : 20,000. The result is $7,200. which subtracted from $20,000. leaves $12,800. Now the deduction has been considerably reduced.

But this is only the beginning. Deductions for charitable bequests, specific exemption and general claims under Schedules J, K, L and M must be considered.

The property previously taxed, the residence, which is subject to general claims, is $15,000. This is because the $25,000. value in Benson's estate is actually taxable only at $15,000., the balance after Benson's $9,000. mortgage and $1,000. homestead exemption. Stating this as a proportion,—the equity in the residence subject to general claims ($15,000.) is to its appraised value ($25,000.) as the reduction is to $20,000. Stripped of verbiage, the formula is 15,000 : 25,000 :: X : 20,000. The result is $12,000., the amount otherwise deductible for the purposes of computing further reductions.

The property of Benson subject to general claims must also be considered. This includes other property ($105,000.) and $15,000. the equity in the residence, a total of $120,000. On the debit side are general claims ($4,000.), unpaid mortgage balance of mortgage on other real estate ($5,000.), a total of $9,000. Added to this are charitable gifts ($6,000.) and the personal exemption ($100,000.). This brings the total deductions to $115,-000. The proportion based on this is as follows: The amount otherwise deductible for purposes of computing further deductions ($12,000.) is to the total property of Benson subject to general claims ($120,000.) as the total reduction is to the total deductions $115,000. Mathematically stated this is 12,000 : 120,-000 :: X : 115,000. The result is $11,500.

Thus, the primary deduction of $20,000. is reduced by $18,700. the sum of the two reductions, namely $7,200. and $11,500., leaving a final deductible allowance of $1,300.

When the additional tax is computed, the specific exemption is $60,000. in place of $100,000. On the foregoing basis, the reductions will be $7,200. and $7,500. instead of $7,200. and $11,500.

If in the above example there was also a marital deduction the amount of such deduction would be added to the other deductions and the computation made.

It will be observed that a separate computation is required for the basic tax and the additional tax in effect under the 1939 Code.

§ 280. Deduction for Property Previously Taxed; Return.

Since the deduction for property previously taxed does not apply to the estates of decedents dying on and after August 17, 1954, the Estate Tax Return, Form 706, now in use, does not contain any provision therefor. As the present form points out, for estates of persons dying before August 17, 1954 Form 706 (Revised December 1953) should be used. The present Schedule I refers to annuities.[1]

Former Schedule I providing for the report of property previously taxed is understandably more complex than other schedules. In the first place, it has five columns so that items of principal and of income may be reported separately, either according to the value at the date of death or according to the optional value. The fifth column must show the value of the item in the prior estate. The instructions provide as to this that the value of each item of property and any income thereon determined as of the applicable date or dates for inclusion in the value of the gross estate of the present decedent should be entered under the appropriate columns A, B, C, and D. It will be noted that column A is provided for the value under the option, of the principal of each item of property, column B, for any income thereon under the option, column C is provided for the value at the date of the decedent's death of the principal of each item of property, and column D is provided for any income thereon

---

1. §§ 178 et seq, supra.

accrued to the date of death. The value finally determined in
the prior estate or gift of each item of property should be entered in column E.[2] The description should be the same description given in the prior estate. It should identify the items by
cross-referencing to the item number previously used. It should
also show the true story as to mortgages and liens on the premises. The description should show the schedule and item number
of the property as it appeared in the prior return. To make it
clear that the schedule and item number relate to the prior return, they should be included in parentheses. If only a portion
of an item in the prior estate is reflected in the present estate,
that fact should be indicated and only a proportionate part of
the value of the item in the prior estate, as finally determined,
should be entered in column E.[3] As to the description, it should
also be noted that in accordance with the foregoing second limitation, any amount paid before the death of the present decedent
in discharge of a mortgage or other lien on the property previously taxed, provided such mortgage or other lien was deducted in
the prior case, should be shown last under the column headed
"Description," together with an identification of the item of
property involved and the item deducted in the prior case. The
total of such amounts paid should be entered at item (b).[4]

As to preparation of the totals, the instructions provide that
the "Total included in gross estate" (included in the value of the
gross estate utilized for the computation of the tax) is the total
of columns A and B if the optional valuation is adopted, or the
total of columns C and D if the optional valuation is not adopted.
However, if the optional valuation is adopted, both such totals
should be entered under the appropriate columns under the
Recapitulation, Schedule O.[5]

In addition to this, it should be noted that the amount of the
gross deduction for property previously taxed, in accordance
with the first limitation, is entered at item (a). If the optional
valuation is adopted, the amount of the gross deduction is the
total of column A or the total of column E, whichever is the
lower. If the optional valuation is not adopted, the amount of
the gross deduction is the total of column C or the total of

2. Instructions, Schedule I, Form 706
(Revised Dec 1953); Reg 105, § 81.41.
3. Instructions, Schedule I, Form 706
(Revised Dec 1953); Reg 105, § 81.42.

4. Note 2, supra.
5. Note 2, supra.

column E, whichever is the lower. The amount of item (b) is subtracted from the amount of the item (a); and the difference, which is entered at item (c) is the amount of the deduction as reduced in accordance with the second limitation. The amount of the net deduction for property previously taxed, as reduced by a certain proportion of the total other deductions in accordance with the third limitation, is finally computed under Schedules P and Q or under Schedule R.[6]

6. Note 2, supra.

FORM NO. 37

Schedule I; Property Previously Taxed

Name of donor or prior decedent   Charles Hall
If a donor, show date of gift ....

If a decedent, show date of death .... October 31, 1951 .... St. Louis, Mo.
Residence of donor at time of gift, or of prior decedent at time of death

Item No.	Description of property, subsequent valuation dates, and description and amounts of mortgages or other liens paid	(Column A) Value under option	(Column B) Income under option	(Column C) Value at date of death	(Column D) Income accrued at date of death	(Column E) Finally determined value in prior estate or gift
1	Residence of WINTHROP BENSON (described as in prior return including schedule and item number whether the whole item or only part, data on discharge of mortgages or liens, if any).	$ 0	$ 0	$25,000	$ 0	$20,000
	TOTALS	$ 0	$ 0	$25,000	$ 0	$20,000

Total included in gross estate (total of columns A and B, or total of columns C and D, whichever is applicable) (also enter under Recapitulation, Schedule O) $25,000

(a) Gross deduction (total of applicable column A or C, or total of column E, whichever is lower) $20,000
(b) Total amount paid on mortgages or other liens deducted in prior estate or gift (enter detailed information at bottom of column headed "Description") .... $ 0
(c) Deduction for property previously taxed without proportionate reduction (item (a) minus item (b)) (also enter under Schedules P and Q, or Schedule R) $20,000
(If more space is needed, insert additional sheets of same size)

Estate of WINTHROP BENSON

Schedule I—Sheet XII

370

[Harris]

§ 281. Transfers for Public, Charitable, or Religious Uses; Generally.

Where there is a legacy of a stated amount to a public, charitable, or religious organization, there is no problem in determining the amount to be allowed as a deduction from the gross estate. But it is a common situation, particularly when the decedent has but one near relative, to leave his estate in trust for the benefit of that person for life, and then provide that the remainder after the termination of the life estate be given to a charity.

In such case, the computation of the value of the remainder runs up against the statutory provision which we have previously discussed,[7] that if the Federal Estate tax or any death tax, is, either by the terms of the will, by the law of the jurisdiction under which the estate is administered, or by the law of the jurisdiction imposing the particular tax, payable in whole or in part out of the charitable bequest, legacy, or devise, otherwise deductible, *then the amount deductible shall be the amount of such bequest, legacy, or devise, reduced by the amount of such taxes.*[8]

The problem is further complicated when the decedent's domiciliary state has a similar provision. If taxes are payable out of the charitable bequest, they must first be determined before the amount of the bequest can be determined. But if the amount of the bequest is unknown it is impossible to determine the amount of the taxes. The objection to the original statute was that this involved two mutually dependent indeterminates and its solution required the use of an algebraic formula.[9] While Congress was at first persuaded by this argument to abandon the provision, it subsequently changed its mind and restored it.[10] The result is that that is exactly what is required for solution of the problem. Such formula was devised and is known as the Greeley formula, named after its author.[11]

As the Regulation points out, it should be noted that if the Federal Estate Tax is payable out of a charitable transfer so that the amount of the transfer otherwise passing to charity is reduced by the amount of the tax, the resultant decrease in the amount passing to charity will further reduce the allowable deduction. In such case, the amount of the charitable deduction

---

7. § 255, supra.

8. IRC, § 2055(c) (1954 Code).

9. Edwards v Slocum, 264 US 61, 68 L ed 564, 44 S Ct 293 (1924).

10. Note 7, supra.

11. See Journal of Accountancy, May, June, July, 1938 by Harold D. Greeley, Esq, also see Journal of Accountancy, March 1940, by Ellen E. Eastman.

can be obtained only by a series of trial and error computations, or by a formula. If, in addition, interdependent State and Federal taxes are involved, the computation becomes highly complicated. Examples of methods of computation of the charitable deduction and the marital deduction (with which similar problems are encountered) in various situations are contained in supplemental instructions to the Estate Tax return.[12]

§ 282. Transfers for Public, Charitable, and Religious Uses; Operation.

As the Regulation referred to, points out, when the amount of the charitable deduction is reduced by the amount of the tax, the amount of the deduction can only be obtained by a series of trial and error computations. If the gift is $100,000. and is reduced by a tax of $5,000., the gift becomes only $95,000., and the tax on this amount is less than $5,000. It therefore becomes necessary to make a series of computations until it is determined at what point the tax and the amount actually receivable total $100,000. This is comparatively simple. But when the bequest is reduced by both State and Federal taxes, neither dependent on the other, the formula referred to[13] must be resorted to. This is not the only complication, since in one case the will may provide for exoneration of some bequests and not of others and in other cases the marital deduction may also be involved. As a practical matter, unless one dotes on mathematics, a rough computation of the deduction should be made and the job of making the exact computation left to the Estate Tax Examiner. The Supplemental Instructions for Computation of Interrelated Death Taxes and the Marital Deduction contains some excellent practical advice. If any difficulty is experienced in computation, a request for solution of the problem may be submitted a reasonable time before the due date of the return to the Commissioner of Internal Revenue, Washington, 25, D. C. The request should be accompanied by a copy of the will, a statement showing the distribution of the estate under the decedent's will or under State Law, a computation of the State death tax showing the amount payable and such documents as may be necessary or convenient in the analysis of the legal situation. A visit to the nearest office of the Estate Tax Audit group will find them similarly helpful.

To those who insist upon independent solution of the problem,

12. Reg, § 20.2055–3(b).   13. Greeley Formula, § 281, supra.

the involved formula referred to will be found in both Commerce Clearing House and Prentice Hall Estate and Gift Tax services. As we have noted, such computation to the last decimal point may well be love's labor lost, since it is the rare estate in which upon audit of the return there are not changes made, so that an entirely new computation is required.

§ 283. Death Taxes Payable Out of Transfers for Public, Charitable, or Religious Uses.

We have previously discussed the 1956 amendment to the Internal Revenue Code of 1954 which allows a deduction for the amount of death taxes imposed by a state upon transfers for public, charitable, or religious uses.[14]

If a state death tax is imposed upon the transfer of the decedent's entire estate and not upon a transfer of a particular share thereof, the State death tax imposed upon a transfer for charitable, etc., uses is deemed to be an amount, E, which bears the same ratio to F (the amount of the State death tax imposed with respect to the transfer of the entire estate) as G (the value of the charitable, etc., transfer, reduced as provided in the next sentence) bears to H (the total value of the properties, interests, and benefits subjected to the State death tax received by all persons interested in the estate, reduced as provided in the last sentence of this paragraph). In arriving at amount G of the ratio, the value of the charitable, etc., transfer is reduced by the amount of any deduction or exclusion allowed with respect to such property in determining the amount of the State death tax. In arriving at amount H of the ratio, the total value of the properties, interests, and benefits subjected to State death tax received by all persons interested in the estate is reduced by the amount of all deductions and exclusions allowed in determining the amount of the State death tax on account of the nature of a beneficiary or a beneficiary's relationship to the decedent.[15]

The Regulation furnishes examples of the application of the section.[16]

§ 284. Marital Deduction; Elements Basic to Computation.

As we have seen in our previous discussion the marital deduction is allowable (1) in an amount equal to the value of any

14. § 214, supra.
15. Reg, § 20.2053–9(d).
16. Reg, § 20.2053–9(e).

interest in property which passes or has passed from the decedent to his surviving spouse,[17] (2) but only to the extent that such interest is included in determining the gross estate,[18] and (3) in an amount not to exceed 50% of the adjusted gross estate,[19] (4) taking into account the effect which State death taxes and incumbrances and obligations have on the net value to the surviving spouse of such interest.[20] Each of these must be considered in computing the amount of the deduction.

Even where all of the decedent's property passes to his surviving spouse, the maximum amount allowed as the marital deduction cannot exceed the statutory limitation of 50% of the adjusted gross estate. In the case of community property, a different rule applies, which is discussed in the succeeding section.

Thus, if the decedent's gross estate is $200,000., and the total deductions for funeral and administration expenses, claims against the estate, encumbrances, and losses are $50,000., the adjusted gross estate is $150,000. The *maximum* marital deduction would therefore be half of this amount, or $75,000. It does not follow that this is the amount allowable. If the spouse in fact receives less than such amount, *only the net amount received* will be deductible.

§ 285. Marital Deduction; Community Property Rule.

As we have seen, the purpose of the marital deduction was to equalize the tax status of citizens of community property law states and noncommunity property law states, so that in order that there might not be a double deduction, it was necessary to provide a special rule to apply in the case of residents of community property law states.[1] The adjusted gross estate is determined in such cases by deducting from the entire value of the gross estate

(1) The value of any property included in the gross estate held as community property.

(2) The value of lifetime transfers included in the gross estate, which at the time of the transfer were community property.

17. §§ 227, 228, supra.   20. § 233, supra.
18. § 226, supra.   1. § 243, supra.
19. § 238, supra.

(3) The amount receivable as insurance under policies on the life of the decedent purchased with premiums or other consideration paid out of community property.

(4) An amount which bears the same ratio to the aggregate of deductions for funeral and administration expenses, claims against the estate, and losses, which the value of the property included in the gross estate, diminished by the total of (1), (2), and (3), bears to the entire value of the gross estate.[2]

What is and what is not considered community property for the purposes of the statute has been treated heretofore.[3]

The operation of the statute is as follows:[4] Benson's gross estate consists of $200,000. in *separate* property and $100,000., his interest in *community* property. Deductions for debts, funeral and administration expenses, and losses total $45,000.

Gross Estate		$300,000
Community Property (his share)	$100,000	
Allowable Deductions		
(Separate Property) $\frac{200}{300}$ of $45,000		30,000
(Gross Estate)		
Total Reduction		130,000
Adjusted Gross Estate		$170,000
Maximum Marital Deduction		$ 85,000

If in the above example, lifetime transfers of community property were included in the gross estate, and insurance on the decedent's life purchased with community property, the total of these items would be added to the $130,000. and that total deducted from the gross estate.

If Benson's gross estate was the same as above, but he and his wife partitioned community property of the value of $224,-000., and part of the property of the value of $160,000. was *converted* into Benson's separate property, and the balance of $64,000. was converted into his wife's separate property, and assuming that at his death the property is valued at $200,000., the marital deduction would be computed as follows: First it is necessary to determine the portion of the separate property

2. Reg, § 20.2056(c)–2(a).　　4. Reg, § 20.2056(c)–2(j).
3. Note 1, supra.

acquired by Benson which will be considered to be held as community property. That would be

$$\frac{64,000}{160,000} \times \$200,000 = \$80,000$$

The computation would then proceed as follows:

Gross Estate $300,000

Community Property ($100,000 + $80,000) $180,000

Allowable Deductions $\dfrac{(200 - 80}{300} \times \$45,000)$ ... 18,000

Total Deduction 198,000

Adjusted Gross Estate $102,000
Maximum Marital Deduction 51,000

§ 286. Marital Deduction; Valuation.

The *amount* of the marital deduction is affected by whether the fiduciary values the gross estate as of the date of death or elects the alternate valuation. The *right* to the deduction is not affected thereby.[5] Thus, if a property interest passing to the surviving spouse has a value at the date of death of $20,000., but is sold within a year of death for $30,000., if the fiduciary takes date of death valuation, the amount of the marital deduction is computed on the basis of the property valued at $20,000. If he elects the alternate valuation, the marital deduction is computed on the basis of the property valued at $30,000. The fact that the property is worth more or less than either of these amounts at any other time has no bearing on the basis of valuation.[6] If the maximum deduction is sought, it is necessary to compute the value of the gross estate as of the date of death and as of the alternate dates. Many wills today provide for the fiduciary to select a valuation date which will result in the lower tax. In such case the computation is mandatory.

The amount of the marital deduction is also affected by any encumbrance or obligation on the property passing.[7] Thus, if the decedent devises his residence worth $25,000. to his wife with direction that she pay $5,000. to his sister, the value of the property passing is only $20,000. If he devises it to her in satisfac-

5. Reg, § 20.2056(b)-4(a).
6. See Committee Reports on addition of Subsection (e) to IRC, § 812 by Rev Act of 1948.

7. § 233, supra.

tion of a claim, the amount of the claim would have to be deducted from its value.[8]

The amount of the marital deduction, as we shall see in the succeeding sections, may be considerably affected by death taxes, if any are required to be paid therefrom.

§ 287. Marital Deduction; Effect of Death Taxes.

In the determination of the value of any property interest which passed from the decedent to his surviving spouse, there must be taken into account the effect which the Federal Estate Tax, or *any* estate, succession, legacy, or inheritance tax has upon the net value to the surviving spouse of the property interest.[9]

If the only bequest to the surviving spouse is $100,000. and she is required to pay a State inheritance tax of $1,500. but no other death taxes, then the value of her bequest is $98,500. for the purposes of the marital deduction.[10] As previously noted,[11] the marital deduction is based upon the amount a spouse actually receives.

If the decedent devises real property to his wife having a value for Federal Estate Tax purposes of $100,000., and a non-deductible life estate, and the State values the property at $90,000. and the life estate at $30,000. and imposes an inheritance tax of $4,800. (at graduated rates), which is required to be paid by the wife, the value of the property for the purpose of the marital deduction is computed as follows:

$$\frac{\text{(State valuation of realty)} \quad 90,000}{\text{(State valuation of wife's entire interest)} \quad 120,000} \times \$4,800 \text{ (Tax paid)} = \$3,600$$

If no other taxes affect the interest of the wife, the value of the realty for purposes of the marital deduction is $100,000. less $3,600., or $96,400.[12]

The above problems are simple ones and easy of solution. They require no great mathematical skill except knowledge of simple subtraction and division. But computation of the amount of the marital deduction abounds with complexities when Federal, or State and Federal taxes, and the marital deduction

8. Reg, § 20.2056(b)–4(b).
9. Reg, § 20.2056(b)–4(c)(1).
10. Reg, § 20.2056(b)–4(c)(2).

11. Note 7, supra.
12. Reg, § 20.2056(b)–4(c)(3).

are interrelated. Methods of computation in such case are considered in the succeeding sections.

§ 288. Marital Deduction and Death Taxes; Interrelation; Generally.

Where the devise or bequest to the surviving spouse is a fixed pecuniary amount, or specific property, and part of the estate tax or other death duty is chargeable to it, the only problem is to compute the proportion of such property to the taxable estate, the value of such property being reduced by its share of the tax. But this is not only not usually the case, but in fact, rarely so. If the decedent bequeaths his residuary estate, or a portion of it, to his surviving spouse, and his will contains a direction that all death taxes shall be payable out of the residuary estate, the value of the bequest, for the purpose of the marital deduction, is based upon the amount of the residue as reduced pursuant to such direction. If by local law the Federal Estate Tax is payable out of the residue, the value of the bequest, for the purpose of the marital deduction, may not exceed its value as reduced by the Federal Estate Tax.[13]

The result is, that in such cases, the marital deduction cannot be determined until the taxes are determined, and the taxes cannot be determined until the marital deduction is known. As one writer[14] says of this provision, "if you had some ham, you could have some ham and eggs, if you had some eggs." The solution is not as impossible as would appear. Methods of solving the problems presented may be found in many sources. In particular states, the solution depends upon the nature of the death tax, if any. One state has no such tax, others have an estate tax or an inheritance tax, in some the Federal tax is deductible and in others it is not. In many wills drawn today there is a provision for the spouse's share to be a portion of the residue computed before estate taxes, and further provision that no part of the tax be paid from such share. It is not, however, the happy lot of every lawyer to be able to avoid the computations necessary otherwise.

The Treasury Department is not unaware of the fact that not all lawyers are mathematicians and has therefore prepared Supplemental Instructions for Computation of Interrelated

---

13. Reg, § 20.2056(b)–4(c)(4).   14. I. A. Powers, Marital Deduction Formulas, 27 Taxes 726 (1949).

Death Taxes and Marital Deduction. In such cases as these may be inadequate, there are several practical solutions. As the Supplemental Instructions advise, if any difficulty is experienced, a request for solution may be submitted to the Commissioner of Internal Revenue. If the reader insists on his own solution, examples of further methods of computation are furnished in Commerce Clearing House, Federal Estate and Gift Tax Reporter, covering every combination of circumstances, including the situation where there may be property in two states. A third solution is to follow the unofficial recommendation of the Estate Tax examiners and in filing the return approximate the marital deduction. This practical advice is based on their experience that there are invariably adjustments on audit of the return which will require re-computation of the marital deduction.

In the examples given in the Supplemental Instructions and set forth in succeeding sections it is assumed

(1) The Federal Estate Tax is a charge against the general estate.

(2) All claims against the estate (other than death taxes) are deductible in computing the taxable estate.

(3) No deduction for charitable, etc., bequests or credit for tax on prior transfers, gift tax or foreign death taxes are allowed.

Inherent in the Treasury's assumptions are a host of further complicated situations which may arise.

§ 289. Marital Deduction and Death Taxes; Interrelation; When Nonexistent.

There are several situations in which the problem of interrelation of death taxes and the marital deduction does not arise. The first is the case previously referred to in which the testator directs that such portion as passes to his wife be exonerated from the payment of any tax.

In states which have apportionment statutes which provide for exemptions and deductions being credited to the person entitled to such deduction or exemption, if a spouse's share in the estate is one half or less of the gross estate, there results a statutory exoneration.

A third situation is where the amount passing to the surviving spouse exceeds one half of the adjusted gross estate by such an amount that in no event can the taxes chargeable to her share reduce the share to less than one half the adjusted gross estate.

In none of these cases will it be necessary to compute the effect of death taxes on the spouse's share. But it is pointed out that if at the outset, it is doubtful whether one half the adjusted gross estate will be smaller than the net marital deduction, a computation of the amount of the tax affecting the net benefit to the surviving spouse can be made upon the assumption that the marital deduction is one half the adjusted gross estate. If such computation shows that (due consideration being given to both Federal and State death taxes) the deduction is, in fact, less than one half the adjusted gross estate, the computations set forth in the Instructions will be necessary.[15]

§ 290. Marital Deduction and Death Taxes; Interrelation; Estate Subject to the Gross Estate Tax; No Credit for State Death Taxes.

The first example in the Supplemental Instructions[16] deals with the estate of a resident or citizen of the United States. The gross estate is $200,000. Total deductions for the purpose of determining the adjusted gross estate are $40,000. The decedent bequeathed $80,000. to his son and the residue to his widow. She paid a State inheritance tax of $700. The Federal Estate Tax is payable out of the general estate. The computation, as in all of the examples, is divided into six parts: (1) distributing the estate and determining the gross property interests passing to the surviving spouse; (2) assuming a taxable estate in the correct bracket; (3) the trial computation; (4) determining the factor to be used in adjusting the discrepancy in the assumed taxable estate; (5) adjusting the discrepancy; and (6) proof that the adjustment is correct.

15. Supplemental Instructions for Computation of Interrelated Death Taxes and Marital Deduction.

16. Note 15, supra, (C).

(1) *Distributing the estate:*

Gross estate	$200,000
Debts and charges	40,000
Adjusted gross estate	160,000
Bequest to son	80,000
Gross property passing to spouse	80,000
State inheritance tax payable by spouse	700
Marital deduction before Federal tax	79,300

(2) *Assuming a taxable estate in the correct bracket:*

Gross estate		$200,000
Debts and charges	$40,000	
Marital deduction before Federal tax	79,300	
Specific exemption	60,000	179,300
Taxable estate before Federal tax		$20,700

Consideration of the facts of the example shows that when the gross marital deduction is reduced by death taxes, the taxable estate will be increased by the amount of such tax, since the taxable estate above before reduction by the state tax is $20,000. Referring to Table A on page 40 of Form 706 it is noted that the gross tax on a taxable estate of $20,000. is $1,600., and on a taxable estate of $30,000. is $3,000. The result of adding either amount of Federal Estate Tax to the above taxable estate of $20,700. produces a figure still within the $20,000. to $30,000. bracket. Therefore, an assumed taxable estate of $20,000. and a tax rate of 14% (the amount in column 4 of Table A) may be used as a basis for the computation.

Note that it is necessary to determine by trial and error or otherwise, the tax bracket within which the true taxable estate lies. A satisfactory method, illustrated above, is to start with the bracket which contains the *taxable estate before Federal tax* and proceed to higher brackets, if necessary, until a bracket is found which satisfies the following test: *Both the taxable estate based on the highest tax in the bracket and the taxable estate based on the lowest tax in the bracket must fall within the bracket itself. Only the bracket containing the true taxable estate will satisfy this test.*

(3) *Trial computation:*

Assumed taxable estate for Federal tax .... $ 20,000
Net Federal tax thereon 1,600

Gross estate $200,000
Debts and charges $40,000
Gross property passing to spouse ... $80,000
Less taxes payable by spouse
    State tax $700
    Federai tax on assumed taxable
      estate 1,600   2,300

Trial marital deduction   77,700
Specific exemption   60,000
                                177,700

Trial taxable estate .... $ 22,300
Assumed taxable estate 20,000

Discrepancy in assumed taxable estate .... $ 2,300

(4) *Corrective factor:*

Highest rate of Federal tax .... .14
Portion of Federal tax chargeable to spouse 100%
Subtractive term (100% × .14) .... .14
Divisor (1.00 minus .14) .... .86

This method is the "One Dollar Rule," which is based upon determining how much of the discrepancy would be eliminated by an adjustment of $1.00 in the assumed deduction of $80,000.

(5) *Adjusting the discrepancy:*

Assumed taxable estate $20,000.00
Adjustment (Discrepancy of $2,300 ÷ .86, the divisor) 2,674.42

True taxable estate $22,674.42
Net Federal tax thereon (Table A, page 40) .... $ 1,974.42

(6) *Proof:*

Gross estate		$200,000.00
Debts and charges		$40,000.00
Gross property passing to spouse	$80,000.00	
Less taxes payable by spouse		
State tax	$700.00	
Federal tax	1,974.42	2,674.42
Net marital deduction		77,325.58
Specific exemption		60,000.00
		177,325.58
Taxable estate		$ 22,674.42
Net Federal estate tax, same as true taxable estate		$ 1,974.42

In entering the figures above on Schedule M of the return, there is entered in the value column the amount of the *gross property interests* passing to the spouse, in this case, $80,000., and under item (a) at the bottom of page 29, the sum of $700., the State tax paid by the spouse, and under item (b) the above amount of $1,974.42. The net value of such property interests, $77,325.58 is entered at the bottom of the schedule and also under Schedule O, the Recapitulation.[17]

§ 291. Marital Deduction and Death Taxes; Interrelation; Estate Subject to the Gross Estate Tax; Maximum Credit for State Death Taxes; Portion of Residue Bequeathed to Spouse.

The second example in the Supplemental Instructions[18] deals with more involved factors and with inter vivos and nontestamentary transfers. The decedent's gross estate in the amount of $1,100,000. consists of real property $80,000., stocks and bonds $650,000., mortgages and cash $85,000., insurance payable to the spouse $75,000., property held jointly with the spouse $15,000., miscellaneous property $30,000., and inter vivos transfers included in the gross estate, $175,000., of which the spouse is the income beneficiary with a general power of appointment. Allowable deductions are $35,000. The decedent bequeathed $60,000. to his children and the residue equally to his wife and five children. The widow paid a State death tax of $8,650. The Federal

17. Instructions, Schedule M, Form 706.   18. Note 15, supra, (D).

tax is payable out of the general estate. In this case the State death tax exceeds the maximum amount of the credit for State death taxes, commonly known as the 80% credit,[19] and since there is no credit for Gift Tax, tax on prior transfers, or foreign death duties, Table K may be used in computing the Federal Estate Tax.[20]

(1) *Distributing the estate:*

Gross estate		$1,110,000.00
Debts and charges		35,000.00
Adjusted gross estate		$1,075,000.00
Specific bequests	$60,000.00	
Insurance payable to spouse	75,000.00	
Property held jointly with spouse	15,000.00	
Transferred property passing to spouse	175,000.00	
		325,000.00
Residue before Federal tax		$ 750,000.00
One sixth to spouse		125,000.00
Insurance payable to spouse		75,000.00
Property held jointly with spouse		15,000.00
Transfer qualifying for marital deduction		175,000.00
Gross property passing to spouse		$ 390,000.00
State death tax payable by spouse		8,650.00
Marital deduction before Federal tax		$ 381,350.00

(2) *Assuming a taxable estate in the correct bracket:*

Gross estate		$1,110,000.00
Debts and charges	$35,000.00	
Marital deduction before Federal tax	381,350.00	
Specific exemption	60,000.00	
		$ 476,350.00
Taxable estate before Federal tax		$ 633,650.00

Referring to Table K[1] it will be noted that the above taxable estate is in the $500,000. to $640,000. bracket. Since the Federal

---

19. See § 309, infra, for discussion of credit.

20. See § 293, infra, for Table K.

1. § 293, infra.

Estate Tax is payable from the general estate, the one sixth share of the residue bequeathed to the spouse will be reduced by one sixth of the net Federal Estate Tax. The reduction of the marital deduction will increase the taxable estate by a similar amount. One sixth of the tax on $500,000., $133,300., is $22,216.-67. which, added to the above taxable estate of $633,650., produces a figure *outside* of the $500,000. to $640,000. bracket. However, one sixth of the tax on $640,000., $176,700., is $29,450., and one sixth of the tax on $750,000., $209,920., is $34,986.67., and the addition of either amount of tax to $633,650. produces a figure within the $640,000. to $750,000. bracket. It will be recalled that in the prior example[2] it was pointed out that both the taxable estate based on the highest tax in the bracket and the lowest tax in the bracket must fall within the bracket itself, and only the bracket containing the true taxable estate will satisfy the test. The above demonstrates the application of the test. Therefore an assumed taxable estate of $640,000. and a tax rate of .302 may be used as a basis for the computation.

(3) *Trial computation:*

Assumed taxable estate		$ 640,000.00
Net Federal tax thereon		176,700.00
One sixth thereof		29,450.00
Gross estate		$1,110,000.00
Debts and charges	$35,000.00	
Gross property passing to spouse $390,000.00		
Less taxes payable by spouse		
State tax $8,650.00		
One sixth of Federal tax on assumed estate ... 29,450.00		
	38,100.00	
Trial marital deduction	351,900.00	
Specific exemption	60,000.00	
		446,900.00
Trial taxable estate		$ 663,100.00
Assumed taxable estate		640,000.00
Discrepancy in assumed taxable estate		$ 23,100.00

2. § 290, supra.

(4) *Corrective factor:*

Highest rate of Federal tax (Table K)	.302
Portion of Federal tax chargeable to spouse	⅙
Subtractive term (⅙ × .302)	.050333333
Divisor (1.00 minus .050333333)	.94966667

(5) *Adjusting the discrepancy:*

Assumed taxable estate	$ 640,000.00
Adjustment ($23,100.00 ÷ .94966667)	24,324.32
True taxable estate	$ 664,324.32
Net Federal tax thereon	184,045.94
One sixth thereof payable by spouse	30,674.32

(6) *Proof:*

Gross estate		$1,110,000.00
Debts and charges	$35,000.00	
Gross property passing to spouse $390,000.00		
Less taxes payable by spouse		
State tax $8,650.00		
Federal tax 30,674.32		
	39,324.32	
Net marital deduction	350,675.68	
Specific exemption	60,000.00	
	445,675.68	
Taxable estate		$ 664,324.32
Net Federal Estate Tax		$ 184,045.94

§ 292. Marital Deduction and Death Taxes; Interrelation; Estate Subject to the Gross Estate Tax; Maximum Credit for State Death Taxes; Federal Tax Deductible as Administration Expense for State Tax.

The third example in the Supplemental Instructions[3] deals with a case in which the Federal tax is payable out of the general estate, but the portion of it chargeable to the spouse's share is deductible as an administration expense in determining the spouse's inheritance for State tax purposes. It is assumed that the decedent's estate in the amount of $532,000. consists of real property held as tenant by the entirety and not taxable under State law, personal property held jointly with the spouse, one half of which is taxable under State law, insurance payable to the spouse and not taxable under State law, and other personal

3. Note 15, supra, (E).

property. Debts and charges amount to $22,000. The spouse and each of the decedent's two children received bequests of $100,000., and the residue was divided between the three equally. It is assumed that the State death tax will exceed the 80% credit, so that Table K will apply.

(1) *Distributing the estate:*

Gross estate		$532,000.00
Debts and charges		22,000.00
Adjusted gross estate		$510,000.00
Property held by entirety	$ 8,000.00	
Property held jointly with spouse	12,000.00	
Insurance payable to spouse	25,000.00	
Specific bequest to spouse	100,000.00	
Specific bequests to children	200,000.00	
		$345,000.00
Residue before Federal tax		$165,000.00
One third thereof to spouse		$ 55,000.00
Property held by entirety		8,000.00
Jointly held property		12,000.00
Insurance payable to spouse		25,000.00
Specific bequest to spouse		100,000.00
Gross property passing to spouse		$200,000.00
Property not taxable for State tax purposes		
Property held by entirety	$ 8,000.00	
One half joint property	6,000.00	
Insurance payable to spouse	25,000.00	
		39,000.00
Spouse's inheritance for State tax before deduction of Federal tax		$161,000.00

(2) *Assuming a taxable estate in the correct bracket:*

Gross estate		$532,000.00
Debts and charges	$ 22,000.00	
Marital deduction before taxes	200,000.00	
Specific exemption	60,000.00	
		282,000.00
Taxable estate before taxes		$250,000.00

Referring to Table K[4] it will be noted that the above taxable estate of $250,000. is at the lower boundary of the $250,000. to $440,000. bracket. One third of the tax on a taxable estate of $440,000. is $38,833.33., and one third of the tax on a taxable estate of $250,000. is $20.593.33. Adding either amount of tax to the taxable estate before taxes produces a figure still *within* the $250,000. to $440,000. bracket, and the result will not be changed by the further addition of the spouse's trial State death tax, below. Therefore an assumed taxable estate of $250,000. and a Federal tax rate of .288 may be used as the basis for the computation, the bracket satisfying the test discussed heretofore.[5]

(3) *Trial computation (State tax):*

Assumed taxable estate for Federal tax	$250,000.00
Net Federal tax thereon (Table K)	61,780.00
One third thereof	20,595.33

Spouse's inheritance for State tax before deduction of Federal tax	$161,000.00
One third of Federal tax on assumed taxable estate	20,593.33

Spouse's trial inheritance for State tax purposes	$140,406.67

In the individual case the particular State law must be consulted. In the example, a spouse is allowed a specific exemption of $5,000. and tax is computed on the excess at the rate of 1% on the first $50,000., 2% on the next $50,000., and 3% on the next $400,000.

Tax on first $50,000 less $5,000 exemption at 1%	$ 450.00
$50,000 at 2%	1,000.00
$40,406.67 at 3%	1,212.20

Trial State tax on spouse's inheritance	$2,662.20

It is clear that the spouse's true inheritance for State tax purposes will fall within the State bracket of $100,000. to $500,000. and the 3% rate. Should the spouse's trial inheritance fall outside the correct tax bracket, the proof (6) will fail, and it will be necessary to repeat the computation, commencing at (2), with an assumed taxable estate sufficiently close to the true taxable estate to insure that the spouse's trial inheritance falls in the correct State bracket.

4. § 293, infra.   5. § 290, supra.

(4) *Trial Computation (Federal tax):*

Gross estate $532,000.00
Debts and charges .... $ 22,000.00
Gross property passing to spouse .. $200,000.00
Less taxes payable by spouse
  One third Federal tax $20,593.33
  State tax 2,662.20

23,255.53

Trial marital deduction 176,744.47
Specific exemption 60,000.00

$258,744.47

Trial taxable estate $273,255.53
Assumed taxable estate 250,000.00

Discrepancy in assumed taxable estate .... $ 23,255.53

(5) *Corrective factor:*

Highest rate of State inheritance tax .... .03
Highest rate of Federal tax (Table K) .... .288
Portion of federal tax chargeable to spouse .... ⅓
Product (⅓ × .288) .... .09600

In the previous examples,[6] any increase in the amount of Federal tax payable by the spouse reduced the marital deduction by a similar amount. In this example an increase of $1.00 in the amount of the spouse's Federal tax causes a reduction of 3¢ in the spouse's State inheritance tax, so that the net effect is a decrease of only 97¢ in the marital deduction. This interrelation is reflected by subtracting from .09600 the product of (.09600 × .03) or .00288.

Subtractive term (.09600 minus .00288) .... .09312
The divisor (1.00 minus .09312) .... .90688

(6) *Adjusting the deficiency:*

Assumed taxable estate $250,000.00
Adjustment ($23,255.53 ÷ .90688) 25,643.45

True taxable estate for Federal tax $275,643.45
Net Federal tax thereon (Table K) 69,165.31
One third thereof payable by spouse 23,055.10

6. §§ 290, 291, supra.

(7) *Proof:*

Spouse's inheritance for State tax before deduction of Federal tax	$161,000.00
Federal tax deduction	23,055.10
Spouse's inheritance for State tax purposes	$137,944.90
Tax (State) on spouse's inheritance	$ 2,588.35

Gross estate for Federal tax $532,000.00
Debts and charges .... $ 22,000.00
Gross property passing to spouse .. $200,000.00
Less taxes payable by spouse
    State .... $ 2,588.35
    Federal 23,055.10   25,643.45

Net marital deduction 174,356.55
Specific exemption 60,000.00

                                                    $256,356.55

Taxable estate $275,643.45
Net Federal tax .... $ 69,165.31

§ 293. Marital Deduction and Death Taxes; Interrelation; Use of Table K.

Since the computations demonstrated in the preceding sections would become even more involved if it were necessary in each case to compute the tax and then make allowance for the 80% credit[7] for State death taxes, the Treasury Department prepared Table K for use in the computation of the marital deduction, which gives effect to that credit by making allowance for the maximum credit, i.e., 80%, for State death taxes. The table cannot be used if the taxable estate is less than $40,000., or if the amount of the State death taxes paid is less than the maximum credit under the statute, or if credits are claimed for Gift Tax, taxes on prior transfers, or foreign death duties.

7. § 309, infra.

FORM NO. 38

Table K

(A) Net estate (for additional tax) equalling—	(B) Net estate (for additional tax) not exceeding—	Net tax on amount in column (A)	Rate of net tax on excess over amount in column (A)
$ 40,000	$ 50,000	$ 4,800	$0.212
50,000	60,000	6,920	.242
60,000	90,000	9,340	.272
90,000	100,000	17,500	.264
100,000	140,000	20,140	.284
140,000	240,000	31,500	.276
240,000	250,000	59,100	.268
250,000	440,000	61,780	.288
440,000	500,000	116,500	.280
500,000	640,000	133,300	.310
640,000	750,000	176,700	.302
750,000	840,000	209,920	.322
840,000	1,000,000	238,900	.314
1,000,000	1,040,000	289,140	.334
1,040,000	1,250,000	302,500	.326
1,250,000	1,500,000	370,960	.356
1,500,000	1,540,000	459,960	.386
1,540,000	2,000,000	475,400	.378
2,000,000	2,040,000	649,280	.418
2,040,000	2,500,000	666,000	.410
2,500,000	2,540,000	854,600	.450
2,540,000	3,000,000	872,600	.442
3,000,000	3,040,000	1,075,920	.472
3,040,000	3,500,000	1,094,800	.464
3,500,000	3,540,000	1,308,240	.494
3,540,000	4,000,000	1,328,000	.486
4,000,000	4,040,000	1,551,560	.526
4,040,000	5,000,000	1,572,600	.518
5,000,000	5,040,000	2,069,880	.558
5,040,000	6,000,000	2,092,200	.550
6,000,000	6,040,000	2,620,200	.580
6,040,000	7,000,000	2,643,400	.572
7,000,000	7,040,000	3,192,520	.602
7,040,000	8,000,000	3,216,600	.594
8,000,000	8,040,000	3,786,840	.624
8,040,000	9,040,000	3,811,800	.616
9,040,000	10,000,000	4,427,800	.608
10,000,000	10,040,000	5,011,480	.618
10,040,000		5,036,200	.610

§ 294. Marital Deduction and Death Taxes; Interrelation; Alternate Methods.

The Supplemental Instructions advise that the method explained in the preceding sections is adaptable to most of the situations which will arise. In applying such method, care must be taken to see that each factor actually used in the computation of the true tax is reflected in the corrective factor. If difficulty is experienced, two alternative methods are outlined.[8]

The first of these is designated "successive approximation." It is also known as the trial and error method. It is assumed that the gross estate is $200,000., debts and charges $40,000., so that the adjusted gross estate is $160,000. Decedent bequeathed $80,000. to his son and the residue to his widow. No State death tax is payable out of the general estate or with respect to the bequest to the widow. The first trial computation is as follows:

Gross estate		$200,000.00
Debts and charges	$40,000.00	
Assumed marital deduction	80,000.00	
Specific exemption	60,000.00	
		$180,000.00
Trial taxable estate		$ 20,000.00
Trial tax (Table A, page 40, Form 706)		$ 1,600.00

Since the Estate Tax is payable out of the general estate, this trial computation results in a trial marital deduction of $78,400. ($80,000. minus the $1,600. trial tax). The discrepancy, ($1,600.), between the assumed marital deduction ($80,000.) and the trial marital deduction ($78,400.) computed on the basis of such assumption could be eliminated by further trial computations. Thus, a second computation would be made on the assumption that the marital deduction is $78,400. ($80,000., the deduction first assumed, less $1,600., the first trial tax). There would thus be obtained a second trial taxable estate of $21,600. and a second trial tax of $1,824., thereby reducing the discrepancy to $224. If this process were continued, there would finally be obtained an assumed deduction of $78,139.53., which would agree with the marital deduction computed on the basis of such assumption, thus eliminating the discrepancy. This would require two more computations.

8. Note 15, supra, (F).

A second alternate method is designated the "proportion" method. In this method the computation commences with an assumed taxable estate, using round numbers to even tens of thousands. The trial taxable estate thereby determined, is almost certain to differ from the assumed taxable estate, possibly $5,000. less. A second computation should be made with a second assumed taxable estate which probably will be too small, so that the second trial taxable estate will be greater than the assumed amount. It may be $1,000. greater. Then recourse may be had to simple proportion. The adjustment to be made to the second assumed taxable estate is an amount (A) which bears the same ratio to (B), the second discrepancy, as (C), the difference between the two taxable estates bear to (D), the sum of the two discrepancies. This may be expressed as:

$$\frac{\text{Adjustment to second assumed taxable estate}}{\text{Second discrepancy}} = \frac{\text{Difference between assumed taxable estates}}{\text{Sum of discrepancies}}$$

In the above example, computations based on trial taxable estates of $20,000. and $30,000., respectively, result in discrepancies of plus $1,600. and of minus $7,000., respectively. Thus, the adjustment will be expressed mathematically as follows:

$$\text{Adjustment} = \frac{\text{(Second discrepancy) } \$7,000 \times \text{(Difference between taxable estates) } \$10,000, \text{ or } \$70,000,000}}{\text{(Sum of discrepancies) (\$7,000 plus \$1,600) } \$8,600}$$

The adjustment equals $8,139.53.
The true taxable estate is, therefore, $30,000. minus $8,139.53, or $21,860.47.

§ 295. Marital Deduction and Estate Tax; Interrelation; Summary.

The information and examples furnished in the preceding sections have as their purpose the familiarization of brother members of the bar with the mathematics of computation of the marital deduction, not as an exercise, but so that it will be possible to apply the facts of a particular situation to such examples and thus arrive at a solution with the minimum of effort. In applying the examples, the case requiring solution must be carefully analyzed to determine which elements are present. As previously noted, the different states have different statutes, some having a transfer tax, some having an estate tax, some merely having a statute based on absorbing the Federal credit, and one at least having no death tax. There must also be determined the manner in which taxes are chargeable. If in any given case the attorney experiences difficulty, any of the local Estate and Gift Tax units of the Internal Revenue Service will be found most helpful and cooperative. If that is not convenient, a request to the Commissioner at Washington will receive attention, and the problem solved.[9]

§ 296. Specific Exemption.

For purposes of the Estate Tax imposed *upon the estates of residents or citizens of the United States,* there is allowed as a deduction from the value of the gross estate a specific exemption of $60,000.[10]

Under the 1939 Code there were two Estate Taxes, the basic tax, as against which there was allowable an exemption of $100,-000.,[11] and the additional tax, as against which there was an exemption of $60,000.[12] The 1954 Code made no practical change, the difference being one of method of computation, not result. As we shall see,[13] the amount of tax is the same under the 1954 Code as under the 1939 Code. Under statutes prior to the 1939 Code the exemption for the purpose of the additional Estate Tax was $40,000. prior to 1942, but at that time there was also not includible in the gross estate insurance payable to designated beneficiaries to the extent of $40,000.[14] The additional Estate Tax has been preserved with respect to members of the armed forces, discussed in the succeeding section.

In the case of a *decedent nonresident not a citizen* of the United States, the allowable exemption is only $2,000.,[15] unless a death duty convention provides for another amount, such as a prorated part of the exemption allowed in the case of estates of citizens or residents.[16] This was the same under the 1939 Code.[17] The difference between the exemption for a citizen or resident and that for a nonresident not a citizen is substantial and has been worth litigating.[18]

9. See § 288, supra.
10. IRC, § 2052 (1954 Code).
11. IRC, § 812(a) (1939 Code).
12. IRC, § 935(c) (1939 Code).
13. § 317, infra.

14. See §§ 73, 74, supra.
15. IRC, § 2106(a)(3) (1954 Code).
16. Reg, § 20.2106–1(a)(3).
17. IRC, § 861(a)(4) (1939 Code).
18. See Rogers, 17 BTA 570 (1929);

§ 297. Members of the Armed Forces Dying During an Induction Period.

We have previously discussed the statutory provisions affecting the estates of members of the Armed Forces of the United States who die during an induction period.[19] While the additional Estate Tax has been eliminated for all other purposes, the statute provides that the additional Estate Tax shall not apply to the estates of citizens or residents of the United States dying during an induction period, while in active service as a member of the Armed Forces of the United States as defined in the statute.[20] In such cases, there would be no Federal Estate Tax payable unless the decedent's estate before the specific exemption exceeded $100,000. If it exceeded that amount, the excess would be subject only to the basic tax. In all other respects the computation of the amount of tax would be made in the same way as in any other estate, i.e., the same property would be includible in the gross estate and the same deductions would be allowable.

§ 298. Nonresidents Not Citizens.

We have previously discussed the subject of the estates of nonresidents not citizens of the United States with respect to definition of the term,[1] the preliminary notice,[2] the property includible in the gross estate,[3] allowable deductions,[4] and the specific exemption.[5] The preparation of the return has been left to this point, because in the usual nonresident alien estate, the return used is Form 706NA, which it will be seen is a single double faced sheet with all of the information respecting the gross estate, deductions, and computation of the tax, included thereon. It is only when there are lifetime transfers, trusts, powers of appointment, or if charitable deductions, Gift Tax or Estate Tax credits, or a prorated exemption are allowable that the return must be made upon Form 706. In the latter case the taxable estate is determined by the use of Schedule Q of Form 706, except that in the case of a nonresident not a citizen who was domiciled in France or Greece at the time of his death, the determination is made upon Form 706(g) (Schedule Q(2)) instead of Schedule Q.

Fifth Ave Bank of NY, 36 BTA 634 (1937); Farmers Loan & Trust Co v US, 60 F2d 618 (1932).

19. § 195, supra.
20. Note 19, supra.

1. § 12, supra.
2. § 24, supra.
3. §§ 184, 187, supra.
4. § 258, supra.
5. § 296, supra.

Unless the value of the decedent's entire gross estate is disclosed in the return no deductions will be allowed.[6] Valuation may be either as of the date of death or the alternate valuation may be elected. Before demonstrating the manner in which the tax is computed, examination of the return will aid in an understanding of the figures used.

FORM NO. 39

Nonresident Alien Estate Tax Return

(For use only by estates of decedents dying after August 16, 1954)

The return must under certain circumstances be filed on Form 706 instead of this form. For details see section 2 of instructions.

Decedent's name   Henri Bouisson

Date of death   Jan. 10, 1960

Residence (domicile) at time of death   100 Rue Robillard, Paris, France

Citizenship (nationality) at time of death   French

Business or occupation   Railroad plows

Names of persons filing return   Charles Boissevain

Designations (Executor, administrator, beneficiary, custodian, trustee)
    Ancillary Admr.

Mailing address (Number, street, city, zone, State) 980 Park Avenue,
    N. Y.

If the answer to question 6, 7, or 8 is "Yes," use of this form is inappropriate, and the return should be made on Form 706.

1a. Did the decedent die testate? [x] Yes   [ ] No

 b. Were letters testamentary or of administration granted for the
        estate? [x] Yes [ ] No

If granted to persons other than those filing the return, supply names
        and addresses.

2. Did the decedent, at the time of his death, own any—

 a. Real property located in the United States? [x] Yes [ ] No

 b. Stocks of United States corporations? [x] Yes   [ ] No

 c. Bonds, certificates, checks, bills, or notes physically located in the
        United States? [ ] Yes [x] No

 d. Debts owing by persons resident in the United States or by United
        States corporations? [ ] Yes   [x] No

 e. Other property situated in the United States? [ ] Yes   [x] No

3. Was the decedent engaged in business in the United States at date
        of death? [ ] Yes   [x] No

4. Did the decedent and spouse own, at the time of death, any community property situated in the United States? [ ] Yes   [x] No

6. Reg, § 20.2106–1(b).

5. Did the decedent, at the time of his death, own any property situated in the United States as a joint tenant or as a tenant by the entirety with right of survivorship?   [ ] Yes   [x] No

6. Did the decedent make any transfer during his lifetime (without an adequate and full consideration in money or money's worth) of property of an amount of $5,000 or more, any part of which was situated in the United States either at the time of transfer or at the time of the decedent's death?   [ ] Yes   [x] No

7. Were there in existence at the time of the decedent's death any trusts created by him during his lifetime, any part of the property of which was situated in the United States either when the trust was created or at the time of the decedent's death?
[ ] Yes   [x] No

8a. Did the decedent, at the time of his death, possess a general power of appointment over property any part of which was situated in the United States?   [ ] Yes   [x] No

b. Or, at any time, exercise or release such a power?   [ ] Yes   [x] No

(NOTE.—A general power of appointment means any power of appointment exercisable in favor of the decedent, his estate, his creditors, or the creditors of his estate, and includes the right of a beneficiary to appropriate or consume the principal of a trust. See Estate Tax Regulations for complete definition.)

Computation of tax (see sections 10 and 11 of instructions)

1. Taxable estate (item 8, schedule B) $14,371.51
2. Gross tax on taxable estate (use "Table for computing estate tax") .... $ 980.87
3. Credit for State death taxes 0.00

4. Net estate tax payable (item 2 minus item 3) .... $ 980.87

Declaration

We/I declare under the penalties of perjury that this return including the additional sheets attached, if any, has been examined by us/me, and to the best of our/my knowledge and belief, is a true, correct, and complete return. It is understood that a complete return requires the listing herein of all the property constituting the part of the decedent's gross estate (as defined by the Statute) situated in the United States.

Date Oct. 15, 1960   CHARLES BOISSEVAIN
Date ....
Date ....
                                       (Signatures of person(s) filing return)
                                       DANIEL WEBSTER CLAY
                                       (Signature of person preparing return)
Date Oct. 15, 1960   149 Broadway, N.Y. 6, N.Y.
                                       (Address of person preparing return)

SCHEDULE A—Gross Estate in the United States
(see sections 3, 4, 5, 6, and 7 of instructions)

Is election hereby made to have the gross estate of this decedent valued in accordance with values as of a date or dates subsequent to the decedent's death as authorized by section 2032 of the Internal Revenue Code? [ ] Yes   [x] No (This election cannot be exercised unless it is shown upon the return and the return is timely filed. The information in columns (c) and (d) should not be furnished unless the reply to this question is "Yes.")

(a) Item No.	(b) Description of property	(c) Subsequent valuation date	(d) Alternate value	(e) Value at date of death
1	Improved real estate located at 45 Kilburn Road, Garden City, Nassau County, New York, Section 33, Block 74, Lots 9, 10, 11, improved with one family brick veneer and frame dwelling and two car garage. Assessed value land and building, 1960—$7,700. Fair market value as per annexed appraisal			$10,000.00
2	100 shares American Telephone and Telegraph Co., common, N. Y. Exchange @ 173⅜			17,337.50
	(If more space is needed, attach additional sheets of same size)			
	Total			$27,337.50

SCHEDULE B—Taxable Estate (see sections 8 and 9 of instructions)

If adequate proof in support of items 2 and 4 is not submitted, deduction at item 4 will not be allowed. If adequate proof in support of item 2 is not submitted, deduction at item 6 will be limited to $2,000. See section 9 of instructions for circumstances under which "prorated specific exemption" will be allowed. If prorated specific exemption is claimed under Japanese treaty, the numerator of the fraction set forth in item 6 is the value of the property situated in the United States and the subject of tax by both the United States and Japan.

1. Gross estate in the United States (total, schedule A) . . . . . $ 27,337.50
2. Gross estate outside the United States, not including real
    property 126,243.80

3. Total gross estate wherever situated (item 1 plus item 2) . $153,581.30

4. Amount of funeral expenses, administration expenses, debts of decedent, mortgages and liens, and losses during administration (attach itemized schedule) $12,842.65

5. Deduction of expenses, claims, etc. (that proportion of item 4 that item 1 bears to item 3) $2,285.99

6. Specific exemption of $2,000 (in estates qualifying for "prorated specific exemption," use $2,000 or $\dfrac{\text{item } 1}{\text{item } 3} \times$ $60,000, whichever is the greater) 10,680.00

7. Total deductions (item 5 plus item 6) .... $ 12,965.99

8. Taxable estate (item 1 minus item 7) .... $ 14,371.51

It must be stressed that if any deductions are to be allowed, there must be annexed a separate schedule in which must be listed

(1) the value of the estate outside the United States, except real property, and

(2) *all of the deductions,* both those incurred in the United States and those outside the United States.

This must be supported by a copy of the inventory of property filed under the foreign death duty act; or if no such inventory was filed, a certified copy of the inventory filed with the foreign court of probate jurisdiction.[7]

If the items of deduction were not included in the foreign schedules, or if no such schedules were filed, then there should be submitted a written statement of the foreign executor containing a declaration that it is made under the penalties of perjury setting forth the facts relied upon as entitling the estate to the benefit of the particular deduction or deductions.[8]

We have previously noted that there are Death Tax Conventions with twelve countries, with others pending with ten additional countries.[9] In all of these, except those with Ireland, South Africa, and the United Kingdom there is provision for a prorated exemption as in the example demonstrated in the return above. In cases where there is no treaty, or in the case of the three countries named, there is no proration but the amount of the exemption is $2,000. Even in such cases, where the necessary information as to assets and claims and expenses outside

7. Reg, § 20.6018–4(c).   9. See § 185, supra.
8. Reg, § 20.2106–2(b).

the United States is furnished, a proportionate deduction will be allowed, even though there is no proration of the exemption. One further fact should be noted. In the case of charitable gifts for use within the United States, the estate of a nonresident not a citizen is entitled to the *full amount* of the charitable gift as a deduction.[10]

§ 299. Schedule O; Recapitulation.

Having set forth in the schedules all of the property of the decedent includible in his gross estate, and all of the deductions properly allowable, we arrive at the point where we are ready to begin the determination of the tax which will be payable. The first step in this process is to gather all of the information listed in the schedules and set it forth in such manner that such determination may be made. Schedule O is the gathering place. It will be recalled that at the bottom of each schedule of the return there is a total, with instructions that such figure be entered upon the Recapitulation, Schedule O. Each of the items of the gross estate is thus carried forward and totalled, the result being the gross estate.

In entering the items of deductions the transposition is not so mechanical, since there are three matters which must be considered before entering amounts in the deduction column. Items 1, 2, and 3 under deductions are entered from the totals shown on Schedules J and K. If the total of these three items *does not exceed* the value at the time of the decedent's death of the property subject to claims,[11] then the total is entered at item 4. *If the total exceeds* the value of property subject to claims, then the amount to be entered at item 4 is the amount of property subject to claims, *plus* such excess as represents amounts paid before the date prescribed for filing the Estate Tax return.[12]

In the case of the marital deduction, there is carried forward to Schedule O the net value of the bequests to the surviving spouse. This amount is entered as item 9. The adjusted gross estate must be determined, which is computed by deducting from the total of the gross estate, the total of items 5 through 7, the deductions considered in determining the adjusted gross estate.[13] The result is the adjusted gross estate, which is entered at item

10. Reg, § 20.2106–1(a)(2).
11. See § 192, supra.

12. Instructions, Schedule O, Form 706; note 11, supra.
13. See § 238, supra.

10. The question then is as to the amount of the marital deduction. If item 9 is equal to or less than 50% of item 10, then the amount of item 9 is entered at item 11. If it is more than 50% of item 10, then 50% of item 10 is entered at item 11.[14]

If the decedent and his spouse ever held property as community property it is necessary to attach a separate sheet to the return showing how the adjusted gross estate was computed.[15] We have previously discussed the marital deduction in community property law states,[16] and the method of computation.[17]

When these transpositions and computations have been made, the total gross estate and the total allowable deductions are available for further computation of the tax.

FORM NO. 40

Schedule O; Recapitulation

Schedule	Gross estate	Alternate value	Value at date of death
A	Real estate	$	$ 49,600.00
B	Stocks and bonds		117,000.00
C	Mortgages, notes, and cash		17,994.24
D	Insurance		43,761.86
E	Jointly owned property		15,834.64
F	Other miscellaneous property		212,025.53
G	Transfers during decedent's life		5,628.89
H	Powers of appointment		
1	Annuities		74,243.00
	TOTAL GROSS ESTATE	$	$536,088.16

14. Note 13, supra.

15. Instructions, Schedule O, Form 706, pars 3, 4.

16. § 243, supra.

17. § 285, supra.

Sched-ule	Deductions		Amount
J	1. Funeral expenses and expenses incurred in administering property subject to claims	$ 18,395.87	
K	2. Debts of decedent	18,101.79	
K	3. Mortgages and liens	19,920.98	
	4. Total of items 1 through 3	$ 56,418.64	
	5. Allowable amount of deductions from item 4 (see note *)	$ 56,418.64	
L	6. Net losses during administration	1,008.33	
L	7. Expenses incurred in administering property not subject to claims	4,374.34	
	8. Total of items 5 through 7		$ 61,801.31
M	9. Bequests, etc., to surviving spouse	$113,014.75	
	10. Adjusted gross estate (see note **) ...	474,286.85	
	11. Net amount deductible for bequests, etc., to surviving spouse (item 9 or one-half of item 10, whichever is smaller)		113,014.75
N	12. Charitable, public, and similar gifts and bequests		101,862.35
	TOTAL ALLOWABLE DEDUCTIONS, except specific exemption (totals of lines 8, 11, and 12)		$276,678.41

* Note.—See paragraph 1 of the instructions.

** Note.—Enter at item 10 the excess of "TOTAL GROSS ESTATE" over item 8, if the decedent and his surviving spouse at no time held property as community property. If property was ever held as community property, compute the "Adjusted gross estate" (item 10) in accordance with the instructions and example on page 32, and attach an additional sheet showing such computation.

Estate of WINTHROP BENSON   Schedule O—Page 33

§ 300. Schedule P; Taxable Estate; Resident or Citizen.

Schedule P of the return is used *only in the estate of a resident or citizen of the United States* for the summarization of the gross estate, deductions, and the specific exemption, so that the amount of the taxable estate, the amount upon which the gross Estate Tax will be computed may be determined. It requires a minimum of mathematical knowledge, but is merely a breathing space before plunging into really involved computations.

FORM NO. 41

Schedule P; Taxable Estate; Resident or Citizen

Instructions.—This Schedule Should Be Used only for the Estate of a Resident or Citizen of the United States

1. Total gross estate $536,088.16
2. Total allowable deductions $276,678.41
3. Specific exemption 60,000.00
4. Total deductions plus specific exemption 336,678.41

5. Taxable estate (item 1 minus item 4) $199,409.75

§ 301. Schedule Q; Taxable Estate; Nonresident Not a Citizen of the United States.

We have previously noted the fact that under certain circumstances the Estate Tax Return of a nonresident not a citizen of the United States cannot be made upon Form 706NA, but must be made upon Form 706.[18] In such cases the taxable estate is set forth in Schedule Q, except that if the decedent was a nonresident domiciled in France or Greece, separate Form 706(g) must be obtained, since the Death Tax Conventions with those countries differ with respect to allowable credits.

18. § 298, supra.

FORM NO. 42

Schedule Q; Taxable Estate; Nonresident Not a Citizen

1. Value of gross estate in the United States (Schedules A, B, C, D, E, F, G, H, and I) .... $ 27,337.50
2. Value of gross estate outside the United States, not including real property (must be supported by proof described in instructions under "Deduction of administration expenses, claims, etc., on page 39) 126,243.80

3. Value of total gross estate wherever situated (item 1 plus item 2) $153,581.30

4. Gross deductions under Schedules J, K, and L .... $ 12,842.65

5. Net deductions under Schedules J, K, and L (that proportion of item 4 that item 1 bears to item 3) .... $ 2,285.99
6. Charitable, public, and similar gifts and bequests (Schedule N) ....
7. Specific exemption of $2,000 (in estates qualifying for "prorated specific exemption," use $2,000 or $\frac{\text{item 1}}{\text{item 3}} \times$ $60,000, whichever is the greater) 10,680.00

8. Total deductions plus specific exemption (item 5 plus items 6 and 7) .... $ 12,965.99

9. Taxable estate (item 1 minus item 8) .... $ 14,371.51

§ 302. Schedule R; Credit For Tax on Prior Transfers; Comparison to Deduction for Property Previously Taxed.

There are allowable as possible credits against the gross Estate Tax four different credits. Although not listed first among the sections of the 1954 Code, the first credit to be computed in the Estate Tax Return is that for taxes paid on prior transfers. The provision is new to the 1954 Code and replaces the deduction for property previously taxed under the 1939 Code, which we have previously discussed.[19] Its purpose is the same as that of the prior provision, namely, to prevent subjecting the same property to the Estate Tax twice within a relatively short period of time.

A credit is allowed for the tax paid on property in the estate

19. §§ 276 et seq, supra.

of the prior decedent, but it can never be larger than if the current decedent had not received the property. It provides more equitable results and removes the difficult task of tracing the property. To eliminate the tracing, the credit is based upon the value of the property at the time of the death of the prior decedent. Moreover, property transferred between spouses, to the extent no marital deduction was available, is eligible for this credit. The credit is allowed in full for two years following the death of the prior decedent and then decreases by 20% every two years thereafter until no credit is allowed after the tenth year. Since the purpose of the provision is to prevent the diminution of an estate by the imposition of successive taxes on the same property within a brief period of time, the credit for Gift Tax paid on a prior transfer is omitted from the statute.[20]

The credit for prior transfers is substantially different from the deduction for property previously taxed. In addition to the facts noted, that it is a credit and not a deduction, so that it is related to the prior decedent's estate and its benefits are not measured by the rate of tax applicable to the current decedent's estate; it extends for ten years at a graduated rate, instead of five years; tracing of the property is eliminated; it applies to property transferred between spouses; and there is no credit for prior Gift Tax paid; it is also to be noted that it applies where two or more decedents die within ten years, a limited credit is allowed where the transferor dies within *two years after* the transferee, and the term "property" is defined, as well as valuation is clarified.[1]

Each of the subdivisions of the statute will be separately treated in succeeding sections, and the method of computation of the credit demonstrated. While the statute is considered to be, and is in fact, a simplification of the subject of prior transfers, it is by no means simple.

§ 303. Schedule R; Credit for Tax on Prior Transfers; General Rule.

A credit is allowed against the Federal Estate Tax imposed on the present decedent's estate for Federal Estate Tax paid on the transfer of property to the present decedent from a trans-

---

20. House Committee Report 1337, Senate Report 1662, Conference Report 2543, Internal Revenue Code of 1954 on § 2013.

1. Note 20, supra.

feror who died *within ten years before,* or *within two years after,* the present decedent's death. There is no requirement that the transferred property be identified in the estate of the present decedent or that the property be in existence at the time of the decedent's death. It is sufficient that the transfer of the property was subjected to tax in the estate of the transferor.[2] This removes one of the greatest problems which existed under the deduction allowed under the 1939 Code, the necessity for identification of the property.[3]

The credit is limited to the *smaller* of (1) the amount of tax attributable to the transferred property in the transferor's estate, and (2) the amount of tax attributable to the transferred property in the decedent's estate.[4]

The credit is reduced by a percentage which depends upon the time between deaths. If the transferor died within two years *before or after* the present decedent, the full credit is allowable. The amount of the credit then is reduced to 80% if the transferor died within the third or fourth years preceding the decedent, to 60% if the transferor died within the fifth or sixth years preceding the decedent's death, to 40% if the transferor died within the seventh or eighth years preceding the decedent's death, and to 20% if the transferor died within the ninth or tenth years preceding the decedent's death. The word "within" means "during". Therefore, if a death occurs on the second anniversary of another death, the first death is considered to have occurred within the two years before the second death.[5]

Since the credit applies when there are two or more transfers within the statutory period, the transfer from each must be separately computed, the aggregate limitation determined being apportioned in accordance with the value of property transferred to the decedent by each transferor.[6]

The credit applies only to the estates of decedents dying on and after August 17, 1954, except as previously noted,[7] that in the case of property transferred by a decedent to his spouse within two years of his death, if the decedent died after December 31, 1951, the credit here discussed may be taken.

---

2. IRC, § 2013(a) (1954 Code); Reg, § 20.2013–1(a).

3. See § 277, supra.

4. IRC, § 2013(c)(1) (1954 Code); Reg, § 20.2013–1(b).

5. IRC, § 2013(a) (1954 Code); Reg, § 20.2013–1(c).

6. IRC, § 2013(c)(2) (1954 Code).

7. § 276, supra.

§ 304. Schedule R; Credit for Tax on Prior Transfers; "Property" and "Transfer" Defined.

The statute defines the words "property" and "transfer" as used in it. The Regulation expands upon the statutory definition and furnishes examples of the meaning of the terms.

The term "property" means any beneficial interest in property, including a *general* power of appointment. It does not include an interest in property consisting of bare legal title, such as that of a trustee. It does not include a nongeneral power of appointment. Examples of property described, are annuities, life estates, estates for terms of years, vested *or contingent* remainders and other future interests.[8]

The term "transfer" of property by or from a transferor means any passing of property or an interest in property under circumstances which were such that *the property or interest was included in the gross estate of the transferor.* If the decedent receives property as the result of the exercise or nonexercise of a power of appointment, the *donee* of the power (and not the creator) is deemed to be the transferor of the property if the property subject to the power is includible in the donee's gross estate. Thus, notwithstanding the designation by local law of the capacity in which the decedent takes, property received from the transferor includes interests in property held by or devolving upon the decedent: (1) as spouse under dower or curtesy laws or laws creating an estate in lieu of dower or curtesy; (2) as surviving tenant of a tenancy by the entirety or joint tenancy with survivorship rights; (3) as beneficiary of the proceeds of life insurance; (4) as survivor under an annuity contract; (5) as donee of a general power of appointment; (6) as appointee under the exercise of a general power of appointment; or (7) as remainderman under the release or nonexercise of a power of appointment by reason of which the property is included in the gross estate of the donee of the power.[9]

The application of the provision is illustrated by the following example: A devises property to B, as trustee, with directions to pay the income to C for life. Upon C's death the property is to be sold. C is given a general testamentary power to appoint one third of the proceeds, and a nongeneral power to appoint two thirds to such issue of D as he may choose. D has a son and a daughter. C exercises the general power by appointing the

8. Reg, § 20.2013–5(a).   9. Reg, § 20.2013–5(b).

one third to D, and the nongeneral power by appointing the two thirds to D's daughter. Since B's interest is that of a trustee it is not a beneficial interest and is not property for the purposes of the credit. On the other hand, C's life estate and his testamentary *general power* over the one third interest in the remainder constitute "property" for the purposes of the credit in C's estate. Likewise, D's one third interest in the remainder received through the exercise of C's *general power* is "property" received from C. No credit is allowed in the estate of D's daughter for property passing to her from A, since her interest was not susceptible of valuation at the time of A's death.[10]

§ 305. Schedule R; Credit for Tax on Prior Transfers; Valuation of Property Transferred.

The statute provides that the value of property transferred to the decedent shall be *the value used for the purpose of determining the Federal Estate Tax liability of the estate of the transferor* but—

(1) there shall be taken into account the effect of the Federal Estate Tax, or any estate, succession, legacy, or inheritance tax, on the net value to the decedent of such property;

(2) where such property is encumbered in any manner, or where the decedent incurs any obligation imposed by the transferor with respect to such property, such encumbrance or obligation shall be taken into account in the same manner as if the amount of a gift to the decedent of such property was being determined; and

(3) if the decedent was the spouse of the transferor at the time of the transferor's death, the net value of the property transferred to the decedent shall be reduced by the amount allowed as a marital deduction, in the estate of the transferor.[11]

It is to be noted that it is the value as fixed in the Estate Tax proceedings in the prior decedent's estate, which is taken as the value in the current decedent's estate for the purpose of the credit, and further that such value is to be reduced so as to reflect the net value of the property received by the decedent. If the transfer from spouse to spouse is involved the value is reduced by the amount thereof allowed as a marital deduction in order that there may not be a double credit.

If the decedent received a life estate or remainder or other

10. Reg, § 20.2013–5(c).   11. IRC, § 2013(d) (1954 Code).

limited interest in property included in the transferor's gross estate, the value of the interest is determined as of the date of the transferor's death on the basis of recognized actuarial principles.[12] If the interest cannot be so valued, it is considered for purposes of the credit to have no value.[13] Thus, if property is bequeathed to B by A, and it was included in A's estate at a value of $100,000., but is sold by B for $150,000., its value in B's estate for computation of the credit is $100,000.[14] If A grants B a life estate in property, at which time B is 56 years old, with remainder to C, and the property is included in A's estate at a value of $100,000., the value of the life estate is $44,688. and of the remainder $55,312. If B and C die within the statutory period, for the purpose of computing the credit for tax on prior transfers, the values in B's and C's estates are respectively $44,688. and $55,312.[15]

For the purposes of the section an obligation imposed by the transferor and incurred by the decedent with respect to the property includes a bequest in lieu of the interest of the surviving spouse under community property laws, unless such interest was, immediately prior to the transferor's death a mere expectancy.[16] However, an obligation imposed by the transferor and incurred by the decedent with respect to property does not include a bequest, devise, or other transfer in lieu of dower, curtesy, or other marital rights.[17] If the transferor devises property subject to a mortgage, the value is the equity. If the transferor directs the executor to satisfy the mortgage, the value is the full value. If a bequest or devise is subject to a condition that the recipient make payment to another of $1,000., the value of the property is reduced by that amount. Where the transferor bequeaths property to his wife, the decedent, in lieu of her interest in community property, and she elects to relinquish her community property interest and take the bequest, the value of the bequest must be reduced by the value of the community property interest relinquished, for the purpose of the computation of the credit. If the transferor bequeaths his entire residuary estate to the decedent, out of which certain claims are to be satisfied and the entire distributable income during administration is applied to pay the claims and the decedent pays the

12. See §§ 114, 115, supra.
13. Reg, § 20.2013-4(a).
14. Note 13, supra, Example 1.

15. Note 13, supra, Example 2.
16. See §§ 41, 48, supra.
17. Reg, § 20.2013-4(b)(3)(ii).

balance of the claims out of his own funds, so that he receives a larger sum out of the transferor's estate than he was actually bequeathed, the value of the property transferred to the decedent is the value at which such property was included in the transferor's gross estate, reduced by the amount of the estate income and the decedent's own funds paid to satisfy the claims.[18]

§ 306. Schedule R; Credit for Tax on Prior Transfers; Limitation on Credit.

As previously observed, the credit for tax on prior transfers is limited to the *smaller* of (1) the amount of tax attributable to the transferred property in the transferor's estate, and (2) the amount of tax attributable to the transferred property in the decedent's estate.[19]   This means that it is necessary to determine the amount of tax in the prior estate which was incurred by the inclusion of the transferred property, and then determine the amount of tax on the current decedent's estate, including and then excluding the transferred property.

Under the first limitation, the credit is limited to an amount expressed by the formula

$$\frac{\text{value of transferred property}}{\text{transferor's adjusted taxable estate}} \times \begin{array}{c}\text{transferor's adjusted}\\ \text{Federal Estate Tax}\end{array}$$

As we have seen, the *value of transferred property* in the above ratio is the value of the property in the prior estate.[20] *The transferor's adjusted Federal Estate Tax* is the amount of the Federal Estate Tax paid with respect to the transferor's estate *plus:*

(1) Any credit allowed the transferor's estate for Gift Tax, *and*

(2) Any credit allowed the transferor's estate for tax on prior transfers, but only if the transferor acquired property from a person who died within ten years before the death of the present decedent.[1]

The transferor's adjusted taxable estate is the amount of the transferor's taxable estate (or net estate if the transferor died before the 1954 Code) *decreased* by the net amount of Federal Estate Tax and all other estate, succession, legacy, inheritance,

---

18. Reg, § 20.2013–4(b)(3)(iii).
19. IRC, § 2013(b)(1954 Code); Reg, § 20.2013–1(b).
20. § 305, supra.
1. Reg, § 20.2013–2(a)(b).

or similar death taxes imposed by and paid to any taxing authority, whether within or without the United States, with respect to the transferor's gross estate, *and increased* by the amount of the exemption allowed in computing his taxable estate.[2]

If the credit for tax on prior transfers relates to property received from two or more transferors, the provisions of the section are to be applied *separately* with respect to the property received from each transferor.[3]

The second limitation is the amount of the Federal Estate Tax resulting from the inclusion of the transferred property in the current decedent's estate.[4] Thus the credit is limited to the difference between—

(1) The net estate tax payable with respect to the present decedent's estate, determined without regard to any credit for tax on prior transfers, or any credit for foreign death taxes claimed under the provisions of a death duty convention, and

(2) The net Estate Tax determined as provided in (1) above, but computed by *subtracting* from the present decedent's estate the value of the property transferred, and by making the adjustment for any charitable deduction, if one is allowable to the estate of the present decedent.[5] In other words, the tax in the present decedent's estate is first computed with the transferred property included, and it is then computed with the transferred property excluded.

If the amount of difference between the two taxes is smaller than the amount of the tax attributable to the transferred property in the prior decedent's estate, such smaller amount will be the amount of the credit.

If a charitable deduction is allowable to the estate of the present decedent, for the purpose of computing the tax in his estate, the charitable deduction otherwise allowable is reduced by an amount which is equal to the result of the following formula:[6]

$$\text{charitable deduction otherwise allowable} \times \frac{\text{value of transferred property}}{\text{value of present decedent's gross estate} - \text{amount of deductions for expenses, indebtednesses, taxes, losses}}$$

If the credit for tax on prior transfers relates to property re-

2. Reg, § 20.2013–2(c).
3. IRC, § 2013(c)(2) (1954 Code); Reg, § 20.2013–2(d).
4. IRC, § 2013(c)(1) (1954 Code).
5. Reg, § 20.2013–3(a).
6. Reg, § 20.2013–3(b).

ceived from two or more transferors, the property received from all transferors is aggregated in determining the second limitation. However, the limitation so determined is apportioned to the property received from each transferor in the ratio that the property received from each transferor bears to the total property received from all transferors.[7]

As with other provisions of the Estate Tax statute which involve complicated computations, the Regulations present examples of the operation of the statute, which help to make its complexities intelligible, and which are illustrated in the succeeding section.

§ 307. Schedule R; Credit for Tax on Prior Transfers; Operation of the Statute.

The Commissioner of Internal Revenue is apparently of the same mind as the writer that one example is worth thousands of words, since after explaining at great length the meaning of the statute granting the credit for tax on prior transfers, the Regulations conclude with two examples of its application.[8]

In the first example A died December 1, 1953, leaving a gross estate of $1,000,000. Expenses, indebtednesses, etc., amounted to $90,000. A bequeathed $200,000. to B, his wife, $100,000. of which qualifies for the marital deduction. B died November 1, 1954, leaving a gross estate of $500,000. Expenses, indebtednesses, etc., amounted to $40,000. B bequeathed $150,000. to charity. A and B were both citizens of the United States. The estates of A and B both paid State death taxes equal to the maximum credit allowable for State death taxes. Death taxes were not a charge on the bequest to B.

7. Reg, § 20.2013–3(c).   8. Reg, § 20.2013–6.

"First limitation" on credit for B's estate:

A's gross estate		$1,000,000.00
Expenses, indebtedness, etc.		90,000.00
A's adjusted gross estate		$ 910,000.00
Marital deduction	$100,000.00	
Specific exemption	60,000.00	160,000.00
A's taxable estate		$ 750,000.00
A's gross estate tax		233,200.00
Credit for State death taxes		23,280.00
A's net estate tax payable		$ 209,920.00

$$\text{``First limitation''} = \frac{\$209,920.00 \times (\$200,000.00 - \$100,000.00)}{\$750,000.00 - \$209,920.00 - \$23,280.00 + \$60,000.00}$$

The figures above represent the formula heretofore treated.[9] The sum of $209,920.00 is the transferor's adjusted Federal Estate Tax. The value of the transferred property is the bequest of $200,000. in A's estate reduced by $100,000., the amount of the marital deduction allowed in A's estate.[10] The transferor's adjusted taxable estate is the amount of the transferor's taxable estate, $750,000., decreased by the net amount of Federal and State death taxes paid, $209,920. and $23,280., and increased by the specific exemption of $60,000. The result of the equation is $36,393.90.

9. § 306, supra.   10. See § 305, supra.

"Second limitation" on credit for B's estate:

(1) B's net estate tax payable computed, *including* previously taxed transfer

B's gross estate		$500,000.00
Expenses, indebtedness, etc.	$ 40,000.00	
Charitable deduction	150,000.00	
Specific exemption	60,000.00	250,000.00

B's taxable estate	$250,000.00

B's gross estate tax	65,700.00
Credit for State death taxes	3,920.00

B's net estate tax payable	$ 61,780.00

(2) B's net estate tax payable, *excluding* previously taxed transfer

B's gross estate		$400,000.00
Expenses, indebtedness, etc.	$ 40,000.00	
Charitable deduction		

$$\$150,000 - \left(\$150,000 \times \frac{\$200,000 - \$100,000}{\$500,000 - \$40,000}\right) = 117,391.30$$

Specific exemption	60,000.00	217,391.30

B's taxable estate	$182,608.70

B's gross estate tax	45,482.61
Credit for State death taxes	2,221.61

B's net estate tax payable	$ 43,261.00

It will be observed that in the second computation, the gross estate excludes only the amount of the bequest which was taxable in the prior estate and not the entire bequest, $100,000. of the total having qualified for the marital deduction. The charitable deduction of $150,000. otherwise allowable is reduced by the amount of the deduction multiplied by the value of the transferred property, i.e., $200,000.–$100,000. and divided by the value of the present decedent's estate, $500,000. less expenses, indebtedness, etc., $40,000.[11]

11. See § 306, supra.

"Second limitation"
B's net estate tax payable including transferred property .. $61,780.00
B's net estate tax payable excluding transferred property . 43,261.00

$18,519.00

Since the credit under the "first limitation" is $36,393.90 and under the second limitation is $18,519.00, and the credit is limited to the smaller of the amounts computed under the two limitations, the credit in the instant example is $18,519.00. If the present decedent had died within the third or fourth year after the prior decedent, the credit would be 80% of $18,519.00.

The second example deals with the same estates as in the first example, but in addition with the situation where the present decedent's estate relates to property received from two prior transferors. B, in addition to the bequests from A, also receives a bequest from C in the amount of $50,000. C died December 1, 1950, leaving a gross estate of $250,000. Expenses, indebtedness, etc., of C's estate were $50,000. C was a citizen of the United States and his estate paid death taxes equal to the maximum 80% credit. Death taxes were not a charge on the bequest to B.

(1) *With respect to the property received from A:*

The first limitation would be the same as in the preceding example, namely, $36,393.90

(2) *With respect to the property received from C:*

C's gross estate $250,000.00
   Expenses, indebtedness, etc. $50,000.00
   Specific exemption 60,000.00 110,000.00

C's taxable estate $140,000.00

C's gross estate tax 32,700.00
   Credit for State death taxes 1,200.00

C's net estate tax payable .... $ 31,500.00

"First limitation" = $31,500.00 × $50,000.00 ÷ ($140,000.00 — $31,500.00 — $1,200.00 + $60,000.00) = ... $ 9,414.23

Here again the adjusted Federal Estate Tax of C, $31,500.00, is multiplied by the value of the transferred property in C's estate, $50,000.00, there having been no marital deduction, and the product is divided by C's taxable estate, $140,000.00, reduced by the net amount of Federal and State death taxes paid, $31,500.00 and $1,200.00, and increased by the amount of the specific exemption, $60,000.00. The divisor is C's adjusted taxable estate.

"Second limitation" on credit for B's estate:

(1) The computation of B's net estate tax payable, *including* the transferred property would be the same as in the preceding example, namely, $61,780.00.

(2) B's net estate tax payable, *excluding* the transferred property

B's gross estate		$350,000.00
Expenses, indebtedness, etc.	$ 40,000.00	
Charitable deduction $150,000.00 — ($150,-000.00 × $200,000.00 — $100,000.00 + $50,000.00) ÷ ($500,000.00 — $40,000-.00)	101,086.96	
Specific exemption	60,000.00	201,086.96
B's taxable estate		$148,913.04
B's gross estate tax		$ 35,373.91
Credit for State death taxes		1,413.91
B's net estate tax payable		$ 33,960.00

Here again the charitable deduction of $150,000. otherwise allowable is reduced by the amount of the deduction multiplied by the value of the transferred property, in this example the $200,000. bequest from A less the marital deduction of $100,000., and the $50,000. received from C's estate, and this product is divided by the value of the present decedent's estate, $500,000. less expenses, indebtedness, etc., $40,000.

"Second limitation"

B's net estate tax payable including transferred property ..	$61,780.00
B's net estate tax payable excluding transferred propery .	33,960,00
	$27,820.00

Since the "second limitation" is less than the "first limitation," that figure is used for further computations. In this example there have been two prior estates involved, so that it is necessary to apportion the credit between the transfers from each prior decedent.[12]

Apportionment:

Transfer from A	$100,000.00
Transfer from C	50,000.00
Total	$150,000.00
Portion of "second limitation" attributable to transfer from A (100/150 of $27,820.00)	$ 18,546.67
Portion of "second limitation" attributable to transfer from C (50/150 of $27,820.00)	9,273.33

It will have been observed that A died within two years of B, so that 100% of the credit is allowable on the transfer from A. C, however, died more than two years before B, but within four years of B, so that the percentage reduction is applicable and 80% of the credit is allowable on the transfer from C.[13]

Credit for tax on transfer from A $18,546.67 × 100%	$18,546.67
Credit for tax on transfer from C $9,273.33 × 80%	7,418.66
Total credit for tax on prior transfers	$25,965.33

§ 308. Schedule R; Credit for Tax on Prior Transfers; Return.

Schedule R of the Estate Tax return is divided into three parts. The first part deals with the transferor's estate. The first item is the net value of the transfer in the prior estate. The second item is the transferor's adjusted taxable estate. Item 3 is the transferor's adjusted Federal Estate Tax. Item 4 is the proportion of the adjusted Federal Estate Tax which the value of the transferred property bears to the transferor's adjusted taxable estate. This is the "first limitation."

Part II consists of six items. Item 5 is the amount of the present decedent's tax including the transferred property. Item 6 is the gross estate of the decedent excluding the transferred property. Item 7 is the total of deductions and the specific exemption, adjustment being made for charitable deduction, if any. Item 8 is item 6 minus item 7. Item 9 is the net estate tax payable on the decedent's estate with the transferred property excluded. Item 10 is the difference between the net estate tax payable on the decedent's estate, including and excluding the transferred property. This is the "second limitation."

---

12. Note 11, supra.   13. See § 303, supra.

Part III deals with the determination of the credit. Item 11 is the maximum amount of credit allowable before the percentage reduction. This will be the smaller of the amount computed under the first and second limitation, items 4 and 10. Item 12 is the percent of the credit allowable depending upon the time lapse between deaths. The final item, 13, is the credit allowable.

Where there are transfers from two or more transferors the method used is to make the computations in *Part I* on a separate Schedule R *for each transferor*. The computations in *Part II* are made *only once* on the copy in the return. The amount entered in Item 6 is the total gross estate less the total of the amounts entered in items 1 of the computations made for all the transferors. The amount entered in item 10 is apportioned to each transferor.[14] *Part III is computed separately for each transferor.* There is entered in item 11 the amount shown in item 4 or the amount from item 10 which is apportioned to that transferor, whichever is the smaller, and the computation completed. The total amount of the credit allowable is the total of the amounts entered in items 13 of *all the computations*.[15]

The figures in the following schedule are those used in the computations illustrated in the first example in the preceding section.

FORM NO. 43

Schedule R; Credit for Tax on Prior Transfers

Name of transferor　　KATHERINE BENSON
Date of transferor's death　　December 1, 1958
Transferor's residence at time of death　　Binghamton, New York

COMPUTATION OF THE CREDIT

Part I—Transferor's Tax on Prior Transfers

1. Net value of transfers $100,000.00
2. Value of transferor's estate (adjusted in accordance with instructions for item 2) $576,800.00
3. Tax on transferor's estate (adjusted in accordance with instructions for item 3) $209,920.00
4. Transferor's tax on prior transfers (proportion of item 3 which item 1 bears to item 2) .... $ 36,393.90

---

14. See apportionment, § 307, supra.　　15. Instructions, Schedule R, Form 706, par 6.

Part II—Transferee's Tax on Prior Transfers

5. Transferee's tax computed without regard to credit allowed under this schedule .... $ 61,780.00
6. Transferee's reduced gross estate $400,000.00
7. Transferee's deductions (adjusted in accordance with instructions for item 7) $217,391.30
8. Transferee's reduced taxable estate (item 6 minus item 7) $182,608.70
9. Tax on reduced taxable estate .... $ 43,261.00
10. Transferee's tax on prior transfers (item 5 minus item 9) $ 18,519.00

Part III—Credit Allowable

11. Maximum amount before application of percentage requirement (item 4 or item 10, whichever is smaller) .. $ 18,519.00
12. Percent allowable is 100%
13. Credit allowable (item 12 × item 11) .... $ 18,519.00

§ 309. Schedule S; Credit for Foreign Death Taxes; In General.

The final schedule of the Estate Tax return, Schedule S, deals with the credit for foreign death duties. This credit is allowed against the Federal Estate Tax for any inheritance, legacy, or succession taxes actually paid to any foreign country. It is allowed *only for foreign death taxes paid*

(1) with respect to property situated within the country to which the tax is paid,

(2) with respect to property included in the decedent's gross estate, and

(3) with respect to the decedent's estate.

The credit is allowable to the estate of a decedent who was a citizen of the United States at the time of his death, and also to a resident not a citizen of the United States *if* the country of which he was a national, in imposing death taxes, allows a similar credit to the estates of citizens of the United States resident in that country. The credit is *not allowable* in the estates of non-residents not citizens of the United States. The credit is allowable not only for death taxes paid to foreign countries which are states in the international sense, but also for death taxes paid to possessions or political subdivisions of foreign states. No credit is allowable for interest or penalties paid in connection with foreign death taxes.[16]

16. IRC, § 2014(a) (1954 Code); Reg, § 20.2014-1(a); See Rev Rul 55-381, 1955-1 CB 464.

The Technical Amendments Act of 1958 added a subdivision to the statute dealing with credit for foreign death taxes as part of an overall pattern which involved amendments to other sections of the law and the addition of a new section[16a] dealing with a citizen of the United States who acquires citizenship in a possession of the United States.[16b] For purposes of the credits authorized for foreign death taxes, each possession of the United States shall be deemed to be a foreign country.[16c] *The amendment is effective as to estates of decedents dying after September, 2, 1958.*

As in the case of the credit for prior transfers, there are two limitations on the credit, discussed hereafter.[17]

The statute provides for the method of valuation to be used in applying the limitations,[18] the proof required for the allowance of the credit,[19] and the time within which the credit may be claimed.[20] Each of these are discussed in the succeeding sections.

The credit for foreign death duties was introduced into the Estate Tax in 1951 in order to eliminate double taxation where the entire property is taxed under the Federal statute and also part of the assets are taxed in a foreign country because of their situs there. The 1939 Code provisions[1] apply to the estates of decedents dying after October 20, 1951. The 1954 Code combined the two sections of the 1939 Code into a single section[2] without making any substantive changes. However, in applying the statute there must be taken into account the changes made by the 1954 Code in the situs rules.[3] For the purposes of the credit the determination of the country within which property is situated is made in accordance with the rules applicable for the estates of nonresidents not citizens in determining whether property is situated within or without the United States.[4] Thus, under the 1954 Code, stock issued by a foreign corporation would not be considered situated within the United States although

16a. IRC, § 2208 (1954 Code), as added by Technical Amendments Act of 1958, § 102(a), HR 8381, 85th Cong, 2nd Sess.

16b. § 12, supra.

16c. IRC, § 2014(f) (1954 Code), added by Technical Amendments Act of 1958, § 102(c)(2), HR 8381, 85th Cong, 2nd Sess.

17. § 310, infra.

18. IRC, § 2014(c) (1954 Code).

19. IRC, § 2014(d) (1954 Code).

20. IRC, § 2014(e) (1954 Code).

1. IRC, §§ 813(c), 936(c) (1939 Code) as added by Rev Act 1951, § 603.

2. IRC, § 2014 (1954 Code).

3. See §§ 184, 185, supra.

4. IRC, § 2014(a) (1954 Code); Reg, § 20.2014–1(a)(3).

physically located here, whereas under the 1939 Code it would be.

§ 310. Schedule S; Credit for Foreign Death Duties; Limitations on Credit.

The credit for foreign death duties is limited to the smaller of the following amounts:

(1) The amount of a particular foreign death tax attributable to property situated in the country imposing the tax and included in the decedent's gross estate for Federal Estate Tax purposes; and

(2) The amount of the Federal Estate Tax attributable to particular property situated in a foreign country, subjected to foreign death tax in that country, and included in the decedent's gross estate for Federal Estate Tax purposes.[5]

The "first limitation", the amount of the foreign death tax attributable to property situated in the country imposing the tax and included in the decedent's gross estate for Federal Estate Tax purposes is an amount which equals

$$\frac{\text{Value of property in foreign country subjected to foreign death tax and included in gross estate}}{\text{value of all property subjected to foreign death tax}} \times \text{amount of foreign death tax}$$

The values used in this proportion are the values determined for the purpose of the foreign death tax.[6] *The amount of the foreign death tax for which credit is allowable must be converted into United States money.*

Application of the provision is illustrated in the Regulation. At the time of his death, the decedent, a citizen of the United States owned real property in Country X valued at $80,000. and Stock in Y Corporation (a corporation organized under the laws of Country X) valued at $80.000. Decedent left by will $50,000. of the real property and $20,000. of the Y Corporation stock to his surviving spouse. He left the rest of the real property and stock to his son. The real property was not included in his gross estate. There is no death duty convention in existence between the United States and Country X. Under the inheritance tax laws of Country X the tax is computed as follows:

5. IRC, § 2014(b) (1954 Code); Reg, § 20.2014-1(b).

6. IRC, § 2014(c)(1) (1954 Code).

Inheritance tax of surviving spouse:

Value of real property in Country X $50,000

Value of stock in Corporation Y 20,000

Total value $70,000

Tax (16% rate) 11,200

Inheritance tax of son:

Value of real property in Country X $30,000

Value of stock in Corporation Y 60,000

Total value $90,000

Tax (16% rate) 14,400

The "first limitation" on the credit for foreign death taxes is

$$\frac{\$20,000 + \$60,000}{\$70,000 + \$90,000} \times (\$11,200 + \$14,400) = \ldots\ldots\ldots \$12,800$$

It will be observed that $80,000. is the value of the property in the foreign country subjected to foreign death tax *and included in the gross estate.* The foreign real estate is not taxable in the gross estate. The total value of all property subjected to the foreign death tax is $160,000. The total foreign death tax is $25,600., but only $12,800. of this amount is attributable to property situated in the country imposing the tax and included in the gross estate, so that this is the amount for the "first limitation."[7]

If a foreign country imposes more than one kind of death tax or imposes taxes at different rates upon the several shares of an estate, or if a foreign country and a political subdivision or possession thereof each imposes a death tax, a "first limitation" is to be computed *separately* for each tax or rate and the results added in order to determine the total "first limitation". Thus, if in the preceding example the tax rate of the spouse were 10% with a tax of $7,000. and the tax rate of the son were 20%, with a tax of $18,000., the computation of the "first limitation" would be made as follows:

"First limitation" for tax of spouse =

$$\frac{\$20,000}{\$70,000} \times \$7,000 = \ldots\ldots\ldots \$ 2,000$$

"First limitation" for tax of son =

$$\frac{\$60,000}{\$90,000} \times \$18,000 = \ldots\ldots\ldots \$12,000$$

Total "first limitation" for credit for foreign death taxes $14,000

7. IRC, § 2014(b)(1) (1954 Code); Reg, § 20.2014-2(a).

The same situation would result if a foreign country and one of its provinces both imposed death taxes.

The "second limitation", the amount of the Federal Estate Tax attributable to property situated in the country imposing the tax and included in the decedent's gross estate for Federal Estate Tax purposes is an amount which equals

$$\frac{\text{adjusted value of the property situated in the foreign country, subjected to foreign death taxes, and included in the gross estate}}{\text{value of entire gross estate, less charitable and marital deductions}} \times \begin{array}{c}\text{gross Federal Estate}\\ \text{Tax, less credits for}\\ \text{State death taxes and}\\ \text{gift tax}\end{array}$$

The values used in this proportion, are the values determined for the purpose of the Federal Estate Tax.[8]

If a charitable or marital deduction is allowed with respect to the foreign property, the adjusted value of the property situated in the foreign country, subjected to foreign death tax and included in the gross estate, is the value of the property so situated *reduced* as follows:

(1) If a charitable deduction or a marital deduction is allowed to a decedent's estate with respect to any part of the foreign property specifically bequeathed, devised, or otherwise specifically passing to a charitable organization or to the decedent's spouse, by the amount of the charitable deduction or marital deduction allowed with respect to such specific transfer.

(2) If a charitable deduction or a marital deduction is allowed to a decedent's estate with respect to a bequest, devise, or other transfer of an interest in a group of assets including both the foreign property and other property, by an amount which bears the same ratio to the amount of the charitable deduction or marital deduction allowed with respect to such transfer of an interest in a group of assets, as the value of the foreign property included in the group of assets bears to the value of the entire group of assets. "Group of assets" has reference to those assets which could be utilized in satisfying the charitable or marital transfer.

Any reduction on account of the marital deduction must proportionately take into account the limitation on the aggregate

---

8. IRC, § 2014(c)(2) (1954 Code); Reg, § 20.2014–3(a).

amount of the marital deduction.[9] This latter refers to the maximum allowable marital deduction.[10]

The Regulation furnishes three examples of the computation of the "second limitation".[11] In each one, any credit under a death duty convention is not considered.

In the first example, decedent, a citizen and resident of the United States at the time of his death, left a gross estate of $1,000,000. which includes: shares of stock issued by a United States corporation, valued at $750,000.; bonds issued by the government of Country X physically located in the United States, valued at $50,000.; and shares of stock issued by a Country X corporation, valued at $200,000. Expenses, indebtedness, etc., amounted to $60,000. Decedent specifically bequeathed $40,000. of the stock of the foreign corporation to a United States charity and left the residue of his estate to his son and daughter in equal shares. The gross Federal Estate Tax is $266,500. and the credit for State death taxes is $27,600. Under the situs rules, the shares of stock of the foreign corporation comprise the only property deemed to be situated in Country X. The "second limitation" on the credit for foreign death taxes is

$$\frac{\$200,000 - \$40,000}{\$1,000,000 - \$40,000} \times (\$266,500 - \$27,600) = \$39,816.67$$

It will be seen that the adjusted value of the property situated in the foreign country, is the value of such property less the charitable deduction, i.e., $200,000.—$40,000. The divisor is the value of the entire gross estate, $1,000,000. less the charitable deduction, $40,000. The quotient is then multiplied by the gross Estate Tax, $266,500., less the credit for State death taxes, $27,600., there being no gift tax involved.

In the second example, decedent, a citizen and resident of the United States at the time of his death, left a gross estate of $1,000,000, which includes: shares of stock issued by a United States corporation, valued at $650,000.; shares of stock issued by a Country X corporation, valued at $200,000.; and life insurance in the amount of $150.000., payable to a son. Expenses, indebtedness, etc., amounted to $40,000. The decedent made a specific bequest of $25,000. of the Country X corporation stock to Charity A and a general bequest of $100,000. to Charity B. The resi-

---

9. IRC, § 2014(b)(2) (1954 Code); 10. See § 238, supra.
Reg, § 20.2014–3(b).   11. Reg, § 20.2014–3(c).

due of his estate was left to his daughter. The gross Federal Estate Tax is $242,450. and the credit for State death taxes is $24,480. Under these facts, neither the stock of the Country X corporation specifically bequeathed to Charity A, nor the insurance payable to the son could be utilized in satisfying the bequest to Charity B. Therefore, the "group of assets" which could be so utilized is limited to stock of the Country X corporation valued at $175,000. and stock of the United States corporation valued at $650,000.

In determining the adjusted value of the property situated in the foreign country, the reductions above referred to are computed as follows:

Value of property situated in Country X $200,000.00
Less: Reduction in (1) above $25,000.00
    Reduction in (2) above

$$\frac{\$175,000}{\$175,000 + \$650,000} \times \$100,000 \ldots \quad 21,212.12 \quad 46,212.12$$

$153,787.88

In this computation the specific bequest to Charity A is the full amount of the bequest without reduction. The reduction for the bequest to Charity B is that portion of the total bequests in the proportion that the value of the foreign property included in the group of assets *and which could be utilized for satisfaction of the bequest,* namely, $200,000. minus $25,000., the specific bequest to Charity A, bears to the value of the entire group of assets which could be utilized for payment of the bequest, namely, $650,000., the United States corporation stock, plus $175,000. of the Country X corporation stock.

The reduction having been determined and the adjusted value of the property situated in the foreign country fixed, the computation of the "second limitation" proceeds as in the previous example.

$$\frac{\$153,787.88}{\$1,000,000 - \$125,000} \times (\$242,250 - \$24,480) = \$38,309.88$$

The third example adds the marital deduction as a factor to be considered in the determination of the "second limitation". Decedent, a citizen and resident of the United States at the time of his death, left a gross estate of $850,000. which includes: shares of stock issued by United States corporations, valued at

$440,000.; real estate located in the United States, valued at
$110,000.; and shares of stock issued by Country X corporations,
valued at $300,000. Expenses, indebtedness, etc., amounted to
$50,000. Decedent devised $40,000. in real estate to a United
States charity. In addition he bequeathed to his wife $200,000.
in United States stocks and $300,000. in Country X stocks. The
residue of his estate passed to his children. The gross Federal
Estate Tax is $81,700. and the credit for State death taxes is
$5,520.

Decedent's adjusted gross estate is $800,000. (i.e., $850,000.,
gross estate less $50,000. expenses., indebtedness, etc.). The
aggregate marital deduction allowed to his estate is limited to
one half of this amount, or $400,000. The adjusted value of the
property situated in the foreign country, subjected to foreign
death taxes, and included in the gross estate is computed as follows:

Value of property situated in Country X $300,000
Less: Reductions (1) and (2) above
    Total amount of bequests qualifying for marital
      deduction
    Specific bequest of Country X stock $300,000
    Specific bequest of United States stock 200,000

                                       $500,000
    Limit on aggregate marital deduction 400,000
    Part of specific bequest of Country X stock
      with respect to which the marital deduction
      is allowed
$$\frac{400,000}{500,000} \times \$300,000 \dots\dots\dots \$240,000$$

      Adjusted value .... $ 60,000

The proportion is that stated in (2) above. $400,000. is the
amount of the marital deduction, $500,000. is the value of the
entire group of assets from which the marital deduction could
be satisfied, and $300,000. is the value of the foreign property.
The adjusted value having been determined, the computation of
the "second limitation" proceeds.

$$\frac{\$60,000}{\$850,000 - \$40,000 - \$400,000} \times (\$81,700 - \$5,520) = \$11,148.29$$

Where the foreign country imposes more than one kind of

death tax or imposes taxes at different rates upon the several shares of an estate, or where the foreign country and a political subdivision or possession thereof each impose a death tax, the "second limitation" is still computed by applying the ratio set forth above. The first factor of the ratio, the adjusted value of the foreign property, is determined by taking into consideration the combined values of the foreign property which is subjected to each different tax or different rate. The combined value, however, cannot exceed the value at which such property was included in the gross estate for Federal Estate Tax purposes. Thus, if Country X imposes a tax on the inheritance of a surviving spouse at 10% and on that of a son at 20%, the combined value of their inheritances is taken into consideration in determining the first factor of the ratio, which is then used in computing the "second limitation."

The *lesser* of the "first limitation" and the "second limitation" is the credit for foreign death taxes.[12]

§ 311. Schedule S; Credit for Foreign Death Taxes; Where Death Duty Convention.

We have previously referred to the fact that there are in effect Death Tax Conventions with twelve countries, and negotiations pending for such treaties with ten other countries.[13] Most of these treaties provide for reciprocal credit for taxes paid to the countries parties to the convention. In such cases as credit is authorized by a death duty convention for a particular foreign death tax, there is allowed *either* the credit provided for in the convention *or* the credit for foreign death taxes, whichever is the more beneficial to the estate.[14]

Decedent, a citizen of the United States and a domiciliary of Country X at the time of his death, left a gross estate of $1,000.-000, which includes: shares of stock issued by a Country X corporation, valued at $400,000.; bonds issued by a Country X corporation physically located in the United States, valued at $350,000.; and real estate located in the United States, valued at $250,000. Expenses, indebtedness, etc., amounted to $50,000. Decedent left his entire estate to his son. There is in effect a death duty convention between the United States and Country X which provides for allowance of credit by the United States for

---

12. IRC, § 2014(b) (1954 Code); Reg, § 20.2014–3(d).

13. §§ 185, 258, supra.

14. Reg, § 20.2014–4(a)(1).

succession duties imposed by the national government of Country X. The gross Federal Estate Tax is $307,200. and the credit for State death taxes is $33,760. Country X imposed a net succession duty on the stocks and bonds of $180,000. Under the situs rules, the shares of stock comprise the only property deemed to be situated in Country X. Under the convention, both the stocks and the bonds are deemed to be situated in Country X.[15]

The credit authorized by the convention for death taxes imposed by Country X is computed as follows:

(1) Country X tax attributable to property situated in Country X and subjected to tax by both countries

$$\frac{\$750,000}{\$750,000} \times \$180,000 = \ldots\ldots\ldots\ldots\ldots\ldots\ldots\ldots\ldots\ldots \$180,000$$

(2) Federal Estate Tax attributable to property situated in Country X and subjected to tax by both countries

$$\frac{\$750,000}{\$1,000,000} \times \$273,440 = \ldots\ldots\ldots\ldots\ldots\ldots\ldots\ldots \$205,080$$

(3) Credit, lesser of (1) or (2) $180,000

The credit authorized under the Federal statute is computed as follows:

(1) "First limitation"

$$\frac{\$400,000}{\$750,000} \times \$180,000 = \ldots\ldots\ldots\ldots\ldots\ldots\ldots\ldots\ldots\ldots \$ 96,000$$

(2) "Second limitation"

$$\frac{\$400,000}{\$1,000,000} \times \$273,440 = \ldots\ldots\ldots\ldots\ldots\ldots\ldots\ldots \$109,376$$

(3) Credit .... $ 96,000

It will be observed that all of the decedent's estate is deemed to be situated in Country X, except the United States real estate, and is taxable there. All of the property is taxable in the United States.[16]

On the basis of the facts contained in the example the credit authorized under the convention is the more beneficial to the estate.

It should be noted that the greater of the treaty credit and the statutory credit *is not necessarily* the more beneficial to

15. Note 14, Example (i).   16. § 38, supra.

the estate. Such is the situation, for example, where there is involved both a credit for foreign death taxes and also for prior transfers. The reason is that the amount of the credit for tax on prior transfers may differ depending upon whether the credit for foreign death taxes is taken under the treaty or under the statute. Therefore, under certain circumstances, the advantage of taking the greater of the treaty credit and the statutory credit may be more than offset by a resultant smaller credit for tax on prior transfers. The solution is to compute the net estate tax payable, first on the assumption that the treaty credit will be taken, and then on the assumption that the statutory credit will be taken, and determine which is more beneficial.[17]

In any case in which tax is imposed by a foreign country or political subdivision, as in the case where the Dominion of Canada and one of the provinces both impose death taxes, the particular treaty must be consulted.

The credits under the treaties are in general more comprehensive than under the statute.[18]

§ 312. Schedule S; Credit for Foreign Death Taxes; Where Death Duty Convention; Tax by Foreign Country and Political Subdivision.

In some instances a tax may be imposed by the foreign country and also by one of its political subdivisions. Such is the case of property in the Province of Ontario, Dominion of Canada. Both the Dominion and the Province impose a tax. Where there is a death duty convention with the foreign country, there is allowed *either* the credit provided for by the convention *or* the credit for foreign death taxes, whichever is more beneficial to the estate. Thus, if a portion of the estate of a United States citizen is situated in Canada, with which the United States has a death duty convention allowing a credit for Canadian death duties and the property is subjected to tax by both the Dominion and the Province of Ontario, there is allowed either the credit for the national death tax computed under the convention, or a credit for both the Dominion and provincial death duties computed under the statute, whichever is more beneficial. However, unless the convention provides otherwise, credit may not be claimed

17. Reg, § 20.2014–4(a)(2).
18. See Outline of Death Duty and Gift Tax Treaties, U. S. Treasury Dept. IRS Publication No 228.

separately under the convention for the Dominion tax and under the statute for the provincial tax.[19]

The Dominion Succession Duty Act will be effective only as to persons dying prior to Jan. 1, 1959, at which time an Estate Tax Act is anticipated to become effective. Since this will affect the United States-Canadian Death Tax Convention, further word from the Treasury must be awaited as to estates of persons dying after Dec. 31, 1958. The following example applies to decedents dying before Jan. 1, 1959.

Thus, decedent, a citizen of the United States, and a domiciliary of Country X at the time of his death, left a gross estate of $225,000. which includes: bonds issued by a United States corporation physically located in Y, a province of Country X, valued at $100,000.; bonds issued by a Country X corporation physically located in the United States, valued at $75,000.; and shares of stock issued by a Country X corporation, valued at $50,000. Expenses, indebtedness, etc., amounted to $10,000. Decedent left his entire estate to his son. There is in effect a death duty convention between the United States and Country X which provides for allowance of credit by the United States for succession duties imposed by the national government of X. The gross Federal Estate Tax is $55,200. and the credit for State death taxes is $3,000. Country X imposed a net succession duty on the Country X stock and the Country X bonds of $18,000. Province Y imposed a net succession duty on the United States bonds of $16,000. Under the situs rules the United States bonds and the Country X stock are deemed to be situated in Country X. Under the convention, the Country X bonds and the Country X stock are deemed to be situated in Country X.[20]

The credit authorized by the convention for death taxes imposed by Country X is computed as follows:

(1) Country X tax attributable to property situated in Country X and subjected to tax by both countries

$$\frac{\$125,000}{\$125,000} \times \$18,000 = \dots\dots\dots\dots\dots\dots\dots \$18,000$$

(2) Federal Estate Tax attributable to property situated in Country X and subjected to tax by both countries

$$\frac{\$125,000}{\$225,000} \times \$52,200 = \dots\dots\dots\dots\dots\dots\dots \$29,000$$

(3) Credit, lesser of (1) or (2) $18,000

19. Reg, § 20.2014–4(b).   20. Note 19, Example.

The credit authorized under the Federal statute is computed as follows:

(1) "First limitation" with respect to Country X tax

$$\frac{\$50,000}{\$125,000} \times \$18,000 = \dots\dots\dots\dots\dots\dots\dots\dots\dots \$\ 7,200$$

(2) "First limitation" with respect to Province Y tax

$$\frac{\$100,000}{\$100,000} \times \$16,000 = \dots\dots\dots\dots\dots\dots\dots\dots\dots \$16,000$$

Total "first limitation" $23,200

(3) "Second limitation"

$$\frac{\$150,000}{\$225,000} \times \$52,200 = \dots\dots\dots\dots\dots\dots\dots\dots\dots \$34,800$$

(4) Credit, lesser of total of (2) or (3) $23,200

On the basis of the facts contained in this example the credit under the statute is more beneficial to the estate.

§ 313. Schedule S; Credit for Foreign Death Taxes; Where Death Duty Convention; Property Taxed by Two or More Countries.

If credits against the Federal Estate Tax are allowable under the statute, or under the statute and one or more death duty conventions, for death taxes paid to more than one country, the credits are combined and the aggregate amount is credited against the Federal Estate Tax.[1] This rule may result in credit being allowed for taxes imposed by two different countries upon the same item of property. If such is the case, the total amount of the credits with respect to such property is limited to the amount of the Federal Estate Tax attributable to the property, determined in accordance with the rules prescribed for computing the "second limitation" set forth heretofore.[2] The Regulation furnishes an example of the application of the provision.[3]

The decedent, a citizen of the United States and a domiciliary of Country X at the time of his death, left a taxable estate which included bonds issued by Country X corporations, physically located in Country Z. Each of the three countries involved imposed death taxes on the Country X bonds. Assume that under the provisions of a treaty between the United States and Country X, the estate is entitled to a credit against the Federal Estate

1. Reg, § 20.2014–1(a)(2).   3. Reg, § 20.2014–4(c).
2. § 310, supra.

Tax for death taxes imposed by Country X on the Country X bonds in the maximum amount of $20,000. Assume, also, that under the provisions of the Federal statute, the estate is entitled to a credit against the Federal Estate Tax for death taxes imposed by Country Z on the Country X bonds in the maximum amount of $10,000. Finally, assume that the Federal Estate Tax attributable to the Country X bonds is $25,000. Under such circumstances, the credit allowed the estate with respect to the Country X bonds would be limited to $25,000.

§ 314. Schedule S; Credit for Foreign Death Taxes; Proof of Credit.

The credit provided in the statute shall be allowed *only if the taxpayer establishes to the satisfaction of the Secretary or his delegate—*

(1) the amount of taxes actually paid to the foreign country,

(2) the amount and date of each payment thereof,

(3) the description and value of the property in respect of which such taxes are imposed, and

(4) all other information necessary for the verification and computation of the credit.[4]

If the foreign death tax has not been determined and paid by the time the Federal Estate Tax return is filed, credit may be claimed on the return in an estimated amount. However, before credit for the foreign death tax is finally allowed, satisfactory evidence, such as a statement by an authorized official of each country, possession, or political subdivision thereof, imposing the tax, must be submitted certifying: (1) the full amount of the tax (exclusive of any interest or penalties), as computed before allowance of any credit, remission or relief; (2) the amount of any credit, remission, or relief, and other pertinent information, including the nature of the allowance and a description of the property to which it pertains; (3) the net foreign death tax payable after any such allowance; (4) the date on which the death tax was paid, or if not all paid at one time, the date and amount of each partial payment; and (5) a list of the property situated in the foreign country and subjected to its tax, showing a description and the value of the property. Satisfactory evidence must also be submitted showing that no refund of the tax is pending and none authorized, or if any refund is pending or

4. IRC, § 2014(d) (1954 Code).

has been authorized, its amount and other pertinent information.[5]

The following information shall also be submitted wherever applicable:

(1) If any of the property subjected to the foreign death tax was situated outside of the country imposing the tax, the description of each item of such property and its value.

(2) If more than one inheritance or succession tax is involved with respect to which credit is claimed, or where the foreign country, possession, or political subdivision thereof imposes more than one kind of death tax, or where both the foreign country and a possession or political subdivision thereof each imposes a death tax, *a separate computation* with respect to each inheritance or succession tax.

(3) In addition to the above information, the District Director may require the submission of any further proof deemed necessary to establish the right to the credit.[6]

Certification of the payment of the foreign death tax or taxes is made upon Form 706CE. The form is prepared in triplicate, one copy being retained by the estate fiduciary and two copies forwarded to the office of the foreign authority administering the tax. It is advisable to enclose a post paid envelope addressed to the District Director of Internal Revenue, with the request that the foreign authority certify the amount of taxes paid to it. If taxes have been paid to more than one such authority, separate forms should be sent to each.

5. Reg, § 20.2014–5(a).   6. Reg, § 20.2014–5(b)(c).

FORM NO. 44

Certification of Payment of Foreign Death Tax

For credit against United States estate tax in the estate of a
decedent domiciled in or a citizen of the United States
(*See instructions on reverse side before using this form*)

> Estate tax return filed with
> District Director of Inter-
> nal Revenue,
> City
>   210 Livingston Street
>   Brooklyn, N. Y.
> State
>   New York, U. S. A.
> Date of Death
>   January 10, 1959

Name of decedent   WINTHROP BENSON
Citizenship (Nationality) at time of death   United States
Domicile at time of death   Brooklyn, N. Y.
Last address   25 Plaza Street

(a) Name of foreign government imposing the tax   Republic of France
Amount of death tax as finally determined by such government, excluding any interest or penalty (*Express amount in the foreign
currency*). 2,000,000 francs

(b) The preceding amount was computed in accordance with the provisions of any applicable death tax convention.

(c) The amounts paid (excluding any interest or penalty) and payment
dates of the death tax are (*Express amount in foreign currency*)
2,000,000 francs. Jan. 12, 1960.

(d) The description, location and value (as established and accepted by
the death tax officials of the government named above) of property
subjected to the death tax are as follows:

Item No.	Description and Location	Value expressed in the foreign currency
1	100 shares of common stock of Charbonais Fils, S. A. par value 100,000 francs	Fr. 12,000,000

(Attach additional sheets, if necessary)

(e) Check Statement Applicable:

    [x] No refund of the death tax indicated in item (a), or any portion thereof, has been claimed or allowed (or)

    [ ] Refund of the death tax indicated in item (a), or a portion thereof, has been claimed and (check one)

        [ ] Claim was rejected in full.   [ ] Consideration is pending.

        [ ] Refund was allowed in the amount of ——————.

(f) In case (1) any credit against or diminution of the death tax indicated in item (a) is pending or was allowed, (2) property was subjected to tax at more than one rate, or (3) more than one inheritance was subjected to tax, an explanation should be furnished herein or on an attached sheet.

(g) A reduction in the amount of the death tax indicated in item (a) by credit, refund, or otherwise, except as may be indicated in item (e) above, [ ] will be claimed (or)

    [x] is not contemplated. (Check applicable statement)

I/We declare that the information contained in this statement, including any attached schedules, is true and correct.

Katherine Benson
(Signature)

Executrix
(Title: Executor, Administrator, etc.)

100 Main Street, Duluth, Minn.
(Address)

April 15, 1960
(Date)

CERTIFICATION

(For use of authorized tax official of the foreign government imposing the death tax)

The information contained in items (a) through (f) above, including any attached schedules pertaining thereto, is hereby certified to be correct [x] without exception (or) [ ] except as indicated in my attached statement.

Pierre Printemps   ....
(Signature)   (Title)

....
(Government)   (Date)

(Please forward a certified copy to the District Director indicated in upper right corner)

INSTRUCTIONS

Death tax conventions are in effect with the countries listed below. Where optional date is shown, personal representative may elect to have convention apply if decedent died prior to effective date but on or after optional date.

Country	Effective Date	Optional Date
Canada	June 14, 1941	None
United Kingdom	July 25, 1946	January 1, 1945
France	October 17, 1949	None
Norway	December 11, 1951	None
Ireland	December 20, 1951	January 1, 1951
Union of South Africa	July 15, 1952	July 1, 1944
Switzerland	September 17, 1952	None
Finland	December 18, 1952	None
Greece	December 30, 1953	None
Australia	January 7, 1954	None
Japan	April 1, 1955	None
Italy	October 26, 1956	None

Under certain circumstances credit against the United States estate tax for death taxes paid to foreign national governments and political subdivisions thereof may be allowed under section 2014 of the Internal Revenue Code. This credit is available to estates of domiciliaries or citizens of the United States. If the decedent was domiciled in, but not a citizen of the United States, credit is not allowable unless the country of which the decedent was a national allows a similar credit to estates of United States citizens domiciled in such country.

This statement must be prepared in triplicate. One copy is to be retained by the estate's representative. For certification of estate, inheritance, legacy or succession tax paid to a foreign government, two copies must be forwarded to the office which administers such tax. Upon certification, that office should forward a certified copy to the District Director of Internal Revenue indicated on the reverse side of this form. Separate certification should be obtained for each foreign death tax for which credit is claimed.

If after the allowance of credit for the death tax shown in item (a), a reduction is made in the amount of such tax, the estate's representative is required to notify the appropriate District Director of Internal Revenue of the reduction and pay any additional United States estate tax resulting from any reduction in the credit.

§ 315. Schedule S; Credit for Foreign Death Taxes; Period of Limitation on Credit.

The credit for foreign death taxes is allowed only for such taxes as were *actually paid and credit therefor claimed* within four years after the filing of the return, *except* that

(1) If a petition for redetermination of a deficiency has been filed with the Tax Court within the statutory time, then within such four year period or before the expiration of sixty days after the decision of the Tax Court becomes final.

(2) If an extension of time has been granted for payment of the tax, or of a deficiency, then within such four year period or before the date of the expiration of the period of the extension.[7]

Under Death Tax Conventions the period of limitation differs.

§ 316. Schedule S; Credit for Foreign Death Taxes; Return.

The Instructions for the preparation of Schedule S are detailed and helpful. It is pointed out that if more than one foreign death tax is involved, the computations for the credit with respect to each should be made on separate copies of Schedule S.[8] Under item 1 there should be entered the amount of the tax paid to the foreign country, and there should not be included any tax paid to such country with respect to property *not included in the gross estate.* This is the "first limitation."[9] If only part of the property is included in the gross estate, an additional sheet showing the computation of the amount entered must be attached. Item 2 is the value of the gross estate less the total of deductions shown on lines 11 and 12 of Schedule O, i.e., the marital deduction and charitable bequests. Item 3 is the value of the property situated in the foreign country subject to its taxes, less the portion of deductions attributable to such property. Item 4 is the difference between the Net Federal Estate Tax payable and any credit for Gift Tax. Item 5 is the "second limitation".[10] Item 6 is the lesser of the "first limitation" or the "second limitation", i.e., item 1 or item 5.[11]

All of the countries with whom there are death tax conventions are listed, except Italy, the present form having been revised

---

7. IRC, § 2014(e) (1954 Code); Reg, § 20.2014-6.

8. Instructions Schedule S, Form 706, par 1.

9. See § 310, supra.

10. Note 9, supra.

11. Instructions, Schedule S, Form 706, par 2.

before that treaty became effective.[12] But Form 706CE, revised September 1957, refers to such treaty.

The Instructions then furnish an example of the computation of the credit under the statute. In the example, the gross estate consisted of stock of United States corporations, $90,000.; bonds of M country corporations, $45,000.; stocks of M country corporations, $75,000. Owned by the decedent but not included in the gross estate was real estate in M country valued at $60,000. All of the stocks and bonds were in vaults in the United States. Debts, etc., total $20,000. The real estate and the stock of the M country corporations passed to the surviving spouse, and qualified for the marital deduction. The gross Federal Estate Tax less credit for State death taxes was $25,820. The M country inheritance tax imposed on the widow's inheritance of $70,000. is $21,000. The decedent's daughter inherited $65,000. consisting entirely of M country corporations stock, and the M country tax on the daughter's inheritance was $19,500. No tax was imposed by M country on the M country corporation bonds.

FORM NO. 45

Schedule S; Credit for Foreign Death Taxes

List all of the foreign countries to which death taxes have been paid, credit for the payment of which is claimed on this return: Country M. If credit is claimed for death taxes paid to more than one foreign country, compute the credit for taxes paid to one country on this sheet and use a separate copy of Schedule S for each of the other countries. The copies of Schedule S on which the additional computations are made should be attached hereto.

The credit computed on this sheet is for   Succession Tax
(Name of death tax or taxes)
imposed in   Country M   Credit is computed under
(Name of country)
Section 2014 of the Internal Revenue Code of 1954
(Insert "treaty" or "statute")

COMPUTATION OF THE CREDIT

(All amounts and values shown hereunder must be entered in United States money)

1. Amount of estate, inheritance, legacy and succession taxes imposed in the above country attributable to property situated in that country, and subjected to such taxes, and included in the gross estate (as defined by statute) $ 22,500.00

2. Value of the gross estate (adjusted, if necessary, in accordance with instructions for item 2) $200,000.00

3. Value of property situated in that country, and subjected to death taxes imposed in that country, and included in the gross estate (adjusted, if necessary, in accordance with instructions for item 3) .... $ 65,000.00

4. Federal estate tax before allowance of credit for foreign death taxes .... $ 25,820.00

5. Amount of Federal estate tax attributable to property specified at item 3 (proportion of item 4 that item 3 bears to item 2) .... $ 8,391.50

6. Credit for death taxes imposed in the above country (item 1 or item 5, whichever is the smaller) .... $ 8,391.50

Estate of WINTHROP BENSON   Schedule S—Page 37

In the foregoing schedule, while the total tax paid to Country X was $40,500, it was not all attributable to property situated in that country *and included in the gross estate.* All of the tax paid on the daughter's inheritance was so attributable, but of the $70,000. received by the widow, only $10,000. was included in the gross estate, the rest being real property situated outside the United States. Therefore, only 1/7 of the $21,000. paid on the widow's inheritance was so attributable. The total tax so attributable to property included in the gross estate is thus $19,-500. and $3,000., or $22,500. The gross estate is $210,000., but there must be deducted therefrom the $10,000. marital deduction allowed to the widow, so that the gross estate as adjusted becomes $200,000. The only property taxed in the foreign country *and included in the gross estate* is the stock of Country M corporations valued at $75,000. This must be adjusted by the reduction of $10,000. for the marital deduction, so that the amount reportable at Item 3 is $65,000. The Federal Estate Tax after credit for State death taxes is $25,820. The "second limitation" is 65,000/200,000 of $25,820., or $8,391.50. Since this is less than the "first limitation" of $22,500, the credit for foreign death taxes is $8,391.50.[13] Where additional computations are necessary, as in the determination of item 1 above, a separate sheet should be annexed to the return showing how the figure was arrived at. Any other information which may be required by the Estate Tax examiner to determine the manner

13. Note 9, supra.

in which the credit was computed should be furnished by affidavit with the return.

§ 317. Gross Estate Tax.

Having completed all of the schedules of the Estate Tax Return we have arrived at the point where we are ready to determine the amount of tax payable. This requires that there first
be determined the gross Estate Tax, which is computed by the
application of progressively graduated rates to the value of the
decedent's taxable estate.[14] For ease of computation there is
set forth on the last page of Form 706 two tables. Table A is
the table used for computation of the gross Estate Tax.

Prior to the 1954 Code, since there was a basic tax[15] and an
additional tax,[16] it was necessary to compute the tax under each
provision of the statute separately. The 1954 Code eliminated
this *method* of computation, but did not change the amount of
tax payable. Instead of first determining the tentative tax,
and if the estate exceeded $100,000., subtracting the basic tax
separately computed, to determine the additional tax, deducting
the 80% credit as against the basic tax, and adding that result
to the additional tax, as was required under the 1939 Code, it is
now possible to determine the tax in two steps. The first step
is to determine the gross estate tax by applying the rates from
the following table to the amount of the taxable estate shown in
Schedule P.

14. IRC, § 2001 (1954 Code); Reg,
§ 20.2001–1(a).

15. IRC, § 810 (1939 Code).

16. IRC, § 935 (1939 Code).

FORM NO. 46

Table A; Computation of Gross Estate Tax

Taxable estate equaling (1) (Dollars)	Taxable estate not exceeding (2) (Dollars)	Tax on amount in column (1) (3) (Dollars)	Rate of tax on excess over amount in column (1) (4) (Percent)
. . .	5,000	. . .	3
5,000	10,000	150	7
10,000	20,000	500	11
20,000	30,000	1,600	14
30,000	40,000	3,000	18
40,000	50,000	4,800	22
50,000	60,000	7,000	25
60,000	100,000	9,500	28
100,000	250,000	20,700	30
250,000	500,000	65,700	32
500,000	750,000	145,700	35
750,000	1,000,000	233,200	37
1,000,000	1,250,000	325,700	39
1,250,000	1,500,000	423,200	42
1,500,000	2,000,000	528,200	45
2,000,000	2,500,000	753,200	49
2,500,000	3,000,000	998,200	53
3,000,000	3,500,000	1,263,200	56
3,500,000	4,000,000	1,543,200	59
4,000,000	5,000,000	1,838,200	63
5,000,000	6,000,000	2,468,200	67
6,000,000	7,000,000	3,138,200	70
7,000,000	8,000,000	3,838,200	73
8,000,000	10,000,000	4,568,200	76
10,000,000	. . . .	6,088,200	77

Thus, if we assume that the taxable estate is $525,000., we see that the amount falls within the $500,000. to $750,000. bracket. The tax on $500,000. in column (1) is shown in column (3) to be $145,700. The excess amount of $25,000. is taxable as shown in column (4) at the rate of 35%, and the tax on such excess is $8,750. Adding this to the sum of $145,700., we find that the gross Estate Tax is $154,450. That amount is entered as item 1, in Part I, on Page 1 of the return.

§ 318. Credit for State Death Taxes; Generally.

The next item in the computation of the tax is the credit for state death taxes. The statute allows a credit against the gross Estate Tax for estate, inheritance, legacy or succession taxes actually paid to any State, Territory, or possession of the United States, or the District of Columbia. It is allowed *only* for State death taxes paid

(1) with respect to property included in the decedent's gross estate, and

(2) with respect to the decedent's estate.[17]

Note that the credit will not be allowed if the property was not included in the decedent's gross estate,[18] nor if the State tax is paid on the estate of one other than the decedent.[19]

This credit is referred to as "the 80% credit" because under the former statute[20] it was computed on the basis of 80% of the basic estate tax. Under the present statute, while the result is the same, the method of computation is simplified by the use of Table B on the last page of Form 706.

There is no credit allowed if the taxable estate does not exceed $40,000. Furthermore, the credit is not automatic. Proof of payment of State death taxes is required, and the proof must be submitted within the statutory period.[1] The tax must actually have been paid.[2] It has recently been held that where a deposit on account of the State tax was made, and the State tax would exceed the permissible credit, the credit was allowable.[3] And the credit has been allowed even though there was the possibility of a refund.[4] The credit allowable may not exceed the amount paid.[5] It does not include the amount allowed as a discount.[6] Thus, if the credit as computed under the statute were $800. and the amount paid to the State was $700., only $700. would be allowable as a credit. Some states, such as New York

---

17. IRC, § 2011(a) (1954 Code); Reg, § 20.2011–1(a).

18. Morsman, 14 BTA 108 (1928); Brock, 16 BTA 1358 (1929).

19. See Fletcher, 29 BTA 503 (1934); compromised by stipulation 74 F2d 1014 (CCA 5) (1935).

20. IRC, § 813(b) (1939 Code).

1. IRC, § 2011(c) (1954 Code).

2. Moore, 21 BTA 279 (1930); but see Walker v Blacklidge, 35–2 USTC ¶ 9550; Aronauer v US, 37–1 USTC ¶ 9052.

3. Goyette v US, 57–2 USTC ¶ 11,710.

4. Phillips, 36 BTA 1102 (1937); Weisberger, 29 TC 217 (1957).

5. Smith v Comm, 59 F2d 533 (CCA 7) (1932); Commonwealth Trust Co v Driscoll, 43–1 USTC ¶ 10,016, aff'd 137 F2d 653 (CCA 3), cert den 321 US 764, 88 L ed 1061, 64 S Ct 521.

6. Note 5, supra; but see Markle, 311 Pa 472, 166 A 884 (1933).

provide for an alternative tax equal to the maximum credit, so
that in all events the full credit is allowable.

FORM NO. 47

Table B; Computation of Maximum Credit for State Death Taxes

Taxable estate equaling (1) (Dollars)	Taxable estate not exceeding (2) (Dollars)	Credit on amount in column (1) (3) (Dollars)	Rate of credit on excess over amount in column (1) (4) (Percent)
40,000	90,000	. . .	0.8
90,000	140,000	400	1.6
140,000	240,000	1,200	2.4
240,000	440,000	3,600	3.2
440,000	640,000	10,000	4.0
640,000	840,000	18,000	4.8
840,000	1,040,000	27,600	5.6
1,040,000	1,540,000	38,800	6.4
1,540,000	2,040,000	70,800	7.2
2,040,000	2,540,000	106,800	8.0
2,540,000	3,040,000	146,800	8.8
3,040,000	3,540,000	190,800	9.6
3,540,000	4,040,000	238,800	10.4
4,040,000	5,040,000	290,800	11.2
5,040,000	6,040,000	402,800	12.0
6,040,000	7,040,000	522,800	12.8
7,040,000	8,040,000	650,800	13.6
8,040,000	9,040,000	786,800	14.4
9,040,000	10,040,000	930,800	15.2
10,040,000	. . . .	1,082,800	16.0

Thus, if the decedent's taxable estate is $525,000., it is in the
$440,000. to $640,000. bracket. The credit on $440,000. in column
(1) is $10,000. as shown in column 2. The credit on the excess
of $200,000. is computed at the 4% rate, shown in column (4),
and is $8,000. The *maximum* credit allowable, therefore, is $18,-
000. If such amount or more has been paid to the State, the
entire amount is the amount of the credit. If a lesser amount has
been paid to the State, such lesser amount is the amount of the
credit.

We have previously referred to charitable bequests which may be taxable by particular states and the 1956 amendment to provide for such situation.[7] In such cases there is a limitation on the credit, discussed hereafter.[8]

§ 319. Computation of the Tax; Credit for State Death Taxes; Period of Limitations on Credit.

The credit allowed for State death taxes includes only such taxes as were actually paid and credit therefor claimed *within four years* after the filing of the Estate Tax Return, *except*

(1) If a petition for redetermination of a deficiency has been filed with the Tax Court within the statutory time, then within four years or before the expiration of sixty days after the decision of the Tax Court becomes final.

(2) If an extension of time has been granted for payment of the tax, or of a deficiency, then within four years or before the date of the expiration of the period of extension.

(3) If a claim for refund or credit of an overpayment of the tax has been filed within the statutory time, then within four years or before the expiration of 60 days of the mailing by certified mail or registered mail by the Secretary or his delegate to the taxpayer of a notice of the disallowance of any part of such claim, or before the expiration of 60 days after a decision by any court of competent jurisdiction becomes final with respect to a timely suit instituted upon such claim, whichever is later.

Refund based on the credit may (despite the provisions of Sections 6511 and 6512) be made if claim therefor is filed within the period above provided. Any such refund shall be made without interest.[9]

Subdivision (3) above was added by the Technical Amendments Act of 1958[9a] and *applies to decedents dying on and after August 17, 1954.*

An exception to this period is made in the rare instance where an election is made to postpone the tax on a remainder or reversionary interest.[10] In such case the credit attributable to such part of the tax must be claimed within sixty days after the termination of the precedent interest.[11]

By the Technical Amendments Act of 1958 the Secretary or his delegate is authorized to extend the time for payment for

7. §§ 214, 255, supra.
8. § 321, infra.
9. IRC, § 2011(c) (1954 Code).
9a. Technical Amendments Act of
1958, § 65(a), HR 8381, 85th Cong, 2nd Sess.
10. See § 328, infra.
11. IRC, § 2015 (1954 Code).

a reasonable period not in excess of two years from the expiration of the period of postponement.[11a]

The fact that a notice of deficiency is mailed before the credit is claimed does not affect the right to it if the claim is made, for payment made before the expiration of the statutory period.[12] The United States District Court is without authority to extend the four year limit.[13]

The usual procedure is that if upon the audit of the return, evidence of payment of the State death tax is not presented, the Estate Tax Examiner disallows the credit and assesses a deficiency, with a notation that if the proof is presented before the expiration of the statutory period, the deficiency will be satisfied. Normally there is no problem about obtaining the credit.

§ 320. Computation of the Tax; Credit for State Death Taxes; Evidence of Payment.

Before the credit for State death taxes is allowed, evidence that such taxes have been paid must be submitted to the District Director. The District Director *may* require the submission of a certificate from the proper officer of the taxing State, showing

(1) the total amount of tax imposed (before adding interest and penalties and before allowing discount);

(2) the amount of any discount allowed;

(3) the amount of any interest and penalties imposed or charged;

(4) the total amount actually paid in cash; and

(5) the date of payment.

If the amount of the tax has been redetermined, the amount finally determined should be stated. The evidence should be filed with the return, but if not convenient or possible, it should be submitted as soon after as practicable. Additional proof *may* be required, such as whether a claim for refund is pending, and whether a refund has been authorized, and if there has been a refund, its date, amount, and description of the property in respect of which the refund was made. There *may* also be required an itemized list of the property on which the State death tax was imposed, and an affidavit by the fiduciary whether any litiga-

---

11a. IRC, § 6163(b) (1954 Code), as added by Technical Amendments Act of 1958, § 66(b), HR 8381, 85th Cong, 2nd Sess.

12. Bonnetti, 7 TCM 268 (1946).

13. Howard v US, 40 F Supp 697 (1941).

tion is pending or contemplated which may affect the amount of the tax paid.[14]

Rigorous as these requirements sound, all that is actually required in the ordinary case is a certificate from the State taxing authority certifying the amount of tax paid and the fact that no claim for refund on any part of such tax has been authorized or is pending. In New York for example, Form TT66C is furnished by the New York State Tax Commission, certifying such facts. The certificate is obtainable upon payment of a fee of $1.00.

While the State tax must be *paid* within the statutory period and the claim for the credit must be made within the statutory period, the time limit does not apply to the submission of evidence of payment.

§ 321. Computation of the Tax; Credit for State Death Taxes; Limitation on Credit When State Death Taxes Paid on Charitable Gift.

We have previously discussed the amendment of the statute in 1956, effective as to estates of persons dying *after December 31, 1953,* which permits as a deduction from the gross estate of State death taxes imposed upon charitable bequests.[15] The result is that the deduction and the credit for State death taxes become interrelated.

The credit for State death taxes cannot exceed the least of

(a) The amount of State death taxes paid other than those for which a deduction is allowed under Section 2053(d);

(b) The amount of the maximum credit for State death taxes; and

(c) An amount, A, which bears the same ratio to B (the amount of the maximum credit for State death taxes if the deduction under Section 2053(d) were not allowed in computing the decedent's taxable estate) as C (the amount of State death taxes paid other than those for which a deduction is allowed under Section 2053 (d)) bears to D (the total amount of State death taxes paid).

For the purpose of the computation, in determining what the decedent's taxable estate would be if the deduction under Section 2053(d) were not allowed, adjustment must be made for the decrease in the deduction for charitable gifts by reason of any

14. Reg, § 20.2011–1(c)(2).   15. Note 7, supra.

increase in Federal Estate Tax which would be chargeable against the charitable gifts.[16]

The Regulation illustrates the application of the provision. It is assumed that the decedent died January 1, 1955, leaving a gross estate of $925,000. Expenses, indebtedness, etc., amounted to $25,000. The decedent bequeathed $400,000 to his son with the direction that the son bear the State death taxes on the bequest. The residuary estate was left to a charitable organization. Except as noted, all Federal and State death taxes were payable out of the residuary estate. The State imposed death taxes of $60,000. on the son's bequest and death taxes of $75,-000. on the bequest to charity. The taxable estate is computed as follows:

Gross estate				$925,000.00
Expenses, indebtedness, etc.		$25,000.00		
Exemption		60,000.00		
Deduction under 2053(d)		75,000.00		
Charitable deduction:				
Gross estate	$925,000.00			
Expenses, etc. . $25,000.00				
Bequest to son . 400,000.00				
State death tax paid from residue 75,000.00				
Federal Estate Tax paid from residue 122,916.67	622,916.67	302,083.33	462,083.33	
Taxable estate				$462,916.67

16. Reg, § 20.2011–2.

If the deduction under Section 2053(d) were not allowed, the decedent's taxable estate would be computed as follows:

Gross estate $925,000.00
    Expenses, indebtedness, etc. $25,000.00
    Exemption 60,000.00
    Charitable deduction:
      Gross estate $925,000.00
        Expenses, etc. .. $25,000.00
        Son's bequest .. 400,000.00
        State death tax
          from residue . 75,000.00
        Federal Estate
        Tax from resi-
        due .... 155,000.00　655,000.00　270,000.00　355,000.00

Taxable estate $570,000.00

Under these facts, the credit for State death taxes is determined as follows:

(1) Amount of State death taxes paid other than those for which a deduction is allowed under Section 2053(d) ($135,000 — $75,000) $60,000.00
(2) Maximum credit allowable for State death taxes on taxable estate of $462,916.67 .... 10,916.67
(3) As per ratio above

$$\frac{(1) \text{ above, } \$60,000}{\text{total State tax, } \$135,000} \times \begin{array}{c}\text{(maximum credit if}\\ \text{deduction not al-}\\ \text{lowed) } \$15,200 \text{ on}\\ \$570,000\end{array} = 6,755.56$$

Since (3) is the least amount, it is the amount of the credit.

§ 322. Deduction for State Death Taxes.

We have seen that the allowance of a deduction for State death taxes imposed upon a charitable gift is not allowed unless the entire decrease in the Federal Estate Tax resulting from the allowance of the deduction inures solely to the benefit of the charitable transferee, or the Federal Estate Tax is equitably apportioned among all the transferees of property included in the gross estate.[17]

17. § 214, supra.

The tax is considered to be equitably apportioned only if each transferee is required to bear the burden of the Federal tax in an amount equal to

$$\frac{\text{the value of the transfer reduced by } any \text{ charitable deductions and the marital deduction}}{\text{the sum of the taxable estate and the exemption allowed in computing the taxable estate}} \times \begin{array}{l} \text{the Federal Estate Tax payable} \\ \text{after the allowance of the credits} \\ \text{for foreign and State death taxes} \end{array}$$

In determining the amount of State death tax imposed upon a transfer for charitable purposes, where the State tax is imposed upon the entire estate and not upon the transfer of a particular share, the State death tax is equal to

$$\frac{\text{the value of the charitable gift, reduced by the amount of any deduction or exclusion allowed with respect to such property in determining the State death tax}}{\text{the total value of the property received by all beneficiaries and subjected to the State death tax, reduced by the amount of all deductions and exclusions allowed by the State on account of the nature or relationship of the beneficiary}} \times \begin{array}{l} \text{the amount of the State death tax} \\ \text{imposed with respect to the} \\ \text{entire estate} \end{array}$$

The Regulation illustrates the application of the provisions.[18]
The decedent's gross estate was $200,000. He bequeathed $90,-000. to a nephew, $10,000. to Charity A, and the remainder to Charity B. State death tax was paid in the amount of $13,500. by the nephew, $1,500. by Charity A, and $15,000. by Charity B. The State tax was payable by each beneficiary and the Federal tax out of the residue. Since the Federal tax is payable entirely by Charity B, and allowance of the deduction for State taxes paid on the Charitable transfers would inure solely for the benefit of Charity B, deduction is allowed for both the $1,500. and the $15,000. paid by the charities.

18. Reg, § 20.2053-9(e).

The decedent's gross estate was $350,000. Expenses, indebtedness, etc., were $50,000. The estate was bequeathed equally to a son, daughter, and Charity A. State death tax was paid by the son and daughter each in the amount of $2,000. and $5,000. by Charity A. Each beneficiary was required by local law to pay has own State tax and a proportionate share of the Federal tax after considering the net amount of each bequest subject thereto. Since the deductions under Sections 2053(d) and 2055 are to be taken into account in determining the share of Charity A's Federal tax, the tax is considered to be equitably apportioned. Thus a deduction is allowed for $5,000. paid by Charity A and $95,000. is allowed as a charitable deduction, so that Charity A pays no part of the tax and it is borne entirely by the son and daughter.

If in the example immediately above the Federal tax were payable as an expense of administration, the deduction would not be allowable, since some part of the deduction would inure to the benefit of the son and daughter. In addition, the deduction could not be allowed because the Federal tax is not equitably apportioned.

The decedent bequeathed his entire residuary estate in trust to pay the income to X for life with remainder to charity. The State tax on X's bequest was $2,000. and $10,000. on the bequest to charity. All State and Federal taxes are payable out of the residue. If the deduction for the State tax is allowed, some portion of the decrease in the Federal tax would benefit X, since the income would be received by X on the corpus increased by the deduction. Also, the Federal tax is not considered equitably apportioned, since each legatee's share of the Federal tax is not based on the net amount of his bequest subject to the tax. Since some part of the deduction would inure to the benefit of X, and since there is no equitable apportionment, no deduction is allowable.

Decedent's gross estate was $750,000. Expenses, indebtedness, etc., were $50,000. Decedent bequeathed $350,000. to his spouse and the remainder equally to his son and a charity. State taxes were $7,000. on the wife's bequest, $26,250. on the son's bequest, and $26,250. on the charity's bequest. Local law provided for each legatee to pay his share of the State tax and for the Federal tax to be apportioned, but the wife was not required to pay any part of the Federal tax. The marital deduction allowed is limited to $343,000. ($350,000. bequest less $7,000. State tax payable by the wife). Thus, the bequest to the wife is subjected to the Federal tax in the net amount of $7,000. If the deduction for State death tax on the charitable bequest is allowed, some portion would inure to the benefit of the son. The Federal tax is also not equitably apportioned for the same reason as in the preceding example. For both of these reasons, no deduction is allowable.

§ 323. Credit for Gift Taxes; In General.

In the case of the fourth credit allowable, the amount thereof is entered as item 4 on Part II of the computation of the tax on Page 1 of the return. This is the credit for Federal Gift Taxes. As we have seen, the decedent in his lifetime may have made transfers of property on which he may have paid a Gift Tax. Upon his death these transfers may be included in his gross estate because made in contemplation of death, or for any of the reasons which would subject lifetime transfers to the Estate Tax.[19] In such case a credit is allowed against the Federal Estate Tax for the Gift Tax paid. The credit is allowable even though the Gift Tax is paid by the fiduciary after the decedent's death and the amount of the Gift Tax is deductible from the gross estate as a debt of the decedent.[20] The amount of the credit for Gift Tax paid on property included in the gross estate is limited to the smaller of the limitations discussed in the succeeding section.[1]

§ 324. Credit for Gift Taxes; Limitations on Credit.

The credit for Gift Taxes paid on property of the decedent included in the gross estate is subject to two limitations, the lesser of which is the amount allowable. When more than one gift is included in the gross estate, a separate computation of the two limitations on the credit must be made for each gift.[2]

The "first limitation" is the amount of the Gift Tax paid on the gift. Thus, if only one gift was made during a certain calendar year, and the gift is wholly included in the gross estate, the credit is limited to the amount of Gift Tax paid for that calendar year. On the other hand, if more than one gift was made during

19. See §§ 118 et seq, supra.
20. § 215, supra.

1. IRC, § 2012(a) (1954 Code); Reg, § 20.2012–1(a)(b).
2. Reg, § 20.2012–1(b).

a certain calendar year, the credit is limited to an amount which equals

$$\frac{\text{amount of the gift}}{\substack{\text{total taxable gifts,}\\ \text{plus specific ex-}\\ \text{emption allowed}}} \times \text{ total Gift Tax paid}$$

The *amount of the gift* does not mean the total gift, but the total included in computing the Gift Tax. This requires that there be excluded the amount of the annual exclusion, and any charitable or marital deduction which may have been taken. The values taken are the Gift Tax values, not the Estate Tax values. If part of the gift only is included in the gross estate, a similar computation is made. Thus, if the decedent in 1955 made gifts to his son of $13,000., to his wife of $86,000., and to a charity of $10,000., the total of gifts is $109,000. On each of the three gifts there was an annual exclusion of $3,000., the gift to the wife was entitled to a marital deduction of $43,000., and the charitable gift was deductible to the extent of $7,000., the amount of the gift, less the annual exclusion. The decedent had used $20,000. of his specific Gift Tax exemption and used the remaining $10,-000. in reporting the above gifts. The total of deductions and the balance of the specific exemption was $60,000., which deducted from the included amount of gifts of $100,000., left the amount of taxable gifts as $40,000. A Gift Tax of $3,600. was paid on this amount. The gift to the wife was included in the gross estate. Applying the above ratio to the facts, the "first limitation" is computed as follows:

$$\frac{\substack{\$86,000 - \$3,000 - \$43,000 \text{ (gift to}\\ \text{wife, less annual exclusion, less marital}\\ \text{deduction)}}}{\substack{\$40,000 + \$10,000 \text{ (taxable gifts, plus}\\ \text{specific exemption allowed)}}} \times \;\; \$3,600 \text{ (total gift tax paid)}$$

Under the "first limitation", therefore, the credit with respect to the gift cannot exceed $2,880.[3]

In making the computation it is important to bear in mind that the amount of the annual exclusion and the specific exemption has varied. From 1932 to 1938 the annual exclusion was $5,000. From 1939 through 1942 it was $4,000., and since 1943 it has

3. Reg, § 20.2012–1(c).

been $3,000. The specific exemption was $50,000. from 1932 to 1935, $40,000. from 1936 to 1942, and has been $30,000. since 1943.

The "second limitation" is the amount of Estate Tax attributable to the inclusion of the gift in the gross estate. The "second limitation" equals[4]

$$\frac{\text{value of the gift}}{\substack{\text{value of gross estate, less} \\ \text{marital deduction and} \\ \text{charitable deduction}}} \times \substack{\text{gross estate tax, less} \\ \text{credit for State} \\ \text{death taxes}$$

The value of the gift is the value of the property transferred by gift and included in the gross estate, as determined for the purpose of the Gift Tax *or* for the purpose of the Estate Tax, *whichever is lower, and adjusted* as follows:

The appropriate value is reduced by all or a portion of any annual exclusion allowed for Gift Tax purposes. If the Gift Tax value is lower than the Estate Tax value, it is reduced by the entire amount of the exclusion. If the Estate Tax value is lower than the Gift Tax value, it is reduced by an amount which bears the same ratio to the Estate Tax value as the annual exclusion bears to the total value of the property as determined for Gift Tax purposes. Thus, if a donor transferred in contemplation of death property valued for the Gift Tax at $300,000., to his five children, with annual exclusions totalling $15,000., and the same property was included in his gross estate at a value of $270,000., the reduction is

$$\frac{\$15,000 \text{ (annual exclusions)}}{\$300,000 \text{ (Gift Tax value)}} \times \$270,000 \text{ (Estate Tax value)}$$

The first reduction is $13,500.[5]

The appropriate value is *further reduced* if any portion of the value of the property is allowed as a marital deduction or as a charitable deduction. The amount of the reduction is an amount which bears the same ratio to the value determined as above as the portion of the property allowed as a marital deduction or as a charitable deduction bears to the total value of the property as determined for Estate Tax purposes. Thus, if a gift is made solely to the decedent's surviving spouse and is included in the gross estate, but an Estate Tax marital deduction is allowed for the full value of the gift, no credit for Gift Tax on the gift will be allowed since the reduction under this pro-

4. Reg, § 20.2012–1(d).   5. Reg, § 20.2012–1(d)(2)(i).

vision together with the reduction above will have the effect of reducing the value of the gift to zero, which applied to the equation for determining the "second limitation" will result in a zero credit. If, however, by reason of the limitation on the aggregate marital deduction to 50% of the value of the adjusted gross estate, the aggregate marital deduction allowed is less than the aggregate marital deduction computed without regard to that limitation, then the reduction under this provision is an amount which bears the same ratio to the value determined above as the aggregate marital deduction allowed bears to the aggregate marital deduction computed without regard to the 50% limitation.[6]

The application of the preceding paragraph is illustrated by the following example: In 1955, a donor transferred to his wife in contemplation of death property valued for the Gift Tax at $86,000. He was allowed an annual exclusion of $3,000. On death, his gross estate was $350,000. Expenses, indebtedness, etc., were $50,000. The gift was included in the gross estate and valued at $100,000. It qualified for the marital deduction. The wife received the major part of the estate. The aggregate marital deduction was $150,000. The amount of the marital deduction computed without regard to the 50% limitation would have been $250,000. The gross Estate Tax was $17,900., and the credit for State death taxes was $400. The value of the gift which is used in computing the "second limitation" is computed as follows:

Value of gift to wife for the purpose of the Gift Tax or for
the purpose of the Estate Tax, whichever is lower $86,000.00
Less: Portion of annual exclusion allowed in determining
the Gift Tax 3,000.00

Net value $83,000.00
Less: Portion of the net value allowed as a marital deduction

$$\frac{\$150{,}000 \text{ (aggregate marital deduction allowed for the purpose of the Estate Tax)}}{\$250{,}000 \text{ (aggregate marital deduction computed without regard to statutory limitation)}} \times \begin{array}{c}(\$86{,}000 - \$3{,}000) \text{ (value of gift to wife for the purpose of the Gift Tax or for the purpose of the Estate Tax, whichever is lower, less portion of annual exclusion allowed in determining Gift Tax}\end{array}$$

6. Reg, § 20.2012–1(d)(2)(ii).
454

The result of the ratio is $49,800. Deducting this from the net value of the gift, the value of the gift for the purpose of computing the "second limitation" is $33,200.

The computation of the "second limitation" then proceeds as follows:

$$\frac{\$33,200 \text{ (value of gift as reduced above)}}{\$350,000 - \$150,000} \times (\$17,900 - \$400) \text{ (gross estate tax less credit for State death taxes)}$$
(value of gross estate less marital deduction allowed)

The "second limitation" therefore, is $2,905. The amount of the credit is the smaller of the amounts as computed under the "first limitation" and the "second limitation".[7]

§ 325. Credit for Gift Taxes; Split Gifts.

As we shall see in the chapters dealing with the Gift Tax hereafter, a gift made by one spouse may be considered as made by each spouse to the extent of one half thereof, if the other spouse consents thereto.[8] In such case if the property which was the subject of the gift is included in the gross estate, the credit allowed for Gift Taxes is allowed with respect to both halves of the gift. The "first limitation" is separately computed with respect to *each half* of the gift in the same manner as previously illustrated.[9] The "second limitation" is computed with respect to the *entire gift* in the same manner as previously illustrated.[10] Thus, a donor in contemplation of death, transferred property valued at $106,000. to his son on January 1, 1955, and he and his wife consented that the gift be considered a split gift. The property was included in his gross estate. Under the "first limitation" the amount of Gift Tax paid by him with respect to the gift is $11,250. and the amount of the Gift Tax paid by his wife is $1,200. Under the "second limitation", the amount of the Estate Tax attributable to the property is $28,914. Therefore, the credit for Gift Tax allowed is the Gift Tax paid by him and his wife ($11,250. + $1,200.) since it is smaller than the amount computed under the "second limitation".[11]

7. Reg, § 20.2012–1(d)(3).
8. IRC, § 2513 (1954 Code).
9. § 324, supra.
10. Note 9, supra.
11. Reg, § 20.2012–1(e).

§ 326. Credit for Death Taxes on Remainders.

Where the value of a reversionary or remainder interest is included in the gross estate, the fiduciary may elect to postpone the payment of the tax on that part of the estate until six months after the termination of the precedent interest.[12] The Technical Amendments Act of 1958 added a further provision applicable where the precedent interest did not terminate before the beginning of the six month period which ends on the date of enactment, September 2, 1958, permitting the Secretary or his delegate, if he finds that the payment of the tax at the expiration of the period of postponement would result in undue hardship to the estate, to extend the time for payment for a reasonable period not in excess of two years from the expiration of the period of postponement.[12a] In such case, credit for State and foreign death taxes attributable to such remainder or reversionary interest is allowable if claimed either within the statutory period or within sixty days after the termination of the precedent interest, except that if an extension is granted, as above noted, the time is extended to the period covered by the hardship extension.[13] The allowance of the credit is subject to the limitations affecting each of such credits.[14]

In applying the statute, credit for either tax paid within the time required in each case is applied first to the portion of the Federal Estate Tax payment which is not postponed, and any excess is applied to the balance of the Federal Estate Tax. However, credit for either or both taxes not paid within the time required in each case is allowable only against the portion of the Federal Estate Tax attributable to the reversionary or remainder interest, and only for either or both taxes attributable to that interest. If either or both taxes are imposed upon both a reversionary or remainder interest and other property, without a definite apportionment of the tax, the amount of the tax deemed attributable to the reversionary or remainder interest is an amount which bears the same ratio to the total tax as the value of the reversionary or remainder interest bears to the value of the entire property with respect to which the tax was imposed.

---

12. IRC, § 6163(a) (1954 Code).
12a. IRC, § 6163(b) (1954 Code), as added by Technical Amendments Act of 1958, § 66(b), HR 8381, 85th Cong, 2nd Sess.

13. IRC, § 2015 (1954 Code).
14. Reg, § 20.2015–1(a).

In applying the ratio, adjustments must be made consistent with those required by Section 6163.[15]

The Regulation[16] furnishes three examples of the operation of the provision. In the first, one third of the Federal Estate Tax was attributable to a remainder interest in real property located in State Y, and two thirds of the Federal Estate Tax was attributable to other property located in State X. The payment of the tax attributable to the remainder interest was postponed. The maximum credit allowable for State death taxes is $12,000. Therefore, of the maximum credit allowable, $4,000. is attributable to the remainder interest and $8,000. is attributable to the other property. Within the statutory period for State death tax credit, inheritance tax of $9,000. was paid to State X in connection with the other property. With respect to this, the maximum credit of $8,000. is allowed as a credit against the Federal Estate Tax attributable to the other property, and $1,000. is allowed as a credit against the postponed tax. After the expiration of the four year period but before the expiration of 60 days after termination of the life estate, inheritance tax of $5,000. was paid to State Y on the remainder interest. As the maximum credit allowable with respect to the remainder interest is $4,000., and $1,000. has already been allowed, an additional credit of $3,000. will be credited against the Federal Estate Tax attributable to the remainder.

The other examples offer variations of the first.

§ 327. Completion of Computation of Tax.

In the preceding sections we have seen the manner in which the gross Estate Tax is determined, and the credits allowable against the gross Estate Tax. In order that the amount of the net Estate Tax payable may be easily seen, Page 1 of Form 706 provides for the entry of all the ultimate figures in the determination of the tax.

There are two parts to the "Computation of the Tax". Part I is made up of three items, which are the ones found in the great majority of all estates. Item 1 is the gross Estate Tax which is computed as we have shown.[17] Item 2 is the credit for State death taxes.[18] Deducting this latter amount from the gross Estate Tax determines item 3, the net amount payable unless there

---

15. Reg, § 20.2015–1(b).
16. Reg, § 20.2015–1(c).

17. § 317, supra.
18. §§ 318 et seq, supra.

are credits for Federal Gift Taxes, for tax on prior transfers, or for foreign death taxes. If there be such credits, they are entered respectively as items 4, 5, and 6, and totalled under item 7. There is then deducted from the net amount payable, item 3, the total of such credits, the balance being the net Estate Tax payable, item 8.

FORM NO. 48

Computation of Tax

Part I

1. Gross estate tax (use table A, page 40) $65,700.00
2. Credit for State death taxes (use table B, page 40) 3,920.00

3. Gross estate tax less credit for State death taxes (item 1 minus item 2). This is the net amount payable unless credit for Federal gift taxes, tax on prior transfers, or foreign death taxes is claimed in Part II $61,780.00

Part II

4. Credit for Federal gift taxes $1,200.00
5. Credit for tax on prior transfers 847.65
6. Credit for foreign death taxes 285.60

7. Total of credits under Part II (total of items 4, 5, and 6) .. 2,333.25

8. Net estate tax payable (item 3 minus item 7) $59,446.75

§ 328. Vestiges of Basic Estate Tax and Additional Estate Tax.

We have previously noted that for all practical purposes, the terms "basic estate tax" and "additional estate tax" have little application under the 1954 Code. The statute still retains a definition of each of the terms for two reasons.

It provides that the basic Estate Tax and the Estate Tax imposed by the Revenue Act of 1926 shall be 125% of the amount determined to be the maximum credit for State death taxes. The additional Estate Tax shall be the difference between the tax imposed by Section 2001 (citizens or residents) or 2101 (nonresidents not citizens) and the basic Estate Tax.[19]

The reason for the definition is that, as we have seen,[20] the statute provides in the case of members of the Armed Forces

19. IRC, § 2011(d) (1954 Code).   20. § 297, supra.

dying during an induction period, that the additional Estate Tax does not apply to their estates. The second reason for retention of the terms in the statute is to supply a means of computing State death taxes under local statutes using those terms.[1]

1. Reg, § 20.2011–1(d).

CHAPTER 5

PRACTICE AND PAYMENT

§ 329. Scope of Chapter.

Other than appellate procedure, there remains for consideration under the subject of Federal Estate taxation the manner in which the taxing authorities arrive at the determination of the tax and the matters in connection with payment of the tax, liability therefore, and refunds, if any. This involves the procedure in filing the return, the audit and fixation of the tax, and payment. The latter in turn requires consideration of the many features bound up in the matter of payment. It has been our purpose to conduct the lawyer step by step through the preparation of the return, and now we are ready to conclude those matters necessary to complete the tax proceedings administratively.

§ 330. Declaration of Fiduciary and Attorney.

All of the schedules having been completed and the tax computed, it is necessary that the return be signed by all of the fiduciaries, if there be more than one,[1] and be verified by a written declaration that it is made under the penalties of perjury.[2] The 1939 Code required verification under oath. It may still be required to be made under oath.[3] The Secretary

1. § 29, supra.   3. IRC, § 6065(b) (1954 Code).
2. IRC, § 6065(a) (1954 Code).

of the Treasury is authorized to provide the manner of signing.[4] The return must also be signed by the attorney or agent preparing the return and similarly verified under the penalties of perjury. These declarations appear at Page 40 of Form 706.

A recent Revenue Ruling[4a] permits returns prepared by a firm to so indicate. If a firm is responsible for preparation of the return the statement of verification must be signed with the firm name and if the firm name is stamped or typed, it must be followed by the signature of a person authorized to sign the verification on behalf of the firm.

FORM NO. 49

Declaration

We/I declare under the penalties of perjury that this return (including any accompanying statements) has been examined by us/me, and is, to the best of our/my knowledge and belief, a true, correct, and complete return, made in good faith pursuant to the Internal Revenue Code and the regulations thereunder.

April 15, 1960   KATHERINE BENSON   100 Catalpa Avenue, Detroit, Mich.
   (Date)   (Signature)   (Address)

FORM NO. 50

Declaration of Attorney or Agent Preparing Return

I declare under the penalties of perjury that I prepared this return for the person or persons named herein; and that this return (including any accompanying schedules and statements) is, to the best of my knowledge and belief, a true, correct, and complete return based on all the information relating to the matters required to be reported in this return of which I have any knowledge.

April 15, 1960   DANIEL WEBSTER CLAY   250 Dearborn Street,
                                          Detroit, Mich.

   (Date)   (Signature)   (Address)

§ 331. Transfer Certificates in Nonresident Estates.

Many states require the procurement of a waiver from its taxing authorities, before they will permit stock owned by a nonresident of the State in a corporation of the State to be transferred. So far as the Federal Estate Tax is concerned, the only time that such a document is required is in the case of a nonresident decedent under the circumstances hereafter set forth.

---

4. IRC, § 6061 (1954 Code).   4a. Rev Rul 58–390, IRB 1958–31 p 15.

The Regulation provides that a transfer certificate is a certificate permitting the transfer of property of a nonresident decedent (*regardless of citizenship*) without liability. No domestic corporation or its transfer agent should transfer stock registered in the name of a nonresident decedent, regardless of citizenship, *except* such shares which have been submitted for transfer by a duly qualified executor or administrator who has been appointed and is acting in the United States, without first requiring a transfer certificate covering all of the decedent's stock of the corporation and showing that the transfer may be made without liability. Corporations, transfer agents of domestic corporations, transfer agents of foreign corporations (*except* as to shares held in the name of a nonresident decedent not a citizen of the United States), banks, trust companies, or other custodians in actual or constructive possession of property of such a decedent can insure avoidance of liability for taxes and penalties only by demanding and receiving transfer certificates before transfer of property of nonresident decedents. *However,* a transfer certificate need not be required for bonds owned by a decedent who was a nonresident not a citizen, if it is known that the bonds were not physically situated in the United States at the time of death. A transfer certificate will be issued by the District Director when he is satisfied that the tax imposed upon the estate, if any, has been fully discharged. The tax will be considered fully discharged for purposes of the issuance of a transfer certificate, only when investigation has been completed and payment of the tax, including any deficiency finally determined, has been made. If the tax liability has not been fully discharged, transfer certificates may be issued permitting the transfer of particular items of property without liability upon the filing with the District Director of such security as he may require. *No transfer certificate is required in the case of a resident decedent.* Further in the case of a nonresident decedent (*regardless of citizenship*) a transfer certificate is not required with respect to property which is being administered by an executor or administrator appointed, qualified, and acting within in the United States.[5]

5. Reg, § 20.6325–1.

FORM NO. 51

United States Certificate Releasing Estate Tax Lien

District of 1st New York   Date of Death   Jan. 15, 1960

Estate of WINTHROP BENSON

Residence at time of death Copiague, L.I. N.Y.

By direction of the Commissioner of Internal Revenue, and in accordance with the provisions of the laws applicable to the collection of internal revenue, I do hereby certify that the estate tax with respect to the above-named estate, has been fully discharged or duly provided for, wherefore and by reason whereof, I do hereby issue this certificate releasing the lien of the United States imposed by Section 6324 of the Internal Revenue Code of 1954 on the following described property:

100 shares Chase Manhattan Bank

Date   July 18, 1960   Thomas E. Scanlon
                                   District Director of Internal Revenue

§ 332. Authorization of Attorney.

An attorney will not be recognized as representing an estate or executor unless he is enrolled to represent claimants before the Treasury Department.[6] If he asks a ruling on a question of law arising in a particular case, the Commissioner will require satisfactory evidence of the right to obtain such ruling. In all cases in which information is sought regarding an estate, or an interview is asked by an attorney, the information or interview will be denied unless the attorney presents a duly executed power of attorney from the executor or administrator authorizing the attorney to act in his behalf. Powers of attorney should be filed in the office of the Supervising Estate Tax Examiner in which the case is under consideration.[7]

What this means is that if the attorney intends to represent his client before the Treasury Department, Internal Revenue Service, he must first obtain Form 24, which is the so-called "green card." A written request to the Secretary of the Committee on Practice, Treasury Department, Washington, D. C. for a copy of Department Circular 230, governing the recognition of agents and attorneys and for Form 23 should be made. Upon completion the form may now be sent to the District Director of Internal Revenue. There is no difficulty about an attorney

---

6. Reg 105, § 81.72.

7. Note 6, supra; see also Policy of Internal Revenue Service, 1954–33, pp 21, 22, 24; Policy of Internal Revenue Service, 1954–49, p 25; Rev Rul 212, 1953-2 CB 449.

being admitted to practice. All that is required is the execution and delivery of the form referred to and payment of a fee of $25.00. There will then be issued the enrollment card which is valid for five years and is periodically renewable thereafter for five year periods upon payment of a fee of $5.00.[8]

In filing the Estate Tax Return there should be filed at the same time Form 711, which is a power of attorney and statement relative to fees, which appears on the reverse side of the form.

FORM NO. 52

Power of Attorney

If the taxpayer desires to be represented by an attorney or agent by correspondence or otherwise, a power of attorney is required. See Treasury Department Circular No. 230 as revised relative to admission to practice before the Treasury Department, and also Conference and Practice Requirements as revised, Internal Revenue Service. Application for admission should be directed to the Director of Practice, Internal Revenue Building, Washington 25, D. C., who will, upon request, supply the necessary forms and information. If specifically requested, a copy of the Bureau Conference and Practice Requirements as revised will also be furnished. The use of the following form of power of attorney is entirely optional with the executor.

I—We, KATHERINE BENSON the undersigned executrix (administrat—) of the estate of WINTHROP BENSON, Deceased have made, constituted, and appointed, and, by these presents, do make, constitute, and appoint DANIEL WEBSTER CLAY of 250 Dearborn Street, Detroit, Mich. my—our true and lawful attorney for me—us and in my—our name, place, and stead to appear for and represent me—us before the Internal Revenue Service or any office, division, or agent or employee thereof, relative to the estate tax liability of said estate, giving and granting to said attorney. . . . full power and authority to do and perform any and every act and thing relative to the estate tax liability of this estate as full and to all intent and purposes as I—we might do if personally present.

Dated at Detroit, Mich. this 15th day of April, 1960

KATHERINE BENSON

. . . .
Executed in presence of:

Alfred A. Adams
Kenneth P. Gross

The power of attorney must be *witnessed by two disinterested individuals or acknowledged before a notary public,* in which case there should

8. 31 CFR 10, amended Nov. 26, 1958.

be pasted or securely affixed a certificate of acknowledgment in the form provided by the law of the place where instrument is executed. *An authenticated copy of the power of attorney* must be submitted with the original.

The power of attorney must be *accompanied by a short-form certificate* (or authenticated copies of letters testamentary or letters of administration) showing that the authority of the executor or administrator who gave it is in full force and effect.

The power of attorney should be filed with the District Director of Internal Revenue in whose office the estate tax return has been or will be filed. If, prior to the filing of the return, a ruling is requested from the Commissioner of Internal Revenue, Washington, D. C., it will expedite matters if a power of attorney accompanies the request.

A statement signed by the attorney or agent must accompany the power of attorney showing whether the fee agreement is contingent in whole or in part. The form on the reverse of this sheet may be used for this purpose.

When filing the above power of attorney make certain that

(1) the power of attorney is witnessed by *two* persons;

(2) an authenticated copy is submitted with the original;

(3) a certificate of letters is filed with it; *and*

(4) the statement relative to fees on the reverse side of the power of attorney is executed.

The Internal Revenue Service is insistent upon compliance with its requirements. If not, the attorney will not receive a copy of the Estate Tax Examiner's report.

If a contingent fee, or a partially contingent fee has been arranged, the statement which follows should indicate the agreement in full. Contingent fees are not encouraged.[9]

FORM NO. 53

Statement Relative to Fees to Be Filed With Power of Attorney

Detroit, Mich.
(Place)
April 15, 1960
(Date)

This is to certify that I (have) (have not) entered into a contingent or partially contingent fee agreement for the representation of Katherine Benson, Executrix under the Last Will and Testament of Winthrop Benson, Deceased before the Treasury Department in the matter of

9. See Treasury Dept. Circular 230 (Revised).

estate taxes, under the terms of a power of attorney filed with the Treasury Department on April 18, 1960, and (in case a contingent or partially contingent fee agreement has been made) that a report of such fee agreement (has) been made to the Director of Practice.

DANIEL WEBSTER CLAY

(Signature of attorney or agent)

§ 333. Examination of Return.

The return having been completed and executed, it, together with the power of attorney and statement relative to fees is filed in the office of the District Director in which the decedent was domiciled. The return is then checked for clerical errors and if such be found the attorney will be advised. It is then forwarded to the audit branch of the Estate and Gift Tax Unit of the District Director's office for assignment to an Estate Tax examiner, formerly called Revenue agents.[10]

In order to expedite the audit of the return and obtain discharge of the executor from personal liability, it is advisable to take advantage of the provision of the Code that if the executor makes written application to the Secretary or his delegate for determination of the amount of the tax and discharge from personal liability therefor, the Secretary or his delegate (as soon as possible, and in any event within one year after the making of such application, or, if the application is made before the return is filed, then within one year after the return is filed, but not after the expiration of the period prescribed for the assessment of the tax in Section 6501) shall notify the executor of the amount of the tax. The executor, on payment of the amount of which he is notified, shall be discharged from personal liability for any deficiency in tax thereafter found to be due and shall be entitled to a receipt or writing showing such discharge.[11] There is no particular form for the application. The customary method is to write a letter to the District Director requesting that pursuant to the provisions of Section 2204 of the Internal Revenue Code of 1954 the executor requests that the amount of the Estate Tax upon the estate of the named decedent be determined and the executor be discharged from personal liability therefor.

At this point, there may be one of three procedures adopted. In cases, which although exceeding the gross amount of $60,000,

10. See Mim 4261, XIII-2 CB 371; Mim 6125, 1947-1 CB 116; Mim 6293, 1948-2 CB 59; Rev Rul 54-172, 1954-1 CB 394.

11. IRC, § 2204 (1954 Code).

the estate is not liable for the payment of any tax, as where the amount of the marital deduction is in such an amount that there is no possibility of tax, the attorney will be advised that there is no tax payable and the Estate Tax proceeding completed. In other cases in which a field audit is not necessary, the attorney will be asked to bring his file to the office of the Estate and Gift Tax Unit and the audit completed there. In the greater number of cases, however, the Estate Tax examiner to whom the case has been assigned will arrange an appointment at the office of the attorney for the fiduciary, at which time he will request that there be available for his inspection such documents and records as he may require to complete his audit. This will usually consist of the decedent's check books, income tax records, and proof of payment of items claimed as deductions, among other things.

At the time of the audit, if valuations are questioned, the examiner sends the items to the Valuation Section of the Internal Revenue Service, which in due course reports its opinion as to value. The examiner may also request further information. The audit may be completed in one visit or in several. After the examiner has determined whether or not he agrees with the return as filed, he will advise the attorney. If at that time there are differences of opinion as to valuation, inclusion of property, or deductions, which cannot be compromised, an informal conference procedure has been adopted.

§ 334. Informal Conference.

When the attorney is advised by the Estate Tax examiner of proposed adjustments to which he is unwilling to agree and he so advises the examiner, there will then be received Form L-19 offering an informal conference for the purpose of reviewing the proposed adjustments.

FORM NO. 54

Statement of Examining Officer's Proposed Adjustments

U. S. Treasury Department

Internal Revenue Service

District Director

210 Livingston Street

Brooklyn 1, N. Y.

Au:CC:WSM

Katherine Benson, Executrix

100 Elm Street

Copiague, L. I., N. Y.

Dear Madam:

You previously indicated that you did not agree to the adjustment(s) marked(*) listed on the reverse hereof which were proposed during a recent examination of your estate tax liability.

IF YOU DESIRE AN INFORMAL CONFERENCE with a representative of this office for the purpose of securing an impartial review of these adjustments, please so advise within the next TEN DAYS by telephoning or writing to the person whose name and address are shown below. Upon receipt of your request, a mutually convenient time and place for the conference will be arranged. You may be accompanied by any person or persons, acting solely in the capacity of witnesses, who may have knowledge of facts or can furnish information in support of the contentions on which you rely.

In the event that you desire to appear with a representative, or if you do not wish to attend the conference personally, your representative must be enrolled to practice before the Treasury Department, and a Power of Attorney in his name must be filed in duplicate with an additional conformed copy for each taxable year in excess of one, together with a contingent fee statement.

IF YOU DO NOT REQUEST AN INFORMAL CONFERENCE within the time stated above, a report of the examination will be forwarded to you after which the prescribed procedure toward asserting the correct income tax liability will be followed. Should you decide to accept the proposed adjustments at this time, it will be appreciated if you so notify this office at the address shown below.

Very truly yours,

Thomas E. Scanlon

(Name)

District Director

(Title)

Name and address of person to contact

W. S. Molloy, Conference Coordinator

Box 991, General Post Office

Brooklyn 1, New York

Telephone No.

ULster 2-5100

Extension

229

469

U. S. Treasury Department — Internal Revenue Service

Statement of Examining Officer's Proposed Adjustments

Year Ended (*or period*)

Taxable estate per return ...... $	$49,008.11	$
Net adjustments as computed below		
Proposed adjusted taxable estate . $	$67,766.84	$
Proposed increase and explanation $	$	$
Unallowable deductions and additional assets		
Schedule B, Item 3	12,328.80	
Schedule E, Item 1	2,000.00	
Schedule G, Item 2	3,835.00	
	——————	
	18,163.80	
Executor's commissions, Increase ..	93.54	

Upon receipt of this letter, if a conference is desired it can be arranged by telephone. Except in an unusual case, it is desirable to have such conference. As the letter indicates, the conference is informal. It will be attended by the Group Supervisor, the Estate Tax examiner and the estate attorney. Its informality is no excuse for lack of preparation. Where there are factual questions involved, if all of the facts have not been presented, as they should have been, the conference offers an opportunity to remedy this. When valuation is concerned, it will often be found that a reasonable adjustment can be made with the conferee. In many cases the conferences are horse-trading sessions and a compromise is achieved which is satisfactory.

If, on the other hand, there is involved a close question of law, the conference is unlikely to serve any useful purpose, in which case it is the writer's practice to advise the examiner that he does not desire a conference. *Unless it has been determined to go through the various agencies of the Internal Revenue Service, but if unsuccessful, to then pay the tax, Form 890, the Waiver of Restrictions on Assessment and Collection of Deficiency and Acceptance of Overassessment should not be executed.*

§ 335. Estate Tax Examiner's Report.

If the informal conference has been refused, or if after the conference no satisfactory compromise is achieved, the examiner will prepare his report which will be sent to the fiduciary and the attorney representing him. The report accompanies the so-called thirty day letter, which refers to other enclosures. These latter consist of the Waiver of Restrictions, which will be one of two forms, depending upon whether there is a credit for State death taxes or not, a Receipt of Estate Tax Examiner's Report, and detailed Instructions as to the Preparation of Protests Against Findings of Examining Officers. The report shows the amounts as reported in the Estate Tax return and as recommended by the examiner. Where there are credits for prior transfers, or a charitable or marital deduction, the computation will be included, as well as the computations showing the manner in which the deficiency has been determined.

FORM NO. 55

Thirty Day Letter

U. S. Treasury Department
Internal Revenue Service
District Director
210 Livingston Street
Brooklyn 1, N. Y.

In replying refer to:
BKN:A:FA:EG:First New York

Jan. 10, 1960

Katherine Benson, Executrix
100 Elm Street
Copiague, L. I., N. Y.
Dear Madam:

The attached report, which has been carefully reviewed by this office, discloses certain adjustments or conclusions resulting from the examination of the return for the estate indicated therein.

If you accept the findings, please execute the enclosed agreement form and return it to this office promptly. If you do not accept the findings, you may, WITHIN 30 DAYS from the date of this letter, file a protest in accordance with the enclosed instructions. Any protest filed will be given careful consideration and a conference will be granted by the Appellate Division of the Regional Commissioner's office, if requested.

Submission of the agreement form will expedite assessment of the proposed deficiency and stop the running of interest thereon thirty days after receipt of the form, or on the date of assessment, or on the date of payment, whichever is earlier. If desired, payment of the proposed deficiency may be made without awaiting assessment by making remittance therefor payable to the District Director of Internal Revenue, 210 Livingston Street, Brooklyn 1, N. Y. enclosing this letter or a copy thereof.   The remittance should include interest on the additional tax (exclusive of penalties, if any) computed at 6% per annum from the due date of the return to the date of the payment.

This is not a statutory notice of deficiency.   If, however, upon the expiration of the 30-day period you have not submitted the agreement form or a written protest or advised that the deficiency has been paid or will be paid upon notice and demand, a statutory notice will then be sent you as provided by law.

Prompt execution and return of the enclosed receipt form indicating your position with respect to the findings disclosed by the report will be greatly appreciated.

Very truly yours,
Thomas E. Scanlon
District Director of Internal Revenue

Enclosures:
    Report of Examination
    Agreement Form
    Receipt Form
    Instructions

Enclosed in the thirty day letter will be the line adjustments made by the Estate Tax examiner, which indicates schedule by schedule the totals as returned, the changes made in the schedules by the examiner, and the corrected totals as adjusted. There is also a recomputation of the tax showing the amount as returned, the corrected amount, and the deficiency or over-assessment, as the case may be.   When there have been credits for prior transfers,[12] or the charitable deduction,[13] or marital deduction,[14] is interrelated to death taxes, the computations showing how these have been affected by the changes are also annexed to the report.

12. See §§ 302 et seq, supra.   14. See §§ 287 et seq, supra.
13. See §§ 281 et seq, supra.

FORM NO. 56

Line Adjustments

Estate of WINTHROP BENSON   Date of Death   Schedule 1
March 15, 1959

Item	Return (a)	Additions to Value of Estate (b)	Deductions from Value of Estate (c)	Corrected (d)
A Real estate	$ 38,083.00			$ 38,083.00
B Stocks and bonds	74,233.60	$12,328.80		86,462.40
C Mortgages, notes, and cash	17,994.24			17,994.24
D Insurance	57,770.00			57,770.00
E Jointly owned property	5,006.00	2,000.00		7,006.00
F Other miscellaneous property	156,220.00			156,220.00
G Transfers during decedent's life .	2,001.11	3,835.00		5,836.11
H Powers of appointment	14,397.80			14,397.80
I Annuities				
Total Gross Estate	$365,705.75	$18,163.80		$383,869.55
J 1. Funeral expenses and expenses incurred in administering property subject to claims	$ 18,070.87	93.54		$ 18,164.41
K 2. Debts of decedent	14,062.07			14,062.07
K 3. Mortgages and liens	15,025.00			15,025.00
4. Total of items 1 through 3 ...	$ 47,157.94			$ 47,251.48
5. Allowable amount of above deductions	$ 47,157.94			$ 47,251.48
L 6. Net losses during administration				
L 7. Expenses incurred in administering property not subject to claims				
8. Total of items 5 through 7 ...	$ 47,157.94			$ 47,251.48
M 9. Bequests, etc., to surviving spouse	$144,010.64			$144,010.64
10. Adjusted gross estate	318,547.81			336,618.07
11. Net amount deductible for bequests, etc., to surviving spouse (item 9 or ½ of item 10, whichever is smaller)	$144,010.64			$144,010.64
N 12. Charitable, public, and similar gifts and bequests	23,544.00			23,544.00
Total Allowable Deductions, except specific exemption (totals of lines 8, 11, and 12)	$214,712.58			$214,806.12
Specific exemption	60,000.00			60,000.00
Total deductions	$274,712.58			$274,806.12
Taxable Estate	$ 90,993.17			$109,063.43

473

FORM NO. 57

Computation of Estate Tax

Estate of   WINTHROP BENSON   Date of Death   Schedule 2
                                    March 15, 1959

Part I

Item	Return	Corrected
1. Gross estate tax	$17,248.29	$23,419.03
2. Credit for State death taxes	415.89	705.01
3. Gross estate tax less credit for State death taxes	16,832.40	22,714.02

(*item 1 minus item 2*)

Part II

4. Credit for Federal gift taxes ....
5. Credit for tax on prior transfers ....
6. Credit for foreign death taxes ....
7. Total of credits under Part II (*total of items 4, 5, and 6*) ....
8. Net estate tax payable (*item 3 minus item 7*) $16,832.40 $22,714.02
9.
10. Deficiency/overassessment 5,888.62

Remarks   (*Explain if the tax determination may be adjusted due to credit evidence*)

(Note: If at the time of the audit evidence of the payment of State death taxes had not been submitted, the amount of the deficiency would be increased by the above credit, with a notation that if the evidence be furnished by a specific date, the deficiency would be reduced accordingly)

FORM NO. 58

Credit for Tax on Prior Transfers

Estate of   WINTHROP BENSON   Date of Death   March 15, 1959

Part I—Transferor's Tax on Prior Transfers

1. Value of transfers in transferor's estate
Insurance, jointly owned property, annuities, transfers, etc. ....
Specific bequests ....
Interest in residuary estate ....
Life estates, remainder interests, etc. ....

    Total value of prior transfers ....
Less: Reductions:
    Transferee's share of taxes of prior estate
      Fed. estate tax ....
      State taxes ....
      Foreign taxes ....
    Mortgages, liens, etc. ....
    Obligations assumed ....
    Marital deduction ....

Net value of transfers (Item 1, Schedule R) ....

2. Value of transferor's estate
Taxable estate ....
Add: Specific exemption ....

    Total ....
Deduct:
    Federal estate tax ....
    State taxes ....
    Foreign taxes ....

Value of transferor's estate as adjusted (Item 2, Schedule R) ....

3. Tax on transferor's estate
Federal estate tax paid by transferor's estate ....
Add: Credits allowed transferor's estate:
    Gift tax credit ....
    Credit for tax on prior transfers received from
    a prior transferor who died within 10 years of
    decedent. ....

Taxes on transferor's estate as adjusted (Item 3, Schedule R) ....

4. Transferor's tax on prior transfers
   Enter that portion of Item 3 which Item 1 bears to Item 2.
   (Item 4, Schedule R) ....

Part II—Transferee's Tax on Prior Transfers

5. Transferee's tax computed without regard to credit allowed
   under this schedule. *If charitable or marital deductions
   are affected by the tax, then, for purposes of Item 5, such
   deductions shall be determined as though no credit were
   allowed for tax paid by the transferor's estate.* ....
   Less: Credits allowed for
   State taxes ....
   Foreign taxes ....
   Gift tax ....

   Transferee's tax without credit (Item 5, Schedule R) ....

6. Transferee's reduced gross estate
   Gross estate as corrected ....
   Less: Item 1, Schedule R ....

   Transferee's reduced gross estate (Item 6, Schedule R) ....

7. Transferee's deductions
   Debts and charges not affected by transferred property ....
   Marital deduction computed after eliminating property
      shown as Item 1, Schedule R ....
   Charitable deduction (reduced by that proportion of amount
      otherwise deductible which Item 1, Schedule R bears to
      gross estate, less debts and charges). ....
   Specific exemption ....
   Transferee's deductions as adjusted (Item 7, Schedule K) . ...

8. Transferee's reduced taxable estate
   Item 6 (above) ....
   Less: Item 7 (above) ....
   Transferee's reduced taxable estate (Item 8, Schedule R) ... .

9. Tax on reduced taxable estate
   Federal estate tax on Item 8 (after credit for State taxes) ....
   Less:
      Credit for gift taxes ....
      Foreign death duties under the Statute ....

   Tax on the reduced taxable estate (Item 9, Schedule K) ... .

10. Transferee's tax on prior transfers

    Item 5 (above) ....

    Less: Item 9 (above) ....

    Transferee's tax on prior transfers (Item 10, Schedule R) .. ..

Part III—Credit Allowable

11. Item 4 of Part I ....

    Item 10 of Part II ....

    Enter the smaller amount (Item II, Schedule R) ....

12. Date of Death

    Transferor:

    Transferee:

    Time Lapse   Yrs.

    Percentage allowable (Item 12, Schedule R) ....%

13. Credit allowable (Item 12 × Item 11) ....

FORM NO. 59

Computation of Marital and/or Charitable Deduction

Estate of WINTHROP BENSON   Date of Death   March 15, 1959

Item	Trial	True
1. Gross estate	$........	$........
Less: Funeral expenses, administration expenses, debts, liens, etc.	....	....
2. Adjusted gross estate	....	....
Less: Specific bequests and assets not administered by executors		
Life insurance (not to estate) .. $........		
Jointly owned assets		
Transfers and powers of appointment		
Specific bequests to other than spouse		
Specific bequests to spouse		
Specific bequests to charities	....	....
Residue before taxes	....	....
Less: Fixed State and Foreign Taxes	....	....

Item	Trial	True
Net residue before Federal and unfixed State Taxes	....	....

3. By reference to tax tables insert in the trial col. an estimated New York and Federal tax in an amount slightly less than the approximate amount of both taxes

Federal tax ....

N. Y. State tax ....

_____   _____

4. Net residue after deducting estimated taxes .. ..
5. Amount of residue passing to

	Trial	True		
spouse ....% $........ $........				
charity ....%	....	....	....	....

6. Specific bequests, life insurance, jointly owned property, etc. passing to

spouse ....

charity ....

_____   _____

7. Total passing to spouse and/or charity (Item 5 plus Item 6) ....
8. Adjusted gross estate (Same as Item 2) ....
9. Less:

Charitable bequests ... $........ $........

Amount passing to spouse (Limit to ½ of Item 8) ....

_____   _____

10. Net estate (Item 8 minus Item 9) ....
11. Specific exemption ....

_____   _____

12. Net taxable estate (Item 10 minus Item 11) ... .
13. Complete block from Table K, Col. 1 ....

_____   _____

14. Excess (Item 12 minus Item 13) ....
15. Rate of tax on excess (from Table K, Col. 4) .. ..% ......%

_____   _____

16. Net tax on excess (Item 14 multiplied by Item 15) ....

Item	Trial	True
17. Tax on complete block (from Table K, Col. 3)	....	....
18. Net Federal tax before foreign tax credits or gift tax credit (Item 16 plus Item 17)	....	....
19. Credits		
Foreign tax .... $........ $........		
Gift tax	....	....
20. Net Federal tax after credits (Item 18 minus Item 19)	$........	$........
21. Net N. Y. State Tax (from Table below, Line K)	....	....
22. Total Estate taxes	....	....
23. Assumed total taxes (same as Item 3)	....	....
24. Excess over assumed tax (Item 22 minus Item 23)	....	....

25. Formula for corrective figure:

$$1.00 - \frac{\text{Item } 24}{\dfrac{\text{Item } 5}{\text{Item } 4} \times (\text{Item } 15 + \text{F})} =$$

If "Amount passing to spouse", Item 9 above, was reduced to ½ of Item 8, substitute for Item 5 in the formula the part of Item 5 passing only to charity. ....

26. Assumed taxes (same as Item 3) ....

27. Net true Federal and N. Y. State taxes (Item 25 plus Item 26) *Insert this amount in Item 3, True col. and continue computation in True col. to Item 22. Proof: Item 22, True col. should equal Item 27, Trial col.* ....

Computation of New York State Tax

	Item	Trial	True
A.	Adjusted gross income (Same as Item 2) ...	....	....
B.	Less		
	Charitable bequests Same as		
	Amount passing to Item 9		
	spouse	....	....
C.	Net estate (A minus B)	....	....
D.	Complete block from N. Y. State Tax Table .	....	....
E.	Excess (C minus D)	....	....

479

Item		Trial	True
F.	Rate of tax on excess from N. Y. State Tax Table	......%	......%
G.	Net tax on excess (E multiplied by F)	....	....
H.	Tax on complete block from N. Y. State Tax Table	....	....
I.	Net N. Y. State Tax before discounts and exemptions	....	....
J.	Credits		
	Discount allowed	....	....
	Exemptions	....	....
K.	Net N. Y. State tax after discounts and exemptions (I minus J)	....	....

FORM NO. 60
When No Credit for State Death Taxes

Estate Tax

Waiver of Restrictions on Assessment and Collection
of Deficiency and Acceptance of Overassessment

Pursuant to the provisions of section 6213(d) of the Internal Revenue Code of 1954 or corresponding provisions of prior internal revenue laws, the undersigned executor or administrator waives the restrictions provided in sections 6212(a) and 6213(a) of the Internal Revenue Code of 1954, or corresponding provisions of prior internal revenue laws, and consents to the assessment and collection of the following deficiency, together with interest on the tax as provided by law, and accepts the following overassessment as correct:

	Deficiency	*Overassessment*
TAX	$3986.24	$............
PENALTY	$ 14.26	$............
TOTAL	$3996.90	$............

Estate of WINTHROP BENSON

By ....

Executor or Administrator.

Jan. 5, 1960   100 Elm Street, Copiague, L. I., N. Y.
(Date)   (Address)

NOTE.—The execution and filing of this form will expedite the adjustment of the tax liability as indicated above. It is not, however, a final closing agreement under section 7121 of the Internal Revenue Code of 1954, and does not, therefore, preclude the assertion of a deficiency or a further deficiency in the manner provided by law should it subsequently be determined that additional tax is due; nor does it extend the statutory period of limitation for refund, assessment, or collection of the tax.

FORM NO. 61

When Credit for State Death Taxes

Estate Tax

Waiver of Restrictions on Assessment and Collection of
Deficiency and Acceptance of Overassessment

Pursuant to the provisions of section 6213(d) of the Internal Revenue
Code of 1954 or corresponding provisions of prior internal revenue laws,
the undersigned executor or administrator waives the restrictions provided in sections 6212(a) and 6213(a) of the Internal Revenue Code of
1954, or corresponding provisions of prior internal revenue laws, and
consents to the assessment and collection of the following deficiency,
together with interest on the tax as provided by law, and accepts the
following overassessment as correct:

	Deficiency	Overassessment
TAX	$3,982.64	$............
PENALTY	$ 14.26	$............
TOTAL	$3,996.90	$............

It is understood that evidence of payment of estate inheritance, legacy
or succession taxes to any of the several States, Territories or the District
of Columbia (or if the decedent died after June 29, 1939, to any possession of the United States), as required by Section 81.9 of Regulations 105
will be filed with the District Director of Internal Revenue, 210 Livingston Street, Brooklyn 1, N. Y., as promptly as practicable. In the event
that such evidence is not filed on or before March 15, 1960 the undersigned executor or administrator waives the restrictions provided in
Section 308(a) of the Revenue Act of 1926, or Section 871(a) of the
Internal Revenue Code, and consents to the assessment and collection of
a deficiency in estate tax in the sum of $4,650.91. together with in-
terest thereon at the statutory rate to the 30th day after April 10, 1960
or until the deficiency is assessed, whichever is the earlier.

Estate of WINTHROP BENSON
By ....
Executor or Administrator.

Jan. 5, 1960   100 Elm Street, Copiague, L. I., N. Y.
(Date)   (Address)

NOTE.—The execution and filing of this form will expedite the adjustment of the tax liability as indicated above. It is not, however, a final
closing agreement under section 7121 of the Internal Revenue Code of
1954, and does not, therefore, preclude the assertion of a deficiency or a
further deficiency in the manner provided by law should it subsequently
be determined that additional tax is due; nor does it extend the statutory
period of limitation for refund, assessment, or collection of the tax.

FORM NO. 62

Receipt of Estate Tax Examiner's Report

Please sign and return immediately

Office of District Director of Internal Revenue

City and State   First New York

Date   Jan. 10, 1960

Receipt is hereby acknowledged of your letter dated ....
enclosing report prepared by Estate Tax Examiner Samuel A. Brander,
covering the Estate Tax, showing a deficiency of $3,996.90.

Signed Agreement Form ...... has already been forwarded to
your office .... [ ]*

A signed Agreement Form has not previously been forwarded to
your office, and the position of the undersigned is indicated by
the check mark(s) hereunder:

1. Estate Tax Examiner's findings are accepted .... [ ]
   (a) Signed Agreement Form ...... is enclosed herewith .... [ ]
   (b) Payment of any deficiency in tax indicated above has
       already been made to the District Director of Internal
       Revenue .... [ ]
   (c) Payment of any deficiency in tax indicated above will be
       made to the District Director of Internal Revenue upon
       receipt of notice and demand, and no objection will be
       made to the immediate assessment of the tax .... [ ]
2. Estate Tax Examiner's findings are not accepted .... [ ]
3. Protest will be filed within the allotted time .... [ ]
4. I do not intend to protest these findings .... [ ]
                    Taxpayer ....**
                    By ....

* If signed agreement form has already been forwarded, check this block only,
    disregard the balance of the form, and sign and return it to this office.
** If taxpayer is a corporation, the corporate name should be typed and signature
    should be by duly authorized officer of the corporation.

IMPORTANT: It is essential that communications transmitting this
form, or protests, or agreements, relative to the above-mentioned determination should be addressed to the District Director of Internal Revenue, Audit Division.

FORM NO. 63

Instructions as to the Preparation of Protests Against Findings of Examining Officers

The protest and any additional statement of facts must be submitted to this office within 30 days of the date of the letter with which these instructions are enclosed. Such protest and statement must be submitted in triplicate under oath of the taxpayer (in the case of a corporation, the oath of a duly constituted officer). The oath requirement may be satisfied by executing the original of the protest under oath and conforming the remaining copies to the original, that is, by making the copies identical with the original except that, in lieu of the signatures of the executing parties appearing on the original, the names of the executing parties may be inserted on the copies by typewriter or otherwise. The protest must contain the following information:

(a) The name and address of the taxpayer (in the case of an individual, the residence, and in the case of a corporation, the principal office or place of business);

(b) The designation by date and symbol of the letter advising of the proposed adjustments in tax liability with respect to which the protest is made;

(c) The designation of the year or years involved;

(d) An itemized schedule of the findings to which the taxpayer takes exception;

(e) A statement of the facts upon which the taxpayer relies with respect to each issue it is desired to contest. No reduction in taxes proposed nor increases in allowance of claims will be made unless the facts relied upon are submitted in writing and in verified form. All evidence except that of a supplementary or incidental character shall be submitted over the sworn signature of the taxpayer;

(f) In case the taxpayer desires a hearing, a statement to that effect;

(g) In case the protest is prepared or filed by an attorney or agent, in addition to the signature of the taxpayer, it shall have thereon a statement signed by such attorney or agent showing whether or not he prepared it and whether or not the attorney or agent knows of his own knowledge that the facts therein are true.

In case the taxpayer is represented by an attorney or agent, it is essential that such representative be admitted to practice before the United States Treasury Department and be provided with a power of attorney, signed by the taxpayer, authorizing him to act for the taxpayer. Powers of attorney must be furnished in duplicate with one additional copy for each taxable year in excess of one. If a power of attorney covering pertinent years is presently on file, a new power of attorney will not be necessary unless the taxpayer employs a different representative.

Attention of representatives is called to the necessity of filing with this office a "Statement Relative to Fees" as required by Treasury Department Circular No. 230 (revised).

Your Appellate Rights

Upon receipt of a letter from the office of the District Director of Internal Revenue advising you of a proposed adjustment of your tax, you may execute an agreement form consenting to the adjustment or file a protest with the office from which the letter was received, and request a hearing before the Appellate Division of the Regional Commissioner's Office, if one is desired, in accordance with the above instructions. At such a hearing you may appear personally or be represented by an attorney or agent, also as provided in the instructions.

In the event an agreement or a written protest is not filed with the District Director of Internal Revenue, or in case a written protest is filed with the District Director of Internal Revenue, and an agreement is not reached in the Appellate Division of the Regional Commissioner's Office, and your case involves a deficiency, a final notice of the deficiency will be issued in which you will be granted 90 days within which to file a petition with The Tax Court of the United States.

If a petition is filed and docketed, the Appellate Division of the Regional Commissioner's Office will afford you an opportunity to settle your case without the necessity of a trial before The Tax Court. If a settlement cannot be reached, your case will be set down for a hearing before The Tax Court.

Appeal from the decision of The Tax Court may be made to the U. S. Court of Appeals.

If an overassessment only is proposed, the procedure is the same as above, except that your appellate rights do not extend beyond the Appellate Division of the Regional Commissioner's Office, unless the case involves a claim for refund disallowed in whole or in part. In such case, you may file suit with the United States District Court or the United States Court of Claims.

§ 336. Definition of Deficiency.

When the adjustments made by the Estate Tax examiner result in a greater amount of tax than shown in the return filed, the excess is known as a deficiency. The Code defines the term "deficiency" as the amount by which the tax imposed by subtitles A and B (subtitle B covering Estate and Gift Tax) exceeds the excess of—

(1) the sum of

(A) the amount shown as the tax by the taxpayer upon his

return, if a return was made by the taxpayer and an amount was shown by the taxpayer thereon, plus

(B) the amounts previously assessed (or collected without assessment) as a deficiency, over—

(2) the amount of rebates, as defined in subsection (b)(2), made.[15]

The term "rebate" means so much of an abatement, credit, refund, or other repayment, as was made on the ground that the tax imposed was less than the excess of the amount specified above in (1) over the rebates previously made.[16]

§ 337. Procedure After Report; Protest.

Upon receipt of the thirty day letter and the Estate Tax examiner's report, acknowledgment of its receipt is made on the enclosed receipt.[17] It is also necessary at that time to determine whether to pay the tax at that point or pursue the matter further. This involves a matter of judgment. If the amount of the deficiency does not merit further legal expense, the fiduciary will execute the Waiver of Restrictions on Assessment and Collection of Deficiency, referred to in the thirty day letter as Agreement Form, and return it with the receipt to the Estate Tax Examiner. In due course, the executor will receive a notice of assessment of the deficiency.

If, however, the executor is dissatisfied and desires to continue further, then he may either file a protest and present the matter further before the Appellate Division of the Regional Commissioner's office, or wait for the ninety day letter before going to the Tax Court. As we shall see, he may also pay the tax, without executing the waiver, and after application for refund, institute action for recovery of the tax paid.

In many cases it is advantageous to file the protest, since many cases are settled in the Appellate Division. In preparing the protest, the instructions should be followed carefully. The protest must be *in triplicate,* and *under oath.* The attorney should not act as notary. There must also be attached a statement by the attorney preparing the protest, of such fact, and whether he knows of his own knowledge that the facts therein are true. If the attorney is not admitted to practice before the Treasury Department he may not appear, and in all events, if a

15. IRC, § 6211(a) (1954 Code).   17. Form 62, § 335, supra.
16. IRC, § 6211(b)(2) (1954 Code).

power of attorney and statement relative to fees has not theretofore been filed, it must be done so before he can appear.[18]

FORM NO. 64

Protest

Feb 2, 1960

District Director of Internal Revenue
210 Livingston Street,
Brooklyn 1, N. Y.
Re : Katherine Benson, as
    Executrix of Winthrop Benson, Dcsd.
    100 Elm Street, Copiague, L. I., N. Y.
        Reference : AU :F :EG :SAB—1st New York

Sir :

In accordance with the permission granted in your letter of Jan. 10, 1960, reference above, advising that the examination of the Estate Tax Return in the above estate discloses a deficiency in the Federal Estate Tax liability of the above named estate of $5,888.62, protest is hereby made against such determination and the following facts are submitted in support thereof:

A. Name and address of taxpayer.
    Katherine Benson, as Executrix of the Estate of Winthrop Benson, 100 Elm Street, Copiague, L. I., N. Y.

B. Date and symbols of your letter.
    Jan. 10, 1960, AU :F :EG :SAB—1st New York

C. Tax involved and tax disputed.
    The tax involved is the net estate tax payable, and the amount thereof disputed is the deficiency, to wit, $5,888.62 is protested by the taxpayer.

D. Findings to which taxpayer takes exception.
    The taxpayer takes exception to the findings of the report including in the gross estate the value of item 1, of the joint property of the decedent and Katherine Benson, and the value of the alleged transfer of 100 shares of the stock of Winthrop Benson, Inc.
    Exception is taken to the finding that $2,000 of the joint account in the name of the decedent and Katherine Benson is taxable under the provisions of Section 2040 of the Internal Revenue Code of 1954.
    Exception is taken to the finding that 100 shares of the stock of

18. Instructions, Form 63, § 335, supra.

Winthrop Benson, Inc. is includible in the gross estate of the decedent under the provisions of Section 2037 of the Internal Revenue Code of 1954.

E. Statement of facts upon which taxpayer relies.

The joint account consisted of funds, no part of which were contributed by the decedent.

The transfer of the stock of Winthrop Benson, Inc. was concededly not made in contemplation of death, and the evidence submitted with the return establishes that the transfer was a completed gift, the decedent retaining no interest, dominion, or control over the property.

The taxpayer further incorporates herein the memoranda of law submitted simultaneously with the Estate Tax Return herein, with the same force and effect as if set forth at length herein.

F. Oral hearing requested.

The taxpayer requests an oral hearing before the Appellate Division of the Regional Commissioner's Office.

> Respectfully submitted,
>
> KATHERINE BENSON, Executrix of the Estate of Winthrop Benson, Dcsd.

STATE OF NEW YORK
COUNTY OF SUFFOLK } ss:

KATHERINE BENSON, being first duly sworn, says that she is the above named Executrix of the Estate of Winthrop Benson, deceased, and as such is duly authorized to execute this protest; that she has read the foregoing protest and is familiar with the statements contained therein and that the facts stated are true to the best of her knowledge, information and belief.

> KATHERINE BENSON

Subscribed and sworn to before me
this 2nd day of Feb. 1960
ANDREA HAYS
Notary Public
Suffolk County

The above protest was prepared by the undersigned DANIEL WEBSTER CLAY, attorney for the above named taxpayer, who is informed and believes that the facts contained therein are true, although he does not know the same of his own knowledge.

> DANIEL WEBSTER CLAY
> Attorney for Taxpayer

§ 337A. Procedure After Report; Hearing in Appellate Division.

After the protest to the thirty day letter has been received by the District Director, the case will be transferred to the Appellate Division of the Regional Commissioner's Office. In spite of its imposing title, it is a branch of the Internal Revenue Service operating as an appeal bureau or agency of the Service. This branch was formerly known as the Technical Staff. A conference will be arranged for a mutually agreeable time. Briefs may be submitted at least five days before the date of the hearing. Additional facts not presented theretofore will not be considered. Although designated a hearing, it is in fact a conference, and informal. No testimony is taken. The attorney representing the Commissioner is thoroughly versed in the matters to be discussed. He will be found to be reasonable. He can be convinced, but the facts or law involved must be clearly presented. Unless the attorney representing the taxpayer has prepared his case, the hearing is likely to be a waste of time. On the other hand, it will be found that an adjustment may be made at this level, which was not possible until such time.

§ 337B. Procedure After Report; Ninety Day Letter.

If the hearing in the Appellate Division does not result in an adjustment, or if no protest was filed to the thirty day letter, within a short time there will be received the ninety day letter which advises that a deficiency has been determined. There will be enclosed the notice of deficiency, the waiver referred to,[19] and a notice advising of the procedure if an appeal to the Tax Court of the United States is determined upon. If no appeal is to be taken, then the waiver is executed and returned and an assessment will be received shortly thereafter. If an appeal is determined upon to the Tax Court, the procedure thereupon is treated hereafter in the chapters dealing with such appeals.

19. Forms 60 and 61, § 335, supra.

FORM NO. 65

Ninety Day Letter

U. S. Treasury Department
Internal Revenue Service
Brooklyn, N. Y.

Office of District Director of Internal Revenue

In Replying Refer To:
AU:F:EG:SAB—1st New York

March 15, 1960

Katherine Benson, Executrix
100 Elm Street
Copiague, L. I., N. Y.

Dear Madam:

In accordance with the provisions of existing internal revenue laws, notice is hereby given of the deficiency or deficiencies mentioned.

Within 90 days from the date of the mailing of this letter you may file a petition with The Tax Court of the United States, at its principal address, WASHINGTON 4, D. C., for a redetermination of the deficiency. In counting the 90 days you may not exclude any day unless the 90th day is a Saturday, Sunday, or legal holiday in the District of Columbia in which event that day is not counted as the 90th day. Otherwise Saturdays, Sundays, and legal holidays are to be counted in computing the 90-day period.

Should you not desire to file a petition, you are requested to execute the enclosed form and forward it to the District Director of Internal Revenue, Audit Division, 210 Livingston Street, Brooklyn 1, N. Y. The signing and filing of this form will expedite the closing of your return(s) by permitting an early assessment of the deficiency or deficiencies, and will prevent the accumulation of interest, since the interest period terminates 30 days after receipt of the form, or on the date of assessment, or on the date of payment, whichever is the earliest.

Very truly yours,
RUSSELL C. HARRINGTON
Commissioner,
By THOMAS E. SCANLON
District Director of Internal
Revenue.

Enclosures:
Statement
IRS Publication No. 160
Agreement Form

FORM NO. 66

Notice of Requirements for Appeal to Tax Court

Publication No. 160 (Rev. 6-55)
U. S. Treasury Department
Internal Revenue Service

NOTICE

Appeals Should Be Addressed To
The Tax Court of the United States
Washington 4, D. C.

IF YOU DECIDE TO INITIATE A PROCEEDING BEFORE THE TAX COURT OF THE UNITED STATES, an original and four carbon copies of your petition, embodying a copy of the deficiency notice enclosed herewith, should be prepared in accordance with the Rules of Practice of said Tax Court (especially rules 4, 5, 6, 7, and 26). (A copy of the Rules of Practice will be furnished free upon request to the Tax Court.) Under the Internal Revenue Code of 1954 and the rules of the Tax Court, a petition (together with a filing fee of $10) must be delivered in sufficient time to be RECEIVED AND FILED OF RECORD BY THE TAX COURT, at its principal address, WASHINGTON 4, D. C., within the number of days indicated in attached notice after the attached registered notice is mailed (not counting Saturday, Sunday, or legal holiday in the District of Columbia as the last day of the time specified). If the petition is mailed, the date of the United States postmark, or the date of registration if sent by United States registered mail, shall be deemed to be the date of delivery. THE NUMBER OF DAYS WITHIN WHICH A PETITION MAY BE FILED WITH THE TAX COURT CANNOT BE EXTENDED.

The Tax Court of the United States is in no way connected with the Internal Revenue Service or the Treasury Department. Under no circumstances should a petition for redetermination be forwarded to the Commissioner of Internal Revenue or a district director of internal revenue.

§ 338. Payment; Time and Place.

The Estate Tax is payable at the time fixed for filing the return.[20] The time fixed for the filing of the return is, as we have seen,[1] fifteen months from the date of death. The tax is therefore payable fifteen months after the decedent's death. The time for such payment may be extended.

If the tax is due fifteen months after the decedent's death, the

---

20. IRC, § 6151(a) (1954 Code).   1. § 28, supra.

due date is the day of the fifteenth calendar month after his death, numerically corresponding to the day of the calendar month on which death occurred, except that if there is no numerically corresponding day in the fifteenth month, the last day of the fifteenth month is the due date. Thus, if the decedent died on August 31st, the due date is November 30th, fifteen months later.[2]

There is no discount for prepayment,[3] so that if the amount of tax is substantial, it is advisable not to pay the tax at the time of filing the return, so that the tax payment may earn interest until the due date.

The place at which payment is made is at the office of the principal Internal Revenue officer for the Internal Revenue district in which the return is required to be filed.[4]

§ 339. Extension of Time for Payment; Hardship; Generally.

If the Secretary or his delegate finds that the payment on the due date of any part of the amount determined by the executor as the tax would result in undue hardship to the estate, he may extend the time for payment for a reasonable period, not in excess of ten years from the date fixed for payment of the tax.[5]

In the case of the amount determined as a deficiency, the amount thereof can be extended for a period not to exceed four years from the date otherwise fixed for payment of the deficiency.[6]

The extension will not be granted upon a general statement of hardship. The term "undue hardship" means more than an inconvenience to the estate. It must appear that substantial financial loss, for example, due to the sale of property at a sacrifice price, will result to the estate from making payment of the tax at the due date. If a market exists, a sale of property at the current market price is not ordinarily considered as resulting in an undue hardship.[7] The application is not pro forma. It is necessary to make a real showing that a sale cannot be made at current market prices to provide the money for payment of the tax or the deficiency and that the money cannot be borrowed upon reasonable terms.[8]

2. Reg, § 20.6075-1.
3. Reg, 105, § 81.75.
4. Note 20, supra.
5. IRC, § 6161(a)(2) (1954 Code).
6. IRC, § 6161(b)(2) (1954 Code).
7. Reg, § 20.6161-1(b).
8. See Mim 4303, CB XIV-1, 133.

The application for the extension must be in writing and must contain, or be supported by, information under the penalties of perjury showing the undue hardship that would result to the estate if the request were refused. The application is filed with the District Director, who has discretion to grant or deny the extension, or impose conditions. A determination will usually be made within thirty days. The application must be made before the due date. No single extension for more than a year will be granted, and if a further extension is requested, application must be made before the date of the expiration of the previous extension.[9]

If the extension is granted a bond may be required. This cannot exceed double the amount of the tax.[10] The amount of tax for which an extension is granted must be paid on or before the expiration of the period of the extension without the necessity of notice and demand from the Director. Payment of the amount for which the extension was granted and the additions thereto will not relieve the fiduciary from paying the entire amount of interest provided for in the extension, nor will the extension relieve the fiduciary from filing the return within the required time, nor will it operate to prevent the running of interest. The running of the statute of limitations for assessment and collection is suspended for the period of the extension, and the extension may extend the time within which the credit for foreign death duties or State death taxes are required to be paid and credit claimed.[11]

The application for extension is made by affidavit reciting fully and completely *the facts* which will establish undue hardship. The bond is executed upon Form 1127-B, which will be furnished by the District Director's office if the extension is granted. Not many extensions are granted.

The Small Business Tax Revision Act of 1958 added two subdivisions[12] to the provision for extension of time for payment of the tax, and enacted a new section[12a] providing for installment payments of the Estate Tax where the estate consists largely of

9. Reg, §§ 20.6161–1(a)(c); 20.6161–2(a)(c).

10. IRC, § 6165 (1954 Code); Reg, § 20.6161–1(a).

11. Reg, §§ 20.6161–1(d)(e); 20.6161–2(d)(e); IRC, § 6503(d) (1954 Code).

12. IRC, § 6161(a)(2)(B)(C) (1954 Code), as added by Small Business Tax Revision Act of 1958, § 206(c), HR 8381, 85th Cong, 2nd Sess.

12a. IRC, § 6166 (1954 Code), added by Small Business Tax Revision Act of 1958, § 206(a), HR 8381, 85th Cong, 2nd Sess.

an interest or interests in a closely held business or businesses. The provisions of the new section are treated in the succeeding section.

The same general requirements exist with respect to extension of time to pay a deficiency, except as to the time period, as noted above.

§ 340. Extension of Time for Payment; Where Estate Consists Largely of Interest in Closely Held Business.

Where the estate of the decedent consisted largely of an interest in a closely held business, the heirs were often faced with the necessity of either breaking up the business or selling it to strangers in order to raise the funds necessary for the payment of the Estate Tax imposed upon and resulting from the decedent's ownership of such interest. In order to make it possible to keep together such a business enterprise, Congress enacted in the Small Business Tax Revision Act of 1958 a new section to be added to the 1954 Code, granting to the fiduciary an election to make payment of the tax in installments. In order to take advantage of the provision, however, all of the requirements of the section must be met, *since the statute does not apply to every case in which a closely held business is an estate asset.*

If the value of an interest in a closely held business which is included in determining the gross estate of a decedent who was (at the date of his death) a citizen or resident of the United States exceeds *either*

(1) *35 percent of* the value of the *gross estate* of such decedent, *or*

(2) *50 percent* of the *taxable estate* of such decedent, the executor may elect to pay part or all of the tax in two or more (but not exceeding 10) equal installments. Any such election shall be made not later than the time prescribed for the filing of the return (including extensions thereof), and shall be made in such manner as the Secretary or his delegate shall by regulation prescribe. If an election under the section is made, the provisions of the subtitle shall apply as though the Secretary or his delegate were extending the time for payment of the tax. For the purposes of the section, value shall be value determined for Federal Estate Tax purposes.[12b]

12b. IRC, § 6166(a) (1954 Code), added by Small Business Tax Revision   Act of 1958, § 206(a), HR 8381, 85th Cong, 2nd Sess.

The maximum amount of tax which may be paid in installments shall be an amount which bears the same ratio to the tax imposed as the value of the interest in a closely held business which qualifies, bears to the value of the gross estate.[12c] Thus, if the gross estate is $1,000,000. and the decedent's interest in a closely held business is $400,000., since it exceeds 35% of the gross estate, the estate qualifies for installment payment, but only to the extent of $400,000./$1,000,000. or 40% of the tax.

For the purposes of the section, the term "interest in a closely held business" means—

(1) an interest as a proprietor in a trade or business carried on as a proprietorship,

(2) an interest as a partner in a partnership carrying on a trade or business, *if*

(A) the decedent owned 20% or more of the total capital interest in such partnership, *or*

(B) such partnership had 10 or less partners,

(3) ownership of any stock in a corporation carrying on a trade or business, *if*

(A) the decedent owned 20% or more in value of the *voting stock* of such corporation, *or*

(B) such corporation had 10 or less shareholders.

For the purposes of the subsection, determinations shall be made as of the time immediately before the decedent's death.[12d]

There is a special rule where the decedent owned interests in two or more closely held businesses, with respect to each of which there is included in determining the value of the decedent's gross estate more than 50% of the total value of each such business. In such case the aggregate amount is treated as an interest in a single closely held business. For purposes of this 50% requirement, an interest in a closely held business which represents the surviving spouse's interest in property held by the decedent and the surviving spouse as community property shall be treated as having been included in determining the value of the decedent's gross estate.[12e]

If an election is made to pay the tax in installments, the first installment must be paid on or before the date prescribed for payment of the tax (fifteen months from the date of death),

12c. IRC, § 6166(b) (1954 Code).   12e. IRC, § 6166(d) (1954 Code).
12d. IRC, § 6166(c) (1954 Code).

and each succeeding installment must be paid annually thereafter.[12f]

If an election is made to pay the tax in installments and a deficiency has been assessed, the deficiency shall be prorated to such installments. The part of the deficiency so prorated to any installments *the date for payment of which has not arrived* shall be collected at the same time as, and as a part of, such installment. The part of the deficiency so prorated to any installment *the date for payment of which has arrived* shall be paid upon notice and demand from the Secretary or his delegate. The subsection does not apply if the deficiency is due to negligence, to intentional disregard of rules and regulations, or to fraud with intent to evade tax.[12g]

Interest is payable annually on the unpaid balance of tax at the rate of 4% and at the same time as an installment is paid.[12h]

Since the statute is intended to relieve hardship, in order to avoid the section being used improperly, it provides for acceleration of the tax under certain circumstances.

(1) *If*—

(A) aggregate withdrawals of money or other property from the trade or business, an interest in which qualifies, equal or exceed 50% of the value of such trade or business, *or*

(B) 50% or more of an interest in a closely held business which qualifies, is distributed, sold, exchanged, or otherwise disposed of,

then the extension of time for payment of the tax provided in the section shall cease to apply, and any unpaid portion of the tax payable in installments shall be paid upon notice and demand from the Secretary or his delegate. Subparagraph (B) does not apply to an exchange of stock pursuant to a plan of reorganization described in subparagraph (D), (E), or (F) of section 368 (a)(1), nor to an exchange to which section 355 (or so much of section 356 as relates to section 355) applies; but any stock received in such an exchange shall be treated for purposes of subparagraph (B) as an interest which qualifies under the statute.

(2) (A) If an election is made to make payment in installments *and the estate has undistributed net income for any taxable year after its fourth taxable year,* the executor shall, on or before the date prescribed by law for filing the income tax return

12f. IRC, § 6166(e) (1954 Code).   12h. IRC, § 6166(g) (1954 Code).
12g. IRC, § 6166(f) (1954 Code).

for such taxable year (including extensions thereof), pay an amount equal to such undistributed net income in liquidation of the unpaid portion of the tax payable in installments.

(B) For purposes of subparagraph (A), the undistributed net income of the estate for any taxable year is the amount by which the distributable net income of the estate for such taxable year (as defined in section 643) exceeds the sum of—

(i) the amounts for such taxable years specified in paragraphs (1) and (2) of section 661(a) (relating to deduction for distributions, etc.);

(ii) the amount of tax imposed for the taxable year on the estate under chapter 1; and

(iii) the amount of the Federal Estate Tax (including interest) paid by the executor during the taxable year (other than any amount paid pursuant to this paragraph).

(3) If any installment under the section is not paid on or before the date fixed for its payment by the section (including any extension of time for the payment of such installment), the unpaid portion of the tax payable in installments shall be paid upon notice and demand from the Secretary or his delegate.[12i]

Since the section was enacted and became law on September 2, 1958, it was necessary to enact transitional rules for estates pending before its enactment. Thus it is provided

(1) IN GENERAL—*If—*

(A) a deficiency in the tax imposed is assessed after the date of the enactment of the section, *and*

(B) the estate qualifies under the 35% or 50% provision, the executor may elect to pay the deficiency in installments. The provision does not apply if the deficiency is due to negligence, intentional disregard of rules and regulations, or to fraud with intent to evade tax.

(2) TIME of ELECTION—An election under this subsection must be made not later than 60 days after issuance of notice and demand by the Secretary or his delegate for the payment of the deficiency, and shall be made in such manner as the Secretary or his delegate shall by regulations prescribe.

(3) EFFECT of ELECTION on PAYMENT—If an election is made under this subsection, the deficiency shall (subject to the limitation provided by subsection (b) be prorated to the installments which would have been due if an election had been

12i. IRC, § 6166(h) (1954 Code).

timely made under the section at the time the Estate Tax return was filed. The part of the deficiency so prorated to any installment the date for payment of which would have arrived shall be paid at the time of the making of the election under this subsection. The portion of the deficiency so prorated to installments the date for payment of which would not have so arrived shall be paid at the time such installments would have been due if such an election had been made.

(4) APPLICATION of SUBSECTION(h)(2)—In the case of an election under this subsection, subsection (h)(2) shall not apply with respect to undistributed net income for any taxable year ending before January 1, 1960.[12j]

This new section applies to the estates of decedents dying after the enactment of the 1954 Code, namely, August 17, 1954, but only where the date for filing the Federal Estate Tax return is after September 2, 1958. It also applies to the estates of such persons in the case of a deficiency assessed after the date of the enactment of the Act, where the date for filing the Estate Tax return (including extensions) expired before the date of the enactment of the Act.[12k]

It will be observed that the section is complex and will require not only a thorough examination of the facts in each case to determine whether the estate qualifies to elect to make payment in installments, but also computation of the amount of tax or deficiency attributable to the closely held interest, filing of the election in time, and after the election has been made, keeping in mind the circumstances under which there may be an acceleration of the installments.

Temporary Regulations have been promulgated pending the issuance of final Regulations covering the subject.[121]

§ 341. Payment; Liability for.

The statute bluntly says, "the tax imposed by this chapter shall be paid by the executor."[13] As we have seen, the term executor is not used in the strict sense of that fiduciary relationship, but means not only the executor, but the administrator, or if there be neither appointed, qualified, and acting within the

---

12j. IRC, § 6166(i) (1954 Code).

12k. Small Business Tax Revision Act of 1958, § 206(f), HR 8381, 85th Cong, 2nd Sess.

121. Reg, § 24.1–1 (TD 6321, 1958–43, p 45).

13. IRC, § 2002 (1954 Code).

United States, then any person in actual or constructive possession of any property of the decedent.[14]

The Regulation[15] provides that the duty to pay the tax applies to the entire tax, regardless of the fact that the estate consists in part of property which does not come into the possession of the executor or such other person. If the executor pays a debt or distributes any portion of the estate before all the Estate Tax is paid, he is personally liable, to the extent of the payment or distribution, for so much of the Estate Tax as remains due and unpaid.

The ordinary procedure is for the fiduciary to pay the tax, and as we shall see, there are adequate remedies to effect collection.

§ 342. Payment; How Made; Receipts.

Payment of the tax may be made by check or money order, or by United States notes and certificates of indebtedness.

District Directors may accept checks drawn on any bank or trust company incorporated under the laws of the United States, any State, Territory, or possession of the United States, or money orders, *provided* such checks or money orders are collectible in United States currency at par. A check or money order is payable at par only if the full amount thereof is payable without any deduction for exchanges or other charges. The District Director may refuse to accept any personal check when he has good reason to believe that such check will not be honored upon presentment.[16]

Payment may also be made by Treasury certificates of indebtedness, Treasury notes, or Treasury bills of any series (not including interim receipts issued by Federal Reserve banks in lieu of definitive certificates, notes, or bills). All interest coupons should be detached.[17] The bonds are not delivered to the District Director, but are assigned to "The Secretary of the Treasury for redemption, the proceeds to be paid to the Director of Internal Revenue at .... for credit on Federal Estate Taxes due from the Estate of ...." The bonds must be accompanied by Form PD1782 properly completed and a certificate of letters. The Federal Reserve Bank and the Treasury Department have issued various rulings and circulars delineating the procedure and the bonds which are so redeem-

14. IRC, § 2203 (1954 Code).   16. Reg, § 301.6311–1.
15. Reg, § 20.2002–1.   17. Reg, § 301.6312–1.

able.[18] In New York, a waiver from the State Tax Commission is also required.

While the District Director is required to give a receipt when payment is made in cash, upon request he will do so when payment is made by check, and will also issue the receipt in duplicate when so requested.[19] It is advisable to request duplicate receipts in all cases. The receipt will be sufficient evidence of the payment to entitle the executor to be credited with the amount by any court having jurisdiction to audit or settle his accounts.[20]

§ 343. Collection of Unpaid Tax; Remedies.

If any person liable for payment of the tax neglects or refuses to pay the same within ten days after notice and demand the tax authorities may levy upon all property belonging to such person or on which there is a lien for the tax. If there is a finding that the collection of the tax is in jeopardy, upon notice and demand and failure or refusal to pay the tax, the levy may be made without regard to the ten day limitation.[1] The term "levy" includes the power of distraint and seizure by any means. Thereupon the property may be sold.[2] There may be successive seizures until the amount due is fully paid.[3]

There is also the authority to bring a civil action in the name of the United States to subject the property of the decedent to be sold under the judgment or decree of the court, pay the amount due, and deposit the balance, if any, according to the order of the court.[4]

§ 344. Collection of Unpaid Tax; Reimbursement out of Estate.

While the normal procedure is for the fiduciary to make payment of the tax out of the estate assets, that is not so in all cases. If any portion of the tax is paid by or collected out of that part of the estate passing to, or in the possession of, any person other than the duly qualified executor or administrator, that person may be entitled to reimbursement, either out of the undistributed

---

18. Treasury Dept Circulars, 956, 1000, 1005; Federal Reserve Bank of Chicago, Supplement F to Operating Circular No 15; Appendix to Operating Circular No 17 of Federal Reserve Bank of New York.

19. Reg, § 301.6314-1.

20. Reg, § 301.6314-1(b).

1. IRC, § 6331(a) (1954 Code).

2. IRC, § 6331(b) (1954 Code); but see § 4636, infra.

3. IRC, § 6331(c) (1954 Code).

4. IRC, § 7404 (1954 Code).

estate or by contribution from other beneficiaries whose shares or interests in the estate would have been reduced had the tax been paid before the distribution of the estate, or whose shares or interests are subject either to an equal or prior liability for the payment of taxes, debts, or other charges against the estate. These provisions, however, are not designed to curtail the right of the District Director to collect the tax from any person, or out of any property, liable for its payment.[5]

The District Director cannot be required to apportion the tax among the persons liable nor to enforce any right of reimbursement or contribution.[6]

This is not an apportionment statute. The statute specifically provides that it is the purpose and intent of the statute that so far as is practicable and unless otherwise directed by the will of the decedent, the tax shall be paid out of the estate before its distribution.[7] The purpose is to prevent the tax being paid out of the share of a particular beneficiary. The question of apportionment of the tax is entirely within the jurisdiction of the several states.[8]

There are two exceptions to this in the case of life insurance beneficiaries and appointees, which are discussed in the succeeding sections.

§ 345. Collection of Unpaid Tax; Liability of Life Insurance Beneficiaries.

The first exception to the rule against apportionment of the tax under the Federal statute is in the case of life insurance beneficiaries. *Unless the decedent directs otherwise in his will,* if any part of the gross estate on which tax has been paid consists of proceeds of policies of insurance on the life of the decedent receivable by a beneficiary other than the executor, the executor shall be entitled to recover from such beneficiary such portion of the total tax paid as the proceeds of such policies bear to the sum of the taxable estate and the amount of the exemption allowed in computing the taxable estate, determined under Section 2051. If there is more than one such beneficiary, the executor shall be entitled to recover from such beneficiaries in the same ratio. In the case of such proceeds receivable by the surviving

---

5. IRC, § 2205 (1954 Code); Reg, § 20.2205–1.

6. Reg, § 20.2205–1.

7. IRC, § 2205 (1954 Code).

8. Riggs v Del Drago, 317 US 95, 87 L ed 106, 63 S Ct 109 (1942).

spouse for which a marital deduction is allowed, the section does not apply to such proceeds, except as to the amount thereof in excess of the aggregate amount of the marital deductions allowed.[9]

It should be noted that the statute only applies where there is no stipulation against apportionment. In determining the proportion, the amount of the specific exemption is added to the taxable estate. Where the spouse is the beneficiary of the insurance, the statute applies only to the excess of insurance over the marital deduction.

The reason for the provision was said to stem from the elimination of the exclusion for insurance payable to designated beneficiaries to the extent of $40,000.[10] under the 1942 Revenue Act.[11] *The statute does not apply to insurers.*[12] It is held that the executor cannot sue to recover until after payment of the tax.[13]

Whether the executor has a duty to recover the share of tax from the beneficiary, or merely has the power to do so, depends upon the State in which the estate is administered.[14]

§ 346. Collection of Unpaid Tax; Liability of Appointees.

The second exception to the rule against apportionment of the tax under the Federal statute is the case of recipients of property over which the decedent had power of appointment. In such case the appointive property never comes into the possession of the fiduciary but is taxable in the decedent's estate. Thus it is provided that *unless the decedent directs otherwise in his will,* if any part of the gross estate on which the tax has been paid consists of the value of property included in the gross estate under Section 2041, the executor shall be entitled to recover from the person receiving such property by reason of the exercise, nonexercise, or release of a power of appointment, such portion of the total tax paid as the value of such property bears to the sum of the taxable estate and the amount of the exemption allowed in computing the taxable estate, determined

9. IRC, § 2206 (1954 Code).

10. See § 70, supra.

11. Hancock Mutual Life Ins Co v Helvering, 128 F2d 745 (CA–DC) (1942).

12. Zahn, 300 NY 1, 87 NE2d 558 (1949); Commercial Trust Co of NJ v Thurber, 136 NJ Eq 471, 42 A2d 571, affd 137 NJ Eq 457, 45 A2d 672 (1945);

West Coast Life Ins Co v Twogood, 83 F Supp 710 (1949).

13. West Coast Life Ins Co v Twogood, note 12, supra.

14. See Act No 291, Acts of 1951, Alabama; Pearce v Citizens Bank & Trust Co of Bloomington (Est. of Day), Indiana Appellate Court, Mar. 2, 1951.

under Section 2052, or Section 2106(a), as the case may be. If there is more than one such person, the executor shall be entitled to recover from such persons in the same ratio. In the case of such property received by the surviving spouse of the decedent for which a marital deduction is allowed, the section does not apply to such property except as to the value thereof reduced by an amount equal to the excess of the aggregate amount of the marital deductions over the amount of proceeds of insurance upon the life of the decedent receivable by the surviving spouse for which proceeds a marital deduction is allowed.[15]

Here, it should be noted, that if the spouse receives the appointive property and the proceeds of insurance, in excepting the amount of the marital deduction, it is necessary to reduce the amount of the marital deduction by the amount of the proceeds of insurance received by the spouse. To do otherwise would be to allow a deduction under both Section 2206 of the amount of the marital deduction, and then again under Section 2207.

§ 347. Discharge of Executor.

We have previously referred to the fact that in order to expedite the audit of the return it is advisable to make written application for determination of the tax.[16] The primary purpose, however, of such application is to obtain the discharge of the executor from personal liability. Within one year after making such application, or if the application is made before the return is filed, then within one year after the return is filed, but not after the expiration of the period prescribed for the assessment of the tax, the Secretary or his delegate must notify the executor of the amount of the tax. The executor, on payment of the amount of which he is notified, shall be discharged from personal liability for any deficiency in tax thereafter found to be due and shall be entitled to a receipt or writing showing such discharge.[17] If no such notification is received, the executor is discharged at the end of such one year period from personal liability for any deficiency thereafter found to be due.[18]

The statute does not apply to the trustee of an inter vivos trust included in the gross estate of a decedent.[19] Further, the dis-

---

15. IRC, § 2207 (1954 Code).
16. § 333, supra.
17. IRC, § 2204 (1954 Code).

18. Reg, § 20.2204–1.
19. Rev Rul 57–424, IRB 1957–38 p 16.

charge of the executor does not bar assessment of a deficiency against the transferee.[20]

§ 348. Lien of Tax; Generally and Special Lien for Estate Taxes.

The statute provides for a lien in favor of the United States upon all property and rights to property belonging to any person liable to pay any tax, who neglects or refuses to pay the same after demand. This includes any interest, additional amount, addition to tax, or assessable penalty, together with any costs that may accrue in addition thereto.[1]

Unless another date is specifically fixed by law, such lien arises at the time the assessment is made and continues until the liability for the amount so assessed is satisfied or becomes unenforceable by reason of lapse of time.[2] *Such lien is not valid* against any mortgagee, pledgee, purchaser, or judgment creditor *until notice thereof has been filed* in the place provided by the statute.[3]

There is also a special lien for Estate Taxes. Unless the Estate Tax is sooner paid in full, it is a lien for ten years upon the gross estate of the decedent, *except* that such part of the gross estate as is used for the payment of charges against the estate and expenses of its administration allowed by any court having jurisdiction thereof, is divested of such lien.[4] This is an acknowledgment of the fact that administration expenses are a primary charge upon a decedent's estate.

Other subdivisions of the statute deal with the liability of transferees and others, continuance of the lien after discharge of the executor, and an exception in the case of pledged securities, which are discussed in the succeeding sections, as well as the release of the lien.

This special lien attaches at the date of the decedent's death to every part of the gross estate, whether or not the property comes into the possession of the duly qualified executor or administrator. It attaches to the extent of the tax shown to be due by the return and of any deficiency in tax found to be due upon review and audit.[5]

20. Brainard, 47 BTA 947 (1942).
1. IRC, § 6321 (1954 Code).
2. IRC, § 6322 (1954 Code).
3. IRC, § 6323 (1954 Code).
4. IRC, § 6324(a)(1) (1954 Code).
5. Reg, § 301.6324–1(a).

The lien continues for a period of ten years after the decedent's death, *except that such lien shall be divested with respect to*

(1) such portion of the gross estate as is used for the payment of charges against the estate and expenses of its administration allowed by the court;

(2) such property as is transferred to a bona fide purchaser, mortgagee, or pledgee, for an adequate and full consideration in money or moneys worth, by the spouse, transferee, trustee, surviving tenant, person in possession of the property by reason of the exercise, nonexercise, or release of a power of appointment, or beneficiary, who receives, or has on the date of the decedent's death, property included in the gross estate, or such property as is transferred by the transferee of such person;

(3) such portion of the gross estate (or any interest therein) as has been transferred to a bona fide purchaser, mortgagee, or pledgee for an adequate and full consideration in money or money's worth, if payment is made of the full amount of the tax determined by the District Director pursuant to a request of the executor for discharge from personal liability;

(4) such property as to which the District Director has issued a certificate releasing the lien.[6]

The general lien noted above, and the special lien for the Estate Tax are not exclusive of each other, but are cumulative. Each lien will arise when the conditions precedent to the creation of such lien are met and will continue in accordance with the provisions applicable to the particular lien. Thus, the special lien may exist without the general lien being in force, or the general lien may exist without the special lien being in force, or the general lien and the special lien may exist simultaneously, depending upon the facts and pertinent statutory provisions applicable to the respective liens.[7] It must be remembered that the general lien depends upon filing, to be effective against a mortgagee, pledgee, purchaser, or judgment creditor.

The statute applies to liens arising under the 1939 Code.[8]

§ 349. Lien of Tax; Liability of Transferees and Others.

If the Estate Tax is not paid when due, then the spouse, transferee, trustee (except the trustee of an employee's trust which meets the requirements of Section 401(a)),[9] surviving tenant,

6. Reg, § 301.6324–1(a)(2).
7. Reg, § 301.6324–1(c).
8. Reg, § 301.6324–1(d).
9. See § 181, supra.

person in possession of the property by reason of the exercise, nonexercise, or release of a power of appointment, or beneficiary, who receives, or has on the date of the decedent's death, property included in the gross estate, to the extent of the value, at the time of the decedent's death, of such property, is personally liable for such tax.[10]

Any part of such property transferred by any of such persons, to a bona fide purchaser, mortgagee, or pledgee, *for an adequate and full consideration* in money or money's worth, *shall be divested of the special lien,* and a like lien then attaches to all the property of such spouse, transferee, trustee, surviving tenant, person in possession, beneficiary, or transferee of any such person, *except* any part transferred to a bona fide purchaser, mortgagee, or pledgee, for an adequate and full consideration in money or money's worth.[11] What is an adequate and full consideration has been treated under many subjects heretofore.[12]

Similar provisions under prior statutes have been enforced against transferees described in the statute.[13]

As used in the statute, a bona fide purchaser, mortgagee, or pledgee is one who, in acquiring the particular property, deals at arm's length, as between strangers, and pays a full and adequate consideration in money or money's worth. This conclusion is not affected by the fact that the purchaser, mortgagee, or pledgee of property from a surviving tenant is presumed to have knowledge of the Estate Tax lien by reason of the recital of death of a joint tenant in the chain of title.[14]

§ 350. Lien of Tax; Continuance after Discharge of Executor.

We have seen that by proper application the executor may receive a discharge from personal liability.[15] This discharge does not operate as a release of any part of the gross estate from the lien for any deficiency that may thereafter be determined to be due, unless such part of the gross estate (or any interest therein) has been transferred to a bona fide purchaser, mortgagee, or pledgee for an adequate and full consideration in money, or money's worth, in which case such part (or such interest) shall

10. IRC, § 6324(a)(2) (1954 Code).
11. Note 10, supra.
12. See §§ 89, 130, 158, 218, supra.
13. See McCue, 5 TCM 141 (1945); Goar, 9 TCM 854 (1947); Vandenhoeck, 4 TC 125 (1944); Atwater, 3 TCM 1223 (1944); Cutler, Jr, 5 TC 1304 (1945); US v Klipple, 57-2 USTC ¶11,712.
14. Rev Rul, 56-144, 1956-1 CB 563.
15. § 347, supra.

not be subject to a lien or to any claim or demand for any such deficiency, but the lien shall attach to the consideration received from such purchaser, mortgagee, or pledgee by the heirs, legatees, devisees, or distributees.[16]

§ 351. Lien of Tax; Exception in Case of Securities.

Both the provisions providing for a lien for unpaid taxes and a special lien for Estate Taxes include an exception in case of securities, in addition to any other exceptions. The special lien is not valid with respect to a security as defined in Section 6323 (c) (2), as against any mortgagee, pledgee, or purchaser of any such security, for an adequate and full consideration in money or money's worth, *if* at the time of such mortgage, pledge, or purchase such mortgagee, pledgee, or purchaser is without notice or knowledge of the existence of such lien.[17]

Section 6323(c)(2) defines "security" as any bond, debenture, note, or certificate or other evidence of indebtedness, issued by any corporation (including one issued by a government or political subdivision thereof), with interest coupons or in registered form, share of stock, voting trust certificate, or any certificate of interest or participation in, certificate of deposit or receipt for, temporary or interim certificate for, or warrant or right to subscribe to or purchase, any of the foregoing; negotiable instrument; or money.

The Regulation points out that the consideration must have been an adequate and full equivalent reducible to a money value. As in all other cases, a relinquishing or promised relinquishment of dower, curtesy, or of a statutory estate created in lieu thereof, or of other marital rights is not an adequate consideration. Neither is love and affection, promise of marriage, or any other consideration not reducible to a money value.[18]

§ 352. Lien of Tax; How Release Obtained.

The provisions for release of the lien of the tax treats first with complete release, and then with the subject of partial discharge of the lien.[19]

The District Director will issue a release whenever he finds that the liability for the tax has been satisfied *or* has become *unenforceable as a matter of law* (and not merely uncollectible

---

16. IRC, § 6324(a)(3) (1954 Code).   18. Reg, § 301.6323–1(b)(1).
17. IRC, § 6324(c) (1954 Code).   19. IRC, § 6325 (1954 Code).

or unenforceable as a matter of fact). If he finds that the tax has been adequately provided for, he may issue a release for particular items of property. The issuance of the certificate of release is *within his discretion*. The primary purpose of the release is to clear title and not to evidence payment of the tax. The application should be filed with the District Director. It should be made in writing under the penalties of perjury and

(1) Explain the circumstances requiring the release (such as that title to real property is closing and cannot be conveyed without the release).

(2) Fully describe the particular items for which the release is desired.

(3) The applicant's relation to the estate, such as executor, heir, devisee, legatee, beneficiary, transferee, or purchaser.

(4) If the return has not been filed a showing of

(a) the value of the property to be released,

(b) the basis for such valuation,

(c) the approximate value of the gross estate and the approximate value of the total real property included in the gross estate,

(d) if the property is to be sold or otherwise transferred, the name and address of the purchaser or transferee and the consideration, if any, paid or to be paid by him.[20]

It is advisable to furnish a metes and bounds description in the case of real property, which is the item for which releases are most often required.

The procedure thereafter depends upon the factual situation. If the fair market value of the property *remaining* subject to the lien is at least double the sum of the amount of the unsatisfied liability secured by such lien and of the amount of all other liens upon the property which have priority to such lien, the release will be issued promptly.[1] If the tax is not so secured, there will be required a part payment of the tax to cover the amount due on the property for which the release is sought.[2]

The District Director may, in his discretion, issue a certificate of release of any tax lien if he is furnished and accepts a bond that is conditioned upon the payment of the amount assessed (together with all interest in respect thereto), within the time agreed upon in the bond, but not later than six months be-

---

20. Reg, § 301.6325–1(a)(1)(2). 2. Reg, § 301.6325–1(b)(2).
1. Reg, § 301.6325–1(b)(1).

fore the expiration of the statutory period for collection, including any period for collection agreed upon in writing by the District Director and the taxpayer.[3]

Where the interest of the United States in any property subject to the lien is valueless, as is frequently the case in mortgage foreclosures, the 1954 Code permits the District Director to issue a release upon a proper showing of the facts.[4]

Under the 1939 Code certain Estate and Gift Tax liens which were indefinite in amount or which could not be determined until a later time might be released without requiring that property remaining subject to the lien be of a value at least double the amount of the unsatisfied liability. By inadvertence this provision was omitted from the 1954 Code. This oversight has been remedied by the amendment of the statute.[4a] The present subdivision (d) was formerly subdivision (c).

A certificate of release or of partial discharge issued under the statute is conclusive that the lien upon the property covered by the certificate is extinguished.[5]

§ 353. Jeopardy Assessments; Authority for.

If a District Director believes that the assessment or collection of a deficiency will be jeopardized by delay, he is required to assess such deficiency immediately, together with the interest, additional amounts, and additions to the tax provided by law, and notice and demand made for the payment thereof.[6]

The District Director may believe that collection of the tax is in jeopardy because the statute of limitations on assessment will bar the assessment, or because the acts of the taxpayer indicate that he is taking means to evade the payment of the tax.

§ 354. Jeopardy Assessments; Deficiency Letters.

Normally, when there is a deficiency, notice thereof must be given to the taxpayer by certified mail or registered mail.[7] A jeopardy assessment, however, may be made either before or

3. Reg, § 301.6325–1(a)(3).

4. IRC, § 6325(b)(2) (1954 Code); Reg, § 301.6325–1(b)(3).

4a. IRC, § 6325(c) (1954 Code), added by Technical Amendments Act of 1958, § 77, HR 8381, 85th Cong, 2nd Sess.

5. IRC, § 6325(d) (1954 Code), as amended by Technical Amendments Act of 1958, § 77, HR 8381, 85th Cong, 2nd Sess.

6. IRC, § 6861(a) (1954 Code); Reg, § 301.6861–1(a).

7. IRC, § 6212 (1954 Code), as amended by §§ 76, 89(b) of Technical Amendments Act of 1958, HR 8381, 85th Cong, 2nd Sess.

after the mailing of the deficiency letter, but if made before the mailing of the notice of deficiency, then it is required that the notice of deficiency be mailed within sixty days after the making of the assessment.[8]

Prior to September 2, 1958 it was required that the notice of deficiency be mailed by registered mail. The Technical Amendments Act of 1958 amended the statute to permit mailing either by certified or registered mail.[8a] Notices mailed prior to the amendment must have been sent by registered mail to comply with the statute.[8b]

§ 355. Jeopardy Assessments; Amount Assessable before and after Decision of Tax Court.

The amount of the jeopardy assessment is limited by whether or not the Tax Court of the United States has made a decision, as is the time within which such assessment may be made.

The jeopardy assessment may be made in respect of a deficiency greater or less than that notice of which has been mailed to the taxpayer, despite the provisions of Section 6212(c) prohibiting the determination of additional deficiencies, and whether or not the taxpayer has theretofore filed a petition with the Tax Court. The Tax Court must be notified of the assessment when it is made after the filing of the petition with the Tax Court. The Tax Court has jurisdiction to redetermine the entire amount of the deficiency and of all amounts assessed at the same time in connection therewith.[9] Thus, *before the decision of the Tax Court* the amount of the jeopardy assessment may be more or less than the amount of the deficiency.

If the jeopardy assessment is made *after the decision of the Tax Court* is rendered, such assessment may be made only in respect of the deficiency determined by the Tax Court in its decision.[10]

A jeopardy assessment may not be made after the decision of the Tax Court has become final, or after the taxpayer has filed a petition for review of the decision of the Tax Court.[11]

---

8. IRC, § 6861(b) (1954 Code); Reg, § 301.6861–1(c).

8a. Technical Amendments Act of 1958, § 89(b), HR 8381, 85th Cong, 2nd Sess.

8b. § 577, infra.

9. IRC, § 6861(c) (1954 Code); Reg, § 301.6861–1(b)(c).

10. IRC, § 6861(d) (1954 Code); Reg, § 301.6861–1(b).

11. IRC, § 6861(e) (1954 Code).

§ 356. Jeopardy Assessments; Abatement.

There are two provisions in the statute with respect to abatement of the jeopardy assessment. At any time before the decision of the Tax Court is rendered, the District Director may abate such assessment, or any unpaid portion thereof, to the extent that he believes the assessment to be excessive in amount. Notice thereof must be given to the Tax Court if the petition is filed with the Tax Court before the making of the assessment, or is subsequently filed.[12]

The District Director may abate a jeopardy assessment in whole or in part, if it is shown to his satisfaction that jeopardy does not exist. An abatement may not be made under the paragraph, after a decision of the Tax Court in respect of the deficiency has been rendered, or, if no petition is filed with such court, after the expiration of the period for filing such petition.[13]

After abatement of a jeopardy assessment in whole or in part, the District Director may proceed to assess and collect a deficiency in the manner authorized by law as if the jeopardy assessment or part thereof so abated had not existed. The period of assessment and limitation applies as if the jeopardy assessment had not been made, except that it is suspended from the date of the jeopardy assessment until the tenth day after the date of abatement.[14]

Request for abatement of a jeopardy assessment, because jeopardy does not exist, must be filed with the District Director, and must state fully the reasons for the request, and be supported by such evidence as will enable the District Director to determine that the collection of the deficiency is not in jeopardy.[15]

§ 357. Jeopardy Assessments; Stay of Collection.

The 1954 Code made a number of changes with respect to stay of collection of jeopardy assessments, which will be noted.

When a jeopardy assessment has been made, the collection of the whole or any amount of such assessment may be stayed by filing with the District Director a bond to be furnished by him on request. The bond may be filed—

(1) At any time before the time collection by levy is authorized under Section 6331(a), *or*

---

12. IRC, § 6861(e) (1954 Code); Reg, § 301.6861–1(e).

13. Reg, § 301.6861–1(f)(1).

14. IRC, § 6861(g) (1954 Code); Reg, § 301.6861–1(f)(2).

15. Reg, § 301.6861–1(f)(3).

(2) After collection by levy is authorized, and before levy is made on any property or rights to property, *or*

(3) In the discretion of the District Director, after any such levy has been made and before the expiration of the period of limitations on collection.[16]

The bond must be in an amount *equal to* the portion (including interest thereon to the date of payment as calculated by the District Director) of the jeopardy assessment collection of which is sought to be stayed. The bond must be conditioned upon the payment of the amount (together with interest thereon), the collection of which is stayed, at the time at which, but for the making of the jeopardy assessment, such amount would be due.[17] It is further required in the case of an Estate Tax jeopardy assessment, that the bond be conditioned upon the payment of so much of the amount included therein as is not abated by a decision of the Tax Court which has become final, together with the interest on such amount. If the Tax Court determines that the amount assessed is greater than the correct amount of the tax, the bond will be proportionately reduced at the request of the taxpayer after the Tax Court renders its decision. If the bond is given before the taxpayer has filed his petition with the Tax Court, it must contain a further condition that if a petition is not filed before the expiration of the period provided in Section 6213(a) for the filing of such petition, the amount stayed by the bond will be paid upon notice and demand at any time after the expiration of such period, together with interest thereon at the rate of six percent per annum from the date of the jeopardy notice and demand to the date of the notice and demand made after the expiration of the period for filing the petition with the Tax Court.[18]

Under the 1939 Code, the amount of the bond was double the amount of the tax.[19] The statute applies to taxes imposed under the 1954 Code.[20] The bond is executed upon Form 1129.

The 1954 Code added a provision with respect to the stay of the sale of seized property pending the decision of the Tax Court.[1] As we have noted previously, one of the remedies for

16. Reg, § 301.6863–1(a)(1)(2).

17. IRC, § 6863(a) (1954 Code); Reg, § 301.6863–1(a)(3).

18. IRC, § 6863(b)(1)(2) (1954 Code); Reg, § 301.6863–1(b).

19. IRC, §§ 872(f)(g), 1013(f)(g) (1939 Code).

20. IRC, § 7851(a)(6)(A) (1954 Code).

1. IRC, § 6863(b)(3) (1954 Code).

collection of the tax is the right to levy upon and sell property.[2] Where, notwithstanding the provisions of Section 6213(a) (restriction on assessment when petition filed to Tax Court), a jeopardy assessment has been made, the property seized for the collection of the tax shall not be sold.

(1) *if* the jeopardy assessment was made before a deficiency letter has been mailed, prior to the issuance of the notice of deficiency and the expiration of the time provided for the filing of a petition with the Tax Court, and

(2) *if* petition is filed with the Tax Court (whether before or after the making of such jeopardy assessment), prior to the expiration of the period during which the assessment of the deficiency would be prohibited if there were no authority for making a jeopardy assessment, *except*

such property may be sold if

(a) the taxpayer consents to the sale, *or*

(b) the District Director determines that the expenses of conservation and maintenance of the property will greatly reduce the net proceeds from the sale of such property, *or*

(c) if the property is of a type to which Section 6336 (relating to sale of perishable goods) is applicable.[3]

The stay of sale provision applies only with respect to a jeopardy assessment *made on or after January 1, 1955,* but applies with respect to taxes imposed under the 1939 Code as well as the 1954 Code.[4]

§ 358. Jeopardy Assessments; Collection of Unpaid Amounts; Claim in Abatement.

When a petition has been filed with the Tax Court and when the amount which should have been assessed has been determined by a decision of the Tax Court which has become final, then any unpaid portion, the collection of which has been stayed by bond shall be collected as part of the tax upon notice and demand of the District Director, and any remaining portion of the assessment shall be abated. If the amount already collected exceeds the amount determined as the amount which should have been assessed, such excess shall be credited or refunded to the taxpayer, *without the filing of claim therefor.* If the amount determined as the amount which should have been

2. § 343, supra.
3. Reg, § 301.6863–2.
4. IRC, § 6863(b)(3)(c) (1954 Code).

assessed is greater than the amount actually assessed, then the difference shall be assessed and collected as part of the tax upon notice and demand.[5]

It may be noted that no claim for abatement may be filed with respect to Income, Gift, or Estate Tax.[6]

§ 359. Limitations; on Assessment and Collection.

The statutory period within which assessment of the tax must be made, with the exceptions noted in the succeeding section, is within three years *after the return was filed* (whether or not such return was filed on or after the date prescribed), and no proceeding in court without assessment for the collection of the tax may be begun after the expiration of such period.[7]

It will be noted that the time begins to run from the date of the filing of the return and not from the date of death. But the Code provides that for purposes of the section a return filed *before the last day* prescribed by law or by Regulations for the filing thereof, *shall be considered as filed on such last day.*[8] Thus, in the case of the Estate Tax, the statute begins to run from a date fifteen months after the date of death.[9]

§ 360. Limitations; Exceptions.

There are a number of exceptions to the three year period. These are:

(1) Where the person required to make the return fails to do so but discloses the information on which the return is then made by a District Director or other Internal Revenue officer,[10] the execution of such return does not begin the running of the statute.[11]

(2) Where a false or fraudulent return with intent to evade the tax is filed, proceedings for collection without assessment may be begun at any time.[12]

(3) The same is true when there is a failure to make and file a return within the statutory period.[13]

(4) Where the taxpayer and the District Director or an As-

5. IRC, § 6861(f) (1954 Code); Reg, § 301.6861-1(d).
6. IRC, § 6404(b) (1954 Code); Reg, § 301.6404-1(b).
7. IRC, § 6501(a) (1954 Code); Reg, § 301.6501(a)-1.
8. IRC, § 6501(b)(1) (1954 Code); Reg, § 301.6501(b)-1(a).
9. § 28, supra.
10. IRC, § 6020 (1954 Code).
11. IRC, § 6501(b)(3) (1954 Code).
12. IRC, § 6501(c)(1)(2) (1954 Code).
13. IRC, § 6501(c)(3) (1954 Code).

sistant Regional Commissioner so agree prior to the expiration of the statutory period, the time for assessment may be extended, *but this applies only to the Gift Tax and not the Estate Tax*.[14]

(5) Where the taxpayer omits from the gross estate, or total gifts during the year in the case of the Gift Tax, an item or items properly includible therein, the amount of which is in excess of 25% of the gross estate or of the total amount of gifts during the year, the period of limitations is six years after the return was filed.[15]

(6) Where a credit for State death taxes,[16] or foreign death taxes[17] has been allowed and thereafter a refund of such tax has been received, any Federal tax found to be due by reason of the refund is payable upon notice and demand and the statutory period of limitation does not apply.[18]

§ 361. Limitations; Collection after Assessment.

In any case in which a tax has been assessed within the statutory period of limitation properly applicable thereto, such tax may be collected by levy or by a proceeding in court, *but only if* the levy is made or the proceeding begun.

(1) within six years after the assessment of the tax, *or*

(2) prior to the expiration of any period for collection agreed upon *in writing* by the taxpayer and the District Director before the expiration of such six year period (or if there is a release of levy under Section 6343 after such six year period, then before such release). The period so agreed upon may be extended by subsequent agreements in writing made before the expiration of the period previously agreed upon.[19]

The date on which a levy on property or rights to property is made is the date on which the notice of seizure is given.[20]

§ 362. Limitations; Suspension of Running of Period.

The 1954 Code made several changes with respect to suspension of the running of the period of limitations on assessment and collection, which apply to the estates of decedents dying on and after August 17, 1954 and gifts made in 1955 or later.

(1) The running of the period of limitations on the making of

---

14. IRC, § 6501(c)(4) (1954 Code).

15. IRC, § 6501(e)(2) (1954 Code); Reg, § 301.6501(e)–1(b).

16. §§ 318 et seq, supra.

17. §§ 309 et seq, supra.

18. IRC, §§ 6501(c)(5), 2016 (1954 Code).

19. IRC, § 6502(a) (1954 Code); Reg, § 301.6502–1(a).

20. IRC, § 6502(b) (1954 Code).

assessments or the collection by levy or a proceeding in court, in respect of any Estate or Gift Tax deficiency, after the mailing of the notice of deficiency, is suspended for the period of *ninety days* if the notice is addressed to a person within the United States and the District of Columbia, *or one hundred and fifty days* if such notice is addressed to a person outside the United States and the District of Columbia, *plus an additional sixty days* thereafter in either case. If a proceeding in respect of the deficiency is placed on the docket of the Tax Court, the period of limitations is suspended *until the decision of the Tax Court becomes final, and* for an additional *sixty days* thereafter.[1]

(2) Where the assets of a taxpayer (*other than the estate of a decedent* or of an incompetent) are in the control or custody of the court in any proceeding before any court of the United States, or any State or Territory of the United States, or of the District of Columbia, the period of limitation on collection after assessment is suspended for the period such assets are in the control or custody of the court and for six months thereafter.[2]

(3) The running of the period of limitation on collection after assessment is suspended for the period of time that collection is hindered or delayed because property of the taxpayer is situated or held outside the United States or is removed from the United States. The total suspension of time under this provision shall not in the aggregate exceed six years.[3]

(4) Where an estate is granted an extension of time for payment of the Estate Tax, the running of the period of limitations for assessment or collection of such tax is suspended for the period of time for which the extension is granted.[4]

(5) The running of the period of limitations for assessment or collection of the Estate Tax is suspended in respect of a decedent claiming a deduction under Section 2055(b)(2) until thirty days after the expiration of the period for assessment or collection of the tax imposed on the estate of the surviving spouse.[5] This was added to the statute in 1956 at the same time that there was added the special deduction in the case of charity where

1. IRC, § 6503(a)(1) (1954 Code); Reg, § 301.6503(a)–1(a).

2. IRC, § 6503(b) (1954 Code); Reg, § 301.6503(b)–1.

3. IRC, § 6503(c) (1954 Code); Reg, § 301.6503(c)–1.

4. IRC, § 6503(d) (1954 Code).

5. IRC, § 6503(e) (1954 Code); Reg, § 301.6503(e)–1.

the donee of a power is eighty years of age, and which has been treated previously.[6]

The statute also provides that if the Regulations issued pursuant to Section 6035 require the giving of notice by any fiduciary in any proceeding under the Bankruptcy Act, or by a receiver in any other court proceeding, of his qualification as such, the running of the period of limitations on the making of assessments shall be suspended for the period from the date of the institution of the proceeding to a date thirty days after the date upon which the notice from the receiver or other fiduciary is received by the District Director; but the suspension shall in no case be for a period in excess of two years.[7]

There is also provision for the suspension of the running of the statute in the case of transferees, discussed hereafter.[8]

§ 363. Interest; General Rule.

The general rule with respect to underpayments or nonpayment of Income, Estate, or Gift Taxes is that interest is payable on any unpaid amount at the rate of six percent per annum from the last date prescribed for payment to the date of payment.[9]

In the case of the Estate Tax there are exceptions to the general rule where an extension of time for payment of the tax has been granted or there is an option to pay in installments.[10]

§ 364. Interest; Extension of Time for Payment of Estate Tax.

As we have seen,[11] upon a showing of undue hardship, an extension of time for payment of the Estate Tax may be granted for a period not in excess of ten years from the date fixed for payment of the tax. We have also seen,[12] where the value of a reversionary or remainder interest is included in the gross estate, the fiduciary may elect to postpone the payment of the tax on that part of the estate until six months after the termination of the precedent interest, and the Secretary may grant a further extension for two years. Most recently, there has been added a provision that the tax on an interest in a closely held business may be paid in installments over a period of not more than ten years, upon compliance with the requirements of the

6. § 245, supra.

7. IRC, § 6872 (1954 Code); see also IRC, § 6871(a) (1954 Code).

8. § 372, infra.

9. IRC, § 6601(a) (1954 Code); Reg, § 301.6601-1(a).

10. See § 364, infra.

11. § 339, supra.

12. § 326, supra.

statute, previously discussed.[12a] In all of these cases, the rate of interest payable on the tax so postponed is payable at the rate of four percent per annum instead of six percent.[13]

It will be noted, that unlike the provisions of the 1939 Code, except in one instance, discussed hereafter, there are no separate provisions with respect to the tax shown on the return and a deficiency tax.

§ 365. Interest; Last Date Prescribed for Payment.

Since interest begins to run from the last date prescribed for payment to the date of payment,[14] the statute defines the method of determining the former.

The due date for payment of tax is determined without regard to any extension of time, and interest continues to run during the period of extension and for any further period during which the tax remains unpaid.[15]

Where there has been a jeopardy assessment[16] and payment was demanded before the due date prescribed otherwise, interest does not begin to run prior to the prescribed due date.[17]

§ 366. Interest; Suspension; Waiver of Restrictions.

We have previously referred to the waiver of restrictions on assessment and collection of a deficiency.[18] If such waiver has been filed, and if notice and demand for payment of the deficiency is not made within thirty days after the filing of the waiver, interest will not be imposed on the deficiency for the period beginning after such thirtieth day and ending with the date of notice and demand.[19] The 1939 Code terminated the period with the date of assessment or the filing of the waiver, whichever was earlier.[20]

§ 366A. Interest; Applicable Rules; No Interest on Interest.

In re-writing and combining the provisions of the 1939 Code in the 1954 Code, a number of changes were made in existing law with respect to interest. One of the most important was

---

12a. § 340, supra.

13. IRC, § 6601(b) (1954 Code); Reg, § 301.6601–1(b).

14. Note 9, supra.

15. IRC, § 6601(c)(1) (1954 Code); Reg, § 301.6601–1(c)(1).

16. §§ 353 et seq, supra.

17. IRC, § 6601(c)(3) (1954 Code);

Rev Rul 54–426, IRB 1954–2 CB 39; Reg, § 301.6601–1(c)(3).

18. §§ 334, 335, supra.

19. IRC, § 6601(d) (1954 Code); Rev Rul 54–426, IRB 1954–2 CB 39; Reg, § 301.6601–1(d).

20. IRC, §§ 891, 1021 (1939 Code).

the elimination of the system of charging interest upon interest. The statute provides

(1) Interest shall be paid upon notice and demand, and shall be assessed, collected, and paid in the same manner as taxes. Any reference to any tax (except that relating to deficiency procedures) imposed by the title shall be deemed to also refer to interest imposed by the section on such tax.

(2) No interest under the section shall be imposed on the interest provided by the section.

(3) Interest shall be imposed under subsection (a)[1] in respect of any assessable penalty, additional amount, or addition to the tax only if such assessable penalty, additional amount, or addition to the tax is not paid within ten days from the notice and demand therefor, and in such case interest shall be imposed only for the period from the date of notice and demand to the date of payment.

(4) If notice and demand is made for payment of any amount, and if such amount is paid within ten days after the date of such notice and demand, interest under the section on the amount so paid shall not be imposed for the period after the date of such notice and demand.[2]

Under the 1939 Code, in the case of deficiencies, interest ran from the date prescribed for payment of the tax to the date of assessment of the deficiency and then interest on the amount assessed ran from the date of assessment. Therefore, interest was payable on the interest from the date prescribed for payment to the date of assessment.

§ 367. Penalties; Additions to the Tax.

The Revenue Act of 1954, like its predecessors, provides for three different kinds of penalties. The first of these is an addition to the tax. Failure to file a return required by the statute, unless such failure is due to reasonable cause, results in addition to the tax of five percent thereof for each month of delinquency, to a maximum of twenty-five percent.[3]

Negligence or intentional disregard of rules and regulations with respect to Income or Gift Taxes, if without intent to defraud, will cause an addition to any underpayment to the extent of five percent thereof.[4] If the underpayment is due to fraud, there

1. § 363, supra.
2. IRC, § 6601(f) (1954 Code); Reg, § 301.6601–1(f).

3. § 34, supra.
4. IRC, § 6653(a) (1954 Code); Reg, § 301.6653–1(a).

may be added to the tax fifty percent of the underpayment, and in the case of Income and Gift Taxes this is in lieu of the five percent penalty for negligence or intentional disregard of rules or regulations.[5] If this penalty is imposed, then the delinquency penalty of twenty-five percent is not.[6]

The additions to the tax, additional amounts, and penalties provided, are payable upon notice and demand and are assessed and collected and paid in the same manner as taxes.[7]

This makes the maximum penalty fifty percent, whereas under the 1939 Code both the delinquency penalty and the fraud penalty could be imposed and result in a total of seventy-five percent.

Since the statute refers to underpayment, it defines such term, as the deficiency.[8]

§ 368. Penalties; Civil.

It will be recalled that in the instructions for preparation of the return there were repeated references to the penalties for failing to comply with the various provisions of the statute. The 1954 Code brought all of these together in Chapter 75. There is but one relating to a civil penalty, all the others providing for fine, imprisonment, or both.

Whoever fails to comply with any duty imposed upon him by Section 6018, 6036 (in the case of an executor), or 6075(a), or, having in his possession or control any record, file, or paper, containing or supposed to contain any information concerning the estate of the decedent, or, having in his possession or control any property comprised in the gross estate of the decedent, fails to exhibit the same upon request to the Secretary or his delegate who desires to examine the same in the performance of his duties under Chapter 11 (relating to Estate Taxes), shall be liable to a penalty not exceeding $500, to be recovered with costs of suit, in a civil action in the name of the United States.[9]

§ 369. Penalties; Criminal.

While there is but one civil penalty, there are five criminal penalties provided by the statute.

The first penalty is for any *wilful* attempt to evade or defeat the tax or payment thereof, which is a felony and punishable

---

5. IRC, § 6653(b) (1954 Code); Reg, § 301.6653–1(b).

6. IRC, § 6653(d) (1954 Code); Reg, § 301.6653–1(b)(2).

7. IRC, § 6659 (1954 Code); Reg, § 301.6659.

8. IRC, § 6653(c) (1954 Code).

9. IRC, § 7269 (1954 Code).

by a fine of not more than $10,000, imprisonment for not more than five years, or both.[10]

The second provides that any person required to collect, account for, and pay over any tax imposed by the title who *wilfully* fails to do so, shall be guilty of a felony, punishable by a fine of not more than $10,000, imprisonment for not more than five years, or both.[11]

The third penalty provided is in the case of failure to make a return, keep any records, or supply any information, and *wilfully* failing to do so, at the time required by law or regulations. Such failure is a misdemeanor punishable by a fine not to exceed $10,000, imprisonment for not more than one year, or both, together with the costs of prosecution.[12]

In all three cases the penalty is in addition to other penalties provided by law, i.e., the civil penalties.

The fourth penalty among the criminal penalties deals with fraud and false statements. These are in connection with declarations under the penalties of perjury, aiding or assisting in the preparation or presentation of such, fraudulent bonds, permits and entries, removal or concealment with intent to defraud, and concealment, withholding, falsifying, and destroying records in connection with compromises and closing agreements. Such crime is a felony punishable by fine not to exceed $5,000, imprisonment for not more than three years, or both, together with the costs of prosecution.[13]

Finally, any person who *wilfully* delivers or discloses to the Secretary or his delegate any list, return, account, statement, or other document, known to him to be fraudulent or to be false as to any material matter, shall be fined not more than $1,000, or imprisoned not more than one year, or both.[14]

It will be observed that the element of intent must be found for the criminal penalties to apply.[15] It will also be observed that in each instance the statute refers to "any person" as subject to its provisions, and not merely the taxpayer.[16]

10. IRC, § 7201 (1954 Code).
11. IRC, § 7202 (1954 Code).
12. IRC, § 7203 (1954 Code).
13. IRC, § 7206 (1954 Code).
14. IRC, § 7207 (1954 Code).

15. See Sen Fin Comm Report on §§ 7201, 7202, 7203, 7206, 7207, Revenue Act of 1954.
16. Note 15, supra.

§ 370. Transferred Assets; Method of Collection.

As we have seen, collection of the tax can not be defeated by transfer of a decedent's assets for less than an adequate and full consideration, but the transferee becomes liable for the tax.[17] In such case the statute provides for the method of collection.

The amount for which the transferee of property of a decedent, in the case of the Estate Tax, or of a donor, in the case of the Gift Tax, is liable at law or in equity, and the amount of the personal liability of a fiduciary under Section 3647 of the Revised Statutes, as amended (31 U.S.C. 192), in respect of the payment of such taxes, whether shown on the return of the taxpayer or determined as a deficiency in the tax, is assessed against such transferee or fiduciary and paid and collected in the same manner and subject to the same provisions and limitations as in the case of a deficiency in the tax with respect to which such liability is incurred, except as noted in the succeeding sections hereof.[18]

The provisions of the Code made applicable by Section 6901 (a) to the liability of a transferee or fiduciary include the provisions relating to:

(1) Delinquency in payment after notice and demand and the amount of interest attaching because of such delinquency;

(2) The authorization of distraint and proceedings in court for collection;

(3) The prohibition of claims and suits for refund; and

(4) In any instance in which the liability of a transferee or fiduciary is one for Income, Estate, or Gift Taxes, the filing of a petition with the Tax Court and the filing of a petition for review of the Tax Court's decision.[19]

The term "transferee" includes donee, heir, legatee, devisee, and distributee, and with respect to Estate Taxes, also includes any person who under Section 6324(a)(2),[20] is personally liable for any part of such tax.[1]

§ 371. Transferred Assets; Period of Limitation.

The period of limitations for assessment of the liability of a transferee or fiduciary is as follows:

(1) In the case of the liability of an *initial transferee* within

---

17. § 349, supra.
18. IRC, § 6901(a) (1954 Code); Reg, § 301.6901–1(a)(1)(2).

19. Reg, § 301.6901–1(a)(3).
20. § 348, supra.
1. IRC, § 6901(h) (1954 Code).

one year after the expiration of the period of limitations for assessment against the transferor.[2]

(2) In the case of the liability of the *transferee of a transferee, within one year after* the expiration of the period of limitation for assessment against the preceding transferee, *but not more than three years* after the expiration of the period of limitation for assessment against the initial transferor; *except* that if, before the expiration of the period of limitation for the assessment of the liability of the transferee, a court proceeding for the collection of the tax or liability in respect thereof has been begun against the initial transferor or the last preceding transferee, respectively, then the period of limitation for assessment of the liability of the transferee shall expire one year after the return of execution in the court proceeding.

(3) In the case of the liability of a *fiduciary, not later than one year after* the liability arises or not later than the expiration of the period for collection of the tax in respect of which such liability arises, whichever is the later.[3]

If before the expiration of the time prescribed in the three cases above, the Secretary or his delegate and the transferee or fiduciary have agreed to an extension of time for the assessment, the time for assessment is accordingly extended, and such extension is deemed an agreement and extension for purposes of Section 6511(c) relating to limitations on credits or refunds in case of extension of time by agreement.[4]

For the purposes of the section, if any person is deceased, or is a corporation which has terminated its existence, the period of limitation for assessment against such person shall be the period that would be in effect had death or termination of existence not occurred.[5]

§ 372. Transferred Assets; Suspension of Running of Period of Limitations.

The running of the period of limitations upon the assessment of the liability of a transferee or fiduciary, is, after the mailing to the transferee or fiduciary of the notice of deficiency, suspended for the period during which the Secretary or his delegate is prohibited from making the assessment in respect of the liability of the transferee or fiduciary (and in any event, if a proceeding

2. See §§ 359 et seq, as to limitations on assessment.

3. IRC, § 6901(c) (1954 Code).

4. IRC, § 6901(d) (1954 Code); Reg, § 301.6901-1(d).

5. IRC, § 6901(e) (1954 Code).

in respect of the liability is placed on the docket of the Tax Court, until the decision of the Tax Court become final), and for sixty days thereafter.[6] No assessment may be made until the mailing of the notice of deficiency and the expiration of the period of ninety or one hundred and fifty days, depending upon whether mailed to a person in the United States or without it.[7]

§ 373. Transferred Assets; Burden of Proof and Evidence.

The statute recognizes the handicaps under which a transferee labors when claim is made that he is liable for payment of the tax. It provides that in proceedings before the Tax Court the burden of proof shall be upon the Secretary or his delegate to show that a petitioner is liable as a transferee of property of a taxpayer, *but not* to show that the taxpayer was liable for the tax.[8]

It is further provided that upon application to the Tax Court, a transferee of property of a taxpayer shall be entitled, under rules prescribed by the Tax Court, to a preliminary examination of books, papers, documents, correspondence, and other evidence of the taxpayer or a preceding transferee of the taxpayer's property, if the transferee making the application is a petitioner before the Tax Court for the redetermination of his liability in respect of the tax (including interest, additional amounts, and additions to the tax provided by law) imposed upon the taxpayer. Upon such application, the Tax Court may require by subpoena, ordered by the Tax Court or any division thereof and signed by a judge, the production of all such books, papers, documents, correspondence, and other evidence, within the United States the production of which, in the opinion of the Tax Court or division thereof, is necessary to enable the transferee to ascertain the liability of the taxpayer or preceding transferee and will not result in undue hardship to the taxpayer or preceding transferee. Such examination shall be had at such time and place as may be designated by the subpoena.[9]

§ 374. Transferred Assets; Prohibition of Injunctions.

The statute[10] under the title "Prohibition of Injunctions" refers to another section which provides that no suit shall be main-

---

6. IRC, § 6901(f) (1954 Code).
7. IRC, § 6213 (1954 Code).
8. IRC, § 6902(a) (1954 Code).

9. IRC, § 6902(b) (1954 Code).
10. IRC, § 6904 (1954 Code).

tained in any court for the purpose of restraining the assessment or collection of—

(1) the amount of the liability, at law or in equity, of a transferee of property of a taxpayer in respect of any Internal Revenue tax, or

(2) the amount of the liability of a fiduciary under Section 3467 of the Revised Statutes (31 U.S.C. 192) in respect of any such tax.[11]

The theory on which such relief is barred is that there is an adequate remedy at law.[12]

§ 375. Notice of Fiduciary Relationship.

Every person acting for another person in a fiduciary capacity is required to give notice thereof to the District Director in writing. As soon as such notice is filed with the District Director such fiduciary must except as otherwise specifically provided, assume the powers, rights, duties, and privileges of the taxpayer with respect to the taxes imposed by the Code. If the person is acting as a fiduciary for a transferee or other person specified in Section 6901, such fiduciary is required to assume the powers, rights, duties, and privileges of the transferee or other person under that section. The amount of the tax or liability is ordinarily not collectible from the personal estate of the fiduciary but is collectible from the estate of the taxpayer or from the estate of the transferee or other person.[13] These rights and obligations continue until notice is given that the fiduciary capacity has terminated.[14]

The statute provides that the notice shall be given in accordance with the Regulations.[15] The Regulation prescribes the requirements for the notice and for the notice of termination.

The notice must be signed by the fiduciary and filed with the District Director for the district where the return of the person for whom the fiduciary is acting is required to be filed. It must state the name and address of the person for whom the fiduciary is acting, and the nature of the liability of such person; that is, whether it is a liability for tax, and, if so, the type of tax, the year or years involved, or a liability at law or in equity of a transferee of property of a taxpayer, or a liability of a fiduciary under Sec-

---

11. IRC, § 7421(b) (1954 Code).
12. See Polk v Page, 281 F 74 (CCA 1) (1922); Nichols v Gaston, 281 F 67 (CCA 1) (1922).
13. Reg, § 301.6903–1(a).
14. IRC, § 6903(a) (1954 Code).
15. IRC, § 6903(b) (1954 Code).

tion 3467 of the Revised Statutes, as amended (31 U.S.C. 192), in respect of the payment of any tax from the estate of the taxpayer. Satisfactory evidence of the authority of the fiduciary to act for any other person in a fiduciary capacity must be filed with and made a part of the notice. If the fiduciary capacity exists by order of court, a certified copy of the order may be regarded as satisfactory evidence.

When the fiduciary capacity has terminated, the fiduciary, in order to be relieved of any further duty or liability as such, must file with the District Director written notice that the fiduciary capacity has terminated as to him, accompanied by satisfactory evidence of the termination of the fiduciary capacity. The notice should state the name and address of the person, if any, who has been substituted as fiduciary.[16]

Any written notice disclosing a fiduciary relationship which has been filed under the 1939 Code is sufficient notice under the present statute. Any satisfactory evidence of the authority of the fiduciary to act for another person already filed need not be resubmitted.

"Fiduciary" as defined by the statute means a guardian, trustee, executor, administrator, receiver, conservator, or any person acting in any fiduciary capacity for any person.[17]

The provisions of Section 6903 do not abridge in any way the powers and duties of fiduciaries provided for in other sections of the Code.[18]

§ 376. Credit or Refund; Period of Limitations on Filing Claim.

Heretofore we have been discussing the cases where there has been an underpayment of the tax. But it is also possible to overpay the amount of tax due where the tax has been illegally assessed and collected,[19] or where it is determined that there is no liability for the tax.[20] In such cases it is provided that the overpayment shall be credited against any liability for an Internal Revenue tax and the balance refunded.[1] However, claim for the credit or refund must first be filed.[2] Where the payment made is in excess of the amount shown on the return, the District Director may make refund without waiting for the filing of a claim for refund. The Regulation points out, however, that

16. Reg, § 301.6903-1(b).
17. IRC, § 7701(a)(6) (1954 Code).
18. Reg, § 301.6903-1(e).
19. IRC, § 6401(a) (1954 Code).

20. IRC, § 6401(c) (1954 Code).
1. IRC, § 6402 (1954 Code).
2. Reg, § 301.6402-2.

taxpayers should submit claims for refunds to protect themselves in the event the District Director fails to make such refund.[3]

A claim for credit or refund of an overpayment of the tax in respect of which the taxpayer is required to file a return *must be filed by the taxpayer within three years from the time the return was filed or two years from the time the tax was paid, whichever of such periods expires the later,* or if no return was filed by the taxpayer, within two years from the time the tax was paid.[4] The section was amended by the Technical Amendments Act of 1958 to correlate the rule with respect to assessments[4a] with that relating to refunds.[4b]

The provision must be read in conjunction with the further provision that for the purposes of the section, any return filed before the last day prescribed for the filing thereof shall be considered as filed on such last day, and payment of any portion of the tax made before the last day prescribed for payment of the tax shall be considered made on such last day. Also, the last day in either case is determined without regard to any extension of time granted the taxpayer.[5] Thus, in the case of the Estate Tax, the maximum time is three years and fifteen months from the date of death.

Where there has been an extension agreement in respect to assessment of the Gift Tax,[6] the period for filing the claim is extended for six months after the expiration of the agreed period for assessment.[7] The provision does not apply to the Estate Tax.

The period of limitations is strictly applied,[8] and if the application for refund is not filed within the statutory period no refund may be had.[9]

The application for refund is made upon Form 843. While it has been held that it is not necessary that the claim be filed on

3. Reg, § 301.6402–4.

4. IRC, § 6511(a) (1954 Code), as amended by Technical Amendments Act of 1958, § 82(a), HR 8381, 85th Cong, 2nd Sess.

4a. § 359, supra.

4b. Senate Finance Committee Report on Technical Amendments Act of 1958, § 82(a), HR 8381, 85th Cong, 2nd Sess.

5. IRC, § 6513(a) (1954 Code).

6. See § 360, supra.

7. IRC, § 6511(c)(1) (1954 Code).

8. See Fawcett v US, 164 F2d 696 (CCA 9) affg 70 F Supp 742 (1947); Braun v Lewellyn, 38 F2d 477 (1930); Ordway v US, 37 F2d 19 (CCA 2) (1930); Dysart v US, 95 F2d 652 (CCA 8), cert den 305 US 608, 83 L ed 386, 59 S Ct 67 (1938); St. Aubin v Sheehan, 138 F Supp 154 (1956); but see Walkden v US, 58–2 USTC ¶ 11,802, affd 58–2 USTC ¶ 11,803 (CA 6) (1958).

9. IRC, § 6514 (1954 Code).

such form,[10] informal claims have resulted in the loss of refund.[11] It must be remembered that a civil action for refund may not be instituted unless a claim has been filed within the statutory period.[12] The claim, together with appropriate supporting evidence, must be filed in the District Director's office where the tax was paid. The claim must set forth in detail each ground upon which a credit or refund is claimed, *and facts sufficient to apprise the Commissioner of the exact basis thereof.* The statement of the grounds and facts must be verified by a written declaration that it is made under the penalties of perjury.[13] In the case of the Gift Tax a separate claim should be filed for each taxable year.[14] A fiduciary of a deceased taxpayer must file a certificate of letters, but if the fiduciary filed the original return this is not required.[15] Caution dictates that Form 843 be used in filing a claim for refund and that it be full and complete in every particular.

FORM NO. 67

Claim for Credit or Refund

To Be Filed With the District Director Where
Assessment Was Made or Tax Paid

District Director's Stamp
(Date received)

The District Director will indicate in the block below the kind of claim filed, and fill in, where required.

[x] Refund of Taxes Illegally, Erroneously, or Excessively Collected.

[ ] Refund of Amount Paid for Stamps Unused, or Used in Error or Excess.

[ ] Abatement of Tax Assessed (not applicable to estate, gift, or income taxes).

Please Type or Print Plainly

Name of taxpayer or purchaser of stamps
  Katherine Benson, Executrix under Last Will and Testament of Winthrop Benson
Number and street
  100 Elm Street
City, town, postal zone, State
  Copiague, L. I., N. Y.

---

10. Hoyt v US, 21 F Supp 353 (1937).

11. Hansen, 9 TC 108 (1947); McFadden, 3 TCM 155 (1944).

12. IRC, § 7742 (1954 Code).

13. Reg, § 301.6402–2(a)(2),(b)(1).

14. Reg, § 301.6402–2(d).

15. Reg, § 301.6402–2(e).

1. District in which return (if any) was filed
   First New York

2. Name and address shown on return, if different from above

3. Period—If for tax reported on annual basis, prepare separate form
   for each taxable year
   From ...., 19..... To ...., 19.....

4. Kind of tax
   Estate Tax

5. Amount of assessment
   $3,468.12
   Date of payment
      March 10, 1958

6. Date stamps were purchased from the Government

7. Amount to be refunded
   $3,468.12

8. Amount to be abated (not applicable to income, estate, or gift taxes)
   $.......

9. The claimant believes that this claim should be allowed for the following reasons:

The above assessment was made as a deficiency assessment predicated
on the contention of the Commissioner that inter vivos transfers made by
the decedent within three years of his death were made in contemplation
of death within the meaning of the statute. As appears from the annexed
documents, said transfers were not within the purview of the statute
and the assessment and collection of the tax was erroneous.

Attach letter size sheets if space is not sufficient.

I declare under the penalties of perjury that this claim (including any
accompanying schedules and statements) has been examined by me and to
the best of my knowledge and belief is true and correct.

Signed KATHERINE BENSON

Dated Jan. 15, 1960

For District Director's Use Only

TRANSCRIPT OF CLAIMANT'S ACCOUNT

(Complete only as to Miscellaneous Excise Taxes and Alcohol, Tobacco, and Certain Other Excise Taxes Imposed Under Subtitles D and E, Internal Revenue Code)

The following is a transcript of the records of this office covering the liability that is the subject of this claim.

A—Assessed Taxes

Taxable Period and Class of Tax (a)	Account Number (b)	Reference and Date (c)	Amount Assessed (d)	Paid, Abated, or Credited Date or Sched. No. (e)	Amount (f)	PD. AB. CR. (g)	Remarks (h)

B—Purchase of Stamps

To Whom Sold Or Issued (i)	Kind (j)	Number (k)	Denomination (l)	Date of Sale (m)	Amount (n)	If Special Tax Stamp, State: Serial No. (o)	Period Commencing (p)

Prepared By (*Initials*)   Date   District

§ 377. Credit or Refund; State Death Taxes; Foreign Death Taxes.

It will be recalled that in the discussion of the credit for State death taxes and foreign death taxes, the statute prescribed a period of limitations in both cases.[16] The statute of limitations in such cases differs from the general statute for credit or refund. It is provided with respect to the credit for State death taxes that refund based on the credit may (*despite the provisions of Sections 6511 and 6512*) be made if claim therefor is filed within the period provided by Section 2011, but that any such refund shall be made without interest.[17] Identical language is used in respect to the credit for foreign death taxes.[18]

§ 378. Credit or Refund; Limitation on Allowance.

The statute provides that no credit or refund may be allowed after the period of limitations for filing a claim, unless a claim has been filed within the statutory period.[19]

It then provides for limitations on the amount of the credit or refund, namely;

(1) If the claim was filed during the three year period, the amount of credit or refund shall not exceed the portion of the tax

16. §§ 315, 319, supra.

17. IRC, § 2011(c) (1954 Code); Rev Rul 56–568, 1956 2 CB 1001.

18. IRC, § 2014(e) (1954 Code).

19. IRC, § 6511(b)(1) (1954 Code).

paid within the three years immediately preceding the filing of the claim, equal to three years plus the period of any extension of time for filing the return.

(2) If the claim was not filed within the three year period, the amount of the credit or refund shall not exceed the portion of the tax paid during the two years immediately preceding the filing of the claim.

(3) If no claim was filed, the credit or refund shall not exceed the amount which would be allowable under (1) or (2), as the case may be, if claim was filed on the date the credit or refund is allowed.[20]

§ 379. Credit or Refund; Interest.

With the exception of the credit for State death taxes or foreign death taxes,[1] interest is allowed and paid upon any overpayment in tax at the rate of six percent per annum.[2] In the case of a credit, it is payable from the date of the overpayment to the due date of the amount against which the credit is taken.[3] In the case of a refund, it is payable from the date of the overpayment to a date determined by the District Director, which shall be not more than thirty days prior to the date of the refund check. The acceptance of a refund check does not deprive the taxpayer of the right to make a claim for any additional overpayment and interest thereon, provided the claim is made within the applicable period of limitations. If a taxpayer does not accept a refund check, no additional interest on the amount of the overpayment included in the check will be allowed.[4]

"Due date" means the last day fixed by law or regulations for the payment of the tax (determined without regard to any extension of time), and not the date on which the District Director makes demand for the payment of the tax.[5]

Prior to the amendment of the section by the Technical Amendments Act of 1958 in the case of a credit it was payable as presently provided, but if the amount against which the credit was taken was an additional assessment, payment of interest was

---

20. IRC, § 6511(b)(2) (1954 Code), as amended by Technical Amendments Act of 1958, § 82(b), HR 8381, 85th Cong, 2nd Sess.

  1. § 377, supra.

  2. IRC, § 6611(a) (1954 Code).

  3. IRC, § 6611(b)(1) (1954 Code), as

amended by Technical Amendments Act of 1958, § 83(b), HR 8381, 85th Cong, 2nd Sess.

  4. IRC, § 6611(b)(2) (1954 Code); Reg, § 301.6611–1(f).

  5. Reg, § 301.6611–1(g)(2).

up to the date of the assessment of that amount.[6] The term "additional assessment" meant a further assessment for a tax of the same character previously paid in part, and included the assessment of a deficiency (as defined in Section 6211[7]).[7a] The amendment has removed the previous difference between interest on an overpayment credited against the original tax and that credited against an additional assessment. *The amendment applies only in respect of overpayments credited after December 31, 1957.*[7b]

§ 380. Credit or Refund; Effect of Petition to Tax Court.

If the taxpayer files a petition with the Tax Court for redetermination of the deficiency, no credit or refund may be allowed or made, and no suit for the recovery of any part of the tax shall be instituted by the taxpayer, *except* as to the following:

(1) An overpayment determined by a decision of the Tax Court which has become final.

(2) Any amount collected in excess of an amount computed in accordance with the decision of the Tax Court which has become final.

(3) Any amount collected after the expiration of the period of limitation upon levying or beginning a proceeding in court for collection.[8]

§ 381. Credit or Refund; Overpayment Determined by Tax Court.

If the Tax Court finds that there is no deficiency and further finds that the taxpayer has made an overpayment, or finds that there is a deficiency, but that the taxpayer has made an overpayment of such tax, the overpayment determined by the Tax Court shall be credited and refunded to the taxpayer when the decision of the Tax Court has become final. No such credit or refund shall be allowed or made of any portion of the tax *unless the Tax Court determines as part of its decision that such portion was paid*—

(1) After the mailing of the notice of deficiency, or

---

6. IRC, § 6611(b)(1) (1954 Code) before amendment.

7. § 336, supra.

7a. IRC, § 6611(c) (1954 Code) before repeal by Technical Amendments Act of 1958, § 83(c), HR 8381, 85th Cong, 2nd Sess.

7b. Technical Amendments Act of 1958, § 83(d), HR 8381, 85th Cong, 2nd Sess.

8. IRC, § 6512(a) (1954 Code); Reg, § 301.6512–1(a).

(2) Within the period which would be applicable under Section 6511 (b)(2), (c), or (d), if on the date of the mailing of the notice of deficiency a claim had been filed (whether or not filed) stating the grounds upon which the Tax Court finds that there is an overpayment.[9]

In the case of a jeopardy assessment made under Section 6861 (a), if the amount which should have been assessed as determined by a decision of the Tax Court which has become final is less than the amount already collected, the excess payment shall be credited or refunded subject to a determination being made by the Tax Court with respect to the time of payment as above stated.[10]

If the amount of the deficiency as determined by the Tax Court (in a case where collection has not been stayed by the filing of a bond) is disallowed in whole or in part by the reviewing court, then the overpayment resulting from such disallowance shall be credited or refunded without the making of claim therefor, *subject to a determination being made by the Tax Court with respect to the time of payment* as above stated.[11]

Where the amount collected is in excess of the amount computed in accordance with the decision of the Tax Court which has become final, the excess payment shall be credited or refunded within the period of limitation provided in Section 6511.[12]

Where an amount is collected after the statutory period upon the beginning of levy or a proceeding in court for collection has expired, the taxpayer may file a claim for refund of the amount so collected within the period of limitation provided in Section 6511. In any such case, the decision of the Tax Court as to whether the statutory period upon collection of the tax expired before notice of deficiency was mailed shall, when the decision becomes final, be conclusive.[13]

It should be noted that the decision of the Tax Court must determine the time of payment.

§ 382. Waiver of Restrictions on Assessment; Closing Agreements; Compromises.

There are three terms used in the statute which are frequently confused. The first of these is a waiver of restrictions on assessment and collection of deficiency, heretofore referred to.[14] A

---

9. IRC, § 6512(b) (1954 Code); Reg, § 301.6512-1(b).
   10. Reg, § 301.6512-1(c).
   11. Reg, § 301.6512-1(d).

12. Reg, § 301.5612-1(e).
   13. IRC, § 6512(a)(3) (1954 Code); Reg, § 301.6512-1(f).
   14. § 334, supra.

taxpayer at any time has the right, by a signed notice in writing, to waive the restrictions of the Code[15] on the assessment and collection of the whole or any part of the deficiency.[16] This may be signed either before or after a notice of deficiency is mailed. Form 890 upon which the waiver is indicated refers to the fact that such waiver is *not a closing agreement* and does not preclude the assertion of a deficiency or further deficiency nor extend the statutory period of limitation for refund, assessment or collection of the tax. It does not however point out the fact that the filing of the waiver stops the running of interest on the deficiency if notice and demand for payment of the tax is not made within thirty days.[17] It also does not point out that the waiver does not bar an action for refund, but *if it is signed before* the notice of deficiency has been mailed, and none is mailed, as is customary in such cases, the right to seek a redetermination in the Tax Court is lost.[18]

The second term is "closing agreement". The Secretary or his delegate is authorized to enter into an agreement in writing with any person relating to the liability of such person (or of the person or estate for whom he acts) in respect of any Internal Revenue tax for any taxable period.[19]

If such agreement is approved by the Secretary or his delegate (within such time as may be stated in such agreement, or later agreed to) such agreement shall be final and conclusive, and, except upon a showing of fraud or malfeasance, or misrepresentation of a material fact—

(1) the case shall not be reopened as to the matters agreed upon or the agreement modified by any officer, employee, or agent of the United States, and

(2) in any suit, action, or proceeding, such agreement, or any determination assessment, collection, payment, abatement, refund, or credit made in accordance therewith, shall not be annulled, modified, set aside, or disregarded.[20]

The important provision to note is that the agreement must be signed not only by the taxpayer, but must be approved by the Secretary or his delegate. There is much authority to the effect

15. IRC, § 6213(a) (1954 Code).
16. IRC, § 6213(d) (1954 Code).
17. IRC, § 6601(d) (1954 Code); § 366, supra.
18. Note 15, supra; Monge v Smyth,

229 F2d 361 (CA 9) (1956); Associated Mutual v Delaney, 176 F2d 179 (CA 1) (1949).
19. IRC, § 7121(a) (1954 Code).
20. IRC, § 7121(b) (1954 Code).

that if this not be present the agreement is not effective.[1] Attempts have been made to obtain the effect of a closing agreement by incorporating the statutory language into the waiver on restrictions. Such attempts have been unsuccessful.[2] The form used for the agreement is Form 866.

The statute also provides for compromises. The Secretary or his delegate may compromise any civil or criminal case arising under the Internal Revenue laws prior to reference to the Department of Justice for prosecution or defense; and the Attorney General or his delegate may compromise any such case after reference to the Department of Justice for prosecution or defense. The statute further provides for the filing of the opinion of the General Counsel of the Treasury with his reasons for making the compromise, together with a statement of the amount of tax assessed, interest, additional amounts and penalties and the amount actually paid. Such opinion is not required in any civil case where the unpaid tax is less than $500.[3] In order for an offer in compromise to be accepted there must be uncertainty as to liability or collection,[4] but there is no statutory authority to compromise solely because a hard case which excites sympathy or is appealing from the standpoint of equity is presented.[5]

An offer in compromise is made either on Form 656 or 656C, depending on whether the offer is made to pay in full the amount of the compromise, or in installments. The Internal Revenue Service has promulgated rules of procedure. Either form must be accompanied by Form 433, a financial statement of the taxpayer. After the offer has been filed with the District Director, the procedure followed depends upon the amount involved and the prior history of the case. If the offer is accepted it is binding on the taxpayer and the Treasury.[6]

§ 383. Reversionary or Remainder Interests; Extension of Time for Payment of Tax.

We have previously discussed the subject of extension of time

1. Botany Worsted Mills v US, 278 US 282, 73 L ed 379, 49 S Ct 129 (1939); US v Lustig, 163 F2d 85 (CCA 2) (1947); Bank of NY v US, 141 F Supp 364 (1956); Bennett v US, 231 F2d 465 (CA 7) (1956).

2. Bank of NY v US, note 1, supra.

3. IRC, § 7122 (1954 Code).

4. Op Atty Gen 7, XIII-2 CB 445.

5. Op Atty Gen 6, XIII-2 CB 442; 7, XIII-2 CB 445.

6. Walker v Alamo Foods, 16 F2d 694 (CCA 5) (1927); Backus v US, 59 F2d 242 (1932); Ely & Walker Dry Goods Co. v US, 34 F2d 429 (CCA 8) (1929); Ayer v White, 62 F2d 921 (CCA 1) (1933).

for payment of the tax generally,[7] and the right of the fiduciary to elect postponement of payment of the tax in the case of a reversionary or remainder interest.[8] In the case of inclusion of a reversionary or remainder interest in property, the payment of the part of the tax attributable to that interest may, at the election of the executor, be postponed until six months after the termination of the precedent interest or interests in the property.[9] The provision is limited to cases in which the reversionary or remainder interests are included in the decedent's gross estate as such and does not extend to cases in which the decedent creates future interests by his own testamentary act.[10]

If the Secretary or his delegate finds that the payment of the tax at the expiration of the period of postponement provided for in the statute would result in undue hardship to the estate, he may extend the time for payment for a reasonable period not in excess of two years from the expiration of such period of postponement.[10a] Thus authorization for further extension was added by the Technical Amendments Act of 1958 and applies where the precedent interest or interests did not terminate before the beginning of the six month period which ended on the date of the enactment of the Act, namely, September 2, 1958.[10b]

Notice of the exercise of the election to postpone the payment of the tax must be filed with the District Director before the date prescribed for payment of the tax. The notice of election may be made in the form of a letter addressed to the District Director. There should be filed with the notice of election a certified copy of the will or other instrument under which the reversionary or remainder interest was created, or a copy verified by the executor if the instrument is not filed of record. The District Director may require the submission of such additional proof as he deems necessary to disclose the complete facts. If the duration of the precedent interest is dependent upon the life of any person, the notice of election must show the date of birth of that person.[11]

If the decedent's gross estate consists of both a reversionary or remainder interest in property and other property, the tax

7. § 339, supra.

8. §§ 326, 364, supra.

9. IRC, § 6163(a) (1954 Code).

10. Reg, § 20.6163–1(a).

10a. IRC, § 6163(b) (1954 Code), added by Technical Amendments Act of 1958, § 66(b)(1), HR 8381, 85th Cong, 2nd Sess.

10b. Technical Amendments Act of 1958, § 66(b)(3), HR 8381, 85th Cong, 2nd Sess.

11. Reg, § 20.6163–1(b).

attributable to the reversionary or remainder interest, is an amount which bears the same ratio to the total tax as the value of the reversionary or remainder interests reduced by (1) the amount of claims, mortgages, and indebtedness which is a lien on such interest; (2) losses during the settlement of the estate; (3) charitable deductions; and (4) the portion of the marital deduction allowed on account of bequests of such interest to the decedent's surviving spouse, bears to the entire gross estate reduced by such deductions having similar relationship to the items comprising the gross estate.[12]

Before a postponement may be granted, as in the case of an extension of time for payment,[13] a bond must be furnished for double the amount of the tax and estimated interest for the duration of the precedent interest, conditioned upon the payment of the tax and interest accrued, within six months after the termination of the precedent interest. If after the acceptance of the bond it is determined that the amount of the tax attributable to the reversionary or remainder interest was understated in the bond, a new bond or a supplemental bond may be required, or the tax, to the extent of the understatement may be collected. The bond must be conditioned upon the principal or surety promptly notifying the District Director when the precedent interest terminates and upon the principal or surety notifying the District Director during the month of September of each year as to the continuance of the precedent interest, if the duration of the precedent interest is dependent upon the life or lives of any person or persons, or is otherwise indefinite.[14]

As has been noted, the rate of interest payable on the amount of tax postponed is not at the usual rate of six percent, but at the reduced rate of four percent.[15]

§ 384. Bonds; Form; Single Bond in Lieu of Multiple Bonds.

We have seen that there are many cases in which bonds are required, such as for extension of time for payment of the tax,[16] to stay the collection of a jeopardy assessment,[17] where the tax on a reversionary or remainder interest is postponed,[18] and for release of lien.[19] We shall see that a bond is also required when

12. Reg, § 20.6163–1(c).
13. Note 7, supra.
14. Reg, § 20.6165–1(b).
15. § 364, supra.

16. Note 7, supra.
17. § 357, supra.
18. § 383, supra.
19. § 352, supra.

a review of the decision of the Tax Court is sought in the Court of Appeals.[20]

Whenever a bond is required it must be in such form and with such surety or sureties as may be prescribed by the Regulations, except that in lieu of such bond a deposit of bonds or notes of the United States may be made.[1] In any case in which two or more bonds are required or authorized, a single bond may be provided for.[2] The bond is usually that of a surety company holding a certificate of authority from the Secretary of the Treasury as an acceptable surety on Federal bonds.

§ 385. Time for Performing Certain Acts Postponed by Reason of War.

The 1939 Code contained provision for the suspension of the various time limitations which we have been discussing in the case of persons in the Armed Forces of the United States in a combat zone. We have seen that there are special exemptions for such personnel.[3] The 1954 Code provides for the time within which certain acts are otherwise required to be performed or there are statutes of limitation, the time otherwise provided is extended during the period of such service, or hospitalization outside the United States and the District of Columbia as a result of injury received while serving in such area, and the next 180 days thereafter. The statute provides that such period of time shall be disregarded in determining whether any of the following acts were performed within the time prescribed: filing a return, paying the tax, filing a petition with the Tax Court, allowance of credit or refund, filing claim for credit or refund, bringing suit for credit or refund, assessment of any tax, giving or making any notice or demand for payment of tax, collection of the tax, bringing suit for collection, any other act required or permitted. The suspension also applies to the amount of any credit or refund.[4]

There are excepted, jeopardy assessments, bankruptcy and receiverships, transferred assets, and action taken before ascertainment of the fact that the person was entitled to the benefits of the statute.[5]

20. IRC, § 7485 (1954 Code).
1. IRC, § 7101 (1954 Code).
2. IRC, § 7102 (1954 Code).
3. §§ 195, 297, supra.
4. IRC, § 7508(a) (1954 Code).
5. IRC, § 7508(b) (1954 Code).

§ 386. Estates of Nonresidents Not Citizens.

The provisions of the statute dealing with returns and procedure apply in all substantial respects to the estates of nonresidents not citizens, except as we have observed with respect to the preliminary notice,[6] usual return,[7] place of filing and payment of the tax,[8] transfer certificates in such estates,[9] and the suspension of the period of limitations on assessment when notice of deficiency is mailed outside the United States.[10] The procedure for assessment, collection, and appeal, are the same in the estates of nonresidents not citizens as in estates of residents or citizens.

§ 387. Review of Deficiency; Actions for Refund.

We have been concerned up to this point with the procedures before the Internal Revenue Service. This having been completed, if the taxpayer is dissatisfied with the result, he has a choice of seeking a review of the administrative action either before the Tax Court of the United States, the Court of Claims, or the United States District Court. In the first instance, without paying the tax, he files a petition with the Tax Court within the statutory period. In the others, he pays the tax and then after application for refund and denial thereof or failure to act by the tax authorities, he is authorized to institute action for refund. The procedures in all such cases are treated hereafter.[11]

6. § 24, supra.
7. § 27, supra.
8. § 28, supra.
9. § 331, supra.
10. § 362, supra.
11. Chaps 11 et seq.

CHAPTER 6

GENERAL PRINCIPLES OF FEDERAL GIFT TAX

§ 388. Scope of Chapter.

From the very beginning of the Estate Tax in 1916, fertile minds began exploring methods of avoiding its effects. One of the most effective means is not to possess property at death. Persons possessed of large fortunes thereupon began to make lifetime gifts of substantial portions of their property, as a result of which the Estate Tax impact was considerably lessened. In order to prevent this frustration of the Estate Tax, there was introduced into the tax law a Gift Tax, which imposed a tax upon lifetime transfers. A knowledge of probate or estate law without an understanding of the Gift Tax is not possible. It is, therefore, necessary to the practicing lawyer to know not only

539

the effect of Estate Taxes on the disposition of a client's property, but also the effect of Gift Taxes.

This chapter will treat of the general principles of gift taxation under the Federal statutes, so that preliminarily there may be developed an understanding of the nature, purpose, applicability and procedures involved in the Federal Gift Tax. With this foundation established we may then proceed to the details of the tax.

§ 389. Nature.

As in the case of the Estate Tax, although the tax is designated a Gift Tax, it is not a direct tax on the property which is the subject of the gift, but on the exercise of the power of transmitting property.[1] Its imposition does not rest upon general ownership, but is an excise tax based upon the use made of property, or the privilege of transmitting property.[2] It is not the receipt of property which is taxed, but the transfer.[3] The fact that the statute creates a lien does not change it from an excise tax to a direct tax on property.[4] In some cases, it has been said, it amounts to a down payment on the Estate Tax.[5]

§ 390. Constitutionality.

As might have been anticipated, the first Gift Tax, that of 1924, was attacked as a direct tax unapportioned, and also on the ground that it was a deprivation of property without due process of law. The United States Supreme Court, by a divided court, held that the tax was not a direct tax but an excise tax, and that it did not deprive of property without due process.[6] It was also attacked on the ground that it was an encroachment

---

1. Brown v Deputy, 30 F Supp 860 (1940).

2. Phipps v Comm, 91 F2d 627 (CCA 10), cert den 302 US 742, 82 L ed 574, 58 S Ct 144 (1937); Bromley v Mc-Caughn, 280 US 124, 74 L ed 226, 50 S Ct 46 (1929).

3. Smith v Shaughnessy, 318 US 176, 87 L ed 690, 63 S Ct 545 (1943); US v Ryerson, 114 F2d 150 (CCA 7), revd other grounds 312 US 260, 85 L ed 819, 61 S Ct 479, affd 312 US 405, 85 L ed 917, 61 S Ct 656 (1940); note 1, supra.

4. Blodgett v Holden, 11 F2d 180,

revd other grounds 27 F2d 1016 (CCA 6), mod 275 US 142, 72 L ed 206, 48 S Ct 105 (1926).

5. Smith v Shaughnessy, note 3, supra.

6. Bromley v McCaughn, note 2, supra; see also Anderson v McNeir, 16 F2d 970 (CCA 1), revd other grounds 275 US 577, 72 L ed 435, 48 S Ct 204 (1927); note 4, supra; O'Connor v Anderson, 28 F2d 873 (CCA 1), affd 280 US 615, 74 L ed 656, 50 S Ct 81 (1928); Means v US, 39 F2d 748, cert den 282 US 849, 75 L ed 753, 51 S Ct 28 (1930).

on state rights and an abuse of Congressional powers,[7] and that it provided for unreasonable and capricious classification.[8] None of these attacks were successful.

The 1932 Gift Tax statute was similarly subjected to test of its constitutionality and it too was sustained.[9]

The original statute was also attacked because it sought to make the tax apply to gifts effective before the enactment of the statute. The Supreme Court held that to the extent that the statute sought to do so it was arbitrary and invalid.[10] In the enactment of the 1932 statute Congress specifically provided that the tax did not apply to transfers made prior to the date of the act,[11] and that the calendar year for purposes of the act included only that portion of the year after the date of enactment.[12]

§ 391. Statutory Structure and History.

The first Federal Gift Tax statute was enacted in 1924[13] and was in effect only from June 2, 1924 to December 31, 1925. It was repealed as of January 1, 1926.[14] Its repeal was due to its ineffectiveness and the difficulty of administering it. Since there was an annual exemption as well as exclusion it produced little revenue and was easily overcome.[15]

With the increase in the methods of avoiding Estate and Income Taxes by means of lifetime gifts and the tax authorities' lack of success in including such transfers in the donor's gross estate as transfers in contemplation of death, Congress decided to stop this drain on the revenue by the enactment of a new Gift Tax statute.[16] Among its purposes it has been stated that it was intended to discourage family settlements so as to avoid high income surtaxes,[17] not only to prevent Estate Tax avoidance, but also to prevent Income Tax avoidance through reducing yearly income and thereby escaping the effect of

7. Note 4, supra; Bowers v Taft, 20 F2d 561 (CCA 1), cert den 275 US 520, 72 L ed 404, 48 S Ct 121 (1927).

8. Anderson v McNeir, note 6, supra.

9. Housman v Comm, 105 F2d 973 (CCA 2), affg 38 BTA 1007, cert den 309 US 656, 84 L ed 1005, 60 S Ct 469 (1939); Dupont v Deputy, 26 F Supp 773 (1939).

10. Blodgett v Holden, 275 US 142, 72 L ed 206, 48 S Ct 105 (1928); Anderson v McNeir, 275 US 577, 72 L ed 435, 48 S Ct 204 (1927); Untermeyer v Ander-

son, 276 US 440, 72 L ed 645, 48 S Ct 353 (1928).

11. Rev Act 1932, § 501(b).

12. Rev Act 1932, § 531(a), effective June 6, 1932.

13. Rev Act 1924, §§ 319–324.

14. Rev Act 1926, § 1200.

15. See Sen Fin Com Rep 52, 69th Cong, 1st Sess p 9.

16. Rev Act 1932, §§ 501–532.

17. Merrill v Fahs, 324 US 308, 89 L ed 963, 65 S Ct 655, rehg den 324 US 888, 89 L ed 1436, 65 S Ct 863 (1945).

progressive surtax rates,[18] and to prevent or compensate for the loss of surtax on income when large estates were split up by gifts to numerous donees.[19] As was also said, it was in the nature of a down payment on the Estate Tax.[20]

Having learned from the infirmities of the 1924 Gift Tax statute, the tax was applied at graduated rates, which are three quarters those applying to the Estate Tax in the same bracket, allowing but one lifetime exemption, with an annual exclusion, and providing for cumulative computation of the tax in a particular year, so that prior gifts are not disregarded, but must be considered in the computation of tax on the gifts made in the particular year.

It is this statute which was the progenitor of the Gift Tax under the 1939 Code,[1] and is the basis of Chapter 12 of the 1954 Code.

This recitation of historical events is for the purpose of impressing the fact that the statute in effect at the time of a gift is applicable. The 1954 Code provisions apply only to transfers by gift made during the calendar year 1955 and thereafter.[2] The 1939 Code provisions apply to transfers made for the calendar years 1940 to and including 1954.[3] Transfers prior to that time are controlled by the 1932 Act.[4]

§ 392. Outline of the Tax.

We will discover that the Gift Tax statute has many refinements and complexities. Before delving into these it is necessary to have a general understanding of what the tax is and how it operates. While the tax is not imposed upon property as such, the amount of tax is measured by the value of the property transferred. It is not applicable to transfers by corporations or other persons than individuals, but it is applicable to transfers by individuals to corporations or other persons.[5] A transfer by a corporation may, however, be considered a gift by the stockholders.[6] The tax applies to all transfers by gift of property, wherever situated, by an individual who is a citizen or

18. Smith v Shaughnessy, note 3, supra.

19. Sanford v Comm, 308 US 39, 84 L ed 20, 60 S Ct 51, rehg den 308 US 637, 84 L ed 529, 60 S Ct 258 (1939).

20. Smith v Shaughnessy, note 3, supra.

1. IRC, §§ 1000–1031 (1939 Code).
2. IRC, § 2501 (1954 Code).
3. IRC, § 1000 (1939 Code).
4. IRC, § 501 (1932 Act).
5. Reg, § 25.0–1(a).
6. Reg, § 25.2511–1(h)(1).

resident of the United States, to the extent the value of the transfer exceeds the amount of the exclusions authorized by the statute, and the deductions similarly authorized.[7] A citizen is subject to the tax whether or not a resident, as is a resident, whether or not a citizen. A resident is one who has his domicile in any of the states of the United States, the Territories of Alaska and Hawaii, and the District of Columbia.[8] In the case of nonresidents not citizens, different rules apply as to taxability.[9] The admission of Alaska will not change the effect of the Regulation.

The tax is imposed separately for each calendar year on the total taxable gifts made by a donor during that year, *but the rate of tax* depends not only on the amount of gifts made in the year in question, but on the total amount of gifts made in that year and in previous years.[10] The failure of the 1924 Act was in not tying the rate of tax to the total of gifts.

As we shall see, "gift" within the meaning of the Federal Gift Tax does not have the same meaning as under common law, since a gift may result for purposes of the statute from transfers not generally considered such.

As in the case of the Estate Tax there is a specific exemption which may be used at any time during a donor's lifetime applying to the total of gifts made by him. A nonresident not a citizen is not entitled to this exemption unless there is a tax convention permitting it.[11] In addition, the first $3,000. of gifts made to any one donee during the year is excluded from consideration in determining the amount of gifts for the calendar year.[12] This means that gifts may be made to any number of different individuals in any year and if each does not exceed $3,000., there will be no tax payable. The catch in this provision is that the annual exclusion is allowable only for gifts of *present interests*. This has been the subject of protracted litigation. In computing the amount of gifts subject to the tax there are also allowed deductions for gifts to charitable and similar purposes,[13] and as to gifts between spouses there is a marital deduction.[14] When husband or wife make a gift to a third person, it is also possible for the gift to be considered made one half by each upon proper consent by the other spouse.[15]

7. Note 5, supra.
8. Reg, § 25.0–1(b).
9. Reg, § 25.2511–3.
10. Reg, § 25.2502–1(a).
11. Reg, § 25.2521–1(a).

12. Reg, § 25.2503–2.
13. Reg, § 25.2522(a)–1.
14. Reg, § 25.2523(a)–1.
15. Reg, § 25.2513–1.

Each of these matters will be separately treated in greater detail hereafter.

The amount of tax payable for any calendar year is computed in six steps. First the amount of taxable gifts for the calendar year involved is determined. "Taxable gifts" is the total amount of gifts made during the calendar year, less the amount of specific exemption available, and the charitable and marital deduction, if any. "Total amount of gifts" is the total of gifts for the calendar year, less the total of annual exclusions. Next the aggregate sum of taxable gifts for each of the preceding years is determined. This is the total of such gifts less the annual exclusions applying in such year and any allowable deductions, but not the specific exemption. The results of the first and second step are added and the tax computed thereon. The tax is similarly computed on the total amount of taxable gifts for the years preceding the calendar year in question. The tax payable for the calendar year involved is the difference between these two taxes.[16] The actual computation will be illustrated in the chapter on computation.

§ 393. Statutory Construction.

In the construction of the Gift Tax statute any ambiguity in the statute is resolved by reference to Congressional statements made at the time of enactment.[17] Since the purpose of the statute was to reach every type and kind of transfer by gift, the terms used in the statute will be interpreted in their broadest and most comprehensive sense.[18] Since the Gift and Estate Tax laws are closely related, the provisions of the former will be read in the light of related provisions of the latter.[19] While the statutes must be read as in pari materia, where the Gift Tax statute is unambiguous, so that external aids are unnecessary, the rule must yield.[20] Of course, the ultimate construction of the statute

16. Note 10, supra.

17. Brier v Comm, 108 F2d 967 (CCA 3) (1939).

18. Comm v Hogle, 165 F2d 352 (CCA 10) (1947); Hardenburgh v Comm, 198 F2d 63 (CA 8), cert den 344 US 836, 97 L ed 650, 73 S Ct 45 (1952); Comm v Wemyss, 324 US 303, 89 L ed 958, 65 S Ct 652 (1945); Horst v Comm, 150 F2d 1 (CCA 9), cert den 326 US 761, 90 L ed 458, 66 S Ct 141 (1945).

19. Comm v Barnard, 176 F2d 233

(CA 2) (1949); Sanford v Comm, 308 US 39, 84 L ed 20, 60 S Ct 51, rehg den 308 US 637, 84 L ed 529, 60 S Ct 258 (1939); Comm v Walston, 168 F2d 211 (CCA 4) (1948); Hesslein v Hoey, 91 F2d 954 (CCA 1), cert den 302 US 756, 82 L ed 585, 58 S Ct 284 (1937).

20. Harris v Comm, 178 F2d 861 (CA 2), rehg den 339 US 946, 94 L ed 1360, 70 S Ct 795, revd other grounds 340 US 106, 95 L ed 111, 71 S Ct 181 (1949).

is that placed on it by the Supreme Court.[1] The Gift Tax being supplementary to the Estate Tax, the two are in pari materia and must be construed together.[2]

§ 394. Correlation of Gift Tax, Estate Tax, and Income Tax.

As we have seen, the purpose of the enactment of the Gift Tax was to prevent both Income Tax avoidance and Estate Tax avoidance.[3] It was also said to be a kind of down payment on the Estate Tax.[4] That being so, the question arises whether subjecting property to one tax will relieve it from payment of either of the others, or, whether the Gift Tax and the Estate Tax and the Gift Tax and the Income Tax are mutually exclusive.

It has been held that the Income Tax is not to be construed as though in pari materia with either the Estate Tax or the Gift Tax.[5] The Gift Tax and the Income Tax are separate and distinct, and neither is dependent upon the other for imposition of the tax.[6] As the court there noted, the Gift Tax is imposed not upon property but on the right of transfer, while the Income Tax is imposed on income at the time of realization. Income, Estate, and Gift Taxes are not mutually exclusive,[7] so that the fact that income from the transferred property is taxable to the donor neither prevents the imposition of a Gift Tax,[8] nor does it require the imposition of a Gift Tax.[9] The completeness of a transfer for Income Tax purposes has no effect on its completeness for Gift Tax purposes.[10]

So far as the Gift Tax and the Estate Tax is concerned they are not mutually exclusive.[11] Generally a transfer which is incomplete from the Estate Tax point of view is regarded as incomplete for Gift Tax purposes.[12] It does not follow, however,

1. Sanford v Comm, note 19, supra.

2. Sanford v Comm, note 19, supra; Merrill v Fahs, 324 US 308, 89 L ed 963, 65 S Ct 655, rehg den 324 US 888, 89 L ed 1436, 65 S Ct 863 (1945); Galt v Comm, 216 F2d 41 (CA 7), cert den 348 US 951, 99 L ed 743, 75 S Ct 438 (1954); Uhl v Comm, 241 F2d 867 (CA 7) (1957); Heringer v Comm, 235 F2d 149 (CA 9), cert den 352 US 927, 1 L ed 2d 162, 77 S Ct 225 (1956); Comm v Converse, 163 F2d 131 (CCA 2) (1947); Comm v Stewart, 153 F 2d 17 (CCA 3) (1946).

3. § 391, supra.

4. Smith v Shaughnessy, 318 US 176, 87 L ed 690, 63 S Ct 545 (1943).

5. Farid-Es-Sultanah v Comm, 160 F 2d 812 (CCA 2) (1947).

6. Galt v Comm, note 2, supra.

7. Whayne v Glenn, 59 F Supp 517 (1945).

8. Goulder v US, 45–2 USTC ¶10,210; Comm v Beck, 129 F2d 243 (CCA 2) (1942).

9. Blass, 11 TCM 622 (1948).

10. Comm v Prouty, 115 F2d 331 (CCA 1) (1940); Penn, 11 TCM 776 (1948).

11. Note 4, supra.

12. Higgins v Comm, 129 F2d 237

[Harris]—35 **545**

that a transfer which is complete for Gift Tax purposes may not also be subjected to the Estate Tax.[13] As we saw in our discussion of the Estate Tax, many transfers which are complete for purpose of the Gift Tax may nonetheless be subject to the Estate Tax.[14] In such case a credit is allowable for the Gift Tax paid.[15]

§ 395. Law Applicable.

While it is held that whether a taxpayer took the necessary steps to complete a gift is a question of Federal law and not State law,[16] it has also been held that if under State law the taxpayer could not make a gift, a tax could not be levied thereon.[17] Generally it may be said that whether a gift is of a present or future interest is a matter of Federal law and local law has no application,[18] unless the statute by express language or necessary implication makes its application dependent or local law.[19] The court will not be concerned with distinctions and technicalities of common law rules governing estates in land.[20] But State law will be applicable in determining the nature of an interest under a trust agreement to be administered under its law.[1] It will not, however, control the question of whether or not there is consideration within the meaning of the statute.[2]

§ 396. Domicile; Residence.

As in the case of the Estate Tax, the importance of whether the donor is a citizen or resident of the United States looms large in relation to the Gift Tax, since there is a difference in taxability, the specific exemption, some deductions, split gifts and the marital deduction, dependent on such fact.

(CCA 1), cert den 317 US 658, 87 L ed 529, 63 S Ct 57 (1942); Burnet v Guggenheim, 288 US 280, 77 L ed 748, 53 S Ct 369 (1933).

13. Comm v Procter, 142 F2d 824 (CCA 4), cert den 323 US 756, 89 L ed 606, 65 S Ct 90 (1944); Herzog v Comm, 116 F2d 591 (CCA 2) (1941).

14. §§ 118, et seq, supra; § 173, supra.

15. § 323, supra.

16. Richardson v Comm, 126 F2d 562 (CCA 2) (1942).

17. Bedford, 5 TC 726 (1945).

18. French v Comm, 138 F2d 254 (CCA 8) (1943); Charles v Hassett, 43 F Supp 432 (1942).

19. US v Pelzer, 312 US 399, 85 L ed 913, 61 S Ct 659 (1941); Comm v Greene, 119 F2d 383, cert den 314 US 641, 86 L ed 514, 62 S Ct 80 (1941); Allen, 3 TC 1224 (1944).

20. Wisotskey v Comm, 144 F2d 632 (CCA 3) (1944).

1. Cannon v Robertson, 98 F Supp 331 (1951); Ashcraft v Allen, 90 F Supp 543 (1950).

2. Greene, 1 TCM 758 (1942); Comm v Greene, note 19, supra.

The Regulations point out that the tax applies to all transfers by gift of property, wherever situated, by any individual who is a citizen or resident of the United States.[3] The Proposed Regulation provided that if the donor was a citizen of the United States, *whether or not a resident,* or a resident of the United States, whether or not a citizen, the tax applied regardless of where the property was situated.[4] A resident is one who has his domicile in any of the States of the United States, the Territories of Alaska or Hawaii, and the District of Columbia. A person acquires a domicile in a place by living there, for a brief period of time, with no definite present intention of moving therefrom. Residence without the requisite intention to remain indefinitely will not constitute domicile, nor will intention to change domicile effect such change unless accompanied by an actual removal.[5] In the case of the Gift Tax there has been little litigation on the subject.[6] The determination of the question would be made in the same way as in other cases.[7] The admission of Alaska will not change the effect of the Regulation.

The 1954 Code made certain changes with respect to gifts by alien nonresidents, which will be treated hereinafter.[8] It having been held that a citizen of the United States who at the time of his death resided in a possession of the United States was not a citizen for purposes of the Estate Tax,[8a] Congress added a new section to the Estate Tax statute[8b] and a new subdivision to the Gift Tax statute[8c] to overcome these decisions. The latter provides that a donor who is a citizen of the United States and a resident of a possession thereof shall, for purposes of the Gift Tax, be considered a "citizen" of the United States within the meaning of that term wherever used in the statute unless he acquired his United States citizenship *solely* by reason of (1) his being a citizen of such possession of the United States, or (2) his birth or residence within such possession of the United States. The provision applies only to gifts made after September 2, 1958. The effect is that a United States citizen who moves

3. Reg, § 25.2501–1(a).

4. Reg, § 25.2501–2(a).

5. Reg, § 25.2501–1(b).

6. See Forni, 22 TC 975 (1954); De-Goldschmidt-Rothschild v Comm, 9 TC 325, affd 168 F2d 975 (CCA 2) (1947).

7. § 7, supra.

8. §§ 428, 476, infra.

8a. Fairchild, 24 TC 408 (1956);

Smallwood, 11 TC 740 (1949); Rivera, 214 F2d 60 (CA 2), affg 19 TC 271 (1954).

8b. IRC, § 2208 (1954 Code).

8c. IRC, § 2501(b) (1954 Code), as added by Technical Amendments Act of 1958, § 102(b), HR 8381, 85th Cong, 2nd Sess.

from the United States to one of the possessions will be treated for Gift Tax purposes in the same manner in which he would have been treated if he had remained in the United States.

§ 397. Authority for Proceedings.

While the Gift Tax statute is the basis for all procedure under it, the procedure and administration of the tax has been grouped together with the Income Tax and Estate Tax under general provisions for procedure and administration, with authority granted to the Secretary of the Treasury or his delegate to promulgate regulations.[9] Pursuant thereto there have been issued Regulations which in minutest detail prescribe the administrative procedure to be followed. The Regulations follow the statutory numbering of the sections of the law and are of great aid in clarifying involved provisions of the statute and leading the way for those not too well acquainted with the Gift Tax. They also serve in many cases to clear up questions that have been raised by the statute, by stating the position the Internal Revenue Service will take on some of these. While they are helpful, they must not be taken in every case as determinative of a question. As we shall see in the succeeding section, not every Regulation is necessarily a correct exposition of the law, and in some instances the courts have disagreed with the position expressed in a Regulation. It is only fair to say, however, that it is a rare instance in which the courts have done so, and for the most part the Regulations are a statement of case law.

Another source of information is the instructions which are part of the Gift Tax Return.[10] The Donee's or Trustee's Information Return of Gifts,[11] which was formerly in use, also contained helpful instructions. *The final Gift Tax Regulations eliminated the requirement for the latter return.*

§ 398. Applicable Statutes and Regulations.

Although the Gift Tax statute was enacted on August 17, 1954, unlike the Estate Tax statute, it did not become operative on that date, but was expressly made applicable to gifts made during the calendar year *1955* and each calendar year thereafter.[12] To have made it applicable as of the date of enactment would have presented many administrative difficulties. The provisions of

9. IRC, §§ 6001 et seq.
10. Form 709.

11. Form 710.
12. IRC, § 2501(a) (1954 Code).

the 1939 Code apply to gifts for the calendar years 1940 to 1954 inclusive, and the provisions of the 1932 Act apply to gifts from June 6, 1932 to and including December 31, 1939.[13] These dates are important, since the annual exclusion differed, as we shall see.

The present Gift Tax statute is Chapter 12 of the Internal Revenue Code of 1954. Subchapter A deals with the determination of liability for the tax. Subchapter B treats of transfers which are deemed taxable gifts and exceptions thereto, and Subchapter C treats of the specific exemption and allowable deductions.

Since gifts made in prior years are considered in the computation of the tax for the current calendar year, it is important to bear in mind that the statute in effect at the time of prior transfers to some extent controls the present tax. It is also necessary to keep in mind the fact that the law has been amended from time to time, and transfers taxable at one time may no longer be so, as in some instances in the cases of nonresidents, and on the other hand deductions now allowable, such as the marital deduction, were not allowable under prior statutes. *Where there have been gifts at a prior time the statute in effect then must be consulted.*

With each of the Gift Tax statutes there have been corresponding Regulations promulgated.[14] Some of the Regulations promulgated under prior statutes have been held to be in conflict with the statute and have been rejected by the courts.[15] Others have been sustained.[16] The courts have also interpreted a Reg-

13. IRC, § 1000(a) (1939 Code).

14. 1954 Code, Reg, § 25.2501 et seq; 1939 Code, Reg 108; 1932 Act, Reg 79.

15. Rasquin v Humphrey, 308 US 54, 84 L ed 77, 60 S Ct 77 (1939); Wemyss v Comm, 144 F2d 78 (CCA 6), revd other grounds 324 US 303, 89 L ed 958, 65 S Ct 652 (1944); Higgins v Comm, 129 F2d 237 (CCA 1), cert den 317 US 658, 87 L ed 529, 63 S Ct 57 (1942); Comm v Wells, 88 F2d 339 (CCA 7) (1937); Comm v Powers, 115 F2d 209 (CCA 1), cert den 311 US 640, 85 L ed 408, 61 S Ct 141, affd 312 US 259, 85 L ed 817, 61 S Ct 509 (1940); Comm v Shattuck, 97 F2d 790 (CCA 7) (1938); Essick v US, 88 F Supp 23 (1949);

Comm v Walston, 168 F2d 211 (CCA 4) (1948).

16. Herrmann v Comm, 235 F2d 440 (CA 5) (1956); Zanuck v Comm, 149 F2d 714 (CCA 9) (1945); US v Ryerson, 114 F2d 150 (CCA 7), revd other grounds 312 US 260, 85 L ed 819, 61 S Ct 479, affd 312 US 405, 85 L ed 917, 61 S Ct 656 (1940); Helvering v Cronin, 106 F2d 907 (CCA 8) (1939); Comm v Haines, 104 F2d 854 (CCA 3) (1939); Affelder v Comm, 7 TC 1190 (1946); Edwards v Comm, 46 BTA 815, affd 135 F2d 574 (CCA 7) (1942); Fondren v Comm, 324 US 18, 89 L ed 668, 65 S Ct 499 (1945); US v Pelzer, 312 US 399, 85 L ed 913, 61 S Ct 659 (1941);

ulation differently than intended by the Treasury.[17] Generally it may be said that Regulations cannot create a tax or enlarge a taxing statute.[18] Reasonably clear revenue statutes cannot be extended or restricted by administrative regulations. When they do not explain, but legislate, they will be rejected by the courts.[19]

§ 399. Definitions; Residents; Nonresidents.

The statute provides that the Gift Tax shall be imposed on the transfer of property by gift during a calendar year *by any individual,* resident or nonresident, *except* transfers of tangible property by a nonresident who is not a citizen of the United States and who was not engaged in business in the United States during such calendar year.[20]

The statute defines neither resident, nonresident, nor citizen. However, the Regulations, as we have seen, defines a resident as one who has his domicile in any of the States of the United States, the Territories of Alaska and Hawaii, and the District of Columbia.[1] The Estate Tax Regulation[2] and the Gift Tax Regulation correspond. All others are declared to be nonresidents.[3] For the purposes of the Regulations the term "nonresident alien" means a person who is a nonresident not a citizen of the United States at the time of the gift.[4] The admission of Alaska will not affect this.

The Technical Amendments Act of 1958 made an important change in the Gift Tax statute with respect to citizens of the United States residing in one of the possessions, which has been treated previously.[4a]

§ 400. Definitions; Calendar Year; Preceding Calendar Years; Taxable Gifts.

While the statute contains definitions of other terms used, the primary ones requiring definition for the purposes of the com-

Latta v Comm, 212 F2d 164 (CA 3), cert den 348 US 825, 99 L ed 650, 75 S Ct 40 (1954).

17. Roberts v Comm, 143 F2d 657 (CCA 5), cert den 324 US 841, 89 L ed 1403, 65 S Ct 585 (1944); Comm v Barnard, 176 F2d 233 (CA 2) (1949); Guggenheim v Rasquin, 312 US 254, 85 L ed 813, 61 S Ct 507 (1941).

18. Missouri Packing Co. v Hellmich,

12 F2d 978 (CCA 8), 273 US 242, 71 L ed 628, 47 S Ct 395 (1926).

19. See Comm v Clark, 202 F2d 94 (1953).

20. IRC, § 2501(a) (1954 Code).
1. Reg, § 25.2501–1(b).
2. Reg, § 20.0–1(b).
3. Note 13, supra.
4. Note 3, supra.
4a. See § 396, supra.

putation of the tax are "calendar year", "preceding calendar year", and "taxable gifts".

The term "calendar year" includes only the calendar year 1932 and succeeding calendar years, and, in the case of the calendar year 1932, includes only the portion of such year after June 6, 1932.[5] The significance of the date is that the 1932 Act became effective on that date and applied only to transfers on and after that date.[6]

The term "preceding calendar years" means the calendar year 1932 and all calendar years intervening between the calendar year 1932 and the calendar year for which the tax is being computed.[7]

The term "taxable gifts" means the total amount of gifts made during the calendar year, less the deductions provided in Subchapter C.[8] The deductions referred to are the specific exemption, and the charitable and marital deductions. Under the 1939 Code the term used was "net gifts".[9] There is no difference in meaning between the two terms.

§401. Outline of Procedure.

The procedure under the Gift Tax resembles the procedure under the Estate Tax only in some particulars. Just as in the case of the Estate Tax all estates are not required to file a return, so in the case of the Gift Tax, a return is required to be made only for such gifts as exceed the amount of the annual exclusion, except that *in all cases where the gift is of a future interest* a return is required.[10] *Until November 1958* it was required not only that the donor file a return, but also that an information return be filed by the donee. This was provided for by the Regulations under the 1939 Code, and the Proposed Gift Tax Regulations for the 1954 Code contained explicit instructions for such a return.[11] *Such return, which was required to be made upon a specific form, is no longer required for gifts made after the calendar year 1954.* The requirement therefor has been deleted from the final Gift Tax Regulations.[11a] There is also required that where a gift is made by husband and wife as a split-gift that a consent be filed.[12]

5. IRC, § 2502(b) (1954 Code).
6. Comm v Copley, 194 F2d 364 (CA 7) (1952).
7. IRC, § 2502(c) (1954 Code).
8. IRC, § 2503(a) (1954 Code).
9. IRC, § 1003(a) (1939 Code).
10. Reg, § 25.6019–1(a).
11. Proposed Reg, § 25.6011–1.
11a. Reg, § 25.6011–1.
12. Reg, § 25.6019–2.

The return is required to be filed on or before the due date, usually April 15th of the year following the calendar year in which the gifts were made, unless an extension has been granted.[13] Unless there is an error in the return, or there is some question with respect to valuation, the annual exclusion, or a deduction, there is no field audit and the matter is concluded. If the Internal Revenue Service determines that additional tax is due, the procedure thereafter is the same as in the case of the Estate Tax.

In succeeding sections we shall treat of each of the preliminary procedural details in connection with the returns and filing thereof, as well as payment of the tax.

§ 402. Returns; Statutory Provisions.

The 1954 Code made no changes in substance in the requirement for Gift Tax returns. Any individual who in any calendar year makes any transfer by gift (except those which under Section 2503(b) are not to be included in the total amount of gifts for such year) is required to make a Gift Tax return.[14] Section 2503(b) excludes the first $3,000. to each donee of a gift of a present interest, from the total amount of gifts.

In the case of the election to treat a tenancy by the entirety as a gift in the year of its creation, a return is required whether or not the gift exceeds $3,000.[15]

There is no specific provision in the Code for the filing of the donee or trustee information return, which was required until the promulgation of the Gift Tax Regulations in November 1958. The Secretary of the Treasury is authorized to require such other returns as he deems sufficient to show liability for tax.[16] However, ever since the inception of the Gift Tax it had been required that a donee or trustee information return be filed, and in fact the Proposed Gift Tax Regulations dealt specifically and at great length with the requirements thereof.[16a] Prior Regulations had done likewise.[16b] When the final Gift Tax Regulations were issued in November 1958, the Treasury eliminated the requirement for the donee or trustee return.[16c] *Therefore, as to gifts made in the calendar year 1955 and thereafter, the donee or trustee is no longer required to file an information return.* In

---

13. Reg, § 25.6075–1.
14. IRC, § 6019(a) (1954 Code).
15. IRC, § 6019(b) (1954 Code); IRC, § 2515(c) (1954 Code).

16. IRC, § 6001 (1954 Code).
16a. Proposed Reg, § 25.6011–2.
16b. Reg, § 108, § 86.21.
16c. Reg, § 25.6011–1.

any particular case, however, the Commissioner would be authorized to require such a return if he felt it necessary.

§ 403. Returns; When Required.

Any *individual citizen or resident* of the United States, who within the calendar year 1955, or within any calendar year thereafter, makes a transfer or transfers by gift to *any one donee of a value* or total value *in excess of $3,000. (or regardless of value* in the case of a gift of a *future interest* in property) must file a gift tax return on Form 709 for that year. A nonresident not a citizen of the United States who made such a gift must also file a return if under Regulation § 25.2511–3[17] the transfer is subject to the Gift Tax.[18]

The return is required even though because of deductions no tax may be payable. *Individuals only* are required to file returns and not trusts, estates, partnerships or corporations. Only one copy of the return is required.[19] Thus, if a donor made a gift of $10,000. to one donee, and the donor had used none of his specific exemption, while no tax would be payable, a return would be required. The same would be true if he made a gift of $6,000. to his wife.

Where the gift is made by husband or wife, and the other spouse consents that the gift be considered a split-gift, the section applies separately to each spouse.[20] Thus, if the gift is of a future interest, both spouses would be required to file returns. If the husband made a gift of $5,000. as a split-gift, and the wife made none to the donee, since each would be considered as making a gift of $2,500., neither would be required to file a return. If the wife made a gift to the same donee of an additional $2,000., she would be required to make a return, but not the husband.

When an election is made to treat the creation of a tenancy by the entirety as a gift in the year in which it is effected, even though the amount of the gift does not exceed the amount of the annual exclusion, a return must be filed.[1]

Prior to the issuance of the final Gift Tax Regulations in November, 1958, it was required that in every case in which a donor was required to make a return, the donee or trustee receiving the gift file an information return on Form 710. When

17. § 428, infra.
18. Note 10, supra.
19. Note 10, supra.

20. Reg, § 25.6019–2.
1. Reg, § 25.2515–2(a).

the gift was for a statutory charitable or similar purpose, the organization receiving it was not required to make a return if the gift was made by a citizen or resident of the United States, and if the gift was made by a nonresident not a citizen, the information return was not required if the gift was to a United States organization or for use in the United States.[2] When the final Regulations were issued, the requirement for information returns was deleted. *There is no longer any requirement for an information return by a donee or trustee,* as to gifts made in the calendar year 1955 and thereafter.[3]

§ 404. Returns; Timeliness.

The 1954 Code changed the date for filing the Gift Tax return from the 15th day of March to the 15th day of April following the close of the calendar year.[4] The District Director, may however, grant a reasonable extension.[5] The time is extended as to persons serving in the Armed Forces in a combat zone.[6]

The due date is the date on or before which the return is required to be filed. However, when the due date falls on a Saturday, Sunday, or a legal holiday, the due date is the next succeeding day which is not a Saturday, Sunday, or a legal holiday. If the return is placed in the mails, it should be posted in ample time to reach the office of the District Director under ordinary handling of the mails, on or before the date on which the return is required to be filed. If a return is made and placed in the mails in due course, properly addressed and postage paid, in ample time to reach the office of the District Director on or before the due date, no penalty will attach should the return not actually be received by the District Director until after that date. If a question may be raised as to whether the return was posted in ample time to reach the office of the District Director on or before the due date, the envelope will be preserved and attached to the return.[7]

As we have seen the requirement for filing a donee or trustee information return being no longer required, the provisions for the due date of filing thereof are no longer required.[8]

As the Instructions for Form 709 point out, the required return cannot be filed prior to the close of the calendar year in which

2. Proposed Reg, § 25.6001–2.
3. Reg, § 25.6001–1.
4. IRC, § 6075(b) (1954 Code).
5. Reg, § 25.6081–1.

6. See § 385, supra.
7. Reg, § 25.6075–1(b).
8. § 401, supra.

the gifts were made unless the return is for a deceased donor.[9] The statute specifically provides for the return to be made following the close of the calendar year and on or before April 15th.[10]

As we shall see, failure to file the donor's return within the statutory time will result in additions to the tax, since the donor is primarily liable for its payment.[11]

§ 405. Returns; Who Files.

In the case of the donor's return it is required that the individual donor file the same, and not trusts, estates, partnerships, or corporations.[12] If the donor dies before filing his return, his fiduciary is required to do so. If the donor becomes legally incompetent before filing his return, his guardian or committee is required to do so.[13]

As we have seen, the donee or trustee information return is no longer required as to gifts made in the calendar year 1955 and thereafter.[14]

Where there is a split gift, depending upon whether each or both donors come within the requirements of the statute,[15] either, neither, or both may be required to file a donor's return.

In the case of the election to treat a tenancy by the entirety as a gift in the year of its creation, the donor spouse will be required to file a return.[16]

§ 406. Returns; Nonresident Not a Citizen.

As we have seen[17] a nonresident not a citizen of the United States who made a gift to any one donee of a value in excess of $3,000. during the calendar year, is required to file a return if the transfer is subject to the Gift Tax. To determine whether a transfer is subject to the Tax, two separate sections of the Code must be consulted. First it is provided that for the calendar year 1955 and each calendar year thereafter the tax is imposed on transfers by gift *by any individual, resident or nonresident,* *except* transfers of intangible property by a nonresident who is not a

9. Instructions, Form 709.
10. Note 4, supra.
11. §§ 552, 558, infra.
12. Reg, § 25.6019-1(a).
13. Reg, § 25.6019-1(b).

14. § 401, supra.
15. § 403, supra.
16. § 402, supra.
17. § 403, supra.

citizen of the United States and who was not engaged in business in the United States during such calendar year.[18]

As to a donor who is a citizen of the United States and a resident of a possession thereof, for the purposes of the Gift Tax he is considered a "citizen" of the United States within the meaning of that term whenever used in the statute unless he acquired his United States citizenship *solely* by reason of (1) his being a citizen of such possession of the United States, or (2) his birth or residence within such possession of the United States.[18a] This provision was added to the statute by the Technical Amendments Act of 1958 and applies to gifts made *after the date of the enactment of the Act, namely, September 2, 1958.* This was a substantial change from the 1939 Code,[19] since under it, intangibles which were the subject of a gift were taxed, if situated in the United States.[20] It is further provided that the tax applies in the case of a nonresident not a citizen of the United States *only if the property is situated within the United States.*[1] Shares of stock owned and held by a nonresident not a citizen are deemed property within the United States only if issued by a domestic corporation.[2] This too is a substantial change from the provisions of the 1939 Code, which considered stock as having a situs in the United States either if it was stock of a domestic corporation or was physically located here.[3]

The Regulation has combined these two sections of the Code and summarizes the rules applicable.

(1) If the nonresident alien donor was *not engaged in business* in the United States during the calendar year in which the gift was made, the tax applies *only to the transfer of real property and tangible personal property situated in the United States.*

(2) If the nonresident alien donor was *engaged in business* in the United States during the calendar year in which the gift was made, the tax applies to the *transfer of all property* (whether real or personal, tangible or intangible) *situated in the United States.*[4]

Since taxability is dependent upon where the property is sit-

---

18. IRC, § 2501(a) (1954 Code).

18a. IRC, § 2501(b) (1954 Code), as added by Technical Amendments Act of 1958, § 102(b), HR 8381, 85th Cong, 2nd Sess.

19. IRC, § 1000(a)(b) (1939 Code).

20. Harris v Comm, 178 F2d 861 (CA 2) revd other grounds 340 US 106, 95 L ed 111, 71 S Ct 181 (1949).

1. IRC, § 2511(a) (1954 Code).

2. IRC, § 2511(b) (1954 Code).

3. Sen Fin Comm Report, § 2511, 1954 Code.

4. Reg, § 25.2511-3(a).

uated, it is necessary to lay down situs rules, which the Regulation[5] does.

(1) Real property, tangible personal property, and, except as otherwise provided in (2) below, the written evidence of intangible personal property which is treated as being the property itself are within the United States if physically situated therein. For example, a bond for the payment of money is not within the United States unless physically situated therein. Intangible personal property the written evidence of which is not treated as being the property itself constitutes property within the United States if consisting of a property right issuing from or enforceable against a resident of the United States or a domestic corporation (public or private) irrespective of where such written evidence is physically located.

(2) Shares of stock owned and held by a nonresident alien donor constitute property within the United States if issued by a domestic corporation, irrespective of where the certificates are physically located. However, since a share of stock is intangible property, the transfer by a nonresident alien donor of a share of stock issued by a domestic corporation would, under the provisions of the rules for determining taxability above, be subject to the tax *only if the donor was engaged in business* in the United States during the calendar year in which the gift was made.[6]

(3) Shares of stock owned and held by a nonresident alien donor do not constitute property within the United States if issued by a corporation which is not a domestic corporation, *irrespective of where the certificates are physically located.* Therefore, the tax will not under any circumstances apply to the transfer of a share of such stock by a nonresident alien donor.

The similarity of the situs rules for the Gift Tax to those for the Estate Tax will be noted.[7]

Having determined whether or not a transfer by gift by a nonresident alien is subject to the Gift Tax, a return, if necessary, is made in the same way as in the case of a resident or citizen.

§ 407. Returns; Contents; Regulations.

The Regulations dealing with the preparation of Gift Tax returns are detailed and instructive. The Gift Tax return must

5. Reg, § 25.2511–3(b).
6. Rev Rul 56–438, 1956–2 CB 604.
7. §§ 185, 186, supra.

be made on Form 709, the same form being used for citizens or residents and nonresidents not citizens.[8] When life insurance is the subject of a gift, the life insurance statement must be made on Form 938.[9] Prior to November 1958 it was also required that the donee or trustee information return be made upon Form 710. As we have seen, this is no longer required as to gifts made in the calendar year 1955 and thereafter.[9a]

Copies of the forms may be obtained from the District Director, and the fact that a person required to file a form has not been furnished with copies is no excuse for failing to file a required form.

In the case of the Gift Tax return there must be set forth: (1) each gift made during the calendar year which is included in computing taxable gifts; (2) the deductions claimed and allowable; (3) the taxable gifts made for each of the preceding calendar years. In addition the return must set forth the fair market value of all gifts not made in money, including gifts resulting from sales and exchanges of property made for less than full and adequate consideration in money or money's worth, giving as of the date of the sale or exchange, both the fair market value of the property and that of the consideration received by the donor. If a donor contends that his retained power over property is of such nature as to render the gift incomplete and hence not subject to tax as of the calendar year of the initial transfer, the transaction should be disclosed in the return for the calendar year of the initial transfer and evidence showing all relevant facts, including a copy of the instrument of transfer, should be submitted with the return. *The instructions printed on the return should be carefully followed.* All documents and vouchers used in preparing the return should be retained by the donor so as to be available for inspection by representatives of the Internal Revenue Service whenever required. A certified or verified copy of each document required by the instructions on the return, or any documents the donor may desire to submit, should be filed with the return.[10] In substance, this is the same general advice given by the Estate Tax Regulations. The taxpayer should not take it upon himself to determine borderline cases, but if he believes that a transfer is not subject to the tax, he should report it and substantiate his claim.

8. Reg, § 25.6019–1(a).
9. Reg, § 25.6001–1(b).

9a. § 401, supra.
10. Reg, § 25.6019–3(a).

Instructions are also given as to the requirements of the return when there is a property settlement incident to divorce,[11] which will be discussed hereafter under that subject.[12]

The Regulation sets forth the manner in which property which is the subject of a gift should be listed upon the return.[13] That will be demonstrated in the sections dealing with transfers of different kinds of property.

Since the Gift Tax return consists of a two-sided single sheet, containing all of the information required for the computation of the tax, a completed return will be illustrated in the chapter on computation of the tax.[14]

The requirement in the Proposed Gift Tax Regulations[15] for an information return by donee or trustee, including the donee of a split gift between husband and wife to a third party, has been deleted from the final Regulations and is no longer required.

§ 408. Returns; Contents; Form 709.

As noted, the donor is required to make his return upon Form 709. This is a double sheet, the first and second page containing the actual return and the second sheet being severable and containing the instructions for preparation of the return.

There is first required to be stated the name, address, residence and citizenship of the donor. This is followed by Part A, which consists of eight questions designed to determine whether a taxable gift has been made either by trust or otherwise, and whether of a present or future interest.

Part B deals with gifts by husband and wife under the split-gift provisions of the statute, and it is followed by a consent to be signed in such case.

There then follow the details considered in computation of the tax. But as in the case of the Estate Tax, although the computation appears on the first page of the return, it cannot be completed until the entire return is completed.

The second page of the return contains Schedule A and Schedule B, the first for a description of the amount of gifts during the calendar year, with the date of the gift or gifts and its value at the date of the gift, followed by the items to be considered in determining the amount of taxable gifts to be reported

11. Reg, § 25.6019–3(b).
12. §§ 455, 456, infra.
13. Reg, § 25.6019–4.

14. Chapter 9, infra.
15. Proposed Reg, § 25.6001–2.

on the first page for the amount of taxable gifts for the calender year for which the return is being made. Schedule B contains the details of taxable gifts for preceding years, and there must be reported therein the year in which the prior gift was made, the Internal Revenue District in which the prior return was filed, the amount of the specific exemption claimed with respect to each year, and the amount of taxable gifts for each preceding year. From this is determined the amount of taxable gifts for preceding years to be considered in the computation of the tax for the year of the return being filed.[16]

It will be recalled that gifts made in prior years are considered in the computation of the tax for the calendar year being reported.[17]

Having determined the amount of taxable gifts for the current year and the total amount of taxable gifts for preceding years, the tax is computed for each, and the difference is the amount of tax on taxable gifts for the year. As noted, these items are set forth on the first page of the return.

§ 409. Returns; Contents; Form 710.

The donee's or trustee's information return is now only a matter of historical interest. The final Gift Tax Regulations issued in November 1958 deleted the requirement for such return as to gifts made in the calendar year 1955 and thereafter. It is necessary to know the procedure theretofore, since such return was required from the inception of the Gift Tax until recently, and the reader will see many references thereto from time to time. Reference will therefore be made to the former requirements, so that some familiarity may be had therewith.

The return was made upon Form 710, and consisted of a single sheet. The information required was set forth on the front of the form and Instructions set forth on the reverse side. It required the name and address of the donor and of the donee or trustee, a description of the property received, the date of the gift and the approximate value of the subject of the gift.[18]

The return was required to be filed by every donee or trustee in any case where the donor was required to file a return.[19] The due date was April 15th of the year following the year in which

16. Form 709.
17. § 398, supra.
18. Form 710.

19. Proposed Reg, § 6001–2; Reg, 108 § 86.21.

the gift was made.[20] The return was filed either by the beneficiary of a trust or the trustee, but only one return was required, and if the donee died, by his legal representative.[1] The general requirements for reporting the information were also detailed.[2] No such particularity of detail was required as in the case of the Gift Tax return. It was only required that a general description of the property transferred be given. The form then used follows:

FORM NO. 68

Donee's or Trustee's Information Return of Gifts

Calendar Year 1954

Donor's name   WINTHROP BENSON
    Donor's address   200 Catalpa Avenue, Dallas, Texas
Donee's name   GEORGE BENSON
    Donee's address   189 Lincoln Drive, Augusta, Maine
Trustee's name
    Trustee's address

Item No.	Description of property received	Date of gift	Approximate value at date of gift
1	100 shares American Telephone & Telegraph Company, common stock	Aug. 8	$17,825.00

Pursuant to the Gift Tax Regulations of the Treasury Department, I hereby give notice of the herein-described property received from the above-named donor, and certify that I have carefully read the instructions on the reverse side of this form and that all the information given herein is correct, to the best of my knowledge and belief.

                (Signature) GEORGE BENSON
                (Designation) Donee

                . . . .
                (Address of donee's executor
                      or administrator)

Date   Jan. 15, 1955

§ 410. Returns; Execution.

The Gift Tax return must be executed by the donor, and if dead or incompetent, by his legal representative.[3] The return shall not be made by an agent unless by reason of illness, absence, or nonresidence, the person liable for the return is unable to make it within the time prescribed. Mere convenience is not

---

20. Proposed Reg, § 25.6071–1; Reg, 108 § 86.22.
  1. Note 19, supra.

2. Note 19, supra.
3. Reg, § 25.6019–1(a)(b).

[Harris]—36

sufficient reason for authorizing an agent to make the return. If by reason of illness, absence, or nonresidence, a return is made by an agent, *the return must be ratified* by the donor or other person liable for its filing *within a reasonable time* after such person becomes able to do so. If the return filed by the agent is not so ratified, it will not be considered the return required by the statute.[4] Supplemental data may be submitted at the time of ratification. The ratification may be in the form of a statement, executed under the penalties of perjury and filed with the District Director, *showing specifically* that the return made by the agent has been carefully examined and that the person signing ratifies the return as the donor's. If the return is signed by an agent, a statement fully explaining the inability of the donor must accompany the return.[5]

Returns are now signed under the penalties of perjury, and an oath is no longer required unless the Secretary or his delegate requires it, which he is authorized to do.[6]

When the return is prepared by another, such person must execute the declaration appearing on the return.[7] A recent Revenue Ruling[7a] permits returns prepared by a firm to so indicate. If a firm is responsible for preparation of the return the statement of verification must be signed with the firm name and if the firm name is stamped or typed, it must be followed by the signature of a person authorized to sign the verification on behalf of the firm.

When the return is filed by an agent it is important that it be ratified by the donor within a reasonable time after the donor is able to do so, since otherwise the period of limitation to assess a deficiency does not begin to run.[8]

When there is a split-gift by husband and wife, the consent upon the return must be signed *before the return is filed.*[9]

§ 411. Returns; Place of Filing.

If the donor is a resident of the United States, the Gift Tax return must be filed with the District Director for the district in which the legal residence or principal place of business of the donor is located.

If the donor is a nonresident (whether or not a citizen), and

---

4. See Rohmer, 21 TC 1099 (1954).

5. Reg, § 25.6019–1(c).

6. IRC, § 6065 (1954 Code).

7. Instruction 19, Form 709.

7a. Rev Rul 58–390, IRB 1958–31 p 15.

8. Note 4, supra.

9. IRC, § 2513(b)(2) (1954 Code).

his principal place of business is located in an Internal Revenue district, the Gift Tax return must be filed with the District Director for the Internal Revenue district in which the donor's principal place of business is located. If he does not have such a place of business, the return must be filed with the Director of International Operations, Internal Revenue Service, Washington 25, D. C., or with such other official as the Commissioner may designate.[10]

§ 412. Returns; Extension of Time.

While it is important that the donor file on or before the due date a return as nearly complete and final as it is possible for him to prepare, if he is unable to do so, the District Director is authorized to grant a reasonable extension of time, which shall not be more than six months, except in the case of taxpayers who are abroad.

Applications for extensions of time should be addressed to the District Director for the district in which the donor files his returns and must contain *a full recital of the causes for delay.*

An extension of time for filing a return does not operate to extend the time for payment of the tax, or any part thereof, unless so specified in the extension.

No extension of time for filing a return will be granted unless the application is received by the District Director before the expiration of the time within which the return otherwise must be filed. The application should, when possible, be made sufficiently early to permit the District Director to consider the matter and reply before what otherwise would be the due date of the return.[11] It may be observed that the District Directors are reasonable in the matter of extensions of time to file returns when there is a *legitimate* excuse.

§ 413. Returns; Failure to File; Delinquency.

The failure to file the Gift Tax return has, with the exception of the loss of the right of alternate valuation in the case of the Estate Tax, the same penalties as attach to failure to file an Estate Tax return.[12] Willful failure is subject to both criminal and monetary penalties. The average taxpayer, however, is not concerned with these, but with the additions to the tax for failure

10. Reg, § 25.6091–1.
11. Reg, § 25.6081–1.

12. See § 34, supra.

to file the return in time. Five percent of the tax is added for each month of late filing, up to a maximum of twenty five percent.[13] In addition, the limitations on assessment and collection of the tax do not apply in the case of failure to file the return.[14]

The imposition of the penalty is mandatory.[15] But this is only so when the delinquency in filing the return is willful. Upon a showing that the delinquency was due to a reasonable cause and not to willful neglect, the addition to the tax will not be assessed. If the taxpayer exercised ordinary business care and prudence and was nevertheless unable to file the return within the prescribed time, then the delay is due to a reasonable cause.[16]

Failure to file in reliance on an attorney has usually been held to be reasonable cause.[17] In recent years, however, there appears a tendency to find that a taxpayer is required to know or learn the time within which various tax returns must be filed and not to consider reliance on an attorney reasonable cause for failure to file a return on time.[18] The Regulation notes that the taxpayer wishing to avoid the addition to the tax for failure to file the return must make an affirmative showing of all facts alleged as a reasonable cause for failure to file.[19] Failure to file the return because the taxpayer was too busy, or he thought the return had been filed,[20] or he believed that the gift was worthless,[1] will not be considered reasonable cause.

§ 414. Returns; Supplemental Data.

Every person liable for the tax or the collection thereof is required by the Code to keep such records, render such statements, and make such returns as prescribed by Regulations.[2] The Regulation provides for the donor to furnish such supplemental data as may be required by the District Director. It is the duty of the donor to furnish upon request copies of all documents relating to his gift or gifts, appraisal lists of any items included in the total amount of gifts, copies of balance sheets, or other

13. IRC, § 6651 (1954 Code).

14. IRC, § 6501(c) (1954 Code).

15. Fleming, 3 TC 974 (1944); Ginsberg, 24 TC 273 (1955).

16. Reg, § 301.6651–1(a)(3).

17. Note 4, supra; Fisk v Comm, 203 F2d 358 (CA 6) (1953); Reichers, 9 TCM 403 (1947); McColgan, 10 BTA 958 (1928); Collino, 25 TC 1026 (1956).

18. Sochalski, 14 TCM 72 (1955); Ferrando v US, 245 F2d 582 (CA 9) (1957).

19. Note 16, supra.

20. Reinhold, 7 TCM 697 (1946).

1. Powers, 13 TCM 1189 (1954).

2. IRC, § 6001 (1954 Code).

financial statements obtainable by him relating to the value of stock constituting the gift, and any other information obtainable by him that may be necessary in the determination of the tax. For every policy of life insurance listed on the return, the donor must procure a statement from the insurance company on Form 938 and file it with the District Director who receives the return. The District Director may require the insurance company to file the form directly with him.[3]

Where a settlement of marital rights is followed by divorce within two years, upon the agreement becoming effective, the Gift Tax return filed at such time must have annexed a copy of the agreement and a certified copy of the final decree of divorce.[4]

This itemization of required documents will be treated at greater length in connection with the kinds of transfers with which they are used. It should hardly be necessary to point out that taxability in many cases depends upon the proof submitted in support of a claim of nontaxability. If the question is one of valuation, the evidence to support the valued claimed should be adequate. No return can be considered properly prepared which does not contain as part of it the necessary documents from which the tax may be determined.

The Instructions set forth the documents required to be filed with the return. A certified or verified copy of each is required.[5]

§ 415. Returns; Records Required to Be Kept.

To aid in the determination of the tax, the donor is required to keep such permanent books of account or records as are necessary to establish the amount of his total gifts, the deductions, and the other information required to be shown in the return.[6] All documents and vouchers used in preparing the return must be retained by the donor so as to be available for inspection by representatives of the Internal Revenue Service whenever required.[7]

3. Reg, § 25.6001–1(b).
4. Reg, § 25.6019–3(b).
5. Reg, § 25.6019–3(a).

6. Reg, § 25.6001–1(a).
7. Note 4, supra.

CHAPTER 7

TRANSFERS SUBJECT TO FEDERAL GIFT TAX

§ 416. Scope of Chapter.

Having been introduced to the Federal Gift Tax in the preceding chapter, we now approach the details required in the preparation of the return. The first of these deals with the transfers which are considered gifts for the purpose of the statute. These are the items which are required to be set forth in Schedule A of the return, and with respect to which the questions in Part A of the return are directed, namely, the total gifts during the calendar year.

In and of itself, the statute is not particularly helpful, since it merely states that the tax is imposed on the transfer of property by gift during a calendar year, by any individual, resident or nonresident, except transfers of intangible property by a nonresident who is not a citizen of the United States and who was not engaged in business in the United States during such calendar year.[1] The Technical Amendments Act of 1958 added a further provision, effective as to gifts made after September 2, 1958, that a donor who is a citizen of the United States and a resident of a possession thereof, for the purposes of the Gift Tax is considered a "citizen" of the United States within the meaning of that term whenever used in the statute unless he acquired his United States citizenship *solely* by reason of (1) his being a citizen of such possession of the United States, or (2) his birth or residence within such possession of the United States.[1a] The statute also provides for the valuation of gifts.[2]

It is therefore necessary to know what transfers are deemed gifts within the meaning of the statute. As we shall see, the statute sets its own standard for the determination of the question, so that many transfers not usually considered gifts, are such for the purposes of the tax. We shall, therefore, treat generally with the subject of gifts and then proceed to the various subjects of gifts and their valuation.

§ 417. What a Gift is, Generally.

A gift is a voluntary transfer of property by one to another without any consideration or compensation therefor. It is a gratuity and not only does not require consideration but there can be none.[3] Its essential elements are: (1) an intention on the part of the donor to make the gift; (2) delivery by the donor of the subject matter of the gift; and (3) acceptance of the gift by the donee.[4] As has been said, there must be a donor competent to make the gift, a clear and unmistakable intention on his part to make it, a donee capable of taking the gift, a conveyance, assignment, or transfer sufficient to vest the legal title in the donee, without power of revocation at the will of the donor, and a relinquishment of dominion and control of the subject matter of the gift by delivery to the donee.[5]

Within the meaning of the Internal Revenue Code and the decisions, the word "gift", for the purpose of the imposition of

---

1. IRC, § 2501(a) (1954 Code).
1a. IRC, § 2501(b) (1954 Code), as added by Technical Amendments Act of 1958, § 102(b), HR 8381, 85th Cong, 2nd Sess.
2. IRC, § 2512 (1954 Code).

3. Comm v Montague, 126 F2d 948 (CCA 6) (1942).
4. Botchford v Comm, 81 F2d 914 (CCA 9) (1936); Ross, 28 BTA 39 (1933).
5. Edson v Lucas, 40 F2d 398 (CCA 8) (1930).

the tax, has a much broader meaning. Taxable gifts are not restricted to the most usual and obvious kinds, such as gifts of cash, real property, chattels, stocks and bonds and the like. As the Regulation notes, the Gift Tax applies to a transfer by way of gift whether the transfer is in trust or otherwise, whether the gift is direct or indirect, and whether the property is real or personal, tangible or intangible. A taxable transfer may be effected by the creation of a trust, the forgiving of a debt, the assignment of a judgment, or of the benefits of a contract of insurance.[6] It may also result from indirect gifts whereby property or property rights or interests are gratuitously passed to or conferred upon another, such as renunciation of one's rights in intestacy.[7]

Donative intent on the part of the transferor is not an essential element in the application of the Gift Tax to the transfer. The application of the tax is based on the objective facts of the transfer and the circumstances under which it is made, rather than on the subjective motives of the donor.[8]

The Regulation furnishes many examples of transfers considered taxable gifts. Thus transfer of corporate property to a stockholder, not as earnings or in liquidation, a gift to a donee upon his agreeing to pay an annuity to a third party, a withdrawal from a joint bank account by the co-owner who was not the creator of the account, the creation of certain joint titles, the payment of premiums on life insurance owned by one other than the insured, are all transfers which the average taxpayer might not consider gifts, but which for the purposes of the statute are.[9]

A gift may also result from a transfer which is incomplete at one time but which by a subsequent act becomes a completed gift. Where a transfer in trust reserves to the donor grantor a power to alter, amend, modify, or revoke, there has been no completed gift. When the power is relinquished, however, a gift takes place.[10] The release or termination of a power to change the disposition of transferred property, otherwise than by the death of the donor, completes a gift.[11]

Transfers reached by the Gift Tax are not confined to those only which, being without a valuable consideration, accord with the common law concept of gifts, but embrace as well sales,

6. Reg, § 25.2511–1(a).
7. Reg, § 25.2511–1(c).
8. Reg, § 25.2511–1(g)(1).
9. Reg, § 25.2511–1(g).
10. Burnet v Guggenheim, 288 US 280,

77 L ed 748, 53 S Ct 369 (1933); Sanford v Comm, 308 US 39, 84 L ed 20, 60 S Ct 51, rehg den, 308 US 637, 84 L ed 529, 60 S Ct 258 (1939).

11. Reg, § 25.2511–2.

exchanges, and other dispositions of property for a consideration to the extent that the value of the property transferred by
the donor exceeds the value in money or money's worth of the
consideration given therefor.   It does not reach transfers by
sale, exchange, or otherwise, made in the ordinary course of
business, at arm's length and free from any donative intent.[12]
Where the value of the consideration is less than the value of
the transfer, the difference is a gift.[13]   Prior to the 1954 Code
many marital settlements no longer treated as gifts, were so
considered.[14]

A gift may also arise by reason of the exercise or release of
a power of appointment, creation of another power or lapse of
a power under certain circumstances.[15]

Where a tenancy by the entirety or a joint tenancy between
husband and wife with right of survivorship is created, a gift may
arise at the creation of the tenancy or upon its termination, at
the option of the donor.   But the election must be made at the
time of the creation of the tenancy.[16]

These differences between the common law concept of gift
and its meaning within the Gift Tax statute are here pointed out,
so that the reader may remove from his thinking any prior im-
pressions as to the elements of a gift and consider the subject in
the light of the statute.   In succeeding sections we will treat of
specific situations to which the Gift Tax is applicable.

§ 418. Parties to Gift.

As previously noted, the Gift Tax is imposed on individuals.[17]
It is not applicable to transfers by corporations or other persons
than individuals.[18]   This does not mean that transfers ostensibly
by partnerships or corporations escape the tax.   When a partnership interest is transferred by gift the transfer is a gift by
the individual partners.[19]   A transfer of property by a corporation is considered a gift from the stockholders of the corporation.   If the donee is a stockholder, the transfer is a gift to him
from the other stockholders to the extent that it is not a distribu-

12. Reg, § 25.2512–8.

13. Bergan, 1 TC 543 (1942); Hooker,
10 TC 388, aff'd 174 F2d 863 (CA 5)
(1949); Converse, 5 TC 1014 (1945);
Gross, 7 TC 837 (1946).

14. See §§ 454 et seq, infra.

15. See §§ 456 et seq, infra.

16. See §§ 449 et seq, infra.

17. Note 1, supra.

18. Reg, § 25.0–1(b).

19. See Gross, note 13, supra; Lippert,
11 TC 783 (1948); also Lippert v Comm,
184 F2d 672 (CA 8) (1950).

tion from earnings or in liquidation to which he is entitled as a stockholder.[20]

Since one of the essential elements of a valid gift is a donor competent to make the gift, if mental competency is lacking there can be no gift subject to the tax.[1] In the case of a gift by an infant, since the infant may disaffirm before attaining his majority, it would appear that there is not a completed gift. Where the tax took effect after the infant attained her majority, it was held that the gift was complete.[2] Where the gift is made by the committee of an incompetent,[3] or the guardian of an infant,[4] pursuant to court order, it is held the tax attaches.

It is a further element of a valid gift that there be a donee capable of taking. A gift cannot, therefore, be made to an incompetent. In the case of an infant, the gift may be made to the guardian, and the 1954 Code specifically provides for the allowance of the annual exclusion in such case.[5] The statute further recognizes that a gift can be made to a trustee.[6]

While the statute limits the imposition of the tax to gifts *by* individuals, it does not so limit the recipient or donee. There is no question about the fact that a transfer to a corporation without consideration is subject to the Gift Tax.[7] The question in such case has been the extent of the gift and the number of annual exclusions. The Regulation states that a transfer of property by a donor to a corporation represents gifts by the donor to the other individual shareholders of the corporation to the extent of their proportionate interests, but that a gift by an individual to a charitable, public, political or similar organization may constitute a gift to the organization as a single entity.[8] The Tax Court appears not to agree with this position.[9] Gifts to a partnership would presumably be considered gifts to the individual members of the partnership, as in the case of gifts by a partnership.

20. Reg, § 25.2511–1(g)(1).

1. Crawley, 9 TCM 286 (1947).

2. Comm v Allen, 108 F2d 961 (CCA 3), cert den 309 US 680, 84 L ed 1023, 60 S Ct 718 (1940).

3. ET4, XIII–2 CB 368; City Bank Farmers Trust Co. v Hoey, 101 F2d 9 (CCA 2), affg 23 F Supp 831 (1939); Comm v Greene, 119 F2d 383 (CCA 9), cert den 314 US 641, 86 L ed 514, 62 S Ct 80 (1941); Lester, 1 TCM 758 (1942).

4. Stokowski v Pedrick, 52–2 USTC ¶ 10,861.

5. IRC, § 2503(c) (1954 Code).

6. IRC, § 2511(a) (1954 Code).

7. Heringer, 21 TC 607 (1954); Thompson, 42 BTA 121 (1940); Scanlon, 42 BTA 997 (1940); Collins, 1 TC 605 (1942).

8. Note 20, supra.

9. Note 7, supra.

§ 419. Donative Intent.

The question of donative intent has been confused by the statements made in many cases that there must be donative intent on the part of the donor for the gift tax to apply. The statements have either been made in cases where the question involved consideration,[10] or where the question was whether the donee relinquished dominion or control at a particular time so as to subject to tax.[11]

Except in such cases, as the Regulation states, donative intent is not an essential element in the application of the Gift Tax.[12] The Regulation is a statement of the purpose of Congress in enacting the 1932 Act to dispense with the test of donative intent.[13]

§ 420. Delivery and Date of Transfer.

The question of delivery is chiefly important in the determination of the time at which a gift takes place so as to be subject to the tax. Where there is the intent to make a gift but no action taken to consummate it, no gift will have taken place.[14]

The Regulation notes that the Gift Tax is not imposed upon the receipt of the property by the donee and attaches even though the identity of the donee may not be known at the date of the transfer.[15] While it is said that delivery is an essential element of a gift, examination of the decided cases indicate that what is meant is that the question is when the gift becomes effective. Thus, separation of securities into three bundles at the request of the donor, even though not delivered to the donees at the time, became effective at such time.[16] Delivery of a deed although not recorded effected a transfer.[17] Where an agreement provided for stock to be delivered at a future time, the delivery date was the date of the gift and not the agreement date.[18] A number of cases

---

10. Wemyss v Comm, 144 F2d 78 (CCA 6), revd other grounds 324 US 303, 89 L ed 958, 65 S Ct 652 (1944); Comm v Greene, note 3, supra; Sportswear, Hosiery Mills v Comm, 129 F2d 376 (CCA 3) (1942).

11. Schwarzenbach v Comm, 4 TC 179 (1944); Comm v Prouty, 115 F2d 331 (CCA 1) (1940); Latta v Comm, 212 F2d 164 (CA 3), cert den 348 US 825, 99 L ed 650, 75 S Ct 40 (1954).

12. Reg, § 25.2511–1(f).

13. Comm v Wemyss, 324 US 303, 89 L ed 958, 65 S Ct 652 (1945); Merrill v Fahs, 324 US 308, 89 L ed 963, 65 S Ct 655 (1945).

14. Staley, 41 BTA 752 (1940); Larson v Comm, 117 F2d 821 (CCA 9) (1941).

15. Reg, § 25.2511–2(a).

16. Ross, 28 BTA 39 (1933).

17. Macomber, 10 TCM 539 (1948).

18. Gruen, 1 TC 130 (1942).

have been decided on whether the facts evidenced an intention that the gift take place at the time of execution of the instrument of gift or at the time of delivery.[19] Where there is a legal impediment to the transfer, the gift does not take place until it has been removed.[20]

In the case of stock transfers the date of transfer depends upon whether the stock is delivered to the donee or to a bank or transfer agent. If delivered to the donee, the gift takes place at the time of delivery,[1] while if delivered to a bank or transfer agent the gift does not take place until transfer on the corporate books.[2]

§ 421. Property Interests Subject to the Tax.

The statute is both general and specific with respect to the imposition of the Gift Tax. It first provides for the imposition of the tax on the transfer by gift of property by any individual, resident or nonresident, except transfers of intangible property by nonresidents not citizens and not engaged in business in the United States.[3] It then provides that the tax shall apply whether the transfer is in trust or otherwise, whether the gift is direct or indirect, and whether the property is real or personal, tangible or intangible, but in the case of a nonresident not a citizen of the United States, only if the property is situated in the United States, shares of stock in the case of the latter being deemed property within the United States only if issued by a domestic corporation.[4] A more comprehensive definition would be difficult to find. That was the purpose of Congress in enacting the 1932 statute, which was the basis for the present statute. As the framers of the Act stated at the time, the terms "property", "transfer", "gift", and "indirectly" were used in the broadest and most comprehensive sense; the term "property" reaching every species of right or interest protected by law and having an exchangeable value. The words "transfer by gift" and

19. See De Forest, 27 BTA 373 (1933); Herrmann, 9 TC 1055 (1947); Comm v Copley, 194 F2d 364 (CA 7) (1952); Galt v Comm, 216 F2d 41 (CA 7) (1954).

20. Jorgensen v US, 152 F Supp 73 (1957); Newman v Comm, 222 F2d 131 (CA 9), affg 19 TC 708 (1955); First Union Trust & Sav. Bank v US, 5 F Supp 143 (1933).

1. Rev Rul 54-554, 1954-2 CB 317.

2. Rev Rul 54-135, 1954-1 CB 205; Richardson v Comm, 126 F2d 562 (CCA 2) (1942); but see Mein, 5 TCM 713 (1945).

3. IRC, § 2501(a) (1954 Code).

4. IRC, § 2511 (1954 Code).

"whether direct or indirect" was designed to cover and comprehend all transactions (subject to certain express conditions and limitations) whereby and to the extent that property or a property right is donatively passed to or conferred upon another, regardless of the means or the device employed in its accomplishment. The courts have so interpreted it.[5]

In addition to the general provisions for the imposition of the tax the statute provides for taxation when a transfer is made for less than adequate and full consideration,[6] the exercise or release of powers of appointment,[7] and the creation or termination of tenancies by the entirety.[8]

The statute refers to property, so that it must be assumed that gratuitous services rendered are not subject to gift, unless they are rendered to a third person.[9] In such case the consideration received by the third party is the equivalent of the consideration received by the party performing the services. As between donor and donee it would appear there is no gift.[10]

When the gift is direct there is no problem in determining the property which is the subject of the gift. Thus, accrued interest,[11] an annuity for an inadequate consideration,[12] a check,[13] forgiveness of an indebtedness,[14] insurance,[15] bank accounts,[16] jointly owned property,[17] tenancy by the entirety,[18] and interest in a partnership,[19] notes,[20] interest paid on an unenforceable note,[1] a share in intestacy,[2] income from trust property,[3] life estates,[4] a pension,[5] a possibility of reverter,[6] a remainder,[7] contingent

5. Comm v Hogle, 165 F2d 352 (CCA 10) (1947); Hardenbergh v Comm, 198 F2d 63 (CA 8), cert den 344 US 836, 97 L ed 650, 73 S Ct 45 (1952).

6. IRC, § 2512(b) (1954 Code).

7. IRC, § 2514 (1954 Code).

8. IRC, § 2515 (1954 Code).

9. Reg, § 25.2511-1(g)(3).

10. Fisher, 8 TC 732 (1947).

11. Affelder, 7 TC 1190 (1946).

12. Bartman, 10 TC 1073 (1948).

13. GCM 16460, XV-1 CB 369.

14. Reg, § 25.2511-1(a).

15. Note 14, supra.

16. Harris v Comm, 178 F2d 861 (CA 2) (1950).

17. Reg, § 25.2511-1(g)(4).

18. Lilly v Smith, 96 F2d 341 (CCA 7), cert den 305 US 604, 83 L ed 383, 59 S Ct 64 (1938).

19. Gross, 7 TC 837 (1946).

20. Note 13, supra.

1. French v Comm, 138 F2d 254 (CCA 8) (1943).

2. Note 5, supra; Maxwell, 17 TC 1589 (1952).

3. Adams, 12 TCM 1103 (1949); Cerf v Comm, 141 F2d 564 (CCA 3) (1944).

4. Mack, 39 BTA 220 (1939).

5. Morrow, 2 TC 210 (1943).

6. McLean, 41 BTA 1266, mod other grounds, 127 F2d 942 (CCA 5) (1940).

7. Robinette v Helvering, 318 US 184, 87 L ed 700, 63 S Ct 540 (1943); Comm v Proctor, 142 F2d 824 (CCA 4), cert den 323 US 756, 89 L ed 606, 65 S Ct 90 (1944); Comm v Marshall, 125 F2d 943 (CCA 2) (1942).

or vested, and tax exempt bonds[8] have all been held subject to the tax upon transfer by gift. It will be noted that in many of the above cases the subject of the gift is easily identifiable. In others, the gift arises not by an actual delivery of the subject of the gift, but by an act which indirectly results in a gift being made. There are many other instances in which this arises. Where stock, intended as a gift was sold by the donees before receipt, the stock was the subject of the gift and not the money received for its sale.[9] Payment by a husband for a joint and survivor annuity to a charitable organization is a gift to the wife of the portion of the fund paid for the annuity to the wife.[10]

§ 422. Transfers by Gift; When Transferred; Generally.

The statute provides for the taxation of transfers by gift. There is thus presented at the very outset of the determination of taxability, the question whether there has been such a transfer. The question arises chiefly in connection with a gift in trust where the donor retains dominion and control over the subject of the gift although transferring the legal title to the trustee. But the essence of a transfer as respects taxation is the passage of control over the economic benefits of property rather than any technical change in title.[11] *The Gift Tax applies only when there is a completed gift.* There is a completed gift only when the donor has so parted with dominion and control as to leave in him no power to change its disposition, whether for his own benefit, or for the benefit of another.[12] Therefore, it becomes important in every case to determine whether the donor has so parted with dominion and control. Because of the multiplicity of powers over a transfer which may be retained, the determination has not been easy.

In the 1932 Act it was provided with respect to transfers in trust that the tax should not apply to them where the power to revest title to the property was vested in the donor, either alone or in conjunction with any person not having a substantial adverse interest in the disposition of the property or the income therefrom. The relinquishment or termination of such a power (except by the donor's death) was considered to be a transfer by

8. Hamersley v US, 16 F Supp 768 (1936); Mim 5202, 1941-2 CB 241.
9. Gruen, 1 TC 130 (1942).
10. Rev Rul 55-388, 1955-1 CB 233.
11. Sanford v Comm, 308 US 39, 84 L

ed 20, 60 S Ct 51, rehg den 308 US 637, 84 L ed 529, 60 S Ct 258 (1939); Comm v Marshall, note 7, supra.
12. Reg, § 25.2511-2(b).

gift of the property subject to the power, and the payment of
income therefrom to a beneficiary was considered a transfer by
the donee of the income by gift.[13] The Supreme Court then decided that if the donor retained the power of revocation over a
trust created by him there was no completed gift and the transfer was not subject to the Gift Tax.[14] The case was decided under
the 1924 statute. The court having so decided, however, Congress decided the provision noted above in the 1932 Act was
unnecessary,[15] and repealed the same.[16]

But the decision did not answer many other questions. It
dealt with only the power of revocation and not with other powers. It was six years before the court decided that a retained
power to alter or amend a trust prevented a gift from being
complete so as to be subject to the tax.[17] In fact, the Treasury
was as confused about the matter as the taxpayer, holding that
a gift took place at the time of the creation of the trust in one
instance,[18] and that it took place upon relinquishment of the
power in the other.[19]

Because of the dichotomous position taken by the Treasury,
many taxpayers had paid a Gift Tax upon creating an irrevocable
trust. In the light of the court's decisions, if they then relinquished the power to alter or amend the trust they would be subject again to a tax. In order to remedy this injustice, the Regulations[20] and the statute[1] were amended to provide that the
relinquishment of power or control with respect to the distribution of the property or income therefrom of trusts created before
January 1, 1939, where the grantor had no power to revest title
in himself which could be exercised by himself or by himself and
one not having a substantial adverse interest, was not taxable
as a gift, if the relinquishment took place between January 1,
1940 and December 31, 1947.

Examination of the factual details in the decided cases will
be found helpful in the determination of powers which will be

13. Rev Act 1932, § 501(a).
14. Burnet v Guggenheim, 288 US 280, 77 L ed 748, 53 S Ct 369 (1933).
15. HR Rep No. 704, 73rd Cong, 2nd Sess 40 (1934); Sen Rep No. 558, 73rd Cong, 2nd Sess 40 (1934).
16. Rev Act 1934, § 511.
17. Sanford v Comm, note 11, supra; Rasquin v Humphreys, 308 US 54, 84 L ed 77, 60 S Ct 60 (1939).
18. Rasquin v Humphrey, note 17, supra.
19. Sanford v Comm, note 11, supra.
20. Reg 108, § 86.3(b) as amended by TD 5366, 1944 CB 583.
1. IRC, § 1000(e), as added by § 502(a) Rev Act of 1943, enacted Feb. 25, 1944.

considered either the continuance or cessation of the donor's dominion and control, and when there is a relinquishment of powers so as to subject to the Gift Tax. These will be considered in the succeeding sections.

§ 423. Transfers by Gift; When Transferred; Retained Powers.

The Regulation is a codification of case law. Thus, it is stated that if upon a transfer of property (whether in trust or otherwise) the donor reserves any power over its disposition, the gift may be wholly incomplete, or may be partially complete and partially incomplete, depending upon all the facts in the particular case. Accordingly, in every case of a transfer of property subject to a reserved power, the terms of the power must be examined and its scope determined.[2] For example, if a donor transfers property to another in trust to pay the income to the donor or accumulate it in the discretion of the trustee, and the donor retains a testamentary power to appoint the remainder among his descendants, no portion of the transfer is a completed gift.[3] On the other hand if the donor had not retained the testamentary power of appointment, but instead provided that the remainder should go to another or his heirs, the entire transfer would be a completed gift. However if the exercise of the trustee's power in favor of the grantor is limited by a fixed or readily ascertainable standard, enforceable by or on behalf of the grantor, then the gift is incomplete to the extent of the ascertainable value of any rights thus retained by the grantor.[4]

A gift is incomplete in every instance in which a donor reserves the power to revest the beneficial title to the property in himself.[5] A gift is also incomplete if and to the extent that a reserved power gives the donor the power to name new beneficiaries or to change the interests of the beneficiaries as between themselves unless the power is a fiduciary power limited by a fixed or readily ascertainable standard.[6] Thus if an estate for life

2. Camp v Comm, 195 F2d 999 (CA 1) (1952); Publicker v Niles, 55–1 USTC ¶ 11,531.

3. Rosenau, 37 BTA 468 (1938).

4. Note 12, supra; Rev Rul 54–538, 1954–2 CB 316.

5. Smith v Shaughnessy, 318 US 176, 87 L ed 690, 63 S Ct 545 (1943); Comm

v Warner, 127 F2d 913 (CCA 9) (1942); Hettler, 5 TC 1079 (1945).

6. Smith v Shaughnessy, note 5, supra; Rasquin v Humphreys, note 17, supra; Higgins v Comm, 129 F2d 237 (CCA 1), cert den 317 US 658, 87 L ed 529, 63 S Ct 57 (1942); Cockrell v US, 39 F Supp 148 (1941); Brown v Deputy, 30 F Supp

is transferred, but, by an exercise of the power, the estate may be terminated or cut down by the donor to one of less value, and without restriction upon the extent to which the estate may be so cut down, the transfer constitutes an incomplete gift. If in this example the power was confined to the right to cut down the estate for life to one for a term of five years, the certainty of an estate for not less than five years results in a gift to that extent complete.[7]

Not every retained power prevents a gift being complete. A gift is not considered incomplete, merely because the donor reserves the power to change the manner or time of enjoyment. Thus, the creation of a trust the income of which is to be paid annually to the donee for a period of years, the corpus being distributable to him at the end of the period, and the power reserved by the donor being limited to a right to require the income to be accumulated and paid at the same time as the corpus, is a completed gift.[8]

Since a gift is not consummate until put beyond recall,[9] it is clear that so long as the donor retains any power to alter, amend, revoke, or terminate the interest granted, there is no completed gift.[10] It will be recalled that this is also the test for inclusion of transferred property in the estate of the donor.[11]

Irrevocability alone is not the touchstone, but whether the donor retained dominion and control in any form.[12] There are, however, two exceptions to the rule that retention of control prevents a gift from being complete so as to be subject to the Gift Tax. They are not so much exceptions as distinctions. Thus, if the donor has a power to change the enjoyment of a transfer, but the power is subject to exercise only in conjunction with a person having a substantial adverse interest in the disposition

860 (1940); Sherman, 41 BTA 898 (1940); Mack, 39 BTA 220 (1937); Paolozzi, 23 TC 182 (1955); Gramm, 17 TC 1063 (1951); Vander Weele, 27 TC 340 (1956).

7. Reg, § 25.2511–2(c).

8. Reg, § 25.2511–2(d).

9. Note 14, supra.

10. Note 14, supra; Sanford v Comm, 308 US 39, 84 L ed 20, 60 S Ct 51, rehg den 308 US 637, 84 L ed 529, 60 S Ct 258 (1939); Fletcher Trust Co. v Comm, 141 F2d 36 (CCA 7), cert den 323 US 711,

89 L ed 572, 65 S Ct 36 (1944); Higgins v Comm, note 6, supra; Latta v Comm, 212 F2d 164 (CA 3), cert den 348 US 25, 99 L ed 650, 75 S Ct 40 (1954); Comm v Prouty, 115 F2d 86 (CCA 1) (1940); Comm v Solomon, 124 F2d 86 (CCA 3) (1941); Means v US, 39 F2d 748, cert den 282 US 849, 75 L ed 753, 51 S Ct 28 (1930).

11. § 149, supra.

12. Note 3, supra; Rev Rul 54–342, 1954–2 CB 315; Higgins v Comm, note 6, supra.

of the property or the income,[13] or the power is limited by a fixed or readily ascertainable standard,[14] then there is a completed gift. The theory back of this is that in the first instance, the donor no longer has any control, since his power is subject to veto by another, and in the second instance, since the retained interest may be valued, it may be severed from the entire interest, and the remainder is a completed transfer. It will be recalled that the 1932 Act provided that the tax did not apply when the power to revest title was vested in the donor either alone or in conjunction with a person not having a substantial adverse interest.[15] While the section was repealed, it was not done because it was no longer the law, but because it was not required. Under the then statute the term was defined as meaning a direct legal or equitable interest in the trust property and not merely a sentimental or parental interest in seeing the trust fulfilled for the advantage of other beneficiaries.[16] It was held that the provisions of the Income Tax law could not be read into the Gift Tax statute so as to exclude as one having an adverse interest members of the donor's family, but that in determining whether there was in fact such an adverse interest the court was bound to give weight to the formal rights granted by the trust instrument, bearing in mind the admonition that where the grantor is the trustee and the beneficiaries are members of his family group, special scrutiny of the arrangement is necessary.[17]

The Regulation states that a donor is considered as himself having a power if it is exercisable by him in conjunction with any person not having a substantial adverse interest in the disposition of the property or the income therefrom, and that neither a trustee has an adverse interest, nor does the spouse or relative of the donor have such interest solely by reason of his relationship.[18] Just what is a substantial adverse interest. Unlike the Income Tax statute, which defines "adverse party" and "non-adverse party",[19] neither the Gift Tax statute nor the Regulation above defines the term. The term has been passed upon

13. Comm v Prouty, note 10, supra; Rohnert, 3 TCM 985 (1944); Camp v Comm, note 2, supra; Hernstadt v Hoey, 47 F Supp 874 (1942); Gilette, 7 TC 219 (1946); Cerf v Comm, 141 F2d 564 CCA 3) (1944); Herzog v Comm, 116 F2d 591 (CCA 2) (1941); Wood, 40 BTA 905 (1939).

14. Plummer, 2 TC 263 (1943); Rev Rul 54-538, 1954-2 CB 316.
15. § 422, supra.
16. Comm v Prouty, note 10, supra.
17. Note 16, supra.
18. Reg, § 25.2511-2(e).
19. IRC, § 672(a) (1954 Code); IRC, § 672(b) (1954 Code).

in both Gift Tax and Estate Tax cases.[20]   Where the power is granted to another, and the donor retains no power, there is a completed gift even though the trustee may return the property to the donor,[1] or where the donor has the right to veto changes by the trustee.[2]

The Regulation further notes that if a donor transfers property to himself as trustee (or to himself and some other person, not possessing a substantial adverse interest, as trustees), and retains no beneficial interest in the trust property, and no power over it except fiduciary powers, the exercise or nonexercise of which is limited by a fixed or readily ascertainable standard, to change the beneficiaries of the transferred property, the donor has made a completed gift and the entire value of the transferred property is subject to the Gift Tax.[3]

While the Regulation dealing with cessation of the donor's dominion and control does not go into the question of adverse interest, in treating of the gift taxation of general powers of appointment, the Regulation states that an interest adverse to the exercise of a power is considered as substantial unless its value in relation to the total value of the property subject to the power is insignificant. For this purpose, the interest is to be valued in accordance with the actuarial principles set forth in the Regulations. In this connection it is further stated that a taker in default of appointment under a power has an interest which is adverse to an exercise of the power. A coholder of the power has no adverse interest merely because of his joint possession of the power nor merely because he is a permissible appointee under a power. However, a coholder of a power is considered as having an adverse interest where he may possess the power after the possessor's death and may exercise it at that time in favor of himself, his estate, his creditors, or the creditors of his estate. Thus, for example, if X, Y, and Z held a power jointly to appoint among a group of persons which includes themselves, and on the death of X the power will pass to Y and Z jointly, then Y and Z are considered to have interests adverse

20. See note 13, supra; Thorp v Comm, 164 F2d 966 (CCA 3) (1948); Comm v Kaplan, 102 F2d 329 (CCA 1) (1939); Stewart, 28 BTA 256, revg 27 BTA 593, affd 70 F2d 696 (CCA 2) cert den 293 US 582, 79 L ed 678, 55 S Ct 96 (1934); Mackay v Comm, 94 F2d 558 (CCA 2) (1938); Comm v Flanders, 111 F2d 117 (CCA 2) (1940); Wheeler, 20 BTA 1377 (1930); Stone, 26 BTA 379 (1932); Fish, 45 BTA 120 (1941).

1. Herzog v Comm, note 13, supra.
2. Wood, note 13, supra.
3. Reg, § 25.2511-2(g).

to the exercise of the power in favor of X. Similarly, if on Y's death the power will pass to Z, Z is considered to have an interest adverse to the exercise of the power in favor of Y. The application of the Regulation is illustrated by the following examples:

(1) The taxpayer and R are trustees of a trust under which the income is to be paid to the taxpayer for life and then to M for life, and R is remainderman. The trustees have power to distribute corpus to the taxpayer. Since R's interest is substantially adverse to an exercise of the power in favor of the taxpayer, the latter does not have a general power of appointment. If M and the taxpayer were trustees, M's interest would likewise be adverse.

(2) The taxpayer and L are trustees of a trust under which the income is to be paid to L for life and then to M for life, and the taxpayer is remainderman. The trustees have power to distribute corpus to the taxpayer during L's life. Since L's interest is adverse to an exercise of the power in favor of the taxpayer, the taxpayer does not have a general power of appointment. If the taxpayer and M were trustees, M's interest would likewise be adverse.

(3) The taxpayer and L are trustees of a trust under which the income is to be paid to L. The trustees can designate whether corpus is to be distributed to the taxpayer or to A after L's death. L's interest is not adverse to an exercise of the power in favor of the taxpayer, and the taxpayer therefore has a general power of appointment.[3a]

§ 424. Transfers by Gift; When Transferred; Relinquishment of Power.

As we have seen, a gift becomes subject to the tax when it is complete. Until the donor has relinquished dominion and control over the transfer, so far as the Gift Tax is concerned, there is no transfer. As has been said, the statute is aimed at transfers of the title that have the quality of a gift and a gift is not consummate until put beyond recall, but where the donor reserves in a trust a power to alter, amend, revoke, or modify, so that there is no completed gift at the time of the transfer to the trust, when he later relinquishes such rights *he makes a gift as of the date of the relinquishment,* and *the law in effect at that date* applies, no matter when the trust was created.[4] The date is of

---

3a. Reg, § 25.2514–3(b)(2).   4. Burnet v Guggenheim, 288 US 280,

significance when there has been a change in the law between the creation of the trust and the relinquishment. In many of the cases decided, the general principle that the date of relinquishment controls was enunciated in connection with the claim that a tax was not payable because at the date of the original transfer in trust there was no Gift Tax, or where there had been a change in the rates and the law between such dates.

The date is also important, however, in determining when the Gift Tax is payable. Liability for the tax accrues on the date of a completed transfer. Thus the relinquishment of the right to designate new beneficiaries,[5] to consent to the change of beneficiaries,[6] to change beneficiaries of insurance,[7] and of trusteeship with power to terminate,[8] were held to be the determining act for the purpose of the tax, and the date on which it took place, the date for imposition of the tax.

It should be noted that the receipt of income or of other enjoyment of the transferred property by the transferee or by the beneficiary (other than by the donor himself) during the interim between the making of the initial transfer and the relinquishment or termination of the power operates to free such income or other enjoyment from the power, and constitutes a gift of such income or of such other enjoyment taxable as of the calendar year of its receipt.[9] Where there is a joint power, and one of the parties holding the power dies, a gift takes place at that time.[10] It is not the relinquishment of every power which results in a gift. If the power is one, which retained, would not prevent the gift being complete at the time of the original transfer, the subsequent release of such power has no effect on the date of the gift.[11]

77 L ed 748, 53 S Ct 369 (1933); Helvering v Hutchings, 312 US 653, 85 L ed 909, 61 S Ct 653 (1941); Sanford v Comm, note 10, supra; Comm v Warner, 127 F2d 913 (CCA 9) (1942); Comm v Prouty, note 10, supra; Latta v Comm, note 10, supra; Helvering v McCormack, 135 F2d 294 (CCA 2) (1943); Higgins v Comm, note 6, supra; Lit v US, 18 F Supp 435 (1937).

5. Sanford v Comm, note 10, supra.

6. Cerf v Comm, note 13, supra.

7. Fletcher Trust Co. v Comm, note 10, supra.

8. Blumberg v Smith, 138 F2d 956 (CCA 7) (1943); Helvering v McCormack, note 4, supra; Higgins v Comm,

129 F2d 237, cert den 317 US 658, 87 L ed 529, 63 S Ct 57 (1942); Camp v Comm, 15 TC 412, revd other grounds 195 F2d 999 (CA 1) (1952); DuPont, 12 TC 246 (1943).

9. Reg, § 25.2511-2(f); Comm v Warner, note 4, supra; Helvering v McCormack, note 4, supra; Brown, 3 TCM 148 (1944); Warburg, 6 TCM 789 (1946); Fleming, 3 TC 974 (1944); Roeser, 2 TC 298 (1943); Yerkes, 47 BTA 431 (1942).

10. Noble v Rogan, 49 F Supp 370 (1943); Goodman, 4 TC 191 (1944).

11. Wood, note 13, supra; Kolb, 5 TC 588 (1945).

The relinquishment of a power to alter or amend, which is not one retained by a donor, but granted by another, is not within the contemplation of the statute.[12]

Where a gift is made upon condition, such as the consent of the beneficiary at a future time,[13] or upon survival and remarriage,[14] not until the event takes place is the tax incurred.

As a matter of historical interest it may be noted that the 1932 Act specifically provided that the relinquishment or termination of a power by the donor to revest title in the transferred property in himself should be deemed to be the transfer subject to the tax. That is the origin of the present interpretation.

§ 425. Transfers by Gift; When Transferred; Reversionary Interests.

As we discovered in our discussion of the Estate Tax, when a person creates an irrevocable trust and retains no interest which would otherwise cause the property to be included in his gross estate, but has a possible reversionary interest in a value in excess of 5% of the value of the property, it will be taxable as a transfer taking effect at death.[15] Many taxpayers were led to believe that if a transfer was taxable under the Estate Tax, unless it was in contemplation of death, there was not a completed transfer at the time of the transfer where the donor retained a possible reversionary interest.[16] This position was taken before the Supreme Court decided that the retention of a reversionary interest subjected to the Estate Tax.[17]

After that decision, there came before the court a case in which a 72-year-old husband created a trust for his 44-year-old wife, with the income payable to her, and the remainder to revert to him if he were living, and if not to such persons as his wife should appoint. The Supreme Court then held that in such a case, where the grantor had neither the form nor substance of control unless he outlived his wife, he had lost all economic control and the gift was complete except for the value of his reversionary interest.[18] It also held that if the value of

---

12. Clark, 47 BTA 865 (1942); Nunnally, 5 TCM 562 (1945).

13. Dresselhuys, 40 BTA 30 (1939).

14. McLean, 11 TC 543 (1948).

15. §§ 144 et seq, supra.

16. Schmidlapp, 43 BTA 29 (1941); Trevor, 40 BTA 1241 (1939); McLean,

41 BTA 1266, mod other grounds 127 F 2d 942 (CCA 5) (1940).

17. Helvering v Hallock, 309 US 106, 84 L ed 604, 60 S Ct 444 (1939).

18. Smith v Shaugnessy, 318 US 176, 87 L ed 690, 63 S Ct 545 (1943).

the reversionary interest was incapable of valuation, the entire value of the property transferred would be subjected to Gift Tax.[19]

These cases have therefore settled the question, so that when an irrevocable trust is created in which the settlor retains a reversionary interest, a Gift Tax is payable at the time of the creation of the trust on the value of the transferred property, less the value of the reversionary interest. If it cannot be valued, the tax will be payable on the entire interest.

§ 426. Transfers by Gift; When Transferred; Short Term Trusts.

While the tax authorities main attention with respect to short term trusts, has been directed to the taxation of the income therefrom to the donor or settlor of the trust, such trusts have also received consideration under the Gift Tax with respect to the transfer of the income. These so-called "Clifford Trusts" were arrangements by which the income tax was sought to be avoided by creating a trust for one other than the settlor, to pay the income therefrom for a stated period, with the corpus reverting to the settlor. The trust derived its name from the case of Helvering v. Clifford[20] in which Clifford created a trust for his wife, to terminate within five years or the sooner death of either. The income could be accumulated at his discretion, and upon termination of the trust the income was payable to the wife, and the corpus reverted to him.

At this time we are not concerned with the Income Tax aspects of such a trust. But the question arises in such case, since there is a gift of income, whether the gift is completed at the time of creation of the trust, or at the time the income is paid. It is held that taxable gifts of future income are made at the time of the creation of the trust, or a transfer to it thereafter, since after the transfer the settlor has no economic interest in the income.[1] The fact that the income is taxable to the settlor[2] does not affect the completion of the gift of income when the trust is created.[3]

19. Robinette v Helvering, 318 US 184, 87 L ed 700, 63 S Ct 540 (1943).

20. 309 US 331, 84 L ed 788, 60 S Ct 554 (1940).

1. Comm v Hogle, 165 F2d 352 (CA 10) (1947); Lockard, 7 TC 1151, affd 166 F2d 408 (CCA 1) (1946).

2. IRC, §§ 671 et seq (1954 Code).

3. Note 1, supra.

§ 427. Transfers by Gift; When Transferred; Disclosure of Retained Power.

We have referred previously to the Regulation dealing with the contents of the return and the advice that if a donor contends that his retained power over property is of such nature as to render the gift incomplete and hence not subject to tax as of the calendar year of the initial transfer, the transaction should be disclosed in the return for the calendar year of the initial transfer.[4] This advice is repeated in the Regulation dealing with incomplete transfers, with the same requirement that there should be filed with the return evidence showing all relevant facts, including a copy of the instrument of transfer.[5]

The advice is sound, since if the facts be not reported and subsequently it be determined that the transfer was complete at the time of the initial transfer, penalties will have been incurred. In any instance in which the donor retains a power and does not report the transaction he is taking a needless risk.

§ 428. Transfers by Nonresidents Not Citizens.

We have previously discussed the fact that the Gift Tax applies to nonresidents not citizens of the United States, but while in the case of a resident or citizen, the tax applies regardless of where the property is situated,[6] in the case of the nonresident not a citizen of the United States, the tax does not apply to transfers of intangible property if such person *was not engaged in business in the United States* during the calendar year.[7] If the property which is the subject of the transfer is not situated within the United States the tax does not apply.[8] As noted, this is a substantial change from the provisions of the 1939 Code.

The changes in the statute by the 1939 Code also provided that only shares of stock in domestic corporations should be considered situated in the United States. Because of these changes, it is likely that many more trusts will be created by nonresident aliens not engaged in business in the United States, since it will be possible to do so without incurring Gift Tax.[9] It will also permit foreign securities to be held here and transferred by a nonresident alien without being subject to the Gift Tax, even though he be engaged in business here.

4. § 407, supra; Reg, § 25.6019-3 (a).
5. Reg, § 25.2511-2(j).
6. § 396, supra.
7. § 399, supra.
8. § 406, supra.
9. See Rev Rul 56-438, 1956-2 CB 604.

There are Gift Tax treaties between the United States and Australia and Japan. Since these change some of the situs rules, when a gift by the nationals of either country is involved, the particular treaty should be consulted.

§ 429. Community Property.

Until the enactment of the Revenue Act of 1942, the statute was silent as to community property, and gifts from community property were considered made half by the husband and half by the wife. The Revenue Act of 1942 amended the 1939 Code taxing gifts on community property as gifts by the husband, except to the extent that it could be shown that the property had been received as compensation for personal services actually rendered by the wife, or derived originally from such compensation, or from separate property of the wife.[10] The constitutionality of the statute was sustained.[11]

The Revenue Act of 1948, whose purpose was to extend the tax advantage which taxpayers in community property states enjoyed, to the citizens of noncommunity property states, introduced the concept of the marital deduction, conformed the statute accordingly,[12] and re-established the rule prior to 1942, so that all gifts from community property prior to January 1, 1943 and subsequent to April 2, 1948 were treated as half from the husband and half from the wife.[13]

In all gifts in community property law states two facts must be borne in mind. The first is that the laws controlling the question are not the same. The second is that there may be community property, separate property, and community property which was converted into separate property after January 1, 1943. In California, a determining date is July 28, 1927. Different taxability results, depending upon whether the subject of a gift is one or the other.

The *general* theory of community property is that all property acquired and the income and increase thereof, or exchanges during the marriage, is community property, and to be managed by the husband pursuant to the particular statute, which varies from state to state. Each spouse may have separate property,

10. IRC, § 1000(d) (1939 Code) as added by § 453 Rev Act 1942.

11. Beavers v Comm, 165 F2d 208 (CCA 5), cert den 334 US 811, 92 L ed 1743, 68 S Ct 1017 (1948).

12. Rev Act of 1948, § 371.

13. IRC, § 1000(d) (1939 Code) as added by § 453, Rev Act 1942 and amended by §371, Rev Act 1948.

which consists of property owned by either prior to the marriage, and property acquired after the marriage by gift, descent, or devise, together with the income, increase, and exchanges. In some states the income from separate property is considered community property. For purposes of the marital deduction, community property which was converted into separate property after December 31, 1941 is considered held as community property. As to community property acquired in California before July 29, 1927, the interest of the wife was not a vested interest, so that for Estate Tax purposes the entire property was includible in the husband's estate on his death. It is questionable that a gift of such property would be so considered. The conversion of community property after December 31, 1941 and before April 3, 1948 is not a gift from one spouse to the other.[14]

Insofar as separate property is concerned, it is treated for Gift Tax purposes the same as property transferred by gift by residents of noncommunity property states. The exclusions, exemption, and the marital deduction and split-gift provisions apply to gifts of such property.

In the case of community property, however, all gifts are considered as made one half by each spouse.[15] Where community property is used to purchase insurance on the life of the husband and a third party is the beneficiary, upon the death of the husband the wife is considered to have made a gift of one half of the proceeds.[16]

It will be seen from the foregoing that community property requires consideration, since it may arise in connection with various types of assets. It will be adverted to as necessary hereafter.

§ 430. Valuation of Gifts; Generally.

The statute provides that if the gift is made in property, the value thereof at the date of the gift shall be considered the amount of the gift.[17] The word property includes money, so that the gift of a rare coin would be measured by the value of the coin at the time of the gift.[18]

The value of the property is the price at which such property would change hands between a willing buyer and a willing

14. Essick v US, 88 F Supp 23 (1950).

15. Letter of Deputy Commissioner D. S. Bliss, Nov. 22, 1935.

16. Reg, § 25.2511–1(g)(9).

17. IRC, § 2512(a) (1954 Code).

18. Comm, Report, Rev Act 1932.

seller, neither being under any compulsion to buy or to sell, and both having reasonable knowledge of relevant facts. The value of a particular kind of property is not the price that a forced sale of the property would produce. The value is generally to be determined by ascertaining as a basis the fair market value at the time of the gift of each unit of the property. For example, in the case of shares of stocks or bonds, such unit of property is generally a share or a bond. Property shall not be returned at the value at which it is assessed for local tax purposes unless that value represents the fair market value thereof on the date of the gift. All relevant facts and elements of value as of the time of the gift should be considered.[19]

The Regulation is identical with the Estate Tax Regulation, and states the rules generally applicable to valuation. The value furnished should be fair and reasonable.[20] What is market value is a question of fact.[1] The Regulations prescribe the method of valuing various kinds of property and with rare exceptions have been sustained.[2] But the criterion for determining the value of a gift for purposes of the tax is a question of law.[3] If the criterion is incorrect, before there will be a reversal it must appear that the taxpayer has been prejudiced.[4] It must be remembered that the determination of the Commissioner is presumptively correct.[5] The burden of proving the value to be less than that fixed by the Commissioner is upon the taxpayer.[6] The valuation of gifts does not differ from the valuation under the Estate Tax.[7] The rules laid down in the Regulations are not formulae, but factors which furnish a fair basis for valuation.

Valuation of particular assets are dealt with at length in the Regulations and will be dealt with hereafter in connection with such items of property. As we advised in connection with the

19. Reg, § 25.2512–1.

20. Hunt v Comm, 12 BTA 396 (1928).

1. Minnesota Rate Cases, 230 US 352, 57 L ed 1511, 33 S Ct 729 (1912); Zanuck v Comm, 149 F2d 714 (CCA 9) (1945); Spitzer v Comm, 153 F2d 967 (CCA 8) (1946); US v Frank, 133 F2d 1009 (CCA 7) (1943).

2. § 398, supra.

3. Powers v Comm, 312 US 259, 85 L ed 817, 61 S Ct 519 (1941); Zanuck v Comm, note 1, supra.

4. Maytag v Comm, 187 F2d 962 (CA 10) (1951).

5. Lockard v Comm, 166 F2d 409 (CCA 1) (1948); Hyman v Numan, 143 F2d 425 (CCA 2) (1944).

6. James v Comm, 148 F2d 236 (CCA 2) (1945); Schlegel v US, 71 F Supp 495, affd 164 F2d 276 (CCA 1) (1947); Groff v Smith, 34 F Supp 319 (1940).

7. See Chapter 2, supra, in connection with Estate Tax valuation of various assets.

Estate Tax, many of the disagreements as to value are adjusted by compromise in conference. Placing absurdly low values on assets which are the subject of a gift will result in the Gift Tax Examiner in turn placing an absurdly high value thereon for bargaining purposes. Common sense dictates that the values submitted be not unreasonable.

§ 431. Valuation of Real Estate.

All which was said about the valuation of real estate under the Estate Tax[8] is generally applicable to valuation of such property under the Gift Tax. But while the Estate Tax does not apply to real property situated outside the United States,[9] it has been held that in the case of a citizen or resident the Gift Tax applies to foreign real estate.[10] Under the 1924 Act there was a holding to the contrary.[11]

The principles of valuation are the same under both taxes. Neither the Estate Tax nor the Gift Tax Regulations specifically refer to the valuation of real property. The usual method of using the opinion of an expert witness is employed and all the relevant factors which affect value are considered. Thus, in particular cases there have been considered proof of experts and actual sales,[12] testimony of experts, sales, and the size of lots,[13] and the description of the property and its condition, testimony of experts, possibility of a tax assessment, the price bid for adjoining property, and all other relevant factors.[14]

If the property is transferred subject to a mortgage, the mortgage must be deducted from the valuation.[15] A dower interest is not considered in fixing value,[16] nor is a curtesy interest.[17]

§ 432. Real Estate; Description.

The Regulation provides that there should be given for each parcel of real estate a legal description, its area, a short statement of the character of any improvements, and if located in a city, the name of street and number.[18] The Instructions on Form 709 provide similarly.[19]

8. §§ 43, 51, supra.
9. § 43, supra.
10. MacDonald v US, 139 F Supp 598 (1956).
11. Lyman, 23 BTA 540 (1931).
12. Carlton v Comm, 190 F2d 183 (CA 5) (1951).
13. Smith, 8 TCM 586 (1947).
14. Cullers, 14 TCM 925, revd 237 F 2d 729 (CA 8) (1955).
15. Janos, 11 TCM 1211 (1948).
16. Rev Rul 58-13, IRB 1958-2 p 10; Bartman, 10 TC 1073 (1948).
17. Thompson, 37 BTA 793 (1938).
18. Reg, § 25.6019-4.
19. Instruction 11, Form 709.

Form 709 contains no example of the method of reporting real estate as does Form 706, but it is customary to report gifts of real estate in the same manner as for Estate Tax. Since there is no separate schedule for mortgages affecting the property, when there is a mortgage, the amount is shown and deducted, and the equity transferred, is reported.[20] It will save time, if there is filed with the return, an appraisal by a real estate expert, since the Examiner will request it before auditing the return.[1]

§ 433. Stocks and Bonds; Valuation; Generally.

The principles of valuation of securities which are listed on a stock exchange, in the over-the-counter market, either on a selling price or bid and asked basis, is the same for Gift Tax purposes as for Estate Tax purposes.[2] The Regulations for both are identical in language. The Gift Tax Regulation provides for the method of valuing stocks and bonds based on selling prices,[3] based on bid and asked prices,[4] where selling prices and bid and asked prices are not available for dates both before and after the date of the gift,[5] where selling prices or bid and and asked prices do not represent fair market value,[6] and where the selling prices and bid and asked prices are unavailable.[7] The Estate Tax Regulations contain the same provision with respect to situations where the sales price or bid and asked price does not reflect the fair market value.[8] For some strange reason the Gift Tax Regulation uses the word "represent" instead of "reflect".

The major source of litigation concerning valuation under the Gift Tax has involved the so-called "blockage theory" and stock of closely held corporations. We shall treat of these in the succeeding sections.

§ 434. Stocks and Bonds; Valuation; Closely Held Corporation.

Unlike the Estate Tax statute,[9] there is no reference in the Gift Tax statute to unlisted securities. But the Regulation provides that if the provisions for valuation of securities regularly

20. See Form 5, § 45, supra.
1. See Form 7, § 49, supra.
2. See §§ 54, 56, 57, supra.
3. Reg, § 25.2511–2(b).
4. Reg, § 25.2511–2(c).

5. Reg, § 25.2511–2(d).
6. Reg, § 25.2511–2(e).
7. Reg, § 25.2511–2(f).
8. See § 58, supra.
9. IRC, § 2031(b) (1954 Code).

traded are inapplicable because actual sale and bid and asked prices are lacking, then the fair market value is to be determined by taking the following factors into consideration:

(1) In the case of corporate or other bonds, the soundness of the security, the interest yield, the date of maturity, and other relevant factors; and

(2) In the case of shares of stock, the company's net worth, prospective earning power and dividend-paying capacity, and other relevant factors.

Some of the other relevant factors are stated to be the value of the business; the economic outlook in the particular industry; the company's position in the industry and its management; and the values of securities of corporations engaged in the same or similar lines of business which are listed on a stock exchange.

However, the weight to be accorded such comparisons or any other evidentiary factors considered in the determination of a value depends upon the facts of each case. Complete financial and other data upon which the valuation is based must be submitted with the return, including copies of reports in any case in which examinations of the company have been made by accountants, engineers, or any technical experts as of or near the date of the gift.[10]

The language is identical with that of the Estate Tax Regulation for the valuation of closely held stock. Unlike former Regulations, there is no reference to close corporations, but a Revenue Ruling defines the term as meaning a corporation in which the stock is held in few hands, or in few families, and wherein it is not at all, or only rarely dealt in by buying or selling.[11] It has previously been noted that the same Ruling sets forth some of the fundamental factors in evaluation of such stock, which are:

(1) The nature of the business and the history of the enterprise.

(2) The economic outlook in general and the condition and outcome of the specific industry.

(3) Book value and financial condition.

(4) Earning capacity.

(5) Dividend paying capacity.

(6) Good will.

(7) Sales of the stock and the size of the block.

---

10. Note 7, supra.   11. Rev Rul 54-77, IRB 1954-1 CB 187.

(8) Market price of similar stocks which are listed on an exchange.

It will be observed that the Regulation has incorporated only some of these factors.

As observed heretofore, there are rules for valuation, but no formulae. "Relevant factors" will be found to cover a multitude of items. Valuation can only be determined by applying the general rules to the *facts of each case.* As the Revenue Ruling referred to points out, often an appraiser will find wide differences of opinion as to the fair market value of a particular stock. In resolving such differences he should maintain a reasonable attitude in recognition of the fact that *valuation is not an exact science.* A sound valuation will be based upon all the relevant facts, but the elements of common sense, informed judgment and reasonableness must enter into the process of weighing those facts and determining their aggregate significance. This advice to appraisers may equally well be regarded by the taxpayer when evaluating a gift. Valuations have been based upon the following in particular cases: fair market value of corporate assets,[12] earnings, assets, good will, and possible future,[13] past and prospective earnings, assets, expert testimony, possible effects of pending litigation, and other facts,[14] net worth, earnings, dividend paying capacity, record of dividends, position in the industry, indebtedness, good will, tangible assets, and net working capital, as well as the fact the stock was not voting stock, arrears of dividends on preferred stock, and the fact that the stock was pledged,[15] the asset value of stock of an investment company,[16] balance sheets,[17] and earning power, dividends paid, book value, nature of business, adequacy of reserves, size of holding, surplus for dividends, sales of stock and restrictions thereon, management's ability, the corporation's reputation, its position in the industry, distribution and method, opportunity for promoting a new product, competitive position, condition of plant and equipment, business volume, prosperity and depression, balance sheet and earnings ratio, tariffs, taxes, transportation regulations, and other legal restrictions, and length of time

12. Rosenthal, BTA mem op, Dec. 11, 622–E (1941).

13. Aufiero, 13 TCM 182 (1949).

14. Rollman, BTA memo op, Dec. 12, 184–D (1941).

15. Morse, 10 TCM 636 (1948).

16. Richardson v Comm, 151 F2d 102 (CCA 2), cert den 326 US 796, 90 L ed 485, 66 S Ct 490 (1945).

17. Schwabacher, 5 TCM 971 (1945).

the corporation was in business.[18] There have also been considered net worth, earning power, dividend paying capacity, prospects for the future, lack of depth in management, the fact that the stock represented a minority interest, no dividend payment record, two other transfers of stock, and the history of the company.[19] If these cases prove anything, they establish that fair market value is a question of fact and not of formula.[20] In fixing values for the Gift Tax, of closely held stock, no factor which may affect the value should be overlooked.

In Gift Tax cases, while restriction on the right to transfer the stock in and of itself does not reduce value, it must be considered along with other relevant factors.[1]

While the Regulation makes no reference to good will in the valuation of closely held stock, the Revenue Ruling referred to[2] lists this as one of the factors to be considered. That subject has been treated heretofore, and the methods for determination of the same enumerated.[3]

The important thing in any matter of valuation is to submit adequate evidence to substantiate the value claimed, for otherwise the value fixed by the Commissioner will be sustained.[4]

§ 435. Stocks and Bonds; Valuation; Blockage.

The Gift Tax Regulation,[5] as does the Estate Tax Regulation,[6] for the first time recognizes the effect of "blockage." As was noted in connection with the Estate Tax,[7] the Commissioner vigorously opposed for many years the contention that the size of a block of stock listed on an exchange had any effect on its value. In fact it was attempted to be outlawed by a Gift Tax Regulation that the size of a block of securities was not a relevant factor in determining value.[8] The court struck it down.[9]

The Regulation provides that in certain exceptional cases, the

18. Baltimore Nat. Bank v US, 136 F Supp 642 (1955).

19. Kieckhefer v US, 56–2 USTC ¶ 11,618.

20. Burda, 2 TCM 497 (1944).

1. Kline v Comm, 130 F2d 743 (CCA 3) (1942); Krauss v US, 140 F2d 510 (CCA 5) (1940); Comm v McCann, 141 F2d 385 (CCA 2) (1945); Spitzer v Comm, 153 F2d 967 (CCA 8) (1946); Moore, 3 TC 1205 (1944); note 18, supra; Bartram v Graham, 157 F Supp 757 (1957).

2. Note 11, supra.

3. § 59, supra; note 15, supra.

4. James v Comm, 148 F2d 236 (CCA 2) (1945); Groff v Smith, 34 F Supp 319 (1940).

5. Reg, § 25.2511–2(e).

6. Reg, § 20.2031–2(e).

7. § 55, supra.

8. Reg, 79, Art 19.

9. Comm v Shattuck, 97 F2d 790 (CCA 7) (1938).

[Harris]—38

size of the block of securities made the subject of each separate gift in relation to the number of shares changing hands in sales may be relevant in determining whether selling prices reflect the fair market value of the block of stock to be valued. If the donor can show that the block of stock to be valued, with reference to each separate gift, is so large in relation to the actual sales on the existing market that it could not be liquidated in a reasonable time without depressing the market, the price at which the block could be sold as such outside the usual market, as through an underwriter, may be a more accurate indication of value than market quotations. On the other hand, if the block of stock to be valued represents a controlling interest, either actual or effective, in a going business, the price at which other lots change hands may have little relation to its true value.[10]

It will be observed that while the Internal Revenue Service is compelled to recognize size of holdings as a factor to be considered in valuation, it does so reluctantly, by also giving the Regulation a reverse twist which will increase value if the interest is a controlling one.

As has been said, blockage is not a law of economics, a principle of law, nor a rule of evidence. If the value of a given number of shares is influenced by the size of the block, *this is a matter of evidence* and not of doctrinaire assumption.[11] The size of the block which is the subject of a gift *may* have a bearing on its value. *But merely proving that it is a large block is not sufficient.* Expert testimony will be required that it cannot be sold at the quoted price, and evidence must be presented of all factors which it is claimed result in a valuation lower than its selling price or bid and asked price. The courts have fixed a value lower than the quoted price *when the facts warranted,*[12] and have refused to do so when they did not.[13]

10. Note 6, supra.

11. Walters, 35 BTA 259 (1936).

12. Whitmore v Fitzpatrick, 54-2, USTC ¶ 10,976; Soss BTA memo op, Dec. 11, 371-B (1940); Sensenbrenner, BTA memo op, Dec 9215-A (1936); Helvering v Maytag, 125 F2d 55 (CCA 8), cert den 316 US 689, 86 L ed 760, 62 S Ct 1280 (1942); Fleming, 10 TCM 764 (1948), Lunken, 4 TCM 610 (1944); Avery, 3 TC 963 (1944); Havemeyer v US, 59 F Supp 537 (1943), cert den 326

US 776, 90 L ed 456, 66 S Ct 138 (1945); Standish, 8 TC 1204 (1947).

13. Mott v Comm, 139 F2d 317 (CCA 6) (1944); Newberry, 39 BTA 1123 (1939); Groff v Smith, 34 F Supp 319 (1943); Bull v Smith, 119 F2d 490 (CCA 2) (1941); Phipps v Comm, 12 F 2d 214 (CCA 10), cert den 317 US 645, 87 L ed 519, 63 S Ct 38 (1942); Richardson v Comm, 151 F2d 102 (CA-DC), cert den 326 US 796, 90 L ed 485, 66 S Ct 490 (1945); Clause, 5 TC 647, affd 154

§ 436. Stocks and Bonds; Description.

The Regulation provides that the description of bonds should include the number transferred, principal amount, name of obligor, date of maturity, rate of interest, date or dates on which interest is payable, series number where there is more than one issue, and the principal exchange upon which listed, or the principal business office of the corporation, if unlisted.

Description of stocks should include number of shares, whether common or preferred, and, if preferred, what issue thereof, par value, quotation at which returned, exact name of the corporation, and, if the stock is unlisted, the location of the principal business office, the State in which incorporated and the date of incorporation, or if the stock is listed, the principal exchange upon which sold.[14]

§ 437. Interest in Business; Valuation.

An interest in a sole proprietorship by the creation of a partnership is frequently the subject of a gift, particularly between a parent and child, because of the income splitting benefits it offers. In such case the Regulation advises that care should be taken to arrive at an accurate valuation of any interest in a business which the donor transfers without an adequate and full consideration in money or money's worth. The fair market value of any interest in a business, whether a partnership or a proprietorship, is a net value equal to the amount which a willing purchaser, whether an individual or a corporation, would pay for the interest to a willing seller, neither being under any compulsion to buy or sell. The net value is determined on the basis of all relevant factors including—

(1) A fair appraisal as of the date of the gift of all the assets of the business, tangible and intangible, *including good will;*

(2) The demonstrated earning capacity of the business; and

(3) The other factors relating to the valuation of stock of a closely held corporation, *to the extent applicable.*

The Regulation specifically points out that special attention should be given to determining an adequate value of the good will of the business. Complete financial and other data upon which the valuation is based must be submitted with the return, including copies of reports in any case in which examination of

F2d 655 (CCA 3) (1945); Allen, 3 TC   14. Reg, § 25.6019.4.
1224 (1944).

the business has been made by accountants, engineers, or any technical experts as of or near the date of the gift.[15]

Since gifts of business interests for the most part involve as donor and donee, members of the same family, they are particularly suspect not only for Income Tax purposes, but also with respect to valuation for Gift Tax purposes. We have previously discussed the valuation of business interests for Estate Tax purposes.[16] The same principles and methods of valuation apply when a business interest is the subject of a gift, except that there is no need to consider the effect of the owner's death. Whether good will is present depends upon the facts of the individual case. As in the case of valuation of stock in closely held corporations, no relevant factor which may affect value should be overlooked. Examination of the cases disclose that the courts determine each case upon the facts of that case, and that book value will be taken in one instance,[17] good will considered in one case,[18] and not in another,[19] each case being decided on the factors present.[20]

§ 438. Notes; Valuation.

The fair market value of notes, secured or unsecured, *is presumed to be* the amount of unpaid principal, plus accrued interest to the date of the gift, *unless the donor establishes* a lower value. Unless returned at face value, plus accrued interest, *it must be shown by satisfactory evidence* that the note is worth less than the unpaid amount (because of the interest rate, or date of maturity, or other cause), or that the note is uncollectible in part (by reason of the insolvency of the party or parties liable, or for other cause), and that the property, if any, pledged or mortgaged as security is insufficient to satisfy it.[1]

The question of valuation of notes at less than face value is less likely to occur in the case of gifts than when such note is an asset of the decedent's estate. The same evidence, however, is required.[2] A note may be valued at less than face value for Gift Tax.[3]

15. Reg, § 25.2512–3.

16. §§ 102, 103, supra.

17. Kelly, 8 TCM 1108 (1947); Cohn, 6 TCM 865 (1946).

18. Grimes, 13 TCM 1119 (1954).

19. Lippert, 11 TC 783 (1949), also Lippert v Comm, 184 F2d 672 (CA 8) (1950).

20. See Harvey, 11 TCM 773 (1949); Scherer, 3 TC 776 (1944).

1. Reg, § 25.2512–4.

2. See § 65, supra.

3. Blackburn, 20 TC 204 (1953).

§ 439. Notes; Description.

Description of notes should include name of maker, date on which given, date of maturity, amount of principal, amount of principal unpaid, rate of interest and whether simple or compound, and date to which interest has been paid. If the gift includes accrued income to the date of the gift, the amount of such accrued income should be separately set forth.[4]

§ 440. Annuities, Life Estates, Terms for Years, Remainders and Reversions; Valuation.

The Gift Tax Regulation[5] with respect to the valuation of annuities, life estates, terms for years, remainders and reversions is identical with the Estate Tax Regulation[6] for valuation of such interests in the estate of a decedent, except for reference to donor instead of decedent, and the statement that where the donor transfers property in trust or otherwise and retains an interest therein, the value of the gift is the value of the property transferred less the value of the donor's retained interest. If the donor assigns or relinquishes an annuity, life estate, remainder or reversion which he holds by virtue of a transfer previously made by himself or another, the value of the gift is the value of the interest transferred.[7]

The necessity for valuing such interests in connection with gifts arises frequently, since many gifts are made in trust with a separation of income and principal, and the separate interests payable to different persons. Thus, if the donor transfers property in trust to pay the income to A for life, or for a term of years, and the remainder to B, the value of A's life estate or term for years must be valued separately, and the value of B's remainder interest valued separately. In the valuation of such interests tables have been prepared for use in computation. Use of such tables has been sustained by the courts.[8] The method of computing the value of annuities, life estates, terms for years, remainders and reversions has been previously illustrated.[9]

4. Note 14, supra.

5. Reg, § 25.2512–5.

6. Reg, § 20.2031–7.

7. Reg, § 25.2512–5(a)(1).

8. Wisotskey v Comm, 144 F2d 632 (CCA 2) (1944); O'Malley-Keyes, 4 TC 976 (1944); Dupont, 2 TC 246 (1943); Affelder, 7 TC 1190 (1946); Bowden, 14 TCM 1102, affd 234 F2d 937 (CA 5), cert den 352 US 916, 1 L ed 2d 123, 77 S Ct 215 (1955); Bartman, 10 TC 1073 (1948); McMurtry v Comm, 203 F2d 659 (CA 1) (1953); Comm v Procter, 142 F 2d 824 (CCA 4) cert den 323 US 756, 89 L ed 606, 65 S Ct 90 (1944); Comm v Marshall, 125 F2d 943 (CCA 2) (1942); Dumaine, 16 TC 1035 (1951).

9. §§ 112 et seq, supra.

These tables are not used for the valuation of commercial annuity contracts.[10] The method of valuation of such contracts will be demonstrated hereafter.[11]

Since January 1, 1952, the tables applicable to gifts made thereafter are based on a $3\frac{1}{2}\%$ rate, whereas before that date the rate used was 4%.

In the taxation of the gifts, the valuation of the differing interests is important not only because the tax is based thereon, but also as we shall see, because the annual exclusion applies only to gifts of present interests. Thus, an increase in the value of a present interest may reduce the amount of tax payable on the gift. The amount of tax may also be affected by valuation when there is a gift to charity, since the larger the value of the interest given to charity, the smaller the tax.

When the gift is conditioned upon remarriage,[12] or there is a power of invasion,[13] the value of the transferred interest may be computed by the use of the tables provided. As we have noted, a remainder is reduced by the amount of a retained reversionary interest, if the latter is capable of valuation.[14]

§ 441. Life Insurance and Annuity Contracts; Valuation.

Prior to 1941 it was held that the value of a life insurance contract or of a contract for the payment of an annuity issued by a company regularly engaged in the selling of contracts of that character, which was the subject of a gift, was the cash surrender value.[15] The Supreme Court then decided that the valuation of such contracts for the purpose of the Gift Tax was not the cash surrender value, but the cost of duplicating them at the date of the gift.[16] It was pointed out that in the absence of more cogent evidence, the one criterion which reflects both the insurance value and the investment value of such contracts was the cost of duplication, since cash surrender value reflects only part of the value of the contract.[17]

10. Note 7, supra.

11. § 441, infra.

12. Lingo, 13 TCM 436 (1949).

13. Lockard, 7 TC 1151 (1946); McMurtry v Comm, note 8, supra.

14. § 425, supra.

15. Blaffer v Comm, 103 F2d 489 (CCA 5), cert den 308 US 559, 84 L ed 469, 60 S Ct 91 (1939); Helvering v Bryan, 109 F2d 907 (CCA 8) (1940); Farish v Comm, 103 F2d 1011 (CCA 5), cert den 308 US 559, 84 L ed 469, 60 S Ct 91 (1939); Comm v Haines, 104 F 2d 854 (CCA 3) (1939); Helvering v Comm, 106 F2d 907 (CCA 8) (1939).

16. Guggenheim v Rasquin, 312 US 254, 85 L ed 813, 61 S Ct 507 (1941); Powers v Comm, 312 US 259, 85 L ed 817, 61 S Ct 509 (1941).

17. US v Ryerson, 312 US 260, 85 L ed 819, 61 S Ct 479 (1941).

The Regulation states the effect of the decisions in providing that the value of a life insurance contract or of a contract for the payment of an annuity issued by a company regularly engaged in the selling of contracts of that character is established through the sale of the particular contract by the company, or through the sale by the company of comparable contracts. As valuation through sale of comparable contracts is not readily ascertainable when the gift is of a contract which has been in force for some time and on which further premium payments are to be made, the value may be approximated by adding to the interpolated terminal reserve at the date of the gift the proportionate part of the gross premium last paid before the date of the gift which covers the period extending beyond that date. If, however, because of the unusual nature of the contract such approximation is not reasonably close to the full value, this method may not be used.[18]

With the removal of the payment of premiums test in the taxation of insurance in a decedent's estate, the number of gifts of policies of insurance has increased greatly, and therefore the need for valuation of such policies. The Regulation furnishes examples of the method of valuation, which have been followed in many cases.

If a donor purchases from a life insurance company for the benefit of another a life insurance contract or a contract for the payment of an annuity, the value of the gift is the cost of the contract.[19]

If an annuitant purchased from a life insurance company a single payment annuity contract by the terms of which he was entitled to receive payments of $1,200 annually for the duration of his life, and five years later at the age of 50 makes a gift of the policy, the value of the gift is the amount the company would charge for a similar annuity for the life of a person, age 50.[20]

If a donor makes a gift of a paid up policy on his life, the value of the gift is the cost of a single premium policy on the life of the donor at his age at the date of the gift.[1]

If the donor makes a gift of a policy on his life, four months after the last premium due date of a policy issued nine years and four months prior to the date of the gift, and the donor is

18. Reg, § 25.2512–6(a).
19. Reg, § 25.2512–6(b) Example (1).
20. Reg, § 24.2512–6(b) Example (2).
1. Reg, § 25.2512–6(b) Example (3).

35 years old at the time of the gift, the gross annual premium being $2,811., the value of the gift is computed as follows:[2]

Terminal reserve at end of 10th year	$14,601.00
Terminal reserve at end of 9th year	12,965.00
Increase	1,636.00
4/12 of increase	545.33
Terminal reserve at end of 9th year	12,965.00
Interpolated terminal reserve at date of gift	13,510.33
8/12 of gross premium ($2,811)	1,874.00
Value of the Gift	$15,384.33

The interpolated reserve is the reserve which the insurance company enters on its books against its liability on the contract, or the insurer's valuation of the contract. The word "interpolated" simply indicates adjustment of the reserve to the specific date in question.[3]

Even though the particular policy may no longer be available, the interpolated terminal reserve value of the policy is used as the value of the gift.[4]

We have previously discussed combination annuity and life insurance contracts,[5] whereunder the annuitant purchases a single premium life insurance and annuity contract, neither of which contracts would be sold separately by the company, and thereafter the assignment by the purchaser of the insurance contract. The Supreme Court has held recently that such contracts are severable.[6] Even though the Commissioner contended that the proceeds of such policies were not insurance, he has ruled that for Gift Tax purposes the value thereof is the replacement value at the date of the gift.[7]

When part of the premium is paid by another, the value of the gift is that proportionate part thereof paid for by the donor.[8]

When community property life insurance is the subject of a gift it has been held that the full value thereof is taxable,[9] but

2. Reg, § 25.2512–6(b) Example (4).
3. Comm v Edwards, 135 F2d 574 (CCA 7) (1943).
4. Note 3, supra.
5. § 152, supra.
6. Fidelity Philadelphia Trust Co. v Smith, 58–1 USTC ¶ 11,761.

7. Letter of Deputy Comm, D. S. Bliss, Mar. 27, 1941.
8. Kirk, 39 BTA 902 (1939); Helvering v Supplee, 118 F2d 347 (CA 3) (1947).
9. Blaffer v Comm, note 15, supra; Farish v Comm, note 15, supra.

it has also been held that only one half thereof is taxable.[10] It would appear that if the wife does not join in the gift and she has a vested interest in community property, that unless she joined in the gift, there would be a transfer of only one half. In any event, whether the gift be all or half, the *method* of valuation of the policy is the same as in the case of separate property.[11]

§ 442. Annuities, Life Estates, Terms for Years, Remainders, Reversions, Life Insurance and Annuity Contracts; Description.

Description of life insurance policies must show the name of the insurer and the number of the policy.[12] It is also required that *for every policy* of life insurance listed on the return, the donor must procure a statement from the insurance company on Form 938 and file it with the District Director, who may also require that the form be filed directly with him.[13] A separate form is required for each policy which is the subject of a gift. The insurance company will issue the form on request.

In describing an annuity, the name and address of the issuing company must be given, or, if payable out of a trust or other fund, such a description as will fully identify the trust or fund. If the annuity is payable for a term of years, the duration of the term and the date on which it began must be given, and if payable for the life of any person, the date of that person must be stated.[14]

All of the information upon which the donor fixed the value of the gift should be furnished with the return so that the tax authorities may determine whether the valuation and computation of the tax is correct.

10. Perkins, 1 TC 982 (1942).
11. Note 9, supra.
12. Reg, § 25.6019–4.

13. Reg, § 25.6001–1(b).
14. Note 12, supra.

FORM NO. 69

Life Insurance Statement

Valuation data with respect to assignment of policy or irrevocable designation of beneficiary during the calendar year 1960

(This statement should be filed by the donor with the Federal Gift Tax Return, Form 709)

Intercontinental Insurance Co., St. Louis, Mo.

(Name and address of insurance company)

1. (*a*) Name of insured Winthrop Benson   Date of birth   Jan. 10, 1925

   (*b*) Number of policy 246,857   Face amount, $15,000.00   Date of issue Sept. 18, 1950

   (*c*) Kind of policy Ordinary Life Preferred Class

   (*d*) Gross premium $281.10 payable annually (state frequency of payment)

2. (*a*) If an assignment—give date Jan. 15, 1960, and name of assignee Katherine Benson

   (*b*) If an irrevocable designation of beneficiary—give date . . . ., name of beneficiary and (if known) his date of birth . . . . and if other than a simple designation, quote in full (attach additional sheet if necessary) . . . .

3. If the policy is not paid-up—furnish the following:

   (*a*) Interpolated terminal reserve on date of assignment or irrevocable designation of beneficiary $1,351.03

   (*b*) Proportion of gross premium paid beyond date of assignment or irrevocable desig- nation of beneficiary . . . . $ 187.40 $1,538.43

   (*c*) Adjustment on account of dividends to credit of policy and any outstanding indebtedness against policy (dividends $. . . . . . ., net indebtedness $. . . . . . .) . . $. . . . . . .

   (*d*) Net total value of the policy (for gift tax purposes) . . $1,538.43

4. If the policy is a paid-up or a single-premium contract— furnish the following:

   (*a*) Total cost, on date of assignment or irrevocable desig- nation of beneficiary, of a single-premium policy on life of insured and at his attained age, for original face amount plus any additional paid-up insurance (additional face amount $. . . . . . .) (see footnote*) $. . . . . . .

(*b*) Adjustment on account of dividends to credit of policy and any outstanding indebtedness against policy (dividends $......, net indebtedness $......) .. $......

_____

(*c*) Net total value of policy (for gift tax purposes) ...... $......

The undersigned officer of the above-named insurance company hereby certifies that this statement sets forth true and correct information.

June 8, 1960   T. V. Evans, Asst. Secy.

<small>(Date of certification)</small>   <small>(Signature and title)</small>

* If a single-premium policy for the total face amount would not have been issued on the life of the insured as of the date specified, nevertheless assume that such a policy could then have been purchased by the insured and state the cost thereof, using for such purpose the same formula and basis employed, on the date specified, by the company in calculating single premiums.

§ 443. Certain Annuities under Qualified Plans.

Under Section 2039(c) of the 1954 Code the portion of survivor benefits payable under a qualified plan which is attributable to the employer's contributions are excluded from the employee's gross estate for purposes of the Estate Tax.[14a] There was some doubt as to whether the exercise of an option or election to have the benefits payable to a beneficiary who survived the employee, or the failure to exercise such election, resulted in a taxable gift of that portion of the benefits attributable to the contributions of the employer. Congress has resolved the doubt by enacting a new section of the Gift Tax statute which provides that a gift does not occur in such cases.

The exercise or nonexercise by an employee of an election or option whereby an annuity or other payment will become payable to any beneficiary at or after the employee's death will not be considered a transfer for purposes of the Gift Tax if the option or election and annuity or other payment is provided for under—

(1) an employee's trust (or under a contract purchased by an employee's trust) forming part of a pension, stock bonus, or profit-sharing plan which, at the time of such exercise or non-exercise, or at the time of termination of the plan if earlier, met the requirements of Section 401(a);

(2) a retirement annuity contract purchased by an employer (and not by an employee's trust) pursuant to a plan which, at

---

14a. See §§ 178 et seq, supra.

the time of such exercise or nonexercise, or at the time of termination of the plan if earlier, met the requirements of Section 401(a)(3), (4), (5), and (6); or

(3) a retirement annuity contract purchased for an employee by an employer which is an organization referred to in Section 503(b)(1), (2), or (3), and which is exempt from tax under Section 501(a).[14b]

If the annuity or other payment referred to above is attributable to any extent to payments or contributions made by the employee, then the provision above shall not apply to that part of the value of such annuity or other payment which bears the same proportion to the total value of the annuity or other payment as the total payments or contributions made by the employee bear to the total payments or contributions made. For purposes of the preceding sentence, payments or contributions made by the employee's employer or former employer toward the purchase of an annuity described in (3) above shall, to the extent not excludable from gross income under Section 403(b), be considered to have been made by the employee.[14c]

For purposes of the section, the term "employee" includes a former employee.[14d]

The provisions of (1) and (2) above apply with respect to the calendar year *1955 and* all calendar years *thereafter.* For the calendar years *before 1955,* the determination of whether the exercise or nonexercise by an employee of an election or option described above is a transfer for purposes of the Gift Tax under the *1939 Code* shall be made as if the present section had not been enacted and without inferences drawn from the fact that the section is not made applicable with respect to calendar years before 1955.[14e] *The provisions of (3) above apply* with respect to calendar years *after 1957.*[14f]

This new section provides for Gift Tax purposes, a rule which is similar to that provided for Estate Tax purposes by Section 2039(c).[14g] The principles followed under Section 2039 in con-

14b. IRC, § 2517(a) (1954 Code), as added by Technical Amendments Act of 1958, § 68, and amended by § 23(f), HR 8381, 85th Cong, 2nd Sess.

14c. IRC, § 2517(b) (1954 Code) as added and amended.

14d. IRC, § 2517(c) (1954 Code) as added and amended.

14e. Technical Amendments Act of 1958, § 68(c), HR 8381, 85th Cong, 2nd Sess.

14f. Technical Amendments Act of 1958, § 23(g), HR 8381, 85th Cong, 2nd Sess.

14g. Note 14a, supra.

nection with determining the value of survivor benefits and the amount of employee's and employer's payments or contributions are equally applicable under the above new section.[14h]   The extension of the provisions of the section to employees of educational, charitable and religious organizations corresponds with the amendments to the Estate Tax statute.[14i]

§ 444. Miscellaneous Property; Valuation and Description.

The variety of property which may be the subject of a gift would preclude the possibility of the Regulations making specific mention of each.   Where particular property is not referred to in the Regulations, the general rule applies that the value is the price at which such property would change hands between a willing buyer and a willing seller, neither being under any compulsion to buy or to sell, and both having reasonable knowledge of relevant facts.[15]

It may be helpful to consider factual situations in particular cases for reference, when an item of property needs to be valued.

The value of land contracts and judgments is arrived at in the same way as they are valued for Estate Tax purposes.[16]   If the donor forgives an indebtedness of the donee, the amount thereof is the value of the gift.[17]   When property is pledged or subject to an indebtedness, the value of the gift is the value of the property reduced by the debt.[18]

When there is a conversion of a tenancy by the entirety into a tenancy in common, if the ages of the parties differ, the amount of the gift from the younger to the older is to the extent of the value of the rights of the younger under the tenancy by the entirety less one half the value of the property, based upon the Actuaries' or Combined Experience Table of Mortality.[19]

Upon a sale of literary works it was held that a gift of part thereof was reducible by the proportionate part of the agent's commission paid on the sale.[20]   Where the gift is made subject to the payment of taxes, the amount of such taxes are properly deducted from the value of the gift.[1]

14h. Senate Finance Committee Report on IRC, § 2517 (1954 Code), as added and amended; see § 4504C, supra, as to includible amounts.

14i. §§ 180, 181, supra.

15. Reg, § 25.2512–1.

16. §§ 66, 106, supra.

17. Ogle, BTA mem op, Dec. 9831–A.

18. Cohen, 44 BTA 709 (1941); Comm v Procter, 142 F2d 824, cert den 323 US 756, 89 L ed 606, 65 S Ct 90 (1944).

19. Special Ruling, Oct. 1, 1948.

20. Rohmer, 21 TC 1099 (1954).

1. Harrison, 17 TC 1350 (1952); Lingo, 13 TCM 436 (1949); Gruen, 1 TC 130 (1942).

We have previously treated of the valuation of various mineral interests and the like.[2]

Description of the seller's interest in land contracts transferred must include the name of the buyer, date of contract, description of property, sale price, initial payments, amounts of installment payments, unpaid balance of principal, interest rate and date prior to gift to which interest has been paid. Judgments must be described by giving the title of the cause and the name of the court in which rendered, date of judgment, name and address of judgment debtor, amount of judgment, rate of interest to which subject, and stating whether any payments have been made thereon, and, if so, when and in what amounts.[3]

§ 445. Effect of Excise Tax on Valuation.

The Regulations devote a special provision to the effect of excise tax on the valuation of a gift. This is the result of several cases which have held that the best evidence of value is the cost of an article subject to excise tax, plus the excise tax paid thereon.[4] A Revenue Ruling is to similar effect.[5]

This is incorporated in the form of a provision that if jewelry, furs or other property, the purchase of which is subject to an excise tax, is purchased at retail by a taxpayer and made the subject of gifts within a reasonable time after purchase, the purchase price, including the excise tax, is considered to be the fair market value of the property on the date of the gift, *in the absence of evidence* that the market price of similar articles has increased or decreased in the meantime. Under other circumstances, the excise tax is taken into account in determining the fair market value of property to the extent, and only to the extent, that it affects the price at which the property would change hands between a willing buyer and a willing seller.[6] The Regulation thus creates a presumption in favor of cost price plus excise tax as the value. This presumption, however, will not stand in the face of proof to the contrary. When such value is determined in any case where there has been a change for the worse in value between the date of the gift and the purchase, the

---

2. § 51, supra.
3. Note 12, supra.
4. Gould, 14 TC 414 (1950); Duke v Comm, 200 F2d 82 (CA 2), cert den 345 US 906, 97 L ed 1342, 73 S Ct 645 (1952); Publicker v Comm, 206 F2d 250 (CA 3), cert den 346 US 924, 98 L ed 418, 74 S Ct 312 (1953).
5. Rev Rul 55–71, 1955–1 CB 110.
6. Reg, § 25.2512–7.

result is due entirely to a lazy taxpayer who fails to present proper proof to rebut the presumption.

§ 446. Relation of Consideration to Valuation of Gift; Generally.

We observed that the refrain of transfers for less than an adequate and full consideration in money or money's worth ran through the estate taxation of jointly owned property,[7] lifetime transfers in contemplation of death,[8] transfers taking effect at death,[9] and the allowance of claims against the estate.[10] The same question presents itself in connection with the Gift Tax. The statute provides that where property is transferred for less than an adequate and full consideration in money or money's worth, then the amount by which the value of the property exceeded the value of the consideration shall be deemed a gift, and shall be computed in computing the amount of gifts made during the calendar year.[11]

The Regulation provides that transfers reached by the Gift Tax are not confined to those only which being without a valuable consideration accord with the common law concept of gifts, but embrace as well sales, exchanges, and other dispositions of property for a consideration to the extent that the value of the property transferred by the donor exceeds the value in money or money's worth of the consideration given therefor. However, a sale, exchange, or other transfer of property made in the ordinary course of business (a transaction which is bona fide, at arm's length, and free from any donative intent), will be considered as made for an adequate and full consideration in money or money's worth.[12]

The Regulation and the statute is a reflection of the intent of Congress in the enactment of the 1932 Act. That intent was to dispense with the test of donative intent[13] and to substitute a test which could be administered more easily, namely, to consider any transfer to the extent that it exceeded a full consideration, as a gift. It was not intended thereby to affect business transactions within the meaning of ordinary speech.[14]

While it would appear that it would be simple to apply the

7. § 89, supra.
8. § 130, supra.
9. § 155, supra.
10. § 218, supra.
11. IRC, § 2512(b) (1954 Code).

12. Reg, § 25.2512–8.
13. § 419, supra.
14. Comm v Wemyss, 324 US 303, 89 L ed 958, 65 S Ct 652 (1945).

test established by the statute, not all cases present a black or white picture, but there are many which are grey. Any transfer of property is treated as a gift to the extent that the transferor does not receive in return an adequate and full equivalent in money or something which can be valued in money.[15] "Consideration" as used in the statute is not the same as common law consideration, but means that when the transferor gives something away and does not at the same time replace it with money or equal value or some goods or services capable of being evaluated in money, he is deemed to have made a gift within the statute. Mutual promises may be common law consideration, but may not be so for purposes of the Gift Tax.[16] A moral obligation is not consideration.[17] There must be a money consideration which benefits the donor for there to be consideration.[18]

There are many transactions which are ostensibly business transactions, but which are not so in fact. Many of these occur in connection with family settlements of one kind or another, or marital arrangements, which under the common law concept of gifts may be sufficient consideration to support a contract, but which for the purposes of the Gift Tax do not constitute consideration. Thus the transfer of a business interest for some consideration, but not one equal to the value of the interest received, will result in a gift having been made as to the difference.[19] Subterfuges intended to disguise the real nature of the transaction are unlikely to be successful.[20] A transaction which concerns a business is not necessarily a business transaction which is bona fide, at arm's length and free from any donative intent.[1] On the other hand, a transfer in return for a promise of support has been held adequate consideration.[2] The purchase of an annuity for a retiring employee has been held to be additional compensation and not a gift,[3] as has a business subsidy given to a firm to induce it to locate its plant on certain property.[4]

Many of the problems which arise in connection with consid-

15. Comm v Bristol, 121 F2d 129 (CCA 1) (1941).

16. Note 15, supra.

17. Lester v US, 35 F Supp 535 (1946).

18. Note 14, supra.

19. Bergan, 1 TC 543 (1943); Hoffman, 2 TC 1160 (1943); Hunkele, 3 TCM 426 (1944); Bartman, 10 TC 1073 (1948).

20. Lampert, 14 TCM 1184 (1956).

1. See Kelly, 8 TCM 1108 (1947); Housman v Comm, 105 F2d 973 (CCA 2), affg 38 BTA 1007, cert den 309 US 656, 84 L ed 1005, 60 S Ct 469 (1939); note 19, supra.

2. Bergan, note 19, supra.

3. Morrow, 2 TC 210 (1943).

4. GCM 16952, 1937-1 CB 133.

eration result from intrafamily transactions or settlement of marital rights, which will be discussed in the succeeding sections.

§ 447. Relation of Consideration to Valuation of Gift; Matrimonial Transfers; Antenuptial Gifts.

The Regulation states that a consideration not reducible to a value in money or money's worth, as love and affection, promise of marriage, etc., is to be wholly disregarded, and the entire value of the property transferred constitutes the amount of the gift.[5]

As a result, antenuptial transfers are deemed to be gifts and are taxable as such.[6] At one time there was doubt on the question.[7] By applying the rule that the Estate and the Gift Tax were in pari materia, the Supreme Court read the provisions of the Estate Tax statute,[8] that a relinquishment or promised relinquishment of dower or curtesy, or of a statutory estate created in lieu of dower or curtesy, or of other marital rights in the decedent's property or estate, shall not be considered to any extent a consideration in "money or money's worth", into the Gift Tax statute.

It has been held, however, that to the extent that a transfer is in satisfaction of the spouse's right of support, it is for an adequate consideration.[9] The Proposed Gift Tax Regulation provided that a transfer of property which, or the income from which, was to be used in the future to discharge a donor's obligation to support a dependent, was not a transfer for a consideration in money or money's worth, unless under local law the transfer operated completely to discharge the donor's obligation.[10] This sentence has been deleted from the final Gift Tax Regulation, as it was from the Proposed Estate Tax Regulation. The significance of the deletion remains to be seen.

There is one exception to the rule that the release of marital rights is not consideration, which was added by the 1954 Code, and deals with property settlements followed by divorce.[11]

---

5. Note 12, supra.

6. Merrill v Fahs, 324 US 308, 89 L ed 963, 65 S Ct 655 (1945); note 15, supra; note 14, supra; Krause v Yoke, 89 F Supp 91 (1950).

7. See Lasker v Comm, 138 F2d 989 (CCA 7) (1943).

8. IRC, § 2043(b) (1954 Code).

9. McWilliams v Harrison, 44-1 USTC ¶ 10,119; Rosenthal, 17 TC 1047, revd other grounds 205 F2d 505 (CA 2) (1951).

10. Proposed Reg, § 25.2512-8.

11. IRC, § 2516 (1954 Code).

There is a further provision, also added by the 1954 Code, granting an election to defer the gift when it is without consideration, and which results from the creation of a tenancy by the entirety or a joint tenancy in real property.[12] Each will be discussed hereafter.

§ 448. Relation of Consideration to Valuation of Gift; Intrafamily Transfers.

Intrafamily transactions are particularly suspect under the Gift Tax. It does not follow, however, that because the transaction is between members of the same family, that there can not be such a one in the ordinary course of business, which is bona fide, at arm's length, and free from donative intent.[13]

Definite rules for the income taxation of family partnerships have been promulgated, since as the Senate Finance Committee's Report on the 1951 Act pointed out, "transactions between persons in a close family group, whether or not involving partnership interests, afford much opportunity for deception and should be subject to close scrutiny." Gift taxation in intrafamily transactions is subject to the test of consideration and whether the transfer is made in the ordinary course of a business transaction.[14]

If it is shown that there was a sufficient consideration there is no gift within the meaning of the statute.[15] On the other hand, if it be shown that the transaction was not in the ordinary course of business and for less than an adequate and full consideration, the difference between the price paid and the value is deemed a gift.[16] Many such transactions are sought to be covered up by claims that they were for services rendered,[17] or by creation of joint or reciprocal trusts,[18] or other devices.[19] None such, which do not meet the tests of the statute and Regulations will pass muster.

12. IRC, § 2515 (1954 Code).

13. Rosenthal v Comm, 205 F2d 505 (CA 2) (1953).

14. Reg, § 25.2512-8.

15. Myers v Magruder, 15 F Supp 488 (1936); Rothrock, 7 TC 848 (1946).

16. Friedman, 10 TC 1145 (1948); Gross, 7 TC 837 (1946); Robinette v Helvering, 318 US 184, 87 L ed 700, 63 S Ct 540 (1943).

17. Rohmer, 21 TC 1099 (1954).

18. Robinette v Helvering, note 16, supra; Comm v McLean, 127 F2d 942 (CCA 5) (1942); Giannini v Comm, 148 F2d 285 (CCA 9), cert den 326 US 730, 90 L ed 434, 66 S Ct 38 (1945).

19. French v Comm, 138 F2d 254 (CCA 8) (1943); Deal, 29 TC 730 (1958).

§ 449. Community Property; Consideration.

We have previously noted that for purposes of the Gift Tax marital deduction, as well as the Estate Tax marital deduction, community property which was converted into separate property after December 31, 1941 is considered held as community property.[20] The Treasury at one time tried to tax such conversion as a gift,[1] but it was held that the Regulation was invalid.[2] The court held that the transfer by each spouse was in consideration of the other's transfer.[3]

While the transfer of half of community income to one spouse by the other is not a gift for purposes of the Gift Tax,[4] a gift subject to the tax may arise when one spouse transfers community property to a trust, reserving income for the joint lives of the spouses, and the corpus being payable to others. On the death of the first spouse, if the survivor does not disaffirm the trust, she makes a gift of her interest in one half the remainder reduced by her life estate.[5] Where the widow accepts an amount in lieu of her interest in community property, the amount received is partial consideration, and the balance is a gift.[6]

§ 450. Tenancies by the Entirety; Generally.

Prior to the 1954 Code, *which is effective only as to gifts made after January 1, 1955,* the creation of a tenancy by the entirety constituted a taxable gift when one spouse paid the entire consideration, to the extent of the value of the property less the present worth of the retained rights of such spouse.[7] A gift might also arise on the termination of the tenancy if the proceeds were not divided between husband and wife. Furthermore, upon the death of one tenant, prima facie the entire property was part of the decedent's gross estate, except to the extent that it could be shown that the survivor paid value therefor.[8] The Estate Tax effect is the same under the 1954 Code.[9]

An estate by the entirety in real property is essentially a joint tenancy between husband and wife with the right of sur-

---

20. § 429, supra.

1. Reg 108, § 86.2(c), prior to amendment by TD 6015.

2. Comm v Mills, 183 F2d 32 (CA 9) (1950); Essick v US, 88 F Supp 23 (1949).

3. Comm v Mills, note 2, supra.

4. Rev Rul 55-46, 1955-2 CB 608.

5. Chase Nat. Bank of City of NY, 25 TC 617 (1955).

6. Siegel, 26 TC 743, affd 250 F2d 339 (CA 9) (1956).

7. Reg 108, § 86.2(a)(6).

8. IRC, § 811(e) (1939 Code); Reg 105, § 81.22.

9. IRC, § 2040 (1954 Code).

vivorship. As used in the statute and Regulations, the term includes a joint tenancy between husband and wife in real property with right of survivorship, or a tenancy which accords to the spouses rights equivalent thereto, regardless of the term by which such a tenancy is described in local law.[10] This provision is inserted because in some states tenancies by the entirety are not permitted.

The 1954 Code provides for an election by the donor to treat the transaction as a gift at the time of the creation of the tenancy, or at the termination of the tenancy other than by death of a spouse.[11]

The contribution made by either or both spouse in the creation of such a tenancy during the calendar year 1955 and thereafter, *is not deemed a gift* by either spouse, regardless of the proportion of the total consideration furnished by either spouse, *unless* the donor spouse elects to treat such event as a gift in the calendar year in which the transaction is effected. However, there is a gift upon the termination of such a tenancy, other than by the death of a spouse, if the proceeds received by one spouse on termination of the tenancy are larger than the proceeds allocable to the consideration furnished by that spouse to the tenancy. The creation of a tenancy by the entirety takes place if either the husband or wife purchases property and causes the title thereto to be taken as tenants by the entirety, or both join in such a purchase, or if either or both cause such tenancy to be created in property already owned by either or both of them. The rule also applies to contributions made in making additions to the property by improvements or reduction of indebtedness, regardless of the proportion of the consideration furnished by each spouse.[12]

Since the gift may take place at different times, as may the termination, the contribution may differ, the value be different at different applicable dates, and there may be improvements, additions and appreciation in value, there are presented many different factors in the determination of the amount of the gift. In the light of these possible complexities, the Regulations are extremely detailed and attempt to provide for every possible contingency. They will be discussed in the succeeding sections.

10. IRC, § 2515(d) (1954 Code); Reg, § 25.2515–1(a).

11. IRC, § 2515 (1954 Code).

12. IRC, § 2515(a) (1954 Code); Reg, § 25.2515–1(b).

§ 451. Tenancies by the Entirety; Consideration.

Where the donor does not elect to have the creation of a tenancy by the entirety treated as a gift, but awaits the termination of the tenancy, it is necessary at that time to determine the proportions of the total consideration furnished by each of the spouses in order to determine the value of the gift which then takes place.[13] The Regulation, therefore, deals with the method of determination of the amount and proportion of consideration to be used in computing the value of the gift.

The consideration furnished by a person in the creation of a tenancy by the entirety or the making of additions thereto is the amount contributed by him. The contribution may be made by either spouse or by a third party. It may be in the form of money, property, or an interest in property. If the latter two, the amount of the contribution is the fair market value of the property at the time of transfer to the tenancy, or its exchange for the property which became the subject of the tenancy. If a decedent devises property to the spouses as tenants by the entirety valued at his death at $30,000., that is the amount of his contribution. If a husband takes title in his own name to property at a cost of $25,000. and creates a tenancy by the entirety later at a time when it is worth $40,000., the latter amount is his contribution. If he purchases stock for $25,000., and when it has a fair market value of $35,000. exchanges it for real property, taking title with his wife as tenant by the entirety, his contribution is $35,000.[14]

Whether consideration derived from a third party is furnished by the third party or by the spouses depends upon the manner of transfer. If a decedent devises real property to the spouses as tenants by the entirety, the decedent is the person who furnished the consideration. If the decedent's will directs his executor to discharge an indebtedness of the tenancy, the decedent is the person who furnished the consideration for the addition to the tenancy. If the husband and wife received a bequest and used it to reduce the indebtedness, they are the persons who furnished the consideration for the addition to the tenancy.[15]

Where part of the property subject to the tenancy is sold to a third party, or the original property sold and other property of

13. IRC, § 2515(b) (1954 Code).
14. Reg, § 25.2515–1(c)(1)(i).
15. Reg, § 25.2515–1(c)(1)(ii).

lesser value acquired through reinvestment so that there is not a termination, the proportionate contribution to the remaining tenancy is in general the same as the proportionate contribution to the original tenancy, and the character of the contribution remains the same. These proportions are applied to the cost of the remaining or substituted property. Thus, if the total contribution to the cost of the property was $20,000. and a fourth of the property was sold, the contributions to the remaining portion of the tenancy is $15,000. However, if it is shown that at the time of the contribution more or less than one fourth thereof was attributable to the portion sold, the contribution is divided between the portion sold and the portion retained in the proper proportion. If the portion sold was acquired as a separate tract, it is treated as a separate tenancy. Thus, assume X, a third party gave real property to H and W as tenants by the entirety, having a then value of $15,000., and 5 years later H spent $5,000. thereon in improvements and elected to treat it as a gift, and subsequently W spent $10,000. on improvements, but did not so elect. The property then appreciated $30,000. in value, was sold for $60,000., and $45,000. of this was invested in another tenancy by the entirety. Since X contributed one half of the consideration for the original property and the additions, i.e., $15,000. out of $15,000. + $5,000. + $10,000., he is considered as having contributed $22,500. ($\frac{1}{2}$ of $45,000.) toward the creation of the remaining portion of the tenancy and additions thereto. H is considered as having furnished one sixth, i.e., $5,000. out of $30,000., or $7,500. (1/6 of $45,000.), and W is considered as having contributed one third, or $15,000.[16]

Any general appreciation (appreciation due to fluctuations in market value) in the value of the property occurring between two successive contribution dates which can be readily measured and which can be determined with reasonable certainty to be allocable to any particular contribution or contributions previously furnished, is to be treated, for the purpose of the computations upon termination[17] as though it were additional consideration furnished by the person who furnished the prior consideration. Successive contribution dates are the two consecutive dates on which any contributions to the tenancy are made, not necessarily by the same party. Further, appreciation allocable to the prior consideration falls in the same class as the prior

16. Reg, § 25.2515-1(c)(1)(iii).   17. Reg, §§ 25.2515-3, 25.2515-4.

consideration to which it relates.[18] The Regulation furnishes three examples of its application.

In 1940, H purchased real property for $15,000. which he caused to be transferred to his wife and himself as tenants by the entirety. In 1956 when the fair market value was $30,000. he made improvements in the amount of $5,000., and sold the property in 1957 for $35,000. The appreciation of $15,000. constitutes an additional contribution by H, having the same characteristics as his original contribution.[19]

In 1955 H and W purchased property as tenants by the entirety, H contributing $10,000. and W, $5,000. to the total price of $15,000. In 1960 when the property had a fair market value of $21,000., W made improvements of $5,000. The property is sold for $26,000. The appreciation of $6,000. results in an additional contribution by H of $4,000. (10,000/15,000 of $6,000.), and by W of $2,000. (5,000/15,000 of $6,000.). H's total contribution is $14,000. ($10,000. + $4,000.) and W's contribution is $12,000. ($5,000. + $2,000. + $5,000.).[20]

In 1956 H and W purchase real property as tenants by the entirety. The purchase price is $15,000., with a down payment of $3,000., the balance to be paid monthly over a period of fifteen years. H contributed $2,000. and W, $1,000. H paid all the monthly installments, the property appreciating in value to $24,000. Here the appreciation is so gradual and the contributions so numerous, that the amounts allocable to any particular contribution cannot be ascertained with any reasonable certainty. Accordingly, the appreciation in value may be disregarded in determining the amount of the consideration furnished, in making the computations upon termination.[1]

§ 452. Tenancies by the Entirety; Termination.

As we have seen, upon the creation of a tenancy by the entirety, the donor may elect to have the transaction treated as a gift. But if he does not do so it will not be considered such. But when he does not do so at that time, the termination of the tenancy (except where the other spouse dies first) results in a gift to the extent that the proportion of the total consideration furnished by such spouse multiplied by the proceeds of the termination exceeds the value of such proceeds of termination received by him.[2]

18. Reg, § 25.2515–1(c)(2).
19. Note 18, Example 1.
20. Note 18, Example 2.

1. Note 18, Example 3.
2. Note 13, supra.

This raises a number of questions which the Regulations proceed to answer. Upon the termination of a tenancy by the entirety, whether created before, during, or subsequent to the calendar year 1955, a gift may result, depending upon the disposition made of the proceeds of the termination (whether the proceeds be in the form of cash, property, or interests in property). A gift may result notwithstanding the fact that the contributions of either spouse to the tenancy was treated as a gift.[3] As previously noted, even before the present statute, if upon termination of the tenancy the proceeds were not divided between the tenants a gift would result.[4]

Except as indicated below, a termination of a tenancy is effected when all or a portion of the property so held by the spouses is sold, exchanged, or otherwise disposed of, by gift or in any other manner, or when the spouses through any form of conveyance or agreement become tenants in common of the property or otherwise alter their respective interests in the property formerly held by them as tenants by the entirety. In general, any increase in the indebtedness on a tenancy constitutes a termination of the tenancy to the extent of the increase in the indebtedness. However, such an increase will not constitute a termination of the tenancy to the extent that the increase is offset by additions to the tenancy within a reasonable time after such increase. Such additions (to the extent of the increase in the indebtedness) shall not be treated by the spouses as contributions within the meaning of the Regulations.[5]

A termination is not considered as effected to the extent that the property subject to the tenancy is exchanged for other real property, the title to which is held by the spouses in an *identical* tenancy. For this purpose, a tenancy is considered identical if the proportionate values of the spouse's respective rights (other than any change in the proportionate values resulting solely from the passage of time) are identical to those held in the property which was sold. *In addition,* the sale, exchange (other than an exchange described above), or other disposition of property held as tenants by the entirety *is not considered as a termination if all three* of the following conditions are satisfied:

(1) There is no division of the proceeds of the sale, exchange

3. Reg, § 25.2515–1(d)(1).
4. § 450, supra.

5. Reg, § 25.2515–1(d)(2)(i).

or other disposition of the property held as tenants by the entirety;

(2) On or before the due date for the filing of a Gift Tax return for the calendar year in which the property held as tenants by the entirety was sold, exchanged, or otherwise disposed of, the spouses enter into a binding contract for the purchase of other real property; and

(3) After the sale, exchange, or other disposition of the former property and *within a reasonable time* after the date of the contract referred to in (2) above, such other real property actually is acquired by the spouses and held by them in an identical tenancy.

To the extent that *all three* of these conditions are not met (whether by reason of the death of one of the spouses or for any other reason), the provisions of the preceding sentence shall not apply, and the sale, exchange, or other disposition of the property will constitute a termination of the tenancy. "A reasonable time" means the time which, under the particular facts in each case, is needed for those matters which are incident to the acquisition of the other property (i.e., perfecting of title, arranging for financing, construction, etc.). The fact that proceeds of a sale are deposited in the name of one tenant or of both tenants separately or jointly as a convenience does not constitute a division within the meaning of (1) above, if the other requirements are met.[6]

When the proceeds on termination are in money, computation is based upon that fixed value. But there must also be considered the case where there is a sale, exchange, or other disposition in which the proceeds are received in the form of property or an interest in property, as provided in the statute[7] and expanded by the Regulation. Where the proceeds are received in the form of property or an interest in property, the value of the proceeds received by that spouse is the fair market value, on the date of termination of the tenancy by the entirety, of the property or interest received. Thus, if a tenancy by the entirety is terminated so that thereafter each spouse owns an undivided half interest in the property as tenant in common, the value of the proceeds of termination, received by each spouse is one half the value of the property at the time of the termination of the tenancy by the entirety. If under local law one spouse without the consent

---

6. Reg, § 25.2515–1(d)(2)(ii).   7. Note 13, supra.

of the other, can bring about a severance of his or her interest in a tenancy by the entirety and does so by making a gift of his or her interest to a third party, that spouse is considered as having received proceeds of termination in the amount of the fair market value, at the time of the termination, of his severable interest as determined in accordance with the Regulation.[8] He has in addition, made a gift to the third party of the fair market value of the interest conveyed to the third party. In such case, the other spouse also is considered as having received as proceeds of termination the fair market value, at the time of termination, of the interest which she thereafter holds in the property as tenant in common with the third party. However, since Section 2515(b) contemplates that the spouses may divide the proceeds of termination in some proportion other than that represented by the values of their respective legal interests in the property, if both spouses join together in making a gift to a third party of property held by them as tenants by the entirety, the value of the proceeds of termination which will be treated as received by each is the amount which each reports (on his or her Gift Tax return filed for the calendar year in which the termination occurs) as the value of his or her gift to the third party. This amount is the amount which each reports without regard to whether the spouses elect to treat the gifts as made one half by each under the split-gift provisions of the statute. Thus, if H and W hold real property as tenants by the entirety which they gift to their son in 1956 when the property has a fair market value of $60,000., and H reports it as a gift of $36,000. on his return for that year, and W reports it as a gift of $24,000. on her return, H is considered to have received proceeds of termination of $36,000., and W to have received $24,000.[9]

Except where the sale, exchange, or other disposition of the property is not considered a termination because meeting the three conditions noted above, where the proceeds of a sale, exchange, or other disposition of the property are not actually divided between the spouses but are held (whether in a bank account or otherwise) in their joint names or in the name of one spouse as custodian or trustee for their joint interests, *each spouse is presumed,* in the absence of a showing to the contrary, to have received, as of the date of termination, proceeds of

8. Reg, § 25.2512–5.   9. Reg, § 25.2515–1(d)(3)(i).

termination equal in value to the value of his or her enforceable property rights in respect of the proceeds.[10]

Since the section is new to the statute, the Regulations are necessarily specific and detailed and attempt to treat of every transaction in which a gift takes place upon termination of a tenancy by the entirety. Because of the election to treat not only the creation of such a tenancy as a gift, but also additions in the same manner, many complex situations will arise which will require involved computations. These will be treated in the chapter on computation of the tax.[11]

§ 453. Tenancies by the Entirety; Election to Treat Creation as Gift; Manner of Election.

The 1954 Code granted a person creating a tenancy by the entirety to treat it as a gift, as was the practice under the 1939 Code, upon the creation of the tenancy, or to wait until the termination of the tenancy. It also granted the same right with respect to additions made to the property. It is true that under the 1939 Code, few of the persons creating tenancies by the entirety realized that a gift had been made.

If the election is made to treat the creation of the tenancy as a gift, or if that be not done, to treat additions as gifts, the statute provides that the election must be made in a particular way.[12] The election to treat the creation of a tenancy by the entirety in real property, or additions to its value made thereto, as constituting a gift in the year in which effected, must be exercised by including the value of such gifts in the Gift Tax return of the donor for the calendar year in which the tenancy was created, or the additions in value were made to the property. The election *may be exercised only* in a return filed within the time prescribed by law, or before the expiration of any extension of time granted pursuant to law for the filing of the return. *In order to make the election, a Gift Tax return must be filed for the calendar year in which the tenancy was created, or additions in value thereto made, even though the value of the gift involved does not exceed the amount of the annual exclusion.*[13]

This means that if the election is to be exercised it must be done on the return filed on or before the 15th day of April following the close of the calendar year in which the tenancy was

---

10. Reg, § 25.2515–1(d)(3)(ii).   12. IRC, § 2512(c) (1954 Code).
11. Chapter 9, infra.   13. Reg, § 25.2512–2(a).

created or the additions made,[14] unless an extension of time for filing the return has been granted.[15] It will be noted, that unlike other gifts, where no return need be filed if the gift to a donee does not exceed the amount of the annual exclusion, if the election is to be made, no matter what the amount of the gift, the gift must be reported. This does not affect the tax, but does serve as notice that the election has been exercised. All that is required is that Form 709 set forth the details as to the creation of the tenancy.

§ 454. Tenancies by the Entirety; Election to Treat Creation as Gift; Valuation; Generally.

Where the donor spouse elects to treat the creation of a tenancy by the entirety as a gift, the amount thereof is determined in the same way as it was under the 1939 Code. The amount of his contribution less the value of his retained interest is the amount of the gift.[16] What that retained interest is, however, depends upon State law. The Regulations, therefore, provide that the value of the retained interest is determined as follows:

(1) If under the law of the jurisdiction governing the rights of the spouses, either spouse, acting alone, can bring about a severance of his or her interest in the property, the value of the donor's retained interest is one half the value of the property.

(2) If, under the law of the jurisdiction governing the rights of the spouses each is entitled to share in the income or other enjoyment of the property but neither, acting alone, may defeat the right of the survivor of them to the whole of the property, the amount of the retained interest of the donor is determined by multiplying the value of the property by the appropriate actuarial factor for the donor spouse at his attained age at the time the transaction is effected.[17]

Factors representing the respective interests of the spouses, under a tenancy by the entirety, at their attained ages at the time of the transaction may be found, or readily computed with the use of the tables referred to previously.[18] State law may provide that the husband only is entitled to all of the income or other enjoyment of the real property held as tenants by the entirety, and the wife's interest consists only of the right of sur-

14. § 404, supra.
15. § 412, supra.
16. Reg, § 25.2512–2(b).

17. Note 16, supra.
18. Pamphlet "Actuarial Values for Estate and Gift Tax", § 112, supra.

vivorship with no right of severance. In such a case a special factor may be needed to determine the value of the interest of the respective spouses.[19] This will be furnished by the Commissioner upon request, accompanied by a statement of the date of birth of each person, the duration of whose life may affect the value of the interest, and the pertinent facts.[20]

The method of computing the value of the gift when an election is made to treat the creation of the tenancy by the entirety as a gift will be illustrated in the chapter on computation of the tax.[1]

§ 455. Certain Property Settlements Arising Out of Marriage.

We have previously noted that there is one exception to the rule that a transfer in settlement of a spouse's dower, curtesy, or other property rights arising out of a marriage is not deemed to be for an adequate and full consideration in money or money's worth, and is therefore subject to the Gift Tax on the full value of the property transferred.[2]

This exception was added by the 1954 Code because of the decision of the Supreme Court that a transfer of property pursuant to a decree of divorce was deemed a transfer for an adequate and full consideration in money or money's worth and not subject to the Gift Tax.[3] The courts had great difficulty in applying the rationale of Harris v. Commissioner[4] and determined taxability or nontaxability in most instances on whether the terms of the agreement between the spouses were incorporated in the decree. In some cases the question hinged on whether the agreement itself provided for its becoming effective upon entry of a decree.[5]

As the Senate Finance Committee pointed out in creating the exception to be discussed hereafter, prior to the 1954 Code there was substantial uncertainty as to whether a gift resulted from transfers to the wife under a property settlement incident to a divorce. The uncertainty was resolved for Gift Tax purposes, by providing that where husband and wife enter into a written

---

19. Reg, § 25.2515–2(c).
20. Reg, § 25.2512–5(e).
1. Note 11, supra.
2. § 447, supra.
3. Harris v Comm, 340 US 106, 95 L ed 111, 71 S Ct 181 (1950).

4. Note 3, supra.
5. See Rosenthal v Comm, 205 F2d 505 (CA 2) (1953); Metcalf, 9 TCM 884 (1947); McMurtry v Comm, 203 F 2d 659 (CA 1) (1953); Grigg, 20 TC 420 (1953).

agreement relative to their marital and property rights *and divorce occurs within two years thereafter* (whether or not such agreement is approved by the divorce decree), any transfers of property or interests in property made pursuant to such agreement—

(1) to either spouse in settlement of his or her marital or property rights, *or*

(2) to provide a reasonable allowance for the support of issue of the marriage *during minority,*

shall be deemed to be transfers made for full and adequate consideration in money or money's worth.[6]

The statute applies to such transfers for Gift Tax, but there is no corresponding provision of the Estate Tax statute. However, the effect thereof is recognized to a limited extent.[7]

The *Proposed* Gift Tax Regulations provided that when a transfer of property between spouses in settlement of their dower, curtesy, or other property rights arising out of the marriage did not qualify under Section 2516, it might nevertheless be exempt from Gift Tax, *but only* if the transfer was effected by a court decree rather than by a promise or agreement between the spouses. It further provided that a transfer was deemed to be effected by decree if:

(1) the transfer was pursuant to an agreement which was binding only upon the entry of a decree of divorce, separate maintenance, or annulment, and such decree was subsequently granted incorporating the terms of the agreement, *or*

(2) the transfer was solely pursuant to a divorce, separation, maintenance, or annulment decree as, for example where there had been no prior out of court agreement between the spouses.[8]

This appeared to be an acknowledgment of defeat, since the Commissioner attempted to tax such transfers,[9] but was defeated by the courts.[10]

This provision has been deleted from the final Gift Tax Regulations,[10a] as was the introductory paragraph of the Proposed Regulation.[10b] The significance of the deletion remains to be determined.

Transfers to provide a reasonable allowance for the support

---

6. IRC, § 2516 (1954 Code).
7. See § 158, supra.
8. Proposed Reg, § 25.2516–1(c).
9. ET 19, 1946–2 CB 166.
10. Comm v Converse, 163 F2d 131

(CCA 2) (1947); Harding, 11 TC 1051 (1948); McLean, 11 TC 543 (1948); Jones, 1 TC 1207 (1943).
10a. Reg, § 25.2516–1.
10b. Proposed Reg, § 25.2516–1(a).

of children (including legally adopted children) of a marriage during minority are not subject to the Gift Tax if made pursuant to an agreement which satisfies the requirements of Section 2516.[11] This would not include adult children.[12] The Proposed Gift Tax Regulation provided that current expenditures by an individual on behalf of his spouse or minor child in satisfaction of his legal obligation to provide for their support were not taxable gifts, but that the extent of the donor's legal obligation to support his spouse or minor child was to be ascertained from the facts and circumstances of the individual case.[13] This provision has been deleted from the final Regulation.[13a] We have previously discussed support of a dependent.[14]

§ 456. Certain Property Settlements Arising Out of Marriage; Disclosure on Return.

When spouses have entered into a property settlement incident to divorce, it is probable that the divorce will not take place within the same calendar year as that in which the agreement becomes effective. Where the divorce is not granted on or before the due date for the filing of the Gift Tax return for the calendar year in which the agreement became effective, the transfer must be disclosed by the transferor upon a Gift Tax return filed for the calendar year in which the agreement became effective and a copy of the agreement must be attached to the return. In addition, a certified copy of the divorce decree must be furnished to the District Director not later than sixty days after the divorce is granted. Pending receipt of evidence that the final decree of divorce has been granted (but in no event for a period of more than two years from the effective date of the agreement), the transfer will be tentatively treated as one made for full and adequate consideration in money or money's worth.[15]

§ 457. Powers of Appointment; General Considerations.

We have discussed previously in connection with powers of appointment under the Estate Tax, the nature of a power of appointment,[16] the statutory provisions of that statute,[17] the evolution of the statute,[18] its constitutionality,[19] the definition

11. Proposed Reg, § 25.2511–1(f)(1).
12. Widemann, 26 TC 565 (1956).
13. Reg, § 25.2511–1(f).
13a. Reg, § 25.2511–1(g)(1).
14. § 447, supra.

15. Reg, § 25.6019–3(b).
16. § 160, supra.
17. § 161, supra.
18. § 160, supra.
19. § 163, supra.

of a general power of appointment,[20] exceptions to the definition,[1] powers created prior to October 21, 1942,[2] and thereafter,[3] the date of the creation of a power,[4] the effect of the exercise[5] or lapse[6] of a power, and of release or partial release,[7] and disclaimer or renunciation[8] of a general power of appointment.

The Gift Tax statute follows the Estate Tax statute in all substantial particulars and in certain instances is identical with the latter. Section 2541 of the 1954 Code treats as a taxable gift the *exercise* of a *general* power of appointment created *on or before October 21, 1942*, as well as the *exercise or complete release* of a *general* power created *after October 21, 1942*. Under certain circumstances the exercise of a power created after October 21, 1942, by the creation of another power is taxable. The *lapse* of a power created *after October 21, 1942* may also be treated as a gift under certain circumstances.[9] The significance of the 1942 date is that prior to that time the Gift Tax statute contained no reference to powers of appointment. There were conflicting decisions as to whether the exercise of a general power resulted in a gift, some cases holding that it did,[10] and others that it did not.[11] The relinquishment or release of a power was held not subject to the tax,[12] and also the contrary.[13] These conflicts were attempted to be resolved by the enactment of a provision for the taxation of powers of appointment in the Gift Tax statute in the Revenue Act of 1942.[14] It resulted in the addition to the 1939 Code of Section 1000(c). The statute was unsatisfactory and resulted in the Powers of Appointment Act of 1951 which we have discussed previously.[15] The 1954 Code made no change in substance in the statute as it existed in the 1939 Code after the amendment by the Powers of Appointment Act of 1951.

It must be noted that the statute in using the term "power of

20. § 164, supra.

1. § 165, supra.

2. § 166, supra.

3. § 167, supra.

4. § 168, supra.

5. § 169, supra.

6. § 170, supra.

7. § 171, supra.

8. § 172, supra.

9. Reg, § 25.2514–1(a).

10. Richardson v Comm, 151 F2d 102 (CCA 2), cert den 326 US 796, 90 L ed 485, 66 S Ct 490 (1945); Cerf v Comm, 141 F2d 564 (CCA 3) (1944).

11. Comm v Walston, 168 F2d 211 (CCA 4) (1948); Grasselli, 7 TC 255 (1946); Clark, 47 BTA 865 (1942); Nunally, 5 TCM 562 (1946).

12. Comm v Solomon, 124 F2d 86 (CCA 3) (1941); Du Pont, 2 TC 246 (1944).

13. Clark, note 11, supra.

14. Rev Act 1942, § 452.

15. § 162, supra.

appointment" does not include powers reserved by a donor to *himself.* No provision of Section 2514 is to be construed as in any way limiting the application of other sections of the Internal Revenue Code of 1954 or the Regulations. The power of the owner of property to dispose of his interest is not a power of appointment, and the interest is includible in the amount of his gifts to the extent that it would be includible under Section 2511 or other provisions. For example, if a trust created by S provides for payment of the income to A for life with the power in A to appoint the entire trust estate by deed during her lifetime to a class consisting of her children, and a further power to dispose of the entire corpus by will to anyone, including her estate, and A exercises the inter vivos power in favor of her children, she has made a taxable gift of the income, and has also relinquished her general power to appoint by will, so that she has also made a gift under the provisions for taxing powers of appointment.[16]

§ 458. Powers of Appointment; Statutory Provisions.

As noted, the Gift Tax statute follows the terms of the Estate Tax statute. The statute divides powers into those created prior to October 21, 1942 and those created thereafter. In either case *only general powers of appointment are taxable.*

As to *pre-1942* powers *only the exercise* is a gift, and if the general power was reduced to a nongeneral power before November 1, 1951, or the donee was under a legal disability and reduced the power within six months after the termination of the disability, subsequent exercise is not a gift. The failure to exercise such powers or the complete release thereof is not an exercise.[17]

As to *post-1942* powers, exercise or release is a gift, but disclaimer or renunciation is not deemed a release.[18]

The statute then defines the meaning of general power of appointment and creates three exceptions to it.[19] A further exception is provided in the case of a nongeneral power of appointment, if it is exercised by creating another power which, under local law can be validly exercised to suspend the power of alienation for a period ascertainable without regard to the date of the

16. Reg, § 25.2514–1(b)(2); but see Self v US, 142 F Supp 939 (1956).

17. IRC, § 2514(a) (1954 Code); Reg, § 25.2514–2.

18. IRC, § 2514(b) (1954 Code); Reg, § 25.2514–3.

19. IRC, § 2514(c) (1954 Code).

[Harris]—40

creation of the first power.[20]   This provision is directed to the situation in Delaware where such powers may be created.

The statute then provides for the taxation of post-1942 powers to a limited extent,[1] and also for fixing the date of the creation of a power.[2]

These statutory provisions will be treated in succeeding sections.

§ 459. Powers of Appointment; Definition and Exceptions.

As noted in connection with the Estate Tax, the Gift Tax statute does not use the terms general and special power of appointment.[3] It refers only to general powers of appointment, except in the single case of the creation of another power, in which case the term power of appointment is used. The first thing to be noted, therefore, is that taxability is determined under the statutory definition and not under State laws of property.[4] Powers other than general powers are nongeneral powers.

The statute defines a general power of appointment as a power which is exercisable in favor of the individual possessing the power (called the possessor), his estate, his creditors, or the creditors of his estate.[5] The Regulation further defines "power of appointment."[6] The definition follows the terms of the Estate Tax Regulation.[7]

The statute then creates three exceptions, namely, (1) a power to consume, invade, or appropriate property for the benefit of the possessor which is limited by an *ascertainable standard* relating to the health, education, support, or maintenance of the possessor; (2) a power of appointment created on or *before October 21, 1942,* which is exercisable by the possessor *only in conjunction* with another person; and (3) a power of appointment created after October 21, 1942, which is exercisable by the possessor *only in conjunction* with another person who is the creator of the power, or who has a substantial adverse interest to its exercise, a person who, after the death of the possessor has the power to appoint to himself being deemed to have an

20. IRC, § 2514(d) (1954 Code); Reg, § 25.2514–3(d).

1. IRC, § 2514(e) (1954 Code).

2. IRC, § 2514(f) (1954 Code).

3. § 161, supra.

4. Rogers v Helvering, 320 US 410, 88 L ed 134, 64 S Ct 172 (1943); Morgan v Comm, 309 US 78, 84 L ed 585, 60 S Ct 424 (1940); Stratton v US, 50 F2d 48 (CCA 1), cert den 284 US 651, 76 L ed 552, 52 S Ct 31 (1931).

5. Note 19, supra; Reg, § 25.2514–1 (c).

6. Reg, § 25.2514–1(b)(1).

7. See § 164, supra.

adverse interest.[8]   None of these are considered general powers of appointment.

If such other person does have such adverse interest against the exercise of the power, it will be deemed a general power of appointment only in respect of a fractional part of the property subject to the power, to be determined by dividing the value of the property by the number of persons, including the possessor, in favor of whom the power is exercisable.[9]

The question of what is an ascertainable standard[10] and a substantial adverse interest[11] has been previously discussed.

There is a further exception in the taxation of powers of appointment. While only general powers of appointment come within the statute, in a single case, a nongeneral power of appointment created after October 21, 1942 is taxable, if it is exercised by creating another power, which under the applicable local law, can be validly exercised so as to postpone the vesting of any estate or interest in the property which was subject to the first power, or suspend the absolute ownership or power of alienation of such property, for a period ascertainable without regard to the date of the creation of the first power.[12]   As the framers of the Powers of Appointment Act of 1951 noted, in at least one State it is possible to suspend the power of alienation in the manner referred to in the statute.[13]   That State is Delaware.

§ 460. Powers of Appointment; Created Prior to October 21, 1942.

An exercise of *a general power of appointment created on or before October 21, 1942,* is deemed a transfer of property by the individual possessing such power; but the failure to exercise such power or the complete release of such a power is not deemed an exercise thereof. If a general power of appointment created on or before October 21, 1942, has been partially released so that it is no longer a general power of appointment, the subsequent exercise of such power is not deemed the exercise of a general power of appointment *if*

(1) such partial release occurred before November 1, 1951, *or*

(2) the donee of such power was under a legal disability to

---

8. Note 19, supra; Reg, § 25.2514–1 (c)(2), § 25.2514–2(b), § 25.2514–3(b).

9. IRC, § 2514(c)(3)(C) (1954 Code).

10. § 164, supra.

11. §§ 164, 423, supra.

12. IRC, § 2514(d) (1954 Code).

13. Sen Fin Comm Report, Powers of Appointment Act of 1951.

release such power on October 21, 1942, and such partial release occurred not later than six months after the termination of such legal disability.[14] The date of November 1, 1951 resulted from the exception in the Revenue Act of 1942 which permitted the tax free release of general powers if made before January 1, 1943, with the cut-off date extended yearly, the last date being November 1, 1951, fixed by the Powers of Appointment Act of 1951.[15]

Thus as to powers of appointment created prior to October 21, 1942, the only way in which they can become subject to the Gift Tax is if they are general powers *and* they are exercised. If a nongeneral power and exercised, or a general power and, not exercised, or released or permitted to lapse, there is no transfer subject to the tax. The lapse and release of powers is discussed hereafter.[16]

§ 461. Powers of Appointment; Created Subsequent to October 21, 1942.

The exercise or release of a *general power* of appointment created *after October 21, 1942,* is deemed a transfer of property by the individual possessing such power. A disclaimer or renunciation of such a power of appointment is not deemed a release of such a power.[17] A nongeneral power of appointment is also deemed a transfer in one situation, discussed heretofore.[18]

As we have seen, the release of a pre-1942 power is not taxable, whereas it will be observed that the release of a post-1942 power is.

We shall also see that the lapse of a post-1942 power may be subject to the tax.[19]

It must be borne in mind that only general powers of appointment within the meaning of the statute are affected.

§ 462. Powers of Appointment; Date of Creation of Power.

When it is granted by will, the question might arise as to whether the date of death or the execution of the will controlled. The statute provides that a power of appointment created by a will executed on or before October 21, 1942, shall be considered a power created on or before such date, if the person executing

---

14. Note 17, supra.
15. Note 13, supra; Reg, § 25.2514–2.
16. §§ 463, 464, infra.
17. Note 18, supra.
18. § 459, supra.
19. § 463, infra.

such will died before July 1, 1949, without having republished such will, by codicil or otherwise.[20] This is an exception to the general rule that a will speaks as of the date of death.

Inter vivos instruments create additional questions. Whether or not a power of appointment created by an inter vivos instrument executed on or before October 21, 1942, is considered a power created on or before that date depends upon the facts and circumstances of the particular case. For example, assume that A created a revocable trust before October 21, 1942, providing for payment of income to B for life with remainder as B shall appoint by will. If A dies after October 21, 1942, without having exercised his power of revocation, B's power of appointment is considered a power created after October 21, 1942. On the other hand, assume that C created an irrevocable inter vivos trust before October 21, 1942, naming T as trustee and providing for payment of income to D for life with remainder to E. Assume further that T was given the power to pay corpus to D and the power to appoint a successor trustee. If T resigns after October 21, 1942, and appoints D as successor trustee, D is considered to have a power of appointment created before October 21, 1942. As another example assume that F created an irrevocable inter vivos trust before October 21, 1942, providing for payment of income to G for life with remainder as G shall appoint by will, but in default of appointment, income to H for life with remainder as H shall appoint by will. If G dies after October 21, 1942, without having exercised his power of appointment, H's power of appointment is considered a power created before October 21, 1942, even though it was only a contingent interest until G's death. If, in this last example, G had exercised his power of appointment by creating a similar power in I, I's power of appointment would be considered a power created after October 21, 1942. A power is not considered as created after October 21, 1942, merely because the power is not exercisable or the identity of its holders is not ascertained until after that date.[1]

§ 463. Powers of Appointment; Exercise and Nonexercise or Lapse.

It is only the *exercise* of a general power of appointment created before *October 21, 1942,* which makes such transfers

---

20. IRC, § 2514(f) (1954 Code).   1. Reg, § 25.2514–1(e).

taxable under the Gift Tax.[2] The complete release of such powers or the failure to exercise such does not constitute a transfer.

So far as general powers of appointment created after October 21, 1942, the exercise of such powers subjects to the tax.[3]

These rules apply to the taxation of powers held by an individual, but when the power is held jointly with another there is a difference in taxability upon exercise, depending upon whether it is a pre-1942 or post-1942 power. In the case of a *pre-1942 power,* it is only necessary that the power be required to be exercised *jointly* with another person.[4] If it is *post-1942 power,* not only must the power be *joint* to avoid taxation upon exercise, but the other person must be either the *creator of the power* or have a *substantial adverse interest* to its exercise.[5]

The exercise of a post-1942 power will also not result in tax if it is a power to consume, invade, or appropriate property for the benefit of the possessor and is limited by an ascertainable standard relating to the health, education, support, or maintenance of the possessor.[6]

Both of these results, in the case of joint powers, and those limited by an ascertainable standard, are caused by the statutory exceptions in the definition of general powers.

Since taxation of pre-1942 powers depends upon exercise, the question may arise when there is a partial exercise, whether the entire property or only a part is subject to the tax. If such a power is partially exercised as to a portion of the property subject to the power, the exercise is considered to be a transfer only as to the value of that portion. However, if the exercise of the power creates or changes any beneficial interest in a portion subject to the power, the power is considered exercised with respect to the entire portion. Thus, if the possessor of a pre-1942 power, exercised it by directing the income from the property to be paid to his wife for life, and did not otherwise exercise his power, it would be considered exercised as to the entire property.[7]

We have seen that in the case of *pre-1942* general powers of appointment, the statute specifically provides that the failure to exercise the power shall not be deemed an exercise thereof.[8] In the case of *post-1942 powers,* the failure to exercise a power,

2. § 460, supra.
3. § 461, supra.
4. § 459, supra.
5. Note 4, supra.
6. Note 4, supra.
7. Reg, § 25.2514–2(e).
8. IRC, § 2514(a) (1954 Code).

resulting in a lapse, is considered a release of the power,[9] which is expressly made subject to the tax.[10] In order to provide an exemption which would not be subject to abuse, in enacting the Powers of Appointment Act of 1951, Congress provided that the lapse of a power during any taxable year would be subject to Gift Tax, only to the extent that the property which could have been appointed exceeded $5,000. or five percent of the aggregate value of the assets out of which or the proceeds of which the exercise of the lapsed powers could be satisfied.[11] Thus, if an individual has a noncumulative right to withdraw $10,000. a year from a fund, and the right is not exercised, and the fund at the end of any calendar year equals or exceeds $200,000., there is no gift. If the fund is $100,000. at the end of the calendar year and the right is not exercised, there is a gift of $5,000.[12]

§ 464. Powers of Appointment; Release or Partial Release.

The statute provides that as to *pre-1942* general powers of appointment a *complete release* thereof shall not be deemed an exercise thereof, nor if there has been a *partial release,* so that it is no longer a general power, and the partial release took place before November 1, 1951, or if the donee was under a legal disability on October 21, 1942, if partially released within six months after the termination of such disability, the exercise shall not be deemed the exercise of a general power.[13] This was the opportunity afforded holders of general powers to reduce the same to nongeneral powers and thus escape the effect of the Revenue Act of 1942.[14]

It will be noted the statute uses the term "complete release." This means a release of all powers over all or a portion of the property subject to the power as distinguished from the reduction of the power to a lesser power. Thus, if the possessor completely relinquished a power over one half of the property subject to the power, the power is completely released as to that half. However, if at or before the time the power is relinquished, the holder of the power exercises the power in such a manner or to such an extent that the relinquishment results in the reduction, enlargement, or shift in a beneficial interest in property, the relinquishment will be considered to be an exercise and not a release of the power. Thus, if A created a trust in 1940 to pay

9. IRC, § 2514(e) (1954 Code).
10. IRC, § 2514(b) (1954 Code).
11. Note 9, supra.
12. Reg, § 2514–3(c)(4).
13. Note 8, supra.
14. See § 460, supra.

the income to B for life, B having power to amend the trust, and the remainder payable to such persons as B should appoint, and in default to C, and B amended the trust in 1948, by providing for the payment of the remainder to C, and in 1955 amended the trust by relinquishing his power to amend the trust, if the 1948 amendment remained in effect, the relinquishment is considered an exercise of B's power and not a release of his general power. On the other hand, if the 1948 amendment became ineffective before or at the time of the 1955 amendment, or if B merely amended the trust by changing the purely ministerial powers of the trustee, his relinquishment of the power in 1955 will be considered as a release of the power of appointment.[15]

So far as post-1942 general powers of appointment are concerned, the statute specifically provides that a release shall be deemed a transfer of property subject to the tax.[16]

Where a post-1942 general power of appointment is partially released so that thereafter the donor may still appoint among a limited class of persons not including himself, the partial release does not effect a complete release, since the possessor of the power has retained the right to designate the ultimate beneficiaries of the property over which he holds the power and since it is only the termination of such control which completes a gift.[17] The determination of whether there has been a completed gift is made under the principles which have been discussed previously.[18] Thus the reduction of a post-1942 general power to a nongeneral power does not incur Gift Tax at the time of the reduction, but when there is an exercise or release of the reduced power.

The Regulation provides that a release of a power of appointment need not be formal or express in character.[19] Where the donee of a general power created before 1942 amended the trusts before 1951, and reduced her general power to a nongeneral one, after 1942, the court held that substance was more important than form, and the release was not a taxable transfer.[20]

§ 465. Powers of Appointment; Disclaimer or Renunciation.

The statute specifically provides that a disclaimer or renun-

15. Reg, § 25.2514–2(c).
16. Note 10, supra.
17. Reg, § 25.2514–3(c)(1).
18. §§ 422, 427, supra.
19. Note 12, supra.
20. Emery v US, 153 F Supp 248 (1957).

ciation of a general power of appointment shall not be deemed a release of such power.[1]

While in effect, a disclaimer or renunciation is a release of the right to exercise the power, the reason for the exception is that the donee of a power of appointment, particularly under an inter vivos trust, often does not learn of the power until long after the creation of the trust. Living trusts and wills frequently grant powers of appointment to a person not born, or ascertainable at the time of the creation of the trust.[2]

While the statute does not so provide, both the Regulation and the Senate Finance Committee Report on the Powers of Appointment Act of 1951 state that a disclaimer or renunciation must be unequivocal and effective under local law. A disclaimer is a complete and unqualified refusal to accept the rights to which one is entitled. Such rights refer to the incidents of the power and not to other interests of the possessor of the power in the property. If *effective under local law,* the power may be disclaimed or renounced without disclaiming or renouncing such other interests. There can be no disclaimer or renunciation of a power after its acceptance. A disclaimer of a power over only a portion of the property subject to the power is not a complete and unqualified refusal to accept the rights to which one is entitled. In the absence of facts to the contrary, the failure to renounce or disclaim within a reasonable time after learning of its existence will be presumed to constitute an acceptance of the power.[3]

Where property passes under intestate statutes, there is no right to renounce in order to avoid vesting of title in oneself.[4] The two exceptions are in Louisiana[5] and Rhode Island.[6] In such case renunciation results in a Gift Tax.[7] On the other hand a testamentary benefit may be renounced without incurring Gift Tax.[8] Since a power of appointment may only be granted by testamentary or inter vivos instrument, no problems of local law arise.

1. Note 10, supra.

2. Sen Fin Comm Report, Powers of Appointment Act of 1951.

3. Reg, § 25.2514–3(c)(5).

4. Bostian v Milens, 239 Mo App 555, 193 SW2d 797 (1946); Coomes v Finegan, 233 Ia 448, 7 NW2d 729 (1943).

5. L.S.A.—C.C., Arts 976, 977, 1018.

6. L 1947, Ch 1947, §§ 24–33.

7. Hardenbergh v Comm, 198 F2d 63 (CA 8), cert den 344 US 836, 97 L ed 650, 73 S Ct 45 (1952); Maxwell, 17 TC 1589 (1952).

8. Brown v Routzahn, 63 F2d 914 (CCA 6), cert den 290 US 641, 78 L ed 557, 54 S Ct 60 (1933).

There has been much discussion as to whether there may be a partial disclaimer. This has applied particularly to the marital deduction. The Regulation flatly refuses to recognize a partial disclaimer.[9] The Regulation further creates a presumption. Neither of these appear in the statute.

§ 466. Powers of Appointment; Amount of Gift.

If a power of appointment exists as to a part of an entire group of assets or only over a limited interest in property, the section applies only to such part or interest.[10]

If a general power of appointment created on or before October 21, 1942, is exercised only as to a portion of the property subject to the power, the exercise is considered to be a transfer only as to the value of that portion. The subject of partial exercise has been previously discussed.[11]

There has also been discussed the extent to which a gift occurs when there is a lapse of a post-1942 power.[12]

When a post-1942 power is exercisable in conjunction with another person, but such other person is not either the creator of the power or one having a substantial interest adverse to its exercise, so that it comes within the exception to the definition of a general power, the possessor of the power is treated as possessed of a general power of appointment over an aliquot share of the property, to be determined with reference to the number of joint holders. Thus, if X, Y, and Z hold an unlimited power jointly to appoint among a group of persons, including themselves, but on the death of X the power does not pass to Y and Z jointly, then Y and Z are not considered to have adverse interests and X is considered to have a general power of appointment as to one third of the property subject to the power.[13]

We have referred to the one case in which a nongeneral power of appointment created after October 21, 1942 may be subjected to the tax.[14] That is the case in which a power can be exercised by creating another power and suspend the right of alienation for a period without regard to the date of the creation of the first power. In such case the value of the property subject to the second power is considered to be its value unreduced by any precedent or subsequent interest which is not subject to the

9. Note 3, supra.
10. Reg, § 25.2514–1(b)(3).
11. § 463, supra.

12. Note 11, supra.
13. Reg, § 25.2514–3(b)(3).
14. § 459, supra.

second power. Thus, if the donor has the power to appoint $100,-000. among a group consisting of his children or grandchildren, and during his lifetime exercises the power by making an outright appointment of $75,000. and giving one appointee a power to appoint $25,000., no more than $25,000. is considered a gift under the section. But if the donor appoints the income from the entire fund to a beneficiary for life with power in the beneficiary to appoint the remainder, the entire $100,000. will be considered a gift, if the exercise of the second power can validly postpone the vesting of any estate or interest in such property, or can suspend the absolute ownership or power of alienation of such property for a period ascertainable without regard to the date of the creation of the first power.[15]

§ 467. Powers of Appointment; Summary of Taxability.

For ease of reference and testing of questions involving the application of the Gift Tax statute to powers of appointment, the taxability thereof may be summarized as follows:

With one exception,[16] *only general powers* of appointment are taxable. Nongeneral powers are not.

A power is subject to the Gift Tax if

it is exercisable in favor of (a) the donee, (b) his creditors, (c) his estate, or (d) the creditors of his estate, *and*

(a) it is not limited by an ascertainable standard, *or*

(b) it is a *pre-1942* power, and can be exercised by the donee alone, *or*

(c) it is a *post-1942* power and can be exercised by the donee without the consent of the donor or other person having a substantial adverse interest to its exercise,[18] *and*

1. it is a *post-1942* power and *is exercised.*[19]

2. whether or not a general power created after October 21, 1942, it is exercised by creating another power as provided in the statute;[20]

3. it is a *pre-1942* power and is released after November 1, 1951, unless the donee was under a legal disability and released the power within six months after the disability terminated.[1] But a disclaimer or renunciation is not deemed a release.[2]

---

15. Reg, § 25.2514-3(d).
16. Note 14, supra.
17. § 458, supra.
18. Note 14, supra.

19. §§ 461, 462, supra.
20. Note 14, supra.
1. §§ 460, 464, supra.
2. § 465, supra.

4. the power was created after October 21, 1942 and lapses, but only to the extent that the amount the donee may draw exceeds the greater of $5,000. or 5% of the appointive property in any year.[3]

§ 468. Powers of Appointment; Examples of Operation of Statute.

The Proposed Gift Tax Regulation furnished nine examples of the operation of the statute, which are here set forth in the belief that they will be found helpful, even though the final Regulation[3a] reduces the number of examples to five. They illustrate the difference between a power of appointment and a right of disposition which adds nothing to the rights which a person otherwise has of disposing of his income or property. In any case where a person has a beneficial interest in income or property and a fiduciary power to dispose of the income or property to another person measurable by a fixed or readily ascertainable standard, the disposition by the former of the income or property does not constitute the making of a gift to the extent that the disposition is pursuant to the exercise of such power. Further, in each instance in which it is indicated that the donor has a power of appointment, its exercise, release or lapse would not constitute a taxable gift unless it is a *general* power of appointment, and for this purpose a power limited by an ascertainable standard relating to health, etc., is not a general power of appointment. In each of the following examples it is assumed, unless otherwise stated, that S has transferred property in trust *after* October 21, 1942, with the remainder payable to R at L's death, and that neither L nor R has any interest in or power over the enjoyment of the trust property except as is indicated separately in each example.[4]

(1) The income is payable to L. L has the power to cause the income to be paid *to R*. The exercise of the right constitutes the making of a taxable gift. L's power does not constitute a power of appointment, since it is only a power to dispose of his income interest, a right otherwise possessed by him.[5]

(2) The income is to be accumulated during L's life. L has the power to have the income distributed *to himself*. L has a general power of appointment over the income, the lapse or release

3. §§ 461, 463, supra.
3a. Reg, § 25.2514–3(e).

4. Proposed Reg, § 25.2514–3(e).
5. Note 4, Example 1.

of which during his life may constitute a taxable transfer. For example, if his power in any year extends only to the income of that year, so that his power lapses at the end of that year as to that year's income, the accumulation for the year will constitute a transfer to the extent that the year's accumulation which he could have caused to be paid to himself (in excess of the value of his power to receive income on the accumulation) exceeds the greater of $5,000. or 5% of the income for that year.[6]

(3) The income is to be paid to L. L has the right to have the income accumulated and added to corpus. The result is the same as in (1) above (except that no gift is made of the value of L's right to receive income from the accumulations) at the time L's power over the accumulations ceases. Thus, if L's power in any year extends only to that year's income, any accumulation of the income of any one year constitutes a taxable transfer (with the same exception) at the end of the year.[7]

(4) The income is to be paid to L. L has a power, exercisable at any time, to cause corpus to be distributed *to himself*. L has a general power of appointment over the remainder interest, the release of which constitutes the making of a taxable gift to the extent of the value of the remainder.[8]

(5) The income is payable to L. L has the power to cause the corpus to be distributed *to R* at any time. To the extent that L's income interest is affected, the result is the same as in (1) above. L's power over the value of the remainder interest after his death does not constitute a general power of appointment and the exercise thereof does not constitute the making of a taxable gift.[9]

(6) The income is to be accumulated and added to corpus. R has a right to appoint the income *to L*. R has a power to dispose of his remainder interest in the income, the exercise of which constitutes the making of a taxable gift of the value, if any, of the interest.[10]

(7) The income is payable to L. R has the right to cause the corpus to be distributed *to L* at any time. R's power is not a power of appointment, but merely a right to dispose of his remainder interest, a right already possessed by him. In such case, the exercise of the right constitutes the making of a taxable gift of the value, if any, of his remainder interest.[11]

6. Note 4, Example 2.   9. Note 4, Example 5.
7. Note 4, Example 3.   10. Note 4, Example 6.
8. Note 4, Example 4.   11. Note 4, Example 7.

(8) The income is to be paid to L. R has the right to appoint the corpus *to himself* at any time. R's general power of appointment over the corpus includes a general power to dispose of L's income interest therein. The lapse or release of R's general power over the income interest during his life may constitute a taxable transfer. For example, if the income in any year is paid to L, R's power lapses at the end of the year as to that year's income, and the amounts paid to L during the year will constitute a transfer to the extent they exceed the greater of $5,000. or 5% of the income of that year. R's right to take the remainder interest is not a power of appointment, but merely a power to accelerate the receipt of his own property. The result is therefore the same as if R had only a power during L's lifetime to appoint the income to himself for the duration of L's life.[12]

(9) S transfers property in trust. So much of each year's income as is needed to support, educate, and maintain R shall be applied for his benefit; the balance of the yearly income is to be paid *to L*. L transfers his rights in the income to R. L's disposition of his income interest to R is a gift to R to the extent that the value of L's interest in the income exceeds the value of R's right to support, education, and maintenance.[13]

These nine examples in the Proposed Regulation, as noted, have been reduced to five in the final Regulations. In the above Example (1) is the same as Example (1) adopted, Example (4) is the same as Example (3) adopted, Example (7) is the same as Example (4) adopted, and Example (8) is substantially the same as Example (5) adopted. Example (2) in the final Regulation[13a] deals with income to be accumulated during L's life, with the power in L to have the income distributed to himself. If L's power is limited by an ascertainable standard (relating to health, etc.) as defined in paragraph (c)(2) of Section 25.2514–1,[13b] the lapse of such power will not constitute a transfer of property for Gift Tax purposes. If L's power is not so limited, its lapse or release during L's lifetime may constitute a transfer of property for Gift Tax purposes.

In each of these examples the distinction must be observed between a disposition of an interest which the holder of the power already has, which may be a power, but not a general power of appointment, and the case where the holder of the

12. Note 4, Example 8.
13. Note 4, Example 9.
13a. Note 3a, supra.
13b. § 459, supra.

power has the right to appoint to himself, his creditors, his estate, or the creditors of his estate, in which case he has a general power of appointment. In the first instance a transfer of his interest is taxable under the general provisions of the statute,[14] while in the latter case the transfer is taxable under the powers of appointment provisions of the statute.[15]

§ 469. Powers of Appointment; Description.

The Regulation prescribes no method for the reporting of the exercise or release of a power of appointment. Form 709, the Gift Tax Return, asks whether the taxpayer made any transfer by the exercise or release of a power of appointment, except as provided in the Regulations.[16] If the answer be yes, it is required that such transfer be fully disclosed under Schedule A. The Instructions state that the exercise or release of a power of appointment may constitute a gift by the individual possessing the power, and advise that in such case the Gift Tax Regulations should be consulted.[17]

When there has been an exercise or release of a power of appointment, a certified or verified copy of the trust instrument must be annexed to the return and a complete statement of the facts made. If it is claimed that such exercise or release was not taxable, the facts should be stated and the basis for non-taxability set forth. A certified or verified copy of the instrument of exercise or release, or of disclaimer or renunciation, should also be filed with the return. The taxpayer or his counsel should not take it upon himself to determine that a transfer does not fall within the statute.

§ 470. Jointly Owned Property.

Many gifts arise as the result of the creation of a joint tenancy. In the case of real estate, as between husband and wife, the 1954 Code has made special provision therefor, which has been treated previously.[18] When that relationship does not exist, if A with his own funds purchases property and has the title conveyed to himself and B as joint owners with rights of survivorship, but which rights may be defeated by either party severing his interest, there is a gift to B in the amount of one half the value of the property.[19]

14. IRC, §§ 2501, 2511 (1954 Code).
15. IRC, § 2515 (1954 Code).
16. Form 709, question 7.
17. Instruction 6, Form 709.

18. §§ 450 et seq, supra.
19. Reg, § 25.2511–1(h)(5); Mim 5202, 1941–2 CB 241.

The same situation would result in the case of the creation of a joint tenancy in personal property, *whether or not the other party were the wife.* An exception is made, however, in the case of bank accounts and United States Savings Bonds. If A creates a joint bank account for himself and B (or a similar type of ownership by which A can regain the entire fund without B's consent), there is a gift to B *when B draws* upon the account for his own benefit, to the extent of the amount drawn. Similarly, if A purchases a United States savings bond registered as payable "to A or B," there is a gift to B when B surrenders the bond for cash without any obligation to account for a part of the proceeds to A.[20]

If a joint Income Tax return is filed by a husband and wife for a taxable year, the payment by one spouse of all or part of the Income Tax liability for such year is not treated as resulting in a transfer which is subject to Gift Tax. The same rule is applicable to the payment of a Gift Tax for a calendar year in the case of a husband and wife who have consented to have the gifts made considered as made one half by each of them.[1] The same rule does not apply so far as the Estate Tax is concerned.[2]

§ 471. Gift by Husband or Wife to Third Party; Generally.

As we have seen, in 1948 Congress created the marital deduction in order to equalize the tax status of residents of community property law states and noncommunity property law states.[3] But the marital deduction was not sufficient for this purpose where gifts were made to third parties, since in community property law states, such property, if community property, would be considered as a gift to the extent of one half by each spouse, while that would not be the result in noncommunity property law states. There was therefore enacted at the same time as the marital deduction the provision for the so-called "splitting" between spouses of gifts made to third parties.[4] That provision was continued in the 1954 Code.[5]

The statute provides that a gift made by one spouse to any person other than his spouse, shall be considered as made one half by him and one half by his spouse, *but only if*

20. Reg, § 25.2511–1(h)(4); Mim 5202, 1941–2CB241.

1. Reg, § 25.2511–1(d).

2. See §§ 215, 216, supra.

3. §§ 284 et seq, supra.

4. IRC, § 1000(f) (1939 Code), as added by § 314 Rev Act 1948; Sen Fin Comm Report, Public Law 471, 80th Cong, Apr 2, 1948.

5. IRC, § 2513 (1954 Code).

(1) At the time of the gift *each spouse* is a citizen or resident of the United States.

(2) He does not create in his spouse a general power of appointment over such interest.

(3) A donor is married to the other spouse *at the time of the gift* and *does not remarry* during the remainder of the calendar year.[6]

(4) *Both spouses* have signified their consent to the application of (1), (2), (3), in the case of *all gifts* made during the calendar year by either while married to the other.[7]

(5) The consent of the other spouse is not revoked.[8]

It must be observed that the statute has numerous conditions. In the first place, its provisions do not apply automatically. A gift by a spouse to a third party will only be treated as made one half by each spouse if they so elect by executing the consent. It is not mandatory[9] and *may* be so considered.[10] Both spouses must be either citizens or residents of the United States. If either spouse was a nonresident not a citizen of the United States during any portion of the calendar year, the consent is not effective with respect to·any gift made during that portion of the calendar year.[11]

An individual is considered the spouse of another only if he was married to such individual *at the time of the gift* and does not remarry during the calendar year.[12] If the consenting spouses were not married to each other during a portion of the calendar year the consent is not effective with respect to any gifts made during such portion of the calendar year. Where the consent is signified by the fiduciary of a deceased spouse, the consent is not effective with respect to gifts made by the surviving spouse during the portion of the calendar year that his or her spouse was deceased.[13] The fact that the parties entered into a pre-nuptial agreement under which each spouse waived all marital rights in the property of the other does not deprive of the right to take advantage of the split-gift provisions.[14]

A consent is not effective with respect to any gift by one spouse

6. IRC, § 2513(a)(1) (1954 Code).

7. IRC, § 2513(a)(2) (1954 Code).

8. IRC, § 2513(c) (1954 Code).

9. Note 4, supra.

10. Reg, § 25.2513–1(a).

11. Reg, § 25.2513–1(b)(2).

12. Note 10, supra.

13. Reg, § 25.2513–1(b)(1).

14. Rev Rul 55–241, 1955–1 CB 470.

of a property interest over which he created in his spouse a general power of appointment.[15]

The consent applies alike to gifts made by one spouse alone and to gifts made partly by each spouse, provided such gifts were to third parties. The consent may not be applied only to a portion of the property constituting such gifts. For example, a wife may not treat gifts made by her spouse from his separate property to third parties as having been made one half by her if her spouse does not consent to treat gifts made by her to third parties during the same calendar year as having been made one half by him. If the consent is effectively signified on either the husband's return or the wife's return, *all gifts* made by the spouses to third parties during the calendar year will be treated as made one half by each spouse.[16] Thus, one spouse may not treat gifts by him to third parties as split-gifts, while his spouse treats her gifts to third parties as made by herself alone. Nor can the parties treat some gifts as individual gifts and others as split-gifts. The statute provides for all or nothing in any calendar year. Each calendar year, however, is separate, so that a consent to treat gifts as split-gifts in one calendar year does not require the same treatment in any other year.

As in all other transfers by gift the amount thereof must be ascertainable, for the application of the statute. If one spouse transfers property in part to his spouse and in part to third parties, the consent is effective with respect to the interest transferred to third parties only insofar as such interest is ascertainable at the time of the gift and hence severable from the interest transferred to his spouse.[17] Where such severance is not possible, split-gift treatment will be denied.[18]

The subject of consent is discussed in the succeeding sections.

§ 472. Gift by Husband or Wife to Third Party; Manner and Time of Signifying Consent.

The statute provides that it shall only apply if both spouses signify their consent to have all gifts to third parties made by either during the calendar year while married to each other[19] and that the consent shall be signified in such manner as provided by the Regulations.[20] The latter require that in order for such con-

---

15. Reg, § 25.2513-1(b)(3); see also §§ 4462B.40 et seq.

16. Reg, § 25.2513-1(b)(5); Rev Rul 146, 1953-2 CB 292.

17. Reg, § 25.2513-1(b)(4).

18. Whittall, 24 TC 808 (1955).

19. Note 7, supra.

20. IRC, § 2513(b)(1) (1954 Code).

sent to be effective, it be signified by both spouses. If both spouses file Gift Tax returns within the time for signifying consent it is sufficient if the consent of both spouses is signified on one of the returns, or if the consent of the husband is signified on the wife's return, and the consent of the wife is signified on the husband's return. If only one spouse files a Gift Tax return within the time for signifying consent, the consent of both spouses shall be signified on that return. However, wherever possible, the notice of consent is to be shown on both returns. If one spouse files more than one Gift Tax return for a calendar year on or before the 15th day of April following the close of the calendar year, *the last return* so filed will, for the purpose of determining whether a consent has been signified, be considered as the return.[1] Where prior to her marriage a spouse made gifts and filed a return, and during the same year married and filed a consent to split-gifts, the latter was considered timely.[2] Where one spouse signs a consent or return for the other as the other's agent, it must be ratified by the other within a reasonable time.[3]

The consent may be signified at any time following the close of the calendar year, subject to the following limitations:

(1) The consent may not be signified after the 15th day of April following the close of the calendar year, unless before such 15th day no return has been filed by either spouse, in which case the consent may not be signified after a return for the year has been filed for the year by either spouse; and

(2) The consent may not be signified for a calendar year after a notice of deficiency in Gift Tax for that year has been sent to either spouse.[4]

The executor or administrator of a deceased spouse, or the guardian or committee of a legally incompetent spouse, as the case may be, may signify the consent.[5] Three states have adopted legislation authorizing such action.[6]

If the donor and spouse consent to the application of the split-gift provisions, the return or returns for the calendar year must set forth, to the extent provided thereon, information relative to the transfers made by each spouse.[7]

1. Reg, § 25.2513–2(a); Rev Rul 188, 1953–2 CB 292.
2. Frieder, 28 TC 1256 (1957).
3. Rev Rul 54–6, 1954–1 CB 205.
4. IRC, § 2513(b)(2) (1954 Code);
Reg, § 25.2513–2(b).
5. Reg, § 25.2513–2(c).
6. Arkansas, Colorado, Illinois.
7. Reg, § 25.2513–2(d).

§ 473. Gift by Husband or Wife to Third Party; Revocation of Consent.

The statute permits the revocation of a consent previously signified, if made as provided.[8] If the consent to the application of the provisions of Section 2513 for a calendar year was effectively signified on or before the 15th day of April following the close of the calendar year, either spouse may revoke the consent by filing *in duplicate* with the District Director of Internal Revenue a signed statement of revocation, but only if the statement is filed on or before such 15th day of April. Therefore, a consent which was not effectively signified until after the 15th day of April following the close of the calendar year to which it applies may not be revoked.[9]

While the Gift Tax Return, Form 709, contains the form of the consent to be used under the section, there is no form for the revocation. All that is required is that a statement be filed. This may be in the form, "The undersigned hereby revokes her consent to have the gifts made by herself and her spouse, Winthrop Benson, to third parties during the calendar year 1960, considered as having been made one half by each of them. (Signed) Katherine Benson." The revocation should be executed in duplicate and filed with the District Director of the district where the consent was filed. The address of the taxpayer should also be indicated.

§ 474. Gift by Husband or Wife to Third Party; Return.

We have previously discussed to some extent the requirements of the return when there is a split-gift.[10] Form 709 in part B on the first page of the return deals with such gifts. There must first be indicated whether the spouses consent thereto, and if so, the name of the spouse, whether married during the entire calendar year, and if not, the date of marriage, divorce or being widowed, and whether a Gift Tax return will be filed by the other spouse for the calendar year must be stated. There then follows the form of consent.

While the administrative provisions of the Regulations treat generally of returns required in case of consent,[11] those dealing with gifts by spouses to third parties are more specific and fur-

8. IRC, § 2513(c) (1954 Code).
9. Reg, § 25.2513–3.

10. §§ 401, 403, 405, 408, 409, 410, supra.
11. Reg, § 25.6019–2.

nish examples of when a return is required. If a husband and wife consent to split-gifts and only one spouse makes gifts during the year, the other spouse is not required to file a Gift Tax return if the total value of the gifts made to *each* third party is not in excess of $6,000. *and no portion of the property transferred constitutes a gift of a future interest.* If the gift is of a future interest and the spouses consent to a split-gift, *each spouse* must file a return.[12] In such case the amount of the transfer is of no importance.

In the following cases each spouse is required to file a return: the husband makes gifts to a third party of $7,000. and the wife makes none; the husband makes gifts to a third party of $5,000. and the wife makes a gift of $2,000. to the same party; the husband makes gifts to third parties of $2,000. and the wife makes none, but the gift is of a future interest.[13] In these cases splitting the gifts results in a gift by each spouse of an amount in excess of the $3,000. annual exclusion, or it is of a future interest.

In the following cases, only the husband donor is required to file a return: the husband makes gifts valued at $5,000. to each of two third parties and the wife makes none; the husband makes gifts of $5,000. to a third party and the wife makes gifts of $3,000. to a different third party.[14]

Even though the other spouse is not required to file a return, information relative to the transfers made by each spouse must be furnished.[15]

§ 475. Gift by Husband or Wife to Third Party; Joint and Several Liability for Tax.

If husband and wife elect to treat gifts made by them to third parties during a calendar year as having been made one half by each by signifying their consent, and the consent is not revoked, the liability of the spouses for the *entire* Gift Tax for the calendar year is joint and several.[16]

§ 476. Gifts by Nonresidents Not Citizens.

When a gift is made by a nonresident not a citizen of the

12. Reg, § 25.2513–1(c).

13. Reg, § 25.2513–1(d), Examples 1, 3, 5.

14. Reg, § 25.2513–1(d), Examples 2, 4.

15. Note 7, supra.

16. IRC, § 2513(d) (1954 Code); Reg, § 25.2513–4.

United States the problem presented is whether the gift is subject to the tax. There has previously been discussed the matters which determine whether transfers by nonresidents not citizens are subject to the Gift Tax.[17] If such person was not engaged in business in the United States during the calendar year, the tax affects only transfers of real estate and tangible personal property situated in the United States. If he was engaged in business in the United States during the calendar year, the tax affects all transfers of property situated in the United States. Shares of stock, being an intangible, are only subject to the tax if issued by a domestic corporation, and the donor was engaged in business in the United States during the calendar year.[18]

It having been determined that the transfer is subject to the tax then the provisions of the statute apply to nonresidents not citizens in exactly the same way as in the case of a resident or citizen. Acts deemed to result in a completed gift which affects property subject to the tax are treated the same. An exception is made in the case of gifts by husband and wife to third parties, since the statute provides that each spouse must be a citizen or resident, as we have seen.[19] We shall also see that neither the specific exemption nor the marital deduction is allowed to a nonresident not a citizen. It must also be remembered that a gift of moneys on deposit in United States banks was subject to the tax, even though the alien was not engaged in business in the United States, if the transfer took place prior to 1955.[20] Transfers of property outside the United States are not and were not subject to the tax.[1]

There are in effect between the United States and Australia and Japan respectively, Gift Tax conventions which establish rules of domicile and situs. These conventions should be consulted when nationals of these countries are concerned.

§ 477. Gifts Taxable in Donor's Estate.

When a donor makes a lifetime gift, the fact that the gift is subject to the Gift Tax and that a Gift Tax is paid thereon does not remove the possibility that the same property will be in-

17. § 406, supra.
18. Reg, § 25.2511-3.
19. § 471, supra.

20. Harris v Comm, 178 F2d 861 (CA 2) (1949).
1. IRC, § 2511(a) (1954 Code); Wodehouse, 19 TC 487 (1953).

cluded in his gross estate upon his death. We have seen that the Gift Tax and the Estate Tax are not mutually exclusive.[2]

Thus, a transfer may be complete for purposes of the Gift Tax and still be incomplete for purposes of the Estate Tax. Such transfers are those in which the donor made the transfer in contemplation of death,[3] or in which he retained a life estate,[4] or which take effect at death.[5] When the Gift Tax has been paid and the property is included in the donor's gross estate, the Estate Tax statute provides for a credit against the Estate Tax for the Gift Tax paid.[6]

2. § 394, supra.
3. See §§ 121 et seq, supra.
4. See §§ 139 et seq, supra.

5. See §§ 144 et seq, supra.
6. §§ 323 et seq, supra.

CHAPTER 8

FEDERAL GIFT TAX EXCLUSIONS
AND DEDUCTIONS

§ 478. Scope of Chapter.

The Gift Tax statute bases the amount of tax upon the aggregate sum of taxable gifts.[1] The term "taxable gifts" in turn is stated to be the total amount of gifts made during the calendar year, less the statutory deductions.[2] At the same time it provides that except in the case of a gift of a future interest a specific amount shall not be included in the total amount of gifts.[3]

In the preceding chapter we have dealt with all the kinds of transfers which are subject to the Gift Tax. But this is merely the beginning in the determination of the amount of tax ultimately payable, since the taxable gifts are only those remaining after there has been deducted the statutory deductions as well as such amounts as are not included in the total amount of gifts. In this chapter, therefore, we shall consider all those items which reduce the amount upon which the tax is computed.

§ 479. Taxable Gifts; Definition.

The term "taxable gifts" means the total amount of gifts made during the calendar year, less the deductions provided for in the statute.[4] The 1939 Code used the term "net gifts", but there is no difference in meaning between the two terms.[5] While the statute does not designate the amount of the annual exclusion as a deduction, it is in fact deducted in computing the total amount of gifts, since it is provided that in the case of gifts (*other than gifts of future interests in property*) made to any person by the donor during the calendar year 1955 and subsequent calendar years, the first $3,000. of such gifts *shall not be included* in the total amount of gifts made during such year.[6] This is the annual *exclusion*. The difference in nomenclature affects only the question of reporting gifts, but has the same effect taxwise as a deduction has.

1. IRC, § 2502(a) (1954 Code).
2. IRC, § 2503(a) (1954 Code).
3. IRC, § 2503(b) (1954 Code).
4. Note 2, supra.
5. IRC, § 1003(a) (1939 Code).
6. Note 3, supra.

The *deductions* referred to are the specific exemption,[7] the charitable deduction,[8] and the marital deduction.[9]

The amount of taxable gifts is therefore determined by deducting from the total amount of gifts made by the donor during the calendar year

(1) A specific exemption of $30,000., less the sum of the amounts claimed and allowed as an exemption in prior calendar years.

(2) Gifts for public, charitable, etc., purposes.

(3) The marital deduction.[10]

(4) The annual exclusion for each donee.[11]

§ 480. The Annual Exclusion; Generally.

The Gift Tax statute provides that in the case of gifts (*other than gifts of future interests in property*) *made to any person* by the donor during the calendar year 1955 and subsequent calendar years, *the first $3,000. of such gifts to such person shall not,* for purposes of determining taxable gifts, *be included* in the total amount of gifts made during such year.[12]

Few provisions of the statute have been as productive of litigation as the annual exclusion. The amount of the exclusion has varied from time to time. Between 1932 and 1938 it was $5,000.[13] From 1939 to and including 1942 it was $4,000.,[14] and from 1943 to date it has been $3,000.[15] The amounts are of importance, since in computing gifts for any calendar year, the amount of gifts in prior years must be considered.

It will be observed that the exclusion is permitted as to present interests and does not apply to future interests. The distinctions are fine, and will be discussed in succeeding sections.

It has been stated that in providing the exclusion in the original Act Congress intended to obviate the necessity of keeping an account of and reporting numerous small gifts and to fix an amount sufficiently large to cover in most cases wedding and Christmas gifts and occasional gifts of relatively small amounts.[16] The purpose in denying the benefit to gifts of future

7. IRC, § 2521 (1954 Code).
8. IRC, § 2522 (1954 Code).
9. IRC, § 2523 (1954 Code).
10. Reg, § 25.2503–1.
11. Reg, § 25.2503–2.
12. Note 3, supra.

13. Rev Act of 1932, § 504(a); IRC, § 1003(b)(1) (1939 Code).
14. IRC, § 1003(b)(2) (1939 Code).
15. IRC, § 1003(b)(3) (1939 Code).
16. Welch v Paine, 130 F2d 990 (CCA 1) (1942).

interests was the protection of the revenue and the appropriate administration of the tax immunity provided by the Act.[17]

§ 481. The Annual Exclusion; Number and Amount Allowable.

It will have been observed that the annual exclusion is allowed for the *gifts* made *to any person* and that the first $3,000. of such *gifts to such persons* shall not be included in the total amount of gifts made during the year.[18]

Thus, the exclusion is not measured by the number of gifts but by the number of persons. It is further limited to the actual amount of the gift. If the donor makes a gift of a present interest to ten different persons, and each received $3,000. or more, the total excluded amount would be $30,000. But if half received $2,000. each and the others $3,000. each, the total exclusions would be $25,000. (5 × $2,000. + 5 × $3,000.). Further, if one person received two separate gifts totalling $5,000., $2,000. of that total amount would be included in the donor's taxable gifts.

A question which soon arose under the original statute was whether when a gift was made to a trustee for the benefit of more than one person, the gift was to the trustee or to the beneficiaries. If the gift was to the trustee, then a donor could completely avoid any tax by creating numerous trusts. Several lower courts did in fact so hold.[19] This prompted Congress in the Revenue Act of 1938 to deny the allowance of the annual exclusion to gifts in trust.[20] When in 1941 the Supreme Court determined that gifts in trust were gifts to the beneficiaries of the trust,[1] and that an exclusion was permissible for each beneficiary, Congress restored the right of the exclusion to gifts in trust, at the same time reducing still further the amount of the exclusion which it had reduced to $4,000. in the 1938 Act, to $3,000. in the 1942 Act.[2]

Prior to the decision of the Supreme Court holding that when there was a gift of a present interest to a trust the number of

17. US v Pelzer, 312 US 399, 85 L ed 913, 61 S Ct 659 (1941).

18. Note 3, supra.

19. Comm v Wells, 88 F2d 339 (CCA 7) (1937); Comm v Krebs, 90 F2d 880 (CCA 3) (1937); Noyes v Hassett, 20 F Supp 31 (1937).

20. Rev Act of 1938, § 505(a).

1. Helvering v Hutchings, 312 US 393, 85 L ed 909, 61 S Ct 653 (1941); US v Pelzer, note 17, supra; Ryerson v US, 312 US 405, 85 L ed 917, 61 S Ct 656 (1941).

2. Rev Act of 1942, § 454.

exclusions was measured by the number of beneficiaries of the trust, many courts had held similarly.[3]

It has been noted that in computing the tax for the current year, gifts for prior years must be considered. Where an exclusion is improperly allowed in a prior year, even though the statute of limitations may prevent an assessment of a deficiency for the prior year, in computing the current year's tax the erroneous exclusion may be disallowed.[4]

We have previously discussed the question of the exclusion in the case of a gift to a corporation or a partnership.[5]

In order to determine the number and the amount of exclusions it is necessary that the donee be identified[6] and the amount of the interest be ascertainable.[7] The latter question arises frequently in connection with invasion provisions in trust instruments and will be treated hereafter.[8]

§ 482. The Annual Exclusion; Future Interests; Generally.

The statute provides that the annual exclusion is allowable for *other than future interests* in property.[9] This provision has been the source of major litigation. While the Regulation is quite specific on the subject, it does not begin to answer all the questions which may arise.

"Future interests" is a legal term, and includes reversions, remainders, and other interests or estates, whether vested or contingent, and whether or not supported by a particular interest or estate, which are limited to commence in use, possession or enjoyment at some future date or time. The term has no reference to such contractual rights as exist in a bond, note (though bearing no interest until maturity), or in a policy of life insurance, the obligations of which are to be discharged by payments in the future. But a future interest or interests in such contrac-

---

3. Christian v Comm, 110 F2d 851 (CCA 8) (1940); McBrier v Comm, 108 F2d 967 (CCA 3) (1940); Rheinstrom v Comm, 105 F2d 642 (CCA 8) (1939); Roberston v Nee, 105 F2d 651 (CCA 8) (1939); Welch v Davidson, 102 F2d 100 (CCA 1) (1939); Loew, 42 BTA 17 (1940); Early v Reid, 112 F2d 718 (CCA 4) (1940).

4. Comm v Disston, 325 US 442, 89 L ed 1720, 65 S Ct 1328 (1945); Winton v Reynolds, 57 F Supp 565 (1944); Farish, 2 TCM 699 (1943); Goodhart,

2 TCM 267 (1943); Roberts, 2 TC 679 (1943); Wallerstein, 2 TC 542 (1943); Winterbothan, 46 BTA 972 (1942).

5. § 418, supra.

6. Barneson, BTA memo op, Dec. 11, 842-H (1941) and BTA mem op, Dec. 11, 874-C (1941).

7. Smyth, 2 TCM 4 (1943); Polk, 5 TCM 357 (1945); Riter, 3 TC 301 (1944); Geller, 9 TC 484 (1947).

8. § 486, infra.

9. IRC, § 2503(b) (1954 Code).

tual obligations may be created by the limitations contained in a trust or other instrument of transfer used in effecting a gift.[9a]

The Regulation is a statement of the definitions placed on the term by Congress,[10] and has been repeated in prior Regulations.[11]

The determination of whether an interest is future or present is not dependent upon local state law,[12] but state law is applicable in determining whether the donee has the present right to use, possession and enjoyment.[13] The term is not used in the same sense as in the law of conveyancing.[14] The motive of the donor is of no importance, except as it bears upon whether there is a right to, or postponement of, the immediate enjoyment of the gift.[15] In determining the nature of the rights conferred by a trust instrument, the words used are important,[16] but the court is not bound to refer only to the four corners of the instrument, and may look to facts apart from it.[17]

The usual concepts of the law of property are not those used in determining whether an interest is a future interest. When title vests,[18] the fact that title has vested,[19] the donor's complete divestiture of title,[20] or the fact that an interest is subject to the claims of creditors,[1] are not determinative. *If the donee does not have the right to presently use, possess, or enjoy the interest donated, the gift is one of a future interest.*[2] While it would seem that this is a simple test to apply, the large number of cases in which the question has been litigated, indicates that it is not.

Another factor entering into the determination of whether an

9a. Reg, § 25.2503–3(a).

10. House Comm Rep No 708, 72nd Cong, 1st Sess, p 29; Senate Comm Rep No 665, 72nd Cong, 1st Sess, p 41.

11. Reg, 78, Art XI; Reg 108, § 86.11.

12. US v Pelzer, note 17, supra; Wisotskey, 144 F2d 632 (CCA 3) (1944); Charles v Hassett, 43 F Supp 432 (1942); French v Comm, 138 F2d 254 (CCA 8) (1943).

13. Ashcraft v Allen, 90 F Supp 543 (1950); Munger v US, 154 F Supp 417 (1957).

14. Comm v Wells, 132 F2d 405 (CCA 6) (1942).

15. Fondren v Comm, 324 US 18, 89 L ed 668, 65 S Ct 499 (1945).

16. Wisotskey, note 12, supra.

17. Stifel v Comm, 197 F2d 107 (CA 2) (1952).

18. Comm v Sharpe, 153 F2d 163 (CCA 9) (1946).

19. Note 15, supra; Comm v Glos, 123 F2d 548 (CCA 7) (1941); Welch v Paine, 120 F2d 141 (CCA 1) (1941); Hessenbruch v Comm, 178 F2d 785 (CA 3) (1950); Brody, 19 TC 126 (1952); Phillips, 12 TC 216 (1949).

20. Phillips, note 19, supra; Geller, 9 TC 484 (1947).

1. Welch v Paine, note 19, supra.

2. Note 15, supra; note 18, supra; Comm v Gardner, 127 F2d 929 (CCA 7) (1942); French v Comm, 138 F2d 254 (CCA 8) (1943); note 14, supra; Charles v Hassett, note 12, supra; Hessenbruch v Comm, note 19, supra; Shefner v Knox, 131 F Supp 936 (1955).

interest is a present or future interest is the question of whether the number of eventual donees and the value of their respective gifts is ascertainable. As Congress pointed out in enacting the provision, the exemption being available only insofar as the donees are ascertainable, the denial of the exemption in the case of gifts of future interests was dictated by the apprehended difficulty, in many instances, of determining the number of eventual donees and the values of their respective gifts.[3]

§ 483. The Annual Exclusion; Future Interests; Present Interest Distinguished.

The Regulation notes that *an unrestricted right to the immediate use, possession, or enjoyment of property or the income from property* (such as a life estate or term certain) *is a present interest* in property. If a gift is made of an interest which does not commence immediately or is not unrestricted, or the value of which is not ascertainable by accepted actuarial methods, no exclusion is allowable. However, if a donee has received a present interest in property, the possibility that such interest may be diminished by the transfer of a greater interest in the same property to the donee through the exercise of a power is disregarded in computing the value of the present interest, to the extent that no part of such interest will at any time pass to any other person.[4]

This latter provision was written into the 1954 Code because of certain decisions[5] in which it had been held that although a gift might be made in trust of the present right to receive income, if power was given to the trustee in his uncontrolled discretion to pay over the trust principal to the income beneficiary, the income interest was not susceptible of determination and was therefore a gift of a future interest.[6] But where there is a gift of income and the remainder to the same person, the remainder interest is a future one.[7]

The question of whether gifts are those of a present or future interest largely arises in connection with gifts of income and lim-

---

3. Note 10, supra.

4. Reg, § 25.2503–3(b).

5. Evans, 17 TC 206, affd 198 F2d 435 (CA 3) (1951); Rev Rul 54–92, IRB 1954–1 CB 207; Tyler, 12 TCM 407 (1949); Reinfeld, 14 TCM 1326 (1955).

6. Sen Fin Comm Report, § 2503 (1954 Code).

7. Note 15, supra; Wisotskey, note 12, supra; Brody, 19 TC 126 (1953); Pope, 12 TCM 646 (1949); Newmaker, 12 TCM 232 (1949); but see Kinney v Anglim, 43 F Supp 431 (1941).

itations thereon, as well as in the case of gifts to minors, both of which are treated hereafter.

§ 484. The Annual Exclusion; Future Interests; Gifts of Income.

Where a gift is made outright, no question arises as to the donee's right to the immediate use, possession, or enjoyment of the property. When the gift is in trust, however, whether the donee has the right to its immediate use depends upon the terms of the trust instrument. There may be many reasons why such essential to a present interest is lacking.

When the gift is of an immediate life interest in income it is a present interest,[8] nor need the interest be for life, but may be for a lesser period.[9] The fact that the trust contains a spend-thrift clause,[10] or that the interest is subject to payment of specific amounts from the income to others,[11] does not affect the determination. If the trust is revocable there is a gift of a present interest in each year in which the income is paid to the donee.[12]

There is immediate payment when income is required to be started at once and not postponed to a future time at the discretion of the trustee. But this does not mean upon the completion of the gift or the day after. It means at fairly regular intervals of reasonable length.[13] Thus payment as soon as reasonably practicable,[14] or convenient,[15] or upon demand of the beneficiary within thirty days after the end of the trust year,[16] all meet the standard. If the right to the income depends upon surviving to a particular time,[17] the act of some other person,[18] or attaining a certain age,[19] the gift is of a future interest.

8. Comm v Brandegee, 123 F2d 58 (CCA 1) (1941).

9. Charles v Hassett, note 12, supra; Fisher v Comm, 132 F2d 383 (CCA 9) (1942).

10. Charles v Hassett, note 12, supra; Gilmore, 213 F2d 520 (CA 6) (1954); Rev Rul 54–344, IRB 1954–2 CB 319.

11. Comm v Lowden, 131 F2d 127 (CCA 7) (1942).

12. Roeser, 2 TC 298 (1943).

13. Helvering v Rubinstein, 124 F2d 969 (CCA 8) (1942).

14. Kempner v Comm, 126 F2d 853 (CCA 5) (1942).

15. Edwards, 46 BTA 815 (1942).

16. Hallowell, BTA memo op, Dec. 12, 244–A (1942).

17. US v Pelzer, 312 US 399, 85 L ed 913, 61 S Ct 659 (1941); Ryerson v US, 312 US 405, 85 L ed 917, 61 S Ct 656 (1941); Comm v Boeing, 123 F2d 86 (CCA 9) (1941); Hopkins v Magruder, 122 F2d 693 (CCA 4) (1941); Comm v Warner, 127 F2d 913 (CCA 9) (1942); Sensenbrenner, 46 BTA 713, affd 134 F2d 883 (CCA 7) (1943).

18. McIlvain, 1 TCM 558 (1942).

19. Comm v Disston, 325 US 442, 89 L ed 1720, 65 S Ct 1328 (1945); Welch v Paine, 120 F2d 141 (CCA 1) (1941); Winton v Reynolds, 57 F Supp 565

When the trust provides for accumulation of the income, there is obviously no right to immediate enjoyment and the gift is not a present one.[20] If the income may be used for purposes other than for the benefit of the beneficiary, such as the payment of mortgages, insurance premiums and taxes, there is no right to immediate use,[1] but not if the amount to be paid is a fixed amount.[2]

Where there is not the absolute right to the income, but its distribution is within the discretion of another such as a trustee,[3] another person,[4] or a joint beneficiary,[5] the gift has consistently been held to be that of a future interest. It must be noted, however, that many of these cases involved gifts to minors, the determination of when such gifts are future interests having been changed by the 1954 Code, and which changes are discussed hereafter.[6]

§ 485. The Annual Exclusion; Future Interests; Remainders and Reversions.

In considering remainder and reversionary interests we must bear in mind the definition of a future interest as used in the statute. The fact that the interest is a vested one, so that the holder thereof may alienate it, is as we have seen,[7] not the determining factor. The test is whether the owner thereof has an interest which is limited to commence in use, possession, or enjoyment at a future time.

A remainder or reversionary interest comes squarely within the definition and it has therefore been held consistently from the very inception of the Gift Tax statute that such interests are future interests.[8]

(1944); Burrell, 3 TCM 489 (1944); Laughlin, 3 TCM 1038 (1944); Scherer, 3 TC 776 (1944); Crane, 16 TCM 12 (1957).

20. Hopkins v Magruder, note 17, supra; US v Pelzer, note 17, supra.

1. Note 8, supra; Nelson, 46 BTA 653 (1942); Comm v Boeing, note 17, supra; Bristol v Welch, 45 F Supp 676 (1942).

2. Frank, 3 TCM 1180 (1944); note 11, supra.

3. Welch v Paine, note 19, supra; Hessenbruch v Comm, 178 F2d 785 (CA 3) (1950); Welch v Paine, 130 F2d

990 (CCA 1) (1942); Allen, 3 TC 1224 (1944); Geller, 9 TC 484 (1947); Guggenheim, 1 TC 845 (1942); Rev Rul 55–303, IRB 1955–1 CB 471; Fondren v Comm, 324 US 18, 89 L ed 668, 65 S Ct 499 (1945); French v Comm, 138 F2d 254 (CCA 8) (1943).

4. Wood, 16 TC 962 (1951).

5. Smyth, 2 TCM 4 (1943); Ryerson v US, note 17, supra; Howe v US, 142 F2d 310 (CCA 7) (1944).

6. §§ 491 et seq, infra.

7. § 482, supra.

8. Warner, BTA memo op, Dec. 11, 306–L (1940); Block, BTA memo op,

§ 486. The Annual Exclusion; Future Interests; Where Power of Invasion.

When income is payable to a beneficiary, even though an interest may be a present interest, its value must be determinable in order for the annual exclusion to be allowed.[9] Where there is a power of invasion granted, the question arises whether the value of the present interest is ascertainable. As two Revenue Rulings point out, generally, the Gift Tax exclusion is not allowable, unless the number of eventual donees is ascertainable or unless the interest of each beneficiary is susceptible of valuation. However, the allowance of the exclusion is determined by the facts in each particular case.[10] If after taking into consideration all possible future contingencies, it can be shown that the present interest has some ascertainable value, based upon sound actuarial principles, the exclusion is allowable to the extent of the minimum value of such interest, or $3,000., whichever is the lesser. In such cases it is not necessary that the exact value of the gift of the present interest in property be determinable on the basis of recognized actuarial principles.[11] This may sound like a contradiction in terms. But applying the statement to a set of facts makes it clear that it is not. If the donor transfers $2,000,000. in trust for ten years to pay the income in equal shares to such of the donor's grandchildren as may be living at the time of payment and to the then living issue of such of the donor's grandchildren who shall then be dead, the then living issue of any grandchild not then living to receive in equal shares per stirpes that share of the net income which the said grandchild would have received if living at the time, and the donor had four married children and ten grandchildren, computation of the present interest of the oldest beneficiary in the income, even assuming that there might be sixty beneficiaries, would indicate that his interest was more than $3,000.[12] Under the circumstances, the full exclusion would be allowable.

Dec. 11, 083–A(1940); Brody, 19 TC 126 (1952); note 18, supra; Polk, 5 TCM 357 (1945); Rev Rul 54–401, IRB 1954–2 CB 320; Hutchings Sealy Nat Bank v Comm, 141 F2d 422 (CCA 5) (1944); Gould, 6 TCM 755 (1946); Tyler, 12 TCM 407 (1949); Ashcraft v Allen, 90 F Supp 543 (1950).

9. Smyth, note 5, supra; Polk, note 8, supra.

10. Rev Rul 55–679, IRB 1955–2 CB 390.

11. Rev Rul 55–678, IRB 1955–2 CB 388.

12. Note 10, supra.

[Harris]—42

This method has been followed by the courts. Where the interest was capable of valuation the exclusion has been allowed,[13] and where it has not been possible to do so it has been disallowed.[14] In considering cases decided under the 1939 Code, two things must be kept in mind. As we have seen, the 1954 Code expressly negated decisions which had held that where the income and remainder were payable to the same person, no exclusion would be allowed if the remainder could be accelerated for the benefit of the life tenant by the exercise of a power.[15] We shall also see[16] that certain gifts for the benefit of minors for which no exclusion was allowable under the 1939 Code, are specifically held not to be future interests under the 1954 Code.

Since when there is a power of invasion, the question is not primarily whether the interest is a present one or a future one, but whether the amount or value of the interest is ascertainable, if under all of the facts in the particular case it appears that the invasion cannot reduce the interest below the statutory amount, as where the encroachment is limited by ascertainable standards, or there does not appear that there will be need to encroach, the exclusion will be allowed.[17]

§ 487. The Annual Exclusion; Future Interests; Insurance and Annuities.

With the removal of the payment of premiums test for includibility of the proceeds of insurance in the gross estate of a decedent, gifts of insurance and annuity policies have flourished. Further impetus to such gifts will be given by the determination by the Supreme Court that a gift of insurance purchased as part of a combination annuity and insurance contract will not result in the inclusion of the insurance in the estate of the donor.[18]

The Regulation states that the term "future interests" has no reference to such contractual rights as exist in a policy of life insurance, the obligations of which are to be discharged by payments in the future.[19]

13. Kniep v Comm, 172 F2d 755 (CA 8) (1949); Gilmore v Comm, 213 F2d 520 (CA 6) (1954).

14. Riter, 3 TC 301 (1944); Geller, note 3, supra; Evans v Comm, 198 F2d 435 (CA 3) (1952); Rev Rul 54-92, IRB 1954-1 CB 207; Tyler, note 8, supra.

15. § 483, supra.
16. § 491, infra.
17. Jones, 29 TC —, No 25 (1958).
18. Fidelity-Philadelphia Trust Co v Smith, 356 US 274, 2 L ed 2d 765, 78 S Ct 730 (1958).
19. Reg, § 25.2503-3(a).

Where there is an irrevocable assignment of a life insurance policy to the beneficiary there is a gift of a present interest, as there is of any premiums thereafter paid by the donor thereon.[20] But if there is a limitation so that the donee cannot presently enjoy the policy by surrendering it or borrowing upon it,[1] or if the donee cannot exercise his rights in the policy without the joint action of another,[2] the gift is of a future interest. Although it was held that where insurance was assigned before it had any cash surrender value, the payment of premiums thereon in the year of the gift and the following year were gifts of future interests,[3] a Revenue Ruling[4] points out that such statement was obiter dicta and that a gift of an insurance policy having no cash value is not a gift of a future interest merely because the policy has no cash value, and that a gift of an insurance policy, whether or not it has a cash value, may or may not be a gift of a future interest, *depending upon whether, by the terms of the gift, the interests of the donee in the policy are in some manner restricted.*

One of the ways in which restrictions may be placed upon the donee's present enjoyment of an assigned policy most commonly used, is by the creation of an insurance trust. While the term "future interests" has no reference to an insurance policy ipso facto, a future interest in such obligation may be created by the limitations contained in a trust or other instrument of transfer.[5] When policies are transferred to a trust and the rights of the beneficiaries are contingent on survivorship;[6] the trustees can acquire ownership only by joint action terminating the trust;[7] the trust can be invaded for the beneficiary only in a contingency which might never arise;[8] the income is to be accumulated;[9] the donor reserves the right to change beneficiaries;[10] the proceeds are not to be distributed until after the donor's death;[11] the trus-

20. Baer, 2 TCM 285 (1943); Chittenden v Comm, 43–1 USTC ¶ 10,047.

1. Perkins, 1 TC 982 (1942); Skouras, 14 TC 523 (1950).

2. Skouras v Comm, 188 F2d 831 (CA 2) (1951); Smyth, 2 TCM 4 (1943).

3. Nashville Trust Co, 2 TCM 992 (1943).

4. Rev Rul 55–408, 1955–IRB 1 CB 113.

5. Note 19, supra.

6. Ryerson v US, 312 US 405, 85 L ed 917, 61 S Ct 656 (1941).

7. Note 6, supra.

8. Phillips, 12 TC 216 (1949).

9. Watkins, 2 TCM 254 (1943).

10. Fletcher Trust Co, 1 TC 798, affd 141 F2d 36 (CCA 7) (1942).

11. Comm v Warner, 127 F2d 913 (CCA 9) (1942); Comm v Boeing, 123 F2d 86 (CCA 9) (1941); Candle, 4 TCM 324 (1944).

tee has discretion to distribute income and corpus;[12] or the income on the proceeds is not payable until after the donor's death;[13] the gift is of a future interest. But if the dividends are distributable annually, while the proceeds are a future interest, the dividends are a present interest.[14] And when the beneficiary has the right to call for the corpus of the trust at any time, premiums paid by the donor on policies in the trust are gifts of a present interest.[15] The effect of the statute cannot be avoided by directing the payment of the income to the beneficiaries of an insurance trust, when the only asset of the trust consists of the policies of insurance.[16]

In the case of annuities, the question hinges on whether the annuitant has a present and immediate right to the benefits of the contract, or enjoyment is to begin in the future. In the latter case, the gift is of a future interest.[17]

§ 488. The Annual Exclusion; Burden of Proof.

The right to the annual exclusion is not automatic. The taxpayer has the burden of establishing not only the right to the exclusion but the value of the interest. The burden of establishing that the gift is of a present interest must first be met.[18] We have also seen that the value of the interest must be ascertainable before the exclusion will be allowed.[19]

The determination of the Commissioner as to the amounts allowable as exclusions is presumptively correct and the taxpayer has the burden of proving not only his right to the claimed exclusion, but also the amount of it.[20]

§ 489. The Annual Exclusion; Operation of the Statute.

The Regulation[1] furnishes six illustrations of the operation

12. Bolton, 1 TC 717 (1942).

13. Fidelity Trust Co, 2 TCM 89, aff'd 141 F2d 54 (CCA 3) (1943); Candle, note 11, supra.

14. Tideman, 1 TC 968 (1942); Frank, 3 TCM 1180 (1944).

15. Halsted, 28 TC 1069 (1957).

16. Note 8, supra.

17. Ream, 2 TCM 1067 (1943); Morrow, 2 TC 210 (1943); Roberts v Comm, 143 F2d 557 (CCA 5), cert den 324 US 841, 89 L ed 1403, 65 S Ct 585 (1944).

18. Smyth, note 2, supra; Comm v Sharp, 153 F2d 163 (CCA 9) (1946);

Comm v Disston, 325 US 442, 89 L ed 1720, 65 S Ct 1328 (1945).

19. Robinette v Helvering, 318 US 184, 87 L ed 700, 63 S Ct 540 (1943); Helvering v Blair, 121 F2d 945 (CCA 2) (1941); Brody, 19 TC 126 (1952); Evans, 17 TC 206, aff'd 198 F2d 435 (CA 3) (1951); Affelder, 7 TC 1190 (1946); Riter, 3 TC 364 (1944).

20. Kniep v Comm, 172 F2d 755 (CA 8) (1949); Herrmann v Comm, 235 F2d 440 (CA 5) (1956).

1. Reg, § 25.2503-3(c).

of the statute, which may be found helpful in an understanding of it. These examples are as follows:

(1) Under the terms of a trust created by A the trustee is directed to pay the net income to B, so long as B shall live. The trustee is authorized *in his discretion to withhold payments of income* during any period he deems advisable and add such income to the trust corpus. Since B's right to receive the income payments is subject to the trustee's discretion, it is not a present interest and no exclusion is allowable with respect to the transfer in trust.[2]

(2) C transfers certain insurance policies on his own life to a trust created for the benefit of D. *Upon C's death* the proceeds of the policies are to be invested and the net income therefrom paid to D during his lifetime. Since the income payments to D will not begin until after C's death, the transfer in trust represents a gift of a future interest in property against which no exclusion is allowable.[3]

(3) Under the terms of a trust created by E the net income is to be distributed to A's three children *in such shares* as the trustee, *in his uncontrolled discretion,* deems advisable. While the terms of the trust provide that all of the net income is to be distributed, the amount of the income any one of the three beneficiaries will receive rests entirely within the trustee's discretion and cannot be presently ascertained. Accordingly, no exclusions are allowable with respect to the transfers to the trust.[4]

(4) Under the terms of a trust the net income is to be paid to F for life, with the remainder payable to G on F's death. The trustee has the uncontrolled power *to pay over the corpus to F* at any time. Although F's present right to receive the income may be terminated, *no other person has the right to such income* interest. Accordingly, the power in the trustee is disregarded in determining the value of F's present interest. The power is not disregarded to the extent the trustee during F's life can distribute corpus to persons other than F.[5] This example demonstrates the change made by the 1954 Code, previously referred to.[6]

(5) The corpus of a trust created by J consists of certain real

2. Note 1, Example (1); see § 484, supra.

3. Note 1, Example (2); see § 487, supra.

4. Note 1, Example (3); see § 484, supra.

5. Note 1, Example (4).

6. § 483, supra.

property, subject to a mortgage. The terms of the trust provide that *the net income from the property is to be used to pay the mortgage.* After the mortgage is paid in full the net income is to be paid to K during his lifetime. Since K's right to receive the income payments will not begin until after the mortgage is paid in full the transfer in trust represents a gift of a future interest in property against which no exclusion is allowable.[7]

(6) L pays premiums on a policy of insurance on his life, all the incidents of ownership of which (including the right to surrender the policy) are vested in M. The payment of premiums constitutes a gift of a present interest.[8]

The Regulation furnishes no example where there is a power of invasion measured by a standard. This is understandable, since each case is determined by its own facts. The Revenue Rulings which we have previously referred to,[9] however, indicate the manner of operation of the statute in such cases.

§ 490. The Annual Exclusion; Description of Gifts Subject to.

While where the gift is one of a present interest the first $3,000. of gifts made to any one donee is excluded in computing the tax, the *entire value* of gifts totaling more than $3,000. to any one donee during the year must be listed in the return.[10] Thus, in Schedule A of the return the gift is described in the manner required for the particular kind of transfer and its full value at the date of the gift shown. Item (f) of Schedule A has provision for showing the total amount of exclusions.

If the gift is of a present interest and does not exceed $3,000. in the calendar year for each donee, then no matter how many donees there may be, no return need be filed, except where there is an election to treat the creation of a tenancy by the entirety as a gift.[11]

§ 491. The Annual Exclusion; Gifts to Minors; History of the Statute.

Prior to the 1954 Code there was much litigation on the question of whether particular gifts for the benefit of a minor constituted present interests or future interests. It was settled that

7. Note 1, Example (5); see § 484, supra.

8. Note 1, Example (6); see § 487, supra.

9. § 486, supra.

10. Instruction 9, Form 709.

11. § 453, supra.

a trust created to accumulate income for the minority of an infant, with payment of the accumulated income to him upon his attaining his majority, was a gift of a future interest and not entitled to the annual exclusion.[12] A similar result was reached where the trustee had the discretion to use income and principal for the beneficiary.[13] A power of invasion was held to deny the exclusion because the interest could not be valued.[14] If the amount of the invasion was specified, evaluation was possible and the exclusion allowed.[15]

There then ensued a conflict between the courts, with the Tax Court refusing to follow the court favorable to the taxpayer. The Court of Appeals for the Seventh Circuit held that the right in the infant or guardian to terminate the trust for his benefit was sufficient to create a present interest of both income and principal.[16] The Court of Appeals for the Second Circuit held to the contrary.[17] The Tax Court, as has been noted, refused to follow the Seventh Circuit.[18]

It was to resolve this conflict that in enacting the Internal Revenue Code of 1954 Congress added a new provision[19] describing a type of gift to a minor which will not be treated as a gift of a future interest.[20]

§ 492. The Annual Exclusion; Gifts to Minors; Statutory Provision.

The statute provides that no part of a gift to an individual who has not attained the age of 21 years on the date of such transfer shall be considered a gift of a future interest in property for purposes of the annual exclusion *if the property and income therefrom*

(1) *may be* expended by, or for the benefit of, the donee before his attaining the age of 21 years, *and*

(2) *will* to the extent not so expended—

(A) *pass to the donee* on his attaining the age of 21 years, *and*

---

12. US v Pelzer, 312 US 399, 85 L ed 913, 61 S Ct 659 (1941); Ryerson v US, 312 US 405, 85 L ed 917, 61 S Ct 656 (1941).

13. Fondren v Comm, 324 US 18, 89 L ed 668, 65 S Ct 499 (1945); Comm v Disston, note 18, supra.

14. Evans v Comm, note 19, supra; Brody, note 19, supra.

15. Note 20, supra.

16. Kieckhefer v Comm, 189 F2d 118 (CA 7), revg 15 TC 111 (1951).

17. Stifel v Comm, 197 F2d 107 (CA 2), affg 17 TC 647 (1952).

18. Stifel, 17 TC 647 (1952).

19. IRC, § 2503(c) (1954 Code).

20. House and Senate Comm Reports, § 2503 of 1954 Code.

(B) in the event the donee dies before attaining the age of 21 years, be payable to the estate of the donee, or as he may appoint under a general power of appointment.[1]

Thus, to qualify under the statute the gift must meet the following conditions:

(1) Both the property itself *and* its income may be expended by or for the benefit of the donee before he attains the age of 21 years.

(2) Any portion of the property and its income not disposed of for his benefit before he attains the age of 21 years will pass to the donee when he attains the age of 21 years.

(3) Any portion of the property and its income not disposed of for his benefit before he attains the age of 21 years will be payable either to the estate of the donee or as he may appoint under a general power of appointment as defined in Section 2514(c) if he dies before attaining the age of 21 years.[2]

The statute has settled many questions, but others still remain to be answered. Some of these relate to the power of appointment which may be granted, and are discussed in the succeeding section.

§ 493. The Annual Exclusion; Gifts to Minors; Requirements of Power of Appointment.

The statute provides that if the donee dies before attaining the age of 21 years, unexpended principal and income must be payable to his estate or be subject to a general power of appointment by him as defined in Section 2514(c).[3] The definition of a power of appointment under the statute, and the exceptions has been treated previously.[4]

The Regulation expands upon the kind of power of appointment which will satisfy the requirements of the statute. Either a power of appointment exercisable by the donee by will or a power of appointment exercisable by the donee during his lifetime will suffice. However, if the transfer is to qualify for the exclusion under the statute, *there must be no restrictions of substance* (as distinguished from formal restrictions referred to in the Regulations dealing with the marital deduction power of appointment[5]) by the terms of the instrument of transfer on the

---

1. Note 19, supra.
2. Reg, § 25.2503-4(a).
3. Note 19, supra.

4. § 459, supra.
5. Reg, § 25.2523(e)-1(g)(4).

exercise of the power by the donee. However, if the minor is given a power of appointment exercisable during lifetime or is given a power of appointment exercisable by will, the fact that under the local law a minor is under a disability to exercise an inter vivos power or to execute a will does not cause the transfer to fail to satisfy the conditions of the statute. Further, a transfer does not fail to satisfy the conditions of the statute by reason of the mere fact that—

(1) There is left to the discretion of a trustee the determination of the amounts, if any, of the income or property to be expended for the benefit of the minor and the purpose for which the expenditure is to be made, provided there are no substantial restrictions under the terms of the trust instrument on the exercise of such discretion.

(2) The donee, upon reaching age 21, has the right to extend the term of the trust; or

(3) The governing instrument contains a disposition of the property or income not expended during the donee's minority to persons other than the donee's estate in the event of the default of appointment by the donee.[6]

This latter removes from the realm of speculation, the question of whether a gift over in default of appointment would be a limitation disqualifying the gift.

The Proposed Regulation had provided that a power of appointment granted to a minor which under local law could not be exercised by him, did not satisfy the requirements of the statute.[7] Happily, this has been deleted from the final Regulation.

The provision of the Regulation that there must be no restrictions of substance is a significant one. If the trust provided for accumulation of the income, the lack of the requisite discretion to expend for the benefit of the minor would make the statute inapplicable. The same result would follow if *either* the income or the principal were subject to expenditure, *but not both*. The accumulation of income will make the gift one of a future interest, no matter how short the time of accumulation. So short a period as three months was held sufficient.[8]

6. Reg, § 25.2503–4(b).

7. Proposed Reg, § 25.2503–4(b).

8. Hessenbruch v Comm, 178 F2d 785 (CA 3) (1950).

§ 494. The Annual Exclusion; Gifts to Minors; Decisions Prior to 1955.

It must not be assumed that the provisions added to the 1954 Code makes all previously decided cases involving gifts to infants inapplicable. Section 2503(c) applies only to gifts which comply with the requirements of the section. A gift which does not satisfy the requirements of the section may be either a present or future interest under the general rules. Thus for example, a transfer of property in trust with income required to be paid annually to a minor beneficiary and corpus to be distributed to him upon his attaining the age 25, is a gift of a present interest with respect to the right to income, but is a gift of a future interest with respect to the right to corpus.[9]

An outright gift to a minor is not a gift of a future interest.[10] When the gift is in trust it is not necessary that the trust terminate upon the minor attaining majority,[11] but it is only required that the donee have the right to present enjoyment, for the exclusion to be allowable. When the income is to be used for the benefit of the minor,[12] or is payable to a parent or guardian for the benefit of the minor[13] the exclusion is allowable under the 1954 Code as it was prior thereto. When the gift is outright to the minor, it is a gift of a present interest whether or not under state law the appointment of a guardian is required.[14] When it was trust, in the absence of the appointment of a legal guardian, the gift was of a future interest, where the trustee had the uncontrolled discretion to use the principal and income for the welfare of the donor's minor children, under the 1939 Code.[15]

9. Reg, § 25.2503–4(c).

10. Rev Rul 54–400, IRB, 1954, 2 CB 319.

11. Wisotskey v Comm, 144 F2d 632 (CCA 3) (1944); Smith v Comm, 131 F2d 254 (CCA 8) (1942); Davidson v Welch, 22 F Supp 726, aff'd 102 F2d 100 (CCA 1) (1938); Phillips, 12 TC 216 (1949); Deeds, 37 BTA 293 (1938).

12. Sensenbrenner, 46 BTA 713 (1942); Stifel, 46 BTA 568 (1942); Smith v Comm, 131 F2d 254 (CCA 8) (1942), note 16, supra; Comm v Sharp,

153 F2d 163 (CCA 9) (1946); Kelly, 19 TC 27 (1952); McCoy, 6 TCM 1097 (1946).

13. Fisher v Comm, 132 F2d 383 (CCA 9) (1942); Kinney v Anglim, 43 F Supp 431 (1941); Phillips, note 11, supra; Gates, 1 TCM 354 (1942); Strekalovsky v Delaney, 78 F Supp 556 (1948).

14. Note 10, supra.

15. Rev Rul 54–91, IRB, 1954–1 CB 207.

§ 495. The Annual Exclusion; Gifts to Minors; Transfers Under "Gifts to Minors" Statutes; Gift, Estate and Income Tax Effect.

A large number of states have adopted statutes permitting gifts of securities, and in many cases gifts of money to minors, without the appointment of a guardian, but providing for reservation of management powers by the donor or an adult member of the minor's family. It is held that the Gift Tax exclusion is allowable in the case of such gifts.[16] But when the donor is the trustee, if he dies before the minor attains his majority, his control over the property would make it includible in his estate.[17] The enthusiasm over these statutes has been further dampened by a ruling that if the income is used to discharge a legal obligation to support the minor, the income will be taxable to the obligor.[18]

§ 496. Deductions; Specific Exemption; Generally.

It will be recalled that the Gift Tax is based upon the amount of taxable gifts, which is the total amount of gifts made during the calendar year, less the statutory deductions.[19] The first of these deductions is the specific exemption.

In computing taxable gifts for the calendar year, there is allowed as a deduction *in the case of a citizen or resident* an exemption of $30,000., less the aggregate of the amounts claimed and allowed as specific exemption in the computation of Gift Taxes for the calendar year 1932 and all calendar years intervening between that calendar year and the calendar year for which the tax is being computed under the laws applicable to such years.[20]

Several matters must be noted in considering the specific exemption. As in the case of the Estate Tax, residents or citizens are treated differently than nonresidents not citizens. Except as otherwise provided in a tax convention between the United States and another country, a donor who was a nonresident not a citizen of the United States at the time a gift or gifts were made is not entitled to the exemption.[1] There are Gift Tax conventions between the United States and Australia and Japan. It will have been noted that the annual exclusion is not so limited.

16. Rev Rul 56–86, IRB, 1956–1 CB 449.

17. Lober v US, 346 US 335, 98 L ed 15, 74 S Ct 98 (1953).

18. Rev Rul 56-484, 1956–2 CB 23.

19. § 479, supra.

20. IRC, § 2521 (1954 Code).

1. Reg, § 25.2521–1(a); De Goldschmidt-Rothschild, 9 TC 325 (1947); Fara Forni, 22 TC 975 (1954).

It must then be noted that the exemption is not limited to the calendar year, but is a lifetime exemption, and at the option of the donor, may be taken in the full amount of $30,000. in a single calendar year, or be spread over a period of years in such amounts as the donor sees fit, but after the limit has been reached, no further exemption is allowable.[2] Here again, unlike the annual exclusion, there is no question of whether the interest is a present or future one, nor the number of persons to whom gifts have been made. The exemption may be applied to future interests as well as present interests, and to any number of gifts to any number of donees. Where the taxpayer in error takes no part of the exemption in a particular year, he may thereafter recompute his return,[3] and may do so even in a proceeding before the Tax Court.[4] If on the other hand, the taxpayer uses part of his exemption in the belief that there has been a completed gift, when in fact there has been none, the part so used is still available.[5] But where the taxpayer made gifts in 1932, 1933 and 1934 and used her exemption in the returns for 1932 and 1934, which were timely filed, but did not file the 1933 return until 1941, it was held that she could not claim the exemption in the 1933 return.[6] The specific exemption was $50,000. for the years prior to 1936, $40,000. for the years 1936 through 1942, and has been $30,000. since.

Finally, it must be noted, that the specific exemption to be used in the computation of the tax is $30,000. The amount by which the specific exemption claimed and allowed in Gift Tax returns for prior calendar years exceeds $30,000. is includible in determining the aggregate sum of taxable gifts for preceding calendar years.[7] As has been noted,[8] gifts made in prior calendar years must be taken into consideration in computing the tax on gifts made in the current calendar year. Therefore, when gifts were made at a time when the specific exemption was greater than $30,000., in determining the aggregate sum of the taxable gifts for preceding years, the total of the amounts allowed as

2. Reg, § 25.2521–1(a).

3. Richardson v Comm, 126 F2d 569 (CCA 2) (1942).

4. Crellin, 46 BTA 1152 (1942); Danner, 3 TC 638 (1944).

5. Schmidlapp, 43 BTA 829 (1941); Schuhmacher, 8 TC 453 (1947); Special Ruling, Aug 9 and Sept 6, 1955, Carl T. Palmer; Rev Rul 55–709, IRB, 1955–2 CB 609.

6. Meyer, 2 TC 291, aff'd 149 F2d 642 (CCA 8) (1943).

7. Reg, § 25.2521–1(c); Blaffer, BTA mem op, Dec. 12, 218–C (1941).

8. § 398, supra.

deductions, for the specific exemption, under Section 2521 and the corresponding provisions of prior laws may not exceed a total of $30,000. Thus, if the only preceding years during which the donor made gifts were 1940 and 1941 (at which time the specific exemption allowable was $40,000.) and in his return for those years the donor claimed deductions totaling $40,000. for the specific exemption and reported taxable gifts totaling $110,000., nevertheless, in determining the aggregate sum of the taxable gifts for preceding years, the deductions for the specific exemption may not exceed a total of $30,000., and the aggregate sum of his taxable gifts for preceding years will be $120,000., instead of the $110,000. reported on his returns for preceding years.[9] The practical effect of this is to reduce the specific exemption applicable in former years to that in effect at the present time, not by increasing the amount of tax due in the prior year or years, but by increasing the tax due on gifts made after 1942. As we shall see, the Tax Court is not bound by the determination of the tax in a prior year.[10] The fact that the statute of limitations has run on the prior year does not affect the right to make the correct computation for the current year.[11] The statute creates a special rule in the case of valuation of certain gifts for preceding years.[12] It will be discussed in the chapter on computation of the tax.[13]

§ 497. Deductions; Specific Exemption; Gifts by Husband or Wife to Third Party.

The specific exemption is a personal exemption. No part of a donor's lifetime specific exemption of $30,000. may be deducted from the value of a gift attributable to his, or her, spouse where a husband and wife consent to have the gifts made during a calendar year considered as made one half by each of them.[14] The gift-splitting provisions of Section 2513 do not authorize the filing of a joint Gift Tax return nor permit a donor to claim any of his, or her, spouse's specific exemption. For example, if a husband has no specific exemption remaining available, but his wife does, and the husband makes a gift to which his wife consents (or the wife makes a gift to which the husband consents), the specific exemption remaining available may be claimed only

9. Reg, § 25.2504–1(b).
10. Farish, 2 TC 291 (1943).
11. Note 10, supra.

12. IRC, § 2504(c) (1954 Code).
13. Chap 9, infra.
14. See §§ 471 et seq, supra.

on the return of the wife, with respect to one half of the gift. The husband may not claim any specific exemption, since he has none available.[15]

It is this situation which may determine whether spouses should treat gifts to third parties as split-gifts. Since such gifts may be separately treated for each calendar year, being treated in one year as split-gifts, and in another as individual gifts, in a particular year it may be less costly to treat a gift as an individual one.

§ 498. Deductions; Charitable and Similar Gifts; Citizens or Residents.

The second deduction referred to in the Gift Tax statute is that for charitable and similar gifts. The statute divides such gifts into those made by citizens or residents[16] and those made by nonresidents not citizens.[17]

In computing taxable gifts for the calendar year, there may be deducted *in the case of a citizen or resident* the amount of all gifts made during such calendar year to or for the use of—

(1) the United States, any State, Territory, or any political subdivision thereof, or the District of Columbia, for *exclusively* public purposes;

(2) a corporation, or trust, or community chest, fund, or foundation, organized and operated *exclusively* for religious, charitable, scientific, literary, or educational purposes, including the encouragement of art and the prevention of cruelty to children or animals, *no part of the net earnings* of which inures to the benefit of any private shareholder or individual, and no *substantial* part of the activities of which is carrying on *propaganda,* or otherwise attempting to *influence legislation;*

(3) a fraternal society, order, or association, operating under the lodge system, but only if such gifts are to be used *exclusively* for religious, charitable, scientific, literary, or educational purposes, including the encouragement of art and the prevention of cruelty to children or animals;

(4) posts or organizations of war veterans, or auxiliary units or societies of any such posts or organizations, if such posts, organizations, units, or societies *are organized in the United States* or any of its possessions, and if *no part of their net earn-*

15. Reg, § 25.2521–1(b).   17. IRC, § 2522(b) (1954 Code).
16. IRC, § 2522(a) (1954 Code).

ings inures to the benefit of any private shareholder, or individual.[18]

The provision, while not identical with that under the Estate Tax statute,[19] is substantially the same, except that gifts to veterans organizations must be to those organized in the United States instead of incorporated by Act of Congress, and there is omitted from the Gift Tax statute the provision with respect to the termination of a power of appointment. The omission is due to the fact that it is not required in the Gift Tax statute, since the exercise or release of a power is a taxable transfer,[20] and if for a charitable beneficiary would be deductible.

In the case of citizens or residents of the United States there is no limitation that the gifts must be used within the United States, or that the beneficiaries be domestic corporations or societies,[1] as we shall see there is in the case of nonresidents not citizens.

§ 499. Deductions; Charitable and Similar Gifts; Uses Qualifying.

As in the case of the Estate Tax, the Gift Tax statute prescribes definite tests for the allowance of the deduction in the case of citizens or residents. There is provided the organizations qualifying, the purpose of the gift, and actions which will disqualify. The right to the deduction is controlled by the same principles applicable in the case of the Estate Tax.[2] It will be noted that exclusivity is the test for all except veterans organizations.[3] In the case of religious, charitable, scientific, etc., organizations, and veterans organization, no part of the net earnings may inure to the benefit of any private shareholder or individual,[4] and in the case of organizations engaged in religious, charitable, scientific etc. purposes, other than fraternal societies so engaged, no substantial part of their activities must be engaging in propaganda or influencing legislation.[5] The statute differs in this respect from the Estate Tax statute, which applies such limitation also to fraternal societies.[6]

While cases decided under the Estate Tax are generally ap-

---

18. Note 16, supra.
19. See § 245, supra.
20. § 463, supra.
1. Reg, § 25.2522(a)–1(b).
2. § 246, supra.

3. IRC, § 2522(a)(1)(2)(3) (1954 Code).
4. IRC, § 2522(a)(2)(4) (1954 Code).
5. IRC, § 2522(a)(2) (1954 Code).
6. IRC, § 2055(a)(3) (1954 Code).

plicable,[7] the differences noted above must be considered in a particular case. Under the Gift Tax statute, gifts to the following have been held qualified for the deduction: the Foundation of the New York State Bar Association,[8] the Birth Control League of Massachusetts,[9] a private corporation entirely devoted to making charitable donations, help being given in small amounts to relatives of the principal donor,[10] the United States Olympic Association,[11] the Pacific War Memorial Commission,[12] a charitable foundation whose legislative activities were not substantial,[13] and a nonprofit organization organized exclusively for educational purposes whose only activity was the renting of its property at cost to an exempt school association.[14]

On the other hand gifts to the following have been held not to be allowable as deductions: for the promotion of "Lumia", the art of light in motion, where the money could be withdrawn and used by an individual,[15] a trust for the education of named relatives of the settlor, with provision that any funds not so expended be used for the education of members of a church of which the relatives were not members,[16] and the Foundation for World Government.[17]

There are special statutory provisions with respect to gifts to certain Federal agencies and organizations.[18]

Certain gifts for charitable and similar purposes which would otherwise be deductible, may be disallowed because of prohibited transactions by the beneficiary. The provision in the Gift Tax statute[19] and Regulations[20] is the same as that in the Estate Tax and has been discussed previously.[1]

§ 500. Deductions; Charitable and Similar Gifts; Transfers Not Exclusively for Charitable Etc., Purposes.

When a gift is made for the benefit of one or more individuals for life or a term of years, and the remainder gifted to charity, or the charity is to receive a gift only in certain contingencies, the same questions arise under the Gift Tax as under the Estate

7. Note 2, supra.
8. Special Ruling, Oct 17, 1950.
9. Faulkner, 42 BTA 1019 (1940).
10. Mallery, 40 BTA 778 (1939); Murphy, 13 TCM 17 (1949).
11. Special Ruling, Apr. 15, 1952.
12. Rev Rul 54–220, IRB, 1954–1 CB 65.
13. Davis, 22 TC 1091 (1954).
14. Simpson, 2 TC 963 (1943).
15. Bolton, 1 TC 717 (1943).
16. Crellin, 46 BTA 1152 (1942).
17. Blaine, 22 TC 1195 (1954).
18. IRC, § 2522(d) (1954 Code).
19. IRC, § 2522(c) (1954 Code).
20. Reg, § 25.2522(c)–1.
1. § 248, supra.

Tax.[2] Those questions concern valuation of the gift and determination of whether the charity will ever receive anything.

If a trust is created or property is limited for both a charitable and a private purpose, deduction may be taken of the value of the charitable beneficial interest only insofar as that interest is presently ascertainable, and hence severable from the noncharitable interest. Thus, if money or property is placed in trust to pay the income to an individual during his life or for a term of years, and then to pay the principal to a charitable organization, the present value of the remainder is deductible.[3] But if the amount of the beneficial interest cannot be determined, no deduction can be allowed.[4] This latter situation arises largely in connection with contingent gifts.

If as of the date of the gift a transfer for charitable purposes is dependent upon the performance of some act or the happening of a precedent event in order that it might become effective, no deduction is allowable unless the possibility that the charitable transfer will not become effective is so remote as to be negligible. If an estate or interest passes to or is vested in charity on the date of the gift and the estate or interest would be defeated by the performance of some act or the happening of some event, the occurrence of which appeared to be highly improbable on the date of the gift, the deduction is allowable. If the donee or trustee is empowered to divert the property or fund, in whole or in part, to a use or purpose which would have rendered it, to the extent that it is subject to such power, not deductible had it been directly so given by the donor, the deduction will be limited to that portion of the property or fund which is exempt from the exercise of the power. The deduction is not allowed in the case of a transfer in trust conveying a present interest in income if by reason of all the conditions and circumstances surrounding the transfer it appears that the charity may not receive the beneficial enjoyment of the interest. For example, assume that assets placed in trust consist of stock in a corporation the fiscal policies of which are controlled by the donor and his family, that the trustees and remaindermen are likewise members of the donor's family, and that the governing instrument contains

2. See §§ 250, 251, supra.

3. Reg, § 25.2522(a)–2(a); Dumaine, 16 TC 1035 (1951); Thatcher, 38 BTA 336 (1938); ET 15, 1940–1 CB 234; Brown v Deputy, 30 F Supp 860 (1940);

Rev Rul 57–506, IRB, 1957–44 p. 10; Rev Rul 55–275, IRB, 1955–1 CB 295.

4. Mason, 46 BTA 682 (1942); Guggenheim, 1 TC 845 (1943).

[Harris]—43

no adequate guarantee of the requisite income to the charitable organization. Under such circumstances, no deduction will be allowed. Similarly, if the trustees were not members of the donor's family but had no power to sell or otherwise dispose of closely held stock, or otherwise insure the requisite enjoyment of income to the charitable organization, no deduction would be allowed.[5]

Thus, where the remainder interest which a charity may receive under the terms of an irrevocable trust is based upon the contingency that the life tenants, aged 40 and 50 years, respectively on the date of the gift, die without either being survived by issue, the gift to the charity is so wholly uncertain that no deduction may be allowed.[6] The same result would follow where the donor could increase the amounts payable to life beneficiaries out of the corpus.[7] Even though at the time the case reached the Tax Court the contingency had been determined, since it was not determinable at the date of the gift, the deduction was disallowed.[8] The question has arisen more frequently in Estate Tax cases which have been referred to.[9]

§ 501. Deductions; Charitable and Similar Gifts; Nonresidents Not Citizens.

The statute deals separately with charitable and similar gifts by nonresidents not citizens.[10] The deduction is governed by the same rules as those applying to gifts by citizens or residents, *subject, however, to the following exceptions:*

(1) If the gift is made to or for the use of a corporation, *the corporation must be one created or organized under the laws of the United States* or of any State or Territory thereof.

(2) If the gift is made to or for the use of a trust, community chest, fund, or foundation, or a fraternal order or association operating under the lodge system, the gift must be *for use within the United States* exclusively for religious, charitable, scientific, literary or educational purposes, including encouragement of art and the prevention of cruelty to children or animals.[11]

The Estate Tax statute has similar limitations with respect to the estates of nonresidents not citizens.[12]

5. Reg, § 25.2522(a)–2(b).
6. Rev Rul 55–483, IRB, 1955–2 CB 391.
7. ET 6, XIV–1 CB 381; see also Mason, note 4, supra.

8. Guggenheim, note 3, supra.
9. § 250, supra.
10. IRC, § 2522(b) (1954 Code).
11. Reg, § 25.2522(b)–1.
12. § 258, supra.

§ 502. Deductions; Marital Deduction; Generally.

As we have seen,[13] in order to remove the inequality which existed between residents of community property law states and noncommunity property law states, the Revenue Act of 1948 initiated the marital deduction as applicable to the Estate Tax. At the same time the concept was introduced to the Gift Tax statute, by allowing the marital deduction in the case of interspouse gifts and permitting gifts to third parties by either spouse to be treated at their election as made one half by each. The latter provision has been discussed heretofore.[14] The statute was amended by the 1954 Code, applying to gifts made in the calendar year 1955 and thereafter, to permit the deduction for legal life estates and a portion thereof, if coupled with the required general power of appointment.

As Congress pointed out at the time of the introduction of the marital deduction, it was allowed with respect to gifts *only for gifts made after the date of the enactment of the bill.*[15] *It is not allowed in the case of gifts by nonresident aliens,* but is allowed in the case of a gift by a citizen or resident to his nonresident alien spouse. It was further noted that while the *Estate Tax* marital deduction was allowed *for the entire value* of an interest in property passing, with a limitation on the aggregate of 50% of the adjusted gross estate, the *Gift Tax* marital deduction is limited to *half the value of the gift* of an interest in property.[16]

The 1954 Code also applied to community property, the rules respecting conversion thereof into separate property, which were in effect except between 1943 and the date of the enactment of the original marital deduction. Some of the provisions of the Estate Tax statute are not carried into the Gift Tax because they do not apply to inter vivos gifts.

The statute is complex, but most of the problems which it presents have been determined in connection with the Estate Tax rather than the Gift Tax.[17]

§ 503. Deductions; Marital Deduction; Deductible and Nondeductible Interests; Generally.

The statute does not use the terms "deductible" and "nondeductible" interests, but states that where a donor who is a citizen

---

13. § 225, supra.
14. §§ 471 et seq, supra.
15. § 372, Rev Act 1948, effective Apr. 2, 1948.
16. Sen Fin Comm Report, § 372, Rev Act 1948.
17. See §§ 226 et seq, supra.

or resident transfers during the calendar year by gift an interest
in property to a donee who at the time of the gift is the donor's
spouse, there shall be allowed as a deduction in computing taxable gifts for the calendar year an amount with respect to such
interest equal to one half of its value.[18] It then proceeds to
enumerate interests which will not be entitled to the deduction.[19]
These are nondeductible interests, as is any interest not included
in the total amount of gifts made during the calendar year. Examples of the latter are tenancies by the entirety, where an election is not made to treat its creation as a gift,[20] and certain property settlements,[1] which are not included in the total amount of
gifts.[2]

§ 503A. Deductions; Marital Deduction; Life Estate or Other Terminable Interests; Generally.

The statute[3] denies the marital deduction with respect to gifts
to a spouse which are "terminable interests," under the circumstances noted unless such interest comes within one of the exceptions[4] of the statute.

If a donor transfers a terminable interest in property to the
donee spouse, the marital deduction is disallowed with respect
to the transfer *if the donor spouse also—*

(1) Transferred an interest in the same property to another
donee,[5] *or*

(2) Retained an interest in the same property in himself,[6] *or*

(3) Retained a power to appoint an interest in the same property.[7]

Under these circumstances, if the other donee, the donor, or
the possible appointee, may, by reason of the transfer or retention, possess or enjoy any part of the property after the termination or failure of the interest therein transferred to the donee
spouse, no marital deduction may be taken with respect to the
transfer to the donee spouse.[8]

For the purposes of the section a distinction is to be drawn
between "property" as such term is used in the section, and an
"interest in property." The "property" referred to is the under-

18. IRC, § 2523(a) (1954 Code).
19. IRC, § 2523(b) (1954 Code).
20. §§ 450 et seq, supra.
1. §§ 455, 456, supra.
2. Reg, § 25.2523(a)–1(b).
3. IRC, § 2523(b) (1954 Code).

4. IRC, § 2523(d)(e) (1954 Code).
5. § 504, infra.
6. § 505, infra.
7. § 506, infra.
8. Reg, § 25.2523(b)–1(a)(2).

lying property in which various interests exist; each such interest is not, for this purpose, to be considered as "property." A "terminable interest" in property is an interest which will terminate or fail on the lapse of time or on the occurrence or failure to occur of some contingency. Life estates, terms for years, annuities, patents, and copyrights are therefore terminable interests. However, a bond, note, or similar contractual obligation, the discharge of which would not have the effect of an annuity or term for years, is not a terminable interest.[9] The statement that annuities, patents and copyrights are terminable interests stems from the examples given in the Senate Finance Committee's Report on the 1948 Act, but the Regulations concede in the examples furnished, that a nonrefund annuity, or with refund payable to the holder of the annuity, and a patent which expires at the time of the termination of the interest of the donee, will qualify for the marital deduction.[10] The Estate Tax Regulation provides that if a decedent transfers to his spouse all the interest he ever had in a term for years, a patent, or any other terminable interest, the interest of the spouse is a deductible interest if it is not otherwise disqualified.[11]

§ 504. Deductions; Marital Deduction; Property Which Another Donee May Possess or Enjoy.

The statutory definition of nondeductible terminable interests contains but two subdivisions.[12] The first subdivision, however, treats of two different situations. These are transfers in which either the donor or a person other than the donor's spouse may possess or enjoy any part of the property after the termination of the spouse's interest.[13]

No marital deduction is allowable with respect to the transfer to the donee spouse of a terminable interest, *in case*—

(1) The donor transferred (for less than an adequate and full consideration in money or money's worth) an interest in the same property to any person other than the donee spouse (or the estate of such spouse), *and*

(2) By reason of such transfer, such person (or his heirs or assigns) may possess or enjoy any part of such property

---

9. Reg, § 25.2523(b)–1(a)(3).
10. Reg, § 25.2523(b)–1(b)(6)(iii)
(vi).
11. Reg, § 20.2056(b)–1(c).
12. Note 3, supra.
13. IRC, § 2523(b)(1) (1954 Code).

after the termination or failure of the interest therein transferred to the donee spouse.[14]

In determining whether the donor transferred an interest in property to any person other than the donee spouse, it is immaterial whether the transfer to the person other than the donee spouse was made at the same time as the transfer to such spouse or at any earlier time.[15]

Except in the case of a life estate with power of appointment in the donee, *if at the time of the transfer it is impossible to ascertain the particular person or persons who may receive a property interest* transferred by the donor, *such interest is* considered as transferred *to a person other than the donee spouse* for the purpose of the section. This rule is particularly applicable in the case of a transfer of a property interest by the donor subject to a reserved power.[16] Under this rule, any property interest over which the donor reserved a power to revest the beneficial title in himself, or over which the donor reserved the power to name new beneficiaries or to change the interests of the beneficiaries as between themselves, is for the purposes of the section, considered as transferred to a "person other than the donee spouse". Thus an irrevocable transfer with the income payable to the wife for ten years, the corpus thereafter to be distributed to the wife and children in such proportions as the trustee determined, would be a transfer to a person other than the donee spouse. The same would be true if at the termination of the trust the corpus was payable to the wife, but the donor retained the power to revest title in himself.[17]

The term "person other than the donee spouse" includes the possible unascertained takers of a property interest, as, for example, the members of a class to be ascertained in the future. If the donor created a power of appointment over a property interest, other than the life estate with power of appointment in the donee spouse, the term "person other than the donee spouse" refers to the possible appointees and takers in default (other than the spouse) of such property interest.[18]

An exercise or release at any time by the donor (either alone or in conjunction with any person) of a power to appoint an interest in property, even though not otherwise a transfer by him,

14. Reg, § 25.2523(b)–1(b)(1).
15. Reg, § 25.2523(b)–1(b)(2).
16. See §§ 422 et seq, supra.

17. Reg, § 25.2523(b)–1(b)(3).
18. Reg, § 25.2523(b)–1(b)(4).

shall, in determining for the purpose of the section whether he transferred an interest in such property to a person other than the donee spouse, be considered as a transfer by him.[19]

§ 505. Deductions; Marital Deduction; Property Which the Donor May Enjoy.

The second kind of transfer of a terminable interest to a donee spouse for which no marital deduction is allowable, is one in which—

(1) The donor retained in himself an interest in the same property, *and*

(2) By reason of such retention, the donor (or his heirs or assigns) may possess or enjoy any part of the property after the termination or failure of the interest transferred to the donee spouse. However, this would not be so if the transfer was the creation of a joint tenancy or tenancy by the entirety the creation of which was treated as a gift.[20]

§ 506. Deductions; Marital Deduction; Retention by Donor of Power to Appoint.

The third kind of transfer of a terminable interest to a donee spouse for which no marital deduction is allowable, is one in which—

(1) The donor had, immediately after the transfer, the power to appoint an interest in the same property, *and*

(2) The donor's power was exercisable (either alone or in conjunction with any person) in such manner that the appointee may possess or enjoy any part of the property after the termination or failure of the interest transferred to the donee spouse.[1]

For the purposes of the section the donor is to be considered as having, immediately after the transfer to the donee spouse, such power to appoint even though the power cannot be exercised until after the lapse of time, upon the occurrence of an event or contingency, or upon the failure of an event or contingency to occur. It is immaterial whether the power retained by the donor was a taxable power of appointment[2] under the statute.[3]

19. Reg, § 25.2523(b)–1(b)(5).
20. Reg, § 25.2523(b)–1(c).
1. Reg, § 25.2523(b)–1(d)(1).
2. §§ 457 et seq, supra.
3. Reg, § 25.2523(b)–1(d)(2).

§ 507. Deductions; Marital Deduction; Interest in Unidentified Assets.

The statute provides that where the assets out of which, or the proceeds of which, the interest transferred to the donee spouse may be satisfied include a particular asset or assets with respect to which no deduction would be allowed if such asset or assets were transferred from the donor to such spouse, then the value of the interest transferred to such spouse shall, for purposes of the statute, be reduced by the aggregate value of such particular assets.[4] These are commonly referred to as "tainted assets".

In order for the section to apply, *two circumstances must co-exist, as follows:*

(1) The property transferred to the donee spouse must be payable out of a group of assets. An example of a property interest payable out of a group of assets is a right to a share of the corpus of a trust upon its termination.

(2) The group of assets out of which the property interest is payable must include one or more particular assets which, if transferred to the donee spouse would not qualify for the marital deduction. Therefore, the provision is not applicable merely because a group of assets includes a terminable interest, but would only be applicable if the terminable interest were non-deductible.[5]

If both of these circumstances are present, the marital deduction with respect to such property interest may not exceed one half of the excess, if any, of its value over the aggregate value of the particular asset or assets which, if transferred to the donee spouse, would not qualify for the marital deduction.[6]

§ 508. Deductions; Marital Deduction; Joint Interests.

A joint interest created by the donor between his spouse and himself is a terminable interest for which no marital deduction would be allowable, *except that the statute provides* that if the interest is transferred to the donee spouse as sole joint tenant with the donor, or as tenant by the entirety, the interest of the donor in the property which exists solely by reason of the possibility that the donor may survive the donee spouse, or that there may occur a severance of the tenancy, shall not for the purposes of determining whether the interest is a nondeductible termi-

4. IRC, § 2523(c) (1954 Code).   6. Reg, § 25.2523(c)-1(c).
5. Reg, § 25.2523(c)-1(b).

nable interest, be considered as an interest retained by the donor in himself.[7]

This exception would only apply if at the time of the creation of the tenancy the donor spouse elected to treat it as a gift, or at the time of an addition the addition was treated as a gift, or upon termination of the tenancy. If prior to termination transfers were not treated as gifts, no marital deduction could be claimed at the time of contribution.[8]

§ 509. Deductions; Marital Deduction; Life Estate With Power of Appointment in Donee.

A second exception to the terminable interest rule is created by the statute where the donor transfers an interest in property, if by such transfer his spouse is entitled for life to *all the income from the entire interest, or all the income from a specific portion thereof,* payable annually, or at more frequent intervals, with power in the donee spouse *to appoint the entire interest, or such specific portion* (exercisable in favor of such donee spouse, or of the estate of such donee spouse, or in favor of either, whether or not in each case the power is exercisable in favor of others), and with *no power in any other person* to appoint any part of such interest, or such portion, to any person other than the donee spouse. The provision applies only if, by such transfer, such power in the donee spouse to appoint the interest, or such portion, whether exercisable by will or during life, is exercisable by such spouse alone and in all events.[9]

This provision is in all substantial respects identical with the Estate Tax provision[10] except for the substitution of the words surviving spouse for the words donee spouse. The Gift Tax Regulations[11] follow the wording of the Estate Tax Regulations, and the provisions thereof have been previously discussed[12] and are equally applicable.

It must be noted that the 1954 Code made two substantial changes with respect to the allowance of the marital deduction. In the case of the marital deduction, *gifts made prior to the calendar year 1955* did not qualify for the marital deduction if the gift was a legal life estate with power of appointment. It

7. IRC, § 2523(d) (1954 Code).
8. See §§ 450 et seq, supra.
9. IRC, § 2523(e) (1954 Code).
10. IRC, § 2056(b)(5) (1954 Code).

11. Reg, § 25.2523(e)–1(a)(e)(f)(g)(h).
12. See § 234, supra.

was required under the former statute that the gift be in trust.[13] Under that statute, even though the gift was made in trust, it did not qualify if it consisted of a portion of the transferred property. The 1954 Code removed both of these limitations. As we have noted, the Technical Amendments Act of 1958 amended the Estate Tax provisions of the 1939 Code so as to permit refunds in certain cases where the marital deduction was denied to legal life estates and portion trusts.[13a] It did not amend the Gift Tax statute.

The effect of this exception is that if the donee spouse is given either a legal life estate or is the income beneficiary of a trust, *and in addition* she has the sole and unlimited power to appoint her interest *to herself or her estate,* the interest will qualify for the marital deduction.

§ 510. Deductions; Marital Deduction; Entire Interest or Specific Portion.

One of the exceptions to the terminable interest rule, is, as we have seen in the preceding section, the case where the donee spouse receives for life all the income from the entire interest or a specific portion of the entire interest, or a specific portion of all the income from the entire interest.

It has also been noted that the qualification of a portion was new to the 1954 Code and *applies only to gifts made in the calendar year 1955 and thereafter.* Under the 1939 Code the marital deduction was disallowed under the Estate Tax in a number of cases in which the spouse was entitled to a portion.[14] As noted above, the Technical Amendments Act of 1958 amended the Estate Tax provisions of the 1939 Code.

Here again the Gift Tax statute and the Estate Tax statute are identical except for the substitution of donee spouse for surviving spouse. The Gift Tax Regulation,[15] therefore, follows the wording of the Estate Tax Regulations,[16] the terms of which have been treated previously.[17]

§ 511. Deductions; Marital Deduction in Community Property Law States.

Because the purpose of the Revenue Act of 1948 was to equalize the tax status of citizens of community property law states and

13. IRC,   § 1004(a)(3)(E)   (1939 Code).
13a. See § 225, supra.
14. § 237, supra.

15. Reg, § 25.2523(e)–1(b)(c)(d).
16. Reg, § 20.2056(b)–5(b)(c)(d).
17. Note 14, supra.

the other states, it became necessary to establish a special rule for the allowance of the Gift Tax marital deduction in the case of community property, such states having in their statutes a built-in marital deduction, since gifts in community property law states from one spouse to another are considered made of only one half of the property. The allowance of the marital deduction on that half would result in a double marital deduction. Therefore, as in the case of the Estate Tax,[18] the Gift Tax statute provides a special rule for the marital deduction.

The marital deduction is allowable with respect to any transfer by a donor to his spouse *only to the extent* that such transfer can be shown to represent a gift of property which was not, at the time of the gift, held as "community property". The burden of establishing the extent to which a transfer represents a gift of property not so held rests upon the donor.[19]

Any property held by the donor and his spouse as community property under the law of any State, Territory, or possession of the United States, or of any foreign country, except property in which the donee spouse had at the time of the gift merely an expectant interest is "community property". The donee spouse is regarded as having, at any particular time, merely an expectant interest in property at that time held by the donor and herself as community property under the laws of any State, Territory, or possession of the United States, or of any foreign country, if, in case such property were transferred by gift into the separate property of the donee spouse, the entire value of such property (and not merely one half of it), would be treated as the amount of the gift.[20]

Separate property acquired by the donor as a result of a "conversion", after December 31, 1941, of property held by him and the donee spouse as community property (except such property in which the donee spouse had at the time of the conversion merely an expectant interest), into their separate property, subject to the limitation with respect to value hereafter, is "community property".[1]

Property acquired by the donor in exchange (by one exchange

18. IRC, § 2056(f) (1954 Code).

19. IRC, § 2523(f)(1) (1954 Code); Reg, § 25.2523(f)–1(a).

20. IRC, § 2523(f)(2) (1954 Code); Reg, § 25.2523(f)–1(b)(i).

1. IRC, § 2523(f)(3) (1954 Code); Reg, § 25.2523(f)–1(b)(ii).

or a series of exchanges) for separate property resulting from such conversion is "community property".[2]

The characteristics of property which acquired a noncommunity instead of a community status by reason of an agreement (whether antenuptial or postnuptial) are such that the statute classifies the property as community property of the donor and his spouse in the computation of the marital deduction. In distinguishing property which thus acquired a noncommunity status from property which acquired such a status solely by operation of the community property law, the statute refers to the former category of property as "separate property" acquired as a result of a "conversion" of property held as such "community property". As used in the section the phrase "property held as such community property" is used to denote the body of property comprehended within the community property system; the expression "separate property" includes any noncommunity property, whether held in joint tenancy, tenancy by the entirety, tenancy in common, or otherwise; and the term "conversion" includes any transaction or agreement which transforms property from a community status into a noncommunity status.[3]

The separate property which the statute classifies as community property is not limited to that which was in existence at the time of the conversion. Thus all of the following are within the meaning of the statute: a partition of community property, whereby a portion of the property becomes the separate property of each; a transfer of community property into some other form of ownership, such as a joint tenancy; an agreement that future earnings and gains which would otherwise be community property shall be shared by the spouses as separate property; a change in the form of ownership which causes future rentals which would otherwise have been acquired as community property, to be acquired as separate property.[4]

The statutory rules apply only if the conversion took place after December 31, 1941, and only to the extent stated in the section. The historical background of this provision has been discussed heretofore.[5]

Where the value of the separate property acquired by the donor on conversion exceeds the amount acquired by the donee

2. IRC, § 2523(f)(3) (1954 Code); Reg, § 25.2523(f)–1(b)(iii).

3. Reg, § 25.2523(f)–1(b)(2).

4. Reg, § 25.2523(f)–1(b)(3).

5. §§ 41, 48, supra.

spouse, the statute requires an apportionment to determine the amount held as separate property.[6] The method of computation is illustrated in the succeeding chapter.[7]

When the gift by a spouse is of his or her separate property, it is not within the special rule applying to community property, since the statute specifically provides that a gift otherwise allowable shall be allowed only to the extent that the transfer can be shown to represent property which is not community property.[8] This is an oblique way of saying that noncommunity property is qualified for the marital deduction, if otherwise complying with the requirements of the statute. A gift of separate property, therefore, is treated in the same way as a gift by a spouse in a noncommunity property law state.

§ 512. Deductions; Marital Deduction; Application of Statute.

To those not acquainted with the refinements of the marital deduction, there is encountered difficulty in applying the language thereof to particular facts. The Regulations will be found extremely helpful in such case, since they offer many examples of the application of the various provisions. Thus as examples of nondeductible interests because one other than the donee spouse may possess or enjoy the property after the termination of the spouse's interest, are: a gift to wife for life of income and remainder to A or issue, but if A die without issue the remainder to wife; a refund annuity to wife, with further payments, if any, to A; conveyance to wife for life with remainder to A; gift to A for life with remainder to wife if she survives A, otherwise to B and his heirs; a transfer to wife of rentals reserved out of a prior transfer of real property.[9] On the other hand the purchase of a nonrefund annuity for wife, or refund payable to her estate, or transfer of a patent to wife and A as *tenants in common*, would be deductible because no one other than the spouse could enjoy the interest after the spouse.[10]

An example of an interest in property which the donor may possess or enjoy would be where the donor purchased three annuities for the benefit of his wife and himself. One was payable to the wife for life with refund to the donor, the second provided

6. IRC, § 2523(f)(4) (1954 Code).
7. Chap 9, infra.
8. Note 18, supra.

9. Reg, § 25.2523(b)–1(b)(6)(i–v).
10. Reg, § 25.2523(b)–1(b)(6)(iii, vi).

for payments to the donor for life and, to his wife for life if she survived him, and the third was for the joint lives of the spouses and to the survivor. In each case the interest is nondeductible because the donor may possess or enjoy the interest after the wife.[11]

An example of a nondeductible interest because of the retention of a power to appoint by the donor, is the granting of a power of appointment to the wife for life, on property over which the husband possessed a power of appointment.[12]

An example of a life estate with a power of appointment in the donee spouse which fails to fully qualify because the power is not exercisable by the donee spouse alone and in all events, is a trust for the benefit of the wife for life with power to appoint the entire corpus, but with the right in the trustee to distribute 30% of the corpus to the son at age 35. The marital deduction applies to only 70% of the trust. If the wife had power to appoint one half of the corpus, under similar facts, the marital deduction would apply to one half of 70%, or 35%.[13]

There have been few cases decided under the marital deduction provisions of the Gift Tax statute. An interest in the income of a trust containing only insurance policies does not qualify for the deduction.[14] Gifts of United States Savings Bonds registered in the name of the donee spouse and payable on death to the other spouse are nondeductible terminable interests.[15] A gift of a remainder interest which would be includible in the donee's estate if she died during the term of the trust is entitled to the marital deduction,[16] as is a gift to the committee of an incompetent spouse.[17]

§ 513. Deductions; Marital Deduction; Valuation.

The valuation of property which is the subject of a gift for which the marital deduction is allowable differs in no respect from the valuation of any other gift. The same principles apply as have been treated heretofore.[18]

The Regulation refers only to a remainder interest.[19] If the

---

11. Reg, § 25.2523(b)–1(c)(2).
12. Reg, § 25.2523(b)–1(d)(3).
13. Reg, § 25.2523(e)–1(h), Example 2.
14. Halsted, 28 TC 1069 (1957); Smith, 23 TC 367 (1954).
15. Rev Rul 54–410, IRB, 1954–2 CB 321.
16. Rev Rul 54–470, IRB, 1954–2 CB 320.
17. Letter Ruling, Mar. 16, 1950.
18. §§ 430 et seq, supra.
19. Reg, § 25.2523(a)–1(c).

income from property is made payable to the donor or another individual for life, or for a term of years, with remainder absolutely to the donor's spouse or to her estate, the marital deduction is equal to one half the present value of the remainder. As in all cases, the claim for deduction must be supported by a full statement of the present worth of the interest. Computation of such interests is treated hereafter.[20]

§ 514. Deductions; Extent of Deduction.

The statute provides that the deduction for charitable and similar gifts and the marital deduction shall be allowed *only to the extent that such gifts are included in the amount of gifts against which such deductions are applied.*[1] In the case of the marital deduction, particularly, this has the effect of reducing the amount which would be allowable otherwise. Thus, if a husband makes gifts of present interests in the calendar year to his wife of $5,000., the marital deduction, were it not for the above provision would be $2,500., since the marital deduction is applied before the annual exclusion is taken. But the statute limits the deduction to the extent that the gift to the wife is included in the amount of gifts against which the deduction is applied. Only $2,000. of the $5,000. is so included, because there is excluded $3,000. from such gift. Therefore, the amount of the marital deduction in this case is $2,000. instead of $2,500.[2]

§ 515. Deductions; Marital Deduction; Return.

In reporting gifts for which the marital deduction is claimed, the same information as to value is furnished as in the case of other gifts and entered on Schedule A of Form 709. That form furnishes no specific directions for the manner of reporting property for which the deduction is claimed. Affidavits of value should be furnished in any case where required.[3] If there is a question whether property is or is not community property the supporting affidavits should accompany the return, since the burden is on the donor to establish that the property transferred is not such.[4]

If the gift was made by means of a trust, a certified or verified copy of the trust instrument must be submitted.[5] In such case

---

20. §§ 534, 537, infra.
1. IRC, § 2524 (1954 Code).
2. Reg, § 25.2524–1(a).

3. Note 18, supra.
4. Reg, § 25.2523(f)–1(a).
5. Instruction 13, Form 709.

the District Director will want to ascertain whether the trust complies with the statutory requirements.

The amount of the marital deduction is set forth in Item (h)(2). This amount is *one half of the total* gifts to the spouse which qualify for the deduction, unless the total gifts, less the annual exclusion, if allowable with respect to such gifts, is less in amount than such one half. In that case the amount of the marital deduction, is, as we have seen,[6] limited. Thus, if the gift is of a future interest of a value of $5,000., there is no exclusion, and the marital deduction would be reported as $2,500.

§ 516. Deductions; Nonresidents Not Citizens.

Since in the case of nonresidents not citizens of the United States different treatment is accorded in the matter of the deductions, it may be helpful in conclusion, to summarize the applicable provisions.

Except as otherwise provided in a Gift Tax convention, there being presently but two, with Australia and Japan, respectively, there is no specific exemption.[7]

The deduction for charitable and similar gifts is available to nonresidents not citizens if the gift is made to or for the use of a corporation organized or created in the United States, and in other cases the gift must be for use in the United States.[8] Within these limitations, such gifts are treated the same for citizens or residents as for nonresidents not citizens.

The marital deduction is not allowed in the case of nonresidents not citizens, but the donee spouse may be a nonresident alien, and so long as the gift is made by a citizen or resident, the deduction is allowable.[9]

6. § 513, supra.   8. § 501, supra.
7. § 496, supra.   9. § 502, supra.

CHAPTER 9

COMPUTATION OF FEDERAL GIFT TAX

§ 517. Scope of Chapter.

The ultimate determination in any question involving taxation is the amount of tax payable. In order to arrive at that point many other matters must be considered before computing the tax. It has been our purpose, therefore, to acquaint those concerned with the determination with that which must be known in order to arrive at the point where it is possible to make the computation. Thus, we have considered the nature of the Gift Tax, its relation to the Estate and Income Tax, the preliminary requirements with respect to procedure under the statute, the principles upon which the tax is based, transfers which are taxable as gifts, and those items permissible to reduce the tax payable. Having ascertained the taxable transfers and allowable deductions we are in a position to begin the computations necessary to determine the amount of tax which will be payable.

But computation of the tax is not the only computation required in the preparation of the Gift Tax return. Many other mathematical problems are presented in the return. Some of these of a minor nature have been considered in connection with particular transfers treated heretofore. The more complex situations are grouped in this chapter, concluding with the actual computation of the tax. There will also be demonstrated the manner in which the Gift Tax return is prepared.

§ 518. Real Estate.

Gifts of real estate present first the necessity for valuation which has been treated heretofore.[1] In addition, however, since many gifts of real estate are made in trust, with the gift of either a present or future interest, mathematical computations are required to determine the value of the interest transferred. Those computations are treated hereafter.[2] In the case of tenancies by the entirety, two series of computations may be required. If the creation or subsequent additions are treated as gifts, we have seen that it is necessary to determine the proportionate share of the owners.[3] Upon termination of the tenancy, more involved computations are required, and are discussed hereafter.[4] If the gift is a split-gift, other computations will be necessary, as will be demonstrated.[5]

§ 519. Stocks and Bonds.

In the case of securities listed upon an exchange the only

1. § 431, supra.
2. § 524, infra.
3. §§ 451, 452, supra.
4. §§ 526 et seq, infra.
5. § 532, infra.

computation is averaging of prices as required by the Regulations.[6] If the stock is that of a closely held corporation or the question of blockage enters into the valuation, computations are necessary to fix value, and the method of so doing has been demonstrated.[7]

§ 520. Interests in Business.

Since interests in a business are frequently the subjects of gifts and intrafamily gifts thereof are particularly suspect,[8] computation of the value of the interest transferred will be required. The method of so doing is the same as in the case of the valuation of the stock of a closely held corporation and has been illustrated.[9]

§ 521. Notes; Mortgages.

The primary problem in gifts of notes or mortgages is that of valuation. While it is unusual for a donor to make a gift of a note which is worth less than its face value, such a note may be so valued.[10] It is more usual that a mortgage, the subject of a gift, may be claimed to be worth less than face value. In such case the problem of computation is one of percentage, or the reduction of the mortgage to the equity value. It will also be necessary to compute the interest on either the note or mortgage to the date of the gift.[11]

§ 522. Future Interests; Generally.

As we have seen, in the application of the annual exclusion, the question of whether a gift is of a present interest or a future one is important.[12] So far as taxation of a gift is concerned, however, future interests are subject to the Gift Tax and the specific exemption applies to such interests.[13] Therefore, when there is a gift of a future interest, it becomes necessary to compute its value. We have also seen that even though the gift be of a present interest, where there is a power of invasion, the value of the interest must be ascertainable for the annual exclusion to be allowable. In such case, it becomes necessary to compute the value of the interest. That computation has been

6. § 434, supra.
7. §§ 58, 434, 435, supra.
8. § 448, supra.
9. § 58, supra.

10. § 438, supra.
11. § 65, supra.
12. §§ 480 et seq, supra.
13. § 496, supra.

demonstrated,[14] and is made by the use of actuarial tables, as is the computation of the value of a present interest and a remainder or reversion.

Since many gifts are in trust, a single gift may consist of several parts, such as a life estate for one or more lives and a remainder or reversionary interest. The same may be true of an annuity. The method of computing the value of such separate interests is considered in the succeeding sections.

§ 523. Life Insurance and Annuity Contracts.

Where the donor makes a gift of a life insurance or annuity contract issued by a company regularly engaged in the selling of contracts of that character, the person preparing a Gift Tax return is relieved of any necessity for computation of its value. As we have seen,[15] the computation is made by the insurance company which issued the contract.

When the annuity is not issued by a company regularly engaged in selling such contracts, then the value must be computed by the use of the actuarial tables discussed in the succeeding section.

§ 524. Annuities, Life Estates, Terms for Years, Remainders, Reversions.

In the preceding chapters relating to the Gift Tax, we have discussed many factual situations in which the donor created a trust with income payable to A for life, and the remainder to B, or the donor retains either a life interest or a reversionary interest. The computation in such case of the value of the life estate and of the remainder or reversionary interest is comparatively simple. The same is true of the valuation of the gift of an annuity. By the use of the actuarial tables set forth in the Estate Tax and Gift Tax Regulations, simple mathematics produces the answer. Whether the valuation be for the purpose of either tax, the computation is the same and has been previously demonstrated.[16]

More involved computations may be required, however, when two lives are involved, as where there is a gift of income for the life of A and B, with remainder to charity at the death of the survivor, or the first to die. There may be a contingent joint

14. § 486, supra.   16. §§ 113, 114, 115, supra.
15. § 440, supra.

life remainder. An annuity may be payable for a fixed number of years or until the prior death of the annuitant, or a joint and survivor annuity. There may even be involved many lives, as we have seen.[17] The computation in all such cases is made by the use of the actuarial tables contained in IRS Publication No. 11, the pamphlet to which reference has been made previously.[18] It not only contains such tables, but illustrates the methods to be used in making all of these various computations. No one who is charged with the preparation of Estate or Gift Tax returns should be without it. It is available from the Superintendent of Documents, Washington 25, D. C. at a cost of 35 cents.

§ 525. Community Property.

In the case of community property, the first computation is division of the value of the gift between the spouses. The involved computation arises in determining the amount of the marital deduction when there has been a conversion of community property into separate property after December 31, 1941.[19] The method of computation in such case will be demonstrated hereafter.[20]

§ 526. Tenancy by the Entirety; One Half Income to Each Spouse.

In 1954 and prior years, if a husband transferred property to his wife and himself as tenants by the entirety, he having paid the entire consideration, there was a gift to the wife. As we have seen,[1] under the 1954 Code, such a transaction in 1955 and thereafter, may at the election of the donor be treated as a gift upon creation of the tenancy or upon its termination. As to such gifts prior to 1955, and those treated as gifts thereafter, the value of the gift must be determined. This is done by the use of the tables referred to previously.[2] The computation differs, depending upon whether under the law of the jurisdiction of the property each tenant is entitled to half of the income from the property, or the husband is entitled to all of the income and the wife has only the right of survivorship. The following is the method of computation when each tenant is entitled to half of the income. The computation when the husband is entitled

17. § 486, supra.
18. § 112, supra.
19. §§ 429, 510, supra.

20. § 536, infra.
1. §§ 450 et seq, supra.
2. § 524, supra.

to the entire income is illustrated in the succeeding section.

A husband with $1,000. of his own funds purchases property and causes the title to be taken in himself and his wife as tenants by the entirety. The husband is 45 and the wife 40. The difference in age is five years. By reference to Table IX in the pamphlet referred to,[3] the factor for the combined income and survivorship rights of the older tenant is .44971. The value of the husband's rights in the property is, therefore, $449.71 and the value of the gift to the wife is $550.29.

If the wife is the older, the amounts are reversed, i.e., the factor in the table would be used for her interest.

The table runs from age 25 to age 74, and for differences in age up to 14 years. If the ages or difference in ages is outside the tables it is then necessary to compute the value of the present worth of the right to receive the use of $1,000. until the death of the first to die of two persons of the ages of the spouses. This is the value of the combined right to income, and one half is the right of each. The present worth of $1,000. due at the death of the younger provided the older survives is then computed. This is the value of the husband's right of survivorship. Adding this to half of the value of the right to income gives the husband's interest. The balance is the value of the gift.

§ 527. Tenancy by the Entirety; All Income to Husband.

In some states[4] the husband is entitled to all the income of property held as tenants by the entirety. In such case the value of the wife's right of survivorship must be determined. This is done by the use of the tables in the pamphlet referred to.[5] Table IV is used in the computation.

A wife with $1,000. of her own funds purchases property and takes title in herself and her husband as tenants by the entirety. The wife is 65 and the husband is 72. The present worth of $1,000. due at the death of a person aged 72, provided a person aged 65 survives is .52010 × $1,000., or $520.10. This is the present worth of the wife's right of survivorship. The value of the gift to the husband is therefore the difference between $1,000. and this amount, or $479.90.

---

3. Note 2, supra.   5. Note 2, supra.
4. Massachusetts, North Carolina.

§ 528. Tenancy by the Entirety; Entire Value of Gift Determined Upon Termination of Tenancy.

There has been discussed previously the election afforded a donor spouse of treating a tenancy by the entirety as a gift upon its creation or upon its termination.[6] In such case, upon termination of the tenancy the entire amount of the gift may be required to be determined upon termination, or if part was treated as a gift and part not, that part terminated must be determined. There will be considered in this section the computation of the amount of the gift when the entire value is determined upon termination, and the other cases in the succeeding sections.

In any case in which—

(1) The creation of a tenancy by the entirety (including additions in value thereto), was not treated as a gift, and

(2) The entire consideration for the creation of the tenancy, and any additions in value thereto, was furnished solely by the spouses,[7] the termination of the tenancy (other than by the death of a spouse) always results in the making of a gift by a spouse who receives a smaller share of the proceeds of the termination (whether received in cash, property, or interests in property) than the share of the proceeds attributable to the total consideration furnished by him.[8] Thus, a gift is effected at the time of termination of the tenancy by the spouse receiving less than one half of the proceeds of termination, if such spouse (regardless of age) furnished one half or more of the total consideration for the purchase and improvements, if any of the property held in the tenancy. Also, if one spouse furnished the entire consideration, a gift is made by such spouse to the extent that the other spouse receives any portion of the proceeds of termination.[9]

In computing the value of the gift under these circumstances, it is necessary first to determine the spouse's share of the proceeds attributable to the consideration furnished by him. This share is computed by multiplying the total value of the proceeds of termination by a fraction, the numerator of which is the total consideration furnished by the donor spouse and the denominator of which is the total consideration furnished by both spouses. From this amount there is subtracted the value

6. Note 1, supra.
7. § 451, supra.
8. Note 7, supra.
9. Reg, § 25.2515–3(a).

of the proceeds of termination received by the donor spouse. The amount remaining is the value of the gift. In arriving at the "total consideration furnished by the donor spouse" and the "total consideration furnished by both spouses", for purposes of the computation, the consideration furnished[10] is not reduced by any amounts which otherwise would have been excludable, i.e., the amount of the annual exclusion, in determining the amounts of taxable gifts for the years in which the consideration was furnished. Thus, if in 1955, real property was purchased for $30,000., the husband and wife each contributing $12,000., with a mortgage of $6,000., and in each of the years 1956 and 1957, the husband paid $3,000. on the mortgage, which he did not disclose on his return as a gift in such years, the total consideration furnished by the husband is $18,000. and that by the wife, $12,000.[11]

The section applies as follows: In 1956 the husband furnished $30,000. and the wife furnished $10,000. for the purchase and subsequent improvement of real property held by them as tenants by the entirety. Neither spouse elected to treat the consideration furnished as a gift. The property later sold for $60,000., the husband receiving $35,000. and the wife $25,000. The termination of the tenancy results in a gift to the wife of $10,000., based on the following computation:[12]

$$\frac{\$30,000 \text{ (consideration furnished by husband)}}{\$40,000 \text{ (total consideration furnished by both)}} \times \$60,000 \text{ (proceeds of termination)} = \$45,000$$

$$\$45,000 - \$35,000 \text{ (proceeds received by husband)} = \$10,000 \text{ gift by husband to wife}$$

Where there is a part termination, and a reinvestment of part of the proceeds,[13] it is necessary to determine the value of the gift as to the part terminated, and the share of the tenants in the remainder. Thus, the husband purchases stock of a value of $10,000. When it has a value of $30,000. he and his wife purchase real property as tenants by the entirety, he transferring his shares of stock and she contributing $10,000. The property is sold for $60,000. and the proceeds to the extent of $24,000. is divided between them, the balance being reinvested in a ten-

10. § 450, supra.
11. Reg, § 25.2515–3(b).
12. Reg, § 25.2515–3(c).
13. § 452, supra.

ancy by the entirety. The original tenancy has been terminated only to the extent of $24,000., at which time there is a gift of $6,000. to the wife, computed as follows:

$$\frac{\$30,000 \text{ (consideration furnished by husband)}}{\$40,000 \text{ (total consideration furnished by both)}} \times \$24,000 \text{ (proceeds of termination)} = \$18,000$$

$$\$18,000 - \$12,000 \text{ (proceeds received by husband)} = \$6,000 \text{ gift by husband to wife}$$

Since the tenancy was terminated only in part, with respect to the remaining portion of the tenancy each spouse is considered as having furnished that proportion of the total consideration for the remaining portion of the tenancy as the consideration furnished by him before the sale bears to the total consideration furnished by both spouses before the sale. The consideration furnished by the husband for the reduced tenancy created by the reinvestment of $36,000. of the proceeds is computed as follows:[14]

$$\frac{\$30,000 \text{ (consideration furnished by husband before sale)}}{\$40,000 \text{ (total consideration furnished by both before sale)}} \times \$36,000 \text{ (consideration for reduced tenancy)} = \$27,000$$

The consideration furnished by the husband for the reduced tenancy is, therefore, $27,000. and that furnished by the wife $9,000.

§ 529. Tenancy by the Entirety; Value of Gift on Termination When Entire Consideration Treated as Gift.

When all of the consideration furnished for the creation of a tenancy by the entirety is treated as a gift, upon termination of the tenancy a gift may result if the spouse surrenders a property interest in the tenancy and receives an amount less than the value of the property interest surrendered. Such situation may occur where the tenancy was created by one spouse with his own funds prior to the calendar year 1955, or if the tenancy was created after 1954 and the election was made to

14. Note 12, supra.

treat it as a gift. In the example illustrated previously,[15] the husband's interest in the property was $449.71 and that of the wife $550.29. If upon the termination of the tenancy, there were received $1,000., of which each received half, there would take place at that time a gift from the wife to the husband of $50.29.[16] If the termination took place five years after the gift, the factors would be different, so that the respective interests would differ.

If it is assumed that at the date of the sale of the property, the respective spouses were 50 and 45, and the property was sold for $2,000., then the value of the husband's interest would be $2,000. $\times$ .44284 or $885.68, and the wife's interest $1,114.32. In such case an equal division of the proceeds would result in a gift to the husband of $114.32.

§ 530. Tenancy by the Entirety; Value Upon Termination Where Both Types of Consideration.

A more complex kind of computation is required when the consideration furnished for the creation of the tenancy by the entirety consists in part of consideration furnished by the spouses after 1954 and not treated as a gift at that time and in part of consideration furnished by the spouses and treated as a gift or furnished by a third party. In that case the amount of the gift is determined.

(1) By determining the value of the gift as to that portion of the proceeds of termination which the consideration not treated as a gift bears to the total consideration;

(2) By determining the value of the gift as to that portion of the proceeds of termination which was treated as a gift;

(3) By subtracting the proceeds of termination received by the donor from the total of the amounts which are to be compared with the proceeds of termination received by a spouse in determining whether a gift was made by that spouse.[17]

For example, assume that consideration of $30,000. was furnished in 1954, and that in 1955 the husband contributed $12,000. and the wife $8,000., the husband's contribution not being treated as a gift. Assume further that between 1957 and 1965 the property appreciated in value by $40,000. and was sold in 1965 for $90,000., of which the husband received $40,000. and the wife

15. § 526, supra.   17. Reg. § 25.2515–4(c).
16. Reg, § 25.2515–4(b).

$50,000. The principles for valuation on termination when all the proceeds are treated as the result of contributions not treated as gifts[18] are applied to $36,000. (20,000/50,000 × $90,000.) in arriving at the amount which is compared with the proceeds of termination received by a spouse. Applying these same principles, this amount in the case of the husband is $19,800. (12,000/20,000 × $36,000.). Similarly the principles for valuation when the entire consideration is treated as a gift[19] are applied to $54,000. ($90,000.—$36,000.), the remaining portion of the proceeds of termination, in arriving at the amount which is compared with the proceeds of termination received by a spouse. If in this case either spouse, without the consent of the other spouse, can bring about a severance of his interest in the tenancy, the amount so determined in the case of the husband would be $27,000. ($\frac{1}{2}$ of $54,000.). The total of the two amounts which are to be compared with the proceeds of termination received by the husband is $46,800. ($19,800. + $27,000.). This sum of $46,800. is then compared with the $40,000. proceeds received by the husband, and the termination of the tenancy has resulted, for Gift Tax purposes, in a transfer of $6,800. by the husband to the wife in 1965.[20]

A further example of the application of the provision follows. X died in 1948 and devised real property to Y and Z (Y's wife) as tenants by the entirety. Under the law of the jurisdiction both spouses are entitled to share equally in the income from, or the enjoyment of, the property, but neither spouse, acting alone, may defeat the right of the survivor of them to the whole of the property. The fair market value at the date of X's death was $100,000. and this amount is the consideration which X furnished toward the creation of the tenancy. In 1955, at which time the fair market value of the property was the same as at the time of X's death, improvements of $50,000. were made to the property, of which Y furnished $40,000. out of his own funds and Z furnished $10,000. out of her funds. Y did not elect to treat his transfer to the tenancy as resulting in the making of a gift in 1955. In 1956 the property was sold for $300,000. and Y and Z each received half of the proceeds. At the time of the sale Y and Z are respectively 45 and 40 on their birthdays nearest the

18. § 528, supra.   20. Note 17, supra.
19. § 529, supra.

date of the gift. The value of the gift made by Y to Z is $19,842, computed as follows:[1]

Amount determined under principles applying when entire amount not treated as gift

(1)

$$\frac{\$50,000 \text{ (consideration not treated as gift in year furnished)}}{\$150,000 \text{ (total consideration furnished)}} \times \$300,000 \text{ (proceeds of termination)} = \begin{array}{c}\$100,000 \text{ (proceeds of termination to which principles for valuation apply when no part of consideration treated as gift)}\end{array}$$

(2)

$$\frac{\$40,000 \text{ (consideration furnished by Y and not treated as gift)}}{\$50,000 \text{ (total consideration not treated as gift)}} \times \$100,000 = \$80,000$$

Amount determined under principles applying when portion of consideration furnished by third party

(3)

$$\$300,000 \text{ (total proceeds of termination)} - \$100,000 \begin{array}{c}\text{(proceeds to which principles for valuation apply when no part of consideration treated as gift)}\end{array} = \$200,000 \begin{array}{c}\text{(proceeds to which principles apply when entire consideration treated as gift)}\end{array}$$

(4)
.44971 (factor for Y's interest) × $200,000 = $89,842.

Amount of gift

Amount determined under (2) .... $ 80,000

Amount determined under (4) 89,842

Total $169,842

Less: Proceeds received by Y $150,000

Amount of gift by Y to Z .... $ 19,842

§ 531. Powers of Appointment.

The mathematical problems in connection with powers of appointment are comparatively simple. Thus, if the power exists as to part of an entire group of assets, or a limited interest in

1. Reg, § 25.2515–4(d).

property, it is merely necessary to compute the fractional share to which the power applies.[2] The same is true when there is a partial exercise of a pre-1942 power.[3]

When there is a lapse of a post-1942 power it is necessary to compute the amount by which the amount as to which there has been a lapse exceeds 5% of the aggregate value of the assets out of which or the proceeds of which the exercise of the lapsed power could be satisfied.[4] In the case of joint powers created after 1942 it is necessary to compute the fractional share of the joint owners.[5] The single case in which a nongeneral power of appointment is taxable has been discussed[6] and the method of computation illustrated.

§ 532. Gifts by Husband or Wife to Third Parties.

The primary computation in the case of gifts by husband and wife to third parties, is as we shall see,[7] the determination of whether such gift is advisable. Once that has been determined, the computations in connection with such gifts are the same as those in the case of other gifts, and then a simple process of division.

§ 533. Deduction for Charitable and Similar Gifts.

When a charitable gift is an outright one, no problems of computation are presented. Many such gifts, however, are remainder interests after one or more intervening lives have terminated. In such case the computation of the value of the remainder interest is made by the use of the actuarial tables which have been treated previously.[8]

When there is a remainder to charity, with a power of invasion for the benefit of the life tenant, and the amount of the invasion is fixed by an ascertainable standard, it is necessary to compute from the standard set the extent to which invasion will be necessary in order to determine the amount ultimately receivable by the charity.[9]

§ 534. The Marital Deduction; Generally.

In the computation of the Gift Tax marital deduction there are not presented the problems which exist with respect to the Estate

2. Reg, § 25.2514–1(b)(3).
3. Reg, § 25.2514–2(e).
4. § 463, supra.
5. Reg, § 25.2514–3(b)(3).

6. § 466, supra.
7. § 545, infra.
8. § 524, supra.
9. § 256, supra.

Tax marital deduction, since there is no interrelation of taxes to the deduction.[10] Except in the case of tenancy by the entirety[11] and certain property settlements arising out of matrimonial agreements,[12] if the gift by one spouse to the other is a deductible interest the computation of the amount of the marital deduction, ordinarily merely requires division by two of the amount of the gift.

If the total gifts by a donor to his spouse during a calendar year have a value of $6,000. or more, the amount of the marital deduction is determined *without regard to the amount of the exclusion, if any, allowable.* Thus, if in a particular calendar year a donor made a gift to his spouse of a present interest of $10,000., the amount of the marital deduction is $5,000. The exclusion is taken after one half of the gift is computed, so that in this case the total amount of included gifts would be $2,000.[13] The first exception to the application of this method is where the amount of the marital deduction would, if computed as above, exceed the amount of the gifts against which the deduction is applied, and which has been treated previously.[14] The other two apply in the case where included in the assets qualifying for the marital deduction there are some which do not qualify, and in the case of community property. These exceptions are discussed in the succeeding sections.

§ 535. The Marital Deduction; Tainted Assets.

It has been noted that where the assets out of which, or the proceeds of which, the interest transferred to the donee spouse may be satisfied include a particular asset or assets with respect to which no deduction would be allowed if such asset or assets were transferred from the donor to such spouse, then the value of the interest transferred to such spouse, shall for purposes of the statute, be reduced by the aggregate value of such particular assets.[15] In such case, these so-called "tainted assets" must be computed and deducted from the interest transferred, before the marital deduction is computed.

Assume that the husband is the owner of a rental property and on July 1, 1950 transferred it to A by gift, reserving the income for a period of 20 years. On July 1, 1955 he created a trust

10. §§ 286 t seq, supra.
11. §§ 450 et seq, supra.
12. § 455, supra.

13. Reg, § 25.2523(a)–1(b)(ii).
14. § 514, supra.
15. § 507, supra.

to last for a period of ten years. He was to receive the income from the trust and at its termination the trustee was to turn over to the settlor's wife, property having a value of $100,000. The trustee has absolute discretion in deciding which properties in the corpus he shall turn over to the wife in satisfaction of the gift to her. The trustee received two items of property from the husband. Item (1) consisted of shares of corporate stock, and Item (2) consisted of the right to receive the income from the rental property during the unexpired portion of the 20-year term. Assume that the value of the right to receive the income for the unexpired term of 5 years on July 1, 1965 will be $30,000. Item (2) is a nondeductible interest because the donor may enjoy the interest after the termination of the wife's interest,[16] and since the trustee can turn it over to the wife in partial satisfaction of her gift, only $70,000. of the $100,000. receivable by her on July 1, 1965, will be considered as property with respect to which a marital deduction is allowable. The present value on July 1, 1955 of the right to receive $70,000. at the end of 10 years is $49,573.93 (70,000 × .708199).[17] The value of the property qualifying for the marital deduction, therefore, is $49,573-.93, and a marital deduction is allowed for one half of that amount, or $24,786.97.[18]

§ 536. The Marital Deduction; Cases Involving Community Property.

When community property was converted into separate property after December 31, 1941, as has been noted,[19] if thereafter a spouse makes a gift to the other spouse of any part of such separate property, it is necessary to determine the portion of the transferred property which is considered to be community property.

Thus, during 1942 the donor and his spouse partitioned certain real property held by them under community property laws. The real property then had a value of $224,000. A portion of the property, then having a value of $160,000., was converted into the donor's separate property, and the remaining portion, then having a value of $64,000., was converted into his spouse's separate property. In 1955 the donor made a gift to his spouse of

16. § 505, supra.
17. From Table II, Column 4, § 112, supra.

18. Reg, § 25.2523(c)-1(c).
19. § 511, supra.

the property acquired by him as a result of the partition, which property then had a value of $200,000. The portion of the property transferred by gift which is considered as community property is:

$$\frac{\$ 64,000 \text{ (value of property acquired by donee spouse)}}{\$160,000 \text{ (value of property acquired by donor spouse)}} \times \$200,000 = \$80,000$$

Since $80,000. is considered to be community property under the statute, the difference between the amount of the gift, $200,-000., and such amount, or $120,000. qualifies for the marital deduction, and the amount of the marital deduction is, therefore, $60,000.[20]

§ 537. The Marital Deduction; Gift of Portion.

When an excepted terminable interest is one in which the donee spouse receives for life all the income from a specific portion of the entire interest, or a specific portion of all the income from the entire interest,[1] in order to determine the amount of the marital deduction it is necessary to compute the value of the interest, and then determine the proportionate amount thereof to which the spouse's interest applies. The rules for determining this proportion have been previously set forth.[2]

Assume that a wife is given a life interest in a fund of $100,000., with the entire income payable to her, but with a general power of appointment over one half of the fund. Since her power relates to only half of the interest, $50,000. is a deductible interest, and the marital deduction is one half thereof.

§ 538. Computation of the Tax; General Rule.

The statute states that the Gift Tax for each calendar year shall be an amount equal to the excess of—

(1) a tax, computed in accordance with the rate schedule set forth in the section, on the aggregate sum of the taxable gifts for such calendar year and for each of the preceding calendar years, over

(2) a tax computed in accordance with such rate schedule, on the aggregate sum of the taxable gifts for each of the preceding calendar years.[3]

While the Gift Tax is imposed separately for each calendar

20. Reg, § 25.2523(f)–1(b)(5).
1. § 510, supra.
2. § 237, supra.
3. IRC, § 2502(a) (1954 Code).

year on the total taxable gifts made by a donor during that year, the rate of tax is determined by the total of all gifts made by the donor during the year *and in all previous years* since June 6, 1932.[4] This cumulative method of fixing the rate of tax was one of the lessons learned from the infirmities of the 1924 Act.[5] The 1932 date is that of the enactment of the Gift Tax statute from which the present one is derived.

The Regulation sets forth the six steps to be followed in computing the tax, as follows:

(1) *First step.* Ascertain the amount of "taxable gifts"[6] for the calendar year for which the return is being prepared.

(2) *Second step.* Ascertain "the aggregate sum of the taxable gifts for each of the preceding calendar years",[7] considering only those gifts made after June 6, 1932.

(3) *Third step.* Ascertain the total amount of the taxable gifts, which is the sum of the amounts determined in the first and second steps.

(4) *Fourth step.* Compute the tax on the total amount of taxable gifts (as determined in the third step) using the rate schedule set forth in the statute.[8]

(5) *Fifth step.* Compute the tax on "the aggregate sum of the taxable gifts for each of the preceding calendar years" (as determined in the second step), using the rate schedule set forth in the statute.

(6) *Sixth step.* Subtract the amount determined in the fifth step from the amount determined in the fourth step. The amount remaining is the Gift Tax for the calendar year for which the return is being prepared.[9]

The terms "calendar year" and "preceding calendar year" are defined in the statute[10] and have been treated previously.[11]

The statutory provision is simple, and the Regulation for the method of computation is most explicit. The problems which arise in the computation of the tax are not primarily created by the method of fixing the tax payable, but in determining the amount of the items to be considered in each step. That has been the purpose of our consideration of the items which must be included as transfers under the Gift Tax and those items which are

---

4. Reg, § 25.2502–1(a).
5. See § 391, supra.
6. § 479, supra.
7. § 539, infra.

8. § 541, infra.
9. Note 4, supra.
10. IRC, § 2502(b)(c) (1954 Code).
11. § 400, supra.

deductible. The remaining questions will be considered in the succeeding sections.

§ 539. Computation of the Tax; Taxable Gifts for Preceding Years.

The second step in the computation of the tax requires that there be ascertained "the aggregate sum of the taxable gifts for each of the preceding calendar years" considering only those gifts made after June 6, 1932.

The words "aggregate sum of the taxable gifts for each of the preceding years" means the *correct aggregate* of such gifts, not necessarily that returned for those years and in respect of which tax was paid. All transfers which constituted gifts in prior calendar years under the laws, *including the provisions of law relating to exclusions* from gifts, in effect *at the time* the transfers were made *are included* in determining the amount of taxable gifts for preceding years. The *deductions other than for the specific exemption* allowed by the laws in effect at the time the transfers were made also are taken into account in determining the aggregate sum of the taxable gifts for preceding years.[12]

This presents three matters for consideration. First, in the computation of the tax for the calendar year for which the return is being filed, the correct aggregate for preceding calendar years must be used. Thus, if in a prior year or years an exclusion was erroneously taken,[13] or a transfer was erroneously held nontaxable,[14] and the statute of limitations has run as to the tax, nonetheless, in the computation of aggregate gifts, such transfers are taken in the correct amount. This does not apply in the case of valuation.[15]

Next, the exclusions applicable in the year of the prior transfers applies to such gifts. The annual exclusion was $5,000. before 1939, $4,000. for the calendar years 1939 through 1942, and $3,000. thereafter.[15a]

Finally, the *deductions* in effect at the time of the prior gifts are applicable. This means that as to gifts by one spouse to another prior to the calendar year 1949, no marital deduction

12. IRC, § 2504(a)(b) (1954 Code); Reg, § 25.2504–1(a).

13. Comm v Disston, 325 US 442, 89 L ed 1720, 65 S Ct 1328 (1945); Winton v Reynolds, 57 F Supp 565 (1944).

14. McMurtry v Comm, 203 F2d 659 (CA–1) (1953).

15. IRC, § 2504(c) (1954 Code); § 540, infra.

15a. § 480, supra.

would be allowable.[16] The same would be true with respect to portion gifts or life estates prior to the calendar year 1955.[17]

It will be noted that *while deductions in effect at the time* of prior transfers *apply, the specific exemption in effect at such time does not.* We have seen that the specific exemption may not exceed $30,000. in the determination of the aggregate sum of taxable gifts for preceding years, even though the tax paid in such year or years was based upon a greater exemption in effect at the time.[18]

§ 540. Computation of the Tax; Valuation of Certain Gifts for Preceding Calendar Years.

Due to the cumulative nature of the Gift Tax and the progression in Gift Tax rates, the tax liability for gifts in a particular year is dependent on the correct valuation of gifts in prior years, as we have seen.[19] Therefore, a taxpayer's Gift Tax liability for 1953, for example, might be dependent on whether the valuation of a gift made in 1935 is larger, or smaller, or the same as previously reported, although the statute of limitations has run on the tax paid on the 1935 transfer. Congress believed that once the value of a gift has been accepted for purposes of the tax by both the government and the taxpayer, this value should be acceptable to both in measuring the tax to be applied to subsequent gifts,[20] and therefore in the 1954 Code added specific provisions relating to the computation of taxable gifts in preceding years, just discussed,[1] and also added a provision that if the time has expired within which a tax may be assessed for a gift, and *if a tax has been assessed or paid* on the gift, the *value* of the gift which was used in computing the tax for that year shall be the *value* for computing the tax in years subsequent to 1954.[2]

It should be noted, that the provision applies only to the value of the prior gift. The rule will not prevent an adjustment when no tax was paid on the prior gift, and will not prevent adjustment if issues other than valuation of property are involved.[3]

16. § 502, supra.
17. Note 16, supra.
18. § 496, supra.
19. § 539, supra.

20. Committee Reports, IRC, § 2504 (1954 Code).
1. Note 19, supra.
2. IRC, § 2504(c) (1954 Code).
3. Reg, § 25.2504–2.

§ 541. Computation of the Tax; Rate of Tax; Table for Computing Gift Tax.

The rate schedule for computation of the tax is set forth in the statute.[4] The Regulation contains a table incorporating the statutory rates.[5]

FORM NO. 70

Table for Computing Gift Tax

(A) Amount of taxable gifts equaling—	(B) Amount of taxable gifts not exceeding—	Tax on amount in column (A)	Rate of tax on excess over amount in column (A) *Percent*
.....	$5,000	......	$2\frac{1}{4}$
$5,000	10,000	$112.50	$5\frac{1}{4}$
10,000	20,000	375.00	$8\frac{1}{4}$
20,000	30,000	1,200.00	$10\frac{1}{2}$
30,000	40,000	2,250.00	$13\frac{1}{2}$
40,000	50,000	3,600.00	$16\frac{1}{2}$
50,000	60,000	5,250.00	$18\frac{3}{4}$
60,000	100,000	7,125.00	21
100,000	250,000	15,525.00	$22\frac{1}{2}$
250,000	500,000	49,275.00	24
500,000	750,000	109,275.00	$26\frac{1}{4}$
750,000	1,000,000	174,900.00	$27\frac{3}{4}$
1,000,000	1,250,000	244,275.00	$29\frac{1}{4}$
1,250,000	1,500,000	317,400.00	$31\frac{1}{2}$
1,500,000	2,000,000	396,150.00	$33\frac{3}{4}$
2,000,000	2,500,000	564,900.00	$36\frac{3}{4}$
2,500,000	3,000,000	748,650.00	$39\frac{3}{4}$
3,000,000	3,500,000	947,400.00	42
3,500,000	4,000,000	1,157,400.00	$44\frac{1}{4}$
4,000,000	5,000,000	1,378,650.00	$47\frac{1}{4}$
5,000,000	6,000,000	1,851,150.00	$50\frac{1}{4}$
6,000,000	7,000,000	2,353,650.00	$52\frac{1}{2}$
7,000,000	8,000,000	2,878,650.00	$54\frac{3}{4}$
8,000,000	10,000,000	3,426,150.00	57
10,000,000	....	4,566,150.00	$57\frac{3}{4}$

By the use of the table the tax may be quickly computed. Thus, if the amount of taxable gifts is $63,000., referring to

4. IRC, § 2502(a) (1954 Code).   5. Reg, § 25.2502–1(b).

column A, we see that the amount of taxable gifts equalling $60,000. is subject to a tax of $7,125. The excess of $3,000. is subject to tax at the rate of 21%, or $630. The total tax is, therefore, $7,125. + $630., or $7,755.

These rates must be applied twice, first to determine the tax on the total amount of taxable gifts, and then to determine the tax on the aggregate sum of the taxable gifts for each of the preceding calendar years. The difference between the two amounts, is the amount of tax payable for the calendar year for which the return is being prepared. The methods of computation will be demonstrated in various factual situations in the succeeding sections.

§ 542. Computation of the Tax; No Taxable Gifts for Prior Years.

The simplest computation is when the donor made no gifts in prior years. In such case but one computation is required. The rates in the table above[6] are applied to the amount of taxable gifts for the year of the report. After totaling the amount of gifts and reducing that amount by the exclusions applicable, if any, and the deductions, if any, and using so much of the specific lifetime exemption as may be applicable, the remainder is the amount of taxable gifts for the calendar year. Thus if the donor makes two gifts of $50,000 each, one being a charitable gift, the tax would be computed as follows:

Total gifts		$100,000
Less exclusions (2 × $3,000)	$6,000	
Deduction ($50,000 — 3,000)	47,000	
Specific exemption	30,000	83,000
Taxable gifts		$ 17,000

Referring to the table,[7] the tax on $10,000. is $375. and the tax on the excess of $7,000. at the rate of 8¼% is $577.50., the total tax being $952.50.

§ 543. Computation of the Tax; No Specific Exemption Available.

When the donor has utilized his specific exemption in prior years, there must be considered the exclusions applicable in such years and the amount of exemption which was taken in such

6. § 541, supra.   7. Note 6, supra.

prior years. Thus, a donor makes gifts during the calendar year 1955 of present interests to A of $30,000. and to B of $33,000. An exclusion is allowable as to each gift, so that the amount of included gifts is $57,000. Specific exemption was claimed and allowed in a total amount of $50,000. in the donor's Gift Tax return for the calendar years 1934 and 1935,[8] so there remains no specific exemption to be claimed for the 1955 gifts. The total amount of gifts made by the donor during preceding years, *after excluding* the then annual exclusion of $5,000.[9] for each donee for each calendar year is computed as follows:

Calendar year 1934 .... $120,000
Calendar year 1935 25,000

Total amount of included gifts for preceding calendar years .. $145,000

The aggregate sum of the taxable gifts for the preceding calendar years is $115,000., which is determined by deducting *a specific exemption of $30,000.* from $145,000., the total amount of included gifts for preceding calendar years. The deduction from the 1934 and 1935 gifts for the specific exemption cannot exceed $30,000. for purposes of computing the tax on the 1955 gifts even though a specific exemption in a total amount of $50,000. was allowed in computing the donor's Gift Tax liability for 1934 and 1935.[10] The computation of the tax for the calendar year 1955 is then as follows:[11]

(1) Amount of taxable gifts for year .... $ 57,000
(2) Total amount of taxable gifts for preceding years 115,000

(3) Total taxable gifts $172,000
(4) Tax computed on item (3) 31,725
(5) Tax computed on item (2) 18,900

(6) Tax for year 1955 (item 4 minus item 5) .... $ 12,825

§ 544. Computation of the Tax; Charitable and Marital Deductions; Split-Gifts; Part of Exemption Available.

The computations become more complex when other factors such as the deduction for charity, the marital deduction, and split-gifts are present, as well as when the respective spouses have utilized part of their specific exemption in prior years.

8. § 496, supra.
9. § 539, supra.
10. Note 8, supra.
11. Reg, § 25.2502–1(c), Example (2).

Thus, during the calendar year 1955, the husband makes the following gifts:

To his daughter	$40,000
To his son	5,000
To his wife	5,000
To a charitable organization	10,000

The gifts to the wife qualify for the marital deduction, and husband and wife consent to treat the gifts to third parties as split-gifts.[12] The amount of the husband's taxable gifts for preceding years is $50,000. and he has used only $25,000. of his specific exemption, claiming the balance for the calendar year 1955.[13] The wife made no gifts during the calendar year 1955 nor during any preceding calendar year. The wife claims sufficient specific exemption on her return to eliminate tax liability.[14] In this case it is necessary for both spouses to file a return,[15] and to compute the tax for both. The computation of the husband's tax is as follows:

(a) Total gifts of husband $60,000
    Less: Portion of items treated as split-gifts ($\frac{1}{2}$ of gifts to
        daughter, son, and charity) 27,500

    Balance $32,500
    Less: Exclusions ($3,000 each for daughter, wife, and
        charity. The exclusion for the son is limited to
        $2,500, the amount of his gift included[16]) 11,500

    Total amount of included gifts for year $21,000
    Less: Deductions:
        Charity ($5,000 — $3,000) $2,000
        Marital ($5,000 — $3,000) 2,000
        Specific exemption (balance) 5,000

    Total deductions $9,000

    Amount of taxable gifts for year $12,000

12. §§ 471 et seq, supra.   15. § 474, supra.
13. §§ 496, 497, supra.   16. § 514, supra.
14. Reg, § 25.2502–1(c), Example (3).

(b) (1) Amount of taxable gifts for year $12,000
     (2) Total taxable gifts for preceding years 50,000

     (3) Total taxable gifts $62,000
     (4) Tax on item (3)   7,545
     (5) Tax on item (2)   5,250

     (6) Tax for calendar year .... $ 2,295

The computation of the wife's tax is as follows:

Gifts of spouse to be included $27,500
Total gifts for year $27,500
Less: Exclusions ($3,000 each for gift to daughter and
       charity and $2,500 for gift to son)   8,500

Balance $19,000
Less: Deductions:
      Charity $2,000
      Specific exemption 17,000

Total deductions $19,000
Amount of taxable gifts for year   0

The wife has used enough of her specific exemption to eliminate any tax, and there will then remain available to her for use
in subsequent years the balance of $11,000. of her specific ex-
emption. In the succeeding section we shall see that a split-gift
may be more costly when the donor spouse has not used the
specific exemption and the other has.

§ 545. Computation of the Tax; Split-Gifts; Effect When Donor Spouse Has Available Exemption.

In many cases, before treating a gift by a spouse to a third
party as a split-gift, computation is required to determine whether it should be so treated. We have seen that *all gifts* made by
both spouses to third parties during the calendar year must be
treated as split-gifts if the parties consent that gifts for the
year be so treated.[17] Therefore, if one spouse has used all or part
of his specific exemption in a prior year, since the Gift Tax rates
are applied to the aggregate amount of taxable gifts for prior
years, plus the taxable gifts for the current year, the rate for
the current year is determined by the previous gifts.[18] Thus, if
the donor spouse has made no gifts during preceding calendar

17. § 451, supra.   18. § 538, supra.

years and the other spouse has, treating a gift by the donor spouse as a split-gift may result in a larger tax. If a father has made gifts after deducting annual exclusions and deductions in prior years, of $200,000., and his wife has made no prior gifts, if she makes a gift of $56,000. in the current calendar year, treating the gift as a split-gift will result in a tax greater by $4,110. than if the wife returned the gift as her own. The computation follows:

Husband's Gift Tax

(1) Amount of taxable gifts for year .... $ 25,000
(2) Total taxable gifts for preceding years 170,000

(3) Total taxable gifts $195,000
(4) Tax computed on item (3) 36,900
(5) Tax computed on item (2) 31,275

(6) Tax for year .... $ 5,625

Wife's Gift Tax

(1) Amount of taxable gifts for year 0

By treating the $56,000. as a split-gift, the amount of the gift is reduced to $28,000. Deducting an annual exclusion of $3,000., and applying $25,000. of the wife's specific exemption, there would be no tax payable by her.

If the gift is not made as a split-gift, the wife's tax on the gift would be computed as follows:

(1) Amount of taxable gifts for year ($56,000 less the annual exclusion of $3,000 and $30,000 exemption) $23,000
(2) Total taxable gifts for preceding years 0

(3) Total taxable gifts $23,000
(4) Tax on item (3) 1,515
(5) Tax on item (2) 0

(6) Tax for year .... $ 1,515

§ 546. Specimen Gift Tax Return; Details of Return.

All of the matters which we have considered up until this point have had the same purpose, i.e., to furnish all of the facts and the law necessary for the preparation of the Gift Tax return. The return itself is comparatively simple, consisting of but two pages for information as to taxable gifts for the year of the return and preceding calendar years, the deductions and the exemption, and the computation of the tax. It is knowing what is required to fill in in the return that presents the problems. These problems it has been our purpose to solve.

Proceeding to the return,[19] the first page requires first that the name, address, residence, and citizenship of the donor be given. There follows in Part A a series of eight questions designed to elicit information which will determine the amount of gifts for the calendar year of the return.

The first question deals with the creation of trusts, and whether by the creation of the trust there was a completed gift, or whether there were additions to a trust previously created, or by the relinquishment of rights in a trust there was completed a gift, which at the time of the creation of the trust was not complete.[20]

The second question concerns transfers in trust under which the donor did not relinquish dominion and control. Such transfers may or may not be subject to the tax.[1]

The third question deals with gifts of insurance, or payment of premiums on previously issued policies.[2]

The fourth question concerns permitting the joint owner of a bank account who was not the creator of the account to withdraw funds from it.[3]

The fifth and sixth questions deal with the creation of joint tenancies[4] or such tenancies in real property, as well as tenancies by the entirety.[5]

The seventh question treats with powers of appointment and the exercise or release thereof which may be subject to the tax.[6]

The eighth question in Part A is all-inclusive, and requires a statement as to whether the donor has made a transfer by any other method, direct or indirect.

All of these questions are predicated upon the donor, during the calendar year for which the return is filed, without an adequate and full consideration in money or money's worth,[7] making a transfer exceeding $3,000. in value (or regardless of value if a future interest).[8]

19. Form 709.
20. §§ 422 et seq, supra.
1. § 422, supra.
2. § 441, supra.
3. § 470, supra.

4. Note 3, supra.
5. Note 12, supra.
6. §§ 457 et seq, supra.
7. §§ 446 et seq, supra.
8. §§ 482 et seq, 403, supra.

It will be observed that the questions are designed to uncover any gift which may be subject to the Gift Tax.

Part B deals with split-gifts and requires disclosure of whether the spouses consent to such treatment, the name of the spouse other than the one making the return, whether the parties were married during all of the calendar year, and if not, the date of marriage, divorce, or death. It will be recalled that the provision may only be applied to gifts made during the portion of the year when the necessary status obtained.[9] Information is also required as to whether the other spouse will file a Gift Tax return for the calendar year in which split-gift treatment is elected.[10] There is also the consent to be signed by the other spouse.[11]

The first page, as in the Estate Tax return, contains the computation of the tax. This computation cannot be made, however, until the second page of the return is completed. The signing of the return under the penalties of perjury, by the taxpayer and of the person preparing the return, if any, is required on the first page.[12]

The reverse side of Form 709 contains Schedule A in which is listed each item which was the subject of a gift, with the donee's name and address, the date of the gift, and its value at such date. These items and the method of reporting and valuing the same have been treated previously.[13] There then follow ten lettered items from which the amount of the taxable gifts for the year of the return may be determined. From the total gifts set forth in Schedule A (a), there is first deducted the portion thereof which is treated as a split-gift and reported by the other spouse (b). To the balance (c), there is added the portion of split-gifts of the other spouse to be included in the taxpayer's return (d). This leaves the total of the gifts for the year (e). From this total there is deducted the total of allowable exclusions (f). The deductions, charitable gifts reduced by exclusions (h)(1), the marital deduction (h)(2), and the specific exemption claimed in the year of return (h)(3) are then totaled (i), and deducted from the total included amount of gifts for the year (g). The result is the amount of taxable gifts for the year (j), which is carried over as the first item in the computation of the tax on the first page.

Schedule B contains the items required in order to determine

9. § 471, supra.
10. § 474, supra.
11. § 472, supra.

12. § 410, supra.
13. Chapter 7, supra.

the total amount of taxable gifts for preceding years. The calendar year of the prior gift, the Internal Revenue district where the prior return was filed, the amount of specific exemption claimed and the amount of the taxable gifts in each year must be stated. The total amount of the specific exemption claimed theretofore and the total amount of prior taxable gifts, without adjustment for any reduced specific exemption applicable is obtained (a). To the amount of taxable gifts is added the amount by which the specific exemption claimed in prior years exceeds $30,000. (b).[14] The result is the total amount of taxable gifts for preceding years (c), which in turn is carried over to the first page as the second item in the computation of the tax.

14. § 496, supra.

FORM NO. 71

Gift Tax Return

Donor   WINTHROP BENSON
(Given name, middle name or initial, surname)
Address   200 Catalpa Avenue, Estes Park, Colorado
Residence   Same
Citizenship   U. S. A.

A. Have you (the donor), during the calendar year indicated above, without an adequate and full consideration in money or money's worth, made any transfer exceeding $3,000 in value (or regardless of value if a future interest) as follows? (Check whether "Yes" or "No.")

1. By the creation of a trust   [x] Yes [ ] No *or* the making of additions to a trust previously created   [x] Yes   [ ] No   in either case for the benefit of a person or persons other than yourself, and with respect to which you retained no power to revest the beneficial title to the property in yourself or to change the beneficiaries or their proportionate benefits; or by relinquishing every such power that was retained in a previously created trust.   [x] Yes   [ ] No

2. By permitting a beneficiary, other than yourself, to receive the income from a trust created by you and with respect to which you retained the power to revest the beneficial title to the property in yourself or to change the beneficiaries or their proportionate benefits.   [ ] Yes   [x] No

3. By the purchase of a life insurance policy   [x] Yes   [ ] No *or* the payment of a premium on a previously issued policy   [ ] Yes   [x] No, the proceeds of which are in either case payable to a beneficiary other than your estate, and with respect to which you retained no power to revest the economic benefits in yourself or your estate or to change the beneficiaries or their proportionate benefits; or by relinquishing every such power that was retained in a previously issued policy.   [ ] Yes   [x] No

4. By permitting another to withdraw funds from a joint bank account which were deposited by you.   [x] Yes   [ ] No

5. By conveying title to another and yourself as joint tenants.   [ ] Yes   [x] No

6. By conveying title to your spouse and yourself as tenants by the entirety or as joint tenants with right of survivorship.   [x] Yes   [ ] No   If "Yes," see section 8 of the instructions.

7. By the exercise or release of a power of appointment, except as provided in the Gift Tax Regulations.   [x] Yes   [ ] No

8. By any other method, direct or indirect.   [x] Yes   [ ] No   If the answer is "Yes" to any of the foregoing, such a transfer (other than the creation of a joint tenancy with your spouse in real prop-

717

erty with right of survivorship, or addition thereto, which you do not elect to treat as a gift) should be fully disclosed under Schedule A.

B. Gifts of husband and wife to third parties.—Do you consent to have the gifts made by both you and your spouse to third parties during the calendar year considered as having been made one-half by each of you? [x] Yes [ ] No   (See section 7 of instructions.)

If the answer is "Yes" the following information must be furnished and the consent shown below signed by your spouse.

1. Name of spouse, KATHERINE BENSON   2. Were you married during the entire calendar year? [x] Yes [ ] No   3. If the answer to 2 is "No," check whether [ ] married, [ ] divorced, or [ ] widowed. Give date ....   4. Will a gift tax return for this calendar year be filed by your spouse? [x] Yes [ ] No

CONSENT OF SPOUSE

I consent to have the gifts made by both me and my spouse to third parties during the calendar year considered as having been made one-half by each of us.

Feb. 18, 1961
    (Date)

KATHERINE BENSON
(Signature of spouse)

COMPUTATION OF TAX (See section 18 of instructions)

1. Amount of taxable gifts for year (line j, Schedule A) .. $ 66,242.53
2. Total amount of taxable gifts for preceding years (line c, Schedule B) 76,000.00

3.   Total taxable gifts (item 1 plus item 2) $142,242.53

4. Tax computed on item 3 .... $ 25,029.57
5. Tax computed on item 2 ....   10,505.00

6. Tax on taxable gifts for year (item 4 minus item 5) .... $ 14,524.57

I declare under the penalties of perjury that this return (including any accompanying schedules and statements) has been examined by me and to the best of my knowledge and belief is a true, correct, and complete return.

DANIEL WEBSTER CLAY	WINTHROP BENSON
(Signature of person, other than taxpayer, preparing this return)	(Signature of taxpayer or other person filing return)
185 Ridge Street, Estes Park, Colo.	200 Catalpa Ave., Estes Park, Colo.
(Address of person preparing return)	(Address of taxpayer or other person filing return)
April 10, 1961	April 10, 1961
(Date)	(Date)

SCHEDULE A—Total Gifts During Year and Computation of Taxable Gifts.

Item No.	Description of Gift, and Donee's Name and Address	Date of Gift	Value at Date of Gift
1.	To Colorado Trust Company, Estes Park, Colo., as Trustee under agreement dated June 15, 1960, for Katherine Benson, donor's wife, life interest in income, and remainder to Sylvia Benson	6/15/60	$75,000.00
	Age of Katherine Benson at date of gift 45 (Copy of agreement annexed)		
2.	To Colorado Trust Company, Estes Park, Colo., as Trustee under agreement dated Sept. 1, 1955, for George Benson, with income payable to him for life with remainder to Sylvia Benson	9/1/55	25,000.00
	Age of George Benson at date of gift 28		
3.	To Estelle Benson, 308 Capa Drive, San Diego, Cal., by purchase of policy of insurance on the life of the donor from The Life Insurance Co., for the benefit of the donee.		1,266.90
4.	To Katherine Benson, by withdrawal by her from joint account created by the donor in the Colorado Savings Bank, payable to donor and Katherine Benson, with right of survivorship	8/31/60	2,500.00
5.	To William Benson, Grand Lake, Colo., by lapse of power of appointment under the will of Winthrop Benson, Sr., who died Mar. 12, 1947. (Will and computation annexed)	3/12/60	5,000.00
6.	To Helen Benson, 47 Circle Drive, Chicago, Illinois, cash	6/8/60	5,000.00

(a) Total gifts of donor $113,766.90
(b) Less portion of items 2 to 6 reported by spouse (see section 10 of instructions) 19,383.45

(c) Balance .... $ 94,383.45
(d) Gifts of spouse to be included (from line b of spouse's return) (see section 10 of instructions) 5,000.00

(e) Total gifts for year .... $ 99,383.45
(f) Less total exclusions not exceeding $3,000 for each donee (except gifts of future interests) 10,266.90

(g) Total included amount of gifts for year .... $ 89,116.53
(h) Deductions (see sections 14, 15, and 16 of instructions):
   (1) Charitable, public, and similar gifts (based on items .... to ...., less exclusions) .... $ ....
   (2) Marital deduction (based on items 1 and 4) 22,874.00
   (3) Specific exemption claimed 0.00

(i) Total deductions (total of lines 1, 2, and 3) 22,874.00

(j) Amount of taxable gifts for year (line g minus line i) .... $ 66,242.53

SCHEDULE B—Returns, Amounts of Specific Exemption, and Taxable Gifts for Preceding Years (subsequent to June 6, 1932).

Calendar Year	Internal Revenue District in which prior return was filed	Amount of Specific Exemption	Amount of Taxable Gifts
1942	1st New York	$40,000.00	$66,000.00

(a) Totals for preceding years (without adjustment for reduced specific exemption). $40,000.00 $66,000.00

(b) Amount, if any, by which total specific exemption, line a, exceeds $30,000 (see section 17 of instructions) 10,000.00

(c)   Total amount of taxable gifts for preceding years (total, last column, line a, plus amount, if any, line b) $76,000.00

(If more space is needed, attach additional sheets of same size)

In the preparation of the return it was necessary to evaluate the life interests in item 1 and 2 of Schedule A to determine the amount of item 1 applicable to the marital deduction and whether the amount of the life interest exceeded $3,000. for the purpose of the annual exclusion. This was done by the use of the tables for valuing life estates.[15] The value of the policy of insurance is furnished by the insurance company.[16] The exclusion allowable on that gift is the amount thereof, $1,266.90. Although the donor took a specific exemption of $40,000. on prior gifts, that being the amount of the exemption at the time, $10,000. of that amount is required to be added to the total amount of taxable gifts for preceding years in the computation of the tax for the year of the return.[17]

15. § 112, supra.
16. § 441, supra.

17. § 496, supra.

CHAPTER 10

PRACTICE AND PAYMENT OF FEDERAL GIFT TAX

§ 547. Scope of Chapter.

We have now proceeded through all of the steps in the preparation of the Gift Tax return, and have arrived at the point where the return is ready for execution and filing, and the payment of the tax made. There then follows the administrative procedure in the Internal Revenue Service of the Treasury Department. Much of this procedure is identical with respect to the Estate Tax and the Gift Tax. There has been treated previously the Estate Tax administrative procedure.[1] In such cases as they differ the differences will be considered, and where they are identical, reference will be made to the discussion under the Estate Tax.

§ 548. Verification of Returns.

The Gift Tax return has a single verification for the taxpayer and the person preparing the return, in place of the double form

---

1. Chapter 5, supra.

in the case of the Estate Tax. In all other respects the requirements are the same, with the same statutory provisions applying.[2]

The former donee's return required no verification. The final Gift Tax Regulations eliminated the need for such return.[3]

§ 549. Payment; Time and Place.

As in the case of the Estate Tax the Code does not fix a specific date for payment of the tax, but provides that the tax shall be payable to the principal Internal Revenue officer of the district in which the return is required to be filed and at the time required for filing the return.[4] Since the Gift Tax return is required to be filed on or before April 15th following the close of the calendar year,[5] that is the time for payment of the tax. An exception is made when an extension of time has been granted for payment of the tax or the taxpayer is serving in the Armed Forces in a combat zone.[6]

The customary procedure is to make payment of the tax at the time of filing the return. Payment is made to the District Director of the district where the return is filed.[7]

§ 550. Extension of Time for Payment.

The provisions for extension of time for payment of the Gift Tax differ from those under the Estate Tax. If it is shown to the satisfaction of the District Director that the payment of all or any part of the amount determined as the tax due by the donor upon the due date will result in undue hardship to the donor, the District Director, at the written request of the donor, may grant an extension of time for the payment of all or any part of the tax. The period of the extension *shall not exceed six months* from the date fixed for payment thereof except in the case of a donor who is abroad.[8] Under the Estate Tax the extension may be for a period up to ten years.[9]

The time for payment of the amount of Gift Tax determined as a deficiency may be extended for a period not to exceed 30

2. §§ 330, 410, supra.
3. § 409, supra.
4. IRC, § 6151 (1954 Code); § 338, supra.
5. § 404, supra.
6. Reg, §§ 25.6075-1, 25.6151-1; 25.6161-1; § 385, supra.

7. § 411, supra.
8. IRC, § 6161(a)(1) (1954 Code); Reg, § 25.6161-1(a).
9. § 339, supra.

months,[10] whereas under the Estate Tax the time limit is four years, except where a closely held interest is concerned.[11]

So far as the definition of undue hardship,[12] the requirements of the application for extension,[13] the conditions thereof,[14] and the form of bond where an extension is granted for the payment of the tax or a deficiency,[15] the Gift Tax Regulations follow the Estate Tax Regulations.[16] In the case of the Gift Tax the donor must furnish a statement of his assets and liabilities, together with a record of all receipts and disbursements for each of the three months immediately preceding the month in which falls the date prescribed for payment of the tax.[17]

§ 551. Audit of Return and Procedure.

The office procedure in the case of the Gift Tax will differ from that under the Estate Tax, depending upon the return filed. Whereas, in every case in the Estate Tax there will be either a notification that there is no tax due, or that the tax as fixed in the return is correct, or there will be an office audit or field audit, the person filing the Gift Tax return will only be notified if an audit is necessary. In that case the examiner to whom the case has been assigned will go through the same procedure as in the case of the Estate Tax. The same unit or group of examiners in the office of the District Director process both Estate and Gift Tax returns.

If the taxpayer wishes to be represented by an attorney, he must file a power of attorney and the attorney must be authorized to practice before the Treasury Department.[18] There is no provision under the Gift Tax statute for release from liability. When the examiner disagrees with the return as filed,[19] the same informal conference procedure may be followed as in the Estate Tax.[20] The examiner, who is still designated an Estate Tax Examiner, makes his report and it is sent with the thirty day letter and other documents[1] to the taxpayer and his representative. Many of the forms are interchangeable, the same forms being used for Income, Estate and Gift Tax. The line adjustments for the Gift Tax will differ. After receiving the

10. IRC, § 6161(b)(1) (1954 Code).
11. Note 9, supra.
12. Reg, § 25.6161–1(b).
13. Reg, § 25.6161–1(c).
14. Reg. § 25.6161–1(c).
15. Reg. § 25.6165–1.
16. Note 9, supra.
17. Note 13, supra.
18. § 332, supra.
19. § 333, supra.
20. § 334, supra.
1. § 335, supra.

report of the proposed deficiency, the protest,[2] Appellate Division procedure,[3] and ninety day letter,[4] are the same as in the case of the Estate Tax.

§ 552. Payment; Liability for.

The statute is succinct. It states "the tax imposed by Section 2501 shall be paid by the donor."[5] The tax is *primarily payable by the donor* on his transfers by gift and not by the donees on their receipt.[6] The making of a gift by the donor does not carry with it any implied promise by the donor to pay the tax.[7]

If the donor dies before the tax is paid the amount of the tax is a debt due the United States from the decedent's estate and his executor or administrator is responsible for its payment out of the estate. If there is no duly qualified executor or administrator, the heirs, legatees, devisees and distributees are liable for and required to pay the tax to the extent of the value of their inheritance, bequests, devises, or distributive shares of the donor's estate. If a husband and wife effectively signify consent to have the gifts made during any calendar year considered as made one half by each,[8] the liability with respect to the Gift Tax for that calendar year is joint and several.[9]

We shall see that although the primary liability for the payment of the Gift Tax is that of the donor, the donee or transferee may be liable when the donor has failed to pay the tax.[10]

Every executor, administrator, or assignee, or other person, who pays, in whole or in part, any debt due by the person or estate for whom or for which he acts before he satisfies and pays the debts due to the United States from such person or estate, is answerable in his own person and estate to the extent of such payments for the debts so due to the United States, or for so much thereof as may remain due and unpaid.[11]

§ 553. Payment; How Made; Receipts.

The provisions with respect to the manner of payment of the Estate Tax and the Gift Tax are identical.[12] However, in the

2. § 337, supra.
3. § 337A, supra.
4. § 337B, supra.
5. IRC, § 2502(d) (1954 Code).
6. Helvering v Robinette, 129 F2d 832 (CCA 3), cert den 318 US 184, 87 L ed 700, 63 S Ct 540 (1942).
7. Fidelity Union Trust Co. v An-
thony, 71 A2d 191, 13 NJ Super 596, affd 86 A2d 594, 18 NJ Super 49 (1951).
8. §§ 471 et seq, supra.
9. Reg, § 25.2502-2.
10. §§ 555, 559, supra.
11. Revised Statutes, § 3467 (31 USC 192).
12. § 342, supra.

case of the Gift Tax there is no provision for duplicate receipts as there is in the case of the Estate Tax.[13]

§ 554. Collection of Unpaid Tax; Remedies.

In the case of the Gift Tax, the same remedies of levy, and of civil action exist as under the Estate Tax.[14] The provisions of the Estate Tax statute as to reimbursement out of the estate,[15] and liability of life insurance beneficiaries[16] and appointees[17] does not apply to the Gift Tax, since these situations do not arise in the case of gifts.

§ 555. Lien of Tax; Generally; Donees and Transferees.

The general provisions of the statute with respect to the lien for taxes applies to both the Gift Tax and the Estate Tax,[18] but with respect to the special lien for Estate and Gift Taxes, the provisions are separately stated for each.

The Gift Tax is a lien upon all gifts made during the calendar year, for 10 years from the time the gifts are made. If the tax is not paid when due, the donee of any gift shall be personally liable for such tax *to the extent of the value of such gift*. Any part of the property comprised in the gift transferred by the donee (or by a transferee of the donee) to a bona fide purchaser, mortgagee, or pledgee for an adequate and full consideration in money or money's worth shall be divested of the lien imposed and the lien, *to the extent of the value of such gift,* attaches to all the property (including after-acquired property) of the donee (or the transferee) except any part transferred to a bona fide purchaser, mortgagee, or pledgee for an adequate and full consideration in money or money's worth.[19]

The meaning of bona fide purchaser is the same for purposes of the Estate and Gift Tax.[20] Similar provisions of prior statutes have been applied to impose liability on the donee to the extent of the value of the gift.[1]

13. IRC, § 6314(a) (1954 Code).

14. § 343, supra.

15. § 344, supra.

16. § 345, supra.

17. § 346, supra.

18. §§ 348, 351, 352, supra.

19. IRC, § 6324(b) (1954 Code); Reg, § 301.6324–1(b).

20. § 349, supra.

1. Baur v Comm, 145 F2d 338 (CCA 3) (1944); Winton v Reynolds, 57 F Supp 565 (1944); Ream, 2 TCM 1067 (1943); Mississippi Valley Trust Co. v Comm, 145 F2d 186 (CCA 8) (1945); Burrell, 3 TCM 489 (1944); Fidelity Philadelphia Trust Co, 3 TC 670 (1943); Moore, 1 TC 14, affd 146 F2d 824 (1945); Vogel, 3 TCM 306 (1943); Gray, 3 TCM 552 (1943); Moore v Comm, 146 F2d 824 (1945); La Fortune, 29 TC 479 (1957).

The liability of transferees is similar under both the Gift and Estate Tax.[2] A donee is in fact a transferee.[3] A trustee is liable for unpaid Gift Taxes of the donor to the extent of the trust property.[4]

§ 556. Jeopardy Assessments.

All of the provisions of the statute with respect to jeopardy assessments apply alike to Income, Estate, and Gift Taxes. There has been discussed previously the authority for such assessments,[5] deficiency letters in such case,[6] the amount assessable before and after the decision of the Tax Court,[7] abatement thereof,[8] stay of collection,[9] and collection of unpaid amounts.[10]

§ 557. Limitations on Assessment and Collection.

In the case of limitations on the assessment and collection of the tax, in all respects except two, the statutory provisions are identical with respect to both the Estate and Gift Tax. The general limitations,[11] are the same, except that in the case of the Gift Tax the time begins to run from the 15th day of April of the year following the calendar year for which the return is filed.

The exceptions to the limitations[12] are the same, except that that in connection with extension by agreement does not apply to the Estate Tax, but only to the Gift Tax,[13] and credits for State or foreign death taxes do not apply to the Gift Tax.

While the limitations on collection after assessment[14] are the same under both taxes, the provisions for suspension of the running of the period of limitations[15] have two which apply only to the Estate Tax.[16]

2. Note 20, supra.

3. Baur v Comm, note 1, supra; Evans, 4 TCM 198 (1944); Vogel, note 1, supra.

4. Fidelity Trust Co. v Comm, 141 F 2d 54 (CCA 3) (1944); Burrell, note 1, supra; Myer, 2 TC 291 (1943); Springfield Nat. Bank, 4 TCM 211 (1944); Fletcher Trust Co, 1 TC 798 (1942); Fidelity Philadelphia Trust Co, note 1, supra; Watkins, 2 TCM 254 (1943); Fidelity Union Trust Co. v Anthony, 81 A2d 191, 13 NJ Super 596, affd 86 A2d 594, 18 NJ Super 49 (1951).

5. § 353, supra.

6. § 354, supra.

7. § 355, supra.

8. § 356, supra.

9. § 357, supra.

10. § 358, supra.

11. § 359, supra.

12. § 360, supra.

13. IRC, § 6501(c)(4) (1954 Code).

14. § 361, supra.

15. § 362, supra.

16. IRC, § 6503(d)(e) (1954 Code).

§ 558. Interest and Penalties.

The general rule with respect to underpayments or nonpayment of the Gift Tax is that interest is payable on such amounts at the rate of six percent per annum from the last date prescribed for payment of the tax.[17] There is no reduction in the amount of interest in case of extension of time of payment as in the case of the Estate Tax.[18] Interest begins to run from the last date prescribed for payment,[19] and the suspension of interest in the case of the execution of a waiver of restrictions.[20] The rule that there shall be no interest on interest,[1] applies equally to the Estate and Gift Tax.

The provisions for penalties in the form of additions to the tax[2] and the criminal penalties,[3] are the same for both the Gift and Estate Tax. In the case of the Estate Tax, however, there are certain civil penalties[4] which do not apply in the case of the Gift Tax.

§ 559. Transferred Assets.

The provisions with respect to transferred assets apply equally to Income, Estate, and Gift Taxes. The method of collection,[5] period of limitations for assessment,[6] suspension of such period,[7] burden of proof and evidence,[8] and prohibiting restraining actions in such cases,[9] are the same under the Estate Tax and the Gift Tax.

There has been treated previously the liability of transferees,[10] a donee being such.

§ 560. Notice of Fiduciary Relationship.

In the case of the Gift Tax the only time a notice of fiduciary relationship is required is when the donor has died before the return has been filed and the tax paid.[11] Such notice and notice of termination of the relationship have been discussed previously.[12] When the donor has died it is important that the notice be filed, since failure to do so may result in the deficiency notice

17. § 363, supra.
18. § 364, supra.
19. § 365, supra.
20. § 366, supra.
1. § 366A, supra.
2. § 367, supra.
3. § 369, supra.
4. § 368, supra.
5. § 370, supra.
6. § 371, supra.
7. § 372, supra.
8. § 373, supra.
9. § 374, supra.
10. §§ 552, 555, supra.
11. § 552, supra.
12. § 375, supra.

not being received, with the resultant loss of the right to seek a redetermination of the tax.[13]

§ 561. Credit or Refund.

In all substantial particulars the provisions concerning credit or refund[14] are the same in the case of the Gift Tax as in the case of the Estate Tax. While, in the case of the period of limitations for filing claims for refund under the Estate Tax the maximum time is three years and fifteen months, under the Gift Tax it is three years from April 15th of the calendar year following the year for which the return is filed, and in the case of the latter tax, when there has been an extension agreement in respect to assessment of the tax, the period for filing the claim is extended for six months after the expiration of the agreed time for assessment. The provisions for credit or refund with respect to credit for State or foreign death taxes, does not, of course, apply to the Gift Tax.[15] The limitation on the allowance of credit or refund,[16] interest thereon,[17] the effect of a petition to the Tax Court,[18] and overpayments determined by that court,[19] are the same for both taxes.

§ 562. Waiver of Restrictions on Assessments; Closing Agreements; Compromises.

The provisions respecting waivers, closing agreements, and compromises are the same for Income, Estate, and Gift Taxes and have been discussed heretofore.[20]

§ 563. Miscellaneous Procedural Provisions.

There are certain general procedural provisions of the statute which apply equally to Income, Estate, and Gift Taxes. These relate to bonds,[1] the time for performance of certain acts postponed by reason of war,[2] and the review of a deficiency in any of such taxes, or an action for refund thereof.[3] They have been treated under the chapter on practice and payment in the case of the Estate Tax.

13. IRC, § 6212(b)(1) (1954 Code); see also Chap 12, infra.
14. § 376, supra.
15. § 377, supra.
16. § 378, supra.
17. § 379, supra.
18. § 380, supra.
19. § 381, supra.
20. § 382, supra.
1. § 384, supra.
2. § 385, supra.
3. § 387, supra.

§ 564. Nonresidents Not Citizens.

The provisions of the statute dealing with returns and procedure apply in all substantial respects to nonresidents not citizens of the United States who are subject to the Gift Tax,[4] except as to the place for filing the return[5] and paying the tax,[6] extension of time for payment,[7] and suspension of the period of limitations on assessment when the notice of deficiency is mailed outside the United States.[8] The procedure for assessment, collection, and appeal is the same in the case of donors who are citizens or residents and those who are nonresidents not citizens of the United States.

4. § 428, supra.
5. § 411, supra.
6. § 549, supra.

7. § 550, supra.
8. § 557, supra.

CHAPTER 11

PRELIMINARIES TO ESTATE OR GIFT TAX LITIGATION

§ 565. Scope of Chapter.

In preceding chapters we have proceeded through all of the steps necessary to process an estate for Federal Estate Tax purposes or a gift for purposes of the Federal Gift Tax. The tax fixed by the taxing authorities is satisfactory to the taxpayer in the great majority of all cases, and in such event it is paid and the matter concluded. Where, however, the taxpayer believes that the imposition of the tax is unwarranted either because of the factual situation or the law applicable, after final determination of the tax at the administrative level, i.e., in the Internal Revenue Service of the Treasury Department, there are further opportunities for judicial review of the deficiency assessment.

In this chapter we will consider the desirability of such review, the forums available therefor, and the requirements of practice therein. Since the greater number of tax cases are reviewed by the Tax Court of the United States, we shall treat primarily with the nature and jurisdiction of that Court.

§ 566. Whether or Not to Litigate.

As we have seen, after all means have been taken to settle the amount of tax at the informal conference,[1] and again with the Appellate Division,[2] and a result satisfactory to the taxpayer

---

1. § 334, supra.   2. § 337A, supra.

has not been attained, a notice of deficiency and the ninety-day letter is sent to the taxpayer.[3] It is at this point that a determination must be made whether to pay the tax and conclude the matter, or to continue further with litigation.

The determination of the question is entirely a matter of judgment. First, is the economic consideration of whether the amount of the deficiency warrants the cost in time and money. An important consideration is the merit of the particular issue. If it is believed that either the Tax Court or other tribunal will have a more understanding or sympathetic approach to the question involved, then further litigation should be considered. Where a substantial amount is involved, since an appeal to the Tax Court stays the assessment of the tax until the final decision by the Tax Court,[4] a petition to the Tax Court defers the payment of the tax. The day of reckoning is therefore put off. The exception to this is where a jeopardy assessment is made.[5]

§ 567. Choice of Forum; Generally.

Upon receipt of a notice of deficiency, the taxpayer has three alternatives. He may pay the tax, and thereafter proceed no further, or after paying the tax, file a claim for refund, and if it is denied or not acted on within six months, sue to recover the tax in either the United States District Court or the Court of Claims.[6] The right to institute such action does not depend upon the deficiency being paid under protest. The third alternative, and that most frequently utilized is by filing a petition with the Tax Court to review the deficiency determination.

The time of payment has an important bearing on the choice of forum. Where the tax is paid *before* the mailing of the notice of deficiency, it is questionable whether the Tax Court has jurisdiction, since its jurisdiction is limited to the review of a deficiency determination.[7] The 1954 Code specifically provides that payment of the tax *after* the mailing of the notice of deficiency shall not deprive the Tax Court of jurisdiction over such deficiency.[8] The effect of payment in such case is to prevent any further interest accumulating on the deficiency.[9] As previously

---

3. § 337B, supra.
4. IRC, § 6213(a) (1954 Code).
5. IRC,   § 6861(a)   (1954   Code); § 354, supra.
6. IRC, § 7422 (1954 Code); CFR, § 601.103(c).

7. IRC, §§ 6213, 6214 (1954 Code).
8. IRC, § 6213(b)(3) (1954 Code).
9. IRC, § 6611 (1954 Code).

noted,[10] if an amount in excess of the deficiency as finally determined by the Tax Court has been paid, the statute provides for refund when the decision of the Tax Court becomes final.[11]

An exception to the effect of payment *before* the mailing of the notice of deficiency is when a jeopardy assessment has been made, in which case the right to apply to the Tax Court is not affected, even though the deficiency notice was mailed before the jeopardy assessment was made.[12]

The taxpayer must determine in his case whether, when dissatisfied with the result before the Internal Revenue Service, he will seek a redetermination of the deficiency by the Tax Court or pay the tax and after refund procedure sue in the Court of Claims or the District Court. There is no calipers within which a case may be fitted and the choice made. All which can be done is present the facts with respect to each Court. The factors present in a particular case will determine which is likely to be more advantageous to the taxpayer. It requires a nice balancing of advantages and disadvantages to make the determination, and even then it is merely an intelligent guess. In a particular case the forum may be determined by whether the Tax Court or the Circuit Court in the district has in other cases supported the position taken by the taxpayer.

§ 568. Choice of Forum; Tax Court.

First, it must be borne in mind that the Tax Court is not part of the Internal Revenue Service. Originally constituted in 1924 it was known as the Board of Tax Appeals. In 1942, it was provided that the body formerly the Board of Tax Appeals be known thereafter as the Tax Court of the United States. It is made up of sixteen judges organized into sixteen divisions of one judge each. One of the judges is designated as a chief judge.

Since one of the choices which the dissatisfied taxpayer has is to file a petition for redetermination of a proposed assessment with the Tax Court, the advantages and disadvantages of doing so must be considered.

One of the advantages noted heretofore is that the tax need not be paid in order to seek review by the Tax Court. It is also the fact that the Tax Court judges, dealing only with taxation are experts who quickly grasp the facts and the law. Whether this

10. § 381, supra.   12. IRC, § 6861 (1954 Code).
11. IRC, § 6512(b) (1954 Code).

is an advantage or disadvantage in the particular case can only be determined upon the facts and the law of the case.

A provision of the Tax Court rule states that the Court expects the parties to stipulate evidence to the fullest extent to which agreement can be reached.[13] The result of this is that before the case reaches trial before the Tax Court, conferences on stipulations result in discussion of the facts and the law and naturally leads to negotiations for settlement. Such discussions are had with a representative of the Appellate Division and the trial attorney from the Regional Counsel's office. It will frequently be found that satisfactory settlements can be made at this time, which were not possible prior thereto. With the recent change in settlement authority in Tax Court cases[14] it is anticipated that settlements will be further expedited. Every reasonable effort is made to settle cases before the Tax Court, since the increasing docket of the Tax Court makes it desirable that its burden be eased. The overwhelming percentage of Estate and Gift Tax cases are settled.

Any impression that the Tax Court is sympathetic to the Treasury is not the fact. The judges of the Tax Court are unusually capable and are not swayed by the fact that a government agency is concerned. But this expertness may be a reason for not taking a case to that court. Tax Court judges are not likely to be influenced by extraneous considerations not directly related to the issues, and are quicker to recognize tax devices. Certain factual questions such as valuation or whether a transfer was in contemplation or death have been decided favorably to the taxpayer more often by juries than by the Tax Court, although it is only fair to say that in the latter type of cases, the success of the Treasury before the Tax Court has not been good.

An important consideration in the selection of the Tax Court as the forum is prior decisions of that court on the particular question.

Many intangibles enter into the determination. All which can be done is to point out some of the factors to be considered.

§ 569. Choice of Forum; Court of Claims.

In determining which court shall be selected for review of the tax, the taxpayer must consider alternatives to the Tax Court.

13. Tax Court, Rule 31(b)(1).　　14. Delegation Order No. 60; Chief Counsel's Order No. 1958-5.

One of these is the Court of Claims.[15] Trial in that court is available only if a claim for refund has been filed and rejected or not acted upon.[16]

The Court of Claims consists of five judges sitting at Washington. However, upon request, testimony of witnesses is taken by commissioners assigned by the court, who will arrange for it to be taken at a time and place convenient to the parties. Upon completion of the proof, the commissioner makes findings of fact and objections may be filed thereto. In most cases submission is made upon agreed facts. If there is to be argument it must be had before the Court in Washington.

There is no right to trial by jury in the court. Since the Federal discovery procedure applies in the court, there may be an advantage in obtaining evidence which is not available under Tax Court procedure. In spite of the fact that decisions of the Court of Claims have been based more on a consideration of the factual situation in the application of the law, comparatively few tax cases are presented to the court. The reason probably is that if a question of fact is presented, the lawyer generally would prefer trial in the District Court before a jury.

§ 570. Choice of Forum; District Court.

The second alternative to trial before the Tax Court, is trial in the U. S. District Court in the district in which the taxpayer resides.[17] Here again, the tax must have been paid and claim for refund filed and rejected or not acted upon before suit may be brought.[18]

Prior to July 30, 1954 unless suit was brought against the District Director to whom the tax was paid, there was no right to trial by jury in the District Court.[19] It was because it was a personal suit against the Director that jury trial was available. Amendment of the statute in 1954 removed the major distinction between a suit against the District Director and a suit against the United States. The chief advantage in still suing the District Director is the difference in taxable costs.[20]

The first and probably greatest advantage of suit in the District Court is the right to trial by jury upon proper demand therefor.[1] The jury being made up of taxpayers, where there is a

15. CFR, § 601.103(c); 28 USC § 1491.
16. Note 6, supra.
17. 28 USC § 1346(a)(1)(3).
18. Note 6, supra.

19. 28 USC § 2402.
20. 28 USC § 2412(a)(b).
1. Note 19, supra.

question of fact, such as valuation, or whether a transfer was in contemplation of death, or a gift or business transaction, juries have been found to favor the taxpayer. The chances are approximately three to one in favor of the taxpayer. Tax Court judges are more dispassionate in their determinations.

Another advantage which trial in the District Court has, as in the case of trial in the Court of Claims, is that the case is under the jurisdiction of the Justice Department. Counsel in charge of the case is less likely to be as technical as the attorneys for the government in the Tax Court, the latter being members of the legal staff of the Regional Counsel or Chief Counsel of the Treasury. Justice Department attorneys have a somewhat different approach to settlement.

There is also the possible advantage of the application of the Federal discovery procedure in the District Court, which is not applicable to the Tax Court.

The chief disadvantage of selecting the District Court as the forum, is the fact that the tax must first be paid. This apparently is a compelling motive in the great majority of cases, since they are brought in the Tax Court.

§ 571. Requirements for Practice; Tax Court.

Practice before the Tax Court of the United States is not limited to lawyers. Any qualified person may be admitted to practice before it.[2] Pursuant to the authority granted to it by statute[3] the Tax Court has promulgated Rules of Practice, among which is Rule 2 relating to admission to practice. The court is authorized to make and enforce reasonable rules for admission and of practice.[4]

While persons other than lawyers must pass a written examination, all an attorney-at-law need do is file a completed application upon the form provided, accompanied by a current certificate from the Clerk of the Appropriate court, showing that he has been admitted to practice before and is a member in good standing of the Bar of the Supreme Court of the United States, or of the highest court of any State or Territory, or of the District of Columbia.[5]

2. IRC, § 7452 (1954 Code).
3. IRC, § 7453 (1954 Code).

4. Goldsmith v US Board of Tax Appeals, 4 F2d 422 (CA DC) (1925).
5. Tax Court Rule 2.

Other applicants must obtain letters from three sponsors and pay a ten dollar examination fee. An applicant who fails the examination three times is not thereafter eligible to take another examination for admission.[6]

Legal firms will not be admitted or recognized. Neither will corporations. But a taxpayer may appear for himself and a taxpayer corporation may be represented by a bona fide officer upon permission of the court.[7]

FORM NO. 72

APPLICATION FOR ADMISSION TO PRACTICE

(Attorney at Law)

I, DANIEL WEBSTER CLAY, a citizen of the United States, hereby apply for admission to practice before the Tax Court of the United States, and submit the following:

1. I reside at (Number—Street) 115 Remada Drive, (City and Zone) Buffalo, (County) Erie, (State) New York.

2. My office address is (Number—Street) 100 Main Street, (City and Zone) Buffalo, (County) Erie, (State) New York.

3. I was admitted to the bar of the (Enter name of highest court) Supreme Court, of the State of New York, on the 29th day of November, 1926 (see attached certificate), and have never been denied admission to or suspended or disbarred from practice before said court or any court of any State, Territory or District of the United States, or any United States court, department, or agency, except as follows: (None), and no action of a disciplinary nature is now pending against me.

4. I am a member (or associate) of the firm of Clay, Calhoun and Stephens.

5. I am a member of (State membership in professional societies) Bar Assn. of Erie County, N. Y., State Bar Assn. and American Bar Assn.

6. I have read the Rules of Practice of the Tax Court of the United States and consider myself qualified to represent parties in proceedings before it.

STATE OF NEW YORK
COUNTY OF ERIE } ss:

DANIEL WEBSTER CLAY, being first duly sworn, says that he is the person named in the foregoing application for admission to practice

6. Note 5, supra.   7. Note 5, supra.

before the Tax Court of the United States and that the statements of fact therein contained are true.

DANIEL WEBSTER CLAY
(Signature of Applicant)

Subscribed and sworn to before me this 14th day of April, 1960.

MARSHALL A. HAHN
(Signature of Officer)

(IMPRESS SEAL HERE)   Notary Public, State of New York
(Official Title)

Enclosures: Clerk's certificate of current date. (See par. 3, above.)
See reverse for Practitioner's Oath, which must be duly executed.

STATE OF NEW YORK
COUNTY OF ERIE } ss:

I, DANIEL WEBSTER CLAY, do solemnly swear (or affirm) that I will support and defend the Constitution of the United States against all enemies, foreign and domestic; that I will bear true faith and allegiance to the same; that I will conduct myself according to law and the Rules and Practice of the Tax Court of the United States; that my conduct will be upright, without misrepresentation by concealment or otherwise, and such, so far as in my power, as will justify the confidence reposed in me by the Court and its judges and by parties whom I may at any time represent and as will promote and maintain respect for the United States, the Court, and those who are entitled to practice before it. SO HELP ME GOD.

DANIEL WEBSTER CLAY
(Signature of Applicant)
100 Main Street, Buffalo, N. Y.
(Business Address)

Subscribed and sworn to before me this 14th day of April, 1960.

ANDREA HAYES
(Signature of Officer)
Notary Public Erie County
(Official Title)

§ 572. Requirements for Practice; Court of Claims.

Any person of good moral character who is a citizen of the United States or of any territory or possession thereof and *who has been admitted to practice* in the Supreme Court of the United States or the highest court of any state, territory, or the District of Columbia, or the United States Court of Customs and Patent Appeals, and is in good standing therein, may be admitted to practice.[8] Thus, only lawyers may practice before the court.

8. Court of Claims Rule 78.

Admission may be had upon oral motion of a member of the bar of the Court, or if the Court is not in session before the Chief Judge or senior Judge,[9] or upon verified application in writing showing the requirements, accompanied by a certificate that he is a member of the bar in good standing, two letters or signed statements of member of the bar of the Court of Claims or of the Supreme Court of the United States, not related to the applicant, stating he is personally known to them, possesses all the required qualifications and that they have examined his application and affirm that his personal and professional character and standing are good.[10]

In either case an oath is required. A fee of $5 is also payable.[11] Foreign attorneys, barristers, or advocates whose country extends a like privilege may be admitted for a particular case.[12]

There may be only one attorney of record who shall be an individual and not a firm.[13]

§ 573. Requirements for Practice; District Courts.

In the case of the District Courts the requirements for admission to practice vary from district to district. In some, admission is had upon motion, while in others petitions and accompanying documents are required. The procedure may be informal or formal, have detailed requirements for admission to practice or otherwise, depending on the particular district.

The simplest way is to write to the Clerk of the District Court in which admission is sought. All details will be furnished, and necessary forms when required.

9. Court of Claims Rule 78(a).
10. Court of Claims Rule 78(b).
11. Court of Claims Rule 78(c).

12. Court of Claims Rule 78(d).
13. Court of Claims Rule 80.

CHAPTER 12

JURISDICTION OF TAX COURT

§ 574. Scope of Chapter.

Since the great majority of all appeals in tax cases are presented to the Tax Court of the United States, we shall treat thereof particularly. While the term "appeal" is generally used, neither in the case of a petition to the Tax Court, nor in an action in the Court of Claims or the District Court is there in terms an appeal. In the Tax Court the proceeding is one for the redetermination of a deficiency, and in the other courts the action is one for recovery of the tax. The effect, however, is the same as in the case of appeal in other proceedings or actions.

The Tax Court being a statutory one, its jurisdiction is only such as the statute grants. We shall, therefore, in this chapter treat of those jurisdictional requirements which must be complied with in order for the Court to consider and determine the questions presented to it, preliminary to the actual initiation of the case.

§ 575. Jurisdiction; Generally.

Such authority as the Tax Court of the United States possesses is limited to that granted by statute. Its primary function is to determine whether a deficiency assessment[1] has been properly determined.[2] As the statute states, the Tax Court has jurisdiction to redetermine the correct amount of the deficiency *even if the amount so redetermined is greater than the amount of the*

---

1. IRC, § 6211(a) (1954 Code).   2. IRC, § 6214(a) (1954 Code).

deficiency, notice of which has been mailed to the taxpayer, and to determine whether any *additional amount, or addition to the tax* should be assessed, if claim therefor is asserted by the Secretary or his delegate at or before the hearing or a rehearing.[3]

If the Tax Court finds that there is no deficiency and further finds that the taxpayer has made an *overpayment of* Income Tax for the same taxable year, of Gift Tax for the same calendar year, or of Estate Tax in respect of the taxable estate of the same decedent, in respect of which the Secretary or his delegate determined the deficiency, or finds that there is a deficiency but that the taxpayer has made an overpayment of such tax, the Tax Court has jurisdiction to determine the amount of such overpayment.[4]

It will be observed that the Tax Court has jurisdiction only with respect to a deficiency in tax or an overpayment, but not with respect to either an overassessment[5] or a refund.[6] Jurisdiction in this respect extends not only to the tax itself, but also to additional amounts or additions to the tax.[7]

In redetermining an Income Tax or Gift Tax deficiency the Court *may consider* such facts with relation to taxes for other years as may be necessary to correctly redetermine the amount of the deficiency, but in so doing has *no jurisdiction* to determine whether or not the tax *for any other year* has been overpaid or underpaid.[8] As we have seen in the case of the Gift Tax it is necessary to consider taxes paid in prior years.

It will also be observed that any additional amount may be asserted by the Commissioner at or before the hearing or a rehearing. In such case the claim is made in an amended answer, the statute of limitations not running while the proceeding is pending before the Court.[9] *The effect is to place the burden of proof as to such new matter upon the Commissioner.*[10]

§ 576. Notice of Deficiency; What It Is.

Preliminary to the Tax Court acquiring jurisdiction a deficiency must have been determined and notice thereof mailed to

3. Note 2, supra.

4. IRC, § 6512(b)(1) (1954 Code); Huntington Natl Bank, 13 TC 760 (1949).

5. Will County Title Co, 38 BTA 1396 (1938); Difco Laboratories, Inc, 10 TC 660 (1948).

6. Fairbanks v Comm, 128 F2d 537 (CCA 5) (1942).

7. See § 367, supra.

8. IRC, § 6214(b) (1954 Code); Scofield, 25 TC 774 (1955).

9. Warburg, 6 TCM 789 (1949); Loew, BTA mem op, Dec 12, 240-F (1942).

10. Tax Court Rule 32.

the taxpayer.[11] We have previously discussed the definition of a notice of deficiency.[12]

There has been much litigation on the subject of the deficiency notice. This has related to what such a notice is and service of the notice, as to form, method and persons.

Since an appeal to the Tax Court rests upon the notice of deficiency and its service, the statute provides for a precise definition of it[13] and the manner and method of service.[14]

Deficiency means the excess of the tax over the sum of the amount shown as such tax by the taxpayer upon his return and the amounts previously assessed (or collected without assessment) as a deficiency; but such sum shall first be reduced by the amount of rebates made. If no return is made, or if the return does not show any tax, for the purpose of the definition "the amount shown as the tax by the taxpayer upon his return" is considered as zero. Accordingly, in any such case, if no deficiencies with respect to the tax have been made, the deficiency is the amount of the tax. Additional tax shown on an "amended return" so-called, filed after the due date of the return, is a deficiency within the meaning of the Code.[15]

The statute provides that the Commissioner must *determine a* deficiency exists.[16] Not every notice respecting additional tax is a determination of a deficiency. Where the tax has been incorrectly computed, notice to that effect is not a determination of deficiency.[17] Whether a particular act of the Commissioner amounts to a determination, is a question of fact.[18] Various communications in the course of the audit are not determinations. Thus, proposed recomputations of the tax,[19] demand from the District Director for payment of an assessment,[20] notice that the audit shows additional tax to be due,[1] or letters such as the invitation to an informal conference or the thirty day letter,[2] are none of them a notice of deficiency within the meaning of the statute.

11. IRC, §§ 6212, 6213 (1954 Code).

12. § 336, supra.

13. IRC, § 6211 (1954 Code).

14. IRC, § 6212(a)(b) (1954 Code).

15. Reg, § 301.6211–1(a).

16. IRC, § 6212(a), as amended by Technical Amendments Act of 1958, § 89(b), HR 8381, 85th Cong, 2nd Sess.

17. IRC, § 6213(b) (1954 Code); Reg, § 301.6213–1(b)(1).

18. Mitchel, 1 BTA 143 (1924).

19. Heafey, 1 BTA 267 (1924).

20. Terminal Wine Co, 1 BTA 697 (1924); Greene, 2 BTA 148 (1925).

1. Moyer, 1 BTA 75 (1924); Sutton, 1 BTA 101 (1924); Musser, 1 BTA 278 (1924).

2. Fidelity Insurance Agency, 1 BTA 86 (1924).

It will be observed that these questions arose at the inception of the Board of Tax Appeals, the predecessor to the Tax Court. Under today's procedures there is little likelihood of such questions arising. The thirty day letter specifically advises that it is not a statutory notice of deficiency[3] and the ninety day letter encloses the notice of deficiency and advises of the procedure on appeal.[4]

While the statute prescribes no form for the deficiency notice, the Internal Revenue Service has adopted the form heretofore illustrated.[5]

§ 577. Notice of Deficiency; Form and Service of.

The statute now provides that if the Secretary or his delegate determines that there is a deficiency in tax he is authorized to send notice of such deficiency to the taxpayer by certified mail or registered mail.[6] Prior to September 2, 1948 the statute specified mailing by *registered* mail. While the statute does not require the notice to be signed,[7] it customarily is, and it may be signed by the District Director,[8] or examiner.[9] It is provided that the Secretary or his delegate is *authorized* to notify the taxpayer of the deficiency by certified mail or registered mail. Under the statute specifying registered mail, the provision was construed by the Tax Court to mean that service must have been made by registered mail.[10] Since September 2, 1958 certified mail will be a compliance with this decision. However, it has recently been held that a notice sent by ordinary mail is sufficient if it is received.[11]

The time within which to file a petition in the Tax Court begins to run from the date of mailing of the deficiency notice, *not the date of receipt.*[12] *Nor is it the date of the letter.*[13]

The statute further provides that in the absence of notice to the Secretary or his delegate of the existence of a fiduciary rela-

---

3. Form No. 55, § 335, supra.
4. § 337B, supra.
5. Form No. 65, § 337B, supra.
6. Note 16, supra.
7. Oswego Falls Corp, 26 BTA 60, affd 71 F2d 673 (CA 2) (1932).
8. Newman, 6 BTA 373 (1927); Smith, 22 F Supp 1011 (1938).
9. Sutton, note 1, supra; Gillespie, 5 TCM 1028 (1945); Wisotskey, 2 TCM 226 (1943).

10. John A. Gebelein, Inc, 37 BTA 605 (1938); Welch v Schweitzer, 106 F2d 885 (CCA 9) (1939); Greve, 37 BTA 450 (1938).
11. Boren, 57–1 USTC ¶ 9426 (CA 9).
12. Note 16, supra.
13. Hurst, Anthony & Watkins, 1 BTA 26 (1924); Southern California Loan Assn, 4 BTA 223 (1926).

tionship,[14] it is sufficient in the case of the Gift Tax that the notice of deficiency be mailed to the taxpayer at his last known address, even if the taxpayer is deceased, or is under legal disability, or, in the case of a corporation, has terminated its existence,[15] and in the case of the Estate Tax, if addressed in the name of the decedent or other person subject to liability, if mailed to his last known address.[16]

The fact that the taxpayer removed from the address given on the return does not affect the sufficiency of the service,[17] unless the taxpayer notifies the District Director of the new address to be used.[18]

If the fiduciary has given notice of his discharge,[19] service of the deficiency notice upon him is ineffective,[20] but even if he has been discharged, if he has not given notice thereof to the District Director the notice mailed to him is adequate.[1]

§ 578. Persons Entitled to File Petition.

The statute merely provides that the taxpayer may file a petition with the Tax Court for a redetermination of the deficiency.[2]

The Rules of the Tax Court provide that a case in that Court shall be brought by and in the name of the person against whom the Commissioner determined the deficiency (or liability, as the case may be), or by and in the full descriptive name of the fiduciary legally entitled to institute a case on behalf of such person. In the event of a variance between the name set forth in the notice of deficiency or liability, and the correct name, a statement of the reasons for such variance shall be set forth in the petition.[3]

Since jurisdiction of the Court depends upon the proper parties, the provisions are strictly construed, and jurisdiction has been denied when petitions have been filed for an estate by a person under a power of attorney from a decedent,[4] trustees instead of executors,[5] fiduciaries instead of beneficiaries,[6] an

---

14. See § 375, supra.

15. IRC, § 6212(b)(1) (1954 Code).

16. IRC, § 6212(b)(3) (1954 Code).

17. Hurd, 9 TC 681 (1947).

18. Clark v Comm, 173 F2d 13 (CA 2) (1949).

19. See § 375, supra.

20. Gillespie v Comm, 5 TCM 1028 (1945).

1. Brandt, 7 TCM 271 (1946).

2. IRC, § 6213(a) (1954 Code).

3. Tax Court Rule 6; see also Rules 4, 7, 23.

4. Miller, BTA, Docket No. 1595.

5. Fifth Third Union Trust Co, 20 BTA 88, revd other grounds, 56 F2d 767 (CA 6) (1932); St. Louis Union Trust Co, 21 BTA 76 (1931).

6. Powers, 20 BTA 753 (1930).

individual who filed both individually and as fiduciary, as against the individual,[7] beneficiaries instead of fiduciary,[8] and life tenant instead of trustee.[9]

However, where the person filing the petition is the proper party even though the deficiency notice is addressed to another, the Court has assumed jurisdiction. Thus, where the notice of deficiency was addressed to decedent after his death,[10] the estate before appointment of the fiduciary,[11] the executor instead of sole devisee and legatee,[12] the beneficiary,[13] or a discharged fiduciary who had not given notice, the Court has taken jurisdiction when the proper party has filed a petition in such case.

§ 579. Transferees.

We have seen that a transferee of assets may become liable for payment of the tax, which is assessed and collected in the same manner and subject to the same provisions and limitations as with respect to a deficiency.[14] A transferee is a taxpayer within the meaning of the statute[15] and may file a petition to the Tax Court.[16]

As heretofore noted,[17] the Commissioner has the burden in transferee cases to establish liability as transferee, and the latter has pre-trial privileges not available in other cases.

§ 580. Time within Which Petition to Be Filed.

Within 90 days or 150 days if the notice is addressed to a person outside the *States of the Union* and the District of Columbia, after the notice of deficiency *is mailed* (not counting Saturday, Sunday, or a legal holiday in the District of Columbia as the last day), the taxpayer may file a petition with the Tax Court for a redetermination of the deficiency.[18] The term "State of the Union" does not include the Territories of

7. Melczer, 23 BTA 124, pet for rev dism 63 F2d 1010 (CCA 9) (1931).

8. Hanify, 21 BTA 379 (1931); Lowrance, 23 BTA 1055 (1931).

9. Shea, 31 BTA 513 (1934).

10. Eisendrath, 28 BTA 744 (1933).

11. Howell, 21 BTA 757, appeal dism 59 F2d 1053 (CA 8) (1931).

12. Helmholz, 28 BTA 165 (1933).

13. New York Trust Co. v Comm, 54 F2d 463 (CA 2), revg 20 BTA 162, cert den 285 US 556, 76 L ed 945, 52 S Ct 457 (1932).

14. §§ 370 et seq, supra.

15. Phillips v Comm, 42 F2d 177 (CA 2), cert den 283 US 589, 75 L ed 1289, 51 S Ct 608 (1930); see also IRC, § 7701 (a)(14) (1954 Code).

16. Duggan, 18 BTA 608 (1929); Roche v Comm, 63 F2d 623 (CA 5) (1933).

17. § 373, supra.

18. Note 2, supra.

Alaska and Hawaii.[19] Alaska's statehood may present a question. It will be noted that the term "United States" is not used, in which case there would be a difference.[20]

Since the statute is applied strictly, it should first be noted that the time limitation is either 90 or 150 *days,* and further that the time begins to run from the *date of mailing* of the notice of deficiency and neither the date of the deficiency letter nor its receipt.[1]

The 150 day period has been held to apply to a taxpayer outside the States of the Union, even though the notice of deficiency was sent to the last known address of the taxpayer within the States of the Union.[2] It has also been held that there is no distinction between persons residing abroad regularly and those temporarily absent.[3] In the light of the statutory language,[4] it appears difficult to reconcile these decisions.

The statute provides that with respect to filing of documents in the Tax Court[5] timely mailing shall be treated as timely filing, so that the postmark stamped on the cover in which the petition is mailed shall be deemed the date of delivery, but only if the postmark date fall within the prescribed period or on or before the prescribed date for the filing of the petition, and only if it was deposited in the mail in the United States in an envelope or other appropriate wrapper, postage prepaid, properly addressed.[6] In the case of mailing or stamp machine, the statute applies only if and to the extent provided by Regulations.[7] Such Regulations have not yet, been promulgated. If the mailing is by registered mail, the date of registration is the postmark date.[8]

There is no provision permitting extension of the time for filing the petition. No action of the Commissioner may be so construed, even an erroneous statement by him of the time for filing.[9]

In computing the time, the date of mailing is excluded and the date of filing is excluded.[10]

19. Reg, § 301.6213–1(a).
20. IRC, § 7701(a)(9) (1954 Code).
1. See § 577, supra.
2. Hamilton, 13 TC 747 (1949).
3. Mindell v Comm, 200 F2d 38 (CA 8) (1952).
4. IRC, § 6213(b) (1954 Code).

5. IRC, § 7502(d) (1954 Code).
6. IRC, § 7502(a) (1954 Code).
7. IRC, § 7502(b) (1954 Code).
8. IRC, § 7502(c) (1954 Code).
9. Ruby, 2 BTA 377 (1925).
10. Chambers v Lucas, 41 F2d 299 (CA DC) (1930).

§ 581. Place of Filing Petition.

The statute provides that the petition must be filed with the Tax Court.[11]   The Rules of the Tax Court provide that the office of the Tax Court of the United States is located on the northeast corner of 12th Street and Constitution Avenue N. W. 1, Washington, D. C. The office of the Clerk of the Court is in Room 2004.[12]

The office of the Clerk is open from 8:45 A.M. to 5:15 P.M. on all days except Saturdays, Sundays and legal holidays in the District of Columbia, for the purpose of receiving petitions, pleadings, motions, and the like.[13]

All mail sent to the Court should be addressed to:

> Tax Court of the United States
>   Box 70
>   Washington 4, D. C.

Other addresses where the Court may be in session should never be used in addressing mail to the Court or to its Clerk.[14]

An exception to this is when the Judge presiding at the trial permits documents to be filed at the particular session of the Court.[15]   The exception does not apply to a petition for redetermination of a deficiency.

§ 582. Fee for Filing Petition.

Pursuant to statutory authority[16] the Tax Court provides that the fee for filing a petition shall be $10, payable at the time of filing.[17]   Checks, money orders, etc. for fees or charges of the Court should be made payable to the *Treasurer of the United States* and mailed or delivered to the Clerk of the Court.[18]

While it is customary and proper to pay the fee at the time of the filing of the petition, and the Rule so provides, it has been held that payment of the fee thereafter did not deprive the Tax Court of jurisdiction.[19]

§ 583. Service of the Petition.

Unlike the practice in civil courts generally, a proceeding in the Tax Court is initiated by filing with the Court a petition, together with the copies required.[20]

11. IRC, § 6213(a) (1954 Code).
12. Tax Court Rule 1(a).
13. Tax Court Rule 1(d).
14. Tax Court Rule 1(b).
15. Tax Court Rule 5.
16. IRC, § 7451 (1954 Code).
17. Tax Court Rule 7(b).
18. Tax Court Rule 1(e).
19. Weaver v Blair, 19 F2d 16 (CCA 3) (1927); Reliance Mfg. Co. v Blair, 19 F2d 789 (CCA 7) (1927).
20. Tax Court Rule 7(a)(1).

The Rules provide for the clerk to make service of a copy of the pleading, motion, notice, brief, or other document to be served on the petitioner and the respondent.[1]

There is, therefore, no need for the petitioner to make service upon the Commissioner.

§ 584. Effect of Payment of Tax.

The Tax Court does not have jurisdiction of an action for refund of tax paid. As we have seen, such action must be instituted in either the Court of Claims or the District Court. Therefore, if the tax was paid, prior to the 1954 Code, whether such payment was made before or after the mailing of the deficiency notice, no petition could be filed in the Tax Court. The 1954 Code, however, specifically provides that in any case where the tax is paid *after the mailing of the notice of deficiency,* such payment shall not deprive the Tax Court of jurisdiction.[2] The purpose of payment after the mailing of the deficiency notice is to stop the running of interest.[3]

If the payment is made before the mailing of the notice of deficiency, under the 1954 Code as under the 1939 Code no notice of deficiency will be mailed and the Tax Court will have no jurisdiction.[4]

There is an additional case in which payment of the tax does not deprive the Tax Court of jurisdiction. We have seen that in any case where the Commissioner believes the assessment or collection of a deficiency will be jeopardized by delay, he may immediately assess a deficiency.[5] In such case, while it is customary to file a bond to stay collection, the taxpayer may pay the tax. In that case, while the procedure differs, depending upon whether the jeopardy assessment is made before or after the filing of a petition,[6] the jurisdiction of the Tax Court exists.[7] If the jeopardy assessment is made before the mailing of the notice of deficiency, then the Commissioner must mail the notice of deficiency within sixty days thereafter.[8] If it is made either before or after the filing of a petition with the Tax Court, then the Commissioner is required to notify the Tax Court of the Assessment.[9]

1. Tax Court, Rule 22.
2. IRC, § 6213(b)(3) (1954 Code).
3. IRC, § 6601(f)(4) (1954 Code).
4. Reg, § 301.6213–1(b)(3).
5. §§ 353, 354, supra.
6. § 355, supra.

7. IRC, § 6861 (1954 Code); see California Associated Raisin Co, 1 BTA 314 (1924); Miller, 2 BTA 72 (1925).
8. IRC, § 6861(b) (1954 Code).
9. IRC, § 6861(c) (1954 Code).

CHAPTER 13

PLEADINGS AND MOTION PRACTICE
IN TAX COURT

§ 585. Scope of Chapter.

The lawyer engaged in general practice, in an action in any civil court, realizes that the issues to be determined by the court must be presented by the pleadings. Because all of the facts have been presented to the Internal Revenue Service before a case reaches the Tax Court, those unfamiliar with the practice may assume that these facts are known to the Tax Court. It is the purpose of this chapter to eliminate any such idea and show the significance of the pleadings, those which are necessary, and the facts which must be alleged in order to properly present one's case to the Court. There will also be considered those motions and other procedural steps connected with pleadings which it is required that the practitioner know.

§ 586. Petition; Significance of.

The Tax Court Rule requires that the petition shall be complete *in itself* so as fully to state the issues.[1] The trial before the Tax Court *is a trial de novo*. None of the proceedings which have taken place in the Internal Revenue Service, nor any of the evidence there presented is before the Court. The only way in which it may learn of these matters is when these facts or documents are offered in evidence upon the trial.[2] The case is decided upon the record made at the hearing, and not upon anything which has gone before which is not presented. If the petition does not set forth the facts upon which the Court may base its decision, the Court not only will not, but cannot, by surmise, supply deficiencies in pleadings for findings of fact.[3] There will, therefore, be considered in the succeeding sections, all of the essential elements of a proper petition.

§ 587. Form and Style of Papers; Generally.

The Rule sets forth the general requirements with respect to papers filed with the Court.

(1) Papers filed with the Court may be prepared by any process provided the information therein is set forth in clear and legible type.

(2) All papers must be bound together *on the left hand side only*.

(3) All papers must have a caption and a signature and copies must be filed as specified below.

(4) *Printed papers* must be printed in 10 or 12 point type, on good unglazed paper, $5\frac{3}{4}$ inches wide by 9 inches long, with inside margin not less than 1 inch wide, and with double-leaded text and single-leaded quotations.

(5) *Typewritten papers* must be typed on only one side of plain white paper, $8\frac{1}{2}$ inches wide by 11 inches long, and weighing not less than 16 pounds to the ream.

(6) *Citations* must be in italics when printed and underscored when typewritten.

(7) *The proper caption*, omitting all prefixes and titles must be placed on all papers. The full name and surname of the taxpayer, such as Winthrop Benson, not Mr. Winthrop Benson, and if an estate, the name of the estate and of the fiduciary,

---

1. Tax Court Rule 7(c)(2).
2. Barry, 1 BTA 156 (1925); Gutterman Strauss Co, 1 BTA 243 (1924).

3. Buffalo Wills-St. Claire Corp, 2 BTA 364 (1925).

with his title, such as Estate of Winthrop Benson, Deceased, Katherine Benson, Executrix.

(8) *The signature* of petitioner or counsel must be subscribed in writing to the original pleading, motion, or brief. Signature must be in individual *and not firm name*. The name must also be typewritten, as well as the mailing address.

(9) *Four conformed copies,* which must be clear and legible, but which may be on any weight paper, must be filed with the signed original except where the Rules provide otherwise. Papers to be filed in more than one case, as in a motion to consolidate, must include one additional copy for each additional case.[4]

The failure of a petition to comply with the Rule is ground for dismissal of the case.[5]

§ 588. Petition; Form; Generally.

The Rules provide the requirements as to the form of the petition.[6]

(1) It must be substantially in accordance with the form in Appendix I of the Rules.

(2) It must be complete in itself so as fully to state the issues.

(3) No telegram, cablegram, radiogram, telephone call, or similar communication will be recognized as a petition.

(4) It must contain:

(A) A caption in the following form:

TAX COURT OF THE UNITED STATES

Estate of WINTHROP BENSON, Deceased,
    KATHERINE BENSON, Executrix,
        Petitioner,
            v.   Docket No. 90,000
COMMISSIONER OF INTERNAL REVENUE,
        Respondent.

PETITION

(B) Numbered paragraphs stating:

1. Petitioner's name and principal office or residence, and the office of the Director, or District Director of Internal Revenue in which the tax return for the period in controversy was filed.

2. The date of mailing of the notice of deficiency on which the

4. Tax Court Rule 4.   6. Tax Court Rule 7(c).
5. Tax Court Rule 7(a)(2).

petition is based, or other proper allegations showing jurisdiction in the Court.

3. The amount of the deficiency (or liability, as the case may be), determined by the Commissioner, the nature of the tax, the year or other period for which the determination was made and, if different from the determination, the approximate amount of taxes in controversy.

4. *Clear and concise assignments of each and every error* which the petitioner alleges to have been committed by the Commissioner in the determination of the deficiency. *Issues in respect of which the burden of proof is by statute placed upon the Commissioner will not be deemed to be raised by the petitioner in the absence of assignment of error in respect thereof.* Each assignment of error must be lettered.

5. *Clear and concise lettered statements of the facts* upon which the petitioner relies as sustaining the assignments of error, except those assignments of error in respect of which the burden of proof is by statute placed upon the Commissioner.

6. A prayer, setting forth relief sought by the petitioner.

It is also required that the petition be verified, and there must be annexed a copy of the deficiency notice.

Each of these requirements will be severally treated in succeeding sections.

§ 589. Petition; Caption and Introduction.

The first statement appearing in the petition is the caption. This is in the form illustrated and prescribed.[7] It is important in this respect to make certain that the petitioner is the proper party.[8] Otherwise, dismissal of the petition will follow.

As noted,[9] if the name set forth in the deficiency notice is incorrect, there should be a statement explaining the variance. Thus, if the deficiency notice was sent to the taxpayer, he having died in the interim, the fiduciary would appear as the petitioner and include in the petition the statement as to the fact of death, the date thereof, and the facts of his appointment as fiduciary.

The form of petition in Appendix I of the Rules of Practice of the Tax Court contains as the introductory statement, "The above named petitioner hereby petitions for a redetermination of the deficiency set forth by the Commissioner of Internal Rev-

7. § 588, supra.
8. § 578, supra.

9. Note 8, supra.

enue in his notice of deficiency (Reference:AU:F:EG:SAB–1st New York) dated March 15, 1960 and as the basis for his case alleges as follows:"

It will be observed that the date of the deficiency notice in the introductory statement is not the date upon which the jurisdiction of the Court depends.[10]

§ 590. Petition; Jurisdictional Allegations.

The first three paragraphs of the petition deal with the allegations necessary to confer jurisdiction on the Court. These must indicate that the petitioner is a person entitled to seek relief. He must state his name, principal office or residence, and the District Director's office in which the return in controversy was filed.[11] If an individual, his full given name and surname, and if acting for a trust or estate, the name of the estate, his name, and his title must be stated.[12] Also as noted,[13] if his name differs from that in the deficiency notice, an explanation is required.

There must then be alleged *the date of the mailing* of the deficiency notice, or other proper allegations showing jurisdiction of the Court.[14] Unless the petition has been filed within the statutory period after the mailing of the notice, the Court is deprived of jurisdiction.[15] *Not only must the date of the mailing of the notice be alleged, but a copy of the deficiency notice must be appended to the petition, and to each copy required.*[16]

There must be alleged the amount of the deficiency (or liability as the case may be), determined by the Commissioner, the nature of the tax, the year or other period for which the determination was made and, if different from the determination, the approximate amount of taxes in controversy.[17] It will be recalled that the Court's jurisdiction is limited to the redetermination of deficiencies and is limited to the year involved.[18]

§ 591. Petition; Assignment of Errors.

The heart of the petitioner's case consists of two parts. The first of these is the assignment of errors. These must be sep-

10. § 580, supra.
11. Tax Court Rule 7(c)(4)(B)(1).
12. Tax Court Rule 4(e).
13. Note 8, supra.
14. Tax Court Rule 7(c)(4)(B)(2).
15. Note 10, supra.
16. Tax Court Rule 7(c)(4)(E).
17. Tax Court Rule 7(c)(4)(B)(3).
18. § 575, supra.

arately lettered. *A clear and concise statement of each and every error* which it is claimed the Commissioner made in the determination of the deficiency is necessary.[19]

These assignments of error present the taxpayer's case in a nutshell. They create the issues upon which the hearing will be held and the Court will make its determination. If the issue is not presented, no matter what evidence is presented the Court will not consider it.[20] Issues not raised by the pleadings cannot be raised for the first time in a brief filed after the hearing.[1]

If the assignment of errors does not present the issues clearly and concisely and in orderly and logical sequence, the task of the Court is increased and the chances of success are lessened.

In the presentation of errors the petitioner is not limited to matters which were previously raised, but may present any valid basis which exists.[2] But he should limit himself to the errors of the Commissioner[3], and not raise issues as to matters which were raised in the audit and review of the tax, but which are no longer present.

Where the statutory burden of proof is on the Commissioner, no issue will be deemed raised by the petitioner in the absence of assignments of error in respect thereto.[4]

If a statement has accompanied the notice of deficiency, so much thereof as is material to the issues set out in the assignments of error must be appended to the petition. If the notice of deficiency refers to prior notices from the Commissioner, which are necessary to elucidate the determination, such parts thereof as are material to the issues set out in the assignments of error must likewise be appended.[5]

§ 592. Petition; Statement of Facts.

Equally important as the assignment of errors, if in fact, not more important, is the statement of facts upon which the

19. Tax Court Rule (7c)(4)(B)(4).
20. Weaver, 2 BTA 709 (1925); Walter & Co, 10 BTA 629 (1928); Camp Wolters Land Co, 5 TC 336 (1945); Kington, 8 BTA 981 (1927); Lowell, 9 BTA 62 (1927); Heckett, 8 TC 841 (1947); Mutual Lumber Co, 16 TC 370 (1951); Toledo Stove Range Co, 16 TC 1125 (1951).
1. Weaver, note 20, supra; North American Coal Corp, 28 BTA 807 (1933); McParrish & Co, 3 TC 119, aff'd

147 F2d 284 (CCA 5) (1944); Houdry, 7 TC 666 (1946); Greenberg, 25 TC 534 (1956).
2. Barry, 1 BTA 156 (1924); Gutterman Strauss Co, 1 BTA 243 (1924); Kling, 1 BTA 1048 (1924).
3. Cleveland Home Brewing Co, 1 BTA 87 (1924); Thomas Shoe Co, 1 BTA 124 (1924).
4. Note 19, supra.
5. Note 16, supra.

[Harris]—48

petitioner relies as sustaining the assignments of error. The assignment of errors presents the questions the Court is asked to determine. But it cannot do so without the facts upon which the determination must be based. As previously observed, the Tax Court has no knowledge of the case other than it obtains from the pleading and the evidence. All which has happened before in the Internal Revenue Service is unknown to it. For a proper presentation by the taxpayer, his petition should acquaint the Court with the facts upon which he relies to sustain his case.

The Rule requires that the statement of facts be *clear and concise.*[6] This is the general rule with respect to pleadings in any court. In the form of petition[7] furnished as an example in the Appendix to the Rules of the Tax Court, it is advised that there should be set forth allegations of the *facts* relied upon— *but not the evidence*—in orderly and logical sequence, so as fully to inform the Court of the issues to be presented and to enable the Commissioner to admit each or deny each specific allegation. This is sound advice.

The statement of facts to a large extent resembles an opening address to a jury. The attorney for the plaintiff in such case will state in chronological order the facts which he intends to present, and will do so in an orderly and logical sequence, so that the jury will be able to understand the evidence as it is presented. The statement of facts may well follow this pattern, without going into the evidence at length. This serves the purpose of permitting the Court to grasp the facts quickly and simplifies the presentation of the case. A well prepared statement of facts also serves the purpose of a trial outline.

The preparation of the statement of facts requires the exercise of discretion. It must neither be too brief to present the facts upon which the petitioner relies, nor must it be so lengthy as to be virtually a resumé of the evidence to be presented. Since the Commissioner's answer must contain a specific admission or denial of each material allegation of fact contained in the petition,[8] if the petitioner's statement of facts is properly drawn, admission of such facts by the Commissioner makes the presentation of the petitioner's case simpler.

In the presentation of the facts, it is advisable to confine

6. Tax Court Rule 7(c)(B)(5).   8. Tax Court Rule 14(b).
7. Tax Court Rules, Appendix 1, a, par 5.

them to the issues raised by the assignment of errors. It is neither necessary nor advisable to trace each step of the proceedings from the filing of the return to the filing of the petition with the Tax Court. Most of such facts have no bearing on the issue before the Court and taxes its patience. Any fact which will sustain the assignment of errors is pertinent, but not every fact in connection with a tax case is.

§ 593. Petition; Prayer for Relief.

The petition must contain a prayer, setting forth the relief sought by the petitioner.[9] The form indicated is "Wherefore, the petitioner prays that this Court may try the case and (here state the relief desired)."[10] The relief desired in the majority of cases is that the Court determine either that there is no deficiency, if it is claimed that there should be none, or redetermine a deficiency in the amount claimed by the taxpayer, where part of the deficiency has been proper.[11]

§ 594. Petition; Signature and Verification.

The allegations of the petition having been completed the petition must be *signed* by the petitioner *or* his counsel.[12]

The petition must be verified *by the petitioner;* provided that where the petitioner is sojourning outside the United States or is a nonresident alien, the petition may be verified by a duly appointed attorney in fact, who must attach to the petition a copy of the power of attorney under which he acts and who must state in his verification that he acts pursuant to such power, that such power has not been revoked, that petitioner is absent from the United States, and the grounds of his knowledge of the facts alleged in the petition. The term "United States" includes only the States and the District of Columbia. *A notary public is not authorized to administer oaths, etc., in matters in which he is employed as counsel.*

Verifications by fiduciaries must contain a statement that the fiduciaries signing and verifying have authority to act for the taxpayer.

Where the petitioner is a corporation, the person verifying must state in his verification that he has authority to act for the corporation.

---

9. Tax Court Rule 7(c)(B)(6).

10. Tax Court Rules, Appendix 1, a, prayer.

11. IRC, § 6214(a) (1954 Code).

12. § 587, supra; Tax Court Rules 7(c)(4)(C), 4(f).

The signature and the verification to the petition is considered the certificate of those performing these acts that there is good ground for the petition, the case has not been instituted merely for delay, and it is not frivolous.[13]

The signature must be followed by the name and address of the person signing the petition and his address must be typed or printed immediately beneath the written signature.[14]

If there is more than one taxpayer, all must verify the petition.[15] When the petition is verified by an attorney in fact or by an agent, if he lacks authority the petition may be dismissed.[16] Verification when the taxpayer is sojourning abroad or is a nonresident alien, by an attorney in fact, is confined to such cases and not to those where the taxpayer is away from the city.

It will be observed that while the petition may be signed by the taxpayer or his counsel, *it must be verified by the taxpayer,* except in the cases noted.

§ 595. Request for Place of Trial.

The Rules provide that the petitioner at the time of filing the petition shall also file a request showing the name of the place where he would prefer the trial to be held. If the petitioner has filed no request the respondent shall file at the time he files his answer, a request showing the name of the place preferred by him.

These requests must be separate from the petition or answer, must have a caption, and must consist of an original and *two* copies.[17]

The Court will fix the time and place for trial to afford reasonable opportunity to a taxpayer to try his case with as little inconvenience and expense as is practicable. A trial may be requested at any place at which suitable courtroom facilities are available and a sufficient number of cases are ready for trial.[18] The Rules partially list the cities in which sessions of the Court are held. In the larger cities there is no problem about obtaining a trial at the place requested, usually the city where, or near where, the District Director's office is located in which the return was filed.

13. Tax Court Rule 7(c)(4)(D).
14. Tax Court Rule 4(f).
15. Greenan, 145 F2d 134 (CA 9) (1944).

16. Hoj, 26 TC 1074 (1956); Stange, 1 BTA 810 (1924).
17. Tax Court Rule 26.
18. Tax Court Rules, Appendix II.

FORM NO. 72A
Request for Place of Trial

TAX COURT OF THE UNITED STATES

Estate of WINTHROP BENSON, Deceased,
KATHERINE BENSON, Executrix,
Petitioner,
v.
COMMISSIONER OF INTERNAL REVENUE,
Respondent.

Docket No. 90,000

Comes now the Petitioner, by her counsel, and requests that the trial of the above entitled case be held at New York City, New York.

DANIEL WEBSTER CLAY

(Signature)

DANIEL WEBSTER CLAY

Attorney for Petitioner
150 Broadway
New York 6, N. Y.

§ 596. Filing the Petition.

The petition having been prepared, it is necessary that the original, together with *four* copies[19] be filed with the Clerk of the Court,[20] and the fee paid.[1] The original and two copies of the request for place of trial should be filed at the same time.[2] It must be remembered that a case in the Tax Court is initiated by the filing of the petition and the copies in accordance with the Rule.[3] Failure of the petition to comply with the Rules is ground for dismissal of the case.[4]

§ 597. Docket Number.

Upon receipt of the petition by the Clerk, the case will be entered upon the docket and assigned a number and the parties notified thereof. The docket number must be placed on all papers thereafter filed in the case and referred to in all correspondence with the court.[5]

19. § 587, supra.
20. § 581, supra.
1. § 582, supra.
2. § 595, supra.

3. Tax Court Rule 7(a)(1).
4. Tax Court Rule 7(a)(2).
5. Tax Court Rule 11.

§ 598. Example of Petition.

There is a substantial difference between an explanation of the requirements of a petition, and the application of the explanation to particular facts. The writer's thesis has always been that a single example is more effective than many words. There follows, therefore, an example of the manner in which a petition is prepared in an actual case.

FORM NO. 73

Petition to Tax Court

TAX COURT OF THE UNITED STATES

Estate of WINTHROP BENSON, Deceased,
  KATHERINE BENSON, Executrix,
     Petitioner,
              Docket No. 90,000
      v.
COMMISSIONER OF INTERNAL REVENUE,
  Respondent.

PETITION

The above-named Petitioner hereby petitions for a redetermination of the deficiency set forth by the Commissioner of Internal Revenue in his notice of deficiency (Reference:AU:F:EG:SAB—1st New York) dated March 15, 1960, and as the basis for her case alleges as follows:

1. The petitioner is the Executrix under the Last Will and Testament of Winthrop Benson, who died a resident of Copiague, Long Island, New York, having duly qualified as such in the Surrogates Court of the County of Suffolk, State of New York on the 15th day of December, 1958, and resides at 100 Elm Street, Copiague, New York. The Estate Tax return involved herein was filed with the District Director of Internal Revenue for the First District of New York.

2. The notice of deficiency (a copy of which is attached hereto and marked Exhibit A) was mailed to the petitioner on the 15th day of March, 1960.

3. The deficiency as determined by the Commissioner is in Estate Tax in the amount of $3,996.90, and the entire amount thereof is in dispute.

4. The determination of tax set forth in the said notice of deficiency is based upon the following errors:

(a) Respondent erroneously determined that the decedent in making a transfer, inter vivos, of 240 shares of Eastman Kodak stock to his wife, Katherine Benson, reserved the income therefrom for life, and that the transfer was consequently one to take effect at the death of the decedent under Section 2036 of the Internal Revenue Code of 1954.

5. The facts upon which the petitioner relies as the basis of this case are as follows:

(a) For purposes of convenience the petitioner, the decedent's wife, with her own funds purchased 240 shares of Eastman Kodak stock on April 14, 1952, and caused the same to be issued in the name of the decedent.

(b) In September 1956, she requested her husband to transfer the stock to her, which was done, but the stock was not transferred on the books of the corporation.

(c) A Gift Tax return was filed for the transfer and thereafter the dividends were received by the decedent and turned over to his wife, or used for the payment of certain requirements of the wife.

(d) The decedent retained no rights in the stock nor in the income therefrom after the transfer.

WHEREFORE the petitioner prays that this Court may try the case and determine that there is no deficiency in Estate Tax.

DANIEL WEBSTER CLAY
(Signature)
Daniel Webster Clay
Attorney for Petitioner
150 Broadway
New York 6, N. Y.

STATE OF NEW YORK   ⎫
                    ⎬ ss:
COUNTY OF NEW YORK ⎭

Katherine Benson, being duly sworn, says that she is the Executrix under the Last Will and Testament of Winthrop Benson, Deceased, the petitioner above named; that she has read the foregoing petition, and is familiar with the statements contained therein, and that the statements contained therein are true, except those stated to be upon information and belief, and that those she believes to be true.

Katherine Benson

Subscribed and sworn to before
  me this 20th day of May, 1960
  ANDREA HAYES
  Notary Public
  New York County

EXHIBIT A.

(This is a copy of the notice of deficiency and the line adjustments which accompanied the notice.)

§ 599. Answer; Time for; Form.

As previously noted,[6] after the petition has been filed, it is served upon the Commissioner by the Clerk of the Court. After

---

6. § 583, supra.

service of the petition, the Commissioner has sixty days within which to file an answer or forty-five days within which to move with respect to the petition.[7]

The answer is required to be drawn so that it will advise the petitioner and the Court fully of the nature of the defense. It must contain a specific admission or denial of each material allegation of fact contained in the petition and a statement of any facts upon which the Commissioner relies for defense or affirmative relief or to sustain any issue raised in the petition in respect of which the burden of proof is, by statute, placed upon him. Paragraphs of the answer are numbered to correspond to those of the petition.[8]

This is not as helpful as it sounds, since in the usual case, the burden of proof being on the taxpayer, the Commissioner follows the advice of the old practitioner to the beginner, "admit nothing, deny everything, and make them prove it." It is not quite as blatant as that, but ordinarily the answer will admit only those facts of which the Commissioner cannot claim lack of knowledge.

Every material allegation of fact set out in the petition and not expressly admitted or denied in the answer, shall be deemed to be admitted.[9]

While the Commissioner need not plead the reason for disallowing a deduction,[10] if he raises any new matter, such as a claim for an additional amount, or addition to the tax,[11] as to which he seeks affirmative relief, or matters as to which he has the burden of proof, such as fraud[12] or in transferee cases,[13] then he must state the facts upon which he relies.[14]

§ 600. Reply; Necessity for.

The affirmative allegations of the answer will be deemed denied in the absence of a reply, unless the Commissioner, within 45 days after the expiration of the time for filing a reply, files a motion reciting that a reply required under the Rules was not filed and requesting the Court to enter an order that specified allegations of fact in the answer shall be deemed to be admitted.[15]

7. Tax Court Rule 14(a).

8. Tax Court Rule 14(b).

9. Tax Court Rule 18(a).

10. Bard Parker Co, Inc, 18 TC 1255, affd 218 F2d 52 (CA 2) (1955); Standard Oil Co. v Comm, 129 F2d 363 (CA 7), cert den 317 US 688, 87 L ed 551, 63 S Ct 261 (1942).

11. IRC, § 6214(a) (1954 Code).

12. IRC, § 7454 (1954 Code).

13. IRC, § 6902(a) (1954 Code).

14. Note 8, supra.

15. Tax Court Rule 18(c)(1).

This requires a determination of when a reply is required. A reply is required when an answer served upon the petitioner alleges material facts.[16] Such facts will be alleged where the Commissioner seeks affirmative relief or has the burden of proof by statute.[17]

The safe procedure in such cases is to file a reply. If the motion referred to above is made, the Clerk will serve a copy thereof on the counsel of record and issue notice of a hearing thereon at which hearing the Court may grant the motion unless the required reply is filed on or before the day fixed for such hearing.[18] It saves much wasted energy if the reply is served in all cases where required. If the Commissioner does not move, as we have seen, the affirmative allegations in the answer will be deemed denied. It would be most unusual for the Commissioner to fail to do so. However, the Regional Counsel will ordinarily advise petitioner's counsel of the need for a reply before moving therefor.

The reply may not be used as a means of permitting the petitioner to plead new matter.[19] The proper method of doing this is by amendment of the pleading, considered hereafter.[20]

§ 601. Reply; Time for; Form.

The petitioner, after service upon him of an answer which requires a reply, has 45 days within which to file the same, or 30 days within which to move with respect to the answer.[1]

The reply must contain a specific admission or denial of each material allegation of fact contained in the answer and must set forth any facts upon which *the petitioner* relies for defense. The paragraphs of the reply must be numbered to correspond with the paragraphs of the answer. The original copy of each reply must be signed by the petitioner or his counsel.[2] Upon motion of the Commissioner upon good cause shown, or upon its own motion, the court may require that a reply be verified.[3]

An original and *4 copies* of the reply must be filed with the Clerk of the Court, and each copy must be conformed to the original.[4]

16. Tax Court Rule 15(a).
17. § 599, supra.
18. Tax Court Rule 18(c)(2).
19. Central Nat. Bank, 29 BTA 530 (1933).
20. § 603, infra.
1. Note 16, supra.
2. Tax Court Rule 15(b).
3. Tax Court Rule 15(d).
4. Tax Court Rule 15(c).

A copy of the answer will be served on the petitioner by the Clerk of the Court.

FORM NO. 74

Answer

TAX COURT OF THE UNITED STATES

Estate of WINTHROP BENSON, Deceased,
    KATHERINE BENSON, Executrix,
        Petitioner,

            v.

COMMISSIONER OF INTERNAL REVENUE,
        Respondent.

Docket No. 90,000

ANSWER

Now comes the Commissioner of Internal Revenue, by his attorney, Arch M. Cantrall, Chief Counsel Internal Revenue Service, and for answer to the petition filed in this proceeding, admits and denies as follows:

1. Admits the allegations contained in paragraph 1 of the petition.

2. Admits the allegations contained in paragraph 2 of the petition.

3. Admits that the deficiency as determined by the Commissioner is in Estate Tax in the amount of $3,996.90; denies the remaining allegations contained in paragraph 3 of the petition.

4. (a) Denies the allegations contained in paragraph 4(a) of the petition.

5. (a), (b), (c), (d) Denies the allegations contained in paragraphs (a), (b), (c) and (d) of the petition.

6. Denies generally each and every allegation contained in the petition not hereinabove specifically admitted, qualified or denied.

WHEREFORE, it is prayed that the determination of the Commissioner of Internal Revenue be in all respects approved.

                    ARCH M. CANTRALL
                       (Signature)
                    Chief Counsel
                    Internal Revenue Service

OF COUNSEL;
    Charles B. Smart
    Regional Counsel
    Kenneth Gross
    Alfred A. Adams
    Attorneys
    Internal Revenue Service

§ 602. Joinder of Issue.

There is no necessity for filing any notice or other form, in order to join issue. A case is deemed at issue upon the filing of the answer unless a reply is required, in which event it is deemed at issue upon filing of the reply, or the entry of an order under Rule 18(c).[5]

§ 603. Amended and Supplemental Pleadings.

A motion for leave to amend a pleading must state reasons for granting it and must be accompanied by the proposed amendment.[6]

The petition may be amended at any time before the answer is filed. Thereafter, and up to the commencement of the trial, it may only be done either with the consent of the Commissioner or by leave of the Court.[7]

While the Court is liberal in allowing amendment, the application must be made in time,[8] although the Court may exercise its discretion.[9] Errors which are not jurisdictional may be corrected by amendment,[10] but not otherwise.[11] Amendment may not be used as a device for filing a petition which has not been filed within the statutory time.[12]

The Court upon its own motion, or upon motion of either party, prior to setting of the case for trial, may order a party to file a further and better statement of the nature of his claim, of his defense, or of any matter stated in any pleading. The motion must point out the defects complained of and the details desired.[13] Such a motion may either be set down for hearing or it may be acted on ex parte.[14] If the motion is granted, an amended pleading must be filed within fifteen days or such other time as the Court allows. If the amended pleading is not filed within the time fixed, the Court may strike the pleading or make such other order as it deems just.[15]

---

5. Tax Court Rule 16.
6. Tax Court Rule 17(a).
7. Tax Court Rule 17(b).
8. Bankers Realty Syndicate, 20 BTA 612 (1930).
9. Steele Wedeles Co, 63 F2d 541 (CCA 7) (1933); Second Carey Trust Co. v Helvering, 126 F2d 526 (CA DC), cert den 317 US 642, 87 L ed 517, 63 S St 34 (1942); Peruna Co, 11 BTA 1180 (1928).

10. Lord & Bushwell Co, 7 BTA 86 (1927); note 8, supra.
11. Wald, 8 BTA 1003 (1927); Aldene Club, 1 BTA 710 (1924); Mills, 1 BTA 199 (1924); Guitar, 1 BTA 213 (1924).
12. Satovsky, 1 BTA 22 (1924).
13. Tax Court Rule 17(c)(1).
14. Tax Court Rule 17(c)(2).
15. Tax Court Rule 17(c)(3).

The Court may at any time *during the course of the trial* grant a motion by either party to amend its pleadings to conform to the proof in particulars stated at the time by the moving party. The amendment or amended pleadings thus permitted, must be filed with the Court at the Trial or must be filed in the office of the Clerk of the Court within such time as the Court may fix.[16]

The Rule formerly provided that the motion must be made before the conclusion of the trial. The revision of April 1, 1958 uses the phrase "during the course of the trial". While the Court has said that the former phrase meant that the time did not extend beyond the time when the trial was concluded and the briefs filed,[17] the Fourth Circuit would extend the time for amendment up to the final decision.[18] The 1958 amendment would indicate that the Tax Court adheres to its position, which appears to be reasonable. It is particularly important in the Tax Court to amend the pleadings to conform to the proof, since the Court is limited in its findings to the case pleaded. The Court will ordinarily grant the motion,[19] and even after the trial.[20] But in the view of the amendment of the Rules, it may be questioned whether an amendment of the pleading will be permitted after the trial. Certainly, a new question may not be raised for the first time in the brief filed after the trial.[1]

§ 604. Motions.

During the course of a tax case there may be necessity for various motions. These may be for leave to file an amended pleading, to require the filing of a further and better statement of the nature of a claim or defense, to dismiss the petition, for severance or consolidation, or for a continuance. Such motions must be timely, must fully set forth the alleged reasons for the action sought and must be prepared in the form and style required by the Rule.[2]

The method of moving in the Tax Court is to file the original and *four copies* with the Clerk of the Court. He serves a copy

16. Tax Court Rule 17(d).
17. Pierce Oil Corp, 30 BTA 469 (1934).
18. Helvering v Edison Securities Corp, 78 F2d 85 (CCA 4) (1935).
19. Alexander Mfg. Co, 9 BTA 347 (1928); Sunnyside Coal & Coke Co, 9 BTA 984 (1928); Kelly, 10 BTA 141 (1928).
20. Behr, 30 BTA 1290 (1934); Mitchell, 32 BTA 1093 (1935); McParrish & Co, 3 TC 119 (1944).
1. Note 17, supra.
2. Tax Court Rule 19(a).

on the counsel of record.[3] Motions will be acted on as justice may require and may, in the discretion of the Court, be placed upon the motion calendar for argument. It is suggested that if the motion is one to which there is no objection, that such fact be noted on the motion.[4] If argument is required, the Clerk will notify the parties, and the proceeding will be listed for hearing on a motion calendar which is called in Washington, unless good cause is shown for holding the hearing elsewhere. Ordinarily the calendar is called at 10 A.M. on Wednesdays.[5]

If a party fails to appear at the call of the motion calendar, the Court will hear the proceeding ex parte. However, a memorandum or brief stating the position of the petitioner upon the motion will be accepted when the failure of the petitioner to appear is justified by distance, shortness of time, or other good reason stated in the memorandum or brief.[6]

Where the motion is directed to defects in a pleading, prompt filing of a proper pleading correcting the defects may obviate the necessity of a hearing.[7]

If a motion, other than one relating to the receipt of evidence during trial, is made orally during trial, the maker must promptly reduce it to writing and file it with the Court unless the Judge sitting directs otherwise.[8]

No motion for retrial, further trial, or reconsideration may be filed more than 30 days after the opinion has been served, except by special leave.[9]

No motion to vacate or revise a decision may be filed more than 30 days after the decision has been entered, except by special leave.[10]

Motions for retrial, further trial or reconsideration, and to vacate or revise a decision, must be separate from each other and not joined to or made a part of any other motion.[11]

3. Tax Court Rule 22.
4. Tax Court Rule 19(b).
5. Tax Court Rule 27(a)(1).
6. Tax Court Rule 27(a)(2).
7. Tax Court Rule 27(a)(3).

8. Tax Court Rule 19(d).
9. Tax Court Rule 19(e).
10. Tax Court Rule 19(f).
11. Tax Court Rule 19(f).

FORM NO. 75

Motion

TAX COURT OF THE UNITED STATES

Estate of WINTHROP BENSON, Deceased,
   KATHERINE BENSON, Executrix,
         Petitioner,
            v.   Docket No. 90,000
COMMISSIONER OF INTERNAL REVENUE,
   Respondent.

MOTION FOR LEAVE TO FILE AMENDED PETITION

Comes now the Petitioner, by her counsel, and moves this Court to grant leave to the Petitioner to file an amended petition herein, a copy of which is annexed hereto.

                   Respectfully Submitted,
                   DANIEL WEBSTER CLAY
                      (Signature)
                   Daniel Webster Clay
                   Attorney for Petitioner
                   150 Broadway
                   New York 6, N. Y.

§ 605. Extensions of Time.

With respect to pleadings, an extension of time will ordinarily be granted by the Court. This does not mean that the time for the filing of a petition to the Tax Court may be extended. As we have seen, the time within which a petition may be filed is statutory and the Court has no authority to extend such time.[12]

An extension of time may be granted by the Court within its discretion upon a timely motion filed setting forth good and sufficient cause therefor, or may be ordered by the Court upon its own motion.[13]

If a motion is filed or an order issued in respect to the adequacy of any petition, the time prescribed in Rule 14(a) begins to run from the date upon which the Court takes final action with respect to the motion or order unless the Court orders otherwise. The time for reply is similarly extended in the case of a motion or order directed to the answer.[14]

Any extension of time for filing a brief correspondingly ex-

---

12. § 580, supra.
13. Tax Court Rule 20(a).

14. Tax Court Rule 20(b).

tends the time for filing all other briefs to be filed unless the Court directs otherwise.[15]

While the Court is lenient in the matter of granting extensions of time for pleading, and in fact many such motions are upon consent, we shall see that this leniency does not extend to motions for continuance or adjournment of the trial.[16]

§ 606. Substitution of Parties.

Where subsequent to the filing of a petition the taxpayer dies, or there is a substitution of fiduciaries, a motion must be made to substitute the new parties. This is done by filing the motion and annexing a certificate from the court which appointed the substitute fiduciaries, unless the certificate is waived by the Commissioner.[17] The Court may order the substitution of proper parties upon the death of a petitioner, or where there is a mistake in the name or title of a party.[18] This is done as a matter of course.[19] The failure to substitute the deceased taxpayer's fiduciary is not fatal to the proceeding.[20]

This must not be confused with the case where a person who is not entitled to do so files the petition. That subject has been discussed heretofore.[1] When the person filing the petition is not the person named in the deficiency notice, as we have seen,[2] the petition should contain an explanation of the variance.

§ 607. Appearance, Withdrawal, and Substitution of Counsel.

Ordinarily counsel makes his appearance by subscribing the original petition.[3] He must, of course, be admitted to practice before the Court. Where there is a substitution of parties, counsel who subscribes the motion therefore will be deemed to have entered his appearance for the new party and must promptly file a motion by the new petitioner for the withdrawal of the former counsel, unless the latter is to continue as counsel for the new petitioner.[4]

Otherwise counsel may enter an appearance *only* by filing in

15. Tax Court Rule 20(c).
16. § 617, infra.
17. Tax Court Rule 23(a)(c).
18. Tax Court Rule 23(d).
19. See Rusk, 20 BTA 138, affd 53 F2d 428 (CCA 7) (1932); Paulson, 10 BTA 732 (1928); Hurd, 12 BTA 368 (1928); Hall, 10 BTA 847 (1928).

20. Duggan, 18 BTA 608 (1929); Manton, 7 TCM 937 (1946).
1. § 578, supra.
2. § 589, supra.
3. Tax Court Rule 24(a)(1).
4. Tax Court Rule 24(a)(2).

duplicate Form 305, which must show that counsel is admitted to practice before the Court, and must bear his signature and office address.[5] The forms are obtainable from the Clerk of the Court, but an adequate substitute will suffice.

Counsel not enrolled to practice may be recognized at a hearing or trial, by special leave of the Court, but only where it appears that counsel can and will promptly become enrolled.[6]

Counsel of record may move to withdraw from a case upon notice to the client, and the client has the same remedy upon notice to counsel. The Court may, in its discretion, deny such motion.[7]

Substitution of counsel may likewise be had upon motion on notice to counsel of record, or if he has designated other counsel to receive service,[8] upon notice to such counsel.[9]

If the petitioner or his counsel changes his mailing address, notice thereof must promptly be filed with the Court, *in duplicate*. A separate notice must be filed for each case.[10]

FORM NO. 76

Entry of Appearance

TAX COURT OF THE UNITED STATES

WASHINGTON

Estate of WINTHROP BENSON, Deceased,
    KATHERINE BENSON, Executrix,
            Petitioner,   Docket No. 90,000
                v.
COMMISSIONER OF INTERNAL REVENUE,
    Respondent.

ENTRY OF APPEARANCE

The undersigned, being duly admitted to practice before the **Tax Court** of the United States as Attorney, herewith enters his appearance **for** the Petitioner in the above-entitled case.

B. WASHBURNE FIELDING
(Signature)
B. Washburne Fielding
400 Fifth Avenue
New York 36, N. Y.

5. Tax Court Rule 24(a)(3).   8. Tax Court Rule 22(b).
6. Tax Court Rule 24(a)(4).   9. Tax Court Rule 24(c).
7. Tax Court Rule 24(b).   10. Tax Court Rule 24(d).

CHAPTER 14

PROCEEDINGS PREPARATORY TO TRIAL

§ 608. Scope of Chapter.

Having proceeded through all of the steps necessary to create an issue for determination by the Tax Court, we have now arrived at the point where the case has been docketed and we await the trial. In this respect a tax case is like any other case in any court. It is largely won or lost by the manner in which it is prepared for trial. As any lawyer of experience knows, it is not usually the trial which determines the result, but the thoroughness with which counsel has considered the facts and the law and prepared for the presentation of these to the court.

After the tax case is docketed, many months will go by before the trial. In the intervening period it is the responsibility of counsel to collate the facts and the law, so that presentation of them at the trial is largely pro forma.

In this chapter, therefore, we shall deal with all those matters which should be done to assure a successful result. This will include negotiations for settlement, if that is possible, agreement with counsel for the Commissioner on those facts which may be stipulated, calendar practice, and preparation of outlines of the facts to be presented, if all of the facts have not been stipulated, as well as the preparation of an adequate trial memorandum.

§ 609. Stimulants to Settlement.

If every case docketed in the Tax Court were to be tried, few practitioners before the Court would survive long enough to try their cases. It must be remembered that there are but sixteen judges of the Court. More than 5,000 cases are docketed annually. Less than 1,000 are disposed of by trial. As of June 30, 1957 the number of pending cases was more than 10,000. It can be seen from this that a litigant before the Court would be in the position of the man climbing a hill, who went forward two steps and fell back three. The picture is not hopeless, however, since more than 80% of all the cases docketed are settled before trial. Every effort is made to encourage settlements.[1]

In the first place the Court, six months prior to the anticipated trial date sends Form 30 to the parties. This requests information as to the possibilities of settlement, whether a stipulation of facts required by the Rules has been prepared, whether the case will be ready for trial, and the estimated trial time. This begins the initiation of consideration of possibilities of settlement.

Ninety days before the trial date the trial notices are served on the parties, instead of sixty days as formerly. This is a further stimulus to considering the possibilities of settlement, since the imminence of the trial always energizes lawyers.

Most recently the settlement jurisdiction of the Regional Counsel's office has been extended.[2] Formerly, the Appellate Division had jurisdiction to settle docketed cases, subject to the concurrence of Regional Counsel. The difficulty with this was that while the technical adviser representing the Appellate Division was capable and well informed, he did not have to try the case, and would insist on terms which the trial counsel considered too onerous. Being aware of the many situations which may arise in the trial of a case, the trial attorney is usually readier to arrive at an adjustment. Since this practice was unsatisfactory, the procedure has been changed. Before the opening date of the session at which the case is upon the calendar for trial the responsibility for settlement is joint, as formerly, any differences to be determined by Chief Counsel. But, after

1. Address of J. Edgar Murdock, Chief Judge, to Tax Executives Institute 12th Annual Congress, Journal of Taxation, Vol 8, No 2 p 106 (Feb 1958).

2. Delegation Order No 60 and Chief Council's Order No 1958–5.

the opening of the session, the conclusion of Regional Counsel as to the advisability of settlement is controlling. This should result in many more settlements.

A third stimulant to settlement is the requirement of the Tax Court that the parties stipulate evidence to the fullest extent to which complete or qualified agreement can be reached. That subject is considered in the succeeding section. The negotiations in connection with the stipulation of facts, inevitably leads to discussion of the facts and the law with the trial attorney and is a natural introduction to the subject of settlement.

It is these procedures which have resulted in such a large percentage of all cases docketed in the Tax Court being settled without necessity for trial. As Judge Murdock suggested,[3] the waiting period between docketing and trial, acts as a cooling off period and is conducive to settlements.

§ 610. Stipulation of Facts.

The Rules of the Tax Court provide that the Court *expects* the parties to stipulate evidence *to the fullest extent* to which complete or qualified agreement can be reached including all material facts that are not or fairly should not be in dispute.[4]

The party expecting to introduce any evidence which might possibly be stipulated (as for example, entries or summaries from books of account and other records, documents, and all other evidence, to the extent not disputed) is required to confer with his adversary promptly after receipt of the trial notice, and both are required to endeavor to stipulate all facts not already stipulated.[5]

Shortly after the receipt of the trial notice, the counsel for the petitioner will receive a letter from the special attorney handling the case in the Regional Counsel's office, requesting that counsel make an appointment with the attorney for a conference to discuss the preparation of a stipulation of facts. It may also be suggested that counsel prepare a draft of a proposed stipulation.

Unless the Commissioner has the burden of proof, the attorney for the petitioner should prepare a proposed stipulation of facts containing the maximum amount of facts which may reasonably be expected to be stipulated. A great deal of time and

---

3. Note 1, supra.
4. Tax Court Rule 31(b)(1).

5. Tax Court Rule 31(b)(2).

inconvenience to witnesses is saved by stipulating all possible facts. The special attorney in the office of Regional Counsel will be found most cooperative and will stipulate as many facts as possible. In many cases it will be found that all of the facts can be stipulated and there will be no need for producing any witnesses. A failure to stipulate when it is possible to do so is not looked upon favorably by the Court. If it were not for the widely used stipulation procedure, it would be impossible for the Court to dispose of the number of cases it does.

The stipulation of facts must be reduced to writing and may be filed with the Court in advance or presented at the trial. When it is filed, it need not be offered formally to be considered in evidence. The stipulation must be filed *in duplicate,* except that duplicates of the exhibits attached to the original need not be filed with the copy.[6]

Any objections to all or any part of a stipulation should be noted in the stipulation, but the Court will consider any objection to stipulated facts made at the trial.[7]

The Court may set aside a stipulation in whole or in part where justice requires, but otherwise will not receive evidence tending to qualify, change, or contradict any fact properly introduced into the record by stipulation.[8]

The stipulation need not be in any specific form and does not prevent submission of evidence upon the trial. If the facts cannot be stipulated, the trial proceeds by testimonial proof. It is usual to provide that the right is reserved to offer further evidence not at variance with the stipulated facts, and the right to object to the materiality or relevancy of such facts.

The parties may not stipulate as to the interpretation of a statute,[9] but may stipulate that if upon the facts the Commissioner erred as a matter of law, the computation of the taxpayer is correct.[10]

6. Tax Court Rule 31(b)(3).
7. Tax Court Rule 31(b)(4).
8. Tax Court Rule 31(b)(5).
9. Jamison Coal & Coke Co, 24 BTA 544 (1931); Lewis, 47 F2d 32 (CCA 7) (1931).
10. Forbes, 82 F2d 204 (CCA 2) (1936).

FORM NO. 77

Stipulation of Facts

TAX COURT OF THE UNITED STATES

Estate of WINTHROP BENSON, Deceased,
  KATHERINE BENSON, Executrix,
    Petitioner,
        v.   Docket No. 90,000
COMMISSIONER OF INTERNAL REVENUE,
    Respondent.

STIPULATION OF FACTS

It is hereby stipulated by and between the Commissioner of Internal Revenue and the Petitioner, by their respective counsel, that the following facts shall be taken as true, and that this stipulation shall be without prejudice to the right of either party to introduce other and further evidence upon the trial of this case not inconsistent with the facts stipulated herein, and to object to the introduction in evidence of any such facts on the ground that they are immaterial or irrelevant.

1. The decedent, Winthrop Benson, died on the 22nd day of November, 1958, a resident of Copiague, Long Island, New York.

2. Katherine Benson, the widow of the decedent, on April 14, 1952, with her own funds purchased 240 shares of Eastman Kodak stock, which stock was issued in the name of the decedent.

3. In September 1956 Katherine Benson requested the decedent to transfer said 240 shares of Eastman Kodak stock to her.

4. On the 21st day of September, 1956 the decedent delivered to Katherine Benson, the said shares of stock.

5. That said stock was never transferred on the corporate books of Eastman Kodak Company, and the decedent was the record owner thereof at the date of his death.

6. That the decedent received the dividends on said stock after the said transfer, which dividends were delivered to Katherine Benson or used for payment of her obligations.

7. That the decedent filed a Gift Tax return for the calendar year 1956, and the said transfer of 240 shares of Eastman Kodak stock to Katherine Benson was reported therein, as appears from said return annexed hereto and marked Exhibit 1–A.

DANIEL WEBSTER CLAY
(Signature)
Attorney for Petitioner
ARCH M. CANTRALL
(Signature)
Attorney for Commissioner
of Internal Revenue

§ 611. Depositions; Generally.

The Tax Court Rules are quite detailed with respect to depositions, three rules being devoted to the subject. The Appendix to the Rules contains the form of application and return.

When either party desires to take a deposition, he must file with the Court a *verified* application and *two conformed copies.* The Court will supply the form, but the application may be made on a substitute form, so long as it contains all the information required by the Court's form.[11]

The application must be filed at least 30 days prior to the date the case is set for trial, and the deposition must be completed and filed at least 10 days prior to the trial. *The application will not be regarded as sufficient ground for a continuance,* unless the case has been at issue less than 60 days and the motion for continuance has been filed not less than 20 days prior to the trial date. Under special circumstances, and for good cause shown, the Court may otherwise order.[12]

The officer before whom the deposition is taken must be authorized to administer oaths, and must not have office connection or business employment with either party or his counsel except by consent of the parties and when no other officer is available, and in his certificate of return to the deposition must so certify.[13]

Upon receipt of the application, the Clerk will serve a copy on the opposite party, and allow a reasonable time for objection. Thereafter, the Court will, in its discretion, make an order, a copy of which will be mailed or delivered to the parties or their counsel, wherein the Court will name the witness whose deposition is to be taken and specify the time when, the place where, and the officer before whom the witness is to testify, but such time, place, and officer specified may or may not be the same as set forth in the application. The applicant must thereupon make all necessary arrangements for the taking of the deposition and furnish the officer before whom it is to be taken with a copy of the order.[14]

At any time after issue is joined, the parties or their counsel may stipulate for the deposition, which must be filed and state the name and address of the witness, the time and place of taking, and the name and address of the officer before whom it is to be

11. Tax Court Rule 45(a).
12. Tax Court Rule 45(b).

13. Tax Court Rule 45(c).
14. Tax Court Rule 45(d).

taken. No order is necessary, but the return must be made in the same way as when there is an order.[15]

Each witness must take the oath or affirm and his questions and answers recorded verbatim. Objections must be noted, without unnecessary comment, explanation, or argument.[16] Other witnesses may be excluded.[17] The testimony must be read and signed by the witness.[18]

When the deposition is returned it must show the docket number and caption, the place, date of taking, the name of the witness and by whom called, counsel present and whom they represent, and in the body the name of counsel examining or cross-examining. The sheets must be fastened so they cannot be tampered with, the exact testimony must be returned, and all exhibits must be marked so as to be identified, and attached to the deposition if practicable. There must be attached a certificate of return.[19]

The original deposition and exhibits, together with *two copies* of the depositions must be enclosed by the officer in a sealed packet, with postage or other transportation charges prepaid, and forwarded to the Tax Court. The original *must* be forwarded to the Court, while the copies may be delivered to the parties or their representatives, in which case there should be included the written request of such parties and the return should state the fact of delivery. If this is not done, the Court will make service of the copies.[20]

The sensible way to arrange for depositions is to discuss the matter with your adversary and in most cases the time and place can be agreed upon. In many cases the subject of the testimony may be agreed upon.

The fees and mileage of the witness and the cost of taking the deposition must be paid by the party at whose instance the deposition is taken.[1]

15. Tax Court Rule 45(e).
16. Tax Court Rule 45(f).
17. Tax Court Rule 45(g).
18. Tax Court Rule 45(h).
19. Tax Court Rule 45(i).
20. Tax Court Rule 45(j).
1. Tax Court Rule 60(b).

FORM NO. 78

Application for Order to Take Depositions

TAX COURT OF THE UNITED STATES

Estate of WINTHROP BENSON, Deceased,
   KATHERINE BENSON, Executrix,
       Petitioner,
           v.   Docket No. 90,000
COMMISSIONER OF INTERNAL REVENUE,
   Respondent.

APPLICATION FOR ORDER TO TAKE DEPOSITIONS

To the Tax Court of the United States:

1. Application is hereby made by the above-named Petitioner for an order to take the deposition of the following named person:

Name of witness	Post-office address
Henry B. Coheen	185 Hemlock Drive
	Rochester, N. Y.

2. It is desired to take the depositions of the person above named for the following reasons:

He will testify to the following material matters: On the 21st day of September, 1956 he was present at the home of the decedent and his wife, at which time Katherine Benson, the wife of the decedent received from the decedent, and the decedent delivered to Katherine Benson 240 shares of Eastman Kodak stock. That at the time the said stock was duly endorsed by the decedent, and his signature was witnessed by the witness.

3. The reasons why the Petitioner desires to take the testimony of the above-named person, rather than have him appear personally and testify before the Court are as follows: The witness is 89 years of age and is in poor health. He is confined to his home and is unable to travel, not having left his home for the past 2 years. He will be unable to attend the trial of this case. In view of his advanced age, it is possible that at the time of the trial he may not be available to present his testimony.

4. It is desired to take the testimony of Henry B. Coheen on the 15th day of September, 1960, at the hour of 11 A. M. before Tyrus S. Bloch, a notary public in the City of Rochester, State of New York, at the residence of the witness, 185 Hemlock Drive, Rochester, N. Y.

5. That Tyrus S. Bloch is a notary public in the State of New York,

who has authority to administer oaths but has no office connection or business employment with the Petitioner or her counsel.

Dated, New York, August 10, 1960

DANIEL WEBSTER CLAY
(Signature)
Daniel Webster Clay
150 Broadway
New York 6, N. Y.

STATE OF YORK

COUNTY OF NEW YORK } ss:

KATHERINE BENSON, being duly sworn, says that the foregoing application for order to take deposition is made in good faith and for the reasons therein stated and that the same is not made for purposes of delay.

KATHERINE BENSON

Subscribed and sworn to before
  me this 10th day of August, 1960
     (Seal)
MARSHA HAYES
Notary Public
New York County

§ 612. Depositions upon Written Interrogatories.

Applications to take depositions upon written interrogatories may be made in substantially the same manner as in the case of oral depositions, except as hereinafter noted. An original and *five copies* of the interrogatories must be filed with the verified application. The Clerk will serve a copy of the application and of the interrogatories with notice to the opposite party that objection or cross-interrogatories may be filed within fifteen days thereafter. Cross-interrogatories must consist of an original and *five copies*. The Clerk will serve a copy thereof with notice that any objections thereto may be filed within 15 days. The initial application and interrogatories must be filed in time to allow for service, objections, cross-interrogatories, and objections thereto, and for taking and filing the deposition at least 10 days prior to any trial then scheduled.[2]

As indicated in the form for application for order to take depositions,[3] *the taking of depositions upon written interrogatories is not favored*, except when the depositions are to be taken in foreign countries, in which case any depositions *must be* upon written interrogatories, except as otherwise directed by the

2. Tax Court Rule 46(a).

3. Form 5-A, Tax Court Rules, Appendix I; Tax Court Rule 46(d).

Court for cause shown. As a practical matter, written interrogatories are an unsatisfactory method for the presentation of evidence.

The officer taking the deposition upon written interrogatories must propound the interrogatories and cross interrogatories in their proper order to each witness and cause the testimony to be reduced to writing in the witness's own words by a stenographic reporter, but no person other than the witness, reporter and the officer taking the deposition shall be present at the examination. Otherwise the officer shall conform substantially to the case where there is an oral examination by counsel.[4]

The officer taking the deposition must certify in his return that no person was present at the examination except the witness, the reporter, and himself, and must otherwise comply with the provisions for a return.[5]

§ 613. Tender of and Objections to Depositions.

With respect to depositions taken upon oral examination, objections to the competency of a witness, or to the competency, relevancy, or materiality of testimony, may be made at the trial, even though noted at the examination, unless the ground of objection is one which might have been obviated or removed if presented at or before the time of the taking of the examination.[6] Objections to errors and irregularities in the manner of taking testimony, in the form of the question or answer, the oath or affirmation, or in the conduct of parties, and errors of any kind which might have been obviated, removed, or cured, if promptly presented will not be considered unless made at the taking of the deposition.[7] Errors or irregularities in the manner of transcription of testimony, preparation, signing, certifying, sealing, endorsing, transmitting, or filing the deposition will not form the basis for objections, but questions in respect thereto can be raised on a motion to suppress the deposition in whole or in part made with reasonable promptness after such defect is or with due diligence might have been ascertained.[8]

Objections to written interrogatories or cross-interrogatories will not be considered subsequent to the taking of the deposition

4. Tax Court Rule 46(b).

5. § 611, supra; Tax Court Rule 46(c).

6. Tax Court Rule 47(a)(1).

7. Tax Court Rule 47(a)(2).

8. Tax Court Rule 47(a)(3).

unless they have been made in the manner and within the time prescribed by Rule 46.[9]

§ 614. Depositions; Necessity for Offering in Evidence.

We have seen that in the case of a stipulation of facts, if it is filed with the Court in advance, it need not be offered formally to be considered in evidence.[10] The same is not true, however, of a deposition. Testimony taken by deposition *will not be considered* until offered and received in evidence.[11]

Exhibits annexed to a stipulation or a deposition must be numbered serially, i.e., 1, 2, 3, etc., if offered by the petitioner; lettered serially, i.e., A, B, C, etc., if offered by the respondent; and marked serially, i.e., 1–A, 1–B, 1–C, etc., if offered as a joint exhibit.[12]

§ 615. Subpoenas.

While the need for the issuance of a subpoena in cases before the Tax Court are not as frequent as in other courts, when the need therefor arises, the Court will issue such upon request by a proper party, signed and sealed, but otherwise in blank, counsel completing it before service.[13] The difficulty with such subpoenas, is that while the Tax Court is authorized to issue it, it has no power to punish for contempt, and such relief must be sought in the District Court.

When completed, it must state the caption of the case, the name and last known address of the witness, the time and place where he is called on to appear, and whether the witness may designate someone to appear in his place.[14] If evidence other than oral testimony is required, such as documentary or written data, the subpoena must number, set forth separately, and describe adequately each item to be produced.[15]

Service may be made by any person not less than 18 years of age who is not a party.[16] The witness must be paid the same fees and mileage as witnesses in courts of the United States.[17] No witness, other than one for the Commissioner, is required to testify in any case before the Court until he shall have been tendered the fees and mileage to which he is entitled.[18]

9. Tax Court Rule 47(b); § 612, supra.
10. § 610, supra.
11. Tax Court Rule 31(c).
12. Tax Court Rule 31(d).
13. Tax Court Rule 44(a).
14. Tax Court Rule 44(b).
15. Tax Court Rule 44(c).
16. Tax Court Rule 44(d).
17. Tax Court Rule 60(a).
18. Tax Court Rule 60(b).

§ 616. Trial Calendars.

We have seen that at the time of filing the petition the petitioner has requested the place where he would prefer the trial to be held.[19] If possible, the trial will be held in such place. When the case is at issue it is placed upon a trial calendar. Although the Rule[20] states that the Clerk will send trial notices not less than 30 days before the date set for trial, although formerly such notices were sent 60 days before, they are now sent 90 days before.

The calendar will be called at the time and place noted and counsel must be prepared to state their estimate of the time required for trial or file stipulations in lieu of trial.[1] Ordinarily it is possible to agree with the Commissioner's counsel that the case be set down for a day certain during the session of the Court. If this cannot be arranged, it is necessary to keep in touch with counsel for the Commissioner and ascertain, as in the case of trial calendars in other courts, the length of time preceding cases will require for trial and estimate when to be ready.

Unlike the procedure in many State courts, the Tax Court Judges are not lenient in the matter of continuances or adjournments. The unexcused absence of a party or his counsel when a case is called for trial will not be the occasion for delay. The case may be dismissed for failure to prosecute or the trial may proceed and the case regarded as submitted on the part of the absent party.[2] As will be seen in the succeeding section, the Court is extremely strict in the matter of continuances. We shall also see that there may be no need for a case to be calendared, if the facts have all been stipulated.

A case once at issue may, upon motion, be placed on an inactive list called the reserve calendar. Good cause must be shown, as, for example, that the case will be governed by the decision in a case pending in a higher court. The case may be placed later on a trial calendar by motion of either party or by the Court on its own motion when the reason for inaction no longer exists.[3]

§ 617. Continuances.

It must be remembered that a Division of the Tax Court does

---

19. § 595, supra.
20. Tax Court Rule 27(b)(1).
1. Tax Court Rule 27(b)(2).

2. Tax Court Rule 27(b)(3).
3. Tax Court Rule 27(d).

not sit continually, but usually for about two weeks at a time. Also, a case does not suddenly appear upon a calendar, but the parties have 90 days' notice of the fact that it will appear on a particular calendar. It is for that reason that the Rules provide that Court action on cases set for trial will not be delayed by a motion for continuance unless it is *timely,* sets forth *good and sufficient cause,* and complies with all applicable Rules.[4]

Conflicting engagement of counsel or the employment of new counsel will never be regarded as good ground for a continuance unless set forth in a motion filed promptly after the notice of hearing or trial has been mailed, or unless extenuating circumstances are shown which the Court deems adequate.[5] An extension of time may be granted by the Court within its discretion upon a timely motion filed setting forth good and sufficient cause therefor or may be ordered by the Court on its own motion.[6]

While the Court will not be unreasonable, many of the excuses for delay in trial in State courts are not countenanced in the Tax Court. Counsel are expected to be ready when reached for trial. If it is anticipated that for any reason the petitioner will not be ready on the trial date, caution dictates that a motion be made prior thereto. Applications on the trial date will receive little consideration unless there are extenuating circumstances. The motion is made in accordance with the Rules.[7]

§ 618. Motions for Changing Place of Trial Designated.

If after the petitioner has filed a request designating the place of trial, either party desires a change in designation of the place of trial, he must file a motion (*with 4 copies*) to that effect, stating fully his reasons therefor. Such motions, made after the notice of the time of trial has been mailed, *will not be deemed* to have been timely filed.[8]

§ 619. Submission without Trial or Appearance.

A substantial number of tax cases are determined by the Court without any necessity for the case being calendared, or where it has been, without the necessity for trial. When a trial is not required for the submission of evidence, as, for example, where sufficient facts have been admitted, stipulated, estab-

---

4. Tax Court Rule 27(c)(1).
5. Tax Court Rule 27(c)(2).
6. Tax Court Rule 20.
7. § 604, supra.
8. Tax Court Rule 26(d).

lished by deposition, or included in the record in some other way, the case may be submitted at any time by notice of the parties filed with the Court. The parties need not wait for the case to be calendared and need not appear in person. The Chief Judge will then assign the case to a Division for report, which Division, upon request of the parties, will fix a time for filing briefs or for oral argument.[9] The Court may require appearance for argument or it may accept briefs in lieu of personal appearance.[10]

If the facts have all been stipulated before the case is calendared, all that is required is that the Court be notified thereof. If no trial is required, as for instance when a settlement is agreed upon shortly before the trial, that fact is communicated to the Judge sitting and the case is submitted.

§ 620. Trial before Commissioner of the Tax Court.

The Chief Judge of the Tax Court is authorized to appoint any attorney of the legal staff of the Court as a "commissioner in a particular case."[11] The commissioner conducts the hearing in accordance with the Court's Rules of Practice, rules upon objections and evidence as provided in Section 7453 of the Code, and exercises such further authority as is necessary for the conduct of the hearing.[12]

Each party must file proposed findings of fact and original brief within 60 days after the hearing unless otherwise directed. As to form and contents, the provisions of Rule 35(e) apply, except that the proposed findings must be complete under the evidence and not subject to the limiting provision that the party having the burden of proof must set forth complete statements of the facts based upon the evidence. The number of copies of proposed findings and briefs to be filed and service thereof is the same as in cases before the Court.[13]

Objection to the findings must be filed within 30 days after service.[14] The commissioner then prepares and files a report of his findings of fact based upon the evidence, and a copy is served on each party.[15] Reply briefs and exceptions to the findings must be filed within 30 days from the service of the findings of fact.[16] Upon motion of either party, made not later than

9. Tax Court Rule 30(a).
10. Tax Court Rule 27(b)(4).
11. IRC, § 7456 (1954 Code).
12. Tax Court Rule 48(a)(b).

13. Tax Court Rule 48(c).
14. Tax Court Rule 48(d).
15. Tax Court Rule 48(e).
16. Tax Court Rule 48(f).

the due date for filing his reply brief, or upon its own motion, the Division to which the case is assigned may, in its discretion, direct oral argument and set a date therefor.[17]

The writer has never seen an Estate Tax or Gift Tax case assigned to a commissioner.

§ 621. Outline of Evidence.

As in the trial of any other action, the careful lawyer will prepare an outline of the facts which he will be required to prove in order to establish the right to the relief requested. This means first an examination of the petition to determine those facts which remain to be proven. Such facts as have been admitted by the Commissioner's answer or have been stipulated, of course need not be proven.

Having determined what the facts to be proven are, the next question is whether they are to be established by testimonial proof or by documentary evidence. It is sound practice to prepare an outline in the form of questions to be propounded to each witness and the place at which each document to be offered in evidence will be admissible, with a notation that it be offered in evidence. It is the writer's practice to list each witness with the questions to be asked of each. In this way it can readily be determined whether the facts alleged in the petition are substantiated. When there are many exhibits, it aids in presenting them to have a separate jacket for them with an index, so that they may be obtained without having to search through files to the annoyance of the Court.

It must again be repeated that more tax cases are lost for lack of preparation than for lack of merit. It is certain that counsel for the Commissioner will be thoroughly prepared. Sad to relate, the same may not be said of the great majority of counsel for the petitioner. Argument cannot take the place of evidence. The petitioner's case stands or falls upon the evidence he presents.

Ex parte statements are not evidence.[18] The failure to adduce evidence in support of the material facts alleged by the party having the burden of proof, generally the petitioner, and denied by his adversary, may be ground for dismissal. The Rule permitting submission without trial or appearance[19] does not re-

17. Tax Court Rule 48(g).
18. Tax Court Rule 31(f).

19. Tax Court Rule 30(a).

lieve the party upon whom rests the burden of proof of the necessity of properly producing evidence in support of issues joined on questions of fact.[20]

In preparing an outline of the evidence to be presented it is advisable to confine the proof to the facts necessary to establish the statements of the facts alleged in the petition and not offer much evidence which has no effect upon the assignments of error. The Tax Court Rules stress the necessity for clarity and conciseness in the assignments of error and the statements of the facts upon which the petitioner relies as sustaining the assignments of error.[1] The same clarity and conciseness should be exhibited in preparing the outline of evidence to be presented. Judges of the Tax Court have commented on the necessity therefor and the consequent confusion of the issues when it is lacking.

§ 622. Trial Memorandum.

In addition to the preparation of an outline of the evidence to be presented, it is highly desirable to prepare for use at the trial a memorandum of law on the legal questions presented by the case, as well as objections to evidence which may be anticipated.

It will ordinarily be required that an opening statement be made by the petitioner's counsel. The more cogent it is, the better understanding of the case the trial Judge will have. If the petitioner's counsel has prepared a trial memorandum, he will be infinitely better qualified to state the issues involved, the facts intended to be proven, and the principles of law which apply to the issues. At the conclusion of the trial, the Court may or may not, depending upon the individual Judge, desire oral argument. In the event that he does, again, the preparation of a trial memorandum will be found valuable, since the authorities to support the petitioner's position are immediately available. Such a memorandum further, sharpens the issues in the mind of counsel, and keeps him on a consistent course.

In many cases there will be questions upon the admissibility of evidence necessary to proof of the petitioner's case, or the inadmissibility of evidence which the Commissioner may desire to offer. Such questions should be discernible to counsel if he has properly prepared his case. Citation of authority to support

20. Tax Court Rule 31(g).   1. § 589, supra.

his position will be readily available in his trial memorandum. The time and effort involved in research and preparation may well be the difference between a favorable and an unfavorable result.

CHAPTER 15

TRIAL IN THE TAX COURT

§ 623. Scope of Chapter.

Since trial in the Tax Court differs in many respects from that in State Courts with which the lawyer is familiar, it is necessary to have an understanding of the trial procedure therein and the rules of evidence which apply. The Rules of Practice, Procedure, and Evidence in the Tax Court are prescribed by statute.[1] It will be the purpose in this chapter to consider the rules of evidence, the manner of introducing evidence in accord therewith, and the method generally in which a case is established before the Court.

§ 624. Rules of Practice, Procedure, and Evidence Applicable.

The 1954 Code provides that proceedings of the Tax Court and

---

1. IRC, § 7453 (1954 Code).

its divisions shall be conducted in accordance with such rules of practice and procedure (other than rules of evidence) as the Tax Court may prescribe and in accordance with the rules of evidence applicable in trials without a jury in the United States District Court of the District of Columbia.[2] The latter part of this provision has been incorporated in the Rules of Practice of the Tax Court.[3]

These provisions, therefore, make applicable the District of Columbia Code relating to evidence,[4] and the Federal Rules of Civil Procedure,[5] and the former Supreme Court Equity Rules.[6] The pertinent provisions thereof will be considered in succeeding sections.

§ 625. Burden of Proof.

The Tax Court Rules[7] provide that the burden of proof shall be upon the petitioner, except as otherwise provided by statute, and except that in respect of any new matter pleaded in his answer, it shall be upon the respondent.

The exceptions, in addition to a case where the Commissioner pleads new matter, are:

(1) When the Commissioner claims that the petitioner is liable as a transferee.[8]

(2) Where the Commissioner claims that the petitioner has been guilty of fraud with intent to evade the tax.[9]

With these exceptions, the burden of establishing that the Commissioner erred is upon the petitioner.[10] The finding of the Commissioner is prima facie correct[11] and the petitioner has the burden of overcoming that determination. As in the trial of a case in any court, this means that the party having the burden of proof must produce evidence sufficient to shift the burden of going forward to the Commissioner. When that has been done, the Commissioner must then assume the burden of establishing evidence to overcome the petitioner's proof.[12] If at this point

2. Note 1, supra.

3. Fed Rules Civ Proc, Rule 31(a).

4. Title 14, Chaps 1–5.

5. Fed Rules Civ Proc, Rules 43, 44, 61.

6. Fed Rules Civ Proc, Rule 46.

7. Tax Court Rule 32.

8. § 373, supra.

9. IRC, § 7454(a) (1954 Code).

10. Wilson, 2 TC 1059 (1943); Smails

v O'Malley, 127 F2d 410 (CCA 8) (1942); McGrew v Comm, 135 F2d 158 (CCA 6) (1943); Slifka v Johnson, 63 F Supp 289 (1945).

11. Orvis v Higgins, 80 F Supp 64 (1948).

12. Bruce & Human Drug Co, 1 BTA 342 (1924); Acorn Refining Co, 2 BTA 253 (1925).

the case is in balance, the determination will be for the Commissioner.[13] The petitioner has the burden of establishing his case by a fair preponderance of the credible evidence.[14] The petitioner need not prove what the correct amount of the tax is, but merely that the Commissioner has erred.[15]

Failure to adduce evidence in support of the material facts alleged by the party having the burden of proof and denied by his adversary, may be ground for dismissal. The provision for the submission without trial or appearance where the facts are uncontested does not relieve the party upon whom rests the burden of proof of the necessity of properly producing evidence in support of issues joined on questions of fact.[16]

§ 626. Evidence; Objections to.

We have seen that objections to all or any part of a stipulation of facts should be noted therein, but the Court will consider any objection thereto made at the trial.[17]

The Rules also provide for the interposition of objections to depositions, which has been discussed previously.[18]

So far as objections to the competency of witnesses or the admission of evidence are concerned there are two schools of thought as to whether an exception to the denial of an objection is necessary. Since the Tax Court is not technically a court, but an independent agency in the Executive Branch of the government,[19] although it has been held that it is in fact a court,[20] it has been questioned whether the Rules of Civil Procedure,[1] dispensing with the necessity for exception after the denial of an objection applies to the Tax Court. In practice, some attorneys do so and others do not. The supercautious one will do so. The writer believes that the day of such technicalities has passed, and does not so except. This does not mean that an objection to evidence should not be specifically directed to the respect in which evidence is objectionable.

13. First Trust & Deposit Co. v Shaughnessy, 135 F2d 940 (CCA 2), cert den 320 US 744, 88 L ed 442, 64 S Ct 46 (1943).

14. O'Neal, 6 TCM 713 (1946).

15. Helvering v Taylor, 293 US 507, 79 L ed 623, 55 S Ct 287 (1935).

16. Tax Court Rule 31(g).

17. Tax Court Rule 31(b)(4).

18. § 613, supra.

19. IRC, § 7441 (1954 Code).

20. Stern, 215 F2d 701 (CA 3) (1954); Reo Motors, 219 F2d 610 (CA 6) (1955).

1. Fed Rules Civ Proc, Rule 46.

§ 627. Evidence; Generally.

Since trial before the Tax Court is conducted according to the rules of evidence applicable to non-jury trials in the United States District Court for the District of Columbia, to which the Federal Rules of Civil Procedure are in part applicable, these must be briefly considered, as well as United States Code Judiciary and Judicial Procedure.

The District of Columbia Code[2] provides for evidence to be taken under oath or affirmation,[3] defines perjury,[4] provides for the manner of taking testimony orally or under a commission,[5] and for impeachment of a witness who takes the party producing him by surprise.[6] It provides the procedure for taking depositions,[7] the rules with respect to the competency of witnesses[8] and the admission of certain documentary evidence,[9] and the presumption of death in case of absence.[10]

The pertinent Federal Rules of Civil Procedure provide for testimony to be taken in open court, and the admission of all evidence which is admissible under the statutes of the United States or formerly applied in Equity suits in the United States courts or under the rules of evidence applied in courts of general jurisdiction of the state in which the United States court is held. Evidence is to be presented according to the most convenient method prescribed in such statutes or rules, and competency of witnesses determined similarly.[11]

Unwilling or hostile witnesses may be cross-examined, that is, asked leading questions. Adverse parties called by a party may be asked leading questions, contradicted, or impeached.[12] A record must be made of excluded evidence.[13]

The Rules further provide for the manner of authentication of copies of official records, proof of the lack of a record, and proof of same according to common law proof.[14]

No error in either the admission or exclusion of evidence and

---

2. District of Columbia Code Title 14.

3. District of Columbia Code § 14-101.

4. District of Columbia Code § 14-102.

5. District of Columbia Code § 14-103.

6. District of Columbia Code § 14-104.

7. District of Columbia Code Chapter 2, §§ 14-201 to 204.

8. District of Columbia Code Chapter 3, §§ 14-301 to 309.

9. District of Columbia Code Chapter 4, §§ 14-401 to 406.

10. District of Columbia Code Chapter 4, §§ 14-501, 502.

11. Fed Rules Civ Proc, Rule 43(a).

12. Fed Rules Civ Proc, Rule 43(b); Tax Court Rule 31(a).

13. Fed Rules Civ Proc, Rule 43(c).

14. Fed Rules Civ Proc, Rule 44.

no error or defect in any ruling or order or in anything done or omitted by the court or any of the parties is ground for granting a new trial or for vacating, modifying, or otherwise disturbing a judgment or order, unless refusal to take such action appears to the court inconsistent with substantial justice. The court at every stage of the proceeding must disregard any error or defect in the proceeding which does not affect the substantial rights of the parties.[15]

The United States Code Judiciary and Judicial Procedure provides generally the rules of evidence applicable to documentary evidence.[16]

Particular application of the more important and most frequently used of these provisions will be treated in succeeding sections.

§ 628. Evidence; Documentary; Generally.

An official record may be proven by a copy of the same exemplified under the hand of the keeper of the same and the seal of the court or office where the record is kept.[17] Deeds and wills may be admitted upon proof of a copy under the hand of the clerk or other keeper of the record thereof and the seal of the court or office where the record has been made.[18] The record of a will and of its probate recorded in the office of the Register of Wills in the District of Columbia, or the transcript thereof, probated elsewhere but filed in such office is prima facie evidence of the contents and due execution.[19] Municipal ordinances of the District of Columbia may be proven by a copy certified by the secretary or assistant secretary of the Board of Commissioners.[20]

Copies of government records and papers and other official records and papers may be proven if properly authenticated.[1] In any case in which it may be necessary to offer such, the provisions of the United States Code Judiciary and Judicial Procedure should be consulted. This covers government records and papers, lost or destroyed court records, Congressional

---

15. Fed Rules Civ Proc, Rule 61.

16. United States Code Judiciary and Judicial Procedure, Chapter 115.

17. District of Columbia Code, § 14-401.

18. District of Columbia Code, § 14-402.

19. District of Columbia Code, § 14-403.

20. District of Columbia Code, § 14-406.

1. Note 16, supra.

Journals, Officer's bonds, State and Territorial Statutes and Judicial Proceedings and Nonjudicial records, consular papers, foreign documents, foreign records of land titles, and United States and foreign patent documents.

Appraisals are admissible only if the person making it testifies.[2] Ex parte affidavits, statements in briefs, and unadmitted allegations in pleadings do not constitute evidence.[3]

A copy of any book, record, paper, or document may be offered directly in evidence in lieu of the original, where the original is available or where there is no objection, and, where the original is admitted in evidence, a copy may be substituted later for the original or such part thereof as may be material or relevant, upon leave granted in the discretion of the trial Judge.[4]

Either party desiring the return at his expense of any exhibit belonging to him, after the decision of the Court in any case has become final, must make prompt application in writing to the Clerk, suggesting a practical manner of delivery. Otherwise exhibits may be disposed of as the Court deems advisable.[5]

It will save much time, if before the trial date copies of proposed exhibits are exhibited to the Chief Counsel's representative. It will be found that, with rare exception, he will agree to their admission.

Before a document can be admitted in evidence, proper foundation therefor must be laid by identification and description by a witness, unless it be an official record.

§ 629. Evidence; Documentary; Shop-Book Rule.

By virtue of the application of the Judicial Code to the Tax Court, the shop-book rule applies therein. Any writing or record, whether in the form of an entry in a book or otherwise, made as a memorandum or record of any act, transaction, occurrence, or event, is admissible as evidence of such act, transaction, occurrence or event if made in regular course of any business, and if it was the regular course of such business to make such memorandum or record at the time of such act, transaction, occurrence, or event or within a reasonable time thereafter. All other circumstances of the making of such writing or record, including lack of personal knowledge by the entrant or maker, may be

2. Sturgess, 2 BTA 69 (1925); Alexandria Paper Co, 3 BTA 239 (1925); Montgomery Bros & Co, 5 BTA 258 (1927).

3. Tax Court Rule 31(f).
4. Tax Court Rule 31(e)(1).
5. Tax Court Rule 31(e)(2).

shown to affect its weight, but such circumstances do not affect its admissibility.

The term "business", includes business, profession, occupation, and calling of every kind.[6]

If any business, institution, member of a profession or calling, or any department or agency of government, in the regular course of business or activity has kept or recorded any memorandum, writing, entry, print, representation or combination thereof, of any act, transaction, occurrence, or event, and in the regular course of business has caused any or all of the same to be recorded, copied, or reproduced by any photostatic, microfilm, micro-card, miniature photographic, or other process which accurately reproduces or forms a durable medium for so reproducing the original, the original may be destroyed in the regular course of business unless held in a custodial or fiduciary capacity or unless its preservation is required by law. Such reproduction, when satisfactorily identified, is as admissible in evidence as the original itself in any judicial or administrative proceeding whether the original is in existence or not and an enlargement or facsimile of such reproduction is likewise admissible in evidence if the original reproduction is in existence and available for inspection under direction of court. The introduction of a reproduced record, enlargement, or facsimile does not preclude admission of the original. The provision may not be construed to exclude from evidence any document or copy thereof which is otherwise admissible under the rules of evidence.[7]

It is not sufficient that a document is part of a business file,[8] but the original entry must be produced,[9] and it must indicate that it was properly made,[10] and is correct.[11] Entries made in regular course and kept regularly in other than bound books are admissible.[12] Summaries from such books or records may be

6. United States Code Judiciary and Judicial Procedure, § 1732(a).

7. United States Code Judiciary and Judicial Procedure, § 1732(b).

8. Schmeller v US, 143 F2d 544 (CCA 6) (1944).

9. Reyburn v Queen City Savings Bank, 171 F 609 (CCA 3) (1909); Roffwarg, 2 BTA 332 (1925); Gaukler and Stewart, 1 BTA 578 (1924); Ball, 5 BTA 882 (1926).

10. Wilcox v Downing, 88 Conn 368, 91 A 262 (1914).

11. Insurance Co v Weide, 9 Wall 677 (1869); Greengard v Comm, 29 F2d 502 (CCA 2) (1928).

12. Queen City Savings Bank v Reyburn, 163 F 597, affd 171 F 609 (1909); Haley v Vecchio, 36 SD 64 (1915).

used, if the originals are produced, where the records are voluminous.[13]

§ 630. Evidence; Documentary; Parol Evidence Rule.

It is the established rule that parol evidence is not admissible to qualify, change, or contradict the terms of a written instrument.[14] But the exceptions to the general rule are numerous. Thus, parol evidence is admissible to explain a document.[15] And so far as tax cases are concerned, since the rule only applies to writings to which both parties are a part,[16] it is infrequently applied, unless the writing concerns the petitioner and the Commissioner. In such case the rule will be applied.[17] The Tax Court applies the rule in the case of a stipulation of facts.[18]

§ 631. Evidence; Documentary; Best Evidence Rule.

It is a fundamental rule of evidence that a writing or record is the best evidence of its contents and parol evidence is not admissible to prove its contents unless there is a satisfactory explanation of its absence.[19] But the writing or record must be the original and not a copy.[20]

§ 632. Evidence; Documentary; Tax Examiner's Reports.

Notices from the Internal Revenue Service and reports of the Tax Examiner are not admissible to prove the facts therein contained. The deficiency letter is merely proof of the determination of a deficiency.[1]

Generally the report of the Tax Examiner is not admissible in evidence.[2] However, for limited purposes it may be admissi-

13. US v Kelley, 105 F2d 912 (CCA 2) (1939); Moran v US, 19 F Supp 557, cert den 303 US 643, 82 L ed 1102, 58 S Ct 642 (1938); Clark, 39 BTA 329 (1939).

14. Hutchins v Langley, 27 App DC 234 (1906).

15. American Crystal Sugar Co v Nicholas, 124 F2d 477 (CCA 10) (1942).

16. Indianapolis Glove Co v US, 96 F2d 816 (CCA 7) (1938); Amalgamated Sugar Co, 4 BTA 568 (1926); Converse & Co, 1 BTA 742 (1924); Boone, 27 BTA 1064 (1933); Mitchell, 45 BTA 300 (1941); Stratton Grocery Co, 8 BTA 317 (1927); Combs Lumber Co, 41 BTA 339 (1940); note 15, supra.

17. Wells & Zerweck, 11 BTA 1416 (1928).

18. Tax Court Rule 31(b)(5).

19. Bergdoll v Pollock, 95 US 337, 24 L ed 512 (1877); Ball, 5 BTA 882 (1927); Findlay Dairy Co, 2 BTA 917 (1925); Burke Electric Co, 5 BTA 553 (1927).

20. Security Trust Co v Robb, 142 F 78 (CCA 3) (1906); Jackson v Clifford, 5 App DC 312 (1894); Drumm-Flato Comm Co v Edmisson, 208 US 534, 52 L ed 606, 28 S Ct 367 (1908).

1. Ayer, 7 BTA 324, affd 26 F2d 54 (CA DC) (1927).

2. Hunter Coal Co, 2 BTA 828 (1925); McFetridge, 9 BTA 759 (1928); Pat-

ble, as for instance where the report is necessary to determine the basis upon which the deficiency was determined,[3] or to show the facts agreed upon by the parties.[4] When so admitted it is limited to such purpose and is not available to establish the facts stated therein.[5]

If it is necessary to prove facts stated in such report, the Chief Counsel's representative will normally stipulate such facts. Otherwise the facts must be proven by common law proof.

§ 633. Evidence; Documentary; Tax Returns.

Since the tax return of the petitioner was prepared and filed by him, being a self-serving statement it is not admissible for the purpose of establishing any of the facts stated therein.[6] Certified copies of the return may be introduced for the purpose of establishing the filing, although the necessity therefor would be rare. Certified copies may be obtained from the Commissioner at Washington at a charge of fifty cents.

The returns may, however, be used as admissions against interest as proof of the petitioner's position at the time,[7] and to contradict testimony offered by the petitioner or his witnesses.[8]

§ 634. Evidence; Documentary; Stipulations and Depositions.

It has been noted previously that if the stipulation of facts has been filed with the Court it is considered in evidence.[9] If it has not been filed, but is presented at the trial, it must be offered in evidence to be considered. While objections will be considered to it, no evidence will be received to alter or contradict it.[10]

On the other hand, although a deposition must be filed with the Court, the testimony so taken will not be considered until offered and received in evidence.[11] The subject of objections to depositions has been treated previously.[12]

terson, 16 BTA 716 (1929); Blundon, 32 BTA 285 (1935); McMahon v US, 61 Ct Cl 559 (1926).

3. Alliance Milling Co, 10 BTA 457 (1928); Blundon, note 2, supra.

4. Hotel de France Co, 1 BTA 28 (1924).

5. Note 2, supra.

6. Watab Paper Co, 27 BTA 488 (1932).

7. Jamaica Water Supply Co, 42 BTA

359, aff'd 125 F2d 517 (CCA 2) (1942); Roche v Comm, 63 F2d 623 (CCA 5) (1933).

8. Old Mission Portland Cement Co, 69 F2d 676 (CCA 9) (1934).

9. § 610, supra.

10. Tax Court Rule 31(b)(4)(5).

11. Tax Court Rule 31(c); § 614, supra.

12. § 613, supra.

§ 635. Evidence; Hearsay.

Hearsay evidence is no more admissible in the Tax Court than in other courts. While in one case, the court in its discretion accepted hearsay evidence which did not affect any substantial right of the petitioner,[13] it refused to admit a trade publication in evidence to prove incorporation, an order of court or of a state commission,[14] stating however, that in a few cases, among which were prices paid and pedigree, trade publications whose integrity had been proven, had been admitted in evidence. The Court was of the opinion that it should not extend the exception to the hearsay rule beyond the adjudged cases.

§ 636. Evidence; Presumptions.

The usual rules of presumption apply in the Tax Court, such as regularity of corporate procedure,[15] compliance with the law,[16] that the record owner of stock is the owner thereof,[17] and that property exchanged for other property was of approximately the same value.[18] It has refused to apply a presumption that failure to produce books of account to verify a statement that the taxpayer had received no income from a particular source would have controverted his testimony.[19]

It must also be remembered that many presumptions operate in favor of the Commissioner. Thus, property appearing to belong to a decedent is presumed to belong to him,[20] a transfer within three years of death is presumed to be in contemplation of death,[1] the presumption of the correctness of the Commissioner's determination,[2] that joint property is that of the decedent,[3] and the presumption that the signature signed to a return is authentic,[4] are all such presumptions.

§ 637. Evidence; Admissions.

Any admission against interest which either of the parties in

13. Schwarz, BTA memo op, Dec. 12, 570–J (1942).

14. Commercial Trust Co, 8 BTA 1138 (1927).

15. Parrot, 1 BTA 1 (1924).

16. Washington Post Co, 10 BTA 1077 (1928); Barnes Coal & Mining Co, 3 BTA 891 (1925).

17. Fort Cumberland Hotel Co, 1 BTA 1256 (1924).

18. Minden Lumber Co, 2 BTA 234 (1925).

19. Tracy, 25 BTA 1055, revd other grounds 70 F2d 93 (CCA 6) (1934).

20. Emery, 27 BTA 1038 (1931); McRae, 30 BTA 1087 (1934).

1. IRC, § 2035 (1954 Code).

2. § 625, supra.

3. McGrew v Comm, 135 F2d 158 (CCA 6) (1943).

4. IRC, § 6064 (1954 Code).

a case in the Tax Court has made, may of course, be used against him. An admission in a pleading is binding on the party making it.[5] It is on this basis of an admission that the tax return of the petitioner may be used as proof of his position or to contradict him.[6]

An offer in compromise is not an admission and may not be so used. It is in the nature of an offer to settle a civil action. Such offers are universally regarded as an offer to buy peace and not an admission of liability.

§ 638. Evidence; Judicial Notice.

The Tax Court takes judicial notice of the same matters which other Federal courts do. Thus, the Tax Court will take judicial notice of Federal and State constitutions,[7] and decisions of Federal courts,[8] state statutes,[9] rules and regulations promulgated by the Commissioner,[10] and other departments,[11] information in the archives of the State Department,[12] historical facts, the laws of nature, the measure of time, the succession of the seasons, the days and months of the year and geographical conditions of the world.[13] It will take judicial notice of facts within the knowledge of every person of ordinary understanding and intelligence.

It will not take judicial notice of municipal regulations and ordinances,[14] foreign laws,[15] conditions existing in a business at the time,[16] the proper rate of investment return without proof of the fair rate in the particular business,[17] nor of matters contained in its files in other cases.[18]

The Court will take judicial notice of facts which it should if

5. Mayo, TC Memo, Dec. 22, 216 (M) (1957-9).

6. § 633, supra.

7. Lamar v Micon, 114 US 218 (1855); Hyattsville Assn v Bouic, 44 App DC 408 (1916); Moese v Herman, 17 App DC 52 (1901).

8. International Textbook Co, 35 App DC 307 (1910).

9. Tonawanda Paper Co, 3 BTA 1195 (1925).

10. Prother v US, 9 App DC 82 (1896).

11. Santa Fe Pacific Railroad Co v Payne, 50 App DC 95 (1920).

12. Underhill v Hernandez, 168 US 250, 42 L ed 456, 18 S Ct 83 (1897).

13. Haller v Clark, 10 Mackey 128, 21 App DC 128 (1892); Werk v Parker, 249 US 130, 63 L ed 514, 39 S Ct 197 (1919); Moese v Herman, note 7, supra.

14. DC v Petty, 37 App DC 156, affd 229 US 593, 57 L ed 1343, 33 S Ct 881 (1911).

15. Rowan, 42 BTA 492, affd 120 F2d 515 (CA 5) (1940).

16. Chesapeake & Virginian Coal Co, 13 BTA 323 (1928).

17. Goold, 8 TCM 2, affd and revd other grounds 182 F2d 573 (CA 9) (1950).

18. Edwards, 39 BTA 735 (1939); Igleheart, 77 F2d 704 (CA 5) (1935).

they are called to its attention. In any case where reliance is to be made upon judicial notice to establish a fact the Court should be advised thereof. If it is a matter about which there may be some doubt, the question should be covered in the trial memorandum. If the Court then refuses to take judicial notice, counsel should be prepared to prove the fact.

§ 639. Evidence; Opinion Testimony.

Many of the controversies between the taxpayer and the Commissioner relate to differences as to valuation. In such case the opinion of expert witnesses is admissible to prove value.[19] But the witness must first be qualified as an expert. Testimony such as is furnished in the affidavits heretofore referred to[20] would be sufficient to qualify a witness as an expert. If the witness is not qualified, however, he will not be permitted to testify.[1] The Tax Court is not bound by the testimony of an expert, but may consider the testimony in the light of all the evidence.[2] The Court has repeatedly considered such testimony.[3] While the Court may disregard the opinion of an expert and use its own judgment in arriving at value, it may not reject opinion evidence and make an arbitrary finding of value not supported by any substantial evidence.[4]

In the interrogation of an expert witness, after he has been qualified, he must first testify as to all the facts, and he may then be asked whether on the basis of such facts he has an opinion, and what the opinion is. An opinion which is not based on evidence is of no value.

§ 640. Evidence; Competency of Witnesses.

The competency of witnesses before the Tax Court is controlled by the District of Columbia Code. A party to the case is a competent witness.[5] A modified dead man's statute bars uncor-

19. Shattuck v Stoneham Branch RR, 6 Allin 115 (Mass) (1863); Montana R Co v Warren, 137 US 348, 34 L ed 681, 11 S Ct 96 (1890).

20. §§ 49, 58, supra.

1. Consumers Ice Co v Burnett, 50 F2d 34 (1931), affg 11 BTA 144 (1928).

2. Twin Ports Bridge Co, 27 BTA 346 (1933); Langwell Real Estate Corp, 30 BTA 145 (1934).

3. Maxwell v Comm, 3 TCM 1207 (1944); Walker, 14 TCM 201 (1950); Fincham, 16 BTA 1418 (1929); Hauptfuhrer, 9 TCM 974 (1947); Cary, Jr, 7 TCM 731 (1946).

4. Phipps v Comm, 127 F2d 214 (CCA 10), cert den 317 US 645, 87 L ed 519, 63 S Ct 38 (1942).

5. District of Columbia Code, § 14-301.

roborated testimony of a party or agent.[6] If a party has testified and thereafter dies or becomes incompetent, his testimony may be given in evidence, but the other party may testify in opposition thereto.[7] In the case of partners or joint contractors, the death of one or more, does not prevent the surviving partner or joint contractor, nor the other party from testifying.[8] Conviction of a crime does not disqualify, but evidence thereof may be given by certificate of the clerk of the court where the conviction was had, and it may be used to discredit the witness.[9] Husband and wife are competent but not compellable to testify for or against each other, but not as to any confidential communication.[10]

§ 641. Evidence; Credibility of Witness.

As in other courts, if the testimony of the witness is not inherently improbable, the Tax Court may not disregard it when it is not impeached.[11] That is so, however, only when the testimony is as to facts. If the testimony is the opinion of the witness the court may disregard it.[12]

While the appellate court may review the facts as found by the Tax Court, it will not reverse where the findings depend upon the credibility of the witnesses.[13]

§ 642. Manner of Trial.

The Rules state that trials before the Court and its Divisions (each Judge of the Tax Court being a Division) will be conducted according to the rules of evidence applicable in trials without a jury in the United States District Court for the District of Columbia.[14] Trial before the Division is also conducted in much the same way as a trial without a jury in the United States District Courts. The Court first disposes of applications for adjournment and other preliminary matters and then proceeds to the trial of the case. Before the presentation of evidence, it is usually required that counsel make an opening statement. There-

6. District of Columbia Code, § 14-302.

7. District of Columbia Code, § 14-303.

8. District of Columbia Code, § 14-304.

9. District of Columbia Code, § 14-305.

10. District of Columbia Code, § 14-306, 307.

11. Blackmer v Comm, 70 F2d 255 (CCA 5) (1934).

12. § 639, supra.

13. Friedman v Comm, 234 F2d 459 (CA 6) (1956).

14. Tax Court Rule 31(a).

after the presentation of evidence is had, and at the conclusion of such presentation, the Court may or may not require oral argument.

The lawyer who has prepared his case will have no different problems in the Tax Court than in any other court. The subject of the opening statement, presentation of evidence, and oral argument at the conclusion of the trial is severally considered in the succeeding sections.

§ 643. Opening Statements.

With rare exceptions the Judge will require that the petitioner make an opening statement. This is very much in the nature of an opening address to a jury, its purpose being to acquaint the Court with the issues involved, the facts which the petitioner intends to present to sustain the assignments of error, and a brief statement of the principles of law involved. In this way, the Court may follow the evidence presented understandingly.

The Judge has no knowledge of the case. He may or may not have read the pleadings. He is not acquainted with all the proceedings which have been had in the Internal Revenue Service, and as to many of these he has no interest. He is interested in knowing what the issues are and the facts and law determinative thereof. Such information he should receive from the petitioner's opening statement. The opening statement immediately advises the Court whether counsel has carefully prepared his case, and if he has, earns the respect of the Court.

The Court has noted that a good, clear and concise opening statement goes a long way toward helping the side making it to win the case. It has also pointed out that in too many cases the taxpayer's counsel confines his remarks to tracing the history of the case from the first examination through its ramifications and vicissitudes in the Internal Revenue Service, with emphasis on what an Examiner or conferee said or did, with the result that the Court is left with little or no idea of what the appeal is about.

Part of the requirements for a brief before the Court may well serve as a guide for the opening statement.[15] It should contain:

(1) *A statement of the nature of the controversy, the tax involved, and the issues to be decided.* For example, this case involves a deficiency in estate tax liability in the sum of $3,996.90, contained in a notice of deficiency mailed on the 15th day of

15. Tax Court Rule 35(e)(2).

March, 1960. The issue presented is, was a gift made by the decedent in his lifetime one to take effect at the death of the decedent as a taxable transfer.

(2) *A brief statement of the facts which the petitioner intends to present in support of his case.* This statement should be of conclusory rather than evidentiary facts, but more expanded than the allegation of facts in the petition.

(3) *A statement of the points of law involved and the statutes and regulations applicable.* The points should not be argued, but stated, so that the Court may understand the legal issues it is called upon to decide. The point headings used in the trial memorandum should supply these.

Time spent in boiling this statement down so that it is both comprehensive and concise will serve two purposes. It will crystallize the issues in the mind of counsel and indicate to the Court that he has a clear understanding of the issues involved, both factual and legal, and is prepared to present them and the facts to resolve them. If counsel has not had experience before the Court, setting forth the opening statement in the trial memorandum will be found valuable.

After the petitioner's counsel has completed his opening statement, counsel for the respondent does likewise.

It has been assumed in our discussion above that the petitioner has the burden of proof, which is the usual case. If, however, the case be one in which the Commissioner has the burden of proof,[16] the order of opening statements and proof is reversed.

§ 644. Presentation of Evidence.

After the opening statements the party having the burden of proof proceeds to present the evidence upon which he relies to establish his case. It may be observed that the Judges of the Tax Court are somewhat less formal than District Court Judges. The Court appreciates as few objections as possible. This does not mean that an objection should not be made in that Court if evidence offered is clearly not admissible. Since there is no jury, and the Tax Court Judges are capable and experienced they incline to permit the introduction of any evidence which may have a bearing on the issues, and if it later turns out that it does not, they will disregard it.

16. § 625, supra.

If there is a stipulation of facts which has not been filed with the Court, it should be offered in evidence and marked. If it has been filed, reference should be made to it and the substance directed to the Court's attention. While the Court may have read both the pleadings and the stipulation of facts, the safer procedure is to assume that it has not, and present the case accordingly. It must be stressed again, that except for the evidence presented in the form of stipulation, deposition, and documentary or testimonial proof, the Judge trying the case has no knowledge of the facts. To counsel who has lived for many months and often years with it, there is a tendency to overlook this and assume otherwise.

The testimonial and documentary proof then follows. The trial memorandum will serve as a chart for the direction this is to take. It is the writer's practice to check off the items on his outline as each question is asked and the answer elicited. In this way there is assurance that all documents and testimonial proof necessary to establish the petitioner's contentions have been presented.

The witnesses produced by each party are, of course, subject to examination by his adversary.

When exhibits have been marked in evidence leave should be requested to substitute photostats, if desired.

§ 645. Oral Argument.

After all of the evidence has been presented, the Rule[17] provides that the parties should be prepared to make oral argument at the conclusion of a trial or to file a written citation of authorities at that time if the Judge so directs. The Rule is observed in the breach.

17. Tax Court Rule 35(a).

CHAPTER 16

PROCEEDINGS AFTER TRIAL IN TAX COURT

§ 646. Scope of Chapter.

The conclusion of the trial is not the conclusion of the case. Much is still required to be done before there is a determination. Briefs must be prepared and submitted, for which a transcript of the evidence is required. Matters may develop after the trial which require consideration. When the Court files its opinion, computations under Rule 50 may be required and must be submitted. If the Tax Court decision is not satisfactory to either party an appeal will lie to the United States Court of Appeals. It will be the purpose of this chapter to treat of these matters.

§ 647. Briefs; Generally; Filing; Service; Copies.

Although the Court is authorized to order oral argument and the filing of written citations at the conclusion of the trial, as we have observed,[1] this is rarely done. The filing of briefs and the making of oral arguments must be in accordance with the directions of the Judge presiding at the trial.[2] The Court customarily fixes the time within which briefs must be filed. If he does not, each party must file an original brief within 45 days after the day on which the trial was concluded and a reply brief within another 30 days thereafter. A party who fails to file an original brief, may not file a reply brief, except on

---

1. § 645, supra. 2. Tax Court Rule 35(a).

leave granted by the Court, and if his reply brief is filed, his adversary may have an additional 30 days thereafter to file his reply brief.[3] Extensions of time may be granted on motion timely made.[4] Any extension of time for filing a brief correspondingly extends the time for filing all other briefs yet to be filed unless the Court directs otherwise.[5]

Whether simultaneous briefs or seriatim briefs will be ordered depends largely upon whether the Commissioner's counsel will agree to seriatim briefs. There is some advantage to the petitioner in such case, since the respondent must treat the statement of facts in the order used by the petitioner and cannot present them in a manner which may be more favorable to the respondent. If counsel cannot agree the Court usually orders simultaneous briefs.

Each brief, whether original or reply, will be served promptly upon the opposite party after it is filed, except where it bears a notation that a copy has already been served, and except that where simultaneous briefs are to be filed they will be served upon the other party immediately after the time for filing such briefs (including any extension thereof) has expired. If an extension is granted after the original time for filing has expired and the brief of the opposite party has been filed but not served, it will be served promptly after the extended period.[6]

An original and *two copies* must be filed if briefs are *typewritten,* and *20 copies* must be filed if briefs are *printed.*[7]

§ 648. Brief; Form and Contents.

The Tax Court Rule[8] is specific as to the form and contents of briefs. All briefs must contain the following in the order indicated:

(1) On its first page, a *table of contents* with page references followed by a list of all citations alphabetically arranged as to cases cited together with references to pages. Citations must be in italics when printed and underscored when typewritten.

(2) A statement of the nature of the controversy, the tax involved, and the issues to be decided.

(3) The party having the burden of proof must set forth complete *statements of the facts* based upon the evidence. *Each*

---

3. Tax Court Rule 35(b).
4. Tax Court Rule 20.
5. Tax Court Rule 20(c).

6. Tax Court Rule 35(c).
7. Tax Court Rule 35(d).
8. Tax Court Rule 35(e).

statement must be numbered, must be complete in itself, and must consist of a concise statement of the essential fact *and not a discussion or argument* relating to the evidence or the law. Reference to the pages of the transcript or the exhibits relied upon in support thereof must be inserted after each separate statement.

If the other party disagrees with any or all of the statements of fact, he must set forth each correction which he believes the evidence requires and must give the same numbers to his statements of fact as appear in his opponent's brief. His statement of fact must be set forth in accordance with the requirements above.

(4) A concise *statement of the points* upon which the party relies.

(5) *The argument.* The argument must set forth the points of law relied upon and any discussion of the evidence deemed necessary to support the statement of fact.

(6) The *signature* of counsel or the party filing.

The practice is to set forth on the title page or cover the caption and docket number, the title of whether the brief is that of the petitioner or the respondent, and the name of counsel. On the first page and such following pages as may be necessary the table of contents is set up as follows:

TABLE OF CONTENTS

There then follows an alphabetical list of citations in the brief in accordance with the requirements of the Rule noted above. Two things must be borne in mind. Each statement of fact should be numbered, be complete in itself, and not a discussion or argument. This is so that any disagreement as to facts by the adversary may be related to the original brief. The second, is that the points upon which the party relies should first be stated, and thereafter the argument upon points of law set forth.

Except as to form, the preparation of a brief in the Tax Court is the same as that in any other court. As a matter of fact, many practitioners prepare their briefs in state courts in the same way. It is a logical and orderly method and permits the Court to see at once what is involved, and the facts and law determinative of the questions presented.

The Commissioner's brief will contain a request for findings of fact. On many occasions, where briefs are filed simultaneously the Commissioner will not file a reply brief. This will depend, however, upon the individual case. The right to file a reply brief may be denied by the Court.[9]

§ 649. Transcripts of Proceedings.

We have seen that the brief must contain a statement of the facts based upon the evidence, with reference to the pages of the transcript after each separate statement.[10] It is therefore necessary to have a transcript of the trial.

Hearings or trials before the Tax Court or its Divisions are stenographically reported.[11] Transcripts are ordered from the reporter immediately after the trial. Since the rate is fixed by contract between the Court and the reporter, the charge varies from year to year.

§ 650. Computations under Rule 50.

There is no time limitation on the time for decision, it merely being required that the decision be made as quickly as practicable.[12] It may be months, and in some cases several years before the case is decided. The procedure is for the trial Judge to write his opinion, which is then reviewed by the Chief Judge. If he does not agree with it, it is then reviewed by the entire Court. This does not happen often.

If the opinion determines that there is no deficiency, the decision will be entered at the same time. However, where the Court has filed its opinion determining the issues, it may withhold entry of its decision for the purpose of permitting the

---

9. Dunn v Comm, 220 F2d 323 (CA 9) (1955).

10. § 648, supra.

11. Tax Court Rule 40.

12. IRC, § 7459(a) (1954 Code).

parties to submit computations pursuant to the determination, showing the correct amount of the deficiency or overpayment to be entered as the decision. If the parties are in agreement as to the amount of the deficiency or overpayment to be entered as the decision, they or either of them must file promptly with the Court an original and *2 copies* of a computation showing the amount of the deficiency or overpayment and that there is no disagreement that the figures shown are in accordance with the report of the Court. The Court will then enter its decision.[13]

The Rules do not prescribe the form of computation. It should contain the caption and docket number and be entitled "Computation Under Rule 50". When the Commissioner makes the computation there is attached thereto Form 535, which advises that the case has been placed on the Motion Calendar for the day noted for argument on the computation and objection thereto, with the warning that if no objection be filed, accompanied by an alternative computation, at least five days prior to the date of argument, the Court may enter decision in accordance with the computation. If the petitioner agrees with the computation, such acquiescence is indicated on Form 18, which is furnished by the Tax Court.

If the parties are not in agreement as to the amount of the deficiency or overpayment to be entered, either party may file a computation which he believes to be in accord with the report of the Court. The clerk will serve a copy upon the opposite party, place the matter upon a motion calendar for argument in due course, and serve notice of the argument upon both parties. If the opposite party fails to file objections, accompanied by an alternative computation, at least 5 days prior to the date of such argument, or any continuance thereof, the Court may enter decision in accordance with the computation already submitted. If computations are submitted by the parties which differ as to the amount to be entered as the decision of the Court, the parties will be afforded an opportunity to be heard in argument thereon on the date fixed, and the Court will determine the correct deficiency or overpayment and enter its decision.[14]

Customarily, the Commissioner files his computation under Rule 50 and a copy of this is sent with Form 535 referred to above. If the computation is claimed to be incorrect, the petitioner prepares his computation and files it together with a notice of objection. The procedure corresponds to motions to settle orders in other courts.

FORM NO. 79

Notice of Objection to Computation Under Rule 50

TAX COURT OF THE UNITED STATES

WINTHROP BENSON, Deceased,
 KATHERINE BENSON, Executrix,
  Petitioner,
   v.
COMMISSIONER OF INTERNAL REVENUE,
 Respondent.

Docket No. 90,000

OBJECTION TO COMPUTATION UNDER RULE 50

The Petitioner objects to Respondent's computation pursuant to Rule 50 of the Rules of Practice of this Court.

Respondent's computation is defective in that (*state defect*).

Annexed hereto is the computation of the amount of the deficiency submitted by the Petitioner for entry as the decision of the Court.

DANIEL WEBSTER CLAY
(Signature)
Daniel Webster Clay
Attorney for Petitioner
150 Broadway
New York 6, N. Y.

On the return day of the hearing upon the objection, argument is confined strictly to consideration of the correct computation of the deficiency or overpayment resulting from the report already made, and no argument will be heard upon or consideration given to the issues or matters already disposed of by such report or of any new issues. The Rule is not to be regarded as affording an opportunity for retrial or reconsideration.[15]

§ 651. Estate Tax Deductions Developing after Trial.

At the time of an audit of an Estate Tax return it cannot be anticipated that it will be necessary to seek a redetermination of the tax before the Tax Court. The legal fees subse-

---

15. Tax Court Rule 50(c).

quently incurred in that respect are not allowed as a deduction by the Examiner and do not appear in the proposed deficiency. But when such action is required, the charges incurred, as we have seen,[16] are a proper deduction. However, it is necessary that the claim therefor be made in the petition or in an amended petition. If it is not raised at the trial, it will not be considered by the Court of Appeals.[17]

When it has been raised, but the parties under Rule 50, or under a remand, are unable to agree upon a deduction involving expenses incurred at or after the trial, the petitioner may move to reopen the case for further trial on that issue.[18]

§ 652. Motions for Retrial, Further Trial, Reconsideration, or to Vacate or Revise Decision.

No motion for retrial, further trials, or reconsideration may be filed more than 30 days after the opinion has been served, except by special leave.[19] No motion to vacate or revise a decision may be filed more than 30 days after the decision has been entered.[20]

While the Tax Court has jurisdiction to grant a new trial until its decision becomes final,[1] which is three months after the date of entry of its decision,[2] it may not do so thereafter.[3] The position of the Tax Court does not substantially differ from that of other courts in similar situations. Unless there are substantial reasons therefor, the Court will not grant a new trial.[4] While the granting of such application is within the discretion of the Court,[5] it has been exercised in favor of granting the motion only in rare cases.[6] In general it may be said that an application for retrial, further trial, or reconsideration will re-

16. § 199, supra; Reg, § 20.2053-3 (c)(2).

17. Bank of California v Comm, 133 F2d 428 (CCA 9) (1943).

18. Tax Court Rule 51.

19. Tax Court Rule 19(e).

20. Tax Court Rule 19(f).

1. Washburn Wire Co v Comm, 67 F2d 658 (CCA 1) (1933).

2. IRC, § 7481 (1954 Code).

3. Lasky v Comm, 235 F2d 97 (CA 9), affd 352 US 1027, 1 L ed 2d 598, 77 S Ct 594 (1956).

4. Selwyn Operating Corp, 11 BTA 593 (1928); Buckeye Producing Co, 15 BTA 435 (1929); Pierce Oil Corp, 30 BTA 469 (1934); Crane-Johnson Co, 311 US 54, 85 L ed 35, 61 S Ct 114 (1940); Rubel, 74 F2d 27 (CCA 6) (1935).

5. Jankowsky v Comm, 56 F2d 1006 (CCA 10) (1932); McCarthy v Comm, 139 F2d 20 (CCA 7) (1943); Bankers Pocahontas Coal Co v Burnet, 287 US 308, 77 L ed 325, 53 S Ct 150 (1932).

6. Canyon Lumber Co, 1 BTA 473 (1924); Peninsula Shipbuilding Co, 9 BTA 189 (1927); Waggoner, 9 BTA 629 (1927); Wells v Comm, 132 F2d 405 (CCA 6) (1942); Stock Yards Nat Bank v Comm, 153 F2d 708 (CCA 8) (1946).

ceive little sympathy from the Tax Court. As it has pointed out in substance, it is the function of counsel to make a complete record, and the penalty for failure to do so is an adverse decision, so that except in a clear case of injustice the parties may not have a second try.[7]

In any event, if such motions be made, they must be separate from each other and not joined to or made a part of any other motion.[8]

§ 653. Review by Appellate Court.

If a party is aggrieved by the determination of the Tax Court, there is further right of appeal to a United States Court of Appeals for the Circuit in which the District Director's office is located in which the return was filed, or if no return was filed, in the United States Court of Appeals for the District of Columbia. The parties, however, may stipulate for the appeal to be filed in any United States Court of Appeals.[9]

The petition for review must be filed within three months after the date of the Tax Court *decision*.[10] *The date of the decision is not the date of the opinion.* Where computation under Rule 50 is required, the date of the decision is the date of the order determining the amount of the deficiency. Where one party files a petition for review, any other party then may file a petition for review within four months of the decision.[11] A motion made within the time provided by the Rule[12] for retrial, further trial, or reconsideration, or to vacate or revise a decision, has the effect of suspending the time for review until the determination of the motion.[13] The petition for review is filed with the Clerk of the Tax Court.

In so far as the procedure on an appeal to a United States Court of Appeals the rules in force in the different circuits should be consulted. Details thereof are not within the scope of this work. The Tax Court Rules provide for payment of the costs and charges for preparation, comparison, and certification of the record on review.[14]

---

7. Ohio Clover Leaf Dairy, 9 BTA 433 (1927).
8. Note 20, supra.
9. IRC, § 7482(b) (1954 Code).
10. IRC, § 7483 (1954 Code).
11. Note 10, supra.
12. Tax Court Rule 19(e)(f).

13. Burnet v Lexington Ice & Coal Co, 62 F2d 906 (CCA 4) (1933); Griffiths v Comm, 50 F2d 782 (CCA 7) (1931); Helvering v Continental Oil Co, 68 F2d 750 (CA DC), cert den 292 US 627, 78 L ed 1481, 54 S Ct 629 (1933).
14. Tax Court Rule 52.

§ 654. Review by Appellate Court; Bond to Stay Assessment and Collection of Deficiency.

One of the attractions of appealing to the Tax Court is the fact that, except in the case of a jeopardy assessment, the petitioner does not have to worry about the only part of a tax assessment which is painful, namely, payment. Putting off that fateful day, is, as we have noted, the determining factor in many cases as to whether the review of a tax case shall be through the Tax Court or by means of an action for refund.

Once, however, the Tax Court has decided that there is a deficiency or other tax liability, any other further review cannot be had without the petitioner filing a bond. This bond must be filed with the Tax Court, in a sum not more than double the amount of the portion of the deficiency in respect of which the petition for review is filed. *The assessment and collection of the tax is stayed only if at or before the time of filing of the petition for review,* the petitioner has filed the bond required, with a surety approved by the Tax Court.[15]

The form of bond is furnished by the Tax Court. There is a form when a corporate surety furnishes the bond and also when collateral is furnished.[16] The maximum amount is fixed by the statute at not more than double the amount of the portion of the deficiency in respect of which the petition for review is filed, but if the amount is large, upon motion, the Court will fix the amount of the bond at the deficiency plus interest for $2\frac{1}{2}$ years.

15. IRC, § 7485 (1954 Code).
16. Tax Court Rules, Appendix I, Forms b and c.

CHAPTER 17

ACTIONS FOR REFUND

§ 655. Scope of Chapter.

At the beginning of our discussion of the remedies available to the taxpayer if dissatisfied with the action of the Internal Revenue Service, it was noted that the taxpayer had three alternatives.[1] One of these, an application to the Tax Court for a redetermination of the deficiency, the method selected in the great majority of all cases, we have discussed in the preceding chapters.[2]

The two other remedies both are based upon payment of the tax and an action for refund after compliance with the prerequisites to suit. Choice of suit in either the United States District Court or in the United States Court of Claims has been discussed previously.[3]

It will be the purpose of this chapter to explore in brief fashion the proceedings in suits in either of such courts, so that the lawyer who is unfamiliar with the practice therein may have sufficient information to institute the action and gain some slight understanding as to the manner in which actions in either of the courts are conducted. A detailed discussion

---

1. § 567, supra.
2. Chapters 12, 13, 14, 15, 16, supra.

3. §§ 569, 570, supra.

of the practice, as has been attempted in the case of the Tax Court, would be beyond the scope of this work, involving as it does Federal Court practice and procedure.

§ 656. Prerequisite to Action.

Before an action for refund may be instituted in either the District Court or the Court of Claims, the requirements for such suit must be complied with. Normally, the United States, as a sovereign, cannot be sued without its consent.[4] The right to do so is granted by statute upon certain conditions. It is a prerequisite to action, therefore, that the conditions be met by the litigant.[5]

In order to institute suit for refund of taxes claimed to have been erroneously or illegally assessed or collected, the tax must first have been paid.[6] An application for refund must then have been filed within the statutory period.[7] There must follow either a rejection of the claim or failure to do so by the Commissioner within six months of the filing of the claim for refund.[8] Suit must be instituted within two years from the date of mailing by registered mail by the Commissioner to the taxpayer of a notice of disallowance of the part of the claim to which the suit or proceeding relates, or from the date the taxpayer waives notification of disallowance, except that the time for suit may be extended by agreement between the taxpayer and the Commissioner.[9]

It is also required that the action must be based upon the grounds set forth in the claim for refund.[10] The 1954 Code provides specifically that payment of the tax need not have been made under protest or duress.[11]

§ 657. United States District Court; Parties and Venue.

The action for refund must be brought by the person who made the alleged overpayment. This follows from the require-

---

4. Dalehite v US, 346 US 15, 97 L ed 1427, 73 S Ct 956 (1953); US v Sherwood, 312 US 584, 85 L ed 1058, 61 S Ct 767 (1941); US v Michel, 282 US 656, 75 L ed 598, 51 S Ct 284 (1931).

5. Minnesota v US, 305 US 382, 83 L ed 235, 58 S Ct 292 (1939); US v Michel, note 1, supra.

6. Flora v US, 246 F2d 929, affd 2 L ed 2d 112 (1957).

7. § 376, supra.

8. IRC, § 7422(a); 6532(a)(1) (1954 Code).

9. IRC, § 6532(a) (1954 Code).

10. Red Wing Malting Co v Willcutts, 15 F2d 626 (CCA 8), cert den 273 US 763, 71 L ed 879, 47 S Ct 476 (1926); US v Andrews, 302 US 517, 82 L ed 398, 58 S Ct 315 (1938).

11. IRC, § 7422(b) (1954 Code).

ment that an action must be prosecuted in the name of the real party in interest.[12] This means that the plaintiff is the fiduciary in an Estate Tax case. The defendant may be either the District Director or the United States. Before the 1954 Code, the only method of obtaining a jury trial in an action for refund was to sue the District Director to whom the tax was paid. Since such limitation no longer applies, in an action against the United States for refund, there is the right to trial by jury.[13] In suits against the District Director there is a difference in taxable costs.[14] A judgment against the Director is payable by the Secretary of the Treasury.[15]

If the suit be against the District Director it must be brought in the district where he resides.[16] If the suit be against the United States, it must be brought in the district *where the plaintiff resides.*[17] It should be noted that it is not the district in which a deceased taxpayer resided or his estate is administered.

§ 658. United States District Court; Complaint.

The requirements of any complaint in the United States District Court are (1) a short and plain statement of the grounds upon which the court's jurisdiction depends, (2) a short and plain statement of the claim showing that the pleader is entitled to relief, and (3) a demand for judgment for the relief to which he deems himself entitled.[18]

This means that in an action to recover taxes erroneously or illegally collected the complaint must show that the plaintiff is the real party in interest, his name and residence and his citizenship. There must also be alleged the statute under which the court has jurisdiction and under which the action arises. If the action is against the Director, the place of his residence and the fact that he is still acting as such. There must then be alleged the facts upon which the action is based, namely, the filing of the return, the payment of the tax, the deficiency notice, payment of the deficiency, filing of the claim for refund within the statutory period, that it complied with the statute, and was disallowed or not acted upon within six months, and that suit has

12. Fed Rules of Civ Proc, Rule 17.
13. 28 USC § 2402.
14. 28 USC § 2412(a)(b).
15. 28 USC, § 2006.
16. 28 USC § 1391; Varnedo v Allen, 67 F Supp 152, affd 158 F2d 467 (CCA 5), cert den 330 US 821, 91 L ed 1272, 67 S Ct 771 (1946).
17. 28 USC § 1402.
18. Federal Rules of Civ Proc, Rule 8(a).

not been instituted prematurely. Copies of the 90-day letter, the claim for refund, and the notice of disallowance should be annexed. This establishes jurisdiction.

The statement of the claim will contain the basis for the claimed erroneous and illegal collection of the tax and the fact that such tax was collected. The grounds stated must be the same as those set forth in the claim for refund.[19]

The prayer for relief will be for the amount of the alleged overpayment with interest. If the action is against the District Director there will also be a demand for costs.

The complaint *must be signed* by at least one attorney of record in his individual name and his address must be stated. This signature has the effect of a verification and the usual verification is not required.[20] The action is commenced when the complaint is filed with the Court[1] and the filing fee paid.[2] Service is made by the United States Marshal or his deputy.[3]

FORM NO. 80

Complaint in Action for Refund

DISTRICT COURT OF THE UNITED STATES
EASTERN DISTRICT OF NEW YORK

KATHERINE BENSON, Executrix under the Last Will and Testament of WINTHROP BENSON, Deceased, Plaintiff, v. THE UNITED STATES, Defendant.	Civil No. 37,777

Plaintiff, complaining of the defendant, by Daniel Webster Clay, Esq., her attorney, alleges:

1. Plaintiff is the Executrix under the Last Will and Testament of Winthrop Benson, late of the County of Suffolk, Deceased, having been duly appointed as such by the Surrogate of the County of Suffolk, State of New York, on the 15th day of January, 1958, and duly qualified as such Executrix and has ever since acted and is now acting thereas.

19. IRC, § 7422(a) (1954 Code); Ney v US, 171 F2d 449 (CA 8), cert den 336 US 967, 93 L ed 1119, 69 S Ct 940 (1948); US v Felt & Tarrant Mfg Co, 283 US 269, 75 L ed 1025, 51 S Ct 376 (1931).

20. Federal Rules Civ Proc, Rule 11.
1. Federal Rules Civ Proc, Rule 3.
2. Turkett v US, 76 F Supp 769 (1948).
3. Fed Rules Civ Proc, Rule 4.

Plaintiff resides at Copiague, Suffolk County, New York and is a citizen of the United States and jurisdiction is conferred upon this Court by 28 USC § 1346(a)(1).

2. This action arises under the Internal Revenue Code of 1954, particularly Sections 1346, 2037 and 7422 thereof, and the plaintiff has a just claim against the defendant for the sum of $3,468.12, together with interest as provided by law.

3. That on the 18th day of February, 1959, the plaintiff duly filed the Estate Tax return for the estate of the above named decedent in accordance with the provisions of law for the execution and filing thereof, with the District Director of Internal Revenue for the First District of New York and at such time and place paid to the said Director the sum of $16,832.40, the amount shown by the said return to be due and payable.

4. That said return was duly audited and on the 20th day of September 1959, the Commissioner of Internal Revenue mailed to the plaintiff a notice of deficiency in the sum of $3,468.12, in addition to the amount shown upon the aforesaid return, which sum of $3,468.12 the plaintiff paid to the said District Director of Internal Revenue aforesaid on the 1st day of October, 1959. A copy of said notice of deficiency is annexed hereto and marked Exhibit A.

5. That thereafter and on the 10th day of October, 1959, the plaintiff duly filed with the District Director of Internal Revenue aforesaid in accordance with the statute, a claim for the refund of the said sum of $3,468.12 and interest and duly demanded the refund and payment of said amount, together with interest as provided by law. A copy of said claim for refund is annexed hereto and marked Exhibit B.

6. (On the 12th day of January, 1960, the Commissioner of Internal Revenue notified the plaintiff by registered mail that said claim for refund had been disallowed in its entirety.) *or* (That more than six months have expired since the filing of said claim for refund and the commencement of this suit and no notice of the disallowance of said claim has been mailed to the plaintiff by registered mail by the Commissioner of Internal Revenue.) (*If disallowed*, a copy of said notice of disallowance is annexed hereto and marked Exhibit C.)

7. That said deficiency was based upon the determination by the Commissioner of Internal Revenue that the taxable estate of the decedent for the purposes of the Internal Revenue Code of 1954 was $104,063.43.

8. In the determination of said taxable estate, the Commissioner of Internal Revenue erroneously and illegally included in the gross estate of the decedent property of the value of $14,836.20 as a transfer which took effect at the decedent's death under the provisions of Section 2037 of the Internal Revenue Code of 1954.

9. No part of the said sum of $3,468.12, the amount of tax overpaid by the plaintiff has been refunded to her.

WHEREFORE, plaintiff demands judgment against the defendant for the sum of $3,468.12, together with interest as provided by law.

DANIEL WEBSTER CLAY
(Signature)
Daniel Webster Clay
Attorney for Plaintiff
150 Broadway
New York 6, N. Y.

§ 659. United States District Court; Demand for Jury.

We have previously noted that Congress amended the statute in 1954 to remove the limitations on refund suits, so that it is no longer necessary to sue the District Director to whom the tax was paid in order to have the right to trial by jury.[4]

However, in order to obtain such trial by jury, the party seeking the same must serve a demand therefor in writing at any time after the commencement of the action *and not later than 10 days* after the service of the last pleading. The demand may be indorsed upon a pleading of the party making the demand.[5] Failure to serve the demand as required constitutes a waiver.[6]

Since the primary reason for commencing suit in the United States District Court is usually for the purpose of obtaining a trial by jury, the sensible procedure is to make the demand by endorsing it upon the complaint. Any form is sufficient so long as it gives notice that the party serving the pleading is making a demand that the case be tried by a jury. The words "The plaintiff hereby demands a trial by jury of the issues in the within action.", or any other appropriate language will serve.

§ 660. United States District Court; Proceedings Prior to Trial.

The proceedings in the United States District Court are in most respects similar to those in the Tax Court, except that the Federal Rules of Civil Procedure apply in the former, so that discovery may be had,[7] pre-trial procedures are in effect,[8] and the rules of evidence are applicable which are in effect in courts of the United States on the hearing of suits in equity or in the courts of general jurisdiction of the state in which the United States court is held.[9]

4. 28 USC § 1346(a)(1); 28 USC § 2402.
5. Fed Rules Civ Proc, Rule 38(b).
6. Fed Rules Civ Proc, Rule 38(d).
7. Fed Rules Civ Proc, Rules 26 et seq.
8. Fed Rules Civ Proc, Rule 16.
9. Fed Rules Civ Proc, Rule 43(a).

The usual motions are available and the practice does not differ so substantially from that in the state courts in which the District Court is located as to present any insurmountable problems. To one not familiar with the practice in Federal courts, the Federal Rules of Civil Procedure will be found most helpful, since they deal at length with the subjects of pleadings,[10] amended pleadings,[11] motions,[12] parties,[13] pre-trial procedure,[14] discovery,[15] trial,[16] and judgment,[17] among other things.

§ 661. United States District Court; Trial.

Trial in the District Court with a jury differs from that in state courts in that examination of jurors may be and usually is conducted by the trial Judge, and additional questions may be permitted to be asked of jurors or submitted by the Judge to them.[18] District Court Judges take a far larger part in the trial than state court Judges customarily do.

The verdict may be a general one or a special verdict upon issues framed by the court.[19] If other questions should be submitted, counsel may make demand therefor. A motion for a directed verdict may be made.[20] Requests may be made for instructions to the jury and objections made to those given by the trial Judge.[1]

We have heretofore noted in the preceding section the rules of evidence applicable. Presentation of evidence, both documentary and testimonial is the same as in other courts.

§ 662. United States District Court; Findings by the Court.

In all actions tried upon the facts without a jury or with an advisory jury, the Court must find the facts specially and state separately its conclusions of law thereon and direct the entry of the appropriate judgment. Requests for findings are not necessary for purposes of review. Findings of fact will not be set aside unless clearly erroneous.[2]

The Court may amend its findings upon motion of a party made not later than 10 days after entry of judgment and may

10. Fed Rules Civ Proc, Rules 5–14.
11. Fed Rules Civ Proc, Rule 15.
12. Fed Rules Civ Proc, Rules 7, 12.
13. Fed Rules Civ Proc, Rules 17–25.
14. Note 8, supra.
15. Fed Rules Civ Proc, Rules 26–37.
16. Fed Rules Civ Proc, Rules 38–42.
17. Fed Rules Civ Proc, Rules 54–63.

18. Fed Rules Civ Proc, Rule 47.
19. Fed Rules Civ Proc, Rule 49; De Eugemo v Allis-Chalmers Mfg Co, 210 F2d 409 (CA 3) (1954).
20. Fed Rules Civ Proc, Rule 50.
1. Fed Rules Civ Proc, Rule 51.
2. Fed Rules Civ Proc, Rule 52(a).

amend its findings or make additional findings and amend the judgment accordingly.[3]

§ 663. Court of Claims; Jurisdiction and Pleading.

The jurisdiction of the Court of Claims extends to an action for refund of taxes erroneously or illegally collected.[4] Its jurisdiction is concurrent with that of the United States District Court.[5] Limitations as to amount, as we have seen, no longer apply to District Courts. Not too many tax refund cases are commenced in the Court of Claims.

The action in the Court of Claims is commenced by filing a *petition*. The chief difference between it and a complaint in the District Court is one of nomenclature. *Twenty-five printed copies* must be filed, or 5 typewritten copies and within 20 days thereafter 25 printed copies must be filed.[6] The provision for printed copies may be waived for good and sufficient cause shown upon motion for such relief, in which case, if the motion be granted, mimeographed copies may be filed.[7] The filing fee of $10 must be paid at the time of the filing of the petition.[8] Service is made by the Clerk of the Court.[9]

The petition must contain a caption with the name of the court, the parties, the docket number, and be entitled "Petition".[10] It must be signed by the attorney of record.[11]

The petition must contain:

(1) A clear and concise statement of the facts on which the claim is based, including the facts upon which the Court's jurisdiction depends, the time when and place where the claim arose and the items and amounts claimed.

(2) Any action on the claim taken by Congress or by a department of the Government, or in any judicial proceeding, including any in the Tax Court.

(3) A clear citation of the Act of Congress, regulation of an executive department or agency, or executive order of the President where the claim is founded upon such act, regulation, or order.

(4) The ownership of the claim if held by assignment and the consideration for such assignment.

3. Fed Rules Civ Proc, Rule 52(b).
4. 28 USC § 1491.
5. Jackson v US, 129 F Supp 537 (1955).
6. Court of Claims Rule 1.
7. Court of Claims Rule 1(c).
8. Court of Claims Rule 82.
9. Court of Claims Rule 2.
10. Court of Claims Rule 10.
11. Court of Claims Rule 11.

(5) A demand for judgment.[12]

The petition corresponds to the complaint in the United States District Court in an action for refund, except that the caption differs, and also that it is customary to allege in a petition in the Court of Claims in accordance with the Rule, that no other action has been taken on the claim by Congress or by any department of the Government, or in any judicial proceeding, including any in the Tax Court of the United States, and the further allegation that the plaintiff is justly entitled to the refund of the amount claimed and that there are no offsets or credits against such amount. These latter are matters of defense, and should not have to be pleaded, but are as a matter of custom.

The Rules provide for defenses which may be pleaded,[13] the time for answer or reply and motions with respect to pleadings,[14] and the amendment of pleadings.[15]

FORM NO. 81

Caption, Title and Introduction to Petition

IN THE UNITED STATES COURT OF CLAIMS

KATHERINE BENSON, Executrix under the Last Will and Testament of WINTHROP BENSON, Deceased, Plaintiff, v. THE UNITED STATES, Defendant.	No. 23,987

PETITION

To the Honorable, the United States Court of Claims:

§ 664. Court of Claims; Reference to Commissioner.

Unless otherwise ordered by the Court, every case is referred to a Commissioner for trial. The procedure before the Commissioner parallels trial before a judge. The Commissioner regulates the proceeding before him, takes the evidence, rules upon it and considers motions.[16]

There is provision for pre-trial conferences,[17] and discovery.[18]

12. Court of Claims Rule 12.
13. Court of Claims Rule 15.
14. Court of Claims Rule 16.
15. Court of Claims Rule 18.

16. Court of Claims Rule 37.
17. Court of Claims Rule 28.
18. Court of Claims Rules 29–36.

The rules of evidence applicable are those in effect in courts of the United States in nonjury trials.[19]

The Commissioner communicates with the parties and arranges for testimony to be taken at a convenient time and place.[20] Upon taking of evidence before a Commissioner it is not necessary to take an exception to rulings or orders.[1]

§ 665. Court of Claims; Findings of Fact.

After the Commissioner has taken all of the evidence submitted by the parties, he files a notice of the closing of the evidence. Thereafter the plaintiff has 40 days to request findings of fact and the defendant has 30 days after the plaintiff has filed his request to file findings of fact, including objections to the plaintiff's findings. The Commissioner will allow the plaintiff reasonable time to file objections to the defendant's findings. The requests for findings of fact *need not be printed,* the original and two copies being filed with the Clerk of the Court unless the Commissioner has directed simultaneous submission of requested findings, in which case the plaintiff must mail the original and two copies to the trial Commissioner.[2]

The requests for findings of fact must be distinct numbered propositions of the facts desired to be found, supported by reference to the record. They must be arranged to present a concise statement in orderly and logical sequence of the whole case.[3]

After the expiration of the time for filing requests and objections the Commissioner files a report of his findings. When directed by the Court he will also file recommendations for conclusions of law.[4]

§ 666. Court of Claims; Exceptions to Commissioner's Findings; Briefs.

The plaintiff has 45 days from the time the Commissioner files his report to file exceptions to the findings *and* to file his brief. Each exception should, at the end thereof, refer to the record. The exceptions and brief may be in a single document or may be separate. Unlike the requests *the exceptions and brief must be printed.* Briefs of more than 10 pages must have an index

---

19. Court of Claims Rule 41.
20. Court of Claims Rule 39.
1. Court of Claims Rule 43.

2. Court of Claims Rule 45(a).
3. Court of Claims Rule 45(b).
4. Court of Claims Rule 45(c).

or table of contents and a table of cases and statutes. The defendant has 30 days from the time the plaintiff files his exceptions and brief to file his own exceptions and brief. The plaintiff then has 20 days for reply. If the facts have been stipulated, which is quite common in tax cases in the Court, the Commissioner files a memorandum report and the plaintiff has 30 days instead of 45 days, and the time of the defendant remains the same, with the time for reply the same.[5]

Exceptions and briefs must be printed, as noted, and 25 copies must be filed.[6]

§ 667. Court of Claims; Argument before the Court.

After the exceptions and briefs have been filed, the case is placed upon the monthly calendar called on the first Monday of each month and may be argued when it is reached or it may be submitted.[7]

Many cases in the Court of Claims are submitted without argument. Whether to do so or not in a particular case will depend upon the facts and the law of that case. The same reasoning applies as when deciding to argue or submit a motion or appeal in any other court. The waiver of argument may be made in open court or by filing a waiver in advance with the Clerk. Failure to appear also results in submission.[8]

§ 668. Court of Claims; Finding by the Court.

In all actions tried on the facts, the Court must find the facts specially and state separately its conclusions of law and direct the entry of an appropriate judgment. The Court may adopt the Commissioner's report, including conclusions of fact and of law, or may modify it, or may reject it in whole or in part, or may direct the Commissioner to receive further evidence, or may refer the case back to him with instructions. Due regard will be given to the opportunity of the trial Commissioner to judge of the credibility of the witnesses, and the findings of fact made by the Commissioner will be presumed to be correct.[9]

5. Court of Claims Rule 46(a).
6. Court of Claims Rule 46(b).
7. Court of Claims Rule 47(a)(c).

8. Court of Claims Rule 47(d).
9. Court of Claims Rule 48.

APPENDIX A

Rules of Practice

TAX COURT OF THE UNITED STATES

REVISED APRIL 1, 1958

NOTICE ABOUT INQUIRIES

Inquiries which are made by local or long distance telephone should be made to the following offices of the Court depending upon the nature of the inquiry. The following indicates which office can give particular information directly:

(1) Deputy Clerk in Charge of Dockets, Records, and Calendars, NAtional 8-5771, Extension 3043, regarding:

    (a) Documents filed with the Court;
    (b) Action taken on documents;
    (c) Status of cases.

(2) Deputy Clerk in Charge of Appellate Matters, NAtional 8-5771, Extension 3039, regarding:

    (a) Filing of petitions for review of Tax Court decisions;
    (b) Other procedures relating to appellate review of cases decided by the Tax Court.

(3) Office of the Clerk of the Court, NAtional 8-5771, Extension 3041, 3042, regarding:

    (a) General procedure in and practice before the Court;
    (b) General information.

JUDGES OF THE TAX COURT OF THE UNITED STATES

Chief Judge

J. EDGAR MURDOCK

Judges

BOLON B. TURNER.

MARION J. HARRON.

JOHN W. KERN.

CLARENCE V. OPPER.

NORMAN O. TIETJENS.

ARNOLD RAUM.

J. GREGORY BRUCE.

GRAYDON G. WITHEY.

MORTON P. FISHER.

ALLIN H. PIERCE.

CRAIG S. ATKINS.

JOHN E. MULRONEY.

BRUCE M. FORRESTER.

RUSSELL E. TRAIN.

WILLIAM M. DRENNEN.

Retired judges recalled to perform judicial duties under the provisions of section 7447 of the Internal Revenue Code of 1954.

C. ROGERS ARUNDELL.

ERNEST H. VAN FOSSAN.

EUGENE BLACK.

CLARENCE P. LEMIRE.

HOWARD P. LOCKE, *Clerk of the Court.*

O. W. SCHOENFELDER, *Administrative Officer.*

ELLA C. THOMAS, *Reporter.*

Contents

INTRODUCTION

These revised rules are promulgated pursuant to authority of section 7453, Internal Revenue Code of 1954, which provides that "The proceedings of the Tax Court and its divisions shall be conducted in accordance with such rules of practice and procedure (other than rules of evidence) as the Tax Court may prescribe and in accordance with the rules of evidence applicable in trials without jury in the District Court of the District of Columbia."

Congress in the revenue acts has enacted provisions relating to the organization, jurisdiction, and procedure of the Tax Court of the United States, and to the action of the Internal Revenue Service with respect to the assessment and collection of deficiencies when a petition has been filed with the Court. Reference is made to those statutory provisions in the revenue acts for procedural requirements other than those relating to the conduct of proceedings before the Court and its divisions to which these Rules of Practice are limited. Refer to the Internal Revenue Code of 1954, and particularly to sections 6211 through 6215, 7483, and 7502.

RULES

Rule 1. Location, Address, Telephone Number, and Business Hours of the Court, Fees, and Definitions

(*a*) *Office of the Court.*—The office of the Tax Court of the United States is located on the second floor of the building on the northeast corner of 12th Street and Constitution Avenue NW., Washington, D. C. The office of the Clerk of the Court is in Room 2004.

(*b*) *Mailing address.*—All mail sent to the Court should be addressed to:

> Tax Court of the United States
> Box 70
> Washington 4, D. C.

Other addresses where the Court may be in session should never be used in addressing mail to the Court or to its Clerk.

(*c*) *Telephone number.*—The telephone number of the Tax Court of the United States at its office in Washington, D. C., is NAtional 8–5771. (See notice inside front cover.)

(*d*) *Business hours.*—The Office of the Clerk of the Court at Washington, D. C., shall be open during business hours on all days, except Saturdays, Sundays, and legal holidays, for the purpose of receiving petitions, pleadings, motions, and the like. "Business hours" are from 8:45 a.m. to 5:15 p. m. (For legal holidays in Washington D. C., see Rule 61 (*b*).)

(*e*) *Fees—Method of payment.*—Checks, money orders, etc., for fees or charges of the Court should be made payable to the Treasurer of the United States and mailed or delivered to the Clerk of the Court. (See Rules 2, 7 (*b*), 52, and 53.)

(*f*) *Definitions.*—

(1) *Time.*—Time, as provided in these Rules and in orders and notices of the Court, means standard time in the city mentioned except when advanced time is substituted therefor by law. (See Rule 61.)

(2) *Commissioner.*—Where in these Rules (except in Rule 48) the word "Commissioner" is used, it refers to the Commissioner of Internal Revenue.

(3) *Code of 1954.*—The designation of "Code of 1954" as used in these Rules refers to the Internal Revenue Code of 1954.

830

Rule 2. Admission to Practice

An applicant who establishes to the satisfaction of the Court that he or she is a citizen of the United States, of good moral character and repute, and possessed of the requisite qualifications to represent others in the preparation and trial of cases, may be admitted to practice before the Court subject to the specific requirements stated hereafter in this Rule.

Each application must be on the form provided by the Court. Application forms and other necessary information will be furnished upon request addressed to the Enrollment Clerk of this Court, Box 70, Washington 4, D. C.

An attorney at law may be admitted to practice upon filing with the Enrollment Clerk a completed application accompanied by a current certificate from the Clerk of the appropriate court, showing that the applicant has been admitted to practice before and is a member in good standing of the Bar of the Supreme Court of the United States, or of the highest court of any State, or Territory, or of the District of Columbia.

An applicant, not an attorney at law, as a condition of being admitted to practice, must pass a written examination given by the Court and the Court may require such person, in addition, to take an oral examination. Any person who has thrice failed such examinations shall not thereafter be eligible to take another examination for admission.

An applicant for admission by examination must be sponsored by at least three persons theretofore enrolled to practice before this Court, and each sponsor must send a letter of recommendation directly to the Enrollment Clerk of the Court where it will be treated as a confidential communication. The sponsor shall send in his letter promptly, stating therein fully and frankly the extent of his acquaintance with the applicant, his opinion of the moral character and repute of the applicant, and his opinion of the qualifications of the applicant to practice before this Court. The Court may in its discretion accept an applicant with less than three such sponsors.

The Court will hold an examination for applicants at its offices in Washington, D. C., on the last Wednesday in October of each year, and at such other times and places as it may designate. The Court will notify each applicant, whose application is in order, of the time and place at which he is to present himself for examination, and the applicant must present that notice to the examiner as his authority for taking an examination. An applicant seeking to qualify by examination must accompany his application with a fee of $10; check or money order to be made payable to the "Treasurer of the United States."

Corporations and firms will not be admitted or recognized.

Practitioners before this Court shall carry on their practice in accordance with the letter and spirit of the canons of professional ethics as adopted by the American Bar Association.

831

The Court may deny admission to, suspend, or disbar any person who in its judgment does not possess the requisite qualifications to represent others, or who is lacking in character, integrity, or proper professional conduct. No person shall be suspended for more than 60 days or disbarred until he has been afforded an opportunity to be heard. A Division may immediately suspend any person for not more than 60 days for contempt or misconduct during the course of any trial or hearing.

The Court may require any practitioner before it to furnish a statement under oath of the terms and circumstances of his employment in any case. (See Rule 24.)

Rule 3. Personal Representation in Lieu of Counsel

Any individual taxpayer may appear for himself upon adequate identification to the Court. A taxpayer corporation may be represented by a bona fide officer of the corporation upon permission granted, in its discretion, by the Court or the Division sitting.

Rule 4. Form and Style of Papers

(*a*) *General.—*

(1) *Typing process to be used.*—Papers filed with the Court may be prepared by any process provided the information therein is set forth in clear and legible type.

(2) *Binding.*—All papers shall be bound together on the *left-hand side only* and shall have no backs or covers.

(3) *Caption, signature, and number of copies.*—All papers shall have a caption and a signature and copies shall be filed as specified below.

(*b*) *Printed papers* shall be printed in 10- or 12-point type, on good unglazed paper, 5⅜ inches wide by 9 inches long, with inside margin not less than 1 inch wide, and with double-leaded text and single-leaded quotations.

(*c*) *Typewritten papers* shall be typed on only one side of plain white paper, 8½ inches wide by 11 inches long, and weighing not less than 16 pounds to the ream.

(*d*) *Citations* shall be in italics when printed and shall be underscored when typewritten.

(*e*) *The proper caption omitting all prefixes and titles* shall be placed on all papers filed. The full given name and surname of each individual petitioner shall be set forth in the caption, but *without* any prefix or title, such as "Mrs.," "Dr.," etc. The name of the estate, the trust, or the other person for whom he acts, shall be given first by each fiduciary filing a petition, followed then by his own name and pertinent title, thus: "Estate of John Doe, deceased, Richard Roe, Executor." (See Rules 6 and 7 (*c*) (4) (*A*) and Appendix I, form a.)

(*f*) *The signature,* either of the petitioner or of his counsel, shall be subscribed in writing to the original of all pleadings, motions, and briefs, and shall be in individual and not in firm name, except that the signature of a petitioner corporation shall be in the name of the corporation by one of its active officers, thus: "John Doe, Inc., by Richard Roe, President." The name and the mailing address of the petitioner or counsel actually signing shall be typed or printed immediately beneath the written signature. The mailing address of counsel shall include the firm name if it is an essential part of the accurate mailing address.

(*g*) *Four conformed copies* shall be filed with the signed original of every paper filed, except as otherwise provided in these Rules. Papers to be filed in more than one case (as a motion to consolidate, or in cases already consolidated) shall include one additional copy for each such additional case.

(*h*) *All copies* shall be clear and legible, but they may be on any weight paper.

Rule 5. Filing of All Documents

Any document to be filed with the Court, must be filed in the office of the Clerk of the Court in Washington, D. C., during business hours (see Rule 1); except that the Judge presiding at any trial or hearing in a case may permit documents pertaining thereto to be filed at that particular session of the Court.

Rule 6. Proper Parties

A case in the Tax Court shall be brought by and in the name of the person against whom the Commissioner determined the deficiency (or liability, as the case may be), or by and in the full descriptive name of the fiduciary legally entitled to institute a case on behalf of such person.

In the event of a variance between the name set forth in the notice of deficiency or liability and the correct name, a statement of the reasons for such variance shall be set forth in the petition. (See Rules 4, 7, and 23.)

The Commissioner shall be named as the respondent.

Rule 7. Initiation of a Case—Petition—Filing Fee—Form

(*a*) *Petition.*—

(1) *Filing.*—A case shall be initiated by filing with the Court a petition consisting of an original and 4 complete, accurately conformed, clear copies, either printed or typed. (See Rules 4 and 6.)

(2) *Improper petition—Dismissal.*—Failure of a petition to comply with this Rule or with Rule 4 or 6 shall be ground for dismissal of the case.

See also section 6213 (*a*), and Section 7502, Code of 1954, in regard to absolute statutory time limit on filing.

(*b*) *Fee for filing petition.*—The fee for filing a petition with the Court shall be $10, payable at the time of filing. (See Rule 1 (*e*).)

(*c*) *Form of petition.*—

(1) The petition shall be substantially in accordance with form **a**, shown in Appendix I.

(2) It shall be complete in itself so as fully to state the issues.

(3) No telegram, cablegram, radiogram, telephone call, or similar communication will be recognized as a petition.

(4) The petition shall contain:

(*A*) A caption in the following form:

TAX COURT OF THE UNITED STATES

. . . .,	
Petitioner,	
v.	Docket **No.**
COMMISSIONER OF INTERNAL REVENUE,	
Respondent.	

PETITION

(*B*) Numbered paragraphs stating:

1. Petitioner's name and principal office or residence, and the office of the director or district director of internal revenue in which the tax return for the period in controversy was filed.

2. The date of mailing of the notice of deficiency on which the petition is based, or other proper allegations showing jurisdiction in the Court.

3. The amount of the deficiency (or liability, as the case may be), determined by the Commissioner, the nature of the tax, the year or other period for which the determination was made and, if different from the determination, the approximate amount of taxes in controversy.

4. Clear and concise assignments of each and every error which the petitioner alleges to have been committed by the Commissioner in the determination of the deficiency. Issues in respect of which the burden of proof is by statute placed upon the Commissioner will not be deemed to be raised by the petitioner in the absence of assignments of error in respect thereof. Each assignment of error shall be lettered.

5. Clear and concise lettered statements of the facts upon which the petitioner relies as sustaining the assignments of error, except those assignments of error in respect of which the burden of proof by statute is placed upon the Commissioner.

6. A prayer, setting forth relief sought by the petitioner.

(*C*) The signature of the petitioner or that of his counsel. (See Rule 4 (*f*).)

(*D*) A verification by the petitioner; provided that where the petitioner is sojourning outside the United States or is a nonresident alien, the petition may be verified by a duly appointed attorney in fact, who shall attach to the petition a copy of the power of attorney under

834   [Harris]

which he acts and who shall state in his verification that he acts pursuant to such power, that such power has not been revoked, that petitioner is absent from the United States, and the grounds of his knowledge of the facts alleged in the petition. As used herein the term "United States" includes only the States and the District of Columbia. A notary public is not authorized to administer oaths, etc., in matters in which he is employed as counsel. (See Title 1, ch. 5, D. C. Code (1951) and 26 Op. A. G. 236.)

Verifications by fiduciaries shall contain a statement that the fiduciaries signing and verifying have authority to act for the taxpayer.

Where the petitioner is a corporation, the person verifying shall state in his verification that he has authority to act for the corporation.

The signature and the verification to the petition shall be considered the certificate of those performing these acts that there is good ground for the petition, the case has not been instituted merely for delay, and it is not frivolous.

(E) A copy of the notice of deficiency (or liability, as the case may be), shall be appended to the petition and to each copy required. If a statement has accompanied the notice of deficiency, so much thereof as is material to the issues set out in the assignments of error likewise shall be appended. If the notice of deficiency refers to prior notices from the Commissioner, which are necessary to elucidate the determination, such parts thereof as are material to the issues set out in the assignments of error shall likewise be appended. (See Appendix I, form a. See Rule 22 re service of the petition.)

Rule 11. Docket

Upon receipt of the petition by the Clerk, the case will be entered upon the docket and assigned a number and the parties notified thereof. This docket number shall be placed by the parties on all papers thereafter filed in the case and referred to in all correspondence with the Court. (See Rules 5 and 7 (a) (1).)

Rule 14. Answer

(a) *Time to answer or move.*—The Commissioner, after service upon him of the petition, shall have 60 days within which to file an answer or 45 days within which to move with respect to the petition. (See Rule 22 (a) re service of answer.)

(b) *Form of answer.*—The answer shall be drawn so that it will advise the petitioner and the Court fully of the nature of the defense. It shall contain a specific admission or denial of each material allegation of fact contained in the petition and a statement of any facts upon which the Commissioner relies for defense or for affirmative relief or to sustain any issue raised in the petition in respect of which issue the burden of proof is, by statute, placed upon him. Paragraphs of the answer shall be numbered to correspond to those of the petition to

835

which they relate. The original shall be signed by the Commissioner or his counsel.

(c) *Copies and conformation.*—The original and 3 copies of the answer shall be filed, and each copy shall be conformed.

(d) *Application of Rule to amended answers.*—This Rule shall apply to the filing of answers to amended petitions and to amendments to petitions, except as the Court in a particular case may otherwise direct.

Rule 15. Reply

(a) *Time to reply or move.*—The petitioner, after service upon him of an answer in which material facts are alleged, shall have 45 days within which to file a reply or 30 days within which to move with respect to the answer. (See Rule 22 (a) re service of reply.)

(b) *Contents and form.*—The reply shall contain a specific admission or denial of each material allegation of fact contained in the answer and shall set forth any facts upon which the *petitioner* relies for defense. The paragraphs in the reply shall be numbered to correspond with the paragraphs of the answer. The original copy of each reply shall be signed by the petitioner or his counsel.

(c) *Copies and conformation.*—An original and 4 copies of the reply shall be filed, and each copy shall be conformed to the original by the petitioner or his counsel.

(d) *Verification.*—The Court, upon motion of the Commissioner in which good cause is shown, or upon its own motion, may require the verification of any reply.

Rule 16. Joinder of Issue

A case shall be deemed at issue upon the filing of the answer unless a reply is required under Rule 15, in which event it shall be deemed at issue upon filing of the reply, or the entry of an order under Rule 18 (c).

Rule 17. Amended and Supplemental Pleadings

(a) *General.*—A motion for leave to amend a pleading shall state reasons for granting it and shall be accompanied by the proposed amendment.

(b) *Petition.*—

(1) *Before answer.*—The petitioner may amend his petition at any time before answer is filed.

(2) *After answer.*—A petition may be amended, after answer is filed and up to the commencement of the trial, only with the consent of the Commissioner or by leave of the Court.

(c) *Amendment ordered.*—

(1) *Occasion for.*—The Court upon its own motion, or upon motion of either party showing good cause filed prior to the setting of the case for trial, may order a party to file a further and better statement

of the nature of his claim, of his defense, or of any matter stated in any pleading. Such a motion filed by a party shall point out the defects complained of and the details desired.

(2) *Consideration of such motion.*—The Court, in its discretion, may set such a motion for hearing (see Rule 27 (*a*)) or may act upon it *ex parte.*

(3) *Penalty for failure to amend.*—The Court may strike the pleadings to which the motion was directed or make such other order as it deems just, if an order of the Court to file amended pleadings hereunder is not obeyed within 15 days of the date of the service of said order or within such other time as the Court may fix.

(*d*) *To conform pleadings to proof.*—The Court may at any time during the course of the trial grant a motion of either party to amend its pleadings to conform to the proof in particulars stated at the time by the moving party. The amendment or amended pleadings thus permitted, shall be filed with the Court at the trial or shall be filed in the office of the Clerk of the Court in Washington, D. C., within such time as the Court may fix. (See Rules 4, 5, and 19.)

Rule 18. Admissions and Denials of Pleaded Facts

(*a*) *Effect of answer.*—Every material allegation of fact set out in the petition and not expressly admitted or denied in the answer, shall be deemed to be admitted.

(*b*) *Effect of reply.*—Every material allegation of fact set out in the answer and not expressly admitted or denied in the reply, where a reply is filed, shall be deemed to be admitted. Any new material contained in the reply shall be deemed to be denied.

(*c*) *Effect of failure to reply and motion thereon.*—

(1) *Denial—Motion seeking admission.*—The affirmative allegations of the answer will be deemed denied in the absence of a reply, unless the Commissioner, within 45 days after the expiration of the time for filing a reply, files a motion reciting that a reply required under these Rules was not filed and requesting the Court to enter an order that specified allegations of fact in the answer shall be deemed to be admitted.

(2) *Service of and hearing on motion.*—The Clerk will serve a copy of the Commissioner's motion upon the petitioner and issue notice of a hearing thereon at which hearing the Court may grant the motion unless the required reply is filed on or before the day fixed for such hearing.

Rule 19. Motions

(*a*) Motions must be timely, must fully set forth the alleged reasons for the action sought and must be prepared in the form and style prescribed by Rule 4. (See Rule 22 (*a*) re service.)

(*b*) Motions will be acted upon as justice may require and may, in the discretion of the Court, be placed upon the motion calendar for argument. Disposition of motions will be expedited if the party filing the same, after consultation with his adversary, is able to note on the motion that there is no objection thereto. (See Rule 27 (*a*) and (*c*) and Rule 30 (*b*).)

(*c*) The filing of a motion shall not constitute cause for postponement of a trial from the date set. (See also Rule 27 (*c*) on motions for continuance.)

(*d*) If a motion, other than one relating to the receipt of evidence during trial, is made orally during trial, the maker thereof shall promptly reduce it to writing and file it with the Court unless the Division sitting directs otherwise.

(*e*) No motion for retrial, further trial, or reconsideration may be filed more than 30 days after the opinion has been served, except by special leave.

(*f*) No motion to vacate or revise a decision may be filed more than 30 days after the decision has been entered, except by special leave.

Motions covered by (*e*) and (*f*) shall be separate from each other and not joined to or made a part of any other motion.

Rule 20. Extensions of Time

(*a*) An extension of time (except for the absolute time limit on filing of the petition, see section 6213 (*a*), Code of 1954, and except as otherwise provided in these Rules) may be granted by the Court within its discretion upon a timely motion filed in accordance with these Rules setting forth good and sufficient cause therefor or may be ordered by the Court upon its own motion.

(*b*) If a motion is filed or an order issued in respect to the adequacy of any petition, the time prescribed in Rule 14 (*a*) shall begin to run from the date upon which the Court takes final action with respect to the motion or the order unless the Court orders otherwise. The time for reply shall be similarly extended in the case of a motion or an order with respect to the adequacy of an answer unless the Court orders otherwise.

(*c*) Any extension of time for filing a brief shall correspondingly extend the time for filing all other briefs yet to be filed in that case unless the Court orders otherwise. (See Rules 19, 22, and 35.)

For continuances, see Rule 27 (*c.*)

Rule 21. Dismissal

A case may be dismissed for cause upon motion of either party or of the Court. (See Rule 7 (*a*) (2) and Rule 27 (*b*) (3).)

Rule 22. Service Upon the Parties

(*a*) *Who will serve and method to be used.*—The Clerk shall make service upon the petitioner by mailing to him or to his counsel of record a copy of the pleading, motion, notice, brief, or other document to be served.

838

Service shall be made by the Clerk upon any named respondent in person, upon deputies duly designated by him to accept service, or upon counsel appearing for the respondent in the case. (See Rules 14 and 15.)

(*b*) *Upon first counsel of record.*—Service upon any counsel of record will be deemed service upon the party, but, where there are more than one, service will be made only upon counsel for petitioner whose appearance was first entered of record—unless the first counsel of record, by writing filed with the Court, designates other counsel to receive service, in which event service will be so made.

(*c*) *Where no counsel of record.*—If there is no counsel of record, service will be made upon the petitioner.

Rule 23. Substitution of Parties—Change of Names

(*a*) *Successor fiduciaries—Certificate needed.*—A motion shall be filed to substitute parties who are successor fiduciaries and shall be supported by a certificate of the proper court or official showing the appointment and qualification of the party who seeks to be substituted. (See Rules 4, 19, and 24 (*a*) (2).)

(*b*) *Change in name—Certificate needed.*—A motion shall be filed to amend the pleadings to show a change in the name of a corporation or other party and shall be supported by a proper official certificate or copy of the decree or other document by which the change was effected, duly certified by the official having its custody. (See Rules 4 and 19.)

(*c*) *Waiver of certificate.*—No certificate need be filed, unless required by Court order, if the respondent consents to a change as described in paragraphs (*a*) and (*b*) above.

(*d*) *Court order.*—The Court, on motion of a party or upon its own motion, may order the substitution of proper parties upon the death of a petitioner, where a mistake in the name or title of a party appears, or for other cause.

Rule 24. Counsel—Appearance—Withdrawal—Substitution—Changed Address

(*a*) *Entry of appearance of counsel.*—

(1) Counsel enrolled to practice before this Court may enter his appearance by subscribing the initial petition.

(2) Counsel who subscribes any motion filed under Rule 23 (*a*) will be deemed to have entered his appearance for such new party and he shall promptly file a motion by the new petitioner for the withdrawal of counsel who had previously entered their appearance unless they are to be recognized as counsel for the new petitioner.

(3) Counsel may otherwise enter his appearance *only* by filing, in duplicate, an entry of appearance which shall be signed by counsel individually, shall show his mailing address, and shall state that he is enrolled to practice before this Court. Form 305 may be obtained from the Clerk and used for this purpose but an adequate substitute will suffice. (See Appendix, form 305.)

(4) Counsel not properly enrolled to practice before this Court will not be recognized except by special leave of the Court granted at a hearing or trial and then only where it appears that counsel can and will promptly become enrolled. (See Rules 2, 4 (*f*), and 7 (*c*) (4) (*C*).)

(*b*) *Withdrawal of counsel.*—Counsel of record in any case desiring to withdraw, or any petitioner desiring to withdraw counsel of record, must file a motion with the Court requesting leave therefor reciting that notice thereof has been given to the client or to the counsel being withdrawn, as the case may be. The Court may, in its discretion, deny such motion.

(*c*) *Substitution of counsel.*—New counsel may be substituted by conforming to the provisions of (*a*) (2) or (*a*) (3) and (*b*) above. (See Rules 2, 4, 19, and 27 (*c*).)

(See Rule 22 (*b*) in regard to substitution of "first counsel of record" for purposes of service.)

(*d*) *Change of address.*—Notice of any change in the mailing address of either counsel or petitioner shall be filed promptly with the Court, in duplicate. Separate notices shall be filed for each case.

Counsel may not act as notary. (See Rule 7 (*c*) (4) (*D*).)

Rule 26. Place of Trial—Requests and Designation

(*a*) *Requests for place of trial.*—The petitioner at the time of filing the petition shall also file a request showing the name of the place where he would prefer the trial to be held. If the petitioner has filed no request the respondent shall file at the time he files his answer, a request showing the name of the place preferred by him.

(*b*) *Form and caption.*—These requests shall be separate from the petition or answer, shall have a caption, and shall consist of an original and 2 copies. (See Rule 7 (*c*) (4) (*A*).)

(*c*) *Designation of place of trial.*—The Court will designate the place of trial in accordance with the statutory provision that the time and place of trial shall be fixed "with as little inconvenience and expense to taxpayers as is practicable," and, in all cases, will notify the parties of the place at which or in the vicinity of which the trial will be held.

(*d*) *Motions for changing place designated.*—If either party desires a change in designation of the place of trial he must file a motion (with 4 copies) to that effect, stating fully his reasons therefor. Such motions, made after the notice of the time of the trial has been mailed, will not be deemed to have been timely filed.

(See Appendix II for further information to assist in making requests as to place of trial. See Rule 4.)

Rule 27. Place, Time, and Notice of Hearings and Trials—Attendance and Continuances

(*a*) *Calendars of hearings on motions and other procedural and subsidiary matters.*—

(1) If it is necessary for the Court to hear the parties on matters other than the merits, the proceeding will be listed for such hearing

on a motion calendar which is called in Washington, D. C., unless good cause for holding the hearing elsewhere is shown in a timely motion to the Court. Ordinarily such calendars will be set for call at 10 a. m. (See Rule 1) on Wednesdays throughout the year, but due notice of the time and place in each case will be given to the parties by the Clerk. (See Rule 22.)

(2) *Attendance at hearings on motion calendar.*—If a party fails to appear at the call of the motion calendar, the Court will hear the proceeding *ex parte*. However, a memorandum or brief stating the position of the petitioner upon the pending motion will be accepted, when the failure of the petitioner to appear is justified by distance, shortness of time, or other good reason stated in such memorandum or brief.

(3) Where the motion or order is directed to defects in a pleading, prompt filing of a proper pleading correcting the defects may obviate the necessity of a hearing thereon.

(*b*) *Trial calendars.*—

(1) Each case, when at issue, will be placed upon a calendar for trial in accordance with Rule 26 and the Clerk, not less than 30 days in advance, will notify the parties of the place where and the date and time when it will be called.

(2) *Calendar call.*—Each case appearing on such a calendar will be called at the time and place scheduled. The cases will be called usually in the order listed, and counsel or the parties will state their estimate of the time required for trial or file stipulations in lieu of trial. The cases for trial will thereupon be tried in due course, but not necessarily in the order listed.

(3) *Attendance at trials.*—The unexcused absence of a party or his counsel when a case is called for trial will not be the occasion for delay. The case may be dismissed for failure properly to prosecute or the trial may proceed and the case be regarded as submitted on the part of the absent party or parties.

(4) The Court may require appearance for argument or it may accept briefs in lieu of personal appearance.

(*c*) *Continuances—Motions—Trials.*—

(1) Court action on cases set for hearing on motions or trial will not be delayed by a motion for continuance unless it is timely, sets forth good and sufficient cause, and complies with all applicable Rules.

(2) Conflicting engagements of counsel or the employment of new counsel will never be regarded as good ground for a continuance unless set forth in a motion filed promptly after the notice of hearing or trial has been mailed or unless extenuating circumstances are shown which the Court deems adequate. (See Rule 20.)

(*d*) *Reserve calendar.*—A case once at issue may, upon motion, be placed on an inactive list called the reserve calendar. Good cause must be shown, as, for example, that the case will be governed by the decision in a case pending in a higher court. The case may be placed later on a trial calendar by motion of either party or by the Court on its own motion when the reason for inaction no longer exists.

841

Rule 30. Submission Without Trial or Appearance

(a) *Submission of cases without trial where facts are uncontested.*—
Any case not requiring a trial for the submission of evidence (as, for
example, where sufficient facts have been admitted, stipulated, established by deposition, or included in the record in some other way) may
be submitted at any time by notice of the parties filed with the Court.
The parties need not wait for the case to be calendared and need not
appear in person. The Chief Judge will then assign the case to a
Division for report, which Division, upon request of the parties, will
fix a time for filing briefs or for oral argument. (See, however, Rule
31 (*g*).)

(b) A contested motion, not predicated upon an issue of fact, may
be submitted in the same way. (See Rule 27 (*a*).)

Rule 31. Evidence and the Submission of Evidence

(a) *Rules applicable.*—The trials before the Court and its Divisions
will be conducted in accordance with the rules of evidence applicable
in trials without a jury in the United States District Court for the
District of Columbia. With reference to the examination of unwilling
or hostile witnesses, see Rule 43 (b) of the Rules of Civil Procedure
for the United States District Courts.[1]

(b) *Stipulations.*—

(1) *Stipulations required.*—The Court expects the parties to stipulate
evidence to the fullest extent to which complete or qualified agreement
can be reached including all material facts that are not or fairly should
not be in dispute.

(2) *In preparation for trial.*—The party expecting to introduce any
evidence which might possibly be stipulated (as, for example, entries
or summaries from books of account and other records, documents, and
all other evidence, to the extent not disputed) shall confer with his
adversary promptly after receipt of the trial notice, and both shall
endeavor to stipulate all facts not already stipulated.

(3) *Presentation—Copies—Form.*—Stipulations in writing may be
filed with the Court in advance or presented at the trial and when filed
need not be offered formally to be considered in evidence. They shall
be filed in duplicate except that duplicates of the exhibits attached to
the original of the stipulation need not be filed. (See Rule 4 as to form
and style.)

---

1 Rules of Civil Procedure for the United States District Courts.
Rule 43. Evidence.

*   *   *   *   *   *   *

(b) Scope of Examination and Cross-Examination. A party may interrogate
any unwilling or hostile witness by leading questions. A party may call an adverse
party or an officer, director, or managing agent of a public or private corporation
or of a partnership or association which is an adverse party, and interrogate him by
leading questions and contradict and impeach him in all respects as if he had been
called by the adverse party, and the witness thus called may be contradicted and
impeached by or on behalf of the adverse party also, and may be cross-examined by
the adverse party only upon the subject matter of his examination in chief.

(4) *Objections.*—Any objection to all or any part of a stipulation should be noted in the stipulation, but the Court will consider any objection to stipulated facts made at the trial.

(5) *No evidence received to alter or contradict.*—The Court may set aside a stipulation in whole or in part where justice requires, but otherwise will not receive evidence tending to qualify, change, or contradict any fact properly introduced into the record by stipulation.

(c) *Depositions must be offered.*—Testimony taken by deposition will not be considered until offered and received in evidence.

(d) *Marking exhibits.*—Exhibits attached to a stipulation or a deposition shall be numbered serially, i. e., 1, 2, 3, etc., if offered by the petitioner; shall be lettered serially, i. e., A, B, C, etc., if offered by the respondent; and shall be marked serially, i. e., 1–A, 2–B, 3–C, etc., if offered as a joint exhibit.

(e) *Documentary evidence.*—

(1) *Copies.*—A copy of any book, record, paper, or document may be offered directly in evidence in lieu of the original, where the original is available or where there is no objection, and, where the original is admitted in evidence, a copy may be substituted later for the original or such part thereof as may be material or relevant, upon leave granted in the discretion of the trial Judge.

(2) *Return after final decision.*—Either party desiring the return at his expense of any exhibit belonging to him, after the decision of the Court in any case has become final, shall make prompt application in writing to the Clerk, suggesting a practical manner of delivery. Otherwise exhibits may be disposed of as the Court deems advisable.

(f) *Ex parte statements are not evidence.*—*Ex parte* affidavits, statements in briefs, and unadmitted allegations in pleadings do not constitute evidence.

(g) *Failure of proof.*—Failure to adduce evidence in support of the material facts alleged by the party having the burden of proof and denied by his adversary, may be ground for dismissal. The provisions of Rule 30 do not relieve the party upon whom rests the burden of proof of the necessity of properly producing evidence in support of issues joined on questions of fact.

Rule 32. Burden of Proof

The burden of proof shall be upon the petitioner, except as otherwise provided by statute, and except that in respect of any new matter pleaded in his answer, it shall be upon the respondent.

Rule 35. Briefs

(a) *General.*—The filing of briefs and the making of oral arguments shall be in accordance with the directions of the Judge presiding at the trial. The parties should be prepared to make oral argument at the conclusion of a trial or to file a written citation of authorities at that time if the Judge so directs.

843

(*b*) *Filing.*—Each party shall file an original brief within 45 days after the day on which the trial was concluded and a reply brief within another 30 days thereafter unless the trial Judge directs otherwise. A party, who fails to file an original brief, may not file a reply brief except on leave granted by the Court, and if his reply brief is filed, his adversary may have an additional 30 days thereafter to file his reply brief. (See Rules 19 and 20 re extensions of time.)

(*c*) *Service.*—Each brief, whether original or reply, will be served promptly upon the opposite party after it is filed, except where it bears a notation that a copy has already been served, and except that where simultaneous briefs are to be filed they will be served upon the other party immediately after the time for filing such briefs (including any extension thereof) has expired. If an extension is granted after the original time for filing has expired and the brief of the opposite party has been filed but not served, it will be served promptly after the extended period. (See Rule 20 (*c*).)

(*d*) *Number of copies.*—An original and 2 copies shall be filed if briefs are typewritten and 20 copies shall be filed if briefs are printed. An original and 6 copies shall be filed on Internal Revenue Code of 1939 section 722 and section 721 (a) and (2) (C) issues.

(*e*) *Form and contents.*—All briefs shall contain the following in the order indicated:

(1) On its first page, a *table of contents* with page references followed by a list of all citations alphabetically arranged as to cases cited together with references to pages. Citations shall be in italics when printed and underscored when typewritten. (See Rule 4.)

(2) A statement of the nature of the controversy, the tax involved, and the issues to be decided.

(3) The party having the burden of proof shall set forth complete *statements of the facts* based upon the evidence. Each statement shall be numbered, shall be complete in itself, and shall consist of a concise statement of the essential fact and not a discussion or argument relating to the evidence or the law. Reference to the pages of the transcript or the exhibits relied upon in support thereof shall be inserted after each separate statement.

If the other party disagrees with any or all of the statements of fact, he shall set forth each correction which he believes the evidence requires and shall give the same numbers to his statements of fact as appear in his opponent's brief. His statement of fact shall be set forth in accordance with the requirements above designated.

(4) A concise *statement of the points* upon which the party relies.

(5) *The argument.*—The argument shall set forth the points of law relied upon and any discussion of the evidence deemed necessary to support the statement of fact.

(6) The *signature* of counsel or the party filing. (See Rule 4 (*f*).)

Rule 40. Transcripts of Proceedings

Hearings or trials before the Court or its Divisions shall be stenographically reported and a transcript thereof shall be made if, in the opinion of the Court or of the Division conducting the hearing or trial, a permanent record is deemed necessary. Transcripts shall be supplied to the parties and to the public by the official reporter at such rates as may be fixed by contract between the Court and the reporter.

Rule 44. Subpoenas

(a) *How issued.*—Subpoenas shall be issued to a proper party, upon request, and when issued shall be signed and sealed, but may otherwise be in blank. Subpoenas so issued in blank shall be completed before service by the party receiving them.

(b) *Contents.*—A subpoena when completed shall state the caption of the case, the names and last known addresses of the witnesses to be called, the time and place at which they are to appear and give testimony, and whether a witness may designate someone to appear in his place.

(c) *For production of documentary evidence.*—If evidence other than oral testimony is required, such as documentary or written data, the subpoena shall number, set forth separately, and describe adequately each item to be produced.

(d) *Service.*—The party on whose behalf a subpoena is issued shall be responsible for its service, and service may be made by any person who is not a party and is not less than 18 years of age. Service of a subpoena upon a person named therein shall be made by delivering a copy thereof to such person.

Rule 45. Depositions

(a) *Application to take.*—When either party desires to take a deposition, he shall file with the Court a verified application and 2 conformed copies, together with an additional copy for each additional docket number involved. The Court upon request will furnish forms for this purpose. If the space in the form furnished by the Court is inadequate for setting forth the reasons in support of the application in any particular case, a substitute form may be used, but the substitute must contain all of the information called for on the Court's form. (See Appendix I, form 5–A.)

(b) *Limitation on time for application to take.*—Applications to take depositions must be filed at least 30 days prior to the date set for the trial of the case, and such depositions must be completed and filed with the Court at least 10 days prior to the trial: *Provided,* Such applications will not be regarded as sufficient ground for the granting of a continuance from the date or place of the trial theretofore set, unless the case shall have been at issue less than 60 days and the motion for continuance shall have been filed not less than 20 days prior to said date of trial: *Provided, further,* That under special circumstances, and for good cause shown, the Court may otherwise order.

(c) *Qualification of officer.*—The officer before whom depositions are taken must be authorized to administer oaths. (See section 7622, Code of 1954.) In no case shall a deposition be taken before any person who has any office connection or business employment with either party or his counsel except by consent of the parties and when no other officer is available, and in his certificate of return to such deposition such officer shall so certify.

(d) *Order for taking.*—Upon receipt of such application, the Clerk will serve a copy thereof on the opposite party, and allow a reasonable time for objection thereto. Thereafter, the Court will, in its discretion, make an order, a copy of which will be mailed or delivered to the parties or their counsel, wherein the Court will name the witness whose deposition is to be taken and specify the time when, the place where, and the officer before whom the witness is to testify, but such time, place, and officer specified in the Court's order may or may not be the same as set forth in the application. The applicant shall thereupon make all necessary arrangements for the taking of each deposition and shall furnish the officer before whom it is to be taken with a copy of the order above mentioned.

(e) *By stipulation.*—At any time after issue is joined, the parties or their counsel may, by stipulation duly signed and filed, take depositions. In such cases, the stipulation shall state the name and address of each witness, the time when and the place where such depositions will be taken, and the name, address, and official title of the officer before whom it is proposed to take the depositions. In such cases, no order to take depositions will be issued, but they shall be taken and returned by the officer in accordance with the Rules of the Court.

(f) *Manner of taking.*—Each witness must first take the oath or affirm. The questions propounded to him and his answers must be recorded verbatim.

Objections to questions or answers shall be explicitly but briefly and concisely stated and recorded without any unnecessary comment, explanation, or argument by counsel for either party.

(g) *Other witnesses to be excluded.*—At the request of either party, a person whom either expects or intends to call as a witness in the same or any related case shall be excluded from the room where the testimony of a witness is being taken. If such person remains in the room or within hearing of the examination after such request has been made, he shall not thereafter be permitted to testify except by the consent of the party who requested his exclusion.

(h) *Depositions to be signed.*—The testimony of the witness when transcribed shall be read to or by him and shall be signed by him. (See Appendix I, form 5–re.)

(i) *Form in which depositions must be returned to the Court.*—When a deposition is returned to the Court it must show the docket number and the caption (the names of the parties) of the case as they appear in the Court's records, the place and date of taking, the name of the witness, the party by whom called, the names of counsel present, indicating which party each counsel represents, and (in the body of the deposition) the name of counsel examining or cross-examining the witness.

The officer must so fasten the sheets of the deposition that they cannot be tampered with. He must spare no pains to return to the Court the exact testimony he has taken. All exhibits must be carefully marked so as to be capable of identification, and when practicable must be attached to the deposition.

The officer must properly execute and attach to the deposition a certificate of return in the form prescribed. (See Appendix I, form 5–re.)

(*j*) *Return of.*—The officer must enclose the original depositions and exhibits, together with 2 copies of the depositions, in a sealed packet, with postage or other transportation charges prepaid, and direct and forward the same to the Tax Court of the United States, Box 70, Washington 4, D. C. In each case, the original of the depositions must be directed and forwarded to the Court. The officer may, however, upon written request, deliver a copy of the depositions to either or to both of the parties, or to their representatives, in lieu of sending such copies to the Court as above provided. If one or both of the required copies are delivered by the officer taking the depositions, he shall attach to his return the written request of the party or parties, or of their counsel to whom such copy or copies were delivered, and shall state in his certificate of return the fact of delivery by him of such copy or copies. If copies of the depositions are delivered by the officer taking the same, no service of copies of such depositions upon the party or his counsel of record will be made by the Court.

Rule 46. Depositions Upon Written Interrogatories

(*a*) *Application for, interrogatories, objections, etc.*—Applications to take depositions upon written interrogatories may be made in substantially the same manner as depositions taken under Rule 45 except as hereinafter noted. An original and 5 copies of the interrogatories must be filed with the verified application. The Clerk will serve a copy of the application and of the interrogatories with notice to the opposite party that objections or cross-interrogatories may be filed within 15 days thereafter. Cross-interrogatories shall consist of an original and 5 copies. The Clerk will serve a copy thereof with notice that any objections thereto may be filed within 15 days. The initial application and interrogatories must be filed in time to allow for service, objections, cross-interrogatories, and objections thereto, and for taking and filing the deposition at least 10 days prior to any trial then scheduled.

(*b*) *Manner of taking.*—The officer taking the deposition upon written interrogatories shall propound the interrogatories and cross-interrogatories in their proper order to each witness and shall cause the testimony to be reduced to writing in the witness's own words by a stenographic reporter then present, but no person other than the witness, reporter, and the officer taking the deposition shall be present at the examination. Otherwise said officer shall conform substantially to the provisions of Rule 45.

(c) *Certificate and return of deposition.*—The officer taking the deposition shall certify in his return that no person was present at the examination except the witness, the reporter, and himself and he shall otherwise comply with the pertinent provisions of Rule 45.

(d) *Depositions in foreign countries.*—Depositions obtained in foreign countries must be taken upon written interrogatories except as otherwise directed by the Court for cause shown.

Rule 47. Tender of and Objections to Depositions

(a) *Objections to depositions taken upon oral examination.*—

(1) *Competency, relevancy, or materiality.*—Objections to the competency of a witness or to the competency, relevancy, or materiality of testimony, where depositions are taken upon oral examination, may be made at the trial, even though not noted at or before the taking of the deposition, unless the ground for the objection is one which might have been obviated or removed if presented at or before the time of the taking of the deposition.

(2) *Irregularities as to manner or form.*—Objections directed to errors and irregularities in the manner of taking the deposition, in the form of any question or answer, in the oath or affirmation, or in the conduct of parties, and errors of any kind which might have been obviated, removed, or cured if promptly presented will not be considered unless made at the taking of the deposition. (See Rule 45 (f).)

(3) *Errors re how transcribed, signed, certified, etc.*—Errors or irregularities in the manner in which the testimony is transcribed or the deposition is prepared, signed, certified, sealed, endorsed, transmitted, filed, or otherwise dealt with by the officer under Rules 45 and 46 shall not form the basis for objections but questions in respect thereto shall be raised on a motion to suppress the deposition in whole or in part made with reasonable promptness after such defect is or with due diligence might have been ascertained.

(b) *Objections to written interrogatories or cross-interrogatories.*—No objections to written interrogatories or cross-interrogatories will be considered subsequent to the taking of the deposition unless they have been made in the manner and within the time prescribed therefor by Rule 46. (See Rule 31 (c) and (e).)

Rule 48. Commissioner of the Tax Court

(a) The term "commissioner" as used in this Rule 48 applies to any attorney of the legal staff of this Court who shall have been designated by the Chief Judge as a "commissioner in a particular case" pursuant to section 7456, Code of 1954.

(b) The commissioner shall conduct the hearing in such case in accordance with the Court's Rules of Practice. He shall rule upon objections and other evidentiary matters in accordance with the rules of evidence as provided in section 7453, and shall exercise such further and incidental authority, including the issuance of subpoenas, as may be necessary for the conduct of the hearing.

848

(c) Each party shall file his proposed findings of fact and original brief within 60 days after the date on which the hearing is concluded, unless otherwise directed. As to their form and contents, the provisions of Rule 35 (e) shall apply, except that the proposed findings of fact of each party shall be complete under the evidence and shall not be subject to the limiting provision of the first sentence of Rule 35 (e) (3). The number of copies of proposed findings of fact and briefs to be filed and service thereof shall be as specified in Rules 35 (d) and 35 (c), respectively.

(d) The objections of each party to the proposed findings of fact of the opposing party, prepared in the manner provided in the second paragraph of Rule 35 (e) (3), shall be filed within 30 days after service of the proposed findings.

(e) Thereafter the commissioner shall prepare and file a report of his findings of fact based upon the evidence in the case, and a copy thereof shall be served on each party.

(f) Reply briefs and any exceptions which the parties may have to the commissioner's findings of fact shall be filed within 30 days from the date of service of the said findings of fact.

(g) Upon motion of either party, made not later than the due date for filing his reply brief, or upon its own motion, the Division to which the case is assigned may, in its discretion, direct oral argument and set a date therefor.

Rule 50. Computations by Parties for Entry of Decision

(a) *Agreed computations.*—Where the Court has filed its opinion determining the issues in a case, it may withhold entry of its decision for the purpose of permitting the parties to submit computations pursuant to the Court's determination of the issues, showing the correct amount of the deficiency or overpayment to be entered as the decision. If the parties are in agreement as to the amount of the deficiency or overpayment to be entered as the decision pursuant to the report of the Court, they or either of them shall file promptly with the Court an original and 2 copies of a computation showing the amount of the deficiency or overpayment and that there is no disagreement that the figures shown are in accordance with the report of the Court. The Court will then enter its decision.

(b) *Procedure in absence of agreement.*—If, however, the parties are not in agreement as to the amount of the deficiency or overpayment to be entered as the decision, in accordance with the report of the Court, either of them may file with the Court a computation of the deficiency or overpayment believed by him to be in accordance with the report of the Court. The Clerk will serve a copy thereof upon the opposite party, will place the matter upon a motion calendar for argument in due course, and will serve notice of the argument upon both parties. If the opposite party fails to file objection, accompanied by an alternative computation, at least 5 days prior to the date of such argument, or any continuance thereof, the Court may enter decision in accordance with

[Harris]—54

the computation already submitted. If in accordance with this Rule computations are submitted by the parties which differ as to the amount to be entered as the decision of the Court, the parties will be afforded an opportunity to be heard in argument thereon on the date fixed, and the Court will determine the correct deficiency or overpayment and enter its decision.

(c) *Limits on argument under this Rule.*—Any argument under this Rule will be confined strictly to the consideration of the correct computation of the deficiency or overpayment resulting from the report already made, and no argument will be heard upon or consideration given to the issues or matters already disposed of by such report or of any new issues. This Rule is not to be regarded as affording an opportunity for retrial or reconsideration.

Rule 51. Estate Tax Deduction Developing After Trial

If the parties in an estate tax case are unable to agree under Rule 50, or under a remand, upon a deduction involving expenses incurred at or after the trial, the petitioner may move to reopen the case for further trial on that issue provided it is raised in the petition or by amendment thereto.

Rule 52. Preparation of Record on Review—Costs

(a) Immediately after the contents of a record on review have been settled or agreed to, the Clerk will notify the petitioner of the costs and charges for the preparation, comparison, and certification of said records; such charges to be determined in accordance with the provisions of section 7474, Code of 1954, and the Act of September 27, 1944, 58 Stat. 743.

(b) No transcript will be certified and transmitted to the appellate court until the costs and charges therefor have been paid. (For name of payee, see Rule 1 (e).)

(c) A petitioner for review who requests the Clerk to certify but not to prepare documents for transmission to a United States Court of Appeals shall furnish the Clerk with the copies of the documents to be certified, if duplicates are not already in the record. (See Rules 4 (g) and 31 (b).)

(For statutory provisions relating to appellate court review of Tax Court decisions, see section 7482 et seq., Code of 1954. For forms of bonds, see Appendix I, forms b and c. The rules of the appellate court to which the appeal is being taken should be consulted.)

Rule 53. Court Records—Removal—Fees for Copies

(a) *Original records to be retained by Clerk—Exceptions.*—The Clerk shall not permit any original record, paper, document, or exhibit filed with the Court to be taken from the courtroom or from other offices of the Court, except as ordered by a Judge of the Court, or except as the Clerk may find necessary in furnishing photostat copies of such records

[Harris]

or transmitting originals to higher Courts for appeal purposes, but when a decision of the Court becomes final he shall proceed in accordance with Rule 31 (e) (2).

(b) *Copies obtained from Clerk.*—A plain or a certified copy of any document, record, entry, or other paper pertaining to a case before this Court may be had upon application to the Clerk, the fee to be charged and collected therefor to be determined in accordance with the provisions of section 7474, Code of 1954, and the Act of September 27, 1944, 58 Stat 743. No copy of any exhibit or original document in the files of the Court shall be furnished to other than the parties until the decision in the case becomes final.

Rule 60. Fees and Mileage

Section 7457 of the Internal Revenue Code of 1954 provides:

(a) *Amount.*—Any witness summoned or whose deposition is taken under section 7456 shall receive the same fees and mileage as witnesses in courts of the United States.

(b) *Payment.*—Such fees and mileage and the expenses of taking any such deposition shall be paid as follows:

(1) *Witnesses for Secretary or his delegate.*—In the case of witnesses for the Secretary or his delegate, such payments shall be made by the Secretary or his delegate out of any moneys appropriated for the collection of internal revenue taxes, and may be made in advance.

(2) *Other witnesses.*—In the case of any other witnesses, such payments shall be made, subject to rules prescribed by the Tax Court, by the party at whose instance the witness appears or the deposition is taken.

No witness, other than one for the Commissioner, shall be required to testify in any case before the Court until he shall have been tendered the fees and mileage to which he is entitled in accordance with the above provision of law.

Rule 61. Computation of Time—Saturdays, Sundays, and Holidays

(a) *Computation of time—Exclusions.*—The day of the act, event, or default starting any period of time prescribed or allowed by these Rules or by an order of this Court shall not be counted as a part of the period, but Saturdays, Sundays, and legal holidays in the District of Columbia shall count just as any other days, except that when the period would expire on a Saturday, Sunday, or legal holiday in the District of Columbia, it shall extend to and include the next succeeding day that is not a Saturday, Sunday, or such legal holiday.

(b) *The legal holidays within the District of Columbia are:*

New Year's Day, January 1 (U. S. C., Title 5, sec. 87).

Inauguration Day, every fourth year (48 Stat. 879; D. C. Code (1951), Title 28, sec. 616).

Washington's Birthday, February 22 (U. S. C., Title 5, sec. 87).

Memorial Day, May 30 (U. S. C., Title 5, sec. 87).

Fourth of July (U. S. C., Title 5, sec. 87).

Labor Day, first Monday in September (U. S. C., Title 5, sec. 87).

Veterans Day, November 11 (U. S. C., Title 5, sec. 87).

Thanksgiving Day, fourth Thursday of November (U. S. C., Title 5, sec. 87).

Christmas Day, December 25 (U. S. C., Title 5, sec. 87).

When legal holidays fall on Sunday the next day shall be a holiday (22 Stat. 1; D. C. Code (1951), Title 28, sec. 616).

Rule 63. Cases Based Upon Disallowance of Claims for Refund or Relief

All of the Rules of Practice, with appropriate changes in wording wherever necessary, shall apply to cases involving the disallowance of claims for refund or relief over which this Court has jurisdiction. Petitions in such cases shall have attached to them a copy of the notice of disallowance, together with whatever statements may accompany that notice, and shall also have attached to them a copy of the claim or application for refund or relief. In cases where no appeal lies from the decision of the Tax Court a copy of the claim or application need be attached only to the original and first copy of the petition.

Rule 64. Renegotiation of Contracts Cases

(a) *Applicability of other rules to renegotiation cases.*—Except as otherwise prescribed by this Rule, cases for the redetermination of excessive profits under the Renegotiation Acts[2] shall be governed by the existing Rules of Practice before this Court. Where any of the existing Rules (except Rule 48) or the matter contained in the Appendix refer to the Commissioner, such Rules and the matter in the Appendix, when applied to a case for the redetermination of excessive profits under the Renegotiation Acts, shall refer to the War Contracts Price Adjustment Board (or to the United States when substituted therefor),[3] to the Secretary as defined and used in the Renegotiation Acts, or to the Renegotiation Board. Similarly references to the taxpayer shall refer to the contractor or subcontractor; references to tax shall refer to profits under a contract or subcontract subject to renegotiation, or to excessive profits thereunder, dependent upon context; and references to the determination of a deficiency, or a notice of such determination, shall refer to the order of the Board or the Secretary determining the amount of excessive profits.

[2] Section 403 of the Sixth Supplemental National Defense Appropriation Act, 1942, as amended by section 701, Revenue Act of 1943, and section 108 of the Renegotiation Act of 1951; also, the Renegotiation Act of 1948 (Supplemental National Defense Appropriation Act of 1948, section 3 (e)), Public Law No. 547, 80th Cong., 62 Stat. 260; also, Public Law No. 764, 83d Cong., 68 Stat. 1116.

[3] Section 201 (h) of the Renegotiation Act of 1951, as amended by section 3, Public Law No. 576, 82d Cong., 2d Sess., approved July 17, 1952, and by section 8, Public Law 764, 83d Cong., 2d Sess., approved September 1, 1954, 68 Stat. 1116.

(*b*) *Initiation of cases.*—A case for the redetermination of excessive profits under the Renegotiation Acts shall be initiated by the filing of a petition, as provided in Rules 4, 6, and the pertinent parts of Rule 7, in which the authority making the determination of excessive profits shall be shown as the respondent. (See form a, Appendix I.)

The petition shall be complete in itself so as fully to state the issues. It shall contain:

(*A*) A caption in the following form:

TAX COURT OF THE UNITED STATES

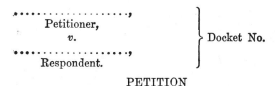

PETITION

(*B*) Proper allegations showing jurisdiction in the Court.

(*C*) A statement of the amount of excessive profits determined by the Board or the Secretary, as the case may be, the period for which determined, and the amount thereof in controversy. If the determination of excessive profits was made on the basis of a specific contract or contracts, the petition shall identify the contract or contracts and shall state the period covered thereby.

(*D*) Clear and concise assignments of each and every error which the petitioner alleges to have been committed by the Board or the Secretary in the determination of excessive profits. Each assignment of error shall be lettered.

(*E*) Clear and concise lettered statements of the facts upon which the petitioner relies as sustaining the assignments of error. The allegations of fact shall contain a statement of the amount received or accrued during the period in question under the contracts or subcontracts subject to renegotiation; the costs paid or incurred with respect thereto and the profits derived therefrom, the type and character of business done, and any other facts pertinent to a determination of the error alleged.

(*F*) A prayer, setting forth relief sought by the petitioner.

(*G*) The signature of the petitioner or that of his counsel. (See Rule 4.)

(*H*) A verification by the petitioner in accordance with the applicable provision of Rule 7 (*c*) (4) (*D*).

(*I*) A copy of the notice and a copy of the order determining the amount of excessive profits, which form the basis for the initiation of the case shall be appended to the petition. If a statement has been furnished to the petitioner by the renegotiating authority setting forth the facts upon which the determination of excessive profits was based and the reasons for such determination, a copy of such statement shall also be appended to the petition.

(*c*) *Claim by respondent for increased amount of excessive profits.*—

853

Any claim for the redetermination of an amount of excessive profits greater than the amount shown in the notice of determination shall be made by the respondent in his answer filed under Rule 14, or in an amendment thereto filed under Rule 17 at or before the time of the trial.

(See statutory references, footnotes 3 and 4, *supra*.)

Rule 65. Bond to Stay Execution of Order of Renegotiation Board

(*a*) *Statute.*—The Renegotiation Act of 1951 provides that execution of the order of the Renegotiation Board may be stayed by filing with the Tax Court a bond, approved as to form and in an amount fixed by the Court, within 10 days after the filing of the petition. See sections 105 (a) and 108 of the Renegotiation Act of 1951. For forms of bonds see Appendix, forms d, e, f, and g.

(*b*) *Fixing amount of bond.*—An application to fix the amount of a bond filed with the petition will be considered prima facie evidence of the proper amount of the bond if it asks that a bond be fixed:

(1) At 112 per cent of the full amount of the excessive profits determined in the unilateral order on which the petition is based, or

(2) At 112 per cent of an amount equal to the full amount of the excessive profits determined in that order reduced by the credit authorized by section 3806 of the Internal Revenue Code of 1939, or section 1481, Code of 1954, and is accompanied by a statement from the district director of internal revenue[4] for the district in which the return for the taxable year was filed, showing the amount of the credit to which the petitioner is entitled as a result of the determination.

The Court will consider other applications differing from the above, but the applicant must have in mind the short time allowed by the statute for the approval of the bond.

(*c*) *Sureties and collateral.*—

(1) The Tax Court will accept as sureties on such bonds companies holding certificates of authority from the Secretary of the Treasury. (See latest U. S. Treasury Form 356.)

(2) If collateral is to be deposited as security for a bond, in lieu of a surety, United States Government marketable public securities fully negotiable by the bearer, owned by the petitioner, in a sum equal at their par value to the amount of the bond to be furnished, will be acceptable. A power of attorney and agreement must accompany such securities. (See Appendix, forms f and g.) For other collateral which may be furnished and documents required therewith see the latest revision of Treasury Department Circular No. 154 (Revised).

[4] Internal revenue agent in charge where no district director has been appointed.

APPENDIX TO RULES OF PRACTICE

I. FORMS

The forms listed below *by small letter* are not printed forms and are not obtainable from the Court. When preparing pleadings or documents involving such forms, be sure to follow Rule 4 carefully as to form, size, type, *and copies* of papers required, unless the number of copies is otherwise specified in the pertinent rule.

The forms identified below *by number* are printed forms, which the Court will furnish upon request. Typed copies of these printed forms may be used instead of the printed forms, except for the subpoena form, which latter must be obtained from the Court.

The forms to be found herein are as follows:

a. Petition.
4. Subpoena.
5–A. Application for order to take depositions.
5–re. Certificate on return of depositions.
305. Entry of appearance.
b. Appeal bond, corporate surety.
c. Appeal bond, approved collateral.
d. Bond with corporate surety in renegotiation cases.
e. Bond with approved collateral in renegotiation cases.
f. Power of Attorney and Agreement by Corporation.
g. Power of Attorney and Agreement by Individuals.

---

a. PETITION
(See Rules 4, 5, 6, and 7)

TAX COURT OF THE UNITED STATES

..................,
Petitioner,
v.   Docket No.
COMMISSIONER OF INTERNAL REVENUE
Respondent.

PETITION

The above-named petitioner hereby petitions for a redetermination of the deficiency set forth by the Commissioner of Internal Revenue in his notice of deficiency (Service symbols) dated ...., 19.., and as the basis for his case alleges as follows:

1. The petitioner is (set forth whether individual, corporation, fiduciary, etc., as provided in Rule 6) with principal office (or residence) at ....
(Street)

............, ... The return for the period here involved was filed
  (City)   (State)
with the collector (director or district director) for the .... district
of ....

855

2. The notice of deficiency (a copy of which is attached and marked Exhibit A) was mailed to the petitioner on ...., 19...

3. The deficiencies (or liabilities) as determined by the Commissioner are in income (profits, estate, or gift) taxes for the calendar (or fiscal) year 19.. in the amount of .... dollars of which approximately .... dollars is in dispute.

4. The determination of tax set forth in the said notice of deficiency is based upon the following errors: (Set forth specifically in lettered subparagraphs the assignments of error in a concise manner and avoid pleading facts which properly belong in the succeeding paragraph.)

5. The facts upon which the petitioner relies as the basis of this case are as follows: (Here set forth allegations of the facts relied upon—but not the evidence—in orderly and logical sequence, with subparagraphs lettered, so as fully to inform the Court of the issues to be presented and to enable the Commissioner to admit each or deny each specific allegation.)

Wherefore, the petitioner prays that this Court may try the case and (here state the relief desired).

(Signed) ....
(Petitioner or counsel)

....
(Post-office address)

STATE OF ....
COUNTY OF .... } ss:

............., being duly sworn, says that he is the petitioner (if a corporation, or fiduciary, state title of office or trust of person verifying and that he is duly authorized to verify the foregoing petition) above named; that he has read the foregoing petition, or had the same read to him, and is familiar with the statements contained therein, and that the statements contained therein are true, except those stated to be upon information and belief, and that those he believes to be true.

(Signed) ....

Subscribed and sworn to before me this .... day of ...., 19...

(Signed) ....
(Official title)

[SEAL]

4. SUBPOENA

(Available—Ask for form 4)
(See Rule 44)

TAX COURT OF THE UNITED STATES

...................,
Petitioner,
v.
COMMISSIONER OF INTERNAL REVENUE
Respondent.

} Docket No.

SUBPOENA

To ....

YOU ARE HEREBY COMMANDED to appear before the Tax Court of the United States .... at ....
(or the name and official title of a person authorized to take depositions)   (Time)

on the .... day of .... at .... then and there to testify
     (Date)   (Month)   (Place)

on behalf of .... in the above-entitled case, and to
          (Petitioner) or (Respondent)

bring with you .... and not to depart without leave of
          (Use reverse if necessary)

the Court.

....
HOWARD P. LOCKE,
Clerk of the Court

Date ....

....
Attorney for (Petitioner) (Respondent)

By ....
                        Deputy Clerk.

RETURN ON SERVICE

The above-named witness was summoned on the .... day of ....,
19.. at .... by delivering a copy of this subpoena to h.... and, if a
witness for the petitioner, by tendering fees and mileage to h.... pursuant to
Rule 60 of the Rules of Practice of the Tax Court.

Dated .... Signed ....

Subscribed and sworn to before me this .... day of ...., 19..

.... [SEAL]

(Name and Title)

5–A. APPLICATION FOR ORDER TO TAKE DEPOSITIONS*

(Available—Ask for form 5–A)

(See Rules 45 and 46)

TAX COURT OF THE UNITED STATES

.................,
Petitioner,
v.
COMMISSIONER OF INTERNAL REVENUE
Respondent.
} Docket No.

APPLICATION FOR ORDER TO TAKE DEPOSITIONS*

To the Tax Court of the United States:

1. Application is hereby made by the above-named ....
                        (Petitioner or respondent)

for an order to take the deposition.. of the following-named person..:

Name of witness	*Post-office address*
(a)	....
(b)	....
(c)	....
(d)	....

* Applications must be filed at least 30 days prior to the date set for trial. When
the applicant seeks to take depositions upon written interrogatories the title of the
application shall so indicate and the application shall be accompanied by an original
and 5 copies of the proposed interrogatories. The taking of depositions upon written
interrogatories is not favored, except when the depositions are to be taken in foreign
countries, in which latter case any depositions taken *must* be upon written interrogatories, except as otherwise directed by the Court for cause shown. (See Rule 46.)
If the parties so stipulate depositions may be taken without application to the
Court. (See Rule 45 (e).)

857

2. It is desired to take the depositions of the persons above named and each of them for the following reasons:

(a) .... will testify to the following material matters:

....

....
(Set forth briefly the matter upon which said witness will be called to testify)

(b) .... will testify to the following material matters:

....

....

(c) .... will testify to the following material matters:

....

....

(d) .... will testify to the following material matters:

....

....

3. The reasons why .... desires to take the testimony of the above-named persons rather than have them appear personally and testify before the Court are as follows: (State specifically reasons for each witness.)

4. It is desired to take the testimony of .... on
(Names of witnesses)
the .... day* of ...., 19.., at the hour of ...... m. before
* (A date sufficiently in advance of the day set for trial of the case to enable the deposition to be completed and filed with the Court at least 10 days prior to the trial)

.... in the City of .... State of
(State name and title of official)

.... at room ....•
(Give number of room, street number, and name of building)

5. That .... is a ....,
(Name of official before whom depositions are to be taken)   (Give official title)
who has authority to administer oaths but has no office connection or business employment with the petitioner or his counsel.

Dated ...., 19...

(Signed) ....•
(Petitioner or counsel)

....................•
(Post-office address)

STATE OF ....⎫
COUNTY OF ....⎬ ss:
                            ⎭

...................., being duly sworn, says that the foregoing applica-
(Petitioner or counsel)
tion for order to take depositions is made in good faith and for the reasons therein stated and that the same is not made for purposes of delay.

(Signed) ....

Subscribed and sworn to before me this .... day of ...., 19...

(Signed) ....
(Official title)

[SEAL]

5–re. CERTIFICATE ON RETURN

(Reverse of form 5)

To the Tax Court of the United States:

I, ..., the person named in the foregoing order to take depositions, hereby certify:

1. That I proceeded, on the .... day of ...., A. D. 19... at the office of ...., in the city of ...., State of ...., at .... m., under the said order and in the presence of .... and .... the counsel for the respective parties, to take the following depositions, viz:

...., a witness produced on behalf of the ....;
(Petitioner or respondent)

...., a witness produced on behalf of the ....;
(Petitioner or respondent)

...., a witness produced on behalf of the ....;
(Petitioner or respondent)

2. That each witness was examined under oath at such times and places as conditions of adjournment required, and that the testimony of each witness (or his answers to the interrogatories filed) was taken stenographically and reduced to typewriting by me or under my direction.

3. That after the testimony of each witness was reduced to writing, the transcript of the testimony was read and signed by the witness in my presence, and that each witness acknowledged before me that his testimony was in all respects truly and correctly transcribed.

4. That, after the signing of the deposition in my presence, no alterations or changes were made therein.

5. That I have no office connection or business employment with the petitioner or his attorney except that of ...., objection to which was
(State connection)
waived by both parties to the case.

[SEAL]

....
(Signature of person taking deposition)

....
(Official title)

....

NOTE.—This form when properly executed, should be attached to and bound with the transcript preceding the first page thereof. It should then be enclosed in a sealed packet, with postage or other transportation charges prepaid, and directed and forwarded to the Tax Court of the United States, Washington 4, D. C.

305. ENTRY OF APPEARANCE

(Available—Ask for form 305)

(See Rule 24)

To Be Filed in DUPLICATE

TAX COURT OF THE UNITED STATES

WASHINGTON

. . . . , *Petitioner,* *v.* COMMISSIONER OF INTERNAL REVENUE *Respondent.*	} Docket **No.**

ENTRY OF APPEARANCE

The undersigned, being duly admitted to practice before the Tax Court of the United States as Attorney C. P. A. Practitioner,* herewith enters his appearance for the petitioner in the above-entitled case.

. . . .

(Signed)

. . . .

(Type signature)

. . . .

(Office address)

(City)

b. APPEAL BOND, CORPORATE SURETY

The following is a satisfactory form of bond for use in case bond with a corporate surety approved by the Treasury Department is to be furnished to stay the assessment and collection of tax involved in an appeal from a decision of the Tax Court. Only the original bond is required. There are no printed forms. Each petitioner must execute the bond, and the corporate seal or a designation of seal in the case of individuals must be affixed.

TAX COURT OF THE UNITED STATES

Washington, D. C.

. . . . , *Petitioner,* *v.* COMMISSIONER OF INTERNAL REVENUE *Respondent.*	} Docket **No.**

BOND

KNOW ALL MEN BY THESE PRESENTS that we . . . . as principal, and . . . . , as surety, are held and firmly bound unto the above-named COMMISSIONER OF INTERNAL REVENUE and/or the UNITED STATES OF AMERICA, in the sum of $. . . . . , (double the deficiency or such sum as the Tax Court has fixed upon petitioner's prior motion), to be paid to the said Commissioner of Internal Revenue and/or the United States of America for the payment of which well and truly to be made we

* Cross out qualification class not applicable.

bind ourselves and each of us and our successors and assigns jointly and severally firmly by these presents. Sealed with our seals and dated the .... day of ...., in the Year of our Lord One Thousand Nine Hundred and ....

WHEREAS, the above named .... is filing or is about to file with the Tax Court of the United States, a petition for review of the said Court's decision in respect of the tax liability of the above petitioner for the taxable year or years ...., by the United States Court of Appeals for the .... Circuit to reverse the decision rendered in the above-entitled cause.

Now, THEREFORE, the condition of this Obligation is such that if the above-named .... shall file its petition for review and shall prosecute said petition for review to effect and shall pay the deficiency as finally determined, together with any interest, additional amounts or additions to the tax provided for by law, then this obligation shall be void, otherwise the same shall be and remain in full force and virtue.

[SEAL]

....
(for an individual petitioner)

....
(for a corporate petitioner)

By ....
Title

(Corporate Seal)   ....
Attest: Surety

....
Secretary

By ....
Title   (Surety corporate seal)

c. APPEAL BOND, APPROVED COLLATERAL

A satisfactory form of bond for use in case an appellant desires to furnish approved collateral (Treasury Department Circular No. 154, Revised), instead of furnishing a corporate surety bond, and also forms of powers of attorney covering the pledged collateral are shown below. Only the original is required in either case. There are no printed forms. Each petitioner must execute the bond, and the corporate seal or a designation of seal in the case of individuals must be affixed.

TAX COURT OF THE UNITED STATES

WASHINGTON, D. C.

.........................,
Petitioner,
v.
COMMISSIONER OF INTERNAL REVENUE
Respondent.

} Docket No.

BOND

KNOW ALL MEN BY THESE PRESENTS that .... is held and firmly bound unto the above-named Commissioner of Internal Revenue and/or the United States of America in the sum of .... ($..............) Dollars, to be paid to the said COMMISSIONER OF INTERNAL REVENUE and/or the UNITED STATES OF AMERICA, for the payment of which, well and truly to be made, the .... binds itself and its successors, firmly by these presents. Sealed with our seals and dated the .... day of ...., in the year of our Lord One Thousand Nine Hundred and ....

WHEREAS, the aboved-named ....
is filing or is about to file with the Tax Court of the United States, a petition for review of the said Court's decision in respect of the tax liability of the above petitioner for the taxable year or years .... by the United States Court of Appeals for the .... Circuit to reverse the decision rendered in the above-entitled cause.

NOW, THEREFORE, the condition of this obligation is such that if the above-named .... shall file its petition for review and shall prosecute said petition for review to effect and shall pay the deficiency as finally determined, together with any interest, additional amounts or additions to the tax provided for by law, then this obligation shall be void, otherwise the same shall be and remain in full force and virtue.

The above-bounden obligor, in order the more fully to secure the Commissioner of Internal Revenue and/or the United States in the payment of the aforementioned sum, hereby pledges as security therefor bonds/notes of the United States in a sum equal at their par value to the aforementioned sum, to wit: ....
.... dollars ($.............), which said bonds/notes are numbered serially and are in denominations and amounts, and are otherwise more particularly described as follows: ....
....
....
which said bonds/notes have this day been deposited with the Clerk of the Tax Court of the United States and his receipt taken therefor.

Contemporaneously herewith the undersigned has also executed and delivered an irrevocable power of attorney and agreement in favor of the Clerk of the Tax Court of the United States, authorizing and empowering him, as such attorney to collect or sell or transfer or assign the above-described bonds/notes so deposited, or any part thereof, in case of any default in the performance of any of the above-named conditions or stipulations.

[SEAL]

....
(for an individual petitioner)

(Corporate Seal)
Attest:

....
(for a corporate petitioner)

.... By ....
Secretary   Title

d. BOND WITH CORPORATE SURETY IN RENEGOTIATION CASES

The following is a satisfactory form of bond for use in case bond with a corporate surety approved by the Treasury Department is to be furnished to stay the execution of an order of the Renegotiation Board (created by the Act of March 23, 1951) involved in a petition to the Tax Court. Only the original bond is required. There are no printed forms. Each petitioner must execute the bond, and the corporate seal or a designation of seal in the case of individuals must be affixed.

TAX COURT OF THE UNITED STATES

Washington, D. C.

. . . . *Petitioner,* *v.* . . . . , *Respondent.*	} Docket **No.**

BOND

KNOW ALL MEN BY THESE PRESENTS: That we . . . . as principal, and . . . . , as surety, are held and firmly bound unto the Renegotiation Board and/or the United States of America, in the sum of $. . . . . (See Rule 65 (*b*) as to amount), to be paid to the Renegotiation Board and/or the United States of America, for the payment of which well and truly to be made we bind ourselves and each of us and our successors and assigns, jointly and severally, firmly by these presents.

SIGNED, sealed, and dated this . . . . day of . . . . , 19. . .

WHEREAS, the Renegotiation Board by its order dated . . . . determined that the above-named principal derived excessive profits from contracts and subcontracts subject to renegotiation, during the fiscal year ended . . . . , in the amount of $. . . . . ; and

WHEREAS, said principal has filed or is about to file a petition in the Tax Court of the United States for a redetermination of the amount of the aforesaid excessive profits,

Now, THEREFORE, the condition of this obligation is such that if the above-named principal shall well and truly pay the amount of profits adjudged by the Tax Court of the United States to be excessive, less any tax credit applicable thereto under section 3806 of the Internal Revenue Code of 1939, or section 1481, Code of 1954, with interest thereon as required by law, or if said principal, in the event that said proposed proceeding in the Tax Court of the United States is not timely filed, or after filing is dismissed or otherwise concluded without an adjudication by said Court as to the amount of excessive profits, shall well and truly pay the amount of profits determined by the Renegotiation Board to be excessive by its said order dated . . . . , less any tax credit applicable thereto under section 3806 of the Internal Revenue Code of 1939, or section 1481, Code of 1954, with interest thereon as required by law, then this obligation shall be void; otherwise it shall be and remain in full force and effect.

[SEAL]

. . . .
(for an individual petitioner)

(Corporate Seal)
Attest:

. . . .
(for a corporate petitioner)

. . . .
Secretary

By . . . .
Title

. . . .
Surety

By . . . .
Title   (Surety corporate seal)

e. BOND WITH APPROVED COLLATERAL IN RENEGOTIATION CASES

A satisfactory form of bond for use in case the petitioner in a renegotiation filed under the Act of March 23, 1951, desires to furnish approved collateral under Rule 65 (c) (2), instead of furnishing a corporate surety bond, follows. Forms of power of attorney covering the pledged collateral for use with bonds secured by collateral, both in appeals from this Court in tax cases and in petitions to this Court in such renegotiation cases, are also shown below. Only the original instrument is required in each instance. There are no printed forms. Each petitioner must execute the bond, and the corporate seal or a designation of seal in the case of individuals must be affixed.

TAX COURT OF THE UNITED STATES

Washington, D. C.

....................,
Petitioner,
v.
....................,
Respondent.

}Docket No.

BOND

KNOW ALL MEN BY THESE PRESENTS: That .... is (are) held and firmly bound unto the Renegotiation Board and/or the United States of America in the sum of .... ($ ....) Dollars (see Rule 65 (b) as to amount), to be paid to the Renegotiation Board and/or the United States of America, for the payment of which, well and truly to be made, the said .... bind(s) himself (herself, itself, or themselves) and his (her, its, or their) successors and assigns, firmly by these presents.

SIGNED, sealed and dated this .... day of ...., 19...

WHEREAS, the Renegotiation Board by its order dated .... determined that the above-named .... derived excessive profits from contracts and subcontracts subject to renegotiation, during the fiscal year ended .... in the amount of $......; and

WHEREAS, the above-named .... has (have) filed or is (are) about to file a petition in the Tax Court of the United States for redetermination of the amount of the aforesaid excessive profits,

NOW, THEREFORE, the condition of this obligation is such that if the above-named .... shall well and truly pay the amount of profits adjudged by the Tax Court of the United States to be excessive, less any tax credit applicable thereunto under section 3806 of the Internal Revenue Code of 1939, or section 1481, Code of 1954, with interest thereon as required by law, or if the above-named ...., in the event that said proposed case in the Tax Court of the United States is not timely filed or after filing is dismissed or otherwise concluded without an adjudication by said Court as to the amount of excessive profits, shall well and truly pay the amount of profits determined by the Renegotiation Board to be excessive by its said order dated ...., less any tax credit applicable thereto under section 3806 of the Internal Revenue Code of 1939, or section 1481, Code of 1954, with interest thereon as required by law, then this obligation shall be void; otherwise it shall be and remain in full force and effect.

864

The above-bounden obligor(s) in order the more fully to secure the Renegotiation Board and/or the United States in the payment of the aforementioned sum, hereby pledge(s) as security therefor bonds/notes of the United States in a sum equal at their par value to the aforementioned sum, to wit: ....
.... ($..........) Dollars, which said bonds/notes are numbered serially and are in the denominations and amounts, and are otherwise more particularly described as follows: ....
....
....
which said bonds/notes are being herewith deposited with the Clerk of the Tax Court of the United States and his receipt taken therefor.

Contemporaneously herewith the undersigned has also executed and delivered an irrevocable power of attorney and agreement in favor of the Clerk of the Tax Court of the United States, authorizing and empowering him, as such attorney to collect or sell or transfer or assign the above-described bonds/notes so deposited, or any part thereof, in case of any default in the performance of any of the above-named conditions or stipulations.

[SEAL]

....
(for an individual petitioner)

(Corporate Seal)   ....
Attest: (for a corporate petitioner)

....   By ....
     Secretary   Title

f. POWER OF ATTORNEY AND AGREEMENT BY CORPORATION

KNOW ALL MEN BY THESE PRESENTS: That ...., a corporation duly incorporated under the laws of the State of ...., and having its principal office in the city of ...., State of ...., in pursuance of a resolution of the Board of Directors of said corporation, passed on the .... day of ...., 19.., a duly certified copy of which resolution is hereto attached, does hereby constitute and appoint the Clerk of the Tax Court of the United States as attorney for said corporation, for and in the name of said corporation to collect or to sell, assign, and transfer certain United States Liberty bonds or other bonds or notes of the United States, the property of said corporation, described as follows:

Title of bonds/notes	Total face amount	Denomination	Serial No.	Interest dates
....	....	....	....	....
....	....	....	....	....
....	....	....	....	....
....	....	....	....	....

such bonds/notes having been deposited by it, pursuant to the Act of July 30, 1947, c. 390, 61 Stat. 646, as security for the faithful performance of any and all of the conditions or stipulations of a certain obligation entered into by it with (here enter "the Commissioner of Internal Revenue and/or the United States" or enter "the Renegotiation Board and/or the United States") under date of ...., which is hereby made a part thereof, and the undersigned agrees that, in case of any default in the performance of any of the conditions and stipulations of such undertaking, its said attorney shall have full power to collect said bonds/notes or any part thereof, or to sell, assign, and transfer said bonds/notes or any part thereof without notice, at public or private sale,

[Harris]—55

865

or to transfer or assign to another for the purpose of effecting either public or private sale, free from any equity of redemption and without appraisement or valuation, notice and right to redeem being waived, and the proceeds of such sale or collection, in whole or in part to be applied to the satisfaction of any damages, demands, or deficiency arising by reason of such default, as may be deemed best, and the undersigned further agrees that the authority herein granted is irrevocable.

And said corporation hereby for itself, its successors and assigns, ratifies and confirms whatever its said attorney shall do by virtue of these presents.

In witness whereof, the ...., the corporation hereinabove named, by .... (Name and title of officer), duly authorized to act in the premises, has executed this instrument and caused the seal of the corporation to be hereto affixed this .... day of ...., 19...

Attest:

....

(Corporate seal)   Secretary

By ....

Title

STATE OF ....
COUNTY OF ....} ss:

Before me, the undersigned, a notary public within and for the said county and State, personally appeared .... (Name and title of officer), and for and in behalf of said ...., corporation, acknowledged the execution of the foregoing power of attorney.

Witness my hand and notarial seal this .... day of ...., 19...

[Notarial seal]

....

Notary Public

My Commission expires ....

g. POWER OF ATTORNEY AND AGREEMENT BY INDIVIDUALS

KNOW ALL MEN BY THESE PRESENTS: That I (we), ..., do hereby constitute and appoint the Clerk of the Tax Court of the United States as attorney for me (us), and in my (our) name to collect or to sell, assign, and transfer certain United States Liberty bonds, or other bonds or notes of the United States, being my (our) property described as follows:

Title of bonds/notes	Total face amount	Denomination	Serial No.	Interest dates
....	....	....	....	....
....	....	....	....	....
....	....	....	....	....
....	....	....	....	....

such bonds/notes having been deposited by me (us) pursuant to the Act of July 30, 1947, c. 390, 61 Stat. 646, as security for the faithful performance of any and all of the conditions or stipulations of a certain obligation entered into by me (us) with (here enter "the Commissioner of Internal Revenue and/or the United States" or enter "the Renegotiation Board and/or the United States") under date of ...., which is hereby made a part thereof, and I (we) agree that, in case of any default in the performance of any of the conditions and stipulations of such undertaking, my (our) said attorney shall have full power to collect said bonds/notes or any part thereof, or to sell, assign, and transfer said bonds/notes or any part thereof without notice, at public or private sale, or to transfer or assign to another for the purpose of effecting either public or private sale, free from any equity of redemption and without appraisement or valuation, notice and right to redeem being waived, and the proceeds of such sale or collection, in whole or in part to be applied to the satisfaction of any damages, demands, or deficiency arising by reason of such default, as may be deemed best, and I (we) further agree that the authority herein granted is irrevocable.

And for myself (ourselves), my (our several) administrators, executors, and assigns, I (we) hereby ratify and confirm whatever my (our) said attorney shall do by virtue of these presents.

In witness whereof, I (we) hereinabove named, have executed this instrument and affixed my (our) seal this .... day of ...., 19....

[SEAL]

....

STATE OF .... } ss:
COUNTY OF .... }

Before me, the undersigned, a notary public within and for the said county and State, personally appeared .... (Name of obligor), and acknowledged the execution of the foregoing power of attorney.

Witness my hand and notarial seal this .... day of ...., 19...
[Notarial seal]

....
Notary Public

My Commission expires ....

II. REQUESTS FOR PLACE OF TRIAL

The Court will fix the time and place for trial to afford reasonable opportunity to a taxpayer to try his case with as little inconvenience and expense as is practicable. A trial may be requested at any place at which suitable courtroom facilities are available and a sufficient number of cases are ready for trial. A partial list of cities in which sessions of the Court are held appears below. This list is published to assist parties in making requests under Rule 26. The grouping of cities indicates that it may be necessary to conduct a trial at another city if there are not sufficient cases for trials at the requested city. Moreover, if sufficient cases are not ready for trial in a city requested by a taxpayer, or if suitable courtroom facilities are not available in that city, the Court may find it necessary to calendar cases for trial in some other city within reasonable proximity of the designated place.

LIST

ALABAMA:
    Birmingham.
    Mobile.
ARIZONA: Phoenix.
ARKANSAS: Little Rock, or Memphis, Tenn.
CALIFORNIA:
    Los Angeles.
    San Francisco.
COLORADO: Denver.
DISTRICT OF COLUMBIA: Washington.
FLORIDA:
    Jacksonville.
    Miami.
    Tampa.
GEORGIA: Atlanta.
HAWAII: Honolulu, or Los Angeles or San Francisco, Calif.
ILLINOIS: Chicago.
INDIANA: Indianapolis.
IOWA: Des Moines.
KENTUCKY: Louisville.
LOUISIANA: New Orleans.
MASSACHUSETTS: Boston.
MICHIGAN: Detroit.
MINNESOTA: St. Paul.
MISSISSIPPI: Jackson.
MISSOURI:
    Kansas City.
    St. Louis.
MONTANA: Helena.
NEBRASKA: Omaha.
NEW JERSEY: Newark.
    (New York City courtroom usually used.)

NEW YORK:
    Buffalo.
    New York City.
NORTH CAROLINA: Greensboro.
OHIO:
    Cincinnati.
    Cleveland.
    Columbus.
OKLAHOMA: Oklahoma City or Tulsa.
OREGON: Portland.
PENNSYLVANIA:
    Philadelphia.
    Pittsburgh.
SOUTH CAROLINA: Columbia.
TENNESSEE:
    Knoxville.
    Memphis.
    Nashville.
TEXAS:
    Dallas.
    Houston, or Galveston, or San Antonio.
UTAH: Salt Lake City.
WASHINGTON:
    Seattle.
    Spokane.
WEST VIRGINIA:
    Charleston.
    Huntington.
WISCONSIN:
    Milwaukee, or Chicago, Ill.

APPENDIX B

NEW FEDERAL
ESTATE TAX REGULATIONS

FILED JUNE 23, 1958

(Under 1954 Code)

(T. D. 6296)

(Filed with the Division of the Federal Register, June 23, 1958.)

TITLE 26—INTERNAL REVENUE, 1954

CHAPTER I—INTERNAL REVENUE SERVICE, DEPARTMENT OF THE TREASURY

SUBCHAPTER B—ESTATE AND GIFT TAXES [ESTATE TAX REGULATIONS]

PART 20—ESTATE TAX; ESTATES OF DECEDENTS DYING AFTER AUGUST 16, 1954

SUBCHAPTER F—PROCEDURE AND ADMINISTRATION

[REGULATIONS ON PROCEDURE AND ADMINISTRATION]

PART 301—PROCEDURE AND ADMINISTRATION

Regulations under provisions of the Internal Revenue Code of 1954 relating to the estate tax.

DEPARTMENT OF THE TREASURY,

Office of the Commissioner of Internal Revenue, Washington 25, D. C.

TO OFFICERS AND EMPLOYEES OF
THE INTERNAL REVENUE SERVICE
AND OTHERS CONCERNED:

On October 16, 1956, notice of proposed rule making regarding (1) the Estate Tax Regulations (26 CFR Part 20) under chapter 11 of subtitle B of the Internal Revenue Code of 1954 and under certain sections of subtitle F of the Internal Revenue Code of 1954, and (2) amendments to conform the Regulations on Procedure and Administration (26 CFR Part 301) to section 2 of the Act of August 6, 1956 (Public Law 1011, 84th Cong., 70 Stat. 1075), was published in the Federal Register (21 F. R. 7850). After consideration of all such relevant matter as was presented by interested persons regarding the rules proposed, the following regulations are hereby adopted. Except as specifically provided otherwise, such regulations are applicable to estates of decedents dying after August 16, 1954:

Estate Tax Regulations (26 CFR Part 20)

Paragraph 1. The following Estate Tax Regulations are hereby prescribed under chapter 11 of subtitle B of the Internal Revenue Code of 1954 and under certain sections of subtitle F of the Internal Revenue Code of 1954:

TABLE OF CONTENTS

ESTATE TAX

Estates of Citizens or Residents

TAX IMPOSED

CREDITS AGAINST TAX

GROSS ESTATE

[Authority: §§ 20.1 to 20.7404, inclusive, issued under sec. 7805, I. R. C. 1954; 68A Stat. 917; 26 . S. C. 7805.]

ESTATE TAX

TAX IMPOSED

§ 20.0-1 **Introduction**—(a) *In general.* The regulations in this part (Part 20, Subchapter B, Chapter I, Title 26, Code of Federal Regulations) are designated "Estate Tax Regulations". These regulations pertain to (1) the Federal estate tax imposed by chapter 11 of subtitle B of the Internal Revenue Code on the transfer of estates of decedents dying after August 16, 1954, and (2) certain related administrative provisions of subtitle F of the Code. It should be noted that the application of many of the provisions of these regulations may be affected by the provisions of an applicable death tax convention with a foreign country. Unless otherwise indicated, references in the regulations to the "Internal Revenue Code" or the "Code" are references to the Internal Revenue Code of 1954, as amended, and references to a section or other provision of law are references to a section or other provision of the Internal Revenue Code of 1954, as amended. Unless otherwise provided, the Estate Tax Regulations are applicable to the estates of decedents dying after August 16, 1954, and supersede the regulations contained in Part 81, Subchapter B, Chapter I, Title 26, Code of Federal Regulations (1939) (Regulations 105, Estate Tax), as prescribed and made applicable to the Internal Revenue Code of 1954 by Treasury Decision 6091, signed August 16, 1954 (19 F. R. 5167, Aug. 17, 1954).

(b) *Scope of regulations*—(1) *Estates of citizens or residents.* Subchapter A of chapter 11 of the Code pertains to the taxation of the estate of a person who was a citizen or a resident of the United States at the time of his death. The term "resident" means a decedent who, at the time of his death, had his domicile in the United States. The term "United States", as used in the Estate Tax Regulations, includes only the States, the Territories of Alaska and Hawaii, and the District of Columbia (see section 7701(a)(9)). A person acquires a domicile in a place by living there, for even a brief period of time, with no definite present intention of later removing therefrom. Residence without the requisite intention to remain indefinitely will not suffice to constitute domicile, nor will intention to change domicile effect such a change unless accompanied by actual removal. The regulations pursuant to subchapter A are set forth in §§ 20.2001-1 through 20.2056(e)-3 of this part.

(2) *Estates of nonresidents not citizens.* Subchapter B of chapter 11 of the Code pertains to the taxation of the estate of a person who was a nonresident not a citizen of the United States at the time of his death. A "nonresident" is a decedent who, at the time of his death, had his domicile outside the United States under the principles set forth in

875

subparagraph (1) of this paragraph. (See, however, section 2202 with respect to missionaries in foreign service). The regulations pursuant to subchapter B are set forth in §§ 20.2101-1 through 20.2106-2 of this part.

(3) *Miscellaneous substantive provisions.* Subchapter C of chapter 11 of the Code contains a number of miscellaneous substantive provisions. The regulations pursuant to subchapter C are set forth in §§ 20.2201-1 through 20.2207-1 of this part.

(4) *Procedure and administration provisions.* Subtitle F of the Internal Revenue Code contains some sections which are applicable to the Federal estate tax. The regulations pursuant to those sections are set forth in §§ 20.6001-1 through 20.7101-1. Such regulations do not purport to be all the regulations on procedure and administration which are pertinent to estate tax matters. For the remainder of the regulations on procedure and administration which are pertinent to estate tax matters, see part 301 of this chapter (Regulations on Procedure and Administration).

(c) *Arrangement and numbering.* Each section of the regulations (except this section and § 20.0-2) is preceded by the section or subsection of the Internal Revenue Code which it interprets. The sections of the regulations can readily be distinguished from sections of the Code since—

(1) The sections of the regulations are printed in larger type;

(2) The sections of the regulations are preceded by a section symbol and the part number, arabic number 20 followed by a decimal point (§ 20.) ; and

(3) The sections of the Code are preceded by "Sec.". Each section of the regulations setting forth law or regulations is designated by a number composed of the part number followed by a decimal point (20.) and the number of the corresponding provision of the Internal Revenue Code. In the case of a section setting forth regulations, this designation is followed by a hyphen (-) and a number identifying such section. By use of these designations one can ascertain the sections of the regulations relating to a provision of the Code. Thus, the section of the regulations setting forth section 2012 of the Internal Revenue Code is designated § 20.2012 and the regulations pertaining to section 2012 are designated § 20.2012-1.

§ 20.0-2 General description of tax—(a) *Nature of tax.* The Federal estate tax is neither a property tax nor an inheritance tax. It is a tax imposed upon the transfer of the entire taxable estate and not upon any particular legacy, devise, or distributive share. Escheat of a decedent's property to the State for lack of heirs is a transfer which causes the property to be included in the decedent's gross estate.

(b) *Method of determining tax; estate of citizen or resident—*(1) *In general.* The following subparagraphs contain a general description of the method to be used in determining the Federal estate tax imposed upon the transfer of the estate of a decedent who was a citizen or resident of the United States at the time of his death.

(2) *Gross estate.* The first step in determining the tax is to ascertain the total value of the decedent's gross estate. The value of the gross estate includes the value of all property (except real property situated outside of the United States) to the extent of the interest therein of the decedent at the time of his death. However, the gross estate also may include property in which the decedent did not have an interest at the time of his death. A decedent's gross estate for Federal estate tax purposes may therefore be very different from the same decedent's estate for local probate purposes. Examples of items which may be included in a decedent's gross estate and not in his probate estate are the following: certain property transferred by the decedent during his lifetime without adequate consideration; property held jointly by the decedent and others; property over which the decedent had a general power of appointment; proceeds of certain policies of insurance on the decedent's life; annuities; and dower or curtesy of a surviving spouse or a statutory estate in lieu thereof. For a detailed explanation of the method of ascertaining the value of the gross estate, see sections 2031 through 2044, and the regulations thereunder.

(3) *Taxable estate.* The second step in determining the tax is to ascertain the value of the decedent's taxable estate. The value of the taxable estate is determined by subtracting from the value of the gross estate the authorized exemption and deductions. Under various conditions and limitations, deductions are allowable for expenses, indebtedness, taxes, losses, charitable transfers, and transfers to a surviving spouse. For a detailed explanation of the method of ascertaining the value of the taxable estate, see sections 2051 through 2056, and the regulations thereunder.

(4) *Gross estate tax.* The third step is the determination of the gross estate tax. This is accomplished by the application of certain rates to the value of the decedent's taxable estate. In this connection, see section 2001 and the regulations thereunder.

(5) *Net estate tax payable.* The final step is the determination of the net estate tax payable. This is done by subtracting from the gross estate tax the authorized credits against tax. Under certain conditions and limitations, credits are allowable for the following (computed in the order stated below):

(i) State death taxes paid in connection with the decedent's estate (section 2011);

(ii) Gift taxes paid on inter-vivos transfers by the decedent of property included in his gross estate (section 2012);

(iii) Foreign death taxes paid in connection with the decedent's estate (section 2014); and

(iv) Federal estate taxes paid on transfers of property to the decedent (section 2013).

Sections 2015 and 2016 contain certain further rules for the application of the credits for State and foreign death taxes. For a detailed explanation of the credits against tax, see sections 2011 through 2016, and the regulations thereunder.

(c) *Method of determining tax; estate of nonresident not a citizen.* In general, the method to be used in determining the Federal estate tax imposed upon the transfer of an estate of a decedent who was a nonresident not a citizen of the United States is similar to that described in paragraph (b) of this section with respect to the estate of a citizen or resident. Briefly stated, the steps are as follows: first, ascertain the value of that part of the decedent's "entire gross estate" which at the time of his death was situated in the United States (see §§ 20.2103-1 and 20.2104-1); second, determine the value of the taxable estate by subtracting from the value of that part of the "entire gross estate" which was situated in the United States at the time of the decedent's death the amount of the allowable deductions (see § 20.2106-1); third, compute the gross estate tax on the taxable estate, using the rates set forth in section 2001 (see § 20.2101-1); and fourth, subtract from the gross estate tax the total amount of any allowable credits in order to arrive at the net estate tax payable (see § 20.2102-1).

§ 20.2001-1 **Rate of tax.** (a) The gross estate tax is computed by the application of progressively graduated rates to the value of the decedent's taxable estate in accordance with the following table:

TABLE FOR COMPUTATION OF GROSS ESTATE TAX

(A) Taxable estate equal to or more than—	(B) Taxable estate less than—	(C) Tax on amount in column (A)	(D) Rate of tax on excess over amount in column (A) Percent
....	$ 5,000	....	3
$ 5,000	10,000	$ 150	7
10,000	20,000	500	11
20,000	30,000	1,600	14
30,000	40,000	3,000	18
40,000	50,000	4,800	22
50,000	60,C00	7,000	25
60,000	100,000	9,500	28
100,000	250,000	20,700	30
250,000	500,000	65,700	32
500,000	750,000	145,700	35
750,000	1,000,000	233,200	37
1,000,000	1,250,000	325,700	39
1,250,000	1,500,000	423,200	42
1,500,000	2,000,000	528,200	45
2,000,000	2,500,000	753,200	49
2,500,000	3,000,000	998,200	53
3,000,000	3,500,000	1,263,200	56
3,500,000	4,000,000	1,543,200	59
4,000,000	5,000,000	1,838,200	63
5,000,000	6,000,000	2,468,200	67
6,000,000	7,000,000	3,138,200	70
7,000,000	8,000,000	3,838,200	73
8,000,000	10,000,000	4,568,200	76
10,000,000	....	6,088,200	77

(b) The application of the table may be illustrated by the following example:

Example. The decedent died January 1, 1955, having a gross estate of $600,000. The exemption and authorized deductions amount to $75,000, thus leaving a taxable estate of $525,000. Reference to the table discloses that the specified amount in column (A) nearest to and less than the value of the decedent's taxable estate is $500,000. The tax upon this amount, as indicated in column (C), is $145,700. The amount by which the taxable estate exceeds the same specified amount is $25,000. The tax upon this amount, computed at the rate of 35 percent indicated in column (D), is $8,750. Thus, the total gross estate tax upon a taxable estate of $525,000 is $154,450. From this amount, the credits authorized by sections 2011 through 2014 are subtracted in order to determine the net estate tax payable.

§ 20.2002-1 **Liability for payment of tax.** The Federal estate tax imposed both with respect to the estates of citizens or residents and with respect to estates of nonresidents not citizens is payable by the executor or administrator of the decedent's estate. This duty applies to the entire tax, regardless of the fact that the gross estate consists in part of property which does not come within the possession of the executor or administrator. If there is no executor or administrator appointed, qualified and acting in the United States, any person in actual or constructive possession of any property of the decedent is required to pay the entire tax to the extent of the value of the property in his possession. See section 2203, defining the term "executor". The personal liability of the executor or such other person is described in section 3467 of the Revised Statutes (31 U. S. C. 192) as follows:

Every executor, administrator, or assignee, or other person, who pays, in whole or in part, any debt due by the person or estate for whom or for which he acts before he satisfies and pays the debts due to the United States from such person or estate, shall become answerable in his own person and estate to the extent of such payments for the debts so due to the United States, or for so much thereof as may remain due and unpaid.

As used in said section, the word "debt" includes a beneficiary's distributive share of an estate. Thus, if the executor pays a debt due by the decedent's estate or distributes any portion of the estate before all the estate tax is paid, he is personally liable, to the extent of the payment or distribution, for so much of the estate tax as remains due and unpaid. In addition, section 6324(a)(2) provides that if the estate tax is not paid when due, then the spouse, transferee, trustee (except the trustee of an employee's trust which meets the requirements of section 401(a)), surviving tenant, person in possession of the property by reason of the exercise, nonexercise, or release of a power of appointment, or beneficiary, who receives, or has on the date of the decedent's death, property included in the gross estate under sections 2034 through 2042, is personally liable for the tax to the extent of the value, at the time of the decedent's death, of such property. See also

879

the following related sections of the Internal Revenue Code: section 2204, discharge of executor from personal liability; section 2205, reimbursement out of estate; sections 2206 and 2207, liability of life insurance beneficiaries and recipients of property over which decedent had power of appointment; sections 6321 through 6325, concerning liens for taxes; and section 6901(a)(1), concerning the liabilities of transferees and fiduciaries.

CREDITS AGAINST TAX

Credit for State Death Taxes

§ 20.2011-1 **Credit for State death taxes**—(a) *In general.* A credit is allowed under section 2011 against the Federal estate tax for estate, inheritance, legacy or succession taxes actually paid to any State, Territory, or possession of the United States, or the District of Columbia (hereafter referred to as "State death taxes"). The credit, however, is allowed only for State death taxes paid (1) with respect to property included in the decedent's gross estate, and (2) with respect to the decedent's estate. The amount of the credit is subject to the limitation described in paragraph (b) of this section. It is subject to further limitations described in § 20.2011-2 if a deduction is allowed under section 2053(d) for State death taxes paid with respect to a charitable gift.

(b) *Amount of credit.* (1) If the decedent's taxable estate does not exceed $40,000, the credit for State death taxes is zero. If the decedent's taxable estate does exceed $40,000, the credit for State death taxes is limited to an amount computed in accordance with the following table:

TABLE FOR COMPUTATION OF MAXIMUM CREDIT
FOR STATE DEATH TAXES

(A) Taxable estate equal to or more than—	(B) Taxable estate less than—	(C) Credit on amount in column (A)	(D) Rates of credit on excess over amount in column (A) Percent
$ 40,000	$ 90,000	. . . .	.8
90,000	140,000	$ 400	1.6
140,000	240,000	1,200	2.4
240,000	440,000	3,600	3.2
440,000	640,000	10,000	4.
640,000	840,000	18,000	4.8
840,000	1,040,000	27,600	5.6
1,040,000	1,540,000	38,800	6.4
1,540,000	2,040,000	70,800	7.2
2,040,000	2,540,000	106,800	8.
2,540,000	3,040,000	146,800	8.8
3,040,000	3,540,000	190,800	9.6
3,540,000	4,040,000	238,800	10.4
4,040,000	5,040,000	290,800	11.2
5,040,000	6,040,000	402,800	12.

(A) Taxable estate equal to or more than—	(B) Taxable estate less than—	(C) Credit on amount in column (A)	(D) Rates of Credit on excess over amount in column (A) Percent
$6,040,000	$7,040,000	$522,800	12.8
7,040,000	8,040,000	650,800	13.6
8,040,000	9,040,000	786,800	14.4
9,040,000	10,040,000	930,800	15.2
10,040,000	....	1,082,800	16.

(2) Subparagraph (1) of this paragraph may be illustrated by the following example:

Example. (i) The decedent died January 1, 1955, leaving a taxable estate of $150,000. On January 1, 1956, inheritance taxes totaling $2,500 were actually paid to a State with respect to property included in the decedent's gross estate. Reference to the table discloses that the specified amount in column (A) nearest to but less than the value of the decedent's taxable estate is $140,000. The maximum credit in respect of this amount, as indicated in column (C), is $1,200. The amount by which the taxable estate exceeds the same specified amount is $10,000. The maximum credit in respect of this amount, computed at the rate of 2.4 percent indicated in column (D), is $240. Thus, the maximum credit in respect of the decedent's taxable estate of $150,000 is $1,440, even though $2,500 in inheritance taxes was actually paid to the State.

(ii) If, in subdivision (i) of this example, the amount actually paid to the State was $950, the credit for State death taxes would be limited to $950. If, in subdivision (i) of this example, the decedent's taxable estate was $35,000, no credit for State death taxes would be allowed.

(c) *Miscellaneous limitations and conditions to credit*—(1) *Period of limitations.* The credit for State death taxes is limited under section 2011(c) to those taxes which were actually paid and for which a credit was claimed within four years after the filing of the estate tax return for the decedent's estate. If, however, a petition has been filed with The Tax Court of the United States for the redetermination of a deficiency within the time prescribed in section 6213(a), the credit is limited to those taxes which were actually paid and for which a credit was claimed within four years after the filing of the return or within 60 days after the decision of the Tax Court becomes final, whichever period is the last to expire. Similarly, if an extension of time has been granted under section 6161 for payment of the tax shown on the return, or of a deficiency, the credit is limited to those taxes which were actually paid and for which a credit was claimed within four years after the filing of the return, or before the date of the expiration of the period of the extension, whichever period is last to expire. See section 2015 for the applicable period of limitations for credit for State death taxes on reversionary or remainder interests if an election is made under section 6163(a) to postpone payment of the estate tax

[Harris]—56

attributable to reversionary or remainder interests. If a claim for refund based on the credit for State death taxes is filed within the applicable period described in this subparagraph, a refund may be made despite the general limitation provisions of sections 6511 and 6512. Any refund based on the credit described in this section shall be made without interest.

(2) *Submission of evidence.* Before the credit for State death taxes is allowed, evidence that such taxes have been paid must be submitted to the district director. The district director may require the submission of a certificate from the proper officer of the taxing State, Territory, or possession of the United States, or the District of Columbia, showing: (i) the total amount of tax imposed (before adding interest and penalties and before allowing discount); (ii) the amount of any discount allowed; (iii) the amount of any penalties and interest imposed or charged; (iv) the total amount actually paid in cash; and (v) the date or dates of payment. If the amount of these taxes has been redetermined, the amount finally determined should be stated. The required evidence should be filed with the return, but if that is not convenient or possible, then it should be submitted as soon thereafter as practicable. The district director may require the submission of such additional proof as is deemed necessary to establish the right to the credit. For example, he may require the submission of a certificate of the proper officer of the taxing jurisdiction showing (vi) whether a claim for refund of any part of the State death tax is pending and (vii) whether a refund of any part thereof has been authorized, and if a refund has been made, its date and amount, and a description of the property or interest in respect of which the refund was made. The district director may also require an itemized list of the property in respect of which State death taxes were imposed certified by the officer having custody of the records pertaining to those taxes. In addition, he may require the executor to submit a written statement (containing a declaration that it is made under penalties of perjury) stating whether, to his knowledge, any person has instituted litigation or taken an appeal (or contemplates doing so), the final determination of which may affect the amount of those taxes. See section 2016 concerning the redetermination of the estate tax if State death taxes claimed as credit are refunded.

(d) *Definition of "basic estate tax".* Section 2011(d) provides definitions of the terms "basic estate tax" and "additional estate tax", used in the Internal Revenue Code of 1939, and "estate tax imposed by the Revenue Act of 1926", for the purpose of supplying a means of computing State death taxes under local statutes using those terms, and for use in determining the exemption provided for in section 2201 for estates of certain members of the Armed Forces. See section 2011 (e)(3) for a modification of these definitions if a deduction is allowed under section 2053(d) for State death taxes paid with respect to a charitable gift.

§ 20.2011-2 **Limitation on credit if a deduction is allowed under section 2053(d).** If a deduction is allowed under section 2053(d) for State death taxes paid with respect to a charitable gift, the credit for State death taxes is subject to special limitations. Under these limitations, the credit cannot exceed the least of the following:

(a) The amount of State death taxes paid other than those for which a deduction is allowed under section 2053(d);

(b) The amount indicated in section 2011(b) to be the maximum credit allowable with respect to the decedent's taxable estate; or

(c) An amount, A, which bears the same ratio to B (the amount which would be the maximum credit allowable under section 2011(b) if the deduction under section 2053(d) were not allowed in computing the decedent's taxable estate) as C (the amount of State death taxes paid other than those for which a deduction is allowed under section 2053(d)) bears to D (the total amount of State death taxes paid). For the purpose of this computation, in determining what the decedent's taxable estate would be if the deduction under section 2053(d) were not allowed, adjustment must be made for the decrease in the deduction for charitable gifts under section 2055 or 2106(a)(2) (for estates of nonresidents not citizens) by reason of any increase in Federal estate tax which would be charged against the charitable gifts.

The application of this section may be illustrated by the following example:

Example. The decedent died January 1, 1955, leaving a gross estate of $925,000. Expenses, indebtedness, etc., amounted to $25,000. The decedent bequeathed $400,000 to his son with the direction that the son bear the State death taxes on the bequest. The residuary estate was left to a charitable organization. Except as noted above, all Federal and State death taxes were payable out of the residuary estate. The State imposed death taxes of $60,000 on the son's bequest and death taxes of $75,000 on the bequest to charity. The decedent's taxable estate (determined without regard to the limitation imposed by section 2011 (e)(2)(B)) is computed as follows:

Gross estate				$925,000.00
Expenses, indebtedness, etc.		$ 25,000.00		
Exemption		60,000.00		
Deduction under section 2053(d)		75,000.00		
Charitable deduction:				
Gross estate	$925,000.00			
Expenses, etc.	$ 25,000.00			
Bequest to son	400,000.00			
State death tax paid from residue	75,000.00			
Federal estate tax paid from residue	122,916.67	622,916.67	302,083.33	462,083.33
Taxable estate				$462,916.67

883

If the deduction under section 2053(d) were not allowed, the decedent's taxable estate would be computed as follows:

Gross estate				$925,000.00
Expenses, indebtedness, etc.		$ 25,000.00		
Exemption		60,000.00		
Charitable deduction:				
Gross estate	$925,000.00			
Expenses, etc.	$ 25,000.00			
Bequest to son	400,000.00			
State death tax paid from residue	75,000.00			
Federal estate tax paid from residue	155,000.00	655,000.00	270,000.00	355,000.00
Taxable estate				$570,000.00

On a taxable estate of $570,000, the maximum credit allowable under section 2011(b) would be $15,200. Under these facts, the credit for State death taxes is determined as follows:

(1) Amount of State death taxes paid other than those for which a deduction is allowed under section 2053(d) ($135,000 — $75,000) .. $60,000.00

(2) Amount indicated in section 2011(b) to be the maximum credit allowable with respect to the decedent's taxable estate of $462,916.67 .. 10,916.67

(3) Amount determined by use of the ratio described in paragraph (c) above

$$\frac{\$ 60,000}{\$135,000} \times \$15,200 \ \ldots\ldots\ldots\ldots\ldots\ldots\ldots\ldots\ldots\ldots\ldots \quad 6,755.56$$

(4) Credit for State death taxes (least of subparagraphs (1) through (3) above) 6,755.56

Credit for Gift Taxes

§ 20.2012-1 **Credit for gift tax**—(a) *In general.* A credit is allowed under section 2012 against the Federal estate tax for gift tax paid under chapter 12 of the Internal Revenue Code, or corresponding provisions of prior law, on a gift by the decedent of property subsequently included in the decedent's gross estate. The credit is allowable even though the gift tax is paid after the decedent's death and the amount of the gift tax is deductible from the gross estate as a debt of the decedent.

(b) *Limitations on credit.* The credit for gift tax is limited to the smaller of the following amounts:

(1) The amount of gift tax paid on the gift, computed as set forth in paragraph (c) of this section, or

(2) The amount of the estate tax attributable to the inclusion of the gift in the gross estate, computed as set forth in paragraph (d) of this section.

When more than one gift is included in the gross estate, a separate computation of the two limitations on the credit is to be made for each gift.

(c) *"First limitation."* The amount of the gift tax paid on the gift is the "first limitation." Thus, if only one gift was made during a certain calendar year, and the gift is wholly included in the decedent's gross estate for the purpose of the estate tax, the credit with respect to the gift is limited to the amount of the gift tax paid for that calendar year. On the other hand, if more than one gift was made during a certain calendar year, the credit with respect to any such gift which is included in the decedent's gross estate is limited under section 2012(d) to an amount, A, which bears the same ratio to B (the total gift tax paid for that calendar year) as C (the "amount of the gift," computed as described below) bears to D (the total taxable gifts for the year, computed without deduction of the gift tax specific exemption). Stated algebraically, the "first limitation" (A) equals

$$\frac{\text{"amount of the gift" (C)}}{\substack{\text{total taxable gifts,} \\ \text{plus specific exemp-} \\ \text{tion allowed (D)}}} \times \text{total gift tax paid (B).}$$

For purposes of the ratio stated above, the "amount of the gift" referred to as factor "C" is the value of the gift reduced by any portion excluded or deducted under section 2503(b) (annual exclusion), 2522 (charitable deduction), or 2523 (marital deduction) of the Internal Revenue Code or corresponding provisions of prior law. In making the computations described in this paragraph, the values to be used are those finally determined for the purpose of the gift tax, irrespective of the values determined for the purpose of the estate tax. A similar computation is made in case only a portion of any gift is included in the decedent's gross estate. The application of this paragraph may be illustrated by the following example:

Example. The donor made gifts during the calendar year 1955 on which a gift tax was determined as shown below:

Gift of property to son on February 1	$ 13,000
Gift of property to wife on May 1	86,000
Gift of property to charitable organization on May 15	10,000
Total gifts	109,000
Less exclusions ($3,000 for each gift)	9,000
Total included amount of gifts	100,000
Marital deduction (for gift to wife) ... $43,000	
Charitable deduction ... 7,000	
Specific exemption ($30,000 less $20,000 used in prior years) ... 10,000	
Total deductions	60,000
Taxable gifts	40,000
Total gift tax paid for calendar year 1955	3,600

The donor's gift to his wife was made in contemplation of death and was thereafter included in his gross estate. Under the "first limitation," the credit with respect to that gift cannot exceed

$$\frac{\$86{,}000 - \$3{,}000 - \$43{,}000 \text{ (gift to wife, less annual exclusion and marital deduction)}}{\$40{,}000 + \$10{,}000 \text{ (taxable gifts, plus specific exemption allowed)}} \times \$3{,}600 \text{ (total gift tax paid)}$$

$$= \$2{,}880.$$

(d) *"Second limitation."* (1) The amount of the estate tax attributable to the inclusion of the gift in the gross estate is the "second limitation". Thus, the credit with respect to any gift of property included in the gross estate is limited to an amount, E, which bears the same ratio to F (the gross estate tax, reduced by any credit for State death taxes under section 2011) as G (the "value of the gift," computed as described in subparagraph (2) of this paragraph) bears to H (the value of the entire gross estate, reduced by the total deductions allowed under sections 2055 or 2106(a)(2) (charitable deduction) and 2056 (marital deduction)). Stated algebraically, the "second limitation" (E) equals

$$\frac{\text{"value of the gift" (G)}}{\substack{\text{value of gross estate,}\\ \text{less marital and chari-}\\ \text{table deductions (H)}}} \times \substack{\text{gross estate tax,}\\ \text{less credit for}\\ \text{State death taxes (F).}}$$

(2) For purposes of the ratio stated in subparagraph (1) of this paragraph, the "value of the gift" referred to as factor "G" is the value of the property transferred by gift and included in the gross estate, as determined for the purpose of the gift tax or for the purpose of the estate tax, whichever is lower, and adjusted as follows:

(i) The appropriate value is reduced by all or a portion of any annual exclusion allowed for gift tax purposes under section 2503(b) of the Internal Revenue Code or corresponding provisions of prior law. If the gift tax value is lower than the estate tax value, it is reduced by the entire amount of the exclusion. If the estate tax value is lower than the gift tax value, it is reduced by an amount which bears the same ratio to the estate tax value as the annual exclusion bears to the total value of the property as determined for gift tax purposes. To illustrate: In 1955, a donor, in contemplation of death, transferred certain property to his five children which was valued at $300,000 for the purpose of gift tax. Thereafter, the same property was included in his gross estate at a value of $270,000. In computing his gift tax, the donor was allowed annual exclusions totalling $15,000. The reduction provided for in this subdivision is

$$\frac{\$15{,}000 \text{ (annual exclusions allowed)}}{\$300{,}000 \text{ (value of transferred property for the purpose of the gift tax)}} \times \substack{\$270{,}000 \text{ (value of transferred}\\ \text{property for the purpose of the}\\ \text{estate tax)}} = \$13{,}500.$$

(ii) The appropriate value is further reduced if any portion of the value of the property is allowed as a marital deduction under section 2056 or as a charitable deduction under section 2055 or section 2106(a) (2) (for estates of nonresidents not citizens). The amount of the reduction is an amount which bears the same ratio to the value determined under subdivision (i) of this subparagraph as the portion of the property allowed as a marital deduction or as a charitable deduction bears to the total value of the property as determined for the purpose of the estate tax. Thus, if a gift is made solely to the decedent's surviving spouse and is subsequently included in the decedent's gross estate as having been made in contemplation of death, but a marital deduction is allowed under section 2056 for the full value of the gift, no credit for gift tax on the gift will be allowed since the reduction under this subdivision together with the reduction under subdivision (i) of this subparagraph will have the effect of reducing the factor "G" of the ratio in subparagraph (1) of this paragraph to zero. However, if by reason of the limitation on the aggregate marital deduction to 50 percent of the value of the adjusted gross estate (see section 2056(c)) the aggregate marital deduction allowed is less than the aggregate marital deduction computed without regard to that limitation, then the reduction under this subdivision is an amount, I, which bears the same ratio to J (the value determined in subdivision (i) of this paragraph) as K (the aggregate marital deduction allowed) bears to L (the aggregate marital deduction computed without regard to the 50-percent limitation). For an illustration, see subparagraph (3) of this paragraph.

(3) The application of this paragraph may be illustrated by the following example:

Example. (i) In 1955, a donor, in contemplation of death, transferred certain property to his wife which was valued, for the purpose of the gift tax, at $86,000. In computing his gift tax the donor was allowed an annual exclusion of $3,000. In 1956, the donor died leaving a gross estate of $350,000. Expenses, indebtedness, etc., amounted to $50,000. The gross estate included the property transferred by the decedent to his wife in 1955. This property was valued, for the purpose of the estate tax, at $100,000 and was property for which a marital deduction may be taken. The decedent was survived by his wife to whom he left the major part of his estate. The estate was allowed an aggregate marital deduction of $150,000. The amount of the marital deduction computed without regard to the 50-percent limitation in section 2056(c) would have been $250,000. The gross estate tax was $17,900, and the credit for State death taxes was $400.

(ii) Factor "G" of the ratio which is used in computing the "second limitation" is computed as follows (see paragraph (d)(2) of § 20.2012-1):

Value of gift to wife for the purpose of the gift tax or for the purpose of the estate tax, whichever is lower	$86,000
Less: Portion of annual exclusion allowed in determining the gift tax (see § 20.2012-1(d)(2)(i))	3,000
Net value	83,000

Less: Portion of the net value allowed as a marital deduction under section 2056 (see § 20.2012-1(d)(2)(ii)) =

$$\frac{\$150{,}000 \text{ (aggregate marital deduction allowed for the purpose of the estate tax)}}{\$250{,}000 \text{ (aggregate marital deduction computed without regard to the limitation stated in section 2056(c))}} \times \begin{array}{l}(\$86{,}000 - \$3{,}000) \text{ (value of gift to} \\ \text{wife for the purpose of the gift tax or} \\ \text{for the purpose of the estate tax, which} \\ \text{ever is lower, less portion of annual exclu-} \\ \text{sion allowed in determining the gift tax} \\ \text{(see § 20.2012-1(d)(2)(i))} \end{array}$$

= $49,800

Factor "G" of the ratio 33,200

(iii) Under the "second limitation", the credit for gift tax on the donor's gift to his wife cannot exceed (see § 20.2012-1(d)(1))

$$\frac{\$33{,}200 \text{ (factor "G" of the ratio;}}{\$350{,}000 - \$150{,}000 \text{ (value of gross}} \times \begin{array}{l}(\$17{,}900 - \$400) \text{ (gross estate tax,} \\ \text{less credit for State death taxes)} \end{array}$$

see subdivision (ii) of this example)

estate, less marital deduction allowed)

= $2,905.

The lesser of the "first limitation" as computed in paragraph (c) of this section and the "second limitation" as computed in this paragraph is the credit for gift tax.

(e) *Credit for "split gifts"*. If a decedent made a gift of property which is thereafter included in his gross estate, and, under the provisions of section 2513 of the Internal Revenue Code of 1954 or section 1000(f) of the Internal Revenue Code of 1939, the gift was considered as made one-half by the decedent and one-half by his spouse, credit against the estate tax is allowed for the gift tax paid with respect to both halves of the gift. The "first limitation" is to be separately computed with respect to each half of the gift in accordance with the principles stated in paragraph (c) of this section. The "second limitation" is to be computed with respect to the entire gift in accordance with the principles stated in paragraph (d) of this section. To illustrate: A donor, in contemplation of death, transferred property valued at $106,000 to his son on January 1, 1955, and he and his wife consented that the gift should be considered as made one-half by him and one-half by her. The property was thereafter included in the donor's gross estate. Under the "first limitation", the amount of the gift tax of the donor paid with respect to the one-half of the gift considered as made by him is determined to be $11,250, and the amount of the gift tax of his wife paid with respect to the one-half of the gift considered as made by

888

her is determined to be $1,200. Under the "second limitation", the amount of the estate tax attributable to the property is determined to be $28,914. Therefore, the credit for gift tax allowed is $12,450 ($11,250 plus $1,200).

Credit for Tax on Prior Transfers

§ 20.2013-1 Credit for tax on prior transfers—(a) *In general.* A credit is allowed under section 2013 against the Federal estate tax imposed on the present decedent's estate for Federal estate tax paid on the transfer of property to the present decedent from a transferor who died within ten years before, or within two years after, the present decedent's death. See § 20.2013-5 for definition of the terms "property" and "transfer". There is no requirement that the transferred property be identified in the estate of the present decedent or that the property be in existence at the time of the decedent's death. It is sufficient that the transfer of the property was subjected to Federal estate tax in the estate of the transferor and that the transferor died within the prescribed period of time. The executor must submit such proof as may be requested by the district director in order to establish the right of the estate to the credit.

(b) *Limitations on credit.* The credit for tax on prior transfers is limited to the smaller of the following amounts:

(1) The amount of the Federal estate tax attributable to the transferred property in the transferor's estate, computed as set forth in § 20.2013-2; or

(2) The amount of the Federal estate tax attributable to the transferred property in the decedent's estate, computed as set forth in § 20.2013-3.

Rules for valuing property for purposes of the credit are contained in § 20.2013-4.

(c) *Percentage reduction.* If the transferor died within the two years before, or within the two years after, the present decedent's death, the credit is the smaller of the two limitations described in paragraph (b) of this section. If the transferor predeceased the present decedent by more than two years, the credit is a certain percentage of the smaller of the two limitations described in paragraph (b) of this section, determined as follows:

(1) 80 percent, if the transferor died within the third or fourth years preceding the present decedent's death;

(2) 60 percent, if the transferor died within the fifth or sixth years preceding the present decedent's death;

(3) 40 percent, if the transferor died within the seventh or eighth years preceding the present decedent's death; and

(4) 20 percent, if the transferor died within the ninth or tenth years preceding the present decedent's death;

The word "within" as used in this paragraph means "during". Therefore, if a death occurs on the second anniversary of another death, the first death is considered to have occurred within the two years before the second death. If the credit for tax on prior transfers relates to property received from two or more transferors, the provisions of this paragraph are to be applied separately with respect to the property received from each transferor. See paragraph (d) of example (2) in § 20.2013-6.

(d) *Examples.* For illustrations of the application of this section, see examples (1) and (2) set forth in § 20.2013-6.

§ 20.2013-2 "First limitation". (a) The amount of the Federal estate tax attributable to the transferred property in the transferor's estate is the "first limitation." Thus, the credit is limited to an amount, A, which bears the same ratio to B (the "transferor's adjusted Federal estate tax", computed as described in paragraph (b) of this section) as C (the value of the property transferred (see § 20.2013-4)) bears to D (the "transferor's adjusted taxable estate", computed as described in paragraph (c) of this section). Stated algebraically, the "first limitation" (A) equals

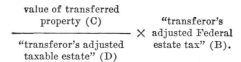

$$\frac{\text{value of transferred property (C)}}{\text{``transferor's adjusted taxable estate'' (D)}} \times \text{``transferor's adjusted Federal estate tax'' (B).}$$

(b) For purposes of the ratio stated in paragraph (a) of this section, the "transferor's adjusted Federal estate tax" referred to as factor "B" is the amount of the Federal estate tax paid with respect to the transferor's estate plus:

(1) Any credit allowed the transferor's estate for gift tax under section 2012, or the corresponding provisions of prior law; and

(2) Any credit allowed the transferor's estate, under section 2013, for tax on prior transfers, but only if the transferor acquired property from a person who died within 10 years before the death of the present decedent.

(c) For purposes of the ratio stated in paragraph (a) of this section, the "transferor's adjusted taxable estate" referred to as factor "D" is the amount of the transferor's taxable estate (or net estate) decreased by the amount of any "death taxes" paid with respect to his gross estate and increased by the amount of the exemption allowed in computing his taxable estate (or net estate). The amount of the transferor's taxable estate (or net estate) is determined in accordance with the provisions of § 20.2051-1 (or the corresponding provisions of prior regulations). The term "death taxes" means the Federal estate tax plus all other estate, inheritance, legacy, succession, or similar death taxes imposed by and paid to any taxing authority, whether within or without the United States. However, only the net amount of such taxes paid is taken into consideration. The amount of the exemption depends upon the citizenship and residence of the transferor at the time of his death. If he was a citizen or resident of the United States, the exemp-

890

tion is the $60,000 authorized by section 2052 (or the corresponding provisions of prior law). If he was not a citizen or resident of the United States, the exemption is the $2,000 authorized by section 2106 (a)(3) (or the corresponding provisions of prior law), or such larger amount as may have been allowed as an exemption pursuant to the prorated exemption provisions of an applicable death tax convention.

(d) If the credit for tax on prior transfers relates to property received from two or more transferors, the provisions of this section are to be applied separately with respect to the property received from each transferor. See paragraph (b) of example (2) in § 20.2013-6.

(e) For illustrations of the application of this section, see examples (1) and (2) set forth in § 20.2013-6.

§ 20.2013-3 "Second limitation". (a) The amount of the Federal estate tax attributable to the transferred property in the present decedent's estate is the "second limitation." Thus, the credit is limited to the difference between—

(1) The net estate tax payable (see paragraph (b)(5) of § 20.0-2) with respect to the present decedent's estate, determined without regard to any credit for tax on prior transfers under section 2013 or any credit for foreign death taxes claimed under the provisions of a death tax convention, and

(2) The net estate tax determined as provided in paragraph (1) of this section, but computed by subtracting from the present decedent's gross estate the value of the property transferred (see § 20.2013-4), and by making only the adjustment indicated in paragraph (b) of this section if a charitable deduction is allowable to the estate of the present decedent.

(b) If a charitable deduction is allowable to the estate of the present decedent under the provisions of section 2055 or section 2106(a)(2) (for estates of nonresidents not citizens), for purposes of determining the tax described in paragraph (a)(2) of this section, the charitable deduction otherwise allowable is reduced by an amount, E, which bears the same ratio to F (the charitable deduction otherwise allowable) as G (the value of the transferred property (see § 20.2013-4)) bears to H (the value of the present decedent's gross estate reduced by the amount of the deductions for expenses, indebtedness, taxes, losses, etc., allowed under the provisions of sections 2053 and 2054 or section 2106(a)(1) (for estates of nonresidents not citizens)). See paragraph (c)(2) of example (1) and paragraph (c)(2) of example (2) in § 20.2013-6.

(c) If the credit for tax on prior transfers relates to property received from two or more transferors, the property received from all transferors is aggregated in determining the limitation on credit under this section (the "second limitation"). However, the limitation so determined is apportioned to the property received from each transferor in the ratio that the property received from each transferor bears to the total property received from all transferors. See paragraph (c) of example (2) in § 20.2013-6.

(d) For illustrations of the application of this section, see examples (1) and (2) set forth in § 20.2013-6.

§ 20.2013-4 **Valuation of property transferred.** (a) For purposes of section 2013 and §§ 20.2013-1 through 20.2013-6, the value of the property transferred to the decedent is the value at which such property was included in the transferor's gross estate for the purpose of the Federal estate tax (see sections 2031, 2032, and the regulations thereunder) reduced as indicated in paragraph (b) of this section. If the decedent received a life estate or remainder or other limited interest in property included in the transferor's gross estate, the value of the interest is determined as of the date of the transferor's death on the basis of recognized valuation principles (see especially § 20.2031-7). The application of this paragraph may be illustrated by the following examples:

Example (1). A died on January 1, 1953, leaving Blackacre to B. The property was included in A's gross estate at a value of $100,000. On January 1, 1955, B sold Blackacre to C for $150,000. B died on February 1, 1955. For purposes of computing the credit against the tax imposed on B's estate, the value of the property transferred to B is $100,000.

Example (2). A died on January 1, 1953, leaving Blackacre to B for life and, upon B's death, remainder to C. At the time of A's death, B was 56 years of age. The property was included in A's gross estate at a value of $100,000. The part of that value attributable to the life estate is $44,688 (see paragraph (c) of § 20.2031-7), and the part of that value attributable to the remainder is $55,312 (see paragraph (d) of § 20.2031-7). B died on January 1, 1955, and C died on January 1, 1956. For purposes of computing the credit against the tax imposed on B's estate, the value of the property transferred to B is $44,688. For purposes of computing the credit against the tax imposed on C's estate, the value of the property transferred to C is $55,312.

(b) In arriving at the value of the property transferred to the decedent, the value at which the property was included in the transferor's gross estate (see paragraph (a) of this section) is reduced as follows:

(1) By the amount of the Federal estate tax and any other estate, inheritance, legacy, or succession taxes which were payable out of the property transferred to the decedent or which were payable by the decedent in connection with the property transferred to him. For example, if under the transferor's will or local law all death taxes are to be paid out of other property with the result that the decedent receives a bequest free and clear of all death taxes, no reduction is to be made under this subparagraph;

(2) By the amount of any marital deduction allowed the transferor's estate under section 2056 (or under section 812 (e) of the Internal Revenue Code of 1939) if the decedent was the spouse of the transferor at the time of the transferor's death; and

(3) (i) By the amount of any encumbrance on the property or by the amount of any obligation imposed by the transferor and incurred by the

decedent with respect to the property, to the extent such charges would be taken into account if the amount of a gift to the decedent of such property were being determined.

(ii) For purposes of this subparagraph, an obligation imposed by the transferor and incurred by the decedent with respect to the property includes a bequest, etc., in lieu of the interest of the surviving spouse under community property laws. unless the interest was, immediately prior to the transferor's death, a mere expectancy. (As to the circumstances under which the interest of a surviving spouse is regarded as a mere expectancy, see the provisions of paragraph (d) of § 20.2056 (c)-2 which arc equally applicable here.) However, an obligation imposed by the transferor and incurred by the decedent with respect to the property does not include a bequest, devise, or other transfer in lieu of dower, curtesy, or of a statutory estate created in lieu of dower or curtesy, or of other marital rights in the transferor's property or estate.

(iii) The application of this subparagraph may be illustrated by the following examples:

Example (1). The transferor devised to the decedent real estate subject to a mortgage. The value of the property transferred to the decedent does not include the amount of the mortgage. If, however, the transferor by his will directs the executor to pay off the mortgage, such payment constitutes an additional amount transferred to the decedent.

Example (2). The transferor bequeathed certain property to the decedent with a direction that the decedent pay $1,000 to X. The value of the property transferred to the decedent is the value of the property reduced by $1,000.

Example (3). The transferor bequeathed certain property to his wife, the decedent, in lieu of her interest in property held by them as community property under the law of the State of their residence. The wife elected to relinquish her community property interest and to take the bequest. The value of the property transferred to the decedent is the value of the property reduced by the value of the community property interest relinquished by the wife.

Example (4). The transferor bequeathed to the decedent his entire residuary estate, out of which certain claims were to be satisfied. The entire distributable income of the transferor's estate (during the period of its administration) was applied toward the satisfaction of these claims and the remaining portion of the claims was satisfied by the decedent out of his own funds. Thus, the decedent received a larger sum upon settlement of the transferor's estate than he was actually bequeathed. The value of the property transferred to the decedent is the value at which such property was included in the transferor's gross estate, reduced by the amount of the estate income and the decedent's own funds paid out in satisfaction of the claims.

§ 20.2013-5 **"Property" and "transfer" defined.** (a) For purposes of section 2013 and §§20.2013-1 through 20.2013-6, the term "property" means any beneficial interest in property, including a general power

893

of appointment (as defined in section 2041) over property. Thus, the term does not include an interest in property consisting merely of a bare legal title, such as that of a trustee. Nor does the term include a power of appointment over property which is not a general power of appointment (as defined in section 2041). Examples of property, as described in this paragraph, are annuities, life estates, estates for terms of years, vested or contingent remainders and other future interests.

(b) In order to obtain the credit for tax on prior transfers, there must be a transfer of property described in paragraph (a) of this section by or from the transferor to the decedent. The term "transfer" of property by or from a transferor means any passing of property or an interest in property under circumstances which were such that the property or interest was included in the gross estate of the transferor. In this connection, if the decedent receives property as a result of the exercise or nonexercise of a power of appointment, the donee of the power (and not the creator) is deemed to be the transferor of the property if the property subject to the power is includible in the donee's gross estate under section 2041 (relating to powers of appointment). Thus, notwithstanding the designation by local law of the capacity in which the decedent takes, property received from the transferor includes interests in property held by or devolving upon the decedent: (1) as spouse under dower or curtesy laws or laws creating an estate in lieu of dower or curtesy; (2) as surviving tenant of a tenancy by the entirety or joint tenancy with survivorship rights; (3) as beneficiary of the proceeds of life insurance; (4) as survivor under an annuity contract; (5) as donee (possessor) of a general power of appointment (as defined in section 2041); (6) as appointee under the exercise of a general power of appointment (as defined in section 2041); or (7) as remainderman under the release or nonexercise of a power of appointment by reason of which the property is included in the gross estate of the donee of the power under section 2041.

(c) The application of this section may be illustrated by the following example:

Example. A devises Blackacre to B, as trustee, with directions to pay the income therefrom to C, his son, for life. Upon C's death, Blackacre is to be sold. C is given a general testamentary power to appoint one-third of the proceeds, and a testamentary power, which is not a general power, to appoint the remaining two-thirds of the proceeds, to such of the issue of his sister D as he should choose. D has a daughter, E, and a son, F. Upon his death, C exercised his general power by appointing one-third of the proceeds to D and his special power by appointing two-thirds of the proceeds to E. Since B's interest in Blackacre as a trustee is not a beneficial interest, no part of it is "property" for purpose of the credit in B's estate. On the other hand, C's life estate and his testamentary power over the one-third interest in the remainder constitute "property" received from A for purpose of the credit in C's estate. Likewise, D's one-third interest in the remainder received through the exercise of C's general power of appointment

894

is "property" received from C for purpose of the credit in D's estate. No credit is allowed E's estate for the property which passed to her from C since the property was not included in C's gross estate. On the other hand, no credit is allowed in E's estate for property passing to her from A since her interest was not susceptible of valuation at the time of A's death (see § 20.2013-4).

§ 20.2013-6 **Examples.** The application of §§ 20.2013-1 through 20.2013-5 may be further illustrated by the following examples:

Example (1). (a) A died December 1, 1953, leaving a gross estate of $1,000,000. Expenses, indebtedness, etc., amounted to $90,000. A bequeathed $200,000 to B, his wife, $100,000 of which qualifies for the marital deduction. B died November 1, 1954, leaving a gross estate of $500,000. Expenses, indebtedness, etc., amounted to $40,000. B bequeathed $150,000 to charity. A and B were both citizens of the United States. The estates of A and B both paid State death taxes equal to the maximum credit allowable for State death taxes. Death taxes were not a charge on the bequest to B.

(b) "First limitation" on credit for B's estate (§ 20.2013-2):

A's gross estate		$1,000,000.00
Expenses, indebtedness, etc.		90,000.00
A's adjusted gross estate		$ 910,000.00
Marital deduction	$100,000.00	
Exemption	60,000.00	160,000.00
A's taxable estate		750,000.00
A's gross estate tax		233,200.00
Credit for State death taxes		23,280.00
A's net estate tax payable		209,920.00

$$\text{"First limitation"} = \frac{\$209,920.00 \ (\S\ 20.2013\text{-}2(b)) \times \$200,000.00 - \$100,000.00 \ (\S\ 20.213\text{-}4)}{\$750,000.00 - \$209,920.00 - \$23,280.00 + \$60,000.00 \ (\S\ 20.2013\text{-}2(c))} = \$ \quad 36,393.90$$

(c) "Second limitation" on credit for B's estate (§ 20.2013-3):

(1) B's net estate tax payable as described in § 20.2013-3(a)(1) (previously taxed transfer included):

B's gross estate		$500,000.00
Expenses, indebtedness, etc.	$ 40,000.00	
Charitable deduction	150,000.00	
Exemption	60,000.00	250,000.00
B's taxable estate		250,000.00
B's gross estate tax		65,700.00
Credit for State death taxes		3,920.00
B's net estate tax payable		61,780.00

(2) B's net estate tax payable as described in § 20.2013-3(a)(2) (previously taxed transfer excluded):

B's gross estate		$400,000.00
Expenses, indebtedness, etc.	$ 40,000.00	
Charitable deduction (§ 20.2013-3(b)) = ($150,000.00 —		
$200,000.00 — $100,000.00)		
$150,000.00 $\times \dfrac{}{\$500,000.00 - \$40,000.00}$ = 117,391.30		
Exemption	60,000.00	217,391.30
B's taxable estate		182,608.70
B's gross estate tax		45,482.61
Credit for State death taxes		2,221.61
B's net estate tax payable		43,260.00

(3) "Second limitation":

Subparagraph (1)	$61,780.00	
Less: Subparagraph (2)	43,260.00	18,520.00

(d) Credit of B's estate for tax on prior transfers (§ 20.2013-1(c)):

Credit for tax on prior transfers = $18,520.00 (lower of paragraphs (b) and (c)) × 100% (percentage to be taken into account under § 20.-2013-1(c)) .... = $ 18,520.00

Example (2). (a) The facts are the same as those contained in example (1) of this paragraph with the following additions. C died December 1, 1950, leaving a gross estate of $250,000. Expenses, indebtedness, etc., amounted to $50,000. C bequeathed $50,000 to B. C was a citizen of the United States. His estate paid State death taxes equal to the maximum credit allowable for State death taxes. Death taxes were not a charge on the bequest to B.

(b) "First limitation" on credit for B's estate (§ 20.2013-2(d))—

(1) With respect to the property received from A:

"First limitation" = $36,393.90 (this computation is identical with the one contained in paragraph (b) of example (1) of this section).

(2) With respect to the property received from C:

C's gross estate		$250,000.00
Expenses, indebtedness, etc.	$50,000.00	
Exemption	60,000.00	110,000.00
C's taxable estate		140,000.00
C's gross estate tax		32,700.00
Credit for State death taxes		1,200.00
C's net estate tax payable		31,500.00

"First limitation" = $\dfrac{\$31,500.00\ (\S\ 20.2013\text{-}2(b)) \times \$50,000.00\ (\S\ 20.2013\text{-}4)}{\$140,000.00 - \$31,500.00 - \$1,200.00 + \$60,000.00\ (\S\ 20.2013\text{-}2(c))}$ = $ 9,414.23

(c) "Second limitation" on credit for B's estate (§ 20.2013-3(c)):

(1) B's net estate tax payable as described in § 20.2013-3(a)(1) (previously taxed transfers included) = $61,780.00 (this computation is identical with the one contained in paragraph (c)(1) of example (1) of this section).

(2) B's net estate tax payable as described in § 20.2013-3(a)(2) (previously taxed transfers excluded):

B's gross estate		$350,000.00
Expenses, indebtedness, etc.	$ 40,000.00	
Charitable deduction (§ 20.2013-3(b)) = $150,000.00 —		

$$(\$150{,}000.00 \times \frac{\$200{,}000.00 - \$100{,}000.00 + \$50{,}000.00)}{\$500{,}000.00 - \$40{,}000.00)} = 101{,}086.96$$

Exemption	60,000.00	201,086.96
B's taxable estate		148,913.04
B's gross estate tax		35,373.91
Credit for State death taxes		1,413.91
B's net estate tax payable		33,960.00

(3) "Second limitation":

Subparagraph (1)	$61,780.00	
Less: Subparagraph (2)	33,960.00	27,820.00

(4) Apportionment of "second limitation" on credit:

Transfer from A (§ 20.2013-4)	$100,000.00
Transfer from C (§ 20.2013-4)	50,000.00
Total	$150,000.00
Portion of "second limitation" attributable to transfer from A (100/150 of $27,820.00)	18,546.67
Portion of "second limitation" attributable to transfer from C (50/150 of $27,820.00)	9,273.33

(d) Credit of B's estate for tax on prior transfers (§ 20.2013-1(c)):

Credit for tax on transfer from A = $18,546.67 (lower of "first limitation" computed in paragraph (b)(1) and "second limitation" apportioned to A's transfer in paragraph (c)(4)) × 100% (percentage to be taken into account under § 20.2013-1(c)) =	$18,546.67
Credit for tax on transfer from C = $9,273.33 (lower of "first limitation" computed in paragraph (b)(2) and "second limitation" apportioned to B's transfer in paragraph (c) (4)) × 80% (percentage to be taken into account under § 20.2013-1(c)) =	7,418.66
Total credit for tax on prior transfers	25,965.33

Credit for Foreign Death Taxes

§ 20.2014-1 **Credit for foreign death taxes**—(a) *In general.* (1) A credit is allowed under section 2014 against the Federal estate tax for any estate, inheritance, legacy, or succession taxes actually paid to any foreign country (hereinafter referred to as "foreign death taxes"). The credit is allowed only for foreign death taxes paid (i) with respect to property situated within the country to which the tax is paid, (ii) with respect to property included in the decedent's gross estate, and (iii) with respect to the decedent's estate. The credit is allowable to the estate of a decedent who was a citizen of the United States at the time of his death. The credit is also allowable to the estate of a decedent who was a resident but not a citizen of the United States at the time of his death if the country of which the decedent was a national, in imposing death taxes, allows a similar credit to the estates of citizens of the United States resident in that country. See paragraph (b)(1) of § 20.0-1 for definition of the term "resident". The credit is not allowable to the estate of a decedent who was neither a citizen nor a resident of the United States at the time of his death. The credit is allowable not only for death taxes paid to foreign countries which are states in the international sense, but also for death taxes paid to possessions or political subdivisions of foreign states. No credit is allowable for interest or penalties paid in connection with foreign death taxes.

(2) In addition to the credit for foreign death taxes under section 2014, similar credits are allowed under death tax conventions with certain foreign countries. If credits against the Federal estate tax are allowable under section 2014, or under section 2014 and one or more death tax conventions, for death taxes paid to more than one country, the credits are combined and the aggregate amount is credited against the Federal estate tax, subject to the limitation provided for in paragraph (c) of § 20.2014-4. For application of the credit in cases involving a death tax convention, see § 20.2014-4.

(3) No credit is allowable under section 2014 in connection with property situated outside of the foreign country imposing the tax for which credit is claimed. However, such a credit may be allowable under certain death tax conventions. In the case of a tax imposed by a political subdivision of a foreign country, credit for such tax shall be allowed with respect to property having a situs in that foreign country, even though, under the principles described in this subparagraph, such property has a situs in a political subdivision different from the one imposing the tax. Whether or not particular property of a decedent is situated in the foreign country imposing the tax is determined in accordance with the same principles that would be applied in determining whether or not similar property of a nonresident decedent not a citizen of the United States is situated within the United States for Federal estate tax purposes. See §§ 20.2104-1 and 20.2105-1. For example, under § 20.2104-1, a bond for the payment of money is not within the United States unless it is physically located in the United States. Accordingly, a bond is deemed situated in the foreign country imposing the tax only if it is physically located in that country. Similarly, under § 20.2104-1, shares of stock are deemed to be situated in the United States only if issued by a domestic (United States) cor-

[Harris]

poration. Thus, a share of corporate stock is regarded as situated in the foreign country imposing the tax only if the issuing corporation is incorporated in that country. Further, under § 20.2105-1, moneys deposited with any person carrying on the banking business by or for a nonresident not a citizen of the United States who was not engaged in business in the United States at the time of death are not deemed situated in the United States. Therefore, an account with a foreign bank in the country imposing the tax is not considered to be situated in that country under corresponding circumstances.

(b) *Limitations on credit.* The credit for foreign death taxes is limited to the smaller of the following amounts:

(1) The amount of a particular foreign death tax attributable to property situated in the country imposing the tax and included in the decedent's gross estate for Federal estate tax purposes, computed as set forth in § 20.2014-2; or

(2) The amount of the Federal estate tax attributable to particular property situated in a foreign country, subjected to foreign death tax in that country, and included in the decedent's gross estate for Federal estate tax purposes, computed as set forth in § 20.2014-3.

§ 20.2014-2 "First limitation". (a) The amount of a particular foreign death tax attributable to property situated in the country imposing the tax and included in the decedent's gross estate for Federal estate tax purposes is the "first limitation." Thus, the credit for any foreign death tax is limited to an amount, A, which bears the same ratio to B (the amount of the foreign death tax without allowance of credit, if any, for Federal estate tax) as C (the value of the property situated in the country imposing the foreign death tax, subjected to the foreign death tax, and included in the gross estate) bears to D (the value of all property subjected to the foreign death tax). Stated algebraically, the "first limitation" (A) equals

$$\frac{\text{value of property in foreign country subjected to foreign death tax and included in gross estate (C)}}{\text{value of all property subjected to foreign death tax (D)}} \times \text{amount of foreign death tax (B)}.$$

The values used in this proportion are the values determined for the purpose of the foreign death tax. The amount of the foreign death tax for which credit is allowable must be converted into United States money. The application of this paragraph may be illustrated by the following example:

Example. At the time of his death, the decedent, a citizen of the United States, owned real property in Country X valued at $80,000 and stock in Y Corporation (a corporation organized under the laws of Country X) valued at $80,000. Decedent left by will $50,000 of the real property and $20,000 of the Y Corporation stock to his surviving spouse. He left the rest of the real property and Y Corporation stock to his son. The real property was not included in his gross estate (see section 2031). There is no death tax convention in existence between the United States and Country X. Under the laws of Country X, the inheritance taxes are computed as follows:

Inheritance tax of surviving spouse:
Value of real property in Country X $50,000
Value of stock in Corporation Y 20,000

Total value 70,000
Tax (16% rate) 11,200

Inheritance tax of son:
Value of real property in Country X $30,000
Value of stock in Y Corporation 60,000

Total value 90,000
Tax (16% rate) 14,400

The "first limitation" on the credit for foreign death taxes is

$$\frac{\$20,000 + \$60,000 \text{ (factor C of the ratio stated at § 20.2014-2 (a))}}{\$70,000 + \$90,000 \text{ (factor D of the ratio stated at § 20.2014-2 (a))}} \times (\$11,200 + \$14,400) \text{ (factor B of the ratio stated at § 20.2014-2(a))} = \$12,800$$

(b) If a foreign country imposes more than one kind of death tax or imposes taxes at different rates upon the several shares of an estate, or if a foreign country and a political subdivision or possession thereof each imposes a death tax, a "first limitation" is to be computed separately for each tax or rate and the results added in order to determine the total "first limitation." The application of this paragraph may be illustrated by the following example:

Example. The facts are the same as those contained in the example set forth in paragraph (a) of this section, except that the tax of the surviving spouse was computed at a 10-percent rate and amounted to $7,000, and the tax of the son was computed at a 20-percent rate and amounted to $18,000. In this case, the "first limitation" on the credit for foreign death taxes is computed as follows:

"First limitation" with respect to inheritance tax of surviving spouse =

$$\frac{\$20,000 \text{ (factor C of the ratio stated at § 20.2014-2(a))}}{\$70,000 \text{ (factor D of the ratio stated at § 20.2014-2(a))}} \times \$7,000 \text{ (factor B of the ratio stated at § 20.2014-2(a))} = \$2,000$$

"First limitation" with respect to inheritance tax of son =

$$\frac{\$60,000 \text{ (factor C of the ratio stated at § 20.2014-2(a))}}{\$90,000 \text{ (factor D of the ratio stated at § 20.2014-2(a))}} \times \$18,000 \text{ (factor B of the ratio stated at § 20.2014-2(a))} = 12,000$$

Total "first limitation" on the credit for foreign death taxes 14,000

§ 20.2014-3 "Second limitation". (a) The amount of the Federal estate tax attributable to particular property situated in a foreign country, subjected to foreign death tax in that country, and included in the decedent's gross estate for Federal estate tax purposes is the "second limitation." Thus, the credit is limited to an amount, E, which bears the same ratio to F (the gross Federal estate tax, reduced by any credit for State death taxes under section 2011 and by any credit for gift tax under section 2012) as G (the "adjusted value of the property situated in the foreign country, subjected to foreign death tax, and included in the gross estate", computed as described in paragraph (b) of this section) bears to H (the value of the entire gross estate, reduced by the total amount of the deductions allowed under sections 2055 (charitable deduction) and 2056 (marital deduction)). Stated algebraically, the "second limitation" (E) equals

$$\frac{\text{"adjusted value of the property situated in the foreign country, subjected to foreign death taxes, and included in the gross estate" (G)}}{\text{value of entire gross estate, less charitable and marital deductions (H)}} \times \frac{\text{gross Federal estate tax, less credits for State death taxes and gift tax (F).}}{}$$

The values used in this proportion are the values determined for the purpose of the Federal estate tax.

(b) Adjustment is required to factor "G" of the ratio stated in paragraph (a) of this section if a charitable deduction under section 2055 or a marital deduction under section 2056 is allowed with respect to the foreign property. In such case, factor "G" is the value of the property situated in the foreign country, subjected to foreign death tax, and included in the gross estate reduced as follows:

(1) If a charitable deduction or a marital deduction is allowed to a decedent's estate with respect to any part of the foreign property specifically bequeathed, devised, or otherwise specifically passing to a charitable organization or to the decedent's spouse, the value of the foreign property is reduced by the amount of the charitable deduction or marital deduction allowed with respect to such specific transfer. See example (1) of paragraph (c) of this section.

(2) If a charitable deduction or a marital deduction is allowed to a decedent's estate with respect to a bequest, devise, or other transfer of an interest in a group of assets including both the foreign property and other property, the value of the foreign property is reduced by an amount, I, which bears the same ratio to J (the amount of the charitable deduction or marital deduction allowed with respect to such transfer of an interest in a group of assets) as K (the value of the foreign property included in the group of assets) bears to L (the value of the entire group of assets). As used in this subparagraph, the term "group of assets" has reference to those assets which, under applicable law, are chargeable with the charitable or marital transfer. See example (2) of paragraph (c) of this section.

901

Any reduction described in subparagraph (1) or (2) of this paragraph on account of the marital deduction must proportionately take into account the 50-percent limitation on the aggregate amount of the marital deduction contained in section 2056(c), if applicable. See example (3) of paragraph (c) of this section.

(c) The application of paragraphs (a) and (b) of this section may be illustrated by the following examples. In each case, the computations relate to the amount of credit under section 2014 without regard to the amount of credit which may be allowable under an applicable death tax convention.

Example (1). (i) Decedent, a citizen and resident of the United States at the time of his death, left a gross estate of $1,000,000 which includes: shares of stock issued by a United States corporation, valued at $750,-000; bonds issued by the government of Country X physically located in the United States, valued at $50,000; and shares of stock issued by a Country X corporation, valued at $200,000. Expenses, indebtedness, etc., amounted to $60,000. Decedent specifically bequeathed $40,000 of the stock issued by the Country X corporation to a United States charity and left the residue of his estate, in equal shares, to his son and daughter. The gross Federal estate tax is $266,500 and the credit for State death taxes is $27,600. Under the situs rules referred to in paragraph (a)(3) of § 20.2014-1, the shares of stock issued by the Country X corporation comprise the only property deemed to be situated in Country X.

(ii) The "second limitation" on the credit for foreign death taxes is

$$\frac{\$200,000 - \$40,000 \text{ (factor G of the ratio stated at § 20.2014-3(a); see also § 20.2014-3(b)(1))}}{\$1,000,000 - \$40,000 \text{ (factor H of the ratio stated at § 20.2014-3(a))}} \times \frac{(\$266,500 - \$27,600)}{\text{(factor F of the ratio stated at § 20.2014-3 (a))}} = \$39,816.67.$$

The lesser of this amount and the amount of the "first limitation" (computed under § 20.2014-2) is the credit for foreign death taxes.

Example (2). (i) Decedent, a citizen and resident of the United States at the time of his death, left a gross estate of $1,000,000 which includes: shares of stock issued by a United States corporation, valued at $650,-000; shares of stock issued by a Country X corporation, valued at $200,000; and life insurance, in the amount of $150,000, payable to a son. Expenses, indebtedness, etc., amounted to $40,000. The decedent made a specific bequest of $25,000 of the Country X corporation stock to Charity A and a general bequest of $100,000 to Charity B. The residue of his estate was left to his daughter. The gross Federal estate tax is $242,450 and the credit for State death taxes is $24,480. Under these facts, and applicable law, neither the stock of the Country X corporation specifically bequeathed to Charity A nor the insurance payable to the son could be charged with satisfying the bequest to Charity B. Therefore, the "group of assets" which could be so charged is limited to stock of the Country X corporation valued at $175,000 and stock of the United States corporation valued at $650,000.

(ii) Factor "G" of the ratio which is used in determining the "second limitation" is computed as follows:

Value of property situated in Country X $200,000.00
Less: Reduction described in § 20.2014-3(b)(1) $25,000.00
    Reduction described in § 20.2014-3(b)(2) =

$$\frac{\$175{,}000 \text{ (factor K of the ratio stated at § 20.2014-3(b)(2))}}{\$175{,}000 + \$650{,}000 \text{ (factor L of the ratio stated at § 20.2014-3(b)(2))}} \times \$100{,}000 \text{ (factor J of the ratio stated at § 20.2014-3(b)(2))} = 21{,}212.12 \quad 46{,}212.12$$

Factor "G" of the ratio $153,787.88

(iii) In this case, the "second limitation" on the credit for foreign death taxes is

$$\frac{\$153{,}787.88 \text{ (factor G of the ratio stated at § 20.2014-3(a); see also subdivision (ii) above)}}{\$1{,}000{,}000 - \$125{,}000 \text{ (factor H of the ratio stated at § 20.2014-3(a))}} \times (\$242{,}450 - \$24{,}480) \text{ (factor F of the ratio stated at § 20.2014-3(a))} = \$38{,}309.88.$$

Example (3). (i) Decedent, a citizen and resident of the United States at the time of his death, left a gross estate of $850,000 which includes: shares of stock issued by United States corporations, valued at $440,000; real estate located in the United States, valued at $110,000; and shares of stock issued by Country X corporations, valued at $300,000. Expenses, indebtedness, etc., amounted to $50,000. Decedent devised $40,000 in real estate to a United States charity. In addition, he bequeathed to his wife $200,000 in United States stocks and $300,000 in Country X stocks. The residue of his estate passed to his children. The gross Federal estate tax is $81,700 and the credit for State death taxes is $5,520.

(ii) Decedent's adjusted gross estate is $800,000 (i.e., $850,000, gross estate less $50,000, expenses, indebtedness, etc.). The aggregate marital deduction allowed to his estate is limited by section 2056(c) to one-half of this amount, or $400,000. Factor "G" of the ratio which is used in determining the "second limitation" is computed as follows:

Value of property situated in Country X $300,000
Less: Reduction described in § 20.2014-3(b)(1) determined as follows (see also end of § 20.2014-3(b))—
    Total amount of bequests which qualify for the marital deduction:
      Specific bequest of Country X stock $300,000
      Specific bequest of United States stock 200,000

                                           500,000
    Limitation on aggregate marital deduction under section 2056(c) 400,000
    Part of specific bequest of Country X stock with respect to which the marital deduction is allowed—

$$\frac{\$400{,}000}{\$500{,}000} \times \$300{,}000 \quad \text{.......................................} \quad 240{,}000$$

Factor "G" of the ratio 60,000

(iii) Thus, the "second limitation" on the credit for foreign death taxes is

$$\frac{\$60,000 \text{ (factor G of the ratio stated at § 20.2014-3(a); see also subdivision (ii) above)}}{\$850,000 - \$40,000 - \$400,000 \text{ (factor H of the ratio stated at § 20.2014-3(a))}} \times \frac{(\$81,700 - \$5,520)}{\text{(factor F of the ratio stated at § 20.2014-3}} = \$11,148.29.$$

(d) If the foreign country imposes more than one kind of death tax or imposes taxes at different rates upon the several shares of an estate, or if the foreign country and a political subdivision or possession thereof each imposes a death tax, the "second limitation" is still computed by applying the ratio set forth in paragraph (a) of § 20.2014-3. Factor "G" of the ratio is determined by taking into consideration the combined value of the foreign property which is subjected to each different tax or different rate. The combined value, however, cannot exceed the value at which such property was included in the gross estate for Federal estate tax purposes. Thus, if Country X imposes a tax on the inheritance of a surviving spouse at a 10-percent rate and on the inheritance of a son at a 20-percent rate, the combined value of their inheritances is taken into consideration in determining factor "G" of the ratio, which is then used in computing the "second limitation." However, the "first limitation" is computed as provided in paragraph (b) of § 20.2014-2. The lesser of the "first limitation" and the "second limitation" is the credit for foreign death taxes.

§ 20.2014-4 **Application of credit in cases involving a death tax convention**—(a) *In general.* (1) If credit for a particular foreign death tax is authorized by a death tax convention, there is allowed either the credit provided for by the convention or the credit provided for by section 2014, whichever is the more beneficial to the estate. The application of this paragraph may be illustrated by the following example:

Example. (i) Decedent, a citizen of the United States and a domiciliary of Country X at the time of his death, left a gross estate of $1,000,000 which includes: shares of stock issued by a Country X corporation, valued at $400,000; bonds issued by a Country X corporation physically located in the United States, valued at $350,000; and real estate located in the United States, valued at $250,000. Expenses, indebtedness, etc., amounted to $50,000. Decedent left his entire estate to his son. There is in effect a death tax convention between the United States and Country X which provides for allowance of credit by the United States for succession duties imposed by the national government of Country X. The gross Federal estate tax is $307,200 and the credit for State death taxes is $33,760. Country X imposed a net succession duty on the stocks and bonds of $180,000. Under the situs rules described in paragraph (a)(3) of § 20.2014-1, the shares of stock comprise the

904

only property deemed to be situated in Country X. Under the convention, both the stocks and the bonds are deemed to be situated in Country X.

(ii)(*a*) The credit authorized by the convention for death taxes imposed by Country X is computed as follows:

(*1*) Country X tax attributable to property situated in Country X and subjected to tax by both countries

$$\frac{(\$750,000}{(\$750,000} \times \$180,000) \dots\dots\dots\dots\dots\dots\dots\dots\dots\dots \$180,000$$

(*2*) Federal estate tax attributable to property situated in Country X and subjected to tax by both countries

$$\frac{(\ \$750,000}{(\$1,000,000} \times \$273,440) \dots\dots\dots\dots\dots\dots\dots\dots\dots 205,080$$

(*3*) Credit (subdivision (*1*) or (*2*), whichever is less) 180,000

(*b*) The credit authorized by section 2014 for death taxes imposed by Country X is computed as follows:

(*1*) "First limitation" computed under § 20.2014-2

$$\frac{(\$400,000}{(\$750,000} \times \$180,000) \dots\dots\dots\dots\dots\dots\dots\dots\dots \$\ 96,000$$

(*2*) "Second limitation" computed under § 20.2014-3

$$\frac{(\ \$400,000}{(\$1,000,000} \times \$273,440) \dots\dots\dots\dots\dots\dots\dots\dots\dots 109,376$$

(*3*) Credit (subdivision (*1*) or (*2*), whichever is less) 96,000

(iii) On the basis of the facts contained in this example, the credit of $180,000 authorized by the convention is the more beneficial to the estate:

(2) It should be noted that the greater of the treaty credit and the statutory credit is not necessarily the more beneficial to the estate. Such is the situation for example, in those cases which involve both a foreign death tax credit and a credit under section 2013 for tax on prior transfers. The reason is that the amount of the credit for tax on prior transfers may differ depending upon whether the credit for foreign death tax is taken under the treaty or under the statute. Therefore, under certain circumstances, the advantage of taking the greater of the treaty credit and the statutory credit may be more than offset by a resultant smaller credit for tax on prior transfers. The solution is to compute the net estate tax payable first on the assumption that the treaty credit will be taken and then on the assumption that the statutory credit will be taken. Such computations will indicate whether the treaty credit or the statutory credit is in fact the more beneficial to the estate.

(b) *Taxes imposed by both a foreign country and a political subdivision thereof.* If a foreign death tax is imposed by both a foreign country with which the United States has entered into a death tax convention and one of its possession or political subdivisions, there is allowed either the credit provided for by the convention or the credit provided for by section 2014, whichever is the more beneficial to the estate. Thus, if a portion of the estate of a United States citizen is situated in X (a country with which the United States has entered into a death tax convention providing for allowance of credit by the United States for death tax imposed by the national government of X) and is subjected to death taxes imposed by both the national government of X and the government of Y, a province of X, there is allowed either a credit for the national death tax computed under the convention or a credit for the combined national and provincial death taxes computed under section 2014, whichever is the more beneficial to the estate. It should be noted that, unless the convention provides otherwise, credit may not be claimed separately under the convention for the national tax and under section 2014 for the provincial tax. The application of this paragraph is illustrated in greater detail in the following example:

Example. (1) Decedent, a citizen of the United States and a domiciliary of Country X at the time of his death, left a gross estate of $225,000 which includes: bonds issued by a United States corporation physically located in Y, a province of Country X, valued at $100,000; bonds issued by a Country X corporation physically located in the United States, valued at $75,000; and shares of stock issued by a Country X corporation, valued at $50,000. Expenses, indebtedness, etc., amounted to $10,000. Decedent left his entire estate to his son. There is in effect a death duty convention between the United States and Country X which provides for allowance of credit by the United States for succession duties imposed by the national government of Country X. The gross Federal estate tax is $55,200 and the credit for State death taxes is $3,000. Country X imposed a net succession duty on the Country X stock and the Country X bonds of $18,000. Province Y imposed a net succession duty on the United States bonds of $16,000. Under the situs rules described in paragraph (a)(3) § 20.2014-1, the United States bonds and the Country X stock are deemed to be situated in Country X. Under the convention, the Country X bonds and the Country X stock are deemed to be situated in Country X.

(2)(i) The credit authorized by the convention for death taxes imposed by Country X is computed as follows:

(*a*) Country X tax attributable to property situated in Country X and subjected to tax by both countries

$$\frac{(\$125,000}{(\$125,000} \times \$18,000) \dots \dots \dots \dots \dots \dots \dots \dots \dots \dots \dots \dots \dots \dots \quad \$18,000$$

(*b*) Federal estate tax attributable to property situated in Country X and subjected to tax by both countries

$$\frac{(\$125,000}{(\$225,000} \times \$52,200) \dots \dots \dots \dots \dots \dots \dots \dots \dots \dots \dots \dots \dots \dots \quad 29,000$$

(*c*) Credit (subdivision (*a*) or (*b*), whichever is less) \dots \dots \dots \dots \dots \dots \dots \quad \$18,000

(ii) The credit authorized by section 2014 for death taxes imposed by Country X (which includes death taxes imposed by Province Y according to § 20.2014-1(a)(1)) is computed as follows:

(a) "First limitation" with respect to tax imposed by national government of Country X computed under § 20.2014-2(b)

$$\left(\frac{\$50,000}{\$125,000} \times \$18,000\right) \quad \dots\dots\dots\dots\dots\dots\dots\dots\dots\dots\dots\dots\dots \quad \$7,200$$

(b) "First limitation" with respect to tax imposed by Province Y computed under § 20.2014-2(b)

$$\left(\frac{\$100,000}{\$100,000} \times \$16,000\right) \quad \dots\dots\dots\dots\dots\dots\dots\dots\dots\dots\dots\dots \quad 16,000$$

(c) Total "first limitation" 23,200

(d) "Second limitation" computed under § 20.2014-3(d)

$$\left(\frac{\$150,000}{\$225,000} \times \$52,200\right) \quad \dots\dots\dots\dots\dots\dots\dots\dots\dots\dots\dots\dots \quad 34,800$$

(e) Credit (subdivision (c) or (d), whichever is less) $23,200

(3) On the basis of the facts contained in this example, the credit of $23,200 authorized by section 2014 is the more beneficial to the estate.

(c) *Taxes imposed by two foreign countries with respect to the same property.* It is stated as a general rule in paragraph (a)(2) of § 20.2014-1 that if credits against the Federal estate tax are allowable under section 2014, or under section 2014 and one or more death tax conventions, for death taxes paid to more than one country, the credits are combined and the aggregate amount is credited against the Federal estate tax. This rule may result in credit being allowed for taxes imposed by two different countries upon the same item of property. If such is the case, the total amount of the credits with respect to such property is limited to the amount of the Federal estate tax attributable to the property, determined in accordance with the rules prescribed for computing the "second limitation" set forth in § 20.2014-3. The application of this section may be illustrated by the following example:

Example. The decedent, a citizen of the United States and a domiciliary of Country X at the time of his death, left a taxable estate which included bonds issued by Country X corporations, physically located in Country Z. Each of the three countries involved imposed death taxes on the Country X bonds. Assume that under the provisions of a treaty between the United States and Country X, the estate is entitled to a credit against the Federal estate tax for death taxes imposed by Country X on the Country X bonds in the maximum amount of $20,000. Assume, also, that under the provisions of section 2014, the estate is entitled to a credit against the Federal estate tax for death taxes imposed by Country Z on the Country X bonds in the maximum amount of $10,000. Finally, assume that the Federal estate tax attributable to the Country X bonds is $25,000. Under such circumstances, the credit allowed the estate with respect to the Country X bonds would be limited to $25,000.

§ 20.2014-5 **Proof of credit.** (a) If the foreign death tax has not been determined and paid by the time the Federal estate tax return required by section 6018 is filed, credit may be claimed on the return in an estimated amount. However, before credit for the foreign death tax is finally allowed, satisfactory evidence, such as a statement by an authorized official of each country, possession or political subdivision thereof imposing the tax, must be submitted on Form 706CE certifying: (1) the full amount of the tax (exclusive of any interest or penalties), as computed before allowance of any credit, remission, or relief; (2) the amount of any credit, allowance, remission, or relief, and other pertinent information, including the nature of the allowance and a description of the property to which it pertains; (3) the net foreign death tax payable after any such allowance; (4) the date on which the death tax was paid, or if not all paid at one time, the date and amount of each partial payment; and (5) a list of the property situated in the foreign country and subjected to its tax, showing a description and the value of the property. Satisfactory evidence must also be submitted showing that no refund of the death tax is pending and none is authorized or, if any refund is pending or has been authorized, its amount and other pertinent information. See also section 2016 and § 20.2016-1 for requirements if foreign death taxes claimed as a credit are subsequently recovered.

(b) The following information must also be submitted whenever applicable:

(1) If any of the property subjected to the foreign death tax was situated outside of the country imposing the tax, the description of each item of such property and its value.

(2) If more than one inheritance or succession is involved with respect to which credit is claimed, or if the foreign country, possession or political subdivision thereof imposes more than one kind of death tax, or if both the foreign country and a possession or political subdivision thereof each imposes a death tax, a separate computation with respect to each inheritance or succession tax.

(c) In addition to the information required under paragraphs (a) and (b) of this section, the district director may require the submission of any further proof deemed necessary to establish the right to the credit.

§ 20.2014-6 **Period of limitations on credit.** The credit for foreign death taxes under section 2014 is limited to those taxes which were actually paid and for which a credit was claimed within four years after the filing of the estate tax return for the decedent's estate. If, however, a petition has been filed with The Tax Court of the United States for the redetermination of a deficiency within the time prescribed in section 6213(a), the credit is limited to those taxes which were actually paid and for which a credit was claimed within four years after the filing of the return, or before the expiration of 60 days after the decision of The Tax Court becomes final, whichever period is the last to expire. Similarly, if an extension of time has been granted under section 6161 for payment of the tax shown on the return, or of a deficiency, the credit is limited to those taxes which were actually paid and for which a credit was claimed within four years after the filing of the return, or before the date of the expiration of the period of the extension, whichever period is the last to expire. See section 2015 for the applicable period of limitations for credit for foreign death taxes on reversionary or remainder interests if an election is made under section 6163(a) to postpone payment of the estate tax attributable to reversionary or remainder interests. If a claim for refund based on the credit for foreign death taxes is filed within the applicable period described in this section, a refund may be made despite the general limitation provisions of sections 6511 and 6512. Any refund based on the credit for foreign death taxes shall be made without interest.

Credit for Death Taxes on Remainders

§ 20.2015-1 **Credit for death taxes on remainders.** (a) If the executor of an estate elects under section 6163(a) to postpone the time for payment of any portion of the Federal estate tax attributable to a reversionary or remainder interest in property, credit is allowed under sections 2011 and 2014 against such portion of the Federal estate tax for State death taxes and foreign death taxes attributable to the reversionary or remainder interest if such State death taxes or foreign death taxes are paid and if credit therefor is claimed either—

(1) Within the time provided for in sections 2011 and 2014, or

(2) Within 60 days after the termination of the preceding interest or interests in the property.

The allowance of credit, however, is subject to the other limitations contained in sections 2011 and 2014.

(b) In applying the rule stated in paragraph (a) of this section, credit for State death taxes or foreign death taxes paid within the time provided in sections 2011 and 2014 is applied first to the portion of the Federal estate tax payment of which is not postponed, and any excess is applied to the balance of the Federal estate tax. However, credit for State death taxes or foreign death taxes not paid within the time provided in sections 2011 and 2014 is allowable only against the portion of the Federal estate tax attributable to the reversionary or remainder interest, and only for State or foreign death taxes attributable to that interest. If a State death tax or a foreign death tax is imposed upon both a reversionary or remainder interest and upon other property, without a definite apportionment of the tax, the amount of the tax deemed attributable to the reversionary or remainder interest is an amount which bears the same ratio to the total tax as the value of the reversionary or remainder interest bears to the value of the entire property with respect to which the tax was imposed. In applying this ratio, adjustments consistent with those required under paragraph (c) of § 20.6163-1 must be made.

(c) The application of this section may be illustrated by the following examples:

Example (1). One-third of the Federal estate tax was attributable to a remainder interest in real property located in State Y, and two-thirds of the Federal estate tax was attributable to other property located in State X. The payment of the tax attributable to the remainder interest was postponed under the provisions of section 6163(a). The maximum credit allowable for State death taxes under the provisions of section 2011 is $12,000. Therefore, of the maximum credit allowable, $4,000 is attributable to the remainder interest and $8,000 is attributable to the other property. Within the 4-year period provided for in section 2011, inheritance tax in the amount of $9,000 was paid to State X in connection with the other property. With respect to this $9,000, $8,000 (the maximum amount allowable) is allowed as a credit against the Federal estate tax attributable to the other property, and $1,000 is allowed as a credit against the postponed tax. After the expiration of the 4-year period but before expiration of 60 days after termination of the life estate or other precedent interest, inheritance tax in the amount of $5,000 was paid to State Y in connection with the remainder interest. As the maximum credit allowable with respect to the remainder interest is $4,000 and $1,000 has already been allowed as a credit, an additional $3,000 will be credited against the Federal estate tax attributable to the remainder interest.

Example (2). The facts are the same as in example (1), except that within the 4-year period inheritance tax in the amount of $2,500 was paid to State Y with respect to the remainder interest and inheritance tax in the amount of $7,500 was paid to State X with respect to the other property. The amount of $8,000 is allowed as a credit against the Federal estate tax attributable to the other property and the amount of $2,000 is allowed as a credit against the postponed tax. After the expiration of the 4-year period but before the expiration of 60 days after the termination of the life estate or other precedent interest, the estate pays additional inheritance taxes of $5,000 to State Y in connection with the remainder interest. Thus, additional credit will be allowed in the amount of $2,000 ($4,000, maximum credit allowable, less $2,000 credit previously allowed) against the Federal estate tax attributable to the remainder interest.

Example (3). The facts are the same as in example (2), except that no payment was made to State Y within the 4-year period. The amount of $7,500 is allowed as a credit against the Federal estate tax attributable to the other property. After termination of the life interest additional credit will be allowed in the amount of $4,000 against the Federal estate tax attributable to the remainder interest. Since the payment of $5,000 was made to State Y following the expiration of the 4-year period, no part of the payment may be allowed as a credit against the Federal estate tax attributable to the other property.

Recovery of Death Taxes Claimed as Credit

§ 20.2016-1 **Recovery of death taxes claimed as credit.** In accordance with the provisions of section 2016, the executor (or any other person) receiving a refund of any State death taxes or foreign death taxes claimed as a credit under section 2011 or section 2014 shall notify the district director of the refund within 30 days of its receipt. The notice shall contain the following information:

(a) The name of the decedent;

(b) The date of the decedent's death;

(c) The property with respect to which the refund was made;

(d) The amount of the refund, exclusive of interest;

(e) The date of the refund; and

(f) The name and address of the person receiving the refund.

If the refund was in connection with foreign death taxes claimed as a credit under section 2014, the notice shall also contain a statement showing the amount of interest, if any, paid by the foreign country on the refund. Finally, the person filing the notice shall furnish the district director such additional information as he may request. Any Federal estate tax found to be due by reason of the refund is payable by the person or persons receiving it, upon notice and demand, even though the refund is received after the expiration of the period of limitations set forth in section 6501 (see section 6501(c)(5)). If the tax found to be due results from a refund of foreign death tax claimed as a credit under section 2014, such tax shall not bear interest for any period before the receipt of the refund, except to the extent that interest was paid by the foreign country on the refund.

GROSS ESTATE

Valuation of Property

§ 20.2031-1 **Definition of gross estate; valuation of property**—(a) *Definition of gross estate.* The value of the gross estate of a decedent who was a citizen or resident of the United States at the time of his death is the total value of the interests described in sections 2033 through 2044, other than real property situated outside of the United States (as defined in paragraph (b)(1)(i) of § 20.0-1) valued as described in §§ 20.2031-1 through 20.2031-9 and § 20.2032-1. The contents of sections 2033 through 2044 are, in general, as follows:

(1) Sections 2033 and 2034 are concerned mainly with interests in property passing through the decedent's probate estate. Section 2033 includes in the decedent's gross estate any interest that the decedent had in property at the time of his death. Section 2034 provides that any interest of the decedent's surviving spouse in the decedent's property, such as dower or curtesy, does not prevent the inclusion of such property in the decedent's gross estate.

(2) Sections 2035 through 2038 deal with interests in property transferred by the decedent during his life under such circumstances as to

911

bring the interests within the decedent's gross estate. Section 2035 includes in the decedent's gross estate property transferred in contemplation of death, even though the decedent had no interest in, or control over, the property at the time of his death. Section 2036 provides for the inclusion of transferred property with respect to which the decedent retained the income or the power to designate who shall enjoy the income. Section 2037 includes in the decedent's gross estate certain transfers under which the beneficial enjoyment of the property could be obtained only by surviving the decedent. Section 2038 provides for the inclusion of transferred property if the decedent had at the time of his death the power to change the beneficial enjoyment of the property. It should be noted that there is considerable overlap in the application of sections 2036 through 2038 with respect to reserved powers, so that transferred property may be includible in the decedent's gross estate in varying degrees under more than one of those sections.

(3) Sections 2039 through 2042 deal with special kinds of property and powers. Sections 2039 and 2040 concern annuities and jointly held property, respectively. Section 2041 deals with powers held by the decedent over the beneficial enjoyment of property not originating with the decedent. Section 2042 concerns insurance under policies on the life of the decedent.

(4) Section 2043 concerns the sufficiency of consideration for transfers made by the decedent during his life. This has a bearing on the amount to be included in the decedent's gross estate under sections 2035 through 2038, and 2041. Section 2044 deals with retroactivity.

(b) *Valuation of property in general.* The value of every item of property includible in a decedent's gross estate under sections 2031 through 2044 is its fair market value at the time of the decedent's death, except that if the executor elects the alternate valuation method under section 2032, it is the fair market value thereof at the date, and with the adjustments, prescribed in that section. The fair market value is the price at which the property would change hands between a willing buyer and a willing seller, neither being under any compulsion to buy or to sell and both having reasonable knowledge of relevant facts. The fair market value of a particular item of property includible in the decedent's gross estate is not to be determined by a forced sale price. The value is generally to be determined by ascertaining as a basis the fair market value as of the applicable valuation date of each unit of the property. For example, in the case of shares of stock or bonds, such unit of property is generally a share of stock or a bond. Livestock, farm machinery, harvested and growing crops must generally be itemized and the value of each item separately returned. Property shall not be returned at the value at which it is assessed for local tax purposes unless that value represents the fair market value as of the applicable valuation date. All relevant facts and elements of value as of the applicable valuation date shall be considered in every case. See §§ 20.2031-2 through 20.2031-8 for further information concerning the valuation of particular kinds of property.

§ 20.2031-2 **Valuation of stocks and bonds**—(a) *In general.* The value of stocks and bonds is the fair market value per share or bond on the applicable valuation date.

(b) *Based on selling prices.* If there is a market for stocks or bonds, on a stock exchange, in an over-the-counter market, or otherwise, the mean between the highest and lowest quoted selling prices on the valuation date is the fair market value per share or bond. If there were no sales on the valuation date, but there were sales on dates within a reasonable period both before and after the valuation date, the fair market value is determined by taking a weighted average of the means between the highest and lowest sales on the nearest date before and the nearest date after the valuation date. The average is to be weighed inversely by the respective numbers of trading days between the selling dates and the valuation date. For example, assume that sales of stock nearest the valuation date (Friday, June 15) occurred two trading days before (Wednesday, June 13) and three trading days after (Wednesday, June 20) and that on these days the mean sale prices per share were $10 and $15, respectively. The price of $12 is taken as representing the fair market value of a share of the stock as of the valuation date

$$\frac{(3 \times 10) + (2 \times 15)}{5}$$

If, instead, the mean sale prices per share on June 13 and June 20 were $15 and $10, respectively, the price of $13 is taken as representing the fair market value

$$\frac{(3 \times 15) + (2 \times 10)}{5}$$

As a further example, assume that the decedent died on Sunday, October 7, and that Saturday and Sunday were not trading days. If sales of stock occurred on Friday, October 5, at mean sale prices per share of $20 and on Monday, October 8, at mean sale prices per share of $23, then the fair market value per share of stock as of the valuation date is $21.50. If stocks or bonds are listed on more than one exchange, the records of the exchange where the stocks or bonds are principally dealt in should be employed. In valuing listed securities, the executor should be careful to consult accurate records to obtain values as of the applicable valuation date. If quotations of unlisted securities are obtained from brokers, or evidence as to their sale is obtained from officers of the issuing companies, copies of the letters furnishing such quotations or evidence of sale should be attached to the return.

(c) *Based on bid and asked prices.* If the provisions of paragraph (b) of this section are inapplicable because actual sales are not available during a reasonable period beginning before and ending after the valuation date, the fair market value may be determined by taking the mean between the bona fide bid and asked prices on the valuation date, or if none, by taking a weighted average of the means between the

[Harris]—58

bona fide bid and asked prices on the nearest trading date before and the nearest trading date after the valuation date, if both such nearest dates are within a reasonable period. The average is to be determined in the manner described in paragraph (b) of this section.

(d) *Based on incomplete selling prices or bid and asked prices.* If the provisions of paragraphs (b) and (c) of this section are inapplicable because no actual sale prices or bona fide bid and asked prices are available on a date within a reasonable period before the valuation date, but such prices are available on a date within a reasonable period after the valuation date, or vice versa, then the mean between the highest and lowest available sale prices or bid and asked prices may be taken as the value.

(e) *Where selling prices or bid and asked prices do not reflect fair market value.* If it is established that the value of any bond or share of stock determined on the basis of selling or bid and asked prices as provided under paragraphs (b), (c), and (d) of this section does not reflect the fair market value thereof, then some reasonable modification of that basis or other relevant facts and elements of value are considered in determining the fair market value. Where sales at or near the date of death are few or of a sporadic nature, such sales alone may not indicate fair market value. In certain exceptional cases, the size of the block of stock to be valued in relation to the number of shares changing hands in sales may be relevant in determining whether selling prices reflect the fair market value of the block of stock to be valued. If the executor can show that the block of stock to be valued is so large in relation to the actual sales on the existing market that it could not be liquidated in a reasonable time without depressing the market, the price at which the block could be sold as such outside the usual market, as through an underwriter, may be a more accurate indication of value than market quotations. Complete data in support of any allowance claimed due to the size of the block of stock being valued shall be submitted with the return. On the other hand, if the block of stock to be valued represents a controlling interest, either actual or effective, in a going business, the price at which other lots change hands may have little relation to its true value.

(f) *Where selling prices or bid and asked prices are unavailable.* If the provisions of paragraphs (b), (c), and (d) of this section are inapplicable because actual sale prices and bona fide bid and asked prices are lacking, then the fair market value is to be determined by taking the following factors into consideration:

(1) In the case of corporate or other bonds, the soundness of the security, the interest yield, the date of maturity, and other relevant factors; and

(2) In the case of shares of stock, the company's net worth, prospective earning power and dividend-paying capacity, and other relevant factors.

Some of the "other relevant factors" referred to in subparagraphs (1) and (2) of this paragraph are: the good will of the business; the economic outlook in the particular industry; the company's position in the industry and its management; the degree of control of the business

914   [Harris]

represented by the block of stock to be valued; and the values of securities of corporations engaged in the same or similar lines of business which are listed on a stock exchange. However, the weight to be accorded such comparisons or any other evidentiary factors considered in the determination of a value depends upon the facts of each case. Complete financial and other data upon which the valuation is based should be submitted with the return, including copies of reports of any examinations of the company made by accountants, engineers, or any technical experts as of or near the applicable valuation date.

(g) *Pledged securities.* The full value of securities pledged to secure an indebtedness of the decedent is included in the gross estate. If the decedent had a trading account with a broker, all securities belonging to the decedent and held by the broker at the date of death must be included at their fair market value as of the applicable valuation date. Securities purchased on margin for the decedent's account and held by a broker must also be returned at their fair market value as of the applicable valuation date. The amount of the decedent's indebtedness to a broker or other person with whom securities were pledged is allowed as a deduction from the gross estate in accordance with the provisions of § 20.2053-1 or § 20.2106-1 (for estates of nonresidents not citizens).

(h) *Securities subject to an option or contract to purchase.* Another person may hold an option or a contract to purchase securities owned by a decedent at the time of his death. The effect, if any, that is given to the option or contract price in determining the value of the securities for estate tax purposes depends upon the circumstances of the particular case. Little weight will be accorded a price contained in an option or contract under which the decedent is free to dispose of the underlying securities at any price he chooses during his lifetime. Such is the effect, for example, of an agreement on the part of a shareholder to purchase whatever shares of stock the decedent may own at the time of his death. Even if the decedent is not free to dispose of the underlying securities at other than the option or contract price, such price will be disregarded in determining the value of the securities unless it is determined under the circumstances of the particular case that the agreement represents a bona fide business arrangement and not a device to pass the decedent's shares to the natural objects of his bounty for less than an adequate and full consideration in money or money's worth.

(j) *Stock sold "ex-dividend."* In any case where a dividend is declared on a share of stock before the decedent's death but payable to stockholders of record on a date after his death and the stock is selling "ex-dividend" on the date of the decedent's death, the amount of the dividend is added to the ex-dividend quotation in determining the fair market value of the stock as of the date of the decedent's death.

§ 20.2031-3 **Valuation of interests in businesses.** The fair market value of any interest of a decedent in a business, whether a partnership or a proprietorship, is the net amount which a willing purchaser, whether an individual or a corporation, would pay for the interest to a willing seller, neither being under any compulsion to buy or to sell and both having reasonable knowledge of relevant facts. The net value is determined on the basis of all relevant factors including—

(a) A fair appraisal as of the applicable valuation date of all the assets of the business, tangible and intangible, including good will;

(b) The demonstrated earning capacity of the business; and

(c) The other factors set forth in paragraphs (f) and (h) of § 20.2031-2 relating to the valuation of corporate stock, to the extent applicable.

Special attention should be given to determining an adequate value of the good will of the business in all cases in which the decedent has not agreed, for an adequate and full consideration in money or money's worth, that his interest passes at his death to, for example, his surviving partner or partners. Complete financial and other data upon which the valuation is based should be submitted with the return, including copies of reports of examinations of the business made by accountants, engineers, or any technical experts as of or near the applicable valuation date.

§ 20.2031-4 Valuation of notes.

The fair market value of notes, secured or unsecured, is presumed to be the amount of unpaid principal, plus interest accrued to the date of death, unless the executor establishes that the value is lower or that the notes are worthless. However, items of interest shall be separately stated on the estate tax return. If not returned at face value, plus accrued interest, satisfactory evidence must be submitted that the note is worth less than the unpaid amount (because of the interest rate, date of maturity, or other cause), or that the note is uncollectible, either in whole or in part (by reason of the insolvency of the party or parties liable, or for other cause), and that any property pledged or mortgaged as security is insufficient to satisfy the obligation.

§ 20.2031-5 Valuation of cash on hand or on deposit.

The amount of cash belonging to the decedent at the date of his death, whether in his possession or in the possession of another, or deposited with a bank, is included in the decedent's gross estate. If bank checks outstanding at the time of the decedent's death and given in discharge of bona fide legal obligations of the decedent incurred for an adequate and full consideration in money or money's worth are subsequently honored by the bank and charged to the decedent's account, the balance remaining in the account may be returned, but only if the obligations are not claimed as deductions from the gross estate.

§ 20.2031-6 Valuation of household and personal effects—(a) *General rule.*

The fair market value of the decedent's household and personal effects is the price which a willing buyer would pay to a willing seller, neither being under any compulsion to buy or to sell and both having reasonable knowledge of relevant facts. A room by room itemization of household and personal effects is desirable. All the articles should be named specifically, except that a number of articles contained in the same room, none of which has a value in excess of $100, may be grouped. A separate value should be given for each article named. In lieu of an itemized list, the executor may furnish a written statement, containing a declaration that it is made under penalties of perjury, setting forth the aggregate value as appraised by a competent appraiser or appraisers of recognized standing and ability, or by a dealer or dealers in the class of personalty involved.

(b) *Special rule in cases involving a substantial amount of valuable articles.* Notwithstanding the provisions of paragraph (a) of this section, if there are included among the household and personal effects articles having marked artistic or intrinsic value of a total value in excess of $3,000 (e.g., jewelry, furs, silverware, paintings, etchings, engravings, antiques, books, statuary, vases, oriental rugs, coin or stamp collections), the appraisal of an expert or experts, under oath, shall be filed with the return. The appraisal shall be accompanied by a written statement of the executor containing a declaration that it is made under the penalties of perjury as to the completeness of the itemized list of such property and as to the disinterested character and the qualifications of the appraiser or appraisers.

(c) *Disposition of household effects prior to investigation.* If it is desired to effect distribution or sale of any portion of the household or personal effects of the decedent in advance of an investigation by an officer of the Internal Revenue Service, information to that effect shall be given to the district director. The statement to the district director shall be accompanied by an appraisal of such property, under oath, and by a written statement of the executor, containing a declaration that it is made under the penalties of perjury, regarding the completeness of the list of such property and the qualifications of the appraiser, as heretofore described. If a personal inspection by an officer of the Internal Revenue Service is not deemed necessary, the executor will be so advised. This procedure is designed to facilitate disposition of such property and to obviate future expense and inconvenience to the estate by affording the district director an opportunity to make an investigation should one be deemed necessary prior to sale or distribution.

(d) *Additional rules if an appraisal involved.* If, pursuant to paragraphs (a), (b), and (c) of this section, expert appraisers are employed, care shall be taken to see that they are reputable and of recognized competency to appraise the particular class of property involved. In the appraisal, books in sets by standard authors shall be listed in separate groups. In listing paintings having artistic value, the size, subject, and artist's name shall be stated. In the case of oriental rugs, the size, make, and general condition shall be given. Sets of silverware shall be listed in separate groups. Groups or individual pieces of silverware shall be weighed and the weights given in troy ounces. In arriving at the value of silverware, the appraisers shall take into consideration its antiquity, utility, desirability, condition, and obsolescence.

§ 20.2031-7 Valuation of annuities, life estates, terms for years, remainders and reversions—(a) *In general.* (1) The fair market value of annuities, life estates, terms for years, remainders and reversions is their present value, determined under this section, except in the case of annuities under contracts issued by companies regularly engaged in their sale. The valuation of such commercial annuity contracts, and of insurance policies on the lives of persons other than the decedent, is determined under § 20.2031-8. (See § 20.2042-1 with respect to insurance policies on the decedent's life.)

(2) The present value of an annuity, life estate, remainder or reversion determined under this section which is dependent on the continuation or termination of the life of one person is computed by the use of Table I in paragraph (f) of this section. The present value of an annuity, term for years, remainder or reversion dependent on a term certain is computed by the use of Table II in paragraph (f). If the interest to be valued is dependent upon more than one life or there is a term certain concurrent with one or more lives, see paragraph (e) of this section. For purposes of the computations described in this section, the age of a person is to be taken as the age of that person at his nearest birthday.

(b) *Annuities*—(1) *Payable annually at end of year.* If an annuity is payable annually at the end of each year during the life of an individual (as, for example, if the first payment is due one year after decedent's death), the amount payable annually is multiplied by the figure in column 2 of Table I opposite the number of years in column 1 nearest the age of the individual whose life measures the duration of the annuity. If the annuity is payable annually at the end of each year for a definite number of years, the amount payable annually is multiplied by the figure in column 2 of Table II opposite the number of years in column 1 representing the duration of the annuity. The application of this subparagraph may be illustrated by the following examples:

Example (1). The decedent received, under the terms of his father's will an annuity of $10,000 a year payable annually for the life of his elder brother. At the time he died, an annual payment had just been made. The brother at the decedent's death was 40 years 8 months old. By reference to Table I, the figure in column 2 opposite 41 years, the number nearest to the brother's actual age, is found to be 17.6853. The present value of the annuity at the date of the decedent's death is, therefore, $176,853 ($10,000 × 17.6853).

Example (2). The decedent was entitled to receive an annuity of $10,000 a year payable annually throughout a term certain. At the time he died, an annual payment had just been made and five more annual payments were still to be made. By reference to Table II, it is found that the figure in column 2 opposite 5 years is 4.5151. The present value of the annuity is, therefore, $45,151 ($10,000 × 4.5151).

(2) *Payable at the end of semiannual, quarterly, monthly, or weekly periods.* If an annuity is payable at the end of semiannual, quarterly, monthly, or weekly periods during the life of an individual (as for example if the first payment is due one month after the decedent's

death), the aggregate amount to be paid within a year is first multiplied by the figure in column 2 of Table I opposite the number of years in column 1 nearest the age of the individual whose life measures the duration of the annuity. The product so obtained is then multiplied by whichever of the following factors is appropriate:

1.0087 for semiannual payments,
1.0130 for quarterly payments,
1.0159 for monthly payments, or
1.0171 for weekly payments.

If the annuity is payable at the end of semiannual, quarterly, monthly, or weekly periods for a definite number of years, the aggregate amount to be paid within a year is first multiplied by the figure in column 2 of Table II opposite the number of years in column 1 representing the duration of the annuity. The product so obtained is then multiplied by whichever of the above factors is appropriate. The application of this subparagraph may be illustrated by the following example:

Example. The facts are the same as those contained in example (1) set forth in subparagraph (1) of this paragraph, except that the annuity is payable semiannually. The aggregate annual amount, $10,000, is multiplied by the factor 17.6853, and the product multiplied by 1.0087. The present value of the annuity at the date of the decedent's death is, therefore, $178,391.62 ($10,000 × 17.6853 × 1.0087).

(3) *Payable at the beginning of annual, semiannual, quarterly, monthly, or weekly periods.* (i) If the first payment of an annuity for the life of an individual is due at the beginning of the annual or other payment period rather than at the end (as, for example, if the first payment is to be made immediately after the decedent's death), the value of the annuity is the sum of *(a)* the first payment plus *(b)* the present value of a similar annuity, the first payment of which is not to be made until the end of the payment period, determined as provided in subparagraph (1) or (2) of this paragraph. The application of this subdivision may be illustrated by the following example:

Example. The decedent was entitled to receive an annuity of $50 a month during the life of another. The decedent died on a day the payment was due. At the date of the decedent's death, the person whose life measures the duration of the annuity was 50 years of age. The value of the annuity at the date of the decedent's death is $50 plus the product of $50 × 12 × 14.8486 (see Table I) × 1.0159 (see subparagraph (2) of this paragraph), or $9,100.82.

(ii) If the first payment of an annuity for a definite number of years is due at the beginning of the annual or other payment period, the applicable factor is the product of the factor shown in Table II multiplied by whichever of the following factors is appropriate:

1.0350 for annual payments,
1.0262 for semiannual payments,
1.0218 for quarterly payments,
1.0189 for monthly payments, or
1.0177 for weekly payments.

919

The application of this subdivision may be illustrated by the following example:

Example. The decedent was the beneficiary of an annuity of $50 a month. On the day a payment was due, the decedent died. There were 300 payments to be made, including the payment due. The value of the annuity as of the date of decedent's death is the product of $50 × 12 × 16.4815 (see Table II) × 1.0189, or $10,075.80.

(c) *Life estates and terms for years.* If the interest to be valued is the right of a person for his life, or for the life of another person, to receive the income of certain property or to use nonincome-producing property, the value of the interest is the value of the property multiplied by the figure in column 3 of Table I opposite the number of years nearest to the actual age of the measuring life. If the interest to be valued is the right to receive income of property or to use nonincome-producing property for a term of years, column 3 of Table II is used. The application of this paragraph may be illustrated by the following example:

Example. The decedent or his estate was entitled to receive the income from a fund of $50,000 during the life of his elder brother. Upon the brother's death, the remainder is to go to X. The brother was 31 years 5 months old at the time of decedent's death. By reference to Table I, the figure in column 3 opposite 31 years is found to be 0.71068. The present value of decedent's interest is, therefore, $35,534 ($50,000 × 0.71068).

(d) *Remainders or reversionary interests.* If a decedent had, at the time of his death, a remainder or a reversionary interest in property to take effect after an estate for the life of another, the present value of his interest is obtained by multiplying the value of the property by the figure in column 4 of Table I opposite the number of years nearest to the actual age of the person whose life measures the preceding estate. If the remainder or reversion is to take effect at the end of a term for years, column 4 of Table II is used. The application of this paragraph may be illustrated by the following example:

Example. The decedent was entitled to receive certain property worth $50,000 upon the death of his elder brother, to whom the income was bequeathed for life. At the time of the decedent's death, the elder brother was 31 years 5 months old. By reference to Table I, the figure in column 4 opposite 31 years is found to be 0.28932. The present value of the remainder interest at the date of decedent's death is, therefore, $14,466 ($50,000 × 0.28932).

(e) *Actuarial computations by the Internal Revenue Service.* If the valuation of the interest involved is dependent upon the continuation or the termination of more than one life or upon a term certain concurrent with one or more lives, a special factor must be used. The factor is to be computed upon the basis of the Makehamized mortality table appearing as Table 38 of United States Life Tables and Actuarial Tables 1939–1941, published by the United States Department of Commerce, Bureau of Census, and interest at the rate of $3\frac{1}{2}$ percent a year, compounded annually. Many such factors may be found in, or readily computed with the use of the tables contained in, a pamphlet entitled "Actuarial Values for Estate and Gift Tax." This pamphlet may be purchased from the Superintendent of Documents, United States Government Printing Office, Washington 25, D. C. However, if a special factor is required in the case of an actual decedent, the Commissioner will furnish the factor to the executor upon request. The request must be accompanied by a statement of the date of birth of each person, the duration of whose life may affect the value of the interest, and by copies of the relevants instruments.

(f) The following tables shall be used in the application of the provisions of this section:

TABLE I

Table, single life, 3½ percent, showing the present worth of an annuity, of a life interest, and of a remainder interest

1 Age	2 Annuity	3 Life Estate	4 Remainder	1 Age	2 Annuity	3 Life Estate	4 Remainder
0	23.9685	.83890	.16110	39	18.2566	.63898	.36102
1	24.9035	.87162	.12838	40	17.9738	.62908	.37092
2	24.8920	.87122	.12878	41	17.6853	.61899	.38101
3	24.8246	.86886	.13114	42	17.3911	.60869	.39131
4	24.7378	.86582	.13418	43	17.0913	.59820	.40180
5	24.6392	.86237	.13763	44	16.7860	.58751	.41249
6	24.5326	.85864	.14136	45	16.4754	.57664	.42336
7	24.4188	.85466	.14534	46	16.1596	.56559	.43441
8	24.2982	.85044	.14956	47	15.8388	.55436	.44564
9	24.1713	.84600	.15400	48	15.5133	.54297	.45703
10	24.0387	.84135	.15865	49	15.1831	.53141	.46859
11	23.9008	.83653	.16347	50	14.8486	.51970	.48030
12	23.7600	.83160	.16840	51	14.5101	.50785	.49215
13	23.6161	.82656	.17344	52	14.1678	.49587	.50413
14	23.4693	.82143	.17857	53	13.8221	.48377	.51623
15	23.3194	.81618	.18382	54	13.4734	.47157	.52843
16	23.1665	.81083	.18917	55	13.1218	.45926	.54074
17	23.0103	.80536	.19464	56	12.7679	.44688	.55312
18	22.8511	.79979	.20021	57	12.4120	.43442	.56558
19	22.6870	.79404	.20596	58	12.0546	.42191	.57809
20	22.5179	.78813	.21187	59	11.6960	.40936	.59064
21	22.3438	.78203	.21797	60	11.3369	.39679	.60321
22	22.1646	.77576	.22424	61	10.9776	.38422	.61578
23	21.9801	.76930	.23070	62	10.6186	.37165	.62835
24	21.7902	.76266	.23734	63	10.2604	.35911	.64089
25	21.5950	.75582	.24418	64	9.9036	.34663	.65337
26	21.3942	.74880	.25120	65	9.5486	.33420	.66580
27	21.1878	.74157	.25843	66	9.1960	.32186	.67814
28	20.9759	.73416	.26584	67	8.8464	.30962	.69038
29	20.7581	.72653	.27347	68	8.5001	.29750	.70250
30	20.5345	.71871	.28129	69	8.1578	.28552	.71448
31	20.3052	.71068	.28932	70	7.8200	.27370	.72630
32	20.0699	.70245	.29755	71	7.4871	.26205	.73795
33	19.8288	.69401	.30599	72	7.1597	.25059	.74941
34	19.5816	.68536	.31464	73	6.8382	.23934	.76066
35	19.3285	.67650	.32350	74	6.5231	.22831	.77169
36	19.0695	.66743	.33257	75	6.2148	.21752	.78248
37	18.8044	.65815	.34185	76	5.9137	.20698	.79302
38	18.5334	.64867	.35133	77	5.6201	.19670	.80330

Table, single life, 3½ percent, showing the present worth of an annuity, of a life interest, and of a remainder interest

1 Age	2 Annuity	3 Life Estate	4 Remainder	1 Age	2 Annuity	3 Life Estate	4 Remainder
78	5.3345	.18671	.81329	92	2.2754	.07964	.92036
79	5.0572	.17700	.82300	93	2.1254	.07439	.92561
80	4.7884	.16759	.83241	94	1.9839	.06944	.93056
81	4.5283	.15849	.84151	95	1.8507	.06477	.93523
82	4.2771	.14970	.85030	96	1.7256	.06040	.93960
83	4.0351	.14123	.85877	97	1.6082	.05629	.94371
84	3.8023	.13308	.86692	98	1.4982	.05244	.94756
85	3.5789	.12526	.87474	99	1.3949	.04882	.95118
86	3.3648	.11777	.88223	100	1.2973	.04541	.95459
87	3.1601	.11060	.88940	101	1.2033	.04212	.95788
88	2.9648	.10377	.89623	102	1.1078	.03877	.96123
89	2.7788	.09726	.90274	103	.9973	.03491	.96509
90	2.6019	.09107	.90893	104	.8318	.02911	.97089
91	2.4342	.08520	.91480	105	.4831	.01691	.98309

TABLE II

Table showing the present worth at 3½ percent of an annuity for a term certain, of an income interest for a term certain, and of a remainder interest postponed for a term certain

1 Number of Years	2 Annuity	3 Term Certain	4 Remainder	1 Number of Years	2 Annuity	3 Term Certain	4 Remainder
1	0.9662	.033816	.966184	16	12.0941	.423294	.576706
2	1.8997	.066489	.933511	17	12.6513	.442796	.557204
3	2.8016	.098057	.901943	18	13.1897	.461639	.538361
4	3.6731	.128558	.871442	19	13.7098	.479844	.520156
5	4.5151	.158027	.841973	20	14.2124	.497434	.502566
6	5.3286	.186499	.813501	21	14.6980	.514429	.485571
7	6.1145	.214009	.785991	22	15.1671	.530849	.469151
8	6.8740	.240588	.759412	23	15.6204	.546714	.453286
9	7.6077	.266269	.733731	24	16.0584	.562043	.437957
10	8.3166	.291081	.708919	25	16.4815	.576853	.423147
11	9.0016	.315054	.684946	26	16.8904	.591162	.408838
12	9.6633	.338217	.661783	27	17.2854	.604988	.395012
13	10.3027	.360596	.639404	28	17.6670	.618346	.381654
14	10.9205	.382218	.617782	29	18.0358	.631252	.368748
15	11.5174	.403109	.596891	30	18.3920	.643722	.356278

§ 20.2031-8 **Valuation of certain life insurance and annuity contracts.** (a) The value of a contract for the payment of an annuity, or an insurance policy on the life of a person other than the decedent, issued by a company regularly engaged in the selling of contracts of that character is established through the sale by that company of comparable contracts. An annuity payable under a combination annuity contract and life insurance policy on the decedent's life (e.g., a "retirement income" policy with death benefit) under which there was no insurance element at the time of the decedent's death (see paragraph (d) of § 20.2039-1) is treated like a contract for the payment of an annuity for purposes of this section.

922

(b) As valuation of an insurance policy through sale of comparable contracts is not readily ascertainable when, at the date of the decedent's death, the contract has been in force for some time and further premium payments are to be made, the value may be approximated by adding to the interpolated terminal reserve at the date of the decedent's death the proportionate part of the gross premium last paid before the date of the decedent's death which covers the period extending beyond that date. If, however, because of the unusual nature of the contract such an approximation is not reasonably close to the full value of the contract, this method may not be used.

(c) The application of this section may be illustrated by the following examples. In each case involving an insurance contract, it is assumed that there are no accrued dividends or outstanding indebtedness on the contract.

Example (1). X purchased from a life insurance company a joint and survivor annuity contract under the terms of which X was to receive payments of $1,200 annually for his life and, upon X's death, his wife was to receive payments of $1,200 annually for her life. Five years after such purchase, when his wife was 50 years of age, X died. The value of the annuity contract at the date of X's death is the amount which the company would charge for an annuity providing for the payment of $1,200 annually for the life of a female 50 years of age.

Example (2). Y died holding the incidents of ownership in a life insurance policy on the life of his wife. The policy was one on which no further payments were to be made to the company (e.g., a single premium policy or a paid-up policy). The value of the insurance policy at the date of Y's death is the amount which the company would charge for a single premium contract of the same specified amount on the life of a person of the age of the insured.

Example (3). Z died holding the incidents of ownership in a life insurance policy on the life of his wife. The policy was an ordinary life policy issued nine years and four months prior to Z's death and at a time when Z's wife was 35 years of age. The gross annual premium is $2,811 and the decedent died four months after the last premium due date. The value of the insurance policy at the date of Z's death is computed as follows:

Terminal reserve at end of tenth year	$14,601.00
Terminal reserve at end of ninth year	12,965.00
Increase	1,636.00
One-third of such increase (Z having died four months following the last preceding premium due date) is	545.33
Terminal reserve at end of ninth year	12,965.00
Interpolated terminal reserve at date of Z's death	13,510.33
Two-thirds of gross premium ($\frac{2}{3} \times$ $2,811)	1,874.00
Value of the insurance policy	15,384.33

§ 20.2031-9 **Valuation of other property.** The valuation of any property not specifically described in §§ 20.2031-2 through 20.2031-8 is made in accordance with the general principles set forth in § 20.2031-1. For example, a future interest in property not subject to valuation in accordance with the actuarial principles set forth in § 20.2031-7 is to be valued in accordance with the general principles set forth in § 20.2031-1.

§ 20.2032-1 **Alternate valuation**—(a) *In general.* In general, section 2032 provides for the valuation of a decedent's gross estate at a date other than the date of the decedent's death. More specifically, if an executor elects the alternate valuation method under section 2032, the property included in the decedent's gross estate on the date of his death is valued as of whichever of the following dates is applicable:

(1) Any property distributed, sold, exchanged, or otherwise disposed of within one year after the decedent's death is valued as of the date on which it is first distributed, sold, exchanged, or otherwise disposed of;

(2) Any property not distributed, sold, exchanged, or otherwise disposed of within one year after the decedent's death is valued as of the date one year after the date of the decedent's death;

(3) Any property, interest, or estate which is affected by mere lapse of time is valued as of the date of the decedent's death, but adjusted for any difference in its value not due to mere lapse of time as of the date one year after the decedent's death, or as of the date of its distribution, sale, exchange, or other disposition, whichever date first occurs.

(b) *Method and effect of election.* (1) While it is the purpose of section 2032 to permit a reduction in the amount of tax that would otherwise be payable if the gross estate has suffered a shrinkage in its aggregate value in the year following the decedent's death, the alternate valuation method is not automatic but must be elected. Furthermore, the alternate valuation method may be elected whether or not there has been a shrinkage in the aggregate value of the estate. However, the election is not effective for any purpose unless the value of the gross estate at the time of the decedent's death exceeded $60,000, so that an estate tax return is required to be filed under section 6018.

(2) If the alternate valuation method under section 2032 is to be used, section 2032(c) requires that the executor must so elect on the estate tax return required under section 6018, filed within 15 months from the date of the decedent's death or within the period of any extension of time granted by the district director under section 6081. In no case may the election be exercised, or a previous election changed, after the expiration of such time. If the election is made, it applies to all the property included in the gross estate, and cannot be applied to only a portion of the property.

(c) *Meaning of "distributed, sold, exchanged, or otherwise disposed of".* (1) The phrase "distributed, sold, exchanged, or otherwise disposed of" comprehends all possible ways by which property ceases to form a part of the gross estate. For example, money on hand at the date of the decedent's death which is thereafter used in the payment of

924

funeral expenses, or which is thereafter invested, falls within the term "otherwise disposed of." The term also includes the surrender of a stock certificate for corporate assets in complete or partial liquidation of a corporation pursuant to section 331. The term does not, however, extend to transactions which are mere changes in form. Thus, it does not include a transfer of assets to a corporation in exchange for its stock in a transaction with respect to which no gain or loss would be recognizable for income tax purposes under section 351. Nor does it include an exchange of stock or securities in a corporation for stock or securities in the same corporation or another corporation in a transaction, such as a merger, recapitalization, reorganization or other transaction described in section 368(a) or 355, with respect to which no gain or loss is recognizable for income tax purposes under section 354 or 355.

(2) Property may be "distributed" either by the executor, or by a trustee of property included in the gross estate under sections 2035 through 2038, or section 2041. Property is considered as "distributed" upon the first to occur of the following:

(i) The entry of an order or decree of distribution, if the order or decree subsequently becomes final;

(ii) The segregation or separation of the property from the estate or trust so that it becomes unqualifiedly subject to the demand or disposition of the distributee; or

(iii) The actual paying over or delivery of the property to the distributee.

(3) Property may be "sold, exchanged, or otherwise disposed of" by: (i) the executor; (ii) a trustee or other donee to whom the decedent during his lifetime transferred property included in his gross estate under sections 2035 through 2038, or section 2041; (iii) an heir or devisee to whom title to property passes directly under local law; (iv) a surviving joint tenant or tenant by the entirety; or (v) any other person. If a binding contract for the sale, exchange, or other disposition of property is entered into, the property is considered as sold, exchanged, or otherwise disposed of on the effective date of the contract, unless the contract is not subsequently carried out substantially in accordance with its terms. The effective date of a contract is normally the date it is entered into (and not the date it is consummated, or the date legal title to the property passes) unless the contract specifies a different effective date.

(d) *"Included property" and "excluded property"*. If the executor elects the alternate valuation method under section 2032, all property interests existing at the date of decedent's death which form a part of his gross estate as determined under sections 2033 through 2044 are valued in accordance with the provisions of this section. Such property interests are hereinafter referred to in this section as "included property". Furthermore, such property interests remain "included property" for the purpose of valuing the gross estate under the alternate valuation method even though they change in form during the alternate valuation period by being actually received, or disposed of, in whole or in part, by the estate. On the other hand, property earned or accrued (whether received or not) after the date of the decedent's death and during the alternate valuation period with respect to any property interest existing at the date of the decedent's death, which does not represent a form of "included property" itself or the receipt of "included property", is excluded in valuing the gross estate under the alternate valuation method. Such property is hereinafter referred to in this section as "excluded property". Illustrations of "included property" and "excluded property" are contained in the subparagraphs that follow:

(1) *Interest-bearing obligations.* Interest-bearing obligations, such as bonds or notes, may compromise two elements of "included property" at the date of the decedent's death, namely, (i) the principal of the obligation itself, and (ii) interest accrued to the date of death. Each of these elements is to be separately valued as of the applicable valuation date. Interest accrued after the date of death and before the subsequent valuation date constitutes "excluded property". However, any part payment of principal made between the date of death and the subsequent valuation date, or any advance payment of interest for a period after the subsequent valuation date made during the alternate valuation period which has the effect of reducing the value of the principal obligation as of the subsequent valuation date, will be included in the gross estate, and valued as of the date of such payment.

(2) *Leased property.* The principles set forth in subparagraph (1) of this paragraph with respect to interest-bearing obligations also apply to leased realty or personalty which is included in the gross estate and with respect to which an obligation to pay rent has been reserved. Both the realty or personalty itself and the rents accrued to the date of death constitute "included property", and each is to be separately valued as of the applicable valuation date. Any rent accrued after the date of death and before the subsequent valuation date is "excluded property". Similarly, the principle applicable with respect to interest paid in advance is equally applicable with respect to advance payments of rent.

(3) *Noninterest-bearing obligations.* In the case of noninterest-bearing obligations sold at a discount, such as savings bonds, the principal obligation and the discount amortized to the date of death are property interests existing at the date of death and constitute "included property". The obligation itself is to be valued at the subsequent valuation date without regard to any further increase in value due to amortized discount. The additional discount amortized after death and during the alternate valuation period is the equivalent of interest accruing during that period and is, therefore, not to be included in the gross estate under the alternate valuation method.

(4) *Stock of a corporation.* Shares of stock in a corporation and dividends declared to stockholders of record on or before the date of the decedent's death and not collected at the date of death constitute "included property" of the estate. On the other hand, ordinary dividends out of earnings and profits (whether in cash, shares of the corporation, or other property) declared to stockholders of record after the date of the decedent's death are "excluded property" and are not to be

valued under the alternate valuation method. If, however, dividends are declared to stockholders of record after the date of the decedent's death with the effect that the shares of stock at the subsequent valuation date do not reasonably represent the same "included property" of the gross estate as existed at the date of the decedent's death, the dividends are "included property", except to the extent that they are out of earnings of the corporation after the date of the decedent's death. For example, if a corporation makes a distribution in partial liquidation to stockholders of record during the alternate valuation period which is not accompanied by a surrender of a stock certificate for cancellation, the amount of the distribution received on stock included in the gross estate is itself "included property", except to the extent that the distribution was out of earnings and profits since the date of the decedent's death. Similarly, if a corporation, in which the decedent owned a substantial interest and which possessed at the date of the decedent's death accumulated earnings and profits equal to its paid-in capital, distributed all of its accumulated earnings and profits as a cash dividend to shareholders of record during the alternate valuation period, the amount of the dividends received on stock includible in the gross estate will be included in the gross estate under the alternate valuation method. Likewise, a stock dividend distributed under such circumstances is "included property".

(e) *Illustrations of "included property" and "excluded property".* The application of paragraph (d) of this section may be further illustrated by the following example in which it is assumed that the decedent died on January 1, 1955:

Description	Subsequent valuation date	Alternate value	Value at date of death
Bond, par value $1,000, bearing interest at 4% payable quarterly on Feb. 1, May 1, Aug. 1, and Nov. 1. Bond distributed to legatee on Mar. 1, 1955	Mar. 1, 1955	$1,000.00	$1,000.00
Interest coupon of $10 attached to bond and not cashed at date of death although due and payable Nov. 1, 1954. Cashed by executor on Feb. 1, 1955	Feb. 1, 1955	10.00	10.00
Interest accrued from Nov. 1, 1954, to Jan. 1, 1955, collected on Feb. 1, 1955	Feb. 1, 1955	6.67	6.67
Real estate, not disposed of within year following death. Rent of $300 due at the end of each quarter, Feb. 1, May 1, Aug. 1, and Nov. 1,	Jan. 1, 1956	11,000.00	12,000.00
Rent due for quarter ending Nov. 1, 1954, but not collected until Feb. 1, 1955	Feb. 1, 1955	300.00	300.00
Rent accrued for November and December 1954, collected on Feb. 1, 1955	Feb. 1, 1955	200.00	200.00
Common stock, X Corporation, 500 shares, not disposed of within year following decedent's death	Jan. 1, 1956	47,500.00	50,000.00
Dividend of $2 per share declared Dec. 10, 1954, and paid on Jan. 10, 1955, to holders of record on Dec. 30, 1954	Jan. 10, 1955	1,000.00	1,000.00

(f) *Mere lapse of time.* In order to eliminate changes in value due only to mere lapse of time, section 2032(a)(3) provides that any interest or estate "affected by mere lapse of time" is included in a decedent's gross estate under the alternate valuation method at its value as of the date of the decedent's death, but with adjustment for any difference in its value as of the subsequent valuation date not due to mere lapse of time. Properties, interests, or estates which are "affected by mere lapse of time" include patents, estates for the life of a person other than the decedent, remainders, reversions, and other like properties, interests, or estates. The phrase "affected by mere lapse of time" has no reference to obligations for the payment of money, whether or not interest-bearing, the value of which changes with the passing of time. However, such an obligation, like any other property, may become affected by lapse of time when made the subject of a bequest or transfer which itself is creative of an interest or estate so affected. The application of this paragraph is illustrated in the following subparagraphs:

(1) *Life estates, remainders, and similar interests.* The values of life estates, remainders, and similar interests are to be obtained by applying the methods prescribed in § 20.2031-7, using (i) the age of each person, the duration of whose life may affect the value of the interest, as of the date of the decedent's death, and (ii) the value of the property as of the alternate date. For example, assume that the decedent or his estate was entitled to receive property upon the death of his elder brother who was entitled to receive the income therefrom for life. At the date of the decedent's death, the property was worth $50,000 and the elder brother was 31 years old. The value of the decedent's remainder interest at the date of his death would, as explained in § 20.2031-7(d), be $14,466 ($50,000 × 0.28932). If, because of economic conditions, the property declined in value and was worth only $40,000 one year after the date of the decedent's death, the value of the remainder interest as of the alternate date would be $11,572.80 ($40,000 × 0.28932).

(2) *Patents.* To illustrate the alternate valuation of a patent, assume that the decedent owned a patent which, on the date of the decedent's death, had an unexpired term of ten years and a value of $78,000. Six months after the date of the decedent's death, the patent was sold, because of lapse of time and other causes, for $60,000. The alternate value thereof would be obtained by dividing $60,000 by 0.95 (ratio of the remaining life of the patent at the alternate date to the remaining life of the patent at the date of the decedent's death), and would, therefore, be $63,157.89.

(g) *Effect of election on deductions.* If the executor elects the alternate valuation method under section 2032, any deduction for administration expenses under section 2053(b) (pertaining to property not subject to claims) or losses under section 2054 (or section 2106(a)(1), relating to estates of nonresidents not citizens) is allowed only to the extent that it is not otherwise in effect allowed in determining the value of the gross estate. Furthermore, the amount of any charitable deduction under section 2055 (or section 2106(a)(2), relating to the estates of nonresidents not citizens) or the amount of any marital

928

deduction under section 2056 is determined by the value of the property with respect to which the deduction is allowed as of the date of the decedent's death, adjusted, however, for any difference in its value as of the date one year after death, or as of the date of its distribution, sale, exchange, or other disposition, whichever first occurs. However, no such adjustment may take into account any difference in value due to lapse of time or to the occurrence or nonoccurrence of a contingency.

§ 20.2033-1 **Property in which the decedent had an interest**—(a) *In general.* The gross estate of a decedent who was a citizen or resident of the United States at the time of his death includes under section 2033 the value of all property, whether real or personal, tangible or intangible, and wherever situated, beneficially owned by the decedent at the time of his death, except real property situated outside of the United States. Real property situated in the United States is included whether it came into the possession anh control of the executor or administrator or passed directly to heirs or devisees. Various statutory provisions which exempt bonds, notes, bills, and certificates of indebtedness of the Federal Government or its agencies and the interest thereon from taxation are generally not applicable to the estate tax, since such tax is an excise tax on the transfer of property at death and is not a tax on the property transferred.

(b) *Miscellaneous examples.* A cemetery lot owned by the decedent is part of his gross estate, but its value is limited to the salable value of that part of the lot which is not designed for the interment of the decedent and the members of his family. Property subject to homestead or other exemptions under local law is included in the gross estate. Notes or other claims held by the decedent are likewise included even though they are cancelled by the decedent's will. Interest and rents accrued at the date of the decedent's death constitute a part of the gross estate. Similarly, dividends which are payable to the decedent or his estate by reason of the fact that on or before the date of the decedent's death he was a stockholder of record (but which have not been collected at death) constitute a part of the gross estate.

§ 20.2034-1 **Dower or curtesy interests.** A decedent's gross estate includes under section 2034 any interest in property of the decedent's surviving spouse existing at the time of the decedent's death as dower or curtesy, or any interest created by statute in lieu thereof (although such other interest may differ in character from dower or curtesy). Thus, the full value of property is included in the decedent's gross estate, without deduction of such an interest of the surviving husband or wife, and without regard to when the right to such an interest arose.

Transfers During Lifetime

§ 20.2035-1 **Transactions in contemplation of death**—(a) *In general.* A decedent's gross estate includes under section 2035 the value of any interest in property transferred by a decedent in contemplation of death within 3 years before his death, except to the extent that the transfer was for a full and adequate consideration in money or money's worth (see § 20.2043-1). With the exception noted in the preceding sentence, the decedent's gross estate includes as a transfer in contemplation of death the value of any interest in property transferred within 3 years before the decedent's death, unless the transfer is shown not to have been made in contemplation of death. The result is not affected by the fact that at the time of the transfer the decedent parted absolutely and immediately with his enjoyment of and title to the property.

(b) *Application of other sections.* If a decedent transfers an interest in property or relinquishes a power in contemplation of death, the decedent's gross estate includes the property subject to the interest or power to the extent that it would be included under section 2036, 2037, or 2038 if the decedent had retained the interest or power until his death. If a decedent exercises or releases a general power of appointment in contemplation of death, the property subject to the power is included in the decedent's gross estate to the extent provided in section 2041 and the regulations thereunder.

(c) *Definition.* The phrase "in contemplation of death," as used in this section, does not have reference to that general expectation of death such as all persons entertain. On the other hand, its meaning is not restricted to an apprehension that death is imminent or near. A transfer "in contemplation of death" is a disposition of property prompted by the thought of death (although it need not be solely so prompted). A transfer is prompted by the thought of death if (1) made with the purpose of avoiding death taxes, (2) made as a substitute for a testamentary disposition of the property, or (3) made for any other motive associated with death. The bodily and mental condition of the decedent and all other attendant facts and circumstances are to be scrutinized in order to determine whether or not such thought prompted the disposition.

(d) *Presumptions.* Any transfer of an interest in property, relinquishment of a power, or exercise or release of a general power of appointment by a decedent within a period of 3 years ending with the date of his death is deemed to have been made "in contemplation of death," unless shown to the contrary. No transfer, relinquishment, exercise, or release made by a decedent more than 3 years before his death is treated as having been made "in contemplation of death."

(e) *Valuation.* The value of an interest in transferred property includible in a decedent's gross estate under this section is the value of the interest as of the applicable valuation date. In this connection, see sections 2031, 2032, and the regulations thereunder. However, if the transferee has made improvements or additions to the property, any resulting enhancement in the value of the property is not considered in ascertaining the value of the gross estate. Similarly, neither income received subsequent to the transfer nor property purchased with such income is considered.

[Harris]

§ 20.2036-1 **Transfers with retained life estate**—(a) *In general.*
A decedent's gross estate includes under section 2036 the value of
any interest in property transferred by the decedent after March 3,
1931, whether in trust or otherwise, except to the extent that the
transfer was for an adequate and full consideration in money or
money's worth (see § 20.2043-1), if the decedent retained or reserved
(1) for his life, or (2) for any period not ascertainable without reference to his death (if the transfer was made after June 6, 1932), or
(3) for any period which does not in fact end before his death—

(i) The use, possession, right to the income, or other enjoyment
of the transferred property, or

(ii) The right, either alone or in conjunction with any other person
or persons, to designate the person or persons who shall possess or
enjoy the transferred property or its income.

If the decedent retained or reserved an interest or right with respect
to all of the property transferred by him, the amount to be included
in his gross estate under section 2036 is the value of the entire property, less only the value of any outstanding income interest which
is not subject to the decedent's interest or right and which is actually
being enjoyed by another person at the time of the decedent's death.
If the decedent retained or reserved an interest or right with respect
to a part only of the property transferred by him, the amount to be
included in his gross estate under section 2036 is only a corresponding proportion of the amount described in the preceding sentence. An
interest or right is treated as having been retained or reserved if
at the time of the transfer there was an understanding, express or
implied, that the interest or right would later be conferred.

(b) *Meaning of terms.* (1) A reservation by the decedent "for
any period not ascertainable without reference to his death" may be
illustrated by the following examples:

(i) A decedent reserved the right to receive the income from transferred property in quarterly payments, with the proviso that no part
of the income between the last quarterly payment and the date of
the decedent's death was to be received by the decedent or his estate;
and

(ii) A decedent reserved the right to receive the income from transferred property after the death of another person who was in fact
enjoying the income at the time of the decedent's death. In such a
case, the amount to be included in the decedent's gross estate under
this section does not include the value of the outstanding income interest of the other person. It may be noted that if the other person
predeceased the decedent, the reservation by the decedent may be
considered to be either for his life, or for a period which does not
in fact end before his death.

(2) The "use, possession, right to the income, or other enjoyment
of the transferred property" is considered as having been retained by
or reserved to the decedent to the extent that the use, possession,
right to the income, or other enjoyment is to be applied toward the
discharge of a legal obligation of the decedent, or otherwise for his

pecuniary benefit. The term "legal obligation" includes a legal obligation to support a dependent during the decedent's lifetime.

(3) The phrase "right . . . to designate the person or persons who shall possess or enjoy the transferred property or the income therefrom" includes a reserved power to designate the person or persons to receive the income from the transferred property, or to possess or enjoy nonincome-producing property, during the decedent's life or during any other period described in paragraph (a) of this section. With respect to such a power, it is immaterial (i) whether the power was exercisable alone or only in conjunction with another person or persons, whether or not having an adverse interest; (ii) in what capacity the power was exercisable by the decedent or by another person or persons in conjunction with the decedent; and (iii) whether the exercise of the power was subject to a contingency beyond the decedent's control which did not occur before his death (e.g., the death of another person during the decedent's lifetime). The phrase, however, does not include a power over the transferred property itself which does not affect the enjoyment of the income received or earned during the decedent's life. (See, however, section 2038 for the inclusion of property in the gross estate on account of such a power.) Nor does the phrase apply to a power held solely by a person other than the decedent. But, for example, if the decedent reserved the unrestricted power to remove or discharge a trustee at any time and appoint himself as trustee, the decedent is considered as having the powers of the trustee.

§ 20.2037-1 **Transfers taking effect at death**—(a) *In general.* A decedent's gross estate includes under section 2037 the value of any interest in property transferred by the decedent after September 7, 1916, whether in trust or otherwise, except to the extent that the transfer was for an adequate and full consideration in money or money's worth (see § 20.2043-1), if—

(1) Possession or enjoyment of the property could, through ownership of the interest, have been obtained only by surviving the decedent,

(2) The decedent had retained a possibility (hereinafter referred to as a "reversionary interest") that the property, other than the income alone, would return to the decedent or his estate or would be subject to a power of disposition by him, and

(3) The value of the reversionary interest immediately before the decedent's death exceeded 5 percent of the value of the entire property.

However, if the transfer was made before October 8, 1949, sction 2037 is applicable only if the reversionary interest arose by the express terms of the instrument of transfer and not by operation of law (see paragraph (f) of this section). See also paragraph (g) of this section with respect to transfers made between November 11, 1935, and January 29, 1940. The provisions of section 2037 do not apply to transfers made before September 8, 1916.

(b) *Condition of survivorship.* As indicated in paragraph (a) of this section, the value of an interest in transferred property is not included in a decedent's gross estate under section 2037 unless possession or enjoyment of the property could, through ownership of such interest, have been obtained only by surviving the decedent. Thus, property is not included in the decedent's gross estate if, immediately before the decedent's death, possession or enjoyment of the property could have been obtained by any beneficiary either by surviving the decedent or through the occurrence of some other event such as the expiration of a term of years. However, if a consideration of the terms and circumstances of the transfer as a whole indicates that the "other event" is unreal and if the death of the decedent does, in fact, occur before the "other event", the beneficiary will be considered able to possess or enjoy the property only by surviving the decedent. Notwithstanding the foregoing, an interest in transferred property is not includible in a decedent's gross estate under section 2037 if possession or enjoyment of the property could have been obtained by any beneficiary during the decedent's life through the exercise of a general power of appointment (as defined in section 2041) which in fact was exercisable immediately before the decedent's death. See examples (5) and (6) in paragraph (e) of this section.

(c) *Retention of reversionary interest.* (1) As indicated in paragraph (a) of this section, the value of an interest in transferred property is not included in a decedent's gross estate under section 2037 unless the decedent had retained a reversionary interest in the property, and the value of the reversionary interest immediately before the death of the decedent exceeded 5 percent of the value of the property.

(2) For purposes of section 2037, the term "reversionary interest" includes a possibility that property transferred by the decedent may return to him or his estate and a possibility that property transferred by the decedent may become subject to a power of disposition by him. The term is not used in a technical sense, but has reference to any reserved right under which the transferred property shall or may be returned to the grantor. Thus, it encompasses an interest arising either by the express terms of the instrument of transfer or by operation of law. (See, however, paragraph (f) of this section, with respect to transfers made before October 8, 1949.) The term "reversionary interest" does not include rights to income only, such as the right to receive the income from a trust after the death of another person. (However, see section 2036 for the inclusion of property in the gross estate on account of such rights.) Nor does the term "reversionary interest" include the possibility that the decedent during his lifetime might have received back an interest in transferred property by inheritance through the estate of another person. Similarly, a statutory right of a spouse to receive a portion of whatever estate a decedent may leave at the time of his death is not a "reversionary interest".

(3) For purposes of this section, the value of the decedent's reversionary interest is computed as of the moment immediately before his death, without regard to whether or not the executor elects the alter-

nate valuation method under section 2032 and without regard to the fact of the decedent's death. The value is ascertained in accordance with recognized valuation principles for determining the value for estate tax purposes of future or conditional interests in property. (See §§ 20.2031-1, 20.2031-7, and 20.2031-9.) For example, if the decedent's reversionary interest was subject to an outstanding life estate in his wife, his interest is valued according to the actuarial rules set forth in § 20.2031-7. On the other hand, if the decedent's reversionary interest was contingent on the death of his wife without issue surviving and if it cannot be shown that his wife is incapable of having issue (so that his interest is not subject to valuation according to the § 20.2031-7 actuarial rules), his interest is valued according to the general rules set forth in § 20.2031-1. A possibility that the decedent may be able to dispose of property under certain conditions is considered to have the same value as a right of the decedent to the return of the property under those same conditions.

(4) In order to determine whether or not the decedent retained a reversionary interest in transferred property of a value in excess of 5 percent, the value of the reversionary interest is compared with the value of the transferred property, including interests therein which are not dependent upon survivorship of the decedent. For example, assume that the decedent, A, transferred property in trust with the income payable to B for life and with the remainder payable to C if A predeceases B, but with the property to revert to A if B predeceases A. Assume further that A does, in fact, predecease B. The value of A's reversionary interest immediately before his death is compared with the value of the trust corpus, without deduction of the value of B's outstanding life estate. If, in the above example, A had retained a reversionary interest in one-half only of the trust corpus, the value of his reversionary interest would be compared with the value of one-half of the trust corpus, again without deduction of any part of the value of B's outstanding life estate.

(d) *Transfers partly taking effect at death.* If separate interests in property are transferred to one or more beneficiaries, paragraphs (a) through (c) of this section are to be separately applied with respect to each interest. For example, assume that the decedent transferred an interest in Blackacre to A which could be possessed or enjoyed only by surviving the decedent, and that the decedent transferred an interest in Blackacre to B which could be possessed or enjoyed only on the occurrence of some event unrelated to the decedent's death. Assume further that the decedent retained a reversionary interest in Blackacre of a value in excess of 5 percent. Only the value of the interest transferred to A is includible in the decedent's gross estate. Similar results would obtain if possession or enjoyment of the entire property could have been obtained only by surviving the decedent, but the decedent had retained a reversionary interest in a part only of such property.

(e) *Examples.* The provisions of paragraphs (a) through (d) of this section may be further illustrated by the following examples. It is assumed that the transfers were made on or after October 8, 1949;

for the significance of this date, see paragraphs (f) and (g) of this section:

Example (1). The decedent transferred property in trust with the income payable to his wife for life and, at her death, remainder to the decedent's then surviving children, or if none, to the decedent or his estate. Since each beneficiary can possess or enjoy the property without surviving the decedent, no part of the property is includible in the decedent's gross estate under section 2037, regardless of the value of the decedent's reversionary interest. (However, see section 2033 for inclusion of the value of the reversionary interest in the decedent's gross estate.)

Example (2). The decedent transferred property in trust with the income to be accumulated for the decedent's life, and at his death, principal and accumulated income to be paid to the decedent's then surviving issue, or if none, to A or A's estate. Since the decedent retained no reversionary interest in the property, no part of the property is includible in the decedent's gross estate, even though possession or enjoyment of the property could be obtained by the issue only by surviving the decedent.

Example (3). The decedent transferred property in trust with the income payable to his wife for life and with the remainder payable to the decedent or, if he is not living at his wife's death, to his daughter or her estate. The daughter cannot obtain possession or enjoyment of the property without surviving the decedent. Therefore, if the decedent's reversionary interest immediately before his death exceeded 5 percent of the value of the property, the value of the property, less the value of the wife's outstanding life estate, is includible in the decedent's gross estate.

Example (4). The decedent transferred property in trust with the income payable to his wife for life and with the remainder payable to his son or, if the son is not living at the wife's death, to the decedent or, if the decedent is not then living, to X or X's estate. Assume that the decedent was survived by his wife, his son, and X. Only X cannot obtain possession or enjoyment of the property without surviving the decedent. Therefore, if the decedent's reversionary interest immediately before his death exceeded 5 percent of the value of the property, the value of X's remainder interest (with reference to the time immediately after the decedent's death) is includible in the decedent's gross estate.

Example (5). The decedent transferred property in trust with the income to be accumulated for a period of 20 years or until the decedent's prior death, at which time the principal and accumulated income was to be paid to the decedent's son if then surviving. Assume that the decedent does, in fact, die before the expiration of the 20-year period. If, at the time of the transfer, the decedent was 30 years of age, in good health, etc., the son will be considered able to possess or enjoy the property without surviving the decedent. If, on the other hand, the decedent was 70 years of age at the time of the transfer, the son will not be considered able to possess or enjoy the property without surviving the decedent. In this latter case, if the value of the decedent's reversionary interest (arising by operation of law) immediately before his death exceeded 5 percent of the value of the property, the value of the property is includible in the decedent's gross estate.

Example (6). The decedent transferred property in trust with the income to be accumulated for his life and, at his death, the principal and accumulated income to be paid to the decedent's then surviving children. The decedent's wife was given the unrestricted power to alter, amend, or revoke the trust. Assume that the wife survived the decedent but did not, in fact, exercise her power during the decedent's lifetime. Since possession or enjoyment of the property could have been obtained by the wife during the decedent's lifetime under the exercise of a general power of appointment, which was, in fact, exercisable immediately before the decedent's death, no part of the property is includible in the decedent's gross estate.

(f) *Transfers made before October 8, 1949.* (1) Notwithstanding any provisions to the contrary contained in paragraphs (a) through (e) of this section, the value of an interest in property transferred by a decedent before October 8, 1949, is included in his gross estate under section 2037 only if the decedent's reversionary interest arose by the express terms of the instrument and not by operation of law. For example, assume that the decedent, on January 1, 1947, transferred property in trust with the income payable to his wife for the decedent's life and, at his death, remainder to his then surviving descendants. Since no provision was made for the contingency that no descendants of the decedent might survive him, a reversion to the decedent's estate existed by operation of law. The descendants cannot obtain possession or enjoyment of the property without surviving the decedent. However, since the decedent's reversionary interest arose by operation of law, no part of the property is includible in the decedent's gross estate under section 2037. If, in the above example, the transfer had been made on or after October 8, 1949, and if the decedent's reversionary interest immediately before his death exceeded 5 percent of the value of the property, the value of the property would be includible in the decedent's gross estate.

(2) The decedent's reversionary interest will be considered to have arisen by the express terms of the instrument of transfer and not by operation of law if the instrument contains an express disposition which affirmatively creates the reversionary interest, even though the terms of the disposition do not refer to the decedent or his estate, as such. For example, where the disposition is, in its terms, to the next of kin of the decedent and such a disposition, under applicable local law, constitutes a reversionary interest in the decedent's estate, the decedent's reversionary interest will be considered to have arisen by the express terms of the instrument of transfer and not by operation of law.

(g) *Transfers made after November 11, 1935, and before January 29, 1940.* The provisions of paragraphs (a) through (f) of this section are fully applicable to transfers made after November 11, 1935 (the date on which the Supreme Court decided *Helvering v. St. Louis Union Trust Co.* (296 U. S. 39) [36–1 USTC ¶ 9005] and *Becker v. St. Louis Union Trust Co.* (296 U. S. 48) [36–1 USTC ¶ 9006]), and before January 29, 1940 (the date on which the Supreme Court decided *Helvering v. Hallock* and companion cases (309 U. S. 106) [40–1 USTC ¶ 9208]), except that the value of an interest in property transferred between these dates is not included in a decedent's gross estate under section 2037 if—

(1) The Commissioner, whose determination shall be final, determines that the transfer is classifiable with the tranfers involved in the *St. Louis Union Trust Co.* cases, rather than with the transfer involved in the case of *Klein v. United States* (283 U. S. 231) [2 USTC ¶ 706], previously decided by the Supreme Court, and

(2) The transfer shall have been finally treated for all gift tax purposes, both as to the calendar year of the transfer and as to subsequent calendar years, as a gift in an amount measured by the value of the property undiminished by reason of a provision in the instrument of transfer by which the property, in whole or in part, is to revert to the decedent should he survive the donee or another person, or the reversion is conditioned upon some other contingency terminable by the decedent's death.

§ 20.2038-1 **Revocable transfers**—(a) *In general.* A decedent's gross estate includes under section 2038 the value of any interest in property transferred by the decedent, whether in trust or otherwise, if the enjoyment of the interest was subject at the date of the decedent's death to any change through the exercise of a power by the decedent to alter, amend, revoke, or terminate, or if the decedent relinquished such a power in contemplation of death. However, section 2038 does not apply—

(1) To the extent that the transfer was for an adequate and full consideration in money or money's worth (see § 20.2043-1);

(2) If the decedent's power could be exercised only with the consent of all parties having an interest (vested or contingent) in the transferred property, and if the power adds nothing to the rights of the parties under local law; or

(3) To a power held solely by a person other than the decedent. But, for example, if the decedent had the unrestricted power to remove or discharge a trustee at any time and appoint himself trustee, the decedent is considered as having the powers of the trustee. However, this result would not follow if he only had the power to appoint himself trustee under limited conditions which did not exist at the time of his death. (See last two sentences of paragraph (b) of this section.)

Except as provided above, it is immaterial (i) in what capacity the power was exercisable by the decedent or by another person or persons in conjunction with the decedent; (ii) whether the power was exercisable alone or only in conjunction with another person or persons, whether or not having an adverse interest (unless the transfer was made before June 2, 1924; see paragraph (d) of this section); and (iii) at what time or from what source the decedent acquired his power (unless the transfer was made before June 23, 1936; see paragraph (c) of this section). Section 2038 is applicable to any power affecting the time or manner of enjoyment of property or its income, even though the identity of the beneficiary is not affected. For example, section 2038 is applicable to a power reserved by the grantor of a trust to accumulate income or distribute it to A, and to distribute corpus to A, even though the remainder is vested in A or his estate, and no other person has any beneficial interest in the trust. However, only the value of an interest in property subject to a power to which section 2038 applies is included in the decedent's gross estate under section 2038.

(b) *Date of existence of power.* A power to alter, amend, revoke, or terminate will be considered to have existed at the date of the decedent's death even though the exercise of the power was subject to a precedent giving of notice or even though the alteration, amendment, revocation, or termination would have taken effect only on the expiration of a stated period after the exercise of the power, whether or not on or before the date of the decedent's death notice had been given or the power had been exercised. In determining the value of the gross estate in such cases, the full value of the property transferred subject to the power is discounted for the period required to elapse between the date of the decedent's death and the date upon which the alteration, amendment, revocation, or termination could take effect. In this connection, see especially § 20.2031-7. However, section 2038 is not applicable to a power the exercise of which was subject to a contingency beyond the decedent's control which did not occur before his death (e. g., the death of another person during the decedent's life). See, however, section 2036(a)(2) for the inclusion of property in the decedent's gross estate on account of such a power.

(c) *Transfers made before June 23, 1936.* Notwithstanding anything to the contrary in paragraphs (a) and (b) of this section, the value of an interest in property transferred by a decedent before June 23, 1936, is not included in his gross estate under section 2038 unless the power to alter, amend, revoke, or terminate was reserved at the time of the transfer. For purposes of this paragraph, the phrase "reserved at the time of the transfer" has reference to a power (arising either by the express terms of the instrument of transfer or by operation of law) to which the transfer was subject when made and which continued to the date of the decedent's death (see paragraph (b) of this section) to be exercisable by the decedent alone or by the decedent in conjunction with any other person or persons. The phrase also has reference to any understanding, express or implied, had in connection with the making of the transfer that the power would later be created or conferred.

(d) *Transfers made before June 2, 1924.* Notwithstanding anything to the contrary in paragraphs (a) through (c) of this section, if an interest in property was transferred by a decedent before the enactment of the Revenue Act of 1924 (June 2, 1924, 4:01 p.m., eastern standard time), and if a power reserved by the decedent to alter, amend, revoke, or terminate was exercisable by the decedent only in conjunction with a person having a substantial adverse interest in the transferred property, or in conjunction with several persons some or all of whom held such an adverse interest, there is included in the decedent's gross estate only the value of any interest or interests held by a person or persons not required to join in the exercise of the power plus the value of any insubstantial adverse interest or interests of a person or persons required to join in the exercise of the power.

(e) *Powers relinquished in contemplation of death*—(1) *In general.* If a power to alter, amend, revoke, or terminate would have resulted in the inclusion of an interest in property in a decedent's gross estate under section 2038 if it had been held until the decedent's death, the relinquishment of the power in contemplation of the decedent's death within 3 years before his death results in the inclusion of the same interest in property in the decedent's gross estate, except to the extent that the power was relinquished for an adequate and full consideration in money or money's worth (see § 20.2043-1). For the meaning of the phrase "in contemplation of death", see paragraph (c) of § 20.2035-1.

(2) *Transfers before June 23, 1936.* In the case of a transfer made before June 23, 1936, section 2038 applies only to a relinquishment made by the decedent. However, in the case of a transfer made after June 22, 1936, section 2038 also applies to a relinquishment made by a person or persons holding the power in conjunction with the decedent, if the relinquishment was made in contemplation of the decedent's death and had the effect of extinguishing the power.

Annuities

§ 20.2039-1 **Annuities**—(a) *In general.* A decedent's gross estate includes under section 2039(a) and (b) the value of an annuity or other payment receivable by any beneficiary by reason of surviving the decedent under certain agreements or plans to the extent that the value of the annuity or other payment is attributable to contributions made by the decedent or his employer. Section 2039(a) and (b), however, has no application to an amount which constitutes the proceeds of insurance under a policy on the decedent's life. Paragraph (b) of this section describes the agreements or plans to which section 2039(a) and (b) applies; paragraph (c) provides rules for determining the amount includible in the decedent's gross estate; and paragraph (d) distinguishes proceeds of life insurance. The fact that an annuity or other payment is not includible in a decedent's gross estate under section 2039(a) and (b) does not mean that it is not includible under some other section of part III of subchapter A of chapter 11. However, see section 2039(c) and § 20.2039-2 for rules relating to the exclusion from a decedent's gross estate of annuities and other payments under certain "qualified plans".

(b) *Agreements or plans to which section 2039(a) and (b) applies.* (1) Section 2039(a) and (b) applies to the value of an annuity or other payment receivable by any beneficiary under any form of contract or agreement entered into after March 3, 1931, under which—

(i) An annuity or other payment was payable to the decedent, either alone or in conjunction with another person or persons, for his life or for any period not ascertainable without reference to his death or for any period which does not in fact end before his death, or

(ii) The decedent possessed, for his life or for any period not ascertainable without reference to his death or for any period which does not in fact end before his death, the right to receive such an annuity or other payment, either alone or in conjunction with another person or persons.

The term "annuity or other payment" as used with respect to both the decedent and the beneficiary has reference to one or more payments extending over any period of time. The payments may be equal or unequal, conditional or unconditional, periodic or sporadic. The term "contract or agreement" includes any arrangement, understanding or plan, or any combination of arrangements, understandings or plans arising by reason of the decedent's employment. An annuity or other payment "was payable" to the decedent if, at the time of his death, the decedent was in fact receiving an annuity or other payment, whether or not he had an enforceable right to have payments continued. The decedent "possessed the right to receive" an annuity or other payment if, immediately before his death, the decedent had an enforceable right to receive payments at some time in the future, whether or not, at the time of his death, he had a present right to receive payments. In connection with the preceding sentence, the decedent will be regarded as having had "an enforceable right to receive payments at some time in the future" so long as he had complied with his obligations under the contract or agreement up to the time of his death. For the meaning of the phrase "for his life or for any period not ascertainable without reference to his death or for any period which does not in fact end before his death", see section 2036 and § 20.2036-1.

(2) The application of this paragraph is illustrated and more fully explained in the following examples. In each example: (i) it is assumed that all transactions occurred after March 3, 1931, and (ii) the amount stated to be includible in the decedent's gross estate is determined in accordance with the provisions of paragraph (c) of this section.

Example (1). The decedent purchased an annuity contract under the terms of which the issuing company agreed to pay an annuity to the decedent for his life and, upon his death, to pay a specified lump sum to his designated beneficiary. The decedent was drawing his annuity at the time of his death. The amount of the lump sum payment to the beneficiary is includible in the decedent's gross estate under section 2039 (a) and (b).

Example (2). Pursuant to a retirement plan, the employer made contributions to a fund which was to provide the employee, upon his retirement at age 60, with an annuity for life, and which was to provide the employee's wife, upon his death after retirement, with a similar annuity for life. The benefits under the plan were completely forfeitable during the employee's life, but, upon his death after retirement, the benefits to the wife were forfeitable only upon her remarriage. The employee had no right originally to designate or ever to change the employer's designation of the surviving beneficiary. The retirement plan at no time met the requirements of section 401(a) (relating to qualified plans). Assume that the employee died at age 61 after the employer started payment of his annuity as described above. The value of the wife's annuity is includible in the decedent's gross estate under section 2039(a) and (b). Includibility in this case is based on the fact that the annuity to the decedent "was payable" at the time of his death. The fact that the decedent's annuity was forfeitable is of no consequence since, at the time of his death, he was in fact receiving payments under the plan. Nor is it important that the decedent had no right to choose the surviving beneficiary. The element of forfeitability in the wife's annuity may be taken into account only with respect to the valuation of the annuity in the decedent's gross estate.

Example (3). Pursuant to a retirement plan, the employer made contributions to a fund which was to provide the employee, upon his retirement at age 60, with an annuity of $100 per month for life, and which was to provide his designated beneficiary, upon the employee's death after retirement, with a similar annuity for life. The plan also provided that (a) upon the employee's separation from service before retirement, he would have a nonforfeitable right to receive a reduced annuity starting at age 60, and (b) upon the employee's death before retirement, a lump sum payment representing the amount of the employer's contributions credited to the employee's account would be paid to the designated beneficiary. The plan at no time met the requirements of section 401(a) (relating to qualified plans). Assume that the employee died at age 49 and that the designated beneficiary was paid the specified lump sum payment. Such amount is includible in the decedent's gross estate under section 2039(a) and (b). Since, immediately before his death, the employee had an enforceable right to receive an annuity commencing at age 60, he is considered to have "possessed the right to receive" an annuity as that term is used in section 2039(a). If, in this example, the employee would not be entitled to any benefits in the event of his separation from service before retirement for any reason other than death, the result would be the same so long as the decedent had complied with his obligations under the contract up to the time of his death. In such case, he is considered to have had, immediately before his death, an enforceable right to receive an annuity commencing at age 60.

Example (4). Pursuant to a retirement plan, the employer made contributions to a fund which was to provide the employee, upon his retirement at age 60, with an annuity for life, and which was to provide his designated beneficiary, upon the employee's death after retirement, with a similar annuity for life. The plan provided, however, that no benefits were payable in the event of the employee's death before retirement. The retirement plan at no time met the requirements of section 401(a) (relating to qualified plans). Assume that the employee died at age 59 but that the employer nevertheless started payment of an annuity in a slightly reduced amount to the designated beneficiary. The value of the annuity is not includible in the decedent's gross estate under section 2039(a) and (b). Since the employee died before reaching the retirement age, the employer was under no obligation to pay the annuity to the employee's designated beneficiary. Therefore, the annuity was not paid under a "contract or agreement" as that term is used in section 2039(a). If, however, it can be established that the employer has consistently paid an annuity under such circumstances, the annuity will be considered as having been paid under a "contract or agreement".

Example (5). The employer made contributions to a retirement fund which were credited to the employee's individual account. Under the plan, the employee was to receive one-half the amount credited to his account upon his retirement at age 60, and his designated beneficiary was to receive the other one-half upon the employee's death after retirement. If the employee should die before reaching the retirement age, the entire amount credited to his account at such time was to be paid to the designated beneficiary. The retirement plan at no time met the requirements of section 401(a) (relating to qualified plans). Assume that the employee received one-half the amount credited to his account upon reaching the retirement age and that he died shortly thereafter. Since the employee received all that he was entitled to receive under the plan before his death, no amount was payable to him for his life or for any period not ascertainable without reference to his death, or for any period which did not in fact end before his death. Thus, the amount of the payment to the designated beneficiary is not includible in the decedent's gross estate under section 2039(a) and (b). If, in this example, the employee died before reaching the retirement age, the amount of the payment to the designated beneficiary would be includible in the decedent's gross estate under section 2039(a) and (b). In this latter case, the decedent possessed the right to receive a lump sum payment for a period which did not in fact end before his death.

Example (6). The employer made contributions to two different funds set up under two different plans. One plan was to provide the employee, upon his retirement at age 60, with an annuity for life, and the other plan was to provide the employee's designated beneficiary, upon the employee's death, with a similar annuity for life. Each plan was established at a different time and each plan was administered separately in every respect. Neither plan at any time met the requirements of section 401(a) (relating to qualified plans). The value of the designated beneficiary's annuity is includible in the employee's gross estate. All rights and benefits accruing to an employee and to others by reason of the employment (except rights and benefits accruing under certain plans meeting the requirements of section 401(a) (see § 20.2039-2)) are considered together in determining whether or not section 2039(a) and (b) applies. The scope of section 2039(a) and (b) cannot be limited by indirection.

(c) *Amount includible in the gross estate.* The amount to be included in a decedent's gross estate under section 2039(a) and (b) is an amount which bears the same ratio to the value at the decedent's death of the annuity or other payment receivable by the beneficiary as the contribution made by the decedent, or made by his employer (or former employer) for any reason connected with his employment, to the cost of the contract or agreement bears to its total cost. In applying this ratio, the value at the decedent's death of the annuity or other payment is determined in accordance with the rules set forth in §§ 20.-2031-1, 20.2031-7, 20.2031-8, and 20.2031-9. The application of this paragraph may be illustrated by the following examples:

Example (1). On January 1, 1945, the decedent and his wife each contributed $15,000 to the purchase price of an annuity contract under the terms of which the issuing company agreed to pay an annuity to the decedent and his wife for their joint lives and to continue the annuity to the survivor for his life. Assume that the value of the survivor's annuity at the decedent's death (computed under § 20.2031-8) is $20,-000. Since the decedent contributed one-half of the cost of the contract, the amount to be included in his gross estate under section 2039(a) and (b) is $10,000.

Example (2). Under the terms of an employment contract entered into on January 1, 1945, the employer and the employee made contributions to a fund which was to provide the employee, upon his retirement at age 60, with an annuity for life, and which was to provide his designated beneficiary, upon the employee's death after retirement, with a similar annuity for life. The retirement fund at no time formed part of a plan meeting the requirements of section 401(a) (relating to qualified plans). Assume that the employer and the employee each contributed $5,000 to the retirement fund. Assume, further, that the employee died after retirement at which time the value of the survivor's annuity was $8,000. Since the employer's contributions were made by reason of the decedent's employment, the amount to be included in his gross estate under section 2039(a) and (b) is the entire $8,000. If, in the above example, only the employer made contributions to the fund, the amount to be included in the gross estate would still be $8,000.

(d) *Insurance under policies on the life of the decedent.* If an annuity or other payment receivable by a beneficiary under a contract or agreement is in substance the proceeds of insurance under a policy on the life of the decedent, section 2039(a) and (b) does not apply. For the extent to which such an annuity or other payment is includible in a decedent's gross estate, see section 2042 and § 20.2042-1. A combination annuity contract and life insurance policy on the decedent's life (e. g., a "retirement income" policy with death benefits) which matured during the decedent's lifetime so that there was no longer an insurance element under the contract at the time of the decedent's death is subject to the provisions of section 2039(a) and (b). On the other hand, the treatment of a combination annuity contract and life insurance policy on the decedent's life which did not mature during the decedent's lifetime depends upon the nature of the contract at the time of the decedent's death. The nature of the contract is generally determined by the relation of the reserve value of the policy to the value of the death benefit at the time

943

of the decedent's death. If the decedent dies before the reserve value equals the death benefit, there is still an insurance element under the contract. The contract is therefore considered, for estate tax purposes, to be an insurance policy subject to the provisions of section 2042. However, if the decedent dies after the reserve value equals the death benefit, there is no longer an insurance element under the contract. The contract is therefore considered to be a contract for an annuity or other payment subject to the provisions of section 2039(a) and (b) or some other section of part III of subchapter A of chapter 11. Notwithstanding the relation of the reserve value to the value of the death benefit, a contract under which the death benefit could never exceed the total premiums paid, plus interest, contains no insurance element.

Example. Pursuant to a retirement plan established January 1, 1945, the employer purchased a contract from an insurance company which was to provide the employee, upon his retirement at age 65, with an annuity of $100 per month for life, and which was to provide his designated beneficiary, upon the employee's death after retirement, with a similar annuity for life. The contract further provided that if the employee should die before reaching the retirement age, a lump sum payment of $20,000 would be paid to his designated beneficiary in lieu of the annuity described above. The plan at no time met the requirements of section 401(a) (relating to qualified plans). Assume that the reserve value of the contract at the retirement age would be $20,000. If the employee died after reaching the retirement age, the death benefit to the designated beneficiary would constitute an annuity, the value of which would be includible in the employee's gross estate under section 2039(a) and (b). If, on the other hand, the employee died before reaching his retirement age, the death benefit to the designated beneficiary would constitute insurance under a policy on the life of the decedent since the reserve value would be less than the death benefit. Accordingly, its includibility would depend upon section 2042 and § 20.2042-1.

§ 20.2039-2 Annuities under "qualified plans"—(a) *In general.* Section 2039(c) excludes from a decedent's gross estate the value of an annuity or other payment receivable under certain "qualified plans" to the extent provided in paragraph (c) of this section. Section 2039(c) applies to estates of all persons dying after December 31, 1953.

(b) *Plans to which section 2039(c) applies.* Section 2039(c) excludes from a decedent's gross estate, to the extent provided in paragraph (c) of this section, the value of an annuity or other payment receivable by any beneficiary (except the value of an annuity or other payment receivable by or for the benefit of the decedent's estate) under—

(1) An employees' trust (or under a contract purchased by an employees' trust) forming part of a pension, stock bonus, or profit-sharing plan which, at the time of the decedent's separation from employment (whether by death or otherwise), or at the time of the earlier termination of the plan, met the requirements of section 401(a), or

(2) A retirement annuity contract purchased by an employer (and

944

not by an employees' trust) pursuant to a plan which, at the time of decedent's separation from employment (by death or otherwise), or at the time of the earlier termination of the plan, met the requirements of section 401(a)(3) through (6).

For the meaning of the term "annuity or other payment", see paragraph (b) of § 20.2039-1. For the meaning of the phrase "receivable by or for the benefit of the decedent's estate", see paragraph (b) of § 20.2042-1. The application of this paragraph may be illustrated by the following examples in each of which it is assumed that the amount stated to be excludable from the decedent's gross estate is determined in accordance with paragraph (c) of this section.

Example (1). Pursuant to a pension plan, the employer made contributions to a trust which was to provide the employee, upon his retirement at age 60, with an annuity for life, and which was to provide his wife, upon the employee's death after retirement, with a similar annuity for life. At the time of the employee's retirement, the pension trust formed part of a plan meeting the requirements of section 401(a). Assume that the employee died at age 61 after the trustee started payment of his annuity as described above. Since the wife's annuity was receivable under a qualified pension plan, no part of the value of such annuity is includible in the decedent's gross estate by reason of the provisions of section 2039(c). If, in this example, the employer provided other benefits under nonqualified plans, the result would be the same since the exclusion under section 2039(c) is confined to the benefits provided for under the qualified plan.

Example (2). Pursuant to a profit-sharing plan, the employer made contributions to a trust which were allocated to the employee's individual account. Under the plan, the employee would, upon his retirement at age 60, receive a distribution of the entire amount credited to his account. If he should die before reaching the retirement age, the amount credited to his account would be distributed to his designated beneficiary. Assume that the employee died before reaching the retirement age and that at such time the plan met the requirements of section 401(a). Since the designated beneficiary's lump sum payment was receivable under a qualified profit-sharing plan, no part of such lump sum payment is includible in the decedent's gross estate by reason of the provisions of section 2039(c).

Example (3). Pursuant to a pension plan, the employer made contributions to a trust which were used by the trustee to purchase a contract from an insurance company for the benefit of an employee. The contract was to provide the employee, upon his retirement at age 65, with an annuity of $100 per month for life, and was to provide his designated beneficiary, upon the employee's death after retirement, with a similar annuity for life. The contract further provided that if the employee should die before reaching the retirement age, a lump sum payment equal to the greater of (a) $10,000 or (b) the reserve value of the policy would be paid to his designated beneficiary in lieu of the annuity described above. Assume that the employee died before reaching the retirement age and that at such time the plan met the requirements of

[Harris]—60

section 401(a). Since the designated beneficiary's lump sum payment was receivable under a qualified pension plan, no part of such lump sum payment is includible in the decedent's gross estate by reason of the provisions of section 2039(c). It should be noted that for purposes of the exclusion under section 2039(c), it is immaterial whether or not such lump sum payment constitutes the proceeds of life insurance under the principles set forth in paragraph (d) of § 20.2039-1.

Example (4). Pursuant to a profit-sharing plan, the employer made contributions to a trust which were allocated to the employee's individual account. Under the plan, the employee would, upon his retirement at age 60, be given the option to have the amount credited to his account (a) paid to him in a lump sum, (b) used to purchase a joint and survivor annuity for him and his designated beneficiary, or (c) left with the trustee under an arrangement whereby interest would be paid to him for his lifetime with the principal to be paid, at his death, to his designated beneficiary. The plan further provided that, if the third method of settlement were selected, the employee would retain the right to have the principal paid to himself in a lump sum up to the time of his death. At the time of the employee's retirement, the profit-sharing plan met the requirements of section 401(a). Assume that the employee, upon reaching his retirement age, elected to have the amount credited to his account left with the trustee under the interest arrangement. Assume, further, that the employee did not exercise his right to have such amount paid to him before his death. Under such circumstances, the employee is considered as having constructively received the amount credited to his account upon his retirement. Thus, such amount is not considered as receivable by the designated beneficiary under the profit-sharing plan and the exclusion of section 2039(c) is not applicable.

(c) *Amount excludable from the gross estate.* (1) The amount to be excluded from a decedent's gross estate under section 2039(c) is an amount which bears the same ratio to the value at the decedent's death of the annuity or other payment receivable by the beneficiary as the employer's contribution (or a contribution made on his behalf) to the plan on the employee's account bears to the total contributions to the plan on the employee's account. In applying this ratio, the value at the decedent's death of the annuity or other payment is determined in accordance with the rules set forth in §§ 20.2031-1, 20.2031-7, 20.2031-8, and 20.2031-9.

(2) In certain cases, the employer's contribution (or a contribution made on his behalf) to a plan on the employee's account and thus the total contributions to the plan on the employee's account cannot be readily ascertained. In order to apply the ratio stated in subparagraph (1) of this paragraph in such a case, the method outlined in the following two sentences must be used unless a more precise method is presented. In such a case, the total contributions to the plan on the employee's account is the value of any annuity or other payment payable to the decedent and his survivor computed as of the time the decedent's rights first mature (or as of the time the survivor's rights first mature if the decedent's rights never mature) and computed in accordance with the

946   [Harris]

rules set forth in §§ 20.2031-1, 20.2031-7, 20.2031-8, and 20.2031-9. By subtracting from such value the amount of the employee's contribution to the plan, the amount of the employer's contribution to the plan on the employee's account may be obtained. The application of this paragraph may be illustrated by the following example:

Example. Pursuant to a pension plan, the employer and the employee contributed to a trust which was to provide the employee, upon his retirement at age 60, with an annuity for life, and which was to provide his wife, upon the employee's death after retirement, with a similar annuity for life. At the time of the employee's retirement, the pension trust formed part of a plan meeting the requirements of section 401(a). Assume the following: (i) that the employer's contributions to the fund were not credited to the accounts of individual employees; (ii) that the value of the employee's annuity and his wife's annuity, computed as of the time of the decedent's retirement, was $40,000; (iii) that the employee contributed $10,000 to the plan; and (iv) that the value at the decedent's death of the wife's annuity was $16,000. On the basis of these facts, the total contributions to the fund on the employee's account are presumed to be $40,000 and the employer's contribution to the plan on the employee's account is presumed to be $30,000 ($40,000 less $10,000). Since the wife's annuity was receivable under a qualified pension plan, that part of the value of such annuity which is attributable to

$$\frac{\$30,000}{\$40,000} \times \$16,000, \text{ or } \$12,000$$

the employer's contributions is excludable from the decedent's gross estate by reason of the provisions of section 2039(c). Compare this result with the results reached in the example set forth in paragraph (b) of this section in which all contributions to the plans were made by the employer.

Jointly-Held Property

§ 20.2040-1 **Joint interests**—(a) *In general.* A decedent's gross estate includes under section 2040 the value of property held jointly at the time of the decedent's death by the decedent and another person or persons with right of survivorship, as follows:

(1) To the extent that the property was acquired by the decedent and the other joint owner or owners by gift, devise, bequest, or inheritance, the decedent's fractional share of the property is included.

(2) In all other cases, the entire value of the property is included except such part of the entire value as is attributable to the amount of the consideration in money or money's worth furnished by the other joint owner or owners. See § 20.2043-1 with respect to adequacy of consideration. Such part of the entire value is that portion of the entire value of the property at the decedent's death (or at the alternate valuation date described in section 2032) which the consideration in money or money's worth furnished by the other joint owner or owners

bears to the total cost of acquisition and capital additions. In determining the consideration furnished by the other joint owner or owners, there is taken into account only that portion of such consideration which is shown not to be attributable to money or other property acquired by the other joint owner or owners from the decedent for less than a full and adequate consideration in money or money's worth.

The entire value of jointly held property is included in a decedent's gross estate unless the executor submits facts sufficient to show that property was not acquired entirely with consideration furnished by the decedent, or was acquired by the decedent and the other joint owner or owners by gift, bequest, devise, or inheritance.

(b) *Meaning of "property held jointly."* Section 2040 specifically covers property held jointly by the decedent and any other person (or persons), property held by the decedent and spouse as tenants by the entirety, and a deposit of money, or a bond or other instrument, in the name of the decedent and any other person and payable to either or the survivor. The section applies to all classes of property, whether real or personal, and regardless of when the joint interests were created. Furthermore, it makes no difference that the survivor takes the entire interest in the property by right of survivorship and that no interest therein forms a part of the decedent's estate for purposes of administration. The section has no application to property held by the decedent and any other person (or persons) as tenants in common.

(c) *Examples.* The application of this section may be explained in the following examples in each of which it is assumed that the other joint owner or owners survived the decedent:

(1) If the decedent furnished the entire purchase price of the jointly held property, the value of the entire property is included in his gross estate:

(2) If the decedent furnished a part only of the purchase price, only a corresponding portion of the value of the property is so included;

(3) If the decedent furnished no part of the purchase price, no part of the value of the property is so included;

(4) If the decedent, before the acquisition of the property by himself and the other joint owner, gave the latter a sum of money or other property which thereafter became the other joint owner's entire contribution to the purchase price, then the value of the entire property is so included, notwithstanding the fact that the other property may have appreciated in value due to market conditions between the time of the gift and the time of the acquisition of the jointly held property;

(5) If the decedent, before the acquisition of the property by himself and the other joint owner, transferred to the latter for less than an adequate and full consideration in money or money's worth other income-producing property, the income from which belonged to and became the other joint owner's entire contribution to the purchase price, then the value of the jointly held property less that portion attributable to the income which the other joint owner did furnish is included in the decedent's gross estate;

948

(6) If the property originally belonged to the other joint owner and the decedent purchased his interest from the other joint owner, only that portion of the value of the property attributable to the consideration paid by the decedent is included;

(7) If the decedent and his spouse acquired the property by will or gift as tenants by the entirety, one-half of the value of the property is included in the decedent's gross estate; and

(8) If the decedent and his two brothers acquired the property by will or gift as joint tenants, one-third of the value of the property is so included.

Powers of Appointment

§ 20.2041-1 **Powers of appointment; in general**—(a) *Introduction.* A decedent's gross estate includes under section 2041 the value of property in respect of which the decedent possessed, exercised, or released certain powers of appointment. This section contains rules of general application; § 20.2041-2 contains rules specifically applicable to general powers of appointment created on or before October 21, 1942; and § 20.2041-3 sets forth specific rules applicable to powers of appointment created after October 21, 1942.

(b) *Definition of "power of appointment"*—(1) *In general.* The term "power of appointment" includes all powers which are in substance and effect powers of appointment regardless of the nomenclature used in creating the power and regardless of local property law connotations. For example, if a trust instrument provides that the beneficiary may appropriate or consume the principal of the trust, the power to consume or appropriate is a power of appointment. Similarly, a power given to a decedent to affect the beneficial enjoyment of trust property or its income by altering, amending, or revoking the trust instrument or terminating the trust is a power of appointment. If the community property laws of a State confer upon the wife a power of testamentary disposition over property in which she does not have a vested interest she is considered as having a power of appointment. A power in a donee to remove or discharge a trustee and appoint himself may be a power of appointment. For example, if under the terms of a trust instrument, the trustee or his successor has the power to appoint the principal of the trust for the benefit of individuals including himself, and the decedent has the unrestricted power to remove or discharge the trustee at any time and appoint any other person including himself, the decedent is considered as having a power of appointment. However, the decedent is not considered to have a power of appointment if he only had the power to appoint a successor, including himself, under limited conditions which did not exist at the time of his death, without an accompanying unrestricted power of removal. Similarly, a power to amend only the administrative provisions of a trust instrument, which cannot substantially affect the beneficial enjoyment of the trust property or income, is not a power of appointment. The mere power of management, investment, custody of assets, or the power to allocate receipts and disbursements as between income and prin-

949

cipal, exercisable in a fiduciary capacity, whereby the holder has no power to enlarge or shift any of the beneficial interests therein except as an incidental consequence of the discharge of such fiduciary duties is not a power of appointment. Further, the right in a beneficiary of a trust to assent to a periodic accounting, thereby relieving the trustee from further accountability, is not a power of appointment if the right of assent does not consist of any power or right to enlarge or shift the beneficial interest of any beneficiary therein.

(2) *Relation to other sections.* For purposes of §§ 20.2041-1 through 20.2041-3, the term "power of appointment" does not include powers reserved by the decedent to himself within the concept of sections 2036 through 2038. (See §§ 20.2036-1 through 20.2038-1.) No provision of section 2041 or of §§ 20.2041-1 through 20.2041-3 is to be construed as in any way limiting the application of any other section of the Internal Revenue Code or of these regulations. The power of the owner of a property interest already possessed by him to dispose of his interest, and nothing more, is not a power of appointment, and the interest is includible in his gross estate to the extent it would be includible under section 2033 or some other provision of Part III of subchapter A of Chapter 11. For example, if a trust created by S provides for payment of the income to A for life with power in A to appoint the remainder by will and, in default of such appointment for payment of the income to A's widow, W, for her life and for payment of the remainder to A's estate, the value of A's interest in the remainder is includible in his gross estate under section 2033 regardless of its includibility under section 2041.

(3) *Powers over a portion of property.* If a power of appointment exists as to part of an entire group of assets or only over a limited interest in property, section 2041 applies only to such part or interest. For example, if a trust created by S provides for the payment of income to A for life, then to W for life, with power in A to appoint the remainder by will and in default of appointment for payment of the remainder to B or his estate, and if A dies before W, section 2041 applies only to the value of the remainder interest excluding W's life estate. If A dies after W, section 2041 would apply to the value of the entire property. If the power were only over one-half the remainder interest, section 2041 would apply only to one-half the value of the amounts described above.

(c) *Definition of "general power of appointment"*—(1) *In general.* The term "general power of appointment" as defined in section 2041 (b)(1) means any power of appointment exercisable in favor of the decedent, his estate, his creditors, or the creditors of his estate, except (i) joint powers, to the extent provided in §§ 20.2041-2 and 20.2041-3, and (ii) certain powers limited by an ascertainable standard, to the extent provided in subparagraph (2) of this paragraph. A power of appointment exercisable to meet the estate tax, or any other taxes, debts, or charges which are enforceable against the estate, is included within the meaning of a power of appointment exercisable in favor of the decedent's estate, his creditors, or the creditors of his estate. A power of appointment exercisable for the purpose of discharging a legal obligation of the decedent or for his pecuniary benefit is considered a power of appointment exercisable in favor of the decedent or his creditors. However, for purposes of §§ 20.2041-1 through 20.2041-3, a power of appointment not otherwise considered to be a general power of appointment is not treated as a general power of appointment merely by reason of the fact that an appointee may, in fact, be a creditor of the decedent or his estate. A power of appointment is not a general power if by its terms it is either—

(a) Exercisable only in favor of one or more designated persons or classes other than the decedent or his creditors, or the decedent's estate or the creditors of his estate, or

(b) Expressly not exercisable in favor of the decedent or his creditors, or the decedent's estate, or the creditors of his estate.

A decedent may have two powers under the same instrument, one of which is a general power of appointment and the other of which is not. For example, a beneficiary may have a power to withdraw trust corpus during his life, and a testamentary power to appoint the corpus among his descendants. The testamentary power is not a general power of appointment.

(2) *Powers limited by an ascertainable standard.* A power to consume, invade, or appropriate income or corpus, or both, for the benefit of the decedent which is limited by an ascertainable standard relating to the health, education, support, or maintenance of the decedent is, by reason of section 2041(b)(1)(A), not a general power of appointment. A power is limited by such a standard if the extent of the holder's duty to exercise and not to exercise the power is reasonably measurable in terms of his needs for health, education, or support (or any combination of them). As used in this subparagraph, the words "support" and "maintenance" are synonymous and their meaning is not limited to the bare necessities of life. A power to use property for the comfort, welfare, or happiness of the holder of the power is not limited by the requisite standard. Examples of powers which are limited by the requisite standard are powers exercisable for the holder's "support," "support in reasonable comfort," "maintenance in health and reasonable comfort," "support in his accustomed manner of living," "education, including college and professional education," "health," and "medical, dental, hospital and nursing expenses and expenses of invalidism." In determining whether a power is limited by an ascertainable standard, it is immaterial whether the beneficiary is required to exhaust his other income before the power can be exercised.

(3) *Certain powers under wills of decedents dying between January 1 and April 2, 1948.* Section 210 of the Technical Changes Act of 1953 provides that if a decedent died after December 31, 1947, but before April 3, 1948, certain property interests described therein may, if the decedent's surviving spouse so elects, be accorded special treatment in the determination of the marital deduction to be allowed the decedent's estate under the provisions of section 812(e) of the Internal Revenue Code of 1939. See § 81.47a(h) of Regulations 105 (26 CFR (1939) 81.47a(h)). The section further provides that property affected by the election shall, for the purpose of inclusion in the surviving

951

spouse's gross estate, be considered property with respect to which she has a general power of appointment. Therefore, notwithstanding any other provision of law or of §§ 20.2041-1 through 20.2041-3, if the present decedent (in her capacity as surviving spouse of a prior decedent) has made an election under section 210 of the Technical Changes Act of 1953, the property which was the subject of the election shall be considered as property with respect to which the present decedent has a general power of appointment created after October 21, 1942, exercisable by deed or will, to the extent it was treated as an interest passing to the surviving spouse and not passing to any other person for the purpose of the marital deduction in the prior decedent's estate.

(d) *Definition of "exercise"*. Whether a power of appointment is in fact exercised may depend upon local law. For example, the residuary clause of a will may be considered under local law as an exercise of a testamentary power of appointment in the absence of evidence of a contrary intention drawn from the whole of the testator's will. However, regardless of local law, a power of appointment is considered as exercised for purposes of section 2041 even though the exercise is in favor of the taker in default of appointment, and irrespective of whether the appointed interest and the interest in default of appointment are identical or whether the appointee renounces any right to take under the appointment. A power of appointment is also considered as exercised even though the disposition cannot take effect until the occurrence of an event after the exercise takes place, if the exercise is irrevocable and, as of the time of the exercise, the condition was not impossible of occurrence. For example, if property is left in trust to A for life, with a power in B to appoint the remainder by will, and B dies before A, exercising his power by appointing the remainder to C if C survives A, B is considered to have exercised his power if C is living at B's death. On the other hand, a testamentary power of appointment is not considered as exercised if it is exercised subject to the occurrence during the decedent's life of an express or implied condition which did not in fact occur. Thus, if in the preceding example, C dies before B, B's power of appointment would not be considered to have been exercised. Similarly, if a trust provides for income to A for life, remainder as A appoints by will, and A appoints a life estate in the property to B and does not otherwise exercise his power, but B dies before A, A's power is not considered to have been exercised.

(e) *Time of creation of power*. A power of appointment created by will is, in general, considered as created on the date of the testator's death. However, section 2041(b)(3) provides that a power of appointment created by a will executed on or before October 21, 1942, is considered a power created on or before that date if the testator dies before July 1, 1949, without having republished the will, by codicil or otherwise, after October 21, 1942. Whether or not a power of appointment created by an intervivos instrument executed on or before October 21, 1942, is considered a power created on or before that date depends upon the facts and circumstances of the particular case. For example, assume that A created a recoverable trust before October 21, 1942, providing for payment of income to B for life with remainder as B shall appoint by will. If A dies after October 21, 1942, without having exercised his power of revocation, B's power of appointment is considered a power created after October 21, 1942. On the other hand, assume that C created an irrevocable inter vivos trust before October 21, 1942, naming T as trustee and providing for payment of income to D for life with remainder to E. Assume further that T was given the power to pay corpus to D and the power to appoint a successor trustee. If T resigns after October 21, 1942, and appoints D as successor trustee, D is considered to have a power of appointment created before October 21, 1942. As another example, assume that F created an irrevocable intervivos trust before October 21, 1942, providing for payment of income to G for life with remainder as G shall appoint by will, but in default of appointment income to H for life with remainder as H shall appoint by will. If G dies after October 21, 1942, without having exercised his power of appointment, H's power of appointment is considered a power created before October 21, 1942, even though it was only a contingent interest until G's death. If, in this last example, G had exercised his power of appointment by creating a similar power in I, I's power of appointment would be considered a power created after October 21, 1942. A power of appointment is not considered as created after October 21, 1942, merely because the power is not exercisable or the identity of its holders is not ascertainable until after that date.

§ 20.2041-2 Powers of appointment created on or before October 21, 1942—(a) *In general.* Property subject to a general power of appointment created on or before October 21, 1942, is includible in the gross estate of the holder of the power under section 2041 only if he exercised the power under specified circumstances. Section 2041(a)(1) requires that there be included in the gross estate of a decedent the value of property subject to such a power only if the power is exercised by the decedent either (1) by will, or (2) by a disposition which is of such nature that if it were a transfer of property owned by the decedent, the property would be includible in the decedent's gross estate under section 2035 (relating to transfers in contemplation of death), 2036 (relating to transfers with retained life estate), 2037 (relating to transfers taking effect at death), or 2038 (relating to revocable transfers). See paragraphs (b), (c), and (d) of § 20.2041-1 for the definition of various terms used in this section.

(b) *Joint powers created on or before October 21, 1942.* Section 2041 (b)(1)(B) provides that a power created on or before October 21, 1942, which at the time of the exercise is not exercisable by the decedent except in conjunction with another person, is not deemed a general power of appointment.

(c) *Exercise during life.* The circumstances under which section 2041 applies to the exercise other than by will of a general power of appointment created on or before October 21, 1942, are set forth in

953

paragraph (a) of this section. In this connection, the rules of sections 2035 through 2038 which are to be applied are those in effect on the date of the decedent's death which are applicable to transfers made on the date when the exercise of the power occurred. Those rules are to be applied in determining the extent to which and the conditions under which a disposition is considered a transfer of property. The application of this paragraph may be illustrated by the following examples:

Example (1). The decedent in 1951 exercised a general power of appointment created in 1940, reserving no interest in or power over the property subject to the general power. The decedent died in 1956. Since the exercise was not made within three years before the decedent's death, no part of the property is includible in his gross estate. See section 2035(b), relating to transfers in contemplation of death.

Example (2). S created a trust in 1930 to pay the income to A for life, remainder as B appoints by an instrument filed with the trustee during B's lifetime, and in default of appointment remainder to C. B exercised the power in 1955 by directing that after A's death the income be paid to himself for life with remainder to C. If B dies after A, the entire value of the trust property would be included in B's gross estate, since such a disposition if it were a transfer of property owned by B would cause the property to be included in his gross estate under section 2036(a)(1). If B dies before A, the value of the trust property less the value of A's life estate would be included in B's gross estate for the same reason.

Example (3). S created a trust in 1940 to pay the income to A for life, remainder as A appoints by an instrument filed with the trustee during A's lifetime. A exercised the power in 1955, five years before his death, reserving the right of revocation. The exercise, if not revoked before death, will cause the property subject to the power to be included in A's gross estate under section 2041(a)(1), since such a disposition if it were a transfer of property owned by A would cause the property to be included in his gross estate under section 2038. However, if the exercise were completely revoked, so that A died still possessed of the power, the property would not be included in A's gross estate for the reason that the power will not be treated as having been exercised.

Example (4). A decedent exercised a general power of appointment created in 1940 by making a disposition in trust under which possession or enjoyment of the property subject to the exercise could be obtained only by surviving the decedent and under which the decedent retained a reversionary interest in the property of a value of more than five percent. The exercise will cause the property subject to the power to be included in the decedent's gross estate, since such a disposition if it were a transfer of property owned by the decedent would cause the property to be included in his gross estate under section 2037.

(d) *Release or lapse.* A failure to exercise a general power of appointment created on or before October 21, 1942, or a complete release of such a power is not considered to be an exercise of a general power of appointment. The phrase "a complete release" means a release of all powers over all or a portion of the property subject to a power of appointment, as distinguished from the reduction of a power of appointment to a lesser power. Thus, if the decedent completely relinquished all powers over one-half of the property subject to a power of appointment, the power is completely released as to that one-half. If at or before the time a power of appointment is relinquished, the holder of the power exercises the power in such a manner or to such an extent that the relinquishment results in the reduction, enlargement, or shift in a beneficial interest in property, the relinquishment will be considered to be an exercise and not a release of the power. For example, assume that A created a trust in 1940 providing for payment of the income to B for life and, upon B's death, remainder to C. Assume further that B was given the unlimited power to amend the trust instrument during his lifetime. If B amended the trust in 1948 by providing that upon his death the remainder was to be paid to D, and if he further amended the trust in 1950 by deleting his power to amend the trust, such relinquishment will be considered an exercise and not a release of a general power of appointment. On the other hand, if the 1948 amendment became ineffective before or at the time of the 1950 amendment, or if B in 1948 merely amended the trust by changing the purely ministerial powers of the trustee, his relinquishment of the power in 1950 will be considered as a release of a power of appointment.

(e) *Partial release.* If a general power of appointment created on or before October 21, 1942, is partially released so that it is not thereafter a general power of appointment, a subsequent exercise of the partially released power is not an exercise of a general power of appointment if the partial release occurs before whichever is the later of the following dates:

(1) November 1, 1951, or

(2) If the decedent was under a legal disability to release the power on October 21, 1942, the day after the expiration of 6 months following the termination of such legal disability.

However, if a general power created on or before October 21, 1942, is partially released on or after the later of these dates, a subsequent exercise of the power will cause the property subject to the power to be included in the holder's gross estate, if the exercise is such that if it were a disposition of property owned by the decedent it would cause the property to be included in his gross estate. The legal disability referred to in this paragraph is determined under local law and may include the disability of an insane person, a minor, or an unborn child. The fact that the type of general power of appointment possessed by the decedent actually was not generally releasable under the local law does not place the decedent under a legal disability within the meaning of this paragraph. In general, however, it is assumed that all general powers of appointment are releasable, unless the local law on the subject is to the contrary, and it is presumed that the method employed to release the power is effective, unless it is not in accordance with the local law relating specifically to releases or, in the absence of such local law, is not in accordance with the local law relating to similar transactions.

(f) *Partial exercise.* If a general power of appointment created on or before October 21, 1942, is exercised only as to a portion of the property subject to the power, section 2041 is applicable only to the value of that portion. For example, if a decedent had a general power of appointment exercisable by will created on or before October 21, 1942, over a trust fund valued at $200,000 at the date of his death, and if the decedent exercised his power either to the extent of directing the distribution of one-half of the trust property to B or of directing the payment of $100,000 to B, the trust property would be includible in the decedent's gross estate only to the extent of $100,000.

§ 20.2041-3 **Powers of appointment created after October 21, 1942—** (a) *In general.* (1) Property subject to a power of appointment created after October 21, 1942, is includible in the gross estate of the holder of the power under varying conditions depending on whether the power is (i) general in nature, (ii) possessed at death, or (iii) exercised or released. See paragraphs (b), (c), and (d) of § 20.2041-1 for the definition of various terms used in this section. See paragraph (c) of this section for the rules applicable to determine the extent to which joint powers created after October 21, 1942, are to be treated as general powers of appointment.

(2) If the power is a general power of appointment, the value of an interest in property subject to such a power is includible in a decedent's gross estate under section 2041(a)(2) if either—

(i) The decedent has the power at the time of his death (and the interest exists at the time of his death), or

(ii) The decedent exercised or released the power, or the power lapsed, under the circumstances and to the extent described in paragraph (d) of this section.

(3) If the power is not a general power of appointment, the value of property subject to the power is includible in the holder's gross estate under section 2041(a)(3) only if it is exercised to create a further power under certain circumstances (see paragraph (e) of this section).

(b) *Existence of power at death.* For purposes of section 2041(a)(2), a power of appointment is considered to exist on the date of a decedent's death even though the exercise of the power is subject to the precedent giving of notice, or even though the exercise of the power takes effect only on the expiration of a stated period after its exercise, whether or not on or before the decedent's death notice has been given or the power has been exercised. However, a power which by its terms is exercisable only upon the occurrence during the decedent's lifetime of an event or a contingency which did not in fact take place or occur during such time is not a power in existence on the date of the decedent's death. For example, if a decedent was given a general power of appointment exercisable only after he reached a certain age, only if he survived another person, or only if he died without descendants,

956

the power would not be in existence on the date of the decedent's death if the condition precedent to its exercise had not occurred.

(c) *Joint powers created after October 21, 1942.* The treatment of a power of appointment created after October 21, 1942, which is exercisable only in conjunction with another person is governed by section 2041(b)(1)(C), which provides as follows:

(1) Such a power is not considered a general power of appointment if it is not exercisable by the decedent except with the consent or joinder of the creator of the power.

(2) Such power is not considered a general power of appointment if it is not exercisable by the decedent except with the consent or joinder of a person having a substantial interest in the property subject to the power which is adverse to the exercise of the power in favor of the decedent, his estate, his creditors, or the creditors of his estate. An interest adverse to the exercise of a power is considered as substantial if its value in relation to the total value of the property subject to the power is not insignificant. For this purpose, the interest is to be valued in accordance with the actuarial principles set forth in § 20.2031-7 or, if it is not susceptible to valuation under those provisions, in accordance with the general principles set forth in § 20.2031-1. A taker in default of appointment under a power has an interest which is adverse to an exercise of the power. A coholder of the power has no adverse interest merely because of his joint possession of the power nor merely because he is a permissible appointee under a power. However, a coholder of a power is considered as having an adverse interest where he may possess the power after the decedent's death and may exercise it at that time in favor of himself, his estate, his creditors, or the creditors of his estate. Thus, for example, if X, Y, and Z held a power jointly to appoint among a group of persons which includes themselves and if on the death of X the power will pass to Y and Z jointly, then Y and Z are considered to have interests adverse to the exercise of the power in favor of X. Similarly, if on Y's death the power will pass to Z, Z is considered to have an interest adverse to the exercise of the power in favor of Y. The application of this subparagraph may be further illustrated by the following additional examples in each of which it is assumed that the value of the interest in question is substantial:

Example (1). The decedent and R were trustees of a trust under the terms of which the income was to be paid to the decedent for life and then to M for life, and the remainder was to be paid to R. The trustees had power to distribute corpus to the decedent. Since R's interest was substantially adverse to an exercise of the power in favor of the decedent the latter did not have a general power of appointment. If M and the decedent were the trustees, M's interest would likewise have been adverse.

Example (2). The decedent and L were trustees of a trust under the terms of which the income was to be paid to L for life and then to M for life, and the remainder was to be paid to the decedent. The trustees had power to distribute corpus to the decedent during L's life. Since

L's interest was adverse to an exercise of the power in favor of the decedent, the decedent did not have a general power of appointment. If the decedent and M were the trustees, M's interest would likewise have been adverse.

Example (3). The decedent and L were trustees of a trust under the terms of which the income was to be paid to L for life. The trustees could designate whether corpus was to be distributed to the decedent or to A after L's death. L's interest was not adverse to an exercise of the power in favor of the decedent, and the decedent therefore had a general power of appointment.

(3) A power which is exercisable only in conjunction with another person, and which after application of the rules set forth in subparagraphs (1) and (2) of this paragraph constitutes a general power of appointment, will be treated as though the holders of the power who are permissible appointees of the property were joint owners of property subject to the power. The decedent, under this rule, will be treated as possessed of a general power of appointment over an aliquot share of the property to be determined with reference to the number of joint holders, including the decedent, who (or whose estates or creditors) are permissible appointees. Thus, for example, if X, Y, and Z hold an unlimited power jointly to appoint among a group of persons, including themselves, but on the death of X the power does not pass to Y and Z jointly, then Y and Z are not considered to have interests adverse to the exercise of the power in favor of X. In this case X is considered to possess a general power of appointment as to one-third of the property subject to the power.

(d) *Releases, lapses, and disclaimers of general powers of appointment.* (1) Property subject to a general power of appointment created after October 21, 1942, is includible in the gross estate of a decedent under section 2041(a)(2) even though he does not have the power at the date of his death, if during his life he exercised or released the power under circumstances such that, if the property subject to the power had been owned and transferred by the decedent, the property would be includible in the decedent's gross estate under section 2035, 2036, 2037, or 2038. Further, section 2041(b)(2) provides that the lapse of a power of appointment is considered to be a release of the power to the extent set forth in subparagraph (3) of this paragraph. A release of a power of appointment need not be formal or express in character. The principles set forth in § 20.2041-2 for determining the application of the pertinent provisions of sections 2035 through 2038 to a particular exercise of a power of appointment are applicable for purposes of determining whether or not an exercise or release of a power of appointment created after October 21, 1942, causes the property to be included in a decedent's gross estate under section 2041(a)(2). If a general power of appointment created after October 21, 1942, is partially released, a subsequent exercise or release of the power under circumstances described in the first sentence of this subparagraph, or its possession at death, will nevertheless cause the property subject to the power to be included in the gross estate of the holder of the power.

958

(2) Section 2041(a)(2) is not applicable to the complete release of a general power of appointment created after October 21, 1942, whether exercisable during life or by will, if the release was not made in contemplation of death within the meaning of section 2035, and if after the release the holder of the power retained no interest in or control over the property subject to the power which would cause the property to be included in his gross estate under sections 2036 through 2038 if the property had been transferred by the holder.

(3) The failure to exercise a power of appointment created after October 21, 1942, within a specified time, so that the power lapses, constitutes a release of the power. However, section 2041(b)(2) provides that such a lapse of a power of appointment during any calendar year during the decedent's life is treated as a release for purposes of inclusion of property in the gross estate under section 2041(a)(2) only to the extent that the property which could have been appointed by exercise of the lapsed power exceeds the greater of (i) $5,000 or (ii) 5 percent of the aggregate value, at the time of the lapse, of the assets out of which, or the proceeds of which, the exercise of the lapsed power could have been satisfied. For example, assume that A transferred $200,000 worth of securities in trust providing for payment of income to B for life with remainder to B's issue. Assume further that B was given a noncumulative right to withdraw $10,000 a year from the principal of the trust fund (which neither increased nor decreased in value prior to B's death). In such case, the failure of B to exercise his right of withdrawal will not result in estate tax with respect to the power to withdraw $10,000 which lapses each year before the year of B's death. At B's death there will be included in his gross estate the $10,000 which he was entitled to withdraw for the year in which his death occurs less any amount which he may have taken during that year. However, if in the above example B had possessed the right to withdraw $15,000 of the principal annually, the failure to exercise such power in any year will be considered a release of the power to the extent of the excess of the amount subject to withdrawal over 5 percent of the trust fund (in this example, $5,000, assuming that the trust fund is worth $200,000 at the time of the lapse). Since each lapse is treated as though B had exercised dominion over the trust property by making a transfer of principal reserving the income therefrom for his life, the value of the trust property (but only to the extent of the excess of the amount subject to withdrawal over 5 percent of the trust fund) is includible in B's gross estate (unless before B's death he has disposed of his right to the income under circumstances to which sections 2035 through 2038 would not be applicable). The extent to which the value of the trust property is included in the decedent's gross estate is determined as provided in subparagraph (4) of this paragraph.

(4) The purpose of section 2041(b)(2) is to provide a determination, as of the date of the lapse of the power, of the proportion of the property over which the power lapsed which is an exempt disposition for estate tax purposes and the proportion which, if the other requirements of sections 2035 through 2038 are satisfied, will be considered

959

as a taxable disposition. Once the taxable proportion of any disposition at the date of lapse has been determined, the valuation of that proportion as of the date of the decedent's death (or, if the executor has elected the alternate valuation method under section 2032, the value as of the date therein provided), is to be ascertained in accordance with the principles which are applicable to the valuation of transfers of property by the decedent under the corresponding provisions of sections 2035 through 2038. For example, if the life beneficiary of a trust had a right exercisable only during one calendar year to draw down $50,000 from the corpus of a trust, which he did not exercise, and if at the end of the year the corpus was worth $800,000, the taxable portion over which the power lapsed is $10,000 (the excess of $50,000 over 5 percent of the corpus), or 1/80 of the total value. On the decedent's death, if the total value of the corpus of the trust (excluding income accumulated after the lapse of the power) on the applicable valuation date was $1,200,000, $15,000 (1/80 of $1,200,000) would be includible in the decedent's gross estate. However, if the total value was then $600,000, only $7,500 (1/80 of $600,000) would be includible.

(5) If the failure to exercise a power, such as a right of withdrawal, occurs in more than a single year, the proportion of the property over which the power lapsed which is treated as a taxable disposition will be determined separately for each such year. The aggregate of the taxable proportions for all such years, valued in accordance with the above principles, will be includible in the gross estate by reason of the lapse. The includible amount, however, shall not exceed the aggregate value of the assets out of which, or the proceeds of which, the exercise of the power could have been satisfied, valued as of the date of the decedent's death (or, if the executor has elected the alternate valuation method under section 2032, the value as of the date therein provided).

(6) A disclaimer or renunciation of a general power of appointment is not considered to be a release of the power. The disclaimer or renunciation must be unequivocal and effective under local law. A disclaimer is a complete and unqualified refusal to accept the rights to which one is entitled. There can be no disclaimer or renunciation of a power after its acceptance. In any case where a power is purported to be disclaimed or renounced as to only a portion of the property subject to the power, the determination as to whether or not there has been a complete and unqualified refusal to accept the rights to which one is entitled will depend on all the facts and circumstances of the particular case, taking into account the recognition and effectiveness of such a disclaimer under local law. Such rights refer to the incidents of the power and not to other interests of the decedent in the property. If effective under local law, the power may be disclaimed or renounced without disclaiming or renouncing such other interests. In the absence of facts to the contrary, the failure to renounce or disclaim within a reasonable time after learning of its existence will be presumed to constitute an acceptance of the power.

(e) *Successive powers.* (1) Property subject to a power of appointment created after October 21, 1942, which is not a general power, is includible in the gross estate of the holder of the power under section 2041(a)(3) if the power is exercised, and if both of the following conditions are met:

(i) If the exercise is (*a*) by will, or (*b*) by a disposition which is of such nature that if it were a transfer of property owned by the decedent, the property would be includible in the decedent's gross estate under sections 2035 through 2037; and

(ii) If the power is exercised by creating another power of appointment which, under the terms of the instruments creating and exercising the first power and under applicable local law, can be validly exercised so as to (*a*) postpone the vesting of any estate or interest in the property for a period ascertainable without regard to the date of the creation of the first power, or (b) (if the applicable rule against perpetuities is stated in terms of suspension of ownership or of the power of alienation, rather than of vesting) suspend the absolute ownership or the power of alienation of the property for a period ascertainable without regard to the date of the creation of the first power.

(2) For purposes of the application of section 2041(a)(3), the value of the property subject to the second power of appointment is considered to be its value unreduced by any precedent or subsequent interest which is not subject to the second power. Thus, if a decedent has a power to appoint by will $100,000 to a group of persons consisting of his children and grandchildren and exercises the power by making an outright appointment of $75,000 and by giving one appointee a power to appoint $25,000, no more than $25,000 will be includible in the decedent's gross estate under section 2041(a)(3). If, however, the decedent appoints the income from the entire fund to a beneficiary for life with power in the beneficiary to appoint the remainder by will, the entire $100,000 will be includible in the decedent's gross estate under section 2041(a)(3) if the exercise of the second power can validly postpone the vesting of any estate or interest in the property or can suspend the absolute ownership or power of alienation of the property for a period ascertainable without regard to the date of the creation of the first power.

(f) *Examples.* The application of this section may be further illustrated by the following examples, in each of which it is assumed, unless otherwise stated, that S has transferred property in trust after October 21, 1942, with the remainder payable to R at L's death, and that neither L nor R has any interest in or power over the enjoyment of the trust property except as is indicated separately in each example:

Example (1). Income is directed to be paid to L during his lifetime at the end of each year, if living. L has an unrestricted power during his lifetime to cause the income to be distributed to any other person, but no power to cause it to be accumulated. At L's death, no part of the trust property is includible in L's gross estate since L had a power to dispose of only his income interest, a right otherwise possessed by him.

Example (2). Income is directed to be accumulated during L's life but L has a noncumulative power to distribute $10,000 of each year's income to himself. Unless L's power is limited by an ascertainable standard (relating to his health, etc.), as defined in paragraph (c)(2) of § 20.2041-1, he has a general power of appointment over $10,000 of each year's income, the lapse of which may cause a portion of any income not distributed to be included in his gross estate under section 2041. See subparagraphs (3), (4), and (5) of paragraph (d) of this section. Thus, if the trust income during the year amounts to $20,000, L's failure to distribute any of the income to himself constitutes a lapse as to $5,000 (i.e., the amount by which $10,000 exceeds $5,000). If L's power were cumulative (i.e., if the power did not lapse at the end of each year but lapsed only by reason of L's death), the total accumulations which L chose not to distribute to himself immediately before his death would be includible in his gross estate under section 2041.

Example (3). L is entitled to all the income during his lifetime and has an unrestricted power to cause corpus to be distributed to himself. L had a general power of appointment over the corpus of the trust, and the entire corpus as of the time of his death is includible in his gross estate under section 2041.

Example (4). Income was payable to L during his lifetime. R has an unrestricted power to cause corpus to be distributed to L. R dies before L. In such case, R has only a power to dispose of his remainder interest, the value of which is includible in his gross estate under section 2033, and nothing in addition would be includible under section 2041. If in this example R's remainder were contingent on his surviving L, nothing would be includible in his gross estate under either section 2033 or 2041. While R would have a power of appointment, it would not be a general power.

Example (5). Income was payable to L during his lifetime. R has an unrestricted power to cause corpus to be distributed to himself. R dies before L. While the value of R's remainder interest is includible in his gross estate under section 2033, R also has a general power of appointment over the entire trust corpus. Under such circumstances, the entire value of the trust corpus is includible in R's gross estate under section 2041.

Life Insurance

§ 20.2042-1 **Proceeds of life insurance**—(a) *In general.* (1) Section 2042 provides for the inclusion in a decedent's gross estate of the proceeds of insurance on the decedent's life (i) receivable by or for the benefit of the estate (see paragraph (b) of this section), and (ii) receivable by other beneficiaries (see paragraph (c) of this section). The term "insurance" refers to life insurance of every description, including death benefits paid by fraternal beneficial societies operating under the lodge system.

(2) Proceeds of life insurance which are not includible in the gross estate under section 2042 may, depending upon the facts of the particular case, be includible under some other section of part III of subchapter A of chapter 11. For example, if the decedent possessed incidents of ownership in an insurance policy on his life but gratuitously transferred all rights in the policy in contemplation of death, the proceeds would be includible under section 2035. Section 2042 has no application to the inclusion in the gross estate of the value of rights in an insurance policy on the life of a person other than the decedent, or the value of rights in a combination annuity contract and life insurance policy on the decedent's life (i.e., a "retirement income" policy with death benefit or an "endowment" policy) under which there was no insurance element at the time of the decedent's death (see paragraph (d) of § 20.2039-1).

(3) The amount to be included in the gross estate under section 2042 is the full amount receivable under the policy. If the proceeds of the policy are made payable to a beneficiary in the form of an annuity for life or for a term of years, the amount to be included in the gross estate is the one sum payable at death under an option which could have been exercised either by the insured or by the beneficiary, or if no option was granted, the sum used by the insurance company in determining the amount of the annuity.

(b) *Receivable by or for the benefit of the estate.* (1) Section 2042 requires the inclusion in the gross estate of the proceeds of insurance on the decedent's life receivable by the executor or administrator, or payable to the decedent's estate. It makes no difference whether or not the estate is specifically named as the beneficiary under the terms of the policy. Thus, if under the terms of an insurance policy the proceeds are receivable by another beneficiary but are subject to an obligation, legally binding upon the other beneficiary, to pay taxes, debts, or other charges enforceable against the estate, then the amount of such proceeds required for the payment in full (to the extent of the beneficiary's obligation) of such taxes, debts, or other charges is includible in the gross estate. Similarly, if the decedent purchased an insurance policy in favor of another person or a corporation as collateral security for a loan or other accommodation, its proceeds are considered to be receivable for the benefit of the estate. The amount of the loan outstanding at the date of the decedent's death, with interest accrued to that date, will be deductible in determining the taxable estate. See § 20.2053-4.

(2) If the proceeds of an insurance policy made payable to the decedent's estate are community assets under the local community property law and, as a result, one-half of the proceeds belongs to the decedent's spouse, then only one-half of the proceeds is considered to be receivable by or for the benefit of the decedent's estate.

(c) *Receivable by other beneficiaries.* (1) Section 2042 requires the inclusion in the gross estate of the proceeds of insurance on the decedent's life not receivable by or for the benefit of the estate if the decedent possessed at the date of his death any of the incidents of ownership in the policy, exercisable either alone or in conjunction with any other person. However, if the decedent did not possess any of such incidents of ownership at the time of his death nor transfer them in contemplation of death, no part of the proceeds would be includible in his gross estate under section 2042. Thus, if the decedent owned a policy of insurance on his life and, 4 years before his death, irrevocably assigned his entire interest in the policy to his wife retaining no reversionary interest therein (see subparagraph (3) of this paragraph), the proceeds of the policy would not be includible in his gross estate under section 2042.

(2) For purposes of this paragraph, the term "incidents of ownership" is not limited in its meaning to ownership of the policy in the technical legal sense. Generally speaking, the term has reference to the right of the insured or his estate to the economic benefits of the policy. Thus, it includes the power to change the beneficiary, to surrender or cancel the policy, to assign the policy, to revoke an assignment, to pledge the policy for a loan, or to obtain from the insurer a loan against the surrender value of the policy, etc. Similarly, the term includes a power to change the beneficiary reserved to a corporation of which the decedent is sole stockholder.

(3) The term "incidents of ownership" also includes a reversionary interest in the policy or its proceeds, whether arising by the express terms of the policy or other instrument or by operation of law, but only if the value of the reversionary interest immediately before the death of the decedent exceeded 5 percent of the value of the policy. As used in this subparagraph, the term "reversionary interest" includes a possibility that the policy or its proceeds may return to the decedent or his estate and a possibility that the policy or its proceeds may become subject to a power of disposition by him. In order to determine whether or not the value of a reversionary interest immediately before the death of the decedent exceeded 5 percent of the value of the policy, the principles contained in paragraph (c)(3) and (4) of § 20.2037-1 in so far as applicable, shall be followed under this subparagraph. In that connection, there must be specifically taken into consideration any incidents of ownership held by others immediately before the decedent's death which would affect the value of the reversionary interest. For example, the decedent would not be considered to have a reversionary interest in the policy of a value in excess of 5 percent if the power to obtain the cash surrender value existed in some other person immediately before the decedent's death and was exercisable by such other person alone and in all events. The terms "reversionary interest" and "incidents of ownership" do not include the possibility that the decedent might receive a policy or its proceeds by inheritance through the estate of another person, or as a surviving spouse under a statutory right of election or a similar right.

(4) A decedent is considered to have an "incident of ownership" in an insurance policy on his life held in trust if, under the terms of the policy, the decedent (either alone or in conjunction with another person

or persons) has the power (as trustee or otherwise) to change the beneficial ownership in the policy or its proceeds, or the time or manner of enjoyment thereof, even though the decedent has no beneficial interest in the trust. Moreover, assuming the decedent created the trust, such a power may result in the inclusion in the decedent's gross estate under section 2036 or 2038 of other property transferred by the decedent to the trust if, for example, the decedent has the power to surrender the insurance policy and if the income otherwise used to pay premiums on the policy would become currently payable to a beneficiary of the trust in the event that the policy were surrendered.

(5) As an additional step in determining whether or not a decedent possessed any incidents of ownership in a policy or any part of a policy, regard must be given to the effect of the State or other applicable law upon the terms of the policy. For example, assume that the decedent purchased a policy of insurance on his life with funds held by him and his surviving wife as community property, designating their son as beneficiary but retaining the right to surrender the policy. Under the local law, the proceeds upon surrender would have inured to the marital community. Assuming that the policy is not surrendered and that the son receives the proceeds on the decedent's death, the wife's transfer of her one-half interest in the policy was not considered absolute before the decedent's death. Upon the wife's prior death, one-half of the value of the policy would have been included in her gross estate. Under these circumstances, the power of surrender possessed by the decedent as agent for his wife with respect to one-half of the policy is not, for purposes of this section, an "incident of ownership", and the decedent is, therefore, deemed to possess an incident of ownership in only one-half of the policy.

Transfers for Insufficient Consideration

§ 20.2043-1 **Transfers for insufficient consideration**—(a) *In general.* The transfers, trusts, interests, rights or powers enumerated and described in sections 2035 through 2038 and section 2041 are not subject to the Federal estate tax if made, created, exercised, or relinquished in a transaction which constituted a bona fide sale for an adequate and full consideration in money or money's worth. To constitute a bona fide sale for an adequate and full consideration in money or money's worth, the transfer must have been made in good faith, and the price must have been an adequate and full equivalent reducible to a money value. If the price was less than such a consideration, only the excess of the fair market value of the property (as of the applicable valuation date) over the price received by the decedent is included in ascertaining the value of his gross estate.

(b) *Marital rights and support obligations.* For purposes of chapter 11, a relinquishment or promised relinquishment of dower, curtesy, or of a statutory estate created in lieu of dower or curtesy, or of other marital rights in the decedent's property or estate, is not to any extent a consideration in "money or money's worth."

§ 20.2044-1 **Applicability to pre-existing transfers or interests.** Sections 2034 through 2042 are applicable regardless of when the interests and events referred to in those sections were created or took place, except as otherwise provided in those sections and the regulations thereunder.

TAXABLE ESTATE

§ 20.2051-1 **Definition of taxable estate.** The taxable estate of a decedent who was a citizen or resident (see paragraph (b)(1)(i) of § 20.0-1) of the United States at the time of his death is determined by subtracting the total amount of the deductions authorized by sections 2052 through 2056 from the total amount which must be included in the gross estate under sections 2031 through 2044. These deductions are in general as follows:

(1) An exemption of $60,000 (section 2052);

(2) Funeral and administration expenses and claims against the estate (including certain taxes and charitable pledges) (section 2053);

(3) Losses from casualty or theft during the administration of the estate (section 2054);

(4) Charitable transfers (section 2055); and

(5) The marital deduction (section 2056).

See section 2106 and the regulations thereunder for the computation of the taxable estate of a decedent who was not a citizen or resident of the United States. See also § 1.642(g)-1 concerning the disallowance for income tax purposes of certain deductions allowed for estate tax purposes.

Exemption

§ 20.2052-1 **Exemption.** An exemption of $60,000 is allowed as a deduction under section 2052 from the gross estate of a decedent who was a citizen or resident of the United States at the time of his death. For the amount of the exemption allowed as a deduction from the gross estate of a decedent who was a nonresident not a citizen of the United States, see paragraph (a)(3) of § 20.2106-1.

Expenses, Indebtedness and Taxes

§ 20.2053-1 **Deductions for expenses, indebtedness, and taxes; in general**—(a) *General rule.* In determining the taxable estate of a decedent who was a citizen or resident of the United States at the time of his death, there are allowed as deductions under section 2053(a) and (b) amounts falling within the following two categories (subject to the limitations contained in this section and in §§ 20.2053-2 through 20.2053-9):

(1) *First category.* Amounts which are payable out of property subject to claims and which are allowable by the law of the jurisdiction,

whether within or without the United States, under which the estate is being administered for—

(i) Funeral expenses;

(ii) Administration expenses;

(iii) Claims against the estate (including taxes to the extent set forth in § 20.2053-6 and charitable pledges to the extent set forth in § 20.2053-5) ; and

(iv) Unpaid mortgages on, or any indebtedness in respect of, property, the value of the decedent's interest in which is included in the value of the gross estate undiminished by the mortgage or indebtedness.

As used in this subparagraph, the phrase "allowable by the law of the jurisdiction" means allowable by the law governing the administration of decedents' estates. The phrase has no reference to amounts allowable as deductions under a law which imposes a State death tax. See further §§ 20.2053-2 through 20.2053-7.

(2) *Second category.* Amounts representing expenses incurred in administering property which is included in the gross estate but which is not subject to claims and which—

(i) Would be allowed as deductions in the first category if the property being administered were subject to claims; and

(ii) Were paid before the expiration of the period of limitation for assessment provided in section 6501.

See further § 20.2053-8.

(b) *Provisions applicable to both categories*—(1) *In general.* If the item is not one of those described in paragraph (a) of this section, it is not deductible merely because payment is allowed by the local law. If the amount which may be expended for the particular purpose is limited by the local law, no deduction in excess of that limitation is permissible.

(2) *Effect of court decree.* The decision of a local court as to the amount and allowability under local law of a claim or administration expense will ordinarily be accepted if the court passes upon the facts upon which deductibility depends. If the court does not pass upon those facts, its decree will, of course, not be followed. For example, if the question before the court is whether a claim should be allowed, the decree allowing it will ordinarily be accepted as establishing the validity and amount of the claim. However, the decree will not necessarily be accepted even though it purports to decide the facts upon which deductibility depends. It must appear that the court actually passed upon the merits of the claim. This will be presumed in all cases of an active and genuine contest. If the result reached appears to be unreasonable, this is some evidence that there was not such a contest, but it may be rebutted by proof to the contrary. If the decree was rendered by consent, it will be accepted, provided the consent was a bona fide recognition of the validity of the claim (and not a mere cloak for a gift) and was accepted by the court as satisfactory evidence upon the merits. It will be presumed that the consent was of this character, and was so accepted, if given by all parties having an interest adverse to the claimant. The decree will not be accepted if it is at variance with the law of the State; as, for example, an allowance made to an executor in excess of that prescribed by statute.

967

On the other hand, a deduction for the amount of a bona fide indebtedness of the decedent, or of a reasonable expense of administration, will not be denied because no court decree has been entered if the amount would be allowable under local law.

(3) *Estimated amounts.* An item may be entered on the return for deduction though its exact amount is not then known, provided it is ascertainable with reasonable certainty, and will be paid. No deduction may be taken upon the basis of a vague or uncertain estimate. If the amount of a liability was not ascertainable at the time of final audit of the return by the district director and, as a consequence, it was not allowed as a deduction in the audit, and subsequently the amount of the liability is ascertained, relief may be sought by a petition to the Tax Court or a claim for refund as provided by sections 6213(a) and 6511, respectively.

(c) *Provision applicable to first category only.* Deductions of the first category (described in paragraph (a)(1) of this section) are limited under section 2053(a) to amounts which would be properly allowable out of property subject to claims by the law of the jurisdiction under which the decedent's estate is being administered. Further, the total allowable amount of deductions of the first category is limited by section 2053(c)(2) to the sum of—

(1) The value of property included in the decedent's gross estate and subject to claims, plus

(2) Amounts paid, out of property not subject to claims against the decedent's estate, within 15 months after the decedent's death (the period within which the estate tax return must be filed under section 6075), or within any extension of time for filing the return granted under section 6081.

The term "property subject to claims" is defined in section 2053(c)(2) as meaning the property includible in the gross estate which, or the avails of which, under the applicable law, would bear the burden of the payment of these deductions in the final adjustment and settlement of the decedent's estate. However, for the purposes of this definition, the value of property subject to claims is first reduced by the amount of any deduction allowed under section 2054 for any losses from casualty or theft incurred during the settlement of the estate attributable to such property. The application of this paragraph may be illustrated by the following examples:

Example (1). The only item in the gross estate is real property valued at $250,000 which the decedent and his surviving spouse held as tenants by the entirety. Under the local law, this real property is not subject to claims. Funeral expenses of $1,200 and debts of the decedent in the amount of $1,500 are allowable under local law. Before the prescribed date for filing the estate tax return, the surviving spouse paid the funeral expenses and $1,000 of the debts. The remaining $500 of the debts was paid by her after the prescribed date for filing the return. The total amount allowable as deductions under section 2053 is limited to $2,200, the amount paid prior to the prescribed date for filing the return.

Example (2). The only two items in the gross estate were a bank deposit of $20,000 and insurance in the amount of $150,000. The insurance was payable to the decedent's surviving spouse and under local law was not subject to claims. Funeral expenses of $1,000 and debts in the amount of $29,000 were allowable under local law. A son was executor of the estate and before the prescribed date for filing the estate tax return he paid the funeral expenses and $9,000 of the debts, using therefor $5,000 of the bank deposit and $5,000 supplied by the surviving spouse. After the prescribed date for filing the return, the executor paid the remaining $20,000 of the debts, using for that purpose the $15,000 left in the bank account plus an additional $5,000 supplied by the surviving spouse. The total amount allowable as deductions under section 2053 is limited to $25,000 ($20,000 of property subject to claims plus the $5,000 additional amount which, before the prescribed date for filing the return, was paid out of property not subject to claims).

(d) *Disallowance of double deductions.* See section 642(g) and § 1.642 (g)-1 with respect to the disallowance for income tax purposes of certain deductions unless the right to take such deductions for estate tax purposes is waived.

§ 20.2053-2 **Deduction for funeral expenses.** Such amounts for funeral expenses are allowed as deductions from a decedent's gross estate as (a) are actually expended, (b) would be properly allowable out of property subject to claims under the laws of the local jurisdiction, and (c) satisfy the requirements of paragraph (c) of § 20.2053-1. A reasonable expenditure for a tombstone, monument, or mausoleum, or for a burial lot, either for the decedent or his family, including a reasonable expenditure for its future care, may be deducted under this heading, provided such an expenditure is allowable by the local law. Included in funeral expenses is the cost of transportation of the person bringing the body to the place of burial.

§ 20.2053-3 **Deduction for expenses of administering estate**—(a) *In general.* The amounts deductible from a decedent's gross estate as "administration expenses" of the first category (see paragraphs (a) and (c) of § 20.2053-1) are limited to such expenses as are actually and necessarily incurred in the administration of the decedent's estate; that is, in the collection of assets, payment of debts, and distribution of property to the persons entitled to it. The expenses contemplated in the law are such only as attend the settlement of an estate and the transfer of the property of the estate to individual beneficiaries or to a trustee, whether the trustee is the executor or some other person. Expenditures not essential to the proper settlement of the estate, but incurred for the individual benefit of the heirs, legatees, or devisees, may not be taken as deductions. Administration expenses include (1) executor's commissions; (2) attorney's fees; and (3) miscellaneous expenses. Each of these classes is considered separately in paragraphs (b) through (d) of this section.

(b) *Executor's commissions.* (1) The executor or administrator, in filing the estate tax return, may deduct his commissions in such an amount as has actually been paid, or in an amount which at the time of filing the estate tax return may reasonably be expected to be paid, but no deduction may be taken if no commissions are to be collected. If the amount of the commissions has not been fixed by decree of the proper court, the deduction will be allowed on the final audit of the return, to the extent that all three of the following conditions are satisfied:

(i) The district director is reasonably satisfied that the commissions claimed will be paid;

(ii) The amount claimed as a deduction is within the amount allowable by the laws of the jurisdiction in which the estate is being administered; and

(iii) It is in accordance with the usually accepted practice in the jurisdiction to allow such an amount in estates of similar size and character.

If the deduction is disallowed in whole or in part on final audit, the disallowance will be subject to modification as the facts may later require. If the deduction is allowed in advance of payment and payment is thereafter waived, it shall be the duty of the executor to notify the district director and to pay the resulting tax, together with interest.

(2) A bequest or devise to the executor in lieu of commissions is not deductible. If, however, the decedent fixed by his will the compensation payable to the executor for services to be rendered in the administration of the estate, deduction may be taken to the extent that the amount so fixed does not exceed the compensation allowable by the local law or practice.

(3) Except to the extent that a trustee is in fact performing services with respect to property subject to claims which would normally be performed by an executor, amounts paid as trustees' commissions do not constitute expenses of administration under the first category, and are only deductible as expenses of the second category to the extent provided in § 20.2053-8.

(c) *Attorney's fees.* (1) The executor or administrator, in filing the estate tax return, may deduct such an amount of attorney's fees as has actually been paid, or an amount which at the time of filing may reasonably be expected to be paid. If on the final audit of a return the fees claimed have not been awarded by the proper court and paid, the deduction will, nevertheless, be allowed, if the district director is reasonably satisfied that the amount claimed will be paid and that it does not exceed a reasonable remuneration for the services rendered, taking into account the size and character of the estate and the local law and practice. If the deduction is disallowed in whole or in part on final audit, the disallowance will be subject to modification as the facts may later require.

(2) A deduction for attorneys' fees incurred in contesting an asserted deficiency or in prosecuting a claim for refund should be claimed at the time the deficiency is contested or the refund claim is prosecuted. A deduction for reasonable attorneys' fees actually paid in contesting an asserted deficiency or in prosecuting a claim for refund will be allowed even though the deduction, as such, was not claimed in the estate tax return or in the claim for refund. A deduction for these fees shall not be denied, and the sufficiency of a claim for refund shall not be ques-

970

tioned, solely by reason of the fact that the amount of the fees to be paid was not established at the time that the right to the deduction was claimed.

(3) Attorneys' fees incurred by beneficiaries incident to litigation as to their respective interests do not constitute a proper deduction, inasmuch as expenses of this character are incurred on behalf of the beneficiaries personally and are not administration expenses.

(d) *Miscellaneous administration expenses.* Miscellaneous administration expenses include such expenses as court costs, surrogates' fees, accountants' fees, appraisers' fees, clerk hire, etc. Expenses necessarily incurred in preserving and distributing the estate are deductible, including the cost of storing or maintaining property of the estate, if it is impossible to effect immediate distribution to the beneficiaries. Expenses for preserving and carrying for the property may not include outlays for additions or improvements; nor will such expenses be allowed for a longer period than the executor is reasonably required to retain the property. A brokerage fee for selling property of the estate is deductible if the sale is necessary in order to (1) pay the decedent's debts, the expenses of administration, or taxes, (2) preserve the estate, or (3) effect distribution. Other expenses attending the sale are deductible, such as the fees of an auctioneer if it is reasonably necessary to employ one.

§ 20.2053-4 **Deduction for claims against the estate; in general.** The amounts that may be deducted as claims against a decedent's estate are such only as represent personal obligations of the decedent existing at the time of his death, whether or not then matured, and interest thereon which had accrued at the time of death. Only interest accrued at the date of the decedent's death is allowable even though the executor elects the alternate valuation method under section 2032. Only claims enforceable against the decedent's estate may be deducted. Except as otherwise provided in § 20.2053-5 with respect to pledges or subscriptions, section 2053(c)(1)(A) provides that the allowance of a deduction for a claim founded upon a promise or agreement is limited to the extent that the liability was contracted bona fide and for an adequate and full consideration in money or money's worth. See § 20.2043-1. Liabilities imposed by law or arising out of torts are deductible.

§ 20.2053-5 **Deductions for charitable, etc., pledges or subscriptions.** A pledge or a subscription, evidenced by a promissory note or otherwise, even though enforceable against the estate, is deductible only to the extent that—

(a) Liability therefor was contracted bona fide and for an adequate and full consideration in cash or its equivalent, or

(b) It would have constituted an allowable deduction under section 2055 (relating to charitable, etc., deductions) if it had been a bequest.

§ 20.2053-6 **Deduction for taxes—**(a) *In general.* Taxes are deductible in computing a decedent's gross estate only as claims against the estate (except to the extent that excise taxes may be allowable as administration expenses), and only to the extent not disallowed by section 2053(c)(1)(B) (see the remaining paragraphs of this section). However, see § 20.2053-9 with respect to the deduction allowed for certain State death taxes on charitable, etc., transfers.

(b) *Property taxes.* Property taxes are not deductible unless they accrued before the decedent's death. However, they are not deductible merely because they have accrued in an accounting sense. Property taxes in order to be deductible must be an enforceable obligation of the decedent at the time of his death.

(c) *Death taxes.* No estate, succession, legacy or inheritance tax payable by reason of the decedent's death is deductible, except as provided in § 20.2053-9 with respect to certain State death taxes on charitable, etc., transfers. However, see sections 2011 and 2014 and the regulations thereunder with respect to credits for death taxes.

(d) *Gift taxes.* Unpaid gift taxes on gifts made by a decedent before his death are deductible. If a gift is considered as made one-half by the decedent and one-half by his spouse under section 2513, the entire amount of the gift tax, unpaid at the decedent's death, attributable to a gift in fact made by the decedent is deductible. No portion of the tax attributable to a gift in fact made by the decedent's spouse is deductible except to the extent that the obligation is enforced against the decedent's estate and his estate has no effective right of contribution against his spouse. (See section 2012 and § 20.2012-1 with respect to credit for gift taxes paid upon gifts of property included in a decedent's gross estate.)

(e) *Excise taxes.* Excise taxes incurred in selling property of a decedent's estate are deductible as an expense of administration if the sale is necessary in order to (1) pay the decedent's debts, expenses of administration, or taxes, (2) preserve the estate, or (3) effect distribution. Excise taxes incurred in distributing property of the estate in kind are also deductible.

(f) *Income taxes.* Unpaid income taxes are deductible if they are on income properly includible in an income tax return of the decedent for a period before his death. Taxes on income received after the decedent's death are not deductible. If income received by a decedent during his lifetime is included in a joint income tax return filed by the decedent and his spouse, or by the decedent's estate and his surviving spouse, the portion of the joint liability for the period covered by the return for which a deduction would be allowed is the amount for which the decedent's estate would be liable under local law, as between the decedent and his spouse, after enforcement of any effective right of reimbursement or contribution. In the absence of evidence to the contrary, the deductible amount is presumed to be an amount bearing the same ratio to the total joint tax liability for the period covered by the return that the amount of income tax for which the decedent would have been liable if he had filed a separate return for that period bears to the total of the amounts for which the decedent and his spouse would have been liable if they had

972

both filed separate returns for that period. Thus, in the absence of evidence to the contrary, the deductible amount equals

$$\frac{\text{decedent's separate tax}}{\text{both separate taxes}} \times \text{ joint tax.}$$

However, the deduction cannot in any event exceed the lesser of—

(1) The decedent's liability for the period (as determined in this paragraph) reduced by the amounts already contributed by the decedent toward payment of the joint liability, or

(2) If there is an enforceable agreement between the decedent and his spouse or between the executor and the spouse relative to the payment of the joint liability, the amount which pursuant to the agreement is to be contributed by the estate toward payment of the joint liability.

If the decedent's estate and his surviving spouse are entitled to a refund on account of an overpayment of a joint income tax liability, the overpayment is an asset includible in the decedent's gross estate under section 2033 in the amount to which the estate would be entitled under local law, as between the estate and the surviving spouse. In the absence of evidence to the contrary, the includible amount is presumed to be the amount by which the decedent's contributions toward payment of the joint tax exceeds his liability determined in accordance with the principles set forth in this paragraph (other than subparagraph (1)).

§ 20.2053-7 **Deduction for unpaid mortgages.** A deduction is allowed from a decedent's gross estate of the full unpaid amount of a mortgage upon, or of any other indebtedness in respect of, any property of the gross estate, including interest which had accrued thereon to the date of death, provided the value of the property, undiminished by the amount of the mortgage or indebtedness, is included in the value of the gross estate. If the decedent's estate is liable for the amount of the mortgage or indebtedness, the full value of the property subject to the mortgage or indebtedness must be included as part of the value of the gross estate; the amount of the mortgage or indebtedness being in such case allowed as a deduction. But if the decedent's estate is not so liable, only the value of the equity of redemption (or the value of the property, less the mortgage or indebtedness) need be returned as part of the value of the gross estate. In no case may the deduction on account of the mortgage or indebtedness exceed the liability therefor contracted bona fide and for an adequate and full consideration in money or money's worth. See § 20.2043-1. Only interest accrued to the date of the decedent's death is allowable even though the alternate valuation method under section 2032 is selected. Inasmuch as real property outside of the United States does not form a part of the gross estate, no deduction may be taken of any mortgage thereon or any other indebtedness in respect thereof.

§ 20.2053-8 **Deduction for expenses in administering property not subject to claims.** (a) Expenses incurred in administering property included in a decedent's gross estate but not subject to claims fall within the second category of deductions set forth in § 20.2053-1, and may be allowed as deductions if they—

(1) Would be allowed as deductions in the first category if the property being administered were subject to claims; and

(2) Were paid before the expiration of the period of limitation for assessment provided in section 6501.

Usually, these expenses are incurred in connection with the administration of a trust established by a decedent during his lifetime. They may also be incurred in connection with the collection of other assets or the transfer or clearance of title to other property included in a decedent's gross estate for estate tax purposes but not included in his probate estate.

(b) These expenses may be allowed as deductions only to the extent that they would be allowed as deductions under the first category if the property were subject to claims. See § 20.2053-3. The only expenses in administering property not subject to claims which are allowed as deductions are those occasioned by the decedent's death and incurred in settling the decedent's interest in the property or vesting good title to the property in the beneficiaries. Expenses not coming within the description in the preceding sentence but incurred on behalf of the transferees are not deductible.

(c) The principles set forth in paragraphs (b), (c), and (d) of § 20.2053-3 (relating to the allowance of executor's commissions, attorney's fees, and miscellaneous administration expenses of the first category) are applied in determining the extent to which trustee's commissions, attorney's and accountant's fees, and miscellaneous administration expenses are allowed in connection with the administration of property not subject to claims.

(d) The application of this section may be illustrated by the following examples:

Example (1). In 1940, the decedent made an irrevocable transfer of property to the X Trust Company, as trustee. The instrument of transfer provided that the trustee should pay the income from the property to the decedent for the duration of his life and, upon his death, distribute the corpus of the trust among designated beneficiaries. The property was included in the decedent's gross estate under the provisions of section 2036. Three months after the date of death, the trustee distributed the trust corpus among the beneficiaries, except for $6,000 which it withheld. The amount withheld represented $5,000 which it retained as trustee's commissions in connection with the termination of the trust and $1,000 which it had paid to an attorney for representing it in connection with the termination. Both the trustee's commissions and the attorney's fees were allowable under the law of the jurisdiction in which the trust was being administered, were reasonable in amount, and were in accord with local custom. Under these circumstances, the estate is allowed a deduction of $6,000.

Example (2). In 1945, the decedent made an irrevocable transfer of property to Y Trust Company, as trustee. The instrument of transfer provided that the trustee should pay the income from the property to the decedent during his life. If the decedent's wife survived him, the trust was to continue for the duration of her life, with Y Trust Company and the decedent's son as co-trustees, and with income payable to the decedent's wife for the duration of her life. Upon the death of both the decedent and his wife, the corpus is to be distributed among designated remaindermen. The decedent was survived by his wife. The property was included in the decedent's gross estate under the provisions of section 2036. In accordance with local custom, the trustee made an accounting to the court as of the date of the decedent's death. Following the death of the decedent, a controversy arose among the remaindermen as to their respective rights under the instrument of transfer, and a suit was brought in court to which the trustee was made a party. As a part of the accounting, the court approved the following expenses which the trustee had paid within 3 years following the date of death: $10,000, trustee's commissions; $5,000, accountant's fees; $25,000, attorney's fees; and $2,500, representing fees paid to the guardian of a remainderman who was a minor. The trustee's commissions and accountant's fees were for services in connection with the usual issues involved in a trust accounting as also were one-half of the attorney's and guardian's fees. The remainder of the attorney's and guardian's fees were for services performed in connection with the suit brought by the remaindermen. The amount allowed as a deduction is the $28,750 ($10,000, trustee's commissions; $5,000 accountant's fees; $12,-500, attorney's fees; and $1,250, guardian's fees) incurred as expenses in connection with the usual issues involved in a trust accounting. The remaining expenses are not allowed as deductions since they were incurred on behalf of the transferees.

Example (3). Decedent in 1950 made an irrevocable transfer of property to the Z Trust Company, as trustee. The instrument of transfer provided that the trustee should pay the income from the property to the decedent's wife for the duration of her life. If the decedent survived his wife the trust corpus was to be returned to him but if he did not survive her, then upon the death of the wife the trust corpus was to be distributed among their children. The decedent predeceased his wife and the transferred property, less the value of the wife's outstanding life estate, was included in his gross estate under the provisions of section 2037 since his reversionary interest therein immediately before his death was in excess of 5 percent of the value of the property. At the wife's request, the court ordered the trustee to render an accounting of the trust property as of the date of the decedent's death. No deduction will be allowed the decedent's estate for any of the expenses incurred in connection with the trust accounting, since the expenses were incurred on behalf of the wife.

Example (4). If, in the preceding example, the decedent died without other property and no executor or administrator of his estate was appointed, so that it was necessary for the trustee to prepare an estate tax return and participate in its audit, or if the trustee required accounting proceedings for its own protection in accordance with local custom, trustees', attorneys', and guardians' fees in connection with the estate tax or accounting proceedings would be deductible to the same extent that they would be deductible if the property were subject to claims. Deductions incurred under similar circumstances by a surviving joint tenant or the recipient of life insurance proceeds would also be deductible.

§ 20.2053-9 Deduction for certain State death taxes—(a) *General rule.* A deduction is allowed a decedent's estate under section 2053(d) for the amount of any estate, succession, legacy, or inheritance tax imposed by a State, Territory, the District of Columbia, or any possession of the United States upon a transfer by the decedent for charitable, etc., uses described in section 2055 or 2106(a)(2) (relating to the estates of nonresidents not citizens), but only if (1) the conditions stated in paragraph (b) of this section are met, and (2) an election is made in accordance with the provisions of paragraph (c) of this section. See section 2011(e) and § 20.2011-2 for the effect which the allowance of this deduction has upon the credit for State death taxes.

(b) *Condition for allowance of deduction.* (1) The deduction is not allowed unless either—

(i) The entire decrease in the Federal estate tax resulting from the allowance of the deduction inures solely to the benefit of a charitable, etc., transferee described in section 2055 or 2106(a)(2), or

(ii) The Federal estate tax is equitably apportioned among all the transferees (including the decedent's surviving spouse and the charitable, etc., transferees) of property included in the decedent's gross estate.

For allowance of the credit, it is sufficient if either of these conditions is satisfied. Thus, in a case where the entire decrease in Federal estate tax inures to the benefit of a charitable transferee, the deduction is allowable even though the Federal estate tax is not equitably apportioned among all the transferees of property included in the decedent's gross estate. Similarly, if the Federal estate tax is equitably apportioned among all the transferees of property included in the decedent's gross estate, the deduction is allowable even though a noncharitable transferee receives some benefit from the allowance of the deduction.

(2) For purposes of this paragraph, the Federal estate tax is considered to be equitably apportioned among all the transferees (including the decedent's surviving spouse and the charitable, etc., transferees) of property included in the decedent's gross estate only if each transferee's share of the tax is based upon the net amount of his bequest subjected to the tax (taking into account any exemptions, credits, or deductions allowed by chapter 11). See examples (2) through (5) of paragraph (e) of this section.

(c) *Exercise of election.* The election to take a deduction for a State death tax imposed upon a transfer for charitable, etc., uses shall be exercised by the executor by the filing of a written notification to that effect with the district director of internal revenue in whose district the estate tax return for the decedent's estate was filed. The notification shall be filed before the expiration of the period of limitation for assessment provided in section 6501 (usually 3 years from the last day for filing the return). The election may be revoked by the executor by the filing of a written notification to that effect with the district director at any time before the expiration of such period.

(d) *Amount of State death tax imposed upon a transfer.* If a State death tax is imposed upon the transfer of the decedent's entire estate and not upon the transfer of a particular share thereof, the State death tax imposed upon a transfer for charitable, etc., uses is deemed to be an amount, E, which bears the same ratio to F (the amount of the State death tax imposed with respect to the transfer of the entire estate) as G (the value of the charitable, etc., transfer, reduced as provided in the next sentence) bears to H (the total value of the properties. interests. and benefits subjected to the State death tax received by all persons interested in the estate, reduced as provided in the last sentence of this paragraph). In arriving at amount G of the ratio, the value of the charitable, etc., transfer is reduced by the amount of any deduction or exclusion allowed with respect to such property in determining the amount of the State death tax. In arriving at amount H of the ratio, the total value of the properties, interests, and benefits subjected to State death tax received by all persons interested in the estate is reduced by the amount of all deductions and exclusions allowed in determining the amount of the State death tax on account of the nature of a beneficiary or a beneficiary's relationship to the decedent.

(e) *Examples.* The application of this section may be illustrated by the following examples:

Example (1). The decedent's gross estate was valued at $200,000. He bequeathed $90,000 to a nephew, $10,000 to Charity A, and the remainder of his estate to Charity B. State inheritance tax in the amount of $13,500 was imposed upon the bequest to the nephew, $1,500 upon the bequest to Charity A, and $15,000 upon the bequest to Charity B. Under the will and local law, each legatee is required to pay the State inheritance tax on his bequest, and the Federal estate tax is to be paid out of the residuary estate. Since the entire burden of paying the Federal estate tax falls on Charity B, it follows that the decrease in the Federal estate tax resulting from the allowance of deductions for State death taxes in the amounts of $1,500 and $15,000 would inure solely for the benefit of Charity B. Therefore, deductions of $1,500 and $15,000 are allowable under section 2053(d). If, in this example, the State death taxes as well as the Federal estate tax were to be paid out of the residuary estate, the result would be the same.

Example (2). The decedent's gross estate was valued at $350,000. Expenses, indebtedness, etc., amounted to $50,000. The entire estate was bequeathed in equal shares to a son, a daughter, and Charity C. State inheritance tax in the amount of $2,000 was imposed upon the bequest to the son, $2,000 upon the bequest to the daughter, and $5,000 upon the bequest to Charity C. Under the will and local law, each legatee is required to pay his own State inheritance tax and his proportionate share of the Federal estate tax determined by taking into consideration the net amount of his bequest subjected to the tax. Since each legatee's share of the Federal estate tax is based upon the net amount of his bequest subjected to the tax (note that the deductions under sections 2053(d) and 2055 will have the effect of reducing Charity C's proportionate share of the tax), the tax is considered to be equitably apportioned. Thus, a deduction of $5,000 is allowable under section 2053(d). This deduction together with a deduction of $95,000 under section 2055 (charitable deduction) will mean that none of Charity C's bequest is subjected to Federal estate tax. Hence, the son and the daughter will bear the entire estate tax.

Example (3). The decedent bequeathed his property in equal shares, after payment of all expenses, to a son, a daughter, and a charity. State inheritance tax of $2,000 was imposed upon the bequest to the son, $2,000 upon the bequest to the daughter, and $15,000 upon the bequest to the charity. Under the will and local law, each beneficiary pays the State inheritance tax on his bequest and the Federal estate tax is to be paid out of the estate as an administration expense. If the deduction for State death tax on the charitable bequest is allowed in this case, some portion of the decrease in the Federal estate tax would inure to the benefit of the son and the daughter. The Federal estate tax is not considered to be equitably apportioned in this case since each legatee's share of the Federal estate tax is not based upon the net amount of his bequest subjected to the tax (note that the deductions under sections 2053(d) and 2055 will not have the effect of reducing the charity's proportionate share of the tax). Inasmuch as some of the decrease in the Federal estate tax payable would inure to the benefit of the son and the daughter, and inasmuch as there is no equitable apportionment of the tax, no deduction is allowable under section 2053(d).

Example (4). The decedent bequeathed his entire residuary estate in trust to pay the income to X for life with remainder to charity. The State imposed inheritance taxes of $2,000 upon the bequest to X and $10,000 upon the bequest to charity. Under the will and local law, all State and Federal taxes are payable out of the residuary estate and therefore they would reduce the amount which would become the corpus of the trust. If the deduction for the State death tax on the charitable bequest is allowed in this case, some portion of the decrease in the Federal estate tax would inure to the benefit of X since the allowance of the deduction would increase the size of the corpus from which X is to receive the income for life. Also, the Federal estate tax is not considered to be equitably apportioned in this case since each legatee's share of the Federal estate tax is not based upon the net amount of his bequest subjected to the tax (note that the deductions under sections 2053(d) and 2055 will not have the effect of reducing the charity's proportionate share of the tax). Inasmuch as some of the decrease in the Federal estate tax payable would inure to the benefit of X, and inasmuch as there is no equitable apportionment of the tax, no deduction is allowable under section 2053(d).

Example (5). The decedent's gross estate was valued at $750,000.

Expenses, indebtedness, etc., amounted to $50,000. The decedent bequeathed $350,000 of his estate to his surviving spouse and the remainder of his estate equally to his son and Charity D. State inheritance tax in the amount of $7,000 was imposed upon the bequest to the surviving spouse, $26,250 upon the bequest to the son, and $26,250 upon the bequest to Charity D. The will was silent concerning the payment of taxes. In such a case, the local law provides that each legatee shall pay his own State inheritance tax. The local law further provides for an apportionment of the Federal estate tax among the legatees of the estate. Under the apportionment provisions, the surviving spouse is not required to bear any part of the Federal estate tax with respect to her $350,000 bequest. It should be noted, however, that the marital deduction allowed to the decedent's estate by reason of the bequest to the surviving spouse is limited to $343,000 ($350,000 bequest less $7,000 State inheritance tax payable by the surviving spouse). Thus, the bequest to the surviving spouse is subjected to the Federal estate tax in the net amount of $7,000. If the deduction for State death tax on the charitable bequest is allowed in this case, some portion of the decrease in the Federal estate tax would inure to the benefit of the son. The Federal estate tax is not considered to be equitably apportioned in this case since each legatee's share of the Federal estate tax is not based upon the net amount of his bequest subjected to the tax (note that the surviving spouse is to pay no tax). Inasmuch as some of the decrease in the Federal estate tax payable would inure to the benefit of the son, and inasmuch as there is no equitable apportionment of the tax, no deduction is allowable under section 2053(d).

Losses

§ 20.2054-1 **Deduction for losses from casualties or theft.** A deduction is allowed for losses incurred during the settlement of the estate arising from fires, storms, shipwrecks, or other casualties, or from theft, if the losses are not compensated for by insurance or otherwise. If the loss is partly compensated for, the excess of the loss over the compensation may be deducted. Losses which are not of the nature described are not deductible. In order to be deductible a loss must occur during the settlement of the estate. If a loss with respect to an asset occurs after its distribution to the distributee it may not be deducted. Notwithstanding the foregoing, no deduction is allowed under this section if the estate has waived its right to take such a deduction pursuant to the provisions of section 642(g) in order to permit its allowance for income tax purposes. See further § 1.642 (g)-1.

Charitable, etc., Transfers

§ 20.2055-1 **Deduction for transfers for public, charitable, and religious uses; in general**—(a) *General rule.* A deduction is allowed under section 2055(a) from the gross estate of a decedent who was a citizen or resident of the United States at the time of his death for the value of property included in the decedent's gross estate and transferred by the decedent during his lifetime or by will—

(1) To or for the use of the United States, any State, Territory, any political subdivision thereof, or the District of Columbia, for exclusively public purposes;

(2) To or for the use of any corporation or association organized and operated exclusively for religious, charitable, scientific, literary, or educational purposes (including the encouragement of art and the prevention of cruelty to children or animals), if no part of the net earnings of the corporation or association inures to the benefit of any private stockholder or individual (other than as a legitimate object of such purposes), and no substantial part of its activities is carrying on propaganda, or otherwise attempting, to influence legislation;

(3) To a trustee or trustees, or a fraternal society, order, or association operating under the lodge system, if the transferred property is to be used exclusively for religious, charitable, scientific, literary, or educational purposes (or for the prevention of cruelty to children or animals), and if no substantial part of the activities of such transferee is carrying on propaganda, or otherwise attempting, to influence legislation; or

(4) To or for the use of any veterans' organization incorporated by Act of Congress, or of any of its departments, local chapters, or posts, no part of the net earnings of which inures to the benefit of any private shareholder or individual.

The deduction is not limited, in the case of estates of citizens or residents of the United States, to transfers to domestic corporations or associations, or to trustees for use within the United States. Nor is the deduction subject to percentage limitations such as are applicable to the charitable deduction under the income tax. However, sections 503(e) and 681(b)(5) provide that no deduction is allowed for transfers to organizations or trusts described in subparagraphs (2) and (3) of this paragraph which have engaged in certain "prohibited transactions" (see § 20.2055-4).

(b) *Powers of appointment*—(1) *General rule.* A deduction is allowable under section 2055(b) for the value of property passing to or for the use of a transferee described in paragraph (a) of this section by the exercise, failure to exercise, release or lapse of a power of appointment by reason of which the property is includible in the decedent's gross estate under section 2041.

(2) *Certain bequests subject to power of appointment.* For the allowance of a deduction in the case of a bequest in trust where the decedent's surviving spouse (i) was over 80 years of age at the date of the decedent's death, (ii) was entitled for life to all of the net income from the trust, and (iii) had a power of appointment over the corpus of the trust exercisable by will in favor of, among others, a charitable organization, see section 2055(b)(2). See also section 6503(e) for suspension of the period of limitations for assessment or collection of any deficiency attributable to the allowance of the deduction.

980

(c) *Submission of evidence.* In establishing the right of the estate to the deduction authorized by section 2055, the executor should submit the following with the return:

(1) A copy of any instrument in writing by which the decedent made a transfer of property in his lifetime the value of which is required by statute to be included in his gross estate, for which a deduction under section 2055 is claimed. If the instrument is of record the copy should be certified, and if not of record, the copy should be verified.

(2) A written statement by the executor containing a declaration that it is made under penalties of perjury and stating whether any action has been instituted to construe or to contest the decedent's will or any provision thereof affecting the charitable deduction claimed and whether, according to his information and belief, any such action is designed or contemplated.

The executor shall also submit such other documents or evidence as may be requested by the district director.

§ 20.2055-2 Transfers not exclusively for charitable purposes—(a) *Remainders and similar interests.* If a trust is created or property is transferred for both a charitable and a private purpose, deduction may be taken of the value of the charitable beneficial interest only insofar as that interest is presently ascertainable, and hence severable from the noncharitable interest. The present value of a remainder or other deferred payment to be made for a charitable purpose is to be determined in accordance with the rules stated in § 20.2031-7. Thus, if money or property is placed in trust to pay the income to an individual during his life, or for a term of years, and then to pay the principal to a charitable organization, the present value of the remainder is deductible. To determine the present value of such remainder use the appropriate factor from column 4 of Table I or Table II of § 20.2031-7, whichever is applicable. If the interest transferred is such that its value is to be determined by a special computation (see paragraph (e) of § 20.2031-7), a request for a specific factor, accompanied by a statement of the date of birth of each person the duration of whose life may affect the value of the remainder, and by copies of the relevant instruments, may be submitted by the executor to the Commissioner who may, if conditions permit, supply the factor requested. If the Commissioner does not furnish the factor, the claim for deduction must be supported by a full statement of the computation of the present value made in accordance with the principles set forth in the applicable paragraph of § 20.2031-7.

(b) *Transfers subject to a condition or a power.* If, as of the date of a decedent's death, a transfer for charitable purposes is dependent upon the performance of some act or the happening of a precedent event in order that it might become effective, no deduction is allowable unless the possibility that the charitable transfer will not become effective is so remote as to be negligible. If an estate or interest has passed to or is vested in charity at the time of a decedent's death and the estate or interest would be defeated by the performance of some act or the happening of some event, the occurrence of which appeared to have been highly improbable at the time of the decedent's death, the deduction is allowable. If the legatee, devisee, donee, or trustee is empowered to divert the property or fund, in whole or in part, to a use or purpose which would have rendered it, to the extent that it is subject to such power, not deductible had it been directly so bequeathed, devised, or given by the decedent, the deduction will be limited to that portion, if any, of the property or fund which is exempt from an exercise of the power. The deduction is not allowed in the case of a transfer in trust conveying to charity a present interest in income if by reason of all the conditions and circumstances surrounding the transfer it appears that the charity may not receive the beneficial enjoyment of the interest. For example, assume that assets placed in trust by the decedent consist of stock in a corporation the fiscal policies of which are controlled by the decedent and his family, that the trustees and remaindermen are likewise members of the decedent's family, and that the governing instrument contains no adequate guarantee of the requisite income to the charitable organization. Under such circumstances, no deduction will be allowed. Similarly, if the trustees are not members of the decedent's family but have no power to sell or otherwise dispose of the closely held stock, or otherwise insure the requisite enjoyment of income to the charitable organization, no deduction will be allowed.

(c) *Disclaimers.* The amount of a bequest, devise, or transfer, for which a deduction is allowable under section 2055, includes an interest which falls into the bequest, devise, or transfer as a result of either—

(1) A disclaimer of a bequest, devise, transfer, or power, if (i) the disclaimer is made within 15 months after the decedent's death (the period of time within which the estate tax return must be filed under section 6075) or within any extension of time for filing the return granted pursuant to section 6081, and (ii) the disclaimer is irrevocable at the time the deduction is allowed, or

(2) The complete termination of a power to consume, invade, or appropriate property for the benefit of an individual (whether the termination occurs by reason of the death of the individual, or otherwise) if the termination occurs (i) within the period described in subparagraph (1)(i) of this paragraph, and (ii) before the power has been exercised.

Ordinarily, a disclaimer made by a person not under any legal disability will be considered irrevocable when filed with the probate court. A disclaimer is a complete and unqualified refusal to accept the rights to which one is entitled. Thus, if a beneficiary uses these rights for his own purposes, as by receiving a consideration for his formal disclaimer, he has not refused the rights to which he was entitled. There can be no disclaimer after an acceptance of these rights, expressly or impliedly. The disclaimer of a power is to be distinguished from the release or exercise of a power. The release or exercise of a power by the donee of the power in favor of a person or object described in paragraph (a) of § 20.2055-1 does not result in any deduction under section 2055 in the estate of the donor of a power (but see paragraph (b)(1) of § 20.2055-1 with respect to the donee's estate).

(d) *Payments in compromise.* If a charitable organization assigns or surrenders a part of a transfer to it pursuant to a compromise agreement in settlement of controversy, the amount so assigned or surrendered is not deductible as a transfer to that charitable organization.

§ 20.2055-3 **Death taxes payable out of charitable transfers.** (a) If under the terms of the will or other governing instrument, the law of the jurisdiction under which the estate is administered, or the law of the jurisdiction imposing the particular tax, the Federal estate tax, or any estate, succession, legacy, or inheritance tax is payable in whole or in part out of any property the transfer of which would otherwise be allowable as a deduction under section 2055, section 2055(c) provides that the sum deductible is the amount of the transferred property reduced by the amount of the tax. Section 2055(c) in effect provides that the deduction is based on the amount actually available for charitable uses, that is, the amount of the fund remaining after the payment of all death taxes. Thus, if $50,000 is bequeathed for a charitable purpose and is subjected to a State inheritance tax of $5,000, payable out of the $50,000, the amount deductible is $45,000. If a life estate is bequeathed to an individual with remainder over to a charitable organization, and by the local law the inheritance tax upon the life estate is paid out of the corpus with the result that the charitable organization will be entitled to receive only the amount of the fund less the tax, the deduction is limited to the present value, as of the date of the testator's death, of the remainder of the fund so reduced. If a testator bequeaths his residuary estate, or a portion of it, to charity, and his will contains a direction that certain inheritance taxes, otherwise payable from legacies upon which they were imposed, shall be payable out of the residuary estate, the deduction may not exceed the bequest to charity thus reduced pursuant to the direction of the will. If a residuary estate, or a portion of it, is bequeathed to charity, and by the local law the Federal estate tax is payable out of the residuary estate, the deduction may not exceed that portion of the residuary estate bequeathed to charity as reduced by the Federal estate tax. The return should fully disclose the computation of the amount to be deducted. If the amount to be deducted is dependent upon the amount of any death tax which has not been paid before the filing of the return, there should be submitted with the return a computation of that tax.

(b) It should be noted that if the Federal estate tax is payable out of a charitable transfer so that the amount of the transfer otherwise passing to charity is reduced by the amount of the tax, the resultant decrease in the amount passing to charity will further

983

reduce the allowable deduction. In such a case, the amount of the charitable deduction can be obtained only by a series of trial-and-error computations, or by a formula. If, in addition, interdependent State and Federal taxes are involved, the computation becomes highly complicated. Examples of methods of computation of the charitable deduction and the marital deduction (with which similar problems are encountered) in various situations are contained in supplemental instructions to the estate tax return.

(c) For the allowance of a deduction to a decedent's estate for certain State death taxes imposed upon charitable transfers, see section 2053(d) and § 20.2053-9.

§ 20.2055-4 **Disallowance of charitable, etc., deductions because of "prohibited transactions."** (a) Sections 503(e) and 681(b)(5) provide that no deduction which would otherwise be allowable under section 2055 for the value of property transferred by the decedent during his lifetime or by will for religious, charitable, scientific, literary, or educational purposes (including the encouragement of art and the prevention of cruelty to children or animals) is allowed if (1) the transfer is made in trust, and, for income tax purposes for the taxable year of the trust in which the transfer is made, the deduction otherwise allowable to the trust under section 642(c) is limited by section 681(b)(1) by reason of the trust having engaged in a prohibited transaction described in section 681(b)(2), or (2) the transfer is made to a corporation, community chest, fund or foundation which, for its taxable year in which the transfer is made, is not exempt from income tax under section 501(a) by reason of having engaged in a prohibited transaction described in section 503(c).

(b) For purposes of section 681(b)(5) and section 503(e), the term "transfer" includes any gift, contribution, bequest, devise, legacy, or other disposition. In applying such sections for estate tax purposes, a transfer, whether made during the decedent's lifetime or by will, is considered as having been made at the moment of the decedent's death.

(c) The income tax regulations contain the rules for the determination of the taxable year of the trust for which the deduction under section 642(c) is limited by section 681(b) and for the determination of the taxable year of the organization for which an exemption is denied under section 503(a). Generally, such taxable year is a taxable year subsequent to the taxable year during which the trust or organization has been notified by the Commissioner of Internal Revenue that it has engaged in a prohibited transaction. However, if the trust or organization during or prior to the taxable year entered into the prohibited transaction for the purpose of diverting its corpus or income from the charitable or other purposes by reason of which it is entitled to a deduction or exemption, and the transaction involves a substantial part of the income or corpus, then the deduction of the trust under section 642(c) for such taxable year is limited by section 681(b), or exemption of the organization for such taxable year is

984

denied under section 503(a), whether or not the organization has previously received notification by the Commissioner of Internal Revenue that it is engaged in a prohibited transaction. In certain cases, the limitation of sections 681 or 503 may be removed or the exemption may be reinstated for certain subsequent taxable years under the rules set forth in the income tax regulations under sections 681 and 503. In cases in which prior notification by the Commissioner of Internal Revenue is not required in order to limit the deduction of the trust under section 681(b) or to deny exemption of the organization under section 503, the deduction otherwise allowable under section 2055 is not disallowed in respect of transfers made during the same taxable year of the trust or organization in which a prohibited transaction occurred or in a prior taxable year unless the decedent or a member of his family was a party to the prohibited transaction. For the purpose of the preceding sentence, the members of the decedent's family include only his brothers and sisters, whether by whole or half blood, spouse, ancestors, and lineal descendants.

Marital Deduction

§ 20.2056(a)-1 Marital deduction; in general. (a) A deduction is allowed under section 2056 from the gross estate of a decedent who was a citizen or resident of the United States at the time of his death for the value of any property interest which passed from the decedent to his surviving spouse, if the interest is a "deductible interest" as defined in § 20.2056(a)-2, and if the total of such interests does not exceed the percentage limitation set forth in §§ 20.2056(c)-1 and 20.2056(c)-2. This deduction is referred to as the "marital deduction." The marital deduction is generally not available if the decedent's gross estate consists exclusively of property held by the decedent and his surviving spouse as community property under the law of any State, Territory, or possession of the United States, or any foreign country. See § 20.2056(c)-2. Except as otherwise provided by a death tax convention with a foreign country, the marital deduction is not allowed in the case of an estate of a nonresident who was not a citizen of the United States at the time of his death. However, if the decedent was a citizen or resident, his estate is not deprived of the right to the marital deduction by reason of the fact that his surviving spouse was neither a resident nor a citizen. For convenience, the surviving spouse is generally referred to in the feminine gender, but if the decedent was a woman the reference is to her surviving husband. Sections 20.2056(b)-1 through 20.2056(b)-6 contain miscellaneous rules for determining the amount of "deductible interests"; §§ 20.2056(c)-1 and 20.2056(c)-2 provide a percentage limitation on the allowable amount of the marital deduction; § 20.2056 (d)-1 states special rules concerning disclaimers of interests in property; and §§ 20.2056(e)-1 through 20.2056(e)-3 define various terms used in the aforementioned sections.

(b) In order to obtain the marital deduction with respect to any property interest, the executor must establish the following facts:

(1) That the decedent was survived by his spouse (see paragraph (e) of § 20.2056(e)-2);

(2) That the property interest passed from the decedent to his spouse (see §§ 20.2056(b)-5, 20.2056(b)-6, 20.2056(d)-1, and 20.2056 (e)-1 through 20.2056(e)-3);

(3) That the property interest is a "deductible interest" (see § 20.2056(a)-2);

(4) The value of the property interest (see § 20.2056(b)-4); and

(5) The value of the decedent's "adjusted gross estate" (see §§ 20.2056(c)-1 and 20.2056(c)-2).

The executor must submit such proof as is necessary to establish these facts, including any evidence requested by the district director.

§ 20.2056(a)-2 Marital deduction; "deductible interests" and "nondeductible interests."

(a) Property interests which passed from a decedent to his surviving spouse fall within two general categories: (1) those with respect to which the marital deduction is authorized, and (2) those with respect to which the marital deduction is not authorized. These categories are referred to in this section and other sections of the regulations under section 2056 as "deductible interests" and "nondeductible interests," respectively (see paragraph (b) of this section). Subject to the percentage limitation set forth in §§ 20.2056 (c)-1 and 20.2056(c)-2, the marital deduction is equal in amount to the aggregate value of the "deductible interests."

(b) An interest passing to a decedent's surviving spouse is a "deductible interest" if it does not fall within one of the following categories of "nondeductible interests":

(1) Any property interest which passed from the decedent to his surviving spouse is a "nondeductible interest" to the extent it is not included in the decedent's gross estate.

(2) If a deduction is allowed under section 2053 (relating to deductions for expenses and indebtedness) by reason of the passing of a property interest from the decedent to his surviving spouse, such interest is, to the extent of the deduction under section 2053, a "nondeductible interest." Thus, a property interest which passed from the decedent to his surviving spouse in satisfaction of a deductible claim of the spouse against the estate is, to the extent of the claim, a "nondeductible interest" (see § 20.2056(b)-4). Similarly, amounts deducted under section 2053(a)(2) for commissions allowed to the surviving spouse as executor are "nondeductible interests." As to the valuation, for the purpose of the marital deduction, of any property interest which passed from the decedent to his surviving spouse subject to a mortgage or other encumbrance, see § 20.2056(b)-4.

(3) If during settlement of the estate a loss deductible under section 2054 occurs with respect to a property interest, then that interest is, to the extent of the deductible loss, a "nondeductible interest" for the purpose of the marital deduction.

(4) A property interest passing to a decedent's surviving spouse which is a "terminable interest," as defined in § 20.2056(b)-1, is a "nondeductible interest" to the extent specified in that section.

§ 20.2056(b)-1 Marital deduction; limitation in case of life estate or other "terminable interest"—(a) *In general.* Section 2056 (b) provides that no marital deduction is allowed with respect to certain property interests, referred to generally as "terminable interests," passing from a decedent to his surviving spouse. The phrase "terminable interest" is defined in paragraph (b) of this section. However, the fact that an interest in property passing to a decedent's surviving spouse is a "terminable interest" makes it nondeductible only (1) under the circumstances described in paragraph (c) of this section, and (2) if it does not come within one of the exceptions referred to in paragraph (d) of this section.

(b) *"Terminable interests."* A "terminable interest" in property is an interest which will terminate or fail on the lapse of time or on the occurrence or the failure to occur of some contingency. Life estates, terms for years, annuities, patents, and copyrights are therefore terminable interests. However, a bond, note, or similar contractual obligation, the discharge of which would not have the effect of an annuity or a term for years, is not a terminable interest.

(c) *Nondeductible terminable interests.* (1) A property interest which constitutes a terminable interest, as defined in paragraph (b) of this section, is nondeductible if—

(i) Another interest in the same property passed from the decedent to some other person for less than an adequate and full consideration in money or money's worth, and

(ii) By reason of its passing, the other person or his heirs or assigns may possess or enjoy any part of the property after the termination or failure of the spouse's interest.

(2) Even though a property interest which constitutes a terminable interest is not nondeductible by reason of the rules stated in subparagraph (1) of this paragraph, such an interest is nondeductible if—

(i) The decedent has directed his executor or a trustee to acquire such an interest for the decedent's surviving spouse (see further paragraph (f) of this section), or

(ii) Such an interest passing to the decedent's surviving spouse may be satisfied out of a group of assets which includes a nondeductible interest (see further § 20.2056(b)-2). In this case, however, full nondeductibility may not result.

(d) *Exceptions.* A property interest passing to a decedent's surviving spouse is deductible (if it is not otherwise disqualified under § 20.2056(a)-2) even though it is a terminable interest, and even though an interest therein passed from the decedent to another person, if it is a terminable interest only because—

(1) It is conditioned on the spouse's surviving for a limited period, in the manner described in § 20.2056(b)-3;

987

(2) It is a right to income for life with a general power of appointment, meeting the requirements set forth in § 20.2056(b)-5; or

(3) It consists of life insurance or annuity payments held by the insurer with a general power of appointment in the spouse, meeting the requirements set forth in § 20.2056(b)-6.

(e) *Miscellaneous principles.* (1) In determining whether an interest passed from the decedent to some other person, it is immaterial whether interests in the same property passed to the decedent's spouse and another person at the same time, or under the same instrument.

(2) In determining whether an interest in the same property passed from the decedent both to his surviving spouse and to some other person, a distinction is to be drawn between "property," as such term is used in section 2056, and an "interest in property." The term "property" refers to the underlying property in which various interests exist; each such interest is not for this purpose to be considered as "property."

(3) Whether or not an interest is nondeductible because it is a terminable interest is to be determined by reference to the property interests which actually passed from the decedent. Subsequent conversions of the property are immaterial for this purpose. Thus, where a decedent bequeathed his estate to his wife for life with remainder to his children, the interest which passed to his wife is a nondeductible interest, even though the wife agrees with the children to take a fractional share of the estate in fee in lieu of the life interest in the whole, or sells the life estate for cash, or acquires the remainder interest of the children either by purchase or gift.

(4) The terms "passed from the decedent," "passed from the decedent to his surviving spouse," and "passed from the decedent to a person other than his surviving spouse" are defined in §§ 20.2056(e)-1 through 20.2056(e)-3.

(f) *Direction to acquire a terminable interest.* No marital deduction is allowed with respect to a property interest which a decedent directs his executor or a trustee to convert after his death into a terminable interest for his surviving spouse. The marital deduction is not allowed even though no interest in the property subject to the terminable interest passes to another person and even though the interest would otherwise come within the exceptions described in § 20.2056(b)-5 and § 20.2056(b)-6 (relating to life estates and life insurance and annuity payments with powers of appointment). However, a general investment power, authorizing investments in both terminable interests and other property, is not a direction to invest in a terminable interest.

(g) *Examples.* The application of this section may be illustrated by the following examples, in each of which it is assumed that the property interest which passed from the decedent to a person other than his surviving spouse did not pass for an adequate and full consideration in money or money's worth:

Example (1). H (the decedent) devised real property to W (his surviving wife) for life, with remainder to A and his heirs. The interest which passed from H to W is a nondeductible interest since it will terminate upon her death and A (or his heirs or assigns) will thereafter possess or enjoy the property.

Example (2). H bequeathed the residue of his estate in trust for the benefit of W and A. The trust income is to be paid to W for life, and upon her death the corpus is to be distributed to A or his issue. However, if A should die without issue, leaving W surviving, the corpus is then to be distributed to W. The interest which passed from H to W is a nondeductible interest since it will terminate in the event of her death if A or his issue survive, and A or his issue will thereafter possess or enjoy the property.

Example (3). H during his lifetime purchased an annuity contract providing for payments to himself for life and then to W for life if she should survive him. Upon the death of the survivor of H and W, the excess, if any, of the cost of the contract over the annuity payments theretofore made was to be refunded to A. The interest which passed from H to W is a nondeductible interest since A may possess or enjoy a part of the property following the termination of the interest of W. If, however, the contract provided for no refund upon the death of the survivor of H and W, or provided that any refund was to go to the estate of the survivor, then the interest which passed from H to W is (to the extent it is included in H's gross estate) a deductible interest.

Example (4). H, in contemplation of death, transferred a residence to A for life with remainder to W provided W survives A, but if W predeceases A, the property is to pass to B and his heirs. If it is assumed that H died during A's lifetime, and the value of the residence was included in determining the value of his gross estate, the interest which passed from H to W is a nondeductible interest since it will terminate if W predeceases A and the property will thereafter be possessed or enjoyed by B (or his heirs or assigns). This result is not affected by B's assignment of his interest during H's lifetime, whether made in favor of W or another person, since the term "assigns" (as used in section 2056(b)(1)(B)) includes such an assignee. However, if it is assumed that A predeceased H, the interest of B in the property was extinguished, and, viewed as of the time of the subsequent death of H, the interest which passed from him to W is the entire interest in the property and, therefore, a deductible interest.

Example (5). H transferred real property to A by gift, reserving the right to the rentals of the property for a term of 20 years. H died within the 20-year term, bequeathing the right to the remaining rentals to a trust for the benefit of W. The terms of the trust satisfy the five conditions stated in § 20.2056(b)-5, so that the property interest which passed in trust is considered to have passed from H to W. However, the interest is a nondeductible interest since it will terminate upon the expiration of the term and A will thereafter possess or enjoy the property.

Example (6). H bequeathed a patent to W and A as tenants in common. In this case, the interest of W will terminate upon the expiration of the term of the patent, but possession or enjoyment of the property by A must necessarily cease at the same time. Therefore, since A's possession or enjoyment cannot outlast the termination of W's interest, the latter is a deductible interest.

Example (7). A decedent bequeathed $100,000 to his wife, subject to a direction to his executor to use the bequest for the purchase of an annuity for the wife. The bequest is a nondeductible interest.

Example (8). Assume that pursuant to local law an allowance for support is payable to the decedent's surviving spouse during the period of the administration of the decedent's estate, but that upon her death or remarriage during such period her right to any further allowance will terminate. Assume further that the surviving spouse is sole beneficiary of the decedent's estate. Under such circumstances, the allowance constitutes a deductible interest since any part of the allowance not receivable by the surviving spouse during her lifetime will pass to her estate under the terms of the decedent's will. If, in this example, the decedent bequeathed only one-third of his residuary estate to his surviving spouse, then two-thirds of the allowance for support would constitute a nondeductible terminable interest.

§ 20.2056(b)-2 Marital deduction; interest in unidentified assets.
(a) Section 2056(b)(2) provides that if an interest passing to a decedent's surviving spouse may be satisfied out of assets (or their proceeds) which include a particular asset that would be a nondeductible interest if it passed from the decedent to his spouse, the value of the interest passing to the spouse is reduced, for the purpose of the marital deduction, by the value of the particular asset.

(b) In order for section 2056(b)(2) to apply, two circumstances must coexist, as follows:

(1) The property interest which passed from the decedent to his surviving spouse must be payable out of a group of assets included in the gross estate. Examples of property interests payable out of a group of assets are a general legacy, a bequest of the residue of the decedent's estate or of a portion of the residue, and a right to a share of the corpus of a trust upon its termination.

(2) The group of assets out of which the property interest is payable must include one or more particular assets which, if passing specifically to the surviving spouse, would be nondeductible interests. Therefore, section 2056(b)(2) is not applicable merely because the group of assets includes a terminable interest, but would only be applicable if the terminable interest were nondeductible under the provisions of § 20.2056(b)-1.

(c) If both of the circumstances set forth in paragraph (b) of this section are present, the property interest payable out of the group of assets is (except as to any excess of its value over the aggregate value of the particular asset or assets which would not be deductible if passing specifically to the surviving spouse) a nondeductible interest.

(d) The application of this section may be illustrated by the following example:

Example. A decedent bequeathed one-third of the residue of his estate to his wife. The property passing under the decedent's will included a right to the rentals of an office building for a term of years, reserved by the decedent under a deed of the building by way of gift to his son. The decedent did not make a specific bequest of the right to such rentals. Such right, if passing specifically to the wife, would be a nondeductible interest (see example (5) of paragraph (g) of § 20.2056(b)-1). It is assumed that the value of the bequest of one-third of the residue of the estate to the wife was $85,000, and that the right to the rentals was included in the gross estate at a value of $60,000. If the decedent's executor had the right under the decedent's will or local law to assign the entire lease in satisfaction of the bequest, the bequest is a nondeductible interest to the extent of $60,000. If the executor could only assign a one-third interest in the lease in satisfaction of the bequest, the bequest is a nondeductible interest to the extent of $20,000. If the decedent's will provided that his wife's bequest could not be satisfied with a nondeductible interest, the entire bequest is a deductible interest. If, in this example, the asset in question had been foreign real estate not included in the decedent's gross estate, the results would be the same.

§ 20.2056(b)-3 **Marital deduction; interest of spouse conditioned on survival for limited period**—(a) *In general.* Generally, no marital deduction is allowable if the interest passing to the surviving spouse is a terminable interest as defined in paragraph (b) of § 20.2056(b)-1. However, section 2056(b)(3) provides an exception to this rule so as to allow a deduction if (1) the only condition under which it will terminate is the death of the surviving spouse within 6 months after the decedent's death, or her death as a result of a common disaster which also resulted in the decedent's death, and (2) the condition does not in fact occur.

(b) *Six months' survival.* If the only condition which will cause the interest taken by the surviving spouse to terminate is the death of the surviving spouse and the condition is of such nature that it can occur only within 6 months following the decedent's death, the exception provided by section 2056(b)(3) will apply, provided the condition does not in fact occur. However, if the condition (unless it relates to death as a result of a common disaster) is one which may occur either within the 6-month period or thereafter, the exception provided by section 2056(b)(3) will not apply.

(c) *Common disaster.* If a property interest passed from the decedent to his surviving spouse subject to the condition that she does not die as a result of a common disaster which also resulted in the decedent's death, the exception provided by section 2056(b)(3) will not be applied in the final audit of the return if there is still a possibility that the surviving spouse may be deprived of the property interest

991

by operation of the common disaster provision as given effect by the local law.

(d) *Examples.* The application of this section may be illustrated by the following examples:

Example (1). A decedent bequeathed his entire estate to his spouse on condition that she survive him by 6 months. In the event his spouse failed to survive him by 6 months, his estate was to go to his niece and her heirs. The decedent was survived by his spouse. It will be observed that, as of the time of the decedent's death, it was possible that the niece would, by reason of the interest which passed to her from the decedent, possess or enjoy the estate after the termination of the interest which passed to the spouse. Hence, under the general rule set forth in § 20.2056(b)-1, the interest which passed to the spouse would be regarded as a nondeductible interest. If the surviving spouse in fact died within 6 months after the decedent's death, that general rule is to be applied, and the interest which passed to the spouse is a nondeductible interest. However, if the spouse in fact survived the decedent by 6 months, thus extinguishing the interest of the niece, the case comes within the exception provided by section 2056(b)(3), and the interest which passed to the spouse is a deductible interest. (It is assumed for the purpose of this example that no other factor which would cause the interest to be nondeductible is present.)

Example (2). The facts are the same as in example (1) except that the will provided that the estate was to go to the niece either in case the decedent and his spouse should both die as a result of a common disaster, or in case the spouse should fail to survive the decedent by 3 months. It is assumed that the decedent was survived by his spouse. In this example, the interest which passed from the decedent to his surviving spouse is to be regarded as a nondeductible interest if the surviving spouse in fact died either within 3 months after the decedent's death or as a result of a common disaster which also resulted in the decedent's death. However, if the spouse in fact survived the decedent by 3 months, and did not thereafter die as a result of a common disaster which also resulted in the decedent's death, the exception provided under section 2056(b)(3) will apply and the interest will be deductible.

Example (3). The facts are the same as in example (1) except that the will provided that the estate was to go to the niece if the decedent and his spouse should both die as a result of a common disaster and if the spouse failed to survive the decedent by 3 months. If the spouse in fact survived the decedent by 3 months, the interest of the niece is extinguished, and the interest passing to the spouse is a deductible interest.

Example (4). A decedent devised and bequeathed his residuary estate to his wife if she was living on the date of distribution of his estate. The devise and bequest is a nondeductible interest even though distribution took place within 6 months after the decedent's death and the surviving spouse in fact survived the date of distribution.

§ 20.2056(b)-4 **Marital deduction; valuation of interest passing to surviving spouse**—(a) *In general.* The value, for the purpose of the marital deduction, of any deductible interest which passed from the decedent to his surviving spouse is to be determined as of the date of the decedent's death, except that if the executor elects the alternate valuation method under section 2032 the valuation is to be determined as of the date of the decedent's death but with the adjustment described in paragraph (a)(3) of § 20.2032-1. The marital deduction may be taken only with respect to the net value of any deductible interest which passed from the decedent to his surviving spouse, the same principles being applicable as if the amount of a gift to the spouse were being determined. In determining the value of the interest in property passing to the spouse account must be taken of the effect of any material limitations upon her right to income from the property. An example of a case in which this rule may be applied is a bequest of property in trust for the benefit of the decedent's spouse but the income from the property from the date of the decedent's death until distribution of the property to the trustee is to be used to pay expenses incurred in the administration of the estate.

(b) *Property interest subject to an encumbrance or obligation.* If a property interest passed from the decedent to his surviving spouse subject to a mortgage or other encumbrance, or if an obligation is imposed upon the surviving spouse by the decedent in connection with the passing of a property interest, the value of the property interest is to be reduced by the amount of the mortgage, other encumbrance, or obligation. However, if under the terms of the decedent's will or under local law the executor is required to discharge, out of other assets of the decedent's estate, a mortgage or other encumbrance on property passing from the decedent to his surviving spouse, or is required to reimburse the surviving spouse for the amount of the mortgage or other encumbrance, the payment or reimbursement constitutes an additional interest passing to the surviving spouse. The passing of a property interest subject to the imposition of an obligation by the decedent does not include a bequest, devise, or transfer in lieu of dower, curtesy, or of a statutory estate created in lieu of dower or curtesy, or of other marital rights in the decedent's property or estate. The passing of a property interest subject to the imposition of an obligation by the decedent does, however, include a bequest, etc., in lieu of the interest of his surviving spouse under community property laws unless such interest was, immediately prior to the decedent's death, a mere expectancy. (As to the circumstances under which the interest of the surviving spouse is regarded as a mere expectancy, see § 20.2056(c)-2.) The following examples are illustrative of property interests which passed from the decedent to his surviving spouse subject to the imposition of an obligation by the decedent:

Example (1). A decedent devised a residence valued at $25,000 to his wife, with a direction that she pay $5,000 to his sister. For the purpose of the marital deduction, the value of the property interest passing to the wife is only $20,000.

Example (2). A decedent devised real property to his wife in satisfaction of a debt owing to her. The debt is a deductible claim under section 2053. Since the wife is obligated to relinquish the claim as a condition to acceptance of the devise, the value of the devise is, for the purpose of the marital deduction, to be reduced by the amount of the claim.

Example (3). A decedent bequeathed certain securities to his wife in lieu of her interest in property held by them as community property under the law of the State of their residence. The wife elected to relinquish her community property interest and to take the bequest. For the purpose of the marital deduction, the value of the bequest is to be reduced by the value of the community property interest relinquished by the wife.

(c) *Effect of death taxes.* (1) In the determination of the value of any property interest which passed from the decedent to his surviving spouse, there must be taken into account the effect which the Federal estate tax, or any estate, succession, legacy, or inheritance tax, has upon the net value to the surviving spouse of the property interest.

(2) For example, assume that the only bequests to the surviving spouse is $100,000 and the spouse is required to pay a State inheritance tax in the amount of $1,500. If no other death taxes affect the net value of the bequest, the value, for the purpose of the marital deduction, is $98,500.

(3) As another example, assume that a decedent devised real property to his wife having a value for Federal estate tax purposes of $100,000 and also bequeathed to her a nondeductible interest for life under a trust. The State of residence valued the real property at $90,000 and the life interest at $30,000, and imposed an inheritance tax (at graduated rates) of $4,800 with respect to the two interests. If it is assumed that the inheritance tax on the devise is required to be paid by the wife, the amount of tax to be ascribed to the devise is

$$\frac{90,000}{120,000} \times \$4,800 = \$3,600.$$

Accordingly, if no other death taxes affect the net value of the bequest, the value, for the purpose of the marital deduction, is $100,000 less $3,600, or $96,400.

(4) If the decedent bequeaths his residuary estate, or a portion of it, to his surviving spouse, and his will contains a direction that all death taxes shall be payable out of the residuary estate, the value of the bequest, for the purpose of the marital deduction, is based upon the amount of the residue as reduced pursuant to such direction. If the residuary estate, or a portion of it, is bequeathed to the surviving spouse, and by the local law the Federal estate tax is payable out of the residuary estate, the value of the bequest, for the

[Harris]

purpose of the marital deduction, may not exceed its value as reduced by the Federal estate tax. Methods of computing the deduction, under such circumstances, are set forth in supplemental instructions to the estate tax return.

(d) *Remainder interests.* If the income from property is made payable to another individual for life, or for a term of years, with remainder absolutely to the surviving spouse or to her estate, the marital deduction is based upon the present value of the remainder. The present value of the remainder is to be determined in accordance with the rules stated in § 20.2031-7. For example, if the surviving spouse is to receive $50,000 upon the death of a person aged 31 years, the present value of the remainder is $14,466. If the remainder is such that its value is to be determined by a special computation (see paragraph (e) of § 20.2031-7), a request for a specific factor may be submitted to the Commissioner. The request should be accompanied by a statement of the date of birth of each person, the duration of whose life may affect the value of the remainder, and copies of the relevant instruments. The Commissioner may, if conditions permit, supply the factor requested. If the Commissioner does not furnish the factor, the claim for deduction must be supported by a full statement of the computation of the present value made in accordance with the principles set forth in the applicable paragraphs of § 20.2031-7.

§ 20.2056(b)-5 **Marital deduction; life estate with power of appointment in surviving spouse**—(a) *In general.* Section 2056(b)(5) provides that if an interest in property passes from the decedent to his surviving spouse (whether or not in trust) and the spouse is entitled for life to all the income from the entire interest or all the income from a specific portion of the entire interest, with a power in her to appoint the entire interest or the specific portion, the interest which passes to her is a deductible interest, to the extent that it satisfies all five of the conditions set forth below (see paragraph (b) of this section if one or more of the conditions is satisfied as to only a portion of the interest):

(1) The surviving spouse must be entitled for life to all of the income from the entire interest or a specific portion of the entire interest, or to a specific portion of all the income from the entire interest.

(2) The income payable to the surviving spouse must be payable annually or at more frequent intervals.

(3) The surviving spouse must have the power to appoint the entire interest or the specific portion to either herself or her estate.

(4) The power in the surviving spouse must be exercisable by her alone and (whether exercisable by will or during life) must be exercisable in all events.

(5) The entire interest or the specific portion must not be subject to a power in any other person to appoint any part to any person other than the surviving spouse.

(b) *Specific portion; deductible amount.* If either the right to income or the power of appointment passing to the surviving spouse pertains only to a specific portion of a property interest passing from

995

the decedent, the marital deduction is allowed only to the extent that the rights in the surviving spouse meet all of the five conditions described in paragraph (a) of this section. While the right over the income and the power must coexist as to the same interest in property, it is not necessary that the rights over the income or the power as to such interest be in the same proportion. However, if the rights over income meeting the required conditions set forth in paragraph (a) (1) and (2) of this section extend over a smaller share of the property interest than the share with respect to which the power of appointment requirements set forth in paragraph (a) (3) through (5) of this section are satisfied, the deductible interest is limited to the smaller share. Correspondingly, if a power of appointment meeting all the requirements extends to a smaller portion of the property interest than the portion over which the income rights pertain, the deductible interest cannot exceed the value of the portion to which such power of appointment applies. Thus, if the decedent leaves to his surviving spouse the right to receive annually all of the income from a particular property interest and a power of appointment meeting the specifications prescribed in paragraph (a) (3) through (5) of this section as to only one-half of the property interest, then only one-half of the property interest is treated as a deductible interest. Correspondingly, if the income interest of the spouse satisfying the requirements extends to only one-fourth of the property interest and a testamentary power of appointment satisfying the requirements extends to all of the property interest, then only one-fourth of the interest in the spouse qualifies as a deductible interest. Further, if the surviving spouse has no right to income from a specific portion of a property interest but a testamentary power of appointment which meets the necessary conditions over the entire interest, then none of the interest qualifies for the deduction. In addition, if, from the time of the decedent's death, the surviving spouse has a power of appointment meeting all of the required conditions over three-fourths of the entire property interest and the prescribed income rights over the entire interest, but with a power in another person to appoint one-half of the entire interest, the value of the interest in the surviving spouse over only one-half of the property interest will qualify as a deductible interest.

(c) *Definition of "specific portion"*. A partial interest in property is not treated as a specific portion of the entire interest unless the rights of the surviving spouse in income and as to the power constitute a fractional or percentile share of a property interest so that such interest or share in the surviving spouse reflects its proportionate share of the increment or decline in the whole of the property interest to which the income rights and the power relate. Thus, if the right of the spouse to income and the power extend to one-half or a specified percentage of the property, or the equivalent, the interest is considered as a specific portion. On the other hand, if the annual income of the spouse is limited to a specific sum, or if she has a power to appoint only a specific sum out of a larger fund, the interest is not a deductible interest. Even though the rights in the surviving spouse may not be

996

expressed in terms of a definite fraction or percentage, a deduction may be allowable if it is shown that the effect of local law is to give the spouse rights which are identical to those she would have acquired if the size of the share had been expressed in terms of a definite fraction or percentage. The following examples illustrate the application of this and the preceding paragraphs of this section:

Example (1). The decedent transferred to a trustee 500 identical shares of X Company stock. He provided that during the lifetime of the surviving spouse the trustee should pay her annually one-half of the trust income or $6,000, whichever is the larger. The spouse was also given a general power of appointment, exercisable by her last will over the sum of $160,000 or over three-fourths of the trust corpus, whichever should be of larger value. Since there is no certainty that the trust income will not vary from year to year, for purposes of paragraphs (a) and (b) of this section, an annual payment of a specified sum, such as the $6,000 provided for in this case, is not considered as representing the income from a definite fraction or a specifice portion of the entire interest if that were the extent of the spouse's interest. However, since the spouse is to receive annually at least one-half of the trust income, she will, for purposes of paragraphs (a) and (b) of this section, be considered as receiving all of the income from one-half of the entire interest in the stock. Inasmuch as there is no certainty that the value of the stock will be the same on the date of the surviving spouse's death as it was on the date of the decedent's death, for purposes of paragraphs (a) and (b) of this section, a specified sum, such as the $160,000 provided for in this case, is not considered to be a definite fraction of the entire interest. However, since the surviving spouse has a general power of appointment over at least three-fourths of the trust corpus, she is considered as having a general power of appointment over three-fourths of the entire interest in the stock.

Example (2). The decedent bequeathed to a trustee an office building and 250 identical shares of Y Company stock. He provided that during the lifetime of the surviving spouse the trustee should pay her annually three-fourths of the trust income. The spouse was given a general power of appointment, exercisable by will, over the office building and 100 shares of the stock. By the terms of the decedent's will the spouse is given all the income from a definite fraction of the entire interest in the office building and in the stock. She also has a general power of appointment over the entire interest in the office building. However, since the amount of property represented by a single share of stock would be altered if the corporation split its stock, issued stock dividends, made a distribution of capital, etc., a power to appoint 100 shares at the time of the surviving spouse's death is not the same necessarily as a power to appoint 100/250 of the entire interest which the 250 shares represented on the date of the decedent's death. If it is shown in this case that the effect of local law is to give the spouse a general power to appoint not only the 100 shares designated by the decedent but also 100/250 of any shares or amounts which are distributed by the corporation and included in the corpus, the requirements of

997

this paragraph will be satisfied and the surviving spouse will be considered as having a general power to appoint 100/250 of the entire interest in the 250 shares.

(d) *Definition of "entire interest"*. Since a marital deduction is allowed for each qualifying separate interest in property passing from the decedent to his surviving spouse (subject to the percentage limitation contained in §§ 20.2056(c)-1 and 20.2056(c)-2 concerning the aggregate amount of the deductions), for purposes of paragraphs (a) and (b) of this section, each property interest with respect to which the surviving spouse received some rights is considered separately in determining whether her rights extend to the entire interest or to a specific portion of the entire interest. A property interest which consists of several identical units of property (such as a block of 250 shares of stock, whether the ownership is evidenced by one or several certificates) is considered one property interest, unless certain of the units are to be segregated and accorded different treatment, in which case each segregated group of items is considered a separate property interest. The bequest of a specified sum of money constitutes the bequest of a separate property interest if immediately following distribution by the executor and thenceforth it, and the investments made with it, must be so segregated or accounted for as to permit its identification as a separate item of property. The application of this paragraph may be illustrated by the following examples:

Example (1). The decedent transferred to a trustee three adjoining farms, Blackacre, Whiteacre, and Greenacre. His will provided that during the lifetime of the surviving spouse the trustee should pay her all of the income from the trust. Upon her death, all of Blackacre, a one-half interest in Whiteacre, and a one-third interest in Greenacre were to be distributed to the person or persons appointed by her in her will. The surviving spouse is considered as being entitled to all of the income from the entire interest in Blackacre, all of the income from the entire interest in Whiteacre, and all of the income from the entire interest in Greenacre. She also is considered as having a power of appointment over the entire interest in Blackacre, over one-half of the entire interest in Whiteacre, and over one-third of the entire interest in Greenacre.

Example (2). The decedent bequeathed $250,000 to C, as trustee. C is to invest the money and pay all of the income from the investments to W, the decedent's surviving spouse, annually. W was given a general power, exercisable by will, to appoint one-half of the corpus of the trust. Here, immediately following distribution by the executor, the $250,000 will be sufficiently segregated to permit its identification as a separate item, and the $250,000 will constitute an entire property interest. Therefore, W has a right to income and a power of appointment such that one-half of the entire interest is a deductible interest.

Example (3). The decedent bequeathed 100 shares of Z Corporation stock to D, as trustee. W, the decedent's surviving spouse, is to receive all of the income of the trust annually and is given a general power, exercisable by will, to appoint out of the trust corpus the sum of

$25,000. In this case the $25,000 is not, immediately following distribution, sufficiently segregated to permit its identification as a separate item of property in which the surviving spouse has the entire interest. Therefore, the $25,000 does not constitute the entire interest in a property for the purpose of paragraphs (a) and (b) of this section.

(e) *Application of local law.* In determining whether or not the conditions set forth in paragraph (a)(1) through (5) of this section are satisfied by the instrument of transfer, regard is to be had to the applicable provisions of the law of the jurisdiction under which the interest passes and, if the transfer is in trust, the applicable provisions of the law governing the administration of the trust. For example, silence of a trust instrument as to the frequency of payment will not be regarded as a failure to satisfy the condition set forth in paragraph (a)(2) of this section that income must be payable to the surviving spouse annually or more frequently unless the applicable law permits payment to be made less frequently than annually. The principles outlined in this paragraph and paragraphs (f) and (g) of this section which are applied in determining whether transfers in trust meet such conditions are equally applicable in ascertaining whether, in the case of interests not in trust, the surviving spouse has the equivalent in rights over income and over the property.

(f) *Right to income.* (1) If an interest is transferred in trust, the surviving spouse is "entitled for life to all of the income from the entire interest or a specific portion of the entire interest," for the purpose of the condition set forth in paragraph (a)(1) of this section, if the effect of the trust is to give her substantially that degree of beneficial enjoyment of the trust property during her life which the principles of the law of trusts accord to a person who is unqualifiedly designated as the life beneficiary of a trust. Such degree of enjoyment is given only if it was the decedent's intention, as manifested by the terms of the trust instrument and the surrounding circumstances, that the trust should produce for the surviving spouse during her life such an income, or that the spouse should have such use of the trust property as is consistent with the value of the trust corpus and with its preservation. The designation of the spouse as sole income beneficiary for life of the entire interest or a specific portion of the entire interest will be sufficient to qualify the trust unless the terms of the trust and the surrounding circumstances considered as a whole evidence an intention to deprive the spouse of the requisite degree of enjoyment. In determining whether a trust evidences that intention, the treatment required or permitted with respect to individual items must be considered in relation to the entire system provided for the administration of the trust.

(2) If the over-all effect of a trust is to give to the surviving spouse such enforceable rights as will preserve to her the requisite degree of enjoyment, it is immaterial whether that result is effected by rules specifically stated in the trust instrument, or, in their absence, by the rules for the management of the trust property and the allocation of receipts and expenditures supplied by the State law. For example, a provision in the trust instrument for amortization of bond premium

999

by appropriate periodic charges to interest will not disqualify the interest passing in trust even though there is no State law specifically authorizing amortization, or there is a State law denying amortization which is applicable only in the absence of such a provision in the trust instrument.

(3) In the case of a trust, the rules to be applied by the trustee in allocation of receipts and expenses between income and corpus must be considered in relation to the nature and expected productivity of the assets passing in trust, the nature and frequency of occurrence of the expected receipts, and any provisions as to change in the form of investments. If it is evident from the nature of the trust assets and the rules provided for management of the trust that the allocation to income of such receipts as rents, ordinary cash dividends, and interest will give to the spouse the substantial enjoyment during life required by the statute, provisions that such receipts as stock dividends and proceeds from the conversion of trust assets shall be treated as corpus will not disqualify the interest passing in trust. Similarly, provision for a depletion charge against income in the case of trust assets which are subject to depletion will not disqualify the interest passing in trust, unless the effect is to deprive the spouse of the requisite beneficial enjoyment. The same principle is applicable in the case of depreciation, trustees' commissions, and other charges.

(4) Provisions granting administrative powers to the trustee will not have the effect of disqualifying an interest passing in trust unless the grant of powers evidences the intention to deprive the surviving spouse of the beneficial enjoyment required by the statute. Such an intention will not be considered to exist if the entire terms of the instrument are such that the local courts will impose reasonable limitations upon the exercise of the powers. Among the powers which if subject to reasonable limitations will not disqualify the interest passing in trust are the power to determine the allocation or apportionment of receipts and disbursements between income and corpus, the power to apply the income or corpus for the benefit of the spouse, and the power to retain the assets passing to the trust. For example, a power to retain trust assets which consist substantially of unproductive property will not disqualify the interest if the applicable rules for the administration of the trust require, or permit the spouse to require, that the trustee either make the property productive or convert it within a reasonable time. Nor will such a power disqualify the interest if the applicable rules for administration of the trust require the trustee to use the degree of judgment and care in the exercise of the power which a prudent man would use if he were owner of the trust assets. Further, a power to retain a residence or other property for the personal use of the spouse will not disqualify the interest passing in trust.

(5) An interest passing in trust will not satisfy the condition set forth in paragraph (a)(1) of this section that the surviving spouse be entitled to all the income if the primary purpose of the trust is

to safeguard property without providing the spouse with the required beneficial enjoyment. Such trusts include not only trust which expressly provide for the accumulation of the income but also trusts which indirectly accomplish a similar purpose. For example, assume that the corpus of a trust consists substantially of property which is not likely to be income producing during the life of the surviving spouse and that the spouse cannot compel the trustee to convert or otherwise deal with the property as described in subparagraph (4) of this paragraph. An interest passing to such a trust will not qualify unless the applicable rules for the administration require, or permit the spouse to require, that the trustee provide the required beneficial enjoyment, such as by payments to the spouse out of other assets of the trust.

(6) If a trust is created during the decedent's life, it is immaterial whether or not the interest passing in trust satisfied the conditions set forth in paragraph (a)(1) through (5) of this section prior to the decedent's death. If a trust may be terminated during the life of the surviving spouse, under her exercise of a power of appointment or by distribution of the corpus to her, the interest passing in trust satisfies the condition set forth in paragraph (a)(1) of this section (that the spouse be entitled to all the income) if she (i) is entitled to the income until the trust terminates, or (ii) has the right, exercisable in all events, to have the corpus distributed to her at any time during her life.

(7) An interest passing in trust fails to satisfy the condition set forth in paragraph (a)(1) of this section, that the spouse be entitled to all the income, to the extent that the income is required to be accumulated in whole or in part or may be accumulated in the discretion of any person other than the surviving spouse; to the extent that the consent of any person other than the surviving spouse is required as a condition precedent to distribution of the income; or to the extent that any person other than the surviving spouse has the power to alter the terms of the trust so as to deprive her of her right to the income. An interest passing in trust will not fail to satisfy the condition that the spouse be entitled to all the income merely because its terms provide that the right of the surviving spouse to the income shall not be subject to assignment, alienation, pledge, attachment or claims of creditors.

(8) In the case of an interest passing in trust, the terms "entitled for life" and "payable annually or at more frequent intervals", as used in the conditions set forth in paragraph (a)(1) and (2) of this section, require that under the terms of the trust the income referred to must be currently (at least annually; see paragraph (e) of this section) distributable to the spouse or that she must have such command over the income that it is virtually hers. Thus, the conditions in paragraph (a)(1) and (2) of this section are satisfied in this respect if, under the terms of the trust instrument, the spouse has the right exercisable annually (or more frequently) to require distribution to herself of the trust income, and otherwise the trust income is to be

1001

accumulated and added to corpus. Similarly, as respects the income for the period between the last distribution date and the date of the spouse's death, it is sufficient if that income is subject to the spouse's power to appoint. Thus, if the trust instrument provides that income accrued or undistributed on the date of the spouse's death is to be disposed of as if it had been received after her death, and if the spouse has a power of appointment over the trust corpus, the power necessarily extends to the undistributed income.

(9) An interest is not to be regarded as failing to satisfy the conditions set forth in paragraph (a)(1) and (2) of this section (that the spouse be entitled to all the income and that it be payable annually or more frequently) merely because the spouse is not entitled to the income from estate assets for the period before distribution of those assets by the executor, unless the executor is, by the decedent's will, authorized or directed to delay distribution beyond the period reasonably required for administration of the decedent's estate. As to the valuation of the property interest passing to the spouse in trust where the right to income is expressly postponed, see § 20.2056(b)-4.

(g) *Power of appointment in surviving spouse.* (1) The conditions set forth in paragraph (a)(3) and (4) of this section, that is, that the surviving spouse must have a power of appointment exercisable in favor of herself or her estate and exercisable alone and in all events, are not met unless the power of the surviving spouse to appoint the entire interest or a specific portion of it falls within one of the following categories:

(i) A power so to appoint fully exercisable in her own favor at any time following the decedent's death (as, for example, an unlimited power to invade); or

(ii) A power so to appoint exercisable in favor of her estate. Such a power, if exercisable during life, must be fully exercisable at any time during life, or, if exercisable by will, must be fully exercisable irrespective of the time of her death (subject in either case to the provisions of § 20.2053(b)-3, relating to interests conditioned on survival for a limited period); or

(iii) A combination of the powers described under subparagraphs (i) and (ii) of this subparagraph. For example, the surviving spouse may, until she attains the age of 50 years, have a power to appoint to herself and thereafter have a power to appoint to her estate. However, the condition that the spouse's power must be exercisable in all events is not satisfied unless irrespective of when the surviving spouse may die the entire interest or a specific portion of it will at the time of her death be subject to one power or the other (subject to the exception in § 20.2053(b)-3, relating to interests contingent on survival for a limited period).

(2) The power of the surviving spouse must be a power to appoint the entire interest or a specific portion of it as unqualified owner (and free of the trust if a trust is involved, or free of the joint tenancy if a joint tenancy is involved) or to appoint the entire interest or a specific portion of it as a part of her estate (and free of the trust

1002

if a trust is involved), that is, in effect, to dispose of it to whomsoever she pleases. Thus, if the decedent devised property to a son and the surviving spouse as joint tenants with right of survivorship and under local law the surviving spouse has a power of severance exercisable without consent of the other joint tenant, and by exercising this power could acquire a one-half interest in the property as a tenant in common, her power of severance will satisfy the condition set forth in paragraph (a)(3) of this section that she have a power of appointment in favor of herself or her estate. However, if the surviving spouse entered into a binding agreement with the decedent to exercise the power only in favor of their issue, that condition is not met. An interest passing in trust will not be regarded as failing to satisfy the condition merely because takers in default of the surviving spouse's exercise of the power are designated by the decedent. The decedent may provide that, in default of exercise of the power, the trust shall continue for an additional period.

(3) A power is not considered to be a power exercisable by a surviving spouse alone and in all events as required by paragraph (a)(4) of this section if the exercise of the power in the surviving spouse to appoint the entire interest or a specific portion of it to herself or to her estate requires the joinder or consent of any other person. The power is not "exercisable in all events", if it can be terminated during the life of the surviving spouse by any event other than her complete exercise or release of it. Further, a power is not "exercisable in all events" if it may be exercised for a limited purpose only. For example, a power which is not exercisable in the event of the spouse's remarriage is not exercisable in all events. Likewise, if there are any restrictions, either by the terms of the instrument or under applicable local law, on the exercise of a power to consume property (whether or not held in trust) for the benefit of the spouse, the power is not exercisable in all events. Thus, if a power of invasion is exercisable only for the spouse's support, or only for her limited use, the power is not exercisable in all events. In order for a power of invasion to be exercisable in all events, the surviving spouse must have the unrestricted power exercisable at any time during her life to use all or any part of the property subject to the power, and to dispose of it in any manner, including the power to dispose of it by gift (whether or not she has power to dispose of it by will).

(4) The power in the surviving spouse is exercisable in all events only if it exists immediately following the decedent's death. For example, if the power given to the surviving spouse is exercisable during life, but cannot be effectively exercised before distribution of the assets by the executor, the power is not exercisable in all events. Similarly, if the power is exercisable by will, but cannot be effectively exercised in the event the surviving spouse dies before distribution of the assets by the executor, the power is not exercisable in all events. However, an interest will not be disqualified by the mere fact that, in the event the power is exercised during administration of the estate, distribution of the property to the appointee will be delayed for the

period of administration. If the power is in existence at all times following the decedent's death, limitations of a formal nature will not disqualify an interest. Examples of formal limitations on a power exercisable during life are requirements that an exercise must be in a particular form, that it must be filed with a trustee during the spouse's life, that reasonable notice must be given, or that reasonable intervals must elapse between successive partial exercises. Examples of formal limitations on a power exercisable by will are that it must be exercised by a will executed by the surviving spouse after the decedent's death or that exercise must be by specific reference to the power.

(5) If the surviving spouse has the requisite power to appoint to herself or her estate, it is immaterial that she also has one or more lesser powers. Thus, if she has a testamentary power to appoint to her estate, she may also have a limited power of withdrawal or of appointment during her life. Similarly, if she has an unlimited power of withdrawal, she may have a limited testamentary power.

(h) *Requirement of survival for a limited period.* A power of appointment in the surviving spouse will not be treated as failing to meet the requirements of paragraph (a)(3) of this section even though the power may terminate, if the only conditions which would cause the termination are those described in paragraph (a) of § 20.2056 (b)-3, and if those conditions do not in fact occur. Thus, the entire interest or a specific portion of it will not be disqualified by reason of the fact that the exercise of the power in the spouse is subject to a condition of survivorship described in § 20.2056(b)-3 if the terms of the condition, that is, the survivorship of the surviving spouse, or the failure to die in a common disaster, are fulfilled.

(j) *Existence of a power in another.* Paragraph (a)(5) of this section provides that a transfer described in paragraph (a) is nondeductible to the extent that the decedent created a power in the trustee or in any other person to appoint a part of the interest to any person other than the surviving spouse. However, only powers in other persons which are in opposition to that of the surviving spouse will cause a portion of the interest to fail to satisfy the condition set forth in paragraph (a)(5) of this section. Thus, a power in a trustee to distribute corpus to or for the benefit of a surviving spouse will not disqualify the trust. Similarly, a power to distribute corpus to the spouse for the support of minor children will not disqualify the trust if she is legally obligated to support such children. The application of this paragraph may be illustrated by the following examples:

Example (1). Assume that a decedent created a trust, designating his surviving spouse as income beneficiary for life with an unrestricted power in the spouse to appoint the corpus during her life. The decedent further provided that in the event the surviving spouse should die without having exercised the power, the trust should continue for the life of his son with a power in the son to appoint the corpus. Since the power in the son could become exercisable only after the death of the surviving spouse, the interest is not regarded as failing to satisfy the condition set forth in paragraph (a)(5) of this section.

Example (2). Assume that the decedent created a trust, designating his surviving spouse as income beneficiary for life and as donee of a power to appoint by will the entire corpus. The decedent further provided that the trustee could distribute 30 percent of the corpus to the decedent's son when he reached the age of 35 years. Since the trustee has a power to appoint 30 percent of the entire interest for the benefit of a person other than the surviving spouse, only 70 percent of the interest placed in trust satisfied the condition set forth in paragraph (a)(5) of this section. If, in this case, the surviving spouse had a power, exercisable by her will, to appoint only one-half of the corpus as it was constituted at the time of her death, it should be noted that only 35 percent of the interest placed in the trust would satisfy the condition set forth in paragraph (a)(3) of this section.

§ 20.2056(b)-6 Marital deduction; life insurance or annuity payments with power of appointment in surviving spouse—(a) *In general.* Section 2056(b)(6) provides that an interest in property passing from a decedent to his surviving spouse, which consists of proceeds held by an insurer under the terms of a life insurance, endowment, or annuity contract, is a "deductible interest" to the extent that it satisfied all five of the following conditions (see paragraph (b) of this section if one or more of the conditions is satisfied as to only a portion of the proceeds):

(1) The proceeds, or a specific portion of the proceeds, must be held by the insurer subject to an agreement either to pay the entire proceeds or a specific portion thereof in installments, or to pay interest thereon, and all or a specific portion of the installments or interest payable during the life of the surviving spouse must be payable only to her.

(2) The installments or interest payable to the surviving spouse must be payable annually, or more frequently, commencing not later than 13 months after the decedent's death.

(3) The surviving spouse must have the power to appoint all or a specific portion of the amounts so held by the insurer to either herself or her estate.

(4) The power in the surviving spouse must be exercisable by her alone and (whether exercisable by will or during life) must be exercisable in all events.

(5) The amounts or the specific portion of the amounts payable under such contract must not be subject to a power in any other person to appoint any part thereof to any person other than the surviving spouse.

(b) *Specific portion; deductible interest.* If the right to receive interest or installment payments or the power of appointment passing to the surviving spouse pertains only to a specific portion of the proceeds held by the insurer, the marital deduction is allowed only to the extent that the rights of the surviving spouse in the specific portion meet the five conditions described in paragraph (a) of this section. While the rights to interest, or to receive payment in installments, and the power must coexist as to the proceeds of the same contract, it is not necessary that the rights to each be in the same proportion. If the rights to interest meeting the required conditions set forth in paragraph (a)(1) and (2) of this section extend over a smaller share of the proceeds than the share with respect to which the power of appointment requirements set forth in paragraph (a)(3) through (5) of this section are satisfied, the deductible interest is limited to the smaller share. Similarly, if the portion of the proceeds payable in installments is a smaller portion of the proceeds than the portion to which the power of appointment meeting such requirements relates, the deduction is limited to the smaller portion. In addition, if a power of appointment meeting all the requirements extends to a smaller portion of the proceeds than the portion over which the interest or installment rights pertain, the deductible interest cannot exceed the value of the portion to which such power of appointment applies. Thus, if the contract provides that the insurer is to retain the entire proceeds and pay all of the interest thereon annually to the surviving spouse and if the surviving spouse has a power of appointment meeting the specifications prescribed in paragraph (a)(3) through (5) of this section, as to only one-half of the proceeds held, then only one-half of the proceeds may be treated as a deductible interest. Correspondingly, if the rights of the spouse to receive installment payments or interest satisfying the requirements extend to only one-fourth of the proceeds and a testamentary power of appointment satisfying the requirements of paragraph (a)(3) through (5) of this section extends to all of the proceeds, then only one-fourth of the proceeds qualifies as a deductible interest. Further, if the surviving spouse has no right to installment payments (or interest) over any portion of the proceeds but a testamentary power of appointment which meets the necessary conditions over the entire remaining proceeds, then none of the proceeds qualifies for the deduction. In addition, if, from the time of the decedent's death, the surviving spouse has a power of appointment meeting all of the required conditions over three-fourths of the proceeds and the right to receive interest from the entire proceeds, but with a power in another person to appoint one-half of the entire proceeds, the value of the interest in the surviving spouse over only one-half of the proceeds will qualify as a deductible interest.

(c) *Applicable principles.* (1) The principles set forth in paragraph (c) of § 20.2056(b)-5 for determining what constitutes a "specific portion of the entire interest" for the purpose of section 2056(b)(5) are applicable in determining what constitutes a "specific portion of all such amounts" for the purpose of section 2056(b)(6). However, the interest in the proceeds passing to the surviving spouse will not be disqualified by the fact that the installment payments or interest to which the spouse is entitled or the amount of the proceeds over which the power of appointment is exercisable may be expressed in terms of a specific sum rather than a fraction or a percentage of the proceeds provided it is shown that such sums are a definite or fixed percentage or fraction of the total proceeds.

1006

(2) The provisions of paragraph (a) of this section are applicable with respect to a property interest which passed from the decedent in the form of proceeds of a policy of insurance upon the decedent's life, a policy of insurance upon the life of a person who predeceased the decedent, a matured endowment policy, or an annuity contract, but only in case the proceeds are to be held by the insurer. With respect to proceeds under any such contract which are to be held by a trustee, with power of appointment in the surviving spouse, see § 20.2056(b)-5. As to the treatment of proceeds not meeting the requirements of § 20.2056(b)-5 or of this section, see § 20.2056(a)-2.

(3) In the case of a contract under which payments by the insurer commenced during the decedent's life, it is immaterial whether or not the conditions in subparagraphs (1) through (5) of paragraph (a) of this section were satisfied prior to the decedent's death.

(d) *Payments of installments or interest.* The conditions in subparagraphs (1) and (2) of paragraph (a) of this section relative to the payments of installments or interest to the surviving spouse are satisfied if, under the terms of the contract, the spouse has the right exercisable annually (or more frequently) to require distribution to herself of installments of the proceeds or a specific portion thereof, as the case may be, and otherwise such proceeds or interest are to be accumulated and held by the insurer pursuant to the terms of the contract. A contract which otherwise requires the insurer to make annual or more frequent payments to the surviving spouse following the decedent's death, will not be disqualified merely because the surviving spouse must comply with certain formalities in order to obtain the first payment. For example, the contract may satisfy the conditions in subparagraphs (1) and (2) of paragraph (a) of this section even though it requires the surviving spouse to furnish proof of death before the first payment is made. The condition in paragraph (a)(1) of this section is satisfied where interest on the proceeds or a specific portion thereof is payable, annually or more frequently, for a term, or until the occurrence of a specified event, following which the proceeds or a specific portion thereof are to be paid in annual or more frequent installments.

(e) *Powers of appointment.* (1) In determining whether the terms of the contract satisfy the conditions in subparagraph (3), (4), or (5) of paragraph (a) of this section relating to a power of appointment in the surviving spouse or any other person, the principles stated in § 20.2056(b)-5 are applicable. As stated in § 20.2056(b)-5, the surviving spouse's power to appoint is "exercisable in all events" only if it is in existence immediately following the decedent's death, subject, however, to the operation of § 20.2056(b)-3 relating to interests conditioned on survival for a limited period.

(2) For examples of formal limitations on the power which will not disqualify the contract, see paragraph (g)(4) of § 20.2056(b)-5. If the power is exercisable from the moment of the decedent's death, the contract is not disqualified merely because the insurer may require proof of the decedent's death as a condition to making payment to

the appointee. If the submission of proof of the decedent's death is a condition to the exercise of the power, the power will not be considered "exercisable in all events" unless in the event the surviving spouse had died immediately following the decedent, her power to appoint would have been considered to exist at the time of her death, within the meaning of section 2041(a)(2). See paragraph (b) of § 20.2041-3.

(3) It is sufficient for the purposes of the condition in paragraph (a)(3) of this section that the surviving spouse have the power to appoint amounts held by the insurer to herself or her estate if the surviving spouse has the unqualified power, exercisable in favor of herself or her estate, to appoint amounts held by the insurer which are payable after her death. Such power to appoint need not extend to installments or interest which will be paid to the spouse during her life. Further, the power to appoint need not be a power to require payment in a single sum. For example, if the proceeds of a policy are payable in installments, and if the surviving spouse has the power to direct that all installments payable after her death be paid to her estate, she has the requisite power.

(4) It is not necessary that the phrase "power to appoint" be used in the contract. For example, the condition in paragraph (a)(3) of this section that the surviving spouse have the power to appoint amounts held by the insurer to herself or her estate is satisfied by terms of a contract which give the surviving spouse a right which is, in substance and effect, a power to appoint to herself or her estate, such as a right to withdraw the amount remaining in the fund held by the insurer, or a right to direct that any amount held by the insurer under the contract at her death shall be paid to her estate.

§ 20.2056(c)-1 Marital deduction; limitation on aggregate of deductions; in general—(a) *In general.* The allowable marital deduction is limited to the smaller of the following amounts:

(1) The aggregate value of the "deductible interests" which passed from the decedent to his surviving spouse (see paragraph (a) of § 20.2056(a)-2).

(2) Fifty percent of the value of the decedent's "adjusted gross estate."

(b) *"Adjusted gross estate".* The "adjusted gross estate" is the entire value of the decedent's gross estate less the aggregate amount of the deductions allowed for expenses, indebtedness, taxes, and losses under sections 2053 and 2054, unless the decedent and his spouse at any time held any property as community property (see § 20.2056 (c)-2). In determining the adjusted gross estate, the gross estate is not reduced by the exemption allowable under section 2052, or by the amount of any charitable deduction allowable under section 2055.

Example. The value of a decedent's gross estate is $200,000 and the aggregate amount of the deductions allowed by sections 2053 and 2054 for expenses, debts, taxes and losses is $30,000. (It is assumed for the purpose of this example that the decedent and his spouse never
1008

held any property as community property.) The decedent left $10,000 to a charitable organization for which a deduction is allowable under section 2055, and left the balance of his estate to his surviving spouse. The value of the adjusted gross estate is, therefore, $200,000 less $30,000, or $170,000. It is assumed that the aggregate value of the deductible interests which passed from the decedent to his surviving spouse is $100,000. The allowable marital deduction is limited to $85,000 (50 percent of the value of the adjusted gross estate).

§ 20.2056(c)-2. **Marital deduction in cases involving community property.** (a) If the decedent and his surviving spouse at any time held property as "community property," as defined in this section, the "adjusted gross estate" referred to in § 20.2056(c)-1 is the entire value of the gross estate less the sum of the following values and amounts:

(1) The value of any property included in the gross estate which was at the time of the decedent's death held by him and his surviving spouse as "community property," as defined in this section.

(2) The value of property (to the extent included in the gross estate) transferred by the decedent during his life, if at the time of such transfer the property was held by him and his surviving spouse as "community property," as defined in this section.

(3) The amount (to the extent included in the gross estate) receivable as insurance under policies upon the life of the decedent, to the extent purchased with premiums or other consideration paid out of property then held by him and his surviving spouse as "community property," as defined in this section.

(4) An amount which bears the same ratio to the aggregate amount of the deductions for expenses, indebtedness, taxes and losses allowed by sections 2053 and 2054 as the value of the gross estate, reduced by the aggregate amount subtracted under subparagraphs (1), (2), and (3) of this paragraph, bears to the entire value of the gross estate. The amount to be subtracted under this subparagraph is

$$\frac{\text{gross estate, less community property}}{\text{entire gross estate}} \times \begin{array}{c} \text{deductions for expenses, indebtedness,} \\ \text{taxes, and losses.} \end{array}$$

(b) If a policy of insurance upon the life of the decedent was purchased partly with property held by him and his surviving spouse as "community property," as defined in this section, and partly with other property, the amount receivable under the policy is considered, for the purpose of paragraph (a)(3) of this section, to have been purchased with such "community property" in the proportion that the payments made with such "community property" bear to the total amount paid.

(c) In determining the "adjusted gross estate" under this section, property held by the decedent and his surviving spouse as "community property," at the time of the death of the decedent (for the purpose

[Harris]—64

of paragraph (a)(1) of this section), at the time of the transfer (for the purpose of paragraph (a)(2) of this section), or at the time of the payment of insurance premiums or other consideration (for the purpose of paragraph (a)(3) of this section), is considered to include—

(1) Any property held by them at such time as community property under the law of any State, Territory, or possession of the United States, or of any foreign country, except property in which the surviving spouse had at such time merely an expectant interest.

(2) Separate property acquired by the decedent as a result of a "conversion" after December 31, 1941, of property held by him and his surviving spouse as community property under the law of any State, Territory, or possession of the United States, or of any foreign country (except such property in which the surviving spouse had at the time of the "conversion" merely an expectant interest), into their separate property, subject to the limitation with respect to value contained in paragraph (h) of this section.

(3) Property acquired by the decedent in exchange (by one exchange or a series of exchanges) for separate property acquired as set forth under subparagraph (2) of this paragraph.

The burden of establishing the extent to which separate property of the decedent was acquired other than as described in subparagraphs (2) and (3) of this section rests upon the executor.

(d) The surviving spouse is regarded as having merely an expectant interest in property held as community property under the law of any State, Territory, or possession of the United States, or of any foreign country (1) at the time of the decedent's death, if the entire value of such property (and not merely one-half of it) is includible in the decedent's gross estate, or (2) at the time of any transfer, payment of insurance premiums or other consideration, or "conversion", if, in case of the death of the decedent at such time, the entire value of the property involved in the transfer, payment, or "conversion" (and not merely one-half of it) would have been so includible without regard to the provisions of section 402(b) of the Revenue Act of 1942 (56 Stat. 942).

(e) The characteristics of property which acquired a noncommunity instead of a community status by reason of an agreement (whether antenuptial or postnuptial) are such that section 2056(c)(2)(C) classifies the property as community property of the decedent and his surviving spouse in the computation of the "adjusted gross estate". In distinguishing property which thus acquired a noncommunity status from property which acquired such a status solely by operation of the applicable property law, section 2056(c)(2)(C) refers to the former category of property as "separate property" acquired as a result of a "conversion" of "property held as such community property". As used in section 2056(c)(2)(C), the phrase "property held as such community property" is used to denote the body of property comprehended within the community property system; the term "sep-

[Harris]

arate property" includes any noncommunity property (whether held in joint tenancy, tenancy by the entirety, tenancy in common, or otherwise); and the term "conversion" includes any transaction or agreement which transforms property from a community status into a noncommunity status.

(f) The separate property which section 2056(c)(2)(C) classifies as community property is not limited to that which was in existence at the time of the conversion. The following are illustrative of the scope of section 2056(c)(2)(C): (1) A partition of community property between husband and wife, in which a portion of such property became the separate property of each, is a conversion of such property; (2) a transfer of community property into some other form of co-ownership, such as a joint tenancy, is a conversion of such property; (3) an agreement (whether made before or after marriage) that future earnings and gains which would otherwise be community property shall be shared by the spouses as separate property effects a conversion of such earnings and gains; and (4) a change in the form of ownership of property which causes the future rentals therefrom, which would otherwise have been acquired as community property, to be acquired as separate property effects a conversion of the rentals.

(g) The rules of section 2056(c)(2)(C) are applicable, however, only if the conversion took place after December 31, 1941, and only to the extent stated in this section.

(h) If the value of the separate property acquired by the decedent as a result of a conversion did not exceed the value of the separate property thus acquired by the surviving spouse, the entire separate property thus acquired by the decedent is to be considered, for the purpose of this section, as held by him and his surviving spouse as community property. If the value (at the time of the conversion) of the separate property so acquired by the decedent exceeded the value (at that time) of the separate property so acquired by the spouse, only a part of the separate property so acquired by the decedent (and only the same fractional part of property acquired by him in exchange for such separate property) is to be considered, for the purposes of this section, as held by him and his surviving spouse as community property. The part of such separate property (or property acquired in exchange therefor) which is considered as so held is the same proportion of it which the value (at the time of the conversion) of the separate property so acquired by the spouse is of the value (at that time) of the separate property so acquired by the decedent.

(j) The application of this section may be illustrated by the following examples:

Example (1). The value of a decedent's gross estate is $300,000, of which $200,000 represents his separate property and $100,000 represents his one-half interest in community property. The decedent's separate property was inherited from his father. The deductions allowed under sections 2053 and 2054 total $45,000. The adjusted gross estate is computed as follows:

Value of gross estate $300,000
Reduction under paragraph (a)(1) $100,000
Reduction under paragraph (a)(4)
  $200,000
  —————— × $45,000 30,000
  $300,000
      Total reduction 130,000
                                                              ————————
      Adjusted gross estate 170,000

The marital deduction will be $85,000 (one-half the value of the adjusted gross estate) in case the aggregate value of the deductible interests which passed from the decedent to his surviving spouse equals or exceeds that amount.

Example (2). The facts are the same as in example (1) except that the decedent's separate property was not inherited from his father, but was acquired under the following transaction: On November 1, 1942, the decedent and his surviving spouse partitioned certain community property then having a value of $224,000. A portion of such property, then having a value of $160,000, was converted into the decedent's separate property, and the remaining portion then having a value of $64,000, was converted into his spouse's separate property. The portion of the separate property so acquired by the decedent which is considered as held as community property at the time of his death is represented by that proportion of $200,000 (the value, at the time of death, of such separate property) which $64,000 (the value, at the time of the conversion, of the separate property so acquired by his spouse) bears to $160,000 (the value, at the time of the conversion, of the separate property so acquired by the decedent), which proportion equals $80,000. The adjusted gross estate is computed as follows:

Value of gross estate $300,000
Reduction under paragraph (a)(1) ($100,000 + $80,000) $180,000
Reduction under paragraph (a)(4)
  $120,000
  —————— × $45,000 18,000
  $300,000
      Total reduction 198,000
                                                              ————————
      Adjusted gross estate 102,000

The marital deduction will be $51,000 (one-half the value of the adjusted gross estate) in case the aggregate value of the deductible interests which passed from the decedent to his surviving spouse equals or exceeds that amount.

§ 20.2056(d)-1 **Marital deduction; effect of disclaimers**—(a) *By a surviving spouse*. If a decedent's surviving spouse makes a disclaimer of any property interest which would otherwise be considered as having passed from the decedent to her, the disclaimed interest is to be considered as having passed from the decedent to the person or persons entitled to receive the interest as a result of the disclaimer. A disclaimer is a complete and unqualified refusal to accept the rights to which one is entitled. It is, therefore, necessary to distinguish between the surviving spouse's disclaimer of a property interest and her acceptance and subsequent disposal of a property interest. For example, if proceeds of insurance are payable to the surviving spouse and she refuses them so that they consequently pass to an alternate beneficiary designated by the decedent, the proceeds are considered as having passed from the decedent to the alternate beneficiary. On the other hand, if the surviving spouse directs the insurance company to hold the proceeds at interest during her life and, upon her death, to pay the principal sum to another person designated by her, thus effecting a transfer of a remainder interest, the proceeds are considered as having passed from the decedent to his spouse. See paragraph (c) of § 20.2056(e)-2 with respect to a spouse's exercise or failure to exercise a right to take against a decedent's will.

(b) *By a person other than a surviving spouse.* It is unnecessary to distinguish, for the purpose of the marital deduction, between a disclaimer by a person other than the surviving spouse and a transfer by such person. If the surviving spouse becomes entitled to receive an interest in property from the decedent as a result of a disclaimer made by some other person, the interest is, nevertheless, considered as having passed from the decedent, not to the surviving spouse, but to the person who made the disclaimer, as though the disclaimer had not been made. If, as a result of a disclaimer made by a person other than the surviving spouse, a property interest passes to the surviving spouse under circumstances which meet the conditions set forth in § 20.2056(b)-5 (relating to a life estate with a power of appointment), the rule stated in the preceding sentence applies, not only with respect to the portion of the interest which beneficially vests in the surviving spouse, but also with respect to the portion over which she acquires a power to appoint. The rule applies also in the case of proceeds under a life insurance, endowment, or annuity contract, which, as a result of a disclaimer made by a person other than the surviving spouse, are held by the insurer subject to the conditions set forth in § 20.2056(b)-6.

§ 20.2056(e)-1 **Marital deduction; definition of "passed from the decedent".** (a) The following rules are applicable in determining the person to whom any property interest "passed from the decedent":

(1) Property interests devolving upon any person (or persons) as surviving coowner with the decedent under any form of joint ownership under which the right of survivorship existed are considered as having passed from the decedent to such person (or persons).

(2) Property interests at any time subject to the decedent's power to appoint (whether alone or in conjunction with any person) are considered as having passed from the decedent to the appointee under his exercise of the power, or, in case of the lapse, release or non-

exercise of the power, as having passed from the decedent to the taker in default of exercise.

(3) The dower or curtesy interest (or statutory interest in lieu thereof) of the decedent's surviving spouse is considered as having passed from the decedent to his spouse.

(4) The proceeds of insurance upon the life of the decedent are considered as having passed from the decedent to the person who, at the time of the decedent's death, was entitled to receive the proceeds.

(5) Any property interest transferred during life, bequeathed or devised by the decedent, or inherited from the decedent, is considered as having passed to the person to whom he transferred, bequeathed, or devised the interest, or to the person who inherited the interest from him.

(6) The survivor's interest in an annuity or other payment described in section 2039 (see §§ 20.2039-1 and 20.2039-2) is considered as having passed from the decedent to the survivor only to the extent that the value of such interest is included in the decedent's gross estate under that section. If only a portion of the entire annuity or other payment is included in the decedent's gross estate and the annuity or other payment is payable to more than one beneficiary, then the value of the interest considered to have passed to each beneficiary is that portion of the amount payable to each beneficiary that the amount of the annuity or other payment included in the decedent's gross estate bears to the total value of the annuity or other payment payable to all beneficiaries.

(b) If before the decedent's death the decedent's surviving spouse had merely an expectant interest in property held by her and the decedent under community property laws, that interest is considered as having passed from the decedent to the spouse. As to the circumstances under which the interest of the surviving spouse under community property laws is regarded as merely expectant, see paragraph (d) of § 20.2056(c)-2.

§ 20.2056(e)-2 **Marital deduction; definition of "passed from the decedent to his surviving spouse"**—(a) *In general.* In general, the definition stated in § 20.2056(e)-1 is applicable in determining the property interests which "passed from the decedent to his surviving spouse". Special rules are provided, however, for the following:

(1) In the case of certain interests with income for life to the surviving spouse with power of appointment in her (see § 20.2056(b)-5);

(2) In the case of proceeds held by the insurer under a life insurance, endowment, or annuity contract with power of appointment in the surviving spouse (see § 20.2056(b)-6);

(3) In case of the disclaimer of an interest by the surviving spouse or by any other person (see § 20.2056(d)-1);

(4) In case of an election by the surviving spouse (see paragraph (c) of this section); and

(5) In case of a controversy involving the decedent's will, see paragraph (d) of this section.

A property interest is considered as passing to the surviving spouse only if it passed to her as beneficial owner, except to the extent otherwise provided in §§ 20.2056(b)-5 and 20.2056(b)-6 in the case of certain life estates and insurance and annuity contracts with powers of appointment. For this purpose, where a property interest passed from the decedent in trust, such interest is considered to have passed from him to his surviving spouse to the extent of her beneficial interest therein. The deduction may not be taken with respect to a property interest which passed to such spouse merely as trustee, or subject to a binding agreement by the spouse to dispose of the interest in favor of a third person. An allowance or award paid to a surviving spouse pursuant to local law for her support during the administration of the decedent's estate constitutes a property interest passing from the decedent to his surviving spouse. In determining whether or not such an interest is deductible, however, see generally the terminable interest rules of § 20.2056(b)-1 and especially example (8) of paragraph (g) of that section.

(b) *Examples.* The following illustrate the provisions of paragraph (a) of this section:

(1) A property interest bequeathed in trust by H (the decedent) is considered as having passed from him to W (his surviving spouse)—

(i) If the trust income is payable to W for life and upon her death the corpus is distributable to her executors or administrators;

(ii) If W is entitled to the trust income for a term of years following which the corpus is to be paid to W or her estate;

(iii) If the trust income is to be accumulated for a term of years or for W's life and the augmented fund paid to W or her estate; or

(iv) If the terms of the transfer satisfy the requirements of § 20.2056 (b)-5.

(2) If H devised property—

(i) To A for life with remainder absolutely to W or her estate, the remainder interest is considered to have passed from H to W;

(ii) To W for life with remainder to her estate, the entire property is considered as having passed from H to W; or

(iii) Under conditions which satisfy the provisions of § 20.2056(b)-5, the entire property is considered as having passed from H to W.

(3) Proceeds of insurance upon the life of H are considered as having passed from H to W if the terms of the contract—

(i) Meet the requirements of § 20.2056(b)-6;

(ii) Provide that the proceeds are payable to W in a lump sum;

(iii) Provide that the proceeds are payable in installments to W for life and after her death any remaining installments are payable to her estate;

(iv) Provide that interest on the proceeds is payable to W for life and upon her death the principal amount is payable to her estate; or

(v) Provide that the proceeds are payable to a trustee under an arrangement whereby the requirements of section 2056(b)(5) are satisfied.

(c) *Effect of election by surviving spouse.* This paragraph contains rules applicable if the surviving spouse may elect between a property interest offered to her under the decedent's will or other instrument and a property interest to which she is otherwise entitled (such as dower, a right in the decedent's estate, or her interest under community property laws) of which adverse disposition was attempted by the decedent under the will or other instrument. If the surviving spouse elects to take against the will or other instrument, then the property interests offered thereunder are not considered as having "passed from the decedent to his surviving spouse" and the dower or other property interest retained by her is considered as having so passed (if it otherwise so qualifies under this section). If the surviving spouse elects to take under the will or other instrument, then the dower or other property interest relinquished by her is not considered as having "passed from the decedent to his surviving spouse" (irrespective of whether it otherwise comes within the definition stated in paragraph (a) of this section) and the interest taken under the will or other instrument is considered as having so passed (if it otherwise so qualifies). As to the valuation of the property interest taken under the will or other instrument, see paragraph (b) of § 20.2056(b)-4.

(d) *Will contests.* (1) If as a result of a controversy involving the decedent's will, or involving any bequest or devise thereunder, his surviving spouse assigns or surrenders a property interest in settlement of the controversy, the interest so assigned or surrendered is not considered as having "passed from the decedent to his surviving spouse."

(2) If as a result of the controversy involving the decedent's will, or involving any bequest or devise thereunder, a property interest is assigned or surrendered to the surviving spouse, the interest so acquired will be regarded as having "passed from the decedent to his surviving spouse" only if the assignment or surrender was a bona fide recognition of enforceable rights of the surviving spouse in the decedent's estate. Such a bona fide recognition will be presumed where the assignment or surrender was pursuant to a decision of a local court upon the merits in an adversary proceeding following a genuine and active contest. However, such a decree will be accepted only to the extent that the court passed upon the facts upon which deductibility of the property interests depends. If the assignment of surrender was pursuant to a decree rendered by consent, or pursuant to an agreement not to contest the will or not to probate the will, it will not necessarily be accepted as a bona fide evaluation of the rights of the spouse.

(e) *Survivorship.* If the order of deaths of the decedent and his spouse cannot be established by proof, a presumption (whether supplied by local law, the decedent's will, or otherwise) that the decedent was survived by his spouse will be recognized as satisfying paragraph (b)(1) of § 20.2056(a)-1, but only to the extent that it has the effect of giving to the spouse an interest in property includible in her gross estate under part III of subchapter A of chapter 11. Under these circumstances, if an estate tax return is required to be filed for the estate of the decedent's spouse, the marital deduction will not be allowed in the final audit of the estate tax return of the decedent's estate with respect to any property interest which has not been finally determined to be includible in the gross estate of his spouse.

§ 20.2056(e)-3 Marital deduction; definition of "passed from the decedent to a person other than his surviving spouse". The expression "passed from the decedent to a person other than his surviving spouse" refers to any property interest which, under the definition stated in § 20.2056(e)-1 is considered as having "passed from the decedent" and which under the rules referred to in § 20.2056(e)-2 is not considered as having "passed from the decedent to his surviving spouse." Interests which passed to a person other than the surviving spouse include interests so passing under the decedent's exercise, release, or nonexercise of a nontaxable power to appoint. It is immaterial whether the property interest which passed from the decedent to a person other than his surviving spouse is included in the decedent's gross estate. The term "person other than his surviving spouse" includes the possible unascertained takers of a property interest, as, for example, the members of a class to be ascertained in the future. As another example, assume that the decedent created a power of appointment over a property interest, which does not come within the purview of §§ 20.2056(b)-5 or 20.2056(b)-6. In such a case, the term "person other than his surviving spouse" refers to the possible appointees and possible takers in default (other than the spouse) of such property interest. Whether or not there is a possibility that the "person other than his surviving spouse" (or the heirs or assigns of such person) may possess or enjoy the property following termination or failure of the interest therein which passed from the decedent to his surviving spouse is to be determined as of the time of the decedent's death.

ESTATES OF NONRESIDENTS NOT CITIZENS

§ 20.2101-1 Estates of nonresidents not citizens; tax imposed. Section 2101 imposes a tax on the transfer of the taxable estate of a nonresident who was not a citizen of the United States at the time of his death. The tax is computed at the same rates as the tax which is imposed on the transfer of the taxable estate of a citizen or resident of the United States. See section 2001. For a general description of the method to be used in determining the net estate tax payable in the case of an estate of a nonresident not a citizen, see paragraph (c) of § 20.0-2. For the meanings of the terms "resident," "nonresident," and "United States," see paragraph (b)(1) and (2) of

§ 20.0-1. For the presumption applying to the residence of missionaries, see section 2202. For the liability of the executor for payment of the tax, see section 2002.

§ 20.2102-1 Estates of nonresidents not citizens; credits against tax. In arriving at the net estate tax payable with respect to the transfer of an estate of a nonresident who was not a citizen of the United States at the time of his death, the following credits are subtracted from the tax imposed by section 2101:

(a) The State death tax credit under section 2011;

(b) The gift tax credit under section 2012; and

(c) The credit for tax on prior transfers under section 2013.

The amount of each of these credits is determined in the same manner as that prescribed for its determination in the estates of citizens and residents of the United States. See §§ 20.2011-1 through 20.2013-6. The provisions of sections 2015 and 2016, relating respectively to the credit for death taxes on remainders and the recovery of taxes claimed as a credit, are applicable with respect to the credit for State death taxes in the case of the estates of nonresidents not citizens. However, the credit for foreign death taxes under section 2014 is not allowed.

§ 20.2103-1 Estates of nonresidents not citizens; "entire gross estate." The "entire gross estate" wherever situated of a nonresident who was not a citizen of the United States at the time of his death is made up in the same way as the "gross estate" of a citizen or resident of the United States. See §§ 20.2031-1 through 20.2044-1. As in the case of a citizen or resident of the United States, it does not include real property situated outside the United States. However, in the case of a nonresident not a citizen, only that part of the entire gross estate which is situated in the United States is included in his taxable estate. In fact, property situated outside the United States need not be disclosed on the return unless certain deductions are claimed or information is specifically requested. See §§ 20.2106-1 and 20.2106-2. For a description of property considered to be situated in the United States, see § 20.2104-1. For a description of property considered to be situated outside the United States, see § 20.2105-1.

§ 20.2104-1 Estates of nonresidents not citizens; property within the United States—(a) *In general.* Property of a nonresident who was not a citizen of the United States at the time of his death is considered to be situated in the United States if it is—

(1) Real property located in the United States.

(2) Tangible personal property located in the United States, except certain works of art on loan for exhibition (see paragraph (b) of § 20.2105-1).

(3) Written evidence of intangible personal property which is treated as being the property itself, such as a bond for the payment of money, if it is physically located in the United States, except

1018

obligations of the United States (but not its instrumentalities) issued before March 1, 1941, if the decedent was not engaged in business in the United States at the time of his death.

(4) Except as specifically provided otherwise in this section or in § 20.2105-1, intangible personal property the written evidence of which is not treated as being the property itself, if it is issued by or enforceable against a resident of the United States or a domestic corporation or governmental unit.

(5) Shares of stock issued by a domestic corporation, regardless of the location of the certificates.

(6) Moneys deposited in the United States by or for the decedent with any person carrying on the banking business, if the decedent was engaged in business in the United States at the time of his death.

(b) *Transfers.* Property of which the decedent has made a transfer taxable under sections 2035 through 2038 is deemed to be situated in the United States if it is determined, under the provisions of paragraph (a) of this section, to be so situated either at the time of the transfer or at the time of the decedent's death. See §§ 20.2035-1 through 20.2038-1.

(c) *Death tax convention.* It should be noted that the situs rules described in this section may be modified for various purposes under the provisions of an applicable death tax convention with a foreign country.

§ 20.2105-1 **Estates of nonresidents not citizens; property without the United States.** Property of a nonresident who was not a citizen of the United States at the time of his death is considered to be situated outside the United States if it is—

(a) Tangible personal property located outside the United States.

(b) Works of art owned by the decedent if they were—

(1) Imported into the United States solely for exhibition purposes,

(2) Loaned for those purposes to a public gallery or museum, no part of the net earnings of which inures to the benefit of any private shareholder or individual, and

(3) At the time of the death of the owner, on exhibition, or en route to or from exhibition, in such a public gallery or museum.

(c) Written evidence of intangible personal property which is treated as being the property itself, such as a bond for the payment of money, if it is not physically located in the United States.

(d) Obligations of the United States issued before March 1, 1941, even though physically located in the United States, if the decedent was not engaged in business in the United States at the time of his death.

(e) Except as specifically provided otherwise in this section or in § 20.2104-1, intangible personal property the written evidence of which is not treated as being the property itself, if it is not issued by or enforceable against a resident of the United States or a domestic corporation or governmental unit.

1019

(f) Shares of stock issued by a corporation which is not a domestic corporation, regardless of the location of the certificates.

(g) Amounts receivable as insurance on the decedent's life.

(h) Moneys deposited in the United States by or for the decedent with any person carrying on the banking business, if the decedent was not engaged in business in the United States at the time of his death.

§ 20.2106-1 **Estates of nonresidents not citizens; taxable estate; deductions in general.** (a) Section 2106(a) provides that the taxable estate of a nonresident who was not a citizen of the United States at the time of his death is determined by subtracting from the value of that part of his gross estate which, at the time of his death, is situated in the United States the total amount of the following deductions:

(1) The deductions allowed in the case of estates of decedents who were citizens or residents of the United States under sections 2053 and 2054 (see §§ 20.2053-1 through 20.2053-9 and § 20.2054-1) for expenses, indebtedness and taxes, and for losses, to the extent provided in § 20.2106-2.

(2) A deduction computed in the same manner as the one allowed under section 2055 (see §§ 20.2055-1 through 20.2055-4) for charitable, etc., transfers, except—

(i) That the deduction is allowed only for transfers to corporations and associations created or organized in the United States, and to trustees for use within the United States, and

(ii) That the provisions contained in paragraph (c)(2) of § 20.2055-2 relating to termination of a power to consume are not applicable.

(3) An exemption of $2,000, unless a death tax convention provides for another amount, such as a prorated part of the exemption allowed in the case of estates of citizens and residents of the United States under section 2052.

(b) Section 2106(b) provides that no deduction is allowed under paragraph (a)(1) or (2) of this section unless the executor discloses in the estate tax return the value of that part of the gross estate not situated in the United States, See § 20.2105-1. Such part must be valued as of the date of the decedent's death, or if the alternate valuation method under section 2032 is elected, as of the applicable valuation date. No marital deduction under section 2056 is allowed.

(c) In connection with the provisions of section 2106(c), see paragraph (a)(3) of § 20.2104-1 and paragraph (d) of § 20.2105-1.

§ 20.2106-2 **Estates of nonresidents not citizens; deductions for expenses, losses, etc.** (a) In computing the taxable estate of a nonresident who was not a citizen of the United States at the time of his death, deductions are allowed under sections 2053 and 2054 for expenses, indebtedness and taxes, and for losses, to the following extent:

(1) A pledge or subscription is deductible if it is an enforceable claim against the estate and if it would constitute an allowable deduc-

1020

tion under paragraph (a)(2) of § 20.2106-1, relating to charitable, etc., transfers, if it had been a bequest.

(2) That proportion of other deductions under sections 2053 and 2054 is allowed which the value of that part of the decedent's gross estate situated in the United States at the time of his death bears to the value of the decedent's entire gross estate wherever situated. It is immaterial whether the amounts to be deducted were incurred or expended within or without the United States.

No deduction is allowed under this paragraph unless the value of the decedent's entire gross estate is disclosed in the estate tax return. See paragraph (b) of § 20.2106-1.

(b) In order that the Internal Revenue Service may properly pass upon the items claimed as deductions, the executor should submit a certified copy of the schedule of liabilities, claims against the estate, and expenses of administration filed under any applicable foreign death duty act. If no such schedule was filed, the executor should submit a certified copy of the schedule of these liabilities, claims and expenses filed with the foreign court in which administration was had. If the items of deduction allowable under section 2106(a)(1) were not included in either such schedule, or if no such schedules were filed, then there should be submitted a written statement of the foreign executor containing a declaration that it is made under the penalties of perjury setting forth the facts relied upon as entitling the estate to the benefit of the particular deduction or deductions.

(c) The application of this section and of § 20.2106-1 may be illustrated by the following example:

Example. The decedent was a nonresident not a citizen of the United States at the time of his death. His gross estate, wherever situated, amounts to $1,000,000, of which $200,000 (or 20 percent) represents the value of the property having its situs within the United States. The funeral expenses, administration expenses, and claims against the estate aggregate $150,000, and there are charitable bequests, for use within the United States, amounting to $25,000. The decedent's taxable estate is determined as follows:

That part of the entire gross estate situated in the United States		$200,000
Deductions for expenses and claims (20 percent of $150,000)	$30,000	
Charitable deduction	25,000	
Exemption	2,000	57,000
Taxable estate		143,000

For the manner of computing the tax on the taxable estate, see § 20.2001-2.

MISCELLANEOUS

§ 20.2201-1 **Members of the Armed Forces dying during an induction period.** (a) The additional estate tax as defined in section 2011 (d) does not apply to the transfer of the taxable estate of a citizen or resident of the United States dying during an induction period as defined in section 112(c)(5) (see paragraph (b) of this section) and while in active service as a member of the Armed Forces of the United States, if the decedent—

(1) Was killed in action while serving in a combat zone, as determined under section 112(c)(2) and (3) (see paragraph (c) of this section), or

(2) Died as a result of wounds, disease, or injury suffered while serving in such a combat zone and while in line of duty, by reason of a hazard to which he was subject as an incident of such service.

(b) Section 112(c)(5) defines the term "induction period" as meaning any period during which individuals are liable for induction, for reasons other than prior deferment, for training and service in the Armed Forces of the United States.

(c) Section 112(c)(2) and (3) provides that service is performed in a combat zone only—

(1) If it is performed in an area which the President of the United States has designated by Executive order for purposes of section 112(c) as an area in which the Armed Forces of the United States are, or have, engaged in combat, and

(2) If it is performed on or after the date designated by the President by Executive order as the date of the commencing of combatant activities in such zone and on or before the date designated by the President by Executive order as the date of termination of combatant activities in such zone.

(d) If the official record of the branch of the Armed Forces of which the decedent was a member at the time of his death states that the decedent was killed in action while serving in a combat zone, or that death resulted from wounds or injuries received or disease contracted while in line of duty in a combat zone, this fact shall, in the absence of evidence establishing the contrary, be presumed to be established for the purposes of the exemption. Moreover, wounds, injuries or disease suffered while in line of duty will be considered to have been caused by a hazard to which the decedent was subjected as an incident of service as a member of the Armed Forces, unless the hazard which caused the wounds, injuries, or disease was clearly unrelated to such service.

(e) A person was in active service as a member of the Armed Forces of the United States if he was at the time of his death actually serving in such forces. A member of the Armed Forces in active service in a combat zone who thereafter becomes a prisoner of war or missing in action, and occupies such status at death or when the wounds, disease, or injury resulting in death were incurred, is considered for purposes of this section as serving in a combat zone.

(f) The exemption from tax granted by section 2201 does not apply to the basic estate tax as defined in section 2011(d).

§ 20.2202-1 **Missionaries in foreign service.** Section 2202 provides that a duly commissioned missionary, dying while in foreign missionary service under a board of foreign missions of a religious denom-

1022

ination in the United States, is presumed to have retained a United States residence (see paragraph (b)(1) of § 20.0-1) held at the time of his commission and departure for foreign service, in the absence of relevant facts other than his intention to remain permanently in such foreign service.

Liability for Tax

§ 20.2203-1 **Definition of executor.** The term "executor" means the executor or administrator of the decedent's estate. However, if there is no executor or administrator appointed, qualified and acting within the United States, the term means any person in actual or constructive possession of any property of the decedent. The term "person in actual or constructive possession of any property of the decedent" includes, among others, the decedent's agents and representatives; safe-deposit companies, warehouse companies, and other custodians of property in this country; brokers holding, as collateral, securities belonging to the decedent; and debtors of the decedent in this country.

§ 20.2204-1 **Discharge of executor from personal liability.** The executor of a decedent's estate may make written application to the district director for the district in which the estate tax return is filed for a determination of the Federal estate tax and discharge from personal liability therefor. Within one year after receipt of the application, or if the application is made before the return is filed then within one year after the return is filed, the executor will be notified of the amount of the tax and, upon payment thereof, he will be discharged from personal liability for any deficiency in the tax thereafter found to be due. If no such notification is received, the executor is discharged at the end of such one year period from personal liability for any deficiency thereafter found to be due.

§ 20.2205-1 **Reimbursement out of estate.** If any portion of the tax is paid by or collected out of that part of the estate passing to, or in the possession of, any person other than the duly qualified executor or administrator, that person may be entitled to reimbursement, either out of the undistributed estate or by contribution from other beneficiaries whose shares or interests in the estate would have been reduced had the tax been paid before distribution of the estate, or whose shares or interests are subject either to an equal or prior liability for the payment of taxes, debts, or other charges against the estate. For specific provisions giving the executor the right to reimbursement from life insurance beneficiaries and from recipients of property over which the decedent had a power of appointment, see sections 2206 and 2207. These provisions, however, are not designed to curtail the right of the district director to collect the tax from any person, or out of any property, liable for its payment. The district director cannot be required to apportion the tax among the persons liable nor to enforce any right of reimbursement or contribution.

§ 20.2206-1 Liability of life insurance beneficiaries. With respect to the right of the district director to collect the tax without regard to the provisions of section 2206, see § 20.2205-1.

§ 20.2207-1 Liability of recipient of property over which decedent had power of appointment. With respect to the right of the district director to collect the tax without regard to the provisions of section 2207, see § 20.2205-1.

PROCEDURE AND ADMINISTRATION

Returns

§ 20.6001-1 Persons required to keep records and render statements. (a) It is the duty of the executor to keep such complete and detailed records of the affairs of the estate for which he acts as will enable the district director to determine accurately the amount of the estate tax liability. All documents and vouchers used in preparing the estate tax return (§ 20.6018-1) shall be retained by the executor so as to be available for inspection whenever required.

(b) In addition to filing a preliminary notice (see § 20.6036-1) and an estate tax return (see § 20.6018-1), the executor shall furnish such supplemental data as may be necessary to establish the correct estate tax. It is therefore the duty of the executor (1) to furnish, upon request, copies of any documents in his possession (or on file in any court having jurisdiction over the estate) relating to the estate, appraisal lists of any items included in the gross estate, copies of balance sheets or other financial statements obtainable by him relating to the value of stock, and any other information obtainable by him that may be found necessary in the determination of the tax, and (2) to render any written statement, containing a declaration that it is made under penalties of perjury, of facts within his knowledge which the district director may require for the purpose of determining whether a tax liability exists and, if so, the extent thereof. Failure to comply with such a request will render the executor liable to penalties (see section 7269), and proceedings may be instituted in the proper court of the United States to secure compliance therewith (see section 7604).

(c) Persons having possession or control of any records or documents containing or supposed to contain any information concerning the estate, or having knowledge of or information about any fact or facts which have a material bearing upon the liability, or the extent of liability, of the estate for the estate tax, shall, upon request of the district director, make disclosure thereof. Failure on the part of any person to comply with such request will render him liable to penalties (section 7269), and compliance with the request may be enforced in the proper court of the United States (section 7604).

(d) Upon notification from the Internal Revenue Service, a corporation (organized or created in the United States) or its transfer agent is required to furnish the following information pertaining to stocks or bonds registered in the name of a nonresident decedent (regardless of citizenship): (1) The name of the decedent as registered; (2) the date of the decedent's death; (3) the decedent's residence and his place of death; (4) the names and addresses of executors, attorneys, or other representatives of the estate, within and without the United States; and (5) a description of the securities, the number of shares or bonds and the par values thereof.

§ 20.6011-1 General requirement of return, statement, or list—
(a) *General rule.* Every person made liable for any tax imposed by subtitle B of the Code shall make such returns or statements as are required by the regulations in this part. The return or statement shall include therein the information required by the applicable regulations or forms.

(b) *Use of prescribed forms.* Copies of the forms prescribed by §§ 20.6018-1 and 20.6036-1 may be obtained from district directors. The fact that an executor has not been furnished with copies of these forms will not excuse him from filing a preliminary notice or making a return. Application for a form shall be made to the district director in ample time for the executor to have the form prepared, verified, and filed with the district director on or before the date prescribed for the filing thereof (see §§ 20.6071-1 and 20.6075-1). The executor shall carefully prepare the preliminary notice and the return so as to set forth fully and clearly the data called for therein. A preliminary notice or a return which has not been so prepared will not be accepted as meeting the requirements of §§ 20.6018-1 through 20.6018-4 and § 20.6036-1.

§ 20.6018-1 Returns—(a) *Estates of citizens or residents.* A return must be filed on Form 706 for the estate of every citizen or resident of the United States whose gross estate exceeded $60,000 in value on the date of his death. The value of the gross estate at the date of death governs with respect to the filing of the return regardless of whether the value of the gross estate is, at the executor's election, finally determined as of a date subsequent to the date of death pursuant to the provisions of section 2032. Duplicate copies of the return are not required to be filed. For the contents of the return, see § 20.6018-3.

(b) *Estates of nonresidents not citizens.* A return must be filed on Form 706 or 706NA for the estate of every nonresident not a citizen if the value of the part of the gross estate situated in the United States exceeded $2,000 on the date of his death. Under certain conditions the return may be made only on Form 706. See the instructions on Form 706NA for circumstances under which that form may not be used. Duplicate copies of the return are not required to be filed. For the contents of the return, see § 20.6018-3.

(c) *Place for filing.* See § 20.6091-1 for the place where the return shall be filed.

(d) *Time for filing.* See § 20.6075-1 for the time for filing the return.

§ 20.6018-2 **Returns; person required to file return.** It is required that the duly qualified executor or administrator shall file the return. If there is more than one executor or administrator, the return must be made jointly by all. If there is no executor or administrator appointed, qualified and acting within the United States, every person in actual or constructive possession of any property of the decedent situated in the United States is constituted an executor for purposes of the tax (see § 20.2203-1), and is required to make and file a return. If in any case the executor is unable to make a complete return as to any part of the gross estate, he is required to give all the information he has as to such property, including a full description, and the name of every person holding a legal or beneficial interest in the property. If the executor is unable to make a return as to any property, every person holding a legal or beneficial interest therein shall, upon notice from the district director, make a return as to that part of the gross estate. For delinquency penalty for failure to file return, see section 6651 and § 301.6651-1 of this chapter (Regulations on Procedure and Administration). For criminal penalties for failure to file a return and filing a false or fraudulent return, see sections 7203, 7206, 7207, and 7269.

§ 20.6018-3 **Returns; contents of returns**—(a) *Citizens or residents.* The return of an estate of a decedent who was a citizen or resident of the United States at the time of his death must contain an itemized inventory by schedule of the property constituting the gross estate and lists of the deductions under the proper schedules. The return shall set forth (1) the value of the gross estate (see §§ 20.2031-1 through 20.2044-1), (2) the deductions claimed (see §§ 20.2052-1 through 20.2056(e)-3), (3) the taxable estate (see § 20.2051-1), and (4) the gross estate tax, reduced by any credits (see §§ 20.2011-1 through 20.2014-6) against the tax. In listing upon the return the property constituting the gross estate (other than household and personal effects for which see § 20.2031-6), the description of it shall be such that the property may be readily identified for the purpose of verifying the value placed on it by the executor.

(b) *Nonresidents not citizens.* The return of an estate of a decedent who was not a citizen or resident of the United States at the time of his death must contain the following information: (1) An itemized list of that part of the gross estate situated in the United States (see § 20.2104-1), (2) an itemized list of any deductions claimed (see §§ 20.2106-1 and 20.2106-2), (3) the amount of the taxable estate (see § 20.2106-1), and (4) the gross estate tax, reduced by any credits (see § 20.2102-1) against the tax. For the disallowance of certain deductions if the return does not disclose that part of the gross estate not situated in the United States, see §§ 20.2106-1 and 20.2106-2.

[Harris]

(c) *Provisions applicable to returns described in paragraphs (a) and (b) of this section.* (1) A legal description shall be given of each parcel of real estate, and, if located in a city, the name of the street and number, its area, and, if improved, a short statement of the character of the improvements.

(2) A description of bonds shall include the number held, principal amount, name of obligor, date of maturity, rate of interest, date or dates on which interest is payable, series number if there is more than one issue, and the principal exchange upon which listed, or the principal business office of the obligor, if unlisted. A description of stocks shall include number of shares, whether common or preferred, and, if preferred, what issue, par value, quotation at which returned, exact name of corporation, and, if the stock is unlisted, the location of the principal business office and State in which incorporated and the date of incorporation, or if the stock is listed, the principal exchange upon which sold. A description of notes shall include name of maker, date on which given, date of maturity, amount of principal, amount of principal unpaid, rate of interest and whether simple or compound, date to which interest has been paid and amount of unpaid interest. A description of the seller's interest in land contracts shall include name of buyer, date of contract, description of property, sale price, initial payment, amounts of installment payments, unpaid balance of principal and accrued interest, interest rate and date prior to decedent's death to which interest had been paid.

(3) A description of bank accounts shall disclose the name and address of depository, amount on deposit, whether a checking, savings, or a time-deposit account, rate of interest, if any payable, amount of interest accrued and payable, and serial number. A description of life insurance shall give the name of the insurer, number of policy, name of the beneficiary, and the amount of the proceeds.

(4) In describing an annuity, the name and address of the grantor of the annuity shall be given, or, if the annuity is payable out of a trust or other funds, such a description as will fully identify it. If the annuity is payable for a term of years, the duration of the term and the date on which it began shall be given, and if payable for the life of a person other than the decedent, the date of birth of such person shall be stated. If the executor has not included in the gross estate the full value of an annuity or other payment described in section 2039, he shall nevertheless fully describe the annuity and state its total purchase price and the amount of the contribution made by each person (including the decedent's employer) toward the purchase price. If the executor believes that any part of the annuity or other payment is excludable from the gross estate under the provisions of section 2039, or for any other reason, he shall state in the return the reason for his belief.

(5) Judgments should be described by giving the title of the cause and the name of the court in which rendered, date of judgment, name and address of the judgment debtor, amount of judgment, and rate

of interest to which subject, and by stating whether any payments have been made thereon, and, if so, when and in what amounts.

(6) If, pursuant to section 2032, the executor elects to have the estate valued at a date or dates subsequent to the time of the decedent's death, there must be set forth on the return: (i) An itemized description of all property included in the gross estate on the date of the decedent's death, together with the value of each item as of that date; (ii) an itemized disclosure of all distributions, sales, exchanges, and other dispositions of any property during the 1-year period after the date of the decedent's death, together with the dates thereof; and (iii) the value of each item of property in accordance with the provisions of section 2032 (see § 20.2032-1). Interest and rents accrued at the date of the decedent's death and dividends declared to stockholders of record on or before the date of the decedent's death and not collected at that date are to be shown separately. (See also paragraph (e) of § 20.6018-4 with respect to documents required to be filed with the return.)

(7) All transfers made by the decedent within 3 years before the date of his death of a value of $1,000 or more and all transfers (other than outright transfers not in trust) made by the decedent at any time during his life of a value of $5,000 or more, except bona fide sales for an adequate and full consideration in money or money's worth, must be disclosed in the return, whether or not the executor regards the transfers as subject to the tax. If the executor believes that such a transfer is not subject to the tax, a brief statement of the pertinent facts shall be made.

§ 20.6018-4   Returns; documents to accompany the return.   (a) A certified copy of the will, if the decedent died testate, must be submitted with the return, together with copies of such other documents as are required in Form 706 and in the applicable sections of these regulations. There may also be filed copies of any documents which the executor may desire to submit in explanation of the return.

(b) In the case of an estate of a nonresident citizen, the executor shall also file the following documents with the return: (1) A copy of any inventory of property and schedule of liabilities, claims against the estate and expenses of administration filed with the foreign court of probate jurisdiction, certified by a proper official of the court; and (2) a copy of any return filed under any applicable foreign inheritance, estate, legacy, or succession tax act, certified by a proper official of the foreign tax department.

(c) In the case of an estate of a nonresident not a citizen, the executor must also file with the return, but only if deductions are claimed, a copy of the inventory of property filed under the foreign death duty act; or, if no such inventory was filed, a certified copy of the inventory filed with the foreign court of probate jurisdiction.

(d) For every policy of life insurance listed on the return, the executor must procure a statement, on Form 712, by the company issuing the policy and file it with the return.

(e) If, pursuant to section 2032, the executor elects to have the estate valued at a date or dates subsequent to the time of the decedent's death, the executor shall file with the return evidence in support of any statements made by him in the return as to distributions, sales, exchanges, or other dispositions of property during the 1-year period which followed the decedent's death. If the court having jurisdiction over the estate makes an order or decree of distribution during that period, a certified copy thereof must be submitted as part of the evidence. The district director may require the submission of such additional evidence as is deemed necessary.

(f) In any case where a transfer, by trust or otherwise, was made by a written instrument, a copy thereof shall be filed with the return if (1) the property is included in the gross estate, or (2) the executor pursuant to the provisions of paragraph (c)(7) of § 20.6018-3 has made a disclosure of the transfer on the return but has not included its value in the gross estate in the belief that it is not so includible. If the written instrument is of public record, the copy shall be certified, or if it is not of record, the copy shall be verified. If the decedent was a nonresident not a citizen at the time of his death, the copy may be either certified or verified.

(g) If the executor contends that the value of property transferred by the decedent within a period of three years ending with the date of the decedent's death should not be included in the gross estate because he considers that the transfer was not made in contemplation of death, he shall file with the return (1) a copy of the death certificate, and (2) a statement, containing a declaration that it is made under the penalties of perjury, of all the material facts and circumstances, including those directly or indirectly indicating the decedent's motive in making the transfer and his mental and physical condition at that time. However, this data need not be furnished with respect to transfers of less than $1,000 in value unless requested by the district director.

§ 20.6036-1 **Notice of qualification as executor**—(a) *Preliminary notice.* A preliminary notice is required to be filed on Form 704 in the case of every citizen or resident of the United States whose gross estate exceeded $60,000 in value at the date of death, and on Form 705 in the case of every nonresident who is not a citizen if that part of his gross estate which was situated in the United States (see § 20.2104-1) exceeded $2,000 in value at the date of death. The value of the gross estate at the date of death governs with respect to the filing of the notice regardless of whether the value of the gross estate is, at the executor's election, finally determined as of a date subsequent to the date of death pursuant to the provisions of section 2032. If there is doubt as to whether the gross estate exceeds $60,000 or $2,000, as the case may be, the notice shall be filed as a matter of precaution in order to avoid the possibility of penalties attaching. The primary purpose of the notice is to advise the Internal Revenue Service of the existence of taxable estates, and filing shall not be delayed beyond the period provided for in § 20.6071-1 merely because of uncertainty as to the exact value of the assets. The estimate of the gross estate called for by the notice shall be the best approximation of value which can be made within the time allowed. Duplicate copies of the preliminary notices are not required to be filed. For criminal penalties for failure to file a notice and filing a false or fraudulent notice, see sections 7203, 7207, and 7269. See § 20.6091-1 for the place for filing the notice. See § 20.6071-1 for the time for filing the notice.

(b) *Persons required to file.* In the case of an estate of a citizen or resident of the United States the preliminary notice must be filed by the duly qualified executor or administrator, or if none qualifies within 2 months after the decedent's death, by every person in actual or constructive possession of any property of the decedent at or after the time of the decedent's death. The signature of one executor or administrator on the preliminary notice is sufficient. In the case of a nonresident not a citizen, the notice must be filed by every duly qualified executor or administrator within the United States, or if none qualifies within two months after the decedent's death, by every person in actual or constructive possession of any property of the decedent at or after the time of the decedent's death.

§ 20.6071-1 **Time for filing of preliminary notice.** If a duly qualified executor or administrator of the estate of a decedent who was a resident or a citizen of the United States qualifies within two months after a decedent's death, or if a duly qualified executor or administrator of the estate of a nonresident not a citizen qualifies within the United States within two months after the decedent's death, the preliminary notice required by § 20.6036-1 must be filed within two months after his qualification. If no such executor or administrator qualifies within that period, the preliminary notice must be filed within two months of the decedent's death.

§ 20.6075-1 **Returns; time for filing estate tax return.** The estate tax return required by section 6018 must be filed on or before the due date. The due date is the date on or before which the return is required to be filed in accordance with the provisions of section 6075(a) or the last day of the period covered by an extension of time granted by the district director as provided in § 20.6081-1. Unless an extension of time for filing has been granted, the due date is the day of the fifteenth calendar month after the decedent's death numerically corresponding to the day of the calendar month on which death occurred, except that, if there is no numerically corresponding day in such fifteenth month, the last day of the fifteenth month is the due date. For example, if the decedent died on August 31, 1955, the due date is November 30, 1956. When the due date falls on Saturday, Sunday, or a legal holiday, the due date for filing the return is the next succeeding day which is not Saturday, Sunday, or a legal holiday. For definition of a legal holiday, see section 7503 and § 301.7503-1 of this chapter (Regulations on Procedure and Administration). As to additions to the tax in the case of failure to file the return within the prescribed time, see section 6651 and § 301.6651-1 of this chapter (Regulations on Procedure and Administration). For rules with respect to the right to elect to have the property valued as of a date or dates subsequent to the decedent's death, see § 20.2032-1, and section 7502 and § 301.7502-1 of this chapter (Regulations on Procedure and Administration).

§ 20.6081-1 **Extension of time for filing the return.** (a) In case it is impossible or impracticable for the executor to file a reasonably complete return within 15 months from the date of death, the district director may, upon a showing of good and sufficient cause, grant a reasonable extension of time for filing the return required by section 6018. Unless the executor is abroad, the extension may not be for more than six months from the date for filing provided by section 6075(a). Therefore, unless the executor is abroad, the due date for filing the return under any extension granted by a district director may not be later than 21 months from the date of the decedent's death. The extension may, of course, be for a lesser period of time.

(b) The application for an extension of time for filing the return shall be addressed to the district director for the district in which the return is to be filed, and must contain a full recital of the causes for the delay. It must be made before the expiration of the time within which the return otherwise must be filed. It shall, where possible, be made sufficiently early to permit the district director to consider the matter and reply before what otherwise would be the due date of the return.

(c) A return as complete as possible must be filed before the expiration of the extension period granted. The return thus filed will be the return required by section 6018(a) and any tax shown thereon will be the "amount determined by the executor as the tax" referred to in section 6161(a)(2), or the "amount shown as the tax by the taxpayer upon his return" referred to in section 6211(a)(1)(A). The return cannot be amended after the expiration of the extension period although supplemental information may subsequently be filed that may result in a finally determined tax different from the amount shown as the tax by the executor on the return. An extension of time for filing the return does not operate to extend the time for payment of the tax. See § 20.6151-1 for the time for payment of the tax, and §§ 20.6161-1 and 20.6163-1 for extensions of time for payment of the tax.

§ 20.6091-1 **Place for filing returns or other documents.** If the decedent was a resident of the United States, the preliminary notice required by § 20.6036-1 and the estate tax return required by § 20.6018-1 must be filed with the district director in whose district the decedent had his domicile at the time of death. If the decedent was a non-resident (whether a citizen or not a citizen), the notice and the return must be filed with the office of the Director of International Operations, Internal Revenue Service, Washington 25, D. C., or with such other office as the Commissioner may designate.

Time and Place for Paying Tax

§ 20.6151-1   Time and place for paying tax shown on the return—
(a) *General rule.* The tax shown on the estate tax return is to be paid at the time and place fixed for filing the return (determined without regard to any extension of time for filing the return). For provisions relating to the time and place for filing the return, see §§ 20.6075-1 and 20.6091-1. For the duty of the executor to pay the tax, see § 20.2002-1.

(b) *Extension of time for paying*—(1) *In general.* For general provisions relating to extension of time for paying the tax, see § 20.6161-1.

(2) *Reversionary or remainder interests.* For provisions relating to extension of time for payment of estate tax on the value of a reversionary or remainder interest in property, see § 20.6163-1.

(c) *Payment with obligations of the United States.* Treasury bonds of certain issues which were owned by the decedent at the time of his death or which were treated as part of his gross estate under the rules contained in § 306.28 of Treasury Department Circular No. 300, Revised (31 CFR Part 306), may be redeemed at par plus accrued interest for the purpose of payment of the estate tax, as provided in said section. Whether bonds of particular issues may be redeemed for this purpose will depend on the terms of the offering circulars cited on the face of the bonds. A current list of eligible issues may be obtained from any Federal reserve bank or branch, or from the Bureau of Public Debt, Washington, D. C. See section 6312 and §§ 301.6312-1 and 301.6312-2 of this chapter (Regulations on Procedure and Administration) for provisions relating to the payment of taxes with United States Treasury obligations.

(d) *Receipt for payment.* For provisions relating to duplicate receipts for payment of the tax, see § 20.6314-1.

§ 20.6161-1   Extension of time for paying tax shown on the return.
(a) In any case in which the district director finds that payment, on the due date, of any part of the tax shown on the return would impose undue hardship upon the estate, he may extend the time for payment for a period or periods not to exceed one year for any one period and for all periods not to extend more than 10 years from the due date.

(b) The extension will not be granted upon a general statement of hardship. The term "undue hardship" means more than an inconvenience to the estate. It must appear that substantial financial loss, for example, due to the sale of property at a sacrifice price, will result to the estate from making payment of the tax at the due date. If a market exists, a sale of property at the current market price is not ordinarily considered as resulting in an undue hardship.

(c) An application for such an extension must be in writing and must contain, or be supported by, information in a written statement declaring that it is made under penalties of perjury, showing the undue hardship that would result to the estate if the requested extension were refused. The application, with the supporting information, must be filed with the district director. When received, it will be examined, and, if possible, within 30 days will be denied, granted, or tentatively granted subject to certain conditions of which the executor will be notified. The district director will not consider an application for such an extension unless it is applied for on or before the due date for payment of the tax. If the executor desires to obtain an additional extension, it must be applied for on or before the date of the expiration of the previous extension. The granting of the extension of time for paying the tax is discretionary with the district director and his authority will be exercised under such conditions as he may deem advisable.

(d) The amount of the tax for which an extension is granted, with the additions thereto, shall be paid on or before the expiration of the period of extension without the necessity of notice and demand from the district director.

(e) The granting of an extension of time for paying the tax will not relieve the executor from the duty of filing the return on or before the date provided for in § 20.6075-1, nor will it operate to prevent the running of interest. See section 6601. An extension of time to pay the tax may extend the period within which State and foreign death taxes allowed as a credit under sections 2011 and 2014 are required to be paid and the credit therefor claimed. See paragraph (c) of § 20.2011-1 and § 20.2014-6.

(f) For provisions requiring the furnishing of security for the payment of the tax for which an extension is granted, see paragraph (a) of § 20.6165-1. For provisions relating to extensions of time for payment of tax on the value of a reversionary or remainder interest in property, see § 20.6163-1.

§ 20.6161-2 **Extension of time for paying deficiency in tax.** (a) In any case in which the district director finds that payment, on the date prescribed therefor, of any part of a deficiency would impose undue hardship upon the estate, he may extend the time for payment for a period or periods not to exceed one year for any one period and for all periods not to exceed four years from the date prescribed for payment thereof.

(b) The extension will not be granted upon a general statement of hardship. The term "undue hardship" means more than an inconvenience to the estate. It must appear that a substantial financial loss, for example, due to the sale of property at a sacrifice price, will result to the estate from making payment of the deficiency at the date prescribed therefor. If a market exists, a sale of property at the current market price is not ordinarily considered as resulting in an undue hardship. No extension will be granted if the deficiency is due to negligence or intentional disregard of rules and regulations or to fraud with intent to evade the tax.

(c) An application for such an extension must be in writing and must contain, or be supported by, information in a written statement declaring that it is made under penalties of perjury showing the undue hardship that would result to the estate if the extension were refused. The application, with the supporting information, must be filed with the district director. When received, it will be examined, and, if possible, within thirty days will be denied, granted, or tentatively granted subject to certain conditions of which the executor will be notified. The district director will not consider an application for such an extension unless it is applied for on or before the date prescribed for payment of the deficiency, as shown by the notice and demand from the district director. If the executor desires to obtain an additional extension, it must be applied for on or before the date of the expiration of the previous extension. The granting of the extension of time for paying the deficiency is discretionary with the district director.

(d) The amount of the deficiency for which an extension is granted, with the additions thereto, shall be paid on or before the expiration of the period of extension without the necessity of notice and demand from the district director.

(e) The granting of an extension of time for paying the deficiency will not operate to prevent the running of interest. See section 6601. An extension of time to pay the deficiency may extend the period within which State and foreign death taxes allowed as a credit under sections 2011 and 2014 are required to be paid and the credit therefor claimed. See paragraph (c) of § 20.2011-1 and § 20.2014-6.

(f) For provisions requiring the furnishing of security for the payment of the deficiency for which an extension is granted, see § 20.6165-1.

§ 20.6163-1 **Extension of time for payment of estate tax on value of reversionary or remainder interest in property.** (a) In case there is included in the gross estate a reversionary or remainder interest in property, the payment of the part of the tax attributable to that interest may, at the election of the executor, be postponed until six months after the termination of the precedent interest or interests in the property. This provision is limited to cases in which the reversionary or remainder interest is included in the decedent's gross estate as such and does not extend to cases in which the decedent creates future interests by his own testamentary act.

(b) Notice of the exercise of the election to postpone the payment of the tax attributable to a reversionary or remainder interest should be filed with the district director before the date prescribed for payment of the tax. The notice of election may be made in the form of a letter addressed to the district director. There shall be filed with the notice of election a certified copy of the will or other instrument under which the reversionary or remainder interest was created, or a copy verified by the executor if the instrument is not filed of record. The district director may require the submission of such additional proof as he deems necessary to disclose the complete facts. If the duration of the precedent interest is dependent upon the life of any person, the notice of election must show the date of birth of that person.

(c) If the decedent's gross estate consists of both a reversionary or remainder interest in property and other property, the tax attributable to the reversionary or remainder interest, within the meaning of this section, is an amount which bears the same ratio to the total tax as the value of the reversionary or remainder interest (reduced as provided in the following sentence) bears to the entire gross estate (reduced as provided in the last sentence of this paragraph). In applying this ratio, the value of the reversionary or remainder interest is reduced by (1) the amount of claims, mortgages, and indebtedness which is a lien upon such interest; (2) losses in respect of such interest during the settlement of the estate which are deductible under the provisions of section 2054 or section 2106(a)(1); (3) any amount deductible in respect of such interest under section 2055 or 2106(a)(2) for charitable, etc., transfers; and (4) the portion of the marital deduction allowed under the provisions of section 2056 on account of bequests, etc., of such interests to the decedent's surviving spouse. Likewise, in applying the ratio, the value of the gross estate is reduced by such deductions having similar relationship to the items comprising the gross estate.

(d) For provisions requiring the payment of interest for the period of the extension, see section 6601(b). For provisions requiring the furnishing of security for the payment of the tax for which the extension is granted, see paragraph (b) of § 20.6165-1. For provisions concerning the time within which credit for State and foreign death taxes on such a reversionary or remainder interest may be taken, see section 2015 and the regulations thereunder.

§ 20.6165-1 Bonds where time to pay tax or deficiency has been extended—(a) *Extensions under section 6161 of time to pay tax or deficiency.* If an extension of time for payment of tax or deficiency is granted under section 6161, the district director may, if he deems it necessary, require the executor to furnish a bond for the payment of the amount in respect of which the extension is granted in accordance with the terms of the extension. However, such bond shall not exceed double the amount with respect to which the extension is granted. For other provisions relating to bonds required where extensions of time to pay estate taxes or deficiencies are granted under section 6161, see the regulations under sections 6165 and 7101 contained in part 301 of this chapter (Regulations on Procedure and Administration).

(b) *Extensions under section 6163 of time to pay estate tax attributable to reversionary or remainder interests.* As a prerequisite to the postponement of the payment of the tax attributable to a reversionary or remainder interest as provided in § 20.6163-1, a bond must be furnished in an amount which is double the amount of the tax and interest for the estimated duration of the precedent interest, conditioned upon the payment of the tax and interest accrued thereon within six months after the termination of the precedent interest. If after the acceptance of a bond it is determined that the amount of the tax attributable to the reversionary or remainder interest was understated in the bond, a new bond or a supplemental bond may be required, or the tax, to the extent of the understatement, may be collected. The bond must be conditioned upon the principal or surety promptly notifying the district director when the precedent interest terminates and upon the principal or surety notifying the district director during the month of September of each year as to the continuance of the precedent interest, if the duration of the precedent interest is dependent upon the life or lives of any person or persons, or is otherwise indefinite. For other provisions relating to bonds where an extension of time has been granted for paying the tax, see the regulations under sections 6165 and 7101 contained in part 301 of this chapter (Regulations on Procedure and Administration).

Collection of Tax

§ 20.6314-1 **Duplicate receipts for payment of estate taxes.** The district director will, upon request, give to the person paying the tax duplicate receipts, either of which will be sufficient evidence of such payment and entitle the executor to be credited with the amount by any court having jurisdiction to audit or settle his accounts.

§ 20.6321-1 **Lien for taxes.** For regulations concerning the lien for taxes, see § 301.6321-1 of this chapter (Regulations on Procedure and Administration).

§ 20.6323-1 **Validity against mortgagees, pledgees, purchasers, and judgment creditors.** For regulations concerning the validity of liens against mortgagees, pledgees, purchasers, and judgment creditors, see § 301.6323-1 of this chapter (Regulations on Procedure and Administration).

§ 20.6324-1 **Special lien for estate tax.** For regulations concerning the special lien for the estate tax, see § 301.6324-1 of this chapter (Regulations on Procedure and Administration).

§ 20.6325-1 **Release of lien or partial discharge of property; transfer certificates in nonresident estates.** (a) A transfer certificate is a certificate permitting the transfer of property of a nonresident decedent without liability. Except as provided in paragraph (b) of this section, no domestic corporation or its transfer agent should transfer stock registered in the name of a nonresident decedent (regardless of citizenship) except such shares which have been submitted for transfer by a duty qualified executor or administrator who has been appointed and is acting in the United States, without first requiring a transfer certificate covering all of the decedent's stock of the corporation and showing that the transfer may be made without liability. Corporations, transfer agents of domestic corporations, transfer agents of foreign corporations (except as to shares held in the name of a non-resident decedent not a citizen of the United States), banks, trust companies, or other custodians in actual or constructive possession of property of such a decedent can insure avoidance of liability for taxes and penalties only by demanding and receiving transfer certificates before transfer of property of nonresident decedents.

(b) A transfer certificate is not required in the case of a nonresident decedent not a citizen of the United States if, as of the date of the decedent's death, the total value of his gross estate situated in the United States is not in excess of $2,000. In this connection, a corporation, transfer agent, bank, trust company or other custodian will not incur liability for a transfer of the decedent's property if the corporation or other person, having no information to the contrary, first receives from the executor or other responsible person, who may be reasonably regarded as in possession of the pertinent facts, a statement that the total value, as of the date of the decedent's death, of that part of his gross estate situated in the United States is not in excess of $2,000. Also, a transfer certificate is not required for bonds owned by a nonresident decedent who was not a citizen of the United States at the time of his death if it is shown that the bonds were not physically situated in the United States at the time of his death.

(c) A transfer certificate will be issued by the district director when he is satisfied that the tax imposed upon the estate, if any, has been fully discharged or provided for. The tax will be considered fully discharged for purposes of the issuance of a transfer certificate only when investigation has been completed and payment of the tax, including any deficiency finally determined, has been made. If the tax liability has not been fully discharged, transfer certificates may be issued permitting the transfer of particular items of property without liability upon the filing with the district director of such security as he may require. No transfer certificate is required in an estate of a resident decedent. Further, in the case of an estate of a nonresident decedent (regardless of citizenship) a transfer certificate is not required with respect to property which is being administered by an executor or administrator appointed, qualified, and acting within the United States. For additional regulations under section 6325, see § 301.6325-1 of this chapter (Regulations on Procedure and Administration).

Interest

§ 20.6601-1 **Interest on underpayment, nonpayment, or extensions of time for payment, of tax.** For regulations concerning interest on underpayments, etc., see § 301.6601-1 of this chapter (Regulations on Procedure and Administration).

§ 20.7101-1 **Form of bonds.** See paragraph (b) of § 20.6165-1 for the form of the bond required in any case in which the payment of the tax attributable to a reversionary or remainder interest has been postponed under the provisions of § 20.6163-1. For further provisions relating to bonds, see § 20.6165-1 of these regulations and the regulations under sections 6165 and 7101 contained in part 301 of this chapter (Regulations on Procedure and Administration).

AMENDMENTS TO ADMINISTRATIVE REGULATIONS

Regulations on Procedure and Administration
(26 CFR Part 301)

Par. 2. Section 301.6503(e) of the Regulations on Procedure and Administration (26 CFR Part 301) is amended—

(A) By redesignating such section as § 301.6503(f).

(B) By redesignating subsection (e) of section 6503, set forth therein, as subsection (f).

(C) By adding at the end of the section a historical note reading:

[Sec. 6503(f) as redesignated by sec. 2, Act of Aug. 6, 1956 (Pub. Law 1011, 84th Cong., 70 Stat. 1075)]

Par. 3. There is inserted after § 301.6503(d)-1 the following new section:

§ 301.6503(e)-1 **Suspension of running of period of limitation; certain powers of appointment.** Where the estate of a decedent is allowed an estate tax charitable deduction under the provisions of section 2055(b)(2) (with respect to property over which the decedent's surviving spouse was given a power of appointment exercisable in favor of charitable organizations) subject to the later disallowance of the deduction if all conditions set forth in section 2055(b)(2) are not complied with, the running of the period of limitation for assessment or collection of any estate tax imposed on the decedent's estate is suspended until 30 days after the expiration of the period for assessment or collection of the estate tax imposed on the estate of the decedent's surviving spouse.

Approved: June 16, 1958

(Signed) FRED C. SCRIBNER, JR.
Acting Secretary of the Treasury

(Signed) RUSSELL O. HARRINGTON
Commissioner of Internal Revenue

(Filed with the Division of the Federal Register June 23, 1958.)

INDEX TO ESTATE TAX REGULATIONS

APPENDIX C
FEDERAL GIFT TAX
REGULATIONS

(Under 1954 Code)

(T. D. 6334)

(Filed with the Division of the Federal Register, November 14, 1958.)

TITLE 26—INTERNAL REVENUE, 1954

**CHAPTER I—INTERNAL REVENUE SERVICE,
DEPARTMENT OF THE TREASURY**

SUBCHAPTER B—ESTATE AND GIFT TAXES

[GIFT TAX REGULATIONS]

FILED NOVEMBER 14, 1958

**PART 25—GIFT TAX; GIFTS MADE AFTER
DECEMBER 31, 1954**

Regulations under provisions of the Internal Revenue Code of 1954
relating to the gift tax.

DEPARTMENT OF THE TREASURY,
Office of Commissioner of Internal Revenue,
Washington 25, D. C.

TO OFFICERS AND EMPLOYEES OF
THE INTERNAL REVENUE SERVICE
AND OTHERS CONCERNED:

On January 3, 1957, notice of proposed rule making regarding the Gift Tax Regulations (26 CFR Part 25) under chapter 12 of subtitle B of the Internal Revenue Code of 1954 and under certain sections of subtitle F of the Internal Revenue Code of 1954 was published in the Federal Register (22 F. R. 53). After consideration of all such relevant matter as was presented by interested persons regarding the rule proposed, the following regulations are hereby adopted. The regulations are applicable to gifts made during the calendar year 1955 and subsequent calendar years:

1044

Table of Contents

GIFT TAX

Determination of Tax Liability

GIFT TAX

Determination of Tax Liability

§ 25.0-1 **Introduction**—(a) *In general.* The regulations in this part (part 25, subchapter B, chapter I, Title 26, Code of Federal Regulations) are designated "Gift Tax Regulations". These regulations pertain to (1) the gift tax imposed by chapter 12 of subtitle B of the Internal Revenue Code on the transfer of property by gift by individuals in the calendar year 1955 and subsequent calendar years, and (2) certain related administrative provisions of subtitle F of the Code. It should be noted that the application of some of the provisions of these regulations may be affected by the provisions of an applicable gift tax convention with a foreign country. Unless otherwise indicated, references in these regulations to the "Internal Revenue Code" or the "Code" are references to the Internal Revenue Code of 1954, as amended, and references to a section or other provision of law are references to a section or other provision of the Internal Revenue Code of 1954, as amended. The Gift Tax Regulations are applicable to the transfer of property by gift by individuals in the calendar year 1955 and subsequent calendar years, and supersede the regulations contained in part 86, subchapter B, chapter I, Title 26, Code of Federal Regulations (1939) (Regulations 108, Gift Tax), as prescribed and made applicable to the Internal Revenue Code of 1954 by Treasury Decision 6091, signed August 16, 1954 (19 F. R. 5167, Aug. 17, 1954).

(b) *Nature of tax.* The gift tax is not a property tax. It is a tax imposed upon the transfer of property by individuals. It is not applicable to transfers by corporations or persons other than individuals. However, see paragraph (h)(1) of § 25.2511-7 with respect to the extent to which a transfer by or to a corporation is considered a transfer by or to its shareholders.

(c) *Scope of regulations*—(1) *Determination of tax liability.* Subchapter A of chapter 12 of the Code pertains to the determination of tax liability. The regulations pursuant to subchapter A are set forth in §§ 25.2501-1 through 25.2504-2 of this part.

(2) *Transfer.* Subchapter B of chapter 12 of the Code pertains to the transfers which constitute the making of gifts. The regulations pursuant to subchapter B are set forth in §§ 25.2511-1 through 25.2516-2 of this part.

(3) *Deductions.* Subchapter C of chapter 12 of the Code pertains to the deductions which are allowed in determining the amount of taxable gifts. The regulations pursuant to subchapter C are set forth in §§ 25.2521-1 through 25.2524-1 of this part.

(4) *Procedure and administration provisions.* Subtitle F of the Internal Revenue Code contains some sections which are applicable to the

gift tax. The regulations pursuant to those sections are set forth in §§ 25.6001-1 through 25.7101-1. Such regulations do not purport to be all the regulations on procedure and administration which are pertinent to gift tax matters. For the remainder of the regulations on procedure and administration which are pertinent to gift tax matters, see part 301 of this chapter (Regulations on Procedure and Administration).

(d) *Arrangement and numbering.* Each section of the Gift Tax Regulations (except this section) is preceded by the section or subsection of the Internal Revenue Code which it interprets. The sections of the regulations can readily be distinguished from sections of the Code since—

(1) The sections of the regulations are printed in larger type;

(2) The sections of the regulations are preceded by a section symbol and the part number, arabic number 25 followed by a decimal point (§ 25.); and

(3) The sections of the Code are preceded by "Sec.".

Each section of the regulations setting forth law or regulations is designated by a number composed of the part number followed by a decimal point (25.) and the number of the corresponding section of the Internal Revenue Code. In the case of a section setting forth regulations, this designation is followed by a hyphen (-) and a number identifying such section. By use of these designations one can ascertain the sections of the regulations relating to a provision of the Code. Thus, the section of the regulations setting forth section 2521 of the Internal Revenue Code is designated § 25.2521 and the regulations pertaining to section 2521 are designated § 25.2521-1.

§ 25.2501-1 **Imposition of tax**—(a) *In general.* The tax applies to all transfers by gift of property, wherever situated, by an individual who is a citizen or resident of the United States, to the extent the value of the transfers exceeds the amount of the exclusions authorized by section 2503 and the deductions authorized by sections 2521, 2522, and 2523. The tax does not apply to a transfer of intangible property by a nonresident who is not a citizen of the United States and who was not engaged in business in the United States during the calendar year in which the transfer was made. For additional rules relating to the application of the tax to transfers by nonresidents not citizens of the United States, see section 2511 and § 25.2511-3.

(b) *Resident.* A resident is an individual who has his domicile in the United States at the time of the gift. For this purpose the United States includes only the States, the Territories of Alaska and Hawaii, and the District of Columbia. See section 7701(a)(9). All other individuals are nonresidents. A person acquires a domicile in a place by living there, for even a brief period of time, with no definite present intention of moving therefrom. Residence without the requisite intention to remain indefinitely will not constitute domicile, nor will intention to change domicile effect such a change unless accompanied by actual removal.

1048

Rate of Tax

§ 25.2502-1 **Rate of tax**—(a) *Computation of tax.* While the gift tax is imposed separately for each calendar year on the total taxable gifts made by a donor during such a year, the rate of tax is determined by the total of all gifts made by the donor during such a year and in all previous years since June 6, 1932. The following subparagraphs set forth the six steps to be followed in computing the tax:

(1) *First step.* Ascertain the amount of the "taxable gifts" for the calendar year for which the return is being prepared. For the meaning of this term see § 25.2503-1.

(2) *Second step.* Ascertain "the aggregate sum of the taxable gifts for each of the preceding calendar years," considering only those gifts made after June 6, 1932. For the meaning of this term see § 25.2504-1.

(3) *Third step.* Ascertain the total amount of the taxable gifts, which is the sum of the amounts determined in the first and second steps.

(4) *Fourth step.* Compute the tax on the total amount of taxable gifts (as determined in the third step) using the rate schedule set forth in paragraph (b) of this section.

(5) *Fifth step.* Compute the tax on "the aggregate sum of the taxable gifts for each of the preceding calendar years" (as determined in the second step), using the rate schedule set forth in paragraph (b) of this section.

(6) *Sixth step.* Subtract the amount determined in the fifth step from the amount determined in the fourth step. The amount remaining is the gift tax for the calendar year for which the return is being prepared.

(b) *Rate of tax.* The tax is computed in accordance with the following table:

TABLE FOR COMPUTING GIFT TAX

(A) Amount of taxable gifts equal to or more than—	(B) Amount of taxable gifts less than—	(C) Tax on amount in Column (A)	(D) Rate of tax on excess over amount in Column (A)
$————	$ 5,000	$————	2¼
5,000	10,000	112.50	5¼
10,000	20,000	375.00	8¼
20,000	30,000	1,200.00	10½
30,000	40,000	2,250.00	13½
40,000	50,000	3,600.00	16½
50,000	60,000	5,250.00	18¾
60,000	100,000	7,125.00	21
100,000	250,000	15,525.00	22½
250,000	500,000	49,275.00	24
500,000	750,000	109,275.00	26¼
750,000	1,000,000	174,900.00	27¾
1,000,000	1,250,000	244,275.00	29¼
1,250,000	1,500,000	317,400.00	31½

1049

(A) Amount of taxable gifts equal to or more than—	(B) Amount of taxable gifts less than—	(C) Tax on amount in Column (A)	(D) Rate of tax on excess over amount in Column (A)
1,500,000	2,000,000	396,150.00	33¾
2,000,000	2,500,000	564,900.00	36¾
2,500,000	3,000,000	748,650.00	39¾
3,000,000	3,500,000	947,400.00	42
3,500,000	4,000,000	1,157,400.00	44¼
4,000,000	5,000,000	1,378,650.00	47¼
5,000,000	6,000,000	1,851,150.00	50¼
6,000,000	7,000,000	2,353,650.00	52½
7,000,000	8,000,000	2,878,650.00	54¾
8,000,000	10,000,000	3,426,150.00	57
10,000,000	———	4,566,150.00	57¾

(c) *Examples.* The following examples illustrate the application of this section with respect to gifts made by citizens or residents of the United States:

Example (1). Assume that the donor made taxable gifts, as ascertained under the first step (paragraph (a)(1) of this section), of $62,500 and that there were no taxable gifts for prior years, with the result that the amount ascertained under the third step is $62,500. Under the fourth step a tax is computed on this amount. Reference to the table discloses that the specified amount in column (A) nearest to and less than $62,500 is $60,000. The tax on this amount, as shown in column (C), is $7,125. The amount by which the taxable gifts exceeds the specified amount is $2,500 and the tax on such excess amount, computed at the rate of 21 percent as shown in column (D), is $525. The tax on taxable gifts of $62,500 is the sum of $7,125 and $525, or $7,650.

Example (2). A donor makes gifts (other than gifts of future interests in property) during the calendar year 1955 of $30,000 to A and $33,000 to B. Two exclusions of $3,000 each are allowable, in accordance with the provisions of section 2503(b), which results in included gifts for 1955 of $57,000. Specific exemption was claimed and allowed in a total amount of $50,000 in the donor's gift tax returns for the calendar years 1934 and 1935 so there remains no specific exemption available for the donor to claim for 1955. The total amount of gifts made by the donor during preceding years, after excluding $5,000 for each donee for each calendar year in accordance with the provisions of section 1003(b)(1) of the 1939 Code, is computed as follows:

Calendar year 1934 .... $120,000

Calendar year 1935 25,000

Total amount of included gifts for preceding calendar years $145,000

The aggregate sum of the taxable gifts for preceding calendar years is $115,000, which is determined by deducting a specific exemption of $30,000 from $145,000, the total amount of included gifts for preceding calendar years. The deduction from the 1934 and 1935 gifts for the

1050

specific exemption cannot exceed $30,000 for purposes of computing the tax on the 1955 gifts even though a specific exemption in a total amount of $50,000 was allowed in computing the donor's gift tax liability for 1934 and 1935. See paragraph (b) of § 25.2504-1. The computation of the tax for the calendar year 1955 (following the steps set forth in paragraph (a) of this section) is shown below:

(1) Amount of taxable gifts for year .... $ 57,000
(2) Total amount of taxable gifts for preceding years 115,000

(3) Total taxable gifts 172,000
(4) Tax computed on item 3 (in accordance with rate schedule in paragraph (b)) 31,725
(5) Tax computed on item 2 (using same rate schedule) 18,900

(6) Tax for year 1955 (item 4 minus item 5) 12,825

Example (3)—(i) *Facts.* During the calendar year 1955, H makes the following gifts of present interests:

To his daughter $40,000
To his son 5,000
To W, his wife 5,000
To a charitable organization 10,000

The gifts to W qualify for the marital deduction, and, pursuant to the provisions of section 2513 (see § 25.2513-1), H and W consent to treat the gifts to third parties as having been made one-half by each spouse. The amount of H's taxable gifts for preceding years is $50,000. Only $25,000 of H's specific exemption was claimed and allowed in preceding years. H's remaining specific exemption of $5,000 is claimed for the calendar year 1955. See § 25.2521-1. W made no gifts during the calendar year 1955 nor during any preceding calendar year. W claims sufficient specific exemption on her return to eliminate tax liability.

(ii) *Computation of H's tax for the calendar year 1955*—(a) *H's taxable gifts for year.*

Total gifts of H $60,000
Less: Portion of items to be reported by spouse (one-half of total gifts to daughter, son and charity) 27,500

Balance 32,500
Less: Exclusions (three of $3,000 each for daughter, wife and charity and one of $2,500 for son) 11,500

Total included amount of gifts for year 21,000
Less: Deductions:
    Charity $2,000
    Marital 2,000
    Specific exemption 5,000

    Total deductions 9,000

Amount of taxable gifts for year 12,000

(b) *Computation of tax.* The steps set forth in paragraph (a) of this section are followed.

(1) Amount of taxable gifts for year $12,000
(2) Total taxable gifts for preceding years 50,000

(3) Total taxable gifts (item (1) plus item (2)) 62,000

(4) Tax computed on item 3 (using rate schedule in paragraph (b) of
      this section) 7,545
(5) Tax computed on item 2 (using rate schedule in paragraph (b) of
      this section) 5,250

(6) Tax for calendar year (item (4) minus item (5)) 2,295

(iii) *Computation of W's tax for calendar year 1955—(a) W's taxable gifts for year.*

Total gifts of W .... $ 0
Less: Portion of items to be reported by spouse   0

Balance   0
Gifts of spouse to be included   27,500

Total gifts for year   27,500
Less: Exclusions (two of $3,000 each for daughter and charity and one of
      $2,500 for son)   8,500

Balance   19,000
Less: Deductions:
      Charity .... $ 2,000
      Marital   0
      Specific exemption 17,000

Total deductions   19,000
Amount of taxable gifts for year   0

(b) *Computation of tax.* Since W had no "taxable gifts" during the year, there is no tax.

Example (4). (i) *Facts.* The facts are the same as in example (3) except that W made outright gifts of $10,000 to her niece and $20,000 to H at various times during the year. The amount of taxable gifts made by W in preceding calendar years is $75,000, and only $20,000 of her specific exemption was claimed and allowed for preceding years. See § 25.2521-1. The remaining specific exemption of $10,000 is claimed for the calendar year 1955.

(ii) *Computation of H's tax for the calendar year 1955—(a) H's taxable gifts for year.*

Total gifts of H	$60,000
Less: Portion of items to be reported by spouse	27,500
Balance	32,500
Gifts of spouse to be included	5,000
Total gifts for year	37,500
Less: Exclusions ($11,500 as shown in example (3) plus $3,000 exclusion for gift to niece)	14,500
Total included amount of gifts for year	23,000

Deductions:

Charity	$2,000	
Marital	2,000	
Specific exemption	5,000	
Total deductions		9,000
Amount of taxable gifts for year		14,000

(b) *Computation of tax.*

(1) Amount of taxable gifts for year	$14,000
(2) Total taxable gifts for preceding years	50,000
(3) Total taxable gifts (item (1) plus item (2))	64,000
(4) Tax computed on item 3	7,965
(5) Tax computed on item 2	5,250
(6) Tax for year (item (4) minus item (5))	2,715

(iii) *Computation of W's tax for the calendar year 1955—(a) W's taxable gifts for year.*

Total gifts of W	$30,000
Less: Portion of items to be reported by spouse (one-half of gift to niece)	5,000
Balance	25,000
Gifts of spouse to be included	27,500
Total gifts for year	52,500
Less: Exclusions (four of $3,000 each for daughter, husband, niece and charity, and one of $2,500 for son)	14,500
Total included amount of gifts for year	38,000

Deductions:

Charity	$ 2,000	
Marital	10,000	
Specific exemption	10,000	
Total deductions		22,000
Amount of taxable gifts for year		16,000

(b) *Computation of tax.*

(1) Amount of taxable gifts for year	$16,000
(2) Total taxable gifts for preceding years	75,000
(3) Total taxable gifts	91,000
(4) Tax computed on item 3	13,635
(5) Tax computed on item 2	10,275
(6) Tax for year (item 4 minus item 5)	3,360

§ 25.2502-2 Donor primarily liable for tax. Section 2502(d) provides that the donor shall pay the tax. If the donor dies before the tax is paid the amount of the tax is a debt due the United States from the decedent's estate and his executor or administrator is responsible for its payment out of the estate. (See § 25.6151-1 for the time and place for paying the tax.) If there is no duly qualified executor or administrator, the heirs, legatees, devisees and distributees are liable for and required to pay the tax to the extent of the value of their inheritances, bequests, devises or distributive shares of the donor's estate. If a husband and wife effectively signify consent, under section 2513, to have gifts made to a third party during any calendar year considered as made one-half by each, the liability with respect to the gift tax of each spouse for that calendar year is joint and several (see § 25.2513-4). As to the personal liability of the donee, see paragraph (b) of § 301.6324-1 of part 301 of this chapter (Regulations on Procedure and Administration). As to the personal liability of the executor or administrator, see section 3467 of the Revised Statutes (31 U. S. C. 192), which reads as follows:

> Every executor, administrator, or assignee, or other person, who pays, in whole or in part, any debt due by the person or estate for whom or for which he acts before he satisfies and pays the debts due to the United States from such person or estate, shall become answerable in his own person and estate to the extent of such payments for the debts so due to the United States, or for so much thereof as may remain due and unpaid.

As used in such section 3467, the word "debt" includes a beneficiary's distributive share of an estate. Thus if an executor pays a debt due by the estate which is being administered by him or distributes any portion of the estate before there is paid all of the gift tax which he has a duty to pay, the executor is personally liable, to the extent of the payment or distribution, for so much of the gift tax as remains due and unpaid.

Taxable Gifts

§ 25.2503-1 General definition of "taxable gifts" and of "total amount of gifts." The term "taxable gifts" means the "total amount of gifts" made by the donor during the calendar year less the deductions provided for in sections 2521, 2522, and 2523 (specific exemption, charitable, etc., gifts and the marital deduction, respectively). The

1054

"total amount of gifts" means the sum of the values of the gifts made during the calendar year less the amounts excludable under section 2503(b).   See § 25.2503-2.

§ 25.2503-2 **Exclusions from gifts.**   Section 2503(b) provides that the first $3,000 of gifts made to any one donee during the calendar year 1955 or any calendar year thereafter, except gifts of future interests in property as defined in §§ 25.2503-3 and 25.2503-4, is excluded in determining the total amount of gifts for the calendar year.   In the case of a gift in trust the beneficiary of the trust is the donee.   The entire value of any gift of a future interest in property must be included in the total amount of gifts for the calendar year in which the gift is made.

§ 25.2503-3 **Future interests in property.**   (a) No part of the value of a gift of a future interest may be excluded in determining the total amount of gifts made during the calendar year.   "Future interests" is a legal term, and includes reversions, remainders, and other interests or estates, whether vested or contingent, and whether or not supported by a particular interest or estate, which are limited to commence in use, possession or enjoyment at some future date or time. The term has no reference to such contractual rights as exist in a bond, note (though bearing no interest until maturity), or in a policy of life insurance, the obligations of which are to be discharged by payments in the future.   But a future interest or interests in such contractual obligations may be created by the limitations contained in a trust or other instrument of transfer used in effecting a gift.

(b) An unrestricted right to the immediate use, possession, or enjoyment of property or the income from property (such as a life estate or term certain) is a present interest in property.   An exclusion is allowable with respect to a gift of such an interest (but not in excess of the value of the interest).   If a donee has received a present interest in property, the possibility that such interest may be diminished by the transfer of a greater interest in the same property to the donee through the exercise of a power is disregarded in computing the value of the present interest, to the extent that no part of such interest will at any time pass to any other person (see example (4) of paragraph (c) of this section).   For an exception to the rule disallowing an exclusion for gifts of future interests in the case of certain gifts to minors, see § 25.2503-4.

(c) The operation of this section may be illustrated by the following examples:

Example (1).   Under the terms of a trust created by A the trustee is directed to pay the net income to B, so long as B shall live.   The trustee is authorized in his discretion to withhold payments of income during any period he deems advisable and add such income to the trust corpus. Since B's right to receive the income payments is subject to the trustee's discretion, it is not a present interest and no exclusion is allowable with respect to the transfer in trust.

Example (2). C transfers certain insurance policies on his own life to a trust created for the benefit of D. Upon C's death the proceeds of the policies are to be invested and the net income therefrom paid to D during his lifetime. Since the income payments to D will not begin until after C's death the transfer in trust represents a gift of a future interest in property against which no exclusion is allowable.

Example (3). Under the terms of a trust created by E the net income is to be distributed to E's three children in such shares as the trustee, in his uncontrolled discretion, deems advisable. While the terms of the trust provide that all of the net income is to be distributed, the amount of income any one of the three beneficiaries will receive rests entirely within the trustee's discretion and cannot be presently ascertained. Accordingly, no exclusions are allowable with respect to the transfers to the trust.

Example (4). Under the terms of a trust the net income is to be paid to F for life, with the remainder payable to G on F's death. The trustee has the uncontrolled power to pay over the corpus to F at any time. Although F's present right to receive the income may be terminated, no other person has the right to such income interest. Accordingly, the power in the trustee is disregarded in determining the value of F's present interest. The power would not be disregarded to the extent that the trustee during F's life could distribute corpus to persons other than F.

Example (5). The corpus of a trust created by J consists of certain real property, subject to a mortgage. The terms of the trust provide that the net income from the property is to be used to pay the mortgage. After the mortgage is paid in full the net income is to be paid to K during his lifetime. Since K's right to receive the income payments will not begin until after the mortgage is paid in full the transfer in trust represents a gift of a future interest in property against which no exclusion is allowable.

Example (6). L pays premiums on a policy of insurance on his life. All the incidents of ownership in the policy (including the right to surrender the policy) are vested in M. The payment of premiums by L constitutes a gift of a present interest in property.

§ 25.2503-4 Transfer for the benefit of a minor. (a) Section 2503 (c) provides that no part of a transfer for the benefit of a donee who has not attained the age of 21 years on the date of the gift will be considered a gift of a future interest in property if the terms of the transfer satisfy all of the following conditions:

(1) Both the property itself and its income may be expended by or for the benefit of the donee before he attains the age of 21 years;

(2) Any portion of the property and its income not disposed of under (1) will pass to the donee when he attains the age of 21 years; and

(3) Any portion of the property and its income not disposed of under (1) will be payable either to the estate of the donee or as he may appoint under a general power of appointment as defined in section 2514(c) if he dies before attaining the age of 21 years.

(b) Either a power of appointment exercisable by the donee by will or a power of appointment exercisable by the donee during his lifetime will satisfy the conditions set forth in paragraph (a)(3) of this section. However, if the transfer is to qualify for the exclusion under this section, there must be no restrictions of substance (as distinguished from formal restrictions of the type described in paragraph (g)(4) of § 25.2523(e)-1) by the terms of the instrument of transfer on the exercise of the power by the donee. However, if the minor is given a power of appointment exercisable during lifetime or is given a power of appointment exercisable by will, the fact that under the local law a minor is under a disability to exercise an inter vivos power or to execute a will does not cause the transfer to fail to satisfy the conditions of section 2503(c). Further, a transfer does not fail to satisfy the conditions of section 2503(c) by reason of the mere fact that—

(1) There is left to the discretion of a trustee the determination of the amounts, if any, of the income or property to be expended for the benefit of the minor and the purpose for which the expenditure is to be made, provided there are no substantial restrictions under the terms of the trust instrument on the exercise of such discretion;

(2) The donee, upon reaching age 21, has the right to extend the term of the trust; or

(3) The governing instrument contains a disposition of the property or income not expended during the donee's minority to persons other than the donee's estate in the event of the default of appointment by the donee.

(c) A gift to a minor which does not satisfy the requirements of section 2503(c) may be either a present or a future interest under the general rules of § 25.2503-3. Thus, for example, a transfer of property in trust with income required to be paid annually to a minor beneficiary and corpus to be distributed to him upon his attaining the age of 25 is a gift of a present interest with respect to the right to income but is a gift of a future interest with respect to the right to corpus.

Taxable Gifts for Preceding Years

§ 25.2504-1 **Taxable gifts for preceding years.** (a) In order to determine the correct gift tax liability for the calendar year 1955 or any calendar year thereafter, it is necessary to ascertain the correct amount, if any, of the aggregate sum of the taxable gifts for each of the preceding calendar years. See paragraph (a)(2) of § 25.2502-1. The words "aggregate sum of the taxable gifts for each of the preceding calendar years" means the correct aggregate of such gifts, not necessarily that returned for those years and in respect of which tax was paid. All transfers which constituted gifts in prior calendar years under the laws, including the provisions of law relating to exclusions from gifts, in effect at the time the transfers were made are included in determining the amount of taxable gifts for preceding years. The deductions other than for the specific exemption (see paragraph (b) of this section) allowed by the laws in effect at the time the transfers were made also are taken into account in determining the aggregate sum of the taxable gifts for preceding years. (The allowable exclusion from a gift was $5,000 for years before 1939, $4,000 for calendar years 1939 through 1942, and $3,000 thereafter.)

(b) In determining the aggregate sum of the taxable gifts for preceding years, the total of the amounts allowed as deductions for the specific exemption, under section 2521 and the corresponding provisions of prior laws, shall not exceed $30,000. Thus, if the only preceding years during which the donor made gifts were 1940 and 1941 (at which time the specific exemption allowable was $40,000), and in his returns for those years the donor claimed deductions totaling $40,000 for the specific exemption and reported taxable gifts totaling $110,000, then in determining the aggregate sum of the taxable gifts for preceding years the deductions for the specific exemption cannot exceed $30,000, and the aggregate sum of the donor's taxable gifts for preceding years will be $120,000 (instead of the $110,000 reported on his returns for preceding years). (The allowable deduction for the specific exemption was $50,000 for calendar years before 1936, $40,000 for calendar years 1936 through 1942, and $30,000 thereafter.)

(c) If, during any preceding calendar year, the donor and his spouse consented to have gifts made to third parties considered as made one-half by each spouse, pursuant to the provisions of section 2513 or section 1000(f) of the Internal Revenue Code of 1939 (which corresponds to section 2513), these provisions shall be taken into account in determining the aggregate sum of the taxable gifts for that preceding calendar year.

(d) If interpretations of the gift tax law in prior calendar years resulted in the erroneous inclusion of property for gift tax purposes which should have been excluded, or the erroneous exclusion of property which should have been included, adjustments must be made in order to arrive at the correct aggregate of taxable gifts for preceding years. However, see section 1000(e) and (g) of the 1939 Code relating to certain discretionary trusts and reciprocal trusts.

§ 25.2504-2 **Valuation of certain gifts for preceding calendar years.** Section 2504(c) provides that if the valuation of a transfer for gift tax purposes with respect to a gift made in a preceding calendar year is at issue, and if the statutory period within which an assessment may be made with respect to the gift has expired and a tax has been actually assessed or paid for such prior calendar year, then the value of the gift for purposes of arriving at the correct amount of the taxable gifts for preceding years is the value which was used in computing the tax for the last preceding calendar year for which a tax was assessed or paid under chapter 12 of the Internal Revenue Code of 1954 or the corresponding provisions of prior laws. However, this rule will not prevent an adjustment in value where no tax was paid or assessed for the prior year. Furthermore, this rule does not apply to adjustments involving issues other than valuation. See paragraph (d) of § 25.2504-1.

Transfers

§ 25.2511-1 **Transfers in general.** (a) The gift tax applies to a transfer by way of gift whether the transfer is in trust or otherwise, whether the gift is direct or indirect, and whether the property is real or personal, tangible or intangible. For example, a taxable transfer may be effected by the creation of a trust, the forgiving of a debt, the assignment of a judgment, the assignment of the benefits of an insurance policy, or the transfer of cash, certificates of deposit, or Federal, State or municipal bonds. Statutory provisions which exempt bonds, notes, bills and certificates of indebtedness of the Federal Government or its agencies and the interest thereon from taxation are not applicable to the gift tax, since the gift tax is an excise tax on the transfer, and is not a tax on the subject of the gift.

(b) In the case of a nonresident alien who was not engaged in business in the United States (see § 25.2501-1) during the calendar year, the tax is imposed only if the gift consisted of real estate or tangible personal property situated within the United States at the time of transfer. See §§ 25.2501-1 and 25.2511-3.

(c) The gift tax also applies to gifts indirectly made. Thus, all transactions whereby property or property rights or interests are gratuitously passed or conferred upon another, regardless of the means or device employed, constitute gifts subject to tax. See further § 25.2512-8. Where the law governing the administration of the decedent's estate gives a beneficiary, heir, or next-of-kin a right to completely and unqualifiedly refuse to accept ownership of property transferred from a decedent (whether the transfer is effected by the decedent's will or by the law of descent and distribution of intestate property), a refusal to accept ownership does not constitute the making of a gift if the refusal is made within a reasonable time after knowledge of the existence of the transfer. The refusal must be unequivocal and effective under the local law. There can be no refusal of ownership of property after its acceptance. Where the local law does not permit such a refusal, any disposition by the beneficiary, heir, or next-of-kin whereby ownership is transferred gratuitously to another constitutes the making of a gift by the beneficiary, heir, or next-of-kin. In any case where a refusal is purported to relate to only a part of the property, the determination of whether or not there has been a complete and unqualified refusal to accept ownership will depend on all of the facts and circumstances in each particular case, taking into account the recognition and effectiveness of such a purported refusal under the local law. In the absence of facts to the contrary, if a person fails to refuse to accept a transfer to him of ownership of a decedent's property within a reasonable time after learning of the existence of the transfer, he will be presumed to have accepted the property. In illustration, if Blackacre was devised to A under the decedent's will (which also provided that all lapsed legacies and devises shall go to B, the residuary beneficiary), and under the local law A could refuse to accept ownership in which case title would be considered as never having passed to A, A's refusal to accept Blackacre within a reasonable time of learning of the devise will not constitute the making of a gift by A to B. However, if a decedent who owned Greenacre died intestate with C and D as his only heirs, and under local law the heir of an intestate cannot, by refusal to accept, prevent himself from becoming an owner of intestate property, any gratuitous disposition by C (by whatever term it is known) whereby he gives up his ownership of a portion of Greenacre and D acquires the whole thereof constitutes the making of a gift by C to D.

(d) If a joint income tax return is filed by a husband and wife for a taxable year, the payment by one spouse of all or part of the income tax liability for such year is not treated as resulting in a transfer which is subject to gift tax. The same rule is applicable to the payment of gift tax for a calendar year in the case of a husband and wife who have consented to have the gifts made considered as made half by each of them in accordance with the provisions of section 2513.

(e) If a donor transfers by gift less than his entire interest in property, the gift tax is applicable to the interest transferred. The tax is applicable, for example, to the transfer of an undivided half interest in property, or to the transfer of a life estate when the grantor retains the remainder interest, or vice versa. However, if the donor's retained interest is not susceptible of measurement on the basis of generally accepted valuation principles, the gift tax is applicable to the entire value of the property subject to the gift. Thus, if a donor, aged 65 years, transfers a life estate in property to A, aged 25 years, with remainder to A's issue, or in default of issue, with reversion to the donor, the gift tax will normally be applicable to the entire value of the property.

(f) If a donor is the owner of only a limited interest in property, and transfers his entire interest, the interest is in every case to be valued by the rules set forth in §§ 25.2512-1 through 25.2512-7. If the interest is a remainder or reversion or other future interest, it is to be valued on the basis of actuarial principles set forth in § 25.2512–5, or if it is not susceptible of valuation in that manner, in accordance with the principles set forth in § 25.2512-1.

(g)(1) Donative intent on the part of the transferor is not an essential element in the application of the gift tax to the transfer. The application of the tax is based on the objective facts of the transfer and the circumstances under which it is made, rather than on the subjective motives of the donor. However, there are certain types of transfers to which the tax is not applicable. It is applicable only to a transfer of a beneficial interest in property. It is not applicable to a transfer of bare legal title to a trustee. A transfer by a trustee of trust property in which he has no beneficial interest does not constitute a gift by the trustee (but such a transfer may constitute a gift by the creator of the trust, if until the transfer he had the power to change the beneficiaries by amending or revoking the trust). The gift tax is not applicable to a transfer for a full and adequate consideration in money or money's worth, or to ordinary business transactions, described in § 25.2512-8.

(2) If a trustee has a beneficial interest in trust property, a transfer of the property by the trustee is not a taxable transfer if it is made pursuant to a fiduciary power the exercise or nonexercise of which is limited by a reasonably fixed or ascertainable standard which is set forth in the trust instrument. A clearly measurable standard under which the holder of a power is legally accountable is such a standard for this purpose. For instance, a power to distribute corpus for the education, support, maintenance, or health of the beneficiary; for his reasonable support and comfort; to enable him to maintain his accustomed standard of living; or to meet an emergency, would be such a standard. However, a power to distribute corpus for the pleasure, desire, or happiness of a beneficiary is not such a standard. The entire context of a provision of a trust instrument granting a power must be considered in determining whether the power is limited by a reasonably definite standard. For example, if a trust instrument provides that the determination of the trustee shall be conclusive with respect to the exercise or nonexercise of a power, the power is not limited by a reasonably definite standard. However, the fact that the governing instrument is phrased in discretionary terms is not in itself an indication that no such a standard exists.

(h) The following are examples of transactions resulting in taxable gifts and in each case it is assumed that the transfers were not made for an adequate and full consideration in money or money's worth:

(1) A transfer of property by a corporation to B is a gift to B from the stockholders of the corporation. If B himself is a stockholder, the transfer is a gift to him from the other stockholders but only to the extent it exceeds B's own interest in such amount as a shareholder. A transfer of property by B to a corporation generally represents gifts by B to the other individual shareholders of the corporation to the extent of their proportionate interests in the corporation. However, there may be an exception to this rule, such as a transfer made by an individual to a charitable, public, political or similar organization which may constitute a gift to the organization as a single entity, depending upon the facts and circumstances in the particular case.

(2) The transfer of property to B if there is imposed upon B the obligation of paying a commensurate annuity to C is a gift to C.

(3) The payment of money or the transfer of property to B in consideration of B's promise to render a service to C is a gift to C, or to both B and C, depending on whether the service to be rendered to C is or is not an adequate and full consideration in money or money's worth for that which is received by B. See section 2512(b) and the regulations thereunder.

(4) If A creates a joint bank account for himself and B (or a similar type of ownership by which A can regain the entire fund without B's

consent), there is a gift to B when B draws upon the account for his own benefit, to the extent of the amount drawn without any obligation to account for a part of the proceeds to A. Similarly, if A purchases a United States savings bond registered as payable to "A or B," there is a gift to B when B surrenders the bond for cash without any obligation to account for a part of the proceeds to A.

(5) If A with his own funds purchases property and has the title conveyed to himself and B as joint owners, with rights of survivorship (other than a joint ownership described in example (4)) but which rights may be defeated by either party severing his interest, there is a gift to B in the amount of half the value of the property. However, see § 25.2515-1 relative to the creation of a joint tenancy (or tenancy by the entirety) between husband and wife in real property with rights of survivorship which, unless the donor elects otherwise, is not considered as a transfer includible for Federal gift tax purposes at the time of the creation of the joint tenancy. See § 25.2515-2 with respect to determining the extent to which the creation of a tenancy by the entirety constitutes a taxable gift if the donor elects to have the creation of the tenancy so treated. See also § 25.2523(d)-1 with respect to the marital deduction allowed in the case of the creation of a joint tenancy or a tenancy by the entirety.

(6) If A is possessed of a vested remainder interest in property, subject to being divested only in the event he should fail to survive one or more individuals or the happening of some other event, an irrevocable assignment of all or any part of his interest would result in a transfer includible for Federal gift tax purposes. See especially paragraph (e) of § 2525.12-5 for the valuation of an interest of this type.

(7) If A, without retaining a power to revoke the trust or to change the beneficial interests therein, transfers property in trust whereby B is to receive the income for life and at his death the trust is to terminate and the corpus is to be returned to A, provided A survives, but if A predeceases B the corpus is to pass to C, A has made a gift equal to the total value of the property less the value of his retained interest. See paragraph (e) of § 25.2512-5 for the valuation of the donor's retained interest.

(8) If the insured purchases a life insurance policy, or pays a premium on a previously issued policy, the proceeds of which are payable to a beneficiary or beneficiaries other than his estate, and with respect to which the insured retains no reversionary interest in himself or his estate and no power to revest the economic benefits in himself or his estate or to change the beneficiaries or their proportionate benefits (or if the insured relinquishes by assignment, by designation of a new beneficiary or otherwise, every such power that was retained in a previously issued policy), the insured has made a gift of the value of the policy, or to the extent of the premium paid, even though the right of the assignee or beneficiary to receive the benefits is conditioned upon his surviving the insured. For the valuation of life insurance policies see § 25.2512-6.

(9) Where property held by a husband and wife as community property is used to purchase insurance upon the husband's life and a third person is revocably designated as beneficiary and under the State law the husband's death is considered to make absolute the transfer by the wife, there is a gift by the wife at the time of the husband's death of half the amount of the proceeds of such insurance.

(10) If under a pension plan (pursuant to which he has an unqualified right to an annuity) an employee has an option to take either a retirement annuity for himself alone or a smaller annuity for himself with a survivorship annuity payable to his wife, an irrevocable election by the employee to take the reduced annuity in order that an annuity may be paid, after the employee's death, to his wife results in the making of a gift. However, see section 2517 and the regulations thereunder for the exemption from gift tax of amounts attributable to employers' contributions under qualified plans and certain other contracts.

§ 25.2511-2 Cessation of donor's dominion and control. (a) The gift tax is not imposed upon the receipt of the property by the donee, nor is it necessarily determined by the measure of enrichment resulting to the donee from the transfer, nor is it conditioned upon ability to identify the donee at the time of the transfer. On the contrary, the tax is a primary and personal liability of the donor, is an excise upon his act of making the transfer, is measured by the value of the property passing from the donor, and attaches regardless of the fact that the identity of the donee may not then be known or ascertainable.

(b) As to any property, or part thereof or interest therein, of which the donor has so parted with dominion and control as to leave in him no power to change its disposition, whether for his own benefit or for the benefit of another, the gift is complete. But if upon a transfer of property (whether in trust or otherwise) the donor reserves any power over its disposition, the gift may be wholly incomplete, or may be partially complete and partially incomplete, depending upon all the facts in the particular case. Accordingly, in every case of a transfer of property subject to a reserved power, the terms of the power must be examined and its scope determined. For example, if a donor transfers property to another in trust to pay the income to the donor or accumulate it in the discretion of the trustee, and the donor retains a testamentary power to appoint the remainder among his descendants, no portion of the transfer is a completed gift. On the other hand, if the donor had not retained the testamentary power of appointment, but instead provided that the remainder should go to X or his heirs, the entire transfer would be a completed gift. However, if the exercise of the trustee's power in favor of the grantor is limited by a fixed or ascertainable standard (see paragraph (g)(2) of § 25.2511-1), enforceable by or on behalf of the grantor, then the gift is incomplete to the extent of the ascertainable value of any rights thus retained by the grantor.

(c) A gift is incomplete in every instance in which a donor reserves the power to revest the beneficial title to the property in himself. A gift is also incomplete if and to the extent that a reserved power gives the donor the power to name new beneficiaries or to change the interests of the beneficiaries as between themselves unless the power is a fiduciary power limited by a fixed or ascertainable standard. Thus, if an estate for life is transferred but, by an exercise of a power, the estate may be terminated or cut down by the donor to one of less value, and without restriction upon the extent to which the estate may be so cut down, the transfer constitutes an incomplete gift. If in this example the power was confined to the right to cut down the estate for life to one for a term of five years, the certainty of an estate for not less than that term results in a gift to that extent complete.

(d) A gift is not considered incomplete, however, merely because the donor reserves the power to change the manner or time of enjoyment. Thus, the creation of a trust the income of which is to be paid annually to the donee for a period of years, the corpus being distributable to him at the end of the period, and the power reserved by the donor being limited to a right to require that, instead of the income being so payable, it should be accumulated and distributed with the corpus to the donee at the termination of the period, constitutes a completed gift.

(e) A donor is considered as himself having a power if it is exercisable by him in conjunction with any person not having a substantial adverse interest in the disposition of the transferred property or the income therefrom. A trustee, as such, is not a person having an adverse interest in the disposition of the trust property or its income.

(f) The relinquishment or termination of a power to change the beneficiaries of transferred property, occurring otherwise than by the death of the donor (the statute being confined to transfers by living donors), is regarded as the event which completes the gift and causes the tax to apply. For example, if A transfers property in trust for the benefit of B and C but reserves the power as trustee to change the proportionate interests of B and C, and if A thereafter has another person appointed trustee in place of himself, such later relinquishment of the power by A to the new trustee completes the gift of the transferred property, whether or not the new trustee has a substantial adverse interest. The receipt of income or of other enjoyment of the transferred property by the transferee or by the beneficiary (other than by the donor himself) during the interim between the making of the initial transfer and the relinquishment or termination of the power operates to free such income or other enjoyment from the power, and constitutes a gift of such income or of such other enjoyment taxable as of the calendar year of its receipt. If property is transferred in trust to pay the income to A for life with remainder to B, powers to distribute corpus to A, and to withhold income from A for future distribution to B, are powers to change the beneficiaries of the transferred property.

(g) If a donor transfers property to himself as trustee (or to himself and some other person, not possessing a substantial adverse interest, as trustees), and retains no beneficial interest in the trust property and no power over it except fiduciary powers, the exercise or nonexercise of which is limited by a fixed or ascertainable standard, to change the beneficiaries of the transferred property, the donor has made a completed gift and the entire value of the transferred property is subject to the gift tax.

(h) If a donor delivers a properly indorsed stock certificate to the donee or the donee's agent, the gift is completed for gift tax purposes on the date of delivery. If the donor delivers the certificate to his bank or broker as his agent, or to the issuing corporation or its transfer agent, for transfer into the name of the donee, the gift is completed on the date the stock is transferred on the books of the corporation.

(j) If the donor contends that a power is of such nature as to render the gift incomplete, and hence not subject to the tax as of the calendar year of the initial transfer, the transaction shall be disclosed in the return and evidence showing all relevant facts, including a copy of the instrument of transfer, should be submitted.

§ 25.2511-3 **Transfers by nonresidents not citizens**—(a) *In general.* Sections 2511 and 2501 contain provisions relating to the taxation of transfers by nonresident alien donors. (See paragraph (b) of § 25.2501-1 for definition of the term "resident.") As combined these rules are—

(1) If the nonresident alien donor was not engaged in business in the United States during the calendar year in which the gift was made, the tax applies only to the transfer of real property and tangible personal property situated in the United States.

(2) If the nonresident alien donor was engaged in business in the United States during the calendar year in which the gift was made, the tax applies to the transfer of all property (whether real or personal, tangible or intangible) situated in the United States.

(b) *Situs of property.* (1) Real property, tangible personal property, and, except as otherwise provided in subparagraph (2) of this paragraph (relating to shares of stock), the written evidence of intangible personal property which is treated as being the property itself are within the United States if physically situated therein. For example, a bond for the payment of money is not within the United States unless physically situated therein. Intangible personal property the written evidence of which is not treated as being the property itself constitutes property within the United States if consisting of a property right issuing from or enforceable against a resident of the United States or a domestic corporation (public or private) irrespective of where such written evidence is physically located.

(2) Shares of stock owned and held by a nonresident alien donor constitute property within the United States if issued by a domestic corporation, irrespective of where the certificates are physically located. However, since a share of stock is intangible property, the transfer by a nonresident alien donor of a share of stock issued by a domestic corporation would, under the provisions of paragraph (a) of this section, be subject to the tax only if the donor was engaged in business in the United States during the calendar year in which the gift was made.

(3) Shares of stock owned and held by a nonresident alien donor do

not constitute property within the United States if issued by a corporation which is not a domestic corporation, irrespective of where the certificates are physically located. Therefore, the tax will not under any circumstances apply to the transfer of a share of such stock by a nonresident alien donor.

Valuation of Gifts

§ 25.2512-1 **Valuation of property; in general.** Section 2512 provides that if a gift is made in property, its value at the date of the gift shall be considered the amount of the gift. The value of the property is the price at which such property would change hands between a willing buyer and a willing seller, neither being under any compulsion to buy or to sell, and both having reasonable knowledge of relevant facts. The value of a particular kind of property is not the price that a forced sale of the property would produce. The value is generally to be determined by ascertaining as a basis the fair market value at the time of the gift of each unit of the property. For example, in the case of shares of stock or bonds, such unit of property is generally a share or a bond. Property shall not be returned at the value at which it is assessed for local tax purposes unless that value represents the fair market value thereof on the date of the gift. All relevant facts and elements of value as of the time of the gift shall be considered. See §§ 25.2512-2 through 25.2512-6 for further information concerning the valuation of particular kinds of property.

§ 25.2512-2 **Stocks and bonds**—(a) *In general.* The value of stocks and bonds is the fair market value per share or bond on the date of the gift.

(b) *Based on selling prices.* If there is a market for stocks or bonds, on a stock exchange, in an over-the-counter market, or otherwise, the mean between the highest and lowest quoted selling prices on the date of the gift is the fair market value per share or bond. If there were no sales on the date of the gift, but there were sales on dates within a reasonable period both before and after the date of the gift, the fair market value is determined by taking a weighted average of the means between the highest and lowest sales on the nearest date before and the nearest date after the date of the gift. The average is to be weighted inversely by the respective numbers of trading days between the selling dates and the date of the gift. For example, assume that sales of stock nearest the date of the gift (Friday, June 15) occurred two trading days before (Wednesday, June 13) and three trading days after Wednesday, June 20) and that on these days the mean sale prices per share were $10 and $15, respectively. The price of $12 is taken as representing the fair market value of a share of the stock as of the date of the gift $\frac{((3\times10)+(2\times15))}{5}$. If, instead, the mean sale prices per share on June 13 and June 20 were $15 and $10, respectively, the price of $13 is taken as representing the fair market value $\frac{((3\times15)+(2\times10))}{5}$.

If stocks or bonds are listed on more than one exchange, the records of the exchange where the stocks or bonds are principally dealt in should be employed. In valuing listed securities, the donor should be careful to consult accurate records to obtain values as of the date of the gift. If quotations of unlisted securities are obtained from brokers, or evidence as to their sale is obtained from officers of the issuing companies, copies of letters furnishing such quotations or evidence of sale should be attached to the return.

(c) *Based on bid and asked prices.* If the provisions of paragraph (b) of this section are inapplicable because actual sales are not available during a reasonable period beginning before and ending after the date of the gift, the fair market value may be determined by taking the mean between the bona fide bid and asked prices on the date of the gift, or if none, by taking a weighted average of the means between the bona fide bid and asked prices on the nearest trading date before and the nearest trading date after the date of the gift, if both such nearest dates are within a reasonable period. The average is to be determined in the manner described in paragraph (b) of this section.

(d) *Where selling prices and bid and asked prices are not available for dates both before and after the date of gift.* If the provisions of paragraphs (b) and (c) of this section are inapplicable because no actual sale prices or quoted bona fide bid and asked prices are available on a date within a reasonable period before the date of the gift, but such prices are available on a date within a reasonable period after the date of the gift, or vice versa, then the mean between the highest and lowest available sale prices or bid and asked prices may be taken as the value.

(e) *Where selling prices or bid and asked prices do not represent fair market value.* In cases in which it is established that the value per bond or share of any security determined on the basis of the selling or bid and asked prices as provided under paragraphs (b), (c), and (d) of this section does not represent the fair market value thereof, then some reasonable modification of the value determined on that basis or other relevant facts and elements of value shall be considered in determining fair market value. Where sales at or near the date of the gift are few or of a sporadic nature, such sales alone may not indicate fair market value. In certain exceptional cases, the size of the block of securities made the subject of each separate gift in relation to the number of shares changing hands in sales may be relevant in determining whether selling prices reflect the fair market value of the block of stock to be valued. If the donor can show that the block of stock to be valued, with reference to each separate gift, is so large in relation to the actual sales on the existing market that it could not be liquidated in a reasonable time without depressing the market, the price at which the block could be sold as such outside the usual market, as through an underwriter, may be a more accurate indication of value than market quotations. Complete data in support of any allowance claimed due to the size of the block of stock being valued should be submitted with the

1067

return. On the other hand, if the block of stock to be valued represents a controlling interest, either actual or effective, in a going business, the price at which other lots change hands may have little relation to its true value.

(f) *Where selling prices or bid and asked prices are unavailable.* If the provisions of paragraphs (b), (c), and (d) of this section are inapplicable because actual sale prices and bona fide bid and asked prices are lacking, then the fair market value is to be determined by taking the following factors into consideration:

(1) In the case of corporate or other bonds, the soundness of the security, the interest yield, the date of maturity, and other relevant factors; and

(2) In the case of shares of stock, the company's net worth, prospective earning power and dividend-paying capacity, and other relevant factors. Some of the "other relevant factors" referred to in subparagraphs (1) and (2) of this paragraph are: the good will of the business; the economic outlook in the particular industry; the company's position in the industry and its management; the degree of control of the business represented by the block of stock to be valued; and the values of securities of corporations engaged in the same or similar lines of business which are listed on a stock exchange. However, the weight to be accorded such comparisons or any other evidentiary factors considered in the determination of a value depends upon the facts of each case. Complete financial and other data upon which the valuation is based should be submitted with the return, including copies of reports of any examinations of the company made by accountants, engineers, or any technical experts as of or near the date of the gift.

§ 25.2512-3 **Valuation of interests in businesses.** (a) Care should be taken to arrive at an accurate valuation of any interest in a business which the donor transfers without an adequate and full consideration in money or money's worth. The fair market value of any interest in a business, whether a partnership or a proprietorship, is the net amount which a willing purchaser, whether an individual or a corporation, would pay for the interest to a willing seller, neither being under any compulsion to buy or to sell and both having reasonable knowledge of the relevant facts. The net value is determined on the basis of all relevant factors including—

(1) A fair appraisal as of the date of the gift of all the assets of the business, tangible and intangible, including good will;

(2) The demonstrated earning capacity of the business; and

(3) The other factors set forth in paragraph (f) of § 25.2512-2 relating to the valuation of corporate stock, to the extent applicable.

Special attention should be given to determining an adequate value of the good will of the business. Complete financial and other data upon which the valuation is based should be submitted with the return, including copies of reports of examinations of the business made by accountants, engineers, or any technical experts as of or near the date of the gift.

§ 25.2512-4 **Valuation of notes.** The fair market value of notes, secured or unsecured, is presumed to be the amount of unpaid principal, plus accrued interest to the date of the gift, unless the donor establishes a lower value. Unless returned at face value, plus accrued interest, it must be shown by satisfactory evidence that the note is worth less than the unpaid amount (because of the interest rate, or date of maturity, or other cause), or that the note is uncollectible in part (by reason of the insolvency of the party or parties liable, or for other cause), and that the property, if any, pledged or mortgaged as security is insufficient to satisfy it.

§ 25.2512-5 **Valuation of annuities, life estates, terms for years, remainders and reversions**—(a) *In general.* (1) The fair market value of annuities, life estates, terms for years, remainders and reversions is their present value, determined under this section, except in the case of annuities and life insurance under contracts issued by companies regularly engaged in their sale. The valuation of such commercial annuity contracts and insurance policies is determined under § 25.2512-6. Where the donor transfers property in trust or otherwise and retains an interest therein, the value of the gift is the value of the property transferred less the value of the donor's retained interest. If the donor assigns or relinquishes an annuity, life estate, remainder or reversion which he holds by virtue of a transfer previously made by himself or another, the value of the gift is the value of the interest transferred.

(2) The present value of an annuity, life estate, remainder or reversion determined under this section which is dependent on the continuation or termination of the life of one person is computed by the use of Table I in paragraph (f) of this section. The present value of an annuity, term for years, remainder or reversion dependent on a term certain is computed by the use of Table II in paragraph (f). If the interest to be valued is dependent upon more than one life or there is a term certain concurrent with one or more lives, see paragraph (e) of this section. For purposes of the computations described in this section, the age of a person is to be taken as the age of that person at his nearest birthday.

(b) *Annuities*—(1) *Payable annually at end of year.* If an annuity is payable annually at the end of each year during the life of an individual (as for example if the first payment is due one year after the date of the gift), the amount payable annually is multiplied by the figure in column 2 of Table I opposite the number of years in column 1 nearest the age of the individual whose life measures the duration of the annuity. If the annuity is payable annually at the end of each year for a definite number of years, the amount payable annually is multiplied by the figure in column 2 of Table II opposite the number of years in column 1 representing the duration of the annuity. The application of this subparagraph may be illustrated by the following examples:

Example (1). The donor assigns an annuity of $10,000 a year payable annually during his life immediately after an annual payment has

1069

been made. The age of the donor on the date of assignment is 40 years and 8 months. By reference to Table I, it is found that the figure in column 2 opposite 41 years is 17.6853. The value of the gift is, therefore, $176,853 ($10,000 multiplied by 17.6853).

Example (2). The donor was entitled to receive an annuity of $10,000 a year payable annually at the end of annual periods throughout a term of 20 years; the donor, when 15 years have elapsed, makes a gift thereof to his son. By reference to Table II, it is found that the figure in column 2 opposite 5 years, the unexpired portion of the 20-year period is 4.5151. The present value of the annuity is, therefore, $45,151 ($10,000 multiplied by 4.5151).

(2) *Payable at the end of semiannual, quarterly, monthly, or weekly periods.* If an annuity is payable at the end of semiannual, quarterly, monthly, or weekly periods during the life of an individual (as for example if the first payment is due one month after the date of the gift), the aggregate amount to be paid within a year is first multiplied by the figure in column 2 of Table I opposite the number of years in column 1 nearest the age of the individual whose life measures the duration of the annuity. The product so obtained is then multiplied by whichever of the following factors is appropriate:

1.0087 for semiannual payments,
1.0130 for quarterly payments,
1.0159 for monthly payments, or
1.0171 for weekly payments.

If the annuity is payable at the end of semiannual, quarterly, monthly, or weekly periods for a definite number of years, the aggregate amount to be paid within a year is first multiplied by the figure in column 2 of Table II opposite the number of years in column 1 representing the duration of the annuity. The product so obtained is then multiplied by whichever of the above factors is appropriate. The application of this subparagraph may be illustrated by the following example:

Example. The facts are the same as those contained in example (1) set forth in subparagraph (1) above, except that the annuity is payable semiannually. The aggregate annual amount, $10,000, is multiplied by the factor 17.6853, and the product multiplied by 1.0087. The value of the gift is, therefore, $178,391.62 ($10,000 x 17.6853 x 1.0087).

(3) *Payable at the beginning of annual, semiannual, quarterly, monthly, or weekly periods.* (i) If the first payment of an annuity for the life of an individual is due at the beginning of the annual or other payment period rather than at the end (as for example if the first payment is to be made immediately after the date of the gift), the value of the annuity is the sum of (*a*) the first payment plus (*b*) the present value of a similar annuity, the first payment of which is not to be made until the end of the payment period, determined as provided in subparagraph (1) or (2) above. The application of this subdivision may be illustrated by the following example:

Example. The donee is made the beneficiary for life of an annuity of $50 a month from the income of a trust, subject to the right reserved by the donor to cause the annuity to be paid for his own benefit or for

1070

the benefit of another. On the day a payment is due, the donor relinquishes his reserved power. The donee is then 50 years of age. The value of the gift is $50 plus the product of $50 x 12 x 14.8486 (see Table I) x 1.0159, or $9,100.82.

(ii) If the first payment of an annuity for a definite number of years is due at the beginning of the annual or other payment period, the applicable factor is the product of the factor shown in Table II multiplied by whichever of the following factors is appropriate:

1.0350 for annual payments,
1.0262 for semiannual payments,
1.0218 for quarterly payments,
1.0189 for monthly payments, or
1.0177 for weekly payments.

The application of this subdivision may be illustrated by the following example:

Example. The donee is the beneficiary of an annuity of $50 a month, subject to a reserved right in the donor to cause the annuity or the cash value thereof to be paid for his own benefit or the benefit of another. On the day a payment is due, the donor relinquishes the power. There are 300 payments to be made covering a period of 25 years, including the payment due. The value of the gift is the product of $50 x 12 x 16.4815 (factor for 25 years, Table II) x 1.0189, or $10,075.80.

(c) *Life estates and terms for years.* If the interest to be valued is the right of a person for his life, or for the life of another person, to receive the income of certain property or to use nonincome-producing property, the value of the interest is the value of the property multiplied by the figure in column 3 of Table I opposite the number of years nearest to the actual age of the measuring life. If the interest to be valued is the right to receive income of property or to use nonincome-producing property for a term of years, column 3 of Table II is used. The application of this paragraph may be illustrated by the following example:

Example. The donor, who during his life is entitled to receive the income from property worth $50,000, makes a gift of such interest. The donor is 31 years old on the date of the gift. The value of the gift is $35,534 ($50,000 x .71068).

(d) *Remainders or reversionary interests.* If the interest to be valued is a remainder or reversionary interest subject to a life estate, the value of the interest should be obtained by multiplying the value of the property at the date of the gift by the figure in column 4 of Table I opposite the number of years nearest the age of the life tenant. If the remainder or reversion is to take effect at the end of a term of years, column 4 of Table II should be used. The application of this paragraph may be illustrated by the following example:

Example. The donor transfers by gift property worth $50,000 which he is entitled to receive upon the death of his brother, to whom the income for life has been bequeathed. The brother at the date of the gift is 31 years of age. By reference to Table I, it is found that the figure in column 4 opposite age 31 is 0.28932. The value of the gift is, therefore, $14,466. ($50,000 x 0.28932.)

(e) *Actuarial computations by the Internal Revenue Service.* If the interest to be valued is dependent upon the continuation or termination of more than one life, or there is a term certain concurrent with one or more lives, or if the retained interest of the donor is conditioned upon survivorship, a special factor is necessary. The factor is to be computed upon the basis of the Makehamized mortality table appearing as Table 38 of United States Life Table and Actuarial Tables 1939-1941, published by the United States Department of Commerce, Bureau of the Census, and interest at the rate of 3½ percent a year, compounded annually. Many such factors may be found in, or readily computed with the use of the tables contained in, a pamphlet entitled "Actuarial Values for Estate and Gift Tax." This pamphlet may be purchased from the Superintendent of Documents, United States Government Printing Office, Washington 25, D. C. However, if a special factor is required in the case of an actual gift, the Commissioner will furnish the factor to the donor upon request. The request must be accompanied by a statement of the date of birth of each person, the duration of whose life may affect the value of the interest, and by copies of the relevant instruments.

(f) The following tables shall be used in the application of the provisions of this section:

TABLE I

Table, single life, 3½ percent, showing the present worth of an annuity, of a life interest, and of a remainder interest

1 Age	2 Annuity	3 Life Estate	4 Remainder	1 Age	2 Annuity	3 Life Estate	4 Remainder
0	23.9685	.83890	.16110	28	20.9759	.73416	.26584
1	24.9035	.87162	.12838	29	20.7581	.72653	.27347
2	24.8920	.87122	.12878	30	20.5345	.71871	.28129
3	24.8246	.86886	.13114	31	20.3052	.71068	.28932
4	24.7378	.86582	.13418	32	20.0699	.70245	.29755
5	24.6392	.86237	.13763	33	19.8288	.69401	.30599
6	24.5326	.85864	.14136	34	19.5816	.68536	.31464
7	24.4188	.85466	.14534	35	19.3285	.67650	.32350
8	24.2982	.85044	.14956	36	19.0695	.66743	.33257
9	24.1713	.84600	.15400	37	18.8044	.65815	.34185
10	24.0387	.84135	.15865	38	18.5334	.64867	.35133
11	23.9008	.83653	.16347	39	18.2566	.63898	.36102
12	23.7600	.83160	.16840	40	17.9738	.62908	.37092
13	23.6161	.82656	.17344	41	17.6853	.61899	.38101
14	23.4693	.82143	.17857	42	17.3911	.60869	.39131
15	23.3194	.81618	.18382	43	17.0913	.59820	.40180
16	23.1665	.81083	.18917	44	16.7860	.58751	.41249
17	23.0103	.80536	.19464	45	16.4754	.57664	.42336
18	22.8511	.79979	.20021	46	16.1596	.56559	.43441
19	22.6870	.79404	.20596	47	15.8388	.55436	.44564
20	22.5179	.78813	.21187	48	15.5133	.54297	.45703
21	22.3438	.78203	.21797	49	15.1831	.53141	.46859
22	22.1646	.77576	.22424	50	14.8486	.51970	.48030
23	21.9801	.76930	.23070	51	14.5101	.50785	.49215
24	21.7902	.76266	.23734	52	14.1678	.49587	.50413
25	21.5950	.75582	.24418	53	13.8221	.48377	.51623
26	21.3942	.74880	.25120	54	13.4734	.47157	.52843
27	21.1878	.74157	.25843	55	13.1218	.45926	.54074

Table, single life, 3½ percent, showing the present worth of an annuity,
of a life interest and of a remainder interest

1	2	3 Life	4	1	2	3 Life	4
Age	Annuity	Estate	Remainder	Age	Annuity	Estate	Remainder
56	12.7679	.44688	.55312	81	4.5283	.15849	.84151
57	12.4120	.43442	.56558	82	4.2771	.14970	.85030
58	12.0546	.42191	.57809	83	4.0351	.14123	.85877
59	11.6960	.40936	.59064	84	3.8023	.13308	.86692
60	11.3369	.39679	.60321	85	3.5789	.12526	.87474
61	10.9776	.38422	.61578	86	3.3648	.11777	.88223
62	10.6186	.37165	.62835	87	3.1601	.11060	.88940
63	10.2604	.35911	.64089	88	2.9648	.10377	.89623
64	9.9036	.34663	.65337	89	2.7788	.09726	.90274
65	9.5486	.33420	.66580	90	2.6019	.09107	.90893
66	9.1960	.32186	.67814	91	2.4342	.08520	.91480
67	8.8464	.30962	.69038	92	2.2754	.07964	.92036
68	8.5001	.29750	.70250	93	2.1254	.07439	.92561
69	8.1578	.28552	.71448	94	1.9839	.06944	.93056
70	7.8200	.27370	.72630	95	1.8507	.06477	.93523
71	7.4871	.26205	.73795	96	1.7256	.06040	.93960
72	7.1597	.25059	.74941	97	1.6082	.05629	.94371
73	6.8382	.23934	.76066	98	1.4982	.05244	.94756
74	6.5231	.22831	.77169	99	1.3949	.04882	.95118
75	6.2148	.21752	.78248	100	1.2973	.04541	.95459
76	5.9137	.20698	.79302	101	1.2033	.04212	.95788
77	5.6201	.19670	.80330	102	1.1078	.03877	.96123
78	5.3345	.18671	.81329	103	.9973	.03491	.96509
79	5.0572	.17700	.82300	104	.8318	.02911	.97089
80	4.7884	.16759	.83241	105	.4831	.01691	.98309

TABLE II

Table showing the present worth at 3½ percent of an annuity for a term certain,
of an income interest for a term certain, and of a remainder
interest postponed for a term certain

1 Number of Years	2 Annuity	3 Term Certain	4 Remainder	1 Number of Years	2 Annuity	3 Term Certain	4 Remainder
1	0.9662	.033816	.966184	16	12.0941	.423294	.576706
2	1.8997	.066489	.933511	17	12.6513	.442796	.557204
3	2.8016	.098057	.901943	18	13.1897	.461639	.538361
4	3.6731	.128558	.871442	19	13.7098	.479844	.520156
5	4.5151	.158027	.841973	20	14.2124	.497434	.502566
6	5.3286	.186499	.813501	21	14.6980	.514429	.485571
7	6.1145	.214009	.785991	22	15.1671	.530849	.469151
8	6.8740	.240588	.759412	23	15.6204	.546714	.453286
9	7.6077	.266269	.733731	24	16.0584	.562043	.437957
10	8.3166	.291081	.708919	25	16.4815	.576853	.423147
11	9.0016	.315054	.684946	26	16.8904	.591162	.408838
12	9.6633	.338217	.661783	27	17.2854	.604988	.395012
13	10.3027	.360596	.639404	28	17.6670	.618346	.381654
14	10.9205	.382218	.617782	29	18.0358	.631252	.368748
15	11.5174	.403109	.596891	30	18.3920	.643722	.356278

§ 25.2512-6 Valuation of certain life insurance and annuity contracts.

The value of a life insurance contract or of a contract for the payment of an annuity issued by a company regularly engaged in the selling of contracts of that character is established through the sale of the particular contract by the company, or through the sale by the company of comparable contracts. As valuation of an insurance policy through sale of comparable contracts is not readily ascertainable when the gift is of a contract which has been in force for some time and on which further premium payments are to be made, the value may be approximated by adding to the interpolated terminal reserve at the date of the gift the proportionate part of the gross premium last paid before the date of the gift which covers the period extending beyond that date. If, however, because of the unusual nature of the contract such approximation is not reasonably close to the full value, this method may not be used.

The following examples, so far as relating to life insurance contracts, are of gifts of such contracts on which there are no accrued dividends or outstanding indebtedness.

Example (1). A donor purchases from a life insurance company for the benefit of another a life insurance contract or a contract for the payment of an annuity. The value of the gift is the cost of the contract.

Example (2). An annuitant purchased from a life insurance company a single payment annuity contract by the terms of which he was entitled to receive payments of $1,200 annually for the duration of his life. Five years subsequent to such purchase, and when of the age of 50 years, he gratuitously assigns the contract. The value of the gift is the amount which the company would charge for an annuity contract providing for the payment of $1,200 annually for the life of a person 50 years of age.

Example (3). A donor owning a life insurance policy on which no further payments are to be made to the company (e. g., a single premium policy or paid-up policy) makes a gift of the contract. The value of the gift is the amount which the company would charge for a single premium contract of the same specified amount on the life of a person of the age of the insured.

Example (4). A gift is made four months after the last premium due date of an ordinary life insurance policy issued nine years and four months prior to the gift thereof by the insured, who was 35 years of age at date of issue. The gross annual premium is $2,811. The computation follows:

Terminal reserve at end of tenth year	$14,601.00
Terminal reserve at end of ninth year	12,965.00
Increase	1,636.00
One-third of such increase (the gift having been made four months following the last preceding premium due date), is	545.33
Terminal reserve at end of ninth year	12,965.00
Interpolated terminal reserve at date of gift	13,510.33
Two-thirds of gross premium ($2,811)	1,874.00
Value of the gift	15,384.33

§ 25.2512-7 **Effect of excise tax.** If jewelry, furs or other property, the purchase of which is subject to an excise tax, is purchased at retail by a taxpayer and made the subject of gifts within a reasonable time after purchase, the purchase price, including the excise tax, is considered to be the fair market value of the property on the date of the gift, in the absence of evidence that the market price of similar articles has increased or decreased in the meantime. Under other circumstances, the excise tax is taken into account in determining the fair market value of property to the extent, and only to the extent, that it affects the price at which the property would change hands between a willing buyer and a willing seller, as provided in § 25.2512-1.

§ 25.2512-8 **Transfers for insufficient consideration.** Transfers reached by the gift tax are not confined to those only which, being without a valuable consideration, accord with the common law concept of gifts, but embrace as well sales, exchanges, and other dispositions of property for a consideration to the extent that the value of the property transferred by the donor exceeds the value in money or money's worth of the consideration given therefor. However, a sale, exchange, or other transfer of property made in the ordinary course of business (a transaction which is bona fide, at arm's length, and free from any donative intent), will be considered as made for an adequate and full consideration in money or money's worth. A consideration not reducible to a value in money or money's worth, as love and affection, promise of marriage, etc., is to be wholly disregarded, and the entire value of the property transferred constitutes the amount of the gift. Similarly, a relinquishment or promised relinquishment of dower or curtesy, or of a statutory estate created in lieu of dower or curtesy, or of other marital rights in the spouse's property or estate, shall not be considered to any extent a consideration "in money or money's worth." See, however, section 2516 and the regulations thereunder with respect to certain transfers incident to a divorce.

Gifts by Husband or Wife to Third Party

§ 25.2513-1 **Gifts by husband or wife to third party considered as made one-half by each.** (a) A gift made by one spouse to a person other than his (or her) spouse may, for the purpose of the gift tax, be considered as made one-half by him and one-half by his spouse, but only if at the time of the gift each spouse was a citizen or resident of the United States. For purposes of this section, an individual is to be considered as the spouse of another individual only if he was married to such individual at the time of the gift and does not remarry during the remainder of the calendar year.

(b) The provisions of this section will apply to gifts made during a particular calendar year only if both spouses signify their consent to treat all gifts made to third parties during that calendar year by both spouses while married to each other as having been made one-half by each spouse. As to the manner and time for signifying consent, see § 25.2513-2. Such consent, if signified with respect to any calendar year, is effective with respect to all gifts made to third parties during such year except as follows:

(1) If the consenting spouses were not married to each other during a portion of the calendar year, the consent is not effective with respect to any gifts made during such portion of the calendar year. Where the consent is signified by an executor or administrator of a deceased spouse, the consent is not effective with respect to gifts made by the surviving spouse during the portion of the calendar year that his spouse was deceased.

(2) If either spouse was a nonresident not a citizen of the United States during any portion of the calendar year, the consent is not effective with respect to any gift made during that portion of the calendar year.

(3) The consent is not effective with respect to a gift by one spouse of a property interest over which he created in his spouse a general power of appointment (as defined in section 2514(c)).

(4) If one spouse transferred property in part to his spouse and in part to third parties, the consent is effective with respect to the interest transferred to third parties only insofar as such interest is ascertainable at the time of the gift and hence severable from the interest transferred to his spouse. See § 25.2512-5 for the principles to be applied in the valuation of annuities, life estates, terms for years, remainders and reversions.

(5) The consent applies alike to gifts made by one spouse alone and to gifts made partly by each spouse, provided such gifts were to third parties and do not fall within any of the exceptions set forth in subparagraphs (1) through (4) of this paragraph. The consent may not be applied only to a portion of the property interest constituting such gifts. For example, a wife may not treat gifts made by her spouse from his separate property to third parties as having been made one-half by her if her spouse does not consent to treat gifts made by her to third parties during the same calendar year as having been made one-half by him. If the consent is effectively signified on either the husband's return or the wife's return, all gifts made by the spouses to third parties (except as described in subparagraphs (1) through (4) of this paragraph), during the calendar year will be treated as having been made one-half by each spouse.

(c) If a husband and wife consent to have the gifts made to third party donees considered as made one-half by each spouse, and only one spouse makes gifts during the year, the other spouse is not required to file a gift tax return provided: (1) The total value of the gifts made to each third party donee is not in excess of $6,000, and (2) no portion of the property transferred constitutes a gift of a future interest. If a transfer made by either spouse during the year to a third party represents a gift of a future interest in property and the spouses consent to have the gifts considered as made one-half by each, a gift tax return for such year must be filed by each spouse regardless of the value of the transfer. (See § 25.2503-3 for the definition of a future interest.)

1076

(d) The following examples illustrate the application of this section relative to the requirements for the filing of a return, assuming that a consent was effectively signified:

(1) A husband made gifts valued at $7,000 during the year to a third party and his wife made no gifts. Each spouse is required to file a return.

(2) A husband made gifts valued at $5,000 to each of two third parties during the year and his wife made no gifts. Only the husband is required to file a return. (See § 25.6019-2.)

(3) A husband made gifts valued at $5,000 to a third party, and the wife made gifts valued at $2,000 to the same third party during the year. Each spouse is required to file a return.

(4) A husband made gifts valued at $5,000 to a third party and his wife made gifts valued at $3,000 to another third party during the year. Only the husband is required to file a return. (See § 25.6019-2.)

(5) A husband made gifts valued at $2,000 during the year to third parties which represented gifts of future interests in property (see § 25.2503-3), and his wife made no gifts during such calendar year. Each spouse is required to file a return.

§ 25.2513-2 Manner and time of signifying consent.

(a) Consent to the application of the provisions of section 2513 with respect to a calendar year shall, in order to be effective, be signified by both spouses. If both spouses file gift tax returns within the time for signifying consent, it is sufficient if—

(1) the consent of the husband is signified on the wife's return, and the consent of the wife is signified on the husband's return;

(2) the consent of each spouse is signified on his own return; or

(3) the consent of both spouses is signified on one of the returns.

If only one spouse files a gift tax return within the time provided for signifying consent, the consent of both spouses shall be signified on that return. However, wherever possible, the notice of the consent is to be shown on both returns and it is preferred that the notice be executed in the manner described in subparagraph (1) of this paragraph. The consent may be revoked only as provided in § 25.2513-3. If one spouse files more than one gift tax return for a calendar year on or before the 15th day of April following the close of the calendar year, the last return so filed will, for the purpose of determining whether a consent has been signified, be considered as the return.

(b) The consent may be signified at any time following the close of the calendar year, subject to the following limitations:

(1) The consent may not be signified after the 15th day of April following the close of the calendar year, unless before such 15th day no return has been filed for the year by either spouse, in which case the consent may not be signified after a return for the year is filed by either spouse; and

(2) The consent may not be signified for a calendar year after a notice of deficiency in gift tax for that year has been sent to either spouse in accordance with the provisions of section 6212.

(c) The executor or administrator of a deceased spouse, or the guard-ian or committee of a legally incompetent spouse, as the case may be, may signify the consent.

(d) If the donor and spouse consent to the application of section 2513, the return or returns for the calendar year must set forth, to the extent provided thereon, information relative to the transfers made by each spouse.

§ 25.2513-3 **Revocation of consent.** If the consent to the application of the provisions of section 2513 for a calendar year was effectively signified on or before the 15th day of April following the close of the calendar year, either spouse may revoke the consent by filing in dupli-cate with the district director of internal revenue a signed statement of revocation, but only if the statement is filed on or before such 15th day of April. Therefore, a consent which was not effectively signified until after the 15th day of April following the close of the calendar year to which it applies may not be revoked.

§ 25.2513-4 **Joint and several liability for tax.** If consent to the application of the provisions of section 2513 is signified as provided in § 25.2513-2, and not revoked as provided in § 25.2513-3, the liability with respect to the entire gift tax of each spouse for such calendar year is joint and several. See paragraph (d) of § 25.2511-1.

Powers of Appointment

§ 25.2514-1 **Transfers under power of appointment**—(a) *Introduc-tory.* (1) Section 2514 treats the exercise of a general power of appoint-ment created on or before October 21, 1942, as a transfer of property for purposes of the gift tax. The section also treats as a transfer of property the exercise or complete release of a general power of appoint-ment created after October 21, 1942, and under certain circumstances the exercise of a power of appointment (not a general power of appoint-ment) created after October 21, 1942, by the creation of another power of appointment. See paragraph (d) of § 25.2514-3. Under certain circumstances, also, the failure to exercise a power of appointment created after October 21, 1942, within a specified time, so that the power lapses, constitutes a transfer of property. Paragraphs (b) through (e) of this section contain definitions of certain terms used in §§ 25.2514-2 and 25.2514-3. See § 25.2514-2 for specific rules applicable to certain powers created on or before October 21, 1942. See § 25.2514-3 for specific rules applicable to powers created after October 21, 1942.

(b) *Definition of "power of appointment"*—(1) *In general.* The term "power of appointment" includes all powers which are in substance and effect powers of appointment received by the donee of the power from another person, regardless of the nomenclature used in creating the power and regardless of local property law connotations. For exam-ple, if a trust instrument provides that the beneficiary may appropriate or consume the principal of the trust, the power to consume or appropriate is a power of appointment. Similarly, a power given to a donee to affect the beneficial enjoyment of a trust property or its income by altering, amending or revoking the trust instrument or terminating the trust is a power of appointment. A power in a donee to remove or discharge a trustee and appoint himself may be a power of appointment. For example, if under the terms of a trust instrument, the trustee or his successor has the power to appoint the principal of the trust for the benefit of individuals including himself, and A, another person, has the unrestricted power to remove or discharge the trustee at any time and appoint any other person including himself, A is considered as having a power of appointment. However, he would not be considered to have a power of appointment if he only had the power to appoint a successor, including himself, under limited conditions which did not exist at the time of exercise, release or lapse of the trustee's power, without an accompanying unrestricted power of removal. Similarly, a power to amend only the administrative provisions of a trust instrument, which cannot substantially affect the beneficial enjoyment of the trust property or income, is not a power of appointment. The mere power of management, investment, custody of assets, or the power to allocate receipts and disbursements as between income and principal, exercisable in a fiduciary capacity, whereby the holder has no power to enlarge or shift any of the beneficial interests therein except as an incidental consequence of the discharge of such fiduciary duties is not a power of appointment. Further, the right in a beneficiary of a trust to assent to a periodic accounting, thereby relieving the trustee from further accountability, is not a power of appointment if the right of assent does not consist of any power or right to enlarge or shift the beneficial interest of any beneficiary therein.

(2) *Relation to other sections.* For purposes of §§ 25.2514-1 through 25.2514-3, the term "power of appointment" does not include powers reserved by a donor to himself. No provision of section 2514 or of §§ 25.2514-1 through 25.2514-3 is to be construed as in any way limiting the application of any other section of the Internal Revenue Code or of these regulations. The power of the owner of a property interest already possessed by him to dispose of his interest, and nothing more, is not a power of appointment, and the interest is includible in the amount of his gifts to the extent it would be includible under section 2511 or other provisions of the Internal Revenue Code. For example, if a trust created by S provides for payment of the income to A for life with power in A to appoint the entire trust property by deed during her lifetime to a class consisting of her children, and a further power to dispose of the entire corpus by will to anyone, including her estate, and A exercises the inter vivos power in favor of her children, she has necessarily made a transfer of her income interest which constitutes a taxable gift under section 2511(a), without regard to section 2514. This transfer also results in a relinquishment of her general power to appoint by will, which constitutes a transfer under section 2514 if the power was created after October 21, 1942.

(3) *Powers over a portion of property.* If a power of appointment exists as to part of an entire group of assets or only over a limited interest in property, section 2514 applies only to such part or interest.

(c) *Definition of "general power of appointment"*—(1) *In general.* The term "general power of appointment" as defined in section 2514(c) means any power of appointment exercisable in favor of the person possessing the power (referred to as the "possessor"), his estate, his creditors, or the creditors of his estate, except (i) joint powers, to the extent provided in §§ 25.2514-2 and 25.2514-3 and (ii) certain powers limited by an ascertainable standard, to the extent provided in subparagraph (2) of this paragraph. A power of appointment exercisable to meet the estate tax, or any other taxes, debts, or charges which are enforceable against the possessor or his estate, is included within the meaning of a power of appointment exercisable in favor of the possessor, his estate, his creditors, or the creditors of his estate. A power of appointment exercisable for the purpose of discharging a legal obligation of the possessor or for his pecuniary benefit is considered a power of appointment exercisable in favor of the possessor or his creditors. However, for purposes of §§ 25.2514-1 through 25.2514-3, a power of appointment not otherwise considered to be a general power of appointment is not treated as a general power of appointment merely by reason of the fact that an appointee may, in fact, be a creditor of the possessor or his estate. A power of appointment is not a general power if by its terms it is either—

(a) Exercisable only in favor of one or more designated persons or classes other than the possessor or his creditors, or the possessor's estate or the creditors of his estate, or

(b) Expressly not exercisable in favor of the possessor or his creditors, the possessor's estate or the creditors of his estate. A beneficiary may have two powers under the same instrument, one of which is a general power of appointment and the other of which is not. For example, a beneficiary may have a general power to withdraw a limited portion of trust corpus during his life, and a further power exercisable during his lifetime to appoint the corpus among his children. The latter power is not a general power of appointment (but its exercise may cause a release of the former power; see example in paragraph (b) (2) of this section).

(2) *Powers limited by an ascertainable standard.* A power to consume, invade, or appropriate income or corpus, or both, for the benefit of the possessor which is limited by an ascertainable standard relating to the health, education, support, or maintenance of the possessor is, by reason of section 2514(c)(1), not a general power of appointment. A power is limited by such a standard if the extent of the possessor's duty to exercise and not to exercise the power is reasonably measurable in terms of his needs for health, education, or support (or any combination of them). As used in this subparagraph, the words "support" and "maintenance" are synonymous and their meaning is not limited to the bare necessities of life. A power to use property for the comfort, welfare, or happiness of the holder of the power is not limited

1080

by the requisite standard. Examples of powers which are limited by the requisite standard are powers exercisable for the holder's "support," "support in reasonable comfort," "maintenance in health and reasonable comfort," "support in his accustomed manner of living," "education, including college and professional education," "health," and "medical, dental, hospital and nursing expenses and expenses of invalidism." In determining whether a power is limited by an ascertainable standard, it is immaterial whether the beneficiary is required to exhaust his other income before the power can be exercised.

(3) *Certain powers under wills of decedents dying between January 1 and April 2, 1948.* Section 210 of the Technical Changes Act of 1953 provides that if a decedent died after December 31, 1947, but before April 3, 1948, certain property interests described therein may, if the decedent's surviving spouse so elects, be accorded special treatment in the determination of the marital deduction to be allowed the decedent's estate under the provisions of section 812(e) of the Internal Revenue Code of 1939. See paragraph (h) of § 81.47a of Regulations 105 (26 CFR (1939) 81.47a(h)). The section further provides that property affected by the election shall be considered property with respect to which the surviving spouse has a general power of appointment. Therefore, notwithstanding any other provision of law or of §§ 25.2514-1 through 25.2514-3, if the surviving spouse has made an election under section 210 of the Technical Changes Act of 1953, the property which was the subject of the election shall be considered as property with respect to which she has a general power of appointment created after October 21, 1942, exercisable by deed or will, to the extent it was treated as an interest passing to the surviving spouse and not passing to any other person for the purpose of the marital deduction in the prior decedent's estate.

(d) *Definition of "exercise."* Whether a power of appointment is in fact exercised may depend upon local law. However, regardless of local law, a power of appointment is considered as exercised for purposes of section 2514 even though the exercise is in favor of the taker in default of appointment, and irrespective of whether the appointed interest and the interest in default of appointment are identical or whether the appointee renounces any right to take under the appointment. A power of appointment is also considered as exercised even though the disposition cannot take effect until the occurrence of an event after the exercise takes place, if the exercise is irrevocable and, as of the time of the exercise, the condition was not impossible of occurrence. For example, if property is left in trust to A for life, with a power in A to appoint the remainder by an instrument filed with the trustee during his life, and A exercises his power by appointing the remainder to B in the event that B survives A, A is considered to have exercised his power if the exercise was irrevocable.

(e) *Time of creation of power.* A power of appointment created by will is in general considered as created on the date of the testator's death. However, section 2514(f) provides that a power of appointment created by a will executed on or before October 21, 1942, is considered a power created on or before that date if the testator dies before July

1, 1949, without having republished the will, by codicil or otherwise, after October 21, 1942. Whether or not a power of appointment created by an inter vivos instrument executed on or before October 21, 1942, is considered a power created on or before that date depends upon the facts and circumstances of the particular case. For example, assume that A created a revocable trust before October 21, 1942, providing for payment of income to B for life with remainder as B shall appoint by will. If A dies after October 21, 1942, without having exercised his power of revocation, B's power of appointment is considered a power created after October 21, 1942. On the other hand, assume that C created an irrevocable inter vivos trust before October 21, 1942, naming T as trustee and providing for payment of income to D for life with remainder to E. Assume further that T was given the power to pay corpus to D and the power to appoint a successor trustee. If T resigns after October 21, 1942, and appoints D as successor trustee, D is considered to have a power of appointment created before October 21, 1942. As another example assume that F created an irrevocable inter vivos trust before October 21, 1942, providing for payment of income to G for life with remainder as G shall appoint by will, but in default of appointment income to H for life with remainder as H shall appoint by will. If G dies after October 21, 1942, without having exercised his power of appointment, H's power of appointment is considered a power created before October 21, 1942, even though it was only a contingent interest until G's death. If, in this last example, G had exercised his power of appointment by creating a similar power in I, I's power of appointment would be considered a power created after October 21, 1942. A power is not considered as created after October 21, 1942, merely because the power is not exercisable or the identity of its holders is not ascertained until after that date.

§ 25.2514-2 **Powers of appointment created on or before October 21, 1942**—(a) *In general.* The exercise of a general power of appointment created on or before October 21, 1942, is deemed to be a transfer of property by the individual possessing the power.

(b) *Joint powers created on or before October 21, 1942.* Section 2514(c)(2) provides that a power created on or before October 21, 1942, which at the time of the exercise is not exercisable by the possessor except in conjunction with another person, is not deemed a general power of appointment.

(c) *Release or lapse.* A failure to exercise a general power of appointment created on or before October 21, 1942, or a complete release of such a power is not considered to be an exercise of a general power of appointment. The phrase "a complete release" means a release of all powers over all or a portion of the property subject to a power of appointment, as distinguished from the reduction of a power of appointment to a lesser power. Thus, if the possessor completely relinquished all powers over one-half of the property subject to a power of appointment, the power is completely released as to that one-half. If at or before the time a power of appointment is relinquished, the holder of the power exercises the power in such a manner or to such an extent that the relinquishment results in the reduction, enlargement, or shift in a beneficial interest in property, the relinquishment will be considered to be an exercise and not a release of the power. For example, assume that A created a trust in 1940 providing for payment of the income to B for life with the power in B to amend the trust, and for payment of the remainder to such persons as B shall appoint or, upon default of appointment, to C. If B amended the trust in 1948 by providing that upon his death the remainder was to be paid to D, and if he further amended the trust in 1955 by deleting his power to amend the trust, such relinquishment will be considered an exercise and not a release of a general power of appointment. On the other hand, if the 1948 amendment became ineffective before or at the time of the 1955 amendment, or if B in 1948 merely amended the trust by changing the purely ministerial powers of the trustee, his relinquishment of the power in 1955 will be considered as release of a power of appointment.

(d) *Partial release.* If a general power of appointment created on or before October 21, 1942, is partially released so that it is not thereafter a general power of appointment, a subsequent exercise of the partially released power is not an exercise of a general power of appointment if the partial release occurs before whichever is the later of the following dates:

(1) November 1, 1951; or

(2) If the possessor was under a legal disability to release the power on October 21, 1942, the day after the expiration of 6 months following the termination of such legal disability.

However, if a general power created on or before October 21, 1942, is partially released on or after the later of those dates, a subsequent exercise of the power will constitute an exercise of a general power of appointment. The legal disability referred to in this paragraph is determined under local law and may include the disability of an insane person, a minor, or an unborn child. The fact that the type of general power of appointment possessed by the holder actually was not generally releasable under the local law does not place the holder under a legal disability within the meaning of this paragraph. In general, however, it is assumed that all general powers of appointment are releasable, unless the local law on the subject is to the contrary, and it is presumed that the method employed to release the power is effective, unless it is not in accordance with the local law relating specifically to releases or, in the absence of such local law, is not in accordance with the local law relating to similar transactions.

(e) *Partial exercise.* If a general power of appointment created on or before October 21, 1942, is exercised only as to a portion of the property subject to the power, the exercise is considered to be a transfer only as to the value of that portion.

§ 25.2514-3 **Powers of appointment created after October 21, 1942** —(a) *In general.* The exercise, release, or lapse (except as provided in paragraph (c) of this section) of a general power of appointment created after October 21, 1942, is deemed to be a transfer of property by the individual possessing the power. The exercise of a power of appointment that is not a general power is considered to be a transfer if it is exercised to create a further power under certain circumstances (see paragraph (d) of this section). See paragraph (c) of § 25.2514-1 for the definition of various terms used in this section. See paragraph (b) of this section for the rules applicable to determine the extent to which joint powers created after October 21, 1942, are to be treated as general powers of appointment.

(b) *Joint powers created after October 21, 1942.* The treatment of a power of appointment created after October 21, 1942, which is exercisable only in conjunction with another person is governed by section 2514(c)(3), which provides as follows:

(1) Such a power is not considered as a general power of appointment if it is not exercisable by the possessor except with the consent or joinder of the creator of the power.

(2) Such power is not considered as a general power of appointment if it is not exercisable by the possessor except with the consent or joinder of a person having a substantial interest in the property subject to the power which is adverse to the exercise of the power in favor of the possessor, his estate, his creditors, or the creditors of his estate. An interest adverse to the exercise of a power is considered as substantial if its value in relation to the total value of the property subject to the power is not insignificant. For this purpose, the interest is to be valued in accordance with the actuarial principles set forth in § 25.2512-5 or, if it is not susceptible to valuation under those provisions, in accordance with the general principles set forth in § 25.2512-1. A taker in default of appointment under a power has an interest which is adverse to an exercise of the power. A coholder of the power has no adverse interest merely because of his joint possession of the power nor merely because he is a permissible appointee under a power. However, a coholder of a power is considered as having an adverse interest where he may possess the power after the possessor's death and may exercise it at that time in favor of himself, his estate, his creditors, or the creditors of his estate. Thus, for example, if X, Y, and Z held a power jointly to appoint among a group of persons which includes themselves and if on the death of X the power will pass to Y and Z jointly, then Y and Z are considered to have interests adverse to the exercise of the power in favor of X. Similarly, if on Y's death the power will pass to Z, Z is considered to have an interest adverse to the exercise of the power in favor of Y. The application of this subparagraph may be further illustrated by the following examples in each of which it is assumed that the value of the interest in question is substantial:

Example (1). The taxpayer and R are trustees of a trust under which the income is to be paid to the taxpayer for life and then to M for life, and R is remainderman. The trustees have power to distribute corpus to the taxpayer. Since R's interest is substantially adverse to an exercise of the power in favor of the taxpayer, the latter does not have a general power of appointment. If M and the taxpayer were trustees, M's interest would likewise be adverse.

Example (2). The taxpayer and L are trustees of a trust under which the income is to be paid to L for life and then to M for life, and the taxpayer is remainderman. The trustees have power to distribute corpus to the taxpayer during L's life. Since L's interest is adverse to an exercise of the power in favor of the taxpayer, the taxpayer does not have a general power of appointment. If the taxpayer and M were trustees, M's interest would likewise be adverse.

Example (3). The taxpayer and L are trustees of a trust under which the income is to be paid to L for life. The trustees can designate whether corpus is to be distributed to the taxpayer or to A after L's death. L's interest is not adverse to an exercise of the power in favor of the taxpayer, and the taxpayer therefore has a general power of appointment.

(3) A power which is exercisable only in conjunction with another person, and which after application of the rules set forth in subparagraphs (1) and (2) of this paragraph, constitutes a general power of appointment, will be treated as though the holders of the power who are permissible appointees of the property were joint owners of property subject to the power. The possessor, under this rule, will be treated as possessed of a general power of appointment over an aliquot share of the property to be determined with reference to the number of joint holders, including the possessor, who (or whose estates or creditors) are permissible appointees. Thus, for example, if X, Y, and Z hold an unlimited power jointly to appoint among a group of persons, including themselves, but on the death of X the power does not pass to Y and Z jointly, then Y and Z are not considered to have interests adverse to the exercise of the power in favor of X. In this case, X is considered to possess a general power of appointment as to one-third of the property subject to the power.

(c) *Partial releases, lapses, and disclaimers of general powers created after October 21, 1942.* (1) The general principles set forth in § 25.2511-2 for determining whether a donor of property (or of a property right or interest) has divested himself of all or any portion of his interest therein to the extent necessary to effect a completed gift are applicable in determining whether a partial release of a power of appointment constitutes a taxable gift. Thus, if a general power of appointment is partially released so that thereafter the donor may still appoint among a limited class of persons not including himself the partial release does not effect a complete gift, since the possessor of the power has retained the right to designate the ultimate beneficiaries of the property over which he holds the power and since it is only the termination of such control which completes a gift.

(2) If a general power of appointment created after October 21, 1942, was partially released prior to June 1, 1951, so that it no longer represented a general power of appointment, as defined in paragraph (c) of § 25.2514-1, the subsequent exercise, release, or lapse of the partially released power at any time thereafter will not constitute the exercise

or release of a general power of appointment. For example, assume that A created a trust in 1943 under which B possessed a general power of appointment. By an instrument executed in 1948 such general power of appointment was reduced in scope by B to an excepted power. The inter vivos exercise in 1955, or in any calendar year thereafter, of such excepted power is not considered an exercise or release of a general power of appointment for purposes of the gift tax.

(3) If a general power of appointment created after October 21, 1942, was partially released after May 31, 1951, the subsequent exercise, release or a lapse of the power at any time thereafter, will constitute the exercise or release of a general power of appointment for gift tax purposes.

(4) A release of a power of appointment need not be formal or express in character. For example, the failure to exercise a general power of appointment created after October 21, 1942, within a specified time so that the power lapses, constitutes a release of the power. In any case where the possessor of a general power of appointment is incapable of validly exercising or releasing a power, by reason of minority, or otherwise, and the power may not be validly exercised or released on his behalf, the failure to exercise or release the power is not a lapse of the power. If a trustee has in his capacity as trustee a power which is considered as a general power of appointment, his resignation or removal as trustee will cause a lapse of his power. However, section 2514(e) provides that a lapse during any calendar year is considered as a release so as to be subject to the gift tax only to the extent that the property which could have been appointed by exercise of the lapsed power of appointment exceeds the greater of (i) $5,000, or (ii) 5 percent of the aggregate value, at the time of the lapse, of the assets out of which, or the proceeds of which, the exercise of the lapsed power could be satisfied. For example, if an individual has a noncumulative right to withdraw $10,000 a year from the principal of a trust fund, the failure to exercise this right of withdrawal in a particular year will not constitute a gift if the fund at the end of the year equals or exceeds $200,000. If, however, at the end of the particular year the fund should be worth only $100,000, the failure to exercise the power will be considered a gift to the extent of $5,000, the excess of $10,000 over 5 percent of a fund of $100,000. Where the failure to exercise the power, such as the right of withdrawal, occurs in more than a single year, the value of the taxable transfer will be determined separately for each year.

(5) A disclaimer or renunciation of a general power of appointment is not considered to be a release of the power. The disclaimer or renunciation must be unequivocal and effective under local law. A disclaimer is a complete and unqualified refusal to accept the rights to which one is entitled. There can be no disclaimer or renunciation of a power after its acceptance. In any case where a power is purported to be disclaimed or renounced as to only a portion of the property subject to the power, the determination as to whether or not there has been a complete and unqualified refusal to accept the rights to which one is entitled will depend on all the facts and circumstances of the particular case, taking

1086

into account the recognition and effectiveness of such a disclaimer under local law. Such rights refer to the incidents of the power and not to other interests of the possessor of the power in the property. If effective under local law, the power may be disclaimed or renounced without disclaiming or renouncing such other interests. In the absence of facts to the contrary, the failure to renounce or disclaim within a reasonable time after learning of its existence will be presumed to constitute an acceptance of the power.

(d) *Creation of another power in certain cases.* Paragraph (d) of section 2514 provides that there is a transfer for purposes of the gift tax of the value of property (or of property rights or interests) with respect to which a power of appointment, which is not a general power of appointment, created after October 21, 1942, is exercised by creating another power of appointment which, under the terms of the instruments creating and exercising the first power and under applicable local law, can be validly exercised so as to (1) postpone the vesting of any estate or interest in the property for a period ascertainable without regard to the date of the creation of the first power, or (2) (if the applicable rule against perpetuities is stated in terms of suspension of ownership or of the power of alienation, rather than of vesting) suspend the absolute ownership or the power of alienation of the property for a period ascertainable without regard to the date of the creation of the first power. For the purpose of section 2514(d), the value of the property subject to the second power of appointment is considered to be its value unreduced by any precedent or subsequent interest which is not subject to the second power. Thus, if a donor has a power to appoint $100,000 among a group consisting of his children or grandchildren and during his lifetime exercises the power by making an outright appointment of $75,000 and by giving one appointee a power to appoint $25,000, no more than $25,000 will be considered a gift under section 2514(d). If, however, the donor appoints the income from the entire fund to a beneficiary for life with power in the beneficiary to appoint the remainder, the entire $100,000 will be considered a gift under section 2514(d), if the exercise of the second power can validly postpone the vesting of any estate or interest in the property or can suspend the absolute ownership or power of alienation of the property for a period ascertainable without regard to the date of the creation of the first power.

(e) *Examples.* The application of this section may be further illustrated by the following examples in each of which it is assumed, unless otherwise stated, that S has transferred property in trust after October 21, 1942, with the remainder payable to R at L's death, and that neither L nor R has any interest in or power over the enjoyment of the trust property except as is indicated separately in each example:

Example (1). The income is payable to L for life. L has the power to cause the income to be paid to R. The exercise of the right constitutes the making of a transfer of property under section 2511. L's power does not constitute a power of appointment since it is only a power to dispose of his income interest, a right otherwise possessed by him.

1087

Example (2). The income is to be accumulated during L's life. L has the power to have the income distributed to himself. If L's power is limited by an ascertainable standard (relating to health, etc.) as defined in paragraph (c)(2) of § 25.2514-1, the lapse of such power will not constitute a transfer of property for gift tax purposes. If L's power is not so limited, its lapse or release during L's lifetime may constitute a transfer of property for gift tax purposes. See especially paragraph (c)(4) of § 25.2514-3.

Example (3). The income is to be paid to L for life. L has a power, exercisable at any time, to cause corpus to be distributed to himself. L has a general power of appointment over the remainder interest, the release of which constitutes a transfer for gift tax purposes of the remainder interest. If in this example L had a power to cause the corpus to be distributed only to X, L would have a power of appointment which is not a general power of appointment, the exercise or release of which would not constitute a transfer of property for purposes of the gift tax.

Example (4). The income is payable to L for life. R has the right to cause the corpus to be distributed to L at any time. R's power is not a power of appointment, but merely a right to dispose of his remainder interest, a right already possessed by him. In such a case, the exercise of the right constitutes the making of a transfer of property under section 2511 of the value, if any, of his remainder interest. See paragraph (e) of § 25.2511-1.

Example (5). The income is to be paid to L. R has the right to appoint the corpus to himself at any time. R's general power of appointment over the corpus includes a general power to dispose of L's income interest therein. The lapse or release of R's general power over the income interest during his life may constitute the making of a transfer of property. See especially paragraph (c)(4) of § 25.2514-3.

Tenancies by the Entirety

§ 25.2515-1 **Tenancies by the entirety; in general**—(a) *Nature of.* An estate by the entirety in real property is essentially a joint tenancy between husband and wife with the right of survivorship. As used in this section and §§ 25.2515-2 through 25.2515-4, the term "tenancy by the entirety" includes a joint tenancy between husband and wife in real property with right of survivorship, or a tenancy which accords to the spouses rights equivalent thereto regardless of the term by which such a tenancy is described in local property law.

(b) *Gift upon creation of tenancy by the entirety; in general.* During calendar years prior to 1955 the contribution made by a husband or wife in the creation of a tenancy by the entirety constituted a gift to the extent that the consideration furnished by either spouse exceeded the value of the rights retained by that spouse. The contribution made by either or both spouses in the creation of such a tenancy during the calendar year 1955, or any calendar year thereafter, is not deemed a gift by either spouse, regardless of the proportion of the total consideration furnished by either spouse, unless the donor spouse elects (see § 25.2515-2) under section 2515(c) to treat such transaction as a gift in the calendar year in which the transaction is effected. However, there is a gift upon the termination of such a tenancy, other than by the death of a spouse, if the proceeds received by one spouse on termination of the tenancy are larger than the proceeds allocable to the consideration furnished by that spouse to the tenancy. The creation of a tenancy by the entirety takes place if (1) a husband or his wife purchases property and causes the title thereto to be conveyed to themselves as tenants by the entirety, (2) both join in such a purchase, or (3) either or both cause to be created such a tenancy in property already owned by either or both of them. The rule prescribed herein with respect to the creation of a tenancy by the entirety applies also to contributions made in the making of additions to the value of such a tenancy (in the form of improvements, reductions in the indebtedness, or otherwise), regardless of the proportion of the consideration furnished by each spouse. See § 25.2516-1 for transfers made pursuant to a property settlement agreement incident to divorce.

(c) *Consideration*—(1) *In general.* (i) The consideration furnished by a person in the creation of a tenancy by the entirety or the making of additions to the value thereof is the amount contributed by him in connection therewith. The contribution may be made by either spouse or by a third party. It may be furnished in the form of money, other property, or an interest in property. If it is furnished in the form of other property or an interest in property, the amount of the contribution is the fair market value of the property or interest at the time it was transferred to the tenancy or was exchanged for the property which became the subject of the tenancy. For example, if a decedent devised real property to the spouses as tenants by the entirety and the fair market value of the property was $30,000 at the time of the decedent's death, the amount of the decedent's contribution to the creation of the tenancy was $30,000. As another example, assume that in 1950 the husband purchased real property for $25,000, taking it in his own name as sole owner, and that in 1956 when the property had a fair market value of $40,000 he caused it to be transferred to himself and his wife as tenants by the entirety. Here, the amount of the husband's contribution to the creation of the tenancy was $40,000 (the fair market value of the property at the time it was transferred to the tenancy). Similarly, assume that in 1950 the husband purchased, as sole owner, corporate shares for $25,000 and in 1956, when the shares had a fair market value of $35,000, he exchanged them for real property which was transferred to the husband and his wife as tenants by the entirety. The amount of the husband's contribution to the creation of the tenancy was $35,000 (the fair market value of the shares at the time he exchanged them for the real property which became the subject of the tenancy).

(ii) Whether consideration derived from third-party sources is deemed to have been furnished by a third party or to have been furnished by the spouses will depend upon the terms under which the transfer is made.

[Harris]—69

If a decedent devises real property to the spouses as tenants by the entirety, the decedent, and not the spouses, is the person who furnished the consideration for the creation of the tenancy. Likewise, if a decedent in his will directs his executor to discharge an indebtedness of the tenancy, the decedent, and not the spouses, is the person who furnished the consideration for the addition to the value of the tenancy. However, if the decedent bequeathed a general legacy to the husband and the wife and they used the legacy to discharge an indebtedness of the tenancy, the spouses, and not the decedent, are the persons who furnished the consideration for the addition to the value of the tenancy. The principles set forth in this subdivision with respect to transfers by decedents apply equally well to inter vivos transfers by third parties.

(iii) Where a tenancy is terminated in part (e.g., where a portion of the property subject to the tenancy is sold to a third party, or where the original property is disposed of and in its place there is substituted other property of lesser value acquired through reinvestment under circumstances which satisfy the requirements of paragraph (d) (2)(ii) of this section), the proportionate contribution of each person to the remaining tenancy is in general the same as his proportionate contribution to the original tenancy, and the character of his contribution remains the same. These proportions are applied to the cost of the remaining or substituted property. Thus, if the total contribution to the cost of the property was $20,000 and a fourth of the property was sold, the contribution to the remaining portion of the tenancy is normally $15,000. However, if it is shown that at the time of the contribution more or less than one-fourth thereof was attributable to the portion sold, the contribution is divided between the portion sold and the portion retained in the proper proportion. If the portion sold was acquired as a separate tract, it is treated as a separate tenancy. As another example of the application of this subdivision, assume that in 1950 X (a third party) gave to H and W (H's wife), as tenants by the entirety, real property then having a value of $15,000. In 1955, H spent $5,000 thereon in improvements and under section 2515(c) elected to treat his contribution as a gift. In 1956, W spent $10,000 in improving the property but did not elect to treat her contribution as a gift. Between 1957 and 1960 the property appreciated in value by $30,000. In 1960, the property was sold for $60,000, and $45,000 of the proceeds of the sale were, under circumstances that satisfy the requirements of paragraph (d)(2)(ii) of this section, reinvested in other real property. Since X contributed one-half of the total consideration for the original property and the additions to its value, he is considered as having furnished $22,500 (one-half of $45,000) toward the creation of the remaining portion of the tenancy and the making of additions to the value thereof. Similarly, H is considered as having furnished $7,500 (one-sixth of $45,000) which was treated as a gift in the year furnished, and W is considered as having furnished $15,000 (one-third of $45,000) which was not treated as a gift in the year furnished.

(2) *Proportion of consideration attributable to appreciation.* Any general appreciation (appreciation due to fluctuations in market value)

in the value of the property occurring between two successive contribution dates which can readily be measured and which can be determined with reasonable certainty to be allocable to any particular contribution or contributions previously furnished is to be treated, for the purpose of the computations in §§ 25.2515-3 and 25.2515-4, as though it were additional consideration furnished by the person who furnished the prior consideration. Any general depreciation in value is treated in a comparable manner. For the purpose of the first sentence of this subparagraph, successive contribution dates are the two consecutive dates on which any contributions to the tenancy are made, not necessarily by the same party. Further, appreciation allocable to the prior consideration falls in the same class as the prior consideration to which it relates. The application of this subparagraph may be illustrated by the following examples:

Example (1). In 1940, H purchased real property for $15,000 which he caused to be transferred to himself and W (his wife) as tenants by the entirety. In 1956 when the fair market value of the property was $30,000, W made $5,000 improvements to the property. In 1957 the property was sold for $35,000. The general appreciation of $15,000 which occurred between the date of purchase and the date of W's improvements to the property constitutes an additional contribution by H, having the same characteristics as his original contribution of $15,000.

Example (2). In 1955 real property was purchased by H and W and conveyed to them as tenants by the entirety. The purchase price of the property was $15,000 of which H contributed $10,000 and W, $5,000. In 1960 when the fair market value of the property is $21,000, W makes improvements thereto of $5,000. The property then is sold for $26,000. The appreciation in value of $6,000 results in an additional contribution of $4,000 (10,000/15,000 x $6,000) by H, and an additional contribution by W of $2,000 (5,000/15,000 x $6,000). H's total contribution to the tenancy is $14,000 ($10,000 + $4,000) and W's total contribution is $12,000 ($5,000 +$2,000 +$5,000).

Example (3). In 1956 real property was purchased by H and W and conveyed to them as tenants by the entirety. The purchase price of the property was $15,000, on which a down payment of $3,000 was made. The remaining $12,000 was to be paid in monthly installments over a period of 15 years. H furnished $2,000 of the down payment and W, $1,000. H paid all the monthly installments. During the period 1956 to 1971 the property gradually appreciates in value to $24,000. Here, the appreciation is so gradual and the contributions so numerous that the amount allocable to any particular contribution cannot be ascertained with any reasonable certainty. Accordingly, in such a case the appreciation in value may be disregarded in determining the amount of consideration furnished in making the computations provided for in §§ 25.2515-3 and 25.2515-4.

(d) *Gift upon termination of tenancy by the entirety*—(1) *In general*. Upon the termination of the tenancy, whether created before, during, or subsequent to the calendar year 1955, a gift may result, depending

1091

upon the disposition made of the proceeds of the termination (whether the proceeds be in the form of cash, property, or interests in property). A gift may result notwithstanding the fact that the contribution of either spouse to the tenancy was treated as a gift. See § 25.2515-3 for the method of determining the amount of any gift which may result from the termination of the tenancy in those cases in which no portion of the consideration contributed was treated as a gift by the spouses in the year in which furnished. See § 25.2515-4 for the method of determining the amount of any gift which may result from the termination of the tenancy in those cases in which all or a portion of the consideration contributed was treated as constituting a gift by the spouses in the year in which furnished. See § 25.2515-2 for the procedure to be followed by a donor who elects under section 2515(c) to treat the creation of a tenancy by the entirety (or the making of additions to its value) as a transfer subject to the gift tax in the year in which the transfer is made, and for the method of determining the amount of the gift.

(2) *Termination*—(i) *In general.* Except as indicated in subdivision (ii) of this subparagraph, a termination of a tenancy is effected when all or a portion of the property so held by the spouses is sold, exchanged, or otherwise disposed of, by gift or in any other manner, or when the spouses through any form of conveyance or agreement become tenants in common of the property or otherwise alter the nature of their respective interests in the property formerly held by them as tenants by the entirety. In general, any increase in the indebtedness on a tenancy constitutes a termination of the tenancy to the extent of the increase in the indebtedness. However, such an increase will not constitute a termination of the tenancy to the extent that the increase is offset by additions to the tenancy within a reasonable time after such increase. Such additions (to the extent of the increase in the indebtedness) shall not be treated by the spouses as contributions within the meaning of paragraph (c) of this section.

(ii) *Exchange or reinvestment.* A termination is not considered as effected to the extent that the property subject to the tenancy is exchanged for other real property, the title to which is held by the spouses in an identical tenancy. For this purpose, a tenancy is considered identical if the proportionate values of the spouses' respective rights (other than any change in the proportionate values resulting solely from the passing of time) are identical to those held in the property which was sold. In addition the sale, exchange, (other than an exchange described above), or other disposition of property held as tenants by the entirety is not considered as a termination if all three of the following conditions are satisfied:

(*a*) There is no division of the proceeds of the sale, exchange or other disposition of the property held as tenants by the entirety;

(*b*) On or before the due date for the filing of a gift tax return for the calendar year in which the property held as tenants by the entirety was sold, exchanged, or otherwise disposed of, the spouses enter into a binding contract for the purchase of other real property; and

(c) After the sale, exchange, or other disposition of the former property and within a reasonable time after the date of the contract referred to in subdivision (b), such other real property actually is acquired by the spouses and held by them in an identical tenancy.

To the extent that all three of the conditions set forth in this subdivision are not met (whether by reason of the death of one of the spouses or for any other reason), the provisions of the preceding sentence shall not apply, and the sale, exchange or other disposition of the property will constitute a termination of the tenancy. As used in subdivision (c) the expression "a reasonable time" means the time which, under the particular facts in each case, is needed for those matters which are incident to the acquisition of the other property (i.e., perfecting of title, arranging for financing, construction, etc.). The fact that proceeds of a sale are deposited in the name of one tenant or of both tenants separately or jointly as a convenience does not constitute a division within the meaning of subdivision (a) if the other requirements of this subdivision are met. The proceeds of a sale, exchange, or other disposition of property held as tenants by the entirety will be deemed to have been used for the purchase of other real property if applied to the purchase or construction of improvements which themselves constitute real property and which are additions to other real property held by the spouses in a tenancy identical to that in which they held the property which was sold, exchanged, or otherwise disposed of.

(3) *Proceeds of termination.* (i) The proceeds of termination may be received by a spouse in the form of money, property, or an interest in property. Where the proceeds are received in the form of property (other than money) or an interest in property, the value of the proceeds received by that spouse is the fair market value, on the date of termination of the tenancy by the entirety, of the property or interest received. Thus, if a tenancy by the entirety is terminated so that thereafter each spouse owns an undivided half interest in the property as tenant in common, the value of the proceeds of termination received by each spouse is one-half the value of the property at the time of the termination of the tenancy by the entirety. If under local law one spouse without the consent of the other, can bring about a severance of his or her interest in a tenancy by the entirety and does so by making a gift of his or her interest to a third party, that spouse is considered as having received proceeds of termination in the amount of the fair market value, at the time of the termination, of his severable interest determined in accordance with the rules prescribed in § 25.2512-5. He has in addition, made a gift to the third party of the fair market value of the interest conveyed to the third party. In such a case, the other spouse also is considered as having received as proceeds of termination the fair market value, at the time of termination, of the interest which she thereafter holds in the property as tenant in common with the third party. However, since section 2515(b) contemplates that the spouses may divide the proceeds of termination in some proportion other than that represented by the values of their respective legal interests in the property, if both spouses join together in making a gift to a third

1093

party of property held by them as tenants by the entirety, the value of the proceeds of termination which will be treated as received by each is the amount which each reports (on his or her gift tax return filed for the calendar year in which the termination occurs) as the value of his or her gift to the third party. This amount is the amount which each reports without regard to whether the spouses elect under section 2513 to treat the gifts as made one-half by each. For example, assume that H and W (his wife) hold real property as tenants by the entirety; that in 1956, when the property has a fair market value of $60,000, they give it to their son; and that on their gift tax returns for the calendar year 1956, H reports himself as having made a gift to the son of $36,000 and W reports herself as having made a gift to the son of $24,000. Under these circumstances, H is considered as having received proceeds of termination valued at $36,000, and W is considered as having received proceeds of termination valued at $24,000.

(ii) Except as provided otherwise in subparagraph (2)(ii) of this paragraph (under which certain tenancies by the entirety are considered not to be terminated), where the proceeds of a sale, exchange, or other disposition of the property are not actually divided between the spouses but are held (whether in a bank account or otherwise) in their joint names or in the name of one spouse as custodian or trustee for their joint interests, each spouse is presumed, in the absence of a showing to the contrary, to have received, as of the date of termination, proceeds of termination equal in value to the value of his or her enforceable property rights in respect of the proceeds.

§ 25.2515-2 **Tenancies by the entirety; transfers treated as gifts; manner of election and valuation.** (a) The election to treat the creation of a tenancy by the entirety in real property, or additions made to its value, as constituting a gift in the year in which effected, shall be exercised by including the value of such gifts in the gift tax return of the donor for the calendar year in which the tenancy was created, or the additions in value were made to the property. See section 6019 and the regulations thereunder. The election may be exercised only in a return filed within the time prescribed by law, or before the expiration of any extension of time granted pursuant to law for the filing of the return. See section 6075 for the time for filing the gift tax return, and section 6081 for extensions of time for filing the return, together with the regulations thereunder. In order to make the election, a gift tax return must be filed for the calendar year in which the tenancy was created, or additions in value thereto made, even though the value of the gift involved does not exceed the amount of the exclusion provided by section 2503(b).

(b) If the donor spouse exercises the election as provided in paragraph (a) of this section, the amount of the gift at the creation of the tenancy is the amount of his contribution to the tenancy less the value of his retained interest in it, determined as follows:

(1) If under the law of the jurisdiction governing the rights of the

spouses, either spouse, acting alone, can bring about a severance of his or her interest in the property, the value of the donor's retained interest is one-half the value of the property.

(2) If, under the law of the jurisdiction governing the rights of the spouses each is entitled to share in the income or other enjoyment of the property but neither, acting alone, may defeat the right of the survivor of them to the whole of the property, the amount of retained interest of the donor is determined by use of the appropriate actuarial factors for the spouses at their respective attained ages at the time the transaction is effected.

(c) Factors representing the respective interests of the spouses, under a tenancy by the entirety, at their attained ages at the time of the transaction may be found in, or readily computed with the use of the tables contained in, the actuarial pamphlet referred to in paragraph (e) of § 25.2512-5. State law may provide that the husband only is entitled to all of the income or other enjoyment of the real property held as tenants by the entirety, and the wife's interest consists only of the right of survivorship with no right of severance. In such a case, a special factor may be needed to determine the value of the interests of the respective spouses. See paragraph (e) of § 25.2512-5 for the procedure for obtaining special factors from the Commissioner in cases requiring their use.

(d) The application of this paragraph may be illustrated by the following example:

Example. A husband with his own funds acquires real property valued at $10,000 and has it conveyed to himself and his wife as tenants by the entirety. Under the law of the jurisdiction governing the rights of the parties, each spouse is entitled to share in the income from the property but neither spouse acting alone could bring about a severance of his or her interest. The husband elects to treat the transfer as a gift in the year in which effected. At the time of transfer, the ages of the husband and wife are 45 and 40, respectively, on their birthdays nearest to the date of transfer. The value of the gift to the wife is $5,502.90, computed as follows:

Value of property transferred $10,000.00
Less $10,000 × .44971 (factor for value of donor's retained rights) 4,497.10

Value of gift .... $ 5,502.90

§ 25.2515-3 **Termination of tenancy by the entirety; cases in which entire value of gift is determined under section 2515(b).** (a) In any case in which—

(1) The creation of a tenancy by the entirety (including additions in value thereto) was not treated as a gift, and

(2) The entire consideration for the creation of the tenancy, and any additions in value thereto, was furnished solely by the spouses (see paragraph (c)(1)(ii) of § 25.2515-1), the termination of the tenancy (other than by the death of a spouse) always results in the making of a

gift by a spouse who receives a smaller share of the proceeds of the termination (whether received in cash, property or interests in property) than the share of the proceeds attributable to the total consideration furnished by him. See paragraph (c) of § 25.2515-1 for a discussion of what constitutes consideration and the value thereof. Thus, a gift is effected at the time of termination of the tenancy by the spouse receiving less than one-half of the proceeds of termination if such spouse (regardless of age) furnished one-half or more of the total consideration for the purchase and improvements, if any, of the property held in the tenancy. Also, if one spouse furnished the entire consideration, a gift is made by such spouse to the extent that the other spouse receives any portion of the proceeds of termination. See § 25.2515-4 for determination of the amount of the gift, if any, in cases in which the creation of the tenancy was treated as a gift or a portion of the consideration was furnished by a third person. See paragraph (d)(2) of § 25.2515-1 as to the acts which effect a termination of the tenancy.

(b) In computing the value of the gift under the circumstances described in paragraph (a) of this section, it is necessary to first determine the spouse's share of the proceeds attributable to the consideration furnished by him. This share is computed by multiplying the total value of the proceeds of the termination by a fraction, the numerator of which is the total consideration furnished by the donor spouse and the denominator of which is the total consideration furnished by both spouses. From this amount there is subtracted the value of the proceeds of termination received by the donor spouse. The amount remaining is the value of the gift. In arriving at the "total consideration furnished by the donor spouse" and the "total consideration furnished by both spouses", for purposes of the computation provided for in this paragraph, the consideration furnished (see paragraph (c) of § 25.2515-1) is not reduced by any amounts which otherwise would have been excludable under section 2503(b) in determining the amounts of taxable gifts for the years in which the consideration was furnished. As an example assume that in 1955, real property was purchased for $30,000, the husband and wife each contributing $12,000 and the remaining $6,000 being obtained through a mortgage on the property. In each of the years 1956 and 1957, the husband paid $3,000 on the principal of the indebtedness, but did not disclose the value of these transfers on his gift tax returns for those years. The total consideration furnished by the husband is $18,000, the total consideration furnished by the wife is $12,000, and the total consideration furnished by both spouses is $30,000.

(c) The application of this section may be illustrated by the following examples:

Example (1). In 1956 the husband furnished $30,000 and his wife furnished $10,000 of the consideration for the purchase and subsequent improvement of real property held by them as tenants by the entirety. The husband did not elect to treat the consideration furnished as a gift. The property later is sold for $60,000, the husband receiving $35,000 and his wife receiving $25,000 of the proceeds of the termination. The termination of the tenancy results in a gift of $10,000 by the husband to his wife, computed as follows:

$$\frac{\$30,000 \text{ (consideration furnished by husband)}}{\$40,000 \text{ (total consideration furnished by both spouses)}} \times \$60,000 \text{ (proceeds of termination)} = \$45,000$$

$45,000 — $35,000 (proceeds received by husband) = $10,000 gift by husband to wife.

Example (2). In 1950 the husband purchased shares of X Company for $10,000. In 1955 when those shares had a fair market value of $30,000, he and his wife purchased real property from A and had it conveyed to them as tenants by the entirety. In payment for the real property, the husband transferred his shares of X Company to A and the wife paid A the sum of $10,000. They later sold the real property for $60,000, divided $24,000 (each taking $12,000) and reinvested the remaining $36,000 in other real property under circumstances that satisfied the conditions set forth in paragraph (d)(2)(ii) of § 25.2515-1. The tenancy was terminated only with respect to the $24,000 divided between them. This termination of the tenancy resulted in a gift of $6,000 by the husband to the wife, computed as follows:

$$\frac{\$30,000 \text{ (consideration furnished by husband)}}{\$40,000 \text{ (total consideration furnished by both spouses)}} \times \$24,000 \text{ (proceeds of termination)} = \$18,000$$

$18,000 — $12,000 (proceeds received by husband) = $6,000 gift by husband to wife.

Since the tenancy was terminated only in part, with respect to the remaining portion of the tenancy each spouse is considered as having furnished that proportion of the total consideration for the remaining portion of the tenancy as the consideration furnished by him before the sale bears to the total consideration furnished by both spouses before the sale. See paragraph (c) of § 25.2515-1. The consideration furnished by the husband for the reduced tenancy is $27,000, computed as follows:

$$\frac{\$30,000 \text{ (consideration furnished by husband before sale)}}{\$40,000 \text{ (total consideration furnished by both spouses before sale)}} \times \$36,000 \text{ (consideration for reduced tenancy)} = \$27,000$$

The consideration furnished by the wife is $9,000, computed in a similar manner.

§ 25.2515-4 **Termination of tenancy by entirety; cases in which none, or a portion only, of value of gift is determined under section 2515(b)**— (a) *In general.* The rules provided in section 2515(b) (see § 25.2515-3) are not applied in determining whether a gift has been made at the termination of a tenancy to the extent that the consideration furnished for the creation of the tenancy was treated as a gift or if the consideration for the creation of the tenancy was furnished by a third party. Consideration furnished for the creation of the tenancy was treated as a gift if it was furnished either (1) during calendar years prior to 1955, or (2) during the calendar year 1955 and subsequent years and the donor spouse exercised the election to treat the furnishing of consideration as a gift. See paragraph (b) of this section for the manner of computing the value of gifts resulting from the termination of the tenancy under these circumstances. See paragraph (c) of this section for the rules to be applied where part of the total consideration for the creation of the tenancy and additions to the value thereof was not treated as a gift and part either was treated as a gift or was furnished by a third party.

(b) *Value of gift when entire consideration is of the type described in paragraph (a) of this section.* If the entire consideration for the creation of a tenancy by the entirety was treated as a gift or contributed by a third party, the determination of the amount, if any, of a gift made at the termination of the tenancy will be made by the application of the general principles set forth in § 25.2511-1. Under those principles, when a spouse surrenders a property interest in a tenancy, the creation of which was treated as a gift, and in return receives an amount (whether in the form of cash, property, or an interest in property) less than the value of the property interest surrendered, that spouse is deemed to have made a gift in an amount equal to the difference between the value, at the time of termination, of the property interest surrendered by such spouse and the amount received in exchange. Thus, if the husband's interest in such a tenancy at the time of termination is worth $44,971 and the wife's interest therein at the time is worth $55,029, the property is sold for $100,000, and each spouse receives $50,000 out of the proceeds of the sale, the wife has made a gift to the husband of $5,029. The principles applied in paragraph (c) of § 25.2515-2 for the method of determining the value of the respective interests of the spouses at the time of the creation of a tenancy by the entirety are equally applicable in determining the value of each spouse's interest in the tenancy at termination, except that the actuarial factors to be applied are those for the respective spouses at the ages attained at the date of termination.

(c) *Valuation of gift where both types of consideration are involved.* If the consideration furnished consists in part of the type described in paragraph (a) of § 25.2515-3 (consideration furnished by the spouses after 1954, and not treated as a gift in the year furnished) and in part of the type described in paragraph (a) of this section (consideration furnished by the spouses and treated as a gift or furnished by a third party), the amount of the gift is determined as follows:

(1) By applying the principles set forth in paragraph (b) of § 25.2515-3 to that portion of the total proceeds of termination which the consideration described in paragraph (a) of § 25.2515-3 bears to the total consideration furnished;

(2) By applying the principles set forth in paragraph (b) of this

section to the remaining portion of the total proceeds of termination; and

(3) By subtracting the proceeds of termination received by the donor from the total of the amounts which under the principles referred to in subparagraphs (1) and (2) of this paragraph are to be compared with the proceeds of termination received by a spouse in determining whether a gift was made by that spouse.

For example assume that consideration of $30,000 was furnished by the husband in 1954. Assume also that on February 1, 1955, the husband contributed $12,000 and the wife $8,000, the husband's contribution not being treated as a gift (see paragraph (b) of § 25.2515-1). Assume further that between 1957 and 1965 the property appreciated in value by $40,000 and was sold in 1965 for $90,000 (of which the husband received $40,000 and the wife $50,000). The principles set forth in paragraph (b) of § 25.2515-3 are applied to $36,000 (20,000/50,000 x $90,000) in arriving at the amount which is compared with the proceeds of termination received by a spouse. Applying the principles set forth in paragraph (b) of § 25.2515-3, this amount in the case of the husband is $21,600 (12,000/20,000 x $36,000). Similarly, the principles set forth in paragraph (b) of this section are applied to $54,000 ($90,000 — 36,000), the remaining portion of the proceeds of termination, in arriving at the amount which is compared with the proceeds of termination received by a spouse. If in this case either spouse, without the consent of the other spouse, can bring about a severance of his interest in the tenancy, the amount determined under paragraph (b) of this section in the case of the husband would be $27,000 ($\frac{1}{2}$ of $54,000). The total of the two amounts which are to be compared with the proceeds of termination received by the husband is $48,600 ($21,600 + 27,000). This sum of $48,600 is then compared with the $40,000 proceeds received by the husband, and the termination of the tenancy has resulted, for gift tax purposes, in a transfer of $8,600 by the husband to his wife in 1965. See paragraph (d) of this section for an additional example illustrating the application of this paragraph.

(d) The application of paragraph (c) of this section may further be illustrated by the following example:

Example. X died in 1948 and devised real property to Y and Z (Y's wife) as tenants by the entirety. Under the law of the jurisdiction, both spouses are entitled to share equally in the income from, or the enjoyment of, the property, but neither spouse, acting alone, may defeat the right of the survivor of them to the whole of the property. The fair market value of the property at the time of X's death was $100,000 and this amount is the consideration which X furnished toward the creation of the tenancy. In 1955, at which time the fair market value of the property was the same as at the time of X's death, improvements of $50,000 were made to the property, of which Y furnished $40,000 out of his own funds and Z furnished $10,000 out of her own funds. Y did not elect to treat his transfer to the tenancy as resulting in the making of a gift in 1955. In 1956 the property was sold for $300,000 and Y and Z each received $150,000 of the proceeds. At the time the property was sold Y and Z were 45 and 40 years of age, respectively, on their birthdays nearest the date of sale. The value of the gift made by Y to Z is $19,942, computed as follows:

Amount determined under principles set forth in § 25.2515-3:

$$\frac{\$50,000 \text{ (consideration not treated as gift in year furnished)}}{\$150,000 \text{ (total consideration furnished)}} \times \$300,000 \text{ (proceeds of termination)} = \$100,000 \begin{array}{l}\text{(proceeds of termination to which principles set forth in § 25.2515-3 apply)}\end{array}$$

$$\frac{\$40,000 \text{ (consideration furnished by H and not treated as gift)}}{\$50,000 \text{ (total consideration not treated as gift)}} \times \$100,000 = \$80,000$$

Amount determined under principles set forth in paragraph (b) of this section:

$$\$300,000 \begin{array}{l}\text{(total proceeds of termination)}\end{array} - \$100,000 \begin{array}{l}\text{(proceeds to which principles set forth in § 25.2515-3 apply)}\end{array} = \$200,000 \begin{array}{l}\text{(proceeds to which principles set forth in paragraph (b) apply)}\end{array}$$

$.44971$ (factor for Y's interest) $\times$ $200,000 = $89,942

Amount of gift

Amount determined under § 25.2515-3	$ 80,000
Amount determined under paragraph (b)	89,942
Total	$169,942
Less: Proceeds received by Y	150,000
Amount of gift made by Y to Z	$ 19,942

Property Settlements

§ 25.2516-1 **Certain property settlements.** (a) Section 2516 provides that transfers of property or interests in property made under the terms of a written agreement between spouses in settlement of their marital or property rights are deemed to be for an adequate and full consideration in money or money's worth and, therefore, exempt from the gift tax (whether or not such agreement is approved by a divorce decree), if the spouses obtain a final decree of divorce from each other within two years after entering into the agreement.

(b) See paragraph (b) of § 25.6019-3 for the circumstances under which information relating to property settlements must be disclosed on the transferor's gift tax return for the calendar year in which the agreement becomes effective.

§ 25.2516-2 **Transfers in settlement of support obligations.** Transfers to provide a reasonable allowance for the support of children (including legally adopted children) of a marriage during minority are not subject to the gift tax if made pursuant to an agreement which satisfies the requirements of section 2516.

Specific Exemption

§ 25.2521-1 **Specific exemption.** (a) In determining the amount of taxable gifts for the calendar year there may be deducted, if the donor was a resident or citizen of the United States at the time the gifts were made, a specific exemption of $30,000, less the sum of the amounts claimed and allowed as an exemption in prior calendar years. The exemption, at the option of the donor, may be taken in the full amount of $30,000 in a single calendar year, or be spread over a period of years in such amounts as the donor sees fit, but after the limit has been reached no further exemption is allowable. Except as otherwise provided in a tax convention between the United States and another country, a donor who was a nonresident not a citizen of the United States at the time the gift or gifts were made is not entitled to this exemption.

(b) No part of a donor's lifetime specific exemption of $30,000 may be deducted from the value of a gift attributable to his spouse where a husband and wife consent, under the provisions of section 2513, to have the gifts made during a calendar year considered as made one-half by each of them. The "gift-splitting" provisions of section 2513 do not authorize the filing of a joint gift tax return nor permit a donor to claim any of his spouse's specific exemption. For example, if a husband has no specific exemption remaining available, but his wife does, and the husband makes a gift to which his wife consents under the provisions of section 2513, the specific exemption remaining available may be claimed only on the return of the wife with respect to one half of the gift. The husband may not claim any specific exemption since he has none available.

(c) The amount by which the specific exemption claimed and allowed in gift tax returns for prior calendar years exceeds $30,000 is includible in determining the aggregate sum of the taxable gifts for preceding calendar years. See paragraph (b) of § 25.2504-1.

Charitable Gifts

§ 25.2522(a)-1 **Charitable and similar gifts; citizens or residents.** (a) In determining the amount of taxable gifts for the calendar year there may be deducted, in the case of a donor who was a citizen or resident of the United States at the time the gifts were made, all gifts included in the "total amount of gifts" made by the donor during the taxable year (see section 2503 and the regulations thereunder) and made to or for the use of:

(1) The United States, any State, Territory, or any political subdivision thereof, or the District of Columbia, for exclusively public purposes.

(2) Any corporation, trust, community chest, fund or foundation organized and operated exclusively for religious, charitable, scientific, literary, or educational purposes, including the encouragement of art and the prevention of cruelty to children or animals, if no part of the net earnings of the organization inures to the benefit of any private

shareholder or individual, and no substantial part of its activities is carrying on propaganda, or otherwise attempting, to influence legislation.

(3) A fraternal society, order, or association, operating under the lodge system, provided the gifts are to be used by the society, order or association exclusively for one or more of the purposes set forth in subparagraph (2) of this paragraph.

(4) Any post or organization of war veterans or auxiliary unit or society thereof, if organized in the United States or any of its possessions, and if no part of its net earnings inures to the benefit of any private shareholder or individual.

The deduction is not limited to gifts for use within the United States, or to gifts to or for the use of domestic corporations, trusts, community chests, funds or foundations, or fraternal societies, orders or associations operating under the lodge system. For the deductions for charitable and similar gifts made by a nonresident who was not a citizen of the United States at the time the gifts were made, see § 25.2522(b)-1.

(b) The deduction under section 2522 is not allowed for a transfer to a corporation, trust, community chest, fund or foundation unless the organization or trust meets the following three tests:

(1) It must be organized and operated exclusively for one or more of the specified purposes.

(2) It must not by a substantial part of its activities attempt to influence legislation by propaganda or otherwise.

(3) Its net earnings must not inure in whole or in part to the benefit of private shareholders or individuals other than as legitimate objects of the exempt purposes.

For further limitations see § 25.2522(c)-1, relating to gifts to trusts and organizations which have engaged in a prohibited transaction described in section 681(b)(2) or section 503(c).

(c) In order to prove the right to the charitable, etc., deduction provided by section 2522, the donor must submit such data as may be requested by the district director. As to the extent the deductions provided by this section are allowable, see section 2524.

§ 25.2522(a)-2 Transfers not exclusively for charitable, etc., purposes—(a) *Remainders and similar interests.* If a trust is created or property is transferred for both a charitable and a private purpose, deduction may be taken of the value of the charitable beneficial interest only insofar as that interest is presently ascertainable, and hence severable from the noncharitable interest. The present value of a remainder or other deferred payment to be made for a charitable purpose is to be determined in accordance with the rules stated in § 25.2512-5. Thus, if money or property is placed in trust to pay the income to an individual during his life, or for a term of years, and then to pay the principal to a charitable organization, the present value of the remainder is deductible. To determine the present value of such remainder use the appropriate factor from column 4 of Table I or II of § 25.2512-5, whichever is applicable. If the interest involved is such that its value is to be determined by a special computation (see paragraph (e) of § 25.2512-5), a request for a specific factor accompanied by a statement of the date of birth of each person, the duration of whose life may affect the value of the remainder, and by copies of the relevant instruments may be submitted by the donor to the Commissioner, who may, if conditions permit, supply the factor requested. If the Commissioner does not furnish the factor, the claim for deduction must be supported by a full statement of the computation of the present value made in accordance with the principles set forth in the applicable paragraph of § 25.2512-5.

(b) *Transfers subject to a condition or a power.* If, as of the date of the gift, a transfer for charitable purposes is dependent upon the performance of some act or the happening of a precedent event in order that it might become effective, no deduction is allowable unless the possibility that the charitable transfer will not become effective is so remote as to be negligible. If an estate or interest passes to or is vested in charity on the date of the gift and the estate or interest would be defeated by the performance of some act or the happening of some event, the occurrence of which appeared to have been highly improbable on the date of the gift, the deduction is allowable. If the donee or trustee is empowered to divert the property or fund, in whole or in part, to a use or purpose which would have rendered it, to the extent that it is subject to such power, not deductible had it been directly so given by the donor, the deduction will be limited to that portion of the property or fund which is exempt from the exercise of the power. The deduction is not allowed in the case of a transfer in trust conveying to charity a present interest in income if by reason of all the conditions and circumstances surrounding the transfer it appears that the charity may not receive the beneficial enjoyment of the interest. For example, assume that assets placed in trust by the donor consist of stock in a corporation, the fiscal policies of which are controlled by the donor and his family, that the trustees and remaindermen are likewise members of the donor's family, and that the governing instrument contains no adequate guarantee of the requisite income to the charitable organization. Under such circumstances, no deduction will be allowed. Similarly, if the trustees were not members of the donor's family but had no power to sell or otherwise dispose of closely held stock, or otherwise insure the requisite enjoyment of income to the charitable organization, no deduction will be allowed.

§ 25.2522(b)-1 **Charitable and similar gifts; nonresidents not citizens.** (a) The deduction for charitable and similar gifts, in the case of a nonresident who was not a citizen of the United States at the time he made the gifts is governed by the same rules as those applying to gifts by citizens or residents, subject, however, to the following exceptions:

(1) If the gifts are made to or for the use of a corporation, the corporation must be one created or organized under the laws of the United States or of any State or Territory thereof.

(2) If the gifts are made to or for the use of a trust, community

1103

chest, fund or foundation, or a fraternal society, order or association operating under the lodge system, the gifts must be for use within the United States exclusively for religious, charitable, scientific, literary or educational purposes, including encouragement of art and the prevention of cruelty to children or animals.

§ 25.2522(c)-1 Disallowance of charitable, etc., deductions because of prohibited transactions. (a) Sections 503(e) and 681(b)(5) provide that no deduction which would otherwise be allowable under section 2522 for a gift for religious, charitable, scientific, literary or educational purposes, including the encouragement of art and the prevention of cruelty to children or animals, is allowed if—

(1) The gift is made in trust and, for income tax purposes for the taxable year of the trust in which the gift is made, the deduction otherwise allowable to the trust under section 642(c) is limited by section 681(b)(1) by reason of the trust having engaged in a prohibited transaction described in section 681(b)(2); or

(2) The gift is made to any corporation, community chest, fund or foundation which, for its taxable year in which the gift is made, is not exempt from income tax under section 501(a) by reason of having engaged in a prohibited transaction described in section 503(c).

(b) For purposes of section 503(e) and section 681(b)(5), the term "gift" includes any gift, contribution, or transfer without adequate consideration.

(c) Regulations relating to the income tax contain the rules for the determination of the taxable year of the trust for which the deduction under section 642(c) is limited by section 681(b), and for the determination of the taxable year of the organization for which an exemption is denied under section 503(a). Generally, such taxable year is a taxable year subsequent to the taxable year during which the trust or organization has been notified by the Internal Revenue Service that it has engaged in a prohibited transaction. However, if the trust or organization during or prior to the taxable year entered into the prohibited transaction for the purpose of diverting its corpus or income from the charitable or other purposes by reason of which it is entitled to a deduction or exemption, and the transaction involves a substantial part of such income or corpus, then the deduction of the trust under section 642(c) for such taxable year is limited by section 681(b), or the exemption of the organization for such taxable year is denied under section 503(a), whether or not the organization has previously received notification by the Internal Revenue Service that it has engaged in a prohibited transaction. In certain cases, the limitation of section 503 or 681 may be removed or the exemption may be reinstated for certain subsequent taxable years under the rules set forth in the income tax regulations under sections 503 and 681.

(d) In cases in which prior notification by the Internal Revenue Service is not required in order to limit the deduction of the trust under section 681(b), or to deny exemption of the organization under section 503, the deduction otherwise allowable under § 25.2522(a)-1 is not disallowed with respect to gifts made during the same taxable year of the trust or organization in which a prohibited transaction occurred, or in a prior taxable year, unless the donor or a member of his family was a party to the prohibited transaction. For purposes of the preceding sentence, the members of the donor's family include only his brothers and sisters (whether by whole or half blood), spouse, ancestors, and lineal descendants.

Gift to Spouse

§ 25.2523(a)-1 **Gift to spouse; in general**—(a) *In general.* In determining the amount of taxable gifts for the calendar year 1955 or any calendar year thereafter, in the case of a donor who was a citizen or resident of the United States at the time the gift was made, there may be deducted an amount equal to one-half the value of any property interest (except as otherwise provided in paragraph (b) of this section) transferred by gift to a donee who at the time of the gift was the donor's spouse. This deduction is referred to as the "marital deduction." No marital deduction is authorized with respect to a gift if the donor, at the time of the gift, was a nonresident not a citizen of the United States. However, if the donor was a citizen or resident of the United States at the time the gift was made, he is not deprived of the right to the marital deduction by reason of the fact that his spouse was a nonresident not a citizen. For convenience the donor's spouse is generally referred to in the feminine gender, but if the donor is a woman the reference is to her husband. The donor must submit such proof as is necessary to establish the right to the marital deduction, including any evidence requested by the district director.

(b) *"Deductible interests" and "nondeductible interests."* The property interests transferred by a donor to his spouse fall within two general categories: (1) those with respect to which the marital deduction is authorized, and (2) those with respect to which the deduction is not authorized. These categories are referred to in this section and §§ 25.2523(b)-1 through 25.2523(f)-1 as "deductible interests" and "nondeductible interests," respectively (see subdivision (ii) of this paragraph). Subject to the limitations set forth in §§ 25.2523(f)-1 (relating to gifts of community property) and 25.2524-1 (relating to cases in which the total value of the gifts made to the donee spouse in any one year is less than $6,000), the marital deduction is equal to one-half of the aggregate value of the "deductible interests." A property interest transferred by a donor to his spouse is a "deductible interest" if it does not fall within one of the two following classes of "nondeductible interest":

(i) A property interest transferred by a donor to his spouse which is a "terminable interest", as defined in § 25.2523(b)-1, is a "nondeductible interest" to the extent specified in that section.

(ii) Any property interest transferred by a donor to his spouse is a "nondeductible interest" to the extent that it is not included in the total amount of gifts made during the calendar year. See §§ 25.2515-1 (relating to tenancies by the entirety) and 25.2516-1 (relating to property settlements, followed by divorce) for some, but not necessarily all, of the situations in which property is transferred by a donor to his spouse and not included in the total amount of gifts made during the calendar year. If the total gifts made by a donor to his spouse during a calendar year have a value of $6,000 or more the amount of the marital deduction is determined without regard to the amount of the exclusion, if any, allowable. For example, assume that in 1955 a donor made a cash gift of $10,000 to his wife. No other gifts were made by the donor in 1955. The amount of the marital deduction is one-half of $10,000, or $5,000; the amount of the exclusion is $3,000; and the total amount of included gifts is $2,000. See § 25.2524-1 with respect to the amount of the marital deduction allowable where the total gifts made in a calendar year by a donor to his spouse have a value of less than $6,000.

(c) *Valuation.* If the income from property is made payable to the donor or another individual for life, or for a term of years, with remainder absolutely to the donor's spouse or to her estate, the marital deduction is equal to one-half the present value of the remainder. The present value of the remainder (that is, its value as of the date of gift) is to be determined in accordance with the rules stated in § 25.2512-5. For example, if the donor's spouse is to receive $50,000 upon the death of a person 31 years of age, the present value of the remainder is $14,466. See the example in paragraph (d) of § 25.2512-5. If the remainder is such that its value is to be determined by a special computation (see § 25.2512-5), a request for a specific factor, accompanied by a statement of the dates of birth of each person, the duration of whose life may affect the value of the remainder, and by copies of the relevant instruments may be submitted by the donor to the Commissioner who, if conditions permit, may supply the factor requested. If the Commissioner does not furnish the factor, the claim for deduction must be supported by a full statement of the computation of the present value, made in accordance with the principles set forth in § 25.2512-5.

§ 25.2523(b)-1 **Life estate or other terminable interest**—(a) *In general.* (1) The provisions of section 2523(b) generally prevent the allowance of the marital deduction with respect to certain property interests (referred to generally as "terminable interests," defined in subparagraph (3) of this paragraph), transferred to the donee spouse under the circumstances described in subparagraph (2) of this paragraph, unless the transfer comes within one of the exceptions set forth in § 25.2523(d)-1, relating to certain joint interests, or § 25.2523-(e)-1, relating to certain life estates with powers of appointment.

(2) If a donor transfers a terminable interest in property to the donee spouse, the marital deduction is disallowed with respect to the transfer if the donor spouse also—

(i) Transferred an interest in the same property to another donee (see paragraph (b) of this section), or

(ii) Retained an interest in the same property in himself (see paragraph (c) of this section), or

(iii) Retained a power to appoint an interest in the same property (see paragraph (d) of this section).

Notwithstanding the preceding sentence, the marital deduction is disallowed under these circumstances only if the other donee, the donor, or the possible appointee, may, by reason of the transfer or retention, possess or enjoy any part of the property after the termination or failure of the interest therein transferred to the donee spouse.

(3) For purposes of this section, a distinction is to be drawn between "property," as such term is used in section 2523, and an "interest in property." The "property" referred to is the underlying property in which various interests exist; each such interest is not, for this purpose, to be considered as "property." A "terminable interest" in property is an interest which will terminate or fail on the lapse of time or on the occurrence or failure to occur of some contingency. Life estates, terms of years, annuities, patents, and copyrights are therefore terminable interests. However, a bond, note, or similar contractual obligation, the discharge of which would not have the effect of an annuity or term of years, is not a terminable interest.

(b) *Interest in property which another donee may possess or enjoy.* (1) Section 2523(b) provides that no marital deduction shall be allowed with respect to the transfer to the donee spouse of a "terminable interest" in property, in case—

(i) The donor transferred (for less than an adequate and full consideration in money or money's worth) an interest in the same property to any person other than the donee spouse (or the estate of such spouse), and,

(ii) By reason of such transfer, such person (or his heirs or assigns) may possess or enjoy any part of such property after the termination or failure of the interest therein transferred to the donee spouse.

(2) In determining whether the donor transferred an interest in property to any person other than the donee spouse, it is immaterial whether the transfer to the person other than the donee spouse was made at the same time as the transfer to such spouse, or at any earlier time.

(3) Except as provided in § 25.2523(e)-1, if at the time of the transfer it is impossible to ascertain the particular person or persons who may receive a property interest transferred by the donor, such interest is considered as transferred to a person other than the donee spouse for the purpose of section 2523(b). This rule is particularly applicable in the case of the transfer of a property interest by the donor subject to a reserved power. See § 25.2511-2. Under this rule, any property interest over which the donor reserved a power to revest the beneficial title in himself, or over which the donor reserved the power to name new beneficiaries or to change the interests of the beneficiaries as between themselves, is for the purpose of section 2523(b), considered as transferred to a "person other than the donee

spouse." The following examples illustrate the application of the provisions of this subparagraph:

(i) If a donor transferred property in trust, naming his wife as the irrevocable income beneficiary for 10 years, and providing that, upon the expiration of that term, the corpus should be distributed among his wife and children in such proportions as the trustee should determine, the right to the corpus, for the purpose of the marital deduction, is considered as transferred to a "person other than the donee spouse."

(ii) If, in the above example, the donor had provided that, upon the expiration of the 10-year term, the corpus was to be paid to his wife, but also reserved the power to revest such corpus in himself, the right to corpus, for the purpose of the marital deduction, is considered as transferred to a "person other than the donee spouse."

(4) The term "person other than the donee spouse" includes the possible unascertained takers of a property interest, as, for example, the members of a class to be ascertained in the future. As another example, assume that the donor created a power of appointment over a property interest, which does not come within the purview of § 25.-2523(e)-1. In such a case, the term "person other than the donee spouse" refers to the possible appointees and takers in default (other than the spouse) of such property interest.

(5) An exercise or release at any time by the donor (either alone or in conjunction with any person) of a power to appoint an interest in property, even though not otherwise a transfer by him is considered as a transfer by him in determining, for the purpose of section 2523(b), whether he transferred an interest in such property to a person other than the donee spouse.

(6) The following examples illustrate the application of this paragraph. In each example it is assumed that the property interest which the donor transferred to a person other than the donee spouse was not transferred for an adequate and full consideration in money or money's worth:

(i) H (the donor) transferred real property to W (his wife) for life, with remainder to A and his heirs. No marital deduction may be taken with respect to the interest transferred to W, since it will terminate upon her death and A (or his heirs or assigns) will thereafter possess or enjoy the property.

(ii) H transferred property for the benefit of W and A. The income was payable to W for life and upon her death the principal was to be distributed to A or his issue. However, if A should die without issue, leaving W surviving, the principal was then to be distributed to W. No marital deduction may be taken with respect to the interest transferred to W, since it will terminate in the event of her death if A or his issue survive, and A or his issue will thereafter possess or enjoy the property.

(iii) H purchased for $100,000 a life annuity for W. If the annuity payments made during the life of W should be less than $100,000, further payments were to be made to A. No marital deduction may be taken with respect to the interest transferred to W, since A may possess or enjoy a part of the property following the termination of W's interest. If, however, the contract provided for no continuation of payments, and provided for no refund upon the death of W, or provided that any refund was to go to the estate of W, then a marital deduction may be taken with respect to the gift.

(iv) H transferred property to A for life with remainder to W provided W survives A, but if W predeceases A, the property is to pass to B and his heirs. No marital deduction may be taken with respect to the interest transferred to W.

(v) H transferred real property to A, reserving the right to the rentals of the property for a term of 20 years. H later transferred the right to the remaining rentals to W. No marital deduction may be taken with respect to the interest since it will terminate upon the expiration of the balance of the 20-year term and A will thereafter possess or enjoy the property.

(vi) H transferred a patent to W and A as tenants in common. In this case, the interest of W will terminate upon the expiration of the term of the patent, but possession and enjoyment of the property by A must necessarily cease at the same time. Therefore, since A's possession or enjoyment cannot outlast the termination of W's interest, the provisions of section 2523(b) do not disallow the marital deduction with respect to the interest.

(c) *Interest in property which the donor may possess or enjoy.* (1) Section 2523(b) provides that no marital deduction is allowed with respect to the transfer to the donee spouse of a "terminable interest" in property, if—

(i) The donor retained in himself an interest in the same property, and

(ii) By reason of such retention, the donor (or his heirs or assigns) may possess or enjoy any part of the property after the termination or failure of the interest transferred to the donee spouse. However, as to a transfer to the donee spouse as sole joint tenant with the donor or as tenant by the entirety, see § 25.2523(d)-1.

(2) In general, the principles illustrated by the examples under paragraph (b) of this section are applicable in determining whether the marital deduction may be taken with respect to a property interest transferred to the donee spouse subject to the retention by the donor of an interest in the same property. The application of this paragraph may be further illustrated by the following example:

Example. The donor purchased three annuity contracts for the benefit of his wife and himself. The first contract provided for payments to the wife for life, with refund to the donor in case the aggregate payments made to the wife were less than the cost of the contract. The second contract provided for payments to the donor for life, and then to the wife for life if she survived the donor. The third contract provided for payments to the donor and his wife for their joint lives and then to the survivor of them for life. No marital deduction may be taken with respect to the gifts resulting from the purchases of the contracts since, in the case of each contract, the donor may possess or enjoy a part of the property after the termination or failure of the interest transferred to the wife.

(d) *Interest in property over which the donor retained a power to appoint.* (1) Section 2523(b) provides that no marital deduction is allowed with respect to the transfer to the donee spouse of a "terminable interest" in property if—

(i) The donor had, immediately after the transfer, a power to appoint an interest in the same property, and

(ii) The donor's power was exercisable (either alone or in conjunction with any person) in such manner that the appointee may possess or enjoy any part of the property after the termination or failure of the interest transferred to the donee spouse.

(2) For the purposes of section 2523(b), the donor is to be considered as having, immediately after the transfer to the donee spouse, such a power to appoint even though the power cannot be exercised until after the lapse of time, upon the occurrence of an event or contingency, or upon the failure of an event or contingency to occur. It is immaterial whether the power retained by the donor was a taxable power of appointment under section 2514.

(3) The principles illustrated by the examples under paragraph (b) of this section are generally applicable in determining whether the marital deduction may be taken with respect to a property interest transferred to the donee spouse subject to retention by the donor of a power to appoint an interest in the same property. The application of this paragraph may be further illustrated by the following example:

Example. The donor, having a power of appointment over certain property, appointed a life estate to his spouse. No marital deduction may be taken with respect to such transfer, since, if the retained power to appoint the remainder interest is exercised, the appointee thereunder may possess or enjoy the property after the termination or failure of the interest taken by the donee spouse.

§ 25.2523(c)-1 **Interest in unidentified assets.** (a) Section 2523(c) provides that if an interest passing to a donee spouse may be satisfied out of a group of assets (or their proceeds) which include a particular asset that would be a nondeductible interest if it passed from the donor to his spouse, the value of the interest passing to the spouse is reduced, for the purpose of the marital deduction, by the value of the particular asset.

(b) In order for this section to apply, two circumstances must co-exist, as follows:

(1) The property interest transferred to the donee spouse must be payable out of a group of assets. An example of a property interest payable out of a group of assets is a right to a share of the corpus of a trust upon its termination.

(2) The group of assets out of which the property interest is payable must include one or more particular assets which, if transferred by the donor to the donee spouse, would not qualify for the marital

1110

deduction. Therefore, section 2523(c) is not applicable merely because a group of assets includes a terminable interest, but would only be applicable if the terminable interest were nondeductible under the provisions of § 25.2523(b)-1.

(c) If the circumstances in the preceding paragraph are both present, the marital deduction with respect to such property interest may not exceed one-half of the excess, if any, of its value over the aggregate value of the particular asset or assets which, if transferred to the donee spouse, would not qualify for the marital deduction. The application of this section may be illustrated by the following example:

Example. H was absolute owner of a rental property and on July 1, 1950, transferred it to A by gift, reserving the income for a period of 20 years. On July 1, 1955, he created a trust to last for a period of 10 years. H was to receive the income from the trust and at the termination of the trust the trustee is to turn over to H's wife, W, property having a value of $100,000. The trustee has absolute discretion in deciding which properties in the corpus he shall turn over to W in satisfaction of the gift to her. The trustee received two items of property from H. Item (1) consisted of shares of corporate stock. Item (2) consisted of the right to receive the income from the rental property during the unexpired portion of the 20-year term. Assume that at the termination of the trust on July 1, 1965, the value of the right to the rental income for the then unexpired term of 5 years (item 2) will be $30,000. Since item (2) is a nondeductible interest and the trustee can turn it over to W in partial satisfaction of her gift, only $70,000 of the $100,000 receivable by her on July 1, 1965, will be considered as property with respect to which a marital deduction is allowable. The present value on July 1, 1955, of the right to receive $70,000 at the end of 10 years is $49,624.33 (70,000 x .708919, as found in Table II of § 25.2512-5). The value of the property qualifying for the marital deduction, therefore, is $49,624.33 and a marital deduction is allowed for one-half of that amount, or $24,812.17.

§ 25.2523(d)-1 Joint interests. Section 2523(d) provides that if a property interest is transferred to the donee spouse as sole joint tenant with the donor or as a tenant by the entirety, the interest of the donor in the property which exists solely by reason of the possibility that the donor may survive the donee spouse, or that there may occur a severance of the tenancy, is not for the purposes of section 2523(b), to be considered as an interest retained by the donor in himself. Under this provision, the fact that the donor may, as surviving tenant, possess or enjoy the property after the termination of the interest transferred to the donee spouse does not preclude the allowance of the marital deduction with respect to the latter interest. Thus, if the donor purchased real property in the name of himself and wife as tenants by the entirety, or as joint tenants with right of survivorship and, pursuant to the provisions of section 2515(c), elected to treat such transaction as a completed gift in the calendar year affected, a marital deduction equal to one-half the value of the interest of the

1111

donee spouse in such property may be taken. See paragraph (c) of § 25.2523(b)-1, and section 2524.

§ 25.2523(e)-1 Marital deduction; life estate with power of appointment in donee spouse—(a) *In general.* Section 2523(e) provides that if an interest in property is transferred by a donor to his spouse (whether or not in trust) and the spouse is entitled for life to all the income from the entire interest or all the income from a specific portion of the entire interest, with a power in her to appoint the entire interest or the specific portion, the interest transferred to her is a deductible interest, to the extent that it satisfies all five of the conditions set forth below (see paragraph (b) of this section if one or more of the conditions is satisfied as to only a portion of the interest):

(1) The donee spouse must be entitled for life to all of the income from the entire interest or a specific portion of the entire interest, or to a specific portion of all the income from the entire interest.

(2) The income payable to the donee spouse must be payable annually or at more frequent intervals.

(3) The donee spouse must have the power to appoint the entire interest or the specific portion to either herself or her estate.

(4) The power in the donee spouse must be exercisable by her alone and (whether exercisable by will or during life) must be exercisable in all events.

(5) The entire interest or the specific portion must not be subject to a power in any other person to appoint any part to any person other than the donee spouse.

(b) *Specific portion; deductible amount.* If either the right to income or the power of appointment given to the donee spouse pertains only to a specific portion of a property interest, the portion of the interest which qualifies as a deductible interest is limited to the extent that the rights in the donee spouse meet all of the five conditions described in paragraph (a) of this section. While the rights over the income and the power must coexist as to the same interest in property, it is not necessary that the rights over the income or the power as to such interest be in the same proportion. However, if the rights over income meeting the required conditions set forth in paragraph (a)(1) and (2) of this section extend over a smaller share of the property interest than the share with respect to which the power of appointment requirements set forth in paragraph (a)(3) through (5) of this section are satisfied, the deductible interest is limited to the smaller share. Conversely, if a power of appointment meeting all the requirements extends to a smaller portion of the property interest than the portion over which the income rights pertain, the deductible interest cannot exceed the value of the portion to which such power of appointment applies. Thus, if the donor gives to the donee spouse the right to receive annually all of the income from a particular property interest and a power of appointment meeting the specifications prescribed in paragraph (a)(3) through (5) of this section as to only one-half of the property interest, then only one-half of the property interest is treated as a deductible interest. Correspondingly, if the income interest of the spouse satisfying the requirements extends to only one-fourth of the property interest and a testamentary power of appointment satisfying the requirements extends to all of the property interest, then only one-fourth of the interest in the spouse qualifies as a deductible interest. Further, if the donee spouse has no right to income from a specific portion of a property interest but a testamentary power of appointment which meets the necessary conditions over the entire interest, then none of the interest qualifies for the deduction. In addition, if, from the time of the transfer, the donee spouse has a power of appointment meeting all of the required conditions over three-fourths of the entire property interest and the prescribed income rights over the entire interest, but with a power in another person to appoint one-half of the entire interest, the value of the interest in the donee spouse over only one-half of the property interest will qualify as a deductible interest.

(c) *Definition of "specific portion"*. A partial interest in property is not treated as a specific portion of the entire interest unless the rights of the donee spouse in income and as to the power constitute a fractional or percentile share of a property interest so that such interest or share in the donee spouse reflects its proportionate share of the increment or decline in the whole of the property interest to which the income rights and the power relate. Thus, if the right of the spouse to income and the power extend to one-half or a specified percentage of the property, or the equivalent, the interest is considered as a specific portion. On the other hand, if the annual income of the spouse is limited to a specific sum, or if she has a power to appoint only a specific sum out of a larger fund, the interest is not a deductible interest. Even though the rights in the donee spouse may not be expressed in terms of a definite fraction or percentage, a deduction may be allowable if it is shown that the effect of local law is to give the spouse rights which are identical to those she would have acquired if the size of the share had been expressed in terms of a definite fraction or percentage. The following examples illustrate the application of this and the preceding paragraphs of this section:

Example (1). The donor transferred to a trustee 500 identical shares of X Company stock. He provided that during the lifetime of the donee spouse the trustee should pay her annually one-half of the trust income or $6,000, whichever is the larger. The spouse was also given a general power of appointment, exercisable by her last will over the sum of $160,000 or over three-fourths of the trust corpus, whichever should be of larger value. Since there is no certainty that the trust income will not vary from year to year, for purposes of paragraphs (a) and (b) of this section, an annual payment of a specified sum, such as the $6,000 provided for in this case, is not considered as representing the income from a definite fraction or a specific portion of the entire interest if that were the extent of the spouse's interest. However, since the spouse is to receive annually at least one-half of the trust income, she will, for purposes of paragraphs (a) and (b) of this section, be considered as receiving all of the income from one-half of the entire interest in the stock. Inasmuch as there is no certainty that the value of the stock will be the same on the date of the donee spouse's death as it was on the date of the transfer to the trustee, for purposes of paragraphs (a) and (b) of this section, a specified sum, such as the $160,000 provided for in this case, is not considered to be a definite fraction of the entire interest. However, since the donee spouse has a general power of appointment over at least three-fourths of the trust corpus, she is considered as having a general power of appointment over three fourths of the entire interest in the stock.

Example (2). The donor transferred to a trustee an office building and 250 identical shares of Y Company stock. He provided that during the lifetime of the donee spouse the trustee should pay her annually three-fourths of the trust income. The spouse was given a general power of appointment, exercisable by will, over the office building and 100 shares of the stock. By the terms of the trust instrument the donee spouse is given all the income from a definite fraction of the entire interest in the office building and in the stock. She also has a general power of appointment over the entire interest in the office building. However, since the amount of property represented by a single share of stock would be altered if the corporation split its stock, issued stock dividends, made a distribution of capital, etc., a power to appoint 100 shares at the time of the donee spouse's death is not the same necessarily as a power to appoint 100/250 of the entire interest which the 250 shares represented on the date of the gift. If it is shown in this case that the effect of local law is to give the spouse a general power to appoint not only the 100 shares designated by the donor but also 100/250 of any shares or amounts which are distributed by the corporation and included in the corpus, the requirements of this paragraph will be satisfied and the donee spouse will be considered as having a general power to appoint 100/250 of the entire interest in the 250 shares.

(d) *Definition of "entire interest"*. Since a marital deduction is allowed for each qualifying separate interest in property transferred by the donor to the donee spouse, for purposes of paragraphs (a) and (b) of this section, each property interest with respect to which the donee spouse received some rights is considered separately in determining whether her rights extend to the entire interest or to a specific portion of the entire interest. A property interest which consists of several identical units of property (such as a block of 250 shares of stock, whether the ownership is evidenced by one or several certificates) is considered one property interest, unless certain of the units are to be segregated and accorded different treatment, in which case each segregated group of items is considered a separate property interest. The bequest of a specified sum of money constitutes the bequest of a separate property interest if immediately following the transfer and thenceforth it, and the investments made with it, must be so segregated or accounted for as to permit its identification as a

1114

separate item of property. The application of this paragraph may be illustrated by the following examples:

Example (1). The donor transferred to a trustee three adjoining farms, Blackacre, Whiteacre, and Greenacre. The trust instrument provided that during the lifetime of the donee spouse the trustee should pay her all of the income from the trust. Upon her death, all of Blackacre, a one-half interest in Whiteacre, and a one-third interest in Greenacre were to be distributed to the person or persons appointed by her in her will. The donee spouse is considered as being entitled to all of the income from the entire interest in Blackacre, all of the income from the entire interest in Whiteacre, and all of the income from the entire interest in Greenacre. She also is considered as having a power of appointment over the entire interest in Blackacre, over one-half of the entire interest in Whiteacre, and over one-third of the entire interest in Greenacre.

Example (2). The donor transferred $250,000 to C, as trustee. C is to invest the money and pay all of the income from the investments to W, the donor's spouse, annually. W was given a general power, exercisable by will, to appoint one-half of the corpus of the trust. Here, immediately following establishment of the trust, the $250,000 will be sufficiently segregated to permit its identification as a separate item, and the $250,000 will constitute an entire property interest. Therefore, W has a right to income and a power of appointment such that one-half of the entire interest is a deductible interest.

Example (3). The donor transferred 100 shares of Z Corporation stock to D, as trustee. W, the donor's spouse, is to receive all of the income of the trust annually and is given a general power, exercisable by will, to appoint out of the trust corpus the sum of $25,000. In this case the $25,000 is not, immediately following establishment of the trust, sufficiently segregated to permit its identification as a separate item of property in which the donee spouse has the entire interest. Therefore, the $25,000 does not constitute the entire interest in a property for the purpose of paragraphs (a) and (b) of this section.

(e) *Application of local law.* In determining whether or not the conditions set forth in paragraph (a)(1) through (5) of this section are satisfied by the instrument of transfer, regard is to be had to the applicable provisions of the law of the jurisdiction under which the interest passes and, if the transfer is in trust, the applicable provisions of the law governing the administration of the trust. For example, silence of a trust instrument as to the frequency of payment will not be regarded as a failure to satisfy the condition set forth in paragraph (a)(2) of this section that income must be payable to the donee spouse annually or more frequently unless the applicable law permits payment to be made less frequently than annually. The principles outlined in this paragraph and paragraphs (f) and (g) of this section which are applied in determining whether transfers in trust meet such conditions are equally applicable in ascertaining whether, in the case of interests not in trust, the donee spouse has the equivalent in rights over income and over the property.

(f) *Right to income.* (1) If an interest is transferred in trust, the donee spouse is "entitled for life to all of the income from the entire interest or a specific portion of the entire interest," for the purpose of the condition set forth in paragraph (a)(1) of this section, if the effect of the trust is to give her substantially that degree of beneficial enjoyment of the trust property during her life which the principles of the law of trusts accord to a person who is unqualifiedly designated as the life beneficiary of a trust. Such degree of enjoyment is given only if it was the donor's intention, as manifested by the terms of the trust instrument and the surrounding circumstances, that the trust should produce for the donee spouse during her life such an income, or that the spouse should have such use of the trust property as is consistent with the value of the trust corpus and with its preservation. The designation of the spouse as sole income beneficiary for life of the entire interest or a specific portion of the entire interest will be sufficient to qualify the trust unless the terms of the trust and the surrounding circumstances considered as a whole evidence an intention to deprive the spouse of the requisite degree of enjoyment. In determining whether a trust evidences that intention, the treatment required or permitted with respect to individual items must be considered in relation to the entire system provided for the administration of the trust.

(2) If the over-all effect of a trust is to give to the donee spouse such enforceable rights as will preserve to her the requisite degree of enjoyment, it is immaterial whether that result is effected by rules specifically stated in the trust instrument, or, in their absence, by the rules for the management of the trust property and the allocation of receipts and expenditures supplied by the State law. For example, a provision in the trust instrument for amortization of bond premium by appropriate periodic charges to interest will not disqualify the interest transferred in trust even though there is no State law specifically authorizing amortization or there is a State law denying amortization which is applicable only in the absence of such a provision in the trust instrument.

(3) In the case of a trust, the rules to be applied by the trustee in allocation of receipts and expenses between income and corpus must be considered in relation to the nature and expected productivity of the assets transferred in trust, the nature and frequency of occurrence of the expected receipts, and any provisions as to change in the form of investments. If it is evident from the nature of the trust assets and the rules provided for management of the trust that the allocation to income of such receipts as rents, ordinary cash dividends and interest will give to the spouse the substantial enjoyment during life required by the statute, provisions that such receipts as stock dividends and proceeds from the conversion of trust assets shall be treated as corpus will not disqualify the interest transferred in trust. Similarly, provision for a depletion charge against income in the case of trust assets which are subject to depletion will not disqualify the interest transferred in trust, unless the effect is to deprive the spouse of the

requisite beneficial enjoyment. The same principle is applicable in the case of depreciation, trustees' commissions, and other charges.

(4) Provisions granting administrative powers to the trustees will not have the effect of disqualifying an interest transferred in trust unless the grant of powers evidences the intention to deprive the donee spouse of the beneficial enjoyment required by the statute. Such an intention will not be considered to exist if the entire terms of the instrument are such that the local courts will impose reasonable limitations upon the exercise of the powers. Among the powers which if subject to reasonable limitations will not disqualify the interest transferred in trust are the power to determine the allocation or apportionment of receipts and disbursements between income and corpus, the power to apply the income or corpus for the benefit of the spouse, and the power to retain the assets transferred to the trust. For example, a power to retain trust assets which consist substantially of unproductive property will not disqualify the interest if the applicable rules for the administration of the trust require, or permit the spouse to require, that the trustee either make the property productive or convert it within a reasonable time. Nor will such a power disqualify the interest if the applicable rules for administration of the trust require the trustee to use the degree of judgment and care in the exercise of the power which a prudent man would use if he were owner of the trust assets. Further, a power to retain a residence for the spouse or other property for the personal use of the spouse will not qualify the interest transferred in trust.

(5) An interest transferred in trust will not satisfy the condition set forth in paragraph (a)(1) of this section that the donee spouse be entitled to all the income if the primary purpose of the trust is to safeguard property without providing the spouse with the required beneficial enjoyment. Such trusts include not only trusts which expressly provide for the accumulation of the income but also trusts which indirectly accomplish a similar purpose. For example, assume that the corpus of a trust consists substantially of property which is not likely to be income producing during the life of the donee spouse and that the spouse cannot compel the trustee to convert or otherwise deal with the property as described in subparagraph (4) of this paragraph. An interest transferred to such a trust will not qualify unless the applicable rules for the administration require, or permit the spouse to require, that the trustee provide the required beneficial enjoyment, such as by payments to the spouse out of other assets of the trust.

(6) If a trust may be terminated during the life of the donee spouse, under her exercise of a power of appointment or by distribution of the corpus to her, the interest transferred in trust satisfies the condition set forth in paragraph (a)(1) of this section (that the spouse be entitled to all the income) if she (i) is entitled to the income until the trust terminates, or (ii) has the right, exercisable in all events, to have the corpus distributed to her at any time during her life.

(7) An interest transferred in trust fails to satisfy the condition set forth in paragraph (a)(1) of this section, that the spouse be entitled

to all the income, to the extent that the income is required to be accumulated in whole or in part or may be accumulated in the discretion of any person other than the donee spouse; to the extent that the consent of any person other than the donee spouse is required as a condition precedent to distribution of the income; or to the extent that any person other than the donee spouse has the power to alter the terms of the trust so as to deprive her of her right to the income. An interest transferred in trust will not fail to satisfy the condition that the spouse be entitled to all the income merely because its terms provide that the right of the donee spouse to the income shall not be subject to assignment, alienation, pledge, attachment or claims of creditors.

(8) In the case of an interest transferred in trust, the terms "entitled for life" and "payable annually or at more frequent intervals", as used in the conditions set forth in paragraph (a)(1) and (2) of this section, require that under the terms of the trust the income referred to must be currently (at least annually; see paragraph (e) of this section) distributable to the spouse or that she must have such command over the income that it is virtually hers. Thus, the conditions in paragraph (a)(1) and (2) of this section are satisfied in this respect if, under the terms of the trust instrument, the donee spouse has the right exercisable annually (or more frequently) to require distribution to herself of the trust income, and otherwise the trust income is to be accumulated and added to corpus. Similarly, as respects the income for the period between the last distribution date and the date of the spouse's death, it is sufficient if that income is subject to the spouse's power to appoint. Thus, if the trust instrument provides that income accrued or undistributed on the date of the spouse's death is to be disposed of as if it had been received after her death, and if the spouse has a power of appointment over the trust corpus, the power necessarily extends to the undistributed income.

(g) *Power of appointment in donee spouse.* (1) The conditions set forth in paragraph (a)(3) and (4) of this section, that is, that the donee spouse must have a power of appointment exercisable in favor of herself or her estate and exercisable alone and in all events, are not met unless the power of the donee spouse to appoint the entire interest or a specific portion of it falls within one of the following categories:

(i) A power so to appoint fully exercisable in her own favor at any time during her life (as, for example, an unlimited power to invade); or

(ii) A power so to appoint exercisable in favor of her estate. Such a power, if exercisable during life, must be fully exercisable at any time during life, or, if exercisable by will, must be fully exercisable irrespective of the time of her death; or

(iii) A combination of the powers described under subdivisions (i) and (ii) of this subparagraph. For example, the donee spouse may, until she attains the age of 50 years, have a power to appoint to herself and thereafter have a power to appoint to her estate. However, the condition that the spouse's power must be exercisable in all events

1118

is not satisfied unless irrespective of when the donee spouse may die the entire interest or a specific portion of it will at the time of her death be subject to one power or the other.

(2) The power of the donee spouse must be a power to appoint the entire interest or a specific portion of it as unqualified owner (and free of the trust if a trust is involved, or free of the joint tenancy if a joint tenancy is involved) or to appoint the entire interest or a specific portion of it as a part of her estate (and free of the trust if a trust is involved), that is, in effect, to dispose of it to whomsoever she pleases. Thus, if the donor transferred property to a son and the donee spouse as joint tenants with right of survivorship and under local law the donee spouse has a power of severance exercisable without consent of the other joint tenant, and by exercising this power could acquire a one-half interest in the property as a tenant in common, her power of severance will satisfy the condition set forth in paragraph (a)(3) of this section that she have a power of appointment in favor of herself or her estate. However, if the donee spouse entered into a binding agreement with the donor to exercise the power only in favor of their issue, that condition is not met. An interest transferred in trust will not be regarded as failing to satisfy the condition merely because takers in default of the donee spouse's exercise of the power are designated by the donor. The donor may provide that, in default of exercise of the power, the trust shall continue for an additional period.

(3) A power is not considered to be a power exercisable by a donee spouse alone and in all events as required by paragraph (a)(4) of this section if the exercise of the power in the donee spouse to appoint the entire interest or a specific portion of it to herself or to her estate requires the joinder or consent of any other person. The power is not "exercisable in all events", if it can be terminated during the life of the donee spouse by any event other than her complete exercise or release of it. Further, a power is not "exercisable in all events" if it may be exercised for a limited purpose only. For example, a power which is not exercisable in the event of the spouse's remarriage is not exercisable in all events. Likewise, if there are any restrictions, either by the terms of the instrument or under applicable local law, on the exercise of a power to consume property (whether or not held in trust) for the benefit of the spouse, the power is not exercisable in all events. Thus, if a power of invasion is exercisable only for the spouse's support, or only for her limited use, the power is not exercisable in all events. In order for a power of invasion to be exercisable in all events, the donee spouse must have the unrestricted power exercisable at any time during her life to use all or any part of the property subject to the power, and to dispose of it in any manner, including the power to dispose of it by gift (whether or not she has power to dispose of it by will).

(4) If the power is in existence at all times following the transfer of the interest, limitations of a formal nature will not disqualify the interest. Examples of formal limitations on a power exercisable during

life are requirements that an exercise must be in a particular form, that it must be filed with a trustee during the spouse's life, that reasonable notice must be given, or that reasonable intervals must elapse between successive partial exercises. Examples of formal limitations on a power exercisable by will are that it must be exercised by a will executed by the donee spouse after the making of the gift or that exercise must be by specific reference to the power.

(5) If the donee spouse has the requisite power to appoint to herself or her estate, it is immaterial that she also has one or more lesser powers. Thus, if she has a testamentary power to appoint to her estate, she may also have a limited power of withdrawal or of appointment during her life. Similarly, if she has an unlimited power of withdrawal, she may have a limited testamentary power.

(h) *Existence of a power in another.* Paragraph (a)(5) of this section provides that a transfer described in paragraph (a) is nondeductible to the extent that the donor created a power in the trustee or in any other person to appoint a part of the interest to any person other than the donee spouse. However, only powers in other persons which are in opposition to that of the donee spouse will cause a portion of the interest to fail to satisfy the condition set forth in paragraph (a)(5) of this section. Thus, a power in a trustee to distribute corpus to or for the benefit of the donee spouse will not disqualify the trust. Similarly, a power to distribute corpus to the spouse for the support of minor children will not disqualify the trust if she is legally obligated to support such children. The application of this paragraph may be illustrated by the following examples:

Example (1). Assume that a donor created a trust, designating his spouse as income beneficiary for life with an unrestricted power in the spouse to appoint the corpus during her life. The donor further provided that in the event the donee spouse should die without having exercised the power, the trust should continue for the life of his son with a power in the son to appoint the corpus. Since the power in the son could become exercisable only after the death of the donee spouse, the interest is not regarded as failing to satisfy the condition set forth in paragraph (a)(5) of this section.

Example (2). Assume that the donor created a trust, designating his spouse as income beneficiary for life and as donee of a power to appoint by will the entire corpus. The donor further provided that the trustee could distribute 30 percent of the corpus to the donor's son when he reached the age of 35 years. Since the trustee has a power to appoint 30 percent of the entire interest for the benefit of a person other than the donee spouse, only 70 percent of the interest placed in trust satisfied the condition set forth in paragraph (a)(5) of this section. If, in this case, the donee spouse had a power, exercisable by her will, to appoint only one-half of the corpus as it was constituted at the time of her death, it should be noted that only 35 percent of the interest placed in the trust would satisfy the condition set forth in paragraph (a)(3) of this section.

§ 25.2523(f)-1 Marital deduction in cases involving community property—(a) *In general.* The marital deduction is allowable with respect to any transfer by a donor to his spouse only to the extent that the transfer can be shown to represent a gift of property which was not, at the time of the gift, held as "community property", as defined in paragraph (b) of this section. The burden of establishing the extent to which a transfer represents a gift of property not so held rests upon the donor.

(b) *Definition of "community property."* (1) For the purpose of paragraph (a) of this section, the term "community property" is considered to include—

(i) Any property held by the donor and his spouse as community property under the law of any State, Territory, or possession of the United States, or of any foreign country, except property in which the donee spouse had at the time of the gift merely an expectant interest. The donee spouse is regarded as having, at any particular time, merely an expectant interest in property held at that time by the donor and herself as community property under the law of any State, Territory, or possession of the United States, or of any foreign country, if, in case such property were transferred by gift into the separate property of the donee spouse, the entire value of such property (and not merely one-half of it), would be treated as the amount of the gift.

(ii) Separate property acquired by the donor as a result of a "conversion", after December 31, 1941, of property held by him and the donee spouse as community property under the law of any State, Territory, or possession of the United States, or of any foreign country (except such property in which the donee spouse had at the time of the "conversion" merely an expectant interest), into their separate property, subject to the limitation with respect to value contained in subparagraph (5) of this paragraph.

(iii) Property acquired by the donor in exchange (by one exchange or a series of exchanges) for separate property resulting from such "conversion."

(2) The characteristics of property which acquired a noncommunity instead of a community status by reason of an agreement (whether antenuptial or postnuptial) are such that section 2523(f) classifies the property as community property of the donor and his spouse in the computation of the marital deduction. In distinguishing property which thus acquired a noncommunity status from property which acquired such a status solely by operation of the community property law, section 2523(f) refers to the former category of property as "separate property" acquired as a result of a "conversion" of "property held as such community property." As used in section 2523(f) the phrase "property held as such community property" is used to denote the body of property comprehended within the community property system; the expression "separate property" includes any noncommunity property, whether held in joint tenancy, tenancy by the entirety, tenancy in common, or otherwise; and the term "conver-

sion" includes any transaction or agreement which transforms property from a community status into a noncommunity status.

(3) The separate property which section 2523(f) classifies as community property is not limited to that which was in existence at the time of the conversion. The following are illustrative of the scope of section 2523(f):

(i) A partition of community property between husband and wife, whereby a portion of the property became the separate property of each, is a conversion of community property.

(ii) A transfer of community property into some other form of co-ownership, such as a joint tenancy, is a conversion of the property.

(iii) An agreement (whether made before or after marriage) that future earnings and gains which would otherwise be community property shall be shared by the spouses as separate property effects a conversion of such earnings and gains.

(iv) A change in the form of ownership of property which causes future rentals, which would otherwise have been acquired as community property, to be acquired as separate property effects a conversion of the rentals.

(4) The rules of section 2523(f) are applicable, however, only if the conversion took place after December 31, 1941, and only to the extent stated in this section.

(5) If the value of the separate property acquired by the donor as a result of a conversion did not exceed the value of the separate property thus acquired by the donee spouse, the entire separate property thus acquired by the donor is to be considered, for the purposes of this section, as held by him and the donee spouse as community property. If the value (at the time of conversion) of the separate property so acquired by the donor exceeded the value (at that time) of the separate property so acquired by the donee spouse, only a part of the separate property so acquired by the donor (and only the same fractional part of property acquired by him in exchange for such separate property) is to be considered, for purposes of this section, as held by him and the donee spouse as community property. The part of such separate property (or property acquired in exchange for it) which is considered as so held is the same proportion of it which the value (at the time of the conversion) of the separate property so acquired by the donee spouse is of the value (at that time) of the separate property so acquired by the donor. The following example illustrates the application of the provisions of this paragraph:

Example. During 1942 the donor and his spouse partitioned certain real property held by them under community property laws. The real property then had a value of $224,000. A portion of the property, then having a value of $160,000, was converted into the donor's separate property, and the remaining portion, then having a value of $64,000, was converted into his spouse's separate property. In 1955 the donor made a gift to his spouse of the property acquired by him as a result of the partition, which property then had a value of

[Harris]

$200,000. The portion of the property transferred by gift which is considered as community property is

$$\frac{\$\ 64{,}000\ \text{(value of property acquired by donee spouse)}}{\$160{,}000\ \text{(value of property acquired by donor spouse)}} \times \$200{,}000 = \$80{,}000$$

The marital deduction with respect to the gift is, therefore, limited to one-half of $120,000 (the difference between $200,000, the value of the gift, and $80,000, the portion of the gift considered to have been of "community property"). The marital deduction with respect to the gift is, therefore, $60,000.

§ 25.2524-1 **Extent of deductions.** Under the provisions of section 2524, the charitable deduction provided for in section 2522 and the marital deduction provided for in section 2523 are allowable only to the extent that the gifts with respect to which those deductions are authorized are included in the "total amount of gifts" made during the calendar year, computed as provided in section 2503 and § 25.2503-1 (i. e., the total gifts less exclusions). The following example illustrates the application of the provisions of this section:

Example. The only gifts made by a donor to his spouse during the calendar year were a gift of $3,000 in May and a gift of $2,000 in August. The first $3,000 of such gifts is excluded under the provisions of section 2503 in determining the "total amount of gifts" made during the calendar year. The marital deduction of $2,500 (one-half of $3,000 plus one-half of $2,000) otherwise allowable is limited by section 2524 to $2,000.

PROCEDURE AND ADMINISTRATION

Records, Statements and Special Returns

§ 25.6001-1 **Records required to be kept**—(a) *In general.* Every person subject to taxation under chapter 12 of the Internal Revenue Code of 1954 shall for the purpose of determining the total amount of his gifts, keep such permanent books of account or records as are necessary to establish the amount of his total gifts (limited as provided by section 2503(b)), together with the deductions allowable in determining the amount of his taxable gifts, and the other information required to be shown in a gift tax return. All documents and vouchers used in preparing the gift tax return (see § 25.6019-1) shall be retained by the donor so as to be available for inspection whenever required.

(b) *Supplemental data.* In order that the district director may determine the correct tax the donor shall furnish such supplemental data as may be deemed necessary by the district director. It is, therefore, the duty of the donor to furnish, upon request, copies of all documents relating to his gift or gifts, appraisal lists of any items included in the total amount of gifts, copies of balance sheets or other financial statements obtainable by him relating to the value of stock constituting the gift, and any other information obtainable by him that may be necessary in the determination of the tax. See section 2512 and the regulations issued thereunder. For every policy of life insurance listed on the return, the donor must procure a statement from the insurance company on Form 938 and file it with the district director who receives the return. If specifically requested by the district director, the insurance company shall file this statement direct with the district director.

§ 25.6011-1 General requirement of return, statement, or list—(a) *General rule.* Every person made liable for any tax imposed by chapter 12 of the Code shall make such returns or statements as are required by the regulations in this part. The return or statement shall include therein the information required by the applicable regulations or forms.

(b) *Use of prescribed forms.* Copies of the forms prescribed by paragraph (b) of § 25.6001-1 and § 25.6019-1 may be obtained from district directors. The fact that a person required to file a form has not been furnished with copies of a form will not excuse him from the making of a gift tax return, or from the furnishing of the evidence for which the forms are to be used. Application for a form should be made to the district director in ample time to enable the person whose duty it is to file, the form to have the form prepared, verified, and filed with the district director on or before the date prescribed for the filing thereof.

Gift Tax Returns

§ 25.6019-1 Persons required to file returns—(a) *In general.* Any individual citizen or resident of the United States who within the calendar year 1955, or within any calendar year thereafter, makes a transfer or transfers by gift to any one donee of a value or total value in excess of $3,000 (or regardless of value in the case of a gift of a future interest in property) must file a gift tax return on Form 709 for that year. A nonresident not a citizen of the United States who made such a gift must also file a return on Form 709 if under § 25.2511-3 the transfer is subject to the gift tax. The return is required even though because of the deductions authorized by sections 2521 (specific exemption), 2522 (charitable, etc., deduction), and 2523 (marital deduction) no tax may be payable. Individuals only are required to file returns and not trusts, estates, partnerships or corporations. Duplicate copies of the return are not required to be filed. See §§ 25.6075-1 and 25.6091-1 for the time and place for filing the gift tax return. For delinquency penalty for failure to file return, see section 6651 and § 301.6651-1 of this chapter (Regulations on Procedure and Administration). For criminal penalties for failure to file a return and filing a false or fraudulent return, see sections 7203, 7206, and 7207.

(b) *Deceased donor.* If the donor dies before filing his return, the executor of his will or the administrator of his estate shall file the return. If the donor becomes legally incompetent before filing his return, his guardian or committee shall file the return.

(c) *Ratification of return.* The return shall not be made by an agent unless by reason of illness, absence, or nonresidence, the person liable for the return is unable to make it within the time prescribed. Mere convenience is not sufficient reason for authorizing an agent to make the return. If by reason of illness, absence or nonresidence, a return is made by an agent, the return must be ratified by the donor or other person liable for its filing within a reasonable time after such person becomes able to do so. If the return filed by the agent is not so ratified, it will not be considered the return required by the statute. Supplemental data may be submitted at the time of ratification. The ratification may be in the form of a statement, executed under the penalties of perjury and filed with the district director, showing specifically that the return made by the agent has been carefully examined and that the person signing ratifies the return as the donor's. If a return is signed by an agent, a statement fully explaining the inability of the donor must accompany the return.

§ 25.6019-2 **Returns required in case of consent under section 2513.** Except as otherwise provided in this section, the provisions of § 25-.6019-1 are applicable with respect to the filing of a gift tax return or returns in the case of a husband and wife who consent (see § 25-.2513-1) to the application of section 2513. In such a case, if both of the consenting spouses are (without regard to the provisions of section 2513) required under the provisions of § 25.6019-1 to file returns, returns must be filed by both spouses. If only one of the consenting spouses is (without regard to the provisions of section 2513) required under § 25.6019-1 to file a return, a return must be filed by that spouse. In the latter case, if after giving effect to the provisions of section 2513 the other spouse is considered to have made any gift (regardless of value) of a future interest in property or any gift or gifts to any one third-party donee exceeding $3,000 in value, then a return must also be filed by such other spouse. Thus, if during any calendar year the husband made a gift of $5,000 to a son (the gift not being a future interest in property) and the wife made no gifts, only the husband is required to file a return for such year. However, if the wife had made a gift of $2,000 to the same son, or if the gift made by the husband had amounted to $7,000, each spouse would be required to file a return if the consent is signified as provided in section 2513.

§ 25.6019-3 **Contents of return**—(a) *In general.* The return shall set forth: (1) each gift made during the calendar year which under sections 2511 through 2515 is to be included in computing taxable gifts; (2) the deductions claimed and allowable under sections 2521 through 2524; and (3) the taxable gifts made for each of the preceding calendar years (see § 25.2504-1). In addition the return shall set forth the fair market value of all gifts not made in money, including gifts resulting from sales and exchanges of property made for less than full and adequate consideration in money or money's worth, giving, as of the date of the sale or exchange, both the fair market value of the property sold or exchanged and the fair market value of the consideration received by the donor. If a donor contends that his retained power over property renders the gift incomplete (see § 25.2511-2) and hence not subject to tax as of the calendar year of the initial transfer, the transaction should be disclosed in the return for the calendar year of the initial transfer and evidence showing all relevant facts, including a copy of the instrument of transfer, should be submitted with the return. The instructions printed on the return should be carefully followed. A certified or verified copy of each document required by the instructions printed on the return form shall be filed with the return. Any additional documents the donor may desire to submit may be submitted with the return.

(b) *Disclosure of transfers coming within provisions of section 2516.* Section 2516 provides that certain transfers of property pursuant to written property settlements between husband and wife are deemed to be transfers for full and adequate consideration in money or money's worth if divorce occurs within two years. In any case where a husband and wife enter into a written agreement of the type contemplated by section 2516, and the final decree of divorce is not granted on or before the due date for the filing of a gift tax return for the calendar year in which the agreement became effective (see § 25.6075-1), the transfer shall be disclosed by the transferor upon a gift tax return filed for the calendar year in which the agreement became effective and a copy of the agreement shall be attached to the return. In addition, a certified copy of the final divorce decree shall be furnished the district director not later than 60 days after the divorce is granted. Pending receipt of evidence that the final decree of divorce has been granted (but in no event for a period of more than two years from the effective date of the agreement), the transfer will tentatively be treated as made for a full and adequate consideration in money or money's worth.

§ 25.6019-4 **Description of property listed on return.** The properties comprising the gifts made during the calendar year shall be listed on the return and shall be described in such a manner that they may be readily identified. Thus, there should be given for each parcel of real estate a legal description, its area, a short statement of the character of any improvements, and, if located in a city, the name of street and number. Description of bonds should include the number transferred, principal amount, name of obligor, date of maturity, rate of interest, date or dates on which interest is payable, series number where there is more than one issue, and the principal exchange upon which listed, or the principal business office of the obligor, if unlisted. Description of stocks shall include number of shares, whether common or preferred, and, if preferred, what issue thereof, par value, quotation at which returned, exact name of corporation, and, if the stock is unlisted, the location of the principal business office, the State in which incorporated and the date of incorporation, or if the stock is listed, the principal exchange upon which sold. Description of notes shall include name of maker, date on which given, date of maturity, amount of principal, amount of principal unpaid, rate of interest and whether simple or compound, and date to which interest has been paid. If the gift of property includes accrued income thereon to the date of the gift, the amount of such accrued income shall be separately set forth. Description of the seller's interest in land contracts transferred shall include name of buyer, date of contract, description of property, sale price, initial payment, amounts of installment payments, unpaid balance of principal, interest rate and date prior to gift to which interest has been paid. Description of life insurance policies shall show the name of the insurer and the number of the policy. In describing an annuity, the name and address of the issuing company shall be given, or, if payable out of a trust or other fund, such a description as will fully identify the trust or fund. If the annuity is payable for a term of years, the duration of the term and the date on which it began shall be given, and if payable for the life of any person, the date of birth of that person shall be stated. Judgments shall be described by giving the title of the cause and the name of the court in which rendered, date of judgment, name and address of judgment debtor, amount of judgment, rate of interest to which subject, and by stating whether any payments have been made thereon, and, if so, when and in what amounts.

§ 25.6075-1 **Returns; time for filing gift tax returns.** The gift tax return required by section 6019 must be filed on or before the due date. The due date is the date on or before which the return is required to be filed in accordance with the provisions of section 6075(b) or the last day of the period covered by an extension of time granted by the district director as provided in § 25.6081-1. Unless an extension of time has been granted, the due date is the 15th day of April following the close of the calendar year in which gifts were made. When the due date falls on Saturday, Sunday, or a legal holiday, the due date for filing the return is the next succeeding day which is not Saturday, Sunday, or a legal holiday. For definition of a legal holiday, see section 7503 and § 301.7503-1 of this chapter (Regulations on Procedure and Administration). As to additions to the tax for failure to file the return within the prescribed time, see section 6651 and § 301.6651-1 of this chapter (Regulations on Procedure and Administration).

§ 25.6081-1 **Extension of time for filing returns.** It is important that the donor file on or before the due date a return as nearly complete and final as it is possible for him to prepare. However, the district director is authorized to grant a reasonable extension of time for filing returns. Applications for extensions of time for filing gift tax returns shall be addressed to the district director for the district in which the donor files his returns and must contain a full recital of the causes for delay. Except in the case of donors who are abroad, no extension for filing gift tax returns may be granted for more than 6 months. An extension of time for filing a return does not operate to extend the time for payment of the tax or any part thereof, unless so specified in the extension. For extensions of time for payment of tax, see § 25.6161-1. No extension of time for filing a return may be granted unless the application is received by the district director before the expiration of the time within which the return must otherwise be filed. The application should, when possible, be made sufficiently early to permit the district director to consider the matter and reply before what otherwise would be the due date of the return.

§ 25.6091-1 **Place for filing returns and other documents.** If the donor is a resident of the United States, the gift tax return required by section 6019 shall be filed with the district director for the district in which the legal residence or principal place of business of the donor is located. If the donor is a nonresident (whether or not a citizen), and his principal place of business is located in an internal revenue district, the gift tax return shall be filed with the district director for the internal revenue district in which the donor's principal place of business is located. If the donor is a nonresident (whether or not a citizen), and he does not have a principal place of business which is located in an internal revenue district, the gift tax return shall be filed with the Director of International Operations, Internal Revenue Service, Washington 25, D. C., or with such other official as the Commissioner may designate.

Payment of Tax

§ 25.6151-1 **Time and place for paying tax shown on return.** The tax shown on the gift tax return is to be paid by the donor at the time and place fixed for filing the return (determined without regard to any extension of time for filing the return), unless the time for paying the tax is extended in accordance with the provisions of section 6161. However, for provisions relating to certain cases in which the time for paying the gift tax is postponed by reason of an individual serving in, or in support of, the Armed Forces of the United States in a combat zone, see section 7508. For provisions relating to the time and place for filing the return, see §§ 25.6075-1 and 25.6091-1.

§ 25.6161-1 **Extension of time for paying tax or deficiency**—(a) *In general*—(1) *Tax shown on return*. A reasonable extension of time to pay the amount of tax shown on the return may be granted by the district director at the request of the donor. The period of such extension shall not be in excess of six months from the date fixed for the payment of the tax, except that if the taxpayer is abroad the period of extension may be in excess of six months.

(2) *Deficiency*. The time for payment of any amount determined as a deficiency in respect of tax imposed by chapter 12 of the Code, or for payment of any part thereof may be extended by the district

1128

director at the request of the donor for a period not to exceed 18 months from the date fixed for the payment of the deficiency, as shown on the notice and demand from the district director, and, in exceptional cases, for a further period not in excess of 12 months. No extension of time for the payment of a deficiency shall be granted if the deficiency is due to negligence, to intentional disregard of rules and regulations, or to fraud with intent to evade tax.

(3) *Extension of time for filing distinguished.* The granting of an extension of time for filing a return does not operate to extend the time for the payment of the tax or any part thereof, unless so specified in the extension.

(b) *Undue hardship required for extension.* An extension of the time for payment shall be granted only upon a satisfactory showing that payment on the due date of the amount with respect to which the extension is desired will result in an undue hardship. The extension will not be granted upon a general statement of hardship. The term "undue hardship" means more than an inconvenience to the taxpayer. It must appear that substantial financial loss, for example, loss due to the sale of property at a sacrifice price, will result to the donor from making payment on the due date of the amount with respect to which the extension is desired. If a market exists, the sale of the property at the current market price is not ordinarily considered as resulting in an undue hardship.

(c) *Application for extension.* An application for an extension of the time for payment of the tax shown on the return, or for the payment of any amount determined as a deficiency, shall be in writing and shall be accompanied by evidence showing the undue hardship that would result to the donor if the extension were refused. The application shall also be accompanied by a statement of the assets and liabilities of the donor and an itemized statement showing all receipts and disbursements for each of the three months immediately preceding the due date of the amount to which the application relates. The application, with supporting documents, must be filed with the district director on or before the date prescribed for payment of the amount with respect to which the extension is desired. The application will be examined by the district director, and within 30 days, if possible, will be denied, granted, or tentatively granted subject to certain conditions of which the donor will be notified. If an additional extension is desired, the request therefor must be made to the district director on or before the expiration of the period for which the prior extension is granted.

(d) *Payment pursuant to extensions.* If an extension of time for payment is granted, the amount the time for payment of which is so extended shall be paid on or before the expiration of the period of the extension without the necessity of notice and demand from the district director. The granting of an extension of the time for payment of the tax or deficiency does not relieve the donor from liability for the payment of interest thereon during the period of the extension.

1129

See section 6601 and § 301.6601-1 of this chapter (Regulations on Procedure and Administration).

§ 25.6165-1 **Bonds where time to pay tax or deficiency has been extended.** For general provisions relating to bonds when extensions of time to pay the gift tax are granted, see the regulations under sections 6165 and 7101 contained in Part 301 of this chapter (Regulations on Procedure and Administration).

§ 25.6321-1 **Lien for taxes.** For regulations concerning the lien for taxes, see § 301.6321-1 of this chapter (Regulations on Procedure and Administration).

§ 25.6323-1 **Validity against mortgagees, pledgees, purchasers, and judgment creditors.** For regulations concerning the validity of liens against mortgagees, pledgees, purchasers, and judgment creditors, see § 301.6323-1 of this chapter (Regulations on Procedure and Administration).

§ 25.6324-1 **Special lien for gift tax.** For regulations concerning the special lien for the gift tax, see § 301.6324-1 of this chapter (Regulations on Procedure and Administration).

§ 25.6601-1 **Interest on underpayment, nonpayment, or extensions of time for payment, of tax.** For regulations concerning interest on underpayment, nonpayment, or extensions of time for payment, of tax, see § 301.6601-1 of this chapter (Regulations on Procedure and Administration).

§ 25.7101-1 **Form of bonds.** For general provisions relating to bonds, see the regulations under sections 6165 and 7101 contained in part 301 of this chapter (Regulations on Procedure and Administration).

INDEX TO GIFT TAX REGULATIONS

1131

INDEX TO FORMS

(Numbers refer to sections)

A

B

[Harris]—72

I

J

L

M

N

S

T

INDEX

(References are to sections)

A

[Harris]—74

1171

I

INTENTION
    donor's, effect on gift tax 419
    element of gift 417

INTEREST—See Also INTEREST IN PROPERTY
    estate tax
        business, in 102
        conditioned on survival of spouse for limited period 232
        deductible 229
        exception to terminable, rule 230
        excluded property, in alternate valuation 261
        includibility in gross estate 63
        in unidentified assets 231
        nondeductible 229
        other, qualified for marital deduction 239
        partnership, not joint property 97
        payment of tax, on
            extension of time for, when 364
            general rule 363
            last date prescribed for 365
            no interest on interest 366A
            suspension of, on 366
            waiver of restrictions 366
        refund, on 379
        terminable 229
    gift tax
        business, in 437
        future 482, 490
        payment of, on 558

INTEREST IN PROPERTY—See Also INTEREST
    marital deduction, definition 227
    passing, definition 228

INTERRELATION OF MARITAL DEDUCTION AND ESTATE TAXES—
See MARITAL DEDUCTION

INTER VIVOS
    transfers—See TRANSFERS DURING LIFE

INVASION
    power of
        as power of appointment 164
        effect on annual exclusion 486
        effect on charitable deduction 251
        limited by ascertainable standard 165, 459, 463

ISSUE
    joinder of, Tax Court.. 602

J

JEOPARDY ASSESSMENT
    abatement 355
    amount assessable before and after decision of Tax Court 355

M

[Harris]—75

[Harris]

S

U